lonely planet

Peru

Amazon Basin
p447

North
Coast
p317

Northern
Highlands
p411

Huaraz & the
Cordilleras
p371

Central
Highlands
p277

Lima
p57

Cuzco & the
Sacred Valley
p203

South
Coast
p109

Arequipa
& Canyon
Country
p145

Lake
Titicaca
p177

Brendan Sainsbury, Alex Egerton, Mark Johanson,
Carolyn McCarthy, Phillip Tang, Luke Waterson

918.5
2021

MARINERA DANCERS, TRUJILLO P26

PISCO SOUR P517

GIBBONS, PARQUE NACIONAL MANU P468

Contents

COVID-19

We have re-checked every business in this book before publication to ensure that it is still open after the COVID-19 outbreak. However, the economic and social impacts of COVID-19 will continue to be felt long after the outbreak has been contained, and many businesses, services and events referenced in this guide may experience ongoing restrictions. Some businesses may be temporarily closed, have changed their opening hours and services, or require bookings; some unfortunately could have closed permanently. We suggest you check with venues before visiting for the latest information.

Contents

ON THE ROAD

MONASTERIO DE SANTA
CATALINA, AREQUIPA P147

Contents

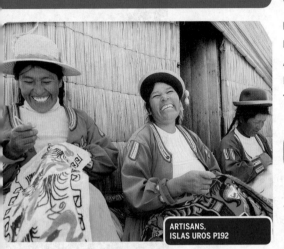

ARTISANS,
ISLAS UROS P192

LLAMA, CUZCO, P204

Right: Cordillera Blanca (p385)

MMPHOTO / GETTY IMAGES©

WELCOME TO

Peru

Ancient, culture-heavy, and complicated, Peru is like several worlds squeezed into one country. For me, Machu Picchu is merely the tip of a massive iceberg. Underneath, it is possible to peel off the layers slowly, piece by piece. From the remote depths of the Cotahausi Canyon to the heady heights of the Cordillera Blanca, from the rolling mists of the arid Pacific coast to the humid rainforests of the Amazon basin, from the mysterious anthropomorphic carvings of Chavín de Huántar to the modern Nikkei restaurants of metro Lima. Welcome to one of the most diverse countries on earth.

By Brendan Sainsbury, Writer

🐦 @sainsburyb

For more about our writers, see p576

Peru

Máncora
Warm waters and
ripping waves (p359)

Chan Chan
The Americas' largest
pre-Columbian city (p331)

Kuélap
An extraordinary
stone fortress (p431)

Parque Nacional Manu
A great rainforest
experience (p468)

Machu Picchu
The planet's most-famous
ruin (p259)

BRAZIL

COLOMBIA

ECUADOR

QUITO ✪

Equator

Río Napo

Río Amazonas

Río Amazonas

Río Tigre

Iquitos

Requena

Río Marañón

Reserva Nacional
Pacaya-Samiria

Contamana

Río Ucayali

Cruzeiro do Sul

Pucallpa

Lagunas

Yurimaguas

Tarapoto

Moyobamba

Chachapoyas

Kuélap

Río Marañón

Tayabamba

Alpamayo
(5947m)

San Ignacio

Bagua

Pedro Ruíz

Celendín

Cajamarca

Chan Chan

Trujillo

Chiclayo

Huancabamba

Zumba

La Tina

Macará

Loja

Machala

Guayaquil

Tumbes

Máncora

Talara

Sullana

Piura

Santa Rosa

Leticia

Tabatinga

200 km
100 miles

68°W
70°W
72°W
74°W
76°W
78°W
80°W

2°S
4°S
6°S
8°S

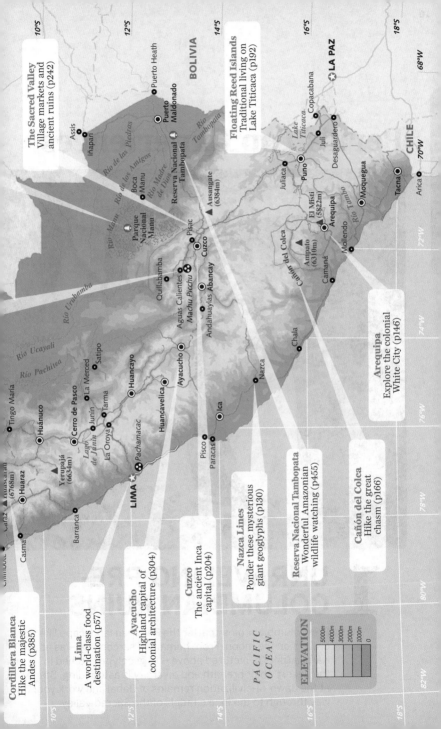

Cordillera Blanca
Hike the majestic Andes (p385)

Lima
A world-class food destination (p57)

Ayacucho
Highland capital of colonial architecture (p304)

Cuzco
The ancient Inca capital (p204)

Nazca Lines
Ponder these mysterious giant geoglyphs (p130)

Reserva Nacional Tambopata
Wonderful Amazonian wildlife watching (p455)

Cañón del Colca
Hike the great chasm (p166)

Arequipa
Explore the colonial White City (p146)

The Sacred Valley
Village markets and ancient ruins (p242)

Floating Reed Islands
Traditional living on Lake Titicaca (p192)

BOLIVIA

CHILE

PACIFIC OCEAN

ELEVATION
5000m
4000m
3000m
2000m
1000m
0

Peru's Top Experiences

1 UNRAVELING PRE-COLUMBIAN RUINS

Pre-Columbian ruins scatter the Peruvian landscape like craters on the moon. From humanoid sarcophagi – as at Karajía (p430), pictured above – to geoglyphs etched in the desert, their breadth and diversity is astounding. Start at the dawn-of-civilization remains of Cabal and work your way through to the Inca citadels of the Sacred Valley.

Machu Picchu

One of the great wonders of the world and a long-standing symbol of Peru, the 'lost' city of the Incas is a little more crowded these days, although no amount of people can detract from its scale and majesty.
p259

Kuélap

The addition of a cable-car in 2017 has improved access to these once-remote ruins in the Northern Highlands that were an erstwhile ceremonial center for the Chachapoya people. Higher than Machu Picchu and older, the massive 20m-tall walls leave an indelible first impression. p431

Chavín de Huántar

Chavín's ruins are an exceptional feat of engineering dating from between 1200 BC and 800 BC. The striking temple-like structures above ground contrast with a labyrinthine complex of underground corridors, ducts and chambers that invite lengthy exploration. p405

2 NOVOANDINA & ITS CULINARY OFFSHOOTS

It's rare to see a 'world's best restaurants' list these days without at least one Peruvian joint in the top ten. The emergence of Novoandina cuisine in the 1980s is hardly surprising in a country that has given the global pantry tomatoes, potatoes, quinoa, and more. Recent developments have seen the growth of gastronomic subgenres including Amazonian and Nikkei cuisine.

GUSTAVO RAMIREZ/SHUTTERSTOCK ©

CRIS BOURONCLE/GETTY IMAGES ©

TOCHIM/SHUTTERSTOCK ©

Central

The outlier in the field of Novoandina is Central in Lima, a restaurant that hit number four in the 'World's Best Restaurants' list in 2017. The key? Don't forget your roots. Chef, Virgilio Martínez (pictured top right) uses ancient foods and growing techniques copied from the Incas. p93

Nikkei

The masters of Peruvian-Japanese Nikkei food are best represented in Lima where restaurants like Matsuei, Hanzo and, most notably Maido ply fried rice, sushi rolls and more creative concoctions like tofu cheesecake ice cream.
p92 Above right: Nikkei food

Iquitos

This steamy riverside jungle city is where you go for unadulterated Amazonian grub including worms, simmered fish intestines and fried ants. Those with weaker stomachs may want to stick to the local *chupín de pollo* (chicken, egg and rice soup). p488

3 TREKKING THE HIGH COUNTRY

The Andes were made for great trekking. Enjoy spectacular mountain scenery and bracing lungfuls of thin air as you navigate paths lined with sporadic ruins, rugged off-the-grid villages and contrasting snippets of indigenous culture that have so far escaped the distractions of the 21st century. Some travelers sally forth independently, others hire an assemblage of guides and *arrieros* (mule-drivers) to smooth their passage.

Cordillera Blanca

The highest mountain range outside the Himalayas with 16 ostentatious summits breeching 6000m, the continent's most challenging trekking country promises glacial lakes, massive Puya raimondii plants and shards of sky-pointed rock. p385 Below: Laguna Parón (p385)

PAUL CLARKE/SHUTTERSTOCK ©

Inca Trail

South America's most famous pedestrian roadway (pictured above left) snakes 43km, up stone steps and through cloud forest mists, to the extravagant ruins of Machu Picchu. p264

Cordillera Huayhuash

The nine-day Huayhuash circuit (pictured right) is a serious undertaking and equal to anything Nepal or Tibet can throw at you. Take it slow and absorb the splendor. p393

4 RIDING THE RIVERS

KIM SCHANDORFF/SHUTTERSTOCK ©

The prime means of transportation in the Amazon basin, rivers are the metaphoric veins of Peru. Isolated jungle lodges use them as their access roads; while choppier waters in the mountains are utilized by for white-water rafting and river running through rapids. The Amazon originates near the Colca Canyon before flowing northeast past the giant river city of Iquitos. Wide and majestic, it's an essential part of Peru's DNA.

Lunahuaná

The not-so-scary rapids of the Río Cañete have established this small town 180km south of Lima as a river running mecca in the rainy season between December and April. p111

Río Apurímac

You could wet yourself in more ways than one on this turbulent river near Cuzco where multi-day trips on class V rapids through deep gorges are for daredevils only. p217

Amazon River Cruises

Fishing and bird-watching are popular pastimes on luxury river cruises that operate out of Iquitos plying the mighty Amazon and its tributaries. p485

5 FABULOUS FESTIVALS

Color and pageantry mix with piety and religion in Peru's busy calendar of festivals. In some instances (eg Semana Santa), what starts off solemn and serious, quickly turns into something more frivolous and fun. While the lion's share of the ceremonies are Catholic in nature honoring important saint's days, there are also some interesting throwbacks to Pre-Columbian and Afro-Peruvian rites and traditions.

MAURO_REPOSSINI/GETTY IMAGES ©

Semana Santa in Ayacucho

Semana Santa in Ayacucho lasts 10 days: and comprises a moving religious spectacle centered on a procession of Christ on a donkey through streets of flowers and palm fronds, followed by fairs, feasts and spectacular predawn fireworks on Easter Sunday. p309

Inti Raymi

The mother of all Inca festivals venerates the sun god 'Inti' and culminates with a celebration of the winter solstice at the citadel of Sacsaywamán just outside Cuzco. p222

6 IMMERSION IN INDIGENOUS CULTURE

PHILIP LEE HARVEY/LONELY PLANET IMAGES ©

TRAVELRLUIS/GETTY IMAGES ©

Cuzco

Mystic, commercial and chaotic, this unique city has been inhabited continuously since pre-Hispanic times. Where else can you find remnants of Inca temples, ornately dressed women walking their llamas on leashes, a museum for magical plants, and the wildest nightlife in the high Andes? p204

Lake Titicaca's Reed Islands

Lake Titicaca's ingenious reed islands were first constructed centuries ago by Uros people to escape more aggressive mainland ethnic groups. The reeds are also used to build thatched homes, elegant boats (pictured left) and archways. Arrange a homestay visit to partake in fishing and learn about some traditional customs. p191

Peru has more indigenous people than any other South American country. Comprising 45% of the total population, their traditions and culture have shaped and enriched the nation. It's in the steeply terraced fields of the Colca Canyon, the ebullient festivals of Cuzco and the musical cadences of Quechua, Aymara and other indigenous languages. Historically, it's reflected in the scattered archaeological sites that tell stories that go back millennia.

7 DIVERSITY IN THE DESERT

Peru's narrow coastal strip is characterized by the extremely dry Sechura desert that runs practically the whole length of the country north to south; its aridity is caused by cold ocean currents colliding with subsiding subtropical air. Far from being boring, this region is alive with interesting features, including large cities, copious archaeological sites, and giant sand dunes. If you can't stand the heat, the Andean foothills are never far away.

Nazca Lines

Made by aliens? Laid out by prehistoric balloonists? Conceived as a giant astronomical chart? No two evaluations of Southern Peru's giant geoglyphs (pictured below), communally known as the Nazca Lines are ever the same. p130

ROBERT CHG/SHUTTERSTOCK ©

Huacachina

It's hard to imagine a more archetypal desert oasis equipped with enough facilities to make it comfortable but not too many gimmicks to render it trite. Added bonus? Sandboarding in the surrounding dunes (pictured above left). p127

Cerro Blanco

Peru's tallest sand dune (pictured right) is usually summited on a hot, arduous three-hour climb on an organized trip from Nazca. p132

8 BIRD BONANZA

In terms of avian diversity, Peru lists over 1800 different types of bird, with new species being discovered all the time. In the Manu area alone, over 360 different species have been spotted – in a single day! Condors utilize the thermal uplifts of the Andes, pelicans drop their valuable guano on rocky coastal islands, while the Andean cock-of-the-rock parades its bright orange plumage in the cloud forests.

Cruz del Cóndor

The famed fly-past for Colca Canyon condors that glide majestically over a spectacular 1200m drop.
p171

Manu National Park

One of the most bird-rich areas in the world, jungle-covered Manu must be accessed on a guided tour. Among over 1000 bird species, you can expect to see all kinds of parrots, macaws, grebes, eagles and pigmy owls. p468

Huembo Interpretation Center

Hummingbird heaven, this attractive spot is the breeding ground for the Marvelous Spatuletail in the Northern Highlands.
p435

Need to Know

For more information, see Survival Guide (p537)

Currency
Nuevo sol (S)

Language
Spanish, Quechua, Aymara

Visas
Visas are generally not not required for travelers entering Peru.

Money
ATMs widely available in larger towns and cities. Credit cards accepted in most establishments.

Cell Phones
In Lima and other larger cities you can buy SIM cards for unlocked phones for about S15. Credit can be purchased in pharmacies and supermarkets. Cell-phone reception may be poor in the mountains or jungle.

Time
Eastern Standard Time (GMT/UTC minus five hours)

When to Go

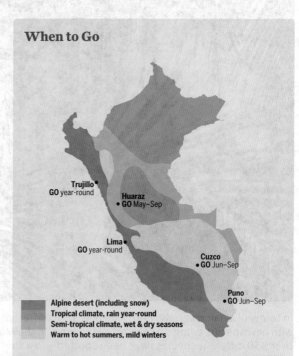

Trujillo
GO year-round

Huaraz
GO May–Sep

Lima
GO year-round

Cuzco
GO Jun–Sep

Puno
GO Jun–Sep

Alpine desert (including snow)
Tropical climate, rain year-round
Semi-tropical climate, wet & dry seasons
Warm to hot summers, mild winters

High Season
(Jun–Aug)

➡ Dry season in Andean highlands and eastern rainforest.

➡ Best time for festivals and highland sports, including treks.

➡ Busiest time due to North American and European holidays.

Shoulder
(Sep–Nov & Mar–May)

➡ Spring and fall weather in the highlands.

➡ Ideal for less-crowded visits.

➡ September to November for good rainforest trekking.

Low Season
(Dec–Feb)

➡ Rainy season in the highlands.

➡ The Inca Trail closes during February for cleanup.

➡ High season for the coast and beach activities.

➡ Very rainy in the Amazon, lasting through May.

Useful Websites

Lonely Planet (www.lonely planet.com/peru) Destination information, hotel bookings, traveler forum and more.

Latin America Network Information Center (www.lanic. utexas.edu/la/peru) Diverse, informative links including academic research.

Living in Peru (www.livingin peru.com) An English-language guide with articles and restaurant reviews.

Peru Reports (www.peru reports.com) Alternative English-language news.

Peruvian Times (www.peruvian times.com) The latest news, in English.

Expat Peru (www.expatperu. com) Useful for government offices and customs regulations.

Important Numbers

Peru's country code	☑51
International access code	4-digit carrier + 00 + country code
Directory assistance	☑103
National tourist information (24hr)	☑511-574-800
Police	☑105

Exchange Rates

Australia	A$1	S2.37
Canada	C$1	S2.54
Europe	€1	S3.85
Japan	¥100	S3.00
New Zealand	NZ$1	S2.17
UK	UK£1	S4.33
USA	US$1	S3.31

For current exchange rates, see www.xe.com.

Daily Costs

**Budget:
Less than S190**

➡ Inexpensive hotel room or dorm bed: S28–165

➡ Set lunches: less than S15; supermarkets have takeout

➡ Entry fee to historic sights: average S10

**Midrange:
S190–650**

➡ Double room in midrange hotel: S85–435

➡ Main dish at midrange restaurant: S40

➡ Group tours: from S120

**Top End:
More than S650**

➡ Double room in top-end hotel: from S250–435

➡ Private city tour: from S200 per person

➡ Fine restaurant dinner: from S60

Opening Hours

Hours are variable and liable to change, especially in small towns, where hours are irregular. Posted hours are a guideline. Lima has the most continuity of services. In other major cities, taxi drivers often know where the late-night stores and pharmacies are located.

Banks 9am–6pm Monday to Friday, some 9am–6pm Saturday

Restaurants 10am–10pm, many close 3pm–6pm

Museums Often close on Monday

Government offices and businesses 9am–5pm Monday to Friday

Shops 9am–6pm, some open Saturday

Arriving in Peru

Aeropuerto Internacional Jorge Chávez (Lima) Many flights arrive in the wee hours, so have a hotel booked ahead. Fast and safe, Airport Express has an hourly shuttle service with seven stops throughout Miraflores. There's no bag limit and it has free wi-fi, USB chargers and bathrooms. Pay via the website or on the bus (cash). *Combi* (minibus) company La S (from S3 per person) runs various routes to Miraflores and beyond. Catch it by walking south of the airport along Av Elmer Faucett. A taxi costs S60 and takes 45 minutes to one hour (rush hour) to Miraflores, Barranco or San Isidro, faster for downtown Lima.

Getting Around

Peru has a constant procession of flights and buses connecting the country. Driving routes to the jungle have improved drastically. Note that poor weather conditions can result in canceled flights and buses. Strikes can be another obstacle in regional travel – consult travel experts on the routes you will be taking.

Public transportation in Peru is cheap, plentiful and frequent.

Light Rail Lima's Metropolitano offers efficient, fast service to downtown.

Train Expensive and geared toward tourists.

Car Useful for traveling at your own pace, though cities can be difficult to navigate and secure parking is a must.

Bus Cheapest option with reclining seats on better long-distance buses.

Taxi A good option for sightseeing, shared taxis are common in the provinces.

For much more on **getting around**, see p548

First Time Peru

For more information, see Survival Guide (p535)

Checklist

➡ Ensure your passport is valid for at least six months past your arrival date

➡ Check the recommended vaccinations and medications

➡ Inform debit and credit card companies of travel plans

➡ Arrange appropriate travel insurance

➡ Charge devices, clear memory and cloud server and find appropriate adapters

➡ Check the airline baggage restrictions

➡ Reserve Inca Trail and Machu Picchu tickets

What to Pack

➡ Good walking shoes or boots

➡ First aid kit with blister care and rehydration salts

➡ Warm waterproof gear

➡ Essentials such as a Swiss Army knife, head lamp and duct tape

➡ Day pack

➡ Earplugs

➡ Toilet paper

➡ Chargers and adapter

Top Tips for Your Trip

➡ In the Cuzco area, start in the lower Sacred Valley and Machu Picchu and work up to Cuzco and higher sites to aid acclimatization.

➡ Book sightseeing flights over the Nazca Lines in advance to avoid waiting around in town for days on end. Try to get an early slot when conditions are calmer.

➡ Shop around for ATMs as fees vary. Banco de la Nación is usually the best for most cardholders.

➡ When you go to higher altitudes, don't book tours for the first few days, stay hydrated and take hiking ascents gradually.

➡ Fly into Cuzco in the morning since afternoon flights can be cancelled due to high winds.

➡ Avoid the cheapest buses which often have safety issues.

What to Wear

Travelers to Peru can get away with casual clothing, but remember to pack for the different climates. For the Andes bring footwear that can tackle cobblestones and mountains, plus a rain jacket and warm layers, as it can be very chilly at altitude. Amazon travelers should presoak an outfit in permethrin for maximum mosquito protection and bring light, long-sleeve clothing and brimmed hats.

Sleeping

Peru has accommodations to suit every budget:

Hotels The most diverse lodging option, from budget to luxury. An overflow in touristy areas means they can be competitively priced.

Hostels Range from huge amenity-oriented party or boutique hostels to run-down backpacker places or family-run guesthouses.

Lodges Stately to rustic lodgings can be found anywhere from the mountains to the Amazon Basin.

Homestays Modest lodgings with families usually arranged through Spanish-language schools.

Camping Campgrounds are rare in Peru and generally not of great quality when you find them.

Shopping

Peru has a bonanza of arts and crafts. Popular souvenirs include alpaca wool sweaters and scarves, woven textiles, ceramics, masks, gold and silver jewelry and the backpacker favorite: Inca Kola T-shirts. While Lima offers a wealth of crafts, highly specialized regional items may be difficult to find. Upscale stores may add a surcharge for credit card transactions.

Bargaining

Bargaining is the norm at street stalls and markets, where it's cash only.

Tipping

Restaurants Tip 10% for good service.

Porters and tour guides Tip each separately at the end of the trip.

Taxis Tip not required (unless drivers have assisted with heavy luggage).

Etiquette

Manners Peruvians are well-mannered. Transactions begin with a formal *buenos días* or *buenas tardes*.

Photos Ask before photographing people in indigenous communities – payment may be requested.

Antiquities It is illegal to buy pre-Columbian antiquities and take them out of Peru.

GORAN BOGICEVIC/SHUTTERSTOCK ©

Woven textiles, Cuzco (p235)

Eating

Cevicherías Lunch restaurants serving fresh fish marinated in lime juice, with many variations on the theme.

Picanterías Informal local restaurants serving hearty portions of Peruvian comfort food.

Novoandina restaurants Gourmet dining that updates old recipes with new techniques and flavor juxtapositions.

Pollerías Rotisserie chicken joints found just about everywhere.

Chifas Usually inexpensive Chinese restaurants, but this wouldn't be Peru if they didn't add their own twist.

Quintas Country-food restaurants serving Andean comfort foods like corn, potatoes and roasted *cuy* (guinea pig).

El Mercado Markets serving hearty soups and other comfort foods with brisk, no-nonsense counter service.

What's New

Despite the tumult of the pandemic, Peru unveiled several surprises in 2020-21, with the country unearthing some important pre-Columbian ruins and discovering a giant cat etched on the Nazca Lines. Quirkier stories helped lighten the mood, including the Japanese tourist who was allowed to enter Machu Picchu on his own after being stranded in Peru for seven months.

Parques Bicentenarios

For Peru's 200th anniversary celebrations in 2021, the country pledged to build 26 special parks, one in each regional capital (and two in Lima). Every park includes five essential components: an ecological area, a cultural center, a library, an esplanade for strolling, and a creative space for local citizens. Leading the way was Lima's two-hectare San Isidro Park, which opened in August 2020. Work began on the capital's second park, Malecón Armendáriz in October 2020. Spread across the cliffs of the Miraflores neighborhood, the 3.8 hectare park costing S20 million, will be beautified with 160,000 plants and criss-crossed by plazas, paths, and a cliff-spanning pedestrian bridge. Although work has been slowed by the pandemic, most of the 26 countrywide parks are expected to be fully operational by 2022.

Puente de la Amistad

Opened in July 2020 as part of the San Isidro Parque Bicentenario project, this pedestrian 'Friendship' bridge traverses Lima's clifftops, linking the waterfront neighborhoods of San Isidro and Miraflores. The 48m bridge, which is illuminated at night, cost S9 million and includes a designated lane for cyclists.

Wat'a Ruins

Thanks to a new form of archaeological technology called Lidar (Light Detection and Ranging), international scientists have been able to gain a better understanding of an ancient Andean settlement near Cuzco that is purportedly older than Machu Picchu. Drones with laser lights have detected man-made features beneath the vegetation and subsequently created a 3D map of the site, which has been christened

LOCAL KNOWLEDGE

WHAT'S HAPPENING

The pandemic was tough on Peru, a fact reflected not just in death rates (which by late 2020 were among the highest in the world), but also in the economic sphere. Tourist arrivals dropped by over three-quarters in 2020, a bitter pill to swallow in a country that employs 1.4 million people in the tourism trade. Psychologically, it couldn't have come at a worse time. 2021 was Peru's bicentennial, with the country celebrating two centuries since its independence from Spain. Some digital celebrations took place in the year's formative months while other real-world events may yet be possible as the vaccine roll-out progresses. Meanwhile, the country faces multiple challenges as it navigates its way through choppy waters post-pandemic still reeling from political protests in November 2020 that saw two presidents deposed in less than a week. At the time of writing the 2021 presidential election had gone to a run-off between Pedro Castillo and Keiko Fujimori. A winner had not been formally announced by electoral authorities in the weeks after the ballet of 6 June.

Wat'a (meaning 'island' in the indigenous language). Perched at 4000m above sea level, the site contains both Inca and pre-Inca ruins. Field information is still being gathered, but early findings suggest it may have acted as a template for Machu Picchu.

Nikkei Food

Still in the midst of a meteoric rise, Peruvian food has recently gained recognition for one of its more inventive subgenres – Nikkei cuisine. Using Peruvian ingredients — such as tropical fish, quinoa, aji and peppers — prepared with traditional Japanese techniques, Nikkei serves up such unusual delights as nigiri sushi, sea urchin rice and 50-hour cooked beef short rib. In the prestigious 2019 William Reed 'World's 50 Best Restaurants' list, Lima's Maido restaurant (p92), captained by chef, Mitsuharu 'Micha' Tsumura, clocked in at an impressive No 10.

Sapiens

Lima's most anticipated post-pandemic restaurant opening is that of Sapiens, a new venture by star Peruvian chef Jaime Pesaque, who has already cemented a legendary reputation at Lima's Mayta. Earmarked for a spring 2021 opening in the capital's San Isidro neighborhood, Sapiens' central thesis revolves around three wood- and charcoal-fired grills dedicated to meat, fish, and vegetables. The business will also be producing its owned cured meats, including an enticing alpaca salami.

'New' Nazca Geoglyph

Excitement hit the famous Nazca Lines in 2020 when a geoglyph in the shape of a cat was discovered by archeologists in the middle of the Covid-19 pandemic. Barely visible and located on a steep hill, the 37m-long figure, thought to date from between 500BC and 200AD, has now been partially restored. Feline symbology was common in Paracas culture and often found on textiles and ceramics.

LISTEN, WATCH & FOLLOW

For inspiration, visit visit www.lonelyplanet.com/peru/articles

Latin America Network Information Center (www.lanic.utexas.edu/la/peru) Diverse, informative links including academic research.

Living in Peru (www.livinginperu.com) An English-language guide with articles and restaurant reviews.

Peru Reports (www.perureports.com) Alternative English-language news.

Peruvian Times (www.peruviantimes.com) The latest news, in English.

FAST FACTS

Food trend Nikkei

Official languages: Spanish, Quechua, Aymara

Life zones 84 (out of 104 worldwide)

Pop 31.8 million

population per sq km

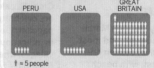

PERU   USA   GREAT BRITAIN

ǂ ≈ 5 people

Taste of the Amazon

Riding on the coattails of Cocina Novoandina, Amazonian food has come in from the jungle and acquired a gourmet touch. The hub of the movement is still in and around the Amazon basin and the Northern Highlands where fried ants and *juane* (rice, meat and egg wrapped in a bijao leaf) are creeping onto gourmet menus.

Month by Month

January

January through March is the busiest (and most expensive) season on the coast, with beach facilities open and festivals rocking. In the mountains and canyons, this is rainy season, best avoided by trekkers and mountaineers.

✯✯ Año Nuevo

New Year's Day, January 1, is particularly big in Huancayo, where a full-blown fiesta continues until Epiphany (January 6).

✯✯ Danza de los Negritos

In the central highlands town of Huánuco, revelers wear costumes with black masks to commemorate slave forefathers who worked the area mines.

✯✯ Fiesta de la Marinera

Trujillo's national dance festival is held during the last week in January, with contest participants decked out in elaborate finery. (p282)

February

The Inca Trail is closed all month. Many Peruvian festivals echo the Roman Catholic calendar and are celebrated with great pageantry, especially in indigenous highland villages, where Catholic feast days are often linked with traditional agricultural festivals.

✯✯ La Virgen de la Candelaria

Held on February 2, this highland fiesta, also known as Candlemas, is particularly colorful around Puno, where folkloric music and dance celebrations last for two weeks.

✯✯ Carnaval

Held on the last few days before Lent (in February or March), this holiday is often celebrated with weeks of water fights, so be warned. It's popular in the highlands – the Cajamarca festival is one of the biggest – and is also busy in the beach towns.

March

Beach resort prices go down and crowds disperse, though the coast remains sunny. Orchids bloom post–rainy season on the Inca Trail and Amazonian birds enact their mating rituals.

✯✯ Verano Negro

A must for anyone with an interest in Afro–Peruvian culture, this festival in Chincha features plenty of music and dancing. It takes place in late February or early March.

✯✯ Fiesta de la Vendimia

A big celebration in the south coast's two main wine regions, Ica and Lunahuaná, these harvest festivals involve some grape stomping.

April

Crowds and high-season prices mark Holy Week, a boon of national tourism in March or April. Hotel prices spike to their highest and availability is low. Reserve well in advance.

🎉 Semana Santa

The week before Easter Sunday, Holy Week is celebrated with spectacular religious processions almost daily; Ayacucho has the biggest celebration in Peru, lasting a full 10 days. Arequipa and Huancayo also have Easter processions.

May

By May the heaviest rains have passed, leaving the highlands lush and green. With the return of drier weather, the trekking season starts to take off in Huaraz and around Cuzco.

🎉 Fiesta de la Cruces

This fascinating religious festival is held on May 3 in various locations including Lima, Apurímac, Ayacucho, Junín, Ica and Cuzco.

🎉 Q'oyoriti

A fascinating indigenous pilgrimage to the holy mountain of Ausangate, outside Cuzco, in May or June. Though known by few outsiders, it's well worth checking out.

🎉 El Señor de Muruhuay

This big annual pilgrimage with an image of a crucified Christ happens in late May – with processions and fireworks to accompany the religious fervor.

June

High season for international tourism runs June through August, with Machu Picchu requiring advance reservations for train tickets and entry.

It's also the busiest time for festivals in and around Cuzco.

🎉 Corpus Christi

Processions of this Catholic celebration in traditional Cuzco are especially dramatic. It's held on the ninth Thursday after Easter.

🎉 Inti Raymi

The Festival of the Sun is the greatest Inca festival, celebrating the winter solstice on June 24. It's certainly the spectacle of the year in Cuzco, attracting thousands of Peruvian and foreign visitors. It's also a big holiday in many jungle towns.

🎉 San Juan

The feast of San Juan is all debauchery in Iquitos, where dancing, feasting and cockfights go on until the wee hours on the eve of the actual holiday of June 24.

🎉 Selvámanos

Reggae, *cumbia* (a Colombian salsa-like dance and musical style) and electronica rock the jungle at this music festival held near Oxapampa in a spectacular national park setting.

🚶 Semana de Andinismo

Mountaineering aficionados descend on the city of Huaraz to celebrate the Andes with hikes, rock climbing, paragliding, skiing and concerts.

🎉 San Pedro y San Pablo

The feasts of Sts Peter and Paul provide more fiestas on June 29, especially

around Lima and in the highlands.

☉ Spot the Marvelous Spatuletail

June is your best opportunity to spot this unique and endangered hummingbird in tracts of forest around the Río Utcubamba valley near Chachapoyas.

July

The continuation of high-season tourism. In Lima the weather is marked by *garúa,* a thick, grey sea mist that lingers over the city for the next few months and brings a chill.

🎉 La Virgen del Carmen

Held on July 16, this holiday is mainly celebrated in the southern sierra – with Paucartambo and Pisac near Cuzco, and Pucará near Lake Titicaca being especially important centers.

🎉 Fiesta del Santiago

Río Mantaro valley towns, especially Huancayo, dress up cattle and parade them through the streets. There's also singing and dancing, in what many believe is an ancient fertility right.

🎉 Fiestas Patrias

The National Independence Days are celebrated nationwide on July 28 and 29; festivities in the southern sierra begin with the Feast of St James on July 25.

August

The last month of high tourist visitation throughout Peru is also typically the most crowded at Machu Picchu. Book reservations for lodging and site tickets well ahead.

🏃 Sierra Andina Mountain Trail

This annual marathon along the Santa Cruz trail to turquoise lakes under snowbound peaks provides hearty athletes with a super-scenic challenge.

🎊 Feast of Santa Rosa de Lima

Commemorating the country's first saint, major processions are held on August 30 in Lima, Arequipa and Junín to honor the patron saint of Lima and of the Americas.

September

Low season everywhere, September and October can still offer good weather to highland trekkers without the crowds, while migrating birds become another attraction for birders.

🍴 Mistura

For one week in September, this massive internationally acclaimed food festival is held in Lima, drawing up to half a million visitors to sample the country's best restaurants and street food.

☆ El Festival Internacional de la Primavera

Not to be missed – the International Spring Festival in Trujillo features supreme displays of horsemanship, as well as dancing and cultural celebrations during the last week of September.

October

The best time to hit the Amazon runs from September to November when drier weather results in better wildlife-watching and easier travel throughout the region.

🏃 Great Amazon River Raft Race

Attracting teams from the world over, the longest raft race in the world flows between Nauta and Iquitos in September or early October.

🎊 La Virgen del Rosario

On October 4, this saint's celebration comes to Lima, Apurímac, Arequipa and Cuzco. Its biggest event is held in Ancash, with a symbolic confrontation between Moors and Christians.

🎊 El Señor de los Milagros

A major religious festival, the Lord of the Miracles celebration is held in Lima on October 18, around which time the bullfighting season starts.

🎊 El Señor de Luren

Travel down to Ica in late October for this religious festival, which is marked by fireworks, processions and plenty of merriment.

November

A good month for festivals, with plenty of events to choose from. It's worth checking out the wild celebrations held in Puno. Waves return, calling all surfers to the coast.

🎊 Todos Santos

All Saints' Day is celebrated on November 1. It's a religious precursor with processions into the following day and Catholic Masses.

🎊 Día de los Muertos

All Souls' Day is celebrated on November 2 with gifts of food, drink and flowers taken to family graves. It's especially colorful in the Andes where some of the 'gift' food and drink is consumed, and the atmosphere is festive rather than somber.

🎊 Puno Week

Starting November 5, this week-long festival involves several days of spectacular costumes and street dancing to celebrate the legendary emergence of the first Inca, Manco Cápac.

December

Beach season returns with warmer Pacific temperatures. Skip the Amazon, where heavy rains start falling from the end of the month through early April.

🎊 Fiesta de la Purísima Concepción

The Feast of the Immaculate Conception on December 8 is a national holiday celebrated with religious processions in honor of the Virgin Mary.

☆ La Virgen del Carmen de Chincha

Frenzied dancing and all-night music in the *peñas* (bars or clubs featuring live folkloric music) of El Carmen on December 27.

Itineraries

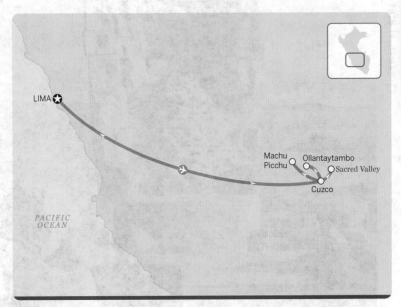

 Greatest Hits Express

This strictly greatest-hits itinerary best suits those with only time enough for a first taste of Peru.

Start your journey in **Lima**; sleep in at cozy Barranco lodgings and find a ceviche restaurant for a leisurely seafood lunch with a touch of pisco. Follow it up by visiting museums in Lima Centro or by renting bikes to pedal the clifftops via the parks of Miraflores.

Fly early the next day to Cuzco, transferring immediately to the lower **Sacred Valley** to acclimatize for several days. Explore the market and ruins of Pisac, tour Moray and Maras, perhaps by mountain bike or on foot. With ancient **Ollantaytambo** as your base, take the train to Aguas Calientes for a day of exploration in the world-famous Inca citadel **Machu Picchu**. From here, take the train to Estación Poroy so you can spend your last day tripping the cobblestones of wonderful **Cuzco**, with museum visits, arts and crafts shops and great restaurants. If you can, squeeze in an evening visit to the planetarium.

Fly back to Lima for your final hurrah, with perhaps a food tour before checking out the club scene before you head back home.

SPARC/SHUTTERSTOCK ©

Top: *Chullpa* (funerary tower), Sillustani (p189)

Bottom: Huacachina (p127)

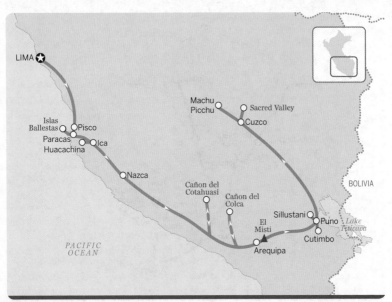

The Gringo Trail

This trip hits some of the preeminent highlights of the continent incorporating an irresistible Peruvian potpourri of ancient ruins, rugged trekking and muscular colonial-era architecture.

Linger briefly in **Lima** before dragging yourself away from the gourmet restaurants and foggy clifftops of Miraflores to journey south to **Pisco** and **Paracas**, where you can boat to the wildlife-rich **Islas Ballestas**, lodging in Paracas. The nearby desert reserve with its archaeological remains and spectacular arid coastline will fill another day of quiet exploration. Then it's on to **Ica**, Peru's wine and pisco capital, and the palm-fringed, dune-lined oasis of **Huacachina**. Famous for sandboarding, this is a good place to overnight. Next is **Nazca** for a flight over the mysterious Nazca Lines.

Turn inland for the 'White City' of **Arequipa**, with its colonial architecture, excellent cuisine and giant monastic complex. Take a bus or car over the 4910m Paso de Patopampa for some trekking in the incredible **Cañon del Colca** with its ancient agricultural terraces or the remote **Cañon del Cotahuasi**, the world's deepest. Alternatively, you can opt to climb **El Misti**, an almost perfectly symmetrical 5822m volcano. Continue upwards to **Puno**, Peru's port on **Lake Titicaca**, the world's highest commercially navigable lake. From here you can boat to traditional islands and explore the strange *chullpas* (ancient funerary towers) at **Sillustani** and **Cutimbo**. It is also possible to make a short (or long) visit to Bolivia by continuing on to the towns and islands on the lake's southern shore.

Wind through the Andes to the former Inca capital of **Cuzco**, South America's oldest continuously inhabited city. Bag a comfortable hotel, browse colorful markets and explore archaeological sites in the **Sacred Valley**, then trek to **Machu Picchu** via an adventurous alternative route. Creative options include a mixture of jungle hiking, mountain biking and even rafting.

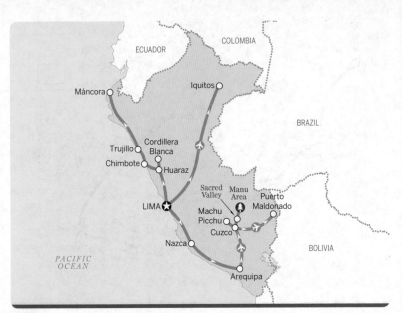

The Best of Peru

If you're set on getting a taste of everything, this whirlwind tour hits Peru's top must-see attractions. Give yourself a full month to take it all in.

Conquer your jet lag by becoming acquainted with the exquisite tastes of Peru in the restaurants of **Lima**, strolling in parks and museums between meals. Head south through the coastal desert for a flyover of the **Nazca Lines** before arriving in stylish, cosmopolitan **Arequipa**, with its mysterious monasteries, deep canyons and smoking volcanoes.

Fly high into the Andes to reach the ancient Inca capital of **Cuzco** for a few days of acclimatization, exploring the cobblestone city and visiting **Sacred Valley** villages to check out colorful markets selling textiles, talismans and dozens of types of tubers. Then board the train to **Machu Picchu**, the most visited archaeological site in South America.

From Cuzco, fly to **Puerto Maldonado** (or brave the 10-hour bus ride) where you can kick back at a wildlife lodge along one of the mighty rivers of the Amazon Basin. Alternatively, take an overland tour from Cuzco to the **Manu area**, with remote tracts of virgin forest holding diverse animals, from kinkajous to caimans; it's one of the most biodiverse areas of the planet. Another option for exploring the Amazonian *selva* (jungle) is to first fly back to Lima, then onward to **Iquitos**, a bustling port that will launch you deeper into the jungle.

Back in Lima, take a bus or fly north to the adventurers' base camp of **Huaraz**, where a short trek will take you to the precipitous peaks of the **Cordillera Blanca**. A day trip to Chavín de Huántar will lead you to one of Peru's oldest ancient sites. Head back down to the coast at **Chimbote**, then dash north to historic **Trujillo**, which offers spicy northern dishes, surrounded by a cornucopia of archaeological sites. These include the ruins of the largest pre-Columbian city in the Americas, Chan Chan, and the fascinating Huacas del Sol y de la Luna. Finish up the journey by taking a seaside break at the bustling surf town of **Máncora**.

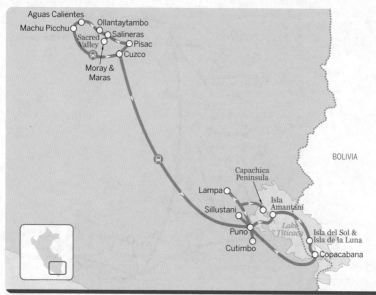

The Inca Heartland

2 WEEKS

Follow this trail to soak in the most potent Inca sites and the altiplano (Andean plateau).

From Lima, fly to Cuzco but travel to the lower **Sacred Valley** to spend your first few days acclimatizing to the altitude. Visit the bustling market of **Pisac**, see the ruins and ride horses at **Moray** and **Maras**. The best accommodations are in the quaint Inca village of **Ollantaytambo**, at a swanky valley resort or area B&B.

From Ollantaytambo, hike the town ruins in the morning or visit the cool salt pans of **Salineras** and take an afternoon train to **Aguas Calientes**. Enjoy a leisurely dinner and go to bed early to take the first bus to the great Inca citadel of **Machu Picchu**.

The following morning, hop on the train to **Cuzco**. Now that you're acclimatized, spend a few days enjoying the charms of this former Inca capital, taking a walking tour, visiting a few museums, admiring the splendors of Qorikancha, the Inca's most spectacular temple, and enjoying the city's outstanding cuisine.

Grab a comfortable tourist bus (or take the historic train) to the altiplano city of **Puno**. If you can coincide with a festival, this is the place to do it, with wild costumes, brass bands and fervent merriment. Otherwise, take in folkloric music at a dinner show or adventure to aquatic accommodations on the retired steamship *Yavari*.

From your base in Puno, the funerary towers of the Colla, Lupaca and Inca cultures can be found at **Sillustani** and **Cutimbo**, an easy day trip, and worth combining with lovely **Lampa** and its historic church. Take a boat tour of **Lake Titicaca**, visiting the famous reed islands and staying overnight in traditional family lodgings on **Isla Amantaní**. If you have a few extra days, take a catamaran tour, which also visits the Bolivian islands of **Isla del Sol** and **Isla de la Luna**, landing you in **Copacabana**, from where you can take a tourist bus back to Puno. Returning to Puno, explore the rural coast of the **Capachica Peninsula**, home to places still steeped in the ancient traditions of the altiplano with nary another traveler in sight.

Get ready for the culture shock of big-city living, and fly back to Lima.

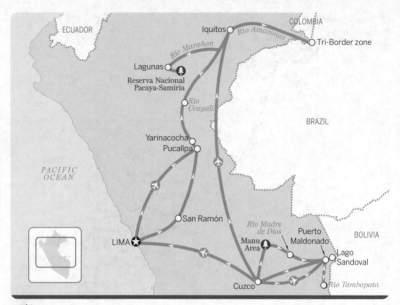

Exploring Amazonia

4 WEEKS

More than half of Peru is jungle, populated by spectacular wildlife and tribal peoples. Go overland and drop dramatically away from the eastern slopes of the Andes to slip deep into the Amazon Basin, which stretches all the way to the Atlantic. This entire itinerary takes a month, or it can be divided by region into one- or two-week segments.

The most popular excursion starts from **Cuzco** and heads to the **Manu area**, itself the size of a small country, albeit one with kingdoms of jungle lodges. Another option is to fly from Cuzco to **Puerto Maldonado** and relax in a thatch-roofed bungalow with a view, either along the **Río Madre de Dios**, the gateway to lovely **Lago Sandoval**, or along the **Río Tambopata**, where a national reserve protects one of the country's largest clay licks. The dry season (July and August) is traditionally the best time to return overland back to Cuzco, although the recent paving of this route means it's now possible outside these months.

Alternatively, return to Lima and turn your focus to the north. The easiest way to get there is to fly from Lima to **Pucallpa**, a city experiencing a resurgence in popularity, and stay in a lodge or a bungalow in the nearby traveler hangout of **Yarinacocha**. The lovely oxbow lake is ringed by tribal villages. You can visit some of these, including those of the matriarchal Shipibo people, renowned for their pottery. Hardcore overland travelers can opt to reach Pucallpa from Lima via a multiday river trip to **San Ramón**, a coffee-growing settlement.

From **Pucallpa**, begin the classic slow riverboat journey north along the **Río Ucayali** to **Iquitos**, the world's largest city with no road access. This northern jungle capital has a buoyant cultural and nightlife scene, a floating market and a bustling port, where you can catch a more comfortable cruise into Peru's largest protected space, **Reserva Nacional Pacaya-Samiria**. You can also access Iquitos flying from Cuzco. It's also tempting to float over into Colombia or Brazil via the unique **Tri-Border Zone**.

It's best to fly if your time is limited; if not, lose yourself for weeks on epic river and road journeys through jungle terrain. Bring bucketloads of patience and self-reliance – and a lot of luck never hurts.

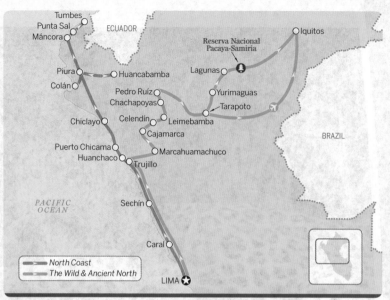

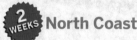

North Coast

2 WEEKS

Explore beaches and ancient civilizations heading toward Ecuador.

Head north from Lima to **Caral**, where South America's oldest known civilization arose. Further north, spy engravings of human sacrifice at **Sechín** and continue to **Trujillo**. Also see the Moche pyramids, the ruins of the once-mighty Chan Chan and the Museo Arqueológico Municipal de Moche. Off the beaches at **Huanchaco** surfers hit the breakers while local fishers trawl the coast. To the north, **Puerto Chicama** boasts one of the world's longest left-hand breaks. The tiny town now has a wonderful new boardwalk overlooking the action.

Then on to **Chiclayo**, with world-class museums showcasing riches from the important archaeological site of Sipán. Craftmarket hub **Piura** boasts great dining, while the witch doctors of **Huancabamba** are tucked into the Andes. Peru's best beaches lie north, with resorts such as **Colán**, **Máncora** and **Punta Sal**; linger here to feast on seafood and dance the balmy nights away.

The journey ends at **Tumbes**, gateway to Ecuador and jumping-off point to Peru's endangered mangrove swamps.

The Wild & Ancient North

2 WEEKS

Explore little-known highland ruins, ending up at the wonders of the Peruvian Amazon.

From **Lima**, head to **Trujillo**, sampling the fiery coastal cuisine and exploring nearby ruins at Chan Chan and Huacas del Sol y de la Luna. From here, take the freshly paved scenic highway to Cajamarca via the mountaintop ruins of **Marcahuamachuco**.

Cajamarca is where the conquistadors captured Inca Atahualpa. In the dry season, travel along the spectacular route to **Celendín** and **Leimebamba** to see the local museum displaying pre-Colombian mummies. Continue on to **Chachapoyas** where the cloud forest obscures the fantastic monolithic fortress of Kuélap.

From Chachapoyas, journey via **Pedro Ruíz** to **Tarapoto**, where you can hike in lush forest to waterfalls. Next, fly to the jungle city of **Iquitos** or continue via **Yurimaguas**, where cargo boats make the rugged two-day trip to Iquitos via the village of **Lagunas**, the western entry point to the **Reserva Nacional Pacaya-Samiria**, for an unforgettable glimpse of the world's greatest river basin. At Iquitos, you can arrange boat trips that go deeper into the rainforest and on to Brazil or Colombia.

Jaguar, Río Tambopata (p2

Plan Your Trip
Peru Outdoors

Scale icy Andean peaks. Raft one of the world's deepest canyons. Surf the heavenly Pacific curlers. Walk the flanks of a smoldering volcano known locally as a living deity. With its breathtaking, diverse landscapes, Peru is a natural adventure hub. So gear up and take the Band-Aids – you're in for one wild ride.

Top Wildlife-Watching Spots

Parque Nacional Manu
Jaguars, tapirs and monkeys inhabit this expansive rainforest park (p468), one of the continent's wildest, deep in the Amazon.

Cañón del Colca
Andean condors glide over this rugged canyon (p166), the second deepest in the world.

Islas Ballestas
Colonies of honking sea lions and penguins claim these rocky Pacific outcrops (p117) off Peru's south coast.

Parque Nacional Huascarán
Giant *Puya raimondii* plants burst with flowers while vicuñas and viscachas bustle around the high alpine landscape of the Cordillera Blanca (p385).

Tumbes
A rare mangrove forest (p365) on the northernmost coast, home to crocodiles, seabirds, flamingos and crabs.

Hiking & Trekking

Pack your hiking boots because the variety of trails in Peru is downright staggering. The main trekking centers are Cuzco and Arequipa in the southern Andes, and Huaraz in the north. Hikers will find many easily accessible trails around Peru's archaeological ruins, which are also the final destinations for more challenging trekking routes.

History goes deep here – you may be hiking through terraced fields along ancient trade routes or trails used by Inca messengers. Yet even then, the fledgling status of some outdoor activities here means that, in certain times and places, you can get a whole mountain, sandy shore or complex of ruins to yourself.

Big plans are in the works for Qhapaq Ñan, the Inca road system which became a World Heritage Site in 2014. It spans a whopping 22,530km from Colombia to Chile and follows one of the most scenic routes possible, proving definitively that the Incas were master road builders. The trail sections above 4000m are in particularly good shape, thanks to a lack of interference. Tourism outfitters hope that the designation will spur investment into these often-neglected trails. **SA Expeditions** (☑ in USA 1-415-549-8049; www.saexpeditions.com) operats a five-day route from Castillo to Huanuco Pampa and plans to add more. Look out for other new trekking opportunities on this route.

Peru's most famous trek is the Inca Trail to Machu Picchu. Limited permits mean this guided-only trek sells out months in advance. For those who haven't planned so far in advance, there are worthwhile alternative routes. In addition, other possibilities around Cuzco include the spectacular six-day trek around the venerated Ausangate (6372m), which will take you over 5000m passes, through huge herds of alpacas and past tiny hamlets unchanged in centuries. Likewise, the isolated Inca site of Choquequirao is another intriguing destination for a trek.

In nearby Arequipa, you can go into some of the world's deepest canyons – the world-famous Cañón del Colca and the Cañón del Cotahuasi. The scenery is guaranteed to knock you off your feet, and it's easier going than some higher altitude destinations. During the wet season, when some Andean trekking routes are impassable, Colca is invitingly lush and green. It's also the best place in Peru for DIY trekking between rural villages. The more remote and rugged Cañón del Cotahuasi is best visited with an experienced local guide and only during the dry season.

Outside Huaraz, the Cordillera Blanca can't be beaten for vistas of rocky, snow-capped mountaintops, while the remote and rugged Cordillera Huayhuash is similarly stunning. The classic and favorite trekking route is the four-day journey from Llanganuco to Santa Cruz, where hardy mountaineers climb the 4760m Punta

RESPONSIBLE TREKKING

➡ Don't depend on open fires. Cook on a lightweight camp stove and dispose of butane cartridges responsibly.

➡ Carry out all rubbish.

➡ Contamination of water sources by human waste can lead to the transmission of diseases. Where there is a toilet, use it. Where there isn't, bury your waste. Dig a small hole 15cm deep and at least 100m from any watercourse. Cover the waste with soil and a rock. Pack out toilet paper.

➡ For washing, use biodegradable soap and a water container at least 50m away from any watercourses. Disperse the waste water widely to allow the soil to filter it fully.

➡ Do not feed the wildlife.

➡ Some trails pass through private property. It's polite to ask residents before crossing their property and to leave all livestock gates as you found them.

➡ Don't give children money, sweets or gifts. This encourages persistent begging, which has become a major problem on some busy routes. If you wish to help, consider donating directly to local schools, NGOs and other volunteer organizations.

➡ Keep a low profile: the gear you are carrying costs more than many locals earn in a month (or a year). Stow everything inside your tent at night.

Union pass, surrounded by ice-clad peaks. Longer treks include the northern route around the dazzling Alpamayo, which requires at least a week. Shorter overnight trips in the area go to mountain base camps, alpine lakes and even along an old Inca road.

Cuzco and Huaraz (and, to a lesser degree, Arequipa) have outfitters that can provide equipment, guides and even *arrieros* (mule drivers). If you prefer to trek ultralight, you might want to purchase your own gear, especially a sleeping bag, as old-generation rental items tend to be heavy. Whether you'll need a guide depends on where you trek. Certain areas of Peru, such as along the Inca Trail, require guides; in other places, such as in the Cordillera Huayhuash, there have been muggings, so it's best to be with a local. Thankfully, scores of other trekking routes are wonderfully DIY. Equip yourself with topographic maps for major routes in the nearest major gateway towns or, better yet, at the Instituto Geográfico Nacional (IGN) or at the South American Explorers Club in Lima.

Whatever adventure you choose, be prepared to spend a few days acclimating to the dizzying altitudes – or face a heavy-duty bout of altitude sickness.

In the Andes, trekking is most rewarding during the dry season (May to September).

Avoid the wet season (December to March), when rain makes some areas impassable.

Mountain, Rock & Ice Climbing

Peru has the highest tropical mountains in the world, offering some absolutely inspired climbs, though acclimatization to altitude is essential. The Cordillera Blanca, with its dozens of snowy peaks exceeding 5000m, is one of South America's top destinations. The Andean town of Huaraz has tour agencies, outfitters, guides, information and climbing equipment for hire. Still, it's best to bring your own gear for serious ascents. Near Huaraz, Ishinca (5530m) and Pisco (5752m) provide two ascents easy enough for relatively inexperienced climbers. For experts, these mountains are also good warm-up climbs for bigger adventures such as Huascarán (6768m), Peru's highest peak. Other challenging peaks include the stunning, knife-edged Alpamayo (5947m) and Yerupajá (6634m), Peru's second-highest mountain, located in the Cordillera Huayhuash. Rock and ice climbing are also taking off around Huaraz, where a few outfitters have indoor climbing walls, rent out technical equipment and organize group trips.

Top: Trekking the
Cordillera Huayhuash
(p393)

Bottom: Machu Picchu
(p259)

In southern Peru, the snowy volcanic peaks around Arequipa can be scaled by determined novice mountaineers. The most popular climb is El Misti (5822m), a site of Inca human sacrifice. Despite its serious altitude, it is basically a very long, tough walk. Chachani (6075m) is one of the easier 6000m peaks in the world – though it still requires crampons, an ice ax and a good guide. Other tempting peaks tower above the Cañón del Colca.

For beginners looking to bag their first serious mountains, Peru may not be the best place to start. Not all guides know the basics of first aid or wilderness search and rescue. Check out a prospective guide's credentials carefully and seek out those who are personally recommended. Carefully check any rental equipment before setting out.

As with trekking, high-elevation climbing is best done during the height of the dry season (mid-June to mid-July).

Rafting, Lunahuaná (p112)

Rafting & Kayaking

Rafting (river running) is growing in popularity around Peru, with trips that range from a few hours to more than two weeks.

Cuzco is the launch point for the greatest variety of rafting options. Choices range from a few hours of mild rafting on the Urubamba to adrenaline-pumping rides on the Santa Teresa to several days on the Apurímac, technically the source of the Amazon (with world-class rafting between May and November). A rafting trip on the Tambopata, available from June through October, tumbles down the eastern slopes of the Andes, culminating in a couple of days of floating in unspoiled rainforest.

Arequipa is another rafting center. Here, the Río Chili is the most frequently run, with a half-day novice trip leaving daily between March and November. Further afield, the more challenging Río Majes features class II and III rapids. On the south coast, Lunahuaná, not far from Lima, is a prime spot for beginners and experts alike. Between December and April, rapids here can reach class IV.

Note that rafting is not regulated in Peru. There are deaths every year and some rivers are so remote that rescues can take days. In addition, some companies are not environmentally responsible and leave camping beaches dirty. Book excursions only with reputable, well-recommended agencies and avoid cut-rate trips. A good operator will have insurance, provide you with a document indicating that they are registered, and have highly experienced guides with certified first-aid training who carry a properly stocked medical kit. Choose one that provides top-notch equipment, including self-bailing rafts, US Coast Guard–approved life jackets, first-class helmets and spare paddles. Many good companies raft rivers accompanied by a kayaker experienced in river rescue.

For more on rafting in Peru, visit www.peruwhitewater.com.

Surfing, Kitesurfing & Paddleboarding

With consistent, uncrowded waves and plenty of remote breaks to explore, Peru has a mixed surfing scene that attracts dedicated locals and international die-hards

Surfers at Playa Lobitos (p357)

alike. Kitesurfing and paddleboarding are also emerging as popular sports.

Waves can be found from the moment you land. All along the southern part of Lima, surfers ride out popular point and beach breaks at Miraflores (known as Wai-kiki), Barranquito and La Herradura. Herradura's outstanding left point break gets crowded when there is a strong swell. In-the-know surfers prefer the smaller crowds further south at Punta Hermosa. International and national championships are held at nearby Punta Rocas as well as Pico Alto, an experts-only 'kamikaze' reef break with some of the largest waves in Peru. Isla San Gallán, off the Península de Paracas, also provides experts with a world-class right-hand point break only accessible by boat; ask local fishers or at hotels.

Peru's north coast has a string of excellent breaks. The most famous is Puerto Chicama, where rides of more than 2km are possible on what's considered the longest left-hand break in the world. Very consistent waves can also be found at Pacasmayo, and outside Chiclayo at Pimentel and Santa Rosa. It's also worth checking out Lobitos and Máncora.

Máncora is a hub for paddleboarding and kitesurfing, which has also caught on in Paracas.

The water is cold from April to mid-December (as low as 15°C/60°F), when wet suits are generally needed. Indeed, many surfers wear wet suits year-round (2/3mm will suffice), even though the water is a little warmer (around 20°C/68°F in the Lima area) from January to March. The far north coast (north of Talara) stays above 21°C (70°F) most of the year.

Though waves are generally not crowded, surfing can be a challenge – facilities are limited and equipment rental is expensive. The scene on the north coast is the most organized, with surf shops and hostels that offer advice, rent boards and arrange surfing day trips. Huanchaco is a great base for these services. Serious surfers should bring their own board.

The best surfing websites include www.peruazul.com, www.vivamancora.com and www.wannasurf.com, with a comprehensive, highly detailed list of just about every break in Peru. Good wave and weather forecasts can be found at www.magicseaweed.com and www.windguru.com.

Sandboarding

Sandboarding down the giant desert dunes is growing in popularity at Huacachina and around Nazca, on Peru's south coast. Nazca's Cerro Blanco (2078m) is among the highest known sand dunes in the world. Some hotels and travel agencies offer tours in *areneros* (dune buggies), where you are hauled to the top of the dunes, then get picked up at the bottom. (Choose your driver carefully; some are notoriously reckless and there has been a fatality.)

For more information on sandboarding worldwide, check out *Sandboard Magazine* at www.sandboard.com.

Mountain Biking & Cycling

Mountain biking is very popular in Peru. It is still a fledgling sport, but there is no shortage of incredible terrain. Single-track trails ranging from easy to expert await mountain bikers outside Huaraz, Arequipa and even Lima. If you're experienced, there are incredible mountain-biking possibilities around the Sacred Valley and downhill trips to the Amazon jungle, all accessible from Cuzco. Easier cycling routes include the wine country around Lunahuaná and in the Cañón del Colca, starting from Chivay.

Mountain-bike rental in Peru tends to be basic; if you are planning on serious biking, it's best to bring your own. (Airline bicycle-carrying policies vary, so shop around.) You'll also need a repair kit and extra parts.

Cycling is popular in Lima, where designated bike lanes in Miraflores and an excellent coastal bike path have made it more accessible than ever.

Swimming

Swimming conditions are ideal along Peru's desert coast from January to March, when the Pacific Ocean waters are warmest and skies are blue. Some of the best spots are just south of Lima. Far more attractive is the stretch of shore on the north coast, especially at laid-back Huanchaco, around Chiclayo and the perennially busy jet-set resorts of Máncora.

Only north of Talara does the water stay warm year-round. Watch for dangerous currents and note that beaches near major coastal cities are often polluted.

Scuba Diving

Scuba diving in Peru is limited. The water is cold except from mid-December to March. During these months the water is at its cloudiest, due to runoff from mountain rivers. Dive shops in Lima offer Professional Association of Diving Instructors (PADI) certification classes, rent scuba equipment and run trips to sea-lion colonies along the coast. Máncora is also a hub for scuba diving.

Horseback Riding

Horse rentals can be arranged in many tourist destinations, but the rental stock is not always treated well, so check your horse carefully before you saddle up. For a real splurge, take a ride on a graceful Peruvian *paso* horse. Descendants of horses with royal Spanish and Moorish lineage, like those ridden by the conquistadors, are reputed to have the world's smoothest gait. Stables around Peru advertise rides for half a day or longer, especially in the Sacred Valley at Urubamba.

Paragliding

Popular paragliding sites include the coastal cliff tops of suburban Miraflores in Lima and various points along the south coast, including Pisco and Paracas. There are few paragliding operators in Peru. Book ahead through the agencies in Lima.

Plan Your Trip
Trekking the Inca Trail

You have pictured its deep, green gorges, the lost citadels and misty peaks that ebb in and out of view. It is nothing less than mind-bending to climb these stone stairways laid millennia ago, following the Andean route that evaded the Spanish for centuries. There is no doubt: trekking the Inca Trail is a traveler's rite of passage. Logistics can be confusing, so preplanning is essential before you get your boots on the trail.

Planning Your Trek
When to Go

Organized groups leave year-round except in February, when the Inca Trail is closed for maintenance and it rains so much that nobody in their right mind goes trekking. The coldest, driest and most popular months are June to August. But those who are well prepared with proper gear can enjoy the trail during any month it's open.

To skip the crowds, consider going before and after the rainy season: from March to May (best vegetation, orchids and birdlife) or September to November.

What to Expect

Even if you are not carrying a full backpack, this trek requires a good level of fitness. In addition to regularly exercising, you can get ready with hikes and long walks in the weeks before your trip (also a good time to test out your gear). Boots should be already worn in before you go. On the trail, you may have to deal with issues such as heat and altitude. Just don't rush; keep a reasonable pace and you should do fine.

Alternative Routes to Machu Picchu
Two-day Inca Trail
A guided overnight route (p46) with the top highlights of the trail. Permits are limited, so book well in advance.

Lares Valley Trek
Best done with a guide, this culturally oriented option (p47) is a flexible multiday trek through quaint Andean villages, combined with train travel from Ollantaytambo to Aguas Calientes.

Salkantay Trek
A scenic, but demanding, five-day hike (p47) that ranges from jungle to alpine terrain, peaking at 4700m. It's possible to do independently or with a guide.

The Inca Jungle Trail
With hiking, biking and rafting options, this guided multisport route (p48) stages to Machu Picchu via Santa Teresa.

Top: Phuyupatamarka (p265)

Bottom: Porters (p47), Inca Trail

BOB POOL/SHUTTERSTOCK ©

Booking Your Trip

It is important to book your trip at least six months in advance for dates between May and August. Outside these months, you may get a permit with a few weeks' notice, but it's very hard to predict. Only licensed operators can get permits, but you can check general availability at www. camino-inca.com.

Consider booking a five-day trip to lessen the pace and enjoy more wildlife and ruins. Other positives include less-crowded campsites and being able to stay at the most scenic one – Phuyupatamarka (3600m) – on the third evening.

Take some time to research your options – you won't regret it. It's best to screen agencies for a good fit before committing. Also make sure you have international travel insurance that covers adventure activities.

Regulations & Fees

The Inca Trail is the only trek in the Cuzco area that cannot be walked independently – you must go with a licensed operator. Prices cost from US$595 to US$6000 and above.

Only 500 people each day (including guides and porters) are allowed to start the trail. Permits are issued to them on a first-come, first-served basis. You will need to provide your passport number to get a permit and carry your passport with you to show at checkpoints along the trail. Be aware that if you get a new passport but had applied for the permit with your old passport, it may present a problem.

Permits are nontransferrable: name changes are not allowed.

Choosing an Inca Trail Operator

While it may be tempting to book your trek quickly and move on to the next item on your to-do list, it's a good idea to examine the options carefully before sending a deposit. If price is your bottom line, keep in mind that the cheapest agencies may cut corners by paying their guides and porters lower wages. Other issues are substandard gear (ie leaky tents) and dull or lackadaisical guiding.

Yet paying more may not mean getting more, especially since international operators take their cut and hire local Peruvian agencies. Talk with a few agencies to get a sense of their quality of service. You might ask if the guide speaks English (fluently or just a little), request a list of what is included and inquire about group size and the kind of transportation used. Ensure that your tour includes a tent, food, a cook, one-day admission to the ruins and the return train fare.

If you have special dietary requirements, state them clearly before the trip and be clear about allergies (versus preference issues). Vegans will meet with a lot of quinoa and lentils. If possible, get confirmation in writing that your specific requirements will be met.

Porters who carry group gear – tents, food etc – are also included. You'll be expected to carry your own personal gear, including sleeping bag. If you are not an experienced backpacker, it may be a good idea to hire a porter to carry your personal gear; this usually costs around US$50 per day for about 10kg.

Part of the fun is meeting travelers from other parts of the world in your trekking group. Keep in mind that individual paces vary and the group dynamic requires some compromise.

For those who prefer more exclusive services, it's possible to organize private trips with an independent licensed guide (US$1250 to US$2000 per person). This can be expensive but for groups of six or more it may in fact be cheaper than the standard group treks. Prices vary considerably, so shop around.

Porter welfare is a major issue in the Cuzco region. Porter laws are enforced through fines and license suspensions by Peru's Ministerio de Trabajo (Ministry of Work).

Lonely Planet only lists operators who haven't been in breach of porter laws at the time of research. Of course, there are other conscientious operators out there, and

WATER TIP

When hiking the Inca Trail, get your next day's water hot in a well-sealed bottle; you can use it as a sleeping bag warmer and it will be cool to drink by the time you're hiking.

some offer other treks and tours around Peru.

Apus Peru (Map p214; ☏084-23-2691; www.apus-peru.com; Cuichipunco 366; ☉9am-1pm & 3-7pm Mon-Sat) A recommended outfitter for the Inca Trail and others, also offering conventional tours. Responsible and popular with travelers. The company joins the Choquequirao trek with the Inca Trail for a total of nine days of spectacular scenery and an ever-more-impressive parade of Inca ruins, culminating in Machu Picchu.

Amazonas Explorer (☏084-25-2846; www.amazonas-explorer.com; Av Collasuyu 910 Miravalle; ☉9am-5pm Mon-Fri) A professional international operator with top-quality equipment and guides, offering rafting trips on the Ríos Apurimac and Tambopata. Also offers trekking the five-day classic and alternative treks. Its two- to 10-day mountain-biking adventures are great for families, with kids' bikes available. Employs socially and environmentally responsible practices.

Aventours (Map p206; ☏084-22-4050; www.aventours.com; Plateros 456; ☉9am-1pm & 4-7pm Mon-Fri) A responsible outfitter with a long-tenured team.

Culturas Peru (Map p206; ☏084-24-3629; www.culturasperu.com; Tandapata 354-A; ☉9am-5pm Mon-Fri) A highly knowledgeable and reputable, locally owned and run outfitter with sustainable practices. Its two-day Inca Trail option is popular.

Mountain Lodges of Peru (☏084-23-6069; www.mountainlodgesofperu.com) Runs luxury lodges in remote trekking locations and offers treks on various routes, including Salkantay and Lares, ending at Machu Picchu. There's no public office. All booking is online or by phone.

Peru Eco Expeditions (☏084-60-7516, 957-349-269; www.peruecoexpeditions.com; Urb San Judas Chico II D-13; ☉9am-4pm Mon-Fri) A small luxury adventure travel company with custom expeditions ranging from day trips to lodge hikes and trips such as the Inca Trail and Rainbow Mountain (with mountain biking or a cultural stop), throughout the region and in the Amazon. Has sustainable tourism practices ranging from filtered water and 100% waste removal on treks to cultural sensitivity toward local communities.

Wayki Trek (Map p204; ☏084-22-4092; www.waykitrek.net; Quera 239; ☉9am-7pm Mon-Fri, to 1pm Sat) A popular Inca Trail outfitter that earns rave reviews. It also does Choquequirao, Salkantay and Ausangate treks. ISO certified.

X-Treme Tourbulencia (Map p206; ☏084-22-5875; www.x-tremetourbulencia.com; Plateros 364; ☉9am-1pm & 4-8pm Mon-Sat) A recommended Cuzco-based tour operator offering multisport access to Machu Picchu via Santa Teresa, the Inca Trail and the Inca Jungle Trail. It also does trips to Ausangate, Salkantay, Choquequirao and a Rainbow Mountain overnight. With multilingual guides.

What to Bring

Trekking poles are highly recommended, as the Inca Trail features a cartilage-crunching number of downhill stone steps. Other items that will come in handy are: a first-aid kit, sunscreen, sandals for camp, a down jacket for cold nights, a waterproof jacket, a warm hat and gloves, sun hat, travel towel, broken-in hiking boots, warm trekking socks, thermal underwear top and bottom, a fleece, water bottle or hydration pack, insect repellent, long pants and sunglasses. Make sure that the weight of your pack is comfortable and that you have enough camera batteries – there are no electrical outlets on the way.

Take cash (in Peruvian soles) for tipping; an adequate amount is S100 for a porter and S200 for a cook.

Alternative Routes to Machu Picchu

For more information on alternative routes to Machu Picchu, the *Alternative Inca Trails Information Packet* from the South American Explorers Club (www.samexplo.org) is a great resource.

Two-Day Inca Trail

This 10km version of the Inca Trail gives a fairly good indication of what the longer trail is like. It's a real workout, and passes through some of the best scenery and most impressive ruins and terracing of the longer trail.

It's a steep three- or four-hour climb from Km 104 to Wiñay Wayna, then another two hours or so on fairly flat terrain to Machu Picchu. You may be on the trail a couple of hours longer, just to enjoy the views and explore. We advise taking the earliest train possible from Cuzco or Ollantaytambo.

The two-day trail means overnighting in Aguas Calientes, and visiting Machu Picchu the next day, so it's really only one day of walking. The average price for this shorter version of the trek is US$400 to US$535.

Lares Valley Trek

This is not a specific track as such, but a walk along any of a number of different routes to Ollantaytambo through the dramatic Lares Valley. Starting at natural hot springs, the route wanders through rural Andean farming villages, lesser known Inca archaeological sites, lush lagoons and river gorges. You'll finish by taking the train from Ollantaytambo to Aguas Calientes. Although this is more of a cultural trek than a technical trip, the mountain scenery is breathtaking, and the highest mountain pass (4450m) is certainly nothing to sneeze at.

Salkantay Trek

A longer, more spectacular trek, with a slightly more difficult approach to Machu Picchu than the Inca Trail. Its highest point is a high pass of over 4700m near the magnificent glacier-clad peak of Salkantay (6271m; 'Savage Mountain' in Quechua). From here you descend in spectacular fashion to the vertiginous valleys of the subtropics. It takes five to seven days to get to Machu Picchu.

For a luxury approach, **Mountain Lodges of Peru** (☏84-26-2640; www.mountainlodgesofperu.com) offers high-quality guiding with accommodations in comfortable lodges with outdoor hot tubs. Prices vary according to high and low seasons.

PLAN YOUR TRIP TREKKING THE INCA TRAIL

PORTER WELFARE

In the past, Inca Trail porters have faced excessively low pay, enormous carrying loads and poor working conditions. Relatively recent laws now stipulate a minimum payment of S170 to porters, adequate sleeping gear and food, and treatment for on-the-job injuries. At checkpoints on the trail, porter loads are weighed (each is allowed 20kg of group gear and 5kg of their own gear).

Yet there is still room for improvement and the best way to help is to choose your outfitter wisely. Conscientious operators do exist, but only a few are confident enough to charge the price that a well-equipped, well-organized, well-guided trip requires. A quality trip will set you back at least US$595. The cheaper trips cut costs and often affect porter welfare – on the Inca Trail and other trekking routes. Go with a well-recommended company.

There's more you can do on the trail:

➡ Don't overpack. Someone will have to carry the extra weight and porters may have to leave their own essential gear behind.

➡ Don't occupy the dining tent until late in the evening if it's where the porters sleep.

➡ Tip the cooks if you liked the food, and always tip your porters.

➡ Tip individuals directly in Peruvian soles. Don't leave it to the company or a guide to distribute tips.

➡ If you don't plan to use your gear again, items such as good sleeping bags are like gold to porters. Warm jackets, pocket tools and headlamps also make thoughtful end-of-trip tips.

➡ If you don't like what you see, complain to your guide and to the agency, and register an official complaint with iPerú (www.peru.info), either at a branch or online.

Though guides and outfitters are subject to annual review, it can take time to deactivate a company that has acted irresponsibly. It is important for trekkers to give feedback. To learn more about the life of porters, look for the documentary *Mi Chacra*, winner of the 2011 Banff Film Festival Grand Prize.

Inca Jungle Trail: Back Door to Machu Picchu

Dreamed up by outfitters and guides, this multisport route between Cuzco and Machu Picchu travels via Santa Teresa with options to bike, hike and raft your way in two to five days. Some call it 'Machu Picchu via the back door.' The number of days and activities vary, but the backbone of tours on offer is the same.

The trip starts with a long, four- to five-hour drive from Cuzco to Abra Málaga – the high (4350m) pass between Ollantaytambo and the Amazon Basin. Somewhere on the Amazon side you'll board mountain bikes for the long ride down to Santa María. Starting on a paved road that turns to dirt after about 20km, it's an incredibly scenic descent from the glacial to the tropical, up to 71km total.

Some operators walk the 23km from Santa María to Santa Teresa; others send you by vehicle (one hour), arguing that it's not a particularly interesting hike, though there is a short section of preconquest *camino de hierro* (iron road) – the Inca version of a superhighway.

Either way you'll arrive in Santa Teresa to the welcome spectacle of the Cocalmayo hot springs. Some companies include rafting near Santa Teresa or the ziplines at Cola de Mono.

From Santa Teresa, you can walk the 20km to Machu Picchu, 12km of it along train tracks. There's nice river scenery but no particular attraction and it's usually dusty and hot. Alternatively, you can catch a bus and a train. You may reverse this route to get back to Cuzco, but it's much quicker to catch the train via the Sacred Valley.

Many varieties of this trip exist, and bare-bones versions may not include hotels or entry fees, so read the fine print. Whether you stay in a tent or a hostel, key factors in the trip price are bike quality, professional English-speaking guides and whether you walk or catch the train to Aguas Calientes. Three-day/two-night trips start from US$465, and usually include a guided tour of Machu Picchu and return train ticket to Ollantaytambo.

Gravity Peru (p218) offers the best-quality bikes. Other respected operators include Reserv Cusco (p222) and X-Treme Tourbulencia (p46).

Plan Your Trip
Family Travel

Traveling to Peru with children can bring some distinct advantages. It is a family-oriented society, and children are treasured. For parents, it makes an easy conversation starter with locals and helps break down cultural barriers. In turn, Peru can be a great place for kids, with plenty of opportunities to explore and interact.

Peru for Kids

Peru is welcoming for kids, though it's best to take all the usual travel precautions. And be sure they have the appropriate vaccinations. Children will often get free or reduced admission rates at events and performances.

Practicalities

Public Transportation Kids are welcome on public transportation. Often someone will give up a seat for a parent and child or offer to put your child on their lap. On buses, children aren't normally charged if they sit on their parent's lap.

Driving Car seats are not widely available with rental cars so it is best to bring one with you.

Expecting & New Mothers Expecting mothers enjoy a boon of special parking spaces and grocery store lines. Breastfeeding in public is not uncommon, but most women discreetly cover themselves.

Babysitting Babysitting services or children's activity clubs tend to be limited to upmarket hotels and resorts.

Public Toilets In general, public toilets are poorly maintained. Always carry toilet paper. While a woman may take a young boy into the ladies' room, it is socially unacceptable for a man to take a girl into the men's room.

Flights Children under the age of 12 may receive discounts on airline travel, while infants under two

Best Regions for Kids

Lima
Kids like the Parque del Amor, Circuito Mágico del Agua, visiting markets and joining outdoor family events.

Cuzco & the Sacred Valley
Whether exploring the narrow passageways of the ancient city of Cuzco, visiting a traditional market or climbing high on the Via Ferrata, there's something here for all ages.

The Coast
Seaside resorts, such as Paracas and Huanchaco, provide beach fun and some surf. A gentle, sunny climate helps keep your plans on target.

Machu Picchu
What could be more intriguing for teens than the mysteries of the Incas? Nearby, smaller sites such as Ollantaytambo, Pisac and Maras also make for exciting explorations.

pay only 10% of the fare provided they sit on their parent's lap.

Health & Safety

The main issue in Peru is diet. Drink only filtered/bottled water. It's also best to avoid raw vegetables unless you are assured they have been properly prepared. When traveling with young children, be particularly careful about their diet, as diarrhea can be especially dangerous for them. Children under two years of age are particularly vulnerable to Hepatitis A and typhoid fever, which can be contracted via contaminated food or water, as they are too young to be vaccinated against them.

Sun exposure can be dangerous, particularly at high altitudes, so make sure kids are adequately covered up and use sunscreen. Altitude sickness can also be an issue, so it's important that the family acclimates slowly. Taking children aged under three to high altitudes is not recommended. Consult your doctor on how to help kids cope with altitude sickness.

Children under nine months should not be taken to lower altitude jungle areas because the yellow-fever vaccine is not safe for this age group.

All travelers to malaria-endemic countries (such as Peru) should visit their physician to obtain appropriate chemoprophylaxis based on their travel risk factors and age. Current guidelines suggest mefloquine, doxycycline and atovaquone-proguanil for travel to Peru, and all of these can be taken by children, with some limitations based on age and drug formulations. Some of these drugs need to be started two weeks before arrival in the country, so plan accordingly.

DEET-containing insect repellents can be used safely, but in concentrations of no higher than 30% for children according to the American Academy of Pediatrics (adults can safely use DEET concentrations of 50%). Insect repellents are not recommended for infants younger than two months of age; use an infant carrier drape with mosquito netting instead.

Since street dogs are common, it's best to be up to date with rabies vaccinations. Most dogs are mild-mannered, but avoid those that seem aggressive.

Dining

While restaurants don't offer special kids' meals, most offer a variety of dishes suitable for children or may accommodate a special request. You can always order food *sin picante* (without spice). It is perfectly acceptable to split a dish between two children or an adult and a child. Don't wait to eat until everyone is too hungry – service can be quite slow. High chairs are available in some larger restaurants.

Adventure

Routine travel, such as train rides or jungle canoe trips, can amount to adventure for kids. In rural areas, community tourism is a great option. Many of the activities aimed at adults can be scaled down for children. Activities such as guided horseback rides and canyoning often have age limits (usually eight and up), but are invariably OK for teenagers. Some rivers may be suitable for children to float or raft; make sure outfitters have life vests and wet suits in appropriate sizes.

Children's Highlights

Adventure

Rafting near Cuzco (p217) Kids enjoy splashing out on the tamer whitewater sections.

Cusco for You, Andean foothills (p246) Horseback riding in the Sacred Valley is ideal for older kids.

La Calera, Cañón del Colca (p169) Splash about in these hot pools.

Action Valley, Sacred Valley (p219) Fun on canopy ziplines.

Mirabici, Lima coast (p77) Cycling the coastal paths of Miraflores.

Kuélap (p431) Ruins galore to explore.

Parque Nacional Manu (p468) Spying wildlife in the Amazon.

Entertainment

Isla Taquile (p192) Stay with a host family on Lake Titicaca.

Festivals throughout Peru Traditional fiestas feature street dancing, parades and merriment.

Sandboarding, Huacachina (p127) These giant dunes make for exhilarating desert fun.

Dining

Quintas in Highland Cities These places serving Andean food have oversized grills and backyard ambience.

Picnics throughout Peru Stock up at a bakery and find a rocky outcrop with a view to the world.

Rainy Day Refuges

Ludotecas in Lima and larger cities Educational centers for children.

Choco Museo Kids can make, decorate and consume their own chocolates in Lima (p61) and Cuzco (p219)

Planning
When to Go

Summer (between December and February) offers the most opportunities for good weather and beach fun, though the coast is enjoyed year-round. Avoid the highlands during the rainiest months (December to March). The highland dry season, between June and August, is ideal for exploring Cuzco and Machu Picchu, though these are also the busiest times.

Accommodations

Most midrange and top-end hotels will have reduced rates for children under 12 years of age, provided the child shares a room with parents. Cots are not normally available, except at the most exclusive hotels. Cabins or apartments, more common in beach destinations, usually make a good choice with options for self-catering.

What to Pack or Rent

➡ If you're traveling with an infant, stock up on diapers (nappies) in Lima or other major cities

before heading to rural areas. Also pack infant medicines, a thermometer and, of course, a favorite toy. Formula and baby food are easily found.

➡ It's handy to have hand sanitizer, as bathrooms may lack soap.

➡ Bring your favorite insect repellent; it's available here but nontoxic items are harder to find.

➡ It's a good idea to have diarrhea medication, just in case.

➡ Kids should have comfortable outdoor clothing, a bathing suit, hats for the sun, a shell jacket and warm clothing for chilly days and nights. Before your trip, make sure everyone has adequate, broken-in shoes. Sandals can also be useful for the coast.

➡ A cheap digital camera or a pair of binoculars can provide lots of entertainment.

➡ It's possible to rent children's bikes with helmets, as well as surf gear.

➡ Strollers are unlikely to be convenient in most places beyond cities.

➡ Baby backpacks are handy for market visits or getting onto the trails with tots or babies over six months old.

➡ Consider carefully the need to bring electronic games, iPads and laptops – they're bound to attract a lot of attention if used in public; it's probably best to limit their use to the hotel.

Before You Go

Keep the kids in mind as you plan your itinerary or include them in the trip planning from the get-go. If renting a car, ask ahead if you can book a child's seat, as they are not always available. For all-round information and advice, check out Lonely Planet's *Travel with Children*.

It's not necessary to be tied down to a schedule while traveling in Peru; plenty of activities can be booked just a few days in advance.

Regions at a Glance

Across its parched coastal desert, jagged Andean peaks and the lush expanse of the Amazon rainforest, the regions of Peru have cultures and landscapes brimming with diversity. In Lima, urban life is among the most sophisticated on the continent. In the provinces and remote areas, communities still follow age-old traditions. Within this dazzling cultural mosaic, solemn pilgrimages honor gods both Christian and indigenous, neon clubs pulse with reveling youth, and ancient ruins lead us back to prehistory. And then there is Peruvian cuisine – sublime creations that alter with the landscape, made with native ingredients and contemporary preparations. Welcome to Peru – it's a real blast to the senses.

Lima

Food
Culture
Nightlife

Novoandina & Beyond

Lima's signature pan-cultural cuisine introduces fresh, indigenous ingredients to sophisticated dishes. Join the half million attending prestigious food festival Mistura, held annually in September.

From Clubs to Catacombs

Founded in the 15th century, Lima has culture in spades, from colonial catacombs and museums to clubs and galleries and design boutiques in funky Barranco.

La Noche

When the sun sets behind the Pacific and a million lights switch on, it's time to enjoy some Latin nightlife. Start with a pisco sour in a weathered bar or a velvet lounge. Later, shake it till the wee hours to *cumbia*, house, techno, Latin rock or *reggaetón*.

p57

South Coast

History
Adventure
Wine

Marked by Legacy

Two pre-Inca civilizations stamped their presence here: Nazca etched geoglyphs into the desert south of Ica while Paracas buried intricate textiles in necropolises near Pisco.

Adrenaline Fix

There's excellent river rafting in Lunahuaná, and sandboarding in Huacachina and Cerro Blanco, the latter one of the world's tallest sand dune. Surfers can rent a 4WD to discover unchartered breaks.

Desert Vineyards

Peru's best grapes grow in its well-irrigated southern desert. Beyond the wine and pisco capital of Ica there are decent wineries in Lunahuaná, close to Lima, and Moquegua, south of Arequipa.

p109

Arequipa & Canyon Country

Trekking
Architecture
Food

Cañón del Colca

For many, trekking in Peru begins and ends on the Inca Trail. But if the crowds make you claustrophobic, come to the spectacular, isolated trails of Colca and Cotahuasi canyons.

The White City

Arequipa is touted as one of the best-preserved Spanish colonial cities in the Americas, crafted uniquely out of white volcanic *sillar* rock. Less heralded are the exquisitely preserved baroque churches in Colca Canyon villages.

La Picantería

Long before Gastón Acurio, Arequipa was fusing Quechua, Spanish and Chinese influences to concoct a unique hybrid cuisine best showcased in the city's traditional restaurants.

p145

Lake Titicaca

Festivals
Culture
Detouring

Like a Virgin

With wild costumes and more than 300 traditional dances, Puno knows festivals. La Virgen de la Candelaria (celebrated February 2) honors the city's patron virgin with a thunderous street party that's the event of the year.

Reed Islands

Community tourism is the best way to understand life on this great blue expanse almost 4000m high. Islanders live in another dimension – from the surreal reed-made Uros to the rural rhythms of Isla Amantani.

Remote Titicaca

Splurge on a visit to the nature preserve of Isla Suasi or spend a few days in rural homestays on the lakeshore to experience timeless Titicaca.

p177

Cuzco & the Sacred Valley

Ruins
Adventure
Culture

Historic Sacred Valley

Overnight in Pisac or Ollantaytambo for full immersion in the Andean culture before the grand finale of Machu Picchu.

High Andean Escapades

Whiz from the high Andes to the jungle on a mountain bike, ascend sheer rock on the via ferrata (iron way) or trek the wilderness around Ausangate. Cuzco rivals Huaraz as Peru's adventure center.

The Quechua World

Inca culture permeates the relics, but living indigenous cultures have just as much of an impact on modern-day Peru. Engage in community tourism, join the fervor of a festival or do Lares trek through remote Andean villages.

p203

Central Highlands

Architecture
Detouring
Festivals

Colonial Backroads

Ayacucho and Huancavelica offer insight into Peru's colonial past. While they lack preservation funds, they haven't been spoiled by Western chain stores either: wander ancient streets and be transported back in time.

Forgotten Andes

Discover the Andes of the good old days: adventure through spectacular gorges on wheezing buses along abysmal roads to cities and ruins seldom seen by tourists.

Holy Week Revelry

Here they take revelry seriously – one valley has a festival every day. Don't miss South America's best Semana Santa (Holy Week) celebrations and the party towns of Río Mantaro.

p277

North Coast

Ruins
Food
Beaches

Civilizations in the Sand

It's not hard to channel your inner Indiana Jones along Peru's north coast, where under nearly every grain of sand this sweeping dune desertscape reveals yet another largely intact ruin.

Ceviche Satisfaction

There's no better stretch of sand for a seafood crusade. Don't miss Peru's iconic dish, ceviche (raw fish marinated in citrus and chili), a major player in the country's gastronomic renaissance.

Big Breaks, Soft Sands

Take on some of South America's best breaks at Lobitos and Puerto Chicama before hitting the beaches of Vichayito and Punta Sal near Mancora for some serious relaxation.

p317

Huaraz & the Cordilleras

Trekking
Outdoors
Ruins

Peru's Trekking Capital

The majestic peaks of the Blanca, Negra and Huayhuash *cordilleras* host the most iconic trails in South America. There is a vast array of treks through with postcard-perfect scenery.

Aire Libre

Beyond trekking, these stately mountains offer a bounty of open-air adventures that range from casual mountain biking, horseback riding and rock climbing to ice climbing and mountaineering endeavors.

Chavín de Huántar

The Unesco ruins at Chavín de Huántar are among Peru's most important and fascinating prehistoric sites, so break up your outdoor lovefest to explore the wonders of this ancient culture.

p371

Northern Highlands

Nature
Ruins
Food

Back to Nature

From the impressive 771m Gocta waterfall to birding opportunities galore and numerous new nature lodges, the Northern Highlands has some of Peru's most impressive landscapes.

Kuélap

Second only to Machu Picchu in awesomeness, the excellently preserved ruins of Kuélap, tucked away in misty cloud forest near Chachapoyas, is reason alone to venture into this neck of the woods.

Lowland Flavors

Jungle-influenced recipes of Tarapoto and Chachapoyas offer original flavors, only just finding their way to renowned Lima restaurants. Wash them down with regional elixirs soaked in wild roots and vines.

p411

Amazon Basin

Adventure
Wildlife
Festivals

Dugout Explorations

Trekking amid foliage so thick you have to slice through it; navigating rivers in dugout canoes like 17th-century explorers; soaring through the canopy on ziplines – it's hard *not* to have an adventure.

Elusive Animals

It's not just anacondas or giant creepy-crawlies, nor is it rose-colored river dolphins, the scarlet flash of cock of the rocks found only in Manu's cloud forests, or jaguars – the search for these creatures makes for one wild adventure.

Hot Celebrations

The Amazon's two premier parties are among Peru's best – conveniently occurring within a week of each other in June: San Juan (Iquitos) and Selvámanos (Oxapampa).

p447

On the
Road

AT A GLANCE

POPULATION
9.75 million

OLDEST HOUSE IN LIMA
Casa Aliaga (p65)

BEST PRE-COLUMBIAN CERAMICS
Museo Larco (p73)

BEST RELIGIOUS BUILDING
Iglesia de Santo Domingo (p65)

BEST PISCO COCKTAILS
Museo del Pisco (p96)

WHEN TO GO
Year-round
A mild and dry climate means comfortable capital visits year-round.

Dec–Mar
The hottest, blue-sky months are ideal for surf and sun on the coast.

Late Aug
Colorful processions mark the festival of Santa Rosa de Lima, the country's first saint.

Miraflores (p69), Lima
<CHRISTIAN VINCES/SHUTTERSTOCK ©

Lima

This capital rises above a long coastline of crumbling cliffs. To enjoy it, climb on the wave of chaos that spans high-rise condos built alongside pre-Columbian temples and fast Pacific breakers rolling toward noisy traffic snarl-ups. Lima is also sophisticated, with a civilization that dates back millennia. Stately museums display sublime pottery; galleries debut edgy art; solemn religious processions recall the 18th century and nightclubs dispense tropical beats. No visitor can miss the capital's culinary genius, part of a gastronomic revolution more than 400 years in the making. This is Lima. Shrouded in history (and sometimes fog), gloriously messy and full of aesthetic delights. Don't even think of missing it.

Lima Highlights

❶ Miraflores dining (p89) Biting into Peruvian delicacies at these innovative restaurants.

❷ Barranco nightlife (p96) Sipping potent pisco (Peruvian grape brandy) cocktails at vintage bars, refurbished mansions and chic lounges.

❸ Museo Larco (p73) Admiring pre-Columbian masterpieces, from sublime tapestries to intricate goldwork.

❹ Pachacamac (p106) Exploring sandy ruins with several civilizations' worth of temples.

❺ Paragliding (p77) Leaping off the Miraflores cliff tops and soaring among the high-rises with the Pacific Ocean filling the horizon.

❻ Iglesia de Santo Domingo (p65) Gazing upon the skulls of some of Latin America's most celebrated saints at this historic church.

❼ Coastal parks (p76) Strolling or cycling the lush cliff tops of Miraflores.

❽ Food tours (p80) Discovering the flavors of Peru, one market and one mouthful at a time.

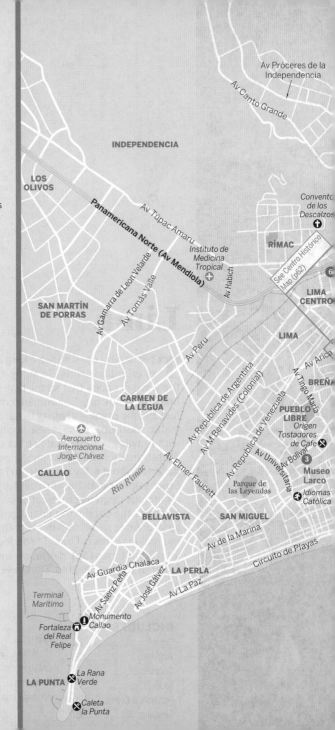

History

As ancient as it is new, Lima has survived apocalyptic earthquakes, warfare and the rise and fall of civilizations. This resilient city has welcomed a rebirth after each destruction. In pre-Hispanic times, the area served as an urban center for the Lima, Wari, Ichsma and the Inca cultures in different periods.

When Spanish conquistador Francisco Pizarro sketched out the boundaries of his 'City of Kings' in 1535, there were roughly 200,000 indigenous people living in the area. By the 18th century, the Spaniards' tumbledown village of adobe and wood had given way to a viceregal capital, where fleets of ships arrived to transport the golden spoils of conquest back to Europe. After a disastrous earthquake wiped out much of the city in 1746, it was rebuilt with splendorous baroque churches and ample *casonas* (large houses). The city's prominence began to fade after independence in 1821, when other urban centers were crowned capitals of newly independent states.

In 1880 Lima was ransacked and occupied by the Chilean military during the War of the Pacific (1879–83). As part of the pillage, the Chileans made off with thousands of tomes from the National Library (they were returned in 2007). Postwar expansion meant that by the 1920s Lima was crisscrossed by a network of broad boulevards inspired by Parisian urban design. When another devastating earthquake struck in 1940, the city again had to rebuild.

By the mid-1900s the population was growing exponentially. An influx of people from rural areas took the metro area from 661,000 inhabitants in 1940 to 8.5 million by 2007. The migration was particularly intense during the 1980s, when armed conflicts in the Andes displaced many people. Shantytowns mushroomed, crime soared and the city fell into a period of steep decay. In 1992 the terrorist group Sendero Luminoso (Shining Path) detonated deadly truck bombs in middle-class Miraflores, marking one of Lima's darkest hours.

Today's Lima has been rebuilt to an astonishing degree. A robust economy and a vast array of municipal improvement efforts have repaved the streets, refurbished parks and created safer public areas to bring back a thriving cultural and culinary life.

◉ Sights

The majority of museums are located in the busy downtown area of Central Lima. If you have a few days here, try visiting them on a weekend morning when traffic is calmer. The neighborhoods of Miraflores and Barranco can be walked in their entirety, and there are pleasant parks and seaside walks to retreat to when you've had your fill of urban attractions.

◉ Lima Centro

The city's historic heart, Lima Centro (Central Lima) is a grid of crowded streets laid out in the 16th-century days of Francisco Pizarro, and home to most of the city's surviving colonial architecture.

Bustling narrow streets are lined with ornate baroque churches in Lima's historic and commercial center, located on the south bank of the Río Rímac. Few colonial mansions remain, as many have been lost to expansion, earthquakes and the perennially moist weather. The best access to the Plaza de Armas is the pedestrian-only street Jirón de la Unión.

Plaza de Armas   PLAZA
(Map p62) Lima's 140-sq-meter Plaza de Armas, also called the Plaza Mayor, was not only the heart of the 16th-century settlement established by Francisco Pizarro, it was a center of the Spaniards' continent-wide empire. Though not one original building remains, at the center of the plaza is an impressive bronze fountain erected in 1650.

Surrounding the plaza are a number of significant public buildings: to the east is the Palacio Arzobispal (Archbishop's Palace; Map p62), built in 1924 in a colonial style and boasting some of the most exquisite Moorish-style balconies in the city. To the northeast is the block-long Palacio de Gobierno.

Palacio de Gobierno   PALACE
(Map p62; ☏ 01-311-3908; www.presidencia.gob. pe; Plaza de Armas; ⊘ tours 9am & 9:45am Sat & Sun) This grandiose baroque-style building from 1937 serves as the residence of Peru's president. Out front stands a handsomely uniformed presidential guard (think French Foreign Legion, c 1900) that changes every day at noon – a ceremonious affair that involves slow-motion goose-stepping and the sublime sounds of a brass band playing 'El Cóndor Pasa' as a military march.

LIMA IN...

Two Days

Start with a **walking tour** (p72) of the city's colonial heart. For lunch, try *chifa* at **Wa Lok** (p87). Afterwards, browse the Chancay pottery inside a pristine historic mansion at the **Museo Andrés del Castillo** (p67) and go for happy-hour pisco cocktails at **Museo del Pisco** (p96). If you've lingered long enough you can see **El Circuito Mágico del Agua** (p67) lit up.

On the second day, go pre-Columbian or contemporary: view breathtaking textiles at the **Fundacíon Museo Amano** (p69) or see a gripping exhibit on the Internal Conflict at the **Museo de la Nación** (p68). Sate your ceviche cravings at **La Mar** (p93), then grab espresso drinks from **Cafe Bisetti** (p94) to stroll through the cliff-top gardens of **Barranco** (p71); or visit **Huaca Pucllana** (p70), the centuries-old adobe temple in the middle of Miraflores. Reboot and spend the evening sampling *novoandina* (nouvelle cuisine) at one of the city's many fine restaurants.

Three Days

In the morning, visit Barranco's exquisite **Museo Pedro de Osma** (p73), which has intriguing Cuzco School canvases and relics from the viceroyalty. Lunch at **Isolina** (p95) or **Colonia & Co** (p95) before browsing through neighborhood galleries and boutiques. Option B: a day trip to **Pachacamac** (p106) to stroll among arid ruins dating back almost two millennia.

The palace is open on weekends for two morning tours that require advance reservation. Book by calling the Office of Tourism (Map p62; ☎01-311-3908; www.presidencia.gob.pe; ⊙visits 9-11am Sat & Sun) between Monday and Thursday. Visitors must bring a valid ID.

Choco Museo   MUSEUM
(Map p62; www.chocomuseo.com/peru; Jirón & Peatonal Carabaya; 45min workshops S50) Housed in a historic 16th-century building where liberator of Peru General San Martín once slept, this cacao museum, with other outlets around the city, offers chocolate-making workshops and sells organic and fair-trade treats.

La Catedral de Lima   CHURCH
(Map p62; ☎01-427-9647; Plaza Mayor s/n; museum S10; ⊙9am-5pm Mon-Fri, 10am-1pm Sat) Next to the Palacio Arzobispal, the cathedral resides on the plot of land that Pizarro designated for the city's first church in 1535. Though it retains a baroque facade, the building has been built and rebuilt numerous times: in 1551, in 1622 and after the earthquakes of 1687 and 1746. The last major restoration was in 1940.

A craze for all things neoclassical in the late 18th century left much of the interior (and the interiors of many Lima churches) stripped of its elaborate baroque decor. Even so, there is plenty to see. The various chapels along the nave display more than a dozen altars carved in every imaginable style, and the ornate wood choir, produced by Pedro de Noguera in the early 17th century, is a masterpiece of rococo sculpture. A museum, in the rear, features paintings, vestments and an intricate sacristy.

By the cathedral's main door is the mosaic-covered chapel with the remains of Pizarro. The authenticity of the remains came into question in 1977, after workers cleaning out a crypt discovered several bodies and a sealed lead box containing a skull that bore the inscription, 'Here is the head of the gentleman Marquis Don Francisco Pizarro, who found and conquered the kingdom of Peru..' After a battery of tests in the 1980s, a US forensic scientist concluded that the body previously on display was of an unknown official and that the brutally stabbed and headless body from the crypt was Pizarro's. The head and body were reunited and transferred to the chapel, where you can also view the inscribed lead box.

Guide services in Spanish, English, French, Italian and Portuguese are available for an additional fee.

Parque de la Muralla   PARK
(Map p62; Amazonas, btwn Lampa & Av Abancay; ⊙9am-9pm) During the 17th century, the heart of Lima was ringed by a *muralla* (city wall), much of which was torn down in the 1870s as the city expanded. However, you

Centro Histórico

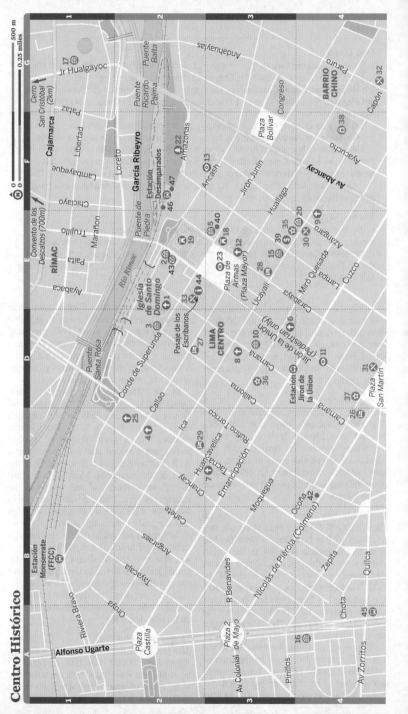

500 m
0.25 miles

Alfonso Ugarte

Plaza Castilla

Plaza 2 de Mayo

Plaza San Martín

Estación Monserrate (FFCC)

Río Rímac

Iglesia de Santo Domingo

Pasaje de los Escribanos

LIMA CENTRO

Plaza de Armas (Plaza Mayor)

RÍMAC

Convento de los Descalzos (700m)

Cerro San Cristóbal (2km)

Cajamarca

García Ribeyro

Estación Desamparados

BARRIO CHINO

Plaza Bolívar

Jiron de la Unión (Pedestrian only)

Estación Jiron de la Union

Puente Santa Rosa

Puente de Piedra

Puente Ricardo Palma

Puente Balta

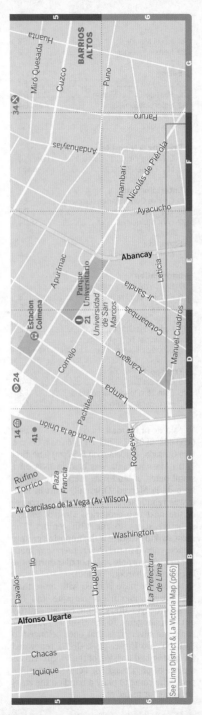

can view a set of excavated remains at the Parque de la Muralla, where, in addition to the wall, a small on-site **museum** (with erratic hours) details the development of the city and holds a few objects.

The park features a bronze **statue** of Francisco Pizarro created by American sculptor Ramsey MacDonald in the early 20th century. The figure once commanded center stage at the Plaza de Armas, but over the years has been displaced as attitudes toward Pizarro have grown critical. The best part: the figure isn't even Pizarro – it's an anonymous conquistador of the sculptor's invention. MacDonald made three copies of the statue. One was erected in the US; the other in Spain. The third was donated to the city of Lima after the artist's death in 1934 (and after Mexico rejected it). So now, Pizarro – or, more accurately, his proxy – sits at the edge of this park, a silent witness to a daily parade of amorous Peruvian teens.

Monasterio de San Francisco   MONASTERY
(Map p62; ☑ 01-426-7377, ext 300; www.museo catacumbas.com; cnr Lampa & Ancash; adult/child under 15 S15/3; ⊙ 9am-8pm) This bright-yellow Franciscan monastery and church is most famous for its bone-lined **catacombs** (containing an estimated 70,000 remains) and its remarkable **library** housing 25,000 antique texts, some of which pre-date the conquest. Admission includes a 30-minute guided tour in English or Spanish. Tours leave as groups gather.

This baroque structure has many other treasures: the most spectacular is a geometric Moorish-style **cupola** over the main staircase, which was carved in 1625 out of Nicaraguan cedar and restored in 1969. In addition, the **refectory** contains 13 paintings of the biblical patriarch Jacob and his 12 sons, attributed to the studio of Spanish master Francisco de Zurbarán.

Iglesia de San Pedro   CHURCH
(Map p62; ☑ 01-428-3010; www.sanpedrode lima.org; cnr Azángaro & Ucayali; ⊙ 8am-noon & 5-8pm Mon-Sat) This small 17th-century church is considered to be one of the finest examples of baroque colonial-era architecture in Lima. Consecrated by the Jesuits in 1638, it has changed little since. The interior is sumptuously decorated with gilded altars, Moorish-style carvings and glazed tiles.

Centro Histórico

Museo Central   MUSEUM
(Map p62; ☑ ext 2655 01-613-2000; www.bcrp.gob.
pe/museocentral; cnr Lampa & Ucayali; ◎10am-
4:30pm Tue-Fri, to 1pm Sat & Sun) FREE Housed
in a graceful bank building, the Museo Central is a well-presented overview of several
millennia of Peruvian art, from pre-Columbian gold and pottery to a selection of 19th-
and 20th-century canvases. Don't miss the
watercolors by Pancho Fierro on the top
floor, which provide an unparalleled view of
dress and class in 19th-century Lima. Identification is required for admittance.

Palacio Torre Tagle   HISTORIC BUILDING
(Map p62; ☑ ext 4584 01-204-2400; Ucayali 363;
◎10am-5pm Sat & Sun) The most immaculate of Lima's historic *casonas* was completed in 1735, and features an ornate baroque
portico (the best one in Lima) and striking
Moorish-style balconies. It's now home to
Peru's Foreign Ministry; entry is very limited.

Iglesia de la Merced   CHURCH
(Map p62; ☑ 01-427-8199; cnr Jirón de la Unión &
Miró Quesada; ◎10am-noon & 5-7pm) The first
Latin Mass in Lima was held in 1534 on a
small patch of land now marked by the Iglesia de la Merced. Originally built in 1541,
it was rebuilt several times over the course
of the next two centuries. Most of today's
structure dates to the 18th century. The
most striking feature is the imposing granite
facade, carved in the *churrigueresque* manner (a highly ornate style popular during the
late Spanish baroque period).

Inside, the nave is lined with more than
two dozen magnificent baroque and Renaissance-style altars, some carved entirely
out of mahogany. To the right as you enter
is a large silver cross that once belonged to
Father Pedro Urraca (1583–1657), renowned
for having had a vision of the Virgin. This is
a place of pilgrimage for Peruvian worshippers, who come to place a hand on the cross
and pray for miracles.

Instituto Riva-Aguero
HISTORIC BUILDING

(Map p62; ☑01-626-6614; Camaná 459; adult/child S12/1; ⊙10am-1pm, 2-7pm Mon-Fri) Toward the center of downtown, this traditional *casona* houses the small Museum of Art & Popular Tradition.

Iglesia de San Agustín
CHURCH

(Map p62; ☑01-427-7548; cnr Ica & Camaná; ⊙8-9am & 4:30-7:30pm Mon-Fri) This church has an elaborate *churrigueresque* facade (completed in 1720), replete with stone carvings of angels, flowers, fruit and, of course, St Augustine. The interiors are drab, but the church is home to a curious woodcarving called *La Muerte* (Death) by 18th-century sculptor Baltazar Gavilán. As one (probably fictional) story goes, Gavilán died in a state of madness after viewing his own chilling sculpture in the middle of the night. The piece sometimes travels, so call ahead.

Be aware that limited opening hours can make the church a challenge to visit.

Iglesia de las Nazarenas
CHURCH

(Map p62; ☑01-423-5718; cnr Tacna & Huancavelica; ⊙7am-1pm & 4-8:30pm) One of Lima's most storied churches was part of a 17th-century shantytown inhabited by former slaves. One of them painted an image of the Crucifixion on a wall here. It survived the devastating earthquake of 1655 and a church was built around it (the painting serves as the centerpiece of the main altar) in the 1700s. The church has been rebuilt many times since but the wall endures.

On October 18 each year a representation of the mural, known as 'El Señor de los Milagros' (p81) is carried around in a tens-of-thousands-strong procession that lasts for days.

Santuario de Santa Rosa de Lima
CHURCH

(Map p62; ☑01-425-1279; cnr Tacna & Callao; ⊙8am-noon & 5-8pm) Honoring the first saint of the Americas, this plain, terracotta-hued church on a congested avenue is located roughly at the site of her birth. The modest adobe sanctuary in the gardens was built in the 17th century for Santa Rosa's prayers and meditation.

Casa-Capilla de San Martín de Porres
CHURCH

(Map p62; ☑01-423-0705; Callao 535; ⊙9am-1pm & 3-6pm Mon-Fri, 9am-1pm Sat) Right across the street from the Santuario de Santa Rosa de Lima, this building (now a center of religious study) commemorates the birthplace of San Martín. Visitors are welcome to view the bright interior patios and diminutive chapel.

Casa de Oquendo
HISTORIC BUILDING

(Map p62; ☑01-427-7987; Conde de Superunda 298; ⊙9am-12:45pm, 2pm-4:45pm Mon-Fri, to noon Sat) The cornflower-blue Casa de Oquendo is a ramshackle turn-of-the-19th-century house (in its time, the tallest in Lima) with a creaky lookout tower that, on a clear day, has views of Callao. Arrange tours for small groups ahead of time with a suggested donation.

★Iglesia de Santo Domingo
CHURCH

(Map p62; ☑01-427-6793; cnr Camaná & Conde de Superunda; church free, convent S7; ⊙9am-1pm & 5-7:30pm Mon-Sat) One of Lima's most historic religious sites, the Iglesia de Santo Domingo and its expansive **convent** are built on land granted to the Dominican friar Vicente de Valverde, who accompanied Pizarro throughout the conquest and was instrumental in persuading him to execute the captured Inca Atahualpa. Originally completed in the 16th century, this impressive pink church has been rebuilt and remodeled at various points since.

It is most renowned as the final resting place for three important Peruvian saints: San Juan Macías, Santa Rosa de Lima and San Martín de Porres (the continent's first black saint). The convent – a sprawling courtyard-studded complex lined with baroque paintings and clad in vintage Spanish tiles – contains the saints' tombs. The church, however, has the most interesting relics: the skulls of San Martín and Santa Rosa, encased in glass, in a shrine to the right of the main altar.

Casa Aliaga
HISTORIC BUILDING

(Map p62; ☑Lima Tours 01-619-6900; www.casa dealiaga.com; Jirón de la Unión 224; admission S30; ⊙9:30am-5pm, by reservation only) Innocuously tucked on a side street by the post office, Casa Aliaga stands on land given in 1535 to Jerónimo de Aliaga, one of Pizarro's followers, and that has been occupied by 16 generations of his descendants. It may not look like much from the outside, but the interiors are lovely, with vintage furnishings and tile work. It can also be visited via organized excursions with Lima Tours (p102).

Jirón de la Unión
HISTORIC SITE

(Map p62) In the late 19th and early 20th centuries, the five pedestrian blocks on Jirón de

Lima District & La Victoria

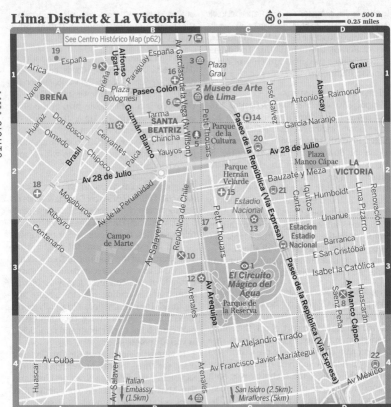

Lima District & La Victoria

◎ Top Sights
1	El Circuito Mágico del Agua	C3
2	Museo de Arte de Lima	B1

◎ Sights
3	Museo de Arte Italiano	B1
4	Museo de Historia Natural	B4
5	Parque de la Cultura	B2

🛏 Sleeping
6	1900 Backpackers	B1
7	Lima Sheraton	B1

🍴 Eating
8	Agallas	D3
9	Cevichería la Choza Nautica	A1
10	Rovegno	B3

✪ Entertainment
11	Brisas del Titicaca Asociacion Cultural	B2

12	Centro Cultural de España	B3
13	Estadio Nacional	C3

🛍 Shopping
14	Polvos Azules	C1

ℹ Information
15	Centro de La Mujer Peruana Flora Tristán	C2
16	Clínica Internacional	B1
17	Conadis	C3
18	Instituto Nacional de Salud del Niño	A2
19	Oficina de Migraciónes	A1

ℹ Transport
20	Civa	C2
21	Móvil Tours	C2
22	Soyuz	D4

la Unión, from the Plaza de Armas to Plaza San Martín, were *the* place to see and be seen. The street has long since lost its aristocratic luster, but the shells of neocolonial and art-deco buildings survive. Watch out for pickpockets who work the crowds during street performances.

Plaza San Martín
PLAZA

(Map p62) Built in the early 20th century, Plaza San Martín has come to life in recent years as the city has set about restoring its park and giving the surrounding beaux-arts architecture a much-needed scrubbing. It is especially lovely in the evenings, when it is illuminated. The plaza is named for the liberator of Peru, **José de San Martín**, who sits astride a horse at the center of the plaza.

At the base of the statue, don't miss the bronze rendering of **Madre Patria**, the symbolic mother of Peru. Commissioned in Spain with the instruction to give the good lady a crown of flames, nobody thought to iron out the double meaning of the word flame in Spanish (llama), so the hapless artisans duly placed a delightful little llama on her head.

The once-stately Gran Hotel Bolívar (p81), built in the 1920s, presides over the square from the northwest.

Museo Andrés del Castillo
MUSEUM

(Map p62; ☑ 01-433-2831; www.madc.com.pe; Jirón de la Unión 1030; S10; ☺ 9am-6pm Mon-Sat, 10am-6pm Sun) Housed in a pristine 19th-century mansion with Spanish tile floors, this worthwhile private museum showcases a vast collection of minerals, as well as breathtakingly displayed Nazca textiles and Chancay pottery, including some remarkable representations of Peruvian hairless dogs.

Panteón de los Próceres
MONUMENT

(Map p62; ☑ 01-427-8157; Parque Universitario; admission S1; ☺ 10am-5pm) Located inside a little-visited 18th-century Jesuit church, this monument pays tribute to Peruvian battle heroes, from Túpac Amaru II, the 18th-century Quechua leader who led an uprising, to José de San Martín, who led the country to independence in the 1820s. The mosaic-lined crypt holds the remains of Ramón Castilla, the four-time Peruvian president who saw the country through a good piece of the 19th century. The impressive baroque altar, carved out of Ecuadorean mahogany, dates from the 1500s.

Museo de la Cultura Peruana
MUSEUM

(Museum of Peruvian Culture; Map p62; ☑ 01-321-5626; www.museos.cultura.pe/museos/museo-nacional-de-la-cultura-peruana; Alfonso Ugarte 650; adult/child S6/3; ☺ 10am-5pm Tue-Sat) About half-a-dozen blocks west of the Plaza San Martín, on a traffic-choked thoroughfare, you'll find the Museo de la Cultura Peruana, a repository of Peruvian folk art. The collection, consisting of elaborate *retablos* (religious dioramas) from Ayacucho, historic pottery from Puno and works in feathers from the Amazon, is displayed in a building whose exterior facade is inspired by pre-Columbian architecture.

Parque de la Cultura
PARK

(Map p66) Originally known as Parque de la Exposición, this revamped park has gardens and a small amphitheater for outdoor performances. Two of Lima's major art museums reside here.

★ Museo de Arte de Lima
MUSEUM

(MALI; Map p66; ☑ 01-204-0000; www.mali.pe; Paseo Colón 125; adult/child S30/15; ☺ 10am-7pm Tue, Thu & Fri, to 5pm Sat & Sun) Known locally as MALI, Lima's principal fine-art museum is housed in a striking beaux-arts building that was renovated in 2015. Subjects range from pre-Columbian to contemporary art, and there are also guided visits to special exhibits. On Sunday entry is just S1. A satellite museum is under construction in Barranco.

Museo de Arte Italiano
MUSEUM

(Italian Art Museum; Map p66; ☑ 01-321-5622; Paseo de la República 250; adult/child S6/1; ☺ 10am-4:30pm Mon-Fri) Just north of MALI, the Museo de Arte Italiano exhibits a tepid collection of 19th- and 20th-century Italian art. Its best attribute is the glittering Venetian mosaics on the exterior walls.

★ El Circuito Mágico del Agua
FOUNTAIN

(Map p66; Parque de la Reserva, Av Petit Thouars, cuadra 5; S4; ☺ 3-10:30pm Wed-Sun) This indulgent series of illuminated fountains is so over the top it can't help but induce stupefaction among even the most hardened travel cynic. A dozen different fountains are capped, at the end, by a laser light show at the 120m-long Fuente de la Fantasía (Fantasy Fountain). The whole display is set to a medley of tunes comprising everything from Peruvian waltzes to ABBA. It has to be seen to be believed.

Access to the area is free by day when the fountains are off.

Museo de Historia Natural MUSEUM
(Natural History Museum; Map p66; ✒ ext 5703 01-619-7000; http://museohn.unmsm.edu.pe; Arenales 1256, Jesús María; adult/child S10/5; ☉ 9am-5pm Mon-Sat, 10am-4:30pm Sun) One block west of *cuadra* 12 off Av Arequipa, south of the Parque de la Reserva, the 100-year-old Museo de Historia Natural, run by the Universidád de San Marcos, has a modest taxidermy collection that provides a useful overview of Peruvian fauna. Guided tours (S50 per group) in Spanish, English and Portuguese are available.

◉ Rímac

Rímac can be a rough neighborhood. Taxis or organized tours are the best options for most sights.

Convento de los Descalzos MUSEUM
(✒ 01-481-0441; Manco Cápac 202A, Alameda de los Descalzos; admission S7; ☉ 9:30am-1pm & 2-5:30pm) At the end of the attractive Alameda de los Descalzos, all but forgotten is this 16th-century convent and museum, run by the Descalzos ('the Barefooted,' a reference to Franciscan friars). Visitors can see old winemaking equipment in the kitchen, a refectory, an infirmary and the monastic cells. There are also some 300 colonial paintings, including noteworthy canvases by renowned Cuzco School artist Diego Quispe Tito. Spanish-speaking guides give 45-minute tours. Taxis from Plaza de Armas start at about S12.

Cerro San Cristóbal VIEWPOINT
This 409m-high hill to the northeast of Lima Centro has a **mirador** (lookout) at its crown, with views of Lima stretching off to the Pacific (in winter expect to see nothing but fog). A huge cross, built in 1928 and illuminated at night, is a Lima landmark and the object of pilgrimages during Semana Santa (Holy Week) and the first Sunday in May. There is a small free **museum**.

Due to a fatal bus accident, tour buses and taxis no longer visit the summit.

Museo Taurino MUSEUM
(Bullfight Museum; Map p62; ✒ 01-481-1467; Hualgayoc 332; adult/child S5/3; ☉ 9am-4:30pm Mon-Fri) Plaza de Acho, Lima's bullring, was built on this site north of the Río Rímac in 1766. Some of the world's most famous toreadors passed through here, among them the renowned Manolete from Spain. A visit includes a free guided tour inspecting cluttered displays of weapons, paintings, photographs and the gilded outfits worn by a succession of bullfighters.

◉ East Lima

The city begins to rise into the foothills of the Andes as you turn east. It's an area strewn with government buildings and teeming with residential districts.

Museo de la Nación MUSEUM
(Museum of the Nation; ✒ 01-618-9393; Av Javier Prado Este 2466, San Borja; ☉ 9am-5pm Tue-Sun) FREE In a brutalist concrete tower, this museum provides a cursory overview of Peru's civilizations, from Chavín stone carvings and the knotted-rope *quipus* (used for record-keeping) of the Incas to colonial artifacts. One must-see is the permanent exhibit **Yuyanapaq**. Quechua for 'to remember,' it's a moving photographic tribute to the Internal Conflict (1980–2000), created by Peru's Truth & Reconciliation Commission in 2003.

From San Isidro, you can catch one of the many buses or *combis* (minibuses) heading east along Av Javier Prado Este toward La Molina.

Museo de Oro del Perú MUSEUM
(Gold Museum of Peru; ✒ 01-345-1292; www.museo roperu.com.pe; Alonso de Molina 1100, Monterrico; adult/child under 11 S33/16; ☉ 10:30am-6pm) The now notorious Museo de Oro del Perú, a private museum, was a Lima must-see until 2001, when a study revealed that 85% of the museum's metallurgical pieces were fakes. It reopened with an assurance that works on display are bona fide, though descriptions classify certain pieces as 'reproductions.' The cluttered, poorly signed exhibits still leave something to be desired.

Of greater interest (and, in all likelihood, of greater authenticity) are the thousands of weapons presented in the **Arms Museum**, on the ground floor. Here, in various jumbled rooms, you'll find rifles, swords and guns from across the centuries, including a firearm that once belonged to Fidel Castro.

Go via taxi or *combi* from Museo de la Nación heading northeast on Angamos toward Monterrico and get off at the Puente Primavera. From there, it's a 15-minute stroll north to the museum.

Asociación Museo del Automóvil MUSEUM
(Automobile Museum; ✒ 01-368-0373; Av La Molina, cuadra 37, cnr Totoritas, La Molina; admission S20; ☉ 10am-7pm) The Asociación Museo del Automóvil has an impressive array of classic

cars, some dating back to 1901, from a Ford Model T to a Cadillac Fleetwood used by four Peruvian presidents.

◎ San Isidro

Well-to-do San Isidro is Lima's banking center and one of its most affluent areas. Its residential neighborhoods offer some important sights.

Espacio Fundacion Telefonica ARTS CENTER
(Map p70; ☑ 01-210-1327; http://espacio.funda ciontelefonica.com.pe; Av Arequipa 1155; ⊙10am-8pm Tue-Sat, noon-7pm Sun) FREE This cultural center focuses on the arts, particularly technology and digital formats. Though it's part of the largest Spanish multinational and housed on the ground level of the corporate building, Espacio is a non-profit that brings some of the most forward-thinking artists (national and international) to the forefront. Entry to exhibits, screenings, lectures and audio performances is free; frequent classes, ranging from animation to how to organize cultural events, have varying costs – see the website for what's coming up.

Bosque El Olivar PARK
(Map p70) This tranquil park, a veritable oasis in the middle of San Isidro, consists of the remnants of an old **olive grove**, part of which was planted by the venerated San Martín de Porres in the 17th century.

Huaca Huallamarca RUINS
(Map p70; ☑ 01-222-4124; www.msi.gob.pe; Nicolás de Rivera 201, San Isidro; adult/child S5/3; ⊙9am-5pm Tue-Sun) Nestled among condominium towers and sprawling high-end homes, the simple Huaca Huallamarca is a highly restored adobe pyramid, produced by the Lima culture, that dates to somewhere between AD 200 and 500. A small on-site **museum**, complete with mummy, details its excavation.

◎ Miraflores

The seaside neighborhood of Miraflores, which serves as Lima's contemporary core, bustles with commerce, restaurants and nightlife. A long greenbelt overlooks the Pacific from a set of ragged cliffs.

★Fundación Museo Amano MUSEUM
(Map p74; ☑ 01-441-2909; www.museoamano. org; Retiro 160; ⊙10am-5pm) FREE The well-designed Fundación Museo Amano features

a fine private collection of ceramics, with a strong representation of wares from the Chimú and Nazca cultures. It also has a remarkable assortment of lace and other textiles produced by the coastal Chancay culture. There's an optional 1.5-hour guided tour in English, Portuguese or Spanish.

Impakto GALLERY
(Map p74; ☑ 01-368-7060; www.galeria-impakto. com; Av Santa Cruz 857; ⊙noon-8pm Mon-Fri, 9am-5pm Sat) Located on the 1st floor of a towering and dark office building, this contemporary-art museum has a glass facade that reveals just enough of the stark white interior to pique your interest. Both national and international artists are continually exhibited here to provide diverse yet always fresh perspectives.

Lugar de la Memoria MUSEUM
(LUM; ☑ 01-719-2065; www.lum.cultura.pe; Bajada San Martin 151; ⊙10am-6pm Tue-Sun) FREE An ambitious state project to preserve the memory of victims of violence during Peru's tumultuous period from 1980 to 2000. This new postmodernist museum features exhibits reflecting on events and commemorating victims, aiming to help Peruvians heal and embrace a strong stance on human rights. It's directed especially at younger generations that didn't experience the period, but will prove fascinating to history-obsessed

San Isidro

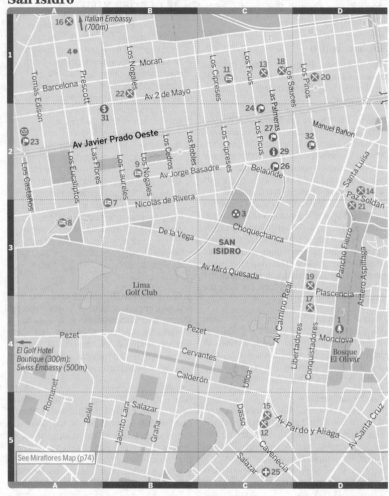

non-nationals as well. Information is in Spanish only.

Huaca Pucllana
RUINS

(Map p74; ☎ 01-617-7138; cnr Borgoño & Tarapacá; adult/child S12/6; ⊙ 9am-4:30pm; ☻) Located near the Óvalo Gutiérrez, this huaca is a restored adobe ceremonial center from the Lima culture that dates back to AD 400. In 2010 an important discovery of four Wari mummies, untouched by looting, was made. Though vigorous excavations continue, the site is accessible by regular guided tours in Spanish (for a tip). In addition to a tiny on-site **museum**, there's a celebrated

restaurant (p92) that offers incredible views of the illuminated ruins at night.

Choco Museo
MUSEUM

(Map p74; ☎ 01-445-9708; www.chocomuseo.com/peru; Berlin 375; adult/child 12 & under 2hr workshops S83/66; ⊙ 11am-8:30pm Sun-Thu, to 9:30pm Fri & Sat) **FREE** On-site chocolate production is the draw of this 'museum' selling fondue and fair-trade hot cocoa. French-owned, it is well known for organic chocolate-making workshops, offered at least twice daily. Truffle workshops must be reserved in advance, but otherwise walk-ins are welcome.

Parque del Amor　　　　　　　　　PARK

(Map p74; Malecón Cisneros) Protected from the ocean breeze by a colorful wall of mosaics, this park in Miraflores is the ideal place to walk hand in hand with that special someone. A monstrously large sculpture of a couple kissing hovers over the area.

◉ Barranco

A tiny resort back at the turn of the 20th century, Barranco is lined with grand old *casonas* (large houses), many of which have been turned into galleries and boutique hotels. With some rough edges, this hip bohemian center has hopping bars and nice areas to stroll.

Museo de Arte Contemporaneo　　MUSEUM

(MAC; Map p78; ☎01-514-6800; www.maclima.pe; Av Grau 1511; adult/child S10/6; ⊗10am-6pm Tue-Sun; ℗⊕) The permanent collection at MAC is a quick study but visiting exhibits, such as a David LaChapelle retrospective, are major draws. There's also a good on-site **cafe** and a **sculpture park** (free access) with shady lawns that provide a good city respite for families. Guided tours available in English.

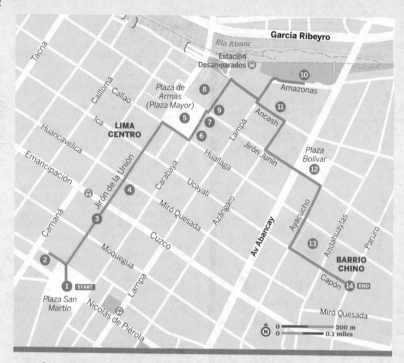

🏃 City Walk
Downtown Lima

START PLAZA SAN MARTÍN
END BARRIO CHINO
LENGTH 3KM; TWO HOURS

Begin in ① **Plaza San Martín** (p67) to imbibe the faded grandeur of ② **Gran Hotel Bolívar** (p81), the city's first fine hotel, which hosted the likes of Clark Gable and Mick Jagger. Walk the pedestrian street of ③ **Jirón de la Unión** (p65); once the heart of aristocratic city life, it's now lined with cinemas and bargain shoe stores. To the right is ④ **Iglesia de la Merced** (p64). Originally built in 1541, it held the first Mass in Lima. Peek inside at the impressive mahogany altars.

The boulevard ends at the ⑤ **Plaza de Armas** (p60), surrounded by palms and ornate canary-yellow buildings. In the era of the viceroys it served as a market, bullpen and even execution site for the condemned. The restored ⑥ **Catedral de Lima** (p61) houses the once-misplaced remains of conquistador Francisco Pizarro in an inscribed lead box. The adjacent ⑦ **Palacio Arzobispal** (p60) has some of the city's best-preserved ornate

Moorish balconies. To the northeast, the grandiose baroque ⑧ **Palacio de Gobierno** (p60) serves as Peru's presidential palace – pass at noon for the ceremonious changing of the guard with a brass band tapping out 'El Condor Pasa.' Across the street, the ⑨ **Museo del Pisco** (p96) merits a stop, though you might want to save it to end your walk with a handcrafted pisco cocktail instead.

The palace backs up against the Río Rímac. Follow behind it to ⑩ **Parque de la Muralla** (p61), a spacious city park alongside remains of the original city wall. Return via Amazonas to Lampa and ⑪ **Monasterio de San Francisco** (p63) to check out the monastery's compelling catacombs, which hold skulls and bones laid out in geometric designs. Cross the avenida to ⑫ **Plaza Bolívar** and Congress. Follow Ayacucho two blocks to the ⑬ **Mercado Central** (Map p62; ☑ 958-849-731; Ucayali 613, Lima Centro; ◷ 7am-9pm Mon-Sat, to 6pm Sun), with stalls of goods from soccer jerseys to piles of tropical and Andean fruit. Take the pedestrian street Capón to ⑭ **El Barrio Chino** (Chinatown) for tea or a sumptuous lunch at a no-nonsense Cantonese eatery.

Museo Pedro de Osma MUSEUM
(Map p78; ☑ 01-467-0141; www.museopedro
deosma.org; Av Pedro de Osma 423; admission
S30; ⊘ 10am-6pm Tue-Sun) Housed in a lovely
beaux-arts mansion surrounded by gardens,
this undervisited museum has an exquisite
collection of colonial furniture, silverwork
and art, some of which dates back to the
1500s. Among the many fine pieces, standouts include a 2m-wide canvas that depicts
a Corpus Christi procession in turn-of-the-
17th-century Cuzco.

Puente de los Suspiros BRIDGE
(Bridge of Sighs; Map p78) A block west of the
main plaza, look for this renovated, narrow
wooden bridge over an old stone stairway
that leads to the beach. Especially popular
with couples on first dates, the bridge has
inspired many a Peruvian folk song.

◉ West Lima & Callao

To the west of downtown, cluttered
lower-middle-class and poor neighborhoods
eventually give way to the port city of Callao,
where the Spanish once shipped gold. Travelers should approach Callao with caution,
since some areas are dangerous, even during
the day.

★ Monumental Callao CULTURAL CENTER
(www.monumentalcallao.com; Jirón Constitución
250; ⊘ 11am-6pm) Superstar graffiti artists
are helping to revive the rough neighborhood surrounding Casa Ronald, a 1920 architectural masterpiece. Now a center for
creatives, Monumental Callao incorporates
restaurants and artists' studios, as well as
galleries, with tenants intermittently donating their time to the surrounding community. Every weekend you can find rooftop
parties with DJs or live salsa concerts, and
even fashion shows using the colorful Spanish-style tiling as the catwalk.

★ Museo Larco MUSEUM
(☑ 01-461-1312; www.museolarco.org; Bolívar 1515,
Pueblo Libre; adult/child under 15 S30/15; ⊘ 9am-
10pm) In an 18th-century viceroy's mansion, this museum offers one of the largest,
best-presented displays of ceramics in Lima.
Founded by pre-Columbian collector Rafael
Larco Hoyle in 1926, the collection includes
more than 50,000 pots, with ceramic works
from the Cupisnique, Chimú, Chancay, Nazca and Inca cultures. Highlights include the
sublime Moche portrait vessels, presented
in simple, dramatically lit cases, and a Wari

weaving in one of the rear galleries that
contains 398 threads to the linear inch – a
record.

There's also gold and jewels. Many visitors are lured here by a separately housed
collection of pre-Columbian erotica illustrating all manner of sexual activity with comi-
cal explicitness. Don't miss the vitrine that
depicts sexually transmitted diseases.

The highly recommended on-site **Café
del Museo** faces a private garden draped
in bougainvillea and is a perfect spot for
ceviche.

Catch a bus marked 'Todo Bolívar' from
Av Arequipa in Miraflores to Bolívar's 15th
block. A painted blue line on the sidewalk
links this building to the Museo Nacional
de Antropología, Arqueología e Historía del
Perú, about a 15-minute walk away.

**Museo Nacional de Antropología,
Arqueología e Historía del Perú** MUSEUM
(National Anthropology, Archaeology & History
Museum; ☑ 01-321-5630; http://mnaahp.cultura.
pe; Plaza Bolívar, cnr San Martín & Vivanco, Pueblo Libre; adult/child S10/1; ⊘ 9am-5pm Tue-Sat,
to 4pm Sun) Trace the history of Peru from
the pre-ceramic period to the early republic. Displays include the famous Raimondi
Stela, a 2.1m Chavín rock carving from one
of the first Andean cultures to have a widespread, recognizable artistic style. Late-colo-
nial and early republic paintings include an
18th-century *Last Supper* in which Christ
and his disciples feast on *cuy* (guinea pig).
The building was home to revolutionary heroes José de San Martín (from 1821 to 1822)
and Simón Bolívar (from 1823 to 1826).

From Miraflores, take a 'Todo Brasil' *combi* from Av Arequipa (just north from Óvalo)
to *cuadra* 22 on the corner of Vivanco, then
walk seven blocks up that street. A blue line
connects this museum with Museo Larco.

◉ La Punta

A narrow peninsula that extends west into
the Pacific Ocean, La Punta was once a fishing hamlet, and later, in the 19th century,
an upscale summer beach resort. Today this
pleasant neighborhood, graced with neocolonial and art-deco homes, is a great spot
to stroll by the ocean and enjoy a seafood
lunch.

You can take a taxi from Miraflores. In
Lima Centro, *combis* (minibuses) traveling
to Callao run west along Av Colonial from
the Plaza 2 de Mayo. Take the ones labeled

Miraflores

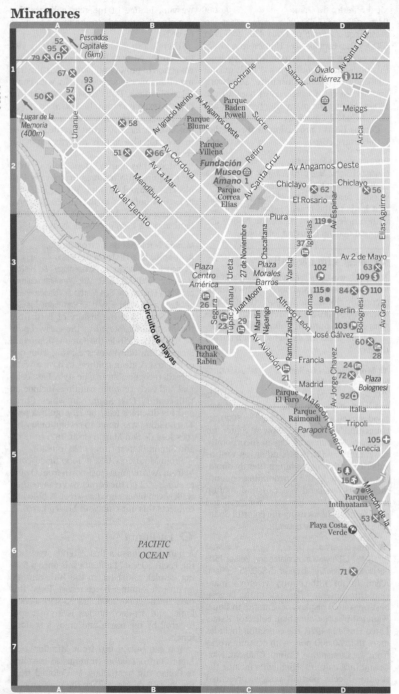

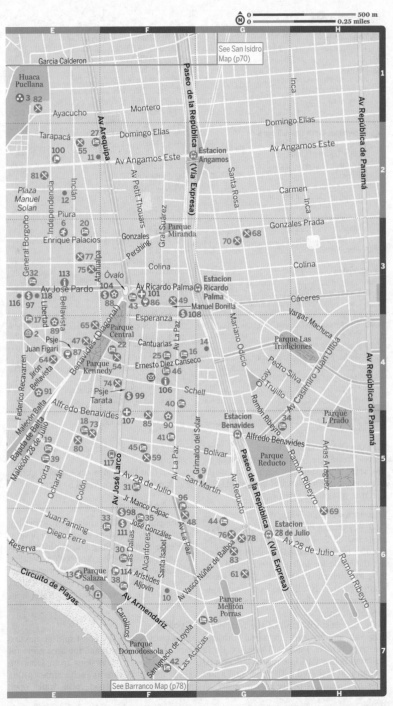

Garcia Calderon

Huaca Pucllana
3 82
Ayacucho
Montero

Av Arequipa
Tarapacá
27
55
100
11
Domingo Elías
Av Angamos Este

Inca
Domingo Elías
Av República de Panamá

Estacion Angamos
Av Angamos Este

81
Plaza Manuel Solan
12
Independencia
Incán
Piura
6 20
Enrique Palacios
Gonzales
Pershing

Santa Rosa

Carmen
Inca
Gonzales Prada

Av Petit Thouars
Gral Suárez
Parque Miranda
70 68

General Borgoño
32
113
75 77
Óvalo
Atahualpa
104
Colina

Colina

Cáceres

Av José Pardo
116
97 118
Libertad
17
2
89
Juan Figari
64
87
91
Bellavista
Jirón
47
Benavides (Diagonal)
65
Parque Central
22
88
43
101
86
108
Manuel Bonilla
Esperanza
49
Cantuarias
25
16
14

Av Ricardo Palma

Estacion Ricardo Palma

Vargas Machuca
Av La Paz

Mariano Odicio

Parque Las Tradiciones
Pedro Silva
Olcay
Trujillo

Av Casimiro Juan Ulloa
Av República de Panamá

Parque Kennedy
54
Ernesto Diez Canseco
46
106
Schell
40

Psje Tarata
74
99
107
85
90
41
Psje

Ramón Ribeyro

Estacion Benavides
Alfredo Benavides
34
Parque L Prado

Alfredo Benavides
18 73
80
19
39
Porta
Ocharán
Colón
45
59
117
31

Av José Larco

Parque Reducto

Paseo de la República (Vía Expresa)
Arias Araguez
Ramón Ribeyro
69

Malecón Balta
Bajada de Balta
Malecón 28 de Julio
Federico Recavarren
Reserva

Juan Fanning
Diego Ferre
33
98
35
111
José Gonzáles
30
Las Dalias
114
38
13
94
Parque Salazar
10
Alcanfores
Aristides Aljovin
Santa Isabel

Av 28 de Julio
Jr Manco Cápac
96
48
Av La Paz
San Martín
Grimaldo del Solar
Bolívar
9
44
76
78
83
61

Estacion 28 de Julio
Av 28 de Julio
Av Vasco Núñez de Balboa
Av Reducto

Circuito de Playas

Av Armendáriz
Carolinos
Parque Domodossola
36
42
San Ignacio de Loyola
Las Acacias
Parque Melitón Porras

See San Isidro Map (p70)

See Barranco Map (p78)

0   500 m
0   0.25 miles

Miraflores

'La Punta.' A good spot to get out is Plaza Gálvez; from here, you can head west along the waterside Malecón Figueredo, which offers magnificent views of craggy Isla San Lorenzo, just off the coast.

Fortaleza del Real Felipe FORT
(☏ 01-429-0532; Plaza Independencia, Callao; adult/child S15/5; ⊙ 9am-2pm) In the 1820s the Spanish royalists made their last stand during the battle for independence at this historic fort, which was built in 1747 to guard against pirates. It still houses a small military contingent. Visits are by guided tours in Spanish only.

On the western flank of the fort, don't miss an opportunity to stroll through the truly bizarre **Parque Tématico de la Policía** (Police Park), a nicely landscaped garden that is dotted with police tanks and life-size statues of police in riot gear – a perfect place for those surreal family vacation photos.

Note that the nearby dock area is quite a rough neighborhood; travel by taxi.

🏃 Activities

Surfing has long been Lima's go-to sport, but with the city becoming more active options are expanding. Cycling and running along coastal paths have become widely popular. The adventurous can paraglide right from coastal Miraflores. Off the coast of Callao, you can dive in waters in which sea lions cavort.

Cycling

Bike paths along the coast and designated lanes in Miraflores make the area great for cycling. Popular excursions from Lima include the 31km ride to Pachacamac (p106), where there are good local trails open between April and December. Expert riders can inquire about the stellar downhill circuit from Olleros to San Bartolo south of Lima. For general information on cycling (in Spanish), try Federación Deportiva Peruana de Ciclismo (p102) or the Facebook page of Ciclismo Sin Fronteras Miraflores.

Mirabici CYCLING
(Map p74; 📞01-673-3908; www.mirabiciperu.pe; Costanera s/n, Miraflores; rentals per hour S23; ⊙9am-7pm) On the coastal paths, this is a convenient stop for bicycle rentals (including tandems) and offers tours of Barranco, Miraflores and San Isidro.

Perú Bike CYCLING
(Map p78; 📞01-260-8225; www.perubike.com; Punta Sal D7, Barranco; ⊙10am-1pm & 4-7pm Mon-Fri, 10am-2pm Sat) A recommended shop that offers repairs. The mountain-biking tours run from conventional to more demanding routes, with downhill options and multiday trips to the Andes and jungle areas.

Paragliding

From the Miraflores cliff tops, tandem flights (S260 for 10 minutes) take off from the cliff-top 'paraport' at the Parque Raimondi to soar over coastal skyscrapers and gaze down at the surfers.

Try **Peru Fly** (Map p74; 📞959-524-940, 01-444-5004; www.perufly.com; Parque del Amor, Miraflores; ⊙10am-6pm), a paragliding school that also offers tandem flights in Miraflores.

Swimming & Water Sports

Despite the newspaper warnings about pollution, *limeños* (inhabitants of Lima) hit the beaches in droves in summer (January through March). **Playa Costa Verde** in Miraflores (nicknamed Waikiki) is a favorite of local surfers and has good breaks year-round. Barranco's beaches have waves

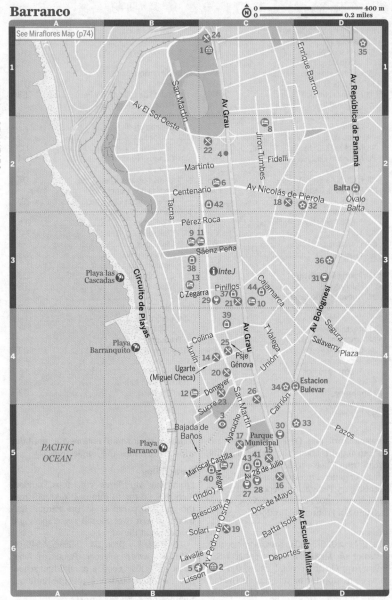

See Miraflores Map (p74)

LIMA ACTIVITIES

that are better for longboards. There are seven other beaches in Miraflores and four more in Barranco. Serious surfers can also try **Playa La Herradura** in Chorrillos, which has waves up to 5m high during good swells. Do not leave your belongings unattended, as theft is a problem.

Wayo Whilar   SURFING

(☎ 01-254-1344; www.wayowhilar.com.pe; Alameda Garzas Reales Mz-FA 7, Chorrillos; ⏰ 9am-7pm Mon-Thu, to 4pm Fri & Sat) The shop of a longtime Peruvian surfer who sells his own line of coveted hand-shaped surfboards.

Barranco

Perú Divers   DIVING
(☏ 997-205-500, 01-251-6231; www.perudivers.
com; Av Defensores del Morro 175, Chorrillos;
⊙ 9am-5pm Mon-Sat) Deep-sea diving off Peru's southern coast is reasonably priced. Luis
Rodríguez, a PADI-certified instructor, owns
this excellent dive shop with equipment for
sale, and offers certification and diving trips.
Regular excursions visit a year-round sea-lion colony at Islas Palomino, off the coast of
Callao.

🍽 Courses

Peru's clear, well-spoken Spanish makes it a
hub for language schools. You will find plenty in Lima.

Centro de Idiomas   LANGUAGE
(Map p70; ☏ 01-219-0151; www.up.edu.pe/idio
mas; Prescott 333, San Isidro; ⊙ 9am-4pm Mon-Fri)
Overseen by the Universidad del Pacífico, it
offers a 40-hour semester-long course, available in five levels.

Idiomas Católica   LANGUAGE
(☏ 01-626-6500; www.idiomas.pucp.edu.pe; Av
Universitaria 888, San Miguel; ⊙ 9am-5pm Mon-Fri)

Managed by the prestigious Catholic University, this program offers five two-hour group
classes per week.

El Sol   LANGUAGE
(Map p74; ☏ 01-242-7763; www.elsol.idiomas
peru.com; Grimaldo del Solar 469, Miraflores)
Private classes are S85 per hour; one-week
courses start at S805.

**Instituto Cultural Peruano-
Norteamericano**   LANGUAGE
(ICPNA; Map p74; ☏ 01-708-2900; www.face
book.com/icpnaoficial; Av Angamos Oeste 160,
Miraflores) ⊙ 9am-4pm Mon-Fri) Offers Spanish
courses from qualified instructors.

👉 Tours

Lima agencies offer guided city tours, visits
to nearby archaeological sites such as Pachacamac, as well as trips around Peru. In
addition, travel agencies organize regional
and national tours. Full-day tours in Lima
usually start at around US$70.

It may be helpful to look for guides registered with **Agotur** (Asociación de Guías Oficiales
de Turismo; www.agoturlima.com), the Peruvian

guide organization. Another resource is www.leaplocal.com. Telephone numbers are for Peruvian daytime use only.

For a fascinating Lima photo day tour (US$75), contact **Andean Photo Expeditions** (📞 960-724-103; www.andeanphoto-expeditions.com), which visits the harbor, Chinatown and the central market.

InkaNatura   ADVENTURE
(Map p70; 📞 in Lima 01-203-5000, in US 1-888-870-7378; www.inkanatura.com; Av Petit Thouars 3811, San Isidro) Offers quality tours throughout Peru, including Chachapoyas and the jungle. Its lodges include Sandoval Lake Lodge (p463) and Heath River Wildlife Center (p464) in the southern Amazon, and (co-owned) Manu Wildlife Center (p469) in the Manu area.

Condor Travel   TOURS
(Map p74; 📞 01-615-3000; www.condortravel.com; Jorge Chávez 154, Miraflores) Recommended for top-end touring and custom itineraries throughout the Andes.

Aqua Expeditions Office   CRUISE
(Map p74; 📞 1-866-603-3687, 965-832-517; www.aquaexpeditions.com; Palacios 335 btwn Independencia & Coronel Inclán) This company runs Amazon cruises out of Nauta near Iquitos.

Lima Tasty Tours   FOOD & DRINK
(Map p78; 📞 958-313-939, 01-249-4594; www.limatastytours.com; Av Grau 1113, Barranco; ⊘ by appointment) Gastronomic tours that reveal Lima as the locals know it, with plenty of sampling at markets. It offers a friendly rapport with clients, tailored options and insider access to lesser-known culinary treasures; tours are available in English.

Jorge Riveros-Cayo   TOURS
(📞 944-367-157; jorge@theperutravelexperience.com) A fluent English speaker and savvy journalist offering private culinary tours, city excursions and tailor-made trips with a cultural bent all around Peru.

Explorandes   ADVENTURE
(Map p74; 📞 01-8423-8380; www.explorandes.com; Aristides Aljovín 484, Miraflores) 🍃 The winner of various green travel awards. Outdoor travel is its focus, with a specialty in trekking, biking and adventure sports. ISO certified.

Lima Vision   TOURS
(Map p74; 📞 01-447-7710; www.limavision.com; Chiclayo 444, Miraflores) Lima Vision has various four-hour city tours (S116), as well as day trips to the ruins at Pachacamac (p106).

Mónica Tours   TOURS
(📞 99-943-0796; www.monicatoursperu.com) Reader-recommended English-speaking tours. There's no street office; contact the company via the website.

Bike Tours of Lima   CYCLING
(Map p74; 📞 01-445-3172; www.biketoursoflima.com; Parque Intihuatana, Miraflores; ⊘ 9:30am-6pm Mon-Sat) Highly recommended for day tours around Barranco, Miraflores and San Isidro, as well as Sunday excursions into downtown. Rentals available.

Peru Expeditions   ADVENTURE
(Map p74; 📞 01-447-2057; www.peru-expeditions.com; Paseo de la Republica 5662, office 1201, Miraflores) Books trips and tours around the region and beyond, and also specializes in 4WD excursions.

⭐ Festivals & Events

Mistura   FAIR
(www.mistura.pe) This weeklong event is one of South America's premier food festivals, attracting international visitors and well-known chefs, showcasing the culinary diversity of Peru. Many small Peruvian businesses have earned acclaim after being 'discovered' here. It offers everything from street food to haute cuisine from Peru's best restaurants. Come hungry!

Festival of Lima   CULTURAL
(⊘ 18 Jan) Celebrates the anniversary of Lima's founding on January 18.

Marcha del Orgullo Lima　　　　LGBT
(www.facebook.com/marchadelorgullolima;
⊙ Jun-Jul) Thousands participate in the
city's festive Gay Pride march. It's held on
the last weekend in June or the first weekend of July.

El Señor de los Milagros　　　　RELIGIOUS
(Lord of Miracles; ⊙ Oct) The city drapes itself
in purple during this massive religious procession through Centro Historico on October 18 in honor of the Christ from the Iglesia
de las Nazarenas (p65); smaller processions
on occur other Sundays in October.

🛏 Sleeping

From family *pensións* to glass towers, Lima
has every type of accommodations. Though
it's one of the most expensive destinations in
the country, an overflow of lodgings means
there's some good value, particularly in the
midrange.

If arriving at night, it's worth contacting
hotels in advance to arrange for airport pickup; even budget hostels can arrange this –
sometimes for a few dollars less than the
official airport service.

🛏 Lima Centro

Offerings in the congested city center lag
behind other neighborhoods. Central Lima
has seen its high-end business slip away as
upscale establishments have shifted to San
Isidro and Miraflores. Some of the city's
cheapest lodgings are near the most storied
attractions. But keep in mind that the area
is mainly alive during the day and can feel
abandoned at night. Although security has
improved greatly, it is advisable to take taxis at night and to never display expensive
camera gear or jewelry.

1900 Backpackers　　　　HOSTEL $
(Map p66; ☎ 01-424-3358; www.1900hostel.com;
Av Garcilaso de la Vega 1588; dm S26-43, s/d incl
breakfast S86/112; @🔊) A downtown hot
spot, this old mansion designed by Gustavo Eiffel is revamped with modern design
touches, though it maintains the marble
floors and other turn-of-the-century flourishes. For a hostel it's downright gorgeous.
Rooms are smart and simple, with bunks
side by side. There's a tiny kitchen and cool
common spaces, such as a pool room with a
bar and a red chandelier.

Though the location is full of with traf-
fic-exhaust fumes during the day, there's

the plus of having a premier museum right
across the street.

Pensión Ibarra　　　　GUESTHOUSE $
(Map p62; ☎ 01-427-8603, 950-149-830; pension-
ibarra@gmail.com; Tacna 359 No 152, 14th fl; s/d
without bathroom from S30/40; 🔊) Inside a
scruffy concrete apartment block, the helpful Ibarra sisters keep seven basic guest
rooms that are clean and have firm beds.
There is a shared kitchen and a laundry service. A small balcony has amazing panoramic views over the noisy city.

Gran Hotel Bolívar　　　　HISTORIC HOTEL $$
(Map p62; ☎ 01-619-7171; www.granhotelbolivar.
com.pe; Jirón de la Unión 958; d incl breakfast S198-
264; @🔊) For aficionados of the gilded age,
this venerable 1924 hotel was where Clark
Gable, Mick Jagger and Robert Kennedy all
stayed. Though now frayed, there's a certain
grand-dame finesse, and it's on Plaza San
Martín. It's also employee-owned, a rarity
in the hotel world, which translates into im-
peccable and entertaining service.

Hotel Maury　　　　HOTEL $$
(Map p62; ☎ 01-428-8188; www.hotelmaury.ho-
teles; Ucayali 201; d/tr incl breakfast S227/263;
🅰@🔊) A longtime Lima outpost renowned
for cultivating a new-fangled cocktail known
as the pisco sour (grape brandy cocktail)
back in the 1930s. While public areas retain
flourishes such as gilded mirrors and Vic-
torian-style furniture, the 76 simple rooms
are more modern, and some feature Jacuzzi
tubs and lockboxes. Credit cards accepted.

Hostal Bonbini　　　　HOTEL $$
(Map p62; ☎ 01-427-6477; www.hostalbon
bini.com; Cailloma 209; s/d/tr incl breakfast
S132/165/198; @🔊) On a street cluttered
with print shops, this comfy, 15-room ho-
tel features simple, carpeted rooms, spick-
and-span bathrooms and cable TV. Service
could be more attentive, but credit cards
are accepted.

Lima Sheraton　　　　HOTEL $$$
(Map p66; ☎ 01-315-5000; www.marriott.com;
Paseo de la República 170; d S492; 🅰@🔊🏊)
Housed in a brutalist high-rise that overlooks the equally dour Palacio de Justicia
(Supreme Court), downtown's top hotel has
more than 400 rooms and suites decorated
in an array of desert tones. In addition to 24-
hour room service, there are concierge services, two on-site restaurants, a bar, a gym, a
swimming pool and a beauty salon.

Non-refundable reservation prices (shown here) are far more economical.

San Isidro

Want to fit into San Isidro? Carry a tennis racket. With a hyper-exclusive golf course at its heart, this is the tree-lined cradle of Lima's elite, who inhabit expansive modernist homes and sip cocktails at members-only social clubs. Accommodations are unapologetically upscale.

Malka Youth Hostel   HOSTEL $
(Map p70; ☎01-222-5589; www.youth-hostel-malka.limaperuhotels.net; Los Lirios 165; dm S40, d with/without bathroom incl breakfast S132/120; @ 🛜) A quiet hostel in a nice neighborhood just a block from a park, Malka is run by an amiable mother-daughter team. The house features 10 clean rooms, a nice garden space and a rock-climbing wall. There is a large shared kitchen and laundry facilities, a TV room with DVD player, luggage storage and a small on-site cafe serving light meals.

It's near the transit hub of Av Arequipa and Av Javier Prado.

Casa Bella Perú   GUESTHOUSE $$
(Map p70; ☎01-421-7354; www.casabellaperu.net; Las Flores 459; d incl breakfast S182-281; @ 🛜) A great midrange option in a relentlessly expensive area, this expansive former 1950s home has contemporary rooms accented by indigenous textiles. Fourteen varied units have comfy beds, firm pillows, oversized plasma TVs and remodeled bathrooms. There is a kitchen, an ample garden and a lounge. Credit cards accepted.

Hotel Basadre Suites   HOTEL $$
(Map p70; ☎01-442-2423; www.hotelbasadre.com; Jorge Basadre 1310; d incl breakfast from S240; ❄@🖼) A good option, this inn has 20 attractive, contemporary rooms, some quite spacious. Built around a former private home, each room has a minibar, hairdryer, cable TV and lockbox. Service is attentive. Breakfast, served in a small room by the garden, is abundant. Credit cards accepted; check the website for excellent special offers.

Suites Antique   APARTMENT $$
(Map p70; ☎01-222-1094; www.suites-antique.com; Av 2 de Mayo 954; d incl breakfast S340; ❄@) Central and low-key, this small hotel features smart, bright decor. The 23 spotless suites are spacious, with small kitchenettes

equipped with microwaves and minifridges. Breakfast is served at the cozy in-house cafe.

Country Club Lima Hotel   LUXURY HOTEL $$$
(Map p70; ☎01-611-9000; www.hotelcountry.com; Los Eucaliptos 590; d incl breakfast from S782; ❄@🛜🖼) Set on a sprawling lawn dotted with palms, this regal hotel occupies one of Lima's finest buildings, a sprawling 1927 structure built in the Spanish tradition. Clad in colorful tiles, wood-beam ceilings and replica Cuzco School paintings, its signature feature is a round stained-glass atrium where breakfast is served. The 83 rooms replete with amenities range from luxurious to opulent. Credit cards accepted.

El Golf Hotel Boutique   BOUTIQUE HOTEL $$$
(☎01-677-8888; www.elgolfhb.com; Valle Riesta 576; s/d incl breakfast from S380/512; ❄@🛜🖼) This intimate hotel features 20 monochromatic rooms outfitted with soft sheets, slippers and marble baths. Service is proper and the on-site restaurant offers the option of lunch or evening meals. It's on a serene residential street, two blocks west of the Lima Golf Club. Credit cards accepted.

Miraflores

The favored neighborhood for travelers is Miraflores, which offers plenty of hostels, inns and upscale hotel chains and vigilant neighborhood security.

Overlooking the ocean, this area's pedestrian-friendly streets teem with cafes, restaurants, hotels, high-rises, banks, shops and nightclubs that pump out everything from disco to *cumbia* (Colombian salsa-like dance music). There are many quiet blocks, too.

★ Quinta Miraflores   BOUTIQUE HOTEL $
(Map p74; ☎01-446-5147; www.quintamiraflores.com; Av 28 de Julio 844; r incl breakfast S120-180; 🛜) Run by an effervescent Italian, this lovely Mediterranean-style home welcomes visitors to enjoy a real retreat in the heart of busy Miraflores. There are just four elegant rooms, each decked out with fun period pieces and thoughtful touches like thick robes, large desks and a cheat sheet of city tips. Breakfast is served in the garden or in your room.

Though central for shopping and restaurants, it's part of only a few remaining *quintas* (tranquil neighborhoods built around a cul de sac) in the city.

Kaclla Healing Dog Hostel
HOSTEL $

(Map p74; 01-241-8977; www.kacllahostel.com; Calle Porta 461; dm incl breakfast S40-45, d/tr without bathroom incl breakfast S110/155;) With its cumbersome name, this pleasant option stakes its claim as an alternative hostel. Shared spaces are cozy and tranquil, with mellow music and a wandering Peruvian hound (the hostel's namesake). All of the 12 rooms have bunks. Reader recommended.

Pariwana
HOSTEL $

(Map p74; 01-242-4350; http://pariwana -hostel.com/hostels/lima; Av Jose Larco 189; dm S40-62, d with/without bathroom S160/140, all incl breakfast;) This well-heeled and central party hostel has proved a hit with the international backpacker crowd. It's full service, with tours on offer, an on-site cafe and a lovely roof deck with shady seating. Doubles with hairdryers feel all grown up. The complimentary earplugs are an unsubtle tip-off, but you probably didn't come here to rest. There are some women-only dorms.

Dragonfly Hostel
HOSTEL $

(Map p74; 01-654-3226; www.dragonfly hostels.com; Av 28 de Julio 190; dm incl breakfast S30-45, d with/without bathroom incl breakfast S149/119;) In a central location, this tiny 2nd-floor hostel proves a popular choice. It's cheerful but a bit cramped. Expect all the usual amenities: lockers, guest kitchen, bar and options for airport transfer. Rooms are brightly appointed and tidy. Guests can also chill on the rooftop.

Flying Dog
HOSTEL $

(Map p74; 01-444-5753; www.flyingdogperu. com; Lima 457; dm incl breakfast S40, s/d incl breakfast S110/140;) Of Flying Dog's four Lima hostels, this is the best, featuring a lovely outdoor garden bar and 3rd-floor lounge area with expansive views over Parque Kennedy. Rooms have hardwood floors and lockers. Two kitchens make for a shorter cooking queue, and the included breakfast is taken at the terrace restaurant across the park.

The biggest branch, across the park, is rather dusty and run down.

Hitchhikers
HOSTEL $

(Map p74; 01-242-3008; www.hhikersperu. com; Bolognesi 400; dm/d/tr without bathroom incl breakfast S35/80/120, d incl breakfast S100;) Occupying an enormous century-old *casona*, this longtime hostel has a wide array of rooms. Secure and sleeper-friendly, it includes a lounge with cable TV and a DVD library, while a bare outdoor patio has barbecue facilities and ping-pong. There are also parking spaces for campers (S20 per person). Overall, a good choice.

Global Family Backpackers
HOSTEL $

(Map p74; 01-389-7374; globalfamilyhs@gmail. com; Juan Moore 304; dm incl breakfast S29, d with/without bathroom incl breakfast S115/87;) A small brick home with parquet floors, a shared kitchen and games such as foosball and ping-pong. It's uncluttered and tranquil, bordering on dull – an advantage if you just crave some rest. The family management is kind but fairly new to tourism. Be warned: the top-floor rooms have bathrooms one flight down.

★ Casa Cielo
BOUTIQUE HOTEL $$

(Map p74; 01-242-1127; www.hotelcasa cielo.com; Berlin 370; s/d/ste incl breakfast S198/333/396;) A beautiful option that's centrally located, offering top-notch service and great value. The look is modern Andino, with ceramic bulls and Mario Testino photographs set against a neutral palette. Rooms feature hypoallergenic pillows, double-pane windows and safe boxes. À la carte breakfasts are served at a top-floor cafe.

Hotel Autor II
BOUTIQUE HOTEL $$

(Map p74; 01-383-4268; http://autor.pe; Av de la Aviacion 316; d incl breakfast S396-495;) Follow the surfer riding the two-story wave up the curving staircase. Mere blocks from the water, this next-generation boutique hotel is elegant without the fuss. In a stately alabaster home with contemporary style and artwork, rooms are on the small side, but well designed with storage areas, convenient lighting and plugs, and small desks. Service is attentive.

It's the sister property to Hotel de Autor (p85).

Libre
DESIGN HOTEL $$

(Map p74; 01-209-0900; https://librehotel.pe; Av La Paz 730; s/d incl breakfast S345/414;) New in 2018, this design hotel is further proof that the renovation of Miraflores is well underway. Guests are greeted by a playful Jade Rivera mural upon entering. Rooms are small but well kitted out, with double-pane windows blocking street noise, coordinated linens, glass showers and big flat-screen TVs. It has an 8th-floor rooftop terrace, a restaurant and 24-hour room service.

Tryp
DESIGN HOTEL **$$**

(Map p74; ☑ 01-571-8100; www.melia.com/en/hotels/peru/lima/tryp-lima-miraflores; Av Ernesto Diez Canseco 344; d/ste S310/450; P❀❀❀) This Melia property updates the international chain hotel with hipster sensibilities: a smart, contemporary style, bicycles to borrow and bluetooth speakers. The 140 rooms are spread over 10 floors, each with a safe, minibar and huge flatscreen TV. There's also 24-hour room service, a gym and heated rooftop lap pool. There is a restaurant in the glass lobby.

IFE Boutique Hotel
BOUTIQUE HOTEL **$$**

(Map p74; ☑ 01-677-2229; www.ifeboutique.com; San Ignacio de Loyola 646; d incl breakfast S324; ❀❀) A little, service-oriented boutique hotel in a convenient neighborhood. It's stylish and elegant, with eight rooms, with styles ranging from classical to pop art. King- and queen-size beds have luxuriant linens. Staff is helpful and amenities include LCD televisions, minibar, iPod docks and safe boxes.

Hotel Ibis
HOTEL **$$**

(Map p74; ☑ 01-634-8888; www.accorhotels.com; Av José Larco 1140; d S225; ❀❀) This French hotel chain is a good option with a great location, a chic Ikea-style look, blackout curtains and soundproof windows. The hotel is cleverly divided into smoking and nonsmoking floors; all rooms are on the small side. Biodegradable toiletries and water-saving policies are a plus. Breakfast is extra, at a full-service 1st-floor cafe.

Inka Frog
HOTEL **$$**

(Map p74; ☑ 01-445-8979; www.inkafrog.com; Iglesias 271; s/d/tr incl breakfast S188/228/264; ❀❀) Targeted at mature hostel-goers wanting private rooms, this subdued and friendly property features ample and spotless modern rooms with fans and flat-screen TVs. Those on a cute roof patio feature air-conditioning at no extra cost. Beware: two rooms have bathrooms accessed via the hallway. Staff is helpful and the street is refreshingly quiet.

Hostal El Patio
GUESTHOUSE **$$**

(Map p74; ☑ 01-444-2107; www.hostalelpatio.net; Ernesto Diez Canseco 341A; s/d/tr incl breakfast from S149/182/248; ❀❀) On a quiet side street just steps from Parque Kennedy, this gem of a guesthouse is named for its plant-filled courtyard with a trickling fountain. With a cheery English- and French-speaking owner, it features small, spotless rooms with cast-iron beds and colonial-style art. A few are equipped with small kitchenettes and minifridges. Check the website for special offers.

El Faro Inn
HOTEL **$$**

(Map p74; ☑ 01-242-0339; www.elfaroinn.com; Francia 857; s/d/tw incl breakfast S165/264/231; ❀❀) You'll find this peaceful option behind a row of international flags (there is no sign) close to the relaxing cliff-top park on the north side of Miraflores. Rooms are small but well appointed, with good value singles steps away from coastal walkways.

Casa San Martín
INN **$$**

(Map p74; ☑ 01-241-4434, 01-243-3900; www.casasanmartinperu.com; San Martín 339; s/d/tr incl breakfast S198/264/314; ❀❀) This Spanish Revival building is modern and uncluttered, with 20 pleasant, high-ceilinged rooms with terracotta tiles and Andean textiles. Breakfast is served in a bright cafe that faces the terrace. Credit cards accepted.

Hotel Antigua Miraflores
INN **$$**

(Map p74; ☑ 01-241-6116; www.antiguamiraflores.com; Av Grau 350; s/d/tr incl breakfast S423/482/640; ❀❀❀) In a converted early-20th-century mansion, this calm, atmospheric inn with a lovely courtyard channels colonial charm, though it's priced well above local competition. Rooms are equipped with the expected modern amenities, but the furnishings display baroque touches. Units vary in size and style; the more expensive ones have Jacuzzi tubs and kitchenettes.

La Paz Apart Hotel
APARTMENT **$$**

(Map p74; ☑ 01-242-9350; www.lapazaparthotel.com; Av La Paz 679; s/d incl breakfast S272/342, 2-bedroom ste S510; ❀❀❀) This modern high-rise may have a businesslike demeanor, but the service is attentive and the rooms comfortable. Twenty-five super-clean suites, all equipped with kitchenette, minifridge and separate sitting area, are tastefully decorated. The most spacious sleeps up to five. The hotel also has a minigym and a small conference room.

Hostal Torreblanca
HOTEL **$$**

(Map p74; ☑ 01-447-3363; www.torreblancaperu.com; Av José Pardo 1453; d/tr incl breakfast S238/291) The lobby may be cramped and the hallways narrow, but the clean, modern rooms in this Spanish-style building are comfortable. A few on the top floor have wood-beamed ceilings, red tilework and fireplaces. Rooms have down duvets and feature cable TV, minibars and telephones. Credit cards are accepted.

Hotel El Doral
HOTEL $$

(Map p74; ☑01-242-7799; www.eldoralhotel. com; Av José Pardo 486; s/d incl breakfast S350/383; ❄@🛜🏊) All business on the outside, these 39 shiny suites (think 1980s) face a plant-filled interior. All units have cable TV, minibar and sitting area – plus double-glazed windows to block out the noise. Breakfast is served on a rooftop terrace that faces the pool.

Hotel Bayview
HOTEL $$

(Map p74; ☑01-445-7321; www.bayviewhotel. com.pe; Las Dalias 276; d/ste incl breakfast S248/413; @🛜) A simple hotel with a restaurant, painted salmon pink. It has carpeted rooms adorned with folksy Peruvian paintings and amenities such as minibars and cable TV. As it's good value, it tends to fill up.

Hotel Señorial
HOTEL $$

(Map p74; ☑01-445-7306, 01-445-1870; www.senorial.com; José González 567; s/d/tr incl breakfast S267/380/462; @🛜) This long-standing hotel features more than 100 rooms and a lovely grassy courtyard. Think standard amenities, with cable TV and perfunctory stabs at decoration. Credit cards accepted.

Hotel San Antonio Abad
HOTEL $$

(Map p74; ☑01-447-6766; www.hotelsanantonioabad.com; Ramón Ribeyro 301; s/d incl breakfast S215/231; ❄@🛜) A bright-yellow mansion from the 1940s houses this reader-recommended hotel. There are 24 ample dark-paneled rooms (some with air-con) with cable TV and soundproofed windows. Breakfast is served on a terrace facing the garden. Free airport pickup can be arranged with advance reservation. Credit cards are accepted.

Hotel Alemán
HOTEL $$

(Map p74; ☑01-445-6999; www.aleman.limaperuhotels.net; Av Arequipa 4704; s/d/tr incl breakfast S165/198/298; @🛜) A rowdy boulevard gives way to this surprisingly charming 23-room hotel built around a Spanish *casona*. Simple, stuccoed rooms are decorated with Peruvian textiles and colonial-style furnishings, and come with cable TV, telephone, desk and minifridge. Credit cards accepted.

★Hotel de Autor
B&B $$$

(Map p74; ☑01-681-8074; http://autor.pe; Av 28 de Julio 562B, Quinta Bustos; d incl breakfast S545;

LIMA FOR FREE

Puente de los Suspiros (p73) A romantic wooden bridge that's inspired many a folk song.

Iglesia de las Nazarenas (p65) One of Lima's most storied churches.

Iglesia de San Agustín (p65) An elaborate facade with a somewhat less impressive interior, save for a chilling woodcarving.

Choco Museo Miraflores (p70) More of a shop than a museum, but worth a visit to be tempted by the on-site chocolate production.

Iglesia de San Pedro (p63) A small baroque church with a sumptuous interior.

Museo Central (p64) Displays centuries of Peruvian art; ID required.

P❄🛜) Why can't every hotel be like this? Service is personal, breakfasts are satisfying, and the style is modern, with authentic travel memorabilia to help guide and inspire your journey throughout Peru. Rooms are spacious, all with king-size beds, luxuriant linens and writing desks. Balconies and claw-foot tubs add a dose of romance on this quiet, centrally located cul-de-sac.

It offers ebikes for rent.

Miraflores Park Hotel
LUXURY HOTEL $$$

(Map p74; ☑01-242-3000; www.miraflorespark. com; Malecón de la Reserva 1035; d incl breakfast from S1419; ❄@🛜🏊) The best of Lima's small luxury hotels, this Belmond property offers a glorious oceanside setting and every frill. The spiral grand staircase, a gorgeous library, spa services and an infinity pool help foster the fairy-tale atmosphere. Tragaluz, the on-site restaurant, is a hot spot for local 30 to 40 year olds, with art-house decor, international cuisine and a champion bar person.

JW Marriott Hotel Lima
HOTEL $$$

(Map p74; ☑01-217-7000; www.marriott.com; Malecón de la Reserva 615; d incl breakfast from S1086; ❄@🛜🏊) The lively five-star Marriott has a superb seafront location by the LarcoMar shopping mall, ideal for watching paragliders floating outside the glass walls. The rooms sparkle and sport every amenity (though wi-fi costs extra): think minibar, plasma TV and whirlpool bath. There is also an executive lounge, restaurants, a bar, a casino and an open-air tennis court, sauna and pool.

Those nervous about their next flight can check the departure and arrival board in the lobby.

Casa Andina
HOTEL $$$

(Map p74; ☑ 01-213-4300; www.casa-andina. com; Av La Paz 463, Colección Privada; d/ste incl breakfast from S1074/1305; ❋@🛜☲) A luxury outpost of Casa Andina, with 148 spacious, chic, earth-palette rooms, which sport pre-Columbian flourishes and organic bath products.

Tierra Viva
HOTEL $$$

(Map p74; ☑ 01-637-1003; www.tierravivahoteles. com/tierra-viva-miraflores-larco; Bolívar 176-180; s/d incl breakfast S509/542) A cheerful addition to Lima, this immaculate Peruvian chain offers good service and modern rooms with lockboxes, berber carpets, king-size beds and woven Andean blankets that add a splash of color. Breakfast is served on the 8th-floor terrace.

🛏 Barranco

At the turn of the 20th century, this was a summer resort for the upper crust. In the 1960s it was a center of bohemian life. Today, it is cluttered with restaurants and bustling bars, its graceful mansions converted into boutique hotels. It is certainly one of the most walkable areas, with lots of gardens and colonial architecture.

Backpackers Inn
HOSTEL $

(Map p78; ☑ 01-247-1326; www.barrancoback packersperu.com; Mariscal Castilla 260; dm incl breakfast S40-49, d incl breakfast S115-165) A British-run backpacker hangout housed in a weathered but essentially clean mansion with 24-hour security on a quiet street. Dorms are ample, some with ocean views. There's a kitchen, eight rooms, a TV lounge and convenient access to Bajada de Baños, leading to the beach. Offers help with trips and tours.

Hostal Gémina
HOTEL $

(Map p78; ☑ 01-477-0712; www.hostalgemina. com; Av Grau 620; s/d/tr incl breakfast S105/150/195; @🛜) Tucked into a small shopping gallery, this welcoming surprise offers 31 spacious units with 1970s style. Think ship-shape, accidental-retro. There's a large living area, and clean rooms feature TVs and folksy textiles. Credit cards accepted.

Casa Nuestra
B&B $$

(Map p78; ☑ 01-248-8091; www.casanuestra peru.com; Jirón Tumbes 270; s/d/tr incl breakfast S132/165/198; @🛜) With cool decor, murals and retro poster art, this sweet home sits on a peaceful, shady side street. It provides a great base for exploring Barranco, and offers discounts for long stays. The 2nd-floor rooms are best – 1st floor digs remain a step behind in terms of renovation. There's kitchen access and a lovely roof deck. By reservation only.

3B Barranco B&B
B&B $$

(Map p78; ☑ 01-719-3868, 01-247-6915; www. 3bhostal.com; Centenario 130; s/d incl breakfast S218/254; @🛜) Cool, clean and modern, this service-oriented lodging is a traveler favorite. A common area charged with Warholesque pastiche art leads to 16 minimalist rooms that feature plush heather-gray bed covers, flatscreen TVs and granite vanities. Windows with blackout curtains open on to lightboxes of tended greenery. Good value, especially if you book direct.

★ Second Home Perú
B&B $$$

(Map p78; ☑ 01-247-5522; www.secondhome peru.com; Domeyer 366; d/ste incl breakfast S446/545; @🛜☲) With a fairy-tale feel, this lovely five-room Bavarian-style *casona* has claw-foot tubs, sculpted ironworks, a swimming pool and breathtaking views of the ocean. Run by the children of artist Victor Delfín, it features private gardens with his taurine sculptures, works of other artists and a sculpting studio that's available for rent. Credit cards accepted.

★ Villa Barranco
BOUTIQUE HOTEL $$$

(Map p78; ☑ 01-396-5418; www.ananay-hotels. com/branches/villa-barranco; Calle Carlos Zegarra 274; d incl breakfast S1706; 🛜) The kind of effortlessly beautiful but comfortable old house that instantly feels like home. This Barranco boutique hotel is brimming with style, from the clever decor to the garden with hummingbirds dive-bombing the honeysuckle. Rooms are spacious, some with claw-foot tubs, and garden access. The best feature is a gorgeous rooftop bar for enjoying pisco sours with friends.

The hotel offers excellent hosts and bicycles for guest use.

Casa Republica
BOUTIQUE HOTEL $$$

(Map p78; ☑ 01-488-6059; www.casarepub lica.com; Av Saez Peña 208; d/ste incl breakfast S627/825; 🛜) On the wide boulevard that evokes Barranco's former grandeur, this stately 1920s Republican-style home sashays onto the hotel scene. Inside, there's a playful tension between classic design and modern accents, with stained glass, chandeliers and marble baths juxtaposed with angular Scandinavian furniture and brash contemporary art. Rooms are very comfortable, with full amenities and king-sized beds; some have bathtubs.

It's worth checking out the rooftop lounge, which has ocean views perfect for evening cocktails. There are plans to add 14 more rooms out back in a new construction.

Hotel B BOUTIQUE HOTEL **$$$**
(Map p78; ☑01-206-0800; www.hotelb.pe; Sáenz Peña 204; d S990-1584; @🛜) This refurbished mansion mixes modern with classical to dramatic effect. There are 17 eclectic rooms (some can feel a bit overstuffed) surrounding a courtyard planted with a living wall of figs. Popular with nonguests, the lovely bar specializes in G&Ts and Gatsby moments. You can also visit the rooftop, which has ocean views.

🛏 West Lima

Mami Panchita INN **$$**
(☑01-263-7203; www.mamipanchita.com; Av Federico Gallesi 198, San Miguel; s/d/tr incl breakfast S139/182/211; @🛜) In a pleasant neighborhood near Miraflores, this Dutch–Peruvian guesthouse occupies a comfortable and sprawling Spanish-style house. The owners run an on-site travel agency. Families can opt for rooms that are large and homey, with a crib option and a flower-bedecked patio ideal for relaxing.

🍴 Eating

The gastronomic capital of the continent, Lima is home to some of the country's most sublime culinary creations: from dishes served at simple *cevicherías* (restaurants serving ceviche) and corner *anticucho* (beef skewer) stands to outstanding molecular cuisine. It has staggeringly fresh seafood, while its status as a centralized capital assures the presence of all manner of regional specialties.

🍴 Lima Centro

Lima's downtown spots offer cheap deals and history, from functional *comedores* (cheap restaurants) packed with office workers to atmospheric eateries that count Peruvian presidents among their clientele.

Pastelería San Martín BAKERY **$**
(Map p62; ☑01-428-9091; Nicolás de Piérola 987; snacks S8; ⏰8:30am-8pm Mon-Sat, 11am-6pm Sun) Founded in 1930, this bare-bones bakery serves what is considered Lima's finest *turrón de doña Pepa,* a dessert associated with the religious feast of El Señor de Los Milagros: flaky, sticky and achingly sweet – pair it with a stiff espresso.

Rovegno DELI **$**
(Map p66; ☑01-424-8465; Arenales 456; mains S10-28; ⏰7am-10pm Mon-Sat) This cluttered bakery-deli-restaurant sells an assortment of decent wines, breads, cheeses, ham and olives, plus plenty of pastries in a rainbow of colors. Restaurant dishes are typical Peruvian specialties such as *lomo saltado* (beef stir-fried with onions and peppers).

Agallas CEVICHE **$$**
(Map p66; ☑01-390-4012; www.facebook.com/agallascantina; Av Manco Cápac 1100; mains S22-28; ⏰12:30-5:30pm Tue-Sun) A country mile from the tourist traps, this hip cantina and *cevichería* in La Victoria serves six heavenly versions of marinated fish with metal cups of beer. It's worth sharing an order of the northern-style seafood rice served in aluminum casserole dishes. The portraits of working *limeños* lining the walls pay homage to the real heart of the city.

Wa Lok CHINESE **$$**
(Map p62; ☑01-447-1314; Paruro 878; mains S15-80; ⏰9am-11pm Mon-Sat, to 10pm Sun; 🌱) Serving seafood, fried rice as light and fresh as it gets, and sizzling meats that come on steaming platters, Wa Lok is among the best *chifas* (Chinese restaurants) in Chinatown. The 16-page Cantonese menu includes dumplings, noodles, stir-fries and a good selection of vegetarian options (try the braised tofu casserole). Portions are enormous; don't over-order.

Tanta PERUVIAN **$$**
(Map p62; ☑01-428-3115; Pasaje Nicolas de Rivera 142; mains S21-50; ⏰9am-10pm Mon-Sat, to 6pm Sun) One of several informal bistros in the Gastón Acurio brand, Tanta serves Peruvian dishes, fusion pastas, generous salads and sandwiches. It's a good bet in the city center, where pickings are slim. The food is generally good but desserts shine: try the heavenly passionfruit cheesecake mousse. There

are other branches in **Miraflores** (Map p74; ☑ 01-444-5231; Av Vasco Núñez de Balboa 660, Miraflores; mains $18-52; ⊗ noon-10pm) and **San Isidro** (Map p70; ☑ 01-421-9708; Pancho Fierro 115, San Isidro; mains $20-45; ⊗ 8am-midnight Mon-Sat, to 10pm Sun).

L'Eau Vive   FRENCH $$

(Map p62; ☑ 01-427-5612; Ucayali 370; mains $32-55, 3-course menús $19; ⊗ 12:30-3pm & 7:30-9:30pm Mon-Sat; ❀) In an 18th-century building, this very simple and unusual eatery is run by French Carmelite nuns. Expect French and other continental specialties (think *coquilles St Jacques*) with Peruvian influences. The food isn't jaw-dropping, but the real reason to come is to enjoy the strange serenade. Every night after dinner (at around 9pm), the nuns gather to sing 'Ave Maria.'

Cevichería la Choza Nautica   CEVICHE $$

(Map p66; ☑ 01-268-1598; Breña 204; mains $19-50; ⊗ noon-11pm) A surprisingly bright spot in a slightly dingy area, this popular *cevichería,* staffed by bow-tied waiters, offers more than a dozen types of ceviches and *tiraditos* (Japanese-style ceviche, without onions). There is also a long list of soups, seafood and rice dishes. Live music plays on busy nights.

Salon Capon   CHINESE $$

(Map p62; ☑ 01-426-9286; Paruro 819; mains $13-48; ⊗ 9am-10pm Mon-Sat, to 7pm Sun) Across the street from Wa Lok, the smaller Salon

Capon has a lengthy Cantonese menu, good dim sum and a traditional bakery that makes scrumptious, flaky egg tarts.

✖ San Isidro

Chic dining rooms, frothy cocktails and fusion haute cuisine: San Isidro is a bastion of fine dining – and not much else.

Coffee Road   CAFE $

(Map p70; ☑ 01-637-2028; Av Prescott 365; mains $6-12; ⊗ 7am-10pm Mon-Fri, 9am-10pm Sat, 2-10pm Sun) Calling all coffee connoisseurs: this cafe of long bars and leather stools will brew you delicious espresso, Chemex, French press, Aeropress and more, using quality Peruvian beans. It's some of the best in town. Also serves quiches and desserts.

★ Barra Chalaca   CEVICHE $$

(Map p70; ☑ 01-422-1465; Av Camino Real 1239; mains $14-39; ⊗ 11am-5pm) This casual ceviche and seafood bar combines masterful cooking and playful rapport for the win. Watching the prep cooks from your bar stool, order *curatodo* (cures everything) – a fishbowl of tropical juices and fresh herbs. There's mouthwatering *tiradito chichuito* (sashimi with capers, avocado and garlic); crisp, lightly battered *pejerrey* (silverside fish), and seafood fried rice that you can't put down.

Come early for lunch, as there's always a wait for tables.

CITY CUISINE

In Lima, food inspires as much reverence as religion. So, the agonizing question is, what to eat? Start by sampling these local staples.

➡ Lima's most tender beef-heart skewers, *anticuchos,* can be found at street carts and a posh Miraflores eatery, Panchita (p93).

➡ Sublime renditions of the country's most seductive dish, ceviche, can be found in places both economical, such as Barra Chalaca, and upscale, such as Pescados Capitales (p93); for something truly different, try it seared at Fiesta (p92).

➡ The country's fusion cuisine, *criollo* cooking – a singular blend of Spanish, Andean, Chinese and African influences – is without parallel at neighborhood eateries Isolina (p95) and El Bodegón (p91), in addition to the super-chic Restaurant Huaca Pucllana (p92).

➡ First-rate service, encyclopedic wine lists, and sculptural dishes that blend the traditional and the nouveau find their apex at Astrid y Gastón Casa Moreyra (p89) and Central (p93).

➡ Celebrating the humble potato, *causas* are cold potato dishes that are as beautiful as they are delectable, and are found in any traditional restaurant.

Matsuei
JAPANESE **$$**

(☎981-310-180; www.matsueiperu.com.pe; Ata-hualpa 195; mains S16-70; ⏱12:30-3:30pm & 7:30-11pm Mon-Sat) Venerated Japanese superchef Nobu Matsuhisa once co-owned this sushi bar. Its new location is posh and atmospheric. Diners come to try some of the most spectacular sashimi and *maki* (sushi rolls) in Lima. A must-have: the *acevichado*, a roll stuffed with shrimp and avocado, then doused in a house-made mayo infused with ceviche broth. Your brain will tingle.

Cafe A Bistro
AMERICAN **$$**

(☎01-264-5856; www.facebook.com/cafeabistro; Av Del Ejercito 2193; mains S25-35; ⏱8am-11pm Fri-Wed, to 4pm Thu) Sandwiched between a gas station and a Chinese restaurant, this restaurant is unexpected, and then some. Serving up classic American breakfasts such as sausage patties, eggs and thick slices of homemade bread, it's a cozy spot with outdoor seating to enjoy a midday brunch or laid-back night out with friends.

Renowned for its hamburgers, this little joint takes pride in using local ingredients and making its bread and sauces from scratch.

Spizza
PIZZA **$$**

(Map p70; ☎01-222-2228; Av 2 de Mayo 455; pizza S31-53; ⏱12:30-11pm Mon-Sat, 12:30-10pm Sun) Never underestimate the value of a thin-crust margherita pizza blistered by a searing wood oven. Upholding Neapolitan tradition, this tiny brick restaurant delivers the goods alongside artisan beer and sangria made with fresh *hierba luisa* mint.

Hanzo
JAPANESE **$$**

(Map p70; ☎01-422-6367; www.hanzo.com.pe; Conquistadores 598; mains S23-58; ⏱12:30-4pm & 7:30-11:30pm Mon-Sat, 12:30-4pm Sun) With a full bar, this atmospheric fusion house is a lively place for sushi but it's not for purists. *Maki acevichado* and butter rolls made with fried rice are playful nods to Peruvian influence.

Segundo Muelle
CEVICHE **$$**

(Map p70; ☎01-717-9998; www.segundomuelle. com; Conquistadores 490; mains S32-58; ⏱noon-5pm) 🍴 A mainstay of impeccable service and renowned ceviches with innovative twists. Try the *ceviche de mariscos a los tres ajíes*, a stack of mixed fish and shellfish bathed in three types of hot pepper sauce. The menu also features rice and other seafood dishes, including a recommended *parrilla marina* (seafood grill).

500 Grados
MEDITERRANEAN **$$**

(Map p70; ☎954-604-536; www.500grados.com; Camino Real 1281; mains S15-45; ⏱7am-midnight) What can't you do with a hot oven, a stack of firewood and a battery of well-oiled cast-iron pans? This restaurant puts that challenge to the test, with mixed results. Bubbly thin-crust pizzas and roasted squash lack seasoning but the pork ribs and roast chicken, served in those pans, are winners. Lots of unique, tasty cocktails, too.

The table service could use some improvement.

Antica
PIZZA **$$**

(Map p70; ☎01-222-9488; www.anticapizzeria.com.pe; Av 2 de Mayo 732; mains S29-48; ⏱noon-midnight) On a street lined with European restaurants, this is one of the most reasonable: a wood-clad, candle-bedecked spot serving house-made pasta, gnocchi and pizza from a wood-fired oven. It's popular with local families. There is antipasto, as well as a decent wine list strong on South American brands.

★Astrid y Gastón Casa Moreyra
FUSION **$$$**

(Map p70; ☎01-442-2775; www.astridygaston. com; Av Paz Soldan 290; mains S53-89; ⏱1-3pm & 7-11pm Mon-Sat) The standard-bearer of *novoandina* cooking in Lima, Gastón Acurio's flagship French-influenced restaurant, run by Lima native Diego Muñoz, remains a culinary tour de force. The seasonal menu features traditional Peruvian fare, but it's the exquisite fusion specialties that make this a sublime fine-dining experience. The 28-course tasting menu showcases the depth and breadth of possibility here – just do it.

Guests may be treated to a kitchen visit to watch white-coated armies assembling plates with tweezer-precision. The setting is a gorgeous mansion with multiple dining rooms, and the service is excellent, including a helpful sommelier.

Punto Italiano
ITALIAN **$$$**

(Map p70; ☎01-349-2278; Av 2 de Mayo 647; mains S30-48; ⏱12:30-4pm & 6-11pm; 🖐) Italian cuisine with a Sardinian twist is dished up at this homey trattoria popular with families. The handmade ravioli is locally renowned while the *carne tagliata* (veal with tagliatelle) with Sardinian cheese is divine.

✕ Miraflores

By far the most varied neighborhood for eating, Miraflores carries the breadth and depth of Peruvian cooking at every price range, from tiny *comedores* with cheap lunchtime *menús* to some of the city's most revered gastronomic outposts. Pavement cafes are ideal for sipping pisco sours and people-watching.

Casual places with cheap *menús* abound on the tiny streets east of Av José Larco just off Parque Kennedy.

La Lucha Sanguachería
SANDWICHES $

(Map p74; ☑01-241-5953; Benavides 308; sandwiches S12-21; ☺8am-1am Sun-Thu, to 3am Fri & Sat) This all-hours corner sandwich shop is the perfect fix for the midnight munchies. *Lechón a la leña* (roasted pork) is its specialty, but there's also roast chicken or ham served in fluffy rolls, and juices are blended on the spot.

El Pan de la Chola
CAFE $

(Map p74; ☑01-221-2138; Av La Mar 918; mains S8-25; ☺8am-10pm Mon-Sat, 9am-7pm Sun; ☜) In South America, finding real, crusty wholegrain bread is rarer than striking gold. Enter this small brick cafe that bakes four scrumptious varieties, and serves organic coffee from the Peruvian Amazon, greek yogurt and sweets. There's European-style seating at big wooden tables; grab a sandwich or share the tasting plate with bread, olives, hummus and fresh cheese.

Ana Avellana
BAKERY $

(Map p74; www.facebook.com/anaavellanalima; Mendiburu 1096; desserts S5-16; ☺8am-9pm Tue-Sat, to 7pm Sun; ☜) A jolly light-blue exterior invites you inside to gaze at Ana Avellana's sweet and savory creations. A dense flourless chocolate cake or luscious Borgoña grape pie is a great pairing for an Americano as you sit on one of the comfy sofas. Herby goat-cheese tarts and rustic quinoa-bread sandwiches filled with roast beef or turkey satisfy those with savory cravings.

Manolo
CAFE $

(Map p74; ☑01-444-2244; www.manolochurros.com; Av José Larco 608; churros S4; ☺7am-1am Sun-Thu, to 2am Fri & Sat) This thriving all-hours sidewalk cafe is best known for its piping-hot churros, which go smashingly well with a *chocolate caliente espeso* (thick hot chocolate) – perfect for dipping. Of course, there's also typical cafe fare.

Helena Chocolatier
SWEETS $

(Map p74; ☑01-715-0000; www.helena.pe; Iglesias 498; chocolates from S3; ☺10:30am-7:30pm Mon-Fri, to 6pm Sat) A longtime artisanal chocolate shop that crafts scrumptious 'Chocolates D'Gala,' each stuffed with fillings made from pecans, marzipan or raspberries and individually gift-wrapped.

Beso Frances
CREPERIE $

(Map p74; ☑01-717-8949; www.besofrances.pe; Malecón de la Reserva, Parque Intihuatana; crepes S10-18; ☺7:30am-11pm) Offering up sweet and savory crepes, this quaint shop is the perfect stop while bike riding or walking along the coastal pathway. Grab a cup of coffee and a crepe filled with fudge, or gooey cheese and roast beef if you need something more filling, and sit at one of the small outdoor tables looking over the Pacific Ocean.

Live violin music everyday at 5pm gives that feeling of a French bistro.

Amore Mio
GELATO $

(Map p74; ☑941-403-377; www.facebook.com/pg/gelatoamoremio; Av La Paz 178; 1/2 scoops S7.50/11; ☺noon-9pm Mon, 11am-9pm Tue-Thu & Sun, to 10pm Fri & Sat; ☎) This two-story artisanal ice-cream shop, just blocks from Parque Kennedy, makes 36 flavors of gelato daily, inspired by Peruvian fruits, and also sells pastries. Limited seating encourages you to choose a treat and keep walking.

Ágora Café y Arte
CAFE $

(Map p74; ☑01-241-4435; www.facebook.com/agoracafeyarte; Diagonal 378, Miraflores; ☺7:30am-9:30pm Mon-Sat, 10am-8pm Sun) Enjoy outdoor seating at this cafe with a view of one of Lima's most popular parks, Parque Kennedy. Sip organic Peruvian coffee (S7 to S12), which pairs so well with a slice of passion-fruit cheesecake, and gaze at the bustling tourists and *limeños* who pass by.

Kulcafé
CAFE $

(Map p74; ☑993-325-5445; Bellavista 370; mains S12-18; ☺8am-11pm Mon-Thu, 11am-midnight Sat & Sun; ☜) For German sweets, coffee drinks and smoothies, this is the spot. Don't go conventional – the 'sweet green' smoothie makes spinach, watermelon and mango delectable together. There are also organic foods and beautiful whole-grain bagels served in a cozy living-room atmosphere where everyone is on their device.

El Enano
SANDWICHES $

(Map p74; ☑01-447-4566; Chiclayo 699; sandwiches S12-18; ☺6am-1am Sun-Thu, to 3am Fri & Sat) Grab a stool at the open-air counter and watch the masters at work. Fresh-roasted chicken, ham, turkey and *chicharrón* (deep-fried pork) sandwiches on French bread are dressed with marinated onions and chilies. After one too many piscos, this is the cure. Exotic fresh juices are served in glass jars.

Anticuchos de la Tía Grimanesa
BARBECUE $

(Map p74; 01-442-1468; Av Ignacio Merino 465; anticucho S15; ⊙5-11pm Mon-Sat) The legendary doña Grimanesa presided over a humble *anticucho* (beef skewer) cart for over 30 years and earned a flock of fans before getting her own place. With tender meat and homemade hot sauces, it's a simple pleasure.

Pastelería San Antonio
CAFE $

(Map p74; 01-241-3001; Av Vasco Núñez de Balboa 770; sandwiches S12-30; ⊙7am-9pm Mon-Thu, to 8pm Fri, 9am-6pm Sat) A cross-section of Miraflores society jams into this 50-year-old institution for an infinite variety of sandwiches, as well as a wide selection of baked goods, including a dreamy chocolate croissant (ask for it warm).

Bodega Miraflores
CAFE $

(Map p74; Diez Canseco 109; coffee S3; ⊙9:30am-1pm & 3:30-7:30pm Mon-Sat) A frumpy spot that serves strong, inky *cortados* (espresso with a dollop of steamed milk) made with coffee grown in Chanchamayo. Bagged, whole-bean coffee is available to take home.

Vivanda
SUPERMARKET $

(Map p74; 01-620-3000; www.vivanda.com.pe; Benavides 487; ⊙7am-midnight) Vivanda is one of the best of Lima's many supermarkets, loaded with both local and imported food, drink, toiletries and medicines. With branches on **José Pardo** (Map p74; Av José Pardo 715, Miraflores; ⊙8am-11pm) and in **San Isidro** (Map p70; 1-620-3000; www.vivanda.com.pe; Av 2 de Mayo 1420, San Isidro; ⊙8am-10pm).

★ámaZ
AMAZONIAN $$

(Map p74; 01-221-9393; www.amaz.com.pe; Av La Paz 1079; mains S20-65; ⊙12:30-11:30pm Mon-Sat, to 4:30pm Sun;) Chef Pedro Miguel's wonder is wholly dedicated to the abundance of the Amazon. Start with tart jungle-fruit cocktails and oversized *tostones* (plantain chips). Banana-leaf wraps, aka *juanes,* hold treasures such as fragrant Peking duck with rice. There's excellent *encurtido* (pickled vegetables) and the generous

LIMA EATING

vegetarian set menu for two is a delicious way to sample the diversity.

ÁmaZ has a popular circular bar and coveted thatched-roof tables.

★El Bodegón
BISTRO $$

(Map p74; 01-444-4704; www.elbodegon.com.pe; Av Tarapaca 197; mains S28-39; ⊙noon-midnight Mon-Sat, 11am-9pm Sun) Dimly lit with polished hardwood and offering snappy service, this corner taverna feels more Buenos Aires than Lima; we're just thankful it's here. This Gastón Acurio enterprise recaptures home-style Peruvian eating. It's worth sharing several dishes to spread your good fortune. Standouts include a creamy roasted cauliflower served whole and an ultradelectable *rocoto relleno* (stuffed pepper) with a nutty, rich sauce.

End your meal with a *suspiro de chirimoya* (custard apple) in decadent *dulce de leche* (caramel sauce).

Bao?
CHINESE $$

(Map p74; 01-483-4180; www.facebook.com/baoacomer; José Domingo Choquehuanca 411; mains S30; ⊙1-4pm & 7-11pm Tue-Fri, 1-11:30pm Sat, 1-4pm Sun) Just as the restaurant scene in Lima began to lean towards the upscale and grandiose, this little steam-bun place found its way into the hearts of many – including Peru's own top chef, Gastón Acurio. Savory pork and chicken sandwiches, rice bowls and dressed-up fries are constant, but the chefs are always experimenting with 'secret menu' items.

Don't miss the *chanchiears* – fried pieces of pork ears that look like crispy fries and are just as addictive.

Mercado 28
FOOD HALL $$

(Map p74; 981-370-730; www.mercado28.pe; Av Vasco Núñez de Balboa 755; mains S12-30; ⊙8am-10pm) This open 2nd-floor market houses more than a dozen restaurant stands attracting a mostly millennial crowd for cheap, informal dining. It's a hit, partially because of the decent quality options, from gourmet burgers to street chicken and poke bowls. In the center of it all, an island bar stocked with beer on tap, cocktails and wine holds it all together.

Maestro Tzu
CHINESE $$

(Map p74; ☑ 01-288-4351; www.maestrotzu.com; LarcoMar; mains S30-50; ⊙noon-11pm) This wonderful upscale restaurant has a prime spot in LarcoMar. It's run by second-generation Chinese restaurateurs using cherished family recipes emphasizing fresh ingredients and sauces without food coloring or additives. The results are delicious, with soups that are light and fragrant; shrimp empanadas with a nice chewy texture; and stir-fries cooked just right. For dessert, try the gelatin with fig honey.

Fiesta Chiclayo Gourmet
PERUVIAN $$

(Map p74; ☑ 01-242-9009; www.restaurantfiesta gourmet.com; Av Reducto 1278; mains S40-65; ⊙12:30pm-midnight Mon-Sat) The finest northern Peruvian cuisine in Lima is served at this busy establishment on Miraflores' eastern edge. The *arroz con pato a la chiclayana* (duck and rice Chiclayo-style) is achingly tender and *ceviche a la brasa* gets a quick sear so it's lightly smoky, yet tender. It has to be eaten to be believed.

La Nacional
PERUVIAN $$

(Map p74; ☑ 01-441-2030; www.lanacional.pe; Av La Mar 1254; mains S26-40; ⊙10am-11pm Mon-Sat, 11am-4pm Sun) If you're looking for traditional Peruvian dishes such as *pastel de choclo* (a savory corn casserole with layers of meat and cheese) or *lomo saltado* (stir-fried beef atop fried potato wedges), this modern kitchen serves them with a fresh twist. A relaxed atmosphere with a touch of class makes it popular for an evening meal accompanied by a glass of wine.

El Mercado
SEAFOOD $$

(Map p74; ☑ 01-221-1322; Unanue 203; mains S35-51; ⊙12:30-5pm Tue-Sun) This hip, barebones ceviche joint just happens to be spearheaded by culinary star Rafael Osterling. Diners pack in for fresh, fusion-style shellfish and eight distinct ceviches but the seared-fish sandwiches are great value. For dessert: cinnamon ice cream perfumed with anise.

Raw Cafe
VEGAN $$

(Map p74; ☑ 01-446-9456; www.facebook.com/ rawcafeclub; Independencia 587; mains S21-34; ⊙9am-9pm Mon-Fri, to 6pm Sat; ☑) The raw-

food movement has arrived in Lima and this popular vegan cafe is proof. Think beet burgers, pizzas with cashew cheese, salads with toasted coconut 'bacon,' green juices and kombucha. Also serves organic coffee.

El Punto Azul
CEVICHE $$

(Map p74; ☑ 01-445-8078; San Martín 595; mains S31-51; ⊙noon-5pm; ☻) Awash in Caribbean blues, this pleasant family eatery dishes up fresh ceviches, *tiraditos* (Japanese-style ceviche, without onions) and family-sized rice dishes. Try its risotto with parmesan, shrimp and *ají amarillo* (yellow chili) – and don't miss the lineup of beautiful desserts. It gets packed, so show up before 1pm if you want a table. Excellent value.

El Rincón del Bigote
CEVICHE $$

(Map p74; ☑ 01-241-2709; José Galvez 529; mains S38-50; ⊙noon-4pm Tue-Sun) Go early. On weekends, locals and tourists line up for seating in this bare-bones ceviche house. The specialty is *almejas in su concha:* pair these marinated clams with a side of crisp yucca fries and a bottle of cold pilsner and you're in heaven.

La Preferida
DELI $$

(Map p74; ☑ 01-445-5180; Arias Araguez 698; mains S18-32, tapas S9; ⊙8am-5pm Mon-Sat) Located a couple of blocks north of Av 28 de Julio, east of the Vía Expresa, this charming take-out place has gorgeous *causas* (whipped potato dishes) and fresh seafood specialties such as *pulpo al olivo* (octopus in olive sauce) and *chupo a la chalaca* (mussels with a corn and tomato salsa) served in tapas-sized portions. A few stools accommodate diners.

Restaurant Huaca Pucllana
PERUVIAN $$

(Map p74; ☑ 01-445-4042; www.resthuacapu cllana.com; Gral Borgoño cuadra 8; mains S24-72; ⊙12:30-4:30pm & 7pm-midnight Mon-Sat, to 4pm Sun) Overlooking the illuminated ruins at Huaca Pucllana, this sophisticated establishment serves a skillfully rendered array of contemporary Peruvian dishes (from grilled *cuy* to seafood chowders), along with a smattering of Italian-fusion specialties. Portions are large. Save room for the pisco and lemon parfait for dessert.

★Maido
JAPANESE $$$

(Map p74; ☑ 01-446-2512; www.maido.pe; San Martín 399; mains S26-110; ⊙12:30-4pm & 7:30-11pm Mon-Sat, 12:30-4pm Sun) ⊘ True artistry and exquisite flavors make Maido an excellent stop for top-notch nikkei (Japanese-Peruvian) fare that has put it on World's Best lists. The menu of chef Mitsuharu 'Micha' Tsumura ranges from sushi to tender 50-hour ribs, *okonomiyaki* (Japanese pancake) and ramen, with a Peruvian accent. Desserts – such as the yucca *mochi* or a white-chocolate egg with sorbet yolk – delight. It supports sustainable fishing.

★ **Central**   PERUVIAN $$$
(Map p78; ☑ 01-242-8515; www.centralrestaurante.com.pe; Av Pedro de Osma 301; mains S52-95; ⊗ seating 12:45-1:15pm & 7:45-8:30pm Mon-Sat)
🍴 Part restaurant, part laboratory, Central reinvents Andean cuisine and rescues age-old Peruvian ingredients not used elsewhere. Dining is an experience, evidenced by tender native potatoes served in edible clay. Chef Virgilio Martinez wants you to taste the Andes. He paid his dues in Europe and Asia's top kitchens, but it's his work here that dazzles.

Seafood – such as the charred octopus starter – is a star, but classics like suckling pig served with pickled vegetables and spiced squash deliver. A menu supplied by sustainable fishing and organic gardens enhance the ultra-fresh appeal.

IK   PERUVIAN $$$
(Map p74; ☑ 01-652-1692; www.ivankisic.pe; Elías Aguirre 179; mains S45-75; ⊗ 6-11pm Mon-Sat)
Combining ancestral traditions with the Peruvian vanguard of molecular gastronomy is a tall order, but most feel that IK pulls it off with style. The restaurant is a tribute to a well-known local chef and its restorative atmosphere of living plants, natural sounds and light projections bring something new to the dining experience. Dishes are well balanced and meticulously presented.

With award-winning bartenders and a master sommelier to assist with the impressive wine selection.

Pescados Capitales   CEVICHE $$$
(Map p74; ☑ 01-421-8808; www.pescadoscapitales.com; Av La Mar 1337; mains S39-70; ⊗ 12:30-5pm) On a street once lined by clattering auto shops, this industrial-contemporary destination serves some of the finest ceviche around. Try the 'Ceviche Capital,' a mix of flounder, salmon and tuna marinated with red, white and green onions, bathed in a three-chili crème. A nine-page wine list offers a strong selection of Chilean and Argentinean vintages.

La Mar   SEAFOOD $$$
(Map p74; ☑ 01-421-3365; www.lamarcebicheria.com; Av La Mar 770; mains S39-79; ⊗ noon-5pm Mon-Fri, 11:45am-5:30pm Sat & Sun) A good-time *cevichería* (restaurant serving ceviche) with outstanding service and wonderful ceviche and *tiraditos* (Japanese version of ceviche), alongside a light and fresh *chifon chaufa* (fried rice). This Gastón Acurio outpost is not much more than a polished cement patio bursting with VIPs. Try the delicious riff on a bloody Mary – the sublime bloody *locho*, seafood shells and all. Desserts deliver too. It does not take reservations.

Panchita   PERUVIAN $$$
(Map p74; ☑ 01-242-5957; www.panchita.pe; Av 2 de Mayo 298; mains S33-76; ⊗ noon-midnight Tue-Sat, to 6pm Sun) A Gastón Acurio homage to Peruvian street food in a contemporary setting ringed by folk art. Skewered meats are grilled over an open flame to melt-in-your-mouth perfection, particularly the charred octopus. Another winner is the crisp suckling pig with *tacu-tacu* (Peruvian fusion dish of rice and beans). There's also a great salad bar. Portions are big and filling so don't come alone. With outstanding service.

Rafael   FUSION $$$
(Map p74; ☑ 01-242-4149; www.rafaelosterling.pe; San Martín 300; mains S48-89; ⊗ 1-3pm & 8-11pm Mon-Wed, to midnight Thu-Sat) A consistent favorite of discerning palates, here chef Rafael Osterling produces a panoply of fusion dishes, such as *tiradito* bathed in Japanese citrus or suckling goat stewed in Madeira wine. For slimmer budgets the crisp pizzas are divine. Make it past the generously poured cocktails and there's a decent and lengthy international wine list.

Las Brujas de Cachiche   PERUVIAN $$$
(Map p74; ☑ 01-444-5310; www.brujasdecachiche.com.pe; Bolognesi 460; mains S44-80; ⊗ noon-midnight Mon-Sat, to 4pm Sun) Quality Peruvian cooking with the live ambience of a tinkling piano. Brujas' menu has wonderfully prepared classics such as *ají de gallina* (spicy chicken and walnut stew), as well as lesser-known specialties such as *carapulcra*, a dried potato stew. To try a bit of everything, hit the lunch buffet. The bar is a popular watering hole for grown-up tastes.

La Rosa Nautica   SEAFOOD $$$
(Map p74; ☑ 01-445-0149; Circuito de Playas; mains S34-72; ⊗ noon-midnight) Location,

LOCAL KNOWLEDGE

MORE, PLEASE

Want to eat like a local? When eating in homes, local *fondas* or *quintas* (informal family restaurants) you can ask for a generous portion by ordering it '*bien taipa.*' If you want seconds, say '*yapa!*' – it roughly translates as 'more, please.'

location, location. Though you can get better seafood deals elsewhere, the views from this eatery on the historic pier are unparalleled. Go during happy hour (5pm to 7pm), when you can watch the last of the day's surfers skim along the crests of the waves. Take a taxi to the pier and walk the last 100m.

✖ Barranco

Even as Barranco has gone upscale in recent years, with trendy restaurants serving everything fusion fare, the neighborhood still holds on to atmospheric, local spots where life is no more complicated than ceviche and beer.

A number of informal restaurants serving *anticuchos* and cheap *menús* line Av Grau around the intersection with Unión.

La Panetteria BAKERY $
(Map p78; ☑01-469-8260; www.facebook.com/lapanetteriabarranco; Av Grau 369; mains S8-22; ☺8am-9pm Tue-Sun; ☏) One of the neighborhood favorites, this bakery serves up a wide variety of breads, from traditional baguettes and French rolls, to playful experiments such as pesto or *aji* (Peru's slightly spicy pepper) loaves and gorgeous pastries. It's busy on weekends with the brunch crowd (eggs aren't on the menu but are available).

Thanks to its wild popularity, it has opened a two-storey extension across the street.

Blu ICE CREAM $
(Map p78; ☑01-247-3791; Av 28 de Julio 202; cones S7-10; ☺11am-10pm) Creamy, dense chocolate, bright herbs, Madagascar vanilla or tart jungle fruit: this is Lima's best gelato, made fresh daily. Keep an eye out for carts set up outside the art shop Dédalo (p100) in Barranco and the popular bread shop La Chola (p90) in San Isidro.

Delifrance BAKERY $
(Map p78; ☑01-247-6760; Av Grau 695; snacks S4-12; ☺9am-8pm Tue-Sat, to 2pm Sun) Stock

your picnic basket with authentic, fresh-baked *pain au chocolat,* baguettes, brioche, top-quality deli meats and cheeses or the lovely French desserts sold at this take-out center.

Burrito Bar MEXICAN $
(Map p78; ☑987-352-120; Av Grau 113; mains S6-18; ☺1-11pm Tue-Sat, noon-5pm Sun) Londoner Stew created this Mexican fast but fresh food sensation after studying tortilla making on YouTube. The experiment was a smash hit, from Baja-style fish tacos to fresh salsas and thirst-quenching mint limeade. Also serves Sierra Andina microbrews. For dessert: sticky toffee pudding.

Cafe Bisetti CAFE $
(Map p78; ☑01-713-9565; Av Pedro de Osma 116; coffee S8-16; ☺8am-9pm Mon-Fri, 10am-11pm Sat, 3-9pm Sun) Locals leave their designer dogs out front of this roasting house where some of the finest lattes in town are served with fresh pastries or bitter chocolate pie. Check out the courses on roasting and tasting.

La Bodega Verde CAFE $
(Map p78; ☑01-247-8804; Sucre 335A; mains S18-28; ☺8am-8pm Mon-Thu, to 10pm Fri-Sun; ☏☑▥) Set in a walled garden, this cafe and gallery is a pleasant spot to linger. Grab the Scrabble (or toys set out for kids) and order up a salad, *lúcuma* milkshake with fruit from the garden tree, tea served in a ceramic pot or organic coffee. Breakfast includes whole-grain breads. It's also vegan-friendly. Sweets, such as carrot cake, are especially good.

There's a second location (p95) at the Museum of Contemporary Art.

Café Tostado PERUVIAN $$
(Map p78; ☑01-247-7133; Av Nicolás de Pierola 222; mains S10-38; ☺12:30-9pm Mon-Sat, 7:30am-6pm Sun) Call it a cultural experience. This barely converted auto-repair shop long ago transformed into a bastion of traditional cooking, with long wooden tables and an open kitchen surrounded by scarred iron pots and drying noodles. Daily specials rotate, but the sought-after signature dish is rabbit, which feeds up to three people.

Award-winning Tunki coffee is served with *chicharrónes* (fried pork belly) on Sunday for a typical Peruvian breakfast.

La 73 BISTRO $$
(Map p78; ☑01-247-0780; Av El Sol Oeste 175; mains S28-55; ☺noon-midnight) ✐ Named for

an iconic local bus, this contemporary bistro serves Peruvian–Mediterranean fare, with sustainable fish. Some dishes seem rushed, but standouts include homemade ravioli with barbecued meat, fluffy rice bowls and duck risotto. The bar serves wine and pisco concoctions, or try the amazing *herba luisa* lemonade. To end on a sweet note, split the crisp, warm churros for dessert.

Colonia & Co
CAFE $$

(Map p78; ☑ 01-489-5459; Av San Martín 131; mains S16-38; ⊙ 8am-11pm; 🖥) For extraordinary coffee, fresh blended juices and wonderful brunch, come to this cheerful modern cafe. Straight from Seattle, the Slayer espresso machine gets heavy play: order a *chapa*, with a touch of milk, allspice and honey; it's pure velvet. The comfort-food menu is short but sweet, with gorgeous eggs Benedict, duck with rice and *pastel de choclo* (corn casserole).

La Bodega Verde
CAFE $$

(Map p78; ☑ 01-248-8559; Av Grau 1511, MAC; mains S18-28; ⊙ 8am-8pm; 🖥🌱) The Museum of Contemporary Art location of this vegan-friendly cafe has an enclosed park setting that's ideal for families. The original location (p94) is in the middle of Barranco.

La Canta Rana
CEVICHE $$

(Map p78; ☑ 01-247-7274; Génova 101; mains S28-47; ⊙ 8am-11pm Tue-Sat) Around for decades, this unpretentious spot draped in flags and plastered in photos packs in the locals with its offering of more than 17 different types of ceviche.

Antica Trattoria
ITALIAN $$

(Map p78; ☑ 01-247-2443; San Martín 201; pastas S20-42; ⊙ noon-11:30pm) A longtime Italian spot with a nouveau-rustic air. Antica serves wood-fired pizza, as well as savory concoctions such as fresh ravioli stuffed with crab and tender osso buco with creamy polenta.

★ Isolina
PERUVIAN $$$

(Map p78; ☑ 01-247-5075; www.isolina.pe; Av San Martín 101; mains S35-78; ⊙ noon-10pm Mon & Tue, to 11pm Wed-Fri, 9am-5pm Sat, 9am-11pm Sun) Go old school. This is home-style *criollo* (spicy Peruvian fare with Spanish and African influences) food at its best. Isolina doesn't shy away from tripe and kidneys, but also offers loving preparations of succulent ribs, *causa escabechada* (whipped potato dishes with marinated onions) and

vibrant green salads on the handwritten menu. Family-sized portions come in old-fashioned tins, but you could make a lighter meal of starters such as marinated clams or ceviche.

You may not havee room for dessert, but it sure looks good. The pisco sours are recommended.

✗ West Lima & Callao

Origen Tostadores de Cafe
CAFE $

(☑ Pueblo Libre 01-261-8280; www.origentostadoresdecafe.com; Av Bolívar 1199, Pueblo Libre; coffee drinks S6-10; ⊙ 8am-10pm Tue-Fri, 10am-10pm Sat & Sun) This artisan coffee shop breaks coffee-making down to a science and has all the chemistry-set-style machines to prove it. Just blocks from Museo Larco, it offers the trifecta of wi-fi, quiet spaces to work or chat and hot or iced caffeinated beverages. Various brewing techniques are used, but the pride is in the beans – Origen works directly with local producers.

There's another location on Calle Las Tiendas in Surquillo offering similar delights.

WORTH A TRIP

SEAFOOD AT LA PUNTA

A quiet residential neighborhood with great views of the water, La Punta is perfect for a leisurely lunch. The gregarious owner of **Caleta la Punta** (☑ 01-453-1380; Malecón Pardo 180, Callao; mains S40-65; ⊙ 10am-5:30pm; 🖥) will lure you in with a complimentary cup of cold *chicha* (blue corn juice). Their mango ceviche won a prize at the prestigious Mistura food festival – seafood fans line up for fresh ceviche and whole fried garlic fish.

Dine in style at the waterfront **La Rana Verde** (☑ 973-752-959; Parque Gálvez s/n, Chorrillos; mains S42-59; ⊙ noon-6pm), ideal for Sunday dinner, with views of Isla San Lorenzo. Dishes are all deftly prepared and the *pulpo al olivo* (octopus in olive oil) is one of the best in Lima. It's located on the pier inside the Club Universitario de Regatas.

While you're here, check out the galleries and street art around nearby Monumental Callao (p73).

Surquillo

La P'tite France
BAKERY $

(Map p74; ☑01-243-1565; www.facebook.com/la ptitefrance.pe; Jirón Gonzales Prada 599; snacks S4-17; ☉10am-6pm Mon-Sat) Traditional French techniques are taken seriously at this small French bakery, yet the bakers get playful with flavors by incorporating native grains and spicy peppers into its loaves. Try its renowned flaky croissant with 36 layers.

La Picantería
PERUVIAN $$$

(Map p74; ☑01-241-6676; www.picanterias delperu.com; Santa Rosa 388, Surquillo; family portions S49-130; ☉noon-5:30pm Mon-Sat) Just blocks from the famous Surquillo market, diners share two long tables to feast on sea urchin omelette, stuffed *rocoto* peppers and stewed osso buco. These traditional plates, hailing from both northern and southern Peru, come with an edge. Chef Héctor Solís knows chiles and doles out just enough heat to leave you at the edge of wanting more.

Few dishes are offered in individual portions. Family portions feed two to four people.

Drinking & Nightlife

Lima is overflowing with establishments of every description, from rowdy beer halls to high-end lounges to atmospheric old bars.

Lima Centro

Nightlife downtown is for the nostalgic, composed largely of vintage hotel bars and period halls. Prices are cheaper here than in other neighborhoods.

★Museo del Pisco
BAR

(Map p62; ☑99-350-0013; www.museodelpis co.org; Jirón Junin 201; ☉10am-midnight) The 'educational' aspect of this wonderful bar might get you in the door, but it's the congenial atmosphere and outstanding original cocktails that will keep you here. We loved the *asu mare* – a pisco martini with ginger, cucumber, melon and basil. A sister bar to the popular original in Cuzco, this one occupies the Casa del Oidor, a 16th-century *casona*.

At lunchtime there's a set menu. Watch the Facebook page for live-music news.

El Bolivarcito
BAR

(Map p62; ☑01-427-2788; Jirón de la Unión 958; ☉7am-9pm Sun-Fri, to 2am Sat) Facing the Plaza San Martín from the Gran Hotel Bolívar, this frayed yet bustling spot is known as 'La Catedral del Pisco' for purveying some of the first pisco sours in Peru. Order the double-sized *pisco catedral* if your liver can take it.

Miraflores

From old-world cafes where suited waiters serve frothy pisco sours to raucous watering holes blaring techno and salsa – Miraflores has a little bit of everything. The area around Parque Kennedy is particularly suited for sipping and people-watching.

Nuevo Mundo Draft Bar
CRAFT BEER

(Map p74; ☑01-241-2762; Calle Manuel Bonilla 103; ☉noon-1am Mon-Thu, to 3am Fri & Sat, 5pm-1am Sun) Nuevo Mundo was one of the first craft breweries to come out of Lima, and it's now a major player on the pub scene, with a wide range of national craft brews on tap. Heavily decorated in what locals call '*chicha*' art (think neon palettes and loud phrases), this is a casual place for happy hour or to catch a soccer game.

Huaringas
LOUNGE

(Map p74; ☑01-243-8151; Bolognesi 460; ☉7pm-midnight Mon-Thu, to 2:30am Fri & Sat) A popular Miraflores bar and lounge located inside the Las Brujas de Cachiche (p93) restaurant, Huaringas serves a vast array of cocktails, including a well-recommended passion-fruit sour. On busy weekends, there are DJs.

Barranco

Barranco's trendy bars and clubs are concentrated around Parque Municipal, which is thronged with revelers on Friday and Saturday nights.

★Dada
COCKTAIL BAR

(Map p78; www.dada.com.pe; Av San Martín 154; ☉7pm-1am Tue & Wed, to 3am Thu-Sat) This chic mansion with themed rooms and a gorgeous patio is Barranco's newest hot spot. You know those locales that are described not as a place but a feeling, perhaps like hugging a friend? That's Dada. Come well dressed and well funded. The cocktails here are not cheap, but they are delicious. Live performances of calypso, jazz and rock.

Reservations accepted online. Events are listed on the website and Facebook page.

Red Cervecera
BEER GARDEN

(Map p78; ☑ 01-396-7944; www.redcervecera. com; Av Francisco Bolognesi 721; ⊙ 11am-8pm Mon, to 1am Tue-Thu, to 3am Fri & Sat; 🖭🕮) An all-encompassing stop for beer connoisseurs and amateurs alike. A well-stocked store at the entrance provides all the ingredients and equipment you'll need to brew up your own craft beer, while the bar toward the back serves up house brews and other domestic beers on tap.

Barra 55
COCKTAIL BAR

(Map p78; www.facebook.com/barr55; Av 28 de Julio 206B; ⊙ 7:30pm-midnight Tue-Thu, to 2:30am Fri & Sat) Specializing in gin, this intimate bar is tucked along one of Barranco's liveliest streets. It's both a chill after-office hangout and a warm-up to a wild night ahead. With jazz beats evolving into funky tunes, an array of international gins and other beverages and tasty tapas to match, this is the spot that Lima was missing.

Arrive as close to opening time as possible to ensure a seat.

Bar Piselli
BAR

(Map p78; ☑ 01-252-6750; Av 28 de Julio 297; ⊙ 10am-11pm Mon-Thu, to 3am Fri & Sat) This neighborhood bar reminiscent of old Buenos Aires beats all rivals for ambience. There's live music on Thursdays provoking boisterous sing-alongs of Peruvian classics.

Juanito's
BAR

(Map p78; ☑ 941-536-016; Av Grau 274; ⊙ 11:30am-2am Mon-Sat, noon-midnight Sun) This worn-in wood-clad bar – it was a leftist hangout in the 1960s – is one of the mellowest haunts in Barranco. Decorated with a lifetime's worth of theater posters, this is where the writerly set arrives to swig *chilcano de pisco* and deconstruct the state of humanity. There's no sign; look for the crowded room lined with wine bottles.

Wahio's
BAR

(Map p74; ☑ 981-342-705; www.facebook.com/ wahiosmiraflores; Calle Berlin 192; cover S20; ⊙ 4pm-5am Thu-Sat) A large and lively bar with slick visuals and fun presentation. You will find a fair share of dreadlocks and a classic soundtrack of reggae, ska and dub in one area and highly danceable Latin music in the other, attracting a young crowd.

⭐ Entertainment

Some of the best events in the city – film screenings, art exhibits, theater and dance – are put on by the various cultural insti-

---

THE CLUB SCENE

The club scene gets started well after midnight and keeps going until the break of dawn. Barranco and Miraflores are the best neighborhoods to go clubbing, but spots come and go, so ask around before heading out. Music styles and cover charges vary depending on the night of the week. For other options, hit 'Pizza Street' (Pasaje Juan Figari) in Miraflores, where a row of raucous clubs regularly spins its wares.

---

tutes, some of which have several branches. Check individual websites or newspapers. *Lima Agenda Cultural* (www.enlima.pe) has event listings.

Cinemas

The latest international films are usually screened with Spanish subtitles, except children's movies, which are always dubbed. Some cinemas offer reduced admission midweek. Listings can be found online or in the cultural pages of the local newspapers.

UVK Multicines
CINEMA

(Map p62; ☑ 01-604-0200; www.uvkmulticines. com; Ocoña 110, Plaza San Martín) San Martín branch of the cinema chain.

Cinerama
CINEMA

(Map p74; ☑ 01-243-0541; www.cinerama.com.pe; Av José Pardo 121, Miraflores) A cramped movie theater.

Cultural Centers

Centro Cultural de España
ARTS CENTER

(CCELIMA; Map p66; ☑ 01-330-0412; www.ccelima.org; Natalio Sánchez 181, Plaza Washington; ⊙ noon-10pm Tue-Sun) A full range of offerings, including a roomy 1st-floor gallery that puts on some of Lima's most intriguing contemporary-art exhibits. Also has a library (closes 7pm).

Centro Cultural
Inca Garcilaso
CONCERT VENUE

(Map p62; ☑ 01-623-2656; www.ccincagarcila so.gob.pe; Ucayali 391; ⊙ 10am-7:30pm Tue-Sat, to 6pm Sun) Part of the Ministry of Foreign Relations, the Centro hosts concerts and exhibits related to Peruvian culture.

Live Music

Many restaurants and bars feature small local acts, while bigger bands tend to play at the casinos or sporting arenas. Most of the following places take table reservations.

Sargento Pimienta   CLUB
(Map p78; ☏01-247-3265; www.sargentopi
mienta.com.pe; Av Bolognesi 757, Barranco; admission from S15; ⊘10pm-4am Tue & Thu-Sat) A
reliable spot in Barranco with a name that
means 'Sergeant Pepper.' The barnlike club
hosts various theme nights and occasional
live bands.

Cocodrilo Verde   LIVE MUSIC
(Map p74; ☏01-444-2381; www.cocodriloverde.
com; Francisco de Paola 226; ⊘7pm-3am Mon-Sat)
With great bands that range from popular
music to jazz and bossa nova, this hip lounge
is good for a night out. Minimum tab S25.

Jazz Zone   CLUB
(Map p74; ☏01-241-8139; www.jazzzoneperu.
com; Av La Paz 656, Miraflores; cover from S8;
⊘3pm-midnight) A variety of jazz, folk, *cumbia* (Colombian salsa-like dance and musical style), flamenco, comedy and other acts
at this intimate, well-recommended club on
the eastern side of Miraflores.

La Noche   LIVE MUSIC
(Map p78; ☏01-247-1012; www.lanoche.com.pe;
Sanchez Carrion 199, Barranco; ⊘7:30pm-3am
Mon-Sat) This well-known tri-level bar is *the*
spot to see rock, punk and Latin music acts
in Lima, though drinks could be better.

El Dragón   LIVE MUSIC
(Map p78; ☏01-715-5043; www.eldragon.com.pe;
Av Nicolas de Pierola 168, Barranco; cover up to
S20; ⊘9pm-midnight Thu-Sat) With live music
or DJs, this popular venue draws a diverse

LGBTIQ+ TRAVELERS

Like in other Latin American countries,
the LGBTIQ+ community in Lima does
not have a substantial public presence.
While social acceptance has grown
exponentially, Peru is a conservative
Catholic country and the generational
gap in acceptance is palpable.

Thousands participate in the city's
Gay Pride march, Marcha del Orgullo
Lima (p81), at the end of June or beginning of July. **Gay Lima** (http://lima.
gaycities.com) lists the latest LGBTIQ+
and gay-friendly spots in the capital and
social media apps can prove helpful for
meeting locals.

---

crowd for Latin rock, *tropicalismo,* soul and
funk.

Peñas

Peruvian folk music and dance is performed
on weekends at *peñas*. There are two main
types of Peruvian music performed at these
venues: *folklórica* and *criollo*. The first is
more typical of the Andean highlands; the
other is a coastal music driven by African-in-
fluenced beats. Admission varies; dinner is
sometimes included in the price.

Brisas del Titicaca Asociacion
Cultural   TRADITIONAL MUSIC
(Map p66; ☏01-715-6960; www.brisasdeltiticaca.
com; Heroes de Tarapacá 168, Lima Centro; admission from S30; ⊘noon-3pm & 9pm-12:30am) A
lauded *folklórica* show near Plaza Bolognesi
downtown, in an enormous venue.

La Peña del Carajo   LIVE PERFORMANCE
(Map p78; ☏01-247-7023; www.delcarajo.com.
pe; Miranda 158; ⊘9am-10pm) Locals recommend this high-energy *peña* that brings
guests to their feet. It offers a variety of
shows.

La Candelaria   TRADITIONAL MUSIC
(Map p78; ☏01-247-1314; www.lacandelariaperu.
com; Av Bolognesi 292, Barranco; admission from
S40) A show that incorporates both *folklórica* and *criollo* music and dancing.

Sport

Estadio Nacional   STADIUM
(Map p66; José Díaz s/n, Lima Centro) *Fútbol*
(soccer) is the national obsession, and Peru's Estadio Nacional, off *cuadras* 7 to 9 of
Paseo de la República, is the venue for the
most important matches and other events.
Teleticket (Map p74; ☏01-613-8888; www.
teleticket.com.pe; Óvalo Gutiérrez s/n; ⊘9am-
9pm) has listings and sales.

Hipódromo de Monterrico   HORSE RACING
(Jockey Club of Peru; ☏01-610-3000; www.hipo-
dromodemonterrico.com.pe) Located at the
junction of the Panamericana Sur and Av
Javier Prado, the horse track has races three
to four days a week; times vary.

Theater

Pickings are slim, but the following theaters
are worth noting.

Microteatro Lima   THEATRE
(Map p78; ☏01-252-8092; www.microteatrolima.
com; Jirón Batallón Ayacucho 271) The theater
is anything but dry or about high society, at

least as far as this tiny space is concerned. A rotating roster of directors and actors changes weekly, offering up plays of just 15 minutes, performed in a 15-sq-meter room in front of 15 audience members. A lively bar makes this a great and unique outing. Plays are in Spanish.

Teatro Británico
THEATRE

(Map p74; ☑01-615-3636; www.britanico.edu.pe; Bellavista 527, Miraflores) This theater hosts a variety of worthwhile productions, including plays in English.

Teatro Segura
THEATRE

(Map p62; ☑01-315-1451; Huancavelica 265, Lima Centro) Built in 1909, the gorgeous Teatro Segura puts on opera, plays and ballet.

🛍 Shopping

Clothing, jewelry and handicrafts from all over Peru can be found in Lima. Shop prices tend to be high, but bargain hunters can haggle their hearts out at craft markets. Credit cards and traveler's checks can be used at some spots, but you'll need to show photo ID.

Quality pisco can be bought duty-free at the airport prior to departure.

★ El Cacaotal
CHOCOLATE

(Map p78; ☑937-595-812; www.elcacaotal.com; Colina 108, 2nd fl; ⊙11am-8pm Mon-Thu & Sat, to 7pm Fri, to 6pm Sun) 🍃 A sustainable chocolate shop with delicious bars and connoisseur expertise. It's the perfect opportunity to appease friends and family back home, and it offers fair-trade compensation for small-scale farmers around Peru. Products are organized by region and portraits of the farmers themselves grace the walls. It also does tastings and excellent workshops in English with an adjacent chocolate lab.

It's run by anthropologist Amanda Wildey, whose studies of turning coca (leaves used in the manufacture of cocaine) producers into cocoa producers has paid off handsomely.

★ Las Pallas
ARTS & CRAFTS

(Map p78; ☑01-477-4629; Cajamarca 212, Barranco; ⊙10am-7pm Mon-Sat) For special gifts, check out this handicrafts shop featuring a selection of the highest-quality products from all over Peru; it's even on the radar of Sotheby's. Ring the bell if the gate is closed during opening hours.

La Zapateria
SHOES

(Map p78; ☑01-249-9609; www.lazapateria handmade.pe; Av Pedro de Osma 135, Barranco; ⊙10am-8pm Mon-Sat, noon-6pm Sun) Though it appears quite small, there's a lot going on inside La Zapateria, one part showroom, one part workshop. Handmade leather shoes can be made to order, and there are plenty of stylish models ready-made on the shelves for both men and women.

Puna
GIFTS & SOUVENIRS

(Map p78; ☑01-477-4065; www.puna.com.pe; Colina 128, 2nd fl; ⊙11am-8pm Mon-Sat) If you want a gift that showcases the innovation of Lima, check out this interior and graphic design studio. Eclectic gifts range from funky handmade clothing and handbags to stylish journals, wallets, textiles, prints and home goods, all Peruvian made.

Flora & Fauna
FOOD & DRINKS

(Map p74; ☑01-727-9678; www.facebook.com/florayfaunape; Av Mariscal La Mar 1110; ⊙9am-9pm) Whole Foods, meet your Peruvian cousin. A friendly, bright space complete with an outdoor eating area welcomes you in to peruse shelf after shelf of organic, all-natural products. All your favorite Peruvian superfoods and super treats (think handcrafted chocolate bars made with Peruvian cacao), fresh produce and poultry, as well as natural beauty products make for healthy retail therapy.

Morphology
FASHION

(Map p74; ☑01-333-4164; www.morphology.com.pe; Av Mariscal La Mar 1332; ⊙11am-7pm Mon-Fri, to 5pm Sat) This towering shop boasts four floors to explore, each providing something different. Designer pieces and jewelry from national and international fashion names, as well as home decor and gush-worthy baby clothes are on display on the 1st and 2nd levels. The top floors include an art gallery and a farm-to-table rooftop restaurant.

Cuatro en un Baúl
VINTAGE

(Map p78; ☑01-247-8882; www.facebook.com/cuatroenunbaul; Jirón Martinez de Pinillos 105, Barranco; ⊙10am-1pm & 2-8pm) With furniture and framed artworks inspired by decades past, as well as small keepsakes such as children's books from national authors and playful figurines, this unique store is perfect for those who like to gifts with a touch of vintage. Many items are upcycled antiques.

El Mundo Papel Artshop
HANDICRAFTS

(Map p74; ☑ 01-445-2343; www.facebook.com/
elmundopapelperu; Av 28 de Julio 552; ☺ noon-
8pm Mon-Fri, 11am-7pm Sat) A quaint space
with plenty of character, this art shop is enjoyed by artists and art appreciators alike.
Screen-printed T-shirts, handmade notebooks and other keepsakes. Ask for upcoming art workshops so you can learn to make
your own designs.

La Sanahoria
FOOD

(Map p78; ☑ 01-249-9488; www.facebook.com/
lasanahoriaoficial; Jirón Centenario 195, Barranco;
☺ 9am-9pm Mon-Fri, to 7pm Sat, 11am-7pm Sun)
Get your fix of national *maca* (a natural
energy booster), bitter chocolate, healthy
grains and organic veggies. Fresh extracts
and grab-and-go options such as vegan,
chicken or steak wraps are available for the
busy health nut or for that next impromptu
picnic.

La Calandria
FOOD

(Map p78; ☑ 01-248-7951; www.facebook.com/la
calandriabarranco; Av 28 de Julio 206; ☺ 9am-8pm
Mon-Sat) Stock up on organic groceries and
sundries in this neighborhood shop. Refrig-
erators hoard fermented drinks and yogurt,
and shelves are lined with bulk grains and
tempting chocolate bars made from Peruvian cacao. You could spend hours gazing at
the jars full of loose-leaf teas, or you could
ask the knowledgeable staff.

El Virrey
BOOKS

(Map p74; ☑ 01-713-0505; www.elvirrey.com; Bolognesi 510, Miraflores; ☺ 9:30am-8:30pm Mon-
Sat, 11am-7pm Sun) A decades-old bibliophile's
paradise, this Lima classic stocks thousands
of rare vintage books and contemporary lit-
erary curiosities.

Dédalo
ARTS & CRAFTS

(Map p78; ☑ 01-652-5400; www.dedalo.pe; Paseo
Sáenz Peña 295, Barranco; ☺ 10am-8pm Mon-Sat,
11am-7pm Sun) A vintage *casona* houses this
contemporary crafts store with a lovely
courtyard cafe. Jewelry, clothes, pottery and
more – this is where handmade objects and
creativity are truly cherished. Come here
looking for a gift for someone else, and you'll
likely leave with something for yourself as
well.

LarcoMar
MALL

(Map p74; ☑ 01-625-4343; www.larcomar.com;
Malecón de la Reserva 610; ☺ 10am-10pm) A well-
to-do outdoor mall wedged into the cliff top

beneath Parque Salazar, full of high-end
clothing shops, trendy boutiques, tourism
services and a wide range of eateries, most
of them very good.

Jade Rivera
ART

(Map p78; ☑ 958-782-860; www.facebook.com/
riverajade; Bajada de Baños 349; ☺ 10am-8pm)
The prints and artwork at this side-street
gallery may look familiar. You can see Jade
Rivera's fantastic street art throughout
Lima; the gallery arranges 2½-hour tours
(S120 per person) at 11am or 3pm.

Polvos Azules
MARKET

(Map p66; ☑ 991-118-294; www.polvosazules.
pe; Av Paseo de la República s/n; ☺ 9am-9pm)
Need a socket wrench, a suitcase and a
T-shirt of Jesus Christ wearing an Alianza
Lima soccer jersey? Then Polvos Azules is
the place for you. This multilevel, popular market attracts people from all social
strata for a mind-boggling assortment of
cheap goods.

ℹ Information

EMERGENCY

Policía de Turismo (Tourist Police, Poltur;
☑ 01-225-8698; Av Javier Prado Este 2465,
5th fl, San Borja; ☺ 24hr) Main division of the
Policía Nacional (National Police) at Museo
de la Nación. English-speaking officers can
provide theft reports for insurance claims or
traveler's-check refunds. In heavily touristed
areas, it is easy to identify members of Poltur
by their white shirts.

Policía Nacional Head Office (☑ 01-460-
0921; Moore 268, Magdalena del Mar; ☺ 24hr)

MEDICAL SERVICES

There are a number of clinics with emergency
services and some English-speaking staff.
Consultations start in the vicinity of S80 and
climb from there, depending on the clinic and
the doctor. Treatments and medications incur
an additional fee, as do appointments with
specialists.

Pharmacies abound in Lima. **Botica Fasa**
(Map p74; ☑ 01-619-0000; cnr Av José Larco
129, Miraflores; ☺ 7am-11pm Mon-Sat, to 10pm
Sun) and **InkaFarma** (Map p74; ☑ 01-315-9000,
deliveries 01-314-2020; www.inkafarma.com.pe;
Alfredo Benavides 425, Miraflores; ☺ 24hr) are
well-stocked chains – open 24 hours; they often
deliver free of charge.

You can have glasses made cheaply by one of
the opticians along Miró Quesada in the vicinity
of Camaná in Central Lima or around Schell and
Av José Larco in Miraflores.

The following medical services are also recommended:

Clínica Anglo-Americana (Map p70; ☑ 01-616-8990; www.clinicaangloamericana.pe; Calle Alfredo Salazar 350; ☺ 24hr) A renowned (but expensive) hospital. There's a walk-in center in La Molina, near the US embassy and a branch in San Isidro.

Clínica Good Hope (Map p74; ☑ 01-610-7300; Malecón Balta 956; ☺ 8:30am-8pm Mon-Fri, to 1pm Sun) Quality care at good prices; there is also a dental unit.

Clínica Internacional (Map p66; ☑ 01-619-6161; www.clinicainternacional.com.pe; Garcilaso de la Vega 1420, Lima Centro; ☺ 8am-9pm Mon-Fri, 8am-5pm Sat) A well-equipped clinic with specialties in gastroenterology, neurology and cardiology.

Clínica Montesur (☑ 01-317-4000; www.clinicamontesur.com.pe; Av El Polo 505, Monterrico; ☺ 24hr) Devoted exclusively to women's health.

Clínica San Borja (☑ 01-635-5000; www.sanna.pe/clinicas/san-borja-lima; Av Guardia Civil 337, San Borja; ☺ 24hr) Another reputable clinic, with cardiology services.

Instituto de Medicina Tropical (Hospital Nacional Cayetano Heredia; ☑ 01-319-0015; Av Honorio Delgado 430, San Martín de Porras; ☺ 9am-8pm Mon-Sat) Good for treating tropical diseases. Located within Hospital Nacional Cayetano Heredia. The immediate area around the hospital is safe, but the surrounding neighborhood can be rough.

Instituto Nacional de Salud del Niño (Map p66; ☑ 01-330-0066; www.insn.gob.pe; Brasil 600, Breña; ☺ vaccination center 8am-4pm Mon-Fri, to noon Sun) A pediatric hospital; administers tetanus and yellow-fever jabs.

MONEY

Banks are plentiful and most have 24-hour ATMs, which tend to offer the best exchange rates.

ATMs

For extra security use ATMs inside banks (as opposed to on the street or in supermarkets); cover the key pad as you enter your password; and graze the whole keypad to prevent infrared tracing of passwords. Avoid making withdrawals late at night.

Banco de Crédito del Perú (BCP; Map p74; www.viabcp.com; cnr Av José Larco & José Gonzales) Has 24-hour Visa and Plus ATMs; also gives cash advances on Visa, and changes Amex, Citicorp and Visa traveler's checks. The **Central Lima** (Map p62; ☑ 01-427-5600; cnr Lampa & Ucayali) branch has incredible stained-glass ceilings. There's another branch at **José Pardo** (Map p74; ☑ 01-445-1259; Av José Pardo 491).

BBVA Continental (Map p74; ☑ 01-595-0000; www.bbvacontinental.pe; Av José Larco 631) A representative of Visa; its ATMs also take Cirrus, Plus and MasterCard.

Citibank (Map p74; ☑ 01-215-2000; www.citibank.com.pe; Av José Larco 127) Has 24-hour ATMs in Miraflores operating on the Cirrus, Maestro, MasterCard and Visa systems; it cashes Citicorp traveler's checks.

Scotiabank (Map p70; ☑ 01-311-6000; www.scotiabank.com.pe; Av 2 de Mayo 1510-1550) ATMs (24-hour) operate on the MasterCard, Maestro, Cirrus, Visa and Plus networks and dispense soles and US dollars. There are also branches at **Miraflores Larco** (Map p74; ☑ 01-311-6000; Av José Larco 1119, Larco) and **Miraflores Pardo** (Map p74; ☑ 01-311-6000; cnr Av José Pardo & Bolognesi, Pardo).

Changing Money

Lima's casas de cambio (foreign-exchange bureaus) give similar or slightly better rates than banks for cash, although not for traveler's checks. They're found downtown on Ocoña and Camaná, as well as along Av José Larco in Miraflores. Consider using street moneychangers carefully, as counterfeit cash is a problem.

LAC Dólar (Map p74; ☑ 01-242-4069; Av La Paz 211; ☺ 9am-2pm & 3-6pm Mon-Fri) A reliable exchange house; can deliver cash to your hotel in exchange for traveler's checks.

Moneygram (Map p74; ☑ 01-445-8671; www.moneygram.pe; Av José Pardo 620, Miraflores) Money transfers.

POST

Serpost, the national postal service, has outlets throughout Lima. Mail sent to you at Lista de Correos (Poste Restante), Correo Central, Lima, can be collected at the main post office in Central Lima.

DHL (Map p70; ☑ 01-221-0816; www.dhl.com.pe; Av 2 de Mayo 635, San Isidro; ☺ 9am-8pm Mon-Fri, to 1pm Sat)

Federal Express (FedEx; Map p74; ☑ 01-517-1600; www.fedex.com/pe_english; Alcanfores 350, Miraflores; ☺ 9am-7pm Mon-Fri, 10am-3pm Sat)

Main Post Office (Map p62; ☑ 01-511-5000; www.serpost.com.pe; Pasaje Piura, Lima Centro; ☺ 8am-9pm Mon-Sat) Poste restante mail can be collected here, though it's not 100% reliable. Bring ID.

SAFE TRAVEL

Like any large Latin American city, Lima is a land of haves and have-nots, which has made stories about crime here the stuff of legend. Yet the city has greatly improved since the lawless 1980s and most travelers have a safe visit. Nonetheless, stay aware.

Airport

The airport attracts crime – watch your belongings closely and beware anyone who approaches you outside gates claiming your flight is delayed, offering transport to the airline office for assistance – this is an express kidnapping tactic used to drain credit cards at various city ATMs. Once you are at the airport, stay inside and don't linger outside the passenger-only area. If you have a middle-of-the-night arrival, ask your hotel to send a driver.

Neighborhoods

Increased police and private security in Miraflores and in the cliff-top parks make them some of the city's safest areas. Barranco is mostly safe and pedestrian-friendly but has seen some evening robberies at a few restaurants and bars. Security may increase by the time you read this, but it doesn't hurt to go out with the minimum of your belongings and leave the rest in a hotel safe. The most dangerous neighborhoods are San Juan de Lurigancho, Los Olivos, Comas, Vitarte and El Agustino.

Precautions

Do not wear flashy jewelry, and keep your camera in your bag when you are not using it. It is best to be discreet with cash and take only as much as you'll need for the day. Unless you need your passport for official purposes, leave it in a hotel safe box; a photocopy will do. Blending in helps, too: *limeños* save their shorts for the beach.

Theft

The most common offense is theft, such as muggings. Do not resist robbery. You are unlikely to be physically hurt, but it is nonetheless best to keep a streetwise attitude.

Touts

Be skeptical of unaffiliated touts and taxi drivers who try to sell you tours or tell you that the hotel you've booked is closed or dodgy. Many of these are scam artists trying to steer you to places that pay them a commission.

Transportation

Be wary at crowded events and the areas around bus stops and terminals. These bring out pickpockets – even in upscale districts. Late at night, it's preferable to take official taxis. The areas of Rímac, Callao, Surquillo and La Victoria can get quite rough, so approach with caution (taxis are best).

TOURIST INFORMATION

Federación Deportiva Peruana de Ciclismo (Map p74; ☑ 01-480-7390; www.fedepeci.pe; Av Aviación s/n puerta 13, La Videna San Luis; ☉ 9am-1pm & 3-5pm Mon-Fri) Has general information (in Spanish) on cycling and events.

iPerú (☑ 01-574-8000; www.peru.travel/iperu; Aeropuerto Internacional Jorge Chávez; ☉ 24hr) The government's reputable tourist bureau dispenses maps, offers good advice and can help handle complaints. The **Miraflores office** (Map p74; ☑ 01-445-9400; www.peru.travel/iperu; LarcoMar; ☉ 11am-1pm & 2-8pm) is tiny but is very useful on weekends. There's another branch in **San Isidro** (Map p70; ☑ 01-421-1627; Jorge Basadre 610; ☉ 9am-6pm Mon-Fri).

Municipal Tourist Office (Map p62; ☑ 01-632-1300; www.munlima.gob.pe; Pasaje de los Escribanos 145, Lima Centro; ☉ 9am-5pm Mon-Fri, 11am-3pm Sat & Sun) Of limited use; check the website for a small number of listings of local events and info on free downtown tours.

TRAVEL AGENCIES

Travel agencies can organize airline bookings and make other arrangements.

Fertur Peru Travel (Map p62; ☑ 01-427-1958, 01-427-2626; www.fertur-travel.com; Jirón Junín 211; ☉ 9am-7pm Mon-Fri, to noon Sat) A highly recommended agency that can book local, regional and international travel, as well as create custom group itineraries. Discounts are available for students. There's another branch in **Miraflores** (Map p74; ☑ 01-242-1900; www.fertur-travel.com; Schell 485; ☉ 9am-7pm Mon-Fri, to 4pm Sat).

InfoPerú (Map p62; ☑ 01-425-0414; http://infoperu.com.pe; Jirón de la Unión 1066, Lima Centro; ☉ 9:30am-6pm Mon-Fri, 10am-2pm Sat) Books bus and plane tickets and dispenses reliable information on hotels and sightseeing.

InteJ (Map p78; ☑ 01-247-3230; www.intej.org; San Martín 240, Barranco; ☉ 9:30am-12:45pm & 2-5:45pm Mon-Fri, 9:30am-12:45pm Sat) The official International Student Identity Card (ISIC) office, InteJ can arrange discounted air, train and bus fares, among other services.

Lima Tours (Map p62; ☑ 01-619-6900; www.limatours.com.pe; Nicolás de Piérola 589, 18th fl, Lima Centro; ☉ 9:30am-6pm Mon-Fri, to 1pm Sat) A well-known, high-end agency that handles all manner of travel arrangements. Also organizes gay-friendly trips and basic gastronomic tours of Lima.

Tika Tours (Map p74; ☑ 01-719-9990; www.tikagroup.com.pe; José Pardo 332-350, Miraflores; ☉ 10am-8pm Mon-Fri, to 1pm Sat) Tour operator and travel agent; helpful for local information, as well as travel all over Peru.

ⓘ Getting There & Away

AIR

Lima's **Aeropuerto Internacional Jorge Chávez** (☑ 01-517-3500, schedules 01-511-6055; www.lima-airport.com; Callao) is stocked with the usual facilities plus a pisco boutique, a post office and luggage storage. Internet access is available on the 2nd floor.

All departure taxes are included in ticket prices. You can get flight information, buy tickets and reconfirm flights online or via telephone, but for ticket changes or problems, it's best to go to the airline office in person.

The following airlines service Lima:

Avianca (Map p74; ☑ 01-511-8222; www.avianca.com; Av José Pardo 831, Miraflores; ⊙ 8:30am-7pm Mon-Fri, 9am-2pm Sat) Flies to Cuzco, Arequipa, Juliaca, Puerto Maldonado and Trujillo.

LATAM (Map p74; ☑ 01-213-8200; www.latam.com; Av José Pardo 513, Miraflores) Goes to Arequipa, Chiclayo, Cuzco, Iquitos, Juliaca, Piura, Puerto Maldonado, Tacna, Tarapoto and Trujillo. Additionally it offers link services between Arequipa and Cuzco, Arequipa and Juliaca, Arequipa and Tacna, Cuzco and Juliaca, and Cuzco and Puerto Maldonado. It offers international services as well.

LC Perú (☑ 01-204-1300; www.lcperu.pe; Av Pablo Carriquirry 857, San Isidro; ⊙ 9am-7pm Mon-Fri, to 5pm Sat) Flies from Lima to Andahuaylas, Ayacucho, Cajamarca, Huánuco, Huaraz, Iquitos and Huancayo (Jauja) on smaller turbo-prop aircraft.

Peruvian Airlines (Map p74; ☑ 01-715-6122; www.peruvianairlines.pe; Av José Pardo 495, Miraflores; ⊙ 9am-7pm Mon-Fri, to 5pm Sat) Flies to Arequipa, Cuzco, Piura, Iquitos, Jauja, Pucallpa, Tarapoto, Tacna and internationally to La Paz, Bolivia.

Star Perú (Map p74; ☑ 01-213-8813; www.starperu.com; Av Espinar 331, Miraflores; ⊙ 9am-6:45pm Mon-Fri, to 1pm Sat) Flies to Ayacucho, Cuzco, Huanuco, Iquitos, Pucallpa, Puerto Maldonado and Tarapoto.

Viva Air (☑ 01-705-0107; www.vivaair.com; Aeropuerto Internacional Jorge Chávez; ⊙ hours vary) This budget airline flies to Arequipa, Cuzco, Iquitos, Piura and Tarapoto.

BUS

There is no central bus terminal; each company operates its ticketing and departure points independently. Some companies have several terminals, so always clarify from which point a bus leaves when buying tickets. The busiest times of year are Semana Santa (the week before Easter Sunday) and the weeks surrounding Fiestas Patrias (July 28–29), when thousands of *limeños* make a dash out of the city and fares double. At these times, book well ahead.

Near the airport, the **Gran Terminal Terrestre** (Terminal Plaza Norte; ☑ 945-018-248; www.granterminalterrestre.com; cnr Av Tomás Valle & Av Túpac Amaru, Plaza Norte Panamericana Norte; ⊙ 6am-midnight), the city's largest bus terminal, has buses to international destinations as well as smaller subsidiaries to northern and southern Peru.

Some stations are in rough neighborhoods. If possible, buy your tickets in advance and take a taxi when carrying luggage.

Bus companies include the following:

Civa (Map p66; ☑ 01-418-1111; www.civa.com.pe; Paso de la Republica 569) For Arequipa, Cajamarca, Chachapoyas, Chiclayo, Cuzco, Ilo, Máncora, Nazca, Piura, Puno, Tacna, Tarapoto, Trujillo and Tumbes. The company also runs a more luxurious sleeper line to various coastal destinations called Excluciva (www.excluciva.com).

Cruz del Sur (Map p62; ☑ 01-424-1003; www.cruzdelsur.com.pe; Quilca 531) One of the biggest companies, serving the coast – as well as inland cities such as Arequipa, Cuzco, Huancayo and Huaraz – with three different classes of service: the cheaper Ideal, and the more luxurious Imperial and Cruzero.

Móvil Tours (Map p66; ☑ 01-716-8000; www.moviltours.com.pe; Paseo de la República 749) For Chachapoyas, Chiclayo, Huancayo, Huaraz and Tarapoto.

Oltursa (☑ 01-708-5000; www.oltursa.pe; Av Aramburu 1160, Surquillo) The main terminal for this very reputable company is located a short distance from San Isidro. Travels to Abancay, Arequipa, Chiclayo, Ica, Máncora, Nazca, Paracas, Piura, Tacna, Trujillo and Tumbes.

Ormeño (☑ 01-472-1710; www.grupo-ormeno.com.pe; Av Javier Prado Este 1057) Specializes in international service to Guayaquil, Ecuador, stopping in Tumbes; to Santiago, Chile, via Tacna; and to Río de Jainero, Brazil, via Cuzco. All buses leave from the terminal in La Victoria.

Peru Hop (Map p74; ☑ 01-242-2140; www.peruhop.com; Av José Larco 812; ⊙ 9am-9pm Mon-Sat, 11am-7pm Sun) A comfortable hop-on, hop-off tourist bus service aimed at the backpacker crowd, traveling throughout Peru to Bolivia. Itineraries are open, with tickets that last one year. Also offers tours.

Soyuz (Map p66; ☑ 01-205-2370; www.soyuz.com.pe; Av México 333, La Victoria) Frequent buses to Cañete, Chincha, Ica and Nazca.

Tepsa (Map p70; ☑ 01-617-9000; www.tepsa.com.pe; Av Javier Prado Este 1091) Comfortable buses that travel to Arequipa, Cajamarca, Chiclayo, Cuzco, Ica, Lambayeque, Máncora, Nazca, Piura, Tacna, Trujillo and Tumbes. There's a bus station at **Javier Prado**.

BUSES FROM LIMA

Prices are general estimates for normal/luxury buses.

DESTINATION	COST (S)	DURATION (HR)
Arequipa	80-170	16-18
Ayacucho	75-110	9-11
Cajamarca	90-150	16
Chiclayo	50-130	12-14
Cuzco	110-185	22-23
Huancayo	40-80	7-8
Huaraz	30-150	8
Ica	30-85	4½-5½
Nazca	50-120	6-8
Piura	90-150	16
Puno	150-170	22
Tacna	120-180	18-22
Trujillo	40-125	9-10
Tumbes	100-200	20

CAR

Lima has major intersections without stoplights, kamikaze bus drivers, spectacular traffic jams and little to no parking. If you are still game, a number of car-rental companies have 24-hour desks at the airport. Prices range from about S99 to S330 per day, not including surcharges, insurance and taxes (of about 19%). Delivery is possible.Options include the following:

Budget (☑ 01-204-4400; www.budgetperu. com; Aeropuerto Internacional Jorge Chávez; ⊘24hr)

Hertz (☑ 01-445-5716; www.hertz.com.pe; Aeropuerto Internacional Jorge Chávez; ⊘24hr)

TRAIN

The **Ferrocarril Central Andino** (Map p62; ☑ 01-226-6363; www.ferrocarrilcentral.com.pe; Estación Desamparados; round-trip adult/child 12 & under tourist class S600/300, standard class S450/225) railway line runs from **Estación Desamparados** (Map p62; ☑ 01-263-1515; Ancash 203) in Lima inland to Huancayo, climbing from sea level to 4829m – the second-highest point for passenger trains in the world – before descending to Huancayo at 3260m. The return is three days later. The journey runs fortnightly from mid-April to mid-November, and includes meals. Confirm schedules in advance as the rail lines aren't always operational. Tickets can be purchased through Teleticket (p98).

ⓘ Getting Around

GETTING TO/FROM THE AIRPORT

The airport is in the port city of Callao, about 12km west of downtown or 20km northwest of Miraflores. In a private taxi, allow at least an hour to the airport from San Isidro, Miraflores or Barranco; by *combi*, expect the journey to take at least two hours – with plenty of stops in between. Traffic is lightest before 6:30am.

Taxi

As you come out of customs, inside the airport to the right is the official taxi service: **Taxi Green** (☑ 01-484-4001; www.taxigreen.com.pe; Aeropuerto Internacional Jorge Chávez; ⊘24hr). Outside the airport perimeter itself, you will find 'local' taxis. Taking these does not always save you money, and safety is an issue – local hustlers use the opportunity to pick up foreign travelers and rob them. It is best to use the official airport taxis, or arrange pickup with your hotel.

Shuttle

Fast and safe, **Airport Express** (☑ 958-130-950, 01-446-5539; www.airportexpresslima. com; Aeropuerto Internacional Jorge Chávez; one-way S25; ⊘7am-midnight; 🛜) has hourly service with seven stops throughout Miraflores. There's no bag limit, free wi-fi, USB chargers and bathrooms on board. Pay via the website or on the bus (cash).

Combi

The cheapest way to get to and from the airport is via the combi company known as La S – a giant letter 'S' is pasted to the front windshields – which runs various routes from the port of Callao to Miraflores and beyond. From the airport, these can be found heading south along Av Elmer Faucett. For the return trip to the airport, La S combis can be found traveling north along Av Petit Thouars and east along Av Angamos in Miraflores. The most central spot to find them is at the paradero (bus stop) on Av Petit Thouars, just north of Av Ricardo Palma. Expect to be charged additional fares for any seats that your bags may occupy. Combi companies change their routes regularly, so ask around before heading out.

BUS

The trans-Lima electric express bus system, El Metropolitano (www.metropolitano.com.pe), is the fastest and most efficient way to get into the city center. Routes are few, though coverage is expanding to the northern part of the city. Ruta Troncal (S2.50) goes through Barranco, Miraflores and San Isidro to Plaza Grau in the center of Lima. Users must purchase a *tarjeta intelligente* (smart card; S4.50) that can be credited for use.

Alternatively, traffic-clogging caravans of minivans hurtle down the avenues with a *cobrador* (ticket taker) hanging out the door and shouting out the stops. Look for the destination placards taped to the windshield. Your best bet is to know the nearest major intersection or landmark close to your stop (eg Parque Kennedy) and tell that to the *cobrador* – they'll let you know whether you've got the right bus. *Combis* are generally slow and crowded, but startlingly cheap: fares run from S1 to S3, depending on the length of your journey.

The most useful bus routes link Central Lima with Miraflores along Av Arequipa or Paseo de la República. Minibuses along Garcilaso de la Vega (also called Av Wilson) and Av Arequipa are labeled 'Todo Arequipa' or 'Larco/Schell/Miraflores' when heading to Miraflores and, likewise, 'Todo Arequipa' and 'Wilson/Tacna' when leaving Miraflores for Central Lima. Catch these buses along Av José Larco or Av Arequipa in Miraflores. To get to Barranco, look for buses along Av Arequipa labeled 'Chorrillos/Huaylas/Metro' (some will also have signs that say 'Barranco'). You can also find these on the Diagonal, just west of Parque Kennedy, in Miraflores.

The principal bus routes connecting Central Lima with San Isidro and Miraflores run along broad avenues such as Tacna, Garcilaso de la Vega and Av Arequipa. These neighborhoods are also connected by the short highway Paseo de la República or Vía Expresa, known informally as *el zanjón* (the ditch).

TAXI

Lima's taxis lack meters, so negotiate fares before getting in. Fares vary depending on the length of the journey, traffic conditions, time of day (evening is more expensive) and your Spanishlanguage skills. Registered taxis or taxis hailed outside a tourist attraction charge higher rates. As a (very) rough guide, a trip within Miraflores costs around S8 to S10. From Miraflores to Central Lima is S20 to S25, to Barranco from S10 to S12, and San Isidro from S15 to S20. You can haggle over fares – though it's harder during rush hour. If there are two or more passengers be clear on whether the fare is per person or for the car.

The majority of taxis in Lima are unregistered (unofficial); indeed, surveys have indicated that no less than one vehicle in seven here is a taxi. During the day, it's usually not a problem to use either. At night, for safety it is important to use registered taxis, which are traceable by the license number painted on their side. Taxis should also have checkers, a rectangular authorization sticker with the word SETAME on the upper left corner of the windshield and may have yellow paint.

Registered taxis can be called by phone or found at taxi stands, such as the one outside the Sheraton in Central Lima or outside the LarcoMar shopping mall in Miraflores. Registered taxis cost about 30% more than regular street taxis but the security is worth it. Recommended taxis include the following:

Easy Taxi (☑ 01-716-4600; www.easytaxi.com/pe) Download the app for fast service and cost estimates from your smartphone.

Taxi Móvil (☑ 01-422-6890)

Taxi Real (☑ 01-215-1414; www.taxireal.com)

AROUND LIMA

On weekends and holidays, *limeños* head for the beach or the hills. From exploring ancient ruins to beach bumming, there is much to do outside of the city that is worthy of exploration if you have a few extra days.

Pachacamac

Situated about 31km southeast of the city center, the archaeological complex of **Pachacamac** (☑ 01-321-5606; http://pachacamac. cultura.pe; Antigua Carr Panamericana Sur Km 31.5, Lurín; adult/child S15/5; ⊙ 9am-5pm Tue-Sat, to 4pm Sun) is a pre-Columbian citadel with adobe and stone palaces and temple pyramids. If you've been to Machu Picchu, it may not look like much, but this was an important Inca site and a major city when the Spanish arrived. It was a ceremonial center for the Lima culture from around AD 100, and was later expanded by the Waris before being taken over by the Ichsma.

The Incas added numerous other structures upon their arrival to the area in 1450. The name Pachacamac, which can be variously translated as 'He who Animated the World' or 'He who Created Land and Time,' comes from the Wari god, whose wooden, two-faced image can be seen in the on-site **museum**.

Most of the buildings are now little more than piles of rubble that dot the desert landscape, but some of the main temples have been excavated and their ramps and stepped sides revealed. You can climb the switchback trail to the top of the **Templo del Sol** (Temple of the Sun), which on clear days offers excellent views of the coast. The most remarkable structure on-site, however, is the Palacio de las Mamacuna (House of the Chosen Women), commonly referred to as the **Acllahuasi**, which boasts a series of Inca-style trapezoidal doorways. Unfortunately, a major earthquake in 2007 left the structure highly unstable. As a result,

WORTH A TRIP

ARTISAN STUDIOS OF LURÍN

Lurín is a working-class enclave 50km south of Central Lima on the Panamericana. At its southern edge, crafts collective **Ichimay Wari** (☎01-430-3674; www.facebook.com/ichimaywari; Antigua Panamericana Sur Km 39.5; ☺8am-1pm & 2-5pm Mon-Sat) has its studios. Here, talented artisans from Ayacucho produce traditional *retablos* (religious dioramas), pottery, Andean-style Christmas decorations and the colorful clay trees known as *arbolitos de la vida* (trees of life). Your best bet is to make an appointment 24 hours in advance to tour individual studios and meet the artisans.

A taxi from Lima costs around S120 round-trip. By bus from the Puente Benavides or Puente Primavera, take one heading to Lurín (S5), San Bartolo or San Miguel. Get off at the main stoplight in Lurín. From there, hail a *mototaxi* (motorcycle taxi) and ask them to take you south to the Barrio Artesano. Parts of Lurín can be rough; take taxis and keep your cameras stowed.

visitors can only admire it from a distance. Without the funding to repair the extensive damage, it has been listed as one of the planet's most endangered sites.

There is a visitors center and cafe at the site entrance, which is on the road to Lurín. A simple map can be obtained from the ticket office, and a track leads from here into the complex. Those on foot should allow at least two hours to explore. (In summer, take water and a hat – there is no shade to speak of once you hit the trail.) Those with a vehicle can drive from site to site.

Various agencies in Lima offer guided tours that include transport and a guide (S120). Mountain-bike tours can be an excellent option.

Alternatively, catch a minibus signed 'Pachacamac' from Av 28 de Julio or the sunken roadway at the corner of Andahuaylas and Grau in Central Lima (S3, 45 minutes); minibuses leave every 15 minutes during daylight hours. From Miraflores, take a bus on Av Benavides headed east to the Panamericana and Puente Primavera, change here for the bus marked 'Pachacamac/Lurín' (S4, 30 minutes). For both services, tell the driver to let you off near the *ruinas* (ruins) or you'll end up at Pachacamac village, about 1km beyond the entrance. To get back to Lima, flag down any bus outside the gate, but expect to stand for the duration of the ride. You can also hire a taxi per hour (from S45) from Lima.

Southern Beaches

Every summer, *limeños* make a beeline for the beaches clustered along the Panamericana to the south. The city exodus peaks on weekends, when, occasionally, the road is so congested that it temporarily becomes one-way. Popular with surfers, this stretch of barren, coastal desert is lapped by cold water and strong currents. Inquire locally before swimming, as drownings occur annually. Surfboard rental is almost nonexistent; it's best to bring your own. The principal beach towns include El Silencio, Señoritas, Caballeros, Punta Hermosa, Punta Negra, San Bartolo, Santa María, Naplo and Pucusana.

Punta Hermosa, with its relentless waves, is *the* surfer spot. The largest waves in Peru (reaching 10m) are found nearby at **Pico Alto** (Panamericana Km 43). **Punta Rocas**, a little further south, holds annual competitions and is popular with experienced surfers.

🛏 Sleeping & Eating

Hostal Hamacas Punta Rocas HOTEL **$**
(☎999-854-766; www.facebook.com/hamacaspuntaroca; Panamericana Km 47, Punta Rocas; d S231, bungalow S363; ☺Dec-Apr) Right on the sand, cute Hostal Hamacas has 15 rooms and five bungalows (which sleep six), all with private bathrooms, hot water and ocean views. There is an on-site **restaurant** during the high season (October to April). The owner is a surfer who also rents boards.

Hostal 110 HOTEL **$$**
(☎01-430-7559; www.hostal110sb.com; Malecón San Martín Nte 110, San Bartolo; d S150-180, apt S240; ☎🅿) Sitting above the bay, Hostal 110 has 14 spacious and neat tiled rooms and apartments – some of which sleep up to six – staggered above a swimming pool on the cliffside. Rooms with a balcony cost slightly more. The stay here is worth it for the sweeping sea views alone. Staff can arrange

surfing classes and scuba diving. Weekday rates are cheaper.

Restaurant Rocío　　　　SEAFOOD **$$**
(☑ 01-430-8184; Urb Villa Mercedes, Mz A, Lte 5-6, San Bartolo; mains S30-50; ☺10am-10pm) On the far southern edge of town facing the soccer field (take a *mototaxi*), this seafood restaurant serves serves delicious *leche de tigre* (seafood broth) and fresh fish grilled or fried and bathed in garlic.

❶ Getting There & Away

To get to these beaches, take a bus signed 'San Bartolo' from the Panamericana Sur at the Puente Primavera in Lima. You can get off at any of the beach towns along the route, but in many cases it will be a 1km to 2km hike down to the beach. Local taxis are usually waiting by the road. A one-way taxi from Lima costs around S150.

Carretera Central

The Carretera Central (Central Hwy) heads directly east from Lima, following the Rímac valley into the foothills of the Andes and on to La Oroya in Peru's central highlands.

In Lima, minibuses to Chosica leave frequently from Arica at the Plaza Bolognesi. These can be used to travel to Puruchuco (S3, 50 minutes). Recognizing sites from the road can be difficult, so let the driver know where you want to get off.

Puruchuco

The site of **Puruchuco** (☑ 01-321-5623; www. visitavirtual.cultura.pe/museos/puruchuco; Av Prolongación Javier Prado Este, cuadra 85, distrito Ate; admission S5; guided groups S20; ☺9am-4:30pm Tue-Sun) hit the news in 2002 when about 2000 well-preserved mummy bundles were unearthed from the enormous Inca cemetery. It's one of the biggest finds of its kind, and the multitude of grave goods included a number of well-preserved quipu (knotted ropes that the Inca used as a system of record-keeping). The site has a highly reconstructed chief's house, with one room identified as a guinea-pig ranch.

Situated amid the shantytown of Túpac Amaru, Puruchuco is 13km from Central Lima. It is best to take a taxi, S35 (S35 one way). A signpost on the highway marks the turn-off, and from here it is several hundred meters along a road to the right.

Cajamarquilla

A pre-Columbian site, **Cajamarquilla** (Sitio Arqueológico Cajamarquilla; ☑ext 4180 01-618-9393; near Av Cajamarquilla; ☺9am-4pm) is a crumbling adobe city that was built up by the Wari culture (AD 700–1100) on the site of a settlement originally developed by the Lima people. It is still undergoing renovation; a visit may be arranged by calling the Ministry of Culture ahead of time.

A road to the left at about Km 10 from Lima (18km from Central Lima) goes to the Cajamarquilla zinc refinery, almost 5km from the highway. The ruins are located about halfway along the refinery road; you take a turn to the right along a short road. There are signs, but ask the locals for the *zona arqueológica* if you have trouble finding them.

AT A GLANCE

POPULATION
Tacna: 262,700

**TALLEST SAND
DUNE**
Cerro Blanco: 1176m

BEST WINERY
Bodega Lazo (p125)

BEST SEAFOOD
Inti-Mar (p122)

**BEST ADVENTUR-
OUS ACTIVITY**
River Running in
Lunahuaná (p112)

**WHEN TO GO
Jan–Mar**
High summer means
the main coastal
beach resorts are
open and pulsating
with energy.

Mar
Grape harvest and
accompanying wine
festivals in Luna-
huaná and Ica.

Jun & Jul
Cooler temperatures,
fewer tourists and
esoteric festivals in
Chincha and Ica.

Brown pelicans and guanay cormorants, Islas Ballestas (p117)
JESS KRAFT/SHUTTERSTOCK©

South Coast

This wild and lonely coast entrances visitors with teetering sand dunes, verdant desert oases, forgotten fishing villages, ancient earth drawings, and plenty of rugged open space for the imagination to run wild. It's a stark, dry corner of earth – caught between the Andes and the sea – that only comes to life in the fertile river valleys that produce wine and fruit. Many adventures begins with rafting in Lunahuaná, wildlife-watching in the Islas Ballestas, sandboarding out of Huacachina and a requisite stop at the mysterious lines and odd geoglyphs that decorate the blank desert canvas outside Nazca. Step off the beaten track to discover unspoiled surf spots, vibrant agricultural villages and spirited and unassuming cultural beats.

INCLUDES

South Coast Highlights

1 Nazca Lines
(p130) Deciphering the mysteries with a once-in-a-lifetime flight-seeing tour.

2 Islas Ballestas
(p117) Taking in the majestic wilderness as you visit sea lion and bird colonies on a boat tour.

3 Huacachina
(p127) Watching the sun set atop a giant sand dune overlooking the desert oasis.

4 Lunahuaná
(p112) Rafting the rip-roarious rapids of Río Cañete in this adventure nexus.

5 Bodega Tacama
(p125) Tasting some of Peru's best wines and piscos at this bodega near Ica.

6 Lagunillas
(p118) Hiking across the deserted Paracas Peninsula for a seafood lunch.

7 Mollendo
(p136) Extending your journey beyond the Gringo Trail with a surf safari to this offbeat town.

8 Reserva Nacional Pampas Galeras (p133) Getting up close to endangered vicuñas (threatened wild relatives of alpacas).

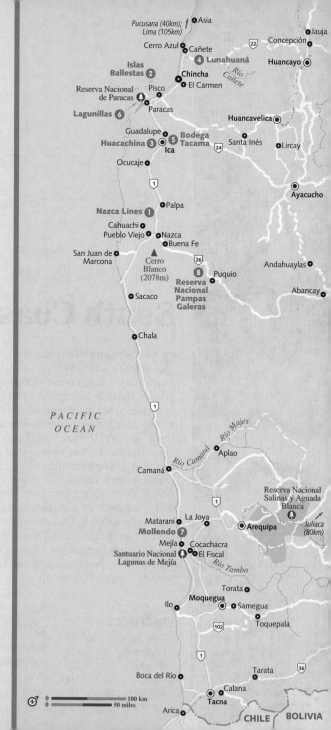

Cerro Azul

 01 / POP 8100

Many Peruvian holidaymakers looking to escape from Lima head to Cerro Azul, a beach popular with experienced surfers. It's a 15-minute walk west of Km 131 on the Panamericana Sur, about 15km north of Cañete, an important transportation hub for the region.

In contrast to the sterile suburban areas full of vacation homes to the north, Cerro Azul is a real town and you'll find life on the streets here even when the weather takes a turn for the worse.

There's a small Inca sea fort in the area, known as **Huarco**.

🏃 Activities

Most of the action takes place south of the pier in Puerto Viejo where, during the high season, a VW bus parks and rents surf boards and gives lessons.

Huarcosurf — SURFING
(📞 977-768-854; Entrada Puerto Viejo; board rental/lesson per hour S20/50; ⊙ 7am-6pm) An ultra-friendly surf school right by the entrance of Puerto Viejo.

🛏 Sleeping & Eating

Hotel Las Palmeras — HOTEL $$
(📞 012-84-6163; www.laspalmerascerroazul.com; Rivera del Mar, Puerto Viejo; r S170-220; ❄ 🞄 ⛱) It doesn't look like much from the road, but step through the original lodge to find a new building containing four floors of spacious modern rooms equipped with king-sized beds and private balconies overlooking the water. The fantastic long pool surrounded by loungers and separated from the sand by a long glass wall seals the deal.

Restaurant Juanito — PERUVIAN $$
(📞 013-35-3710; Rivera del Mar, Puerto Viejo; mains S20-50; ⊙ 9am-6pm) Juanito, located to the south of the pier, is the pick of Cerro Azul's beachfront seafood restaurants, in terms of both ambience and quality. It has a collection of tables on its porch across the road from the town's best break.

It also rents out comfortable rooms upstairs for S180.

❶ Getting There & Away

From Lima, buses headed for Pisco or Ica can drop you at nearby Cañete and sometimes Cerro Azul (S15 to S21, 2½ hours). Buses back to Lima are invariably crowded, especially on Sunday from January to April. There are also *combis* (minibuses) between Cañete and Cerro Azul (S2, 30 minutes) or south to Chincha (S2, one hour).

Lunahuaná

📍 01 / POP 4800 / ELEV 1700M

The small town of Lunahuaná rises like a slice of desert romance above the foggy coastal strip south of Lima. Reached via a winding 38km road that tracks east from the noisy settlement of Cañete, it appears almost magically, a thin strip of broccoli green amid the dusty desert that gleams with a touch of Middle Eastern promise.

Lunahuaná's life and times are split between wine production and river running. Both owe their existence to the seasonally turbulent Río Cañete, whose class IV rapids provide cheap thrills for brave rafters and a vital form of irrigation for the local vineyards.

Some people incorporate Lunahuaná into an overnighter from Lima, and it's certainly worth the effort. The best time to show up is during the second week of March for the grape harvest, **Fiesta de la Vendimia**. An **adventure-sports festival** is usually held in late February or early March.

◉ Sights

Lunahuaná is small with little of architectural significance outside of its main square, which is crowned by the **Iglesia Santiago Apostal** dating from 1690. The square's arched *portales* (walkways) hide bars and shops that specialize in wine and pisco (Peruvian grape brandy). From the square, it's a five-minute walk up to a scenic **mirador** (lookout) with great views of the town and its surrounding greenery.

Catapalla — VILLAGE
A tiny settlement 6km further up the valley from Lunahuaná, Catapalla is a traditional mountain village with quiet, traffic-free streets and a pretty plaza. It's notable for one of the valley's oldest artisanal wineries, La Reyna de Lunahuaná (p112).

The village's other traditional attraction, the **Puente Colgante** (suspension bridge) that used to hang precariously over the Río Cañete's angry rapids, was washed away in the 2017 floods and has yet to be replaced. A one-way taxi ride to Catapalla from Lunahuaná should cost from S6, but you may

WORTH A TRIP

LUNAHUANÁ'S WINERIES

La Reyna de Lunahuaná (☏ 994-777-117; ⏱ 7am-1pm & 2-5pm) A rustic bodega producing both wine and pisco (Peruvian grape brandy), venerable La Reyna de Lunahuaná presides over the main plaza in Catapalla, about 6km east of Lunahuaná. The owners here can teach you the ABCs of pisco and wine production. A one-way taxi ride costs from S6, but you may have to wait until a car shows up for the return.

Bodega Santa Maria (☏ 056-284-1116; www.bodegasantamaria.com; Carr Cañete-Lunahuaná Km 39; ⏱ 8am-6pm) A very well-presented, semi-industrial winery 1km north of the town with flowery grounds and large wooden casks that retain the air of an Andalucian sherry bodega. Free samples of the sweetish wine (red, white and rosé) and powerful pisco varietals are laid out in the outdoor tasting area under the trees or in the aromatic tasting room. It also sells locally made honey.

have to wait until a car shows up for the return.

Incahuasi
RUINS
(☏ 951-359-282; Carr Cañete-Lunahuaná Km 29; ⏱ 8:30am-4pm) **FREE** The most notable archaeological site in the Cañete Valley is Incahuasi, the rough-walled ruins of the military headquarters of the 10th Inca king Túpac Yupanqui, located on the western outskirts of Lunahuaná. Backed by rugged mountains and with views both up and down the valley, it's easy to see why the military rulers chose the site. It is thought that the original buildings date from 1438-ish, soon after the ascension of Emperor Pachacuti.

You won't find a lot of signage or fellow travelers here, but therein lies the attraction. The site is far bigger than it first seems and covers both sides of the highway, though the main structures are in the fenced-off section on the east side of the road. Some walls have been reconstructed but the largest complexes on each end of the site contain original walls which are up to 3m high in some places.

There are no guides on-site but the caretaker will show you around (speaking Spanish); a small tip is appreciated.

The ruins are on the main road 10km west of Lunahuaná. A taxi should cost around S20 round-trip with waiting time.

🏃 Activities

River Running

River running (rafting) can be done year-round, but the best time is between December and April, the rainy months in the Andes when the Río Cañete runs high. For rafting purposes, the river is split into three sections. The hardest (Ruta Alta) is the section east of Lunahuaná up to the village of

Catapalla which is graded III–IV in summer. The easier sections to the west between Lunahuaná and Paullo, and Paullo and Socsi are graded I–III and are only doable in the summer.

Reputable rafting companies include Río Cañete Expediciones, based at Camping San Jerónimo, and **Laberinto Explorer** (☏ 012-84-1057, 996-032-663; lunahuanalaberintoexplorer @gmail.com; Jiron Bolognesi 476), a couple of blocks from Lunahuaná's main plaza. Most trips require a minimum of four people (you'll be paired up on-site), and last between one and three hours. Costs range from S50 to S330.

Zip-Lining

Satisfying a growing international craze for zip-lining (canopy tours), Lunahuaná has a couple of different places to fly through the air including a real corker south of the town. It's fitted out with five cables that shoot vertigo-shunners over the Río Cañete for a total 'zip' distance of 2500m – one of Latin America's longest. The price for the full five lines is S120 with departures at 8am and 4pm. Zippers launch into thin air from Camping San Jerónimo.

Abseiling

You can abseil (rappel) down a cliff face overlooking the Río Cañete approximately 7km north of town. Most agencies in Av Grau organize excursions for around S50.

Cycling

Located high above the car-crazed coast, Luanahuaná is easily cycled; indeed bikes are a handy way of visiting some of the outlying sites and wine bodegas. Decent bikes with gears generally cost S40 for two hours and can be procured from travel companies on Av Grau.

🛏 Sleeping

Camping San Jerónimo CAMPGROUND $
(☎012-84-1271; Carr Cañete-Lunahuaná, Km 33; sites per person S20) This campground borders the river at the far west of town. It has good views and there's a barbecue area where guests can cook. The small restaurant on-site is not always open but there are other options right across the road. Base camp for **Río Cañete Expediciones** (☎012-84-1271; www.riocanete.com).

Hostal Río Alto HOTEL $$
(☎012-84-1125; www.rioaltohotel.com; Carr Cañete-Lunahuaná Km 39; s/d S156/177; 🛜🌊) About 1km along the highway east of Lunahuaná, this friendly guesthouse looks down to the river from a shady terrace overrun with plants that surrounds a pool. Rooms, though plain, are modern and have hot showers and there's a restaurant.

Hostal Prince HOTEL $$
(☎975-270-507; Bolognesi 476; r from S100) Neat and tidy, this new hotel just steps from the plaza has bright modern rooms with small but spotless bathrooms and good mattresses. You can book all your adventures at the agency downstairs.

★ Hotel El Molino HOTEL $$$
(☎013-78-6061; www.hotelelmolino.com.pe; Malecón Araoz, Carr Cañete-Lunahuaná Km 39; r S465; 🅿🛜🌊) Not far from the 'beast' that is Lima's southern suburbs lies the 'beauty' of El Molino, a lovingly tended hotel complex set on the banks of the Río Cañete on the cusp of Lunahuaná. The hotel offers boutique-style rooms encased in glassy river-facing units.

There are two pools, table football and a fine restaurant in the beautifully landscaped grounds where tranquility reigns, bar the odd triumphant whoop of a passing rafter.

Refugio de Santiago HOTEL $$$
(☎991-991-259; www.refugiodesantiago.com; Carr Cañete-Lunahuaná Km 31; r incl breakfast S280; 🌊) This renovated colonial home a few kilometers west of Lunahuaná is the ultimate relaxing getaway. Rooms are rustic but elegant and the grounds feature a fragrant botanical garden and a restaurant that serves textbook local specialties (mains S34 to S54). The rates also include guided walks through the local orchards.

🍴 Eating

Don Ignacio La Casa del Pisco PERUVIAN $
(Plaza de Armas; items from S10) One of the best pisco-biased restaurants on the main square where you can dilute the local 'rocket fuel' with typical food from the area, including memorable crawfish.

El Jardín PERUVIAN $$
(☎989-009-428; Grau 150; mains S25-50; ⊙8am-8pm) Settle in at a table in the thatched-roof dining area or in the garden out the back and enjoy a wide selection of well-prepared traditional plates at this great spot. Also prepares a good set-menu meal for S10.

ℹ Getting There & Away

From Cañete, catch a *combi* to Imperial (S1, 10 minutes), from where *combis* (shared transportation; S4, 45 minutes) and faster *colectivos* (S5, 30 minutes) run to Lunahuaná from Calle 2 de Mayo. In Lunahuaná, *colectivos* wait for passengers on the main road, just downhill from the plaza, and then race back to Imperial.

Chincha

☎056 / POP 217,700

Gloriously chaotic or frustratingly anarchic (depending on your tolerance for dust and noise), Chincha is Peru uncut and unpackaged, an unregulated mess of buses, taxis and jay-walking humanity. On the surface it could be any Peruvian town in any south coast province, but closer scrutiny unearths some engrossing details: sugarcane juice sellers, black African figurines offered as souvenirs, and menus advertising *criolla* (coastal) specialties. Chincha is a stronghold of Afro-Peruvian culture, a small and little-known component of the national whole that testifies to a brutal slave past.

◉ Sights

El Carmen District VILLAGE
A village unlike any other in Peru, El Carmen is a place where African and Latin American cultures collide with hip-gyrating results. It's famed for its rhythm-heavy Afro-Peruvian music heard in the *peñas* (bars and clubs featuring live folkloric music). The best lie about 15km outside town and there are two simple affairs on the town square.

Casa-Hacienda San José MUSEUM
(☎056-31-3332; www.casahaciendasanjose.com; El Carmen; S20; ⊙9am-noon & 3-5 pm Mon-Fri, 9am-noon Sat & Sun) Provoking many visitors

to make the trip all the way down from Lima, this former slave plantation with its stately hacienda offers a window into race and class in the Peruvian historical context. While the buildings and grounds are indeed magnificent, the museum could be orientated less to the opulence of the gentry and more to the horrors endured by their slaves. One-hour tours of the hacienda and its famous catacombs include strolls through the original building, with its fine baroque chapel.

Surviving artifacts include frescoes, agricultural equipment, and brutal remnants of a system once used to subjugate the slaves including an extensive web of catacombs and underground tunnels. A spectacularly ruined cotton factory, dating from 1913, sits next door.

Centro Cultural Amador Ballumbrosio
CULTURAL CENTRE
(☑ 993-574-090; San José 325) The home of El Carmen's most famous dancing family is a museum to Afro-Peruvian culture. Music breaks out here spontaneously most weekends; pop in if you're in the village to view the photos and paintings and see what's up. It's possible to organize homestays with local families here.

🛏 Sleeping

Bare-bones cheap hotels surround Chincha's main plaza. Most fill up and double or triple their prices during festivals. You can always avoid this problem by dancing all night and taking an early morning bus back to Lima or further south along the coast.

In El Carmen, there are a couple of basic *hospedajes* (small, family-owned inns). Alternatively, a few local families will take in overnight guests for around S20 per person per night – ask around.

Casa-Hacienda San José Hotel
HISTORIC HOTEL $$$
(☑ 056-31-3332; www.casahaciendasanjose.com; El Carmen; r with interior/garden view from S510/620; P ❄ 🛜 🏊) Easily the most comfortable hotel in the region, this slick boutique offering on a former slave plantation (p113) is the best-preserved historic hotel on the Peruvian coast, although the neocolonial atmosphere may not appeal to all travelers. The grounds are expansive with small gardens, luxurious hammocks, antiques and a luscious pool.

While the backside bungalows offer all the modern conveniences including air-conditioning, a stay in the historic wing is where it's at. During the week prices are lower.

Casa Andina – Chincha Sausal
BOUTIQUE HOTEL $$$
(☑ 056-26-2451; www.casa-andina.com; Panamericana Sur Km 197.5; r incl breakfast S352-402; ❄ @ 🛜 🏊) A rather odd outpost of Peru's plushest hotel chain, glued to the frankly horrible Panamericana Sur 1km north of Chincha's bus station, the Sausal is aimed at the corporate business market and is thus a bit stuffy and officious. Facilities are nonetheless upper-crust with flowered grounds, luxury bed-linens and a decent restaurant.

🍴 Eating

Restaurante Lorena
PERUVIAN $$
(☑ 056-26-9373; Av Benavides 1030; mains S15-48; ⊗ 11am-4pm) It's a bit of a walk out of the center but this local institution is the best place in town to enjoy traditional dishes. It knocks out good ceviches and the like but is famed for its rich *criollo* flavors. Try the *carapulcra* (mixed meats with Andean potatoes and chili), *seco de rez* (beef in a reduced sauce) or *arroz con pato* (rice with duck).

❶ Getting There & Away

There are a couple of companies based on the old Panamericana Sur with buses running through Chincha en route between Lima (S20 to S23, 2½ hours) and Ica (S7 to S10, two hours). If you're headed to Pisco, most southbound buses can drop you off at the San Clemente turnoff on the Panamericana Sur (S4), from where you can catch frequent *colectivos* and *combis* for the 6km trip into Pisco (S1.50).

Combis and *colectivos* to El Carmen (S2 to S4, 30 minutes) leave from Chincha's central market area, a few blocks from the main plaza.

The plaza is 500m from the old Panamericana Sur where the coastal buses stop.

Pisco

☑ 056 / POP 53,900

The traditional gateway to the wild, wind-swept Paracas region, Pisco was crushed by the devastating 2007 earthquake that destroyed its infrastructure and some of its most attractive buildings – but not its spirit. Gritty resolve has seen the city rebound, though for visits to the Islas Ballestas and Reserva Nacional de Paracas, it has been surpassed by nearby El Chaco, which has a better location and choice of facilities.

Pisco shares its name with the national beverage, a brandy that is made throughout the region. The area is of historical and archaeological interest, having hosted one of the most highly developed pre-Inca civilizations – the Paracas culture from 700 BC until AD 400. Later it acted as a base for Peru's revolutionary fever in the early 19th century.

◉ Sights

Pisco's waterfront, a couple of kilometers west of town, has been given a makeover with a new *malecón* (boardwalk) but due to many businesses in the area closing following the earthquake it remains somewhat desolate and is not particularly safe – especially after dark.

Plaza de Armas   PLAZA
Post-earthquake, Pisco's main Plaza de Armas is a mishmash of the vanquished and the saved. The equestrian statue of **José de San Martín**, hand raised urging the city forward, falls into the latter category. Another survivor is the Moorish **Palacio Municipal** building dating from 1929 whose wrecked shell awaits a major refurb. Pisco's biggest earthquake casualty was the colonial San Clemente Cathedral; a new, red-bricked church has gone up in its place.

Commerce has returned to pedestrianized San Martín, which runs west from the plaza and is beautified with benches, flower-covered trellises and a refreshing fountain.

⮞ Tours

It is perfectly viable to use Pisco as a base for tours of the Paracas Peninsula and the Islas Ballestas. Various agencies dot the central area around the Plaza de Armas.

Aprotur Pisco   TOURS
(☑ 056-50-7156; aproturpisco@hotmail.com; San Francisco 112; ⊙7am-10pm) This laid-back but business-like travel company organizes trips to all the local sights, including the Islas Ballestas (S70) and even the Nazca Lines (US$90 to US$200). Guides speak six languages, including Hebrew.

⏢ Sleeping

Pisco has a limited hotel offering mostly consisting of midrange options catering to business travelers and cheap flophouses favored by young couples. Far more appealing accommodations can be found in nearby Paracas.

Posada Hispana Hotel   HOTEL $
(☑ 056-53-6363; www.posadahispanaperu.com; Bolognesi 222; s/d S50/60; 🅿🛜) This is as good as it gets in Pisco. Rooms feature local textiles and hardwood accents. There's a rooftop terrace for kicking back. The restaurant is one of the best in town, with a good lunchtime *menú* (set meal) served in a two-level bamboo dining room.

Hostal La Casona   HOTEL $
(☑ 056-53-2703; San Juan de Dios 252; s S60-70, d S70-90; 🅿🛜) A massive wooden door serves as a slightly deceiving portal to this hotel half a block from the main square, which, though clean, isn't anywhere near as grand as its entryway suggests. There are three floors of simple rooms that do the job just fine.

Hostal Villa Manuelita   HOTEL $$
(☑ 056-53-5218; San Francisco 227; s/d/tr incl breakfast S110/150/190; 🅿🛜) Unrecognizable from its pre-earthquake colonial incarnation, this modern hotel offers spacious and comfortable (if a little sterile) rooms in a new block at the back that are insulated from the traffic noise. It's very conveniently located only half a block from the plaza.

Pisco

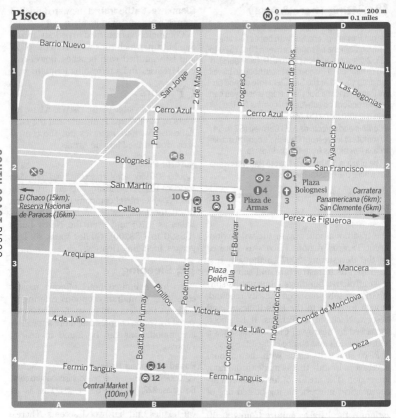

Pisco

◎ Sights
1 Palacio Municipal...................................C2
2 Plaza de Armas C2
3 San Clemente Cathedral......................C2
4 Statue of José de San Martín..............C2

◆ Activities, Courses & Tours
5 Aprotur Pisco C2

🛏 Sleeping
6 Hostal La Casona....................................C2
7 Hostal Villa Manuelita..........................D2
8 Posada Hispana Hotel...........................B2

⊗ Eating
9 As de Oro's...A2

◎ Drinking & Nightlife
10 Taberna de Don Jaime............................B2

ℹ Information
11 Interbank C2

ℹ Transport
12 Colectivos to Paracas and the San
    Clemente turnoff on the
    Panamericana...................................B4
13 Colectivos to San Clemente
    turnoff on Panamericana C2
14 Combis to Paracas..................................B4
15 Flores B2

✕ Eating & Drinking

★ **As de Oro's** PERUVIAN $$
(www.asdeoros.com.pe; San Martín 472; mains S21-46; ⊙ noon-midnight Tue-Sun) Widely considered Pisco's best restaurant, the plush As de Oro serves up spicy mashed potato with octopus, plaice with butter and capers, and grilled prawns with fried yucca and tartare sauce on the back porch overlooking a swimming pool. On Saturdays there's a happening disco here.

Taberna de Don Jaime BAR

(☎ 056-53-5023; San Martín 203; ⏱4pm-2am) This clamorous tavern is a favorite with locals and tourists alike. It is also a showcase for artisanal wines and piscos. On weekends, the crowds show up to dance to live Latin and rock tunes into the small hours.

❶ Information

DANGERS & ANNOYANCES

On its knees after the earthquake, Pisco acquired a reputation for crime, but the curtain is lifting. The commerce-packed streets should be fine during the daytime (there's a notable police presence in the city center). Nonetheless, it is best to use taxis after dark, particularly around the bus stations and market areas. If you arrive late, get the ticket agent at your bus company office to hail you a reputable cab *(taxi de confianza)*.

MONEY

Interbank (San Martín 101) Has a 24-hour global ATM.

❶ Getting There & Away

Pisco is 6km west of the Panamericana Sur, and only buses with Pisco as the final destination actually go there. If you're not on a direct bus to either Pisco or Paracas, ask to be left at the San Clemente turnoff on the Panamericana Sur, where fast and frequent *colectivos* wait to shuttle passengers to central Pisco's Plaza de Armas (S1.50, 10 minutes) or Paracas (S10, 20 minutes). In the reverse direction, **colectivos** for the San Clemente turnoff leave frequently from near Pisco's central market and from the **small terminal** (Callao Cuadra 1) half a block from the Plaza de Armas on Callao. After dark, avoid the dangerous market area.

There are few direct services from Pisco to Nazca; it's often necessary to change buses in Ica or pick up a direct Nazca bus in Paracas.

Flores (☎ 056-79-6643; Pedemonte s/n) offers multiple daily departures from the center of Pisco north to Lima and south to Ica and Arequipa.

At the San Clemente turnoff, **Soyuz** (☎ 056-53-1014; www.soyuzonline.com.pe; Panamericana Sur, Villa los Angeles) has regular bus departures every five minutes to Lima and Ica, as well as some express services.

Transportation from Pisco to Paracas is possible via **combi** (S1.50, 30 minutes), or **colectivo** (20 minutes), which leave frequently from near Pisco's central market (S3) or the **center** (Callao Cuadra 1; S4 to S5).

Pisco's new **airport** has finally opened but at the time of research the only regular scheduled flight was an infrequent service to Cuzco. It's also used for charter sightseeing flights over the Nazca Lines for visitors that don't fancy the long bus ride south to Nazca.

PISCO BUSES

DESTINATION	COST (S)	DURATION (HR)
Arequipa	60-144	12-15
Ica	5-15	1½-2
Lima	20-70	4½

Paracas (El Chaco)

☎ 056 / POP 7000

The Paracas Peninsula's main village, El Chaco – often referred to as 'Paracas' – is the primary embarkation point for trips to the Islas Ballestas and the Reserva Nacional de Paracas. New condos and luxury hotels are found north and south of the village proper. It's a fun place with a lively traveler scene. Most of the action centers on the *malecón* (boardwalk), where you'll find a pretty wide selection of restaurants and bars. Its natural attractions and long beaches stand out from many south-coast destinations, and many travelers end up spending at least two or three nights here, allowing for a day tour to the islands, beach time and an extended foray across the peninsula.

◉ Sights

The region's essential business is the de rigueur boat tour of the Islas Ballestas and the one-day sojourn around the bald, deserted Paracas Peninsula. Birds and sea mammals are the lures here, but, lest we forget, this is also one of Peru's most important archaeological sites, thanks primarily to the pre-Inca treasures unearthed by one of the country's most important archaeologists, Julio Tello, in the 1920s.

◉ Islas Ballestas

Islas Ballestas ISLAND

(tours S35-40, park entrance islands only S11, islands & peninsula S17) Grandiosely nicknamed the 'poor man's Galápagos,' the Islas Ballestas make for a memorable excursion. The only way to get here is on a boat tour, offered by many tour agencies, touts and hotels. Tours leave at 8am, 10am and noon from the **Marina Turística de Paracas** (Malecón s/n, El Chaco). The 8am tour usually has the calmest seas and best wildlife-viewing.

While the two-hour tours do not disembark onto the islands, they do get you startlingly close to an impressive variety of wildlife.

None of the small boats has a cabin, so dress to protect against the wind, spray and sun. The sea can get rough, so sufferers of motion sickness should take medication before boarding. Wear a hat (cheap ones are sold at the harbor), as it's not unusual to receive a direct hit of guano (droppings) from the seabirds.

On the outward boat journey, which takes about 30 minutes, you will stop just offshore to admire the famous Candelabra Geoglyph, a giant three-pronged figure etched into the sandy hills, which is more than 150m high and 50m wide.

A further hour is spent cruising around the islands' arches and caves and watching large herds of noisy sea lions sprawl on the rocks. The most common guano-producing birds in this area are the guanay cormorant, the Peruvian booby and the Peruvian pelican, seen in colonies several thousand strong. You'll see some extraction facilities on a couple of islands. The Peruvian government still extracts guano (it's a great natural fertilizer) from the islands, but only does so every eight years.

You'll also see cormorants, Humboldt penguins and, if you're lucky, dolphins. Although you can get close enough to the wildlife for a good look, some species, especially the penguins, are more visible with binoculars.

In addition to the park entrance fee, boat tour participants are required to pay a S5 boarding fee.

◉ Reserva Nacional de Paracas

This vast desert **reserve** (Carr Punta Pejerrey, Km 27; peninsula only S11, islands & peninsula S17) occupies most of the Península de Paracas. An alternative to tour operators, taxi drivers who function as guides often wait beyond the dock where passengers disembark in Paracas' beach village of El Chaco, and can take groups into the reserve for around S80 to S120 for a three-hour tour. You can also walk or rent a bike from El Chaco – just make sure to allow lots of time, and bring food and plenty of water. To get there, start at the **obelisk** commemorating the landing of the liberator General José de San Martín that lies near the entrance to El Chaco

village, and continue on foot along the tarmac road that heads to the south.

Museo Julio C Tello   MUSEUM
(admission S7.50; ⊙8am-4pm Tue-Sun) Right next to the park visitor center, in front of the Paracas Necropolis burial grounds on Cerro Colorado, this recently expanded museum features interesting archaeological exhibits from the mysterious culture that once dominated the area.

While many top artifacts from the area have been moved to Ica's Museo Regional de Ica and Lima's Museo Larco, it's still well worth a visit. There's a fine collection of textiles, a display of some of the elongated skulls that were used to differentiate the upper classes of the society, pottery and re-creations of Paracas dwellings. Information panels are in Spanish and English.

Centro de Interpretación   VISITOR CENTER
(⊙7am-6pm) **FREE** Located 1.5km south of the entry point to the reserve, this visitor center seems to be aimed for the most part at school groups rather than independent visitors. And while the exhibits on local fauna and geology are interesting enough the real interest lies outside.

The bay in front of the complex is the best spot to view Chilean flamingos, and there's a walkway down to a **mirador** (lookout), from where these birds can best be spotted from June through August.

Keep a lookout for the fossils which can be spotted beside the path on the way down. Staff will lend binoculars if you want to see the birds up close.

Playa Roja   BEACH
This narrow bay southwest of the visitor center features a peculiar reddish sand that contrasts dramatically with the low yellowish cliffs behind and the foamy blue waters lapping at the shore.

Lagunillas   VILLAGE, BEACH
Turkey vultures feast on the washed-up remains of yesterday's marine carcasses on the lonely beach at Lagunillas, 5km south of the visitor centre, where a bunch of almost-identical, salt-of-the-sea restaurants with fishing boats moored in front constitute 'the village'. It's a picturesque spot that looks better from a distance than up close.

There's no running water here so maintaining hygiene standards in the restaurants is a tough task.

Reserva Nacional de Paracas

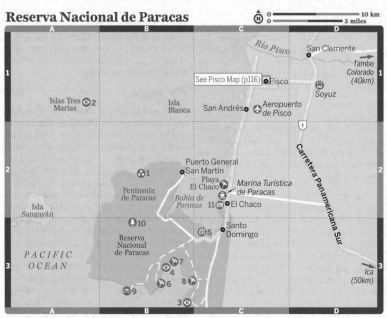

Reserva Nacional de Paracas

◎ Sights

1 Candelabra Geoglyph	B2
Centro de Interpretación	(see 5)
2 Islas Ballestas	A1
3 La Catedral	B3
4 Lagunillas	B3
5 Museo Julio C Tello	C3
6 Playa La Mina	B3
7 Playa Roja	B3
8 Playa Yumaque	B3
9 Punta Arquillo	B3
10 Reserva Nacional de Paracas	B3

⌂ Sleeping

11 Hotel Paracas	C2

Punta Arquillo VIEWPOINT

Just before the Lagunillas turnoff, a spur road branches off the main La Mina road and heads to the southwest for a few kilometers to a parking area near this clifftop lookout. It has grand views of the ocean, with a sea-lion colony on the rocks below and plenty of seabirds gliding by.

Other seashore life around the reserve includes flotillas of jellyfish (swimmers beware), some of which reach about 70cm in diameter with trailing stinging tentacles of 1m. They are often washed up on the shore, where they quickly dry to form mandala-like patterns on the sand. Beachcombers can also find sea hares, ghost crabs and seashells along the shoreline, and the Andean condor occasionally descends to the coast in search of rich pickings.

Playa La Mina BEACH

This beach is a short drive or walk south of Lagunillas on a dirt road and has gentle waters that make it the best swimming area in the reserve. Vacationing Peruvians flock here in summer (January to March) when it can get fairly crowded. If it's busy you may find the odd mobile drinks concession set up. Camping is also allowed. Plan to bring all the water you will need, and never camp alone as robberies have been reported.

Adjacent **El Raspón** beach is usually less busy and is accessed by some stairs running down the rock face.

Candelabra Geoglyph ARCHAEOLOGICAL SITE

A giant three-pronged figure etched into the sandy hills, which is more than 150m high and 50m wide. No one knows exactly who made the glyph, or when, or what it signifies, but theories abound. Some connect it to the Nazca Lines, while others propound that it served as a navigational guide for sailors and was based on the constellation of the Southern Cross. Some even believe it to have been inspired by a local cactus species with hallucinogenic properties.

Playa Yumaque
BEACH, LANDMARK

The reserve protrudes south a fair few kilometers below the Paracas Peninsula. Dirt roads branch off just east of Lagunillas to Yumaque Beach where there is a good bird-watching spot and it's often possible to observe dolphins.

La Catedral
NATURAL FEATURE

This local landmark just south of Playa Yumaque was once a majestic natural arch that jutted out into the sea but was destroyed by the 2007 earthquake. Formed over hundreds of thousands of years by wind and wave erosion, it got toppled in less than a minute. Today it is little more than a sea stack but the panoramas are still impressive and the sunsets here are first class.

Laguna Grande
BEACH

Located around 34km, or an hour's drive, south of the reserve entrance, this remote village has a large inlet protected by a peninsula sand bar that offers optimal conditions for kitesurfing. The village here has no electricity, water or cellular coverage and is a good place to observe the traditional way of life on the peninsula.

Local legend has it that convicts that escape from jail all over the region head here to hide out from the authorities; needless to say pitching a tent nearby is not a great idea.

 Activities

Paracas offers pretty great kitesurfing with limited chop, easy shallow access and good winds. Most outfitters are located at 'Kite Point' south of town near the Hilton.

For private classes expect to pay around S190 for one hour or S1020 for a six-hour course. Group classes are somewhat cheaper.

Kangaroo Kite
KITESURFING

(✆940-472-094; www.kangarookite.net; Urbanización Santo Domingo) A popular kite school offering classes and rental in addition to guided excursions within the Reserva Nacional de Paracas.

Kite Club
KITESURFING

(✆994-831-021; www.kiteclubparacas.com; Urbanización Santo Domingo; ⊙10am-5pm Wed-Sun) A professionally run kite school offering classes and equipment rental. It's located in front of the Double Tree Hilton.

 Tours

Prices and service for tours of the Islas Ballestas and Reserva Nacional de Paracas are usually very similar. The better tours are escorted by a qualified naturalist who speaks Spanish and English. Most island boat tours leave daily at 8am, 10am and noon, and cost around S35 to S40 per person. The number of tours and departure times varies, so it is recommended to reserve a day in advance. Some boats leave from the municipal dock in town but most of the bigger operations depart from the private Marina Turística de Paracas (p117) just to the north.

Less-than-interesting afternoon land tours of the Península de Paracas (S20 to S25) briefly stop at the national reserve's visitor center, breeze by coastal geological formations and spend a long time having lunch in a remote fishing village. Tours of the reserve can be combined with an Islas Ballestas tour to make a full-day excursion (S60).

It's also possible to tour the sights on the peninsula on quad bikes (S100) or in fuel-guzzling mini beach buggies (S120).

If you want to avoid the long road trip to Nazca, it's possible to organize sightseeing flights of the Nazca Lines from the Pisco airport near Paracas, but flights are significantly more expensive than those from the Nazca airfield.

Paracas Explorer
TOURS

(✆056-53-1487; www.paracasexplorer.com; Av Libertadores s/n; ⊙7am-7pm) This busy local travel agency has two offices on the same block and offers the usual island and reserve tours, as well as tours to Tambo Colorado (S200) and multiday trips that take you to Ica and Nazca (from US$200 per person). Can also book flights over the Nazca Lines leaving from Pisco or Ica airports.

Paracas Sights & Tours
BOATING

(✆956-890-301, 056-31-5742; www.paracasights. com; Malecón; ⊙7:30am-8pm) A serious agency offering the usual island tours on its own fleet of modern boats in addition to tours of the Reserva Nacional de Paracas in cars and buses.

📑 Sleeping

El Chaco has an excellent range of hotels with far more options than in Pisco just up the road. Budget and midrange choices are found in the blocks around the Plaza de Armas in town while higher-end resorts are located south of the town.

Paracas Backpackers House   HOSTEL $
(📞 056-53-6700; www.paracasbackpackershouse. com.pe; Av Libertadores s/n; dm S20-30, s without bathroom S45, d with/without bathroom S85/55; 🛜) Of the several 'backpackers hostels' on this strip, this is the original and still the most popular. Most rooms have private baths and look onto the terrace, with hammock and chill area. Dorms sleep seven to 10 people.

It offers all the services travelers could need and organizes tours and onwards transportation. In front two-bed apartments with shared bathrooms offer good value, but don't catch breezes like the upper-storied rooms.

Willy's House   HOSTEL $
(📞 939-281-530; willy.peve16@gmail.com; Av Libertadores s/n; dm/r S20/60; 🛜) This low-key backpackers hostel has four-bed dorms, a back chillaxing area with billiards tables, and clean and spacious private rooms in a new annex. It's no-frills but it's great value and the friendly staff are helpful in organizing activities. Self-caterers will appreciate the shared kitchen.

Bamboo Lodge   HOTEL $$
(📞 999-045-654, 056-50-7017; bamboolodge paracas@hotmail.com; Malecón s/n; r incl breakfast S246-278) If you can score one of the waterfront rooms with their own balconies, this is a top buy. If you only get a room in back, it still ain't half bad. With bamboo everywhere (go figure), simple, light, airy appointments and fab-tiled bathrooms throughout, this is a strong middleweight contender.

Residencial Maria Bonita   HOTEL $$
(📞 056-32-2806; www.residencialmariabonita. com; Av Libertadores s/n; s/d incl breakfast S100/150; 🛜) Bright and friendly, this polished hotel opposite the plaza offers spotless, all-white rooms and common areas adorned with potted plants. Decoration is minimal and showers can be temperamental but all in all it's a good deal. Breakfast is served in the cafe downstairs but with a shut-off of 8:30am it's not great for hard partiers.

Good discounts are available when the town is quiet.

Hostal Santa Maria   HOTEL $$
(📞 056-77-5799; www.hostalsantamariaparacas. com; Plaza de Paracas; s/d incl breakfast S100/120; @🛜) The rooms here are functional and admirably clean, all with cable TV, clean lines and fans to cool off from the considerable heat. There's a rooftop terrace and an annex just down the street. The staff is knowledgeable and can help arrange tours, though they are sometimes preoccupied with looking after the restaurant next door.

Hotel Gran Palma   HOTEL $$
(📞 056-65-5932; www.hotelgranpalma.com; Av Libertadores s/n; s/d incl breakfast S150/230; ❄️🛜) This modern hotel offers brain-surgery-clean rooms, a roadside pool area and breakfast on a pleasant rooftop terrace. The functional minimalist rooms sparkle, but leave little space for embellishment or storage. It's overpriced for what you get, and the service is a bit abrupt.

★**Hotel Paracas**   RESORT $$$
(📞 056-58-1333; www.luxurycollection.com/ hotelparacas; Av Paracas 178; r S2221-2421, ste S2555-3122, all incl breakfast; 🅿️❄️@🛜) A dreamscape plucked from a tourist brochure, with puffed cushions, permanently smiling staff, excellent kids facilities and a luxuriously raked beach, this Starwood resort offers the best high-end rooms in town. The *cabaña*-style rooms have private balconies and massive bathrooms. Unfortunately, ocean views are limited from many rooms. There are three hotels, two pools and a private dock on-site.

Kayaks, paddle boards and catamarans are included.

Nonguests can come for the first-class monster breakfast buffet (S84) that lasts until brunch.

Double-Tree Hilton   RESORT $$$
(📞 016-17-1000; www.doubletree.com; Urbanización Santo Domingo; r S1846/1944; 🅿️❄️@🛜) A super comfortable if somewhat bland choice, this high-end all-suite hotel gives you private patios, a turquoise pool and killer ocean views. The large living areas in the rooms make this a great option for families. Located 2km south of El Chaco.

✕ Eating

★ Inti-Mar
SEAFOOD $$

(www.inti-mar.com; Contiguo Puerto General San Martín, Punto Pejerrey; mains S25-45; ⏱10:30am-3:30pm) One of our favorite places to eat on the entire coast, this breezy spot on the far side of the bay is a working scallop farm with a handful of tables right next to the water. It serves a bunch of different seafood dishes but the fresh scallops served *natural* with lemon and olive oil are phenomenal.

Or try the *conchas a la parmesana*, which are oven-baked in their shell with a Parmesan covering. There are loungers down by the water if you want to stick around for a few drinks after the meal.

It's located just outside the port inside the Reserva Nacional de Paracas. A taxi here costs around S50 but you can incorporate it into a tour of the peninsula. Come early as it gets windy in the afternoon.

Lobo Fino
PERUVIAN $$

(Av Libertadores s/n; mains S26-35, set menus S15-25; ⏱11am-10pm) On the southern edge of town, this unpretentious place with tables on its covered porch prepares quality Peruvian cuisine at fair prices. Locals congregate here at lunch for its excellent set menus, which come in two varieties: *criollo* and *marino*.

Service can be seriously slow – don't come if you have a bus to catch.

Punta Paracas
INTERNATIONAL $$

(Malecón s/n; mains S22-40; ⏱7am-10pm) Coffee and chocolate brownies hit the spot at this open-all-day cafe that remains lively after most other places have closed.

🍷 Drinking & Nightlife

Misk'i
BAR

(Garcia Perez s/n; ⏱5pm-11pm) The best place to begin your evening in Paracas, this chilled-out resto-bar has great wood-fired pizzas (S14-S52), salads and Mexican dishes (mains S16-S26) in addition to an extensive list of cocktails and strong mixed drinks, all accompanied by a perpetual reggae soundtrack that will keep you skankin' it easy.

Fruzion
JUICE BAR

(Garcia Perez s/n; ⏱7am-6pm Mon-Thu, to 8pm Fri-Sat, to 3pm Sun) A bright little modern cafe with a sunny terrace specializing in mixed juices and shakes (S12 to S20) served in massive fish-bowl-like glasses. There's a staggering 80-odd varieties of beverage in addition to quality breakfasts (S12 to S24), real coffee, burgers and pancakes. It's a fine hangout spot although considering the array of wildlife just offshore here, it should really lose the plastic straws.

ℹ Information

MONEY

There are a couple of ATMs in town but during peak periods they may be empty. In Pisco there are many banking options.

BCP (Av Libertadores s/n)

Interbank (Malecón)

TOURIST INFORMATION

iPerú (📞056-638-216; iperunasca@promperu.gob.pe; Av Libertadores s/n; ⏱9am-4pm Wed-Sun)

ℹ Getting There & Away

The fastest way to get to Paracas is via the new airport (p117) at Pisco although at the time of press Cuzco was the only destination with regular flights.

Several buses run daily between Lima and the El Chaco beach district of Paracas (S45 to S68, 3½ hours) before continuing to other destinations south.

Cruz del Sur (📞056-53-6636; www.cruzdelsur.com.pe; Av Libertadores s/n, Ingreso El Chaco) departs from its flash terminal on the northern edge of town and has the most frequent services with departures at 7:30am, 12:30pm, 1:30pm, 3pm, 4pm and 7:10pm. Also runs buses from Paracas to Ica and Nazca at 7:25am, 10:30am, 10:40am, 11:10am, 5:10pm and 5:40pm.

Oltursa (📞056-53-0726; www.oltursa.com.pe; Av Libertadores s/n) has one comfortable bus a day to Lima leaving the office on the main boulevard at 9:50am and one bus south to Ica, Nazca and Arequipa at 10:15am.

Peru Bus (📞056-22-3687; www.perubus.com.pe; Av Libertadores s/n) has the cheapest daily services to Lima at 10:25am and 4:40pm.

Most agencies in El Chaco sell bus tickets including Paracas Explorer (p120).

A cheaper way to get to Lima is to head to Pisco and take a *colectivo* to the Cruce de Pisco from where regular buses run every five minutes to the capital. Transportation from Paracas to Pisco is possible via *combi* (S2, 30 minutes) or *colectivo* (S3 to S5, 20 minutes). Both roam the main boulevard seeking passengers.

There are two daily direct shuttles from Paracas to Huacachina (S20, 1¾ hours) leaving at 10am and 3pm and bookable through most hostels and hotels.

THE BIRD-POO WAR

In the history of pointless wars, the 1864–66 skirmish between Spain and its former colonies of Peru and Chile might seem like the most pointless of them all. Ostensibly, its primary motivation was not self-preservation or saving the world from aliens, but guano, or, to put it less politely, bird poo. Although a thoroughly unpleasant substance when dropped from a great height onto your head, guano has long been a vital contributor to the Peruvian economy, and a resource worth protecting from prying outsiders. In the early 19th century, German botanist Alexander von Humboldt sent samples of it to Europe where innovative British farmers found it to be 30 times more efficient than cow dung when used as a fertilizer. By the 1850s a rapidly industrializing Britain was importing 200,000 tons of the stuff annually to bolster its agriculture. Suddenly the white droppings that covered Peru's bird-filled Pacific Islands were worth the lion's share of the GDP. Spain understood as much in 1864 when, in an act of postcolonial petulance, it occupied the guano-rich Chincha Islands in an attempt to extract reparations from Peru over a small domestic incident in Lambayeque. Peru didn't hesitate to retaliate. A protracted naval war ensued that dragged in Chile, before the islands and their precious bird poo were wrenched back from Spain in 1866.

In the conflict-free present, the industry remains lucrative. Layers of sun-baked, nitrogen-rich guano still cover the Chincha Islands, as well as the nearby Islas Ballestas, although the over-fishing of anchovies (the birds' main food source) in the 1960s and 1970s led to a worrying decline in supplies. Today guano production is closely (and peacefully) regulated by Peru's Ministry of Agriculture.

ℹ️ Getting Around

To get around the Península de Paracas, an alternative to tour operators is taxi drivers who function as guides; they often wait close to the docks where passengers disembark in Paracas' beach village of El Chaco, and can take groups into the reserve for around S80 to S120 for a three-hour tour.

You can also walk or rent a bike from El Chaco – just make sure to allow lots of time, and bring food and plenty of water. To get there, start at the obelisk commemorating the landing of the liberator General José de San Martín that lies near the entrance to El Chaco village, and continue on foot along the tarmac road that heads to the south.

Paracas Backpackers House (p121) rents bikes for S30 (full day).

Some of the tour boats to the Islas Ballestas leave from the municipal dock in town but most leave from the private Marina Turística de Paracas (p117) just to the north.

Ica

🎣 056 / POP 131,000 / ELEV 420M

Just when you thought the landscape was dry enough for martians, out jumps Ica, Peru's agricultural 'miracle in the desert' that churns out bumper crop after bumper crop of asparagus, cotton and fruits, as well as laying claim to being the nation's leading (and best) wine producer. Ica, like Pisco,

sustained significant earthquake damage in 2007 – the graceful cathedral and two other churches were significantly damaged and are undergoing lengthy repairs.

Most people who make it this far bed down in Huacachina 4km to the west, but Ica has reasons to be cheerful too: the south coast's best museum (outside Arequipa) resides here, plus – arguably – the finest winery in Peru. If Nazca seems too much of a circus, it's also possible to organize Nazca Line excursions from Ica – the desert etchings lie 1½ hours to the south.

◎ Sights

Ica's main square has been repainted post-earthquake in generic mustard-yellow to reflect its 'city of eternal sun' moniker. The two sinuous obelisks in its center are supposed to signify the Nazca and Paracas cultures.

The streets surrounding the Plaza de Armas display the odd impressive Spanish colonial mansions while everywhere else bustling commerce reigns.

Museo Regional de Ica   MUSEUM
(Ayabaca cuadra 8; S7.50; ⊙8am-7pm Mon-Fri, 8:30am-6:30pm Sat & Sun) In the suburban neighborhood of San Isidro, Ica pulls out its trump card: a museum befitting a city three times the size. While it might not be the Smithsonian in terms of layout and design,

Ica

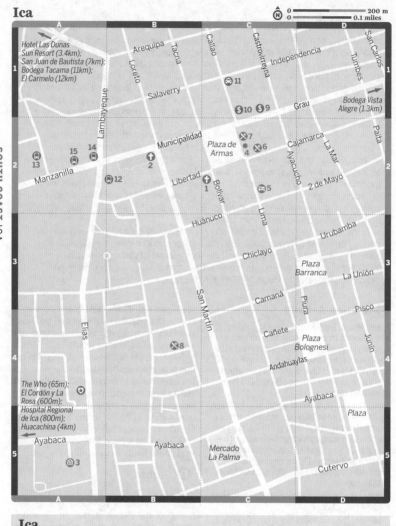

Ica

◎ Sights

1 Iglesia de La Merced	C2
2 Iglesia de San Francisco	B2
3 Museo Regional de Ica	A5

✦ Activities, Courses & Tours

4 Desert Travel	C2

🛏 Sleeping

Hostal Soyuz	(see 15)
5 Hotel Sol de Ica	C2

✕ Eating

6 Helena	C2

7 Plaza 125	C2
8 Restaurant Venezia	B4

ⓘ Information

9 Banco de la Nacion	C1
10 BCP	C1

ⓘ Transport

11 Colectivos to San Juan de Bautista	C1
12 Combis & Colectivos to Pisco/Nazca	B2
13 Cruz del Sur	A2
14 Flores	A2
15 Soyuz/PerúBus	A2

this understated gem catalogs the two key pre-Inca civilizations on Peru's southern coast, namely the Paracas and Nazca cultures, the former famed for its intricate textiles and the latter for its instantly recognizable ceramics.

Any attempt to understand the region's ancient history should begin here where a whole gamut of locally excavated artifacts is on display.

Unfortunately, the museum's famous riches have attracted malign as well as benign interest. In 2004, the building was robbed, with thieves making off with three priceless textiles.

The museum is 2.5km southwest of the city center. Take a taxi from the Plaza de Armas (S5). You could walk, but it's usually not safe to do so alone.

Iglesia de La Merced   CHURCH
(cnr Bolívar & Libertad) Ica's cathedral was the last church the Jesuits built in Peru before their expulsion. It was rebuilt in the late 19th century and contains a finely carved wooden altar. The effects of the 2007 earthquake caused a steeple and part of the roof to collapse. At the time of writing, more than a decade later, it remains in disrepair and closed to visitors.

Iglesia de San Francisco   CHURCH
(cnr Municipalidad & San Martín) This hulking church withstood the 2007 earthquake and continues to show off its fine stained-glass windows.

🏃 Activities

Wineries

Ica is Peru's largest and most revered wine producer, though its desert-defying vineyards are unlikely to get any Euro wine-snobs jumping on a plane anytime soon. The main drawback is 'sweetness.' Even Peru's *semi-seco* (medium-dry) wines are sweet by most yardsticks. Nonetheless, tours around the vineyards can be novel and worthwhile diversions. Most offer free sampling. Bodegas can be visited year-round, but the best time is during the grape harvest from late February until early April.

The countryside around Ica is also scattered with family-owned artisanal bodegas, with many dotted around **San Juan de Bautista** about a 7km taxi (S12 one way) or *colectivo* (S1.50) ride from Ica's center. Colectivos (p127) leave from the corner of Independencia and Callao.

Bodega Lazo   WINE
(📞 056-40-3430; San Juan de Bautista; ⊕9am-1pm Mon-Fri, to 3pm Sat & Sun) 𝐅𝐑𝐄𝐄 One of the best wineries to visit near Ica, Bodega Lazo still uses an artisanal winemaking process to make its traditional piscos, and visitors can observe the entire process before tasting the products.

Bodega Tacama   WINE
(📞 056-58-1030; www.tacama.com; Camino Real s/n, Tinguiña; ⊕9:30am-4:30pm Tue-Sun) 𝐅𝐑𝐄𝐄 Possibly the most professional and lauded of Ica's wineries, Tacama is run out of a sprawling hacienda backed by striped fields lined by vines. Eschewing Peru's penchant for sickly sweet wines, Tacama produces some rather good chardonnays and malbecs that might one day give the Chileans a run for their money.

The half-hour free tour and sampling includes a *mirador* (lookout) and a guide through the aging process (in French oak barrels, no less). Situated 11km northwest of town; you'll have to hire a taxi to get here (S15 each way).

Bodega Vista Alegre   WINE
(📞 056-23-2919; www.vistaalegre.com.pe; Camino a La Tinguiña, Km 2.5; Admission S5; ⊕8am-noon & 1:45-3:45pm Mon-Fri, 9am-noon Sat) About 3km northeast of Ica in the La Tinguiña district, this is the easiest of the large commercial wineries to visit (taxi one way S8). The experience here is more commercial and less traditional than in some of the smaller wineries around town.

☞ Tours

Desert Travel   TOURS
(📞 056-22-7215; desert_travel@hotmail.com; Lima 171; ⊕9am-9pm) Desert Travel is a reliable tour operator offering city tours (S20, four hours), dune-buggy trips in Huacachina (S35), and tours to the Reserva Nacional de Paracas and Islas Ballestas (S50 to S60).

🎉 Festivals & Events

Fiesta de la Vendimia   HARVEST
(⊕early–mid-Mar) This famous grape-harvest festival includes all manner of processions, beauty contests, cockfights and horse shows, music and dancing, and of course, free-flowing pisco and wine.

🛏 Sleeping

Most budget travelers head for Huacachina, 4km west of the city, but Ica has several good midrange and high-end options. Beware that hotels fill up and double or triple their prices during the many festivals.

Hostal Soyuz
HOTEL $

(☏ 056-22-4138; Manzanilla 130; s/d/tr S60/75/95; ❄️🛜) Sitting directly over the Soyuz bus terminal, this handy option for late arrivals or early departures has fairly spacious rooms with air-con and cable TV, but feels institutional, as you'd expect in a bus station, and is only for heavy sleepers on account of the rumpus below. Check-in is beside the bus-ticket desk.

★ El Carmelo
HISTORIC HOTEL $$

(☏ 056-23-2191; www.elcarmelohotelhacienda. com; Carr Panamericana Sur Km 301; s/d/tr/q from S135/190/280/350; @🛜⛱️) This romantic roadside hotel on the outskirts of town inhabits a delightful 200-year-old hacienda that has undeniable rustic charm. Rooms exude a classic elegance but also boast modcons and are very comfortable. However, the stars of the show are the grounds with courtyards, a wonderful wood and cane gazebo and an open fire for the chilly desert nights.

There's a good restaurant plus a winery on-site. Take a taxi from the city center (S5).

Hotel Sol de Ica
HOTEL $$

(☏ 056-23-6168; www.hotelsoldeica.com; Lima 265; s/d/tr incl buffet breakfast S199/249/299; @🛜⛱️) This five-story central hotel is hidden down a long, dark passage behind reception that delivers more than it initially promises. Fairly small rooms have natural wood touches and calm beige curtains and bedspreads, but don't really sparkle. However, it does boast a large garden and swimming pool which is a bit of an oasis from the bustle outside.

A good buffet breakfast is included. We're not sure having to run the water for 20-minutes to get hot water is a good idea in the middle of the desert though.

Hotel Las Dunas Sun Resort
RESORT $$$

(☏ 056-25-6224; www.lasdunashotel.com; Av La Angostura 400, Panamericana Sur Km 300; r from S502; 🅿️❄️@🛜⛱️) By far the most luxurious hotel in town, the sprawling Las Dunas resort is equipped with a swimming pool, a sauna, tennis courts, a minigolf course, a business center, restaurants and bars. Service can be haphazard, however.

It is located a couple of minutes' drive north of the center.

Eating

There are plenty of simple cafes in the center of town while many of Ica's more polished restaurants are found in the surrounding suburbs.

Several shops in the streets east of the plaza sell *tejas* (caramel-wrapped sweets flavored with fruits, nuts etc).

Helena
PERUVIAN $

(☏ 056-22-1844; www.helena.pe; Cajamarca 139; items S4; ⏲️9:30am-8pm) Stop in at this shop half a block from the plaza that is famed around the country for its chocolates and traditional sweets. Try the *tejas* (caramel-wrapped candies flavored with fruits, nuts etc.). You can also visit the factory on the south side of town where you can watch the chocolates being made through a window.

El Cordón y La Rosa
PERUVIAN $$

(☏ 056-21-8012; Los Maestros, Frente Hotel Real; mains S35-55; ⏲️11am-11pm, to 7pm Sun) It's worth the short taxi ride from the center to dine at this modern Peruvian bistro which specializes in seafood but has a wide-ranging menu. It's very popular so tables are a little crammed in. The spotless open kitchen area looks like something straight out of *Masterchef* with neatly uniformed cooks wearing headsets and knocking out plates at lightning speed.

Restaurant Venezia
ITALIAN $$

(Los Manzanos 146, San Isidro; mains S18-32; ⏲️noon-10pm) In a new location fronting a small suburban park a short walk from the Plaza de Armas, this popular family-run Italian restaurant is a good option once you're all ceviched out. It makes a genuine effort at proper Italian flavors unlike many other 'pasta' restaurants around.

Plaza 125
PERUVIAN $$

(Lima 125; mains S17-34, menú S14-16) Your quick stop on the main square backs up homespun *lomo saltado* (strips of beef stir-fried with onions, tomatoes, potatoes and chili) with more internationally flavored chicken fillets. It's riotously popular with locals in a hurry, and the set lunch is a good deal.

Also prepares decent breakfast combos – we prefer the simple *pan con palta* (bread roll with avocado) with freshly squeezed orange juice.

Drinking & Nightlife

There's not much happening in Ica outside of fiesta times, though if it's gringo-dominated nightlife you're after, Huacachina calls like a desert siren. On Ica's Plaza de Armas, you'll find several wine and pisco tasting rooms to pop into for a quick tipple. South of the plaza along Lima local bars and clubs advertise live music, DJs and dancing, but they're pretty rough. The craziest late-night disco, called **The Who** (☑ 056-62-1126; Pacaes s/n; admission S10; ⊙ 10:30pm-7am Fri-Sat), is situated 3km southwest of the plaza; it's a S6 taxi ride.

ℹ Information

DANGERS & ANNOYANCES

Ica experiences some petty theft. Take the normal precautions, particularly around the bus terminals and market areas.

EMERGENCY

Policia (☑ 056-23-5421; Elias, cuadra 5; ⊙ 24hr) At the city center's edge.

MEDICAL SERVICES

Hospital Regional de Ica (☑ 056-23-4798; www.hrica.gob.pe; Prolongación Ayabaca s/n; ⊙ 24hr) For emergency services.

MONEY

Banco de la Nación (Grau 161) Fee-free ATM.

BCP (Plaza de Armas) Has Visa/MasterCard ATMs and changes US dollars.

ℹ Getting There & Away

Ica is a main destination for buses along the Panamericana Sur, so it's easy to get to/from Lima or Nazca. Most of the bus companies are clustered in a high-crime area at the west end of Salaverry, and also Manzanilla west of Lambayeque.

Soyuz (☑ 056-22-4138; www.soyuzonline.com.pe; Manzanilla 130), which is sometimes branded Peru Bus, runs to Lima via Chincha and Cañete with services leaving every 15 minutes. It also has frequent buses south to Nazca via Palpa. Watch your belongings on Soyuz, especially when people get on and off the bus, as petty theft is common.

Flores (☑ 056-21-2266; Manzanilla 152) also runs economic buses to Lima and has services to Nazca. Note that southbound buses leave from a different terminal a block away.

Cruz del Sur (☑ 0801-11111; www.cruzdelsur.com.pe; Fray Ramon Rojas 189) offers more luxurious services going north and south.

Some faster, but slightly more expensive and less safe **colectivos** and *combis* heading for Pisco and Nazca leave when full from near the intersection of Lambayeque and Municipalidad in Ica.

Some small companies may serve destinations around Peru's central highlands, such as Ayacucho and Huancavelica.

Taxis to Huacachina cost S8. **Colectivos** to San Juan de Bautista leave from the corner of Independencia and Callao.

ICA BUSES

DESTINATION	COST (S)	DURATION (HR)
Arequipa	75-160	12
Cuzco	140–165	14
Cañete	8	3
Chincha	6	2
Lima	25–41	4½
Nazca	30	2½
Pisco	5–15	1½–2

Huacachina

☑ 056 / POP 200

Imagine... It's 6pm and you're sitting atop a giant wind-sculpted sand dune watching the sun set psychedelically over a landscape of golden yellows and rusty reds. Two hundred meters below you lies a dreamy desert lagoon ringed by exotic palm trees and furnished with a clutch of rustic yet suitably elegant hotels. It took you an exhausting 20 minutes to climb up to this lofty vantage point, but with a well-waxed sandboard wedged beneath your belly you'll be down in less than one.

While not as famous as Nazca to the south, Huacachina, an aesthetically perfect desert oasis 4km west of Ica, is a firmly established stopover on southern Peru's well-trampled Gringo Trail, and with good reason. Sandboarding, dune-buggie rides and good-old romantic idling are the orders of the day here. This is backpacker central, so expect plenty of late-night parties and international flavors. Many people just make it here for a quick overnight and dune trip the next day, but a few days of relaxed strolls and dune climbs may just channel your inner chi.

🏃 Activities

Sandboarding

You can rent basic sandboards all over town for S5 to S8 an hour to slide, surf or ski your way down the dunes, getting sand lodged into every bodily orifice. Snowboarding this isn't. There are no tow ropes or chairlifts here. Instead you must stagger up the sugary dunes for your 45-second adrenaline rush. Make sure you are given wax (usually in the form of an old candle) when you rent your board as they are pretty useless without regular rubdowns. Start on the smaller slopes and don't be lulled into a false sense of security – several people have seriously injured themselves losing control of their sandboards. Most riders end up boarding belly down with their legs splayed out behind as emergency brakes. Don't forget to keep your mouth shut.

Dune Buggies

Many hotels offer thrill-rides in *areneros* (dune buggies) which head out early morning (8am-ish) and late afternoon (4pm-ish) to avoid the intense sun. They then stop at the top of the soft slopes, from where you can sandboard down and be picked up at the bottom

After a serious accident involving an inexperienced driver claimed the lives of two travelers in mid-2018 and injured many others, buggy rides were prohibited while the authorities looked into the incident.

While it's likely that buggy rides will be given the go ahead again – they are a big part of the local economy – it remains to be seen if the authorities take serious action to regulate the industry and cut out cowboy operators.

If you plan on taking a trip, ask around before choosing an operator. Make sure cameras are well protected, as sand can be damaging.

The going rate for tours is S45 but ask first if sandboard rental is included and how long the tour lasts. Tours do not include a fee of S4, which must be paid upon entering the dunes (this doesn't apply to those entering on foot).

Litter is an issue on Huacachina's dunes, as it is in much of Peru. It ought to go without saying, but pack out all your rubbish when you visit these beautiful, sandy behemoths.

Swimming & Boating

The lagoon's murky waters supposedly have curative properties, which is great because you run a good chance of getting a nasty ear infection if you go in. A more inviting option are the hotel pools (of which there are half a dozen).

You can also hire boats – both rowing and pedal-powered – at a couple of points on the lagoon for S12 an hour.

👉 Tours

Pretty much all the hotels can organize dune-buggy rides. A handful of others run trips to Paracas, Islas Ballestras and Nazca. A reliable option is **Pelican Travel &** **Service** (☑956-385-300; www.pelicanperu.com; Av Perotti s/n; ⏱10am-6:30pm) which has an office on Av Perotti and another one in Ica.

🛏 Sleeping

Huacachina is pretty much just a collection of hotels and hostels so there is a wide range of beds to choose from. It's a popular destination, though, so be sure to make advance reservations.

Hospedaje Mayo HOSTEL $
(☑056-22-9003; hospedajemayo@gmail.com; Av Huacachina s/n; dm/s/d/tr S20/35/70/105; 🛜🖾) Facing the southern dunes, this guesthouse turned hostel has clean, well-maintained rooms with cheery blue and tangerine bed covers. The dorm sleeps 10, and while it has ceiling fans, it can get hot as an armadillo's bottom. There's a tiny pool out back, along with a foosball table.

★**Banana's Adventure** HOSTEL $$
(☑056-23-7129; bananasadventure@hotmail.com; Av Perotti s/n; r per person incl breakfast & excursion S75-110; 🛜🖾) This peaced-out crash pad on the north side of the lagoon only offers packaged stays. They include a room for the night – choose between four-bed dorms with superfirm mattresses or elegant private rooms with glass on all sides and modern fixings – plus a dune-buggy and sandboarding excursion the next day.

We don't love that you are roped into the package tour, but with huge windows, a fun bar and little dip pool, this is the best budget spot in town.

Hostería Suiza HOTEL $$
(☑056-23-8762; www.hosteriasuiza.com.pe; Balneario de Huacachina; s/d/tr incl breakfast S152/249/309; ❄🛜🖾) This formal hotel on the northwest end of the lagoon offers tranquility and some of the best value in Huacachina, with high-ceilinged rooms and Moorish-meets-hacienda architectural features. The rooms looking onto the backyard garden and pool area are the best, with textured green bedspreads and newly remodeled modern bathrooms.

A gentle jazz/bossanova soundtrack rounds out the calm vibe.

Desert Nights HOSTEL $$
(☑056-22-8458; www.huacachinaperu.pe; Balneario de Huacachina s/n; dm S25, r with/without bathroom S90/120; ⏱8am-10pm) While it might not boast the atmosphere of some of the other hostels in town, Huacachina's

HI-affiliate hostel is clean and reliable with top facilities. There's a guest kitchen but you may not need it considering it's fronted by one of the best places to eat in town.

Hostal Curasi
HOTEL $$

(📞 056-21-6989; www.huacachinacurasi.com; Balneario de Huacachina; s/d/q incl breakfast S140/180/210; 🛜 ≋) Right amongst the action at the main entrance to the lagoon, this motel-style place has a garden and pool in the middle to cool off on those hot south-coast days. The rooms have ocean-evoking bedspreads and the odd uber-kitsch oil painting.

El Huacachinero Hotel
HOTEL $$$

(📞 056-21-7435; www.elhuacachinero.com; Av Perotti; s/d incl breakfast S175/280; ❄ 🛜 ≋) Recently upgraded, the Huacachinero logs the finest restaurant in the oasis (by a stretch), a relaxing pool area (no blaring music), and immediate dune access via the back gate if you're up for a 45-degree one-step-forward-two-steps-back climb to the sunset of your dreams. Agreeably rustic rooms have super-comfortable beds and cane accents.

Hotel Mossone
HISTORIC HOTEL $$$

(📞 016-14-3900; www.dematourshoteles.com; Balneario de Huacachina; d/tr/q S378/478/511; ❄ @ 🛜 ≋) The atmospheric central courtyard with its chipped paving stones and wire-mesh aviary looks like something out of Fidel Castro's time-warped Cuba at Huacachina's first hotel. Rooms are huge but unfortunately are poorly prepared and dimly lit, losing the hotel points in the top-tier race. There are free bicycles for guests to explore the area.

✖ Eating

Desert Nights
INTERNATIONAL $

(Blvd de Huacachina; mains S15-25; 🛜) The menu might have been ripped off from anywhere else on the banana-pancake trail, but the cafe restaurant at the front of the hostel of the same name has fantastic views from its rooftop terrace and is somewhere you're guaranteed to meet other travelers.

The excellent Peruvian coffee is backed up by peanut butter and jam sandwiches, burgers, pizzas and brownies.

Nuna Cocina Bar
PERU $$

(📞 954-776-625; Balneario de Huacachina; mains S20-35; ⊙ noon-10pm) Towards the end of the boulevard on the far side of the oasis, this tranquil little spot serves decent Peruvian fare and a wide selection of cocktails on its pleasant porch.

🍷 Drinking & Nightlife

Bars and discos in Huacachina are generally attached to the various hotels, and clientele is mostly foreign. Fame and infamy belong to the boisterous Casa de Arena (Av Perotti s/n; ⊙ 10pm-6am Fri-Sat) disco which fills with a hard partying crowd from Ica.

ℹ Information

SAFE TRAVEL

Though safer than Ica, Huacachina is not a place to be lax about your personal safety or looking after your property. Some guesthouses have reputations for ripping off travelers and also harassing young women with sexual advances. Check out all of your options carefully before accepting a room. Also, the few small stores around the lagoon offer plenty of souvenirs but are often out of the basics; come prepared!

ℹ Getting There & Away

The only way to get to Huacachina from Ica is by taxi (S8 to S10 one way).

Nazca & Around
📞 056 / POP 26,700 / ELEV 590M

'Nazca Lines' refers to the ancient geometric lines that crisscross the Nazca desert and the enigmatic animal geoglyphs that accompany them. Like all great unexplained mysteries, these great etchings on the pampa, thought to have been made by a pre-Inca civilization between AD 450 and 600, attract a variable fan base of archaeologists, scientists, history buffs, New Age mystics, curious tourists, and pilgrims on their way to (or back from) Machu Picchu.

Questions still hang over how they were made and by whom, and the answers are often as much wild speculation as pure science (aliens? prehistoric balloonists?). Documented for the first time by North American scientist Paul Kosok in 1939 and declared a Unesco World Heritage Site in 1994, the lines today are the south coast's biggest tourist attraction, meaning the small, otherwise-insignificant desert town of Nazca can be a bit of a circus.

◉ Sights

The best-known lines are found in the desert 20km north of Nazca, and by far the best way to appreciate them is to get a bird's-eye

Nazca

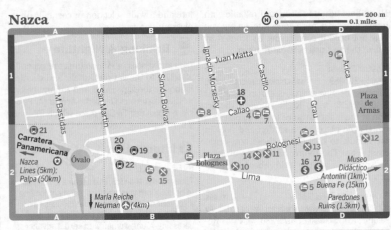

Nazca

Activities, Courses & Tours

Sleeping

Eating

Information

Transport

view from a *sobrevuelo* (overflight). Prices for a standard 30-minute flight taking in 12 of the figures are normally around US$90 but can rise and fall depending on demand. Extended flights taking in more of the lines and including detours to other archaeological sites in the area including the Cantalloc Aqueducts are also offered.

During high season it's a good idea to reserve flights well in advance – either online or through an agency – as they can get booked out. In low season it's possible to just turn up at the airport and shop around.

Nazca Lines & Around

Nazca Lines   RUINS

Spread over 500 sq km (310 sq mi) of arid, rock-strewn plain in the Pampa Colorada (Red Plain), the Nazca Lines are one of the world's great archaeological mysteries. Comprising over 800 straight lines, 300 geometric figures (geoglyphs) and 70 animal and plant drawings (biomorphs), the lines are almost imperceptible on the ground. From above, they form a striking network of stylized figures and channels, many of which radiate from a central axis.

The figures are mostly etched out in single continuous lines, while the encompassing geoglyphs form perfect triangles, rectangles or straight lines running for several kilometers across the desert.

The lines were made by the simple process of removing the dark sun-baked stones from the surface of the desert and piling them up on either side of the lines, thus exposing the lighter, powdery gypsum-laden soil below. The most elaborate designs represent animals, including a 180m-long lizard, a monkey with an extravagantly curled tail, and a condor with a 130m (426ft) wingspan. There's also a hummingbird, a spider and an intriguing owl-headed person on a hillside, popularly referred to as an astronaut because of its goldfish-bowl shaped head, though some believe it's a priest with a mystical owl's head.

Endless questions remain. Who constructed the lines and why? And how did they know what they were doing when the lines can only be properly appreciated from the air? Maria Reiche (1903–98), a German mathematician and long-time researcher of the Lines, theorized that they were made by the Paracas and Nazca cultures between 900 BC and AD 600, with some additions by the Wari settlers from the highlands in the 7th century. She also claimed that the Lines were an astronomical calendar developed for agricultural purposes, and that they were mapped out through the use of sophisticated mathematics (and a long rope). However, the handful of alignments Reiche discovered between the sun, stars and lines were not enough to convince scholars.

Later, English documentary maker Tony Morrison hypothesized that the Lines were walkways linking *huacas* (sites of ceremonial significance). A slightly more surreal suggestion from explorer Jim Woodman was that the Nazca people knew how to construct hot-air balloons and that they did, in fact, observe the lines from the air. Or, if you believe author George Von Breunig, the Lines formed a giant running track.

A more down-to-earth theory, given the value of water in the sun-baked desert, was suggested by anthropologist Johann Reinhard, who believed that the Lines were involved in mountain worship and a fertility/water cult. Recent work by the Swiss-Liechtenstein Foundation (SLSA; www.slsa.ch) agrees that they were dedicated to the worship of water, and it is thus ironic that their theory about the demise of the Nazca culture suggests that it was due not to drought but to destructive rainfall caused by a phenomenon such as El Niño.

About the only thing that is certain is that when the Nazca set about turning their sprawling desert homeland into an elaborate art canvas, they also began a debate that will keep archaeologists busy for many decades, if not centuries to come.

Mirador VIEWPOINT
(Admission S3; ⊘6am-6pm) You'll get only a sketchy idea of the Lines at this lookout on the Panamericana Sur 20km north of Nazca, which has an oblique view of three figures: the lizard, the tree and the hands (or frog, depending on your point of view). It's also a lesson in the damage to which the Lines are vulnerable. The Panamericana Sur runs smack through the tail of the lizard, which from nearby seems all but obliterated.

Signs nearby warn that walking on the Lines is strictly forbidden. It irreparably damages them, and besides, you can't see anything at ground level. To get to the observation tower from Nazca, catch any bus or *colectivo* northbound along the Panamericana Sur (S2, 30 minutes). Some tours (from S50 per person) also combine a trip to the *mirador* with visits to another natural viewpoint and the Maria Reiche Museum. About 1km south of the constructed *mirador* there is a **Mirador Natural** (free) on a small knoll-like hill with a close-up view of one of the geometric lines made by removing reddish pebbles from the gray earth.

Museo Maria Reiche MUSEUM
(Admission S5; ⊘8:30am-5:30pm) When Maria Reiche, the German mathematician and long-term researcher of the Nazca Lines, died in 1998, her house, which stands 5km north of the *mirador* (lookout) along Panamericana Sur, was made into a small museum. Though disappointingly scant on information, you can see where she lived, amid the clutter of her tools and obsessive sketches in addition to a tattooed mummy.

Though the sun can be punishing, it's possible to walk here from the *mirador* in a sweaty hour or so, although the busy highway is not the safest place to walk. Alternatively a passing *colectivo* can sometimes take you (S2). To return to Nazca, just ask the guard to help you flag down any southbound bus or *colectivo*. A visit to the museum can also be arranged as part of a tour to the nearby *mirador*.

Palpa Lines ARCHAEOLOGICAL SITE
Like Nazca, Palpa is surrounded by perplexing geoglyphs, the so-called Palpa Lines, which are serially overshadowed by the more famous, but less abundant, Nazca Lines to the south. The Palpa Lines display a greater profusion of human forms including the Familia Real de Paracas, a group of eight figures on a hillside.

WORTH A TRIP

THE GIANT DUNE

Stand down all other pretenders. **Cerro Blanco**, 14km east of Nazca, is the highest sand dune in Peru and one of the tallest in the world: 2078m above sea level and – more importantly – 1176m from base to summit, that's higher than the tallest mountain in England and numerous other countries. If Huacachina's sand didn't irrevocably ruin your underwear, this could be your bag.

Due to the dune's height and steepness it's best to organize an excursion from Nazca. Trips leave at about 4am to avoid the intense heat. The arduous climb to the top of the dune (buggies can't climb this behemoth) takes approximately three hours. Going down is counted more in minutes with some clear runs of up to 800m. Many agencies in Nazca offer this trip, including Kunan Tours.

It's possible to view some of the Lines from terra firma at a *mirador* (lookout) 8km south of the town of Palpa where a small museum hut offers further explanations in English and Spanish. However, the best way to see more of these lines is on a combined overflight from Nazca.

☉ In Town

Museo Didáctico Antonini   MUSEUM
(📞 056-52-3444; Av de la Cultura 600; S15, plus camera S5; ⊙9am-7pm) On the east side of town, this excellent archaeological museum has an aqueduct running through the back garden, as well as interesting reproductions of burial tombs, a valuable collection of ceramic pan flutes and a scale model of the Lines.

You can get an overview of both the Nazca culture and a glimpse of most of Nazca's outlying sites here. Though the exhibit labels are in Spanish, the front desk lends foreign-language translation booklets for you to carry around. To get to the museum follow Bolognesi to the east out of town for 1km, or take a taxi (S3).

☉ Outlying Sights

Most outlying sights can be visited on tours from Nazca, although individual travelers or pairs may have to wait a day or two before the agency finds enough people who are also interested in going.

Aqueductos de Cantalloc   ARCHAEOLOGICAL SITE
(S10; ⊙9am-6pm) About 4km southeast of town are the 30-plus underground Cantalloc Aqueducts, many of which are still in working order and are essential in irrigating the surrounding fields. The impressive series of stone and wood channels and spiraling access ways were built by the Nazca between AD 200 and 900 and are considered one of the finest examples of pre-Hispanic engineering. Locals say the water here is still good to drink.

Though once possible to enter the aqueducts through the *ventanas* (windows), which local people use to clean the aqueducts each year, it's no longer permitted to go all the way in; instead, you can take note of the Nazca's exceptional stonework from the outside.

It's possible, but not necessarily safe, to walk to the aqueducts; at least, don't carry any valuables. Alternatively you can hire a taxi to take you there for S4 to S5. To get a return taxi you will probably have to walk out a few minutes to the Cooperativa Cantayo.

Admission is via the Boleto Turistica which also covers entry to the nearby Paredones ruins and El Telar, a geoglyph found in the town of Buena Fe. Tours from Nazca take 2½ hours, cost from S30 per person and may be combined with visits to touristy gold and ceramics workshops.

Paredones Ruins   RUINS
(Admission S10; ⊙9am-6pm) The Paredones ruins, 2km southeast of town via Arica over the river, are not very well preserved (primarily because they were constructed from adobe rather than stone) although around 10% of the site has been reconstructed so it's possible to get an idea of how it once looked. Their position on a slope above the town is commanding, which is probably why the Incas used it as an administrative control center between the mountains and the coast.

Admission also covers entry to the nearby Cantalloc Aqueducts.

Chauchilla Cemetery   ARCHAEOLOGICAL SITE
(S8; ⊙8am-5:30pm) The most popular excursion from Nazca, this cemetery, 28km south of Nazca, will satisfy any urges you have to see ancient bones, skulls and mummies. Dating back to the Ica-Chincha culture around AD 1000, the mummies were originally

scattered haphazardly across the desert, left by ransacking tomb-robbers. Now they are seen carefully rearranged inside a dozen or so tombs, though cloth fragments and pottery and bone shards still litter the ground outside the demarcated trail.

The site is located down an 8km unpaved spur road off the highway. Organized tours last three hours and cost S35 to S120 per person depending on whether you wish to take in other attractions on the way.

Cahuachi
RUINS

(⊘9am-4pm) FREE A dirt road travels 25km west from Nazca to Cahuachi, the most important known Nazca center, which is still undergoing excavation. It consists of several pyramids, a graveyard and an enigmatic site called Estaquería, which may have been used as a place of mummification. Tours from Nazca take three hours, cost S50 to S130 per person, and may include a side trip to Pueblo Viejo, a nearby pre-Nazca residential settlement, or sandboarding on nearby dunes.

Going here with advance reservations from a tour agency is recommended as access is complicated. If you want to go independently a round-trip taxi from Nazca costs around S90 to S100.

Reserva Nacional Pampas Galeras
WILDLIFE RESERVE

(☎056-52-2770; www.sernanp.gob.pe/pampa-galeras-barbara-d-achille; Lucanas) This national reserve is a vicuña (threatened wild camelids) sanctuary high in the mountains 90km east of Nazca on the road to Cuzco. It is the best place to see these shy animals in Peru, with about 5000 of the species residing within the reserve boundaries, though tourist services are very limited. The majority of the reserve is located at altitudes between 4000m and 4200m and temperatures can fall to -5°C so be sure to bring suitable clothing.

Every year in June is the *chaccu* (round-up), when hundreds of villagers round up the vicuñas for shearing and three festive days of traditional ceremonies, with music and dancing, and of course, drinking. Full-day tours from Nazca to the reserve begin from S110 per person but it's well worth spending the night up here to fully appreciate the nature. There are three hiking circuits leaving from the visitor's center and basic accommodations are available within the reserve. Resident biology students are often on hand to guide visitors.

Tours

Most people fly over the Lines then leave, but there's more to see around Nazca. If you take one of the many local tours, they typically include a torturously long stop at a potter's and/or gold-miner's workshop for a demonstration of their techniques (tips for those who show you their trade are expected, too).

Hotels tirelessly promote their own tours but it's well worth wandering around town to shop around.

Kunan Tours
TOURS

(☎056-52-4069; www.kunantours.com; Arica 419) Based out of the Kunan Wasi Hotel (p134), this comprehensive travel company offers all the Nazca tours, plus excursions to the Islas Ballestas, Huacachina and Chincha.

Alegría Tours
ADVENTURE

(☎056-52-2497; www.alegriatoursperu.com; Hotel Alegría, Lima 168; ⊘7am-10pm) Behemoth agency offers all the usual local tours, plus off-the-beaten-track and sandboarding options. The tours are expensive for one person, so ask to join up with other travelers to receive a group discount. Alegría can arrange guides in Spanish, English, French and German in some cases.

Sleeping

Despite its importance for tourism in the region, Nazca does not have the best selection of hotels. Prices drop by up to 50% outside of peak season, which runs from May until August.

Hospedaje Yemayá
HOTEL$

(☎056-52-3146; luis.121262@gmail.com; Callao 578; s/d S45/60; @🖲) An indefatigably hospitable family deftly deals with all of the backpackers that stream through their doorway. They offer a few floors of small but well-cared-for rooms with hot showers and cable TV. A sociable terrace and cheap laundry service make it one of the best budget options in town.

Hostal Nasca
HOTEL$

(☎056-52-2085; marionasca13@hotmail.com; Lima 438; s/d/tr S35/45/65, s/d without bathroom 20/25; 🖲) A rock-bottom, bargain-basement place with friendly, elderly owners. Army-barracks-style rooms offer bare-bones facilities; some have private bathrooms.

OVERFLIGHTS OVERVIEW

Bad publicity wracked the Nazca Lines in 2010 when two small aircraft carrying tourists on *sobrevuelos* (overflights) crashed within eight months of each other causing a total of 13 fatalities. The crashes followed an equally catastrophic 2008 accident that killed five French tourists, along with another incident when a plane was forced to make an emergency landing on the Panamericana Sur in 2009.

In reaction to the incidents some changes have been made. All planes now fly with two pilots, more thorough safety inspections have been implemented, and prices have gone up to ensure that companies don't cut corners with poorly maintained aircraft or overfilled flights.

Nonetheless, it still pays to put safety before price when choosing your overflight company. Question anyone who offers prices significantly lower than the other companies and don't be afraid to probe companies on their safety records and flight policies. **Aeroparacas** (☑ 016-41-7000; www.aeroparacas.com; Lima 169) is one of the better airline companies. Other long-standing operators include **Aerodiana** (☑ 014-47-6824; www.aerodiana.com.pe; Aeropuerto Maria Reiche Neuman) and **Alas Peruanas** (☑ 056-52-2444; www.alasperuanas.com; Lima 168). Some countries, including the UK, still place warnings about overflights on their foreign-office websites.

If you do opt for a flight, bear in mind that because the small aircraft bank left and right it can be a stomach-churning experience, so motion-sickness sufferers should consider taking medication. Looking at the horizon may help mild nausea. It's generally best to fly in the morning when there is less wind.

Most airline companies use **Aeropuerto Maria Reiche Neuman** (NZC; ☑ 56-52-3731; Panamericana s/n), 4km southwest of Nazca, although you can also depart from Pisco and Ica if you are not keen on the long bus ride down to Nazca. On top of the tour fee the airport in Nazca normally charges a departure tax of S30.

★ **Hotel Oro Viejo** HOTEL $$
(☑ 056-52-2284; www.hoteلoroviejo.net; Callao 483; s/d/tr/ste incl buffet breakfast S150/200/240/450; ⓟ❄@🛜🏊) There's a decidedly oriental feel to this excellent midrange hotel with its open gardens and glistening swimming pool. Occasional farming artifacts grace the common areas and lounge, while the well-fragranced rooms deliver comfort, quiet and relaxation. The rooms on the ground floor of the original buildling are a bit poky; ask for a new room out back.

Kunan Wasi Hotel HOTEL $$
(☑ 056-52-4069; www.kunanwasihotel.com; Arica 419; s/d/tr S70/90/120; @🛜) Very clean and very bright with each room conforming to a different color scheme. Kunan Wasi is English-speaking, superfriendly, and immaculately clean. Tours can be arranged on-site and travelers will love the top-floor terrace. Welcome to a perfectly packaged Nazca bargain.

Hotel La Encantada HOTEL $$
(☑ 056-52-2930; Callao 592; s/d/tr S105/140/160; @🛜) Offering some of the best value in downtown, this modernish hotel offers two floors of bright, freshly painted rooms and a pleasant terrace out front. Traffic noise can be an issue.

It's often possible to get a good discount off the published prices.

Hotel Alegría HOTEL $$
(☑ 056-52-2702; www.hotelalegria.net; Lima 168; s/d/tr incl breakfast S148/199/231; ❄@🛜🏊) This is a classic travelers' haunt with a restaurant, manicured grounds and pool. It has narrow, tile-floor business-standard rooms. All in all it's an OK bet, but falls a bit short for the price.

DM Hoteles Nazca HOTEL $$$
(☑ 016-14-3900; www.dmhoteles.pe; Bolognesi 147; d/tr/ste incl breakfast S474/507/697; ⓟ❄@🛜🏊) Exceedingly tranquil considering its city-center location, this lauded hotel is arranged around a large courtyard complete with lovely swimming pool and fountain. Classy touches include tilework and arches reminiscent of southern Spain, an on-site planetarium (with daily shows), a comfy lounge, and efficient but not officious service.

Choose between romantic garden-level rooms or more modern affairs on the 2nd floor.

Casa Andina
HOTEL **$$$**

(☎012-13-9718; www.casa-andina.com; Bolognesi 367; s/d incl buffet breakfast S396/451; ❋ @ 🤝 ⛲) This Peruvian chain hotel, poised midway between the bus stations and the Plaza de Armas, offers contemporary Andean touches like leather lampshades and textile bed runners, creating a solid-value proposition in the upmarket hotel category. The palm-filled courtyard and adjacent pool area are small but tasteful.

Eating

West of the Plaza de Armas, Bolognesi is stuffed full of foreigner-friendly pizzerias, restaurants and bars.

Rico Pollo
PERUVIAN **$**

(Lima 190; mains from S16; ⊙11am-11pm) A local lunchtime phenomenon, this very cheap, very crowded *polleria* (roast chicken) joint offers some good barbecued meat cuts in addition to standard rotisserie chicken. For S16 you get a filling meal of chicken breast with fries and vegetables. Fresh cakes provide an excellent supporting act.

La Kasa Rustika
PERUVIAN, INTERNATIONAL **$$**

(Bolgnesi 372; mains S18-40; ⊙7am-11pm) One of the best eateries on the main strip, La Kasa Rustika has a wide menu of Peruvian flavors and international dishes served on an inviting open terrace. Take your pick from steak, seafood, pasta and pizza. Portions are large, prices reasonable and service top-notch.

Mamashana
INTERNATIONAL **$$**

(☎056-21-1286; www.mamashana.com; Bolognesi 270; mains S20-35; ⊙10am-11pm; 🤝) Head upstairs to take advantage of bird's-eye views of the street below at this international-traveler-set favorite. The food is quite good, and prepared with a worldwide audience in mind. Choose from steaks and seafood, to pasta and homestyle hamburgers. The cane-thatched room and exposed wood lend a South American air.

La Encantada Cafe
INTERNATIONAL **$$**

(☎056-52-4216; Bolognesi 282; mains S20-60; ⊙10am-10:30pm) A top spot on the 'Boulevard' (Bolognesi), La Encantada sparkles in Nazca's dusty center with bright and modern dining areas, great coffee, and courteous and friendly waitstaff. The extensive menu mixes Europhile flavors (pasta etc) with Peruvian favorites.

El Portón
PERUVIAN, INTERNATIONAL **$$**

(Ignacio Moreseky 120; mains S20-38; ⊙11:30am-11pm) Fed with a regular diet of Nazca Lines tour groups, this rambling place might be a bit lonely for single diners, but it's well worth visting both for the ambience and quality of the plates. The menu is anchored by above-average Peruvian and international dishes, including great stuffed avocados, which can be enjoyed in the fresh dining rooms or on the terrace.

La Estación Plaza Mayor
STEAK **$$**

(cnr Bolognesi & Arica; mains S21-40) This long-standing spot has a coal grill with a rustic wood-and-bamboo mezzanine seating area overlooking the Plaza de Armas – barbecued meats dominate. Special combination meals with a drink are offered for S20.

ℹ Information

EMERGENCY
Police Station (Panamericana s/n)

MEDICAL SERVICES
Hospital de Apoyo Nazca (☎056-52-2586; www.hospitalnasca.gob.pe; Callao s/n; ⊙24hr) For emergency services.

MONEY
Banco de la Nación (Lima 465) Fee-free ATM in the center.

BCP (Lima 495) Has a Visa/MasterCard ATM and changes US dollars.

SAFE TRAVEL
The town of Nazca is generally safe for travelers, though be wary when walking at night near either bridge to the south of town. Travelers arriving by bus will be met by persistent *jaladores* (agents) trying to sell tours or take arriving passengers to hotels. These touts may use the names of recommended places but are not to be trusted. Never hand over any money until you can personally talk to the hotel or tour-company owner and get a confirmed itinerary in writing. It's best to go with a reliable agency for land tours of the surrounding area, as a few violent assaults and robberies of foreign tourists have been reported.

TOURIST INFORMATION
iPerú (☎016-16-7300, ext 3042; Aerodromo Maria Reiche Neuman; ⊙7am-4pm) Government-run tourism desk at the airfield.

ℹ Getting There & Away

There are no scheduled flights to Nazca as the small airport does not have the facilities to receive larger commercial operations.

Nazca is a major destination for buses on the Panamericana Sur and is easy to get to from Lima, Ica or Arequipa. Bus companies cluster at the west end of Calle Lima, near the *óvalo* (main roundabout). Buses to Arequipa often originate in Lima, and to get a reserved seat you may have to pay the Lima fare.

Most long-distance services leave in the late afternoon or evening. **Cruz del Sur** (0801-11111; www.cruzdelsur.com.pe; Av Los Incas) and **Civa** (056-52-4390; www.civa.com. pe; Lima 155; 6am-2am) have a few luxury buses daily to Lima. Intermediate points such as Ica and Pisco are more speedily served by smaller, *económico* (cheap) bus companies, such as **Flores** (Panamericana s/n) and **Soyuz** (056-52-1464; San Martín 142), which run buses to Ica every half-hour from Av Los Incas. These buses will also drop you at Palpa (S3, one hour).

To go direct to Cuzco, several companies, including Cruz del Sur and Civa, take the paved road east via Abancay. This route climbs over 4000m and gets very cold, so wear your warmest clothes and bring your sleeping bag on board if you have one. Alternatively, some companies also offer direct buses to Cuzco via Arequipa.

For Ica, fast *colectivos* (S15, two hours) and slower minibuses leave when full from near the gas station on the *óvalo*. On the south side of the main roundabout, *colectivos* wait for enough passengers to make the run down to Chala (S15, 2½ hours).

A taxi from central Nazca to the airport, 4km away, costs about S6.

NAZCA BUSES

DESTINATION	COST (S)	DURATION (HR)
Arequipa	70-140	10-12
Camaná	60-120	7
Chala	15	3½
Cuzco	80-140	14
Lima	55-145	8
Ica	30-65	2½
Pisco	30-65	1½-2
Tacna	100-165	15

Chala

054 / POP 2500

The tiny fishing village of Chala, about 170km from Nazca, presents intrepid travelers with an opportunity to break the journey to Arequipa and visit the archaeological site of Puerto Inca.

◉ Sights

Puerto Inca   ARCHAEOLOGICAL SITE

(24hr) FREE This archaeological site marks the spot from where fresh fish was once sent all the way to Cuzco by runners – no mean effort! The ruins include some low stone walls in addition to a seat from which Inca leaders are said to have sat and admired the scenery. While the ruins themselves are not the region's best, it's an atmospheric spot.

The well-marked turnoff is 10km north of the undeveloped fishing village of Chala, about 170km from Nazca, at Km 603 along the Panamericana Sur, from where a dirt road leads 3km west to the ruins.

▣ Sleeping

Hotel Puerto Inka   RESORT $$

(054-63-5362, 054-25-2588; www.puertoinka. com.pe; Panamericana Sur Km 603; camping per person S30, s/d/tr incl breakfast S139/209/319; P ☀) A large resort set on a pretty private bay. It has a campground with a shower complex by the sea. It also offers kayaks and boat tours. The showers are brackish, but the bungalow rooms are pleasant enough. The restaurant is open for nonguests for lunch. Cash only.

It's located right next to the Puerto Inca archaeological site.

❶ Getting There & Away

Colectivos to Chala (S15, 2½ hours) leave when full from the *óvalo* (main roundabout) in Nazca from the early morning until mid-afternoon. Onward buses to Arequipa (S35, eight hours) stop in Chala at small ticket offices along the Panamericana Sur, with most buses departing in the evening.

Mollendo

054 / POP 22.400

Located off the main Panamericana highway, the pleasant beach town of Mollendo doesn't get too many travelers and is mostly visited by a few intrepid surfers, plus a seasonal influx of beach-starved *arequipeños* (inhabitants of Arequipa). It is by far the prettiest beach town of the southern south coast, with a bunch of cool two-story wood buildings dating back 100 years. The village itself slopes down to an arcing beach.

Mollendo's history testifies to occupations by the Incas and the Chileans. More notoriously, it was the birthplace of Abimael

Guzmán, aka Presidente Gonzalo, the philosophy professor turned political agitator who became leader of the Sendero Luminoso (Shining Path) in 1980. Among non-sunbathers, Mollendo is revered for its bird reserve at the nearby Lagunas de Mejía. The town can be a little lacking in atmosphere (and people for that matter) outside of the summer season (January to April).

◉ Sights

Down below the town, the beachfront *malecón* is a pleasant place for a stroll and has a couple of viewpoints set atop rocky outcrops. There are a bunch of bars and *cevicherías* (restaurants serving ceviche) across the road from the beach but many close when things are quiet.

El Castillo de Forga   HISTORIC BUILDING
El Castillo de Forga was built in 1908 on a crag between two of the beaches just south of the city center by a rich *arequipeño* (inhabitant of Arequipa) in love with European architecture. Once an eye-catching stately home, it is currently unoccupied and not open to visitors. There have been proposals to turn it into a casino but nothing has come to fruition.

⊨ Sleeping

El Hostalito   HOTEL $
(☎054-53-4365; www.hotelesdelperu.com.pe; Blondell 169; s/d/tr incl breakfast S60/70/100; ☎) A good budget bet on the top of the hill to the south of the main plaza, this hotel offers small peeks at the ocean from i's top-floor rooms. The rooms are small, but cozy, with flower prints and fans. There's a small terrace out back.

Hotel Bahia del Puerto   HOTEL $$
(☎054-53-2990; hotelbahiadelpuerto@hotmail. com; Ugarte 301; s/d incl breakfast S70/100; ❄@☎☀) Mollendo's best hotel is a bargain. Some rooms have ocean views, big flat-screen TVs and handmade quilts.

✕ Eating

Charlie's Catarindo   PERUVIAN $$
(☎054-53-4297; Malecón Catarindo; mains S29-50; ⊙8am-6pm) Tucked away in a secluded cove framed by rocky mountains just north of town, Charlie's is the local go-to place for a long lunch followed by a couple of drinks. Take a seat out under the umbrellas next to the water or inside the bright dining room

SANTUARIO LAGUNAS DE MEJÍA

About 6km southeast of Mejía along an unbroken line of beaches, the 690-hectare **Santuario Nacional Lagunas de Mejía** (Carr Mollendo, Km 32; Admission S5; ⊙dawn-dusk) protects coastal lagoons that are the largest permanent lakes in 1500km of desert coastline. They attract more than 200 species of coastal and migratory birds, best seen in the very early morning.

The visitor center, which was under refurbishment when we visited and temporarily located in a shipping container, has maps of hiking trails leading through the dunes to *miradors* (lookouts). From Mollendo, *colectivos* (shared transportation) pass by the visitor center (S3, 30 minutes) frequently during the daytime. Ask the staff to help you flag down onward transportation, which peters out by the late afternoon.

with full windows and tuck into a variety of seafood classics.

In high season there is a DJ and volleyball games and it can get a bit overrun. If you want to stay there are a couple of sea-view bungalows for rent from S200. A taxi from town costs around S10.

Marco Antonio   PERUVIAN $$
(Comercio 258; mains S22-52; ⊙8am-8pm Mon-Sat, to 7pm Sun; ☎) This little cafe and eatery scores big on ambience, with classic old-time styling and a few modern touches. The seafood dishes are direct, unpretentious and delicious.

❶ Getting There & Away

The Terminal Terrestre (bus station) is about 2km northwest of the center and is fronted by a rusting old tank; there's a S1 departure tax. **Santa Ursula** (☎054-53-2586; Terminal Terrestre) has frequent bus departures throughout the day for Arequipa (S10, 2½ hours) although it's known to be somewhat unreliable. A better option are the newer buses of **Terra Nova** (☎958-441-855; Terminal Terrestre).

Transportes Moquegua, Cromotex and Oltursa have several direct daily services to Lima via the Costanera highway which avoids the need to take the Panamericana through Arequipa.

Unfortunately, there are only a few direct buses heading south to Ilo, Moquegua and Tacna, with most leaving early in the morning and in high season they may travel full from Lima.

An alternate option is to take a *colectivo* or minivans marked 'El Valle' from the top end of Mariscal Castilla, by a gas station, which pass through Mejía and the Río Tambo Valley to reach Cocachacra (S4, 1½ hours). There you can immediately jump into a *colectivo* heading for El Fiscal (S3, 15 minutes), a flyblown gas station where crowded buses heading to Moquegua, Tacna, Arequipa and Lima regularly stop.

Combis (S2, 20 minutes) and *colectivos* (S3, 15 minutes) to the beach resort of Mejía and the Santuario Nacional Lagunas de Mejía leave from the corner of Commercio and Islay.

Getting Around

Colectivos wait outside the terminal to whisk arriving passengers down to the town's plazas and the beach (S1, 10 minutes) or you can walk.

Moquegua

053 / POP 57,200 / ELEV 1420M

Clinging to the northern limits of the world's driest desert, Moquegua defies near zero annual rainfall by supporting a thriving wine industry and a valley full of green fields replete with grazing cows that look like they might have been peeled off the surface of northern France (it's the rivers, you know). The town itself has a picturesque main square surrounded by well-preserved colonial buildings and makes a very pleasant stopover on the way to or from the southern border.

Sights

The town's small and shady Plaza de Armas boasts a 19th-century wrought-iron fountain, thought by some to have been designed in a workshop run by Gustave Eiffel (of eponymous tower fame), and flower gardens that make it a welcome oasis away from the encroaching desert.

The foreign-funded Museo Contisuyo (053-46-1844; www.museocontisuyo.com; Tacna 294; S1.50; ⊙8am-1pm & 2:30-5:30pm Wed-Mon, 8am-noon & 4-8 pm Tue) is an excellent little repository of local archaeological artifacts, including photographs of recent excavations, along with exhibitions of new works by local artists. The labels are in Spanish and English.

The town's oldest church, Iglesia Matriz (Plaza de Armas), mostly collapsed during a massive earthquake in 1868. You can still

see the ruins today. Opposite you'll find an 18th-century Spanish colonial jail, with intimidating iron-grilled windows. It now houses the government culture department; pop in the day before to arrange an appointment if you want to visit. At one corner of the Plaza de Armas, visitors can enter the Casa Posada de Teresa Podesta (cnr Ancash & Ayacucho; S2; ⊙10am-3pm Mon-Fri), a stately colonial mansion with its innards still intact.

Walk around the town center to see some typical sugarcane thatching, especially along Calle Moquegua, and have a peek inside Catedral Santa Catalina (Ayacucho s/n), which houses the body of 18th-century St Fortunata, whose hair and nails are said to be still growing.

A park on a cliff high above the town is dominated by the Cristo Blanco, a white statue of Christ raised in 2002. There are swinging seats, a small suspension bridge, and expansive views over the Moquegua oasis and the surrounding desert.

Activities

Bodega Biondi   WINE
(053-46-1889; Panamericana Sur Km 1150; ⊙8am-3pm Mon-Fri) One of Moquegua's best wineries is located just south of the town. It's possible to tour the vineyard and sample the locally famous pisco on-site.

Sleeping & Eating

Hostal Plaza   HOTEL $
(053-46-1612; Ayacucho 675; s/d S65/70; 🕸) This is a neat spot by the plaza where some of the upstairs rooms have pretty views of the cathedral. The good-value digs are airy and sport large-screen cable TVs.

Hotel Los Balcones   HOTEL $$
(053-46-3168; www.losbalconeshostal.com; Junin 555; s/d/tr S65/90/120; 🕸) Many hotels in Moquegua offer excellent value but hotel Los Balcones takes it to the next level with bright modern rooms with faux wood floors, top-quality mattresses, big wardobes and large sparkling bathrooms. Throw in friendly service, a good location near the park and fast wi-fi and it's hard to find fault.

Nautica   PERUVIAN $$
(053-46-3854; Arequipa 485; mains S20-57; ⊙11am-11pm) Set in a refurbished old house, this modern bistro is about as chic as it gets in Moquegua. It combines one of the most diverse menus in town with a stylish

yet laid-back ambience. The speciality is seafood but there are also plenty of grill options. It's a great place to hang out after a meal for cocktails.

ℹ️ Information

MONEY

Banco de la Nación Fee-free ATMs a block from the plaza.

BCP (Moquegua 861) Has a 24-hour Visa/MasterCard ATM.

TOURIST INFORMATION

Municipal Tourist Office (Oficina de Turismo; Ayacucho; ⊙7:30am-4:30pm Mon-Fri) Local government-run tourist office. It's located down a passageway next to the cathedral.

ℹ️ Getting There & Away

All buses leave from Moquegua's sparkling new **Terminal Terrestre** (Av Ejercito cuadra 2) which is among the best in Peru; it even boasts a small archaeological museum if you have some extra time between buses. There is a S2 departure tax payable at the small booth in front of the ticket offices.

Quality Oltursa, Civa and Cruz del Sur and cheaper **Flores** (☑053-46-2647; www.floreshnos.net; Terminal Terrestre) buses run north serving Lima via Nazca and Ica. Flores and **Transportes Moquegua** (Terminal Terrestre) run south to Tacna with the latter having better buses and service. Flores occasionally also head west to Ilo but if the bus doesn't fill up it doesn't run. Numerous companies serve Arequipa.

Several smaller companies, including **San Martín** (☑953-521-550; Terminal Terrestre), take the freshly paved route to Puno (S25, nine hours) via Desaguadero on the Bolivian border (S25, six hours), usually departing in the evening.

Faster, though less safe and more expensive, *colectivos* leave when full for Ilo (S10 to S12, one hour) and Arequipa (S30, 3½ hours) from a couple of small terminals downhill southwest of the Plaza de Armas.

MOQUEGUA BUSES

DESTINATION	COST (S)	DURATION (HR)
Arequipa	20-30	3½-4
Cuzco	50	15
Ilo	20	1½
Lima	100–150	16-20
Puno	25	9
Tacna	10	2½

Ilo

☑053 / POP 66,900

The busy departmental port of Ilo, 95km southwest of Moquegua, is not a major tourism destination but does offer a pleasant boardwalk with a couple of outcrops topped with gazebos overlooking the colorful fishing fleet, and trees full of noisy ducks.

The main beach is long and curving but is close to a river mouth and the waters are murky and unappealing for swimming.

There are better beaches to the south of town including **Puerto Ingles**, a secluded cove with gentle waters that locals swear are far colder than those to the north and south, and wide gently curving **Pozo de Lizas** which is the best stretch of sand in the area.

The unattractive port area is used mainly to ship copper from the mine at Toquepala further south, and wine and avocados from Moquegua.

🛏️ Sleeping & Eating

Hotel Kristal Azul · HOTEL $$

(☑053-48-4050; informacion@kristalazul.com.pe; Av 28 de Julio 664; s/d incl breakfast S60/90; 🛜) This 2nd-floor place two blocks from the bus station offers clean, if unremarkable, rooms and helpful management. It's a solid base.

Los Corales · SEAFOOD $$

(Malecón Miramar 504; mains S20-48; ⊙lunch & dinner; 🛜) The prime shorefront position pretty much guarantees fresh seafood including local favorite, *pulpo al olvia* (octopus in olive oil), a cold appetizer. It's a step up from the places in front of the fish market as shown by the quality olives offered alongside the salty corn nibbles.

ℹ️ Getting There & Away

Regional buses leave from private terminals in the town center along Matará, a couple of blocks from the plaza and the beach. Some long-distance buses to Lima and the north depart from the inconveniently located main bus terminal on the hillside to the east of the center, which is fronted by an awesome alien sculpture made from old tyres.

Flores (☑053-48-2512; www.floreshnos.net; cnr Ilo & Matará) covers Tacna (S10, 3½ hours), Moquegua (S8, 1½ hours) and Arequipa (S20, 5½ hours) where you can connect for onward journeys.

Faster, slightly pricier *colectivos* to Tacna and sometimes Moquegua leave when full from the side streets near the small bus stations in the center.

Tacna

 052 / POP 262,700 / ELEV 460M

Patriotism puts up a steely rearguard action in Tacna, Peru's most southerly settlement, a city that belonged to Chile as recently as 1929 (a young Salvador Allende lived here for eight of his childhood years), but is now proudly and unequivocally part of Peru. Just in case you forget, there's an earnest flag-raising ceremony every Sunday morning in the main plaza, plus a raft of heroic statues, leafy avenues and hyperbolic museum exhibits all dedicated to Peru's glorious past.

For outsiders, Tacna's primary role is as a staging post on the way to or from its former nemesis, Chile. Cordial modern relations between the two countries make the border crossing a comparative breeze. If you're delayed in town, some small museums and some Europhile bars and restaurants will smooth the wait.

◎ Sights

Museo Ferroviario MUSEUM

(052-24-5572; Albarracin 402; Admission S5; 8am-6pm) This museum located inside the train station gives the impression of stepping back in time. You can wander amid beautiful, though poorly maintained, 20th-century steam engines and rolling stock. It was closed to visitors when we visited but you might be able to get inside by ringing the bell on the southern gates of the station.

About an 800m walk south of the train station, a British locomotive built in 1859 and used as a troop train in the War of the Pacific is the centerpiece of **El Parque de la Locomotora**, an otherwise empty roadside park.

Paseo Cívico SQUARE

Unlike almost every other town in Peru, Tacna's main plaza is not called the Plaza de Armas because the city was never formally founded by the Spanish. It is studded with palm trees and large pergolas topped by mushroom-like flower domes. The plaza, famously pictured on the front of Peru's S100 note, features a huge arch – a monument to the heroes of the War of the Pacific.

The arch is flanked by larger-than-life bronze statues of Admiral Grau and Colonel Bolognesi, chests puffed out like prizefighting roosters.

Museo Histórico Regional MUSEUM

(Casa de la Cultura, Apurímac 202; Admission S1.50; 7:45am-noon & 1:30-4:30pm Mon-Fri) Patriotic like everything in Tacna, this museum above the town library broadcasts a grand, somewhat triumphant, air. Huge canvases depicting key moments of the region's military history adorn the walls and busts of erstwhile heroes such as Zela, Bolognesi and Ugarte sit among old swords, yellowed letters and details about the War of the Pacific against former foe Chile.

🛏 Sleeping

There's no shortage of hotels catering to Tacna's cross-border traffic. That said, almost all are overpriced and fill up very fast, especially with Chileans who cross the border for weekend shopping and dentistry trips.

Dorado Hotel HOTEL $$

(052-41-5741; www.doradohoteltacna.com; Av Arias Aragüez 145; s/d/tr incl breakfast from S144/187/230; @🛜❄) Posing as Tacna's grandest hotel, the Dorado is the sort of place where the curtains are heavy, the lobby sports shiny balustrades, and a bellhop will carry your bags to your room. While it can't emulate the classy exclusivity of a big-city hotel, it makes a good job of trying.

Hotel Miculla HOTEL $$

(052-24-2477; www.micullahotel.com; Zela 344; r incl breakfast S175; 🛜) A solid midrange choice in the heart of town, Miculla has elegant and comfortable rooms with work desks and good bathrooms although there is no air-conditioning. It puts on a good buffet breakfast spread.

Casa Andina Select Tacna BUSINESS HOTEL $$$

(052-58-0340; www.casa-andina.com; Billinghurst 170; r incl breakfast S345; ❄🛜❄) Part of a popular chain, this large, new hotel tower is not huge on character but offers the most comfort and best facilities in town. It has generic but well finished business-like rooms, and a rooftop pool and gym area with panoramic views of the city. Also has a good restaurant.

One of the few hotels in town with air-conditioning.

🍴 Eating

Popular local dishes include *patasca a la tacneña* (a thick, spicy vegetable-and-meat

Tacna

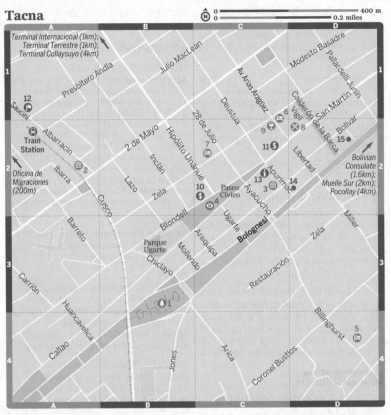

Tacna

◎ Sights

1 El Parque de la Locomotora	B3
2 Museo Ferroviario	A2
3 Museo Histórico Regional	C2
4 Paseo Cívico	C2

⌂ Sleeping

5 Casa Andina Select Tacna	D4
6 Dorado Hotel	C1
7 Hotel Miculla	C2

⊗ Eating

8 Uros Restaurante	D2

☕ Drinking & Nightlife

9 Mushna	C2

ⓘ Information

10 Banco de la Nacion	C2
11 BCP	C2
12 Chilean Consulate	A1
13 iPerú	C2

ⓘ Transport

14 LATAM	D2
15 Peruvian Airlines	D2

soup) and *picante a la tacneña* (hot peppered tripe – better than it sounds). A modern fad here are *hamburguesas de cordero cara negra* – lamb burgers made from the meat of a local breed of sheep from nearby Candarave.

★ **Muelle Sur**   SEAFOOD **$$**
(☎052-24-5106; www.muellesur.com; Los Alamos 1995; mains S29-70) Widely regarded as Tacna's best restaurant, this bustling open-air seafood affair fulfills the hype. It gets crowded with Chilean visitors on weekends who come for their ceviche fix. While the

ceviche and *tiraditos* (Japanese version of ceviche) are the stars here there's also whole fish, rice dishes and reasonably priced whole lobster in addition to beef from the grill. Reservations are advisable.

Uros Restaurante   FUSION **$$**
(☑ 052-41-2851; www.restauranteuros.com; Av San Martín 608; mains S27-48) Tacna's stab at *novoandina* (Peruvian nouvelle cuisine) avoids too many pretensions, if you can get past the (admittedly photogenic) photos of the food on the menu. Try *alpaca a la piedra* – a slab of Andean game meat cooked on a hot volcanic stone.

Drinking & Nightlife

The small pedestrian streets of Libertad and Vigil are ground zero for Tacna's limited nightlife. Be sure to try Tacna's very own drink, the Tacna sour, which is just like a Pisco sour except made with apricot wine.

Mushna   BAR
(Av Arias Araguëz 156; ⊘ 7pm-1am) A postmodern bar that looks like it has drifted across from Arica, Chile, Mushna attracts a fun young crowd and is a good place for a night out in the center. While it's billed as a restobar, it only serves snacks but the cocktail list is

---

WORTH A TRIP

COMPLEJO ARQUEOLÓGICO MICULLA

This 43-hectare archaeological site of **Complejo Arqueológico Miculla** (Admission S1; ⊘ 7am-5pm) is an outdoor gallery of pre-Hispanic art and is considered to be one of the most important collections of rock art in the country. It contains hundreds of petroglyphs carved into large boulders which were left by the Tiahuanaco culture, with the earliest examples being carved around 500 AD. A 3km circuit runs among the boulders passing engravings of anthropomorphic figures hunting, dancing, playing musical instruments and engaged in battle in addition to many representations of animals.

The site is located 23km northeast from Tacna on the road to Palca. Frequent local buses from Tacna will drop you 2km from the trailhead, or a round-trip taxi costs around S70 including waiting time.

---

extensive. The playlist is almost exclusively *reggaetón*.

Information

EMBASSIES & CONSULATES

Bolivian Consulate (☑ 052-25-5121; Bolognesi 1751) Some nationalities may need to solicit a visa up to one month in advance and pay a US$30 to US$160 fee. For some passport holders it's possible to obtain a visa at the border but it will attract an additional fee. US passport holders pay a $160 fee regardless of whether the visa is issued in advance or at the border. Check ahead on the latest regulations.

Chilean Consulate (☑ 052-42-3063; Presbitero Andía s/n) Most travelers don't need a Chilean visa and head straight for the border instead.

IMMIGRATION

Oficina de Migraciones (Immigration Office; ☑ 052-24-3231; Circunvalación s/n, Urb Él Triángulo; ⊘ 8am-4pm Mon-Fri)

MONEY

Chilean pesos, Peruvian nuevos soles and US dollars can all be easily exchanged in Tacna.
Banco de la Nación (San Martín 321) Fee-free ATMs in front of the Paseo Cívico.
BCP (San Martín 574) Has a Visa/MasterCard ATM and gives cash advances on Visa cards.

TOURIST INFORMATION

iPerú (☑ 052-42-5514; San Martín 491; ⊘ 8:30am-6pm Mon-Sat, to 1pm Sun) National tourist office, providing free information and brochures. There are additional branches at the border, airport and bus station.

Getting There & Away

AIR

Tacna's **airport** (TCQ) is 5km southwest of town. **LATAM** (☑ 052-42-8346; www.latam.com; Apurímac 101; ⊘ 8:30am-7pm Mon-Fri, 9am-2pm Sat) and **Peruvian Airlines** (www.peruvian. pe; Av Bolognesi 670) both offer daily passenger services to Lima. Seasonal services to Arequipa and Cuzco are also sometimes offered.

BUS

Most long-distance departures leave from the **Terminal Terrestre** (Hipólito Unánue), at the northeast edge of town, with the exception of some buses to Juliaca, Desaguadero and Puno, which leave from **Terminal Collaysuyo** (Av Emancipación), located in the district of Alta Alianza to the north of town.

Frequent buses (S12) to Arica, Chile, leave between 5am and 7pm from the **international terminal** across the street from the Terminal

ℹ BORDER CROSSING: CHILE VIA TACNA

Border-crossing formalities are relatively straightforward. There are three main transportation options: train, public bus or *colectivo* (shared taxi), with the last proving to be the most efficient. The five-passenger taxis are run by professional companies with desks inside Tacna's international bus terminal. They charge approximately S25 to take you the 65km to Arica in Chile with stops at both border posts. Most of the paperwork is done before you get in the car. On a good day the trip should take little more than an hour. The public bus is cheaper (S12), but slower, as you have to wait for all the passengers to disembark and clear customs.

Note that the border posts are now integrated which means that visitors traveling from Peru into Chile only need to stop at the Chilean building where visiting Peruvian officials stamp travelers out. Coming from Chile to Peru it works in reverse with only a visit to the Peruvian complex required. Both border posts are open 24 hours.

Note that Chile is generally two hours ahead of Peru, or one hour during the period from May until August. From Arica, you can continue south into Chile by air or bus, or northeast into Bolivia by air or bus. For more information, consult Lonely Planet's *South America on a Shoestring, Chile & Easter Island* and/or *Bolivia*.

Terrestre where a S2 terminal tax must also be paid.

San Martín (Terminal Collaysuyo s/n) runs overnight *económico* and luxury bus services to Puno via Desaguadero on the Bolivian border, finally ending up in Cuzco. These mostly leave in the evening from Terminal Collaysuyo. When choosing this route, opt for the nicest bus, or you could be in for a cold, bumpy ride with few bathroom breaks – trust us! Alternatively, you can also return to Arequipa and transfer there.
Julsa (☎ 052-24-7132; Terminal Collaysuyo) also services Cuzco and other destinations in the Sierra Sur.

Long-distance buses are frequently stopped and searched by immigration and/or customs officials not far north of Tacna. Have your passport handy.

A S2 terminal-use tax is levied at the Terminal Terrestre. The usual suspects head to all destinations north including Cruz del Sur, Civa Oltursa and more economical **Flores** (☎ 052-74-1150; www.floreshnos.net; Terminal Terrestre s/n; 🐾).

TACNA BUSES

DESTINATION	COST (S)	DURATION (HR)
Arequipa	20-45	7
Cuzco	50-75	17
Ilo	10-18	3½
Lima	80-144	18-22
Moquegua	10-18	3
Puno	25-45	10

COLECTIVOS

Numerous *colectivos* (S20 to S25, one to two hours) to Arica, Chile, leave from the international terminal across the street from the *terminal terrestre* in order to cross the Chilean border. The vehicles run 24 hours but you may have to wait a while for them to fill off-peak. There's a S2 departure tax from the international terminal.

Fast, though notoriously unsafe, *colectivos* to Moquegua (S15, 2½ hours), and sometimes Ilo, leave when full from Mercado Grau, a short walk uphill from the Terminal Terrestre. Be sure to keep your wits about you in the dangerous market area.

TRAIN

Trains between Tacna's **train station** (☎ 052-61-1824; Av 2 de Mayo) and Arica, Chile (S18/C$3800, 1½ hours) are the most charming but also the slowest way to cross the border. Your passport is stamped at the station before boarding the train in Tacna. There is no stop at the actual border and you receive your entry stamp when you arrive in Chile near Arica's Plaza de Armas. Though this historic railway is a must for train buffs, service can be a little erratic.

At the time of writing two trains a day were departing Tacna at 6am and 4:30pm. Return trains leave Arica at 10am and 8:15pm. Always double check at the station for the latest schedules. It's advised to purchase tickets at least a day in advance.

ℹ Getting Around

A taxi between the airport and the city center costs about S10 or S20 if you take an official airport vehicle. A taxi from the center to the bus terminals costs about S6. There are also direct shared taxis from the airport to Arica in Chile.

AT A GLANCE

POPULATION
Arequipa: 969,300

**HIGHEST PAVED
ROAD**
Paso de Patopampa:
4910m

**BEST NOVOANDINA
CUISINE**
Chicha (p161)

**BEST LUXURY
LODGE**
Colca Lodge (p171)

**BEST CULTURAL
MUSEUM**
Museo Yanque (p170)

**WHEN TO GO
Mar–Apr**
Arequipa puts on
a Semana Santa
parade to rival those
in Spain.

Apr–Dec
Outside rainy sea-
son, hiking in the
Colca and Cotahuasi
canyons is sublime.

Jun–Sep
Your best chance
of seeing Andean
condors gliding
above the Cañón del
Colca.

La Catedral (p150), Arequipa
FLAVIO HUAMANI/SHUTTERSTOCK ©

Arequipa & Canyon Country

Arequipa province is Peru's big combo ticket, with authentic historical immersion and white-knuckle Andean adventure inhabiting the same breathing space. Imagine the cultural riches of one of South America's finest historic cities just a few hours' drive from the world's two deepest canyons and you'll get a hint of the dramatic contrasts here. Ample urban distractions can be found in Arequipa, the arty, audacious, unflappably resilient metropolis that lies in the shadow of El Misti volcano. Beckoning to the northwest are the Colca and Cotahuasi canyons, whose impressive depth is a mere statistic compared to the Andean condors, epic treks and long-standing Spanish, Inca and pre-Inca traditions that lurk in their midst.

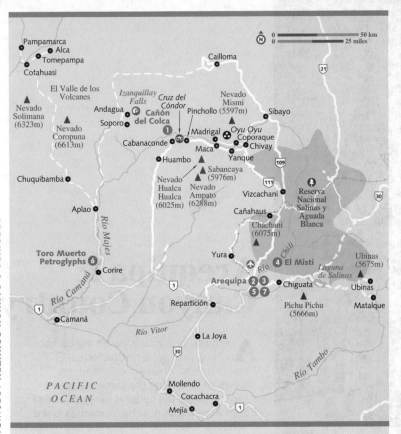

Arequipa & Canyon Country Highlights

1 **Cañón del Colca** (p166)
Watching massive Andean condors glide by as they catch thermal uplifts above the almost-sheer canyon walls.

2 **Monasterio de Santa Catalina** (p147) Getting a glimpse of austere, monastic life behind the high stone walls of the mini citadel in Arequipa.

3 **Picanterías** (p159)
Dining the traditional, communal *arequipeño* way.

4 **El Misti** (p166)
Making a summit attempt on the almost perfectly symmetrical volcano cone that backdrops Arequipa.

5 **Museo Santuarios Andinos** (p150) Studying the frozen remains of Juanita the 'Ice Maiden' mummy.

6 **Toro Muerto Petroglyphs** (p173)
Pondering the meaning of 5000 mysterious desert carvings.

7 **New Cuisine** (p161)
Tasting fusion flavors combining Peru's Inca, Spanish and Asian influences in Arequipa, a driving force in the country's culinary renaissance.

AREQUIPA

♪ 054 / POP 969,300 / ELEV 2350M

Other Peruvians joke that you need a different passport to enter Peru's second-largest city. One-tenth the size of Lima, Arequipa is its pugnacious equal in terms of cuisine, historical significance and confident self-awareness.

Guarded by three dramatic volcanoes, the city's resplendent setting makes an obvious launchpad for trekking, rafting and visiting the Cañón del Colca. The Unesco World Heritage–listed city center is dressed in baroque buildings carved from *sillar* (white volcanic rock) stone, giving Arequipa the nickname 'Ciudad Blanca' (White City). Its centerpiece, a majestic cathedral with the ethereal El Misti (p166) rising behind it, is worth a visit alone.

Pretty cityscapes aside, Arequipa has played a fundamental role in Peru's gastronomic renaissance and dining here – in communal *picantería* eateries or tastebud-provoking fusion restaurants – is a highlight.

The headstrong city has produced one of Latin America's most influential novelists, Mario Vargas Llosa. Juanita, the ice-preserved, sacrificed Inca mummy, is another Arequipan treasure.

History

Evidence of pre-Inca settlement by indigenous peoples from the Lake Titicaca area lead some scholars to think the Aymara people first named the city (*ari* means 'peak' and *quipa* means 'lying behind' in Aymara; hence, Arequipa is 'the place lying behind the peak' of El Misti). However, another oft-heard legend says that the fourth *inca* (king), Mayta Cápac, was traveling through the valley and became enchanted by it. He ordered his retinue to stop, saying, '*Ari, quipay*,' which translates as 'Yes, stay' in Quechua (or an earlier variant of the language). The city was reestablished by the Spaniards on August 15, 1540, a date that is remembered with a weeklong fair (p156).

Arequipa is built in an area highly prone to natural disasters; it was totally destroyed by earthquakes and volcanic eruptions in 1600 and has since been rocked by major earthquakes in 1687, 1868, 1958, 1960 and in 2001. For this reason, many of the city's buildings are built low for stability. Despite the disasters, many fetching historic structures survive.

◉ Sights

★Monasterio de
Santa Catalina   MONASTERY
(📞054-22-1213; www.santacatalina.org.pe; Santa Catalina 301; S40; ⊘9am-5pm, to 7:30pm Tue & Wed, last entry 1hr before closing) This convent shouldn't be missed, even if you've overdosed on colonial edifices. Occupying a whole block and guarded by imposing high walls, it is one of the most fascinating religious buildings in Peru. Nor is it just a religious building – the 20,000-sq-meter complex is almost a citadel within the city. It

was founded in 1580 by a rich widow, doña María de Guzmán. Enter from the southeast corner.

The best way to visit Santa Catalina is to hire one of the informative guides, available for S20 from inside the entrance. Guides speak Spanish, English, French, German, Italian, Portuguese or Japanese. The tours last about an hour, after which you're welcome to keep exploring by yourself until the gates close. The monastery is also open two evenings a week so that visitors can traipse through the shadowy grounds by candlelight as nuns would have done centuries ago.

Alternatively, you can wander around on your own without a guide, soaking up the meditative atmosphere and getting slightly lost (there's a finely printed miniature map on the back of your ticket if you're up for an orienteering challenge). A helpful way to begin is to focus a visit on the three main cloisters. After passing under the *silencio* (silence) arch you will enter the **Novice Cloister**, marked by a courtyard with a rubber tree at its center. Novice nuns entering here were required to zip their lips in a vow of solemn silence and resolve to a life of work and prayer. Nuns lived as novices for four years, during which time their wealthy families were expected to pay a dowry of 100 gold coins per year. At the end of the four years they could choose between taking their vows and entering into religious service, or leaving the convent – the latter would most likely have brought shame upon their family.

Graduated novices passed onto the **Orange Cloister**, named for the orange trees clustered at its center that represent renewal and eternal life. This cloister allows a peek into the **Profundis Room**, a mortuary where dead nuns were mourned. Paintings of the deceased line the walls. Artists were allotted 24 hours to complete these posthumous paintings, since painting the nuns while alive was out of the question.

Leading away from the Orange Cloister, **Córdova St** is flanked by cells that served as living quarters for the nuns. These dwellings would house one or more nuns, along with a handful of servants, and ranged from austere to lavish depending on the wealth of the inhabitants. Ambling down **Toledo St** leads you to the **cafe**, which serves fresh-baked pastries and espressos, and finally to the **communal washing area** where servants

Arequipa

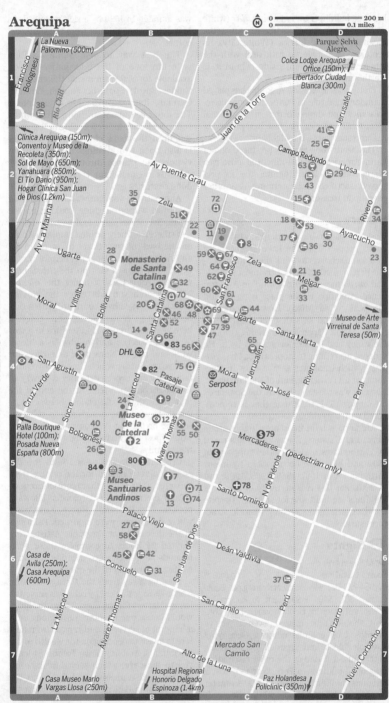

N 0 ——— 200 m
0 ——— 0.1 miles

La Nueva Palomino (500m)

Parque Selva Alegre

Colca Lodge Arequipa Office (150m); Libertador Ciudad Blanca (300m)

Clínica Arequipa (150m); Convento y Museo de la Recoleta (350m); Sol de Mayo (650m); Yanahuara (850m); El Tío Darío (950m); Hogar Clínica San Juan de Dios (1.2km)

Museo de Arte Virreinal de Santa Teresa (50m)

Palla Boutique Hotel (100m); Posada Nueva España (800m)

Casa de Avila (250m); Casa Arequipa (600m)

Casa Museo Mario Vargas Llosa (250m)

Hospital Regional Honorio Delgado Espinoza (1.4km)

Paz Holandesa Policlinic (350m)

Francisco Bolognesi
Río Chili
Juan de la Torre
Av Puente Grau
Jerusalén
Campo Redondo
Llosa
Rivero
Ayacucho
Zela
Av La Marina
Ugarte
Monasterio de Santa Catalina
Moral
Villalba
Bolívar
Santa Catalina
San Francisco
Melgar
Ugarte
Santa Marta
Jerusalén
Rivero
Peral
San Agustín
Cruz Verde
Sucre
La Merced
Pasaje Catedral
Moral
Serpost
San José
Bolognesi
Museo de la Catedral
Álvarez Thomas
Mercaderes
(pedestrian only)
N de Piérola
Museo Santuarios Andinos
Santo Domingo
Palacio Viejo
San Juan de Dios
Deán Valdivia
Consuelo
La Merced
Álvarez Thomas
San Camilo
Perú
Pizarro
Nuevo Corbacho
Mercado San Camilo
Alto de la Luna
DHL
Museo de la Catedral

Arequipa

washed in mountain runoff channeled into huge earthenware jars.

Heading down **Burgos St** toward the cathedral's sparkling *sillar* (white volcanic rock) tower, visitors may enter the musty darkness of the **communal kitchen** that was originally used as the church until the reformation of 1871. Just beyond, **Zocodober Sq** (the name comes from the Arabic word for 'barter') was where nuns gathered on Sundays to exchange their handicrafts, such as soaps and baked goods. Continuing on, to the left you can enter the **cell** of the legendary Sor Ana, a nun renowned for her eerily accurate predictions about the future and the miracles she is said to have performed until her death in 1686.

Finally, the **Great Cloister** is bordered by the **chapel** on one side and the **art gallery**, which used to serve as a communal dormitory, on the other. This building takes on the shape of a cross. **Murals** along the walls depict scenes from the lives of Jesus and the Virgin Mary.

Plaza de Armas
SQUARE

Arequipa's main plaza, unblemished by modern interference, is a museum of the city's *sillar* (volcanic rock) architecture – white, muscular and aesthetically unique. Impressive colonnaded balconies line three sides. The fourth is given over to Peru's widest cathedral, a humongous edifice with two soaring towers. Even this is dwarfed by the dual snowcapped sentinels of El Misti and Chanchani, both visible from various points in the central park.

Arequipeños (inhabitants of Arequipa) are a proud people fond of intellectual debate, especially about their fervent political beliefs, which historically found voice through regular demonstrations in the Plaza de Armas. In mid-2015, protests and traffic were (controversially) banned in and around the plaza to make it more tourist-friendly. Naturally crowds still gather in defiant dissent.

La Catedral
CATHEDRAL

(☑ 054-23-2635; ⊙ 7-10am & 5-7pm Mon-Sat, 11am-noon Sun) FREE This beautiful building on the Plaza de Armas stands out for its stark white *sillar* (volcanic rock) and massive size – it's the only cathedral in Peru that stretches the length of a plaza. It also has a history of rising from the ashes. The original structure, dating from 1656, was gutted by fire in 1844, rebuilt and then flattened by the 1868 earthquake. Most of what you see now has been rebuilt since then. A 'museum' tour is worthwhile.

The interior is simple and airy, with a luminous quality, and the high vaults are uncluttered. The cathedral also has a distinctly international flair; it is one of fewer than 100 basilicas in the world entitled to display the Vatican flag, which is to the right of the altar. Both the altar and the 12 columns (symbolizing the 12 Apostles) are made of Italian marble. The huge Byzantine-style brass lamp

hanging in front of the altar is from Spain and the pulpit was carved in France. In 1870, Belgium provided the impressive organ, said to be the largest in South America, though damage during shipping condemned the devout to wince at its distorted notes for more than a century.

An earthquake in 2001 toppled one enormous tower, and made the other slump precariously, yet by the end of the next year the cathedral looked as good as new.

★ Museo de la Catedral
BASILICA

(☑ 054-21-3149; www.museocatedralarequipa. org.pe; Santa Catalina, Plaza de Armas; admission & tour S10; ⊙ 10am-5pm Mon-Sat) A must for visitors who want to see more of Arequipa's cathedral, the included 45-minute bilingual tour of this 'museum' is actually a peek at the inner workings of the basilica, with an explanation of the impressive 1000-pipe church organ and the symbology and colors employed in religious paintings and ornaments. The rooftop views of Arequipa and its *sillar* (white volcanic rock) buildings are a bonus.

Enter from the Santa Catalina corner of the Plaza de Armas.

Iglesia de La Compañía
CHURCH

(www.jesuitasaqp.pe; Moral cnr Álvarez Thomas; ⊙ 9-11am & 3-6pm) FREE If Arequipa's cathedral seems *too* big, an interesting antidote is this diminutive Jesuit church on the southeast corner of the Plaza de Armas. Proving that small can be beautiful, its facade is an intricately carved masterpiece of the *churrigueresque* style hatched in Spain in the 1660s (think baroque and then some). The equally detailed altar, completely covered in gold leaf, takes the style further and will be eerily familiar to anyone who has visited Seville cathedral in Spain.

To the left of the altar is the **San Ignacio Chapel** (admission S5; ⊙ 9am-1pm & 3-6pm Mon-Sat, 9am-1pm Sun), with a polychrome cupola smothered in unusual jungle-like murals.

Next door, and accessed via Calle Santo Domingo, the beautiful, semi-outdoor shopping center Claustros de la Compañía (p162) continues the ornate theme.

★ Museo Santuarios Andinos
MUSEUM

(☑ 054-28-6613; www.ucsm.edu.pe/museo-santu arios-andinos; La Merced 110; adult S20, child 5-17 S10; ⊙ 9am-6pm Mon-Sat, to 3pm Sun) There's an escalating drama to this theatrically presented museum, dedicated to the preserved

JUANITA – THE ICE MAIDEN

Local climber Miguel Zárate was guiding an expedition on Nevado Ampato (6288m) in 1992 when he found curious wooden remnants, suggestive of a burial site, exposed near the icy summit. In September 1995 he convinced American mountaineer and archaeologist Johan Reinhard to climb the peak, which, following recent eruptions of nearby volcano Sabancaya, had been coated by ash, melting the snow below and exposing the site more fully. Upon arrival, they immediately found a statue and other offerings, but the burial site had collapsed and there was no sign of a body. Ingeniously, the team rolled rocks down the mountainside and, by following them, Zárate was able to spot the bundled mummy of an Inca girl, which had tumbled down the same path when the icy tomb had crumbled.

The girl's body had been wrapped and almost perfectly preserved by the icy temperatures for about 500 years. It was immediately apparent from the remote location of her tomb and from the care and ceremony surrounding her death (as well as the crushing blow to her right eyebrow) that this 12- to 14-year-old girl had been sacrificed to the gods at the summit. For the Incas, mountains were gods who could kill by volcanic eruption, avalanche or climatic catastrophes. These violent deities could only be appeased by sacrifices from their subjects, and the ultimate sacrifice was that of a child.

It took the men days to carry the frozen bundle down to the village of Cabanaconde. From here she was transported on a regal bed of frozen foodstuffs in Zárate's own domestic freezer to the Universidad Católica (Catholic University) in Arequipa to undergo a battery of scientific examinations. Quickly dubbed 'Juanita, the ice maiden,' the mummy was given her own museum in 1998, the Museo Santuarios Andinos. In total, almost two dozen similar Inca sacrifices have been discovered atop various Andean mountains since the 1950s.

body of a frozen 'mummy,' and its compulsory guided tour (free, but a tip is expected at the end). Spoiler: the climax is the vaguely macabre sight of poor Juanita, the 12-year-old Inca girl sacrificed to the gods in the 1450s and now eerily preserved in a glass refrigerator. Tours take about an hour and are conducted in Spanish, English and French.

Before presenting Juanita herself, well-versed student guides from the university lead you through a series of atmospheric, dimly lit rooms filled with artifacts from the expedition that found the 'mummy.' There is a beautifully shot 20-minute film about how Juanita, the so-called 'Ice Maiden,' was unearthed atop Nevado Ampato in 1995. From January to April, Juanita is switched for a different 'mummy' and placed in deep freeze in total darkness for conservation purposes.

Convento y Museo
de la Recoleta   MONASTERY
(☏ 054-27-0966; La Recoleta 117; S10; ☺9am-5pm daily, to 8pm Wed & Fri by appointment) Bibliophiles will delight in this musty monastery's huge library, which contains more than 20,000 dusty books and maps; the oldest volume dates to 1494. Scholarship was an integral part of the Franciscans' order; the library is open for supervised visits, just ask at the entrance.

Also on the premises is a well-known museum of Amazonian artifacts (including preserved jungle animals) collected by the missionaries, and an extensive collection of pre-conquest artifacts and religious art of the *escuela cuzqueña* (Cuzco school).

The monastery was constructed on the west side of the Río Chili in 1648 by Franciscan friars, though now it has been completely rebuilt. Guides speaking Spanish, English, French and Italian are available; a tip is expected.

From the Plaza de Armas, it's an easy 10-minute walk across the river over pleasant Puente Bolognesi on the way to Yanahuara.

Museo de Arte Virreinal
de Santa Teresa   MUSEUM
(☏ 054-28-1188; Melgar 303; admission S20; ☺9am-5pm Mon-Sat) This gorgeous 17th-century Carmelite convent is open to the public as a living museum. The colonial-era buildings are justifiably famed for their decorative painted walls and restored rooms filled with priceless votive objets d'art, murals, precious metalwork, paintings and other historical artifacts. It is all explained by

student tour guides who speak Spanish, English, French, German and Portuguese; tips are appreciated. A charming shop at the front of the complex sells baked goods and rose-scented soaps made by the nuns.

Callejón del Solar   NEIGHBORHOOD

(enter from Bolognesi or San Agustín) **FREE** This magical neighborhood lane is Arequipa's most picturesque with radiant white *sillar* (volcanic rock) houses – people really live here – and pavers, trellis-covered park benches and pots spilling over with flowers. It could easily pass as the tidy set for 'Arequipa: The Stage Production' but has somehow managed to stay off the tourist radar. At night teenagers and lovers are drawn to the privacy of this city oasis; some gates are locked.

Museo de Arte Contemporáneo de Arequipa   GALLERY

(☑054-22-1068; www.facebook.com/museodeart-econtemporaneoarequipa; Sucre 104; admission S3; ⊙10am-3pm Mon-Sat) Set in a wonderfully restored *casona* (large house) and garden dating back to the founding of Arequipa itself in 1540, this museum's small, changing collection of contemporary art by *arequipeño* and international artists is worth a stroll to its central location near the Plaza de Armas.

If your Spanish is up to it, check the website for details of drawing, painting and kids workshops.

★Yanahuara   NEIGHBORHOOD

(cnr Cuesta del Angel & Av Lima) This tranquil neighborhood makes for a pleasant, walkable excursion, with a *mirador* (lookout) as its centerpiece providing excellent views of Arequipa and El Misti through arches inscribed with poetry. To get here, go west on Puente Grau over the namesake bridge, and take the first right along Francisco Bolognesi hugging the park. Take the first left on Cuesta del Ángel and continue four blocks to Plaza Yanahuara with its church and *mirador*.

Casa Ricketts   HISTORIC BUILDING

(Casa Tristán del Pozo; ☑054-21-5060; San Francisco 108; ⊙9am-6pm Mon-Fri, to 1pm Sat) **FREE** The ornate Casa Ricketts has served as a seminary, archbishop's palace, school and home to well-to-do families since it was built in 1738. Today it is the most splendiferous working bank in the city – possibly in all of Peru. Even if you're not here for a transaction, it's worth nosing around its small gallery of Arequipan art, and its dual interior courtyards with their puma-headed fountains.

Casa Museo Mario Vargas Llosa   MUSEUM

(Parra 101; admission & tour S10; ⊙10am-5pm Mon-Sat) The house where Peruvian writer, activist and Nobel Prize in Literature recipient Mario Vargas Llosa was born has been converted into a creative museum. Holograms, rooms-turned-stages of scenes from his novels, original manuscripts and interactive displays illuminate the author's involvement in Latin America's modern history – making the museum not just for his fans. Obligatory tours are in Spanish but self-explanatory enough to be worthwhile.

Museo Histórico Municipal   MUSEUM

(☑054-22-1017; Plazuela San Francisco 407; admission S10; ⊙8am-6pm Mon-Fri) The historical trajectory of both Arequipa and Peru is showcased in this educational, if unexciting, museum, split into different rooms dedicated to different epochs and their heroes. There's pre-Hispanic, the independence era, the republic era and the War of the Pacific.

La Mansión del Fundador   HISTORIC BUILDING

(☑054-44-2460; www.lamansiondelfundador.com; Huasache s/n; admission S15; ⊙9am-5pm) This 17th-century mansion once owned by Arequipa's founder, Garcí Manuel de Carbajal, has been restored with original furnishings and paintings, and even has its own chapel. The mansion is in the village of Huasacache, 9km from Arequipa's city center, most easily reached by taxi (round-trip S20).

Local city tours often stop here, such as the four-hour Mirabus tour with **Tours Class Arequipa** (www.toursclassarequipa.com.pe; Portal de San Agustín 103, Plaza de Armas; 2/4hr tours S35/45; ⊙departures 9:15am, 11am & 2pm, office 8am-8pm).

Casa de Moral   HISTORIC BUILDING

(☑054-21-4907; Moral 318; admission S5; ⊙9am-5pm Mon-Sat) This stylized baroque house built in 1730 is named after the 200-year-old mulberry tree in its central courtyard. Owned by the bank BCP since 2003 it is now a museum notable for its antique maps, heavy furniture, religious art and extensive collection of Peruvian coins and banknotes. Explanations are in Spanish and English.

Iglesia de San Francisco   CHURCH

(☑054-22-3048; Zela 202; admission S10; ⊙9am-noon & 3-6pm Mon-Sat) Originally built in the

16th century, this church has been badly damaged by several earthquakes. It still stands in its *sillar* (white volcanic rock)-brick fusion glory, however, and visitors can see a large crack in the cupola – testimony to the power of quakes. The garden-plaza to its left doubles as a mini-park.

Activities

Arequipa is the center for a slew of outdoor activities dotted around the high country to the north and east of the city. Trekking, mountaineering and river running are the big three, but there are plenty more.

Trekking & Mountaineering

The spectacular canyons and mountains around Arequipa offer many excellent hiking options. Trekking agencies can arrange off-the-beaten-track routes to suit your timeline and fitness level.

The Association of Mountain Guides of Peru warns that many guides are uncertified and untrained, so climbers are advised to go well-informed about medical and wilderness-survival issues. Most agencies sell climbs as packages that include transportation, so prices vary widely depending on the size of the group and the mountain, but the cost for a guide alone is around US$85 per day.

Trekking solo in the well-traveled Cañón del Colca area is popular and easy, but if you're nervous about hiking without guides or want to tackle more untrammeled routes, there are dozens of tour companies based in Arequipa that can arrange guided treks.

Although you can trek year-round, the best (ie driest) time is from April to December. Adequate acclimatization for this area is essential and it's best to have spent some time in Cuzco or Puno immediately before a high-altitude expedition.

Cold temperatures, which sometimes drop to -29°C at the highest camps, necessitate very warm clothing.

Carlos Zárate Adventures and **Peru Adventures Tours** (☎054-22-1658; www.peruadventurestours.com; Zela 209; ⊙8am-5pm Mon-Sat) rent tents, ice axes, crampons, stoves and boots.

Maps of the area can be obtained from Colca Trek in Arequipa or the Instituto Geográfico Nacional (p540) and South American Explorers Club (p46) in Lima.

★**Naturaleza Activa** ADVENTURE SPORTS
(☎968-969-544; naturactiva@yahoo.com; Santa Catalina 211; ⊙office 11am-7pm Mon-Sat) With a full range of trekking, climbing and mountain-biking options on offer, this is a favorite of those seeking adventure tours. A major advantage of going here rather than an agency is that the people you speak to at Naturaleza Activa are actually the qualified guides, not salespeople, so can answer your questions with genuine knowledge. Guides speak English, French and German.

Carlos Zárate Adventures ADVENTURE SPORTS
(☎054-20-2461; www.zarateadventures.com; Jerusalén 505A) This highly professional company offers various treks, and climbs all the local peaks. Founded in 1954 by Carlos Zárate, the great-grandfather of climbing in Arequipa, it's now run by one of his sons, experienced guide Carlos Zárate Flores. Another of Zárate's sons, Miguel, was responsible, along with archaeologists, for unearthing 'Juanita the Ice Maiden' (p151) atop Nevado Ampato in 1995.

Prices depend on group size and transportation method, including S250 per person for a group of four to climb El Misti, and S220 for a three-day trek in the Cañón del Colca, both with private transportation, guide, meals and all equipment.

Zárate's guides generally speak Spanish or English, but French speakers are also available when prearranged. The company also rents all kinds of gear to independent climbers and hikers including ice axes, crampons and hiking boots.

Colca Trek ADVENTURE SPORTS
(☎054-20-6217; www.colcatrek.com.pe; Jerusalén 401B; ⊙office 9am-7pm Mon-Fri, to 4pm Sat, to 1pm Sun) An ecoconscious adventure-tour agency and shop run by the knowledgeable, English-speaking Vlado Soto. In addition to trekking tours away from the crowds, it organizes mountaineering, mountain-biking and river-running trips. It's one of the few shops selling decent topographical maps of the area and is a venerable source of information for those hoping to explore this region on their own.

Be careful of copycat travel agencies that use the Colca Trek name and/or web addresses that are similar to the agency's official site.

Pablo Tour TREKKING
(☎054-20-3737; www.pablotour.com; Jerusalén 400 AB-1; ⊙office 8:30am-8pm) Consistently

recommended by readers, Pablo Tour's guides are experts in trekking and cultural tours in the region, and can furnish trekkers with all the necessary equipment and topographical maps.

River Rafting

Arequipa is one of Peru's premier bases for river rafting and kayaking. Many trips are unavailable during the rainy season (between December and March), when water levels can be dangerously high. For more information and advice, consult www.peru-whitewater.com.

The **Río Chili**, about 7km from Arequipa, is the most frequently run local river, with a half-day trip suitable for beginners leaving almost daily from April to November (from US$40). Further afield, you can also do relatively easy trips on the **Río Majes**, into which the Río Colca flows. The most commonly run stretches include class II and III rapids.

A more off-the-beaten-track possibility is the remote **Río Cotahuasi**, an adventure not for the fainthearted that reaches into the deepest sections of what is perhaps the world's deepest known canyon. Expeditions here are infrequent and only for the experienced, usually taking nine days and including class IV and V rapids. The **Río Colca** was first run back in 1981, but this is a dangerous, difficult trip, not to be undertaken lightly. A few outfitters will do infrequent and expensive river-running trips, and easier sections can be found upriver from the canyon.

Casa de Mauro   RAFTING
(📞 983-839-729; www.facebook.com/lacasade mauroturismoyaventura; Ongoro Km 5) This convenient base camp for river running on the Río Majes is in the village of Ongoro, 190km by road west of Arequipa. The lodge offers 1½-hour trips for beginner to experienced rafters (S100 per person), as well as camping (S20 per person) or triple rooms with private bathrooms (S130 per room).

The cheapest way to get here is to take a Transportes del Carpio bus from Arequipa's Terminal Terrestre to Aplao (S12, three hours, hourly) and then a *combi* (minibus; S2) or a taxi (S15) to Ongoro.

Majes River Lodge   RAFTING
(📞 958-250-220; www.majesriver.com) Offers easy one-hour river-running trips (S70, minimum four people) or more challenging three-hour trips that pass through class IV

rapids (S150, minimum five people) on the Río Majes. Also available are single/double bungalows (S100) with solar hot-water showers, camping, meals of fresh river shrimp and tours to the nearby Toro Muerto petroglyphs (p173).

Get here by taking a taxi (S15) or a *combi* (minibus; S2) from Aplao.

Mountain Biking

The Arequipa area has numerous mountain-biking possibilities. Many of the same companies that offer trekking or mountain-climbing trips also organize downhill volcano mountain-biking trips at **Chachani** and **El Misti** or can arrange tailor-made tours. If you have the experience and wherewithal, these agencies can also rent you high-end bikes and offer expert trip-planning advice to help get you started on your own. Peru Adventures Tours (p153) organizes cycling tours around El Misti for US$50 (half day) including transportation, big-name bikes, helmet, gloves and snacks, with oxygen and first-aid available.

Courses

Want to learn to speak Spanish? Immersion is the best way and Arequipa provides plenty of opportunities for class time, while practicing with the locals in the evenings. Book with a recommended agency and you'll be reading Arequipa-born novelist Mario Vargas Llosa in the original before you know it.

If you recognize the name Gastón Acurio and concur that Peru is the gastronomical capital of Latin America, you may be inspired to enroll in an Arequipa cooking course.

Centro Cultural Peruano Norteamericano   LANGUAGE
(ICPNA; 📞 054-39-1020; www.cultural.edu.pe; Melgar 109) This well-established Peru–North American cultural center offers a range of cultural activities (including theater, music and the like). It's bivouacked in a pleasant *casona* (large house) in the city center.

Rocio   LANGUAGE
(📞 054-22-4568; www.spanish-peru.com; Ayacucho 208) This language school with accommodations options charges US$6 per hour for an individual Spanish class, while small group lessons cost US$116 per 20-hour week. Ring bell number 21 at the communal entrance.

COOKING CLASSES IN AREQUIPA

Local guide and qualified chef Miguel Fernández, who runs **Al Travel Tours** (☑95-939-1436; www.aitraveltours.com; Santa Catalina 203; ⊙ office 10am-6:30pm Mon-Sat), organizes **Peru Flavors**, a four-hour cooking course (S100, minimum two people) where you will learn to prepare a trio of appetizers and mains from the three different geographical regions of Peru: Amazonia, the Andes and the coast. Dishes include *rocoto relleno* (stuffed spicy red peppers), *lomo saltado* (strips of beef stir-fried with onions, tomatoes, potatoes and chili) and *chupe de camarones* (prawn chowder).

Another popular option is the **Peruvian Cooking Experience** (☑054-213-975; www.peruviancookingexperience.com; San Martín 116, Vallecito; 3hr course US$23.50; ⊙11am & 3pm Mon-Sat), based at the Casa de Avila hotel, four blocks southwest of the Plaza de Armas. Courses run Monday to Saturday at 11am and 2pm. You can study the art of ceviche (raw seafood marinated in lime juice) preparation or even opt for vegetarian recipes. Courses are available in Spanish and English. Maximum group size is six.

An excellent excuse to eat chocolate is to make your own artisanal bars at **Chaqchao Chocolates** (☑054-23-4572; www.facebook.com/chaqchao.organic.chocolates; Santa Catalina 204; 2½hr class S65; ⊙11am & 2:45pm). Fun classes held in English guide you through chocolate's history, organic ingredients and stone grinding-tools.

☞ Tours

Dozens of travel agencies line Santa Catalina and Jerusalén offering near-identical excursions to the canyon country, most with daily departures; ho-hum city tours are also pushed. While some agencies are professional, there are also plenty of carpetbaggers muscling in on the action, so shop carefully. Never accept tours from street touts and, where possible, tours should be paid for in cash, as occasional credit-card fraud is reported.

The standard two-day tour of the Cañón del Colca (p166) costs S65 to S225 per person, depending on the season, group size and comfort level of the hotel you stay at in Chivay. Different agencies may sell you tickets for the same tours, so shop around. All tours leave Arequipa between 7am and 9am. Stops include the Reserva Nacional Salinas y Aguada Blanca (p165), Chivay (p167), La Calera Hot Springs (p169), an evening *peña* (bar or club featuring live folkloric music; at an additional fee) trip plus a visit to the Cruz del Cóndor (p171).

While a one-day tour of the Cañón del Colca (really mainly the Cruz del Cóndor) is heavily touted, you will spend most of your time cooped up in a van, missing out on spending significant time in any of the canyon towns and wind up exhausted by the time you return to Arequipa the same day. Departures are at the unholy hour of around 2am.

Free Walking Tour Peru WALKING
(☑998-959-566; www.fwtperu.com; Plaza San Francisco; by donation; ⊙12:20pm) **FREE** A quirky, passionate and knowledgeable guide leads groups on a 2½-hour English/Spanish/French walking tour of Arequipa's landmarks, such as San Lázaro church, and commercial places (with little hard sell) for taste-testing craft beer, chocolate tea and pisco (Peruvian grape brandy). Most participants are happy to tip the guide at the end.

Show up at the plaza of Iglesia de San Francisco (p152) and look for the guide in the green vest.

Ecotours ADVENTURE
(☑054-20-2562; Jerusalén 409; ⊙office 9am-8pm Mon-Sat) In business for 20 years, Arequipa-based Ecotours organizes three-hour river-running trips (S70) on the Río Chili's class II to class IV rapids, or three-day excursions to the Cañón del Colca (S250) with meals and accommodations.

✯ Festivals & Events

Semana Santa RELIGIOUS
(Holy Week; ⊙Mar or Apr) *Arequipeños* claim that their Semana Santa celebrations leading up to Easter are similar to the very solemn and traditional Spanish observances held in Seville. The Maundy Thursday, Good Friday and Holy Saturday processions are particularly colorful and sometimes end with the burning of an effigy of Judas.

Fiesta de la Virgen de Chapi RELIGIOUS
(⊙May 1) Arequipa fills up for this festival, celebrated in the Yanahuara district with a procession where an effigy of the Virgin is held aloft.

Aniversario de Arequipa CULTURAL
(⊙Aug) The reestablishment of Arequipa by the Spaniards in 1540 is celebrated across the city with street parades, dancing, music, beauty pageants, climbing competitions on El Misti and other energetic events peppered through the fortnight leading up to the anniversary on August 15. The fireworks show in the Plaza de Armas on the evening of August 14 is definitely worth catching.

🛏 Sleeping

Stay near the Plaza de Armas for convenience, though away from the bars of San Francisco on weekends if you want quiet. Many accommodations inhabit attractive *sillar* (white volcanic rock) buildings, the thick walls of which often weaken wireless signals. Cable TV and free wi-fi are pretty much a given, as is breakfast – usually merely bread, jam and coffee at cheaper joints. Prices can fluctuate greatly even during high season (June to August).

Misti Inn HOTEL $
(☎054-38-4958; Jerusalén 605; s/d/tr incl breakfast S50/65/92; 🐱) In a handsome, pale-yellow house on the cusp of the colonial center, this old mansion has a more classical feel than the baroque abodes further south. The pattern-heavy decor is a little past its refurb date, but it adds to the homespun charm and service is helpful.

La Posada del Parque B&B $
(☎054-21-2275; www.parkhostel.net; Deán Valdivia 238A; dm/s/d incl breakfast S30/65/85; @🐱) This B&B bargain near the market has high-ceilinged, basic rooms that sit beneath a wonderfully weathered terrace where El Misti appears so close you could almost hug it. There's a kitchen and laundry (additional cost) available and the owners can organize on-site Spanish lessons for US$7 per hour.

La Posada del Cacique HOTEL $
(☎054-20-2170; Jerusalén 404; d/tr S85/98, dm/s without bathroom S33/79; @🐱) This 2nd-floor hostel has rundown but spacious, sunny rooms and a well-equipped shared kitchen, reliable hot water and a tranquil rooftop sitting area. The father-son owners

are great resources for local info and make guests feel right at home.

Hostal Núñez HOSTEL $
(☎054-21-8648; www.hotel-nunez.de; Jerusalén 528; s/d/tr S59/79/156; 🐱) On a street full of not-so-great guesthouses, this secure, friendly hostel is always stuffed with gringos. The colorful rooms sport yesteryear orange decor and cable TV. Note that the singles are a bit of a squeeze.

★**Casa Arequipa** BOUTIQUE HOTEL $$
(☎054-28-4219; www.arequipacasa.com; Av Lima 409, Vallecito; r incl breakfast from US$70; 🐱) Inside a cotton-candy-pink colonial mansion in the gardens of suburban Vallecito, this gay-friendly B&B offers more than half a dozen guest rooms with fine design touches such as richly painted walls, pedestal sinks, antique handmade furnishings and alpaca-wool blankets. There's a sociable cocktail bar in the lobby.

Orkkowasi Casa de Montaña HOSTEL $$
(☎054-21-4518; Álvarez Thomas 208; dm S29, d/tr S88/130, d without bathroom 72; 🐱) Don't let the cramped entrance at this hostel near the Plaza de Armas put you off. The quiet rooms upstairs are clean and spacious with sofas, desks, flat-screen TVs and comfy beds – no springs digging into your ribs! – and modern where it counts, in the (small) bathrooms and speedy wi-fi. There is a kitchen and rooftop lounging space.

Terruño de Yarabaya GUESTHOUSE $$
(☎950-610-077; www.terrunodeyarabaya.weebly.com; cnr Desaguadero 104-106 & Campo Redondo; s/d S100/120; 🐱) All the large rooms here look onto a calming green garden. Rooms and bathrooms are clean and modern with cable TV, microwave and fridge; reclaimed doors give an artistic touch. The attached cafe serves unexpected treats like Japanese curries (the co-owner is Japanese) and the earthy, maple-flavored *lúcuma* fruit, which you can enjoy from your lawn chair.

Casona Terrace Hotel HOTEL $$
(☎054-21-2318; www.hotelcasonaterrace.com; Álvarez Thomas 211; s/d/tw incl buffet breakfast S140/170/170; ❄@🐱) A lovely old colonial home with rooms that are decked out in modern simplicity rather than old-world splendor. The hotel is just one block from the main square but has secure entry and a roof terrace.

Casablanca Hostal
HOTEL **$$**

(☎054-22-1327; www.casablancahostal.com; Puente Bolognesi 104; s/d/tr incl breakfast S111/190/235; @🖵) You might marvel at what you get for your money at this hotel. It has a prime corner location on the main plaza (though with accompanying street noise), beautiful exposed *sillar* (white volcanic rock) brickwork and rooms large enough to keep a horse (or two) in. Service is discreet and breakfast is taken in a lovely sun-filled cafe.

Casa de Avila
HOTEL **$$**

(☎054-21-3177; www.casadeavila.com; San Martín 116, Vallecito; s/d/tr incl breakfast S151/188/271; @🖵) If the spacious courtyard garden doesn't swing it for you, the congenial personalized service ought to – this is not some 'yes sir, no sir' chain hotel. The brown decor and comfy beds emphasize the homey feel. Casa de Avila also hosts Spanish-language courses and a cooking course in the sunny garden three times a week.

Hostal las Torres de Ugarte
HOTEL **$$**

(☎054-28-3532; www.torresdeugarte.com; Ugarte 401A; s/d/tr incl breakfast S163/196/232; @🖵) This friendly hostel in a quiet location behind the Monasterio de Santa Catalina has small, bright modern rooms with blackout curtains, colorful woolly bedspreads and flat-screen TVs. You'll just have to ignore the cacophonous echoing hallways, or head to the rooftop deck chairs. Rates drop considerably in low season.

La Casa de Melgar
HOTEL **$$**

(☎054-22-2459; www.lacasademelgar.com; Melgar 108; s/d incl breakfast US$55/75; 🖵) Housed in an 18th-century building, this scenic hotel is nonetheless fitted out with all the expected modern comforts. High-domed ceilings and unique decor lend the entire place an old-world feel. Comfy beds and tucked-away inner patios help make this a romantic hideaway within the city limits.

Hostal Solar
HOTEL **$$**

(☎054-24-1793; www.hostalsolar.com; Ayacucho 108; s/d incl breakfast S105/120; 🖵) This snazzy pick is clean and airy, with contemporary decor and balconies in the doubles. Prices include a buffet breakfast served on the rooftop terrace. Airport pickup available.

Wild Rover Hostel
HOTEL **$$**

(☎054-21-2830; www.wildroverhostels.com; Calle Ugarte 111; dm/s/d S26/45/89; @🖵🍺) This party hostel is good for scoffing cheap bangers and mash with European backpackers in the attached Irish pub or by the small pool. Wooden floors and odd-tiled bathrooms are old but everything is clean. Opt for a cramped private room if the 20-bed dorm is too much. Beds are comfy, but honestly, expect more socializing than beauty sleep here.

Le Foyer
HOSTEL **$$**

(☎054-28-6473; www.hlefoyer.com; Ugarte 114; d/tr incl breakfast S101/116, dm/d/tr without bathroom incl breakfast S32/72/103; @🖵) There's a distinct New Orleans look to this cheap hostel-like hotel with its wraparound upstairs veranda where you can enjoy a standard bread-and-jam breakfast overlooking busy Jerusalén. Rooms are nothing to brag about but the proximity to plenty of restaurants and nightlife (there's an alluring Mexican place downstairs) means you don't need GPS to find the action.

La Casa de Sillar
HOTEL **$$**

(☎054-28-4249; www.lacasadesillar.com; Rivero 504; s/d/tr incl breakfast S70/90/120; @🖵) Another of those thick-walled colonial mansions made – as the name implies – out of *sillar* (white volcanic rock) hewn from El Misti, this one doesn't pretend to be boutique, but it does offer fine value. Rooms are spacious yet warm and have comfortable beds. Huge maps and an equally huge TV adorn a communal lounge.

Posada Nueva España
HOTEL **$$**

(☎054-25-2941; www.hotelnuevaespana.com; Antiquilla 106, Yanahuara; s/d/tr incl breakfast S91/111/150; @🖵) This distinguished 19th-century colonial house has just more than a dozen rooms with solar-hot-water showers. It's in the quaint, quiet suburb of Yanahuara; call for free pickups from central Arequipa or it's a 20-minute walk. Spanish, French, German and English are spoken.

★ Hotel Casona Solar
HOTEL **$$$**

(☎054-22-8991; www.casonasolar.com; Consuelo 116; s/d/ste S199/319/389; 🖵) This gorgeous 'secret garden' is situated – incredibly given its tranquility – only three blocks from Arequipa's main square. Grand 18th-century rooms are crafted from huge *sillar* (white volcanic rock) stones, some with mezzanine bedrooms. The service (same-day laundry, bus reservations, free airline check-in) is equally dazzling. One of the city's best places to stay.

★**La Hostería** HOTEL **$$$**
(☑054-28-9269; www.lahosteriaqp.com.pe; Bolívar 405; s/d/tr incl breakfast US$66/75/83; ☏) Worth every sol is this picturesque colonial hotel with a flower-bedecked courtyard, light and quiet rooms (with minibar), carefully chosen antiques, a sunny terrace and a lounge. Some rooms do suffer from street noise, so request one in the back. Apartment-style suites on the upper floors have stellar city views.

★**Hotel La Posada del Monasterio** HOTEL **$$$**
(☑054-40-5728; www.hotelessanagustin.com.pe; Santa Catalina 300; s/d/tr incl buffet breakfast from S377/429/514; @☏☳) On a prime corner, this hotel gracefully inhabits an architectural mix-and-match building combining the best of the European and South American style. The comfortable modern rooms have all the expected facilities. The rooftop balcony peers into the Santa Catalina convent across the street. Ask to access the laundry terrace for impressive volcano vistas. It's especially popular with European tour groups.

Palla Boutique Hotel BOUTIQUE HOTEL **$$$**
(☑980-959-990; www.palla.pe; Bolognesi 350; r/ste incl breakfast from S288/374; P☀☏) White *sillar* (volcanic rock) bricks look chic and minimal alongside real wood floors and furniture at gorgeous, central Palla. Rooms are small but suites have freestanding baths and the modern restaurant and rooftop – where an excellent breakfast is served – provide breathing (and posing) room.

Los Tambos Hostal BOUTIQUE HOTEL **$$$**
(☑054-60-0900; www.lostambos.com.pe; Puente Bolognesi 129; r incl breakfast S289-349; ☀@☏) Breaking the mold in historic Arequipa is this modern boutique hotel, a marble roll from the main square, where small but significant extras and above-and-beyond service justify every sol of the asking price. Luring you in are chocolates on your pillow, aromatic soap selections, huge gourmet breakfasts (included), and free transportation to and from the airport or bus terminal.

Libertador Ciudad Blanca LUXURY HOTEL **$$$**
(☑054-21-5110; www.libertador.com.pe; Plaza Bolívar s/n, Selva Alegre; r S502, ste S654-752; ☀@☏☳) The grande dame of Arequipa's hotels, this stylish building 1km north of the center is set in gardens with a pool and playground. Rooms are spacious and public areas opulent, plus its spa boasts a sauna,

Jacuzzi and fitness room. The sedate restaurant serves fine Sunday brunch. Neighboring Selva Alegre park is beautiful; just don't wander far from the crowds.

La Posada del Puente HOTEL **$$$**
(☑054-25-3132; www.posadadelpuente.com; Bolognesi 101; s/d S380/430; @☏) The extensive gardens of this high-end hotel hug the river, making for a tranquil setting with volcano views that's surprisingly removed from the bustling traffic above. Heated rooms look mostly modern but with quirks like ancient TVs with cable. Staying here gives you free access to the sports facilities and swimming pool at the nearby Club Internacional sports complex.

Casa Andina Classic BOUTIQUE HOTEL **$$$**
(☑054-20-2070; www.casa-andina.com; Jerusalén 603; d/tr incl breakfast S291/437; ☀@☏) Flirts with boutique decor, but feels a tad overpriced when you factor in the rather dark restaurant, officious service and rooms that are basically just motel rooms with some deft color accents. The on-site spa claws back a little credibility with massages offered for S120 (one hour). It's part of the Casa Andina chain.

 Eating

Arequipa has a reputation for tasty local dishes like *rocoto relleno* (stuffed spicy red peppers), best enjoyed in the traditional, communal *picantería* restaurants. Trendy upscale spots line San Francisco north of the Plaza de Armas, while touristy outdoor cafes huddle together on Pasaje Catedral. Good, local eateries are in the busy Mercado on San Camilo southeast of the plaza.

La Lucha Sanguchería Criolla SANDWICHES **$**
(☑054-28-4133; www.lalucha.com.pe; Mercaderes 116; sandwiches from S15; ☉8am-midnight) Not your standard sandwiches, the *sánguches* here are panini-like creations with wood-fire-roasted pulled pork, chicken or turkey and creamy sauces such as mild chili *ají*. The hand-cut purple *huayro* potato fries are worth the visit alone. The central location and late hours are useful.

Xarza Mora PERUVIAN **$**
(Álvarez Thomas 211A; menús S11; ☉noon-4pm; ☏☑) Easily the best budget set lunches in Arequipa. Traditional Peruvian dishes, like *causa limeña de pollo* (chicken, avocado and potato stack) are served with generous side salads and greens and a keen sense for

herbs and spices. The bistro vibe is helped by English-speaking staff and a handsome space attached to a *sillar* (white volcanic rock) hotel.

La Despensa
CAFE $

(☑ 054-22-2104; www.facebook.com/ladespensa. aqp; Santa Catalina 302; snacks from S3; ⊗ 8am-1pm Mon-Sat, 9am-4pm Sun; ▣ 🛜) Herby focaccia, delicious brownies, chocolate truffles, handmade pasta, wine and rustic real baguettes filled with arugula and sun-dried tomato are just some of the many homemade treats from 'The Pantry.' The chic *sillar* (white volcanic rock) building and good coffee help make this *the* place to chat or type in Arequipa.

Omphalos
VEGETARIAN $

(www.facebook.com/omphalosaqp; Bolívar 107; mains from S9, menús S10; ⊗ 9:30am-9pm Mon-Sat, to 5pm Sun; 🛜 ✐) A casual and unpretentious place to enjoy a delicious meat-free pesto pasta, spinach risotto or Indian eggplant curry in a lovely courtyard in central Arequipa. The day and night set meals are excellent value.

Hatunpa
PERUVIAN $

(Ugarte 208; dishes S11-16; ⊗ 12:30-9:30pm Mon-Sat, to 4pm Sun; ✐) With the spud as its star ingredient, Hatunpa's cuisine is surprisingly tasty. The trick? Potatoes originate in Peru and the *arequipeños* know how to embellish the varied varieties with imaginative sauces and toppings such as alpaca, *rocoto relleno* (meat-stuffed peppers), chorizo or veg. Even better, they're cheap, casual and filling. Potato haters can substitute with quinoa or *palta* (avocado).

El Turko
TURKISH $

(☑ 959-740-291; www.elturko.com.pe; San Francisco 225; mains S10-17.50; ⊗ 7:30am-11pm Sun-Thu, 24hr Fri & Sat; ✐) This relaxed little joint serves a hungry crowd late-night kebabs, Middle Eastern salads and juicy vegetarian falafel, with excellent coffee, sweet pastries and breakfasts during the day.

Crepísimo
CAFE $

(www.crepisimo.com; Alianza Francesa, Santa Catalina 208; mains S15-34; ⊗ 8am-11pm; 🛜 ✐) All the essential components of a great cafe – food, setting, service, ambience – come together at Crepísimo, located inside Arequipa's French cultural center. In this chic colonial setting, the simple crepe is offered with 100 different types of filling, from Chilean smoked trout to South American fruits and ample vegetarian options, while casual waitstaff serve you Parisian-quality coffee.

Tradición Arequipeña
PERUVIAN $

(☑ 054-42-6467; www.tradicionarequipena.com; Av Dolores 111, José Luis Bustamante y Rivero; meals S18-40; ⊗ 11:30am-6pm Mon-Fri, to 8pm Sat, 8:30am-6pm Sun) This locally famous restaurant has maze-like gardens, live *folklórica* and *criollo* (an upbeat coastal style) music, and does traditional Peruvian fare well, such as seabass ceviche. Sunday breakfast includes *adobo de cerdo,* a traditional slow-cooked pork dish. It's 2km southeast of the center; a taxi ride here costs about S5.

★ La Nueva Palomino
PERUVIAN $$

(☑ 054-25-2393; Leoncio Prado 122; mains S22-69; ⊗ noon-5pm Mon-Sat, 7:30am to noon Sun; 🛜 ✐ ▣) An unmissable local favorite, this long-running *picantería* has old-world formal service but a casual atmosphere that turns boisterous even during the week when family groups descend to eat generous servings of local specialties and drink copious amounts of *chicha de jora* (fermented corn beer) in the courtyard. Solo diners will get full on the excellent *ricoto relleno* (meat-stuffed peppers) alone.

The restaurant is in the Yanahuara (p152) district (2km northwest of the city center), east of the *mirador* (lookout).

★ Zig Zag
PERUVIAN $$

(☑ 054-20-6020; www.zigzagrestaurant.com; Zela 210; mains S36-50; ⊗ noon-11pm; ✐) Upscale but not ridiculously pricey, Zig Zag is a Peruvian restaurant with European inflections. It inhabits a two-story colonial house with an iron stairway designed by Gustave Eiffel (wow, that man must have been busy). The menu classic is a meat selection served on a unique volcano-stone grill with various sauces. The fondues are also good.

Some heretics claim it's even better than famous Peruvian chef Gastón Acurio's Chicha (p161). The various set lunch *menús* (from S55) are an accessible way to taste-test and include a seafood-only or vegetarian option.

Las Gringas
PIZZA $$

(☑ 054-39-9895; www.facebook.com/lasgringaspizza; Santa Catalina 204; pizzas S28/35; ⊗ 10am-3pm & 5-11pm; 🛜 ✐) This pizza cafe stands out for its secluded small courtyard and veggie-friendly pizzas that include

AREQUIPA & CANYON COUNTRY AREQUIPA

LOCAL KNOWLEDGE

AREQUIPA CONCOCTIONS

chicha de jora – fermented corn beer

chupe de camarones – prawn chowder

cuy chactado – spiced, fried guinea pig

ocopa – boiled potato in a creamy, spicy sauce

pastel de papa – baked layers of potato slices and cheese

rocoto relleno – stuffed spicy red peppers

interesting bases like gluten-free *maíz morado* (purple corn), rice, quinoa and yucca cassava. Tasty toppings include smoked red peppers, cranberries, pesto and vegan eggplant 'cheese.' Açaí granola bowls make a fresh brunch.

Part of the proceeds on some pizzas are donated to NGOs working on fighting poverty.

Victoria Picantería   PERUVIAN $$

(☎966-714-119; www.victoriaarequipa.com; San Francisco 227; mains S15-40, shared menús S100-160; ⊙9am-midnight Mon-Sat; ✶🛜) Arequipa's *picanterías* (informal local restaurants) are traditionally communal, and you might be encouraged here to sit at long tables alongside strangers to compare notes on the artfully served alpaca steaks and 'rescued' Arequipan dishes like *camarón al rescoldo* (ember-cooked prawns on wild quinoa). The ample tasting menus cover all the flavors.

Intimate tables provide options for privacy in the beautiful spaces of the *sillar* (white volcanic rock) building.

Los Leños   PIZZA $$

(☎054-28-1818; www.facebook.com/loslenos pizzeria; Jerusalén 407; pizzas S13-46; ⊙5-11pm; 🛜🍴) The indoor smoke from the wood-fired oven and cigarette-puffing diners and staff isn't exactly a sight for sore eyes, but it's worth it for arguably the best pizza in Arequipa. Thin, crispy squares come soaked with flavor; try the quinoa-flour base for a local twist. Besides, the high-domed ceiling keeps the place airy.

El Tío Dario   SEAFOOD $$

(☎054-27-0473; www.tiodario.com; Callejón de Cabildo 100, Yanahuara; mains S30-55; ⊙11am-4pm) Like fish? Like intimate, secret-garden set-

tings? Then grab a taxi (or walk) out to the pleasant Yanahuara (p152) district for the ultimate in ceviches or grilled-fish dishes served in a flower-rich garden that frames superb volcano views. Tío Dario is through the charming archway to the left of Yanahuara *mirador* (lookout).

Zingaro   PERUVIAN $$

(☎054-21-7662; www.zingaro-restaurante.com; San Francisco 309; mains S35-62; ⊙noon-11pm Mon-Sat, to 10pm Sun) Culinary legends are made in this leading font of gastronomic innovation, an ideal place to try outnouveau renditions of Peruvian standards including alpaca ribs, ceviche, or perhaps your first *cuy* (guinea pig). It's in an old *sillar* (white volcanic rock) building with wooden balconies, stained glass and a resident pianist.

Two doors down (San Francisco 315), sister restaurant **Parrilla de Zingaro** specializes in Argentinian-style meats with equally splendid results.

Restaurant on the Top   PERUVIAN $$

(☎054-28-1787; Portal de Flores 102; mains S14-32, menús S20; ⊙11am-10pm; 🍴) The hike up the stairs to this rooftop eatery is well worth it for the view of the Plaza de Armas and mountains beyond. An enormous menu features everything from sandwiches to Alpaca steaks. The lunch and dinner set menus are good value.

Cevichería Fory Fay   CEVICHE $$

(Álvarez Thomas 221; mains S20-35; ⊙10am-4:30pm) This small and to-the-point place serves only the best ceviche (raw seafood marinated in lime juice) and nothing else. Pull up a chair at a rickety table and crack open a beer – limit three per person at this family-oriented joint, though.

The name is a phonetic spelling of how Peruvians say '45' in English. The beers here used to cost 45 cents.

La Trattoria del Monasterio   ITALIAN $$

(☎054-20-4062; www.latrattoriadelmonasterio. com; Santa Catalina 309; mains S23-50; ⊙noon-3pm & 7-11pm Mon-Sat, noon-3pm Sun; 🍴) A helping of epicurean delight can be found just next door to the austere Monasterio de Santa Catalina (p147). The menu of Italian specialties was created with the help of superstar Peruvian chef Gastón Acurio, and is infused with the flavors of Arequipa. Reservations are essential.

Sol de Mayo
PERUVIAN $$

(☑054-25-4148; Jerusalén 207, Yanahuara; mains S28-60) Serving good Peruvian food in the Yanahuara (p152) district, this *picantería* (informal local restaurant) has live *música folklórica* every afternoon from 1pm to 4pm. Book a table in advance. You can combine a visit here with a stop at the *mirador* (lookout) in Yanahuara.

★Salamanto
PERUVIAN $$$

(☑979-394-676; www.salamanto.com; San Francisco 211; mains S48-57, 5-course tasting menus S85; ⏰12:30-3:30pm & 6:30-10:30pm Mon-Sat; 🛜) The innovative, wonderfully plated contemporary Peruvian creations at Salamanto bolster Arequipa's reputation as a foodie destination. The five-dish degustation is unmissable with mushroom and pistachio mousse, trout carpaccio, and alpaca steak with pisco (Peruvian grape brandy) mustard dazzling on artful slabs of stone. There are only three wines (Argentinian and Peruvian) to choose from but they have been carefully chosen.

If you would prefer to concentrate on one dish, the *cuy* (guinea pig) here is glazed in pine fungus and passionfruit alongside amaranth and aloe vera. The delicious duck comes with a *chicha* (fermented corn beer) jelly, hummus and mixed quinoa.

★Chicha
PERUVIAN, FUSION $$$

(☑054-28-7360; www.chicha.com.pe; Santa Catalina 210; mains S44-69; ⏰noon-11pm Mon-Sat, to 8pm Sun; 🛜☑) Peru's most famous chef, Gastón Acurio, owns this experimental place where the menu closely reflects Peru's Inca-Spanish roots. River prawns are a highlight in season (April to December), but Acurio prepares Peruvian staples with equal panache, along with tender alpaca burgers and earthy pastas. Staff can help pair food with pisco (Peruvian grape brandy) cocktails and wines by the glass.

Try the *tacu-tacu* (a Peruvian fusion dish of rice, beans and a protein), *lomo saltado* (strips of beef stir-fried with onions, tomatoes, potatoes and chili), or ceviche. Like many 'celeb' places, Chicha divides opinion between food snobs and purists. Step inside and join the debate.

🍷 Drinking & Nightlife

The nocturnal scene in Arequipa is pretty slow midweek but takes off on weekends, when anyone who's anyone can be seen joining the throng on the corner of San Fran-

cisco and Ugarte sometime after 9pm. Many of the bars there offer happy-hour specials worth enjoying. The 300 block has the highest concentration of places to compare fashion notes.

★Chelawasi Public House
MICROBREWERY

(www.facebook.com/chelawasi; Campo Redondo 102; beers S15-18; ⏰4-11pm Mon-Fri, from noon Sat) Arequipa's first craft-beer bar is a modern but unpretentious pub in the village-like San Lázaro area. The burgers, wings and hand-cut fries are excellent for pacing yourself. New to craft beer? Chelawasi's friendly Canadian-Peruvian owners will step you through the best beers from Peru's microbreweries, with bonus local travel advice, or a chat with other solo drinkers.

Imperio Club
GAY & LESBIAN

(www.facebook.com/imperioclubaqp; Jerúsalen 201; admission S20; ⏰10pm-late Fri & Sat) Arequipa's only central gay club is also its best, with a slick bar and mixed-ages fun crowd that makes it unintimidating to go alone or with company. *Reggaetón,* electronica and dance hits keep the *perreo* (grinding dance) going.

Museo del Pisco
COCKTAIL BAR

(www.museodelpisco.org; cnr Santa Catalina & Moral; drinks S16-32, tastings per person S37; ⏰5pm-midnight Sun-Thu, to 1am Fri & Sat) The name says 'museum,' but the designer slabs of stone and glass, plus the menu of more than 100 pisco (Peruvian grape brandy) varieties, says cocktail bar. Identify your favorite with a tasting of three mini craft piscos, explained in English by knowledgeable staff. Then mix your own (S26) behind the bar. Pace yourself with gourmet burgers and hummus.

Casona Forum
CLUB

(www.casonaforum.com; San Francisco 317; ⏰nightclubs 9pm-late Thu-Sat, bars & restaurant from 7pm daily) A seven-in-one excuse for a good night out in a *sillar* (white volcanic rock) building incorporating a pub (Retro), pool club (Zero), sofa bar (Chill Out), restaurant (Terrasse) and nightclubs (Forum, Club 80s and Latino Salsa Club).

Déjà Vu
COCKTAIL BAR

(San Francisco 319B; ⏰9am-late; 🛜) This eternally popular haunt has a rooftop terrace overlooking the Iglesia de San Francisco, a long list of crazy cocktails and a lethal happy hour every evening. Some of Arequipa's best DJs play electro and house here nightly, but only draw crowds on weekends.

Split
PUB

(Zela 207; ⊙ 5pm-1am Mon-Wed, 6pm-3am Thu-Sat) Two bars split into upstairs and downstairs (with no ground level). Both are dark, narrow and popular with locals who like to kick-start the night with a strong drink such as a 'Misti colado,' a pisco (Peruvian grape brandy) piña colada, or a potluck concoction of alcohol labelled 'tóxicos.' There are pizzas, crepes and pastas to tempt you to stay.

Brujas Bar
BAR

(San Francisco 300; ⊙ 5pm-late) Nordic-style pub with Union Jack flags, happy-hour cocktails and plenty of locals and expats chatting away. Live bands play at 9:30pm and 11pm most nights late in the week.

☆ Entertainment

Salsa and cumbia (a Colombian salsa-like dance and musical style) music and dancing predominate on Av Dolores, 2km southeast of the center (a taxi costs around S5 one way).

Woodstock
LIVE MUSIC

(www.facebook.com/woodstockarequipa; 2nd fl, Ugarte 202B; ⊙ 6pm-midnight Mon-Thu, from 7pm Fri & Sat; 🔊) This clean-cut gourmet burger bar has one thing in common with the namesake festival: live music (mostly jazz, rock and funk), played here most evenings from 9pm. It's loud enough to drown out conversations, the tinkle of craft-beer bottles and the lip-smacking of burgers, which include ample vegetarian options.

Café Art Montréal
LIVE MUSIC

(Ugarte 210; ⊙ 6:30pm-midnight Mon-Wed, to 2am Thu-Sat) This intimate little bar with live bands playing (Thursday to Saturday) on a stage at the back would be equally at home as a bohemian student hangout on Paris' Left Bank.

🛍 Shopping

Arequipa overflows with antique and artisan shops, especially on the streets around Monasterio de Santa Catalina (p147). High-quality leather, alpaca and vicuña (a threatened, wild relative of the alpaca) goods, and other handmade items, are what you'll most often see being sold.

Claustros de la Compañía
SHOPPING CENTER

(118 General Morán; ⊙ most stores 9am-9pm) One of South America's most elegant shopping centers, with a wine bar, ice-cream outlet, numerous alpaca-wool shops and chic cafes and restaurants. Its ornate double courtyard is ringed by cloisters held up by sillar (white volcanic rock) columns, etched with skillful carvings. Couples often dot the upper levels enjoying the romantic setting and southerly views.

Fundo El Fierro
CRAFT MARKET

(San Francisco 200; ⊙ 9am-1:30pm & 3-8:30pm Mon-Thu, to 9pm Fri & Sat) The city's primary craft market occupies a beautiful colonial sillar (white volcanic rock) courtyard next to the Iglesia de San Francisco. Garments, paintings, handmade crafts and jewelry predominate, but you can also procure rare alpaca carpets from Cotahuasi. There's an artisanal fair with special stalls held here in August.

Sol Alpaca
ARTS & CRAFTS

(🖉 054-20-2525; www.michell.com.pe; Juan de la Torre 101; ⊙ 8am-1pm & 1:45-5:30pm Mon-Fri; 🚶) More than just a source for fine alpaca-wool goods and raw thread, this complex functions as a tourist center for international wool-export company Michell (incorporating brands Sol Alpaca and Mundo Alpaca). It includes a well-presented commercial boutique, a museum detailing the process of wool production, a small zoo and a cafe.

Incalpaca Factory
Outlet Claustros
CLOTHING

(🖉 054-205-931; www.incalpaca.com; 118 General Morán; ⊙ 9:30am-7pm Mon-Sat, 11am-3pm Sun) Clearance clothing made from the wool of alpacas – and sometimes vicuñas (threatened, wild relatives of alpaca) – and craftwork from the upmarket Kuna brand. This outlet is within the elegant Claustros de la Compañía plaza; there is another one in Tahuaycani (🖉 ext 303 054-60-300; Av Juan Bustamante de la Fuente s/n; ⊙ 9:30am-7pm Mon-Sat, 11am-3pm Sun; 🚶).

Galería de Artesanías
'El Tumi de Oro'
CRAFT MARKET

(Portal de Flores 126; ⊙ 9:30am-8:30pm Mon-Sat, 10am-7pm Sun) A small artisan market under the portales (stone archways) on Plaza de Armas.

Librería SBS Internacional BOOKS
(☎054-20-5317; www.sbs.com.pe; San Francisco 125; ⏱9:30am-7:45pm Mon-Sat) Chain bookstore with a good selection of titles, including Spanish-learning resources and books in English, French, Italian, Portuguese and German.

ⓘ Information

EMERGENCY

Policía de Turismo (Tourist Police; ☎054-28-2613; Jerusalén 315-317; ⏱24hr) May be helpful if you need an official theft report for insurance claims. English speakers available.

IMMIGRATION

Oficina de Migraciónes (Immigration Office; ☎054-42-1759; www.migraciones.gob.pe; Urb Quinta Tristán, Parque 2, Distrito José Bustamante y Rivero; ⏱8am-4pm Mon-Fri, to noon Sat) Come here to apply for a visa extension.

MEDICAL SERVICES

Clínica Arequipa (☎054-599-000; www.clinicarequipa.com.pe; Bolognesi, near Puente Grau; ⏱8am-8pm Mon-Fri, to 12:30pm Sat) Arequipa's best and most expensive medical clinic.

Hogar Clínica San Juan de Dios (☎054-38-2400, 054-27-2740; www.sanjuandediosarequipa.com; Av Ejército 1020, Cayma; ⏱24hr) Private clinic in the suburb of Cayma, next to Yanahuara.

Hospital Regional Honorio Delgado Espinoza (☎054-23-1818, 054-21-9702; www.hrhdaqp.gob.pe; Av Carreón 505; ⏱24hr) Emergency 24-hour medical services.

InkaFarma (☎054-20-1565; www.inkafarma.com.pe; Santo Domingo 113; ⏱24hr) Well-stocked pharmacy that's part of a large Peruvian chain.

Paz Holandesa Policlinic (☎054-43-2281; www.pazholandesa.com; Av Chávez 527; ⏱8am-8pm Mon-Sat) Vaccinations available at this appointment-only travel clinic where doctors speak English and Dutch.

MONEY

There are money changers and ATMs on streets east of the Plaza de Armas. Global ATMs are easy to find in most areas frequented by travelers, including inside the **Casona Santa Catalina** (☎054-28-1334; www.santacatalina-sa.com.pe; Santa Catalina 210; ⏱most stores 10am-6pm) complex, the bus terminal and the airport. ATM fees charged by each bank vary but are roughly S20 per transaction.

Both BCP and Interbank exchange US traveler's checks.

BCP (San Juan de Dios 123; ⏱9am-6pm Mon-Fri, to 1pm Sat & Sun) Has a Visa ATM and changes US dollars.

Interbank (Mercaderes 217) Has a GlobalNet ATM that accepts most international cards.

POST

DHL (☎054-22-5332; Santa Catalina 115; ⏱8am-6pm Mon-Fri, 9am-noon Sat)

FedEx (☎054-25-6464; Av Belaúnde 121; ⏱9am-5pm Mon-Sat)

Serpost (Moral 118; ⏱8am-8pm Mon-Fri, to 7pm Sat)

SAFE TRAVEL

➡ Petty theft is often reported in Arequipa, so hide valuables and keep your stuff in sight while in bars, cafes and restaurants.

➡ Take great care in Parque Selva Alegre, north of the city center, as muggings have been reported there.

➡ Don't hail taxis from the street. Ask your accommodations or tour operator to call you an official taxi; the extra time and money are worth the added safety.

➡ Only pay for tours at a recognized agency and never trust touts in the street – they bamboozle cash out of a surprisingly high number of travelers.

TOURIST INFORMATION

Indecopi (☎054-42-7495; www.indecopi.gob.pe; cnr Calle 1 & Cultura Tiahuanaco, Urb La Esperanza; ⏱8:30am-4:30pm Mon-Fri) National tourist-protection agency.

iPerú (☎054-22-3265, 24hr hotline 574-8000; iperuarequipa@promperu.gob.pe; Portal de la Municipalidad 110, Plaza de Armas; ⏱9am-6pm Mon-Sat, to 1pm Sun) English-speaking staff give excellent information on local and regional attractions. Also has an office at the **airport** (☎054-44-4564; 1st fl, Main Hall, Aeropuerto Rodríguez Ballón; ⏱10am-7:30pm).

ⓘ Getting There & Away

AIR

Arequipa's **Rodríguez Ballón International Airport** (Aeropuerto Internacional Alfredo Rodríguez Ballón, AQP; ☎054-34-4834; Cerro Colorado) is about 8km northwest of the city center.

LAN (☎054-20-1100; Santa Catalina 118C; ⏱office 9am-7pm, to 2pm Sat) has daily flights to Lima and Cuzco. **LCPeru** (☎054-21-4746; www.lcperu.pe; Moral 225; ⏱office 9am-7pm Mon-Fri, to 1pm Sat) also offers daily flights to Lima. **Sky Airline** (☎054-28-2899; www.skyairline.cl; La Merced 121) flies to Santiago in Chile.

BUS

Most bus companies have departures from the Terminal Terrestre or the smaller Terrapuerto bus terminal, located together on Av Andrés Avelino Cáceres, less than 3km south of the city center (take a taxi for S7). Check in advance which terminal your bus leaves from and keep a close watch on your belongings while you're waiting there. There's a S1.50 departure tax from either terminal, paid separately at a booth. Both terminals have shops, restaurants and left-luggage facilities. The more chaotic Terminal Terrestre also has a global ATM.

Dozens of bus companies have desks at the Terminal Terrestre so shop around. Prices range between superluxury **Cruz del Sur** (☑ 054-42-7375; www.cruzdelsur.com.pe) and **Ormeño** (☑ 054-42-3855; www.grupo-ormeno.com.pe/destinos.html; Terminal Terrestre) with 180-degree reclining 'bed' seats, and no-frills **Flores** (Transportes Flores Hermanos; ☑ 054-43-2228, 01-480-0725; www.floreshnos.pe; Terminal Terrestre) which travels to a greater variety of destinations including Mollendo, Moquegua and Ilo.

Long-Distance Bus Travel

Night buses provide a convenient means to reach many far-off destinations in a city where options for air travel are limited, although some routes do have histories of accidents, hijackings and robberies. Paying a bit extra for a luxury bus service is often worth the added comfort and security. Exercise extreme care with your belongings on cheaper buses and refrain from keeping baggage in overhead luggage racks.

It is also recommended that you carry extra food with you on long bus rides in case of a breakdown or road strike. Bring a warm item of clothing aboard if heading to the canyons, as temperatures drop as you ascend to higher altitudes, even on what starts as a warm day in Arequipa. This is especially essential on tour buses that make stops and let you out.

Regional Services

Many buses useful for sightseeing in the canyon country leave from the Terminal Terrestre and Terrapuerto bus terminal. Travel times and costs vary depending on road conditions. During the wet season (between December and April), expect significant delays.

The best companies serving the Cañón del Colca (Chivay and then on to Cabanaconde) are **Andalucía** (☑ 054-48-0263), from Terrapuerto, and **Reyna** (☑ 054-43-0612; www.reyna.com.pe), from Terminal Terrestre. Catch the earliest daylight departure, usually around 5am, if you want to travel in the canyons the same day. Reserve tickets a day in advance, if possible, by phoning ahead (Spanish only).

Reaching the Toro Muerto petroglyphs (p173) can be difficult with public buses and it is much easier to go with a tour company. It is possible to go first to Corire (S12, three hours, hourly) with Transportes del Carpio, but you need to ask if they will pass near the petroglyphs on that service. From Corire you can continue on to Aplao in the Valle de Majes (S18, 1½ hours) for river running.

Reyna (☑ 054-43-0612; www.reyna.com.pe) has a service departing 4pm to Andagua (S36, 10 hours) to visit El Valle de los Volcanes. The bus leaves Andagua for the return trip to Arequipa at around 5:30pm.

For the Cañón del Cotahuasi (S30, 10 hours), Reyna has a 7am and 5pm departure, and **Cromotex** (☑ 054-42-6836; www.cromotex.com.pe; ⊙ offices 8am-10pm) has a 6pm departure.

Arequipa Buses

DESTINATION	COST (S)	DURATION (HR)
Cabanaconde	17	5
Camaná	12-55	2½
Chivay	13	3½
Cotahuasi	30	10
Cuzco	25-135	10
Ica	75-160	11-15
Juliaca	20-80	5
Lima	50-140	14-17
Mollendo	12-15	2-2½
Moquegua	20-30	6½
Nazca	50-120	10-12
Pisco	40-144	15
Puno	20-82	5
Tacna	30-40	6

⊙ Getting Around

TO/FROM THE AIRPORT

There are no airport buses or shared taxis. An official taxi from downtown Arequipa to the airport costs around S15 to S20; and S20 from the airport. This should include the S7.50 airport entrance fee, but be sure to ask. It is possible to take a *combi* (minibus) marked 'Río Seco' or 'Zamacola' from Puente Grau and Av Ejército that will let you off in a sketchy neighborhood about 700m from the airport entrance.

BUS

Combis (minibuses) go south along Bolívar and Cruz Verde to the Terminal Terrestre (S1, 20 minutes), next door to the Terrapuerto bus terminal, but make sure to ask if they are going *directo* (direct) or it'll be a slower 35-minute trip via the market area. A taxi costs about S7.

TAXI

You can often hire a taxi with a driver for less than renting a car from a travel agency. Local taxi companies include **Tourismo Arequipa** (☑054-45-8888; www.facebook.com/taxi turismoarequipa) and **Taxitel** (☑054-20-0000; www.taxitel.com.pe). A short ride around town costs about S5, while a trip from the Plaza de Armas out to the bus terminals costs about S7. Whenever possible, try to call a recommended company to ask for a pickup as there have been numerous reports of travelers being scammed or even assaulted by taxi drivers. If you must hail a taxi off the street, pick a regular size saloon (sedan) or estate (station wagon) over a compact yellow cab.

CANYON COUNTRY

Going to Arequipa and missing out on the Colca Canyon is like going to Cuzco and neglecting to visit Machu Picchu. For those with more time there's a load of other excursions that merit attention, including climbing the city's guardian volcano El Misti, rafting in the Majes canyon, visiting the petroglyphs at Toro Muerto, exploring El Valle de los Volcanes and trekking down into the world's deepest canyon at Cotahuasi. Most of these places can be visited by a combination of public bus and hiking. Alternatively, friends can split the cost of hiring a taxi or 4WD vehicle and driver.

Reserva Nacional Salinas y Aguada Blanca

One of southern Peru's finest protected reserves, Reserva Nacional Salinas y Aguada Blanca is a vast Andean expanse of dozing volcanoes and brawny wildlife forging out an existence against the odds several kilometers above sea level. Organized Colca Canyon tours unfortunately rush through the area, but drives here take you up to an oxygen-deprived 4910m where, in between light-headed gasps for air, you can ponder weird wind-eroded rock formations, trek on old Inca trails and watch fleet-footed vicuñas run across the desolate pampa at speeds of up to 85km/hour.

As a national reserve, Salinas y Aguada Blanca enjoys better protection than the Colca canyon, primarily because no one lives here bar the odd isolated llama-herder – and a rich variety of high-altitude species

such as vicuñas, tarucas envinados (Andean deer), guanacos and various birds, most notably flamingos. Both El Misti and Chachani volcanoes are part of the reserve.

◉ Sights

Paso de Patopampa   VIEWPOINT

(🅿) The highest point on the road between Arequipa and Chivay is this almost lifeless pass which, at 4910m, is significantly higher than Europe's Mt Blanc and anywhere in North America's Rocky Mountains. If your red blood cells are up to it, disembark into the rarefied air at the **Mirador de los Volcanes** to view a muscular consortium of eight snowcapped volcanoes: Ubinas (5675m), El Misti (5822m), Chachani (6075m), Ampato (6288m), Sabancaya (5976m), Huaca Huaca (6025m), Mismi (5597m) and Chucura (5360m).

Less spectacular but no less amazing is the scrubby yareta, one of the few plants that can survive in this harsh landscape. Yaretas can live for several millennia and their annual growth rate is measured in millimeters rather than centimeters.

Hardy ladies in traditional dress discreetly ply their wares at the *mirador* (lookout) during the day – this must be the world's highest shopping center. It's also usually the last tour-bus stop from Arequipa heading into canyon country.

Pampa de Toccra   WILDLIFE RESERVE

This high plain that lies between El Misti/Chachani and the Colca Canyon has an average height of around 4300m and supports plentiful bird and animal life. You're almost certain to see vicuñas (threatened, wild relatives of alpacas) roadside in the Zona de Vicuñas on the approach to **Patahuasi** (Hwy 34A). At a boggy and sometimes icy lake, waterfowl and flamingos reside in season. Nearby is a bird-watching *mirador* (lookout).

The **Centro de Interpretación de la Reserva Nacional Salinas** (◉9am-5pm) has detailed notes in English and Spanish about the area's geology and fauna. All four members of the South American camelid family thrive on the pampas (high plains) in this region: the domesticated llama and alpaca, and the wild vicuña and (timid and rare) guanaco.

🏃 Activities

🏃 El Misti

Looming 5822m above Arequipa, the city's guardian volcano, **El Misti**, is the most popular climb in the area. It is technically one of the easiest ascents of any mountain of this size in the world, but it's hard work nonetheless and you normally need an ice axe and, sometimes, crampons. Hiring a guide is highly recommended, especially to advise you on any possible recent developments, as in recent years there were signs that the volcano may be awakening slightly from centuries of dormancy (but not about to erupt!). A two-day trip will usually cost between S190 and S270 per person.

The mountain is best climbed from July to November, with the later months being the least cold. Below the summit is a sulfurous yellow crater with volcanic fumaroles hissing gas, and there are spectacular views down to the Laguna de Salinas and back to the city.

The ascent can be approached by many routes, some more worn-in than others, most of which can be done in two days. Beware that the Apurímac route is notorious for robberies. One popular route starts from Chiguata, and begins with a hard eight-hour slog uphill to reach base camp (4500m); from there to the summit and back takes eight hours, while the sliding return from base camp to Chiguata takes three hours or less. The Aguada Blanca route is restricted to a handful of official tour operators and allows climbers to arrive at 4100m before beginning to climb.

Determined climbers can reach the Chiguata route via public transportation. Buses going to Chiguata leave from Av Sepulveda in Arequipa (S10 one way, one hour) hourly beginning at 5:30am and will drop you off at an unmarked trailhead, from where you can begin the long trek to base camp. On the return trip, you should be able to flag down the same bus heading the opposite way. The more common method to reach the mountain is hiring a driver in a 4WD for around S250, who will take you up to 3300m and pick you up on the return.

🏃 Chachani

One of the easiest 6000m peaks in the world is Chachani (6075m), which is as close to Arequipa as El Misti. You will need crampons, an ice axe and good equipment. There are various routes up the mountain, one of which involves going by 4WD to Campamento de Azufrera at 4950m. From there you can reach the summit in about nine hours and return in under four hours. Alternatively, for a two-day trip, there is a good spot to camp at 5200m. Other routes take three days but are easier to get to by 4WD (S400 to S600).

Other Mountains

Nevado Sabancaya (5976m) is part of a massif on the south rim of the Cañón del Colca that also includes extinct **Nevado Hualca Hualca** (6025m) and **Nevado Ampato** (6288m). Sabancaya erupted in 2014 after 15 dormant years and continued spewing ash into 2018, so should only be approached with a guide who understands the geologic activity of the area; neighboring Ampato is a fairly straightforward, if strenuous, three-day ascent, and you get safer views of the active Sabancaya from here.

Other mountains of interest near Arequipa include **Ubinas** (5675m), which is the easiest mountain to summit, but check ahead as in recent years it has spewed enough toxic ash at times that it made climbing unfeasible. **Nevado Mismi** (5597m) is a fairly easy three- or four-day climb on the north side of the Cañón del Colca. You can approach it on public transportation and, with a guide, find the lake that is reputedly the source of the Amazon. The highest mountain in southern Peru is the difficult **Nevado Coropuna** (6613m).

ℹ️ Getting There & Away

Nearly every visitor stops through the reserve on a classic tour from Arequipa, or merely passes by on a public bus without any chance of getting out. Car hire is not recommended for inexperienced drivers on the sharp turns here. Book a longer tour or car with driver in Arequipa, if you want to spend any real time here.

Cañón del Colca

It's not just the vastness and depth of the Colca that make it so fantastical, it's the shifts in its mood. There are more scenery changes along the river canyon's 100km passage than there are in most European countries; from the barren steppe of Sibayo, through the ancient terraced farmland of Yanque and Chivay toward the cruising condors riding warm air currents, into the steep-sided canyon proper beyond Cabanaconde that wasn't thoroughly explored until the 1980s. Of course we shouldn't turn a blind eye to the vital statistics. The Colca is the world's second-deepest canyon, a smidgeon shallower than its near neighbor, the Cotahausi, and twice as deep as the more famous Grand Canyon in the US. But, more than that, it is replete with history, culture, ruins, tradition and – rather like Machu Picchu – intangible Peruvian magic.

Upper Canyon

The Upper Canyon (really still a valley at this stage as it heads northeast) has a colder and harsher landscape than the terraced fields around Chivay and Yanque, and is only lightly visited, meaning you can see handsome traditional villages without any crowds. Pierced by a single road which plies northeast through the village of Tuti to Sibayo, the grassy terrain is inhabited by livestock while the still-young river is ideal for river running and trout fishing. **Tuti** is a tourist-lite village situated only 19km northeast of Colca-hub Chivay. With an economy centered on broad-bean cultivation and clothes-making, it is surrounded by some interesting sights all connected by **hiking trails**.

The easiest excursion is to a couple of **caves** in the hills to the north clearly visible from the main road and accessible via a 3.5km grunt uphill from the village. From the same starting point, you can also hike 8km to an old abandoned village dating from the 1600s known colloquially as **Ran Ran** or 'Espinar de Tuti.' Continue beyond Ran Ran and you'll join the trail to the source of the Amazon (p168) on the north side of Nevado Mismi.

At the head of the Upper Canyon after Tuti and sitting at an altitude of 3900m, **Sibayo** is a traditional rural village little touched by tourism. Many of the adobe houses still have old-fashioned straw roofs unseen elsewhere while the diminutive main plaza is framed by the recently restored Iglesia San Juan Bautista. Northeast of the town, a quiet spot by the river has been embellished by a small suspension bridge crossing the Colca called the Puente Colgante Portillo, much used by alpaca herders, plus a lookout, the **Mirador de Largarta**, named for a lizard-shaped mountain up the valley.

Sibayo has a handful of very basic homestays available in traditional houses,

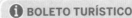

❶ BOLETO TURÍSTICO

To access sites in the Cañón del Colca you need to purchase a *boleto turístico* (tourist ticket; S70) from a booth on the Arequipa road just outside Chivay. If you are taking an organized tour, the cost of the tour usually does not include this additional fee, and you will be asked for this in cash by your guide at the booth. If you are traveling alone, tickets can be purchased on most public buses entering or leaving Chivay, or in the town of Cabanaconde. You will likely also be accosted as you enter the Cruz del Cóndor. Half of the proceeds from this ticket go to Arequipa for general maintenance and conservation of local tourist attractions, while the other half goes to the national agency of tourism.

including **Samana Wasi** (☑ 990-049-5793; Av Mariscal Castilla; r S25).

You can catch a taxi or *colectivo* (shared transportation) from Chivay to Tuti and hike back to Chivay on a well-marked trail alongside the Río Colca. This stretch of the river is popular with rafters.

Combis (minibuses; S10, one hour, hourly) for Sibayo leave from the market area in Chivay. It is possible to hike back southwest down the canyon to Tuti and, ultimately, Chivay from here.

D&M Travel Adventure (p169) on Chivay's Plaza de Armas organizes tours to Sibayo that include walking, fishing, cooking, lunch and an overnight homestay for S100 per person (minimum two people).

Chivay

☑ 054 / POP 7700 / ELEV 3630M

Behold the most accessible and popular segment of the Cañón del Colca, a landscape dominated by agriculture and characterized by some of the most intensely terraced hillsides on earth. The greenery and accessibility has led to this becoming the canyon's busiest region, with the bulk of the business centered in the small town of Chivay. The canyon's nexus, this traditional town has embraced tourism without (so far) losing its high-country identity. Long may it continue!

Around the market area and in the main square are good places to catch a glimpse of the decorative clothing worn by local Colca women. The town itself affords enchanting

ICONIC COLCA CANYON TREKS

Source of the Amazon Trek

For centuries it remained one of the world's greatest mysteries. Humans had landed probes on Mars and split the atom before they got around to finding and – more importantly – agreeing upon the source of the world's most voluminous and (debatably) longest river, the mighty Amazon. Everyone from Alexander von Humboldt to Jean-Michel Cousteau pitched in with their theories (often backed up with expensive expeditions) before the headwaters were finally pinpointed unequivocally in 2007: a fissure in a steep cliff situated at 5170m on the northern slopes of Nevado Mismi, 6992km from the Amazon's river mouth on Brazil's Atlantic coast. Here glacial melt-waters collect in Laguna McInytre before flowing into the Apacheta, Apurímac, Ucayali and Marañón rivers whereupon they form the Amazon proper.

It is surprisingly easy to hike to the Amazon's source (marked inauspiciously by a wooden cross) from the Cañón del Colca. Paths ply north from the villages of Lari or Tuti. It's a two-day out-and-back hike from the latter village, though some people prefer to undertake a three-day route starting in Lari and ending in Tuti, thus making a complete circuit of Nevado Mismi. Alternatively, in the dry season, it is possible to get a 4WD to within 30 minutes' hike of the Apacheta cliff. Carlos Zárate Adventures (p153) in Arequipa organizes memorable guided hikes. Those going it solo should come equipped with maps, food, tents and cold-weather clothing.

El Clásico Trek

Short on time? Confused by the complicated web of Colca paths? Couldn't stand the crowds on the Inca Trail? What you need is 'El Clásico,' the unofficial name for a circular two- to three-day hike that incorporates the best parts of the mid-lower Colca canyon below the Cruz del Cóndor and Cabanaconde.

Start by walking out of Cabanaconde on the Chivay road. At the San Miguel viewpoint (p172), start a long 1200m descent into the canyon on a zigzagging path. Cross the Río Colca via a bridge and enter the village of **San Juan de Chuccho**. Accommodations are available here at the **Casa de Rivelino** (San Juan de Chuccho; r without bathroom S10), with bungalows with warm water and a simple restaurant. Alternatively, you can ascend to the charming village of **Tapay**. Camping or overnight accommodations are available at **Hostal Isidro** – it's owned by a guide and has a shop, satellite phone and rental mules.

On day two descend to the **Cinkumayu Bridge** before ascending to the villages of **Coshñirwa** and **Malata**. The latter has a tiny **Museo Familiar**, basically a typical local home where the owner will explain about the Colca culture. From Malata, descend to the beautiful **Sangalle** oasis (crossing the river again), with more overnight options, before ascending the lung-stretching 4km trail back to Cabanaconde (1200m of ascent).

Though it's easy to do solo, this classic trek can be easily organized with any reputable Arequipa travel agency. In Chivay, Marco Antonio through D&M Travel Adventure charges S100 per person for a tour and one night in Sangalle.

---

views of snowcapped peaks and terraced hillsides, and serves as a logical base from which to explore smaller towns further up the valley.

⦿ Sights

Astronomical Observatory   OBSERVATORY
(Planetario; ☎ 054-53-1020; www.casa-andina. com; Casa Andina, cnr Huayna Cápac & Garcilazo de la Vega; admission S20; ⊙ presentations in English 8pm) No light pollution equals excellent Milky Way vistas. The Casa Andina hotel six blocks southwest of the Plaza de Armas has a tiny observatory which holds nightly sky shows in Spanish and English. The price includes a 30-minute explanation and chance to peer into the telescope. It is open daily but often closes between January and March, when it is hard to catch a night with clear skies.

Activities

La Calera Hot Springs   THERMAL BATHS
(admission S5-15; ⏱5am-6pm) If you've just arrived from Arequipa, you can acclimatize by strolling 3km here and examining the canyon's (surprisingly shallow) slopes alfresco while lying in the naturally heated pools. The setting is idyllic and you'll be entertained by the whooping zipliners as they sail overhead. Free basic padlocked lockers are available.

Colectivos (shared transportation; S1) marked 'Hot Springs' shuttle between Chivay's Plaza de Armas and the springs, leaving when full.

Hiking

Chivay is a good starting point for canyon hikes, both short and long. The view-embellished 7km path to Corporaque on the north side of the canyon starts on the north edge of town. Fork left on the La Calera Hot Springs road, cross the Puente Inca, and follow the fertile fields to the village. Rather than retracing your steps, you can head downhill out of Corporaque past some small ruins and descend to the orange bridge across the Río Colca toward Yanque. From Yanque, on the southern bank, you can catch a passing bus or *colectivo* (shared transportation) for the 7km return to Chivay (or you can walk along the road). For a quicker sojourn rent a mountain bike in Chivay.

To penetrate further west it's possible to continue on up the northern side of the canyon from Corporaque to the villages Ichupampa, Lari and, ultimately, Madrigal. Occasional *combis* (minibuses) run to these villages from the streets around the main market area in Chivay. Another option is to pitch northeast from near the Puente Inca and follow a path along the river to the villages of Tuti and Sibayo.

Zip-lining

Want to dangle terrifyingly over the Río Colca while entertaining bathers relaxing below in La Calera Hot Springs? Then try the canyon's most modern sport – zip-lining. The start point is just past the hot springs, 3.5km from Chivay, but you can organize rides with one of the agencies in town or directly with Colca Zip-Lining (☑95-898-9931; www.colcaziplining.com; 2/4/6 rides S50/100/150; ⏱from 9am Mon-Sat, from 10:30am Sun).

Tours

D&M Travel Adventure   CULTURAL
(☑054-48-0083; Plaza de Armas; ⏱10am-7pm) Runs tours all across the canyon country. It's right next to the police station on Chivay's Plaza de Armas.

🛏 Sleeping

Hostal La Pascana   HOTEL $
(☑054-53-1001; Siglo XX 106; s/d/tr incl breakfast S55/80/110; 🖥) A good old-fashioned crash pad that will probably seem like luxury after a few days hiking in the canyon. Simple rooms have blankets (thank heavens!) and portable heaters, the staff is gracious and there's a small but decent restaurant. It's several notches above the other more modest guesthouses adjacent to the plaza.

⭐**La Casa de Anita**   HOTEL $$
(☑958-911-869; www.facebook.com/hotella casadeanitacolca; Plaza de Armas 785; s/d/tr S80/120/160; @🖥) Just what Chivay needed: a hotel right on the Plaza de Armas where you can rest in clean, spacious rooms with very comfy cotton bedding, spotless modern bathrooms and portable heaters to keep you warm. With the attached restaurant serving good set meals and free tea, and knowledgeable staff (including Chivay's former mayor!), you'd swear you were staying somewhere fancier.

Hotel Colca Inn   HOTEL $$
(☑054-53-1111; www.hotelcolcainn.com; Salaverry 307; s/d/tr incl breakfast S125/158/195; P✳🖥) One of the more comfortable, well-run midrange options in town, for those seeking added creature comforts like heaters and hotel-level service.

⭐**Hotel Pozo del Cielo**   HOTEL $$$
(☑054-34-6547; www.pozodelcielo.com.pe; Calle Huascar s/n; d/tr S320/399; 🖥) 'Heaven's Well,' as the name translates, is all low doorways, high ceilings, weirdly shaped rooms and winding paths. One half expects the seven dwarfs to come marching out. But, surrealism aside, this place works – a functional yet comfortable abode with a boutique-like feel to its individually crafted, heated rooms and fine *'mirador'* restaurant with mountainous views.

⭐**Casa Andina**   BOUTIQUE HOTEL $$$
(☑054-53-1020, 054-53-1022; www.casa-andina. com; cnr Huayna Cápac & Garcilazo de la Vega; d/tr incl breakfast from S288/425; 🖥) The

purposefully rustic rooms here inhabit thatched-roof stone cottages in neatly sculpted grounds. The best features are the unusual extras such as an observatory (p168), oxygen (should you be feeling lightheaded for a lack of it) and nightly culture shows where local musicians and artisans mingle, and a shaman tells fortunes with coca leaves.

✖ Eating & Drinking

Innkas PERUVIAN **$**
(Plaza de Armas 705; mains S12-20; ☺8am-11pm; 🛜) Maybe it's the altitude, but the *lomo saltado* (strips of beef stir-fried with onions, tomatoes, potatoes and chili) here tastes worthy of star chef Gastón Acurio. The sweet service is backed up by even sweeter cakes and great coffee. In an old building with cozy window nooks warmed by modern gas heaters (and boy do you need 'em).

El Balcon De Don Zacarias BUFFET **$$**
(cnr Av 22 de Agosto & Trujillo; buffet S35; ☺11am-3pm; 🛜🍴) There are buffets galore catering to captive tour-group diners but this large restaurant on a corner of the Plaza de Armas stands out for the freshness of dishes such as alpaca steaks and the abundance of meat-free options such as *pastel de papa andina* (potato lasagna) and stuffed eggplant.

The owners have plans to open for dinner also (mains S30).

Aromas Caffee COFFEE
(www.aromascaffee.com; cnr Plaza de Armas & Av 22 de Agosto; coffees S5-9; ☺8am-10pm; 🛜) The tiny cappuccino machine in this diminutive 'three's-a-crowd' cafe takes the conscientious barista about 10 minutes to manipulate, but your Peruvian coffee, when it emerges, is worth the wait.

ℹ Information

Some of the higher-end hotels and a few shops around town exchange US dollars, euros and traveler's checks at unfavorable rates.

Caja Arequipa (Av Salaverry 506) Bank with a 24-hour ATM on the Plaza de Armas.

ℹ Getting There & Away

Chivay is the transportation hub of the canyon region. The bus terminal is a 10- to 15-minute walk from the central Plaza de Armas. There are at least nine daily departures to Arequipa (S13, three hours), the best with Reyna and Andalucia, and four daily with Milagros to Cabanaconde (S8, 2½ hours, from 7:30am), stopping at towns along the southern side of the canyon and at the Cruz del Cóndor.

Combis (minibuses; S2 to S5) and *colectivo* (shared transportation) taxis run to the surrounding villages from street corners in the market area, just north of the main plaza, or you can arrange a private taxi. Mountain bikes in varying condition can be readily hired from travel agencies on the plaza for about S10 a day.

Traveling onward to Cuzco from Chivay is possible on Monday, Wednesday and Friday with the tourist-geared **4M Express** (📞95-974-6330; http://busperu4m.com; Av Siglo XX 118; Chivay to Puno US$50, to Cuzco US$65), departing at 6:45am northwest of Chivay's Plaza de Armas and arriving at Cuzco's Av 28 de Julio at 4:30pm. For those on a budget, some travelers have managed to catch *combis* to Puente Callalli and flag down a bus there, but it's much safer and probably just as fast to return to Arequipa instead.

To get to Puno, it's only slightly cheaper to return to Arequipa but you'll save a few hours by taking a daily direct (stopping for food and photo ops) tourist bus from Chivay with the luxurious 4M Express or comfortable **Rutas del Sur** (📞95-102-4754; chivay@rutasurperu.com; Av 22 de Agosto s/n; Chivay to Puno US$35), all leaving just off Chivay's Plaza de Armas at 1:30pm and arriving at Puno's Plaza de Armas at 7:30pm. If you have taken a tour from Arequipa, let your guide know you don't plan on returning.

It is possible (and cheaper and unsafer) to take a minivan (S7) to outside of Chivay and flag down a regular bus (S15) to Puno, but you might be waiting for over an hour in the cold for a ride.

Yanque

📞054 / POP 2100
Of the Cañón del Colca's dozen or so villages, Yanque, 7km west of Chivay, has the prettiest and liveliest main square, and sports its finest church (from the exterior, at least): the Iglesia de la Inmaculada Concepción, whose ornate baroque doorway has a look that's almost *churrigueresque* (an elaborate and intricately decorated Spanish style).

◉ Sights

Museo Yanque MUSEUM
(📞054-38-2038; www.ucsm.edu.pe/museo-de-yanque; Arequipa 212; admission S7; ☺9am-6pm) This university-run museum is unexpectedly comprehensive for a small village, explaining the culture of the Cañón del Colca in conscientious detail. Exhibits include information on Inca fabrics, cranial deformation,

local agriculture, ecclesial architecture and a mini-exposé on Juanita, the 'Ice Maiden' (p151) now on display in Arequipa. It's opposite the church on the plaza.

Uyo Uyo
RUIN

The remnants of this pre-Inca settlement aren't visible from the road, but can be reached by a half-hour uphill hike from Yanque (or one hour along Carr Coporaque from Coporaque). Giant stone archways and views of patchwork greenery are the reward. Afterwards continue on to a waterfall whose source is the runoff from Nevado Mismi.

Guides are recommended and can be procured at the Colca Lodge. D&M Travel Adventure (p169) on Chivay's Plaza de Armas runs tours (S30, 2:30pm to 5:30pm) to Uyo Uyo.

Baños Chacapi
THERMAL BATHS

(Av Chacapi; admission S10; ☉4am-7pm) These hot springs, a more basic version of La Calera (p169) in Chivay, are a 30-minute walk down to the river from the plaza. The early-bird opening time is mainly for locals, many of whom don't have hot water in their houses.

🛏 Sleeping

Sumaq Huayta Wasi
GUESTHOUSE $

(Casa Bella Flor; ☎929-292-315; www.casabellaflor.com; Arequipa 400; r S35, without bathroom S15; 🛜) A family-run guesthouse in a thatched house set amid a garden in central Yanque. The friendly couple who own it communicate with simple English and plenty of charm. Beds are basic but fine. Excellent home-cooked meals (S15) made with homegrown vegetables offer a chance to help out in the kitchen for a peek into local life.

Casona Plaza Ecolodge
HOTEL $$

(☎054-63-3355; www.casonaplazahoteles.com; Av Collahua Cuadro 7; s/d/tr incl breakfast S182/199/232; 🅿🛜) A fairly upscale option, Casona Plaza Ecolodge has bright, large, heated rooms with safes and cable TV in independent bungalows over spacious grounds where alpacas roam. Unexpected extras include oxygen tanks, horse rental and a travel agency. There's a comprehensive restaurant on-site.

⭐ Colca Lodge
LUXURY HOTEL $$$

(☎054-28-2177; www.colca-lodge.com; Fundo Puye s/n; d/ste incl breakfast S594/735; 🟌🛜🟌) Expensive but utterly romantic, this is the Colca Canyon packaged for the decadent, with artistically manicured grounds spreading majestically aside the rippling Río Colca. Lavish rooms come loaded with dapper dressing gowns, wood-burning stoves, candles, coffee machines and king beds, but the real carrot is the alfresco thermal baths (37°C to 39°C) sculpted into whimsical pools beside the river.

Colca Lodge is just outside of Yanque. For advance reservations, visit the **Arequipa office** (☎054-20-2587, 054-28-2177; Benavides 201, Selva Alegre; ☉8am-1pm & 2-6:30pm Mon-Thu).

ℹ Getting There & Away

Buses from Chivay's bus station stop here on their way to Cabanaconde. Most tours to the Cruz del Cóndor make a brief stop in the plaza. *Colectivos* (shared transportation; S2, 15 minutes) from beside the market depart when full, which is more frequent before 9am and just after 5pm.

Cruz del Cóndor

⭐ Cruz del Cóndor
VIEWPOINT

(Chaq'lla; Carr al Colca; admission with boleto turístico) This famed viewpoint is for many the highlight of their trip to the Cañón del Colca. A large family of Andean condors nests by the rocky outcrop and, with lots of luck, they can occasionally be seen gliding effortlessly on thermal air currents rising from the canyon, swooping low over onlookers' heads. It's a mesmerizing scene, heightened by the spectacular 1200m drop to the river below and the sight of **Nevado Mismi** on the other side of the ravine.

Some much-hyped travel sights are anticlimactic in the raw light of day, but this is not one of them. Recently it has become more difficult to see the condors, mostly due to air pollution, including from travelers' campfires and tour buses. The condors are also less likely to appear on rainy days so it's best to visit during the dry season; they are unlikely to emerge at all in January and February. You won't be alone at the lookout. Expect a couple of hundred people for the 8am 'show' in season.

If you are not part of a tour, large Milagro buses (S8) travel here on the way to Cabanaconde, departing at 7:30am from Chivay's bus station. Afterwards, the only public transportation to Cabanaconde is with the minivan (S5) that transports the women selling *artesanías* (handicrafts) at about

11am, otherwise it's a long 12.5km walk or a long wait until the next large return bus from Cabanaconde materializes.

Cabanaconde

054 / POP 2400 / ELEV 3290M

The narrow lower canyon that runs roughly from Cabanaconde down to Huambo is the Colca at its deepest. Only approximately 20% of Cañón del Colca visitors get as far as ramshackle Cabanaconde (most organized itineraries turn around at the Cruz del Cóndor). For those who make it, the attractions are obvious – fewer people, more authenticity and greater tranquility. Welcome to the *true* canyon experience.

The Colca is significantly deeper here with steep, zigzagging paths tempting the fit and the brave to descend 1200m to the eponymous river. Fruit trees can be found around Tapay and Sangalle, but otherwise the canyon supports no real economic activity. There are no ATMs in Cabanaconde; be sure to bring some cash.

Sights

★ **Mirador de San Miguel**   VIEWPOINT
(Cabanaconde; ⏰24hr) FREE The spectacular views here are a highlight of Cabanaconde, taking in the mountain range, with the villages resembling specks of white dust clinging to its ragged surface, and the canyon below, including the blue-green postage stamp of 'the Oasis.' The descent to the Colca Canyon starts here, but even if you don't make it down, it's worth visiting this *mirador* (lookout).

Walk 15 minutes out of Cabanaconde along the highway; the *mirador* is signposted and next to the snail-like building.

Tours

Local guides can be hired by consulting with your hostel or the *municipalidad* (town hall) in Cabanaconde. The going rate for guides is S30 to S60 per day, depending on the type of trek, season and size of the group. Renting a horse or mule, which is an excellent way to carry water into the canyon and waste out, can be arranged easily for about S60 per day. Ask at Pachamama about guided tours for anywhere in the canyon – highly recommended for safety and not getting lost. D&M Travel Adventure (p169) in Chivay can organize tours

with Marco Antonio, who charges S110 for the 18km of walking and an overnight stay in Sangalle with all food included.

🛌 Sleeping & Eating

Most people eat where they're sleeping, although there are a couple of cheap local restaurants near or on the main plaza.

★ **Pachamama**   HOSTEL $$
(📞054-76-7277, 959-316-322; www.pachamama-home.com; San Pedro 209; d incl breakfast S100, dm/d without bathroom incl breakfast S33/65; @) Pachamama has plenty of room options (doubles, triples and other combos), a pizza oven, a fantastic crepe breakfast and an unexpectedly warm-hearted bar. Run by the ultra-friendly and helpful Ludwig (who's fluent in English), it's also an excellent unofficial information hub for excursions in and around Colca Canyon.

One-way downhill bike excursions from the Cruz del Cóndor to Cabanaconde can be organized for S95, including transportation there with the bikes to see the condors before the ride.

★ **Hotel Kuntur Wassi**   HOTEL $$
(📞054-66-4016; www.arequipacolca.com; Cruz Blanca s/n; s/d/ste incl breakfast S121/140/250; @🛜) As upmarket as Cabanaconde gets, Kuntur Wassi is rather charming. It's built into the hillside above town, with stone bathrooms, trapezoidal windows overlooking the gardens and a nouveau-rustic feel. Suites have enormous bathtubs. There's also a bar, restaurant, library, laundry and foreign-currency exchange. It serves top-notch city-standard food.

Facing the church on the Plaza de Armas, it's on the street on the lower right. There is an office for reservations in central Arequipa at Jerusalén 132B.

La Posada del Conde   HOTEL $$
(📞054-83-0033, 958-310-018; www.facebook.com/laposadadelconde.cabanacondecolcacanyon; San Pedro s/n; d/tr incl breakfast S92/132; 🛜) This small hotel mostly has double rooms, but they are well cared for, with clean bathrooms. The rates often include a welcome *mate* (herbal tea) or pisco sour (Peruvian grape brandy cocktail) in the downstairs restaurant. The same people run a smaller, slightly plusher and pricier lodge up the road.

ⓘ Getting There & Away

Buses for Chivay (S5, 2½ hours) and Arequipa (S17, five hours) via the Cruz del Cóndor leave Cabanaconde from the main plaza (6am, 11am, 11:30am, 1:30pm and 10pm) with three companies, including **Andalucía** (☑ 054-44-5089) and **Reyna** (☑ 054-43-0612; www.reyna.com.pe). Departure times change frequently, though, so check with the bus company office on the main plaza. All buses will stop upon request at towns along the main road on the southern side of the canyon. Morning departures can get full with local farmers toward Chivay, so arrive a little earlier.

The Oasis

At the bottom of the canyon from Cabanaconde, Sangalle lives up to its nickname of 'the Oasis' with mountain walls topped with a blanket of stars at night. Here there are camping grounds and four very similar hostels comprised of basic bungalows, which cost about S15 to S40 per person, some with private bathrooms. Each accommodation has a pool for swimming, most with gardens, such as at **Oasis Paraiso Ecolodge** (☑ 054-79-7485; Sagalle; bungalows per person S40, without bathroom S15; ☒). Check to see which pools currently charge for use, though most are free if you are a guest at their accommodations. There is a local dispute over whether travelers should be charged to use the pools at all.

Activities such as volleyball are available; if you are expecting serenity, know that peace and quiet can be disturbed by music to accompany cocktail sipping. If you arrive late in the day the water will be cold and you are likely to leave before sunshine heats 'the Oasis'; bring warm clothes for the night and be prepared for strong sun on the hike. There's water, food (meals about US$10) and very basic lighting and electricity in Sangalle, but no mobile signal and very weak wi-fi. Do not light campfires as almost half of the trees in the area have been destroyed in this manner, and cart all trash out with you.

OFF THE BEATEN TRACK

TORO MUERTO PETROGLYPHS

A fascinating, mystical site in the high desert, **Toro Muerto** (meaning 'Dead Bull') is named for the herds of livestock that commonly died here from dehydration as they were escorted from the mountains to the coast. A barren hillside is scattered with white volcanic boulders carved with stylized people, animals and birds. Archaeologists have documented more than 5000 such petroglyphs spread over several square kilometers of desert.

Though the cultural origins of this site remain unknown, most archaeologists date the mysterious drawings to the period of Wari domination, about 1200 years ago. Interpretations of the drawings vary widely; a guide can fill you in on some of the most common themes, or you can wander among the boulders yourself and formulate your own elaborate interpretations of the messages these ancient images aim to tell.

Reaching the Toro Muerto petroglyphs can be difficult with public buses and it is much easier to go with a tour company. It is possible to go first to Corire with Transportes del Carpio (S12), or on buses bound for Cotahuasi with Reyna or Cromotex (S30), but you need to ask if they will pass near the petroglyphs on that particular service.

To reach the site by public transportation, take a bus to Corire from Arequipa (S12, three hours, hourly). If you don't want to sleep in Corire, take an early bus (they start as early as 4am). Get off at a gas station just past the sign that denotes the beginning of the town of Corire. From there, you can walk the hot, dusty road about 2km uphill to a checkpoint where visitors must sign in. Otherwise, continue to Corire; from here you can catch a taxi to take you to where the petroglyphs start (from S45 round-trip if the taxi waits).

In Corire, **Hostal Willy** (☑ 054-47-2046; Av Progreso; s/d/tr S40/45/60) has basic accommodations and can provide information on reaching the site. Bring plenty of water, sunblock and insect repellent (as there are lots of mosquitoes en route). Buses return from Corire to Arequipa once an hour, usually leaving at 30 minutes past the hour. The Toro Muerto petroglyphs can also be visited more conveniently on expensive full-day 4WD tours from Arequipa.

The return trek to Cabanaconde is a stiff climb and thirsty work; allow 1½ hours (if super-fit), two to 2½ hours (fit), three to four hours (average fitness) or two hours on a hired mule (S60).

El Valle de los Volcanes

Visitors seeking a destination full of natural wonders and virtually untouched by travelers will rejoice at the remote setting of this broad valley famed for its unusual geological features. The 65km-long Valle de los Volcanes is carpeted with lava flows from which rise many small (up to 200m high) cinder cones, some 80 in total, aligned along a major fissure, with each cone formed from a single eruption.

The valley surrounds the village of **Andagua**, near the snowy summit of Coropuna, a good base for hiking to the top of the perfectly conical twin volcanoes or to a nearby *mirador* (lookout) at 3800m. Also on offer are the 40m-high **Izanquillay Falls**, formed where the Río Andahua runs through a narrow lava canyon to the northeast of town. There are some *chullpas* (funerary towers) at **Soporo**, a two-hour hike to the south of Andagua, passing ruins of pre-Columbian city Antaymarca.

There are several cheap and basic hostels in Andagua, including the recommended **Hostal Volcanes** (☑ 054-83-4065; Calle 15 de Agosto; r S20). Camping is also possible, though you will need plenty of water and sun protection.

❶ Getting There & Away

To get to the valley from Arequipa, take a Reyna bus to Andagua (S45, 10 to 12 hours) which departs from Arequipa around 4pm. Return buses leave Andagua around 2pm. Some tour companies also visit El Valle de los Volcanes as part of expensive tours in 4WDs that may also include visits to the Cañón del Cotahuasi and Chivay.

An alternative way to enter the valley is by hiking from Cabanaconde, crossing the Cañón del Colca, then hiking over a 5500m pass before descending into El Valle de los Volcanes. This trek requires at least five days (plus time for proper acclimatization beforehand), and is best to attempt with an experienced guide and pack mules.

Cañón del Cotahuasi

While the Cañón del Colca has stolen the limelight for many years, it is actually this remote canyon, 200km northwest of Arequipa as the condor flies, that is the deepest known canyon in the world. Cañón del Cotahuasi is around twice the depth of the Grand Canyon, with stretches dropping down below 3500m. While the depths of the ravine are only accessible to experienced river runners, the rest of the fertile valley is rich in striking scenery and trekking opportunities. The canyon also shelters several traditional rural settlements that currently see only a handful of adventurous travelers.

🏃 Activities

Hiking

Cotahuasi is at 2620m above sea level on the southeast side of the canyon. Northeast and further up the canyon are the villages of **Tomepampa** (10km away; elevation 2500m) and **Alca** (20km away; 2660m), which also have basic accommodations. En route you'll pass a couple of **thermal baths** (admission S3).

Buses to the Sipia bridge (S3, one hour) leave the main plaza of Cotahuasi daily at 6:30am, from where you can begin a number of interesting hikes into the deepest parts of the canyon. Forty-five minutes up the trail, the **Sipia waterfall** is formed where the Río Cotahuasi takes an impressive 100m tumble; the viewpoint is from above. Another 1½ hours on a well-trodden track brings you to **Chaupo**, an oasis of towering cacti and remnants of pre-Inca dwellings. Camping is possible. From here a dusty path leads either up to **Velinga** and other remote communities where sleeping accommodations are available, or down to **Mallu**, a patch of verdant farmland at the river's edge where the owner, Ignacio, will allow you to pitch tents and borrow his stove for S12 per night. To get back to Cotahuasi, a return bus leaves the Sipia bridge around 11:30am daily.

Another possible day trip from Cotahuasi is to the hillside community of **Pampamarca**. From here, a two-hour hike up a steep switchbacking trail will bring you to an interesting group of rock formations, where locals have likened shapes in the rocks to mystical figures. A short walk from town brings you to a viewpoint with a view of the rushing 80m-high **Uscune falls**. To get to Pampamarca (S5, two hours), *combis* (minibuses) leave the main square in Cotahuasi twice daily around 7am and 2pm, and return shortly after arriving.

🛏 Sleeping & Eating

Most people eat at their accommodations. There are a few simple restaurants and a market in central Cotahuasi.

Hospedaje Casa Primavera INN **$**
(☏ 054-28-5089; primaverahostal@hotmail.com; Calle Union 112, Tomepampa; d incl breakfast S66, s without bathroom incl breakfast S27) A good find in the tiny village of Tomepampa, this oldish hacienda-style building has a balcony, some floral embellishments and views. There is a variety of simple but clean rooms of different sizes.

Hostal Hatunhuasi GUESTHOUSE **$**
(☏ 054-58-1054, 959-425-769; www.hatunhuasi. com; Centanario 309, Cotahuasi; s/d incl breakfast S35/70) A notch above the other options in town, this friendly guesthouse has plenty of rooms situated around a sunny inner courtyard and has hot water most of the time. Food can be made upon request, and the owners are good sources of hard-to-get information for travelers.

Hotel Vallehermoso HOTEL **$$**
(☏ 054-58-1057; www.hotelvallehermoso.com; Calle Tacna 106, Cotahuasi; s/d/tr incl breakfast S100/145/195) Just what you probably wanted after a dusty 12-hour bus ride, Cotahuasi's poshest joint offers divine comfort in the middle of nowhere while never straying too far from rustic tradition. An on-site restaurant even tries its spin on *cocina novoandina* (New Andean cuisine).

ℹ Getting There & Away

The 420km bus journey from Arequipa to Cotahuasi, much of which is on unpaved roads, takes 10 hours if the going is good. Over three-quarters of the way there, the road summits a 4500m pass between the huge glacier-capped mountains of Coropuna and Solimana (6323m) before dropping down to Cotahuasi. Vicuñas (threatened, wild relatives of alpacas) can also be spotted here running on the high altiplano (Andean plateau). **Reyna** (☏ 054-43-0612; www.reyna.com.pe) operates buses (S30) that leave Arequipa at 7am and 5pm; Cromotex (p164) has a 6pm departure. Buses return to Arequipa from Cotahuasi at around 5pm.

There are hourly *combis* (minibuses) from the Cotahuasi plaza up to Alca (S4, one hour) via Tomepampa (S2, 30 minutes). For Pampamarca, there are two daily buses (S5, two hours) departing in the early morning and again mid-afternoon.

AT A GLANCE

POPULATION
Juliaca: 245,700

BIGGEST FESTIVAL
La Virgen de la
Candelaria (p183)

**BEST ISLAND
HOMESTAY**
Uros Samaraña Uta
Lodge (p192)

**BEST LAKE
TITICACA TOWN**
Luquina Chico (p196)

**BEST LOMO
SALTADO**
La Table del Inca
(p186)

WHEN TO GO
Early Feb
For the marvelous
spectacle of the
festival of La Virgen
de la Candelaria.

Jun–Aug
Winter's dry season
heralds cold, clear
nights and bright
sunny days.

Early Nov
Fiesta Jubilar de
Puno (Puno Week)
celebrates the birth
of Manco Cápac,
the first Inca, in wild
style.

Floating island, Isla Uros (p192)
BERZINA/SHUTTERSTOCK ©

Lake Titicaca

In Andean belief, Titicaca is the birthplace of the sun. Set between Peru and Bolivia, it's the largest lake in South America and the highest navigable body of water in the world. Bright days contrast with bitterly cold nights. Enthralling, deep-blue Lake Titicaca is the unifying, longtime home of highland cultures steeped in the old ways. Pre-Inca Pukara, Tiwanaku and Collas all left their mark on the landscape. Today the region is a mix of crumbling cathedrals, desolate altiplano (Andean plateau) and checkerboard fields backed by rolling hills and high Andean peaks.

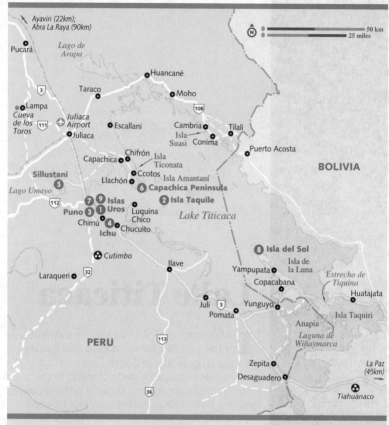

Lake Titicaca Highlights

1 Islas Uros (p192)
Boating the serene blue expanse to mystical islands made entirely of reeds.

2 Isla Taquile (p192)
Drifting along the hills of an island where the men have a talent for knitting and the women for weaving.

3 Puno (p183)
Celebrating festivals with blaring brass bands and crazy costumes in Peru's *capital folklórico*.

4 Ichu (p193) Hiking across farmland and climbing hills to overgrown Inca ruins.

5 Sillustani (p189)
Visiting awe-inspiring funerary towers.

6 Capachica Peninsula (p194) Recharging your batteries in the sunny, somnolent *pueblitos* (tiny towns).

7 Yavari (p183)
Stargazing and sleeping aboard a historic steamship.

8 Isla del Sol (p200) Riding the waters into Bolivia to explore this legendary island.

9 Homestays (p192)
Staying with a local family and learning about lake culture.

Juliaca

♫ 051 / POP 245,700 / ELEV 3826M

The region's only commercial airport makes Juliaca, the largest city on the altiplano, an unavoidable transit hub. The city bustles with commerce (and contraband) due to its handy location near the Bolivian border. Daytime muggings and drunks on the street are not uncommon. Since Juliaca has little to offer travelers, it is advisable to while away some hours in nearby Lampa or move on to Puno.

Hotels, restaurants, *casas de cambio* (foreign-exchange bureaus) and internet cafes abound along San Román, near Plaza Bolognesi. ATMs and banks are nearby on Nuñez.

An excellent, if pricey, choice, the towering **Royal Inn Hotel** (☑ 051-32-1561; www.royalinnhoteles.com; San Román 158; s/d/tr incl breakfast S315/330/420) boasts well-maintained, modern rooms with hot showers, heating and cable TV, plus one of Juliaca's best restaurants with an extensive buffet breakfast (mains from S20).

❶ Getting There & Away

AIR

The **airport** (Inca Manco Capac International Airport, JUL; ☑ 051-32-4248) is 2km west of town. **LAN** (☑ 051-32-2228; San Roman 125; ⊗ office 8am-7pm Mon-Fri, to 4pm Sat) has daily flights to/from Lima, Arequipa and Cuzco. **Avianca** (☑ 051-827-4951; www.avianca.com; Centro Comercial Real Plaza, Tumbes 391, Local LC-105; ⊗ 11am-8pm Mon-Fri, to 6pm Sat & Sun) also flies to Lima.

Official airport taxis go to Puno (S80) and Juliaca (S15). A cheaper option is a *colectivo* (shared transportation; S15), a bus shuttle that goes direct to Puno and drops passengers at their hotels. For the return journey, most hotels in Puno can arrange trips in these minivans.

BUS & TAXI

The **Terminal Terrestre** (San Martín at Av Miraflores) houses long-distance bus companies. Buses leave for Cuzco every two hours from 5am to 11pm, and for Arequipa every two hours from 2:30am to 11:30pm.

Buses to the coast leave from within walking distance of Plaza Bolognesi, on and around San Martín, over the railway tracks; *combis* (minibuses) to Puno leave from Plaza Bolognesi.

Julsa (☑ 051-32-6602, 051-33-1952; www.fb.me/julsaperu) has the most frequent departures to Arequipa; **Power** (☑ 051-32-1952; www.expresopower.com.pe; terminal terrestre, shop C5) has the most frequent to Cuzco. **Civa** (☑ 051-365-882; www.civa.com.pe; Terminal Zonal) and **San Cristobal** run to Lima and Arequipa.

Sur Oriente has a daily bus to Tacna at 7pm. More centrally located and of high quality, **San Martín** and other companies along Tumbes between Moquegua and Piérola go to Tacna (S50 to S60, nine hours, four daily) via Moquegua.

Combis to Puno (S3.50, 50 minutes) leave from Plaza Bolognesi when full. *Combis* for Lampa (S2.50, 30 minutes) leave from Huáscar when full. *Combis* to Huancané (S3.50, one hour) leave every 15 minutes from Ballón and Sucre, about

four blocks east of Apurímac and 1½ blocks north of Lambayeque. *Combis* to Capachica (S4, 1½ hours) leave from the Terminal Zonal (Av Tacna, cuadra 11). *Combis* to Escallani (S3.50, 1½ hours), via an incredibly scenic, unpaved back road, leave from the corner of Cahuide and Gonzáles Prada. All of these terminals are a S4 *mototaxi* (three-wheeled motorcycle rickshaw taxi) ride from the center of town.

JULIACA BUSES

Prices are general estimates for normal/luxury buses.

DESTINATION	COST (S)	DURATION (HR)
Arequipa.	15/50	5
Cuzco	20/40	6-7
Lima	80/170	20
Puno	3.50 (normal only)	1
Tacna	50/60	8-9

❶ Getting Around

Mototaxi is the best option for getting around. A ride to local destinations, including bus terminals, will cost about S4. Bus line 1B cruises around town and down Calle 2 de Mayo before heading to the airport (S0.70).

Lampa

☑ 051 / POP 2500 / ELEV 3860M

This charming little town, 36km northwest of Juliaca, is known as La Ciudad Rosada (the Pink City) for its dusty, pink-colored buildings. A significant commercial center in colonial days, it still shows a strong Spanish influence. It's an excellent place to kill a few hours before flying out of Juliaca, or to spend a quiet night.

◉ Sights

Just out of town is a pretty colonial **bridge**, and about 4km west is **Cueva de los Toros**, a bull-shaped cave with prehistoric carvings of llamas and other animals. The cave is on the right-hand side of the road heading west. Its entrance is part of a large, distinctive rock formation. En route you'll see several *chullpas* (funerary towers), not unlike the ones at Sillustani and Cutimbo.

★**Iglesia de Santiago Apostol**　CHURCH
(Plaza de Armas, Lampa; tour S10; ⊗ 9am-12:30pm & 2-4pm) Worth seeing and the pride of locals, this lime-mortar church includes fascinating features, such as a life-sized sculpture of

The Last Supper; Santiago (St James) atop a real stuffed horse, returning from the dead to trample the Moors; creepy catacombs; secret tunnels; a domed tomb topped by a wonderful copy of Michelangelo's *Pietà*; and hundreds of skeletons arranged in a ghoulishly decorative skull-and-crossbones pattern. It truly has to be seen to be believed. Excellent Spanish-speaking guides are on hand daily.

Museo Kampaq   MUSEUM
(📞951-820-085; cnr Ayacucho & Ugarte; suggested donation S5; ⊗8am-6pm Mon-Fri) Staff at the shop opposite this museum, two blocks west of the Plaza de Armas, will give you a Spanish-language guided tour of the museum's small but significant collection. It includes pre-Inca ceramics and monoliths, plus one mummy. They may also show you a unique vase inscribed with the sacred cosmology of the Incas.

Lampa Municipalidad   NOTABLE BUILDING
(⊗8am-4pm Mon-Fri) **FREE** In the small square beside the Plaza de Armas, the town hall is recognizable by its murals depicting Lampa's history – past, present and future. Inside there's a gorgeous courtyard, a replica of the *Pietà* (a second one is in the church) and a museum honoring noted Lampa-born painter Víctor Humareda (1920–86).

🛏 Sleeping

Hospedaje Estrella   HOSTAL **$**
(Municipalidad 540; s/d/tr S45/65/100) The homely rooms here have mismatched bedding that looks like somebody raided the family linen cabinet, but everything is comfortable and clean. Just two blocks southeast of the main church, the views from the upper rooms are absorbing, which is good because there's no wi-fi.

🛈 Getting There & Away

Combis (minibuses) for Lampa (S2.50, 30 minutes) leave when full from Huáscar (five blocks north of Plaza Bolognesi along San Romàn) in Juliaca. If you have time to kill after checking in at Juliaca airport, get a taxi to drop you off in Lampa (S8, 35 minutes). There is no direct public transportation to/from Puno.

Pucará

📞 051 / POP 675 / ELEV 3860M
More than 60km northwest of Juliaca, the sleepy village of Pucará is famous for its cele-

brations of **La Virgen del Carmen** (The Virgin of Carmen; Plaza de Armas), on July 16, and its earth-colored pottery – including the ceramic *toritos* (bulls) often seen perched on the roofs of Andean houses for good luck. Local workshops are open to the public and offer ceramics classes.

🅞 Sights

Kalasaya   RUINS
(Complejo Arqueológico de Pucará; admission S10; ⊗9am-4pm) These pre-Inca ruins are spread out across a large area above the town and consist of nine pyramid-like structures, the largest of which gives the site its name. Kalasaya is a short way up Lima, west of the main plaza. Just S10 gets you into Kalasaya and the **Museo Lítico Pucará** (⊗8:30am-5pm Tue-Sun) at the Plaza de Armas, though there's nobody to check your ticket at the ruin.

The Kalasaya pyramid is constructed from stone monoliths and human head sculptures jut out from its walls. Other carved creatures include serpents and pumas. The center was used for offerings to the gods and Pucará culture became the central force in the Lake Titicaca region by 200 BC.

🛈 Getting There & Away

Buses to Juliaca (S3.50, one hour) run from 6am to 8pm from Jr 2 de Mayo.

Puno

📞 051 / POP 149,100 / ELEV 3830M
With a regal plaza, concrete-block buildings and crumbling bricks that blend into the hills, Puno has its share of both grit and cheer. It serves as the jumping-off point for Lake Titicaca and is a convenient stop for those traveling between Cuzco and La Paz. But it may just capture your heart with its own rackety charm.

Puno is known as Peru's *capital folklórica* (folkloric capital) – its Virgen de la Candelaria (p183) parades are televised across the nation – and the associated drinking is the stuff of legend. Its urban center can feel contaminated and cold. But Puno's people are upbeat, cheeky and ready to drop everything if there's a good time to be had.

As a commercial (and contraband) hub, its colonial and naval history can be glimpsed in its spots of old architecture, the

Puno

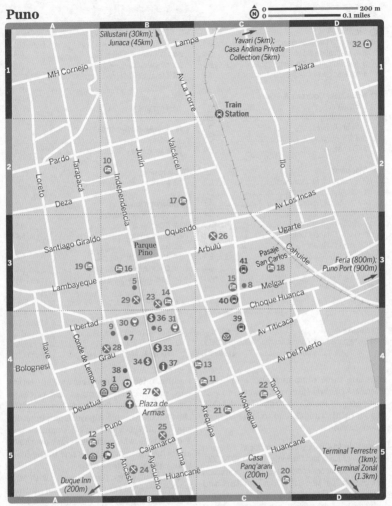

colorful traditional dress worn by many inhabitants and the scores of young cadets in the streets.

◎ Sights

Catedral de Puno CHURCH
(Ayacucho at Deustua; ⊙8am-noon & 3-6pm) FREE Puno's baroque cathedral, on the western flank of the Plaza de Armas, was completed in 1757. The interior is more spartan than you'd expect from the well-sculpted facade, except for the silver-plated altar, which, following a 1964 visit by Pope Paul VI, has a Vatican flag placed to its right.

Casa del Corregidor HISTORIC BUILDING
(☑051-35-1921; www.casadelcorregidor.pe; Deustua 576; ⊙9am-9pm Mon-Sat) FREE An attraction in its own right, this 17th-century house is one of Puno's oldest residences. A former community center, it now houses a small fair-trade arts-and-crafts store and a cafe.

Museo Carlos Dreyer MUSEUM
(Conde de Lemos 289; admission with English-speaking guide S15; ⊙9am-7pm Mon-Fri, to 1pm Sat) This small museum houses a fascinating collection of Puno-related archaeological artifacts and art from pre-Inca, Inca, colonial and the Republic periods. Upstairs

Puno

there are three mummies and a full-scale fiberglass *chullpa* (funerary tower).

It's around the corner from Casa del Corregidor (p181). Guides tend to leave an hour before closing.

Museo de la Coca y Costumbres   MUSEUM
(Museum of Coca and Customs; ☑ 051-977-0360; www.museodelacoca.com; Ilave 581; admission S10; ☺ 9am-7pm Mon-Sat, 3-7pm Sun) Tiny and quirky, this museum offers lots of interesting information – historical, medicinal, cultural – about the coca plant and its many uses. Presentation isn't that interesting, though: reams of text (in English only) are stuck to the wall and interspersed with photographs and old Coca-Cola ads. The display of traditional costumes is what makes a visit here worthwhile.

Though the relation between traditional dress and coca is unfathomable, it's a boon for making sense of the costumes worn in street parades.

☞ Tours

It pays to shop around for a tour operator. Agencies abound and competition is fierce, leading to touting in streets and bus terminals, undeliverable promises, and prices so low as to undercut fair wages. Several of the cheaper tour agencies have reputations for ripping off the islanders of Amantaní and Taquile, with whom travelers stay overnight and whose living culture is one of the main selling points of these tours.

Island-hopping tours, even with the better agencies, are often disappointing: formulaic, lifeless and inflexible, the inevitable result of sheer numbers and repetition. If you only have a day or two though, a reputable tour can give a good taster and insight you might not otherwise get. If you have time, seeing the islands independently is recommended – you can wander around freely and spend longer in the places you like.

Edgar Adventures   CULTURAL
(☑ 051-35-3444; www.edgaradventures.com; Lima 328; ☺ office 7am-8pm) Longtime agency with positive community involvement. More unusual activities include kayaking on Lake Titicaca and visiting remote areas.

SWEET STEAMSHIP DREAMS

The oldest steamship on Lake Titicaca, the famed Yavari (📞 051-36-9329; www.yavari.org; Sesqui Centenario 962; admission by donation; ⏱ 8am-1pm & 3-5:30pm) has turned from British gunship to a museum and recommended bed and breakfast, with bunk-bed lodging and attentive service under the stewardship of its captain. And no, you don't have to be a navy buff reflecting on Titicaca. The Yavari is moored behind the Sonesta Posada Hotel del Inca, about 5km from the center of Puno. It's probably the most tranquil spot in Puno.

Its passage here was not easy. In 1862 the Yavari and its sister ship, the Yapura, were built in Birmingham and shipped as parts around Cape Horn to Arica (now in northern Chile), moved by train to Tacna, and finally hauled by mule over the Andes to Puno. The incredible undertaking took six years.

After its assembly, the Yavari was launched on Christmas Day 1870. The Yapura was later renamed the BAP Puno and became a Peruvian Navy medical ship; it can still be seen in Puno. Both ships had coal-powered steam engines, but due to a shortage of coal, they were fueled with dried llama dung.

After long years of service, the ship was decommissioned by the Peruvian navy and the hull was left to rust on the lakeshore. In 1982, Englishwoman Meriel Larken visited the forgotten boat and decided to attempt to save this piece of Peruvian history. The Yavari Project was formed to buy and restore the vessel.

The devoted crew happily gives guided tours. With prior notice, enthusiasts may even be able to see the engine fired up. Now with a restored engine, the Yavari motors across the lake seven times a year – though you will have to find out for yourself if it's still powered by llama dung.

Leon Tours
BOATING

(📞 051-35-2771; www.peru-titicaca.com; Ayacucho 152, Puno) There are no passenger ferries across the lake from Puno to Bolivia, but Leon Tours offers a 13-hour trip to La Paz on a high-class hydrofoil, visiting Isla del Sol and other sights along the way. Two- and three-day sightseeing tours are also available. In La Paz, its operator is Crillon Tours (📞 Bolivia 591-2-2337533; www.titicaca.com; Av Camacho 1223, La Paz, Bolivia; ⏱ 9am-noon & 2.30-7pm Mon-Sat).

Las Balsas Tours
BOATING

(📞 051-36-4362; www.balsastours.com; Lima 419, 2nd fl, No 213; ⏱ office 9am-noon & 3-8pm Mon-Sat) Offers classic tours on a daily basis.

🎎 Festivals & Events

Many regional holidays and fiestas are celebrated for several days before and after the actual day. Most festivals also feature traditional music and dancing, as well as merry mayhem of all sorts.

El Día de Los Reyes
RELIGIOUS

(Epiphany; ⏱ Jan 6) This celebrates the day that the three wise men visited baby Jesus. Outside every church, and in the Plaza de Armas, you will find women in traditional dress selling dolls for children to lay on church altars at mass.

La Virgen de la Candelaria
RELIGIOUS

(Candlemas; ⏱ Feb 2-18) The region's most spectacular festival spreads out for several days around the actual date (Candlemas), depending upon which day of the week Candlemas falls. If it falls between Sunday and Tuesday, things get underway the previous Saturday; if it occurs between Wednesday and Friday, celebrations will get going the following Saturday.

Fiesta de San Juan
FESTIVAL

(Feast of St John the Baptist; ⏱ Mar 8) St John is the patron saint of the ill and of hospitals and on this feast day his image is carried around the main streets of Puno accompanied by prayers and songs for good health. There is plenty of food, fireworks and music.

Alasitas
FESTIVAL

(⏱ May 2-8) With the blessing of miniature objects, such as cars or houses, suppliants pray that the real thing will be obtained in the coming year. Features a miniature handicrafts fair in Puno on May 2.

Fiesta Jubilar de Puno
CULTURAL

(Puno Week; ⏱ Nov) A huge celebration marking the legendary birth of Manco Cápac, the first Inca. Events are held the first week of November, centered on El Aniversario de Puno (Puno Day; November 5).

🛏 Sleeping

Puma Hostel Puno
HOSTEL $

(☎ 051-36-5300; Cajamarca 154; dm/d/tr incl breakfast S23/47/60; 🛜) The fake 'wood paneling' might make Puma resemble a 1980s business hotel with family beds thrown in, but it's clean, comfortable and excellent value for a hostel near the plaza.

Inka's Rest
HOSTEL $

(☎ 051-36-8720; www.fb.me/inkasrestpuno; Pasaje San Carlos 158; dm/d incl breakfast S16.50/60; @🛜) Tucked into a small alley, this hostel earns high marks for service. Very clean, it features bunks with down duvets, and attractive old tile and parquet floors. There's a cute breakfast area as well as a guest kitchen and huge flat-screen TV. Private rooms are less attractive. There is intercom entry; take a taxi if arriving at night.

Duque Inn
HOSTEL $

(☎ 051-20-5014; Ayaviri 152; s/tr with bathroom S33/99, d without bathroom S/66) Cordial but kooky, this budget lodging is spruced up with satin bedspreads and chandeliers. Archaeologist owner Ricardo Conde is eccentric gold, offering free tours. It's a steal for budget travelers and serious trekkers. From the cathedral, take Ilave (direction Cajamarca) five blocks, then turn right into Ayaviri.

When you see the endless hill, you may want to splurge on taxis.

⭐ Casa Panq'arani
B&B $$

(☎ 051-36-4892, 951-677-005; www.casapanqarani.com; Jr Arequipa 1086; s/tw/d incl breakfast S80/135/145; 🛜) This delightful traditional Puno home has a flower-filled courtyard and inviting rooms lining a 2nd-floor balcony. But the real draw is the sincere hospitality of owners Edgar and Consuelo. Rooms are spacious, with comfortable beds with crocheted bedspreads and fresh flowers. There are ample sunny spots for lounging. Don't miss Consuelo's gourmet altiplano cooking (meals S35 with advance request).

⭐ Intiqa Hotel
HOTEL $$

(☎ 051-36-6900; www.intiqahotel.com; Tarapacá 272; d/tr incl breakfast S247/313; 🛜) Yes, a midrange Puno hotel with a sense of style. The 33 large, heated rooms feature snug duvets and earth tones, extra pillows, desks, flatscreen TVs and a safe box. The elevator is something of a rarity in Puno. Offers free pickups from the Terminal Terrestre. Credit cards are accepted.

Xima Puno Hotel
BOUTIQUE HOTEL $$

(☎ 051-36-5525; www.ximahotels.com; Av Chulluni 195; s/d incl breakfast S189/212; 🅿🛜) This sophisticated hotel has such incredible lake

---

FIESTAS & FOLKLORE AROUND LAKE TITICACA

The folkloric capital of Peru, Puno boasts as many as 300 traditional dances and celebrates numerous fiestas throughout the year. Although dances often occur during celebrations of Catholic feast days, many have their roots in precolonial celebrations, usually tied in with the agricultural calendar. The dazzlingly ornate and imaginative costumes worn on these occasions are often worth more than an entire household's everyday clothes. Styles range from strikingly grotesque masks and animal costumes to glittering sequined uniforms.

Accompanying music uses a host of instruments, from Spanish-influenced brass and string instruments to percussion and wind instruments that have changed little since Inca times. These traditional instruments include *tinyas* (wooden hand drums) and *wankaras* (larger drums formerly used in battle), plus a chorus of *zampoñas* (panpipes), which range from tiny, high-pitched instruments to huge bass panpipes almost as tall as the musician. Keep an eye out for *flautas* (flutes): from simple bamboo pennywhistles called *quenas* to large blocks of hollowed-out wood. The most esoteric is the *piruru*, which is traditionally carved from the wing bone of an Andean condor.

Seeing street fiestas can be planned, but it's often simply a matter of luck. Some celebrations are localized to one town, whilst the whole region lets loose for others. Ask at the tourist office in Puno about any fiestas in the surrounding area while you're in town. The festivals we list are particularly important in the Lake Titicaca region, but many countrywide fiestas are celebrated here, too.

If you plan to visit during a festival, either make reservations in advance or show up a few days early, and expect to pay premium rates for lodgings.

views from every room that you might be tempted to just stay in. Why not when the spacious, neutral-toned rooms are so sleek, with splashes of color?

Posada Luna Azul HOTEL **$$**
(⌨ 951-590-835; www.posadalunaazul.com; Cajamarca 242; s/d incl breakfast S100/128; 🛜) The 'blue moon' name might conjure images of a cozy, tranquil night's rest, and this small hotel is tucked far enough away from the noise that it's true. The petite, clean, carpeted rooms have flat-screen TVs and good heaters, making them impressively warm all night, and the showers are strong and hot. Warmth at last in Puno.

Mosoq Inn HOTEL **$$**
(⌨ 051-36-7518; www.mosoqinnperu.com; Jr Moquegua 673; s/d/tr incl breakfast S175/214/272; @🛜) This modern hotel features 15 rooms distributed across three stories. High-quality mattresses ensure sound sleeping in ample, tangerine-hued rooms. There are also big closets, cable TV and space heaters, plus it has a business center.

Casona Plaza Hotel HOTEL **$$**
(⌨ 051-36-5614; www.casonaplazahoteles.com; Jr Puno 280; d/ste incl breakfast from S135/297; @🛜) This well-run, central hotel with 64 rooms is one of the largest in Puno, but is often full. All rooms are modern and neutral, and the bathrooms are great. They offer *matrimoniales* (matrimonial suites) especially for lovers – most are big enough to dance the *marinera* (Peru's national dance) between the bed and the lounge suite.

Hostal Pukara HOTEL **$$**
(⌨ 051-368-448; www.pukaradeltitikaka.com; Libertad 328; s/d incl breakfast S60/116; @🛜) Bright and cheery, Pukara leaves no corner undecorated, with an eye-catching four-story relief, murals and other touches. Rooms all have cable TV, phones and heating. Street-side rooms can be noisy all night. The buffet breakfast is served in a glass-covered rooftop cafe with a great view.

Hotel El Buho HOTEL **$$**
(⌨ 051-36-6122; www.hotelbuho.com; Lambayeque 144; s/d/tr incl breakfast S181/231/297; @🛜) This quiet hotel features nice (but somewhat dull) rooms with paneled walls and carpets. The staff is helpful and there's a tour agency and good restaurant on-site. Booking on its website can be 25% cheaper.

Conde de Lemos Inn HOTEL **$$**
(⌨ 051-36-9898; www.condelemosinn.com; Puno 675-681; s/d/tr incl breakfast S150/197/214; @🛜) Housed in a startlingly jagged, glass-fronted ziggurat on the Plaza de Armas, this small hotel is recommended by many travelers for its personable staff and high standards. Ask for a corner room with balcony.

Hotel Casona Colón Inn HOTEL **$$**
(⌨ 051-35-1432; www.coloninn.com; Tacna 290 at Libertad; d/tw/tr incl breakfast S150/180/225; @🛜) An elegant European-owned *casona* (large house) with helpful staff. Part of its charm is the Republican-era building with a covered courtyard, and decorated with Cuzco-school paintings and frescos. The on-site restaurant specializes in Belgian and French cuisine; reservations are recommended. Rooms are smallish but with all amenities, including portable heaters and safes, while shared spaces are sumptuously atmospheric.

Hotel Italia HOTEL **$$**
(⌨ 051-36-7706; www.hotelitaliaperu.com; Valcárcel 122; s/d/tr incl breakfast S120/160/210; @🛜) Snug rooms have parquet floors, cable TV, hot showers and heating but vary in quality at this large, well-established spot. There are charming touches, with antique telephones and long-serving staff who are cordial and well-presented. The delicious buffet breakfast includes salty black olives and Puno's own triangular anise bread. Credit cards are accepted.

Hostal La Hacienda HOTEL **$$**
(⌨ 051-35-6109; www.hhp.com.pe; Deustua 297; d/tr S200/332; @🛜) This colonial-style hotel has lovely, airy common spaces, a mind-bending *Vertigo*-style spiral staircase and a 6th-floor dining room with panoramic views. After all that, rooms are a bit generic, but they're warm and comfortable with cable TV and phones. Some have bathtubs.

Casa Andina Premium LUXURY HOTEL **$$$**
(⌨ 051-36-3992; www.casa-andina.com; Av Sesqui Centenario 1970; d incl breakfast from S538; @🛜) On the outskirts of Puno, with lovely lakeside ambience, this upmarket hotel features 46 rooms, gardens and a gourmet restaurant. It even has its own train stop for those coming from Cuzco. The look is rustic chic. Rooms feature impeccable white linens and subtle decor, some with stone fireplaces, and all with oxygen to help acclimatize.

TITILAKA – LUXURY ON TITICACA

Secluded on the rugged shoreline of Lake Titicaca, one hour south of Puno, luxury hotel **Titilaka** (☑ 1-700-5111; www.titilaka.pe; Lake Titicaca; s/d with full board from US$777/1202; @ 🛜) is a destination in itself. Huge picture windows drink in the serene landscapes in every direction. Rooms sport king-sized beds warmed by hot-water bottles, with deep tubs, phone docks and window-ledge seating. There are games for kids, a spa and gourmet restaurant.

The look is whimsical Euro-Andino, with a palette that ranges from neutral to flirty (think blushing rose and purple). Touches of exquisite folk art combine with the sculptures and black-and-white photography of well-known Peruvian artists. The staff is trained to please.

Private guided tours give guests an intimate view of the islands. While most guests go for the three-day packages, the nightly rate also includes full board and local excursions, such as walks and kayaking.

Casa Andina Standard   HOTEL $$$
(☑ 051-213-9739; www.casa-andina.com; Independencia 143; d/tr incl breakfast S307/392; @ 🛜) The classic version of this fashionable Peruvian chain features snappy service and 50 tasteful rooms with muted colors, decorated with Andean folk motifs. Rooms feature heating, safes, blackout curtains and flat-screen TVs. Guests also get free oxygen and *mate de coca* (coca-leaf tea) to help acclimate. A cozy dining space serves pizzas and soups post-excursion.

✗ Eating

Most restaurants geared toward travelers are on Lima. For a cheap snack, try *api* (hot, sweet corn juice) – a serious comfort food found in several places on Calle Oquendo between Parque Pino and the market. Order it with a paper-thin, wickedly delicious envelope of deep-fried dough.

Pushka   PERUVIAN $
(Grau 338; mains S8-15 ménus S8; 🖾) It's hard to imagine that just a couple blocks from Puno's busy tourist street there is a large beer-garden-style restaurant. Yet here it is, with kid's play equipment, astroturf and families enjoying excellent-value *ménus* (set meals) of Peruvian dishes that are of the quality you'll find back on Calle Lima, but without the frills.

La Choza de Oscar   CHICKEN $
(☑ 051-35-1199; www.lachozadeoscar.com; Libertad 354; chicken plate S11; ⏰ 2-10pm Mon-Sat) Peruvian *pollo a la brasa* (roast chicken) has a spiced, crispy exterior and this eatery at the back of a restaurant creates wonders. Vegetarians can opt for a popular nightly salad buffet, and you can even sit in the

main restaurant and enjoy the dance show (7.30pm to 9pm), but tips are encouraged.

Mercado Central   MARKET $
(Oquendo s/n; ⏰ 7am-9.30pm) For self-catering, head to the Mercado Central for fresh fruit, nuts and other produce, but be wary of pickpockets.

⭐ **La Table del Inca**   FUSION $$
(☑ 994-659-357; www.fb.me/latabledelinca; Ancash 239; mains S26-40, 3 courses with wine S80; ⏰ noon-2pm & 6-9.30pm Mon-Thu, 6-9.30pm Sat & Sun; 🛜) If you need a reason to dress up, this fusion restaurant, a little away from the noise, shows off paintings by local artists on its walls, with colorful plating. Peruvian dishes like *lomo saltado* (stir-fried beef with potatoes and chili) hold their own against Euro-Peruvian twists such as quinoa risotto, alpaca carpaccio with *huacatay* (a local aromatic herb), and French desserts.

Reservations are recommended.

⭐ **Mojsa**   PERUVIAN $$
(☑ 051-36-3182; Lima 635; mains S22-30; ⏰ noon-9.30pm; 🛜 🖾) The go-to place for locals and travelers alike, Mojsa lives up to its name, which is Aymara for 'delicious.' Overlooking the plaza, it has a thoughtful range of Peruvian and international food, including innovative trout dishes and a design-your-own salad option. All meals start with fresh bread and a bowl of local olives. In the evening crisp brick-oven pizzas are on offer.

Mareas Ceviche y Más   CEVICHE $$
(www.fb.me/mareassocialpage; Cajamarca 448; mains S13-35; ⏰ 9am-4pm; 🛜) There are dozens of ways to do ceviche and seafood in this

family-filled courtyard restaurant. If you can't decide between seafood pasta, squid fried rice, trout ceviche or ceviche *palteado* (with avocado), try a *combinado* (set combo) of ceviche, *chaufa* (fried rice) and battered fried fish.

Tulipans   PIZZA $$

(☑ 051-35-1796; Lima 394; mains S15-30, menús S20; ◷ 10am-10pm; ☎) Highly recommended for its yummy sandwiches, big plates of meat and piled-high vegetables, this cozy spot is warmed by the pizza oven in the corner. It also has a selection of South American wines. The courtyard patio is attractive for warm days – whenever those happen! Pizzas are only available at night. Tulipans is inside La Casona Parodi.

Balcones de Puno   PERUVIAN $$

(☑ 051-36-5300; Libertad 354; mains S18-35; ◷ 9am-10pm Mon-Sat) Dinner-show venue with traditional local food. The nightly show (7:30pm to 9pm) stands out for its quality and sincerity – no panpipe butchering of 'El Cóndor Pasa' here. Save room for dessert, a major focus of dining here. Reserve ahead for weekends.

Colors   FUSION $$

(☑ 051-36-9254; www.fb.me/raffoalavez; Lima 342; mains S16-30, menús S25; ◷ 10am-10pm; ☎) A couch-cafe with free wi-fi, good brownies and board games. Colors also caters to travelers with its lounge-bar looks and fusion food – set menus not only include trout and alpaca but also curries and falafel, not found elsewhere nearby.

La Casa del Corregidor   CAFE $$

(http://cafebar.casadelcorregidor.pe; Deustua 576; mains S24-34, drinks S6.50-14; ◷ 9am-10pm Mon-Sat; ☎☑) It's just off the plaza but feels like a world and era away. Vinyl records of Peru's yesteryear decorate the walls, while board games and clay teapots are ready to adorn the tables, and a happy yellow courtyard shows off the historical building. Try the good fresh infusions or alpaca BBQ sticks.

🍷 Drinking & Nightlife

Central Puno's nightlife is geared toward tourists, with lively bars scattered around the bright lights on Lima (where touts hand out free-drink coupons), the Plaza de Armas and Parque Pino, where live bands sometimes play on weekend evenings.

Dómino Club   CLUB

(www.fb.me/dominoclubdiscoteca; Libertad 443, near Lima; admission S10; ◷ 8pm-late Mon-Sat) If you want to see how young locals get down, this is the place. Multileveled mayhem, a karaoke lounge, a dance floor that explodes to salsa, *reggaetón* (blending Puerto Rican *bomba*, dancehall and hip-hop) and rock, and *cuba libre* (rum and cola) by the jug: it all adds up to a great night, but it's not for the faint-hearted.

Kamizaraky Rock Pub   PUB

(Grau 158; ◷ 5pm-midnight) With a classic-rock soundtrack, grungy cool bartenders, cocktails, pizzas and liquor-infused coffee drinks essential for staying warm during Puno's bone-chilling nights,this may be a hard place to leave.

🛍 Shopping

Artesanías (handicrafts, from musical instruments and jewelry to scale models of reed islands), wool and alpaca sweaters, and other typical tourist goods are sold in every second shop in the town center. The prices are a bit better at the Feria at the port.

The hypermarket on Los Incas sells not only food but also pisco, electronics and home needs.

Feria   ARTS & CRAFTS

(Av Costanera, Puno port; ◷ 7am-5pm) This craft market sells llama toys, rugs, alpaca sweaters, masks from Puno's La Virgen de la Candelaria festival and other handicrafts you'll see elsewhere in town and on the islands, but at prices more open to haggling. The dozens of nearly identical stalls are at the port entrance, at the end of Av Del Puerto.

Mercado Bellavista   MARKET

(Av El Sol; ◷ 9am-5pm) A market selling household goods and clothes. Watch out for pickpockets.

ℹ Information

EMERGENCY

Policía de Turismo (Tourist Police; ☑ 051-35-3988; Deustua 558; ◷ 24hr) There is a police officer on duty in the Terminal Terrestre – ask around if you need assistance.

IMMIGRATION

Bolivian Consulate (☑ 051-20-5400; www.consuladopuno.simplesite.com; Cajamarca 664; ◷ 8am-4pm Mon-Fri) Can help issue visas for Bolivia.

Oficina de Migraciónes (Immigration Office; ☑ 051-35-7103; www.migraciones.gob.pe;

ETHICAL COMMUNITY TOURISM

There are dozens of tour agencies in Puno, in many cases offering the same thing at wildly different prices. The main difference for this discrepancy is the amount of money the agency pays to the host families. Nearly all the cheaper agencies (and some of the more expensive ones) pay little more than the cost of the visitors' meals. While it's difficult to find out for certain which agencies fairly compensate the host families, the following tips can help you contribute to a better experience.

➡ Use one of our recommended agencies or one recommended by fellow travelers.

➡ Check that your guide rotates both homestays and floating-island visits.

➡ Insist on handing payment for your lodging to the family yourself.

➡ Expect to pay well for your homestay. Visitors must pay at least US$50 for a typical two-day island excursion for the host family to make a profit from your stay.

➡ Travel to the islands independently – it's easy.

➡ Carry out your trash – islanders have no way of disposing of it.

➡ Bring gifts of things the islanders can't grow, such as fresh fruit or school supplies (pens, pencils, notebooks) – not unhealthy snacks.

➡ Don't give candy or money to kids, so they don't learn to beg.

➡ Support communal enterprises, which benefit all. On Taquile (p192), families take turns to run the Restaurante Comunál, on the east side of the main plaza, which gives many people their only opportunity to benefit from the tidal wave of tourism that hits their island daily. Luquina Chico (p196) and Isla Ticonata (p195) run their tourism communally, through rotation of accommodations, profit-sharing, and shared work providing food, transportation, guiding and activities.

➡ Consider visiting one of the communities around the lake. They're harder to get to than the islands but are far more peaceful and less touristed – here you'll see a living, agrarian community.

Ayacucho 270-280; ⊙8am-1pm & 2-4pm Mon-Fri) Helps organize student and business visas but can't arrange extensions on tourist cards.

MONEY

Bolivianos can be exchanged in Puno or at the border. You'll find an ATM inside the Terminal Terrestre that accepts most bank cards and dispenses US dollars and soles. **Scotiabank** (Lima 458; ⊙24hr), **Interbank** (Lima 444), **BCP** (Lima 444) and **Banco Continental** (Lima 418 at Grau) all have branches and ATMs on Lima; there's another Banco Continental at Libertad.

POST

Serpost (Moquegua 267; ⊙8am-8pm Mon-Sat) Peru's national postal service.

SAFE TRAVEL

There are scenic lookouts (Inca, Condor) on the hills above town, but as assaults and robberies have been reported (even by groups), it's not recommended to visit them unless there is a drastic improvement in security.

TOURIST INFORMATION

iPerú (⌨051-36-5088; Plaza de Armas, Lima at Deustua; ⊙9am-6pm Mon-Sat, to 1pm Sun) Patient, English-speaking staff offer good advice here. An excellent first port of call on arrival in Puno. Other useful iPerú offices are at the Terminal Terrestre and Juliaca airport.

ⓘ Getting There & Away

AIR

The nearest airport is in Juliaca, about an hour away. Hotels can book you a comfortable, safe shuttle bus for S15 or you can book directly with **Rossy Tours** (⌨051-36-6709; www.rossytours. com; Tacna 308; ⊙office 9am-8pm). The earliest bus is timed to give you just enough time to check in for the earliest flight, so there is no need to stay in Juliaca. There is a **LAN** (⌨051-36-7227; Tacna 299) office in Puno.

BOAT

There are no passenger ferries across the lake from Puno to Bolivia, but you can get to La Paz via the lake in one or two days on high-class tours that visit Isla del Sol and other sites along the way. **Transturin** (⌨051-35-2771; www.transturin.com; Ayacucho 148; 2-day tour US$181) has a bus/catamaran/bus combination, departing at 6:30am from Puno and arriving in La Paz at 7:30pm, or the following day at noon, with an overnight onboard. Leon Tours (p183) also visits Isla del Sol on the way to La Paz using hydrofoil boats. In total it's a 13-hour trip, though two- and three-day sightseeing tours are available. Crillon Tours is its Bolivian operator.

BUS

The **Terminal Terrestre** (☑ 051-36-4737; Primero de Mayo 703), three blocks down Ricardo Palma from Av El Sol, houses Puno's long-distance bus companies. The terminal has an ATM, and there is a departure tax of S1.50, which you must pay in a separate booth before departure.

Buses leave for Cuzco every two to three hours from 4am to 10pm, and for Arequipa every three to four hours from 2am to 10pm. **Cruz del Sur** (☑ in Lima 01-311-5050; www.cruzdelsur.com. pe; Terminal Terrestre) has the best services to both. **Turismo Mer** (☑ 051-36-7223; www. turismomer.com; Tacna 336; ☺ office 8am-1pm & 3-8pm) buses to Cuzco are also comfortable. Civa (p179) goes to Lima and Arequipa. **Tour Perú** (☑ 051-20-6088; www.tourperu.com.pe; Tacna 285 No 103) goes to Cuzco at 10pm and also has a daily 7am service crossing to La Paz, Bolivia, via Copacabana.

The most enjoyable way to get to Cuzco is via **Inka Express** (☑ 051-36-5654; www.inkaexpress. com; Tacna 346; ☺ office 8am-7pm Mon-Fri, 9am-1pm & 4-7pm Sat & Sun), whose luxury buses with panoramic windows depart every morning at 6.50am. Buffet lunch is included, along with an English-speaking tour guide and oxygen. The sites briefly visited en route include Andahuayllilas, Raqchi, Abra la Raya and Pucará. The trip takes about eight hours and costs US$60.

Local *combis* (minibuses) to Chucuito, Juli, Pomata and the Bolivian border leave from the new, organized **Terminal Zonal** (Branden 415), five blocks south of the Terminal Terrestre. Many *combis* (minibuses; S1) from the center run nearby along Av El Sol or Av Simón Bolívar; ask to 'bajar en Branden' ('get out at Branden') and head towards the lake to find the Terminal.

To get to Capachica (S5, one hour), catch a *combi* from Talara, just off El Sol opposite the Mercado Bellavista. They leave once an hour from about 6am to 2pm.

PUNO BUSES

Prices are general estimates for normal/luxury buses.

DESTINATION	COST (S)	DURATION (HR)
Arequipa	25/75	5
Cuzco	30/80	7-8
Juliaca	3.50/–	1
Lima	150/170	18-21
Copacabana, Bolivia	20/–	3
La Paz, Bolivia	50/–	5-6

TRAIN

The train ride from Puno to Cuzco retains a certain renown from the days – now long gone – when the road wasn't paved and the bus journey was a nightmare. Train fares have skyrocketed in recent years and most travelers now take the bus. There are two train services. The sumptuous Belmond Andean Explorer train is an overnight sleeper service with three meals and cocktails included, coming at a hefty cost for five-star-hotel-like pampering. The cheaper PeruRail Titicaca service is a day trip. Both are for train buffs and well-to-do travellers, since the tracks run next to the road for much of the way, so the scenery, while wonderful through the glass-walled observation car, is comparable to a much cheaper bus ride.

Reservations can be made online at www. perurail.com.

Andean Explorer trains depart from Puno's **train station** (☑ 051-36-9179; www.perurail. com; Av La Torre 224; ☺ train station office 6.30am-noon & 4-6pm Mon-Fri, 6.30am-2.30pm Sat) at noon on Wednesdays, arriving at Cuzco around 7:40am the next day. Tickets cost from US$480 per person; prices rise steeply depending on sleeper cabin type now that the train has been relaunched by luxury hotel brand Belmond.

PeruRail Titicaca trains do not include sleeping and depart Mondays, Thursdays and Saturdays at 7:30am, and arrive in Cuzco at 5:50pm the same day. Tickets are US$260.

❶ Getting Around

Puno is handily compact. If you have energy to spare, you can walk into the center from the port or the bus terminals. To get to the port or lake on foot, walk east from the Plaza de Armas along Jirón Puno, which becomes Avenida Del Puerto to the port. Everything in the town center is within easy walking distance. Lima, the main pedestrian street, fills in the early evening as *puneños* (inhabitants of Puno) come out to promenade.

A short taxi ride anywhere in town (and as far as the transportation terminals) costs S5. *Mototaxis* (three-wheeled motorcycle rickshaw taxis) are a bit cheaper at S2.50, and *triciclos* (three-wheeled cycles) cheapest of all, at S2 – but it's an uphill ride, so you may find yourself wanting to tip the driver more than the cost of the fare!

Around Puno

Sillustani   ARCHAEOLOGICAL SITE

(adult/child S15/2) Sitting on rolling hills on the Lago Umayo peninsula, the *chullpas* (funerary towers) of Sillustani stand out for miles against a desolate altiplano landscape. The ancient Colla people who once

ℹ️ BORDER CROSSING: BOLIVIA

There are two viable routes from Puno to Bolivia. The north-shore route is very much off the beaten track and rarely used. There are two ways to go via the south shore: through either Yunguyo or Desaguadero. The only reason to go via Desaguadero is if you're pressed for time. The Yunguyo route is safer, prettier and far more popular; it passes through the chilled-out Bolivian lakeshore town of Copacabana, from where Isla del Sol – arguably the most significant site in Andean mythology – can be visited.

US citizens have to pay US$160 cash in US dollars for a tourist visa to enter Bolivia. This can be done at the border; shops there can help with the two necessary photos and photocopies. Also, there's a Bolivian Consulate (p187) in Puno. Citizens of the EU, Canada and Australia don't need to pay a fee or provide photos. Everybody needs a return bus/plane ticket and a passport with six months' validity.

Bolivian border agents often try to charge an unofficial B$30 (collaboration fee) to use the border. Politely refuse. Always keep your backpack with you when crossing the border.

Note that Peruvian time is one hour behind Bolivian time.

Via Yunguyo Toward Copacabana

There are two ways to do this.

The quickest and easiest way is with a cross-border bus company such as **Tour Perú** (☑ 051-35-2991; www.tourperu.com.pe; Tacna 285 No 103) or **Ormeño** (☑ 051-36-8176; www.grupo-ormeno.com.pe; Terminal Terrestre). Purchase tickets at the Terminal Terrestre, or the more convenient Tour Perú ticket office in central Puno, at least one day in advance. The services stop at a *casa de cambio* (exchange bureau) at the border and waits for passengers to check through before continuing to Copacabana (S20 to S28, three to four hours). Here, another bus that's waiting can take you straight to La Paz (B$35, 3½ hours), with a changeover of 1½ hours.

The alternative is catching local transportation – *micros* (small buses) – from the Terminal Zonal. This much slower method of transportation is only recommended if you want to stop at some or all of the south-shore towns. Leave as early as 8am to allow enough time. Between towns, *micros* are regular, especially on Sunday, which is the market day in both Juli and Yunguyo. It's a great way to get off the beaten track and rub shoulders with locals.

---

dominated the Lake Titicaca area were a warlike, Aymara-speaking tribe, who later became the southeastern group of the Incas. They buried their nobility in these towers, which can be seen scattered widely around the hilltops of the region.

The most impressive towers are at Sillustani, where the tallest reaches a height of 12m. The cylindrical structures housed the remains of complete family groups, along with plenty of food and belongings for their journey into the next world. Their only opening was a small hole facing east, just large enough for a person to crawl through, which would be sealed immediately after a burial. Nowadays, nothing remains of the burials, but the *chullpas* are well preserved. The afternoon light is the best for photography, though the site can get busy at this time.

The walls of the towers are made from massive coursed blocks reminiscent of Inca stonework, but are considered to be even more complicated. Carved but unplaced blocks, and a ramp used to raise them, are among the site's points of interest, and you can also see the makeshift quarry. A few of the blocks are decorated, including a well-known carving of a lizard on one of the *chullpas* closest to the parking lot.

Sillustani is partially encircled by the sparkling Lago Umayo (3890m), which is home to a wide variety of plants and Andean water birds, plus a small island with vicuñas (threatened, wild relatives of alpacas). Birders take note: this is one of the best sites in the area.

Tours to Sillustani leave Puno at around 2:30pm daily and cost from S30. The round-trip takes about 3½ hours and allows you about 1½ hours at the ruins. If you'd prefer more time at the site, rent a private taxi for S80 with a one-hour waiting time. To save money, catch any bus to Juliaca and ask to be let off where the road splits (S3.50, 25 minutes). From there, taxis (S10) or occasional *combis* (S3, 20 minutes) go to the ruins.

Yunguyo is the end of the line. Catch a *triciclo* (three-wheeled cycle) to Kasani or cross on foot – it's a pleasant 2km along Av Ejército. The *casas de cambio* here offer a better exchange rate than their Bolivian counterparts.

First visit the Peruvian police, followed by the Control Migratorio (Immigration Office) on the left. Walk to the arch and the 'Welcome to Bolivia' sign for Bolivian immigration services.

A *combi* (minibus) to Copacabana is B$3. *Combis* leave more frequently on Sunday; on weekdays you may have to wait up to an hour. If you are inclined to walk the 8km, it's a straightforward stroll around the lake.

The border is open from 7:30am until 6pm, Peruvian time.

Via Desaguadero Toward La Paz

If you're going straight from Puno to La Paz, unsavory Desaguadero is faster, slightly cheaper and more direct than Yunguyo. It's also less scenic and less safe, though perfectly fine if you are traveling via tourist bus, which is only there briefly. Avoid spending the night in Desaguadero.

Combis (minibuses) leave Puno's Terminal Zonal for Desaguadero (S9, 2½ hours) throughout the day.

In Desaguadero, visit the Peruvian Dirección General de Migraciones y Naturalización to get stamped out of Peru. Then head to the building that says 'Migraciones Desaguadero,' to the left of the bridge, to complete Bolivian formalities.

Catch a *triciclo* (three-wheeled cycle) to the Bolivian-side transportation terminal, from where you can get to La Paz in 3½ hours either by *combi* (minibus; B$30/S16) or *colectivo* (shared transportation; B$30/S16).

The border is open from 8:30am to 8:30pm Bolivian time, or one hour earlier by Peruvian time.

Note: the Peruvian police have a bad reputation here, sometimes demanding a nonexistent 'exit tax.' You are not required to visit the Peruvian police station before leaving the country, so if anyone asks you to accompany them there, politely but firmly refuse. There are no ATMs in Desaguadero, so bring cash from Puno if your nationality requires a tourist visa.

Atuncolla (☑ 951-50-2390; Centro Artesanal, Atuncolla; r S25) offers stays with a host family, helping with farming and hiking to lesser-known sites.

Cutimbo   ARCHAEOLOGICAL SITE
(adult/child S15/2) Just over 20km from Puno, this dramatic site has an extraordinary position upon a table-topped volcanic hill surrounded by a fertile plain. Its modest number of well-preserved *chullpas* (funerary towers), built by the Colla, Lupaca and Inca cultures, come in both square and cylindrical shapes. You can still see the ramps used to build them. Look closely and you'll find several monkeys, pumas and snakes carved into the structures.

This remote place receives few visitors, which makes it both enticing and potentially dangerous for independent travelers. Go in a group and keep an eye out for muggers. Thieves are known to hide behind rocks at the top of the 2km trail that leads steeply uphill from the road.

Combis (minibuses) en route to Laraqueri (S3, 30 minutes) leave from the Terminal Zonal in Puno. You can't miss the signposted site, which is on the left-hand side of the road when facing towards Laraqueri – just ask the driver where to get off – from where it's another 20-minute walk uphill. Otherwise, the pricier options from Puno are taking a taxi (about S80 return with a one-hour wait) or a three-hour package tour (S100 per person, minimum two people).

Lake Titicaca's Islands

Lake Titicaca's islands are world famous for their peaceful beauty and the living tradition of their agrarian cultures, which date to pre-Columbian times.

The ever-popular, human-made reed islands of the Islas Uros are the most visited. Isla Taquile is a sleepy island with a unique culture that can suddenly turn festive by night in local dances. **Isla Amantaní** is the least visited as it requires an overnight stay with a family but also can be the most insightful and rewarding. Luxurious Isla Suasi, the only privately owned island, is home to a boutique resort.

Be aware that not all islanders welcome tourism, which only stands to reason since not all benefit from it and may see the frequent intrusions into their daily life as disruptive. It's important to respect the privacy of islanders and show courtesy.

Islas Uros

Just 7km east of Puno, these unique floating islands (admission S5) are Lake Titicaca's top attraction. Their uniqueness is due to their construction. They have been created entirely with the buoyant *totora* reeds that grow abundantly in the shallows of the lake. The lives of the Uros people are interwoven with these reeds. Partially edible (tasting like non-sweet sugarcane), the reeds are also used to build homes, boats and crafts. The islands are constructed from many layers of the *totora*, which are constantly replenished from the top as they rot from the bottom, so the ground is always soft and springy.

Some islands also have elaborately designed versions of traditional tightly bundled reed boats on hand and other whimsical reed creations, such as archways and even swing sets. Be prepared to pay for a boat ride (S10) or to take photographs.

🛏 Sleeping

★ **Cristina Suaña**   HOMESTAY $$
(☑ 951-472-355, 951-695-121; uroskhantati@hotmail.com; Isla Khantati; per person full board S180)
A long-standing accommodation provider on Uros is on Isla Khantati. The tariff is steep but includes top-notch accommodations, three meals, fishing, ample cultural activity and the company of the effervescent Cristina Suaña. Book in advance so she can pick you up from Puno in a private boat – if you catch the ferry you may end up on the wrong island.

Cristina, an Uros native, and her family have built a number of impeccable semi-traditional huts (with solar power, outhouses and shady decks), which occupy half the tiny island. The hyper-relaxed pace means a visit here is not ideal for those with little time on their hands.

★ **Uros Samaraña**
Uta Lodge   HOMESTAY $$$
(☑ 951-826-187; www.fb.me/samaranauta; Islas Uros; d/tr incl 3 meals & boat transfer S435/655)
🍴 Hosts César and Lucy have created a special experience on Islas Uros, and if you wish to deal directly with a Uros family without an agency, this is one of the best choices. Comfortable, large reed huts have private bathrooms, large beds, and those views! Rates include cultural activities like boating, fishing and optionally spending quality time with the family.

Book in advance to arrange free boat transfer to the correct island from Puno.

❶ Getting There & Away

Getting to the Uros is easy – there's no need to go with an organized tour, though you will miss out on the history lesson given by the guides and will be saving just S10 on the cheapest tours, which include admission. Ferries leave from **Puno port** (Puerto de Puno; Av Titicaca) – east of the Plaza de Armas along Jirón Puno, which becomes Avenida Del Puerto – for Uros (return trip S10) when full – at least once an hour from 6am to 4pm. The community-owned ferry service visits two islands, on a rotation basis. Ferries to Taquile and Amantaní can also drop you off in the Uros.

Isla Taquile

Inhabited for thousands of years, the lovely scenery on Isla Taquile (admission S5) is reminiscent of the Mediterranean. In the strong island sunlight, the deep, red-colored soil contrasts with the intense blue of the lake and the glistening backdrop of Bolivia's snowy Cordillera Real on the far side of the lake. Several hills boast Inca terracing on their sides and small ruins on top.

The natural beauty of the tiny island, 35km east of Puno, makes it stand out. Quechua-speaking islanders are distinct from most of the surrounding Aymara-speaking island communities and maintain a strong sense of group identity. They rarely marry non-Taquile people and have a population of about 2000 people.

◉ Sights

Visitors are free to wander around, explore the ruins and enjoy the tranquility. The island is a wonderful place to catch a sunset and gaze at the moon, which looks twice as bright in the crystalline air, rising over the breathtaking peaks of the Cordillera Real.

ICHU

Ten kilometers out of Puno, this rural community, spread across a gorgeous green valley, is home to little-known Inca ruins – Centro Ceremonial Tunuhuire. With superb views, it's a great place for a hike.

Leave the Panamericana at Ichu's second exit (after the service station) and head inland past the house marked 'Villa Lago 1960.' Walk 2km, bearing left at the junction, aiming for the two small, terraced hills you can see in the left of the valley. After bearing left at a second junction (you'll pass the school if you miss it), the road takes you between the two hills. Turn left again and head straight up the first one. Fifteen minutes of stiff climbing brings you to the top, where you'll be rewarded with the remains of a multilayered temple complex, and breathtaking 360-degree views.

This can be done as an easy half-day trip from Puno, arranged by private tour. Take plenty of water and food as there's no store.

Take in the lay of the land while it's still light – with no roads, streetlights or big buildings to use as landmarks, travelers have been known to get so lost in the dark that they end up roughing it for the night.

A stairway of more than 500 steps leads from the dock to the center of the island. The climb takes a breathless 20 minutes if you're acclimatized – more if you're not.

✦ Festivals & Events

Fiesta de San Santiago RELIGIOUS
(Feast of St James; ⊙ Jul 25) The Fiesta de San Santiago is a big feast day on Taquile. Locals in their distinctive colorful dress and knitwear dance and play music to Taquile's patron saint. Celebrations go on for several days until the start of August, when islanders make traditional offerings to Pachamama (Mother Earth). There are also fireworks. It's celebrated mostly on Isla Taquile.

ℹ Getting There & Away

Ferries (round-trip S25; admission to island S5) leave from the Puno port (east of the Plaza de Armas along Av Del Puerto) for Taquile from 7:35am, via Islas Uros. As the ferry stops in Islas Uros, you will also have to pay the admission there. A ferry from Taquile to Puno leaves at 2pm, but this can change so confirm the time with the captain as you arrive on Taquile. There are departures from Amantaní to Taquile (and onwards to Puno) around 4pm every day – check, though, as times vary; it's also possible to get here by ferry from Llachón.

Isla Amantaní

With a population of 4000, remote **Isla Amantaní** (admission S8) is a few kilometers north of the smaller Isla Taquile. Almost all trips to Amantaní involve an overnight stay with islanders. Guests help cook on open fires in the kitchen and the opportunity to engage with different aspects of rural life can create engaging and memorable experiences.

The island is very quiet (no dogs allowed), boasts great views and has no roads or vehicles. Several hills are topped by ruins, among the highest and best-known of which are **Pachamama** (Mother Earth) and **Pachatata** (Father Earth). These date to the Tiwanaku culture, a largely Bolivian culture that appeared around Lake Titicaca and expanded rapidly between 200 BC and AD 1000.

As with Taquile, the islanders speak Quechua, but their culture is more heavily influenced by the Aymara.

🛏 Sleeping

Amantaní Community Lodging HOMESTAY **$**
(☑ 051-36-9714; r per person with full board S45) When you arrive, Amantaní Community Lodging, basically the island families, will allocate you to your accommodations according to a rotating system. Please respect this process, even if you are with a guided group. There's no problem with asking for families or friends to be together.

ℹ Getting There & Away

Ferries (round-trip S30; admission to island S8) leave from the Puno port for Amantaní at 8:30am every day. There are departures from Amantaní to Taquile and Puno around 4pm every day – check, though, as times vary – and sometimes from Amantaní to Puno at around 8am, depending on demand. A private boat taxi between Llachón and Amantaní costs S100 return.

Isla Suasi

On the northeastern part of Lake Titicaca, this beautiful solar-powered island offers a total retreat into nature. The only privately owned island on Titicaca, it has been leased long-term by a luxury hotel, which makes a unique nature retreat.

🛏 Sleeping

★**Hotel Isla Suasi**   RESORT $$$
(☎ 051-35-1102; www.islasuasi.pe; r per person from S586; ❄@☎) 🍴 This is as exclusive as resorts get. Terraced rooms are well-appointed, with down duvets, fireplaces and lake views. The colorful flora, walks, lake swims, kayaking and chance to spot wild vicuña without the crowds make this the paradise island of postcards.

The hotel provides pricey daily transfers (three hours, per person round-trip S660) at 7am for guests from the pier in Puno, with stops to visit the Islas Uros and Isla Taquile: return transfers are at 12.45pm. Ask about the shorter 15-minute transfer, though you need to arrange your own transportion by land first.

ℹ Getting There & Away

The island is a five-hour boat trip from Puno or a more than three-hour drive on dirt roads, with a short boat transfer from Cambria. A S40 entry fee (included in lodging fees) helps local conservation projects.

Capachica Peninsula & Around

Poking far out into the northwestern part of the lake, midway between Juliaca and Puno, the Capachica Peninsula has the same beauty as the lake islands but without the crowds and commercial bent. Each *pueblito* (tiny town) boasts its own glorious scenery, ranging from pastoral and pretty to coweringly majestic. A few days here among the local people – handsome, dignified men in vests and black hats, and shy, smiling women in intricate headgear – with nothing to do but eat well, climb hills and trees, and stare at the lake, can provide a real retreat.

Homestay is the only accommodation on offer in the Capachica Peninsula towns, and homestay-hopping is a major element of the fun. Most of the communities here offer the same deal on food and accommodations, similar to that encountered on Isla Amantaní. Families have constructed or adapted basic rooms for tourists in their homes, and charge around S30 per person per night for a bed, or about S75 for full board.

Llachón and, to a lesser extent, Escallani are set up for travelers just turning up. For other communities, it's very important to arrange accommodations in advance, as hosts need to buy supplies and prepare. It's preferable to call rather than email. Generally, only Spanish is spoken.

The official Turismo Rural Comunitario (www.turismocapachica.wordpress.com) website has more information, including photos, of homestays on the peninsula.

ℹ Information

There is no internet reception on the peninsula, but cell phones work. There are no banks or ATMs and, as elsewhere in Peru, breaking big notes can be very difficult. Bring all the money you need, in bills of S20 or smaller if possible.

ℹ Getting There & Away

Travel agencies in Puno can get you to any of the peninsula's communities.

Strung along the peninsula between the towns of Capachica and Llachón, the villages of Ccotos and Chifrón are linked by deserted, eminently walkable dirt roads and lackadaisical bus services (it's generally quicker to walk over the hill than drive around by the road). Escallani is further north, slightly off the peninsula proper, not far from Juliaca. Locals get to the mainland by *lancha* (small motorboat), which they are happy to hire out.

From Puno, catch a *combi* (minibus) advertising either Capachica or Llachón from east of the Mercado Bellavista. All will stop in Capachica (S5, 60 minutes, hourly). From Capachica's *mercado* (market) continue to Llachón (S2.50, 30 minutes; taxi S25) or other destinations.

For Ccotos (S1, 35 minutes) or Escallani (S2.50, 45 minutes), *combis* leave the *mercado* only on Sundays from 8am to 2pm. You could also take a taxi (S20) or *mototaxi* (three-wheeled motorcycle rickshaw taxi; S15) to Ccotos; it's a bit steeper for Escallani (S85).

The trip from Juliaca to Escallani via Pusi by local *micro* (small bus) is highly recommended for hardy travelers. The scenery on this unpaved, little-traveled road is unparalleled – sit on the left side of the bus if you're heading from Juliaca to Escallani so that you can see the lake.

For Chifrón from Capachica, take a *colectivo* (shared transportation; S1, 13 minutes), taxi (S5, 10 minutes) or *mototaxi* (S4, 10 minutes).

Alternately, you can hike (30 minutes) over the hill from Llachón, or walk the 3km from Capachica.

Llachón is also accessible via the Taquile ferry. The easiest way to combine the two is to arrive by road, then have your host family in Llachón show you where to catch the ferry to Taquile. A private boat taxi between Llachón and Amantaní costs S100 return.

Capachica

All self-guided bus trips from Puno pass through Capachica, the peninsula's forgettable commercial center. Besides very basic restaurants and *hospedajes* (small, family-owned inns), and a pretty church (all visible from the bus), there's no reason to stop here unless you need to switch buses or use the internet or a public telephone (there are a couple around the plaza); these services are unavailable elsewhere on the peninsula.

Llachón

The pretty little village community of Llachón near the peninsula's southern tip, almost 75km northeast of Puno, offers fantastic views and short hikes to surrounding pre-Inca sites. The most developed of the peninsula's communities, thanks to locally managed tourism, it nevertheless feels far from the bright lights of modern Peru. With few cars and no dogs, it's an incredibly peaceful place to sit and enjoy stunning views of Lake Titicaca, while pigs, llamas and kids wander by. From January to March, native birds are also a feature. It's possible to simply turn up in Llachón and ask around for accommodations, or contact **Richard Cahui Flores** (☑951-63-7382; hospedajesamary@hotmail.com; S30 per person, full board S75) who works with lots of families and is the best point of contact for advance bookings. Good direct options are with **Félix Turpo** (Casa de Felix; ☑951-66-4828; www.santamariaturismo.com; S30 per person, full board S75) at his home with incredible views overlooking Isla Taquile; in one of six cozy cabins with **Magno Cahui** (Hospedaje Tika Wasi; ☑951-82-5316; hospedajetikawasi@yahoo.es; S30 per person, full board S75); or in the guesthouse of **Valentín Quispe** (☑951-82-1392; llachon@yahoo.com; S30 per person, full board S75), which is surrounded by an enchanting overgrown cemetery.

Chifrón

If other nearby towns sound a bit too built-up, tiny somnolent Chifrón (population 24), off the main road in the northeast corner of the peninsula, is for you. Drowsing in rustling eucalyptus trees above a deserted beach, accommodations may be basic but on offer is a chance to experience another world. Contact **Emiliano** (☑951-91-9252, 951-91-9652; www.fb.me/emiliano.chifron; Chifrón; S30 per person, full board S75) to arrange a stay.

Ccotos

You can't get much further off the beaten track than Ccotos, two-thirds of the way down the peninsula's east coast. Nothing ever happens here except the annual Miss Playa (Miss Beach) competition, in which the donning of bathing suits stirs much controversy. A good homestay option is on the edge of the lake with friendly **Alfonso Quispe** (Usqay Wasi Inca Samana; ☑951-85-6462; www.turismocapachica.wordpress.com; Ccotos; S30 per person, full board S76) and his family, with easygoing activities on offer.

Isla Ticonata

A couple of hundred meters off Ccotos, Isla Ticonata is home to a fiercely united community and some significant mummies, fossils and archaeological sites. Activities include fishing, dancing, cooking and helping till the family *chakras* (fields). Isla Ticonata is only accessible by organized tour and is a rare example of Lake Titicaca's local communities calling the shots over tour agencies. Tours can be booked in Puno at short notice through travel agencies.

Escallani

In the distant north from the peninsula's other towns, Escallani is the place to spend hours ogling the majestic views of reed beds, patchwork fields, craggy rocks and the perennially snowcapped Illimani (Bolivia's highest mountain, 6438m). The lake takes on a completely different aspect from the settlement, located off the peninsula and on the way to Juliaca. Rock climbers should ask about *escalada en roca* (rock-climbing) spots. This area is a little more ready than other communities to receive guests unannounced – ask around at the plaza to find **Rufino Paucar** (☑Spanish only 97-319-0552;

Escallani; S30 per person, full board S75) and his complex of more than a dozen rustic, straw-thatched cabins high above the town.

South-Shore Towns

The road to Bolivia via Lake Titicaca's southern shore passes through bucolic villages noted for their colonial churches and beautiful views. Traveling this route is an easy way to get a relatively untouristed peek at the region's traditional culture. If you can coordinate the transportation connections, you can visit a few of the south-shore towns in a day trip from Puno or continue on to Bolivia.

For public transportion to any south-shore town, go to Puno's Terminal Zonal. *Combis* (minibuses) leave when full. The route includes Ichu (S2.5, 15 minutes), Chucuito (S3, 30 minutes), Juli (S5, 1¼ hours), Pomata (S8, 1½ hours) and the Bolivian border at Yunguyo (S10, 2¼ hours) or Desaguadero (S11, 2½ hours). Direct transportation to the towns closer to Puno is more frequent, but *combis* to most towns leave at least hourly – more often for closer destinations. It's possible to take a *combi* headed to a more distant location and be let out earlier, but you will probably still have to pay the full fare.

Chucuito

☑ 051 / POP 1100

Quiet Chucuito's claim to fame is the outlandish **Templo de la Fertilidad** (Inca Uyu; Trucos; admission S8; ⊘9am-4.30pm); its grounds are populated with large stone phalluses. The underappreciated, real appeal of Chucuito is staying near a secluded part of Lake Titicaca and eating in the main plaza further uphill from the main road, which has two colonial churches, **Santo Domingo** and **Nuestra Señora de la Asunción**.

With its location so close to Puno, but a world away, weekends are very popular with nostalgic visitors from the big smoke who want a taste of *pueblo* (village) life.

🛏 Sleeping

★ **Taypikala Lago**   HOTEL **$$**

(☑051-79-2266; www.taypikala.com; Calle Sandia s/n; s/d incl breakfast S192/213) It would be hard to miss the museum-like, arched-window exterior of Taypikala Lago at its prime and singular position near the lake. Handsome rustic-modern rooms have impressive water and garden views and staying (luxuriously)

near a secluded part of the lake is a destination in itself, though central Chucuito is a five-minute stroll away across the highway.

ℹ Getting There & Away

For Chucuito and its sights, take a *combi* (minibus; S3, 30 minutes) from Puno's Terminal Zonal and ask to be let out at on the highway for Inca Uyu (or Templo de la Fertilidad). *Combis* leave when full, but if you don't want to wait, *combis* to any south-shore town pass Chucuito.

Luquina Chico

This tiny community, 53km east of Puno on the Chucuito Peninsula, is stunning. If you want to relax in a rural community, Luquina Chico also boasts the best standard of homestay accommodations of any community around the lake. The community is making economic strides thanks to tourism.

Sweeping views of Puno, Juliaca and all the islands of the lake can be taken in from both the headland's heights or the fertile flats by the lake. In the wet season, a lagoon forms that attracts migrating wetland birds.

Chullpitas (miniature burial towers) are scattered all around this part of the peninsula. They are said to house the bodies of *gentiles,* little people who lived here in ancient times, before the sun was born and sent them underground.

Ask around town about renting kayaks. Edgar Adventures (p182) in Puno can also get you here on a mountain bike; a somewhat grueling but extremely scenic three-hour ride along the peninsula.

Homestays offer full board (S80). The participating 35 families are part of a collective Turismo Vivencial Comunitario Luquina Chico (www.fb.me/luquinachicotiticaca) represented by Jimmy (luquinachico@hotmail.com), who speaks basic English; if you don't speak Spanish, tour agencies in Puno can help organize stays.

To get here catch a *combi* (minibus) labeled 'Luquina Chico' (S4.50, two hours), which run every hour or so in the morning from the corner of Jr 1ro Mayo and Banchero Rossi in Puno, just south of the Terminal Terrestre; or take the ferry to or from Isla Taquile and ask the driver to drop you off.

Juli

☑ 051 / POP 8000

Sleepy Juli is a tourist-friendly stop. It's called Peru's *pequeña Roma* (little Rome) on account of its four colonial museum-like churches from the 16th and 17th centuries, which are slowly being restored. Churches are most likely to be open on Sundays, though opening hours here should not be taken as gospel. It's worth knocking on the door if one seems closed.

◉ Sights

Nuestra Señora de la Asunción　　CHURCH
(Cusco; admission S5; ⏰8:30am-5pm) The imposing 1557 church of Nuestra Señora de la Asunción has an expansive courtyard approach that may awaken urges to oratory. Its interior is airy, and the pulpit is covered in gold leaf.

Other churches include Santa Cruz, which has lost half its roof and remains closed for the foreseeable future, but its skeleton and facades are visible. The 1560 stone church of San Pedro, on the main plaza, is in the best condition, with carved ceilings and a marble baptismal font. Mass is celebrated here every Sunday at 8am.

San Juan de Letrán　　CHURCH
(Jr San Juan; admission S5; ⏰8:30am-5pm) Dating from 1570, the adobe baroque church of San Juan de Letrán contains richly framed *escuela cuzqueña* (Cuzco School) paintings that depict the lives of saints. It's two blocks north of the Plaza de Armas.

ℹ Getting There & Away

Micros (small buses; S5, 1¼ hours) from the Terminal Zonal in Puno drop you off near the market, a 10-minute walk downhill from the center. Return transportation leaves from Lima, two blocks up from the plaza; *combis* (minibuses) here also go to Yunguyo (S4, 6am to 7pm).

Pomata

☏ 051 / POP 1800
Just beyond Juli, the road to Pomata runs along the south shore of Lake Titicaca, 105km from Puno. As you arrive, you'll see Dominican church **Templo de Pomata Santiago Apóstolo** (Plaza de Armas; admission S2) – totally out of proportion with the town it dominates, in terms of both size and splendor – dramatically located on top of a small hill. Founded in 1700, it is known for its windows made of translucent alabaster and its intricately carved baroque sandstone facade. Look for the puma carvings – the town's name means 'place of the puma' in Aymara.

ℹ **BORDER CROSSINGS**

Just out of Pomata, the road forks; both routes lead to the Bolivian border (p190). The main road continues southeast through Zepita to the unsavory border town of Desaguadero (p191). The left fork hugs the shore of Lake Titicaca and leads to another, more pleasant border crossing at Yunguyo (p190).

ℹ Getting There & Away

Colectivos (shared transportation) from the Terminal Zonal in Puno stop here (S8, 1½ hours); they are marked with signs for Yunguyo or Desaguadero.

Bolivian Shore

If you are drawn to the idea of staying longer in Bolivia, Lonely Planet's *Bolivia* guidebook has comprehensive information.

Copacabana

Nestled between two hills on the southern shore of Lake Titicaca, Copacabana is a small, bright and enchanting town. It's long been a religious mecca, and local and international pilgrims still flock to its raucous fiestas, but lakeside strolls and meanderings up El Calvario will get you far from the madding crowd. Copa is the launching pad for visiting Isla del Sol and Isla de la Luna, and makes a pleasant stopover between La Paz and Puno or Cuzco.

◉ Sights & Activities

★ **Cathedral**　　CHURCH
(Plaza 2 de Febrero) FREE The sparkling white *mudéjar* (Moorish–style) cathedral, with its domes and colorful *azulejos* (blue Portuguese-style ceramic tiles), dominates the town. Check the noticeboard in front of the entrance for the mass schedule.

The cathedral's black Virgen de Candelaria statue, **Camarín de la Virgen de Candelaria**, carved by Inca Emperor Tupac-Yupanqui's grandson, Francisco Yupanqui, is encased above the altar upstairs in the *camarín* (shrine); visiting hours can be unreliable.

The statue is never moved from the cathedral, as superstition suggests that its disturbance would precipitate a devastating flood of Lake Titicaca. **Museo de la Catedral**

(Murillo s/n; per person B$10, minimum 8) contains some interesting religious art.

Cerro Calvario
MOUNTAIN

The summit can be reached in half an hour and is well worth the climb, especially for a view of the sunset. The **trail** begins near the **church** at the end of 3 de Mayo and climbs past the 14 Stations of the Cross. You can also enter from a longer winding dirt path that begins at the corner of Calles Jáuregui and Costañera.

You'll need sturdy hiking shoes for the long dirt path.

Museo del Poncho
MUSEUM

(www.museodelponcho.org; Baptista, near Costañera; B$15; ⊙ 10am-5:30pm Mon-Sat, to 4pm Sun) A visit to Museo del Poncho will help you unravel the mysteries of the regional textiles. The exhibits, spread over two floors, give a clear insight into the origins and meanings of the poncho – who wears what and why. Labels are in English and Spanish. Hours are irregular and photography is not allowed.

🎎 Festivals & Events

Fiesta de la Virgen de Candelaria
RELIGIOUS

(⊙ Feb 2-5) Honors the patron saint of Copacabana and Bolivia. Copacabana holds an especially big bash, and pilgrims and dancers come from Peru and around Bolivia. There's much music, traditional Aymará dancing, drinking and feasting. On the third day, celebrations culminate with the gathering of 100 bulls in a stone corral along the Yampupata road.

Fiesta de la Cruz
RELIGIOUS

(Feast of the Cross; ⊙ May) This fiesta is celebrated over the first weekend in May all around the lake, but the biggest festivities are in Copacabana. Expect elaborate costumes and traditional dancing.

👉 Tours

To visit Islas del Sol and de la Luna you can either take a ferry or go the luxury route with a La Paz–based tour operator for a guided excursion (adding a night or two in their hotels on Isla del Sol). Recommended operators include the following:

➡ **Crillon Tours** (☑ 233-7533; www.titicaca. com; Av Camacho 1223, La Paz; ⊙ 9am-noon & 2:30-7pm Mon-Fri, to noon Sat)

➡ **Transturin** (☑ 242-2222; www.transturin. com; Achumani Calle 6 No 100, La Paz; ⊙ 9am-7pm Mon-Fri, to noon Sat)

➡ **Magri Turismo** (☑ 244-2727; www. magriturismo.com; Capitán Ravelo 2101, Sopocachi; ⊙ 8:30am-12:30pm & 2:30-6:30pm Mon-Fri, 9am-noon Sat)

🛏 Sleeping

A host of budget options abound, especially along Jáuregui, charging about B$30 to B$40 per person. There are also several midrange options that are well worth the extra bolivianos. During fiestas accommodations fill up quickly and prices increase up to threefold.

⭐ Las Olas
BOUTIQUE HOTEL $$

(☑ 862-2112, cell 7250-8668; www.hostallasolas. com; Pérez 1-3; s/d/tr/q US$41/52/68/79; @ 🛜) To say too much about this place is to spoil the surprise, so here's a taste: quirky, creative, stylish, ecofriendly, million-dollar vistas. Plus there are kitchens, private terraces with hammocks and a solar-powered Jacuzzi. A once-in-a-lifetime experience and well worth the splurge.

Reserve one or two weeks ahead and get here by passing by its partner hotel, La Cúpula.

Hotel La Cúpula
HOTEL $$

(☑ cell 7708-8464; www.hotelcupula.com; Pérez 1-3; s/d/tr from US$17/29/54, s/d/tr ste from US$32/48/60; 🛜) International travelers rave about this inviting oasis, marked by two gleaming-white domes on the slopes of Cerro Calvario, with stupendous lake views. The rooms are basic but stylish. The gardens, hammocks, shared kitchen and friendly atmosphere add to the appeal. The helpful staff speak several languages, and you can even buy the artwork in your room. Best to reserve ahead.

La Aldea Del Inca
GUESTHOUSE $$

(☑ 862-2452; www.hostalaldeadelinca.com; San Antonio 2; s/d/tr/q incl breakfast B$170/280/420/525; 🛜) Themed like the nearby Inca ruins and with spacious rooms replete with Andean art, this hotel makes for a solid mid range option. Most rooms have views and all have heat, TVs and access to the hammock-strewn garden.

Hostal Flores del Lago
HOTEL $$

(☑ 862-2117; Jáuregui s/n; s/d/tr/q B$100/140/210/300; 🛜) This red four-story hotel on the north side of the harbor is a top-tier budget option. The clean rooms are slightly damp, but you'll love the views and the friendly, sunny lobby area, which is the domain of Blanco the cat. Two large 'family-style' rooms for four or more people are available.

Hotel Lago Azul   HOTEL $$
(☑862-2581; cnr Costañera 13 & Jáuregui; s/d B$130/260; @☎) Located right on the lake, this hotel has nicely painted rooms, heaters, small balconies, flat-screen TVs and new mattresses. A bit austere, but you can hardly get a better location.

★ Hotel Rosario del Lago   HOTEL $$$
(☑245-1658, in La Paz 2-277-6286; www.grupo rosario.com; Paredes, near Costañera; @☎) One of the smartest places in town, the hacienda-styled, three-star sister of Hotel Rosario in La Paz has charming modern rooms with solar-heated showers, double-glazed windows and lake views. The polite staff also provide excellent service. The altiplano light streams on a pleasant sun terrace.

A quality restaurant is a plus.

🍴 Eating & Drinking

Some of the best Titicaca fish is served at **beachfront stalls** (Costanera; trout from B$25; ⊙8am-9pm), though hygiene is questionable. The bargain basement is the market *comedor* (dining hall), where you can eat a generous meal of *trucha* (river trout) for a pittance, or an 'insulin shock' breakfast of hot *api morado* (corn drink; B$4) and syrupy *buñuelos* (doughnuts or fritters; B$3).

Several tourist-oriented cafes are situated along Av 6 de Agosto.

El Condor & the Eagle Cafe   CAFE $
(www.facebook.com/elcondorandtheeaglecafe; Av 6 de Agosto s/n; mains B$30; ⊙7am-1pm Mon-Fri; ☎☑) Make this cheery traveler's cafe your breakfast spot with great veggie options, French-press coffee and owners who are more than happy to offer advice on Bolivia. There's also a small bookstore and a great collection of journals where fellow travelers offer tips for onward journeys.

Pan America   BAKERY $
(☑mobile 7881-5278; www.facebook.com/pan americacopacabana; Plaza 2 de Febrero; mains B$20-40; ⊙10am-6:30pm Fri-Mon) 🍴 The American owners of this bakery, which is next to the cathedral (p197), use the profits to fund development projects in nearby rural communities. Come in the morning for coffee and yummy baked goods, and return for wine and pizza (gluten-free, if desired) in the afternoon.

Baguette About It   SANDWICHES $
(Av 16 de Julio s/n; sandwiches B$18-25; ⊙8:30am-2pm & 4:30-7pm) The owners of **Pit Stop** (☑mobile 6323-5727; snacks B$7-15; ⊙8:30am-2pm & 4:30-7pm) have opened this (equally tiny) cafe next door. The focus here is on build-your-own sandwiches and craft beers. It's great for a takeaway as it's right by the tourist buses to La Paz and Peru.

★La Cúpula Restaurant   INTERNATIONAL $$
(www.hotelcupula.com; Pérez 1-3; mains B$24-59; ⊙7:30am-3pm & 6-10pm, closed lunch Tue; ☑) An inventive use of local ingredients makes up the extensive international and Bolivian menu here. The vegetarian range includes a tasty lasagna and there's plenty for carnivores, too. Dip your way through the cheese fondue with authentic Gruyère – it's to die for...which leaves the Bolivian chocolate fondue with fruit platter beyond description.

★La Orilla   INTERNATIONAL $$
(☑862-2267; Av 6 de Agosto s/n; mains B$36-60; ⊙9:30am-2pm & 5-9:30pm; ☑) Some say this cozy maritime-themed restaurant is the best in town, with fresh, crunchy-from-the-vine vegetables and interesting trout creations that incorporate spinach and bacon. They might just be right. Even the high-altitude falafels are pretty good.

ℹ️ Information

MEDICAL SERVICES
You'll likely get the best care at the tourist-friendly **Medical Health Home** (☑cell 7727-8510; www.medicalhome.com.pe; cnr Baptista & Costañera). For serious situations don't think twice – head straight to La Paz.

MONEY
ATMs dot Plaza Sucre. Shops on Av 6 de Agosto will exchange foreign currency (clean dollar bills preferred). Most *artesanías* (crafts stores) sell Peruvian soles.

SAFE TRAVEL
Radiation The thin air, characteristically brilliant sunshine and reflection off the water mean scorching levels of ultraviolet radiation. Wear a hat and sunscreen in this region, and drink lots of water to avoid dehydration.

Crowds Be especially careful during festivals. Stand well back during fireworks displays, when explosive fun seems to take priority over crowd safety, and be wary of light-fingered revelers.

❶ Getting There & Away

AIR

A new airport opened in 2018. At the time of research it was not yet complete, but was planned to have domestic flight connections to La Paz, Rurrenabaque, Trinidad and Uyuni.

BOAT

Buy your tickets for boat tours to Isla de la Luna and Isla del Sol from agencies on Av 6 de Agosto or from beachfront kiosks. If you're traveling in a big group, consider renting a private boat for B$600 to B$900 per day. Separate return services are available from both islands.

BUS

Most buses leave from near Plazas 2 de Febrero or Sucre. The more comfortable nonstop tour buses from La Paz to Copacabana – including those operated by **Titicaca Tourist Transportation** (📞 862-2160; www.titicacabolivia.com; cnr Avs 6 de Agosto & 16 de Julio) – cost about B$30 and are well worth the investment. They depart from La Paz at about 8am and leave Copacabana at 1:30pm and 6:30pm (four hours). You will need to exit the bus at Estrecho de Tiquina (Tiquina Straits) to cross via **ferry** (per person B$2, per car B$30-$40; ⊘ 5am-9pm) between the towns of San Pedro de Tiquina and San Pablo de Tiquina (15 minutes).

Buses to Peru depart and arrive in Copacabana from Av 16 de Julio. You can also get to Puno by catching a public minibus from Plaza Sucre to Kasani (B$4, 15 minutes). Across the border there's frequent, if crowded, onward transportation to Yunguyo (five minutes) and Puno (2½ hours).

A new player in the bus game, Irish-run **Bolivia Hop** (www.boliviahop.com; Linares 940, Rosario; ⊘ office 8:30am-7pm) offers services between Lima, Arequipa, Copa and La Paz, and helps travelers with customs and *hostal* arrangements.

COPACABANA BUSES

DESTINATION	COST (B$)	TIME (HR)
Arequipa (Peru)	80	10-11
Cuzco (Peru)	80	11-12
La Paz	20-30	4
Puno (Peru)	30	3-4

Isla de la Luna

Legend has it that the small Island of the Moon was where Viracocha commanded the

moon to rise in the sky. However, its spiritual significance did not stop the Bolivian government from using this secluded outpost as a political prison for much of the 20th century.

The island is way smaller, way drier and way less touristed than its solar counterpart, and if you only have a day, you are better off heading to Isla del Sol. That said, for slightly more adventurous experiences this is a good alternative, and it's easy enough to tack a half-day here onto your Isla del Sol trip.

Most boats arrive on the eastern side of the island, where you'll find a visitor center, hostel, restaurant and artisan stands. On the other side of the hill, the island's main settlement has basic hostels, a soccer field and a small chapel.

❶ Getting There & Away

Asociación Unión Marines (Costañera, Copacabana; one-way/round-trip to Isla del Sol B$20/40, round-trip to Isla de la Luna B$40; ⊘ departs Copacabana 8:30am & 1:30pm) runs trips from Copacabana at 8:30am, returning from the island at 3pm.

Isla del Sol

Easily the highlight of any Lake Titicaca excursion, Isla del Sol is a large island with several traditional communities, decent tourist infrastructure such as hotels and restaurants, a few worthwhile pre-Columbian ruins, amazing views, great hikes through terraced hills and, well, lots of sun.

The island's permanent residents – a mix of indigenous peoples and émigrés – are distributed between the main settlements of **Cha'llapampa**, near the island's northern end; **Cha'lla**, which backs onto a lovely sandy beach on the central east coast; and **Yumani**, which straddles the ridge above Escalera del Inca in the south and is the biggest town on the island. Unfortunately, due to a conflict between island communities, it is only possible to visit Yumani.

Extensive networks of walking tracks make exploration fairly easy, though the altitude and sun may take their toll: carry lunch and ample water. The sun was born here and is still going strong.

🛏 Sleeping

The most scenic place to stay is Yumani – high on the ridge – where guesthouses are growing faster than coca production. Booking ahead, if possible, can save you the grueling uphill hike with your luggage, as

THE DARK CLOUD OVER SUN ISLAND

Trekking the length of Isla del Sol from the north to the south was once one of the great joys of visiting Lake Titicaca. That's no longer possible. Tourists have been restricted from traveling north of Yumani (and its satellite village of La Estancia) due to an ongoing conflict between the communities of Cha'lla, in the middle, and Cha'llapampa, to the north.

The conflict began in earnest in March 2017 when the people of Cha'lla built a hostel near the ruins of Cha'llapampa in an attempt to cash in on some of the tourism revenue that had long evaded them. This angered the people of Cha'llapampa so much that they blew up the hostel with dynamite. Thing is, the people who now live in Cha'llapampa settled the area from Cha'lla, so the whole ordeal has turned into a family feud writ large.

In retaliation for the hostel incident, the people of Cha'lla instituted a blockade on the north, preventing tourists from traveling there by land or sea. Rather bizarrely (given the cause of the conflict), tourists can't even drop by Cha'lla for a visit, though you should be able to loop around Cerro Palla Khasa.

In theory there should be someone at a guard post stopping you if you walk too far from Yumani. In practice, this doesn't always happen. Either way, do not be tempted to test your fate. A Korean tourist was stabbed and strangled under mysterious circumstances in early 2018 shortly after a heated exchange between the two communities to the north. No one was charged with the murder, but it was suspected at the time that she had unwittingly crossed into the northern half of the island.

These unfortunate events should by no means stop you from visiting Isla del Sol. Stick to Yumani or La Estancia and your trip will likely be perfectly safe and conflict-free. In fact, you may never even realize that there are troubles brewing in the north. As with any conflict, it's best to check with hotels and tour operators in the region (namely Copacabana) before you depart for Isla del Sol to find out the latest, as everything may have been resolved by the time you read this.

many places include a porter service in the price.

Note that prices may double in high season (June to August and during festivals).

If camping, it's best to ask permission from the local authority and then avoid cultivated land (a nominal payment of B$20 should be offered).

★ **La Estancia Ecolodge**　　　LODGE $$$
(☏ 2-244-0989;　www.ecolodge-laketiticaca.com; La Estancia; s/d incl breakfast & dinner US$120/154; ☏) ✿ Magri Turismo's delightful adobe cottages are set above pre-Inca terraces facing snowcapped Illampu. They are authentically ecological with solar-powered showers, sun-powered hot-boxes for heaters and Aymará thatched roofs. Staff can arrange hiking, boat trips and mystic ceremonies.

La Estancia is a 15-minute walk from Yumani.

🛈 Getting There & Around

You can reach Isla del Sol by ferry from either Copacabana or Yampupata, or with a guided tour.

Ferry tickets may be purchased at the **Asociación Unión Marines** (Costañera, Copacabana; one-way/round-trip B$20/30; ⊙ departs Copacabana 8:30am & 1:30pm) ticket kiosks on the beach in Copacabana or from town agencies (save yourself the trouble and buy direct). Boats land at either Pilko Kaina or Escalera del Inca near Yumani. Return trips leave Yumani at 10:30am and between 3pm and 4pm (one-way B$25).

Titicaca Tours (Costañera, Copacabana; round-trip B$30; ⊙ departs Copacabana 8:30am) will take you to both Isla del Sol and Isla de la Luna in half a day – two hours to explore the former and one hour at the latter. However, it's highly recommended to stay overnight or longer on one of the islands.

AT A GLANCE

POPULATION
Cuzco: 427,000

**LARGEST PAINTING
IN SOUTH AMERICA**
Family tree of St
Francis of Assisi in
the Iglesia San
Francisco (p213)

**BEST BOUTIQUE
HOTEL**
Casa Cartagena
(p226)

**BEST EATING
EXPERIENCE**
MIL (p251)

BEST FESTIVAL
Inti Raymi (p222)

WHEN TO GO
Jun–Aug
High season for
tourism, events and
festivals, days are
sunny and nights
cold.

Late Jun
Celebrate the sol-
stice at Inti Raymi,
the largest festival of
the year.

Sep & Oct
Shoulder season for
tourism, with fewer
crowds in Machu
Picchu.

Quechua women, Chinchero (p249)
PHOTOGRAPHY/SHUTTERSTOCK

Cuzco & the Sacred Valley

For Incas, Cuzco was the belly button of the world. A visit to this city and its nearby ruins tumbles you back into the cosmic realm of ancient Andean culture – knocked down and fused with the colonial imprint of Spanish conquest, only to be repackaged as a thriving tourist center. The capital of Cuzco is only the gateway. Beyond lies the Sacred Valley, Andean countryside dotted with villages, high-altitude hamlets and ruins linked by trail and railway tracks to the continent's biggest draw – Machu Picchu.

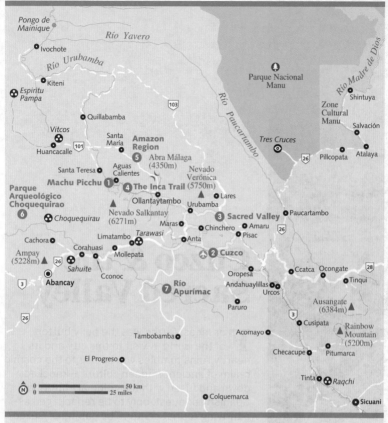

Cuzco & the Sacred Valley Highlights

1 **Machu Picchu** (p262) Drinking in the sublime grandeur of South America's signature ruin.

2 **Cuzco** Exploring the cobblestone streets of San Blas, attending street festivals and sampling the diverse culinary offerings.

3 **Sacred Valley** (p242) Wandering ancient ruins and staying in the charming

lodgings in stunning settings throughout the region.

4 **The Inca Trail** (p264) Taking part in the sublime adventure of hiking to Machu Picchu via the route of its ancient inhabitants.

5 **Mountain biking** (p218) Barreling from the high Andes down into the Amazon on two wheels.

6 **Parque Arqueológico Choquequirao** (p273) Trekking a challenging multiday route to spectacular Inca ruins above the Apurímac River.

7 **Rafting** (p217) Taking on the wild Apurímac or Tampobata Rivers with a rafting trip.

CUZCO

📞 084 / POP 427,000 / ELEV 3326M

Welcome to the navel of the world. The undisputed archaeological capital of the Americas, Cuzco is the continent's oldest continuously inhabited city and the gateway to Machu Picchu. Cosmopolitan Cuzco (also

Cusco, or Qosq'o in Quechua) thrives with a measure of contradiction. Ornate cathedrals squat over Inca temples, massage hawkers ply the narrow cobblestone passages, a rural Andean woman feeds bottled water to her pet llama while the finest boutiques sell pricey alpaca knits.

Visitors to the Inca capital get a glimpse of the richest heritage of any South American city. Married to 21st-century hustle, Cuzco can be a bit disconcerting (note the McDonald's set in Inca stones). Soaring rents on the Plaza de Armas and in trendy San Blas are increasingly pushing locals to the margins. Foreign guests undoubtedly have the run of the roost, so showing respect toward today's incarnation of this powerhouse culture is imperative.

History

According to legend, in the 12th century, the first *inca* (king), Manco Capac, was ordered by the ancestral sun god Inti to find the spot where he could plunge a golden rod into the ground until it disappeared. At this spot – deemed the navel of the earth (*qosq'o* in the Quechua language) – he founded Cuzco, the city that would become the thriving capital of the Americas' greatest empire.

The Inca empire's main expansion occurred in the hundred years prior to the arrival of the conquistadors in 1532. The ninth *inca,* Pachacutec, gave the empire its first bloody taste of conquest, with unexpected victory against the more dominant Chanka tribe in 1438. His was the first wave of expansion that would create the Inca empire.

Pachacutec also proved himself a sophisticated urban developer, devising Cuzco's famous puma shape and diverting rivers to cross the city. He built fine buildings, including the famous Qorikancha temple and a palace on the present Plaza de Armas. Among the monuments he built in honor of Inca victories are Sacsaywamán, the temple-fortress at Ollantaytambo and likely even Machu Picchu.

Expansion continued for generations until Europeans arrived. At that point, the empire ranged from Quito in Ecuador to south of Santiago in Chile. Shortly before the arrival of the Europeans, Huayna Cápac had divided his empire, giving the northern part to Atahualpa and the southern Cuzco area to another son, Huascar. The brothers fought bitterly for the kingdom. As a pure-blooded native *cuzqueño* (inhabitant of Cuzco), Huascar had the people's support, but Atahualpa had the backing of the battle-hardened northern army. In early 1532 Atahualpa won a key battle, capturing Huascar outside Cuzco.

Meanwhile, Francisco Pizarro landed in northern Peru and marched southward. Atahualpa himself had been too busy fighting the civil war to worry about a small band of foreigners, but by 1532 a fateful meeting had been arranged with the Spaniard in Cajamarca. It would radically change the course of South American history: Atahualpa was ambushed by a few dozen armed conquistadors, who succeeded in capturing him, killing thousands of indigenous tribespeople and routing tens of thousands more.

In an attempt to regain his freedom, the *inca* offered a ransom of a roomful of gold and two rooms of silver, including gold stripped from the temple walls of Qorikancha. But after holding Atahualpa prisoner for a number of months, Pizarro murdered him anyway, and soon marched on to Cuzco. Mounted on horseback, protected by armor and swinging steel swords, the Spanish cavalry was virtually unstoppable.

Pizarro entered Cuzco on November 8, 1533, by which time he had appointed Manco, a half-brother of Huascar and Atahualpa, as the new puppet leader. After a few years of towing the line, however, the docile puppet rebelled. In 1536 Manco Inca set out to drive the Spaniards from his empire, laying siege to Cuzco with an army estimated at well over a hundred thousand people. A desperate last-ditch breakout and violent battle at Sacsaywamán saved the Spanish from complete annihilation.

Manco Inca was forced to retreat to Ollantaytambo and then into the jungle at Vilcabamba. After Cuzco was safely recaptured, looted and settled, the seafaring Spaniards turned their attentions to the newly founded colonial capital, Lima. Cuzco's importance quickly waned to that of another colonial backwater. All the gold and silver was gone, and many Inca buildings were pulled down to accommodate churches and colonial houses.

The Spanish kept chronicles in Cuzco, including Inca history as related by the Incas themselves. The most famous of these accounts is *The Royal Commentaries of the Incas,* written by Garcilaso de la Vega, the son of an Inca princess and a Spanish military captain.

◉ Sights

While the city is sprawling, areas of interest to visitors are generally within walking distance, with some steep hills in between. The center of the city is the Plaza de Armas, while traffic-choked Av El Sol nearby is the main business thoroughfare. Walking just a few blocks north or east of the plaza

Central Cuzco

Cusco Planetarium (600m);
Q'enqo (3km);
Pukapukara (7km);
Tambomachay (7km)

Sacsaywamán
(400m)

Don Bosco

Don Bosco

Don Bosco

Arco

Ese

Saphi

40

92

Amargura

Suecia

Coricalle

Kiskapata

Resbalosa

Iris

Huaynapata

34

Tecsecocha

54

122

Saphi

115

72

Suecia

Ataúd

77

27

59

Tigre

132

141

Procuradores

28

58

45

93

Tambo de Montero

48

37

137

Plateros

121

127

155

111

117

157

53

67

Meloc

80

Siete Cuartones

33

46

Santa Teresa

22

139

51

158

19
Plaza de
Armas

49

90

Teatro

130

108

47

123

135

Nueva Alta

89

San Juan de Dios

64

17

Plaza
Regocijo

98

Transport to
Limatambo
(550m)

Granada

Tordo

35

71

29

151

15

Calle del Medio

Espinar

13

Nueva Baja

76

62

32

Garcilaso

149

26

23

Heladeros

Plazoleta
Espinar

Mantas

21

Ceniza

152

6

Plaza San
Francisco

143

Marquez

101

San Bernardo

Almagro

Desamparados

Unión

Santa Clara

82

Mesón de la Estrella

78

Quera

36

San Andrés

7 140

83

Matara

31

74

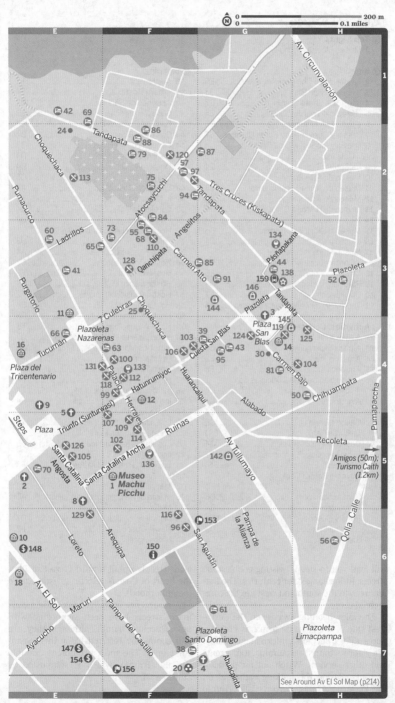

See Around Av El Sol Map (p214)

Central Cuzco

will lead you to steep, twisting cobblestone streets, little changed for centuries. The flatter areas to the south and west are the commercial center.

The alley heading away from the northwest side of the Plaza de Armas is Procuradores (Tax Collectors), nicknamed 'Gringo Alley' for its tourist restaurants, tour agents and other services. Watch out for predatory touts. Beside the hulking cathedral on the Plaza de Armas, narrow Calle Triunfo

leads steeply uphill toward Plaza San Blas, the heart of Cuzco's eclectic, artistic *barrio* (neighborhood).

A resurgence of indigenous pride means many streets have been signposted with new Quechua names, although they are still commonly referred to by their Spanish names. The most prominent example is Calle Triunfo, which is signposted as Sunturwasi.

Central Cuzco

Plaza de Armas   PLAZA
(Map p206) In Inca times, the plaza, called Huacaypata or Aucaypata, was the heart of the capital. Today it's the nerve center of the modern city. Two flags usually fly here – the red-and-white Peruvian flag and the rainbow-colored flag of Tahuantinsuyo. Easily mistaken for an international gay-pride banner, it represents the four quarters of the Inca empire.

Colonial arcades surround the plaza, which in ancient times was twice as large, also encompassing the area now called the Plaza Regocijo. On the plaza's northeastern side is the imposing cathedral (p210), fronted by a large flight of stairs and flanked by the churches of Jesús María and El Triunfo (p210). On the southeastern side is the strikingly ornate church of La Compañía de Jesús (p211). The quiet pedestrian alleyway of Loreto, which has Inca walls, is a historic means of access to the plaza.

It's worth visiting the plaza at least twice – by day and by night – as it takes on a strikingly different look after dark, when it is all lit up.

La Catedral
CHURCH

(Map p206; Plaza de Armas; adult/student S25/12.50; ⊙10am-5:45pm) A squatter on the site of Viracocha Inca's palace, the cathedral was built using blocks pilfered from the nearby Inca site of Sacsaywamán. Its construction started in 1559 and took almost a century. It is joined by the 1536 Iglesia del Triunfo (Map p206; Triunfo s/n) to its right and the 1733 Iglesia de Jesús María to the left.

The cathedral is one of the city's greatest repositories of colonial art, especially for works from the *escuela cuzqueña* (Cuzco school), noted for its decorative combination of 17th-century European devotional painting styles with the color palette and iconography of indigenous Andean artists. A classic example is the frequent portrayal of the Virgin Mary wearing a mountain-shaped skirt with a river running around its hem, identifying her with Pachamama (Mother Earth).

One of the most famous paintings of the *escuela cuzqueña* is *The Last Supper* by Quechua artist Marcos Zapata. Found in the northeast corner of the cathedral, it depicts one of the most solemn occasions in the Christian faith, but graces it with a small feast of Andean ceremonial food; look for the plump and juicy-looking roast *cuy* (guinea pig) stealing the show with its feet held plaintively in the air.

Also look for the oldest surviving painting in Cuzco, showing the entire city during the great earthquake of 1650. The inhabitants can be seen parading around the plaza with a crucifix, praying for the earthquake to stop, which it miraculously did. This precious crucifix, called El Señor de los Temblores (The Lord of the Earthquakes), can still be seen in the alcove to the right of the door leading into El Triunfo. Every year on Holy Monday, the Señor is taken out on parade (p222) and devotees throw *ñucchu* flowers at him – these resemble droplets of blood and represent the wounds of crucifixion. The flowers leave a sticky residue that collects smoke from votive candles lit beneath the statue: this is why he's now black. Legend has it that under his skirt, he's lily white.

The sacristy of the cathedral is covered with paintings of Cuzco's bishops, starting with Vicente de Valverde, the friar who accompanied Pizarro during the conquest. The crucifixion at the back of the sacristy is attributed to the Flemish painter Anthony van Dyck, though some guides claim it to be the work of the 17th-century Spaniard Alonso Cano. The original wooden altar is at the very back of the cathedral, behind the present silver altar, and opposite both is the magnificently carved choir, dating from the 17th century. There are also many glitzy silver and gold side chapels with elaborate platforms and altars that contrast with the austerity of the cathedral's stonework.

The huge main doors of the cathedral are open to genuine worshippers between 6am and 10am. Religious festivals are a superb time to see the cathedral. During the feast of Corpus Christi, for example, it is filled with pedestals supporting larger-than-life statues of saints, surrounded by thousands

---

ⓘ BOLETO TURÍSTICO & BOLETO RELIGIOSO

To visit most sites in the region, you will need Cuzco's official **boleto turístico** (tourist ticket; adult/student S130/70), valid for 10 days. Among the 17 sites included are Sacsaywamán, Q'enqo, Pukapukara, Tambomachay, Piquillacta, Tipón, Museo de Arte Popular, Pisac, Ollantaytambo, Chinchero and Moray, as well as an evening performance of Andean dances and live music at the Centro Qosqo de Arte Nativo. While some inclusions are admitted duds, you can't visit any of them without it.

Three **partial tickets** (adult/student S70/35) cover the ruins immediately outside Cuzco, the museums in Cuzco, and the Sacred Valley ruins. They are valid for one day, except for the Sacred Valley option, which is valid for two.

Purchase *boletos turísticos* from DIRCETUR (p237) or at the sites themselves, except for the Centro Qosqo de Arte Nativo. Students must show valid ID.

The **boleto circuito religioso** (religious circuit ticket; adult/student S30/15), also valid for 10 days, secures entry to Cuzco's churches, the Museo de Arte Religioso and Cuzco's most significant display of contemporary art at Museo Quijote. It's available at any of the sites.

of candles and bands of musicians honoring them with mournful Andean tunes.

Iglesia de La Compañía de Jesús CHURCH
(Map p206; Plaza de Armas; S10; ⊙9am-5pm Mon-Sat, 9-10:30am & 12:45-5pm Sun) Built upon the palace of Huayna Cápac, the last *inca* to rule an undivided, unconquered empire, the church was built by the Jesuits in 1571 and reconstructed after the 1650 earthquake. Two large canvases near the main door show early marriages in Cuzco in wonderful period detail. Local student guides are available to show you around the church, as well as the grand view from the choir on the 2nd floor, reached via rickety steps. Tips are gratefully accepted.

The Jesuits planned to make this the most magnificent of Cuzco's churches. The archbishop of Cuzco, however, complained that its splendor should not rival that of the cathedral, and the squabble grew to a point where Pope Paul III was called upon to arbitrate. His decision was in favor of the cathedral, but by the time word had reached Cuzco, La Compañía de Jesús was just about finished, complete with an incredible baroque facade and Peru's biggest altar, all crowned by a soaring dome.

Museo de Arte Precolombino MUSEUM
(Map p206; ☎084-23-3210; www.map.museo larco.org/museo.html; Plazoleta Nazarenas 231; S20; ⊙8am-10pm) Inside a Spanish colonial mansion with an Inca ceremonial courtyard, this dramatically curated pre-Columbian art museum showcases a stunningly varied, if selectively small, collection of archaeological artifacts previously buried in the vast storerooms of Lima's Museo Larco. Dating from between 1250 BC and AD 1532, the artifacts show off the artistic and cultural achievements of many of Peru's ancient cultures, with exhibits labeled in Spanish, English and French.

Highlights include the Nazca and Moche galleries of multicolored ceramics, *queros* (ceremonial Inca wooden drinking vessels) and dazzling displays of jewelry made with intricate gold- and silver-work.

Museo Inka MUSEUM
(Map p206; ☎084-23-7380; http://museoinka. unsaac.edu.pe; Tucumán near Ataúd; admission S10; ⊙8am-6pm Mon-Fri, 9am-4pm Sat) The charmingly modest Museo Inka, a steep block northeast of the Plaza de Armas, is the best museum in town for those interested in the Incas. The restored interior is jam-packed

STARGAZING WITH THE ANCIENTS

The Incas were the only culture in the world to define constellations of darkness as well as light. Astronomy wasn't taken lightly: some of Cuzco's main streets are designed to align with the stars at certain times of the year. Understanding their interest is a cool way to learn more about the Inca worldview. We recommend a visit to the **Cuzco Planetarium** (☎974-877-776, 084-23-1710; www.planetariumcusco.com; Carr Sacsayhuamán, Km 2; per person with transport S75; ⊙presentations 6pm) before you head out trekking and watching the night sky on your own. Think of how clever you'll feel pointing out the Black Llama to your fellow hikers. Reservations are essential. Price includes transfer from Plaza Regocijo.

with a fine collection of metal- and goldwork, jewelry, pottery, textiles, mummies, models and the world's largest collection of *queros* (ceremonial Inca wooden drinking vessels). There's excellent interpretive information in Spanish, and English-speaking guides are usually available for a small fee.

The museum building, which rests on Inca foundations, is also known as the Admiral's House, after the first owner, Admiral Francisco Aldrete Maldonado. It was badly damaged in the 1650 earthquake and rebuilt by Pedro Peralta de los Ríos, the count of Laguna, whose crest is above the porch. Further damage from the 1950 earthquake has now been fully repaired, restoring the building to its position among Cuzco's finest colonial houses. Look for the massive stairway guarded by sculptures of mythical creatures, and the corner window column that from the inside looks like a statue of a bearded man but from the outside appears to be a naked woman. The ceilings are ornate, and the windows give good views straight out across the Plaza de Armas.

Downstairs in the sunny courtyard, highland Andean weavers demonstrate their craft and sell traditional textiles directly to the public.

Museo de Historia Natural MUSEUM
(Map p206; Plaza de Armas; admission S3; ⊙8:30am-2:30pm Mon-Fri, to 2pm Sat) This university-run natural history museum houses

a somewhat motley collection of stuffed local animals and birds and over 150 snakes from the Amazon. The entrance is hidden off the Plaza de Armas, to the right of Iglesia de la Compañía de Jesús.

Iglesia y Monasterio de Santa Catalina CHURCH

(Map p206; Arequipa s/n; admission S8; ⊙8:30am-1pm & 2-5:30pm Mon-Sat) This convent houses many colonial paintings of the *escuela cuzqueña* (Cuzco school), as well as an impressive collection of vestments and other intricate embroidery. The baroque side chapel features dramatic friezes, and many life-sized (and sometimes startling) models of nuns praying, sewing and going about their lives. The convent also houses 13 real, live contemplative nuns.

Templo y Convento de La Merced CHURCH

(Map p206; ☑084-23-1821; Mantas 121; admission S10; ⊙8am-12:30pm & 2-5:30pm Mon-Sat, cloister 8-11am) Cuzco's third most important colonial church, La Merced was destroyed in the 1650 earthquake, but was quickly rebuilt. To the left of the church, at the back of a small courtyard, is the entrance to the monastery and museum. Paintings based on the life of San Pedro Nolasco, who founded the order of La Merced in Barcelona in 1218, hang on the walls of the beautiful colonial cloister.

The church on the far side of the cloistercontains the tombs of two of the most famous conquistadors: Diego de Almagro and Gonzalo Pizarro (brother of Francisco).

Also on the far side of the cloister is a small religious museum that houses vestments rumored to have belonged to conquistador and friar Vicente de Valverde. The museum's most famous possession is a priceless solid-gold monstrance, 1.2m high and covered with rubies, emeralds and no fewer than 1500 diamonds and 600 pearls. Ask to see it if the display room is locked.

Museo de la Coca MUSEUM

(Map p206; ☑979-711-403; museodelacoca@hotmail.com; Plaza San Blas 618; admission S10; ⊙9am-7pm) A good primer on Andean culture, this is a wonderful and kitschy little museum that traces the uses of the coca leaf, from sacred ritual to its more insidious incarnations. Exhibits are labeled in both English and Spanish. Tips are suggested for guided visits.

★ Museo Machu Picchu MUSEUM

(Casa Concha; Map p206; ☑084-25-5535; Santa Catalina Ancha 320; adult/child S20/10; ⊙8am-7pm Mon-Fri, 9am-5pm Sat) This newish museum exhibits 360 pieces from Machu Picchu taken by Hiram Bingham's expeditions and recently returned by Yale University, including stone tools and metals, ceramics and bones. The collection shows the astounding array of fine handicrafts and ceramics acquired from throughout the vast Incan empire. There's also good background on the Bingham expeditions with informative documentaries (subtitled). Signs are in English and Spanish.

YOUR SACRED VISION FOR SALE

Shamanic ceremonies may be native to the Amazon, but they have become a hot commodity in Cuzco and the Sacred Valley. The psychedelic properties of the San Pedro and *ayahuasca* plants have earned them fame and piqued public curiosity and the interest of psychonauts who travel in search of these experiences.

Extremely powerful drugs, they can be highly toxic in the wrong hands. In 2018 a Canadian man was lynched in the Amazon region by an angry mob who believed he had killed a Shipibo healer. In 2015 a tourist fatally stabbed another tourist while both were under the drug's influence. In some cases, female guests have been attacked while under the influence as well.

Yet the commercial industry is insatiable. In Cuzco, San Pedro is offered alongside massages by street hawkers; *ayahuasca* ceremonies are advertised in hostels. It's important to note that these are not recreational drugs. A real shaman knows the long list of dos and don'ts for practitioners, and may screen participants. Ceremonies can require multiple days for preparation, fasting and extended rituals. Serious operations often use a medical questionnaire.

Many *cuzqueños* (inhabitants of Cuzco) believe that it's a mockery to make these sacred ceremonies into moneymakers. While we don't recommend taking part, research your options and avoid casual opportunities if you do decide to participate.

Casa Concha is a beautiful restored colonial home that belonged to an aristocrat at the time of the conquest.

Museo Histórico Regional   MUSEUM

(Map p206; Garcilaso at Heladeros; boleto turístico adult/student S130/70; ☺8am-5pm) This eclectic museum is housed in the colonial Casa Garcilaso de la Vega, the house of the Inca-Spanish chronicler who now lies buried in the cathedral. The chronologically arranged collection begins with arrowheads from the Preceramic Period and continues with ceramics and jewelry of the Wari, Pukara and Inca cultures. Admission is with the *boleto turístico* (tourist ticket; p210) only, which is valid for 10 days and covers 16 other sites.

There is also a Nazca mummy, a few Inca weavings, some small gold ornaments and a strangely sinister scale model of the Plaza de Armas. A big, helpful chart in the courtyard outlines the timeline and characters of the *escuela cuzqueña*.

Museo Municipal de Arte Contemporáneo   MUSEUM

(Map p206; Plaza Regocijo; boleto turístico adult/student S130/70; ☺9am-6pm Mon-Sat) The small collection of contemporary Andean art on display at this museum in the municipality building is really one for the fans. Museo Quijote (p215) has a much better collection, putting a representative range of Peru's contemporary artists on show, with interpretive information that puts the art in context with history. Admission is with the *boleto turístico* tourist card only.

Iglesia San Francisco   CHURCH

(Map p206; Plaza San Francisco; museum admission S15; ☺9am-6pm) More austere than many of Cuzco's other churches, Iglesia San Francisco dates from the 16th and 17th centuries and is one of the few that didn't need to be completely reconstructed after the 1650 earthquake. It has a large collection of colonial religious paintings and a beautifully carved cedar choir.

The attached museum supposedly houses the largest painting in South America, which measures 9m by 12m and shows the family tree of St Francis of Assisi, the founder of the Franciscan order. Also of macabre interest are the two crypts, which are not totally underground. Inside are human bones, some of which have been carefully arranged in designs meant to remind visitors of the transitory nature of life.

Iglesia y Convento de Santa Clara   CHURCH

(Map p206; Santa Clara s/n) This 16th-century church, part of a strict convent, is difficult to visit but it's worth making the effort to go for morning services, because this is one of the more bizarre churches in Cuzco. Mirrors cover almost the entire interior; apparently, the colonial clergy used them to entice curious indigenous peoples into the church for worship.

The nuns provide the choir during Mass, sitting at the very back of the church and separated from both the priest and the rest of the congregation by an ominous grille of heavy metal bars stretching from floor to ceiling.

Museo de Arte Religioso   MUSEUM

(Map p206; cnr Hatunrumiyoc & Herrajes; admission S10; ☺8am-6pm) Originally the palace of Inca Roca, the foundations of this museum were converted into a grand colonial residence and later became the archbishop's palace. The beautiful mansion is now home to a religious-art collection notable for the accuracy of its period detail, and especially its insight into the interaction of indigenous peoples with the Spanish conquistadors.

There are also some impressive ceilings and colonial-style tile work that's not original, having been replaced during the 1940s.

◉ San Blas

Iglesia de San Blas   CHURCH

(Map p206; Plaza San Blas; adult/student S10/5; ☺10am-6pm Mon-Sat, 2-6pm Sun) This simple adobe church is comparatively small, but you can't help but be awed by the baroque, gold-leaf principal altar. The exquisitely carved pulpit, made from a single tree trunk, has been called the finest example of colonial wood carving in the Americas.

Legend claims that its creator was an indigenous man who miraculously recovered from a deadly disease and subsequently dedicated his life to carving the pulpit for this church. Supposedly, his skull is nestled in the topmost part of the carving. In reality, no one is certain of the identity of either the skull or the woodcarver.

◉ Avenida El Sol & Downhill

Museo de Arte Popular   MUSEUM

(Map p206; ☎084-25-8089; Basement, Av El Sol 103; admission S5; ☺9am-6pm Mon-Sat, 8am-1pm Sun) Winning entries in Cuzco's annual Popular Art Competition are displayed in

Around Av El Sol

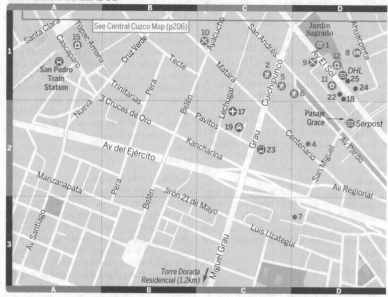

See Central Cuzco Map (p206)

this engaging museum. This is where the artisans and artists of San Blas showcase their talents in styles ranging from high art to cheeky, offering a fascinating, humorous take on ordinary life amid the pomp and circumstance of a once-grandiose culture.

Small-scale ceramic models depict drunken debauchery in a *picantería* (local restaurant), torture in a dentist's chair, carnage in a butcher shop, and even a caesarean section. There's also a display of photographs, many by renowned local photographer Martín Chambi, of Cuzco from the 1900s to the 1950s, including striking images of the aftermath of the 1950 earthquake in familiar streets.

Qorikancha
RUINS

(Map p206; ☎ 084-24-9176; Plazoleta Santo Domingo; admission S15 or boleto turístico; ⏰ 8:30am-5:30pm Mon-Sat, 2-5pm Sun) If you visit only one Cuzco site, make it these Inca ruins forming the base of the colonial church and convent of Santo Domingo. Once the richest temple in the Inca empire, all that remains today is the masterful stonework. The temple was built in the mid-15th century during the reign of the 10th *inca,* Túpac Yupanqui. Postconquest, Francisco Pizarro gave it to his brother Juan who bequeathed it to the Dominicans, in whose possession it remains.

Today's site is a bizarre combination of Inca and colonial architecture, topped with a roof of glass and metal. In Inca times, Qorikancha (Quechua for 'Golden Courtyard') was literally covered with gold. The temple walls were lined with some 700 solid-gold sheets, each weighing about 2kg. There were life-sized gold and silver replicas of corn, which were ceremonially 'planted' in agricultural rituals. Also reported were solid-gold treasures, such as altars, llamas and babies, as well as a replica of the sun. But within months of the arrival of the first conquistadors, this incredible wealth had all been looted and melted down.

Various other religious rites took place in the temple. It is said that the mummified bodies of several previous *incas* (kings) were kept here, brought out into the sunlight each day and offered food and drink, which was then ritually burnt. Qorikancha was also an observatory where high priests monitored celestial activities. Most of this is left to the imagination of the modern visitor, but the remaining stonework ranks with the finest Inca architecture in Peru. A curved, perfectly fitted 6m-high wall can be seen from both inside and outside the site. This wall has withstood all of the violent earthquakes that leveled most of Cuzco's colonial buildings.

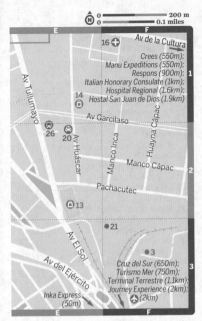

God's guard dogs (*dominicanus* in Latin), hence the name of this religious order.

Iglesia de Santo Domingo   CHURCH

(Map p206) The church of Santo Domingo is next door to Qorikancha. Less baroque and ornate than many of Cuzco's churches, it is notable for its charming paintings of arch-angels depicted as Andean children in jeans and T-shirts. Opening hours are erratic.

Museo Quijote   MUSEUM

(Map p206; Galería Banco la Nacion, Almagro s/n; ⊙9am-6pm Mom-Fri, to 1pm Sun) **FREE** Housed inside a bank, this privately owned muse-um of contemporary art houses a diverse, thoughtful collection of painting and sculp-ture ranging from the folksy to the macabre. There's good interpretive information about 20th-century Peruvian art history, some of it translated into English.

Museo del Sitio de Qorikancha   MUSEUM

(Map p214; Av El Son s/n; boleto turístico adult/student S130/70; ⊙9am-6pm Mon-Sat, 8am-1pm Sun) There are sundry moth-bitten archae-ological displays interpreting Inca and pre-Inca cultures at this small, mangy, un-derground archaeological museum, which is accessed off Av El Sol.

Admission is with the *boleto turístico* tourist card only.

🏃 Activities

Scores of outdoor outfitters in Cuzco offer trekking, rafting and mountain-biking ad-ventures, as well as mountaineering, horse-back riding and paragliding. Price wars can lead to bad feelings among locals, with un-derpaid guides and overcrowded vehicles. The cheaper tours usually take more guests and use guides with a more basic skill set.

Hiking

The department of Cuzco is a hiker's para-dise. Ecosystems range from rainforest to high alpine environments in these enor-mous mountain ranges. Trekkers may come upon isolated villages and ruins lost in the undergrowth. Altitudes vary widely, it is es-sential to acclimatize properly before under-taking any trek.

Of course, most visitors come to hike the famed Inca Trail to Machu Picchu. Be aware that it's not the only 'Inca trail.' What savvy tourism officials and tour operators have christened the Inca Trail is just one of dozens of footpaths that the Incas built to reach Machu Picchu, out of thousands that

Once inside the site, you enter a court-yard. The octagonal font in the middle was originally covered with 55kg of solid gold. Inca chambers lie to either side of the court-yard. The largest, to the right, were said to be temples to the moon and the stars, and were covered with sheets of solid silver. The walls are perfectly tapered upward and, with their niches and doorways, are excellent examples of Inca trapezoidal architecture. The fitting of the individual blocks is so precise that in some places you can't tell where one block ends and the next begins.

Opposite these chambers, on the other side of the courtyard, are smaller temples dedicated to thunder and the rainbow. Three holes have been carved through the walls of this section to the street outside, which scholars think were drains, either for sacrificial *chicha* (fermented corn beer), blood or, more mundanely, rainwater. Alter-natively, they may have been speaking tubes connecting the inner temple with the out-side. Another feature of this side of the com-plex is the floor in front of the chambers: it dates from Inca times and is carefully cob-bled with pebbles.

Colonial paintings around the outside of the courtyard depict the life of St Dominic and contain several representations of dogs holding torches in their jaws. These are

Around Av El Sol

crisscrossed the Inca empire. Some of these overland routes are still being dug out of the jungle by archaeologists. Many more have been developed for tourism, and an ever-increasing number of trekkers are choosing them.

Closer to Cuzco, multiday Sacred Valley trekking itineraries go well off the beaten track to little-visited villages and ruins.

Further afield, recommended treks include Lares and Ausangate and, for archaeological sites, Choquequirao and Vilcabamba.

★ Apus Peru   HIKING
(Map p214; ☎084-23-2691; www.apus-peru.com; Cuichipunco 366; ⊙9am-1pm & 3-7pm Mon-Sat) A recommended outfitter for the Inca Trail and others, also offering conventional tours. Responsible and popular with travelers. The company joins the Choquequirao trek with the Inca Trail for a total of nine days of spectacular scenery and an ever-more-impressive parade of Inca ruins, culminating in Machu Picchu.

★ Alpaca Expeditions   HIKING
(Map p206; ☎084-25-4278; www.alpacaexpeditions.com; Heladeros 157, piso 2 No 24; ⊙9am-7:30pm Mon-Fri, 4:30-7:30pm Sat & Sun) A popular outfitter for the Inca Trail, Sacred Valley treks, Salkantay and Choquequirao, this is one of the few companies to prioritize hiring female guides and porters. Also uses portable bathrooms, plants trees and participates in trail cleanup.

Mountain Lodges of Peru   HIKING
(☎084-23-6069; www.mountainlodgesofperu.com) Runs luxury lodges in remote trekking locations and offers treks on various routes, including Salkantay and Lares, ending at Machu Picchu. There's no public office. All booking is online or by phone.

Llama Path   HIKING
(Map p214; ☎084-24-0822; www.llamapath.com; Cuichipunco 257; ⊙9am-1pm & 3-8pm Mon-Sat, 4-8pm Sun) Friendly trekking company with a solid reputation. Does Inca Trail, Lares, Salkantay, Choquequirao and more.

Peru Eco Expeditions   HIKING
(☎084-60-7516, 957-349-269; www.peruecoexpeditions.com; Urb San Judas Chico II D-13; ⊙9am-4pm Mon-Fri) ⚐ A small luxury adventure travel company with custom expeditions ranging from day trips to lodge hikes and trips, such as the Inca Trail and Rainbow Mountain (with mountain biking or a cultural stop), throughout the region and in the Amazon. With sustainable tourism practices ranging from filtered water and 100% waste removal on treks to cultural sensitivity toward local communities.

Wayki Trek HIKING

(Map p206; ☎ 084-22-4092; www.waykitrek.net; Quera 239; ⊙9am-7pm Mon-Fri, to 1pm Sat) 🏊 A popular Inca Trail outfitter that earns rave reviews. It also does Choquequirao, Salkantay and Ausangate treks. ISO certified.

Peru Treks HIKING

(Map p214; ☎084-22-2722; www.perutreks.com; Av Pardo 540) A longtime operator offering hiking tours to Machu Picchu.

X-Treme Tourbulencia HIKING

(Map p206; ☎084-22-5875; www.x-tremetourbulencia.com; Plateros 364; ⊙9am-1pm & 4-8pm Mon-Sat) A recommended Cuzco-based tour operator offering multisport access to Machu Picchu via Santa Teresa, the Inca Trail and the Inca Jungle Trail. It also does trips to Ausangate, Salkantay, Choquequirao and a Rainbow Mountain overnight. With multilingual guides.

Destiny Peru HIKING

(Map p206; ☎084-437-876; www.destinyperutours.com; Carmen Bajo 184; ⊙9am-2pm & 4-8:30pm Mon-Sat, 9am-2pm Sun) Offers treks including Inca Trail, Salkantay and Ausangate, as well as Rainbow Mountain day trips via the alternative route.

River Rafting

Rafting isn't regulated in Peru – literally anyone can start a rafting company. On top of this, aggressive bargaining has led to lax safety by many cheaper rafting operators. The degree of risk cannot be stressed enough: there are deaths every year. Rafting companies that take advance bookings online are generally more safety conscious (and more expensive) than those just operating out of storefronts in Cuzco.

When choosing an outfitter, it's wise to ask about safety gear and guide training, ask about the quality of the equipment used (ie how old are the flotation devices) and check other traveler comments. It's essential to book a top-notch outfitter employing highly experienced rafting guides with first-aid certification and knowledge of swift-water rescue techniques. Be wary of new agencies without a known track record.

In terms of locations, there are a number of rivers to choose from. Rivers further from Cuzco are days away from help in the event of illness or accident.

Río Urubamba

Rafting the Río Urubamba through the Sacred Valley could offer the best rafting day trip in South America, but Cuzco and all the villages along its course dispose of raw sewage in the river, making for a smelly and polluted trip. Seriously – close your mouth if you fall in.

Despite its unsavory aspects, the **Ollantaytambo to Chilca** (class II to III) section is surprisingly popular, offering 1½ hours of gentle rafting with only two rapids of note. **Huarán** and **Huambutio to Pisac** are other pollution-affected sections.

There are a variety of cleaner sections south of Cuzco on the upper Urubamba (also known as the Vilcanota), including the popular **Chuquicahuana** run (class III to IV+; class V+ in the rainy season). Another less frenetic section is the fun and scenic **Cusipata to Quiquihana** (mainly class II to III). In the rainy season, these two sections are often combined. Closer to Cuzco, **Pampa to Huambutio** (class I to II) is a beautiful section, ideal for small children (three years and over) as an introduction to rafting.

Río Santa Teresa

Río Santa Teresa offers spectacular rafting in the gorge between the towns of Santa Teresa and Santa María, and downstream as far as Quillabamba. One word of warning: the section from Cocalmayo Hot Springs to Santa María consists of almost nonstop class IV to V rapids in a deep, inaccessible canyon. It should only be run with highly reputable operators. Be very aware, if considering a trip here, that guiding this section safely is beyond the powers of inexperienced (cheaper) rafting guides. This is not the place to economize. It's not a bad idea to raft another section in the area with your chosen operator before even considering it.

Other Rivers

Run from May to November, the **Río Apurímac** offers three- to 10-day trips through deep gorges and protected rainforest. Apurímac features exhilarating rapids (classes IV and V) and wild, remote scenery with deep gorges. Sightings of condors and even pumas have been recorded. Four-day trips are the most relaxed and avoid the busier campsites, although three-day trips are more commonly offered. Camping is on sandy beaches, which have become increasingly overused. Sand flies can be a nuisance. Make sure your outfitter cleans up the campsite and practices a leave-no-trace ethic.

An even wilder expedition, the 10- to 12-day trip along the demanding **Río Tambopata** can only be run from May to October. The trip starts in the Andes, north of Lake Titicaca, and descends through the heart of the Parque Nacional Bahuaje-Sonene deep in the Amazon jungle. Just getting to the put-in from Cuzco is a two-day drive. The first days on the river are full of technically demanding rapids (classes III and IV) in wild Andean scenery, and the trip finishes with a couple of gentle floating days in the rainforest. Tapirs, capybara, caiman, giant otters and jaguars have all been seen by keen-eyed boaters.

A popular outfitter, **River Explorers** (☑ 084-431-116; www.riverexplorers.com; Urb Kennedy A, Brillantes B 36; ☺ 8am-1pm & 3-5pm Mon-Fri, to noon Sat) runs all sorts of sections, including trips of up to six days on Río Apurímac.

Mountain Biking

Mountain-biking tours are a growing industry in Cuzco, and the local terrain is superb. Rental bikes are poor quality and it is most common to find *rígida* (single suspension) models, which can make for bone-chattering downhills. Good new or secondhand bikes are not easy to buy in Cuzco either. If you're a serious mountain biker, consider bringing your own bike from home. Selling it in Cuzco is eminently viable.

If you're an experienced rider, some awesome rides are quickly and easily accessible by public transport. Take the Pisac bus (stash your bike on top) and ask to be let off at **Abra de Ccorao**. From here, you can turn right and make your way back to Cuzco via a series of cart tracks and single track; halfway down is a jump park constructed by local aficionados. This section has many variations and is known as **Yuncaypata**. Eventually, whichever way you go, you'll end up in Cuzco's southern suburbs, from where you can easily flag down a taxi to get you home.

If you head off the other side of the pass, to the left of the road, you'll find fast-flowing single track through a narrow valley, which makes it difficult to get lost. It brings you out on the highway in Ccorao. From here, follow the road through a flat section then a series of bends. Just as the valley widens out, turn left past a farmhouse steeply downhill to your left and into a challenging single track through a narrow valley, including a hairy river crossing and some tricky, steep, rocky, loose descents at the end, reaching the village of Taray. From here it's a 10-minute ride along the river to Pisac, where you can catch a bus back to Cuzco.

Many longer trips are possible, but a professionally qualified guide and a support vehicle are necessary. The partly paved road down from **Abra Málaga to Santa María**, though not at all technical, is a must for any cyclist. It is part of the Inca Jungle Trail, offered by many Cuzco operators. **Maras to Salineras** is a great little mission. The **Lares Valley** offers a challenging single track, which can be accessed from Cuzco in a long day. If heading to Manu in the Amazon Basin, you can break up the long bus journey by biking from **Tres Cruces to La Unión** – a beautiful, breathtaking downhill ride – or you could go all the way down by bike. The outfitters of Manu trips can arrange bicycle rental and guides. The descent to the **Río Apurímac** makes a great burn, as does the journey to **Río Tambopata**, which boasts a descent of 3500m in five hours. A few bikers attempt the 500km-plus trip all the way to Puerto Maldonado, a great hot and sweaty challenge.

Gravity Peru ADVENTURE
(Map p214; ☑ 084-22-8032, 984-501-311; www.gravityperu.com; Av Centenario 707; ☺ 8am-6pm) Allied with well-known Gravity Bolivia, this professionally run operator is the only one offering double-suspension bikes for day trips to the so-called 'secret single track.' Its back-door Machu Picchu tour (via adventure options and biking) has become a hugely popular alternative to accessing the ruins. Highly recommended.

TAXI TOURS

If you are short on time to see the sights outside Cuzco, consider taking a taxi tour. If you have two or more people, they can be a particularly good deal, and also allow you to take your time (or not) visiting various ruins and markets. From Cuzco, a tour of the Sacred Valley (possibly including Pisac, Ollantaytambo, Chinchero, Maras and Moray) runs S200 to S240 (for the whole car); to the Southern Valley (with options to Tipón, Pikillacta and Raqcchi) costs around S150.

Reliable options include **Taxi Juan Carlos** (☑ 917-459-192, 910-641-041) and **Virgin Estrella Taxi Tours** (☑ 974-955-374, 973-195-551) in Cuzco.

Horseback Riding

Most agencies can arrange a morning or afternoon's riding. Alternatively, you can walk to Sacsaywamán, where many ranches are located, and negotiate your own terms. Choose carefully, however, as horses may be in a sorry state.

Select agencies will offer multiday trips to the area around Limatambo, and there are some first-rate ranches with highly trained, high-stepping thoroughbred Peruvian *paso* horses in Urubamba.

Bird-Watching

Serious birders should definitely get hold of *Birds of the High Andes* by Jon Fjeldså and Niels Krabbe. One of the best birding trips is from Ollantaytambo to Santa Teresa or Quillabamba, over Abra Málaga. This provides a fine cross section of habitats from 4600m to below 1000m. A good local field guide is *The Birds of Machu Picchu* by Barry Walker.

Other Activities

Action Valley   OUTDOORS
(Map p206; ☑084-24-0835; www.actionvalley. com; Santa Teresa 325; ☺9am-5pm Sun-Fri, closed mid-Jan to mid-Feb) A terror for acrophobes and a blast for kids and juvenile adults. Offerings include paintball (S77), a 10m climbing wall (S34), a 122m bungee jump (S253) and a bungee slingshot (S219). It's also possible to go paragliding (S216) from the *mirador* (lookout) of Racchi. The park is 11km outside Cuzco on Poroy road.

Samana Spa   SPA
(Map p206; ☑084-23-3721; www.samana-spa. com; Tecsecocha 536; 1hr massage S130; ☺10am-6pm Mon-Sat) For some pampering or a post-trekking splurge, visit this pampering spa. No walk-ins, book ahead.

Courses

Cuzco is one of the best places in South America to study Spanish. Shop around – competition is fierce and students benefit with free cultural and social activities. Salsa lessons and cooking nights are more or less ubiquitous.

The standard deal is 20 hours of classes per week, either individual or in groups of up to four people. Most schools will also let you pay by the hour or study more or less intensively.

Visit your school on a Friday to get tested and assigned to a group for a Monday start, or show up any time to start individual lessons. All schools can arrange family homestays and volunteer opportunities.

★**Marcelo Batata Cooking Class** COOKING
(Map p206; ☑984-384-520; www.cuzcodining. com; Calle Palacio 135; 4hr course S297; ☺2pm) If you've fallen for Peruvian cooking, this four-hour course is a worthwhile foray. A fully stocked market pantry demystifies the flavors of the region and the kitchen setup is comfortable. Includes appetizers, a pisco tasting and a main course. In English, Spanish or Portuguese. Accommodates vegetarians, and there's a private-course option.

Proyecto Peru   LANGUAGE
(Map p206; ☑084-24-0278; www.proyecto perucentre.org; Seite Cuartones 290; ☺8am-6pm Mon-Fri) Offers Quechua and business or medical Spanish, with the option of homestays.

Amigos   LANGUAGE
(☑084-22-5053; www.spanishcusco.com; Zaguan del Cielo B-23; ☺9am-5pm Mon-Fri) A long-established nonprofit school with an admirable public-service record.

Fairplay   LANGUAGE
(Map p214; ☑984-78-9252; www.fairservices -peru.org; Pasaje Zavaleta C-5) A unique nonprofit NGO, Fairplay trains Peruvian single mothers to provide Spanish lessons and homestays. Students pay two-thirds of their class fees directly to their teachers. Individual classes only, priced according to the teacher's level of experience.

Excel Language Center   LANGUAGE
(Map p206; ☑084-23-5298; www.excelspanish peru.info; Cruz Verde 336; ☺8am-1pm & 4-9pm Mon-Fri, 9am-noon Sat) A Spanish-language program that has been highly recommended for its professionalism. Also offers lodging.

Choco Museo   COOKING
(Map p206; ☑084-24-4765; www.chocomuseo. com; Garcilaso 210; ☺9am-7pm; ⊕) FREE The wafting aromas of bubbling chocolate will mesmerize you from the start. While the museum aspect here is frankly lite, the best part of this French-owned enterprise is the organic-chocolate-making workshops. You can also come for fondue or a fresh cup of fair-trade hot cocoa. It organizes chocolate farm tours close to Santa María as well. It is multilingual and kid friendly.

Tours

Cuzco has hundreds of registered travel agencies, so ask other travelers for recommendations. Many of the small agencies clustered around Procuradores and Plateros earn

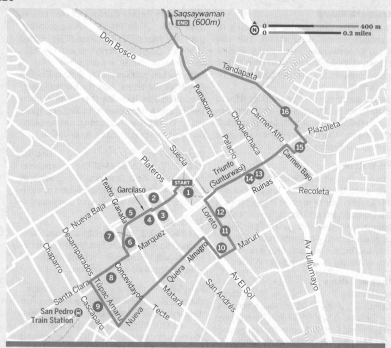

City Walk
Central Cuzco Stroll

START PLAZA DE ARMAS
END SAQSAYWAMÁN
LENGTH 4KM; THREE HOURS

Start from the stunning **1 Plaza de Armas** (p209), stroll up Calle del Medio and head southwest across **2 Plaza Regocijo**. On your left, a beautiful **3 building** houses restaurants and boutiques. Head up Calle Garcilaso, named for the Inca chronicler Garcilaso de la Vega, whose childhood home now houses the **4 Museo Histórico Regional** (p213). Admire the nearby **5 Hotel los Marqueses** (p226), a stunning colonial mansion.

On Sundays, Quechua-speaking country folk meet in **6 Plaza San Francisco**. Drop in to the **7 church and museum of San Francisco** if you're so inclined. Past the colonial archway is the **8 church and convent of Santa Clara**. If it's open, peek inside at the mirrors, used in colonial times to entice curious indigenous people into the church for worship.

Just beyond is the bustling **9 Mercado San Pedro** (p236). Order a juice, then step out onto Calle Nueva and follow to Av El Sol opposite the **10 Palacio de Justicia**. Head up Maruri and take a left into **11 Loreto**, a walkway with Inca walls on both sides. The west wall belongs to Amaruqancha (Courtyard of the Serpents). The east wall is one of the oldest in Cuzco, belonging to the Acllahuasi (House of the Chosen Women). Post-conquest, it became part of the **12 closed convent of Santa Catalina**.

Loreto returns you to the Plaza de Armas. Turn right up Triunfo (signposted as Sunturwasi) and across Palacio into Hatunrumiyoc, another alley named after the **13 12-sided stone**. This belongs to a wall of the palace of the sixth *inca*, Roca, which now houses the **14 Museo de Arte Religioso** (p213).

Hatunrumiyoc ends at Choquechaca. From here it's only a short puff up to **15 Plaza San Blas**, Cuzco's bohemian HQ. Head left along **16 Tandapata** for the classic cobblestone experience. Inca irrigation channels run down ancient stairways, and rock carvings adorn walls and stones in the path.

If you wish, forge uphill to **Saqsaywamán** (p240).

commissions selling trips run by other outfitters, which can lead to mix-ups. If the travel agency also sells ponchos, changes money and has an internet cabin in the corner, chances are it's not operating your tour.

At tourist sites, freelance guides speak some English or other foreign languages. For more extensive tours at major sites, such as Qorikancha or the cathedral, always agree to a fair price in advance. Otherwise, a respectable minimum tip for a short tour is S5 per person in a group and a little more for individuals.

Standard tours often travel in large groups and can be rushed. Classic options include a half-day tour of the city and/or nearby ruins, a half-day trip to the Sunday markets at Pisac or Chinchero and a full-day tour of the Sacred Valley (eg Pisac, Ollantaytambo and Chinchero). It's perfectly feasible to do these at your own pace with a licensed taxi driver or public transport.

Agents also offer expensive Machu Picchu tours that include transport, admission tickets to the archaeological site, an English-speaking guide and lunch. Since you only get to spend a few hours at the ruins, it's more enjoyable (not to mention much cheaper) to DIY and hire a guide at Machu Picchu.

Andean Photo Expeditions   TOUR
(☏960-724-103; www.andeanphotoexpeditions. com; photo tour S248) Run by Peru enthusiasts, this highly personalized guide service offers recommended photo tours in Cuzco and Lima. It also specializes in off-the-beaten-path trips, such as trips to Rainbow Mountain via Cusipata with a homestay, Ausangate mountain treks and jungle trips. The co-owner is an accomplished photographer with work in Cuzco galleries. It offers services in multiple languages.

Habitats Peru   TOUR
(☏984-115-593; www.habitatsperu.com) A recommended birding guide service offering tailored and group trips to wetlands, mountain and jungle environments. It also does conventional tours, and mountain-biking, hiking and jungle tours. Some profits go to preserving the conservation areas visited.

Travel & Healing   OUTDOORS
(☏084-22-7892; www.travelandhealing.com; Av La Cultura 2122, piso 3; ☉8:30am-8pm Mon-Sat) Specializing in spiritual retreats, Ayahuasca ceremonies and Andean cultural wisdom, this outfitter takes a sincere spiritual approach to local tours and treks. Sometimes combined with yoga.

Culturas Peru   ADVENTURE
(Map p206; ☏084-24-3629; www.culturasperu. com; Tandapata 354-A; ☉9am-5pm Mon-Fri) A highly knowledgeable and reputable, locally owned and run outfitter with sustainable practices. Its two-day Inca Trail option is popular.

SAS Travel   TOURS
(Map p206; ☏084-24-9194; www.sastravelperu. com; Calle Garcilaso 270; ☉8am-8pm Mon-Sat) A direct operator with local owners. Offers high-end package tours to Machu Picchu, Inca Trail treks, jungle travel and Cuzco tours. While this outfitter charges more than the competition, traveler satisfaction is generally high.

Amazonas Explorer   OUTDOORS
(☏084-25-2846; www.amazonas-explorer.com; Av Collasuyu 910 Miravalle; ☉9am-5pm Mon-Fri) A professional international operator with top-quality equipment and guides, offering rafting trips on the Ríos Apurimac and Tambopata. Also offers trekking the five-day classic and alternative treks. Its two- to 10-day mountain-biking adventures are great for families, with kids' bikes available. It has socially and environmentally responsible practices.

Alain Machaca Cruz   TOURS
(☏984-056-635; www.alternativeincatrails.com; Belen s/n, Paruro) This independent guide based outside Cuzco leads Laguna Yanahuara and multiday hikes to Choquequierao, Vilcabamba and other areas. He also makes recommended tours to the village of Paruro where you can make *chicha* (fermented corn beer) or see *cuy* (guinea pig) farms. Quechua and English spoken. No set office hours, contact ahead.

SATO   TOURS
(Map p214; ☏084-26-1505; www.southamerica-travelsonline.com; Urbanización Quinta Jardín 288; ☉9am-5pm Mon-Fri, to 1pm Sat) A reputable European agency working with local operators for trekking, hiking and rafting, also a last-minute specialist.

Journey Experience   ADVENTURE
(JOEX; ☏084-24-5642; www.joextravel.com; Av Tupac Amaru V-2-A, Progreso; ☉9am-6pm) A recommended outfitter for hiking and cultural activities.

Aspiring Adventures   ADVENTURE
(☏in US & Canada 1-877-438-1354, in New Zealand 03-489-7474; www.aspiringadventures. com) A small, enthusiastic outfit that's

Kiwi-Australian run with extensive experience in Cuzco and the Sacred Valley. Does biking, classic trips and food-focused tours.

Aventours
ADVENTURE

(Map p206; ☑084-22-4050; www.aventours.com; Plateros 456; ◷9am-1pm & 4-7pm Mon-Fri) A responsible outfitter with a long-tenured team.

Apumayo Expediciones
TOURS

(☑914-169-665; www.apumayo.com; Jr Ricardo Palma Ñ-11, Urb Santa Monica Wanchaq, Cuzco; ◷9am-6pm Mon-Fri) A professional outfitter that takes advance international bookings for Río Tambopata trips. It also specializes in trips to Machu Picchu and other historic sites in the Sacred Valley for disabled travelers.

Respons
CULTURAL

(Responsible Travel Peru; ☑084-59-8331; www.responsibletravelperu.com; Pasaje los Lirios 7A, Urb Mariscal Gamarra; ◷9am-1pm & 3-6pm Mon-Fri) 🌱 High-end sustainable tour operator working with community development in the Sacred Valley. Offers a tour of a weaving community near Pisac and chocolate and coffee tours on the Inca Jungle Trail. Available in English, Spanish and French.

Turismo Caith
CULTURAL TOUR

(☑084-23-3595; www.caith.org; Urb Ucchullo Alto, N4, Pasaje Santo Toribio, Centro Yanapanakusun; ◷9am-7pm Mon-Sat) 🌱 Leader in community tourism as well as standard single and multiday trips. Participants can help with educational projects.

Reserv Cusco
ADVENTURE

(Map p206; ☑084-26-1548; www.reserv-cusco-peru.com; Plateros 327; ◷10am-9pm) This respected tour operator offers a multisport access to Machu Picchu via Santa Teresa and the Inca Jungle Trail.

Peruvian Odyssey
ADVENTURE

(☑84-25-3374; www.peruvianodyssey.com; Calle Panamá K-17; ◷9am-6pm Mon-Fri) Operator with 20 years' experience that also offers alternative route via Santa Teresa.

Antipode
ADVENTURE

(Map p206; ☑084-24-0867; www.antipode-peru.com; Choquechaca 229; ◷9am-12:30pm & 2-6pm Mon-Fri) An attentive, French-run outfit offering classic tours, treks and shorter local adventure outings.

Asociación de Guías Oficiales de Turismo
TOURS

(Agotur; Map p206; ☑084-2334-57; www.agotur-cusco.com; Heladeros 157, 34-F) The official tourism guide association is a good way for travelers to contact guides.

🎊 Festivals & Events

El Señor de los Temblores
CULTURAL

(The Lord of the Earthquakes; ◷Mar/Apr) This procession through the Plaza de Armas takes place on Holy Monday (the Monday before Easter). It dates to the earthquake of 1650. El Señor de los Temblores' crucifix of the savior (now charred with soot) is considered the patron saint of Cuzco, responsible for saving the city from further earthquake damage.

Crucifix Vigil
RELIGIOUS

(◷early May) On May 2 to 3, a Crucifix Vigil is held on all hillsides with crosses atop them.

Q'oyoriti
CULTURAL

(Ausangate; ◷May/Jun) Less well-known than June's spectacular Inti Raymi are the more traditional Andean rites of this festival, which is held at the foot of Ausangate the Tuesday before Corpus Christi, in late May or early June.

Corpus Christi
RELIGIOUS

(◷Jun) Held on the ninth Thursday after Easter, Corpus Christi usually occurs in early June and features fantastic religious processions and celebrations in the cathedral.

Inti Raymi
CULTURAL

(Festival of the Sun; ◷Jun 24) This is Cuzco's most important festival. Visitors from throughout Peru and the world join the whole city celebrating in the streets with dancing and parades. The festival culminates in a reenactment of the Inca winter-solstice festival at Sacsaywamán. Despite its commercialization, it's still worth seeing the pageantry in the city and at Sacsaywamán.

Santuranticuy Artisan Crafts Fair
FESTIVAL

(Plaza de Armas; ◷Dec 24) A crafts fair is held in the Plaza de Armas on Christmas Eve.

🛏 Sleeping

Cuzco has hundreds of lodgings of all types and prices, with some of Peru's highest room rates. Book ahead in peak season (between June and August) especially the 10 days before Inti Raymi on June 24 and Fiestas Patrias (Independence Days) on July 28 and 29.

Prices vary dramatically according to the season and demand. Lonely Planet lists high-season rates.

With advance notice, most hotels offer free airport pickups.

① BUYING MACHU PICCHU TICKETS

You would think accessing the continent's number-one destination might be easier. Get ready. Currently, Machu Picchu tickets can be purchased online (www.machupicchu.gob. pe), though not all foreign credit cards go through. If you reserve online, can't get your card to work and happen to be in Cuzco, you can deposit the amount due at a Banco de la Nación outlet within a three-hour window; later check in via the website to print your ticket.

In Cuzco, you can also purchase tickets from the Dirección Regional de Cultura Cusco (p237) or the Dircetur outlet (p237) in the Museo Histórico. Both outlets accept Peruvian soles, Visa or Mastercard. If you want to risk waiting, you can also purchase them from the Centro Cultural (p258) in Aguas Calientes, but only in Peruvian soles. Note that Aguas Calientes ATMs frequently run out of cash. Student tickets must be purchased in person with valid photo ID from the institution.

For a reasonable fee, travel agencies can also obtain tickets, which some readers recommend. Entry to Machu Picchu requires a valid photo ID. Lastly, ticketing procedures can change, but iPeru (p237) can offer the latest updates. Good luck.

🛌 Central Cuzco

★ Wild Rover
HOSTEL $

(☑ 084-22-7546; www.wildroverhostels.com; Cuesta Santa Ana 782; dm S28-50, d/ste S120/160, all incl breakfast; @ 🛜) In its new, highly fortified hilltop location, Wild Rover is an island – or bubble – unto itself and it's wildly popular. It certainly brings Cuzco hostels to a whole new standard, with a brand-new resort-style compound featuring 201 beds and a separate, soundproof Irish pub. Forget culture shock with these top-notch, modern standards, frequent parties and strict security.

The downside? An inconvenient walking location and a disconnect with local culture, should you spend all your time within the walls.

Intro Hostel
HOSTEL $

(Map p206; ☑ 084-22-3869; www.introhosteles. com; Cuesta Santa Ana 515; dm S28-48, d without bathroom S112, all incl breakfast; 🛜) From the owners of 1900 Backpackers in Lima, this old colonial offers a clean look and good service, an ample courtyard and nice rooms. The mixed stall bathrooms are in good shape. There's a covered outdoor cooking area, billiards and travel-agent services. The reception operates 24 hours; take a taxi if it's late.

Mama Simona
HOSTEL $

(Map p206; ☑ 084-26-0408; www.mamasimona. com; Ceniza 364; dm S36-46, d with/without bathroom S126/102; @ 🛜) Styled for hipsters, with a crushed-velvet sofa and oddball decor. Beds have nice down covers and the shared kitchen with picnic tables is undoubtedly cute. There's also a cute on-site cafe with an excellent, good-value breakfast menu.

Stylish, comfortable and clean, it's two blocks northeast of Plaza San Francisco.

Milhouse
HOSTEL $

(Map p206; ☑ 084-23-2151; www.milhousehostel. com; Quera 270; dm S31-45, d S187, all incl breakfast; 🛜) Booming with backpackers, this busy colonial has all the standard features of a Cuzco hostel: bean bag chairs, ping-pong, travel-agent service and happy hours, with excellent guest treatment. Rooms are a bit airless, but each bed has its own light and plugs. Sports fans will appreciate the coordinated trips to local football matches. On a noisy street.

Pariwana
HOSTEL $

(Map p206; ☑ 084-23-3751; www.pariwana-hostel. com; Av Mesón de la Estrella 136; dm S189/159, with/without bathroom S189/159, ste S240, all incl breakfast; @ 🛜) Resembling spring break, this notably clean, newer hostel is among the better ones, filled with uni-types lounging on poufs and playing ping-pong in the courtyard of a huge colonial. Dorms hold four to 14 beds, priced accordingly. Beds in newish dorms are well spaced and the penthouse suite is well worth the splurge. The chic bar is invite-only. With an on-site travel agency.

Dragonfly
HOSTEL $

(Map p206; ☑ 084-24-7058; www.dragonflyhostels.com; Seite Cuartones 245; dm S28-45, d/tr S149/189, without bathroom S98/149; 🛜) One of several 16th-century colonial buildings redone in candy colors. Guests have use of a kitchen and there are weekly barbecues on the courtyard patio. With friendly staff.

Ecopackers
HOSTEL $

(Map p206; ☑ 084-23-1800; www.ecopackers peru.com; Santa Teresa 375; dm S36-63, d with/

BOOKING JUNGLE TRIPS IN CUZCO

If you plan to hit the Amazon Basin, you will find a lot of tour operators for the region and some lodges have offices based in Cuzco. Check out the following:

Amazon Trails Peru (p469)

Amazonas Explorer (p221)

Crees (☑ 084-26-2433, in UK 0-207-193-8759; www.crees-manu.org; Urb Mariscal Garmarra B-5, Zona 1; ⊗ 9am-5pm Mon-Fri, to noon Sat)

InkaNatura (p468)

Inkaterra (Map p206; ☑ in Cuzco 084-24-5314, in UK 0-800-458-7506, in US & Canada 1-800-442-5042; www.inkaterra.com; Plazoleta Nazarenas 211; ⊗ 8am-6pm Mon-Sat)

Manu Expeditions (☑ 084-22-5990; www.manuexpeditions.com; Los Geranios 2-G, Urb Mariscal Gamarra; 5 days & 4 nights Manu excursion s/d US$2040/3680) ✐

Pantiacolla Tours (p468)

Eco Amazonia Lodge (Map p206; ☑ 084-23-6159; reservas@ecoamazonia.com; Garcilaso 210, Office 206)

without bathroom S218/126; @ �) This big backpacker haven is a stone's throw from Plaza Regocijo. One of the all-inclusives (with bar, pool room and sunbathing), it's thrumming with business but staff can't hide their grumpiness when a line forms at the desk. There are lovely wicker lounges in the courtyard, device plugs located in lockers and sturdy beds that are extra long. With 24-hour security.

Hostal Andrea
GUESTHOUSE $

(Map p206; ☑ 084-23-6713; salemrey@hotmail.com; Cuesta Santa Ana 514; dm/d without bathroom S20/50; @ �) Cuzco's cheapest, this place offers dated but pleasant lodgings with a flower-lined patio and tiny guest kitchen. It's run by an eccentric but welcoming older couple. A reader favorite.

Teatro Inka B&B
GUESTHOUSE $

(Map p206; ☑ 084-24-7372, in Lima 01-976-0523; www.teatroinka.com; Teatro 391; s/d incl breakfast S100/150; @ �) An array of dark but decent doubles sit around an interior courtyard. While it isn't outstanding, it's inexpensive. Service is *meh*.

Hostal Suecia II
HOTEL $

(Map p206; ☑ 084-23-9757; www.hostalsuecia-2cusco.com; Tecsecocha 465; s/d S149/165, without bathroom S116/149; �) This long-standing backpacker favorite continues to offer excellent value with a central location, friendly owners, a light, bright, flowery patio, decent rooms and a book-lending library. Its hostess, Señora Yolanda, has been here for decades.

Hitchhikers
HOSTEL $

(Map p206; ☑ 084-26-0079; www.hhikersperu.com; Saphi 440; dm/d incl breakfast S35/110; �) In a very central location, this hostel is a bit run-down with sloping floors but it's clean and not too busy. Rooms are on the cold side.

★ Niños Hotel
HOTEL $$

(Map p206; ☑ 084-23-1424; www.ninoshotel.com; Meloc 442; s without bathroom S99, d with/without bathroom S198/182; @ �) Long beloved and highly recommended, this hotel is run by a Dutch-founded nonprofit foundation that serves underprivileged children in Cuzco. It is a rambling colonial with sunny courtyard. Refurbished rooms are bordered with bright trim and feature plaid throws and portable heaters. In the coldest months there are hot-water bottles to tuck in bed. A second branch is located at Fierro 476.

The public cafeteria features homemade cakes and breads as well as box lunches.

Tambo del Arriero
HOTEL $$

(Map p206; ☑ 084-26-0709; www.tambodelarriero.com; Nueva Alta 484; s/d/ste incl breakfast S297/396/495; @ �) A spacious and quiet courtyard hotel. Rooms are bordered with floral accents, with heated towel racks and down duvets. Some feature bathtubs. Breakfast comes buffet-style, and the hotel also offers free walking tours. If you like your space it's good value, though the neighborhood remains up-and-coming.

Tierra Viva HOTEL $$
(Map p206; ☑084-60-1317; www.tierraviva hoteles.com; Saphi 766; s/d incl breakfast from S350/376; @🛜) Doubles have hardwood floors or Berber carpets, white linens and colorful throws. Buffet breakfast is available from 5am. The location of this branch, back from the action, makes it a good compromise between central and peaceful.

Other branches are located at San Blas (p229) and Plaza de Armas (Map p206; ☑084-24-5858; www.tierravivahoteles.com; Suecia 345; s/d/ste incl breakfast S330/360/570; 🛜).

Los Andes de America HOTEL $$
(Map p206; ☑084-60-6060; www.cuscoandes. com; Garcilaso 150; s/d incl breakfast S274/310) A Best Western hotel noted for its buffet breakfast, which includes regional specialties such as *mote con queso* (cheese and corn) and *papa helada* (frozen potato). Rooms are warm and comfortable, bathrooms are big and relatively luxurious, and the atrium features a scale model of Machu Picchu.

Hotel Arqueólogo BOUTIQUE HOTEL $$
(Map p206; ☑084-23-2569; www.hotelarqueolo go.com; Pumacurco 408; d incl breakfast S337-349, ste S492; P@🛜) Feeling luxurious but also lived-in, this antique French-owned guesthouse gives a real feel for Cuzco, down to the Inca stonework. Tasteful rooms with original murals and tapestries overlook a vast courtyard paved in river stones. Relax on the back lawn or sip a complimentary pisco sour in the fireplace lounge. The sale of local weavings helps fund public libraries.

French, English and German are spoken. Superior rooms, with chic colonial design, are a significant upgrade.

Hostal Corihuasi GUESTHOUSE $$
(Map p206; ☑084-23-2233; www.corihuasi.com; Suecia 561; s/d incl breakfast S174/210) A brisk walk uphill from the main plaza, this family-feel guesthouse inhabits a mazelike colonial building with postcard views. Amply sized rooms are outfitted in a warm, rustic style with alpaca-wool blankets, handwoven rugs and solid wooden furnishings. Room 1 is the most in demand for its wraparound windows, ideal for soaking up panoramic sunsets. Airport transfer included.

Del Prado Inn HOTEL $$
(Map p206; ☑084-22-4442; www.delprado inn.com; Suecia 310; s/d incl buffet breakfast S225/390; @🛜) Del Prado is a solid option,

with efficient staff and just over a dozen snug rooms reached by elevator. Some have tiny balconies with corner views of the plaza. Check out the original Inca walls in the dining room.

El Balcón Hostal HOTEL $$
(Map p206; ☑084-23-6738; www.balconcusco. com; Tambo de Montero 222; d garden/balcony incl breakfast S228/294; @🛜) A reader favorite, this renovated 17th-century building features regional antiquities and 16 pleasant rooms, all with firm mattresses, balconies, phone and TV. The garden blooms with fuchsias and offers great views over Cuzco. There's also a sauna.

Loreto Boutique Hotel HOTEL $$
(Map p206; ☑084-22-6352; www.loretobou tiquehotel.com; Loreto 115; s/d incl breakfast S285/385) Maybe you're paying for the plaza location, since 'boutique' is an overstatement here. Dimly lit in daytime, Loreto has well-heeled, snug rooms bathed in neutrals. The best features are the four rooms with surviving Inca walls.

Midori HOTEL $$
(Map p206; ☑084-24-8144; www.midori-cus co.com; Ataúd 204; s/d incl breakfast S289/357; @🛜) Popular with small tour groups, this small hotel is classic and comfortable. Enormous rooms feature a living area, brocade fabrics and firm beds. Locally recommended, with some Japanese spoken. Book direct for the cheapest rates.

Hotel Royal Inca I HOTEL $$
(Map p206; ☑084-23-1067; www.royalinka hotel.pe; Plaza Regocijo 299; d incl breakfast S297; @🛜) Quiet as a mausoleum, this central hotel features good-quality rooms. Those in the colonial building are a bit dated but comfortable, while the modern ones are big, bright and cheery. The oddest feature might be the mix of kitsch in the public areas, including gold masks and an oversized wall mural with an indigenous nature scene bordering on soft porn.

Hostal Suecia I HOTEL $$
(Map p206; ☑084-23-3282; www.hostalsuecia1. com; Suecia 332; s/d incl breakfast S149/165; 🛜) Most rooms in this pint-sized guesthouse are very basic, but location and staff are fabulous and there's a sociable, stony, indoor courtyard. The two newer doubles on the top floor (311 and 312) are good value.

> **ⓘ LUXURY LODGES**
>
> For a luxurious, lodge-based experience of Ausangate and other mountain areas, check out **Andean Lodges** (☑ 084-22-4613; www.andeanlodges.com; Av Brasil A-14, Urb Cuzco; 3-day package from US$950; ⏱ 9am-6pm Mon-Fri). Ecofriendly technologies are used in bathrooms and restaurants. Treks range from three-days to a week, with lodging and all meals included.

Andenes de Saphi   HOTEL $$

(Map p206; ☑ 084-22-7561; www.andenesde saphi.com; Saphi 848; s/d S165/198; 🛜) At the far end of Saphi, where the city starts to peter out, this hotel has a rustic wooden construction with skylights and murals in most rooms. Choose yours with care, some feel musty.

Los Angeles B&B   HOTEL $$

(Map p206; ☑ 084-26-1101; www.losangeles cusco.com; Tecsecocha 474; d/tr incl breakfast S165/198; @🛜) Ambient and cheap, this old colonial features worn rooms with gold bedspreads, gelatinous mattresses and dark, carved furniture around a pleasant central courtyard with geraniums.

Hotel los Marqueses   HOTEL $$

(Map p206; ☑ 084-26-4249; www.hotel marqueses.com; Garcilaso 256; s/d incl breakfast from S231/297; 🛜) This colonial villa was built in the 16th century by Spanish conquistadors. Classic features include *escuela cuzqueña* (Cuzco school) paintings, courtyard fountains and balconies overlooking the Plaza de Armas. Rooms have some brass beds, skylights and carved wooden doors, often with odd mismatched furniture – a shame given the history here. Most guests come on package tours.

Wi-fi is available only on the patio.

★ Inkaterra La Casona   BOUTIQUE HOTEL $$$

(Map p206; ☑ Lima 01-610-0400; www.inkaterra. com/inkaterra/inkaterra-la-casona; Atocsaycuchi 616; ste incl breakfast from S1779; @🛜) Hitting the perfect balance of cozy and high style, this renovated grand colonial in tiny Plazoleta Nazarenas is simply debonair. Rustic meets majestic with original features like oversized carved doors; rough-hewn beams and stone fireplaces are enhanced with radiant floors, glittering candelabras, plush divans and gorgeous Andean textiles.

Even though the TV is tucked away, tech isn't far with laptop loans and iPod docks. Service is impeccable and highly personal.

★ Casa Cartagena   BOUTIQUE HOTEL $$$

(Map p206; ☑ in Lima 01-242-3147; www.casa cartagena.com; Pumacurco 336; ste incl breakfast from S825; @🛜🏊) Fusing modern with colonial, this Italian-owned boutique hotel is dripping in style. Its 16 suites feature walls with oversized stripes, king-sized beds, iPod docks, bouquets of long-stemmed roses and enormous bathtubs lit by candles. There's a lovely on-site spa and room service is free.

Management boasts that both Neruda and Che Guevara bedded down in this historic mansion, actually a modest pension half a century ago: no word on how their politics fit in now.

El Mercado   DESIGN HOTEL $$$

(Map p206; ☑ 084-42-1777; www.elmercado hotel.com; Seite Cuartones 306; d/ste incl breakfast S594/772; @🛜) Modern and fresh meets colonial in this playful design hotel adorned with painted rocking horses and market carts. Activity centers on an open stone courtyard with loungers and evening bonfires. Large 2nd-story rooms feature radiant heat – a luxury in these parts – as well as fireplaces. Breakfasts are varied, with made-to-order juices from an old-fashioned cart. With elevator access.

Part of the Mountain Lodges of Peru; most clients come here on package tours covering an active Sacred Valley circuit.

Hotel Monasterio   LUXURY HOTEL $$$

(Map p206; ☑ 084-60-4000; www.belmond. com/hotel-monasterio-cusco; Palacio 136; d incl breakfast from S1914; @🛜) Arranged around graceful 16th-century cloisters, the five-star Monasterio has long been Cuzco's jewel, with majestic public areas and over 100 rooms surrounding genteel courtyards. Jesuit roots show in the irregular floor plans, though some of the renovations (eg a plasma TV that emerges from the foot of the bed) seem a little gauche.

In addition to two high-end restaurants, don't miss the chapel with its original gold-leaf paintings.

🛏 San Blas

La Boheme   HOSTEL $

(Map p206; ☑ 084-23-5694; www.laboheme cusco.com; Carmen Alto 283; dm S40, d with/ without bathroom S120/90, all incl breakfast; 🛜)

With bohemian flair, this inviting, intimate backpacker haunt is perfect for couples or those who want an atmosphere that is a little more intimate. It also has an excellent creperie on-site. There's a cheery courtyard, three small dorms and modest-sized private rooms, with colorful decor designed by the French owner.

San Bleña
GUESTHOUSE $

(Map p206; ☑ 084-22-7570; www.hospedajekun turwasi.com; Tandapata 352; d incl breakfast S132; ☜) Quiet and economical, this stylish family-owned hotel has renovated rooms around a bright interior courtyard. There's attentive service and a buffet breakfast. Interior rooms lack natural light, but feature cozy down duvets and Andean throws. It's a hard bargain to beat.

Pantastico
GUESTHOUSE $

(Map p206; ☑ 084-95-4387; www.pan-tastico.com; Carmen Bajo 226; dm S35, s/d without bathroom S90/100, all incl breakfast; @☜) French-run with a friendly, unkempt air, this bed-and-bakery has good water pressure but beds that are a little bit saggy. Highlights include piping-hot bread at 5am and the residual warmth coming from the big oven. Offers cooking classes and travel-agent services.The one double with a view fetches S20 extra.

Pisko & Soul
HOSTEL $

(Map p206; ☑ 084-22-1998; info@piskoand soul.com; Carmen Alto 294; dm/s incl breakfast S30/120; @☜) This Peruvian hostel goes for the Spanish-language-school formula, with free lessons, evening events and barbecues. Small dorms have snug down covers but the bathrooms could use some bleach.

Samay Wasi
HOSTEL $

(Map p206; ☑ 084-25-3108; www.samaywasi peru.com; Atocsaycuchi 416; d incl breakfast S97-115; @☜) A friendly, rambling hostel clinging precariously to the hillside, hidden up a flight of stairs teetering way above town. There's a proper kitchen and shipshape rooms, though seek yours carefully, as some smell musty. With major city views. Accepts credit cards.

Hospedaje el Artesano de San Blas
GUESTHOUSE $

(Map p206; ☑ 084-28-5909; artesanohostal@hot mail.com; Suytuccato 790; d/tr S60/90, per person without bathroom S20; ☜) If you're wondering why it's such a deal, just try walking here with a full pack. Still, this peaceful and fall-ing-down-charming colonial house has large rooms and a sunny patio with wi-fi reception. Kitchen available.

Ñawin Cusco
APARTMENT $$

(Map p206; ☑ 968-586-106; www.nawincusco.com; Tandapata 357; d S215-248; ☜) On the quiet side of Tandapata, these small garden-level apartments are a home away from home. Cozy rooms with kitchenettes feature plump bedding, Andean weavings, handmade soaps and teas. There are also space heaters, TV and good wi-fi. The attentive owners leave you a map of the city with their own favorite haunts.

Reservation only, no walk-ins.

Quinua Villa Boutique
APARTMENT $$

(Map p206; ☑ 084-24-2646; www.quinua.com.pe; Pasaje Santa Rosa A-8; 2- or 3-person apt S323-545; ☜) A clutch of cozy apartments high up on the hill (staircase-only access), this charmer features suites themed according to historical periods in Peru, with playful touches such as a bedspread completely made of used jeans. With thoughtful touches like fireplaces and kitchens stocked with a basket of cooking supplies. Also has safe boxes, LCD TVs and heaters – one apartment has a sauna.

The staircase access can be a downer if you're not in tip-top shape.

Tika Wasi
BOUTIQUE HOTEL $$

(Map p206; ☑ 084-23-1609; www.tikawasi.com; Tandapata 491; s/d incl breakfast from S221/258; ☜) Behind a tall wall, this modern inn offers a personable option with bright, imaginatively themed rooms, with family photos and colonial accents. Rooms overlook small, sunny decks to hang out on. Breakfast is buffet. Nonnationals should be sure to get the tax subtracted from the room price.

Madre Tierra
B&B $$

(Map p206; ☑ 084-24-8452; www.hostalmadre tierra.com; Atocsaycuchi 647; s/d S156/189; @☜) Warm and very cozy, with plenty of B&B-style luxury comfort touches, Madre Tierra is a vine-entwined, slightly claustrophobic little jewel box. Rooms have skylights and funky dimensions. Good value for money.

Hotel Rumi Punku
HOTEL $$

(Map p206; ☑ 084-22-1102; www.rumipunku.com; Choquechaca 339; s/d incl breakfast S363/429; @☜) Recognizable by the monumental Inca stonework around the entrance, Rumi Punku (Stone Door) is a stylish complex of old colonial houses, gardens and terraces. The rooftop terraces and other outdoor areas are utterly charming. Rooms ooze comfort and class, with central heating, wooden floors and European bedding.

It's probably not worth the upgrade to a superior room unless you want a bigger bed. Sauna and Jacuzzi are available for a minimal charge.

Quinta San Blas
HOTEL $$

(Map p206; ☎084-50-7243; www.ananay-hotels. com/branches/quinta-san-blas/; Carmen Alto 218; d/ste incl breakfast S363/462; ☎) In the heart of busy San Blas, this 20-room colonial offers an oasis of calm. Spare rooms feature king-sized beds with crisp white bedding and walls, with subway-tile bathrooms and central heating. There's also in-room safes and TVs. A minimalist decor makes fine old details like Spanish tiles and the wraparound courtyard balcony stand out even more.

Amaru Hostal
HOTEL $$

(Map p206; ☎084-22-5933; www.amaruhostal. com; Cuesta San Blas 541; s/d incl breakfast S182/231; @☎) In a characterful old building in a prime location, Amaru is deservedly popular. It is certainly the only Cuzco hotel with a complimentary welcome massage (worth it). Flowerpots sit outside well-kept rooms with heating, some with rocking chairs to admire the rooftop view. Rooms in the outer courtyard are noisy, and those at the back are newest.

Hostal Pensión Alemana
HOTEL $$

(Map p206; ☎084-22-6861; www.cuzco-stay.de; Tandapata 260; s/d incl breakfast S256/284; @☎) Attentive and lovely, this polished Swiss-German lodge wouldn't look out of place in the Alps. Nice touches include air purifiers and complimentary tea and fruit. Couples should note there are very few matrimonial beds. Enjoy the tiled garden – rare in Cuzco – and the terraces with sweeping views.

Los Apus Hotel & Mirador
HOTEL $$

(Map p206; ☎084-26-4243; www.losapushotel.com; Atocsaycuchi 515; s/d incl breakfast S327/393; ✸@☎) With understated class, this longtime Swiss-run hotel features central heating, large bedrooms with down duvets and colonial-style art. It may seem overpriced, but you are also paying for the high-tech alarm system and an emergency water supply. A wheelchair-accessible room for travelers with disabilities is available.

La Encantada
BOUTIQUE HOTEL $$

(Map p206; ☎084-24-2206; www.encantada peru.com; Tandapata 354; s/d incl breakfast S313/396; @☎) Bright and cheerful, this modern boutique hotel features terraced gardens and immense views from iron-rail balconies. A circular staircase leads to small, tasteful rooms with soft linens and king-sized beds. The on-site spa helps hikers work out the aches and kinks. Be aware that checkout is at 9am.

Eureka Hostal
HOTEL $$

(Map p206; ☎084-23-3505; www.peru-eureka. com; Chihuampata 591; s/d S180/230; @☎) A funky blend of old and new, Eureka's stylish lobby and sun-soaked cafeteria invite further acquaintance. Rooms are comfortable but a little odd, with a childlike take on traditional motifs. Orthopedic mattresses and down quilts make them as comfortable as they are cool. Flexible tariffs can make it an even better deal.

Casa de Campo Hostal
HOTEL $$

(Map p206; ☎084-24-4404; www.hotelcasa decampo.com; Tandapata 298; s/d incl breakfast S198/231; @☎) The steep climb here might leave you on your knees, but the views will astound. With a warm, friendly vibe, this hillside inn is almost perfect but installations are aging. Some rooms don't even have working electrical outlets (most have just one), so check before settling in. Breakfast includes a sprawling buffet with fresh fruit and cereal. Transfer included.

Casona Les Pleiades
B&B $$

(Map p206; ☎084-50-6430; www.casona-pleiades.com; Tandapata 116; d/tr incl breakfast S198/248; @☎) A pleasant B&B with just seven rooms and a sunny courtyard featuring fresh flowers and balcony seating. Breakfast is served in cozy booths. Heaters and lock-boxes are supplied in rooms.

Hostal El Grial
HOTEL $$

(Map p206; ☎084-22-3012; www.hotelelgrial.com; Carmen Alto 112; s/d incl breakfast S132/198) Good value in a rickety old wood-floored building; all rooms have orthopedic mattresses and the option of heaters; some have views.

★ Tocuyeros Boutique Hotel
BOUTIQUE HOTEL $$$

(Map p206; ☎084-26-2790; www.tocuyeros.com; Tocuyeros 560; d incl breakfast from S825; ☎) A fine addition to San Blas, this hidden treasure sits far off the street, accessed via a long stone tunnel. With only nine rooms, this boutique hotel shines with modern Andean style. Each has double-pane windows, central heating, coffee makers and Netflix on the flat-screen TV. There's also a gorgeous rooftop terrace and low-key on-site restaurant and bar.

Tierra Viva
HOTEL $$$

(Map p206; ☑ 084-23-3070; Carmen Alto 194, San Blas; d incl breakfast S495; @ 🎧) Soaking up the cobbled ambiance of the cool San Blas neighborhood, this chain hotel offers smart rooms with a consistent standard. There's a lovely interior courtyard.

Casa San Blas
BOUTIQUE HOTEL $$$

(Map p206; ☑ 084-23-7900; www.casasanblas. com; Tocuyeros 566; d/apt incl breakfast S488/693; @ 🎧) 🖋 Down a short passageway, this revamped colonial features 18 rooms with nice bedding, hardwood floors and somewhat-kitschy sayings on the walls. Better are the Andean textiles made by local weaving collectives (for sale). Don't miss the lovely rooftop terrace. Filtered water is supplied in a dispenser for easy refills. It has a cozy feel, though service is somewhat impersonal.

🛏 Avenida El Sol & Downhill

Hostal San Juan Masías
GUESTHOUSE $

(Map p214; ☑ 084-43-1563; www.hostalsan juanmasias.com; Ahuacpinta 600; s/d S80/115, without bathroom S60/90, all incl breakfast; @ 🎧) An excellent alternative guesthouse run by Dominican nuns on the grounds of the busy Colegio Martín de Porres. This place is clean, safe and friendly, and overlooks frequent volleyball matches on the courtyard. Simple, spotless rooms with heat are arranged off a long, sunny hallway. Two people will pay more for twin beds than one bed. Continental breakfast.

Los Aticos
HOTEL $

(Map p206; ☑ 084-23-1710; www.losaticos.com; Quera 253, Pasaje Hurtado Álvarez; d/apt incl breakfast S130/260; @ 🎧) Hidden in a small passageway, this sleepy spot is off the radar but worth snagging. Rooms have comfy beds with down duvets and parquet floors. There's also self-service laundry and a full guest kitchen. The three mini-apartments sleep up to four and are good value for self-catering groups or families.

Abittare
BOUTIQUE HOTEL $$

(Map p206; ☑ 084-241-739; www.abittare.cuzco -hotels.com; Santo Domingo 263; s/d incl breakfast from S231/264; 🎧) Facing the flanks of Iglesia Santo Domingo and the Qorikancha, this 44-room boutique hotel is spare in style

but attractively modern. It occupies an attractive colonial building with cobblestone courtyards. Rooms feature rustic oversized headboards, minimalist light fixtures, thick down duvets and latest-generation bathrooms with glass showers. With in-room safe, TVs and heating.

Hostal Inkarri
HOTEL $$

(Map p206; ☑ 084-24-2692; www.inkarrihostal. com; Qolla Calle 204; s/d incl breakfast S218/290; @ 🎧) A roomy place with a pleasant stone courtyard, well-kept colonial terraces and whimsical collections of old sewing machines, phones and typewriters. Decent value, but watch for rooms on the musty side.

Picol Hostal
HOTEL $$

(Map p206; ☑ 084-24-9191; www.picolhostal.com; Quera 253, Pasaje Hurtado Álvarez; s/d incl breakfast S128/172; 🎧) In a bustling commercial district, this small hotel has agreeable staff and tiny, well-kept and airy doubles. The triples are a little too tight.

Hotel Libertador Palacio del Inka
LUXURY HOTEL $$$

(Map p206; ☑ 084-23-1961; www.libertador.com. pe; Plazoleta Santo Domingo 259; d/ste incl breakfast S1023/1224; ❈ @ 🎧 ☒) Opulence bedecks this colonial mansion built over Inca foundations. Parts of the building date back to the 16th century, when Francisco Pizarro was an occupant. It's as luxurious and beautiful as you'd expect, with a fine interior courtyard and ample renovated rooms. Just be aware of the 9am checkout.

It also features a Peruvian restaurant, a bar, a spa and a business center.

🛏 Greater Cuzco

Torre Dorada Residencial
GUESTHOUSE $$

(☑ 084-24-1698; www.torredorada.com; Los Cipreses N-5, Residencial Huancaro; s/d incl breakfast S199/225; @ 🎧) A modern, family-run hotel in a quiet residential district close to the bus terminal. Though it isn't close to the action, guests rave about the high quality of service. It offers free shuttles to the airport, train stations and town center. English is spoken.

Hostal San Juan de Dios
GUESTHOUSE $$

(☑ 084-24-0135; www.hostalsanjuandedios.com; Manzanares 264, Urb Manuel Prado; s/d incl breakfast S149/177; @ 🎧) With wonderful staff, this spotless guesthouse is part of a non-profit enterprise that supports a hospital clinic and also provides job opportunities

REGIONAL CUISINE

Andean cuisine is getting a boost. With the arrival in Moray of world-renowned chef Virgilio Martínez and his restaurant and food laboratory MIL (p251) in Moray, the great diversity of potatoes and other regional produce is being brought from the rural table to mainstream menus. But you don't have to shell out for haute cuisine. Other places, like Ollantaytambo and Cuzco, have taken note and are similarly returning to old roots.

Sunday lunch with a country stroll is a Cuzco ritual. Locals head to the villages south of town: **Tipón** is the place to eat *cuy* (guinea pig), **Saylla** is the home of *chicharrón* (deep-fried pork) and **Lucre** is renowned for duck.

Look for the following foods in local restaurants, on the street and at festivals:

Anticucho Beef heart on a stick, punctuated by a potato, is the perfect evening street snack.

Caldo de gallina Healthy, hearty chicken soup is the local favorite to kick a hangover.

Cañazo Rustic bootleg versions of this potent sugarcane alcohol have long been the life of the village party. New distillery Caña Alta in Ollantaytambo produces a high-quality artisan version to make exquisite cocktails.

Chicharrónes Definitely more than the sum of its parts: deep-fried pork served with corn, mint leaves, fried potato and onion.

Choclo con queso Huge, pale cobs of corn are served with a teeth-squeaking chunk of cheese in the Sacred Valley.

Cuy Guinea pig, raised on grains at home – what could be more organic? The faint of heart can ask for it served as a fillet (without the head and paws).

Grilled alpaca Lean and flavorful, this tender, high-protein meat has gone mainstream in upscale restaurants.

Lechón Suckling pig with plenty of crackling, served with tamales (corn cakes).

for young people with disabilities. The quiet, carpeted rooms have large windows; most have twin beds, though there's one matrimonial double. Staff help with everything from laundry services to making international phone calls.

It's a brisk 30-minute walk from the city center in a nontouristy sector, near shops and amenities.

Turismo Caith GUESTHOUSE $$
(☑ 084-23-3595; www.caith.org; Pasaje Sto Toribio N4, Urb Ucchullo Alto; d/tr incl breakfast S165/231; ☎) This rambling farmhouse-style hostel also runs an on-site girls foundation. Huge picture windows and various balconies and patios look toward the Plaza de Armas, a hearty 20-minute walk or a five-minute taxi ride away. It's great for families – big rooms and cots are available, and the rambling, grassy garden is a perfect place for kids to run around.

✖ Eating

Cuzco's restaurant scene caters for a wide range of tastes and budgets, thanks to its international appeal. Due to its location, Cuzco has access to diverse crops from highland

potatoes and quinoa to avocados, jungle fruit and *ají picante* (hot chiles).

For self-caterers, small, overpriced grocery shops are located near the Plaza de Armas, including **Gato's Market** (Map p206; ☑ 084-23-4026; Santa Catalina Ancha 377; ⊗9:30am-11pm) and **Mega** (Map p214; cnr Matará & Ayacucho; ⊗10am-8pm Mon-Sat, to 6pm Sun).

✖ Central Cuzco

Las Frescas CAFE $
(Map p206; ☑ 940-237-140; Saphi 478; mains S15-25; ⊗noon-8pm Mon-Sat; ☞) Feel good about having a fresh, light lunch in this good food cafe with white bricks with wooden benches. Options are plenty, ranging from poke and quinoa bowls to wraps and salads. There's also great, fresh juices and myriad vegetarian options.

La Rabona BAKERY $
(Map p206; Herrajes 146; mains S15-20; ⊗8am-8pm Mon-Sat, 10am-6pm Sun; ☎☞) Baking Cuzco's best multiseed and sourdough loaves (gold on a multiday trek), wonderful carrot cake and other baked goods including vegan treats, this is a worthy stop for stocking up. It also serves espresso drinks,

matcha tea and golden milk. Pressed juices, like the ginger-apple-beet combo, are liquid energy. Unfortunately, the downstairs seating is a little frumpy.

Deli Monasterio
BAKERY $

(Map p206; Palacio 136; mains S8-19; ⏰8am-9pm; 🛜) Crusty, authentic baguettes are the highlight here (come early), but you can also get nice lunchboxes (perfect for day excursions) with gourmet and veggie options. The mini *pain au chocolat* (chocolate croissants) and passion-fruit cookies aren't bad either. It's added cafe seating so you can stay a while.

La Justina
PIZZA $

(Map p206; ☎084-25-5474; Palacio 110; pizzas S19-36; ⏰6-11pm Mon-Sat) Traipse through an uneven stone courtyard to this little gem of a pizza joint with wooden tables and gorgeous wood-fired pies. Original toppings include tomato, bacon and basil or spinach and garlic. Service can be slow.

Museo del Cafe
CAFE $

(Map p206; ☎084-26-3264; Espaderos 136, piso 2; mains S10-30) With a cozy fireplace, this upstairs cafe has the distinction of serving fresh coffee from its own farm. You can't go wrong with an espresso drink, but there are also lovely soups, light fare and desserts.

Pantastico
BAKERY $

(Map p206; ☎084-25-4387; Tandapata 1024; mains S4-15; ⏰8am-8pm) For a little something sweet, this tiny bakery hits the spot, selling breads, empanadas and fat slabs of tart passion-fruit or coconut bread with fresh juice.

Restaurante Egos
PERUVIAN $

(Map p206; Arequipa 248; menú S12; ⏰7am-9pm Mon-Sat) A bustling restaurant offering typical, filling Andean fare. There's no menu, just blackboard specials in limited supply. Come early for better options, but there's usually a choice of seven main dishes paired with a glass of *chicha de quinoa* or *chicha morada* (fresh blue corn drink).

El Ayllu
CAFE $

(Map p206; Marquez 263; mains S10-18; ⏰6:30am-10pm Mon-Sat, to 1pm Sun) Longtime staff chat up clients and serve traditional pastries like *lengua de suegra* ('mother-in-law's tongue', a sweet pastry confection) and pork sandwiches. Traditional breakfasts are worth trying and coffee is roasted the traditional local way – with orange, sugar and onion peel.

PER.UK
CAFE $$

(Map p206; ☎084-23-3978; Plateros 344; mains S38-60; ⏰noon-10:30pm; 🛜🍴) This love child of a Peruvian-British couple is a low-key cafe serving well-crafted Peruvian fusion dishes, plus pub burgers and oversized salads. Presentation is excellent and the service well above average. It's also kind to vegetarians and celiacs. The delicious *ají de gallina* (spicy chicken and walnut stew) could easily serve two.

★ Cicciolina
INTERNATIONAL $$

(Map p206; ☎084-23-9510; www.cicciolinacuzco.com; Triunfo 393, 2nd fl; mains S38-59; ⏰8am-11pm) On the 2nd floor of a lofty colonial courtyard mansion, Cicciolina may be Cuzco's best restaurant. The eclectic, sophisticated food is divine, starting with house-marinated olives, and continuing with crisp polenta squares with cured rabbit, huge green salads, charred octopus and satisfying mains like red trout in coconut milk, beetroot ravioli and tender lamb. With impeccable service and warmly lit seating.

If you can't get a dinner reservation (try four days ahead in the July–August high season), consider grabbing tapas at the bar or coming back in the morning. Its outstanding breakfasts with homemade bread are great value.

★ La Bodega 138
PIZZA $$

(Map p206; ☎084-26-0272; www.labodega138.com; Herrajes 138; mains S26-37; ⏰11am-10:30pm Mon-Fri, from 10am Sat & Sun; 🍴) Sometimes you are homesick for good atmosphere, uncomplicated menus and craft beer. In comes La Bodega, a fantastic laid-back enterprise run by a family in what used to be their home. Thin-crust pizzas are fired up in the adobe oven, organic salads are fresh and abundant and the prices are reasonable. With weekend brunch. A true find. Cash only.

★ Bojosan
JAPANESE $$

(Map p206; ☎084-24-6502; San Agustin 275; mains S20-26; ⏰12:30-10pm; 🛜🍴) This Tokyo-style noodle shop does right in so many ways. Take a stool and watch the cooks prepare your udon noodles from scratch. Oversized bowls have flavorful broth, you add the protein (duck, chicken and vegetarian options) and a dash of authentic pepper mix. With bottled local artisan beers on offer. Run by the highly regarded Le Soleil (p233) next door.

⭐ **Marcelo Batata** PERUVIAN $$

(Map p206; ☑ 084-22-2424; www.cuscodining.com/marcelo-batata; Palacio 121; mains S43-56; ⏲12:30-11pm) A sure bet for delectable Andean cuisine with a twist. Marcelo Batata innovates with traditional foods to show them at their best – like the humble *tarwi* pea, which makes a mean hummus. The chicken soup with *hierba Luisa* (a local herb), is exquisite, alongside satisfying beet *quinotto* (like risotto), tender alpaca and twice-baked Andean potatoes that offer crispy-creamy goodness.

A daring array of cocktails is best savored on the rooftop deck – the city views make it the top outdoor venue in Cuzco.

⭐ **Limo** SEAFOOD $$

(Map p206; ☑ 084-24-068; www.cuscorestaurants.com/restaurant/limo; Portal de Carnes 236, 2nd fl; mains S20-60; ⏲11am-11pm Mon-Sat) If you must have seafood in Cuzco, make this elegant Nikkei (Japanese-Peruvian) restaurant the place. Don't skip the house pisco sour, tinged with ginger and garnished with a whole chili. *Tiraditos* (raw fish in a fragrant sauce) simply melt on the tongue. Other hits are the creamy potato *causas* and crunchy shrimp rolls with avocado and smoked pepper. With attentive service.

Kion CHINESE $$

(Map p206; ☑ 084-43-1862; www.cuscorestaurants.com/restaurant/kion; Triunfo 370, piso 2; mains S25-60; ⏲11:30am-11pm) This retro-cool Peruvian Chinese restaurant is inviting on all sensory levels. It's also very popular; unfortunately, the dining experience, with clumsy service that includes table changes and wrong dishes delivered, could improve. Come for the housemade *chimichurris* (sauces with a nice bite) and the wonderful *lomo tau si (*thin-sliced beef and vegetables served bubbling in a cast-iron pan).

Mr Soup INTERNATIONAL $$

(Map p206; ☑ 084-38-6073; Saphi 448; mains S20-28; ⏲noon-10pm Tue-Sun) Sometimes you just want a huge bowl of soup. Serving fairly authentic udon curry, Thai *tom kha* (coconut soup), Andean quinoa soup and others, this tiny shop does the trick. Recipes were sourced from families, which helps gives them a homespun taste. For a bargain, go for the soup of the day (S15).

Korma Sutra INDIAN $$

(Map p206; ☑ 084-23-3023; Teatro 382; mains S32-35; ⏲1-10pm; 🛜🍴) If you are craving spice, this London-style curry house will do the trick, with its garlicky naan, lassie and a variety of creamy kormas and curries (try the alpaca chili curry). It's relaxing in the evening, with an open kitchen, low-lit walls and cushioned booths.

Tacomania MEXICAN $$

(Map p206; ☑ 984-132-032; Teatro 394; mains S27-35; ⏲1-10pm Mon-Sat; 🍴) Serving nachos, burritos and tacos, this simple Mexican restaurant is popular with expats. The tortilla chips are fragile but the chunky guacamole with red onion is a home run. If you ask for spicy, it'll deliver. The stylish new location has an open kitchen and ample 2nd-floor dining room. With vegetarian options. Cash only.

Green's Organic CAFE $$

(Map p206; ☑ 084-24-3399; Santa Catalina Angosta 235, 2nd fl; mains S30-58; ⏲11am-10pm; 🛜🍴) 🍴 With all-organic food and a bright farmhouse feel, Green's Organic oozes health. Inventive salads with options like roasted fennel, goat cheese, beets and spring greens are a welcome change of pace and the heartier fare includes pastas and alpaca dishes with attractive presentations. Come early (or late) as it fills up fast and service is notably slow.

Morena Peruvian Kitchen PERUVIAN $$

(Map p206; ☑ 084-43-7832; Plateros 348B; mains S35-50; ⏲noon-10pm) Popular and stylish, this chic cafe bridges the gap between gourmet Peruvian and kinder prices. Serves quinoa, burgers and Peruvian classics like *anticuchos* (beef skewers) in sumptuous sauces and hearty soups.

Papachos BURGERS $$

(Map p206; ☑ 084-22-8205; www.papachos.com; Portal de Belen 115; mains S29-53; ⏲noon-midnight) You could do worse than satisfying your fast-food craving at a Gaston Acurio outlet. Papachos does big, beautiful burgers topped with goodies both creative and comforting. There are veggie options, wings doused in Amazonian pepper sauce, and fish and chips.

A Mi Manera PERUVIAN $$

(Map p206; ☑ 084-22-2219; www.amimanera peru.com; Triunfo 392, 2nd fl; mains S32-52; ⏲10am-10pm) This romantic Cuzco mainstay serves up traditional Peruvian cuisine and pasta. It won't blow your mind with innovation, but offerings like steak in port sauce, spicy yucca or mashed *muña* potatoes comfort and satisfy.

Uchu Peruvian Steakhouse PERUVIAN $$

(Map p206; ☑084-24-6598; www.cuscodining.com/uchu; Palacio 135; mains S48-57; ⊙12:30-10pm) With a cozy, cavernous ambience of low-lit adobe, dark tables and bright turquoise walls, this chic eatery offers meat (steak, alpaca or chicken) and fish cooked on hot volcanic stones at your table, served with delicious sauces. Starters are great – like the BBQ ribs in a smoked elderberry sauce. Staff are knowledgeable and quick, a real treat.

★ Le Soleil FRENCH $$$

(Map p206; ☑084-24-0543; www.restaurantelesoleilcusco.com; San Agustín 275; mains S38-89; ⊙12:30-3pm & 7-11:30pm Thu-Tue) Cuzco's go-to spot for traditional French cooking, this romantic white-linen restaurant delivers with cool precision. Start with trout in a tart mango ginger confit. The duck à l'orange cooked two ways is simply divine. You can also go for a tasting menu (from S145). There's a wonderful selection of French wines and lovely desserts – chocolate fondant being the obvious, happy choice.

Chicha PERUVIAN $$$

(Map p206; ☑084-24-0520; Regocijo 261, 2nd fl; mains S30-65) A Gastón Acurio venture serving up haute versions of Cuzco classics in an open kitchen. Its riff on *anticuchos* is a delectable barbecued octopus with crisp herbed potato wedges. Other contenders include *papas rellenas* (stuffed potatoes), curried alpaca with quinoa, and *chairo* (lamb and barley soup) served in a clay pot.

The *chicha morada* (a nonalcoholic purple maize drink) is beyond fresh.

La Fería PERUVIAN $$$

(Map p206; ☑084-28-6198; www.cuscodining.com/la-feria; Portal de Panes 123, piso 2; mains S40-90; ⊙noon-11pm) For upmarket Andean fare, this cheerful restaurant with killer plaza views is a good bet. Try the *rocotto* soufflé, a twist on the classic stuffed pepper, or *cuy* that's been wood-oven fired. It's also the perfect place to try *chicha de jora*, a traditional fermented corn drink sold on the street, made here with purified water. For dessert: syrupy *picarones* (sweet potato dumplings)!

✗ San Blas

★ Monkey Cafe CAFE $

(Map p206; ☑084-59-5838; Tandapata 300; mains S15-20; ⊙8am-8pm Wed-Mon) Cuzco's finest coffee shop is shoehorned into a tiny locale at the top of San Blas hill. All espresso drinks feature double shots made with Peruvian-origin roasts. There are also very tasty sweets and hearty breakfasts ranging from healthy to heart-stopping.

La Bohème Crepería CRÊPES $

(Map p206; ☑084-23-5694; www.labohemecusco.com; Carmen Alto 283; mains S10-17; ⊙8am-10pm; 🖥🐾) You can't go wrong with the authentic crepes in this Marseillaise-owned cafe, crafted with fusion ingredients like caramelized onions, Andean cheese, mushrooms and béchamel. There's a little patio with great views and firelit evening ambience. The set menu is a great deal. For dessert, try its signature crepe with salted butter and caramel.

Cafeteria 7&7 CAFE $

(Map p206; ☑084-22-6861; Tandapata s/n; mains S7-12; ⊙10am-10pm Mon-Sat, to 2pm Sun; 🖥) This sleek 3rd-story cafe bursts with city views, yet the off-street location means it's quiet and conducive to chilling out. With white leather booths and a nice selection of homemade German cakes, plus light food like quinoa salads and espresso drinks. Also serves ice-cream sundaes.

Meeting Place CAFE $

(Map p206; ☑084-24-0465, 941-445-977; Plaza San Blas; mains S15-29; ⊙8:30am-4pm Mon-Sat; 🖥) This British-Peruvian-owned cafe nails gringo breakfast. Start with organic coffee or nice loose-leaf teas, oversized waffles and egg combinations. The thick milkshakes have their devotees. With swift, friendly service and a good book exchange.

Prasada VEGETARIAN $

(Map p206; ☑084-25-3644; Qanchipata 269; mains S9-15; ⊙10am-9pm Mon-Fri, to 4pm Sat & Sun; 🐾) The best bang for your pesos, serving tacos, tortilla soup and lentil burgers with fresh toppings and generous servings. Pair with a jar of fresh-squeezed juice or kombucha and you're ready for the hike up to Sacsaywamán.

Greenpoint VEGETARIAN $$

(Map p206; ☑084-43-1146; Carmen Bajo 235; mains S22-59; ⊙8am-10pm; 🐾) Even non-vegetarians are repeat customers at this vegan restaurant and bakery offering abundant set-menu lunches (a steal at S15). Highlights include the veggie sushi and mushroom ceviche. Enter through an interior patio. The interior is a little shabby, go for the best seating on the 2nd-floor terrace. Also serves beer and wine.

La Quinta Eulalia
PERUVIAN $$

(Map p206; ☑ 084-22-4951; Choquechaca 384; mains S25-54; ☺12:30-4pm Tue-Sun) This Cuzco classic has been in business for over half a century and its courtyard patio is a score on a sunny day. The chalkboard menu features the tenderest roast lamb, alpaca and traditional sides like the phenomenal *rocotto relleno* (spicy peppers stuffed with beef, peas and carrots topped with dribbling cheese). Among the best places to order *cuy* (guinea pig).

Granja Heidi
CAFE $$

(Map p206; ☑ 084-23-8383; Cuesta San Blas 525, 2nd fl; mains S22-48; ☺11:30am-9:30pm Mon-Sat; ☑) A cozy alpine cafe serving healthy fare that's consistently good, some of it provided from the small farm of the German owner. In addition to wonderful Peruvian fare (*rocoto relleno* is served vegetarian, with stuffed chili and peanuts), there are crepes and huge bowls of soups and salads. The lunchtime set menu (S28) is a deal. Save room for dessert.

Jack's Café
CAFE $$

(Map p206; ☑ 084-25-4606; Choquechaca 509; mains S15-31; ☺7am-11pm) A line often snakes out the door at this consistently good Western-style eatery with Aussie roots. With fresh juices blended with mint or ginger, strong coffee and eggs heaped with smoked salmon or roasted tomatoes, it's easy to get out of bed. Also has nice cafe food, soups and good service.

Pacha Papa
PERUVIAN $$

(Map p206; ☑ 084-24-1318; Plaza San Blas 120; mains S23-45; ☺11:30am-4pm & 7-11pm) Invoking a rustic highland ambience, this open courtyard with wooden tables serves up Peruvian classics, cooked over a wood fire or in clay pots. It's a good spot to try buttered corn in herbs, *ají de gallina* (creamy chicken stew) or oven-fired trout. *Cuy* (guinea pig) should be ordered in advance.

✖ Avenida El Sol & Downhill

La Valeriana
BAKERY $

(Map p214; ☑ 084-50-6941; Av El Sol 576; mains S8-22; ☺7am-10pm Mon-Sat, 8am-9pm Sun; ☜) Facing the sacred garden, this ambient bakery sells truffled cupcakes, whole-wheat sandwiches and good veggie empanadas served on patterned china. There are also coffee drinks and refreshing juices blended with medicinal herbs. A fine stop to charge your batteries.

Drinking & Nightlife

Cuzco has some lively nightlife offerings, ranging from the tame dinner show to late-night clubs. Bars are plentiful and cater to a spectrum of tastes. The European pubs are good places to track down those all-important soccer matches, with satellite TVs more or less permanently tuned to sports.

★Limbus
ROOFTOP BAR

(Map p206; ☑ 084-43-1282; www.limbusresto bar.com; Pasñapakana 133; ☺8am-1am Mon-Sat, noon-midnight Sun) Billed as the best view in Cuzco, it's all that (even after climbing to the top of San Blas). Don't worry, if you come during peak hours you'll have plenty of time to catch your breath while you queue to get in. With gorgeous cocktails and glass-walled panoramas, this was the hottest city spot when we visited.

★Museo del Pisco
BAR

(Map p206; ☑ 084-26-2709; www.museodelpis co.org; Santa Catalina Ancha 398; ☺noon-1am) When you've had your fill of colonial religious art, investigate this pisco museum, where the wonders of the national drink are extolled, exalted and – of course – sampled. Opened by an enthusiastic expat, this museum-bar is Pisco 101, combined with a tapas lounge. Grab a spot early for show-stopping live music (9pm to 11pm nightly).

Ambitions go far beyond the standard pisco sour to original cocktails like *valicha* (pisco with jungle fruit *kion,* spearmint and sour apple). Tapas, such as alpaca miniburgers on sesame buns and *tiradito* (a Japanese-influenced version of ceviche) marinated in cumin-chile, sate your hunger. Look for special tastings and master distiller classes announced on the Facebook page.

Mundo Nuevo
PUB

(Map p206; ☑ 084-24-0594; Portal de Confituria 233; ☺1pm-1am Tue-Sat, from 5pm Sun & Mon) With eye-popping views of the Cathedral, this upstairs bar has a dozen Peruvian microbrews on draft. You could do far worse than watch the sunset on the plaza from here, cold quinoa beer in hand. You can also count on decent pub food and a cheerful atmosphere. With live music from Wednesday to Saturday.

Cholo's Bar
BAR

(Map p206; Palacio 210; ⊘noon-midnight Mon-Sat) Walk through a bumpy inner courtyard to reach this mellow no-frills bar with 15 Peruvian artisan beers on tap – the Intipunku IPA is a sure bet for starters. Away from the fray, it's the perfect place to actually have a conversation. Service can be slow. There's outdoor patio seating too.

Chango
CLUB

(Map p206; ☑990-523-722; www.facebook.com/changoclubcusco; Tecsecocha 429; ⊘9pm-7am) Humming to a techno beat, this happening club with live DJs is the latest of Cuzco's all-night party places. There's also rock, reggae and salsa on rotation. Keep a close eye on your belongings, as there have been reports of pickpocketing.

Republica de Pisco
BAR

(Map p206; ☑084-24-4111; www.facebook.com/republicadelpiscocusco; Plateros 354; ⊘5pm-2am) A wonderful, elegant bar with attentive bartenders and drinks that merit seconds. It's popular with locals and travelers alike. Check the Facebook site for events.

☆ Entertainment

Clubs open early, but crank up a few notches after about 11pm. Happy hour is ubiquitous and generally entails two-for-one on beer or certain mixed drinks.

In popular *discotecas*, especially right on the Plaza de Armas, both sexes should beware of drinks being spiked and of phones and wallets disappearing.

★ Ukuku's
LIVE MUSIC

(Map p206; ☑084-24-2951; Plateros 316; ⊘6pm-2am) The most consistently popular nightspot in town, Ukuku's plays a winning combination of crowd-pleasers – Latin and Western rock, reggae, *reggaetón*, salsa and hip-hop – and often hosts live bands. Usually full to bursting after midnight with as many Peruvians as foreign tourists, it's good, sweaty, dance-a-thon fun. Happy hour is 8pm to 10:30pm.

Centro Qosqo de Arte Nativo
PERFORMING ARTS

(Map p214; ☑084-22-7901; www.centroqosqodeartenativo.com; Av El Sol 604) Has live nightly performances of Andean music and folk dancing at 6:45pm.

THE LUCKY TOAD

Ever wondered what the locals do to relax instead of whiling away the hours over a game of darts or pool in the local bar? Well, next time you're in a *picantería* (local restaurant) or *quinta* (house serving typical Andean food), look out for a strange metal *sapo* (frog or toad) mounted on a large box and surrounded by various holes and slots. Men will often spend the whole afternoon drinking *chicha* (fermented corn beer) and beer while competing at this old test of skill in which players toss metal disks as close to the toad as possible. Top points are scored for landing one smack in the mouth. Legend has it that the game originated with Inca royals, who used to toss gold coins into Lake Titicaca in the hopes of attracting a *sapo*, believed to possess magical healing powers and have the ability to grant wishes.

Km 0
LIVE MUSIC

(Map p206; ☑084-23-6009; www.facebook.com/Cusco.Km.0; Tandapata 100; ⊘11am-late Tue-Sat, from 5pm Sun & Mon) This convivial bar just off Plaza San Blas has a bit of everything. There's live music late regularly – local musicians come here to jam after their regular gigs. Happy hour is 9pm to midnight.

Shopping

The neighborhood of San Blas – the plaza itself, Cuesta San Blas, Carmen Alto and Tandapata – offers Cuzco's best shopping. Traditionally an artisan quarter, it still has some remaining some workshops and showrooms of local craftspeople. Jewelry shops and quirky, one-off designer boutiques are a refreshing reminder that the local aesthetic is not confined to stridently colored ponchos and sheepskin-rug depictions of Machu Picchu.

Center for Traditional Textiles of Cuzco
ARTS & CRAFTS

(Map p214; ☑84-228-117; Av El Sol 603; ⊘7:30am-8pm) This nonprofit organization, founded in 1996, promotes the survival of traditional weaving. You may be able to catch a shop-floor demonstration illustrating different weaving techniques in all their finger-twisting complexity. Products for sale are high end.

Cafe Ricchary
COFFEE

(Map p206; ☑984-305-571; Concevidayoc 116; ⊙8:30am-8:30pm Mon-Sat) This tiny coffee seller near the San Pedro Market sells great local organic roasts, ground and whole bean, for very reasonable prices. You can also get a hot cup but there's only two stools to sit at.

Inkakunaq Ruwaynin
ARTS & CRAFTS

(Map p206; ☑084-26-0942; inside CBC, Tullumayo 274; ⊙9am-7pm Mon-Sat) This weaving co-operative with quality goods is run by 12 mountain communities from Cuzco and Apurimac; it's at the far end of the inner courtyard.

Mercado San Pedro
MARKET

(Map p214; Plazoleta San Pedro; ⊙6am-7pm) Cuz-co's central market is a must-see. Pig heads for *caldo* (soup), frogs (to enhance sexual performance), vats of fruit juice, roast *lechón* (suck-ling pig) and tamales are just a few of the foods on offer. Around the edges are clothes, spells, incense and other random products to keep you entertained for hours.

Jerusalén
BOOKS

(Map p206; ☑084-23-5428; Heladeros 143; ⊙10:30am-7:30pm Mon-Sat) Cuzco's most ex-tensive public book exchange, plus used guidebooks, new titles and music for sale.

Taller Mendivil
ARTS & CRAFTS

(Map p206; ☑084-63-7150; Plazoleta s/n; ⊙9am-7:30pm) A cramped but interesting artisan shop bursting with religious figures and or-nate mirrors.

Himalaya
SPORTS & OUTDOORS

(Map p206; ☑974-233-015, 974-285-336; www.himalayaoutdoorperu.com; Procuradores 398; ⊙9am-10pm) Crammed with new gear and rentals, this gear shop is a handy stop for all your trekking needs, including repellent, equipment and some clothing. There are tents, stoves, hiking poles, sleeping bags and pads for rent, with a deposit (S70) required.

Taller Mendivil
ARTS & CRAFTS

(Map p206; ☑084-23-3247; cnr Hatunrumiyoc & Choquechaca; ⊙8am-9pm Mon-Sat, 10am-7pm Sun) One of several outlets of a well-known artisan shop selling souvenirs, religious fig-ures and ornate mirrors.

Mercado de Huanchac
MARKET

(Mercado de Wanchaq; Map p214; cnr Avs Garcilaso & Huascar; ⊙6am-6pm) Huanchac is the local destination of choice for breakfast the morn-ing after, specializing in the two hangover staples – jolting acid ceviche and greasy *chicharrón* (deep-fried pork).

Taller and Museo Mérida
ARTS & CRAFTS

(Map p206; ☑084-22-1714; Carmen Alto 133, 2nd fl; ⊙9am-5:30pm Mon-Sat) Taller and Museo Mérida offers striking earthenware statues that straddle the border between craft and art.

Centro Artesanal Cuzco
MARKET

(Map p214; ☑974-791-081; Av Tullumayo 28; ⊙9am-8pm) Mass-produced tourist tat from textiles to teapots are sold at the vast Centro Artesanal Cuzco.

ⓘ Information

EMERGENCY

Policía de Turismo (PolTur, Tourist Police; ☑084-24-6088 ext 208; Plaza Túpac Amaru s/n; ⊙24hr)

IMMIGRATION

Most foreign embassies and consulates are located in Lima, though Cuzco does have several honorary consul representatives. If you need a Tarjeta Andina (tourist card), print one from the website of **Oficina de Migraciones** (Immigration Office; Map p214; ☑01-200-1000; www.migraciones.gob.pe; Av El Sol 612; ⊙8am-4:15pm Mon-Fri, 9am-noon Sat).

Belgian Honorary Consulate (☑084-26-1517; alberto@auqui.com.pe; José Gabriel Cosio 307, Urb Magisterial; ⊙9am-noon Mon-Fri)

French Honorary Consulate (Map p206; ☑084-24-9737; Nueva Baja 560)

German Honorary Consulate (Map p206; ☑084-24-2970; San Agustin 307)

Italian Honorary Consulate (☑984-825-400, 084-26-2958; Av Miluska del Castillo Vizcarra, Urbanizacion Mariscal Gamarra 1-B, 1era etapa; ⊙9am-1pm & 3-5pm Mon-Fri)

US Honorary Consulate (Map p206; ☑984-621-369, 084-23-1474; Av El Sol 449, office 201; ⊙appointment only)

MEDICAL SERVICES

Pharmacies abound along Av El Sol. Cuzco's medical facilities are limited; head to Lima for serious procedures.

Clínica Pardo (Map p214; ☑084-24-0997; Av de la Cultura 710; ⊙24hr) Well equipped and expensive – perfect if you're covered by travel insurance.

Clínica Paredes (Map p214; ☑084-22-5265; Lechugal 405; ⊙24hr) Consultations.

Hospital Regional (☑084-23-9792, emergen-cies 084-22-3691; Av de la Cultura s/n; ⊙24hr) Public and free, but wait times can be long and good care is not guaranteed.

MONEY

There are several big bank branches on Av El Sol; go inside for cash advances above daily ATM limits. *Casas de cambio* (foreign-exchange bureaus) give better exchange rates than banks and are scattered around the main plazas and especially along Av El Sol. Money changers can be found outside banks, but rip-offs are common.

BBVA Continental (Map p206; ☑ in Lima 01-440-4553; Av El Sol 368; ☺9am-6pm Mon-Fri, to 1pm Sat)

BCP (Map p206; ☑ 01-458-1230; Av El Sol 189; ☺9am-6:30pm Mon-Thu, to 7:30pm Fri, to 1pm Sat)

Interbank (Map p206; Av El Sol 380; ☺9am-6:30pm Mon-Fri, 9:15am-12:30pm Sat)

POST

DHL (Map p214; ☑ 084-24-4167; Av El Sol 608; ☺8:30am-7pm Mon-Fri, 9am-1pm Sat) International express mail and package courier services.

Serpost (Map p214; ☑ 084-22-5232; Av El Sol 800; ☺8am-8pm Mon-Sat) General delivery (poste restante) mail is held here at the main post office; bring proof of identity.

SAFE TRAVEL

➡ Bags may be stolen from the backs of chairs in public places or from overhead shelves in overnight buses.

➡ Walk around with a minimum of cash and belongings. If you keep your bag in your lap and watch out for pickpockets in crowded streets, transport terminals and markets, you are highly unlikely to be a victim of crime in Cuzco.

➡ Avoid walking by yourself late at night or very early in the morning. Revelers returning late from bars or setting off for the Inca Trail before sunrise are particularly vulnerable to 'choke and grab' attacks.

Taxi Robberies

Robberies and even attacks in cabs have been reported. Use only official taxis, especially at night. (Look for the company's lit telephone number on top of the car.) Lock your doors from the inside and never allow the driver to admit a second passenger. Readers have reported overcharging with *ticos* (taxi rickshaws).

Drugs & Spiked Drinks

Don't buy drugs. Dealers and police often work together and Procuradores is one of several areas in which you can make a drug deal and get busted all within a couple of minutes.

Drink spiking has been reported. Both women and men should keep an eye on their glass and not accept drinks from strangers.

Altitude Issues

Take care not to overexert yourself during your first few days if you've flown in from lower elevations. You may find yourself quickly becoming winded while traipsing up and down Cuzco's narrow streets.

TOURIST INFORMATION

DIRCETUR (Map p206; ☑ 084-58-2030, ext 2000; www.dirceturcusco.gob.pe; Garcilaso s/n, Museo Historico Regional; ☺7am-7:30pm Mon-Sat) (outlet) A central outlet of Dircetur located inside the Museo Historico Regional. Sells Machu Picchu entry tickets and the different versions of the *boleto turístico*. Closed on holidays.

Dirección Regional de Cultura Cusco (Map p206; ☑ 084-58-2030; www.dirceturcusco. gob.pe; Maruri 340; ☺7:15am-6:30pm Mon-Sat) The organizing body for tourism in Cuzco. Sells Machu Picchu entry tickets and the different versions of the *boleto turístico*. Closed on holidays. The website has a useful calendar of regional events and festivals.

iPerú (Map p206; ☑ 084-59-6159; www.peru. travel; Portal de Harinas 177, Plaza de Armas; ☺9am-7pm Mon-Fri, to 1pm Sat) Efficient and helpful. Excellent source for tourist information for both the region and entire country. There's an adjoining section of guarded ATMs. Also has a branch at the **airport** (☑ 084-23-7364; ☺6am-5pm).

Municipalidad del Cusco (www.cusco.gob.pe) The city's official website.

❶ Getting There & Away

AIR

Cuzco's **Aeropuerto Internacional Alejandro Velasco Astete** (CUZ; ☑ 084-22-2611) receives national and international flights. Most arrivals are in the morning, as afternoon conditions make landings and takeoffs more difficult. If you have a tight connection, it's best to reserve the earliest flight available, as later ones are more likely to be delayed or canceled.

There are daily flights to Lima, Juliaca, Puerto Maldonado and Arequipa. Check in at least two hours ahead as overbooking errors are commonplace. During the rainy season, flights to Puerto Maldonado are often seriously delayed. Departure taxes are included in ticket prices.

Avianca (Map p214; ☑ 0800-18-2222; www. avianca.com; Av El Sol 602; ☺8:30am-7pm Mon-Fri, 9am-2pm Sat) Service to/from Lima Monday to Saturday and direct flights to Bogota, Colombia.

LATAM (Map p214; ☑ 084-25-5555; www. latam.com; Av El Sol 627B; ☺9am-7pm Mon-Fri, to 1pm Sat) Direct flights to Lima, Arequipa, Juliaca and Puerto Maldonado, as well as Santiago, Chile.

Peruvian Airlines (Map p214; ☑ 084-25-4890; www.peruvianairlines.pe; Av El Sol 627-A;

9am-7pm Mon-Sat, to noon Sun) To Lima and La Paz, Bolivia.

Star Perú (Map p214; ☑ 01-705-9000; www.starperu.com; Av El Sol 627, oficina 101; ⊙ 9am-1pm & 3-6:30pm Mon-Sat, 9am-12:30pm Sun) Service to Lima.

Viva Air (☑ call center 084-64-4004; www.vivaair.com) Low-cost airline with online booking.

BUS & TAXI

Travel times are approximate and apply only if road conditions are good. Long delays are likely during the rainy season, particularly to Puerto Maldonado or Lima via Abancay. This road is now paved, but landslides can block the road in the rainy season.

International

All international services depart from the **Terminal Terrestre** (☑ 084-22-4471; Vía de Evitamiento 429), about 2km out of town toward the airport. Take a taxi (S30) or walk via Av El Sol. After it turns into Alameda Pachacutec, pedestrians can walk on the median. Straight after the tower and statue of Pachacutec, turn right, and follow the railway lines into a side street that reaches the terminal in five minutes.

To Bolivia, **Transporte Copacabana** (☑ 084-40-2953; www.transcopacabanasa.com.bo; Terminal Terrestre; ⊙ 9am-6pm), **Tour Peru** (☑ 084-23-6463; www.tourperu.com.pe; Terminal Terrestre; ⊙ 9am-6pm), **Transzela** (☑ 084-23-8223; www.transzela.com; Terminal Terrestre; ⊙ 9am-7pm) and **Titicaca** (☑ 084-22-9763; Transporte Terrestre; ⊙ 10am-5pm) offer daily services to Copacabana (10 hours) and La Paz, along with **Transporte Internacional Salvador** (☑ 084-23-3680; www.trans-salvador.com; Terminal Terrestre; ⊙ 9am-7pm), via Desaguadero (12 hours). This is the quickest way to get to La Paz.

Ormeño (☑ 969-933-579; Vía de Evitamiento 429, Terminal Terrestre; ⊙ 9am-7pm) travels to Brazil.

Comfortable backpacker bus **Peru Hop** (Map p206; ☑ in Lima 01-242-2140; www.peruhop.com; Tandapata 100B; ⊙ 9:30am-8:30pm Mon-Fri, to 7:30pm Sat, 10:30am-8:30pm Sun) goes to Bolivia and destinations throughout Peru with hotel pickup and drop-off and multistop hop-on, hop-off service.

Long-Distance

Buses to major cities leave from the Terminal Terrestre. Buses for more unusual destinations leave from elsewhere, so check carefully in advance.

Cruz del Sur (☑ 084-74-0444; www.cruzdelsur.com.pe; Av Industrial 121) has its own terminal but tickets can be purchased at the Terminal Terrestre. Buses are comfortable. Of the cheaper companies, Tour Peru and **Wari** (☑ 084-22-2694; www.grupopalomino.com.pe; Vía de Evitamiento 429, Terminal Terrestre; ⊙ 9am-7pm) have the best buses.

There are hourly departures to Juliaca and Puno from 4am to 11pm, and at random hours through the day. Cheap, slow options like **Libertad** (☑ 084-22-4571; Terminal Terrestre; ⊙ 9am-6pm) stop to let passengers on and off along the way, so you can use them to access towns along the route. Midpriced Transporte Copacabana is faster and more comfortable.

The most enjoyable way to get to Puno is via luxury tourist buses that take the Ruta del Sol. **Inka Express** (☑ 084-63-4838; www.inkaexpress.com; Av Alameda Pachacuteq 499; S165; ⊙ 9am-1pm & 3-7pm Mon-Fri, 9am-1pm & 4-6pm Sat) and **Turismo Mer** (☑ 084-24-5171; www.turismomer.com; El Óvalo, Av La Paz A3; tourist service with entry fees S198; ☎) go every morning. The service includes lunch and an English-speaking tour guide, who talks about the four sites that are briefly visited along the way: Andahuaylillas, Raqchi, Abra la Raya and Pucará. The trip takes about eight hours. Check to see if rates include your site entrance fees.

Departures to Arequipa cluster around 6am to 7am and 7pm to 9:30pm. Ormeño offers a deluxe service at 9am.

Cruz del Sur (☑ 084-74-0444; www.cruzdelsur.com.pe; Av Industrial 121) and **CIVA** (☑ 084-24-9961; www.civa.com.pe; Vía de Evitamiento 429, Terminal Terrestre; ⊙ 9am-6pm) offer relatively painless services to Lima. Wari is the best of the cheaper options. Most buses to Lima stop in Nazca (13 hours) and Ica (16 hours). These buses go via Abancay and can suffer holdups in rainy season. Between January and April, it may be worth going via Arequipa (25 to 27 hours) instead.

Julsa (☑ 951-298-798; Terminal Terrestre) offers direct buses to Tacna, near the Chilean border.

Various companies depart for Puerto Maldonado between 3pm and 4:30pm; CIVA is probably the best option.

For destinations within Cuzco & the Sacred Valley:

Wari and **Expreso Los Chankas** (☑ 084-26-2909; Vía de Evitamiento 429, Terminal Terrestre; ⊙ 9am-6pm) depart every couple of hours through the day for Abancay and Andahuaylas (S70, nine hours). Change at Andahuaylas to get to Ayacucho via rough roads that get very cold at night. If you're going to Ayacucho by bus, wear all of your warm clothes and if you have a sleeping bag, bring it on board the bus.

Buses to Quillabamba via Santa María (S25, 4½ hours) leave from the Santiago terminal, a brisk 20-minute walk from the center. Around the corner in Calle Antonio Lorena, many more companies offer air-conditioned, speedy comfort in the form of modern minivans that cost twice as much and cut a couple of hours off the trip. There are departures of both types of service at 8am, 10am, 1pm and 8pm. Change at Santa María to get to Santa Teresa.

Transportes Siwar ([ ] 993-407-105; Av Tito Condemayta 1613) and other companies have buses to Ocongate (S9, three hours) and Tinqui (S10, three hours), the start of the Ausangante trek, leaving from behind the Coliseo Cerrado every half-hour or when they're full.

Several buses and minivans depart daily to Paucartambo (S9 to S12, three hours) from Paradero Control in distrito de San Jerónimo – a taxi will know where to drop you off.

Regional Services

The government may soon restrict the use of old *colectivos* (shared transportation). Most services run from at least 5am until 7pm. Early and late services may charge more.

➔ Minibuses to Calca (S6, 1½ hours) via Pisac (S4, one hour) leave frequently from the terminal at Tullumayo 207.

➔ Minibuses to Urubamba (S8, 1½ hours) via Pisac leave frequently from the terminal in Puputi 208, just north of Av de la Cultura.

➔ **Minibuses** (Map p214) to Urubamba (S6, 1½ hours) and Ollantaytambo (S12, two hours) via Chinchero (S4, one hour) leave from near the Puente Grau. Just around the corner on Pavitos, faster **colectivos** (Map p214) leave when full for Urubamba (S7, one hour) and Ollantaytambo (S10 to S15, 1½ hours) via Chinchero.

➔ **Colectivos** (Map p214) to Urcos (S5, one hour) via Tipón (S1, 40 minutes), Piquillacta (S5) and Andahuaylillas (S7) leave from the middle of the street outside Tullumayo 207. For S80 they'll drive you into the ruins at Tipón and Piquillacta, wait and bring you back.

➔ You can also get to these destinations, and Saylla, by catching a minibus headed for Urcos (S5) from a terminal just off Av de la Cultura opposite the regional hospital. Shared taxis to Lucre (S3, one hour) depart from Huascar, between Av Garcilaso and Manco Capac, between 7am and 7pm.

➔ Minibuses for Limatambo (S12, two hours) and Curahuasi (S15, three hours) leave Arcopata, a couple of blocks west of Meloc, when full until about 3pm.

Cuzco Buses

Prices are general estimates for normal/luxury buses.

DESTINATION	COST (S)	DURATION (HR)
Abancay	30-50/ -	5
Arequipa	40/135	10
Ayacucho	65/95	16
Copacabana (Bolivia)	60/90	10
Ica	100/155	16
Juliaca	35-40/ -	5
La Paz (Bolivia)	80/120	12
Lima	100/160	21
Nazca	100/150	13
Puerto Maldonado	50/90	10
Puno	40/70	6
Quillabamba	25-35/ -	4½
Tacna	80/120	15

CAR & MOTORCYCLE

Given all the headaches and potential hazards of driving yourself around and finding a place to park, consider hiring a taxi for the day – it's cheaper than renting a car. If you must, you'll find a couple of car-rental agencies in the bottom block of Av El Sol.

Motorcycle rentals are offered by a couple of agencies in the first block of Saphi heading away from the Plaza de Armas.

Traveling by bus from Cuzco to Lima via Abancay and Nazca takes you along a remote route closed from the late 1980s until the late 1990s due to guerilla activity and banditry. It is now much safer, and paved. You should still check recent news reports before heading out this way as rainy-season landslides can really slow a trip. Going west from Abancay to Andahuaylas and Ayacucho is a tough ride on a rough road rarely used except by the most hard-core travelers.

TRAIN

Cuzco has two train stations. **Estación Huanchac** (Wanchaq; Map p214; [ ] 084-58-1414; Av Pachacutec s/n; ⏱ 7am-5pm Mon-Fri, to midnight Sat & Sun), near the end of Av El Sol, serves Juliaca and Puno on Lake Titicaca. **Estación Poroy** (Calle Roldan s/n, Carr Cuzco-Urubamba), east of town, serves Ollantaytambo and Machu Picchu. The two stations are unconnected, so it's impossible to travel directly from Puno to Machu Picchu. (Downtown Estación San Pedro is used only for local trains, which foreigners cannot board.)

You can take a taxi to Poroy (S30) or the station in Ollantaytambo (S90) from Cuzco. Return trips are slightly more expensive.

Tickets are sold at Huanchac station, where there are ATMs, but we recommend purchasing directly through the train companies.

From January through March there is no train service between Cuzco and Aguas Calientes (for Machu Picchu) because of frequent landslides on the route. Instead, there's a bus from Estacion Huanchac to Ollantaytambo, where you can board a train for the remainder of the trip.

To Ollantaytambo & Machu Picchu

To reach Aguas Calientes (and access Machu Picchu) by train takes three hours.

Fares vary according to departure hours: more desirable times are usually more expensive. It is common for trains to sell out, especially at peak hours, so buy your ticket as far ahead of time as possible.

The quickest 'cheaper' way to get from Cuzco to Aguas Calientes is to take a *combi* (minibus) to Ollantaytambo and catch the train from there. In low season (between December and March), service from the Cuzco terminal is discontinued and replaced with a bus from Cuzco to Ollantaytambo, from where you continue by train.

Peru Rail (Map p206; ☎ 084-58-1414; www.perurail.com; Estación Poroy; ☺7am-5pm Mon-Fri, to noon Sat) The flagship service to Aguas Calientes, with multiple departures daily from Estación Poroy, 20 minutes outside of Cuzco. There are three service categories: Expedition (from S232 one way), Vistadome (from S347 one way) and the luxurious Hiram Bingham (from S1736 one way). The Hiram Bingham includes brunch, afternoon tea, entrance to Machu Picchu and a guided tour. It runs daily except Sunday.

Inca Rail (Map p206; ☎ 084-25-2974; www.incarail.com; Portal de Panes 105, Plaza de Armas; 1 way S231-330; ☺8am-9pm Mon-Fri, 9am-7pm Sat, to 2pm Sun) Has three departures daily from Ollantaytambo and four levels of service. For an extra fee, you can add bus service from the Hotel Costa del Sol in Cuzco (called the bimodal service). Children get a significant discount. Environmentally sustainable business practice.

To Puno & Arequipa

An exercise in old-fashioned romance, the **Belmond Andean Explorer** (Map p206; ☎ 084-58-1414; www.perurail.com; Estación Huanchac; to Puno/Arequipa from S5754/13,393; ☺7am-5pm Mon-Fri, to noon Sat) is a gorgeous luxury sleeper train with a glass-walled observation car. It travels across the altiplano to Puno and on to Arequipa. Weekly departures leave Thursdays, arriving at Puno the same evening and Arequipa on Saturday.

Peru Rail also has regular service to Puno on the Titicaca Train (S859, 10½ hours).

ⓘ Getting Around

TO/FROM THE AIRPORT

The airport is about 6km south of the city center. The *combi* lines Imperial and C4M (S0.80, 20 minutes) run from Av El Sol to just outside the airport. A taxi to or from the city center to the airport costs S30. An official radio taxi from within the airport costs S40. With advance reservations, many hotels offer free pickup.

BUS

Local rides on public transportation cost only S1, though it's easier to walk or just take a taxi than to figure out where any given *combi* is headed.

TAXI

There are no meters in taxis, but there are set rates. At the time of research, trips within the city center cost S8 and destinations further afield, such as El Molino, cost S12. Check with your hotel whether this is still correct, and rather than negotiate, simply hand the correct amount to your driver at the end of your ride; he is unlikely to argue if you seem to know what you're doing. Official taxis, identified by a lit company telephone number on the roof, are more expensive than taxis flagged down on the street, but they are safer.

Unofficial 'pirate' taxis, which only have a taxi sticker in the window, have been complicit in muggings, violent assaults and kidnappings of tourists. Before getting into any taxi, do as savvy locals do and take conspicuous note of the registration number.

AloCusco (☎084-22-2222) is a reliable company to call.

AROUND CUZCO

The four ruins closest to Cuzco are Saqsaywamán, Q'enqo, Pukapukara and Tambomachay. They can all be visited in a day – far less if you're whisked through on a guided tour. If you only have time to visit one site, Saqsaywamán is the most important, and less than a 2km trek uphill from the Plaza de Armas in central Cuzco. The cheapest way to visit the sites is to take a bus bound for Pisac and ask the driver to stop at Tambomachay, the furthest site from Cuzco (at 3700m, it's also the highest). It's an 8km walk back to Cuzco, visiting all four ruins along the way. Alternatively, a taxi will charge roughly S70 to visit all four sites. Each site can only be entered with the *boleto turístico* (p210). Local guides hang around offering their services, sometimes quite persistently. Agree on a price before beginning any tour. Robberies at these sites are uncommon but not un-heard of. Cuzco's tourist police recommend visiting between 9am and 5pm.

Saqsaywamán

This immense **ruin** (boleto turístico adult/student S130/70; ⊘ 7am-5:30pm) of both religious and military significance is the most impressive in the immediate area around Cuzco. The long Quechua name means 'Satisfied Falcon,' though tourists will inevitably remember it by the mnemonic 'sexy woman.' Today's visitor sees only about 20% of the original structure. Soon after conquest, the Spaniards tore down many walls and used the blocks to build their own houses in Cuzco, leaving the largest and most impressive rocks, especially those forming the main battlements.

In 1536 the fort was the site of one of the most bitter battles of the Spanish conquest. More than two years after Pizarro's entry into Cuzco, the rebellious Manco Inca recaptured the lightly guarded Sacsaywamán and used it as a base to lay siege to the conquistadors in Cuzco. Manco was on the brink of defeating the Spaniards when a desperate last-ditch attack by 50 Spanish cavalry led by Juan Pizarro, Francisco's brother, succeeded in retaking Sacsaywamán and putting an end to the rebellion. Manco Inca survived and retreated to the fortress of Ollantaytambo, but most of his forces were killed. Thousands of dead littered the site after the Incas' defeat, attracting swarms of carrion-eating Andean condors. The tragedy was memorialized by the inclusion of eight condors in Cuzco's coat of arms.

The site is composed of three different areas, the most striking being the magnificent three-tiered zigzag fortifications. One stone, incredibly, weighs more than 300 tons. It was the ninth inca, Pachacutec, who envisioned Cuzco in the shape of a puma, with Sacsaywamán as the head, and these 22 zig-zagged walls as the teeth of the puma. The walls also formed an extremely effective defensive mechanism that forced attackers to expose their flanks when attacking.

Opposite is the hill called Rodadero, with retaining walls, polished rocks and a finely carved series of stone benches known as the Inca's Throne. Three towers once stood above these walls. Only the foundations remain, but the 22m diameter of the largest, Muyuc Marca, gives an indication of how big they must have been. With its perfectly fitted stone conduits, this tower was probably used as a huge water tank for the garrison. Other buildings within the ramparts provided food and shelter for an estimated 5000 warriors. Most of these structures were torn down by the Spaniards and later inhabitants of Cuzco.

Between the zigzag ramparts and the hill lies a large, flat parade ground that is used for the colorful tourist spectacle of Inti Raymi (p222), held every June 24. To walk up to the site from the Plaza de Armas takes 30 to 50 minutes, so make sure you're acclimatized before attempting it. Arriving at dawn will let you have the site almost to yourself, though solo travelers shouldn't come alone at this time of day.

Q'enqo

The name of this small but fascinating ruin means 'Zigzag.' A large limestone rock, Q'enqo is riddled with niches, steps and extraordinary symbolic carvings, including the zigzagging channels that probably gave the site its name. Scramble up to the top to find a flat surface used for ceremonies: look carefully to see laboriously etched representations of a puma, a condor and a llama. Back below, you can explore a mysterious subterranean cave with altars hewn into the rock. Q'enqo is about 4km northeast of Cuzco, on the left of the road as you descend from Tambomachay.

Pukapukara

Just across the main road from Tambomachay, this commanding structure looks down on the Cuzco valley. In some lights the rock looks pink, and the name literally means 'Red Fort,' though it is more likely to have been a hunting lodge, a guard post and a stopping point for travelers. It is composed of several lower residential chambers, storerooms and an upper esplanade with panoramic views.

Tambomachay

In a sheltered spot about 300m from the main road, this site consists of a beautifully wrought **ceremonial stone bath** (☏ 84-227-037; boleto turístico adult/student S130/70; ⊘ 7:30am-5:30pm) channeling crystalline spring water through fountains that still function today. It is thus popularly known as El Baño del Inca (Bath of the Inca), and theories connect the site to an Inca water cult. It's 8km northeast of Cuzco.

THE SACRED VALLEY

Tucked under the tawny skirts of formidable foothills, the beautiful Río Urubamba Valley, known as El Valle Sagrado (the Sacred Valley), is about 15km north of Cuzco as the condor flies, via a narrow road of hairpin turns. It's worth exploring this peaceful, fetching corner of the Andes with colonial towns and isolated weaving villages. Star attractions are the markets and the lofty Inca citadels of Pisac and Ollantaytambo, but it's also packed with other Inca sites. Its myriad trekking routes are deservedly gaining in popularity. Adrenaline activities range from rafting to rock climbing.

A multitude of travel agencies in Cuzco offer whirlwind tours of the Sacred Valley, stopping at markets and the most significant ruins. It's also worth an in-depth visit. The archaeological sites of Pisac, Ollantaytambo and Chinchero can be visited with a *boleto turístico*, which can be bought directly on-site.

Pisac

📄 084 / POP 9440 / ELEV 2715M

Welcome to the international airport for the cosmic traveler, according to one seasoned local. It's not hard to succumb to the charms of sunny Pisac, a bustling and fast-growing colonial village at the base of a spectacular Inca fortress perched on a mountain spur. Its pull is universal and recent years have seen an influx of expats and New Age followers in search of an Andean Shangri-la. The local tourism industry has responded by catering to spiritual seekers, offering everything from yoga retreats and cleanses to guided hallucinogenic trips. Yet it's also worthwhile for mainstream travelers, with ruins, a fabulous market and weaving villages that should not be missed. Located just 33km northeast of Cuzco by a paved road, it's the most convenient starting point to the Sacred Valley.

◉ Sights

Pisac Ruins

RUINS

(boleto turístico adult/student S130/70; ⊙ 7am-6pm) A truly awesome site with relatively few tourists, this hilltop Inca citadel lies high above the village on a triangular plateau with a plunging gorge on either side. Allow several hours to explore. Taking a taxi up and walking back (4km) is a good option. The most impressive feature is the agricultural terracing, which sweeps around the south and east flanks of the mountain in huge and graceful curves, almost entirely unbroken by steps.

Instead, the terracing is joined by diagonal flights of stairs made of flagstones set into the terrace walls. Above the terraces are cliff-hugging footpaths, watched over by caracara falcons and well defended by massive stone doorways, steep stairs and a short tunnel carved out of the rock. Vendors sell drinks at the top.

This dominating site guards not only the Urubamba Valley below, but also a pass leading into the jungle to the northeast. Topping the terraces is the site's **ceremonial center**, with an *intihuatana* (literally 'hitching post of the sun'; an Inca astronomical tool), several working water channels, and some painstakingly neat masonry in the well-preserved **temples**. A path leads up the hillside to a series of ceremonial baths and around to the military area. Looking across the Kitamayo Gorge from the back of the site, you'll also see hundreds of holes honeycombing the cliff wall. These are **Inca tombs** that were plundered by *huaqueros* (grave robbers), and are now completely off-limits to tourists.

At the time of writing, the trail starting above the west side of the church in town was closed. Check for updates in Pisac. When it's open, it's a two-hour climb and 1½ hours return. Worthwhile but grueling, it's good training for the Inca Trail! The footpath has many crisscrossing trails, but if you aim toward the terracing, you won't get lost. To the west, or the left of the hill as you climb up on the footpath, is the Río Kitamayo Gorge; to the east, or right, is the Río Chongo Valley.

Mercado de Artesania

MARKET

(Plaza Constitución; ⊙ 8am-4pm) Pisac is known far and wide for its market, by far the biggest and most touristy in the region. While there are still some local arts and crafts of note, watch out for mass-produced goods invading from as far as Colombia. Its massive success has it filling the Plaza Constitución and surrounding streets every day.

On Sundays, fruit and vegetable sellers from nearby farming communities come to sell their produce.

The Sacred Valley

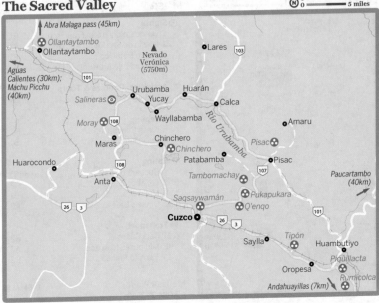

Iglesia de San Pedro Apostol
CHURCH

(Plaza Constitución) Traditionally dressed locals descend from the hills to attend mass in Quechua, including men in highland dress blowing horns, and *varayocs* (local officials) with silver staffs of office. It's held at 11am on Sundays. Travelers can attend but shouldn't take photos. The church recently reopened after its controversial demolition and rebuild in colonial style.

Jardín Botanico
GARDENS

(☎084-63-5563; Grau, cuadra 4; admission S8; ⊙8am-4:30pm) A private enterprise with a huge courtyard full of beautiful specimens and a resident cat.

Horno Colonial San Francisco
LANDMARK

(Mariscal Castilla s/n; snacks S4; ⊙7am-6pm) Huge clay ovens for baking empanadas and other goodies are found in many nooks and crannies, particularly on Mariscál Castilla. But this is the town's most authentic – a colonial oven dating back to 1830. There are also *castillos de cuyes* (miniature castles inhabited by guinea pigs) here.

Amaru
VILLAGE

If you are interested in textiles, it's worth visiting this weaving community that's a 40-minute trip by taxi from Pisac.

⭐ Festivals & Events

La Virgen del Carmen
FESTIVAL

(⊙mid-Jul) Street processions and masked dancing mark the celebration of 'Mamacha Carmen' who defeats demons climbing on rooftops and balconies. This renowned celebration of the Virgin of Carmen takes place from around July 15 to July 18.

☞ Tours

Parque de la Papa
ECOTOUR

(☎084-24-5021; www.ipcca.info/about-parque-de-la-papa; Pisac) Day treks and cooking workshops are some of the offerings of this wonderful nonprofit, which promotes potato diversity and communal farming.

🛏 Sleeping

Lodging ranges from adorable inns to basic backpacker haunts. Foreign-run mystical and spiritual retreats on the outskirts of town offer packages with shamanic ceremonies; some are vastly more commercial than others.

Kinsa Ccocha Inn
HOTEL $

(☎084-20-3101; Arequipa 307A; s/d S50/70; 🛜) With a fertile fig tree in its stony patio, this simple lodging has a nice vibe and thoughtful touches, such as plenty of power plugs, good towels and strong, hot showers. Lest

Pisac

you feel too spoiled, there's no heat, but 2nd-floor rooms are warmer. Breakfast is not offered, but there's an adjoining cafe with good coffee.

★ Pisac Quishu
GUESTHOUSE $$

(☑084-509-106, 942-664-132; www.pisacinca.com; Calle Huayna Picchu F-5; s/d incl breakfast S130/210; ☎❀▣) Talk about sibling rivalry: this excellent new property is next door to the Pisac Inca Guesthouse, which is run by the same family. This one, run by the effervescent sisters Tatiana and Libertad, is slightly more design-conscious, with beautiful, bold-hued rooms around a tranquil courtyard garden. Breakfast includes fruit, plus vegan and gluten-free options. They're adding an on-site ceramic workshop you can visit.

La Casa del Conde
GUESTHOUSE $$

(☑084-78-7818; Andenes de Chihuanco s/n; s/d incl breakfast S205/264; ☎) Guests rave about this lovely country house, nestled into the foothills with blooming flower patches. Family-run and brimming with personality, its lovely rooms feature down duvets, heat and cable TV. There's no car access. It's a 15-minute walk uphill from the plaza, but a *mototaxi* (three-wheeled motorcycle rickshaw taxi) can leave you at the chapel that's five minutes away.

Melissa Wasi
CABAÑAS $$

(☑084-79-7589; www.melissa-wasi.com; Sector Matara s/n; s/d S182/314, 4-person bungalows S429, all incl breakfast; ☎) Guests receive warm treatment at this established lodge, situated on a shady lane, which also serves as a spiritual retreat center. Rooms are in small adobe cabins on a landscaped slope. The restaurant has nightly chef-prepared dinners, though it's drafty and the service can be painfully slow. Wi-fi is only available in common areas. Located 2km from Pisac. English is spoken.

Pisac Inca Guesthouse
GUESTHOUSE $$

(☑084-50-9106; www.pisacinca.com; Huayna Picchu s/n; s/d incl breakfast 153/198; ☎) A few blocks away from the center, this ample guesthouse is a find. Rooms are smart and simple, centered around a large, grassy area with lounge chairs. Some have kitchenettes. There's also a roof deck with views and a glass breakfast room. It's run by the same hospitable family that runs Pisac Quishu.

Pisac Inn
INN $$

(☑084-20-3062; www.pisacinn.com; Plaza Constitución; s/d incl breakfast from S208/250; @☎) Location, location, location! This lovely plaza hotel features an inviting courtyard and romantic rooms with down bedding, dark blue walls and Andean decor. Rooms with king-sized beds are a slight upgrade.It has good off-season discounts. The location means some rooms get noisy early when merchants are setting up outside. It has on-site spa services.

Royal Inka Hotel Pisac   HOTEL $$

(☑ 084-20-3066, 084-20-3064; www.royalinkaho tel.pe; s/d incl breakfast S191/264; ☎⚙) Once a large hacienda, this hotel is surprisingly unpretentious. Rooms are generous, sometimes dated, many with views of the ruins, surrounded by well-tended flower gardens and conservatories. Guests can access the facilities of Club Royal Inka (admission S15; ☺8am-4pm) across the road, plus the on-site spa and Jacuzzi. It's located about 1.5km from the plaza up the road to the ruins.

🍴 Eating

El Sabor   PERUVIAN $

(☑ 990-176-420; Vigil 262; set menu S6; ☺8am-10pm Sun-Fri, to 3pm Sat) This popular local restaurant has the best deal in town: set menus of classic Peruvian fare with three options daily, including a vegetarian option. It's fresh and tasty as the restaurant's name suggests, and great value.

Doña Clorinda   PERUVIAN $$

(☑ 084-20-3051; Urb San Luis, La Rinconada; mains S18-35; ☺9am-5pm) In a lovely colonial home, this longtime Pisac mainstay serves up hearty Andean fare. Order some homemade *chicha morada* (blue corn juice) to go with heaping plates of *arroz chaufa* (Peruvian fried rice), trout, beef and *rocoto relleno* (stuffed peppers) with *kapchi*. A classic.

Mullu   FUSION $$

(☑ 084-20-3073; www.mullu.pe; San Francisco s/n, 2nd fl, Plaza Constitución; mains S30-56; ☺9am-9pm) The balcony of this chill and welcoming place may be the best spot to watch market-day interactions in the plaza below. The menu is fusion (think Thai meets Amazonian while flirting with highland Peruvian). Traditional lamb is tender to falling-off-the-bone; soups, alpaca burgers and blended juices also satisfy. It can also cater for special diets. With homemade chocolates and all-day breakfast (S29).

Ulrike's Café   CAFE $$

(☑ 084-20-3195; Manuel Prado s/s; mains S15-33; ☺9am-9pm; ☎🖧) This sunny cafe is consistently tasty, serving up a great vegetarian *menú* (set meal), plus homemade pasta, house-made bagels and melt-in-the-mouth cheesecake. The fluffy carrot cake is legendary.

There's a book exchange and special events. English, French and German are spoken.

Cuchara de Palo   INTERNATIONAL $$

(☑ 084-20-3062; Plaza Constitución; mains S35-45; ☺7:30-8:30pm) Inside Pisac Inn, this fine-dining restaurant offers organic salads, meats and dishes like pumpkin ravioli drizzled with corn and cream. Service can be slow but it has great ambience, with candle-lit courtyard tables.

ℹ️ Information

Caja Cusco (Amazonas s/n; ☺24hr) has an ATM at the entrance to town. There are mini-markets on Bolognesi.

ℹ️ Getting There & Away

Buses to Urubamba (S5 to S7, one hour) leave frequently from the downtown bridge between 6am and 8pm. **Minibuses to Cuzco** (Amazonas s/n; S5, one hour) leave from Calle Amazonas when full. Many travel agencies in Cuzco also operate tour buses to Pisac, especially on market days.

For the Pisac ruins, minivans (S60 round-trip) near the plaza leave regularly, or hire a **taxi** from near the bridge into town to drive you up the 7.5km paved road.

Pisac to Urubamba

Don't rush the scenic drive between Pisac and Urubamba. The pretty villages of Lamay, Urquillos and Huarán offer boutique accommodations and great day tours for mountain biking, hiking and cultural visits. It's an excellent base from which to leisurely explore the scenic Sacred Valley and its many intriguing side valleys.

🔵 Sights & Activities

⭐ Museo Inkariy   MUSEUM

(☑ 084-79-2819, 984-666-698; www.museoinkariy. com; Carr Pisac-Ollantaytambo Km 53; adult/child 6-17 S35/20; ☺9am-5pm) This wonderful new museum takes visitors into the world of the fascinating pre-Colombian civilizations that came before the Inca. It acknowledges the reality that the Incans built on knowledge developed over millennia of habitation in Peru. Each culture, including the Inca, has its own building with two rooms. One is dedicated to history, with key artifacts and succinct overviews in Spanish and English. The other features a compelling scenario of life-sized figures rendered expertly in action, á la *National Geographic*.

It's also entertaining for children. Reserve ahead for a guided tour in English. There's also an on-site cafe and gift shops.

Patabamba
VILLAGE

A visit to the community of Patabamba offers a fascinating participative demonstration of the weaving process, all the way from picking the plants to making dyes, to shearing sheep and setting up a loom – with explanations of the meanings of colors and patterns. There are also excellent trekking options.

Journey Experience (www.thejoex.com) and other Cuzco agencies offer visits. Campsites and homestays are available with advance notice. Prices vary wildly, depending on group size and transport needed.

Munaycha
ADVENTURE

(984-770-381; www.munaycha.com; Carr Pisac-Ollantaytambo Km 60.2, Huarán) A reputable outfitter offering original active tours around the Sacred Valley, its most popular option is sea kayaking with a picnic. There's also guided Lares treks and a variety of mountain-bike trips. We have heard rave reviews about trek-bike combinations to Huaipo Lake near Chinchero.

Sleeping & Eating

★ Nunu Boutique Hotel
BOUTIQUE HOTEL $$

(981-203-001; www.nunuboutiquehotel.com; Carr Pisac-Ollantaytambo Km 41.5, Lamay; s/d incl breakfast S297/429;) This excellent boutique option with a warm welcome is well worth the detour. Six magical adobe cabins are set in a circle around an expansive lawn with flower paths, hammocks and a swing set. But the real treasures are the colorful two-story cabins, each inventively decorated by theme (cobbler, explorer, seamstress) with whimsical objects, antiquities and Andean weavings.

With solar-heated water. It's on the edge of the village of Lamay, down by the river.

★ Explora
LODGE $$$

(084-30-0000; www.explora.com/machu-picchu-sacred-valley-peru; Urquillos; 4 nights all-inclusive from US$1292;) Surrounded by Inca terraces and fields of corn and quinoa, this luxury lodge creates a fine atmosphere for relaxation – if they let you. Packages come with active tours which are both off the beaten path and personalized, plus a Machu Picchu visit already included in the price. Spacious rooms feature valley views, minimalist style and jacuzzi tubs. Wi-fi is only in the common areas.

At the end of the day, a dip in the gorgeous pool or a walk to the on-site spa and sauna with original colonial mural remnants is a must. There's also a wonderful on-site restaurant with top-notch wine selections. Most visitors book the four-night option.

Viva Peru
CAFE $

(off Carr Pisac-Ollantaytambo, Huarán; mains S8-22; 11am-4pm Mon-Sat;) Just off the main road in Huaran, this adorable cafe hits the spot with oversized sandwiches and fresh fruit juices. There are also vegetarian options and a backyard patio with shady tables.

🛈 Getting There & Away

Buses running between Pisac and Urubamba (S5) pass regularly.

Urubamba

📞 084 / POP 17,800 / ELEV 2870M

A busy and unadorned urban center, Urubamba is a transport hub surrounded by bucolic foothills and snowy peaks. The advantages of its lower altitude and relative proximity to Machu Picchu make it popular with both high-end hotels and package tours. While there is little of historical interest, nice countryside and great weather make it a convenient base from which to explore the extraordinary salt flats of Salineras and the terracing of Moray.

Since Urubamba is quite spread out, the mode of transport of choice are *mototaxis* (three-wheeled motorcycle rickshaw taxis). The Plaza de Armas is five blocks east and four blocks north of the terminal, bounded by Calle Comercio and Jirón Grau.

🏃 Activities

Many outdoor activities that are organized from Cuzco take place near here, including horseback riding, rock climbing, mountain biking, paragliding and hot-air balloon trips.

★ Cusco for You
HORSE RIDING

(987-417-250, 987-841-000; www.cuscoforyou.com; Carr a Salineras de Maras, Pichingoto; 1hr ride S238) Highly recommended for horseback-riding and trekking trips from one to eight days long. Horseback-riding day trips go to Moray and Salineras and other regional destinations. Ask about special rates for families and groups. With an optional transportation service to the ranch, which also has accommodations and dining.

Sacred Wheels
CYCLING

(☑ 984-626-811, 954-700-844; www.sacredwheels. com; 3hr tour from S264) Even the casual rider can enjoy these mountain-bike tours that visit the valley and urban Urubamba, with both gentle and challenging routes.

Perol Chico
HORSEBACK RIDING

(☑ 950-314-065; www.perolchico.com; Carr Urumbamba a Ollantaytambo; overnight packages from US$720) This place is run by Dutch-Peruvian Eduard van Brunschot Vega, with an excellent ranch outside Urubamba with Peruvian *paso* horses. Eduard organizes horseback-riding tours that last up to two weeks. An overnight in the Sacred Valley with rides to Salineras, Maras and Moray includes all meals and luxury accommodations. Advance bookings are required.

🛏 Sleeping

Los Jardines
HOTEL $

(☑ 084-20-1331; www.losjardines.weebly.com; Jr Convención 459; d incl breakfast S152) Noted for its accommodating service, this reader-recommended family hotel occupies a walled compound with a large adobe home and flowering gardens that make it feel like the city isn't even there. Rooms are basic but clean, some feature large picture windows. It's within walking distance of the plaza.

Hostal los Perales
GUESTHOUSE $

(Ecolodge Urubamba; ☑ 084-20-1151, 928-289-566; www.ecolodgeurubamba.com; Pasaje Arenales 102; r per person incl breakfast S45) Tucked down a hidden country lane, this welcoming family-run guesthouse offers good-value, basic rooms around lovely overgrown gardens. Its elderly owners are sweet, serving banana pancakes and *aguaymanto* j(Cape gooseberry) jam from their own tree for breakfast. It's easy to get lost, so take a *mototaxi* (three-wheeled motorcycle rickshaw taxi; S1.50) from the terminal.

Las Chullpas
CABIN $$

(☑ 084-20-1568; www.chullpas.pe; Pumahuanca Valley; d/tr incl breakfast S231/330; @ 🎧) Hidden 3km above town, these rustic woodland cottages make for the perfect getaway. Rooms feature comfortable beds and fireplaces. The site, nestled among thick eucalyptus trees, is spread out with inviting pathways and lounge areas with hammocks. There is also an open kitchen serving vegetarian food, holistic treatments and a sweat lodge (available on request).

Much of the food is grown organically onsite, and efforts are made toward composting and recycling. The affable Chilean owner also guides treks, especially to the Lares Valley. Come with good directions: the roads are unmarked and not all taxi drivers know it.

★ Sol y Luna
BOUTIQUE HOTEL $$$

(☑ 084-20-1620; www.hotelsolyluna.com; Fundo Huincho lote A-5; d/tr incl breakfast from S1492/1848; @ 🎧 ☲) A living fairy tale, this luxury Relais & Chateaux property runs wild with whimsy. Fans of folk art will be overwhelmed – its 43 *casitas* (cabins) feature original murals and comic, oversized sculptures by noted Peruvian artist Federico Bauer. The playful feel spills over to bold tropical hues and a decor of carved wooden beds, freestanding tubs and dainty chandeliers.

French-Swiss owned, it all conspires to charm you. Avant-garde circus productions with former Cirque de Soleil artists provide evening entertainment. For daytime fun, Peruvian *paso* horses can be ridden on the 15 hectares and beyond. With an eccentric atmosphere, its acclaimed restaurant Wayra is the creation of Lima's Malabar-famed chef. There's also a more casual open-air offering featuring food tours and chef visits.

Tambo del Inka
LUXURY HOTEL $$$

(☑ 084-58-1777; www.libertador.com.pe; Carr Urumbamba a Ollantaytambo; d incl breakfast from S1000; @ 🎧 ☲) 🏊 Just like Hogwarts, Tambo del Inka features its own train station – handy for a morning jaunt to Machu Picchu. Stark and commanding, this LEED-certified hotel (with its own water-treatment plant and UV air filters) occupies an immense riverside spread with giant eucalyptus trees. The eucalyptus is a staple of interior decor and even spa treatments.

Rooms are appealing and comfortable. The hotel's best features are a chromo-therapeutic indoor-outdoor pool that changes colors at night, and a hipster lounge with round tables and leather armchairs, backlit by an immense mural of fractured onyx.

Hotel Río Sagrado
LUXURY HOTEL $$$

(☑ 084-20-1631; www.riosagradohotel.com; Carr Urumbamba a Ollantaytambo; d incl breakfast from S1172; @ 🎧) A design haven of cottage-style rooms with rough-hewn beams and exquisite accents of Ayacucho embroidery, this Belmond property is the epitome of understated luxury. The steep hillside location affords privacy for rooms set on terraced pathways perfumed with jasmine blooms. There's also river views from hammocks set amid cascading waterfalls. Facilities include a spa, hot tubs, a sauna and a restaurant.

Casa Andina
LUXURY HOTEL $$$

(☑ in Lima 01-213-9739; www.casa-andina.com; 5th Paradero, Yanahuara; d/ste incl breakfast from S442/663; @ 🛜) In a lovely countryside setting, this good-value Peruvian chain has 92 rooms in town-house-style buildings on manicured lawns. The main lobby and restaurant occupies an inviting high-ceiling glass lodge. Classic rooms offer standard amenities and plasma TVs. Activities include riding, biking and visits to Maras and Moray.

K'uychi Rumi
BUNGALOW $$$

(☑ 084-20-1169; www.urubamba.com; Carr Urumbamba a Ollantaytambo; s/d incl breakfast S396/462; @ 🛜) 'Rainbow Stone' in Quechua, this walled compound of two-story cottages tucked into gardens offers a lost retreat. It's family friendly, small and personable, popular among European travelers. There are various configurations, but most are two bedrooms with kitchenette, fireplace and terrace balcony, linked by a labyrinthine trail with hummingbirds zipping around and very friendly dogs that guard the property.

It's between Km 74 and Km 75 on the main highway, more than 2km west of town.

✖ Eating & Drinking

Kaia
CAFE $

(☑ 991-769-196; Av Mariscal Castilla 563; mains S16-22; ⏱ 11:30am-6pm Tue-Sun; ☑ 🖶) This garden cafe offers flavorful vegetarian and vegan fare, a lunchtime set menu (S18 to S24) and even homemade baby food (S18). There's also falafel, grilled zucchini and recommended roast turkey with passion fruit sauce. Delicious fresh juices come spiked with *maca* (a natural energy booster) or honey. It has a play area for kids with trampoline, and occasional live music.

Tierra Cocina Artesanal
PERUVIAN $$

(☑ 980-728-604; Av Berriozabal 84; mains S35-42; ⏱ noon-8pm Thu-Tue; ☑) 🌱 The gorgeous smells wafting in from the kitchen will lure you into this unassuming restaurant serving hearty country-style Andean dishes in the warm ambience of a small Spanish-tile home. There's slow-cooked beef simmering in the kitchen, homemade alpaca sausage, trout ceviche and corn *pepian* (stew). With organic meats and good vegetarian options.

Huacatay
PERUVIAN $$

(☑ 084-20-1790; Arica 620; mains S32-50; ⏱ 1-9:30pm Mon-Sat) In a little house tucked down a narrow side street, Huacatay makes a lovely night out. Though not every dish is a hit, the tender alpaca steak, served in a port reduction sauce with creamy quinoa risotto and topped with a spiral potato chip, is the very stuff memories are made of. Staff aim to please and there's warm ambience.

Cervecería Valle Sagrado
BREWERY

(Sacred Valley Brewery; ☑ 984-553-892; www. facebook.com/cerveceriadelvalle; Carr Urumbamba a Ollantaytambo, paradero Puente Pachar; mains S5-26; ⏱ noon-8pm Wed-Sun) Located 7km outside of town toward Urubamba, this affable American-style brewery serves its own award-winning brews, including the highly quaffable Inti Punku IPA. You can try a flight of five different beers for S10. It's filled with chilled-out locals and expats. Good pub grub includes deep-fried pickles and cheeseburgers. Check out its Facebook page for news on monthly barbecues.

🔒 Shopping

Seminario Cerámicas
CERAMICS

(☑ 084-20-1002; www.ceramicaseminario.com; Berriozabal 405; ⏱ 8am-7pm) The internationally known local potter Pablo Seminario creates original work with a preconquest influence. His workshop – actually a small factory – is open to the public and offers a well-organized tour through the entire ceramics process.

ℹ Information

Banco de la Nación (☑ 084-20-1291; cnr Ugarte & Jiron Sagrario; ⏱ 8am-5:30pm Mon-Fri, 9am-1pm Sat) changes US dollars and has an ATM. There are more ATMs at the *grifo* (gas station) on the corner of the highway and the main street, Mariscal Castilla, and along the highway to its east.

ℹ Getting There & Away

Urubamba serves as the valley's principal transportation hub. The bus terminal is about 1km west of town on the highway. Buses leave every 15 minutes for Cuzco (S7, two hours) via Pisac (S5, one hour) or Chinchero (S5, 50 minutes). Buses (S1.50, 30 minutes) and *colectivos* (S3, 25 minutes) to Ollantaytambo leave often.

Colectivos to Quillabamba (S40, five hours) leave from the *grifo* (gas station).

A standard *mototaxi* ride around town costs S2.

Salineras de Maras

Salineras de Maras (Salt Pans; admission S10; ⊙9am-4:30pm) is among the most spectacular sights in the whole Cuzco area, with thousands of salt pans that have been used for salt extraction since Inca times. A hot spring at the top of the valley discharges a small stream of heavily salt-laden water, which is diverted into salt pans and evaporated to produce a salt used for cattle licks. It all sounds very pedestrian but the overall effect is beautiful and surreal.

To get here, cross the Río Urubamba over the bridge in Tarabamba (about 4km down the valley from Urubamba) turn right and follow a footpath along the south bank to a small cemetery, where you turn left and climb up a valley to the salt pans. It's about a 500m uphill hike. A rough dirt road that can be navigated by taxi enters Salineras from above, giving spectacular views. Tour groups visit via this route most days. A taxi from Urubamba to visit the Salineras and nearby Moray costs around S120. You can also walk or bike here from Maras. If it's hot, walk the downhill route from Maras and arrange ahead for a taxi pickup.

Chinchero

📞 084 / POP 3754 / ELEV 3762M

Known to the Incas as the birthplace of the rainbow, this typical Andean village combines Inca ruins with a colonial church, some wonderful mountain views and a colorful Sunday market. On a high plain with sweeping views to snow-laden peaks, it's quite beautiful. Since it is very high, it's unwise to spend the night until you're somewhat acclimated. Entry to the historic precinct, where the ruins, the church and the museum are all found, is by the *boleto turístico* (adult/student S130/70), valid for 10 days and covering 17 sites across the region, including Cuzco.

◉ Sights & Activities

Mercado de Chinchero MARKET
(⊙7am-4pm) The Chinchero market, held on Tuesday, Thursday and especially Sunday, is less touristy than its counterpart in Pisac and well worth a special trip. On Sunday, traditionally dressed locals descend from the hills for the produce market, where the ancient practice of *trueco* (bartering) still takes place; this is a rare opportunity to observe genuine bartering.

Iglesia Colonial de Chinchero CHURCH
(boleto turístico adult/student S130/70; ⊙8am-5:30pm) Among the most beautiful churches in the valley, this colonial church is built on Inca foundations. The interior, decked out in merry floral and religious designs, is well worth seeing.

Centro de Textiles Tradicionales HANDICRAFTS
(Chinchero Away Weaving Association; www.textiles cusco.org/index.php/chinchero; ⊙9am-4pm) The best artisan workshop in town.

Wayllabamba HIKING
(Huayabamba) On the far side of the valley, a clear trail climbs upward before heading north and down to the Río Urubamba Valley (about four hours). At the river, the trail turns left and continues to a bridge at Wayllabamba. Cross it for the Sacred Valley road to Calca (turn right, about 13km) or Urubamba (turn left, about 9km).

You can flag down any passing bus until mid-afternoon or continue walking to Yucay, where the trail officially ends. In Yucay you'll find a colonial church, an Inca ruin and more than one charming accommodations option. If you are on a taxi tour from Cuzco, you can have your driver leave you at the trailhead and meet you on the other side.

Ruinas Inca RUINS
(boleto turístico adult/student S130/70; ⊙9am-6pm) The most extensive ruins here consist of terracing. If you start walking away from the village through the terraces on the right-hand side of the valley, you'll also find various rocks carved into seats and staircases.

🛏 Sleeping

Hospedaje Mi Piuray GUESTHOUSE $
(📞946-744-117; www.hospedajemipiuraycusco.com; Garcilaso 187; s/d incl breakfast S30/80; 🛜) A welcoming family hostelry with large, neat rooms with pastel accents and a sunny courtyard. If no one answers the bell, call the cell phone or reserve ahead with your arrival time.

La Casa de Barro INN $$
(📞084-30-6031; www.lacasadebarro.com; cnr hwy & Miraflores; s/d incl breakfast S198/264) A colorful architect-designed adobe with Italian influence, it's a nice retreat for couples or families. There's curvy, rambling stairways and nooks, an overgrown garden, and tasteful rooms with snug quilts. Children can enjoy the playroom and swings. The owners arrange excursions around the region. For lunch, the restaurant offers a set menu (S80), with a vegetarian option.

ℹ Getting There & Away

Traveling between Cuzco and Urubamba, *combis* (S6, 45 minutes) and *colectivos* (S6, 30 minutes) stop on the corner of the highway and Calle Manco Capac II; just flag down whatever comes along for full fare. They will also drop you off at intermediate points, such as the turnoff to Maras.

Moray & Maras

With concentric terraces carved into a huge earthen bowl, the deep amphitheater-like terracing of **Moray** (admission via boleto parcial (partial ticket, adult/student S70/35); ⏰ 8am-5pm), reached via **Maras** village, is a fascinating landscape. The prevailing theory used to be that the Incas used the layers as a kind of laboratory to optimize growing conditions for different crops of each species. It's now thought that the site wouldn't support agriculture without irrigation, of which there's no evidence. Hydrologist investigators think the site may have served as a temple for water ceremonies.

Though refreshingly off the beaten path, this site is easy enough to reach. Take any transportation bound between Urubamba and Cuzco via Chinchero and ask to be let off at the Maras/Moray turnoff known as 'Ramal de Maras.' Taxis usually wait at this turnoff to take tourists to Moray and back for around S40, or both Moray and Salineras and back to the turnoff for around S80.

You could also tackle the 4km walk to the village of Maras yourself. From there, follow the road another 9km to Moray. From Maras, you can walk or bike to Salineras, about 6km away. The trail starts behind the church. The **Maras taxi company** (☑ 084-75-5454) rents out bikes for a fun, fast single-track ride.

Ollantaytambo

☑ 084 / POP 2848 / ELEV 2800M

Dominated by two massive Inca ruins, the quaint village of Ollantaytambo, also called Ollanta, is the best surviving example of Inca city planning, with narrow cobblestone streets that have been continuously inhabited since the 13th century. After the hordes passing through on their way to Machu Picchu die down around late morning, Ollanta is a lovely place to be. It's perfect for wandering the mazy, narrow byways, past stone buildings and babbling irrigation channels, pretending you've stepped back in time. It also offers access to excellent hiking and biking.

◉ Sights

Ollantaytambo Ruins   RUINS

(boleto turístico adult/student S130/70; ⏰ 7am-5pm) Both fortress and temple, these spectacular Inca ruins rise above Ollantaytambo, making a splendid half-day trip. The huge, steep terraces that guard Ollantaytambo's spectacular Inca ruins mark one of the few places where the Spanish conquistadors lost a major battle.

The rebellious Manco Inca had retreated to this fortress after his defeat at Sacsaywamán. In 1536 Hernando Pizarro, Francisco's younger half-brother, led a force of 70 cavalrymen to Ollantaytambo, supported by large numbers of indigenous and Spanish foot soldiers, in an attempt to capture Manco Inca.

The conquistadors, showered with arrows, spears and boulders from atop the steep terracing, were unable to climb to the fortress. In a brilliant move, Manco Inca flooded the plain below the fortress through previously prepared channels. With the Spaniards' horses bogged down in the water, Pizarro ordered a hasty retreat, chased down by thousands of Manco Inca's victorious soldiers.

Yet the Inca victory would be short lived. Spanish forces soon returned with a quadrupled cavalry force and Manco fled to his jungle stronghold in Vilcabamba.

Though Ollantaytambo was a highly effective fortress, it also served as a temple. A finely worked **ceremonial center** is at the top of the terracing. Some extremely well-built walls were under construction at the time of the conquest and have never been completed. The stone was quarried from the mountainside 6km away, high above the opposite bank of the Río Urubamba. Transporting the huge stone blocks to the site was a stupendous feat. The Incas' crafty technique to move massive blocks across the river meant carting the blocks to the riverside then diverting the entire river channel around them.

Pinkulluna   RUINS

(Lari s/n; admission S10; ⏰ dawn-dusk) **FREE** It's a very steep climb up the hillside, but views are magnificent. You will see the Ollantaytambo ruins from the best vantage point, and it's nice to wander around Inca ruins that aren't swamped with tour groups. There's terraces and a handful of constructions in decent shape. Wear sturdy shoes.

Look for the gated entrance to the ruins on Calle Lari.

Inca Quarry
RUINS

The 6km hike to the Inca quarry on the opposite side of the river from the main ruins is a good walk from Ollantaytambo. The trail starts from the Inca bridge by the entrance to the village. It takes a few hours to reach the site, passing several abandoned blocks known as *piedras cansadas* – tired stones.

Looking back towards Ollantaytambo, you can see the enigmatic optical illusion of a pyramid in the fields and walls in front of the fortress. A few scholars believe this marks the legendary place where the original Incas first emerged from the earth.

☞ Tours

Coffee & distillery tours
FOOD

(☑084-20-4014; www.elalbergue.com; Estación de Tren, El Albergue; tours S50) Led by El Albergue B&B, these tours offer a fascinating behind-the-scenes look at a small-scale coffee roaster and distiller of *cañazo, a* sugarcane alcohol that's the oldest spirit in the Americas. Brought by the Spanish colony, the rustic Andean digestif is now taking on new dimensions as a high-end spirit. Participants get a free coffee or cocktail.

✲✲ Festivals & Events

Señor de Choquechilca
FESTIVAL

(☺late May-early Jun) Occurring during Pentecost in late May or early June, the town's most important annual event commemorates the local miracle of the Christ of Choquechilca, when a wooden cross appeared by the Incan bridge. It's celebrated with music, dancing and colorful processions.

🛏 Sleeping

★ Mama Simona
HOSTEL $

(☑084-436-757; www.mamasimona.com/es/ollanta.php; Av Quera Oqllo s/n; dm/s/d incl breakfast S46/117/124) As locations go, this is one of Ollanta's finest, with riverside garden hammocks and papaya trees. Dorms feature individual bed lights and attached bathrooms, with space heaters for rent (S10). There's a large, inviting guest kitchen, cozy TV area and filtered water for drinking. Service, however, could be more enthusiastic. It's on the outskirts of the center.

Casa de Wow
HOSTEL $

(☑984-373-875, 084-20-4010; www.casadewow.com; Patacalle s/n; dm/d incl breakfast S66/169; @ 🖭) A cozy little home away from home run by Wow, a local artist, and managed by

MIL

A lauded Virgilio Martínez restaurant, **MIL** (www.milcentro.pe; Moray; 8-course meal S480; ⊙noon-2pm Tue-Sun) is more an experience than a meal. A set menu showcases the incredibly diverse local Andean ingredients using cutting-edge cooking techniques. Lunch is eight 'moments,' small plates, paired with beverages with alcohol (S269) or without (S124). Built on the flanks of the Moray ruins, its location is superb. Set aside two to three hours.

It's part of a larger, ambitious project that is building a seed bank and reintroducing agricultural biodiversity in local communities, whose organic farms supply the restaurant. It also recycles.

Diners can reserve online with a pre-payment or via a travel agency.

an enthusiastic American. Bunks are snug and couples have a shot at the fantastic handmade Inca royalty bed (though unlike the original, these raw beams are held together with rope, not llama innards). Sign the world's biggest guestbook before leaving.

K'uychi Punku Hostal
HOTEL $

(☑084-20-4175; kuychipunkuhostal@yahoo.com; Kuyuchipunku s/n; s/d incl breakfast S80/150/230; 🖭) Run by the wonderful Bejar-Mejía family, this recommended hotel may be open to bargaining. Lodgings are in an Inca building with 2m-thick walls and a modern section with cute remodeled rooms featuring recycled pallet furniture. A breakfast including eggs and fresh juice is served in Ollanta's most photographed outdoor dining room.

Munay Punku
GUESTHOUSE $

(☑084-21-4813; www.munaypunku.com; Av Quera Oqllo 704; s/d S120/150; 🖭) A spacious, homey three-story place on the outskirts of town toward the ruins of Pumamarca. Ruth and her family are good hosts, rooms are spacious and beds are firm with good bedding. Offers river and countryside views.

Hostal las Orquídeas
HOTEL $

(☑084-20-4032; www.hotellasorquideasllantatambo.com; Av Ferrocarril s/n; s/d incl breakfast S99/149; 🖭) An adequate though dated hotel with a small, grassy courtyard and rooms with parquet floors, down bedding and TVs.

Ollantaytambo

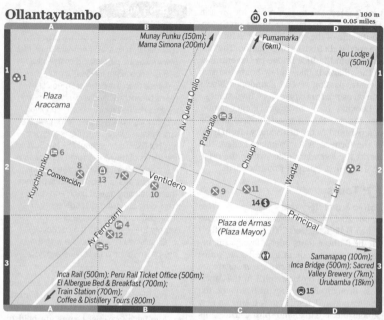

Ollantaytambo

★ **El Albergue Bed & Breakfast**   B&B **$$**
(☎ 084-20-4014; www.elalbergue.com; Estación de Tren; d/tr incl breakfast from S359/393; @🛜) On the train platform, this romantic pit stop exudes Andean charm. Surrounded by green lawns with lush flowerbeds, tasteful tile rooms feature a dark-hardwood trim, tapestries and quality linens in an early-20th-century building. There are portable heaters, games for kids and sauna access. It's 800m (all uphill) from the village center but there's an excellent on-site restaurant.

★ **Apu Lodge**   INN **$$**
(☎ 084-79-7162; www.apulodge.com; Lari s/n; s/d/q incl breakfast S215/248/330; @🛜) 🌿

Backed against the ruins, this modern lodge with a sprawling lawn is a real retreat, thanks to the welcoming staff, big breakfasts and the helpful attention of its Scottish owner. It's great for families. Ample, cozy rooms feature powerful hot showers that melt your muscle aches. The common area has wi-fi and filtered water to fill up on.

Serves wood-fired pizza at night. It can also arrange a sweat lodge or San Pedro ceremony.

Samanapaq   INN **$$**
(☎ 999-583-243, 084-20-4042; www.samanapaq.com; cnr Principal & Alameda de las Cien Ventanas; s/d incl breakfast S254/277, d superior S340; 🛜) This sprawling complex features lawns

for the kids to run on, comfortable shared spaces and 20 motel-style rooms with massage-jet showers. With buffet breakfast and wi-fi in the common areas. There's a pottery workshop on-site.

Hotel Muñay Tika HOTEL **$$**

(☑084-20-4111; www.munaytika.com; Av Ferrocarril s/n; s/d incl breakfast S110/150; @ 🛜) Though the native corn drying in the courtyard might say otherwise, this hotel is modern and spacious. Rooms with tinted windows feature parquet floors and down duvets, somewhat incongruous to some of the particle-board walls throughout! The garden is a nice area to hang out in.

✖ Eating

Il Piccolo Forno ITALIAN **$**

(☑996-400-150; Calle del Medio, also known as Chaupi; mains S15-32; ⊙noon-9pm) Thin-crust pizzas and green salads with crisp chicken chunks are the standouts at this tiny eatery run by an Italian-Peruvian couple. It's a great option when you want to sate your hunger without much ado.

Cafe del Abuelo CAFE **$**

(☑084-21-4871; Convencion 110; mains S12-20; ⊙8am-10pm Mon-Sat, from noon Sun) This cute side-street cafe offers tasty baked goods and desserts and real brewed coffee. It also offers sandwiches and box lunches. The 2nd floor with the mural provides a quiet getaway.

Tutti Amore ICE CREAM **$**

(☑958-272-455; Av Ferrocarril s/n; ice cream S6-15; ⊙9am-6pm) Andres from Rosario, Argentina, serves up homemade gelato-style ice creams, including some exotic jungle-fruit flavors worth a try. It's halfway down the hill to the train station.

★ El Albergue Restaurante INTERNATIONAL **$$**

(☑084-20-4014; Estación de Tren; mains S29-45; ⊙5:30-10am, noon-3pm & 6-9pm; 🍴) 🍃 This whistle-stop cafe serves elegant and well-priced Peruvian fare. It's inviting, with an open kitchen bordered by heaping fruit bowls and candles adorning linen-topped tables. Start with the *causas* (potato dish) or organic greens from the garden. Lamb medallions with *chimichurri* (herb sauce) is a standout, as is as the molle-pepper steak spiced from the tree outside. Access via the train platform.

It also serves local artisan beer. Those less hungry can order homemade pasta in half-portions. For train passengers, it may be worth stopping by the patio option Café Mayu (open at 5am for train passengers) for an espresso or homemade *aguantamayo* cheesecake.

For a twist on a Peruvian barbecue, sign up for its wonderful *pachamanca*, an outdoor feast held at lunchtime on its adjacent organic farm. A variety of meats and potatoes are baked on hot stones in the earth.

Chuncho PERUVIAN **$$**

(☑084-20-4014; www.chuncho.pe; Ventidierio; mains S27-47; ⊙noon-11pm) This concept restaurant connects visitors to the bounty of ancestral Andean foods. It's a great idea, with traditional soups, rehydrated potato dishes, *tarwi* bean salads, tasty alpaca and *cuy*. Sample all with a banquet, the half-portion (S65) easily feeds two. But the real standout is the craft cocktails made with Caña Alta, a locally produced sugarcane spirit.

Cocktails are inventive and addictive. Sample the tart but warming *matacuy* sour with fennel and grapefruit and just try to resist seconds.

Apu Veronica PERUVIAN **$$**

(☑973-214-402; Ventidierio s/n, piso 2; mains S22-45; ⊙1pm-9pm) A good spot for popular Peruvian classics. Light appetites will be satisfied with the quinoa soup with vegetables. If you're hungry you could go for a sizzling steak cooked tableside on a hot stone with native potatoes and green salad. The *cuy* is well prepared too. It's a good value, though service can be sleepy.

Hearts Café CAFE **$$**

(☑084-20-4078; cnr Ventidierio & Av Ferrocarril; mains S11-28; ⊙7am-9pm; 🍴) Serving healthy and hearty food, beer and wine and good coffee, Hearts is a longtime local presence, with some organic produce and box lunches for excursions. Breakfasts like *huevos rancheros* (fried eggs with beans served on a tortilla) target the gringo palette, and the corner spot with outdoor tables was made for people-watching.

🔒 Shopping

Awamaki ARTS & CRAFTS

(☑84-43-6744; www.awamaki.org; Ventidierio s/n; ⊙9am-6pm Mon-Fri, 10am-5pm Sat & Sun) A nonprofit boutique selling gorgeous locally woven sweaters, hats and gloves made with organic dyes, as well as handmade

SACRED VALLEY VIA FERRATA

You can experience the Sacred Valley's *vía ferrata* ('Iron Way' in Italian), a series of ladders, holds and bridges built into sheer rock face, with **Natura Vive** (☑ 974-360-269; www.naturavive. com; vía ferrata or zipline per person S175, both S265). There's a 400m vertical ascent, a heart-hammering hanging bridge and an 80m rappel. The seven ziplines are accessed by a 40-minute hike. Activities run three to four hours. The price includes a round-trip Cuzco transfer.

First developed in the Italian Alps in WWI, the *vía ferrata* is a way for reasonably fit non–rock climbers to have some adrenaline-pumping fun. It was constructed and is operated by rock-climbing and high-mountain professionals. You can also overnight at the on-site **Sky Lodge** (Urubamba Valley; per person with half-pension US$460) clinging to the rock face.

leather handbags and wallets. Products are high quality and design conscious, they're wonderful gifts for those back home. The foundation also runs worthwhile tours to nearby weaving villages.

ⓘ Information

Globalnet ATM (Plaza de Armas; ⊘ 24hr) A streetside ATM.

ⓘ Getting There & Away

BUS & TAXI

Frequent *combis* and taxi *colectivos* shuttle between Urubamba and Ollantaytambo (S2 and S3 respectively, 30 minutes) from 6am to 5pm. Buses are located outside the fruit and vegetable market.

To Cuzco, it's easiest to change in Urubamba, though occasional departures leave direct from the Ollantaytambo train station to Cuzco's Puente Grau (*combis* S15, two hours; *colectivos* S15, 1½ hours).

Even though Ollantaytambo is closer to Santa María (for those traveling on to Santa Teresa) and Quillabamba, buses pass through here already full. Backtrack to Urubamba's bus terminal to get a seat.

TRAIN

Ollantaytambo is a transport hub between Cuzco and Machu Picchu: the cheapest and quickest way to travel between Cuzco and Machu Picchu is to catch a *combi* between Cuzco and Ollantaytambo (two hours), then the train between Ollantaytambo and Aguas Calientes (two hours). Two companies currently offer the service. Rates change according to peak times.

Inca Rail (☑ 084-43-6732; www.incarail.com; Av Ferrocarril s/n; ⊘ 6am-7:45pm Mon-Sat) Three departures daily from Ollantaytambo and four classes (one way S231 to S330). Children get significant discounts.

Peru Rail (www.perurail.com; Av Ferrocarril s/n; ⊘ 5am-9pm) Service to Aguas Calientes with multiple departures daily. With three classes of service, though some trips feature extras. One-way fares: Expedition (from S232), Vistadome (from S315) and the luxurious Sacred Valley (from S581).

ⓘ Getting Around

Ollantaytambo Travel (☑ 975-969-766; www. ollantaytambotravel.com) A reliable taxi service with responsible drivers available for taxi tours throughout the Sacred Valley and private airport transfers.

MACHU PICCHU & THE INCA TRAIL

Aguas Calientes

☑ 084 / POP 1600 / ELEV 2410M

Also known as Machu Picchu Pueblo, this town lies in a deep gorge below the ruins. A virtual island, it's cut off from all roads and enclosed by stone cliffs, towering cloud forest and two rushing rivers. Despite its gorgeous location, Aguas Calientes has the feel of a gold=rush town, with a large itinerant population, slack services that count on one-time customers and an architectural tradition of rebar and unfinished cement. With merchants pushing the hard sell, it's hard not to feel overwhelmed. Your best bet is to go without expectations.

Yet spending the night offers one distinct advantage: early access to Machu Picchu, which turns out to be a pretty good reason to stay.

Note that the footpath from the train station to the Machu Picchu bus stop is stepped. Wheelchairs should be directed across the small bridge to Sinchi Roca and through the center of town.

⊙ Sights & Activities

Museo de Sitio
Manuel Chávez Ballón MUSEUM
(admission S22; ⊙9am-5pm) This museum has superb information in Spanish and English on the archaeological excavations of Machu Picchu and Inca building methods. Stop here before or after the ruins to get a sense of context (and to enjoy the air-conditioning and soothing music if you're walking back from the ruins after hours in the sun).

There's a small botanical garden with orchids outside, down a cool if nerve-testing set of Inca stairs. It's by Puente Ruinas, at the base of the footpath to Machu Picchu.

Las Termas HOT SPRINGS
(admission S20; ⊙5am-8:30pm) Weary trekkers soak away their aches and pains in the town's hot springs, 10 minutes' walk up Pachacutec from the train tracks. These tiny, natural thermal springs, from which Aguas Calientes derives its name, are nice enough but far from the best in the area, and get scummy by late morning.

Towels can be rented cheaply outside the entrance.

Putucusi HIKING
This jagged minimountain sits directly opposite Machu Picchu. Parts of the walk are up ladders, which get slippery in the wet season. The view across to Machu Picchu is worth the trek. Allow three hours. Follow the railway tracks about 250m west of town and you'll see a set of stairs, the start of a well-marked trail.

🛏 Sleeping

Lodgings here are consistently overpriced – probably costing two-thirds more than counterparts in less-exclusive locations. There's a variety of midrange accommodations, alongside some luxury offerings and budget options. Book well ahead for the best selection.

Ecopackers HOSTEL $
(☑084-21-1121; www.ecopackersperu.com/hostel-machu-picchu; Av Imperio de los Incas 136; dm S52-58, d/tw S177/142; ☎) A clean and convenient hostel in a newish building with a moss-covered courtyard featuring a pool table. Staff are welcoming. Dorms have two to three bunks, but if you want women's only, you will pay extra. There's laundry service and a bar-restaurant. Grab those free earplugs at the reception, you will need them!

Supertramp Hostel HOSTEL $
(☑084-43-5830; www.supertramp.com; Chaskatika s/n; dm S36-40, d without bathroom S100, all incl breakfast; ☎) Cloaked in psychedelic murals, this recommended but sometimes cramped hostel has good, helpful staff and a small adjoining cafe that whips up salads and gourmet burgers. Early starters can get egg breakfasts with coffee, toast and jam at 4:30am. Train station pickup available.

Rupa Wasi HOTEL $$
(☑084-21-1101; www.rupawasi.net; Huanacaure s/n; d/ste incl breakfast from S248/413; ☎) Hidden away up a steep flight of stairs, Rupa Wasi clings to the hillside with wooden stairways and moss-strewn stone pathways. It's quaint and a little wild, but the price only reflects its proximity to Machu Picchu. Cabin-style rooms feature down duvets and views; a nice American breakfast is served in the Tree House cafe (p258). Accepts credit cards.

Gringo Bill's HOTEL $$
(☑084-21-1046; www.gringobills.com; Colla Raymi 104; d/tr incl breakfast from S268/471; @🛜🛗) One of the original Aguas Calientes lodgings, friendly Bill's features smart rooms in a multitiered construction. Beds are covered in thick cotton quilts, and bathrooms are large. Suites feature massage-jet tubs and TVs. The mini pool only has space for two. Larger suites easily accommodate families.

Ferre Machu Picchu BOUTIQUE HOTEL $$
(☑084-21-1337; www.hotelferremachupicchu.com; Av Imperio de los Incas 634; d/ste incl breakfast S385/665; ☎) A multistory hotel with a set of attractive riverside rooms with modern decor. It's good value, but we wish they used more gentle cleaning products. There's also an elevator. Takes Visa.

Hotel Presidente HOTEL $$
(☑reservations 084-24-4598; reservas@siahotels.com; Av Imperio de los Incas s/n; s/d incl breakfast from S220/270; @☎) A solid and very secure option featuring small double beds and flat-screen TVs. For the same price it's worth asking for a room with river views, not just for the scenery but to get as far from the train tracks as possible. It's run by the Sierra Andina chain.

Hostal Muyurina HOTEL $$
(☑084-21-1339; www.hostalmuyurina.com; Lloque Yupanqui s/n; d incl breakfast S190; ☎) Sparkling and keen to please, Mayurina is a friendly option. Rooms have phones and TV.

Aguas Calientes

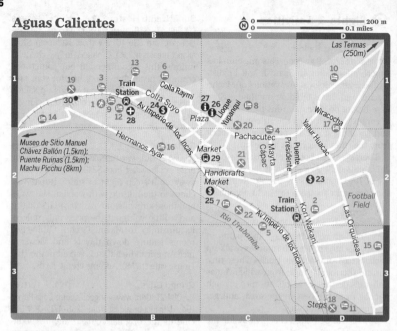

Aguas Calientes

Activities, Courses & Tours
1 Putucusi...A1

Sleeping
2 Casa Andina...D2
3 Ecopackers...A1
4 El Mapi...C2
5 Ferre Machu Picchu..............................C3
6 Gringo Bill's...B1
7 Hatun Inti Boutique.............................C2
8 Hostal Muyurina...................................C1
9 Hotel Presidente..................................B1
10 La Cabaña Hotel.................................D1
11 Machu Picchu Pueblo
    Hotel...D3
12 Machupicchu Hostal............................B1
13 Rupa Wasi...B1
14 Sumaq Machu Picchu
    Hotel...A1
15 Supertramp Hostel.............................D3
16 Tierra Viva..B2
17 Wiracocha Inn.....................................D1

Eating
   Ayasqa...(see 16)
18 Café Inkaterra....................................D3
19 Chullpi..A1
20 Indio Feliz...C1
21 La Boulangerie de Paris......................C2
22 Mapacho...C2
   Tree House.....................................(see 13)

Information
23 ATM..D2
24 Banco La Nacion.................................B1
25 BCP..C2
26 Centro Cultural...................................C1
27 iPerú...C1
28 Medical Center...................................B1

Transport
29 Machu Picchu Bus Tickets & Bus
    Stop...C2
30 Trains to Hydroelectric Station
    (Transport to Santa Teresa)..............A1

Machupicchu Hostal HOTEL $$
(☑ reservations 084-24-4598; reservas@siahotels. com; Av Imperio de los Incas 520; s/d incl breakfast S165/185; @ 🛜) One of the tidy midrange inns by the train tracks, this place has buffet breakfasts and a small flower-festooned interior courtyard. Small, dark rooms echo with sounds of the guesthouse, and you will certainly hear every train. There's wi-fi in the lobby and some of the rooms. Run by the Sierra Andina chain.

La Cabaña Hotel HOTEL $$
(☑ 084-21-1048; www.lacabanamachupicchu.com; Pachacutec 805; s/d incl breakfast S363/429; @ 🛜) Further uphill than most of the

hotels, this welcoming spot features woody, cozy, heated rooms, in part thanks to down duvets decorated with flower petals and chocolates. There's buffet breakfast, plus complimentary tea, filtered water and fruit round the clock.

Wiracocha Inn
HOTEL $$

(☑ 084-21-1088; Wiracocha 206; d/tr/superior incl breakfast S264/330/396) On a side street crowded with midrange hotels, this newer option has well-kept and polished rooms, amiable service and a sheltered patio area near the river. Rooms feature down bedding and TVs.

★ Machu Picchu Pueblo Hotel
LODGE $$$

(☑ in Lima 01-610-0400; www.inkaterra.com; d casitas from US$838, villas from US$1036; ❋ @ 🛜 ♨) 🌿 Luxuriant and set amid tropical gardens, these Andean-style cottages (many with their own private pool) connected by stone pathways are pure indulgence. The devil is in the details: iPod docks, subtle, classy decor and showers with glass walls looking out onto lush vegetation. The on-site spa features a bamboo-eucalyptus sauna, but the best feature is the (included) guided excursions.

Choose from bilingual tours for bird-watching, tea-plantation visits and orchid walks, or take a trip to the hotel's conservation site protecting the rare Andean spectacled bear. Rates include half board and kids under 12 stay for free.

Casa Andina
HOTEL $$$

(☑ 084-21-1017; www.casa-andina.com; Prolongacion Imperio de los Incas E - 34; d/ste incl breakfast S728/862; 🛜) A comfortable classic, this upscale Peruvian chain features truly modern rooms with earthy terra-cotta accents, sparkling installations and glass showers. There are also stunning river views behind the double-pane glass. With flat-screen TVs, safe boxes, an on-site restaurant and all the usual amenities. There is an ATM in the lobby.

Tierra Viva
HOTEL $$$

(☑ 084-21-1201; www.tierravivahoteles.com; Av Hermanos Ayar 401; d/ste incl breakfast from S470/790; @🛜) A respected Peruvian boutique chain has set up shop in this five-story hotel. While the design isn't as smooth as at its other outlets, rooms still work a modern-minimalist charm, displaying Andean weavings (for purchase to benefit a regional foundation). There's elevator access and pleasant staff.

There's a good, unaffiliated **buffet restaurant** (☑ 948-867-217; buffet without drinks S73; ⏰ 5am-10pm) on-site.

Hatun Inti Boutique
HOTEL $$$

(☑ 084-23-4312; www.grupointi.com; Av Camino de los Incas 606; d incl breakfast S606) A well-heeled high-end option with subdued style, wonderful beds and ample rooms. All feature flat-screen TVs, safe boxes and Jacuzzi tubs. A buffet breakfast and dinner or lunch at the on-site restaurant is included.

El Mapi
DESIGN HOTEL $$$

(☑ 084-21-1011; www.elmapihotel.com; Pachacutec 109; d from S726; ❋@🛜) Spare and ultramodern, this design hotel is central and sprawling, with 130 rooms. Lofty ceilings, burnished steel and oversized nature photos create a cool, stripped down atmosphere, though the stark, all-white rooms take it a little too far. It's always busy. Perks include enjoying a welcome pisco sour at the stylish bar and the enormous buffet breakfast.

There's also a warm landscaped pond for dips, a full-service restaurant serving buffet lunch (S74) and an on-site boutique.

Sumaq Machu Picchu Hotel
HOTEL $$$

(☑ 084-21-1059; www.sumaqhotelperu.com; Hermanos Ayar s/n; d half board from S1990; ❋@🛜) This high-end hotel has impeccable service and a soothing interior, thanks to the double-pane windows and neutral palette with splashes of bold color. There are 62 rooms with views of either river and mountains, or a hillside with human-made cascades. Includes an elevator, multiple eating and drinking areas, and a full spa with sauna and Jacuzzi.

The Machu Picchu bus stops conveniently at the door. The hotel offers guests offers a free 45-minute cooking class preparing ceviche and pisco sours.

🍴 Eating

Restaurants range from basic eateries to fine dining. Touts standing in the street will try to herd you into their restaurant, but take your time making a selection. Standards are not very high in most restaurants – if you go to one that hasn't been recommended, snoop around to check the hygiene first. Since refrigeration can be a problem, it's best to order vegetarian if you're eating in low-end establishments.

La Boulangerie de Paris
BAKERY $

(☑ 084-79-7798; Jr Sinchi Roca s/n; snacks S4-12; ⏰ 4am-10pm; 🛜) We don't know how the Frenchmen got here, we're just thankful. This small cafe sells *pain au chocolat,* fresh croissants, espresso drinks and desserts, with a few gluten-free items. You can also order boxed lunches.

★ Indio Feliz
FRENCH $$

(☑ 084-21-1090; Lloque Yupanqui 4; mains S34-48; ⊙ 11am-10pm) Hospitality is the strong suit of French cook Patrik at this multi-award-winning restaurant, but the food does not disappoint. Start with *sopa a la criolla* (mildly spiced, creamy noodle soup with beef and peppers). There are also nods to traditional French cooking – like Provençal tomatoes, crispy-perfect garlic potatoes and a melt-in-your-mouth apple tart.

The candlelit decor shows the imagination of a long-lost castaway with imitation Gauguin panels, carved figurehead damsels, colonial benches and vintage objects. The *menú* (S78) is extremely good value for a decadent dinner. Indio Feliz has good wheelchair access, a fireplace lit on cold days and may eventually add an upstairs bar and terrace, another reason not to leave.

Mapacho
CAFE $$

(☑ 984-759-634; Av Imperio de los Incas 614; mains S20-48; ⊙ 10am-10pm) This friendly streetside cafe is popular with the backpacking set. Perhaps it's all the craft beer and burgers on offer. It's worth checking out the *arroz chaufa* (fried rice) and *lomo saltado* (strips of beef stir-fried with onions, tomatoes, potatoes and chili).

Tree House
FUSION $$

(☑ 084-21-1101; www.thetreehouse-peru.com; Huanacaure s/n; mains S38-60; ⊙ 4:30am-10pm) The rustic ambience of Tree House provides a cozy setting for its fusion menu served alongside South American wines, craft beers and cocktails. Dishes like stuffed wontons with tamarind sauce, alpaca tenderloin and crisp quinoa-crusted trout are lovingly prepared. For dessert, lip-smacking chocolate mousse. With raw and vegan options. Reserve ahead. It's part of the Rupa Wasi hotel (p255).

Chullpi
PERUVIAN $$$

(☑ 914-169-687; Av Imperio de los Incas 140; mains S49-69; ⊙ 11:30am-11pm) Touting *'cocina de autor,'* this stylish shoebox of a restaurant serves beautifully plated food, but in its mass production it might not quite live up to gourmet standards. The fare is classic Andean – including grilled trout, shredded pork and *wallpa chupe* (a chicken-tomato stew). There are also soups and *causas* (creamy potato dishes). Tour groups have a tendency to take over – reserve ahead.

Café Inkaterra
PERUVIAN $$$

(☑ 084-21-1122; Machu Picchu Pueblo Hotel; menú lunch/dinner S93/122; ⊙ 11:30am-4pm & 6-10pm; ☑ 🔊) Upstream from the train station, this tucked-away riverside restaurant is housed in elongated thatched rooms with views of water tumbling over the boulders. There's a set menu (starter, main dish and dessert), with gluten-free and vegetarian options, and a decent kids menu to entice the young ones. The *lomo saltado* bursts with flavor.

❶ Information

MEDICAL SERVICES

Medical Center (☑ 084-21-1005; Av Imperio de los Incas s/n; ⊙ emergencies 24hr) Located by the train tracks.

MONEY

Currency and traveler's checks can be exchanged in various places at highly unfavorable rates. Due to frequent power outages, bank machines can be out of service.

If you are purchasing your Machu Picchu entrance tickets here, you may only do so in Peruvian soles. Bring ample cash!

ATMs run out of cash, especially on the weekends. They include ATMs run by **BCP** (Av Imperio de los Incas s/n) and **Banco La Nacion** (⊙ 24hr).

TOURIST INFORMATION

Centro Cultural (Machu Picchu Tickets; ☑ 084-21-1196; Av Pachacutec s/n; ⊙ 5:30am-8:30pm) The only spot in town selling Machu Picchu entrance tickets, cash only.

iPerú (☑ 084-21-1104; Av Pachacutec, cuadra 1; ⊙ 9am-6pm Mon-Sun) A helpful information center for everything Machu Picchu.

❶ Getting There & Away

There are only three options to get to Aguas Calientes, and hence to Machu Picchu: trek it, catch the train via Cuzco and the Sacred Valley, or travel by road and the Hidroelectrica train via Santa Teresa.

It's a dusty, 12km walk (or taxi ride) from Aguas Calientes along the train tracks to Hidroelectrica, and then a further 9.4km to Santa Teresa (bus and taxi available). Go early and allow two to three hours. Don't bring much luggage and stay alert on the tracks for trains. It is not advisable to do the walk in the rainy season because of the danger of landslides.

BUS

There is no road access to Aguas Calientes. The only buses go from the bus stop (where you can purchase tickets) up the hill to Machu Picchu (round-trip S80, 25 minutes) from 5:30am to 4pm; buses return until 6pm.

TRAIN

Buy a return ticket to avoid getting stranded in Aguas Calientes – outbound trains sell out much quicker than their inbound counterparts. All train companies have ticket offices in the train station, but you can check their websites for up-to-date schedules and ticket purchases.

To Cuzco (three hours), Peru Rail (p240) has service to Poroy and taxis connect to the city, another 20 minutes away.

To Ollantaytambo (two hours), both Peru Rail and Inca Rail (p240) provide service. Inca Rail offers a ticket with connecting bus service to Cuzco.

To Santa Teresa (via Hidroelectrica Station, 45 minutes), Peru Rail travels at 6:45am, 1:30pm and 3:40pm daily, with other departures for residents only. Tickets (US$33) can only be bought from Aguas Calientes train station on the day of departure, but trains actually leave from the west end of town, outside the police station. You can also do this route as a guided multisport tour. Inca Rail has plans to start operating the route too.

Machu Picchu

Shrouded by mist and surrounded by lush vegetation and steep escarpments, the sprawling Inca citadel of Machu Picchu lives up to every expectation. In a spectacular location, it's the most famous archaeological site on the continent, a must for all visitors to Peru. Like the *Mona Lisa* or the pyramids, it has been seared into our collective consciousness, though nothing can diminish the thrill of being here. This awe-inspiring ancient city was never revealed to the Spanish colonisers and was virtually forgotten until the early part of the 20th century.

In the most controversial move in Machu Picchu since Hiram Bingham's explorations, the Peruvian authorities changed entries from daily visits to morning and afternoon turns in 2018. Visitors must plan more carefully than ever to seize the experience. Though an expanded limit of 5940 people are now allowed in the complex (including the Inca Trail) daily, demand remains insatiable.

History

Machu Picchu is not mentioned in any of the chronicles of the Spanish conquistadors. Apart from a couple of German adventurers in the 1860s, who apparently looted the site with the Peruvian government's permission, only the local Quechua people knew of Machu Picchu's existence until American historian Hiram Bingham was guided to it by locals in 1911. You can read Bingham's own account of his 'discovery' in the classic book *Inca Land: Explorations in the Highlands of Peru,* first published in 1922 and now available as a free download from Project Gutenberg (www.gutenberg.org).

Bingham was searching for the lost city of Vilcabamba, the last stronghold of the Incas, and he thought he had found it at Machu Picchu. We now know that the remote ruins at Espíritu Pampa, much deeper in the jungle, are actually the remains of Vilcabamba. The Machu Picchu site was initially overgrown with thick vegetation, forcing Bingham's team to be content with roughly mapping the site. Bingham returned in 1912 and 1915 to carry out the difficult task of clearing the thick forest, when he also discovered some of the ruins on the so-called Inca Trail. Peruvian archaeologist Luis E Valcárcel undertook further studies in 1934, as did a Peruvian-American expedition under Paul Fejos in 1940 and 1941.

Despite scores of more recent studies, knowledge of Machu Picchu remains sketchy. Even today archaeologists are forced to rely heavily on speculation and educated guesswork as to its function. Some believe the citadel was founded in the waning years of the last Incas in an attempt to preserve Inca culture or rekindle their predominance, while others think that it may have already become an uninhabited, forgotten city at the time of the conquest. A more recent theory suggests that the site was a royal retreat or the country palace of Pachacutec, abandoned at the time of the Spanish invasion. The site's director believes that it was a city, a political, religious and administrative center. Its location, and the fact that at least eight access routes have been discovered, suggests that it was a trade nexus between Amazonia and the highlands.

It seems clear from the exceptionally high quality of the stonework and the abundance of ornamental work that Machu Picchu was once vitally important as a ceremonial center. Indeed, to some extent, it still is: Alejandro Toledo, the country's first indigenous Andean president, impressively staged his inauguration here in 2001.

◉ Sights &

Don't miss the Museo de Sitio Manuel Chávez Ballón (p255) by Puente Ruinas at the base of the climb to Machu Picchu. Buses headed back from the ruins to Aguas Calientes will stop upon request at the bridge.

Machu Picchu

CITADEL HIGHLIGHTS

This great 15th-century Inca citadel sits at 2430m on a narrow ridgetop above the Río Urubamba. Traditionally considered a political, religious and administrative center, but new theories suggest that it was a royal estate designed by Pachacutec, the Inca ruler whose military conquests transformed the empire. Trails linked it to the Inca capital of Cuzco and important sites in the jungle. As invading Spaniards never discovered it, experts still dispute when the site was abandoned and why.

At its peak, Machu Picchu was thought to have some 500 inhabitants. An engineering marvel, its famous Inca walls have polished stone fitted to stone, with no mortar in between. The citadel took thousands of laborers 50 years to build – today its cost of construction would exceed a billion US dollars.

Making it habitable required leveling the site, channeling water from high mountain streams through stone canals and building vertical retaining walls that became agricultural terraces for corn, potatoes and coca. The drainage system also helped combat heavy rains (diverting them for irrigation), while east-facing rooftops and farming terraces took advantage of maximum sun exposure.

The site is a magnet to mystics, adventurers and students of history alike. While its function remains hotly debated, the essential grandeur of Machu Picchu is indisputable.

TOP TIPS

➡ Visit before midmorning crowds.

➡ Allow at least three hours to visit.

➡ Wear walking shoes and a hat.

➡ Bring drinking water.

➡ Gain perspective walking the lead-in trails.

ADAMK92/GETTY IMAGES ©

Intihuatana

'Hitching Post of the Sun', this exquisitely carved rock was likely used by Inca astronomers to predict solstices. It's a rare survivor since invading Spaniards destroyed *intihuatanas* throughout the kingdom to eradicate what they considered to be pagan blasphemy.

Western Agricultural Terraces

Sacred Pla

To Hut of the Caretaker of the Funerary Rock

Temple of the Three Windows

Enjoy the commanding views of the plaza below through the huge trapezoidal windows framed by 3-ton lintels. Rare in Inca architecture, the presence of three windows may indicate special significance.

MARCUS DANIEL/GETTY IMAGES ©

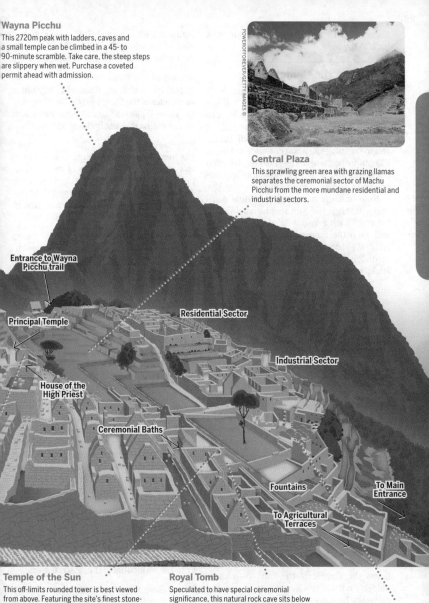

Wayna Picchu
This 2720m peak with ladders, caves and a small temple can be climbed in a 45- to 90-minute scramble. Take care, the steep steps are slippery when wet. Purchase a coveted permit ahead with admission.

POWEROFFOREVER/GETTY IMAGES ©

Central Plaza
This sprawling green area with grazing llamas separates the ceremonial sector of Machu Picchu from the more mundane residential and industrial sectors.

Entrance to Wayna Picchu trail

Principal Temple

Residential Sector

Industrial Sector

House of the High Priest

Ceremonial Baths

Fountains

To Main Entrance

To Agricultural Terraces

Temple of the Sun
This off-limits rounded tower is best viewed from above. Featuring the site's finest stone-work, an altar and trapezoidal windows, it may have been used for astronomical purposes.

OSCAR ESPINOSA/SHUTTERSTOCK ©

Royal Tomb
Speculated to have special ceremonial significance, this natural rock cave sits below the Temple of the Sun. Though it is off-limits, visitors can view its steplike altar and sacred niches from the entrance.

Temple of the Condor
Check out the condor-head carving with rock outcrops that resemble outstretched wings. Behind, an off-limits cavity reaches a tiny underground cell that may only be entered by bending double.

From here it's less than a half-hour walk back to town.

◉ Inside the Complex

Unless you arrive via the Inca Trail, you'll officially enter the ruins through a ticket gate on the south side of **Machu Picchu** (www.machupicchu.gob.pe; adult/student S152/77; ⊙6am-6pm). About 100m of footpath brings you to the mazelike main entrance of Machu Picchu proper, where the ruins lie stretched out before you, roughly divided into two areas separated by a series of plazas.

Note that the names of individual ruins speculate their use – in reality, much is unknown. To get a visual fix of the whole site and snap the classic postcard photograph, climb the zigzagging staircase on the left immediately after entering the complex, which leads to the Hut of the Caretaker.

Hut of the Caretaker
of the Funerary Rock   RUINS
An excellent viewpoint to take in the whole site. It's one of a few buildings that has been restored with a thatched roof, making it a good shelter in the case of rain. The Inca Trail enters the city just below this hut. The carved rock behind the hut may have been used to mummify the nobility, hence the hut's name.

Ceremonial Baths   RUINS
If you head straight into the ruins from the main entry gate, you pass through extensive terracing to a beautiful series of 16 connected ceremonial baths that cascade across the ruins, accompanied by a flight of stairs.

Temple of the Sun   RUINS
Just above and to the left of the ceremonial baths is Machu Picchu's only round building, a curved and tapering tower of exceptional stonework. This structure is off-limits and best viewed from above.

Royal Tomb   RUINS
Below the Temple of the Sun, this almost hidden, natural rock cave was carefully carved by Inca stonemasons. Its use is highly debated; though known as the Royal Tomb, no mummies were actually ever found here.

Sacred Plaza   PLAZA
Climbing the stairs above the ceremonial baths, there is a flat area of jumbled rocks, once used as a quarry. Turn right at the top of the stairs and walk across the quarry on a short path leading to the four-sided Sacred Plaza. The far side contains a small viewing platform with a curved wall, which offers a view of the snowy Cordillera Vilcabamba in the far distance and the Río Urubamba below.

Temple of the Three Windows   RUINS
Important buildings flank the remaining three sides of the Sacred Plaza. The Temple of the Three Windows features huge trapezoidal windows that give the building its name.

Principal Temple   RUINS
The 'temple' derives its name from the massive solidity and perfection of its construction. The damage to the rear right corner is the result of the ground settling below this corner rather than any inherent weakness in the masonry itself.

House of the High Priest   RUINS
Little is known about these mysterious ruins, located opposite the Principal Temple.

Sacristy   RUINS
Behind and connected to the Principal Temple lies this famous small building. It has many well-carved niches, perhaps used for the storage of ceremonial objects, as well as a carved stone bench. The Sacristy is especially known for the two rocks flanking its entrance; each is said to contain 32 angles, but it's easy to come up with a different number whenever you count them.

Intihuatana   RUINS
This Quechua word loosely translates as the 'Hitching Post of the Sun' and refers to the carved rock pillar, often mistakenly called a sundial, at the top of the Intihuatana hill. The Inca astronomers were able to predict the solstices using the angles of this pillar. Thus, they were able to claim control over the return of the lengthening summer days. Its exact use remains unclear, but its elegant simplicity and high craftwork make it a highlight.

Central Plaza   PLAZA
The plaza separates the ceremonial sector from the residential and industrial areas.

Prison Group   RUINS
At the lower end of this area is the Prison Group, a labyrinthine complex of cells, niches and passageways, positioned both under and above the ground.

Temple of the Condor   RUINS
This 'temple' is named for a carving of the head of a condor with rock outcrops as outstretched wings. It is considered the centerpiece of the Prison Group.

⊙ Intipunku

The Inca Trail ends after its final descent from the notch in the horizon called **Intipunku** (Sun Gate; ⊘checkpoint closes around 3pm). Looking at the hill behind you as you enter the ruins, you can see both the trail and Intipunku. This hill, called Machu Picchu (Old Peak), gives the site its name.

Access from the Machu Picchu ruins may be restricted. It takes about an hour to reach Intipunku. If you can spare at least a half-day for the round-trip, it may be possible to continue as far as Wiñay Wayna (p265). Expect to pay S15 or more as an unofficial reduced-charge admission fee to the Inca Trail, and be sure to return before 3pm, which is when the checkpoint typically closes.

⊙ Inca Drawbridge

A scenic but level walk from the Hut of the Caretaker of the Funerary Rock takes you right past the top of the terraces and out along a narrow, cliff-clinging trail to the Inca drawbridge. In under a half-hour's walk, the trail gives you a good look at cloud-forest vegetation and an entirely different view of Machu Picchu. This walk is recommended, though you'll have to be content with photographing the bridge from a distance, as someone crossed the bridge some years ago and tragically fell to their death.

⊙ Wayna Picchu

Wayna Picchu is the small, steep mountain at the back of the ruins. Wayna Picchu is normally translated as 'Young Peak,' but the word *picchu*, with the correct glottal pronunciation, refers to the wad in the cheek of a coca-leaf chewer. Access is limited to 400 people per day – the first 200 in line are let in at 7am, and another 200 at 10am. A ticket (S48) which includes a visit to the Temple of the Moon may only be obtained when you purchase your entrance ticket. These spots sell out a week in advance in low season and a month in advance in high season, so plan accordingly.

At first glance, it would appear that Wayna Picchu is a difficult climb but, although the ascent is steep, it's not technically difficult. However, it is not recommended if you suffer from vertigo. Hikers must sign in and out at a registration booth located beyond the central plaza between two thatched buildings. The 45- to 90-minute scramble up a steep footpath takes you through a short section of Inca tunnel.

Take care in wet weather as the steps get dangerously slippery. The trail is easy to follow, but involves steep sections, a ladder and an overhanging cave, where you have to bend over to get by. Partway up Wayna Picchu, a marked path plunges down to your left, continuing down the rear of Wayna Picchu to the small **Temple of the Moon**. From the temple, another cleared path leads up behind the ruin and steeply onward up the back side of Wayna Picchu.

The descent takes about an hour, and the ascent back to the main Wayna Picchu trail longer. The spectacular trail drops and climbs steeply as it hugs the sides of Wayna Picchu before plunging into the cloud forest. Suddenly, you reach a cleared area where the small, very well-made ruins are found.

Cerro Machu Picchu is a very good alternative if you miss out.

⊙ Cerro Machu Picchu

A more gentle alternative to hiking Wayna Picchu, Cerro Machu Picchu has made strides in popularity recently. While lacking in drama, this 2km walk also happens to be more spectacular than Wayna Picchu, though you won't find archeological remains here. You will find abundant vegetation, including orchids. Allow yourself plenty of time to enjoy the scenery – and catch your breath.

The climb brings you to the top of Machu Picchu (3082m) mountain, to be rewarded with views along the Inca Trail down to the valley floor and across the site of Machu Picchu. There are 800 tickets available daily, with one-hour visits scheduled at 7am and 9am.

> ### ℹ **PREPARATIONS FOR VISITING**
>
> ➡ Tiny sand-fly-like bugs abound. You won't notice them biting, but you may be itching for a week. Bring insect repellent.
>
> ➡ The weather at Machu Picchu seems to have only two settings: heavy rain or bright, burning sunlight. Don't forget rain gear and sunblock.
>
> ➡ Disposable plastic bottles and food are not allowed in the site, though vigilance is a bit lax. It's best to eat outside the gate, use nondisposable water bottles and pack out all trash, even organic waste. Water (in glass bottles) is sold at the cafe just outside the entrance.

☞ Tours

Local guides (per person S150, in groups of six to 10 S30) are readily available for hire at the entrance. Their expertise varies, look for one wearing an official guide ID from DIRCETUR. Agree on a price in advance, clarify whether the fee is per person or group, and agree on the tour length and maximum group size.

🛏 Sleeping

The only lodging onsite is the Machu Picchu Sanctuary Lodge (p263). Most people either arrive on long day trips from Cuzco or Ollantaytambo or stay in nearby Aguas Calientes.

Run by Belmond, **Machu Picchu Sanctuary Lodge** (📞 84-21-1038; www.sanctuary lodgehotel.com; d from US$1600) is an exclusive hotel with one feature no other can match: location. Attention is impeccable and rooms are comfortable, with sober decor, docking stations and eat-in options. Mountain-view rooms cost more. There's also a spa, manicured gardens and personalized Machu Picchu guide service. Among the two restaurants, a popular lunch buffet is open to nonguests (US$40; 11:30am to 3pm).

Though it's the only place to stay at Machu Picchu, the advantage is minor, since buses start running early to the ruins and the early closing time means even hotel guests are denied that cherished panoramic sunset photo. It's often full, so book at least three months ahead.

ℹ Information

SAFE TRAVEL

➤ Inside the ruins, do not walk on any of the walls – this loosens the stonework and prompts a cacophony of whistle-blowing from the guards.

➤ Overnighting here is also illegal: guards do a thorough check of the site before it closes.

➤ Use of the only toilet facilities, just below the cafe, will set you back S1. Validate your ticket before leaving the complex to be allowed back in.

TOURIST INFORMATION

Entrance tickets often sell out: buy them in advance in Cuzco (p223). The ticket booth in Aguas Calientes only accepts cash (soles). Check for changes in online purchasing: it is possible to use debit cards, but only for adult entry (to the ruins, Wayna Picchu and Cerro Machu Picchi). Student and child admission cannot be purchased online. Students must present an official school ID with photograph.

The site is limited to 5940 visitors daily, with 400 paid spots for hiking Wayna Picchu and Cerro Machu Picchu. Visitation is limited to a morning or afternoon ticket: morning tickets are valid between 6am and noon while afternoon tickets are valid between noon and 5:30pm. There is even talk of adding a third turn, which would shorten visits considerably!

Drones, tripods and backpacks over 20L are not allowed into the ruins. Walking sticks are allowed. There are baggage check offices outside the entrance gate (S5 per item; 6am to 4pm). Bringing plastic bottles is frowned upon, so try to bring a reusable bottle, and if you do have food with you, keep it discreet.

For really in-depth information, take along a copy of *Exploring Cuzco* by Peter Frost.

ℹ Getting There & Away

From Aguas Calientes, frequent buses for Machu Picchu (S80 round-trip, 25 minutes) depart from a ticket office along the main road from 5:30am to 3:30pm. Buses return from the ruins when full, with the last departure at 5:45pm. There's a proposal for a tram to eventually replace the bus system, still in the preliminary stages.

Otherwise, it's a steep walk (8km, 1½ hours) up a tightly winding mountain road. First there's a flat 20-minute walk from Aguas Calientes to Puente Ruinas, where the road to the ruins crosses the Río Urubamba, near the museum. A breathtakingly steep but well-marked trail climbs another 2km up to Machu Picchu, taking about an hour to hike (but less coming down!)

The Inca Trail

The most famous hike in South America, the four-day Inca Trail is walked by thousands every year. Although the total distance is only about 39km, the ancient trail laid by the Incas from the Sacred Valley to Machu Picchu winds its way up and down and around the mountains, snaking over three high Andean passes en route, which have collectively led to the route being dubbed 'the Inca Trail.' The views of snowy mountain peaks, distant rivers and ranges, and cloud forests flush with orchids are stupendous – and walking from one cliff-hugging pre-Columbian ruin to the next is a mystical and unforgettable experience.

The Hike

Most trekking agencies run buses to the start of the trail, also known as Piscacucho or Km 82 on the railway to Aguas Calientes.

After crossing the Río Urubamba (2600m) and taking care of registration formalities, you'll climb alongside the river to the trail's first archaeological site, **Llactapata** (Town on Top of the Terraces), before heading south down a side valley of the Río Cusichaca. (If you start from Km 88, turn west after crossing the river to see the little-visited site of **Q'ente** (Hummingbird), about 1km away, then return east to Llactapata on the main trail.)

The trail leads 7km south to the hamlet of **Wayllabamba** (Grassy Plain; 3000m), near which many tour groups will camp for the first night. You can buy bottled drinks and high-calorie snacks here, and take a breather to look over your shoulder for views of the snowcapped **Nevado Verónica** (5750m).

Wayllabamba is situated near the fork of Ríos Llullucha and Cusichaca. The trail crosses the Río Llullucha, then climbs steeply up along the river. This area is known as **Tres Piedras** (Three White Stones; 3300m), though these boulders are no longer visible. From here it is a long, very steep 3km climb through humid woodlands.

The trail eventually emerges on the high, bare mountainside of **Llulluchupampa** (3750m), where water is available and the flats are dotted with campsites, which get very cold at night. This is as far as you can reasonably expect to get on your first day, though many groups will actually spend their second night here.

From Llulluchupampa, a good path up the left-hand side of the valley climbs for a two- to three-hour ascent to the pass of **Warmiwañusca**, also colorfully known as 'Dead Woman's Pass.' At 4200m above sea level, this is the highest point of the trek, and leaves many a seasoned hiker gasping. From Warmiwañusca, you can see the Río Pacamayo (Río Escondido) far below, as well as the ruin of Runkurakay halfway up the next hill, above the river.

The trail continues down a long and knee-jarringly steep descent to the river, where there are large campsites at **Paq'amayo**. At an altitude of about 3600m, the trail crosses the river over a small footbridge and climbs toward **Runkurakay** (Egg-Shaped Building); at 3750m this round ruin has superb views. It's about an hour's walk away.

Above Runkurakay, the trail climbs to a false summit before continuing past two small lakes to the top of the second pass at 3950m, which has views of the snow-laden Cordillera Vilcabamba. You'll notice a change in ecology as you descend from this pass – you're now on the eastern, Amazon slope of the Andes

and things immediately get greener. The trail descends to the ruin of **Sayaqmarka** (Dominant Town), a tightly constructed complex perched on a small mountain spur, which offers incredible views. The trail continues downward and crosses an upper tributary of the Río Aobamba (Wavy Plain).

The trail then leads on across an Inca causeway and up a gentle climb through some beautiful cloud forest and an **Inca tunnel** carved from the rock. This is a relatively flat section and you'll soon arrive at the third pass at almost 3600m, which has grand views of the Río Urubamba Valley, and campsites where some groups spend their final night, with the advantage of watching the sun set over a truly spectacular view, but with the disadvantage of having to leave at 3am in the race to reach the Sun Gate in time for sunrise. If you are camping here, be careful in the early morning as the steep incline makes the steps slippery.

Just below the pass is the beautiful and well-restored ruin of **Phuyupatamarka** (Place Above the Clouds), about 3570m above sea level. The site contains six beautiful ceremonial baths with water running through them. From Phuyupatamarka, the trail makes a dizzying dive into the cloud forest below, following an incredibly well-engineered flight of many hundreds of Inca steps (it's nerve-racking in the early hours, use a headlamp). After two or three hours, the trail eventually zigzags its way down to a collapsed red-roofed white building that marks the final night's campsite.

A 500m trail behind the old, out of use, pub leads to the exquisite little Inca site of **Wiñay Wayna** (Huiñay Huayna), which is variously translated as 'Forever Young,' 'To Plant the Earth Young' and 'Growing Young'

ⓘ AVOIDING THE CROWDS

Avoiding the crowds has become harder than ever, especially since visitors are largely expected to walk a set route through the ruins, instead of spontaneously wandering. Choose the longer route unless you just want to skim – it might be hard to get back to it later.

High season is late May until early September, with June through August being the busiest months. A visit midweek during the rainy season guarantees you more room to breathe, especially during February, when the Inca Trail is closed.

Inca Trail

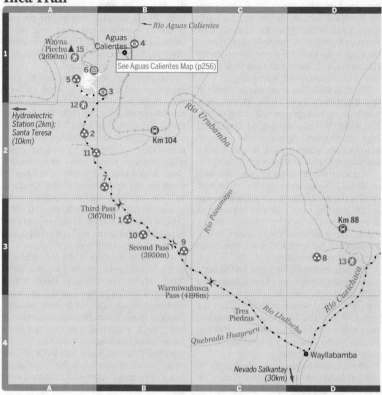

See Aguas Calientes Map (p256)

Hydroelectric Station (2km); Santa Teresa (10km)

Wayna Picchu (2690m) 15

Aguas Calientes 4

6

5

3

12

2

Km 104

11

7

Third Pass (3670m) 1

10

9

Second Pass (3950m)

Warmiwañusca Pass (4198m)

Río Urubamba

Río Pacamayo

Río Cusichaca

Km 88

8   13

Tres Piedras

Río Llulucha

Quebrada Huayruru

Wayllabamba

Nevado Salkantay (30km)

Río Aguas Calientes

(as opposed to 'growing old'). Peter Frost writes that the Quechua name refers to an orchid (*Epidendrum secundum*) that blooms here year-round. The semitropical campsite at Wiñay Wayna boasts one of the most stunning views on the whole trail, especially at sunrise. A rough trail leads from this site to another spectacular terraced ruin, called **Intipata**, best visited on the day you arrive to Wiñay Wayna: consider coordinating it with your guide if you are interested.

From the Wiñay Wayna guard post, the trail winds without much change in elevation through the cliff-hanging cloud forest for about two hours to reach **Intipunku** (Sun Gate) – the penultimate site on the trail, where it's tradition to enjoy your first glimpse of majestic Machu Picchu while waiting for the sun to rise over the surrounding mountains.

The final triumphant descent takes almost an hour. Trekkers generally arrive long before the morning trainloads of tourists,

and can enjoy the exhausted exhilaration of reaching their goal without having to push past enormous groups of tourists fresh off the first train from Cuzco.

CUZCO TO PUNO

A demonstration of the Incas' mastery over their environment, **Tipón** (boleto turístico adult/student S130/70; ⊙ 7am-6pm) consists of some impressive terracing at the head of a small valley with an ingenious irrigation system. It's about 30km from Cuzco, just before Oropesa.

Take any Urcos-bound bus from opposite the hospital in Av de la Cultura in Cuzco, or a *colectivo* from Av Huascar 28, and ask to be let off at the Tipón turnoff (40 minutes). A steep dirt road from the turnoff climbs the 4km to the ruins. You can also contract a taxi tour from Cuzco to drive you into the ruins, wait and bring you back.

N
0 — 5 km
0 — 2.5 miles

E · F

1

2

Km 82

14 ✈

Chilca ●

3

Ollantaytambo
(14km)

Quebrada Sanquchayoc

4

E · F

Inca Trail

stonework contrasts with the Inca blocks. It's interesting to see indigenous people working with the mud that surrounds the area's swampy lakes – the manufacture of adobe (mud bricks) is one of the main industries of this area.

Andahuaylillas

📞 084 / POP 3100 / ELEV 3123M

This pretty Andean village is most famous for its lavishly decorated Iglesia de San Pedro. Near the church is the shop of the Q'ewar Project, a women's cooperative that makes distinctive dolls clad in traditional costumes.

Don't confuse this place with Andahuaylas, west of Cuzco. Andahuaylillas is more than 45km southeast of Cuzco, about 7km before the road splits at Urcos.

◎ Sights

Iglesia de San Pedro   CHURCH

(boleto Ruta del Barocco Andino S20; ⊙7am-5:30pm) Dating from the 17th century, this Jesuit church houses many carvings and paintings, including a canvas of the Immaculate Conception attributed to Esteban Murillo. There are reportedly many gold and silver treasures locked in the church. Is the rumor true or not? All we can tell you is that the 24-hour guards (all villagers) take their job very seriously.

Admission is with the Ruta del Barocco Andino, with tickets available from any of the churches on the route, which also

Admission is with the *boleto turístico* tourist card only.

Piquillacta   RUINS

(boleto turístico adult/student S130/70; ⊙7am-6pm) Meaning 'the Place of the Flea,' Piquillacta is the only major pre-Inca ruin in the area. Built around AD 1100 by the Wari culture, it's a large ceremonial center of crumbling two-story buildings, all with entrances that are strategically located on the upper floor, surrounded by a defensive wall. The stonework here is much cruder than that of the Incas, and the floors and walls were paved with slabs of white gypsum, of which you can still see traces.

Admission is with the *boleto turístico* ticket only, which is valid for 10 days and covers 16 other sites in the region.

Rumicolca   GATE

FREE The huge Inca gate of Rumicolca is built on Wari foundations. The cruder Wari

includes the Capilla de la Vírgen Purificada in Canincunca and the Templo San Juan Bautista in Huaro.

Museo Ritos Andinos   MUSEUM
(Jiron Zubiaga 114; admission by donation; ☉7am-6pm) The eclectic Museo Ritos Andinos has somewhat-random displays including a mummified child, an impressive number of deformed craniums and possibly an alien. You be the judge.

❶ Getting There & Away

To reach Andahuaylillas (up to S7, one hour) from Cuzco, take any Urcos-bound bus from from the middle of the street outside Tullumayo 207.

It's also part of organized tours from Cuzco doing the Ruta del Barrocco Andino.

Raqchi

📞 084 / POP 320 / ELEV 3480M
The little village of Raqchi (125km southeast of Cuzco) is wrapped around Templo de Viracocha, an Inca ruin which was once one of the holiest shrines in the Inca empire.

The people of Raqchi are charming and environmentally conscious, working periodically to eradicate litter left by visitors. And they are famous potters – many of the ceramics on sale in the markets of Pisac and Chinchero come from here.

On the third Sunday in June, Raqchi is the site of a colorful fiesta with much traditional music and dancing.

Looking like an alien aqueduct, the remains of **Templo de Viracocha** (admission S20) were once part of one of the holiest shrines in the Inca empire. Twenty-two columns made of stone blocks helped support the largest-known Inca roof; most were destroyed by Spanish colonisers, but their foundations are clearly seen. The remains of many houses and storage buildings are also visible, and reconstruction is an ongoing process.

Most visitors come here on a day tour from Cuzco that includes other sites in the region.

Buses going between Puno and Cuzco ply this route: it's about 2½ hours to Cuzco, prices vary with bus company.

CUZCO TO THE JUNGLE

There are three overland routes from Cuzco to the jungle. The least developed, cheapest and quickest goes northwest from Ollantaytambo over the Abra Málaga Pass, to the secondary jungle around Quillabamba and into little-visited Ivochote and Pongo de Mainique beyond.

The other two routes are more popular but are rarely accessed by road. You can get to the area around Parque Nacional Manu through Paucartambo, Tres Cruces and Shintuya, or to Puerto Maldonado via Ocongate and Quince Mil. To get deep into these areas, most people go on organized tours which include light-plane flights in and out, or, in some cases, 4WD road transport.

Some of these roads are muddy, slow and dangerous. Think twice before deciding to travel overland and don't even contemplate it in the wettest months (January to April).

Cuzco to Ivochote

Soon after Ollantaytambo, the road leaves the narrowing Sacred Valley and climbs steeply over the 4350m Abra Málaga. From here it's a dizzying, scenic, mostly unpaved descent straight into Amazonia. Dusty **Santa María** has bus-company offices and a couple of very basic *hospedajes* (small, family-owned inns) and restaurants. It marks the junction where you turn off for Santa Teresa and the backdoor route to Machu Picchu, or continue down to Quillabamba.

Santa Teresa
📞 084 / POP 1800 / ELEV 1900M
Long known as the back door to Machu Picchu, Santa Teresa attracts budget tourists hoping to save a few soles. But there are other worthwhile attractions here, namely the Cocalmayo hot springs and the Cola de Mono zipline, both on the outskirts.

❶ BE SAFE IN THE JUNGLE

The activity of narco-traffickers in specific jungle areas in recent times may alter advisable routes for travel and trekking. The government has increased military presence in these areas for security and has added a military base in Kiteni. However, it is always wise to consult with knowledgeable guides and tour operators, or an unaffiliated organization before heading out. Areas that may be of concern include Vilcabamba, Ivochote, Kiteni and beyond, though this is subject to change. It is important to use good, responsible local guides, who can help you interpret any local situation and provide assistance – never go on your own.

Santa Teresa's makeshift feel persists thanks to its repeated flooding, including a landslide in February 2015 which washed out the only bridge into town. Thus vulnerable to the elements, Santa Teresa struggles to position itself in tourism. In the tiny center, most buildings are prefabricated emergency-relief shells and, strangely, the most permanent construction is the puzzling Plaza de Armas statue.

If you are planning to go to Machu Picchu from here, carefully plan your timing with trains or walking the tracks, as tickets can only be purchased for the same day. Machu Picchu usually sells out in high season. Avoid visiting in rainy season when landslides can strand travelers.

🏃 Activities

Cola de Mono   ADVENTURE SPORTS
(☑084-50-9742, 984-992-203; www.canopyperu. com; 2hr zipline S160, rafting S150) South America's highest zipline is a must for thrill-seekers. A total of 2500m of cables with six separate sections whiz high above the spectacular scenery of the Sacsara valley. The owners of Cola de Mono Treehouses, river guides from way back, also run half-day rafting on the spectacular, and so far little-exploited, Santa Teresa river,with treehouse lodgings and camping on site.

To get there, it's a pleasant 2km (half-hour) stroll east – just follow the road out of town or take a taxi.

Baños Termales Cocalmayo   HOT SPRINGS
(admission S10; ⊙7am-11pm Wed, Thu & Sat-Mon, from 1pm Tue & Fri) These stunningly landscaped, council-owned natural hot springs are a fine attraction. As if huge, warm pools and a natural shower straight out of a jungle fantasy weren't enough, you can buy beer and snacks.

It's 4km from town. You can catch a *colectivo* from Santa Teresa to Cocalmayo at around 3pm, when vehicles head down to collect Inca Jungle Trail walkers arriving from Santa María. Otherwise, you may have to brave the unshaded, dusty walk (with cars driving too fast) or take a taxi from Santa Teresa. Pools washed out in the river flooding of 2010 have been rebuilt, though camping areas have not.

🛏 Sleeping

Yellow River Lodge   LODGE **$$**
(☑984-890-028; www.quellomayo.com; Quellomayo; s/d without bathroom incl breakfast S135/270) A cozy place in Quellomayo, 30 minutes from Santa Teresa on the alternative route to Machu Picchu, this welcoming family homestay is an organic farm harvesting coffee, chocolate and tropical fruit. Simple rooms have comfortable beds and colorful walls, but you'll spend most of your time exploring the lush surroundings. Home-cooked meals are available.

To get there, take a bus from Cuzco to Santa María (S30, four hours) and grab a taxi (S50) from there or trek via an old Inca trail; the website has details, including regional transportation options.

Cola de Mono Treehouses   CABIN **$$**
(☑984-992-203, 084-50-9742; www.canopyperu. com; d/f treehouse incl breakfast S200/250, camping per person S25) Sleep in the canopy with views up the Sacsara valley? Yes, please. Rooms with wraparound windows and private bathrooms are suspended 2m up. Campers can bring their own equipment or use tents decked with air mattresses and sheets. Splurge and rent a hot tub (S150) and dine at the lauded on-site restaurant. With an on-site adventure center and excellent hiking.

Eco Quechua   LODGE **$$**
(☑984-756-855, 084-63-0877; www.ecoquechua. com; Sauce Pampa; d incl breakfast S265; 🛜) Staying at this thatched lodge lets you sample jungle living right outside of Santa Teresa, with optional adventure-tour packages that also include Machu Picchu visits. Rooms feature mosquito nets, but still bring repellent. The open-air living room is cloaked in thick vegetation. It's rustic and pricey, but undoubtedly the most ambient spot around. A fine choice for groups.

ℹ Information

There are no banks or ATMs in Santa Teresa – you must bring all the cash you need. You may be able to change dollars at an extremely unfavorable rate.

ℹ Getting There & Away

TO CUZCO

There are no direct public buses from Cuzco to Santa Teresa. From the Santiago terminal in Cuzco, take a bus headed for Quillabamba and get off in Santa María (S25 to S35, five hours), where you can catch a local *combi* or *colectivo* (S15, one hour) to Santa Teresa. These shared vans and wagons take on the winding, dirt road to Santa Teresa like Formula One competitors – try to choose a driver who seems more conservative, as it's a lot to stomach.

Private vans run by Cuzco tour agencies now go direct to Santa Teresa and La Hídroelectrica

(S90 round-trip) from Cuzco most days, with a stop at the plaza in Ollantaytambo. Starts with a hotel pickup in Cuzco. Inquire at your hotel or a reputable agency. Choose your agency carefully – make sure they are licensed and have a reputation for running on time.

Combis going directly to Quillabamba (two hours) depart from Santa María's Plaza de Armas every 15 minutes. *Colectivos* to Santa María leave often from the bus terminal.

TO MACHU PICCHU

To get to Machu Picchu, trains leave from La Hídroelectrica, a hydroelectric station 9.4km from Santa Teresa. Tickets on this route are sold only at the **ticket office** (☉ 5-7:30am & noon-4:30pm daily, plus 7pm-9pm Wed, Fri & Sun) in the Santa Teresa *mercado* (market) on the date of departure or at La Hídroelectrica.

The 13km train ride to Aguas Calientes takes 45 minutes. Most trains are exclusively for locals, who pay a reduced fare. For tourists, **Peru Rail** trains (US$33 one way) go daily at 7:54am, 2:50pm and 5:10pm. Inca Rail plans to add service in the future. Be at the Santa Teresa bus terminal an hour prior to your train to catch a *combi* (S7, 25 minutes).

Though it's considered dangerous, hundreds of travelers walk the train tracks from the Hídroelectrica to Aguas Calientes instead, an outstandingly cheap way to get to Machu Picchu; it takes two to three very dusty and sweaty hours. Not recommended if you're in poor health or with children.

You can also do this route as part of one of the guided multisport tours on offer.

Quillabamba

📞 084 / POP 30.500 / ELEV 1050M

Welcome to the jungle! Quillabamba's tropical vibe is palpable, with heat that becomes oppressive by 9am, music that blares all night, and a land-that-time-forgot feel to most hotels and restaurants.

Quillabamba itself has few attractions and sees little tourism, but there are some outstanding, watery natural attractions nearby. The streets north and south of the Mercado Central, rather than the eternally somnolent Plaza de Armas, are Quillabamba's commercial center.

🏃 Activities & Tours

Balneario de Sambaray　　　SWIMMING

(Sambaray; admission S3; ☉ 9am-5pm) Locals are justifiably proud of Sanbaray, a delightful complex of swimming pools, lawns, bars and a decent trout restaurant. It's a 10-minute *mototaxi* ride (S4) from the center.

Roger Jara　　　TOURS

(rogerjaraalmiron@hotmail.com) Guided trips to all the main attractions, as well as remnant virgin jungle near Quillabamba. Roger can also guide you through the area's big draws, Pongo de Mainique and Vilcabamba. Contact is exclusively via email, and he speaks some English.

🛏 Sleeping & Eating

Hostal Don Carlos　　　HOTEL **$**

(☎ 084-28-1150; www.hostaldoncarlosquillabamba. com; Jirón Libertad 556; s/d S75/110; @ 🛜) With an on-site cafe, this colonial-style hotel features bright, ample rooms around a sunny interior courtyard. Rooms have hot showers and minibars. It's half a block from the Plaza de Armas.

Pizzería Carlo　　　PIZZA **$**

(☎ 084-28-1558; Jr Espinar 309; pizzas from S18; ☉ 6pm-10:30pm Tue-Sun) This restaurant has wood-fired pizzas, and also serves lasagna in big portions. It's a local hangout after dark.

❶ Getting There & Away

Turn right at the end of Plaza de Banderas to find minivans (S35, 4½ hours) to Cuzco in the first block, and the *Terminal Terrestre* (Bus Station) a block later. Buses for Cuzco (S25) leave from here several times a day before 8am and between 1:30pm and 9:30pm. Minivans leave early in the morning and in the evening. All stop at Ollantaytambo and Urubamba en route, but charge full fare wherever you get off.

Walk south along Torre four blocks past Plaza Grau, to Plaza de Banderas, to find transport to Huancacalle (S15, three hours). Minivans leave from Quillabamba's market area for Kiteni (three to six hours) and Ivochote (six to eight hours), further into the jungle.

Huancacalle

📞 084 / POP 300 / ELEV 3200M

Peaceful, pretty Huancacalle is best known as the jumping-off point for treks to Vilcabamba, but many more hikes from three to 10 days long are possible from here, including to Puncuyo, Inca Tambo, Choquequirao and Machu Picchu. Inquire about safety in the area before your hike.

🛏 Sleeping

Hostal Manco Sixpac　　　GUESTHOUSE **$**

(☎ relative in Cuzco 971-823-855; per person without bathroom S20) The town's biggest building, this guesthouse is run by the Cobos family of local guides. There's hot water for showers, a rare find in these parts. You can organize mules and guides here.

ⓘ Getting There & Away

There's no direct transport to Huancacalle from Cuzco. Take a bus to Quillabamba via Santa María (S25, 4½ hours) from the Santiago terminal in Cuzco. In Quillabamba, walk south along Torre four blocks past Plaza Grau, to Plaza de Banderas, to find transport to Huancacalle (S15, three hours), usually leaving in the early morning or late afternoon.

Vilcabamba

The real 'lost city of the Incas,' Vilcabamba – also known as Espíritu Pampa – is what Hiram Bingham was looking for when he stumbled on Machu Picchu. The beleaguered Manco Inca and his followers fled to this jungle retreat after being defeated by the Spaniards at Ollantaytambo in 1536.

The long, low-altitude trek, which takes four to nine days, is very rugged, with many steep ascents and descents before reaching Vilcabamba, 1000m above sea level. You can start at either Huancacalle or Kiteni. This area may be insecure; consult with knowledgeable guides and tour operators in Cuzco before heading out.

Cuzco to Puerto Maldonado

Almost 500km long, this road takes a day to travel in the dry season. Most travelers choose to fly from Cuzco to Puerto Maldonado. Now paved, this route is part of the Interoceánica, a highway that unites the east and west coasts of South America for the first time.

Various companies depart from Cuzco's *Terminal Terrestre* for Puerto Maldonado between 3pm and 4:30pm daily. CIVA (S40 to S70, 10 hours, departs 9pm) is probably the best option. If you want to split up the journey, the best places to stop are Ocongate and Quince Mil, which have basic accommodations.

The route heads toward Puno until soon after Urcos, where the road to Puerto Maldonado begins. About 75km and 2½ hours from Cuzco, you come to the highland town of Ocongate, which has a couple of basic hotels around the plaza.

From here, trucks go to the village of Tinqui, an hour's drive beyond Ocongate, which is the starting point for the spectacular seven-day trek encircling Ausangate (6384m), the highest mountain in southern Peru.

After Tinqui, the road drops steadily to Quince Mil, 240km from Cuzco, less than 1000m above sea level, and the halfway point of the journey. The area is a gold-mining center, and the hotel here is often full. After another 100km the road into the jungle reaches the flatlands, where it levels out for the last 140km into Puerto Maldonado.

Ausangate

Snowcapped Ausangate (6384m), the highest mountain in southern Peru, can be seen from Cuzco on a clear day. Hiking a circuit around its skirts is the most challenging alpine hike in the region. It takes five to six days and crosses four high passes (two over 5000m). The route begins in the rolling brown puna (grasslands of the Andean plateau) and features stunningly varied scenery, including fluted icy peaks, tumbling glaciers, turquoise lakes and green marshy valleys.

Along the way you'll stumble across huge herds of alpacas and tiny hamlets unchanged in centuries. The walk starts and finishes at Tinqui, where there are warm mineral springs and a basic hotel, and mules and *arrieros* (mule drivers) are available for about S50 per day each. Average price is US$750 for an organized, tent-based five-day trek with operators from Cuzco. For a luxurious, lodge-based experience of Ausangate, check out Andean Lodges (p226).

CUZCO TO THE CENTRAL HIGHLANDS

Cuzco to Abancay

Marvellous, little-known ruins and hot springs mark the four-hour, 200km ride from Cuzco to Abancay. It's the perfect opportunity to get off the beaten path. For those not so keen on ruins, it may feel like a long journey with only more incredible Andean scenery to compensate. On the way, there's also the turnoff to Cachora, the starting point to hike to the Choquequirao ruins.

◉ Sights & Activities

Tarawasi RUINS
(Limatambo; ☏ Cuzco 084-58-2030; admission S10)
Named after the Inca site of Rimactambo, Limatambo is popularly known as Tarawasi.

The site was used as a ceremonial center and a resting place for the Inca *chasquis* (Inca runners who delivered messages over long distances). The exceptional polygonal retaining wall, noteworthy for its 28 human-sized niches, is in itself worth the trip from Cuzco. On the wall below it, look for flower shapes and a nine-sided heart amid the patchwork of perfectly interlocking stones.

Limatambo, 80km west of Cuzco, is situated beside the road, about 115km west of Abancay.

Saihuite
ARCHAEOLOGICAL SITE

(☑Abancay 083-32-1664; admission S10) The Inca site of Saihuite, 45km east of Abancay, has a sizable, intricately carved boulder called the Stone of Saihuite, which is similar to the sculpted rock at Q'enqo, near Cuzco,

though it's smaller and more elaborate. The carvings of animals are particularly intricate.

If you are arriving via a Cuzco–Abancay bus, ask to be let off at the turnoff to the ruins, from where it's a 1km walk downhill.

Cconoc
HOT SPRINGS

(☑Abancay 083-32-1664; admission S20; ⊙24hr) The natural thermal baths of Cconoc are 3km downhill from a turnoff 10km east of minor transport hub Curahuasi, around 85km east of Abancay. It has a restaurant, a bar and a basic hotel.

❶ Getting There & Away

It's possible to make a day out of visiting one or two sites, bus-hopping your way to Abancay.

THE Q'OYORITI PILGRIMAGE

Rivers and mountains are *apus* (sacred deities) for the Andean people, possessed of a vital force called *kamaq*. At 6384m, Ausangate (p271) is the Cuzco department's highest mountain and the most important *apu* in the area. The subject of countless legends, it's the *pakarina* (mythical place of sacred origin) of llamas and alpacas, and controls their health and fertility. Condemned souls are also doomed to wander its freezing heights as punishment for their sins.

Ausangate is the site of the traditional festival of Q'oyoriti (p222; Star of the Snow), held in late May or early June between the Christian feasts of the Ascension and Corpus Christi. Despite its overtly Catholic aspect – it's officially all about the icy image of Christ that appeared here in 1783 – the festival remains primarily and obviously a celebration and appeasement of the *apu*, consisting of four or more days of literally nonstop music and dance. Incredibly elaborate costumes and dances – featuring, at the most extreme end, llama fetuses and mutual whipping – repetitive brass-band music, fireworks, and sprinklings of holy water all contribute to a dizzy, delirious spectacle. Highly unusually, no alcohol is allowed. Offenders are whipped by anonymous men dressed as *ukukus* (mountain spirits) wearing white masks that hide their features, who maintain law and order.

Many *cuzqueños* (inhabitants of Cuzco) believe that if you attend Q'oyoriti three times, you'll get your heart's desire. Pilgrims buy an *alacita* (miniature scale model) of houses, cars, trucks, petrol stations, university degrees, driver's licenses or money at stalls lining the pilgrimage pathway. The items are blessed at the church. Repeat three years in a row and see what happens.

Q'oyoriti is a pilgrimage – the only way in is by trekking three or more hours up a mountain, traditionally in the wee hours to arrive around dawn. The sight of a solid, endless line of people quietly wending their way up or down the track and disappearing around a bend in the mountain is unforgettable, as is Q'oyoriti's eerie, otherworldly feel. The majority of attendees are traditionally dressed *campesinos* (peasants) for whom seeing a foreigner may be a novelty (they may even point you out).

Discomfort is another aspect of the pilgrimage. Q'oyoriti takes place at an altitude of 4750m, where glaciers flow down into the Sinakara Valley. It's brutally cold, and there's no infrastructure, no town, just one big elaborate church (complete with flashing lights around the altar) built to house the image of El Señor de Q'oyoriti (The Christ of Q'oyoriti). The temporary toilets are a major ordeal. The blue plastic sea of restaurants, stalls and tents is all carried in, on foot or donkey. The whole thing is monumentally striking: a temporary tent city at the foot of a glacier, created and dismantled yearly to honor two mutually contradictory yet coexisting religions in a festival with dance and costumes whose origins no one can remember.

Start by catching a *colectivo* to Limatambo (S12, two hours) from Arcopata in Cuzco.

Cachora

Sleepy and pleasant Cachora is a traditional agricultural town with colonial roots. It's a whole world away from Cuzco and the crush of tourism. Yet services are sprouting up, since it is now the most common starting point for the hike to Choquequirao. There's no cash machine here so bring all the money you will need for your stay and the trek.

🛏 Sleeping & Eating

With not much on offer here, the best bet is to dine at your lodgings.

Casa Nostra GUESTHOUSE **$**
(☑ 958-349-949; www.choquequiraotrekk.com/en/; sendero a Choquequirao s/n; dm S35-45, d/tr incl breakfast S100/120; ☏) This Peruvian-Italian-run lodge, just beyond the village of Cachora toward Capuliyoc, is a pleasant haven for Choquequirao hikers. With gorgeous views down valley, the rooms are ample and spotless, though unheated, with private bathrooms and electric showers. Breakfast comes with eggs and pancakes, and there are other meals available. It also rents camping equipment and can organize guides and mules.

Hostal Casa de Salkantay GUESTHOUSE **$**
(☑ 984-281-171; www.salkantay.com; sendero a Choquequirao s/n; per person incl breakfast S60; ☏) On the outskirts of Cachora gazing down on the valley below, this two-story lodge offers attractive rooms with electric showers. You can also order meals in advance. It's surrounded by flower gardens with outdoor seating. It's on a hairpin curve on the way out of town toward Capuliyoc.

❶ Getting There & Away

Cachora is 15km from the highway from the same turnoff as Saihuite. From the center, there is sporadic transport to Abancay (S12, two hours).

In Cuzco, shared taxis leave from Arcopata (S50, four hours) to Cachora. You can also take any Abancay-bound bus from Cuzco and get off at Saihuite, where you might find a private taxi (S60 to S90). The spot is isolated, so it's not recommended to arrive after dark, when transport options are few for security reasons.

If you have lodging, arrange your transport ahead of time as there might not be phone service at the drop-off point.

Choquequirao

Remote, spectacular, and still not entirely cleared, the ruins of Choquequirao are often described as a mini–Machu Picchu. This breathtaking site at the junction of three rivers currently requires a challenging two-day hike each way, though you will be happy if you budget more time for it.

Many see it as 'the next big thing' in Inca ruins tourism. In fact, the Peruvian government has already approved controversial plans to put in a tramway, the country's first, with a capacity of 3000 visitors daily. It would bring this remote attraction to within 15 minutes of the nearby highway. Conservationists worry about its potential impact.

For now, you can still go without the crowds. Most Cuzco trekking operators go. Travelers can also organize the walk on their own, but it is remote and its steepness makes it very challenging, especially if you're carrying a heavy pack.

◉ Sights

The many features of this sprawling site take a while to explore. Archaeology fans will not be content with the half-day allotted by a four-day trek.

Take special care exploring these ruins as the site's popularity can cause a huge impact on the infrastructure and there is little funding for its conservation.

Trail guides don't always offer detailed information. It's well worth bringing a copy of *Machu Picchu's Sacred Sisters: Choquequirao & Llactapata* by Gary Ziegler. Peter Frost's *Exploring Cuzco* is also useful.

★**Parque Arqueológico Choquequirao** ARCHAEOLOGICAL SITE
(admission S60) Translating as 'Cradle of Gold,' this remote Incan site (3050m) in the Vilcabamba mountain range over the Apurímac canyon bears a strong resemblance to Machu Picchu. It's enormous, covering 6 sq km, with roughly 30% of the site excavated. Ruins include whole buildings, a leveled ceremonial area and extensive aqueducts and terraces. It was occupied during the 15th and 16th centuries, roughly during the reign of Pachacutec and his son Tupac Yupanqui. Camping is free.

Llama Terraces RUINS
Discovered only in 2002 by archaeologist Percy Paz, these steep terraces on the backside

RAINBOW MOUNTAIN

Also known as Vinicunca, **Rainbow Mountain** (Vinicunca; Pampachiri; admission S10) is a viral hit with travelers thanks to the photogenic nature of its mineral stripes. Getting there requires good physical fitness and proper acclimatization. The 10km round-trip to a high viewpoint facing the mountain is gentle in grade but the high altitude (reaching above 5000m) takes its toll. Try to ascend slowly. With great Ausangate (p271) views.

Be prepared to be one of hundreds hiking the trail – you will find no solitude here. Tour buses from Cuzco go for cheap, but consider whether you want to be herded up the mountain in a large group. Ask other travelers about their experience and look for agencies that offer trips with smaller groups and pay more attention to client needs. Some offer overnights in basic family lodgings nearby. The main access is via Pitumarca, which is a three-hour drive from Cuzco, ending with an hour on a very steep road with sheer drops. A newer alternate access is being developed through Cusipata, on the other side of the mountain, with only an 8km hike that starts at a higher altitude, though infrastructure is more developed on the other side.

Bring plenty of water, wear hiking clothes and bring extra layers. There are small stands along the way selling tea, water and snacks. Horses can be rented (ascent/descent S60/30), led by locals. Nearby Red Valley (S10, two checkpoints) is worth the side trip if you have the time.

of the ruins feature unique stonework resembling that found in the northern Peru ruins of Chachapoyas. The incredible stonework, unique to this site, features 22 white llamas in cascading order, followed at the bottom by the figure of a single herder. They also have a potential astronomical significance.

Access is via the back of the lower plaza. Take extra caution walking here, it's a steep 20-minute descent to the viewpoint.

Activities

Hiking

Outfitters from Cuzco offer a guided, four-day trek (averaging US$500 to US$750 per person). Reputable outfitters include Alpaca Expeditions (p216), Apus Peru (p216), Journey Experience (p221), Llama Path (p216), Peru Eco Expeditions (p216), SAS Travel (p221) and Wayki Trek (p217). Costs for an independent guide can be comparable. Packhorses can be hired in Cachora (per day S50 horse or mule, and S50 for muleteer); make sure that they will be in good condition for the trip, since not all are. Trekking poles are highly recommended.

Independent hikers will find rest stops with organized campgrounds with toilets and some cold showers, expensive bottled water, drinks and basic meals or provisions (such as pasta or instant soup). Bring a water filter, as the water found along the way is not potable. Always carry plenty of water, as sources are infrequent.

Choquequirao

➤ **Start** Capuliyoc

➤ **End** Choquequirao

➤ **Duration** Four to five days round-trip

➤ **Distance** 44km round-trip

➤ **Difficulty** Hard

Perched on the steep slope above the southern side of the Apurimac Canyon, **Capuliyoc** (2915m) is not much more than a campground and a few kiosks selling basic meals, water and drinks. From here, the trail switchbacks down the canyon alongside grassy slopes. This side of the canyon is quite exposed and the small gravel can be loose, so watch your step. There's some guard railings in tight areas, but only on the initial part of the trail. The biggest concern is horses or mules – avoid an unexpected kick by getting well out of their way.

The route follows a 'new' trail, meaning it's not the original access used by the Incas. Descending to **Cocamasana** there's a settler selling basic food and drinks. From the starting point, it's a three-hour descent to **Chiquisca** (1900m), where there are two camping areas. The first offers a kiosk and stone bathrooms with cold showers. The next section of the trail has some steep, short switchbacks with loose sand and rocks (listen for rock fall above). It's 45 minutes further to **Playa Rosalina** (1550m), also with camping, kiosk and stone bathrooms with showers. The mosquitoes are vicious here, but it's a pretty spot alongside the Rio Apurímac, facing the sturdy metal bridge.

If you have camped at Chiquisca or Playa Rosalina, you will want to get a dawn start to avoid blistering heat on the ascent. Cross the bridge over the Rio Apurímac and start the steep switchbacks. With vegetation thicker on this side of the canyon, the trail is a bit more protected from sheer drops. Still, it's hard work. The steep grade starts to let up about 1½ to two hours in, around Santa Rosa I and Santa Rosa II, small settlements 20 minutes apart with camping and basic provisions. From the riverbank it will take around three to four hours to reach Marampata (2850m). This pleasant hillside village has a handful of homes surrounded by geraniums. There are homestay options (with solar-panel electricity), kiosks and campgrounds.

From here the trail levels out quite a bit. It's another one to 1½ hours further to the campsites at Choquequirao (3050m). Upon entering the reserve, visitors must register at the entrance station, where the admission fee is paid. You can see the ridgetop ruins from here, along with the eastern terraces, a breathtakingly steep design in the process of being excavated. Not agricultural in origin, the terracing is thought to be designed to better retain the soil. The campground with bathrooms is a 30-minute walk to the actual ruins.

From the ruins, it's usually a two-day hike back to Capuliyoc, arriving the morning of the second day.

Since the hike is so demanding, it's best to take at least five days for the round-trip visit. You will be glad to have the time to explore the ruins, which are extensive. From Choquequirao, you can also hike the Qhapac Ñan (Inca trail) on to Machu Picchu via Yanama, an eight-day trek.

ⓘ Getting There & Away

The ruins are accessed via a two-day hike starting in Capuliyoc, which lies 12km (two to three hours' walking) from the town of Cachora, the last town with services and public transport, via an exposed, unpaved road. A taxi from Cuzco (S300) may be worthwhile for groups.

Organized tours start at Capuliyoc.

Abancay

☑ 083 / POP 58,750 / ELEV 2378M

This growing rural city is the capital of the department of Apurímac, one of the least explored regions in the Peruvian Andes. There's

little going on here, but travelers may opt to use it as a rest stop on the long, tiring bus journey between Cuzco and Ayacucho.

Jirón Arequipa, with banks, is the main commercial street; its continuation, Av las Arenas, has restaurants and entertainment.

🍽 Sleeping & Eating

Hotel Saywa HOTEL $
(☑083-32-4876; www.hotelsaywa.com; Arenas 302; s/d incl breakfast S65/90; ☏) A friendly spot with good options for solo travelers. Attractive rooms have parquet floors and TV; there's also an onsite tour agency.

Quinta Villa Venecia PERUVIAN $$
(☑083-23-4191; Av Bella Abanquina; mains from S22; ☺9am-5:30pm Mon-Sat) Worth the short taxi ride (it's behind the stadium), Villa Venecia is Abancay's most noteworthy restaurant. Serving up every local food imaginable, it's the living embodiment of the Peruvian mantra *bueno, barato y bastante* (good, cheap and plentiful). The *tallarines* (spaghetti) are an Abancay specialty and the tamales are wonderful. Very family friendly.

ⓘ Information

DIRCETUR (☑83-32-1664; www.dirceturapurimac.gob.pe; Av Arenas 121, 1st fl; ☺8-11am & 12:30-5pm Mon-Fri) Provides information on area attractions, including Cconoc hot springs and Saihuite.

ⓘ Getting There & Away

Streetside **transport to Curahuasi** (Av Nuñez & Garcilazo; S12; ☺6am-4pm) via Saihuite (S12, one hour 40 minutes, 6am-4pm) leave from Av Nuñez & Garcilazo. Several blocks away at the corner of Av Nuñez & Prado Alto you can pick up **transport to Cachora** (cnr Av Nuñez & Prado Alto; S12; ☺6am-5pm) (S12, one hour 40 minutes, 6am-5pm). All *colectivos* leave when full.

Buses toward Cuzco, Andahuaylas and Lima leave from the **Terminal Terrestre** (Av Pachacutec s/n). Various companies go to Cuzco (S30 to S50, five hours), clustered around 6am, 11am and 11pm. Dozens depart to Lima (S60 to S185, 14 to 16 hours) daily, mostly in the afternoon and between 10:30pm and midnight. Departures to Andahuaylas (S15, 3½ hours) cluster around 11:30am and 11:30pm. The faster, more comfortable minibuses to Andahuaylas are a little bit reckless.

Terminal departure tax is S1. Taxis go to the center (S5).

AT A GLANCE

POPULATION
Huancayo: 365,000

HIGHEST TRAIN STATION
La Galera: 4781m

BEST MEAL WITH A VIEW
Via Via (p310)

BEST AYACUCHEÑO ART
Museo de Arte Popular (p305)

BEST BREAKFASTS
Café Coqui (p297)

WHEN TO GO

Jan
Hot but rain-prone weather as Huancayo celebrates Año Nuevo (New Year's) with quirky festivities.

Mar & Apr
Peru's biggest and best Easter party during Ayacucho's Semana Santa.

Jul & Aug
Dry weather with chilly, star-heavy nights; perfect for toddies and thermal-bath relaxation in Huancavelica.

Ferrocarril Central Andino railway (p299)
MARK GREEN/ALAMY ©

Central Highlands

I f it's breathtaking ancient ruins or immersion in uninterrupted wilderness that you crave during your journey, listen up. The rocky, remote Central Highlands can match Peru's better known destinations for these things and more – with the almost absolute absence of other travelers. This sector of the Andes is Peru at its most Peruvian reaching its zenith from Easter to July during its myriad fiestas. Adventure-spirited souls will discover better insights into local life than are possible elsewhere: bonding with fellow passengers on bumpy buses perhaps or hiking into high hills to little-visited Inca palaces.

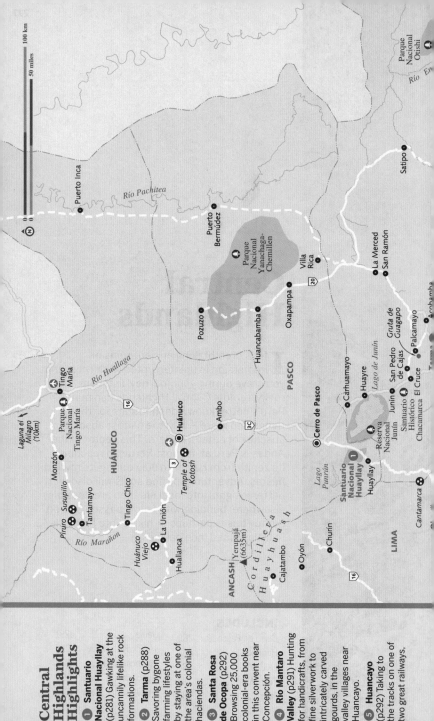

Central Highlands Highlights

1 Santuario Nacional Huayllay
(p281) Gawking at the uncannily lifelike rock formations.

2 Tarma (p288)
Savoring bygone farming lifestyles by staying at one of the area's colonial haciendas.

3 Santa Rosa de Ocopa (p292)
Browsing 25,000 colonial-era books in this convent near Concepción.

4 Río Mantaro Valley (p291) Hunting for handicrafts, from fine silverwork to intricately carved gourds, in the valley villages near Huancayo.

5 Huancayo
(p292) Taking to the tracks on one of two great railways.

JUNIN

Comas

Tingo

Laguna de Paca

Jauja

La Oroya

Pachacayo

Río Mantaro

Reserva Nor Yauyos-Cochas

San Pedro de Casta

Marcahuasi

Chosica

Airport

LIMA

Miraflores

Pucusana • Chilca

Cerro Azul

Cañete

Lunahuaná

PACIFIC OCEAN

Chancay (10km)

Concepción **3**

Mito
Huilhuas
Cochas Grande
4 Río Mantaro
San Jerónimo de Tunán
San Agustín de Cajas
5 Huancayo
Sapallanga
Pucara
Chupaca

Huaytapallana

Pampas

Izcuchaca

6 Huancavelica

HUANCAVELICA

Castrovirreyna

ICA

Chincha Alta
El Carmen

Pisco

Paracas

Ica (50km)

LIMA

Churcampa

Santuario Histórico Pampas de Ayacucho

Quinua

Wari

7 Ayacucho

Andahuaylas **8** (135km)

Julcamarca

Lircay

Laguna de Choclochoca

Santa Inés

Rumichaca

AYACUCHO

Cangallo

Vischongo

Vilcashamán

THE NORTH

Welcome to the least-known zone of Peru's great unknown. On one of the country's most curious thrill rides, you are catapulted up to the breath-sapping mining city of Cerro de Pasco, then plunged down towards Huánuco, jumping-off point for some fabulous archaeological excursions, before dipping down again into tropical Tingo María, poised on the threshold of the jungle.

Canta & Obrajillo

☎01 / POP 2800 / ELEV 2700M

A quaint time-warp, the town of Canta shares some diverting outdoor activities with Obrajillo, its equally dinky neighbor a kilometer down the hill. Families from Lima rock up at weekends for this gentle initiation into Andean life; otherwise it's quiet here.

The towns are reached by traveling northeast from Lima's outskirts on the initially verdant Hwy 20A. You're soon in lush pasture land, one of the key agricultural regions serving the capital, with the valley sides sheering up as you near Canta, the first town of significance.

Highlights in Obrajillo include access to two waterfalls on short trails, as well as horseback riding through this bucolic landscape. The village is renowned for its restaurants, which are invitingly spread along the riverside. An hour's drive north of Canta on the five-hour run up to Huayllay and the Santuario Nacional Huayllay, you'll find the intriguing Inca ruins of Cantamarca.

Sights & Activities

Cantamarca RUIN

FREE The most impressive of numerous Inca ruins peppering the road above Canta, the buildings at Cantamarca – a series of circular dwellings skittering down a mountainside on the right side of the road – date from 1100.

An hour's drive north of Canta, look for the *zona arqueologica* (archaeological zone) roadside signs; the second sign you'll see (on the left) is the one for Cantamarca.

Waterfalls WATERFALL

FREE The hike to these lovely cascades is good for walking off the huge platters of meat at La Choza de Omar at the bottom of the path. Follow the river up a short way from Obrajillo and you will soon encounter the falls.

Horseback Riding HORSEBACK RIDING

(per person per hr from S5) Horseback rides are offered at the point where the road meets the river in Obrajillo, making for a very pleasant activity. The trip up to the village's two waterfalls is perhaps the most popular.

Sleeping & Eating

Hotel Cancayvento HOTEL $$

(☎01-244-7162, 01-422-6344; hotelcancayvento3estrellas@hotmail.com; Av 26 de Junio s/n; s/d incl breakfast from S120/180; P@🛜🏊) High brick walls enclose this pleasant and spacious place at the top of town before the long road winds on up to Huayllay. Simple rooms are of a decent size, a hearty breakfast in the enormous restaurant is included, and there is a pool and grilling area outside. It's owned by a charismatic *limeña* (woman from Lima).

★**La Choza de Omar** PERUVIAN $$

(www.lachozadeomar.com; Obrajillo; mains S25-35; 👪) This rustic outdoor restaurant where the road hits the river in idyllic little Obrajillo entices droves of weekending Lima residents, who go crazy over the huge plates of carnivorous fare while their kids run amok. The emerald-green garden is big enough, fortunately, that this doesn't overly disturb other diners. Try the *pachamanca* (meat baked on hot stones in the ground).

Don't miss a game of *sapo* – Peru's equivalent of a pub sport in which players have to toss coins into a series of holes on a counter, one of which is in the shape of a toad's mouth.

Getting There & Away

Roads in the region are often rough – and it is not uncommon for the main route between any two places to be largely unpaved. Several useful airports (at Tingo María, Jauja and Ayacucho, all with flights to Lima) cut travel time down, but travel within the Central Highlands is exclusively by bus or *colectivo* (shared taxi), which leave only when a minimum of four passengers are ready to go).

Cerro de Pasco

☎063 / POP 66,000 / ELEV 4333M

The highest place of its size in the world, Cerro de Pasco attracts the odd traveler who uses the town as a springboard to visit some of Peru's most spectacular rock formations at Santuario Nacional Huayllay.

MINING OR UNDERMINING? THE TROUBLE WITH THE ALTIPLANO'S MINERAL WEALTH

Mining is Peru's *numero uno* source of income, and the Central Highlands accounts for a sizable chunk of it. But the affluence brought by the extraction of zinc, lead, silver, copper and gold – Peru ranks within the world's top four exporters for each – also raises questions concerning the distribution of that wealth and the detrimental environmental impacts of the extraction. Peru's major mining centers are some of the poorest and most polluted places in the country, if not on the entire continent.

Mining or mineral processing is the economic lifeblood of Cerro de Pasco (one of South America's main zinc and lead mines) and La Oroya (the Central Highlands' main ore-smelting center). Yet it could also be the ruin of these cities. Contamination rates are high: La Oroya constantly appears on 'most- polluted-places-in-the-world' lists. Though Doe Run, the company that owns the La Oroya smelter, has shut down production, there have been clamors from residents to restart operations, despite awareness of the risks.

Huelgas (strikes) over working and living conditions are reported regularly, but also poignantly in evidence are the conditions people are prepared to endure to keep their jobs in this industry. Nowhere is this more apparent than in Cerro de Pasco, where the pit owned by Volcan Compañia Minera is in the middle of the city (and is ironically referred to as Peru's biggest Plaza de Armas). Nine out of 10 children in the town have above-average levels of minerals in their blood, according to research by the US-based Centers for Disease Control and Prevention. And with the mine using the majority of available water, running tap water is only available for limited hours. A significant percentage of the city's population lives in poverty.

Still, there is an even more imminent danger from the mine: houses cluster around its rim, and subsidence from the ever-present hole outside the properties is a problem. In 2008, Volcan was allowed to buy a portion of the historic city center. With the pit poised to eat up the heart of Cerro de Pasco, the Peruvian congress passed a bill proposing an audacious and costly solution: relocating the entire city some 20km away. But this could take an estimated US$500 million and over a decade to execute. And time, for many residents, is running out. Soon, Cerro de Pasco might not be there at all: a victim, like many Peruvian mining towns, of its own success.

First impressions of this dizzyingly-high altiplano (Andean plateau) mining settlement are striking: houses and streets spread haphazardly around a gaping artificial hole in the bare hills that is several miles wide. That's because Spanish colonialists found silver here in the 17th century and this, along with other mineral wealth, has made Cerro a lucrative Peruvian asset.

If you are traveling by *colectivo* (shared transportation) taxi around the altiplano, it is also a handy place to pick up a connecting ride.

◉ Sights

**Santuario Nacional
Huayllay**　　　　　　NATURE RESERVE
(Bosque de Piedras; admission S2, guided tour about S25) Santuario Nacional Huayllay, aka the *bosque de piedras* (forest of stones), is the world's largest and highest rock forest at a chilly 4500m+ with formations looming out of the desolate *pampa* (pampas grass) in such shapes as an elephant, a king's crown and an uncannily lifelike grazing alpaca. The area is highly rated for **rock climbing**. The sanctuary, comprising a vast area of several kilometers, also has **thermal baths**. It's almost an hour outside Cerro de Pasco, just before Huayllay.

It's not a bad idea to hire a guide, both to point out the most striking formations and to direct you to the thermal baths and the nearby **prehistoric cave paintings**. Señor Raul Rojas of **Hostal Santa Rosa** (🖉 963-958-301, 063-42-2120; Libertad 269) in Cerro de Pasco is a recommended guide and charges S50 per person for day trips here. Guides also wait at the site. Going solo, you might miss out on some formations, but it's doable.

Colectivos (shared transportation) traverse the Huayllay–Cerro de Pasco road. In Cerro de Pasco, *colectivos* depart from

Parque Minero, near the bus terminal (S6, 45 minutes).

🛏 Sleeping

Plaza Apart Hotel   HOTEL $$
(☑ 063-42-3391; http://plazaaparthotel.com; Prado 118; s/d from S80/120) Has big, well-appointed, welcoming rooms and cable TV. It's warm, and that's the main thing. On Plaza de Armas.

❶ Getting There & Away

The **bus terminal** (Terminal Terrestre; Arenales s/n), five blocks south of the Plaza de Armas, has buses to Huánuco (S10, three hours), Huancayo (S15, four hours), Lima (S30 to S40, eight hours), La Oroya (S10, 2½ hours) and Tarma.

Faster *colectivos* (shared transportation) from the bus terminal charge S20 to Huánuco. Heading south, for Tarma you may have to change taxis at El Cruce where the Tarma road branches off.

Huánuco

☑ 062 / POP 175,000 / ELEV 1894M

The profusion of archaeological remains in the surrounding mountains is the main reason to linger here. Locals boast Huánuco's perfect elevation gives it the best climate in Peru: indeed, after the tempestuous altiplano (Andean plateau), the city seems positively balmy. It certainly makes a convenient stopover on the Lima–Pucallpa jungle route. Nearby is one of Peru's oldest Andean archaeological sites, the Temple of Kotosh, while up in the hills sit the even more impressive ancient ruins near La Unión and Tantamayo.

Huánuco lies on the important Inca route from Cuzco to Cajamarca, the key settlement in the north of the empire, and developed as a major way station accordingly. The Incas chose Huánuco Viejo, 150km west, as their regional stronghold, but the exposed location prompted the Spanish to move the city to its current scenic setting on the Río Huallaga in 1541. Today, little is left of Huánuco's colonial past.

⊙ Sights

Sights in the city itself are thin on the ground: you might try seeing if **Iglesia San Francisco** (cnr Huallayco & Beraún) is open – it's Huánuco's most appealing church, with lavish baroque-style altars and interesting *escuela cuzqueña* (Cuzco school) paintings – but don't hold your breath.

Temple of Kotosh   RUIN
(admission incl guided tour S5; ⊙ 8am-5:30pm) This ruin is also known as the Temple of the Crossed Hands because of its highlight, a life-sized mud molding of a pair of crossed hands that dates to about 2000 BC. The original is now at Lima's Museo Nacional de Antropología, Arqueología e Historía del Perú (p73), and a replica remains at the site. Little is known about Kotosh, one of the most ancient Andean cultures. The temple, Huánuco's main attraction, is diverting enough, but anticlimactic after seeing the blockbuster Inca sites elsewhere.

Kotosh is about 5km west of town off La Unión road, and the site is easily visited by taxi (S12, including a 30-minute wait and return). In the hills 2km above the site, **Quillaromi** cave has impressive prehistoric paintings.

🎊 Festivals & Events

Danza de los Negritos   TRADITIONAL DANCE
(⊙ Jan) Huánuco's most singular festival sees revelers honoring the memory of the slaves brought to work in the area's mines by donning black masks, dressing up brightly and drinking – lots. It's held January 1, 6 and 18. Now considered a mainly indigenous festival, this was nevertheless originally performed by the slaves themselves.

🛏 Sleeping

Hostal Huánuco   GUESTHOUSE $
(☑ 062-51-1617; www.facebook.com/HOSTALHUA NUCOS.R.L; Huánuco 777; s/d S35/50, s without bathroom S20) This traditional mansion simply exudes character, with old-fashioned tiled floors, a 2nd-floor terrace overlooking a garden and hall walls covered with art and old newspaper clippings. Delightful – if worn – rooms contain characterful old furniture and have comfortable beds. Showers are hot but can take an age to warm up: ask in advance. A gem of a find for backpackers.

Mauri Apart Hotel   APARTMENT $$
(☑ 062-63-5011; www.hotelmauri.com; Valdizán 785; d/apt incl breakfast S110-130/170) Squeaky clean and modern, the Mauri comes as close as Huánuco does to a chic hotel. Color schemes are thought out carefully, service is chilled and understated and many of the rooms have neat little kitchenettes.

Hotel Santorini   HOTEL $$
(☑ 062-51-5130; www.facebook.com/hotelsantorini huanuco; Beraún, btwn Valdizán & Bolivar; s/d

Huánuco

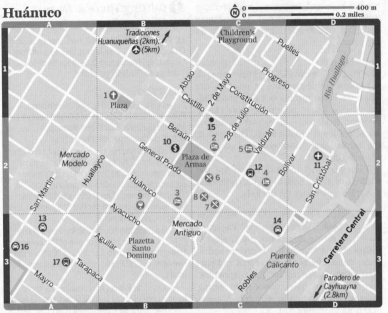

Huánuco

S80/100) The sounds of your own footsteps echo in the immaculate, empty hallways. The rooms (and the cable TV sets within) are big. The drinks in the minibar could be cooler, but at least they're there; ditto for the showers, which could be hotter. A clean, respectable guarantee of a night's sleep. But a Greek Island paradise it ain't.

Grand Hotel Huánuco　　　HOTEL **$$$**
(📞062-51-4222; http://grandhotelhuanuco.com; Beraún 775; s/d/tr incl breakfast S170/240/290; 🅿🛜☒) This grande dame of Huánuco hotels is on the Plaza de Armas. Its public areas are airy and pleasant and its high-ceilinged rooms have solid parquet floors with phone and flat-screen cable TV. The premises include a sauna, gym, billiard room, Jacuzzi, and a pretty good restaurant and bar. Time goes by, and doesn't affect this place much at all.

The hotel's Inka Comfort Restaurant is open from 7am to 10pm.

✖ Eating

Arabica Coffee Cafeteria　　　CAFE **$**
(Calle 28 de Julio 920; coffees from S2; ⊙7am–11:30pm) Serves the city's feistiest coffee by a

country mile, and, for the moment, precious little else. The coffee, though, is enough to make it a popular meeting spot. It's right on the plaza.

Chifa Khon Wa
CHINESE $

(Gral Prado 820; mains S12-22; ⊘ noon-midnight; ⚹) Like a ruthlessly efficient machine the Khon Wa keeps turning out very good Chinese dishes – and these days, more classic Peruvian food, too – in an ever-expanding armory of joints around town. This branch, the largest and most popular, sticks to Chinese-Peruvian.

There's a hotel upstairs if you are too stuffed to stumble back to your accommodation, plus a play park for the kids.

★ Tradiciones Huanuqueñas
PERUVIAN $$

(Huallayco 2444; S20-35; ⊘ 8am-5pm) The quintessential eating experience in Huánuco. Dishes remain true to the Peruvian Andes, prices remain fairly down to earth and portions pose challenges for most appetites. Add on a green, quiet, out-of-town setting and the only question is: why not? A *mototaxi* from the center costs S3.

You might need another fellow eater or two to digest the S50 mountain of meat known as the *ronda huanuqueña*.

Cevicheria El Chalan
CEVICHE $$

(Gral Prado 802; S20-30; ⊘ 10am-4pm) If you're tempted to try ceviche in the Andes just once (many advise against it, because with the fish coming from the coast it is not as fresh) make it at this suave modern place a short hop from the Plaza de Armas. The restaurant has been around for decades, but only recently garnered this great location.

🍷 Drinking & Nightlife

Trapiche
BAR

(Calle 2 de Mayo 924; ⊘ 6pm-1am) Fun, popular and serves a range of cocktails, including some aphrodisiac specials. There's also a branch in Tingo María.

🛈 Information

MEDICAL SERVICES

Clinica Huánuco (☑ 062-51-4026; Constitución 980)

MONEY

Banco Continental (Calle 2 de Mayo at Plaza de Armas) Has a Visa ATM.

🛈 Getting There & Away

AIR

LC Peru (☑ 062-28-0357; www.lcperu.pe; cnr Calles Castillo & 2 de Mayo) flies to and from Lima daily. The airport is 5km north of town. Take a cab (S10) to get there.

BUS & TAXI

Buses go to Lima (S30 to S60, nine hours), Pucallpa (S25 to S35, seven to eight hours), La Merced (S20, six hours) and Huancayo (S20, six hours), with companies all over town.

A *colectivo* (shared transportation) taxi is best for La Unión (S30, four hours) or Tantamayo (S35, five hours), as the ascent is on a narrow corkscrew road. Head to the *cuadra* (block) of Tarapaca between San Martín and Huallayco to find several La Unión *colectivo* companies clamoring for your business.

Take a Pucallpa-bound bus for Tingo María (S10, 2½ to three hours) or one of the **colectivos** (cnr Gral Prado & Robles; S20) from the river end of Gral Prado, which takes around two hours.

For Cerro de Pasco, minibuses (S10, three hours) and *colectivo* taxi (S20, two hours) leave from **Paradero de Cayhuayna** (Carr Central), a 1km *mototaxi* ride from the center, as do *colectivos* to La Oroya and Tarma (S25-30, 4½ hours). You can always catch a ride to Tarma with a La Oroya-bound cab as far as the turnoff at El Cruce (S30-35, 3½ hours) from where other vehicles go down to Tarma.

Bahía Continental (☑ 062-51-9999; Valdizán 718) Luxury buses to Lima.

Colectivos to La Unión (Tarapaca btwn Huallayco & San Martín; S30) Shared transportation for La Unión, to visit the beautiful ruins of Huánuco Viejo.

Transportes Chavín (San Martín btwn Mayro & Tarapaca) *Colectivos* to Tantamayo aren't as common as to La Unión – not least because the road is worse – but these guys offer daily morning services, leaving around 5am. Ideally, come here the day before to book your spot.

Turismo Central (☑ 062-51-1806; www.turismocentral.com.pe; cnr Tarapaca & Abtao) Serves Pucallpa and Huancayo, as well as Lima.

La Unión

🔅 062 / POP 6300 / ELEV 3200M

La Unión is the first (and only) significant community on the bumpy road from Huánuco to Huaraz: and is an exciting way to connect the Central Highlands and the Cordillera Blanca. From here, you can hike to the extensive Inca ruins of Huánuco Viejo.

WORTH A TRIP

TANTAMAYO

Tantamayo was the capital of the pre-Columbian Yarowilca culture, remains of which are scattered throughout the nearby hills. Connected only by rough track to the outside world, the town is ensconced in a green-brown patchwork of fields standing out from the stark, precipitous sides of the Upper Marañon Valley. From this serene, chilly village flows a river that will, hundreds of kilometers downstream, morph into the Amazon itself.

The most impressive ruins around Tantamayo are those at **Piruro** and **Susupillo**. The Yarowilca culture was one of the oldest known in Peru and was architecturally advanced. Buildings were constructed with up to six floors connected via internal spiral staircases, giving them a different appearance to the constructions of the Incas, whom many believe were unable to emulate the superior Yarowilca style.

Both ruins are free to visit. Piruro is easiest to reach, via a 1½ hour walk down from Tantamayo and up the other side of the valley. The path is hard to find; be sure to ask. For Susupillo, vehicles can take you to the village of Florida, a 20-minute drive from Tantamayo, from where you can hike to the site.

There are basic lodgings in Tantamayo, although La Unión has more choice. Tantamayo has public phones (that can't dial internationally) but no listed ones, no cell-phone reception and no banks. Colectivos (shared transportation), minibuses and buses from Huánuco make the journey in anything from five to eight hours (bus S20, colectivo S35). Tantamayo is also connected to La Unión (three hours) from where you can catch onward buses to Huaraz and Lima.

◉ Sights

Huánuco Viejo   RUIN

(admission S5; ⊗8am-6pm) These extensive Inca ruins perch on a swathe of barren *pampa* (pampas grass) at 3700m. There are an incredible 2 sq km of ruins and supposedly more than 1000 buildings and storehouses in total remaining there today. The most impressive structure is the *usnu*, a huge 4m-high ceremonial platform with engravings of animals (monkeys with lion faces) adorning the entrance.

Huánuco Viejo was defended by Illa Tupac, a key figure in the Inca resistance against the Spanish, until 1543, significantly after many Inca settlements had fallen.

Minivans leaving from the market throughout the day (S3) can take you to within a 20-minute walk of the site.

It's a 1½ to two-hour walk from La Unión, starting from behind the central market, where a steep flight of steps lead up to a water tower. From there, the defined path continues through beautiful altiplano (Andean plateau) landscapes. When you've climbed to the plain, look for a road and the ruins visible on open ground to the right. Locals will point you in the right direction.

⌑ Sleeping

Hostal El Viajero   GUESTHOUSE $

(Comercio 1346; r S20-30) This bright red place above a shop, is decent enough by the town of La Unión's basic standards. You really do deserve to be termed a *viajero* (traveler) if you make it all the way out here.

ℹ Getting There & Away

All transport arrives/departs from around the bus terminal on Commercio at the southwest end of town. Companies leave around 6pm to 8pm for Lima (S20 to S30, 10 hours) while a couple of buses daily – plus numerous *colectivos* (shared transportation) – ply the route east to Huánuco (S15-30, five hours) and to Tantamayo (S10, three hours). **El Rapido Bus** (Bus Terminal) has the most user-friendly service to Huaraz, departing at 10:30am (S15, five hours).

Tingo María

🕽 062 / POP 55,000 / ELEV 649M

This languid, humid university and market town lies in the *ceja de la selva* (eyebrow of the jungle), on the cusp between mountains and jungle. Its back rests against the mountains – as the conical, forested hills that flank it testify – but its feet are firmly fixed in the lush, sticky vegetation of the Amazonas region. Tingo María, or Tingo for short, is a popular weekend destination for holidaying *limeños* (inhabitants of Lima), while travelers pause here en route to and from the Amazon.

Around the town, the divine surrounds of Villa Jennifer (p286), open to the public for a fee as well as for guests, are reason enough to stop by. Outside town, the main attraction is Parque Nacional Tingo María:

a lush forested wilderness with caves and great bathing spots.

Sights

Parque Nacional Tingo María PARK

(admission S10) This 180-sq-km park lies to the south of town, around the mouth of the Río Monzón, a tributary of the Río Huallaga. Its most distinguishing feature is the Bella Durmiente (Sleeping Beauty), a hill overlooking the town that, from some angles, resembles a recumbent woman wearing an Inca crown. The park is not without its dangers for tourists, with reports of travelers being robbed and raped at gunpoint in recent years, and it is strongly advised to take a guide with you whichever site you choose to visit.

The main attraction here is one of Peru's biggest show caves, **La Cueva de las Lechuzas** (Parque Nacional Tingo María; admission S10; ⊗8am-6pm). The admission fees gains you access to any of the other park sights, including the waterfalls in the Puente Tres de Mayo area, that you care to see within two days of purchase.

There are many great bathing spots in and around the park. Recommended are the **San Jacintillo Medicinal Springs** (admission S3), 1km before the cave; **Catarata Santa Carmen** (S3) on the southern edge of town; and the waterfalls in the **Puente Tres de Mayo area** (Parque Nacional Tingo María; admission S5) 14km south of Tingo on the Huánuco road.

La Cueva de las Lechuzas has police protection, but the road there is still risky, as are more remote destinations.

☞ Tours

Cesar Manrique de Lara OUTDOORS

(⌨962-086-065; half-day tour S80) A recommended guide for taking you out in his *mototaxi* to the sights of Parque Nacional Tingo María. Cesar is always contactable through Villa Jennifer.

Sleeping

La Gran Muralla I HOTEL $

(⌨062-56-2934; www.hotel-lagranmuralla.com; Raimondi 277; s/d from S50/75) This breezy riverside complex has a light, bright feel to it, exemplified by its welcoming lobby painted with jungle scenes. Its modern rooms are of a decent size and have cable TV, fans and phones. From the 2nd-floor terrace, gaze over a river to the airport and the jungle beyond. About the best hotel in Tingo María center.

★ Villa Jennifer LODGE $$

(⌨062-56-1555; www.villajennifer.com; Castillo Grande Km 3.4; dm S50, s/d from S100/150; P ⊛ ✉) This peaceful tropical enclave is run by a Danish-Peruvian couple who have done wonders with a lush expanse of tropical bushland bounded by rivers on two sides. Suave rustic accommodations range from simple rooms with shared bathrooms to airy mini-homes that can sleep up to 10 people. Common to all is the relaxation space: terraces, sun beds, patios, gardens... paradise.

Listing the other highlights of a stay takes a while. You could spot monkeys capering through the treetops, play table tennis, darts or table soccer, or catch a movie in the DVD lounge. In the excellent **restaurant** (open 7:45am to 9pm), be sure to try the local fruit *anonas* (custard apples) which are delectable. There are also two swimming pools and mini-golf. Not to be missed is the 30-minute hike up to a *mirador* (lookout) on a sheer conical hill above the property. The lodge is located north of Tingo's airport.

Eating

El Encanto de la Selva AMAZONIAN $

(cnr Alameda Perú & Monzón; mains S10-20; ⊗6am-10pm) For local jungle specialties this bright, two-floor establishment ticks all the boxes. Try *tacacho con cecina* (a bed of barbecued banana pummeled into rice-sized grains with dried, smoked meat on top) and wash it down with some cool coconut juice. It's simple, satisfying food. If you need to eat in the center of town, make it here.

❶ Information

SAFE TRAVEL

In recent years there have been reports of travelers being robbed and raped at gunpoint within Parque Nacional Tingo María. We do not recommend venturing into the countryside around Tingo without a guide. Even with a guide, ensure you return before dark. Increased police protection at park attractions has, however, improved security dramatically.

Furthermore, the Huallaga Valley running north of Tingo to Tarapoto is a cocaine-production area and one of the last bastions of the Sendero Luminoso (Shining Path). Risk to tourists from drugs traffickers and the Sendero Luminoso is low but care should still be taken.

MONEY

BCP (Raymondi 249) Changes US cash and has a Visa ATM.

TOURIST INFORMATION

Oficina de Turismo (☑ 999-544-648; Av Alameda Perú s/n, Municipio; ⊙ 8am–noon & 12:30–5:45pm Mon-Fri)

ⓘ Getting There & Away

AIR

LC Peru (☑ 062-56-1672; www.lcperu.pe; Raymondi 571; ⊙ 9am–7pm Mon-Fri, to 6pm Sat) operates daily flights, Monday to Saturda, between Tingo and Lima.

BUS & TAXI

Transport here mostly serves Lima and destinations in between, such as Huánuco, as well as local villages and Pucallpa. The road between Tingo and Pucallpa can be risky and is best done in daylight.

Buses to Lima (S50 to S70, 11 to 12 hours) are operated, among others, by **Transportes León de Huánuco** (☑ 062-56-2030, 962-56-2030; Pimentel 164). Buses usually leave at 7am or 7pm. Some operators, also including León de Huánuco and **Turismo Central** (Raymondi 967-969), go to Pucallpa (S20, nine hours). A faster service to Pucallpa is with **Turismo Ucayali** (Tito Jaime Fernández s/n, cuadra 2) which has *colectivos* (shared transportation; S45, 4 ½ hours).

From around the gas station on Av Raymondi near the León de Huánuco bus terminal, *colectivos* depart to Huánuco (S20, 2½ to three hours) and other destinations. Minivans do the same journey from the same place for about S5 less.

Huallaga Express (☑ 942-607-742; Raymondi cuadra 1 s/n) has cars north to Tocache (S40, three to four hours) and eventually Tarapoto (S95, nine hours). Tarapoto vehicles go direct if there's the demand but normally you'll have to change at Tocache or Janjui or both. Do this journey only in daylight, and only if you must.

ⓘ Getting Around

A *mototaxi* to the Cueva de las Lechuzas is about S25 for the round-trip, including a wait at the cave. The southern part of Parque Nacional Tingo María, Puente Tres de Mayo area, will command a slightly higher *mototaxi* fee, including a wait to visit the waterfalls.

LIMA TO TARMA

This is the most-used artery from Lima up into the heart of the central highlands in the Río Mantaro Valley. However, most travelers whiz straight past the pretty places en route – which include rock formations, Inca ruins, caves and craft villages. Don't join them – make a stop-off here.

ⓘ **ALTITUDE**

Because of the altitude, it's not advisable to go to Marcahuasi from Lima in one day; acclimatize overnight in San Pedro. It takes two hours to hike the 2km to the site; you can sometimes catch a bus (departing 7:30am from the plaza most days) part of the way if it's not engaged on other municipality business, then hike for 45 minutes.

San Pedro de Casta & Marcahuasi

POP 1300

Isolated San Pedro de Casta (elevation 3200m), a mountainside town clustered around a ridge and resounding with the bellows of *burros* (donkeys), is the perfect precursor to your Central Andes adventure. People come here principally to visit the little-known archaeological site of Marcahuasi. The road from Chosica twists spectacularly upward for 40km around a sheer-sided valley before arriving here.

◉ Sights

Marcahuasi   ROCK FORMATION

FREE This little-known archaeological site sits above San Pedro de Casta on a 4-sq-km plateau at 4100m. It's famed for its weirdly eroded rocks shaped into animals, such as camels, turtles and seals. The formations have a mystical significance for some people, who claim they are signs of a pre-Inca culture or energy vortices. The walk up here from San Pedro is breath-sapping, but a delight.

🛏 Sleeping

Gran Hotel Turístico Municipal   HOSTAL **$**
(☑ 963-010-643; r without bathroom S20) San Pedro de Casta's only hotel is not as grand as its name suggests, but it gives you a roof over your head after the exertions of climbing up to Marcahuasi.

ⓘ Getting There & Away

Getting to San Pedro entails taking a bus from Lima to Chosica; minibuses to Chosica can be picked up in Central Lima from Arica at Plaza Bolognesi (S3.50, two hours).

In Choisica ask for Transportes Municipal San Pedro, which leaves from the bus yard by Parque Echenique on Choisica's main drag (Carr Central) at 9am and 3pm (S10, four hours). The bus back to Choisica leaves at 2pm.

Tarma

📍 064 / POP 46,000 / ELEV 3050M

Travelers seldom make it to Tarma, but they should. One of the region's most welcoming cities with a clement climate by altiplano (Andean plateau) standards, this is a great stopover. Surrounded on all sides by scrubby, brown-dirt mountains hiding some intriguing day trips, it's also poised on the cusp of the *ceja de la selva* (eyebrow of the jungle) with a road linking the central Andes to the Amazon Basin and its associated attractions.

Limeños (inhabitants of Lima) come here en route to experience the nearest accessible jungle to their desert capital and the city is now cottoning-on to tourism. Tarma can be used as a base for exploring *la selva central* (Central Amazon) as well as the locales mentioned here.

Idyllic accommodations, and a scattering of nearby Inca ruins, all set around a fertile valley famed for its flower growing, enhance Tarma's allure.

◉ Sights

Astronomical Observatory OBSERVATORY
(www.facebook.com/observatorioafari; Huánuco 614; admission S5) A small astronomical observatory above Hospedaje Central takes advantage of Tarma's high-elevation location, where the clear nights of June, July and August provide ideal opportunities for stargazing (though the surrounding mountains do limit the amount of observable heavens). Admission includes a talk (in Spanish) on constellations and a peek at some stars. The bad news: it only opens sporadically in the aforementioned months.

Try the Facebook page for details of openings, which are often during festival days or holidays.

Tarmatambo ARCHAEOLOGICAL SITE
FREE The best known of the myriad archaeological ruins near Tarma, this was the capital of the Taruma culture and later a major Inca administrative center. The fairly extensive remains include storehouses, palaces and an impressive, still-used aqueduct system. Unlike other Peruvian places with the suffix 'tambo,' this really was a genuine *tambo* (Inca way-station camp). Tarmatambo is 6km south of Tarma.

Ask at the tourist office (p290) about guides to take you there and to other sites: going solo, these ruins are difficult to find. Independent travelers can take a

Jauja-bound bus to Tarmatambo village on the main road below the ruins.

From Tarmatambo, a rarely used **Camino del Inca** (Inca road) forges over the hills down to Jauja: there's basic accommodations in Tarmatambo but it's then a strenuous (but beautiful) all-day hike to Jauja (40km).

☞ Tours

Max Aventura OUTDOORS
(📞 064-32-3908; http://maxaventuraperu.com; Jirón 2 de Mayo 682, cnr Lima) This agency covers the plethora of Tarma's nearby sights – caves, handicrafts, Inca ruins, waterfalls, you name it – as well as la *selva central*. There are many agencies in Tarma with similar offerings, but this one is a little above average, as English is spoken. It's a skip down from the Plaza de Armas.

🛏 Sleeping

Choices in Tarma itself are limited to unspectacular budget options and one expensive resort hotel. A short ride from town, some attractive haciendas (traditional farmhouses, now converted into B&Bs) compensate with atmospheric accommodations.

Most budget hotels have hot water, usually in the morning, though they may claim all day.

Residencial el Dorado GUESTHOUSE $
(📞 064-32-4151; www.hospedajeeldoradotarma. com; Huánuco 488; s/d S40/50) Sizable, clean, occasionally worn rooms face a leafy internal courtyard and come with cable TV and hot showers. Friendly staff and an in-house cafeteria help make this central Tarma's most backpacker-friendly sleeping option.

★Hacienda La Florida HACIENDA $$
(📞 064-34-1041; www.haciendalaflorida.com; s/d/ ste incl breakfast from S125/215/286; P❄🖰) 🐾 This 300-year-old working hacienda is owned by a welcoming Peruvian-German couple, Pepe and Inge. The substantial, prettily decorated rooms flank a large courtyard and boast wooden parquet floors and private bathrooms. There's space for campers (per person S20) and the filling breakfasts (everything homemade!) have a delectable German slant. It's 6km from Tarma on the Acobamba road.

Visitors can stroll the trails on the property, partake in farm life or take various two-day workshops (minimum of six people) on relaxation techniques and cooking classes. El Señor de Muruhuay (p290) shrine is a one-hour hike away, and tours to other

Tarma

Tarma

local sights, such as Yanamarca (p290), are available.

Contact the hacienda by phone; email is not always checked.

Hacienda Santa María HACIENDA $$
(☎ 064-32-1232; www.haciendasantamaria.com; Vista Alegre 1249; s/d incl breakfast from S85/170; ℗) This charming hacienda is a white-walled, 18th-century colonial house with wooden balconies perfect for surveying the surrounding lush, flower-abundant grounds strung with hammocks. Rustic rooms are full of old furniture. There is also a clutch of alternative local tours that the owners can arrange. It's 1km after Calle Vienrich becomes Vista Alegre to the northeast of town.

Los Balcones HOTEL $$
(☎ 064-32-3600; www.balconeshoteltarma.com; Lima, btwn Paucartambo & Moquegua; r incl breakfast S100-195; 🅰) This hotel in a revamped colonial style and a convenient half-block from the Plaza de Armas appears idyllic,

but something is lacking. Despite the rooms ticking all the boxes, a certain soullessness wafts around inside.

Los Portales HOTEL $$$
(☎ 064-32-1411; www.losportaleshoteles.com.pe; Castilla 512; d/ste incl breakfast S210/290; ❄ @ 🅰) The best choice for accommodations in Tarma city itself, the 'LP' is set in secluded gardens in the west of town. Its refined mustard facade conceals 44 standard hotel rooms with cable TV and wi-fi. There's even a children's playground. Rates include continental breakfast and the restaurant provides room service. The two suites have Jacuzzis.

The town's best disco, Kimera, is also on the premises, along with a popular fast-food chicken outlet.

✖ Eating

★**Daylo Cocina Peruana-Fusion** FUSION $
(☎ 064-32-3048; cnr Lima & Jauja; mains S15-30; ⊙noon-11:30pm) With one stylish opening,

LESSER KNOWN SIGHTS AROUND TARMA

El Señor de Muruhuay (near Acobamba; ⊙ dawn-dusk) This white shrine visible on a hill 1.5km from Acobamba is one of Peru's top pilgrimage sites, built around a rock etching of Christ crucified. A small chapel replaced the previous roughly thatched hut at the site in 1835 and the present sanctuary, inaugurated in 1972, is a modern building with an electronically controlled bell tower. It's decorated with huge weavings from San Pedro de Cajas. Acobamba is 9km from Tarma.

San Pedro de Cajas Peaceful San Pedro, some 40km into the hills from Tarma, is the production center for the country's finest *tapices* (tapestries). Most of the village is involved in making these high-quality and highly regarded woven wall hangings, depicting moving scenes from rural Peruvian life. You can watch locals weaving in workshops round the Plaza de Armas: it's one of Peru's best opportunities for witnessing handicraft production – and purchasing the results.

Yanamarca A dramatic hilltop testament to both the power of the pre-Inca peoples and the extent to which their cultures are barely known about. The buildings here, of which there are many, are two or three tiers high, and bear certain similarities to those of the Yarowilka culture found near Tantamayo. It is thought the circular structures were storehouses, and the rectangular ones were used for sleeping. The view from here is superb too.

With no Google Maps pinpoint, no real online information and no on-site noticeboards, it is up to the observer to intuit what Yanamarca, up a twisting dead-end track from Tarma at well over 4000m altitude, was really all about.

Vehicles make the journey up from Tarma from besides Hacienda La Florida (p288). Alternatively, get transport to the village to Pilcoy, just beyond Acobamba, and walk up (three hours).

Gruta de Huagapo (near Palcomayo; ⊙ dawn-dusk) This huge limestone cave ranks among Peru's largest subterranean systems. A proper descent into the Gruta de Huagapo requires caving equipment and experience: tourist facilities consist only of a few ropes. The cave contains waterfalls, squeezes and underwater sections (scuba equipment required). It is possible to enter the cave for a short distance, but you soon need technical gear. It's about 28km up on the way to San Pedro (just past the village of Palcomayo).

Daylo has whirled Tarma's eating scene from the culinary-wasteland category up into refined dining. Food in this intimately designed venue veers away from traditional Peruvian, but doesn't lose sight of these influences. A 'Chinese-style' ceviche goes down a treat with a Chilean wine, for example. And we've rarely seen carpaccio done so well in Peru.

Coffee & Friends CAFE **$**
(Huancayo 347-A; coffees from S3; ⊙ 5-10:30pm daily) The best coffee and cakes in town. Sometimes also open in the morning on Fridays, Saturdays and Sundays.

Restaurant Chavín de Grima PERUVIAN **$**
(Lima 270; meals S17-22; ⊙ 7am-10pm) You won't go far wrong by heading to this veritable institution on the Plaza de Armas for breakfasts and cheap set lunches. A wholesome two-course *menú del día* (set menu of the day) can cost as little as S5. A classic old-school Andes sit-down restaurant.

Hacienda La Florida Restaurant PERUVIAN **$$**
(http://haciendalaflorida.com; mains S20; ⊙ 8am-7pm) This courtyard restaurant serves divine homemade Peruvian-German food that you can enjoy in a peaceful farm setting. Serves breakfast, lunch and dinner, though customers not staying at the hacienda need to reserve in advance.

❶ Information

MONEY

BCP (Lima at Paucartambo) You can change money here; it also has an ATM.

TOURIST INFORMATION

Tourist Office (cnr Jirón 2 de Mayo & Lima; ⊙ 10am-1pm & 3-5:45pm Mon-Fri) On the Plaza de Armas.

❶ Getting There & Away

Most public transport now arrives/departs from the sparkling new **Terminal Terrestre** (cnr Vienrich & Arequipa). There are no shortage of buses to Lima (S30 to S75, six hours). Buses to the central jungle destinations like La Merced (bus S10, *colectivo* S15, two hours) leave from here too, although you can go to Estadio Unión and wait for the frequently passing *colectivos* (shared transportation) and *combis* (minibuses). To forge further into the jungle, La Merced has more transport options.

BUS

Edatur (📞 951-974-261; Terminal Terrestre) Has good services down to the jungle, with San Ramón, La Merced and Satipo served about hourly.

Los Canarios (📞 064-32-3357; Amazonas 694) The best option for going to Huancayo, with small buses (S10, three hours) via Jauja (S7, two hours) leaving almost hourly from 5am to 6pm from their own separate terminal.

OTHER TRANSPORT

On either side of the **gas station** (cnr Castila & Vienrich) at the intersection of Lima, Vienrich and Castilla, **colectivo** (shared transportation) taxis take up to four passengers to Lima (S50 each) or to local destinations, such as Junín and La Oroya (S15). If you want to go to Cerro de Pasco (S25, about four hours), change for onward services to Huánuco, you can take *colectivos* from here, too, though you might have to change at El Cruce (the crossroads of the Tarma and La Oroya–Cerro de Pasco roads).

For colectivos to Huancayo (S20) the departure point is a bit more orderly, opposite the entrance to Terminal Terrestre (on the other side of the chicken restaurant).

From **Estadio Unión** (end of Chanchamayo) (a *mototaxi* here costs S2), Amazon-bound vehicles head via Acobamba (S2, 10 minutes) down to San Ramón and La Merced. The journey to La Merced is spectacular, dropping about 2.5km vertically into the jungle in the space of just over an hour. For destinations beyond La Merced, change at La Merced's convenient bus terminal.

Colectivos for Gruta de Huagapo (S8) and San Pedro de Cajas (S9) leave from the northern end of Moquegua.

RÍO MANTARO VALLEY

The meandering Río Mantaro opens out on a wide, fertile agricultural plain southeast of Tarma, revealing a gentler side to the mostly rugged highlands: undulating pastoral panoramas, the sophisticated city of Huancayo and, dotted in-between, various villages internationally renowned for the quality of their handicrafts.

Festivals are a way of life here. Residents say that there is a festival occurring each day of the year, and chancing upon some colorful celebration is highly likely. Also colorful is the local legend holding that back in the mists of time, two huge snakes had a battle, with the loser falling to earth to form the Río Mantaro.

For those who still crave remoter adventures, there are high-altitude hikes and even kayaking opportunities right down the valley. From Huancayo, some classic Andean travel routes connect through the hard-going but delightfully scenic valleys south to Huancavelica, Ayacucho, Andahuaylas and eventually on to Cuzco.

Jauja

📞 064 / POP 15,000 / ELEV 3250M

This small, bustling colonial town of narrow traffic-swamped streets offers a few basic accommodations, which can be used as a base for sampling area attractions, including a lakeside resort and several interesting hikes.

Jauja was Francisco Pizarro's first capital in Peru, though this honor was short-lived. There are both Inca and pre-Inca associations with Jauja, with remnants of both visible around about.

Coming from Lima, Jauja is the first place you pass along this route; about 60km southeast of Tarma and 50km north of Huancayo.

◉ Sights

Finely carved wooden altars in **Iglesia Matriz de Santa Fe** (Plaza de Armas), the main church, are all that remain of Jauja's early colonial days.

A well-preserved **Camino del Inca** (Inca road) runs from Jauja to Tarma. The most spectacular section begins by Tingopaccha (30 minutes from Jauja by taxi).

Before the Incas, this area was home to an important Huanca indigenous community. **Huanca ruins** can be seen on a hill 3km southeast of Jauja.

✕ Eating

El Paraíso   PERUVIAN $
(Ayacucho 917; mains from S15; ⊙noon-4pm & 6-9pm) The best eatery in town is this vast plant-filled restaurant popular with locals who are attracted by bargain specialties such as *trucha* (river trout) from Laguna de Paca and *picante de cuy* (roast guinea pig

RÍO MANTARO VALLEY VILLAGES

Two main road systems link Huancayo with the villages of the Río Mantaro Valley: *izquierda* is the east and *derecha* is the west side of the river, as you head into Huancayo from the north. It's best to confine your sightseeing on any given day to one side or the other, as few bridges link the two sides.

Perhaps the most interesting excursion on the east side is a visit to the twin villages of Cochas Grande and Cochas Chico, about 11km from Huancayo. These villages are the major production centers for the incised gourds that have made the district famous.

On the west side, the town of Chupaca has an interesting livestock market. Starting early, you can visit and continue by bus to Ahuac, then hike or take a minibus a further 2km up to Laguna Ñahuimpuquio FREE, which offers restaurants and boat rides. From the east shore a path climbs to a ridge for great valley views and Inca ruins.

Other villages known for their handicrafts include San Agustín de Cajas (wicker furniture); Hualhuas (wool products, including ponchos and weavings); and San Jerónimo de Tunán (filigree silverwork).

While most trading is done in Huancayo, the villages are easily visited from the city. They have few facilities but there is no substitute for the experience of seeing the crafts in the villages themselves (plus the quality of the handicrafts is superior to what is available in Huancayo's markets). The key is an ability to speak some Spanish and make friends with the locals.

---

in a spicy sauce). It's just south of the main plaza.

ℹ Getting There & Away

Jauja is well-connected, with the regional airport offering daily flights to Lima, and buses or taxis departing regularly for destinations through the Río Mantaro Valley as well as Lima and Tarma.

Concepción

Set around beautiful gardens and courtyards, Santa Rosa de Ocopa (Ocapa; admission S5, students S2.50; ⏰9am-noon & 3-6pm Wed-Mon) convent was originally built by Franciscans in the early 18th century as a center for missionaries heading into the jungle. The friars accrued an impressive collection of artifacts, now displayed in the museum, and developed a stunning library of some 25,000 volumes (the convent's highlight), with many of its titles dating back to the 15th century.

Admission is by 45-minute guided tour (hourly or once large-enough groups have congregated – seven-person minimum).

Exhibits in the museum include stuffed jungle wildlife, indigenous artifacts, photographs of early missionary work and a large collection of colonial religious art, mainly in the *escuela cuzqueña* style – a combination of Spanish and Andean artistic styles.

Frequent *colectivos* (shared transportation) leave Monday to Saturday from the plaza in Concepción for Ocopa, about 5km

away. *Mototaxis* charge S20 for the return trip, inclusive of an hour's wait.

Concepción is easily visited by taking a Huancayo–Jauja *izquierda* (east side of the valley) bus.

Huancayo

📞 064 / POP 365,000 / ELEV 3244M

The mega-metropolis of the central altiplano (Andean plateau), bustling Huancayo mixes its modern facade with a strong underlying sense of tradition. For many, this self-confident, cosmopolitan city will be their first experience of the Peruvian highlands – it stands within a lush valley on an exciting overland mountain route to Cuzco – and while its charms are less obvious than those of other Andean locales, Huancayo does not disappoint.

The town has some of Peru's finest dining outside of Lima and Cuzco, with well-appointed restaurants serving the region's renowned cuisine. Peru's most interesting handicrafts are sold in the markets here and in the valley beyond, and vibrant, varied fiestas take place almost daily.

There's also Andes trekking and extreme mountain biking and, to top it all off, Huancayo is the terminus for two of Peru's (and South America's) best railway journeys, including the world's second-highest railway over the Andes to and from Lima.

⊙ Sights

Huancayo is a sizable town; you'll end up doing a lot of walking. Most actual attractions lie outside the center. In the city itself, and outside too, the focus is more on experiencing – savoring the taste of seemingly endless quality restaurants, or perhaps trying a language or handicrafts course. The most notable landmark is the Iglesia de La Merced (cnr Castilla & Ayacucho), at the first block of Real, where the Peruvian Constitution of 1839 was approved.

Iglesia de La Inmaculada　　　CHURCH
(cnr Ica & Amazonas) FREE With its duel cupolas capped in sky-blue, this may be a modern place of worship (built 1965), but it is also one of Huancayo's prettier churches.

Cerro de la Libertad　　　VIEWPOINT
(cnr Giráldez & Torre Tagle; ⊙24hr) A popular recreational and dining locale with a great view of the city, as well as artwork stalls and a playground. It's about 2km from the town center; head northeast on Giráldez to get here.

Parque de la Identidad Huanca　　　PARK
This fanciful park is full of stone statues of famous regional personalities, as well as miniature buildings representing the area's culture. It's in the suburb of San Antonio, 3km northeast of the center.

⸚ Activities

Torre Torre　　　HIKING
The eroded geological formations of Torre Torre (*torre* means 'tower'; some outcrops here are thus shaped) lie 2km up in the hills beyond Cerro de la Libertad. Initially head east from Cerro de la Libertad on Taylor, from where a fairly obvious path ascends to the formations.

To make a longer route, continue along the ridge keeping Huancayo to your left (west). You'll eventually reach another rock formation, known as Corona del Fraile (Crown of the Monk), a round-topped rock surrounded by a crown of eucalyptus trees, below which are several waterfalls.

You can return to Huancayo from this end of the ridge. While safe enough during daylight hours, beware of the packs of stray dogs, particularly around the houses below Torre Torre.

☞ Tours

Incas del Perú　　　ADVENTURE
(☏064-39-3298; www.incasdelperu.org; cnr Prolongación Cusco & Federico Galvez Durand) This tour outfitter's ever-active Lucho Hurtado, a local who speaks English and knows the surrounding area well, organizes an incredible array of activities. For the fit, he arranges demanding, multiday Andean mountain-trekking expeditions to the lake and glacier in the nearby mountains (three days & two nights per person S1170). Incas del Perú is located in the La Cabaña (p297) restaurant.

There are also extreme mountain-biking excursions (day trips per person S425) or horse-riding treks (two-person minimum, day trips per person S280) on offer down the eastern slopes of the Andes and into high jungle. It isn't luxurious, but it's a good chance to experience something of the real rural Peru.

Incas del Perú also arrange Spanish and Quechua lessons, including meals and accommodations with a local family (if you wish), for S650 to S1000 per week. Lessons can be modified to fit your interests. You can also learn to cook regional dishes, engage in the local handicraft of gourd carving or discover how to play Andean panpipes.

⚎ Festivals & Events

Año Nuevo　　　TRADITIONAL DANCE
(⊙Jan 1-6) New Year's festivities in Huancayo are some of Peru's most unusual. Dances performed include the *huaconada,* in which revelers dress up to look like quirky old men with big noses, representing village elders who, in times past, would drop by the houses of lazy or mischief-making villagers and whip them into behaving for the coming year. Plenty of butt-whipping still takes place.

Mito, an hour north of Huancayo, and where the *huaconada* originates, also has vivid celebrations.

Semana Santa　　　RELIGIOUS
(⊙Mar or Apr) One of the biggest events in Huancayo, with big religious processions attracting people from all over Peru in the week leading up to Easter.

⸝ Sleeping

La Casa de la Abuela　　　HOSTEL $
(☏064-22-3303; www.incasdelperu.com; Federico Galvez Durand, near cnr Prolongación Cusco; dm/s/d without bathroom incl breakfast S35/60/80; ℙ@⧖) This hostel run by tour operator Incas del Perú makes every effort to welcome tired travelers. The brightly painted house is clean and friendly, with inviting chill-out areas, kitchen facilities, cable TV and

Huancayo

La Tullpa
(700m)

Ferrocarril

J.C Tello

14

Parra del Riego

20

6

Jirón Libertad

Castilla

Arequipa

EL TAMBO

Santa Rosa

Huancavelica

Malecon

Psje.
Salesiano

Río Shulcas

Pasaje
Verand

38
37
36
30
31

Ayacucho

35
3

40
33

Cuzco

17

2

Real

Ancash

5
4

7
16

Puno

12

13

10

Giráldez

Ayacucho

Cuzco

Plaza de la
Constitución

19

Puno

25

26

24

Breña

Moquegua

Lima

Libertad

Loreto

Arequipa

Centro
Cívico

11

Cuzco

21

27

Feria
Dominical

Puno

Junín

Breña

Lima

Loreto

Huancavelica

Ica

Piura

Cajamarca

18

Huánuco

15

Huánuco

Cajamarca

Huánuco

Tarapaca

Angaraes

Parque de la
Identidad Huanca
(1.6km)

Incas del Perú
(350m);
La Casa de la
Abuela (350m)

Cerro de la
Libertad
(700m)

Real
Plaza
Mall

Central
Train
Station

Plaza
Amazonas

Municipalidad

Chilca
(550m)

DVD. It's popular with backpackers for its amenable dorms and compact rooms with shared bathrooms. Now in a new location a 25-minute walk from central Huancayo.

Rates include a great continental breakfast with bread and homemade jam and real, freshly brewed coffee. Good tourist information is available too, on-site and at the nearby La Cabaña (p297) restaurant. It's worth being further from the center to be here.

Hotel los Balcones
HOTEL $

(📞064-21-1041; www.losbalconeshuancayo.com. pe; Puno 282; s/d/tr S/50/60/75; @ 🛜) Sporting plenty of namesake, hard-to-miss balconies, this is an attractive, modern, airy and spacious hotel. Tastefully furnished rooms come with cable TV, phone, alarm clock and reading lights; there's complimentary internet access and a busy in-house restaurant too. Look no further for reasonably priced city-center comfort: when you weigh up price against location and amenities, this place comes out tops.

Hotel Confort
HOTEL $

(📞064-23-3601; Ancash 237; s/d S40/50; 🅿) We'll put our neck on the line here: this is among the best deals in Huancayo city center. As for the *confort* (comfort), 40 nuevo soles won't get you much more anywhere in Peru. Cleaned conscientiously, it's a real survivor, around for decades. In a little-anticipated move, a second branch of the city's smartest cafe, Coqui (p297), has opened underneath.

★ Hotel Turismo
HOTEL $$

(📞064-23-1072; https://turismo.hotelpresidente. com.pe; Ancash 729; s/d from S165/225; 🛜) Where its sister establishment Hotel Presidente (p297) lacks a little in character, this older, more elegant lodging evokes an air of bygone grandeur. The building has wooden balconies, beautiful public areas hung with San Pedro de Cajas tapestries and good views of the plaza outside the Centro Civico. Rooms vary in size and quality, but all will leave you perfectly satisfied.

The on-site restaurant is good, there's a bar with live music at weekends and guests can use the gorgeous antique billiards table, too.

Blub Hotel Spa
HOTEL $$

(📞064-22-1692; www.blubhotelspa.com; Psje Verand 187; s/d incl breakfast S140/200; 🛜) The tucked-away Blub has grown from dithering midrange into one of Huancayo's best sleeps. Its well-appointed, inviting rooms each have

Huancayo

a big flat-screen cable TV, telephone, minibar and '70s-style bathroom. As the name implies, there's a small spa area with a sauna and a nice restaurant too. The hotel overlooks the river (or its bone-dry bed).

Why 'Blub'? It's a crying shame, but the staff we asked didn't have the foggiest idea either.

Hotel Gran Palma HOTEL $$
(☏064-60-3954; http://hotelgranpalma.com/huancayo; Parra del Riego 749, El Tambo; s/d incl breakfast S150/190) This large, sleek white four-floor building in El Tambo is making a bold move, planting an upscale hotel in a district not renowned for such things. But it does everything pretty well. The rooms are none too big, but modern, quiet and very comfortable, with reading lights and flatscreen cable TV, plus there is a restaurant, sauna and conference center.

Isha Hotel BUSINESS HOTEL $$
(☏064-23-1389; Av Giraldez 246; s/d incl breakfast S130/170; @🖧) The best newcomer among Huancayo's central hotels, the Isha attempts to brighten a desperately ugly part of Av Giraldez. Rooms are very smart, although

a fair few don't have outside windows. The hotel is entered, in unorthodox fashion, through a Chinese restaurant (reception is on the 2nd floor).

There's a business center (computers and good wi-fi) and a conference room, which is presumably what prompts the Isha to brand itself a business hotel, rather than the quality of the rooms which is, come crunch time, only a notch above the city average.

Susan's Hotel HOTEL $$
(☏064-20-2251; Real 851; s/d S65/S80-110; 🖧) A clean and cheerful-enough midrange option that hasn't quite shaken off the snarly service from its more budget-focused days, Susan's has a warren of rooms with good-sized bathrooms, cable TV, writing desks and firm mattresses. Rooms can be dark; get one at the rear for peace and quiet, and head to the nice 5th-floor restaurant for light and views.

Hostal El Marquez HOSTAL $$
(☏064-21-9026; www.elmarquezhuancayo.com; Puno 294; s/d/ste incl breakfast S160/190/220; @🖧) The El Marquez is an anomaly. It's outwardly appealing, comfortable and better than most, yet is inexplicably lacking in

character and service, and, price-wise, has a delusional idea of its own worth. Recently renovated, carpeted rooms get all the expected trappings, while several suites feature Jacuzzis, king-sized beds and minibars. A small cafe offers room service.

Hotel Presidente HOTEL $$

(☑ 064-23-1275; https://huancayo.hotelpresidente.com.pe; Real 1138; s/d incl breakfast S195/245; ℗@☎) A good, modern and, perhaps most appealingly, quiet hotel, the Presidente sports large, nicely carpeted rooms and spacious bathrooms. Most rooms have desks and some have minibars. Part of a mini-chain found in Huancavelica and the Central Amazon.

✕ Eating

Huancayo has some fabulous restaurants: regional specialties include *papas a la huancaína* (boiled potatoes in a creamy sauce of cheese, oil, pepper, lemon and egg yolk, served with boiled egg and olives). The city is also known for its *trucha* (trout), reared in nearby lakes.

The cool new area for dining and going out is Parque Túpac Amaru.

Leopardo PERUVIAN $

(cnr Libertad & Huánuco; mains S15-49; ⊙6:30am-5:30pm) Effortlessly combining common-people's cafeteria with upscale restaurant, this joint is *so* Huancayo, right down to the model train in the central dining area. Go Andean with *mondongo* (broth made with maize, tripe, minced pork hoof and vegetables), or go coastal with *tacu tacu* (a concoction of beans, rice and chili fried golden-brown and served with steak).

Leonardo is so popular it's opened an identical restaurant right across the street, and won the undying affection of at least one hungry travel writer.

Café Coqui BAKERY $

(Puno 298; breakfasts S12-16, mains S10-30; ⊙7am-11pm) This modern bakery/coffee shop is a contender for the best breakfast stop in the Central Andes, serving tasty sandwiches, pastries, empanadas, real espresso and other coffees. It's lively from morning until evening and now even does a line in pizzas and other more substantial fare.

You can find other good but less characterful branches under Hotel Confort (p295), a stone's throw away, and on the 2nd floor of Real Plaza Mall (p298).

Zalema Social Coffee CAFE $

(www.facebook.com/Zalemacoffee; Amazonas 461; S5-15; ⊙12:30-11pm Mon-Sat) Keep your eye on this neat little bohemian space: if it keeps on like this, it's really going places. Understated decoration themed around the other passion of the owners (mountain climbing), a laid-back feel, decent coffee, an open fire come evenings and humble but tasty local food, much of it served tapas-style, are just some of the reasons why.

Sofa Café Paris CAFE $

(Puno 252; snacks/light meals from S6-15; ⊙noon-3pm & 4-11pm Mon-Sat; ☎) With the chilled vibe you'd hope from the name, this is a lively venue with a wrap-around mezzanine level to oversee the action below. It favors Nirvana over Andean music and is frequented by trendy young *huancaínos* (Huancayo residents). It does elaborate coffees – in what must be Huancayo's second coffee machine – and cakes, alongside other more substantial Peruvian fare.

The retro pics of London on the walls make one wonder if the decorators ran out of moody Paris images.

★ La Cabaña INTERNATIONAL $$

(mains S20-30; ⊙6-11pm; ☎) This haunt is popular with locals and travelers alike for its relaxed ambience, hearty food and tasty pisco sours (grape brandy cocktails). When you're suitably mellow, order a scrumptious pizza or graze on trout, juicy grills and al dente pastas. It's worth a visit for its wacky decor alone. The soundtrack? Rock-and-roll classics.

Huancahuasi PERUVIAN $$

(☑ 064-24-4826; www.huancahuasi.com; Castilla 2222, El Tambo; mains S20-40; ⊙8am-6pm) This classy establishment is the local eatery of choice in El Tambo district, where Real becomes Castilla northwest of town. A flower-filled courtyard and walls decorated with San Pedro de Cajas tapestries and poems set the ambience for tucking into regional goodies such as *pachamanca*.

Other delights include *papas a la huancaína* (potatoes with a creamy cheese sauce) and *ceviche de trucha* (river-trout ceviche). It's all well presented and the service comes with a smile. Lunchtime is best for a visit; at other times it can be very quiet. A taxi ride from the center is S3.

Detrás de la Catedral PERUVIAN $$

(Ancash 335; mains S10-35; ⊙11am-11pm) This well-run, attractively presented place exudes a woody, warm feeling and has garnered plenty of regular patrons with its broad menu: a flight of steps up from the usual chicken-and-rice choices. Enjoy filling burgers (veggie or meat), specials such as *asado catedral* (barbecued meats done in house style) and very, very lovely *trucha* (river trout).

Save room for the tasty desserts, such as chocolate-drenched *pionono helado* (pastry with caramel filling). Surrealist murals of traditional Andean life grace the walls.

La Tullpa   PERUVIAN **$$**
(☎ 064-25-3649; www.latullpa.com; Atahualpa 145, El Tambo; mains S15-30; ⊙11:30am-5pm) Currently one of the best restaurants in Huancayo, La Tullpa has a simple but attractive wood-floored interior which leads through archways onto a plant-draped courtyard. The gastronomy of the central Andes is showcased here through the likes of *papas a la huancaína* (potatoes with a creamy cheese sauce) and *ceviche de trucha* (river-trout ceviche).

El Consulado   PERUVIAN **$$**
(www.facebook.com/elconsuladorestaurante; Parra del Riego 658, El Tambo; mains S20-30; ⊙10am-6pm) This spacious, high-ceilinged establishment specializes in cuisine from Arequipa, such as the trademark *rocoto relleno* (cheesy stuffed bell peppers), as well as traditional Andean fare.

🍷 Drinking & Nightlife

There are no standout nightclubs – many are outside of the center and can be dangerous late at night. Try the more central disco **Insomnico** (cnr Cajamarca & Moquegua; ⊙9pm-4am Fri & Sat), bars like **Antojitos** (Puno 599; ⊙5pm-late Mon-Sat) or lively restaurants and cafes such as La Cabaña (p297) and Sofa Café Paris (p297).

☆ Entertainment

★ La Cabaña   TRADITIONAL MUSIC
(cnr Prolongación Cusco & Federico Galvez Durand; ⊙6-11pm) Contemplate this: a man collects wondrous and miraculous things, from old fruit machines to antiquated aguardiente-making equipment throughout his life and then arranges them around a lively, cozy restaurant that makes delicious pisco sours (if you're feeling hot) or *calientitos* (if you're feeling cold). Heart-warming and belly-warming. Informal courtyard seating, plus weekly live music, normally at weekends.

Restaurant Peña Turistico
Wanka Wanka   TRADITIONAL MUSIC
(Jirón Parra del Riego 820, El Tambo; ⊙9pm-5am Fri & Sat) This *peña* (bar or club featuring live folkloric music) in El Tambo attracts local bands such as Kjantu and has good *cumbia* and folk music. The food and drinks are pricy though. Take a taxi here (S3).

Shopping

Huancayo is the central altiplano's best shopping destination by a distance, whether you desire traditional markets (there are two main markets here), souvenirs or American-brand jeans. If you have really come to Huancayo for designer clothes, best visit **Real Plaza Mall** (cnr Giraldez & Ferrocarril; ⊙9am-11pm).

Mercado Mayorista   MARKET
(behind Real Plaza Mall; ⊙daily) A colorful produce market spills out from the covered Mercado Mayorista, east along the railway tracks. In the meat section, you can buy Andean delicacies such as frogs, guinea pigs and chickens; an incredible variety of unpronounceable fruits and vegetables also beckon. Don't miss trying the *tokuc* (rotten potato drink). Many stalls open by 4am and stay open until midnight.

Stallholders are friendly and let you try before you buy. Wandering through the different sections, the smells of different products rise up to hit you: it's like a sensory crash course in the ingredients of classic Peruvian dishes. It's one of Peru's most interesting city markets, without doubt. The most important day is Sunday, coinciding with Huancayo's weekly craft market.

Feria Dominical   ARTS & CRAFTS
(Huancavelica; ⊙Sun) This craft market offering weavings, textiles, embroidered items, ceramics and wood carvings occupies numerous blocks along Huancavelica to the northwest of Piura. *Mates burilados* (carved gourds) and many other items from various villages in the Río Mantaro Valley are sold here – handy if you don't have time to trek out to the villages (p292) yourself. Keep an eye on your valuables.

ℹ Information

MEDICAL SERVICES
Clínica Ortega (☎ 064-23-2921; www.clinicaortega.pe; Carrión 1124; ⊙24hr) English is spoken at this clinic southwest of the center.

MONEY

BCP (cnr Real & Breña), **Banco Continental** (Real 631-639) and other banks and **casas de cambio** (foreign-exchange bureaus) are on Real. Most banks open on Saturday morning and have ATMs.

POST

Serpost (Main Post Office; Plaza Huamamarca 350; ⊘8am-7:30pm Mon-Fri, to 3pm Sat)

TOURIST INFORMATION

Incas del Perú (☑064-22-3303; www.incasdelperu.org; cnr Prolongación Cusco & Galvez Durand; ⊘10am-midnight) A recommended source for information on just about anything in the area.

❶ Getting There & Away

Huancayo is well connected by bus and, more than any other city in Peru outside of Cuzco, by train. The regional airport is at **Jauja** (Aeropuerto Francisco Carle; Av Aeropuerto), just under an hour away. **LC Peru** (☑064-21-4514; www.lcperu.pe; Ayacucho 322; ⊘8:30am-6:30pm Mon-Sat) serves Lima from Jauja.

BUS

Huancayo is slowly organizing its bus terminals, with **Terminal Los Andes** (cnr Av Ferrocarril & Los Andes) handling most bus departures north to Tarma and the central jungle.

From Terminal Los Andes, an S4 taxi ride from central Huancayo, there are departures at least hourly for Satipo (S20 to S25, six to seven hours) via Tarma (S10, two hours), San Ramón (S15 to S20, 4¼ hours) and La Merced (S15 to S20, 4½ hours). Many services continue as far as Mazamari (S25 to S27, 7½ hours).

For Lima (west) and destinations in the southern valleys, such as Huancavelica and Ayacucho, bus companies still have their own offices and departure points scattered around the city center.

As it is the most-traveled route, ticket prices to Lima vary wildly. Buses are mainly at night. One-way tickets range from S60 up to about S90. Higher prices will get you a bed seat on a bus-cama (bed bus); bottom-priced seats usually recline a little. Travel time is seven hours.

All companies below are worth noting for the routes they offer – due to the enormous amount of competition, it is worth taking your time deciding if you value the money you shell out or the comfort you travel in.

Cruz del Sur (☑064-22-3367, 064-22-1767; Ayacucho 281) The most luxurious Lima-bound buses. Eight to ten daily services – mainly night-time bus-cama services from S65 to S90.

Expreso Molina (☑064-22-4501; Angaraes 334) The recommended service for Ayacucho (on a still rather bumpy road). Morning departure (S25) and night departures (S30) for the seven-hour journey. There's also a service that takes the longer but safer route via Rumichaca (S40, 10 hours).

Los Canarios (☑064-21-5149; Terminal Los Andes) Serves Tarma almost hourly (S10, three hours), where better connections into the central jungle await, and will stop at Jauja (S7) and Concepción.

Selva Tours (Terminal Los Andes) A surefire bet for services to Satipo via La Merced and on to Mazamari in the central Amazon jungle.

Transportes Ticllas (Ferrocarril 1590) Frequently serves Huancavelica (S15, three to four hours).

Turismo Central (☑064-22-3128; Ayacucho 274) Buses north to Huánuco (S40 to S50, six hours), Tingo María (S60, eight hours) and Pucallpa (S70, 16 hours).

TAXI

Colectivos to Huancavelica leave when full (four-passenger minimum) from the corner of Av Ferrocarril and Ancash (or nearby), by the Transportes Ticllas bus station.

Colectivos for Andean destinations to the north including Tarma (S20) and La Oroya (S18) now leave from a convenient location outside Terminal Los Andes. Colectivos for Jauja (S7, 50 minutes) via San Jerónimo and Concepción (S3, 30 minutes) leave from here too.

TRAIN

Huancayo has two unconnected train stations in different parts of town.

A special tourist train, the **Ferrocarril Central Andino** (www.ferrocarrilcentral.com.pe), runs once or twice per month from Lima's Estación Desamparados (p104) between mid-April and October. In Huancayo, it arrives into (and departs from) the **central train station** (Av Ferrocarril, opposite Real Plaza Mall).

The 12-hour trip leaves Lima at 7am Friday and departs Huancayo for the return trip at the rather inconvenient time of 6pm Sunday. For this return night leg bring along warm clothes and perhaps a blanket.

It's a fabulous run, reaching 4829m and passing La Galera which clocks in as one of the world's highest passenger railway stations (the Tibetans are the record holders, followed by the Bolivians). It operates on a single-gauge track and is popular with train enthusiasts the world over. Either contact Incas del Perú for help with booking or book through the Ferrocarril Centro Andino website. Fares start at S700 for the gorgeous, but overpriced journey.

The **Chilca train station** (Estación Chilca; ☑064-21-6662; Av Leoncio Prado cuadra s/n; first/buffet class S9/13) for Huancavelica is at the southern end of town. The train leaves Huancayo at 6:30am on Monday, Wednesday and

Friday, returning at the same time from Huancavelica on Tuesday, Thursday and Saturday. Buffet class is comfortable, with padded seats and guaranteed seating; 1st class has reserved seats with less padding. The real draw of this train is that it is one used by locals (as opposed to just tourists) and so has plenty of color: umpteen food vendors and a blind violinist who plays for tips. Updates on the service can be obtained from Lucho Hurtado of Incas del Perú (p299).

The ticket office is open from 6am until noon: the station is a fair hike from town so take a taxi.

ⓘ Getting Around

Local buses to nearby villages leave from central street intersections. Show up and wait until a bus appears and wave to flag down: most routes have buses every few minutes. Ask a fellow waiting passenger if unsure. Incas del Perú (p299) provides local bus information.

Taxis charge a standard S4 for rides around town.

BUS

Buses to Cochas (outside Supermercado Plaza Vea) (from outside the Real Plaza Mall) come every 15 minutes.

Combis to Chupaca (cnr Giráldez & Huancas) pass the intersection of Giráldez/Huancas.

THE SOUTHERN VALLEYS

The roads get rougher and are often blocked by impromptu fiestas; the valleys get sheerer and lonelier and, like strange treasures in a chest with the lid only just lifted, the colonial architecture gleams in the sharp mountain light. You have arrived in the most quintessentially Andean swathe of the Central Highlands.

The two outstanding jewels here are the cities of Huancavelica and Ayacucho, both of which developed in magnificent opulence on the back of silver mines discovered in the nearby hills in the 16th and 17th centuries. But the region has a sadder chapter to its history, too, as the stronghold of the Sendero Luminoso (Shining Path) revolutionary group that terrorized Peru in the 1980s and made this entire area off-limits for travelers.

Today these valleys are some of the poorest parts of Peru, but they know how to have a party like no one else: Ayacucho's Semana Santa (p309) is the country's best fiesta.

Huancavelica and Ayacucho, together with Andahuaylas further south, form part of an exciting alternative route down to Cuzco.

Huancavelica

☏ 067 / POP 40,000 / ELEV 3690M

It's a mystery why more travelers don't visit this colonial city, bursting with beautiful churches, charming plazas and mineral springs, all nestling picturesquely within craggy peaks. A good road and a downright fantastic rail journey connect it to Huancayo, 147km north. Still, few people make it here and therein lies another attraction: Huancavelica is a serene spot to take a break from the Gringo Trail and soak up life as locals live it. This might entail partying at one of the frequent fiestas, browsing the markets or just watching the colorful cross-section of society pass by.

⊙ Sights

Minas de Santa Bárbara   MINE

FREE The ghostly mines of Santa Barbara, high in the hills above Huancavelica, and accessed by a tough but rewarding 1½ hour hike, are the city's most poignant site. Closed since a collapse ended two centuries of mineral extraction in 1786, Santa Barbara was once one of the most profitable mines in the Americas. Buildings – including accommodations and a church – enjoy a lonely, lovely location well worth visiting.

The path is accessed from a long flight of steps which heads straight up from above Hospedaje San José in Huancavelica. Above the tree line after the steps end, aim for some TV masts on a hill, just below which the path picks up a stone-surfaced track leading to the mine.

Laguna de Choclococha   LAKE

FREE Dazzling on a sunny day when the surrounding mountains are mirrored in its waters, Laguna de Choclococha at 4700m is one of many lakes adorning the Rumichaca road. Birdlife at the lake includes condors. There is good hiking and fishing, as well as lakeside restaurants.

The lake is located 70km south of Huancavelica and can be visited by taking the Rumichaca-bound bus at 4:30am. It's about two hours to Choclococha 'town', and then a 10-minute walk to the lake; the same bus can pick you up again on its return to Huancavelica at 2pm (check with the driver).

Huancavelica

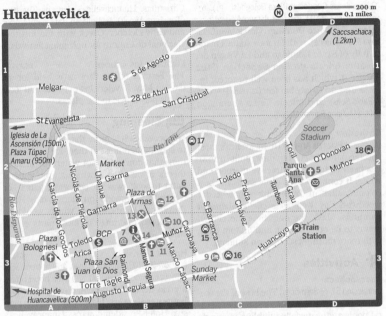

Huancavelica

Instituto Nacional de Cultura MUSEUM
(INC; Raimondi 205, cnr Muñoz; ⊘8:30am-1pm & 3:30-6:30pm Tue-Sun) FREE This museum has displays about the area, plus a bundle of interesting information if you catch the right attendant on the right day and ask. There's a great little **bookshop** here (the volumes look untouched in decades) which you should also ask the attendant to open. A small **museum** features fossils, ceramics and artifacts from the region through the ages. Examples of local costumes are on show in cases. It is in a colonial building on Plaza San Juan de Dios.

Churches

Huancavelica's churches are noted for their silver-plated altars, unlike the gold-plated ones usually found in the rest of Peru's colonial churches. There are several churches of note here, although they are generally closed to tourism. However, you can go as a member of the congregation when they are open for services, usually early in the morning on weekdays, with longer morning hours on Sunday.

The oldest church in Huancavelica is **Iglesia de Santa Ana** (Toril at Parque Santa Ana), founded in the 16th century. Dating from the 17th century are **Iglesia de San Francisco**

(Garcia de las Goodos at Plaza Bolognesi; [P]), renowned for its 11 intricately worked altars; **Iglesia de Santo Domingo** (Toledo btwn Carabaya & S Barranca), with famous statues made in Italy of Santo Domingo and La Virgen del Rosario; **Iglesia de San Sebastián** (Plaza Bolognesi), which has been well restored; **Iglesia de San Cristóbal** (cnr Calles 5 de Agosto & Pablo Solís); and **Iglesia de La Ascensión** (Plaza Mariano Santos Mateo).

Cathedral
CATHEDRAL

(Muñoz at Plaza de Armas) Huancavelica's most spectacular religious building, built in 1673, has been restored in attractive maroon and white. It contains what some say is the best colonial altar in Peru, with ornate cedar woodwork, as well as *escuela cuzqueña* paintings. Mass, the only time the church seems to be open, is 7am and 5:15pm daily, with more morning services on Sundays.

🏃 Activities

Saccsachaca
SPRING

(admission S1; ⊙ 8am-5pm) The best of the scenic springs, Tres Boas, has a spread of natural pools and waterfalls tumbling invitingly down the valley side above the river. The water is not hot, however. You should bring your own swimming gear.

Saccsachaca is the collective name for the springs, but some locals refer to them just as Tres Boas. They are located some 2km east of the center and accessed via the bridge at the end of Javier Heraud off Donovan. Follow the rough road on the other side that climbs above the river via the first of the two pools (Los Incas) and continue to Tres Boas.

San Cristóbal Mineral Springs
BATHHOUSE

(pool/private shower S1.50/3; ⊙ 6am-4pm) These mineral springs feed into two large, slightly murky swimming pools. The lukewarm water supposedly has curative properties. You can rent a towel, soap and a bathing suit if you've forgotten yours (though the selection is limited and unlovely). You can reach the springs via a steep flight of stairs – enjoy the view of the city as you climb.

The baths are often closed on Thursdays for cleaning.

🎊 Festivals & Events

Huancavelica's vibrant fiestas are renowned, due to the influence of the city's mostly indigenous population. Colorful traditional festivities occur on major Peruvian holidays, such as Carnaval, Semana Santa, Todos Santos and Christmas. Huancavelica's Semana Turística (Tourism Week) is held in late September and early October. Check with the Instituto Nacional de Cultura for upcoming festivals.

Fiesta de las Cruces
RELIGIOUS

The Festival of the Crosses is held for six days in May. Revelers bear crosses and local bands play music in the plazas.

🛏 Sleeping

Huancavelica has more than a dozen places to stay, though most of them are budget options that don't offer hot water. Fortunately, there's always the town's natural mineral baths to soak away the aches and pains. For top-end accommodation there is only Hotel Presidente Huancavelica, which would be considered midrange in most parts of the world.

Hotel Ascensión
HOTEL $

(☎ 067-45-3103; Manco Cápac 481; r from S60, without bathroom from S50; 🖥) This hotel offers a great deal, with decent, clean rooms and hot-water showers. It faces the more expensive Hotel Presidente across Huancavelica's delightful Plaza de Armas.

Hospedaje San José
GUESTHOUSE $

(☎ 067-45-1014; Huancayo s/n; s/d S35/45, without bathroom S15/30) A cluttered entrance leads up to surprisingly large rooms with comfortable beds and intermittent hot water. Many rooms get good views over town. It still gets cold here at night, though. It's at the southern end of Baranca by the market.

Hotel Victoria
HOTEL $$

(☎ 067-45-2954; cnr Manco Cápac & Toledo; incl breakfast r S70-120, ste S150) The latest attempt at creating pleasant midrange accommodation in Huancavelica seems OK and has bigger rooms than any other option. It's just down from the Plaza de Armas.

★ Hotel Presidente Huancavelica
HISTORIC HOTEL $$$

(☎ tel/fax 067-45-2760; https://huancavelica.hotelpresidente.com.pe; Plaza de Armas; s/d incl breakfast S260/280; 🖥) Presentable old Hotel Presidente Huancavelica is, truth be told, very pricey for what you actually get, but locations do not get much better. Rooms are much plainer than the gorgeous facade, but do benefit from guaranteed hot showers, telephone, cable TV and a laundry service – not to mention a handy restaurant. There are some suites available, too.

Eating

There are few standout restaurants, but plenty of chicken places and *chifas* (Chinese restaurants). The *menú del día* at lunchtime is what coaxes most locals into eating out: just a few nuevo soles for three courses and a drink.

★ Pollos y Parrilladas El Centro PARRILLA $

(cnr Manuel Segura & Muñoz; mains S15; ⊙11am-11pm) There are two large parts to this plaza-facing restaurant – separated by the kitchen – and at lunchtime every inch of space is needed, as seemingly all of Huancavelica's residents descend here to eat. A good grilled steak is what to go for here – it comes served on its own cooker and it's *muy sabroso* (very tasty).

Killa Cafe CAFE $

(Toledo 315, Plaza de Armas; S5-15; ⊙8am-noon & 3-10pm) The nicest cafe in town has decent coffee, a great *torta de chocolate* (chocolate cake), wi-fi and limited but tasty snacks, such as pancakes, tamales and sandwiches.

🛍 Shopping

Sunday is market day, and the best day to see locals in traditional dress. The main market snakes up Barranca, continuing along Torre Tagle behind the cathedral. Handicrafts are sold daily on the north side of the Plaza de Armas and down the adjoining *pasaje de artesanías*. Colorful wool leggings, hats with earflaps and bootleg CDs are especially popular purchases.

ℹ Information

MEDICAL SERVICES

Hospital de Huancavelica (Hospital Regional Zacarías Correa Valdivia; ☑ 067-45-2990; www.hdhvca.gob.pe; Av Andrés Céceres s/n; ⊙24hr)

MONEY

BCP (Toledo s/n) Has a Visa ATM and changes money.

POST

Main Post Office (Pasaje Ferrua 105) Near Iglesia de Santa Ana.

TOURIST INFORMATION

Tourist Office (Manuel Segura 140; ⊙9am-1:30pm & 3:30-6:30pm Mon-Fri, 9am-1:30pm Sat) Provides good directions (in Spanish) for local hikes, such as the 6km tramp to Santa Barbara mines, as well as transport information. Can arrange tours on request for groups.

ℹ Getting There & Away

Road or rail: in Huancavelica the choice for arrival and departure is yours.

The town now sports a paved road to Huancayo (the easiest approach). Other roads reach Huancavelica directly from Pisco via a 4850m pass, and from Ayacucho via Rumichaca or Lircay.

The most interesting way to Huancavelica, however, is by train from Huancayo. For the time-poor, it's best to take a *colectivo* (shared transportation) here from Huancayo.

BUS

Lima- and Ayacucho-bound buses usually depart from the **Terminal Terrestre**, inconveniently located about 2km to the west of the town center. A taxi here costs S3. Buy your bus tickets in the downtown offices spread along the seventh to 10th blocks of Muñoz, and be sure to ask about exactly where your bus departs from – which seems to change on a whim.

From the Terminal Terrestre, several companies offer nightly departures to Lima (S30 to S60, 10 to 13 hours). The higher price tag is for more luxurious *bus-camas* (bed buses).

Companies go via Huancayo or via Pisco, although if Huancayo is your intended destination, daytime departures run much more frequently from the center. The Pisco route is freezing at night: bring warm clothes. Several companies with offices clustering along Muñoz between Parque Santa Ana and the crossroads with Hwy 26 offer this trip.

Also from Terminal Terrestre, there are bus departures for Ayacucho via Rumiachaca (S30 to S40, seven to eight hours). Some smaller buses leave for the same run from **Plaza Túpac Amaru**.

Companies serving Huancayo (S15, three hours) include **Transportes Ticllas** (☑ 067-36-8264; Muñoz 954) with almost hourly daily departures, as well as a **combi terminal** on Muñoz close to the center with smaller vans for this ride.

Buses tend to be of the ponderous local variety, filled with locals and their goods.

TAXI

Colectivos (shared transportation) taxis are the quickest means of transport out of Huancavelica.

Colectivos to Huancayo (S25, 2½ hours) leave when full (four-passenger minimum). They mostly hang around on Muñoz between Carabaya and Barranca. **Colectivos to Lircay** also run.

Colectivos are is not necessarily the best method of transport to destinations further afield.

TRAIN

Trains currently leave for Huancayo at 6:30am on Tuesday, Thursday and Saturday. Fares are S9 in first class and S13 in buffet class. It takes five or six hours for this scenic trip, one of Peru's last real train journeys.

Ayacucho

📞 066 / POP 181,000 / ELEV 2750M

Travelers are only just rediscovering Ayacucho's treasures. Richly decorated churches dominate the vivid cityscape alongside peach- and pastel-colored colonial buildings hung with wooden balconies. Among numerous festivities, Ayacucho boasts Peru's premier Semana Santa celebrations, while in the surrounding mountains lie some of the country's most significant archaeological attractions.

Yet this mesmerizing colonial city has a dark past. Its name, originating from the Quechua *aya* (death, or soul) and *cuchu* (outback), offers a telling insight. Ayacucho's status as isolated capital of a traditionally poor department provided the breeding ground for Professor Abimael Guzmán to nurture the Sendero Luminoso (Shining Path) Maoist revolutionary movement (p314) that caused thousands of deaths in the region during the 1980s and 1990s. But the city's historically poor links with the outside world also fostered a proud, independent spirit evident in everything from its unique festivals to its booming cultural self-sufficiency.

History

Some of Peru's first signs of human habitation were purportedly discovered in the Pikimachay caves, near Ayacucho (though today there is nothing of interest to be seen there).

Five hundred years before the rise of the Incas, the Wari dominated the Peruvian highlands and established their capital 22km northeast of Ayacucho. The city's original name was San Juan de la Frontera de Huamanga (locals still call it Huamanga) and it grew rapidly after its founding in 1540 as the Spanish sought to defend it against attack from Manco Inca. Ayacucho played a major part in the battles for Peruvian independence, commemorated by an impressive nearby monument.

After the dark days during the 1980s and '90s when the city was terrorized by Sendero Luminos, Ayacucho's first paved road connection with the outside world came only in 1999, to Lima.

Ayacucho has long since turned to face the 21st century and welcomes travelers with good cheer.

👁 Sights

The **Plaza de Armas** (Plaza Mayor de Huamanga; Plaza de Armas) in Ayacucho is one of Peru's most beautiful, and should be a starting point for your explorations. The four sides of the plaza, clockwise from the east, are Portal Municipal, Portal Independencia, Portal Constitución and Portal Unión. Around here, you'll find many gorgeous colonial

---

AYACUCHO: THE TOUGH WAY

Sometimes life is too easy, right? Well, if you are moving on from Huancavelica in the direction of Ayacucho, there are opportunities to make proceedings a little more of a challenge. Besides, the main buses run at night, and who wants to travel in the dark and miss all that cracking scenery?

The 'easiest' daytime option to Ayacucho is to take a 4:30am minibus to Rumichaca. In the west of Huancavelica from Plaza Túpac Amaru (p303), minibuses depart daily (S10, six hours). Then wait for an Ayacucho-bound bus coming from the coast. Most day buses from Lima don't get to Rumichaca until about 2pm.

Another possibility, involving still more stunning scenery and more amounts of time on still more bone-jarring transport, is to take a *colectivo* (shared transportation) from outside Hospedaje San José in Huancavelica to Lircay (S15, two hours), on mostly paved roads. From the market In Lircay, pick up another *colectivo* bound to Julcamarca and then to Ayacucho (S30, four hours) on what is half-track, half-road.

The caveat with Ayacucho-bound *colectivos* in Lircay is that few people want to take them (it's too far) so you might wind up having to pay for the whole car (S120). Ensure you get to Lircay early to maximize your chances of onward transportation to either Julcamarca or Ayacucho.

mansions, including the **Prefectura** (Jirón 28 de Julio) `FREE`. Ask at the tourist office for details on how to visit these buildings.

Other sights in Ayacucho are mostly churches and museums.

★ Museo de la Memoria   MUSEUM

(Prolongación Libertad 1229; S2; ⊙9am-1pm & 3-6pm Mon-Fri, 9am-1pm Sat) Ayacucho's most haunting museum, remembers the impact the Sendero Luminoso (p314) had on Peru in the city that was most deeply affected by the conflict. Its simple displays (in Spanish) are moving: there are eyewitness accounts of the horrors that occurred and a particularly poignant montage of photos by mothers whose children were killed in the fighting.

Some of the mothers still staff the museum, and may talk to you about this terrible time, if your Spanish is up to it. Donations are gratefully accepted. The museum is located 1.5km northwest of the city center.

★ Museo de Arte Popular   MUSEUM

(Portal Independencia 72; ⊙8am-1pm & 2-4:15pm Mon-Fri) `FREE` Displays popular art covering the *ayacucheño* (natives of Ayacucho) spectrum – silverwork, rug- and tapestry-weaving, stone and woodcarvings, ceramics (model churches are especially popular) and the famous *retablos* (ornamental religious dioramas). The latter are colorful wooden boxes varying in size and containing intricate papier-mâché models: Peruvian rural scenes or the nativity are favorites, but interesting ones with political or social commentary can be seen here. Photographs show how Ayacucho changed during the 20th century. Opening hours here change almost as frequently.

Casa Museo
Joaquín López Antay   ART STUDIO

(Cuzco 424; admission adult/child S4/2; ⊙3-6pm Mon-Sat) This captivating little museum is really part art gallery and part an explanation of the process of *retablo* making. *Retablos*, ornamental, originally religious dioramas, are notoriously complex, as is demonstrated here, and often contain hundreds of human and animal figures. Joaquín Lopez Antay was Ayacucho's most famous *retablo* maker and many of his creations are displayed here.

Ask about *retablo*-making classes, which run if there is sufficient interest.

Otto Malena   MUSEUM

(Bellido 548; ⊙6pm-midnight) Officially a restaurant, this surreal Aladdin's Cave is more a museum of curios than anything else, for the owner is primarily a collector of magical things. Artifacts, paintings and busts (some quite rare) are distributed throughout the rambling rooms here, and the owner has 1001 stories about his collection to whet your curiosity while you wait for your Peruvian-Chinese meal (mains S15 to S30).

Plaza Moré   SQUARE

(Jirón 28 de Julio 262) A square of shops and restaurants tucked back from the pedestrian street, with a better quality of establishments than the similar Centro Turístico Cultural San Cristóbal (p310) that is just up the hill.

Mirador de Carmen Alto   VIEWPOINT

`FREE` This *mirador* (lookout) offers fabulous views of Ayacucho, as well as decent restaurants. Taxis here charge S5, otherwise catch a bus from the Mercado Central or walk (one hour).

Museo Arqueológico
Hipólito Unanue   MUSEUM

(☎066-31-2056; Av Independencia s/n; admission S4; ⊙9am-1pm & 3-5pm Tue-Sun) Wari ceramics make up most of the small exhibition here, along with relics from the region's other various civilizations. The museum buildings are set in a botanical garden in the Centro Cultural Simón Bolívar at the university, located more than 1km north of the city center along Independencia – you can't miss it. While there, visit the university library for a free exhibition of mummies, skulls and other niceties.

The best time to visit the museum is in the morning: afternoon hours aren't always adhered to.

Museo Andrés Avelino Cáceres   MUSEUM

(Jirón 28 de Julio 508-512; admission S2; ⊙9:30am-1pm & 3-6pm Mon-Fri, 9:30am-1pm Sat) This museum in the Casona Vivanco, a gorgeous 16th-century mansion, houses maps and military paraphernalia from the period of its namesake, a local man who commanded Peruvian troops during the War of the Pacific (1879–83) against Chile. Displays also include intriguing *retablos* and colonial art: check out the painting of the Last Supper – complete with *cuy*!

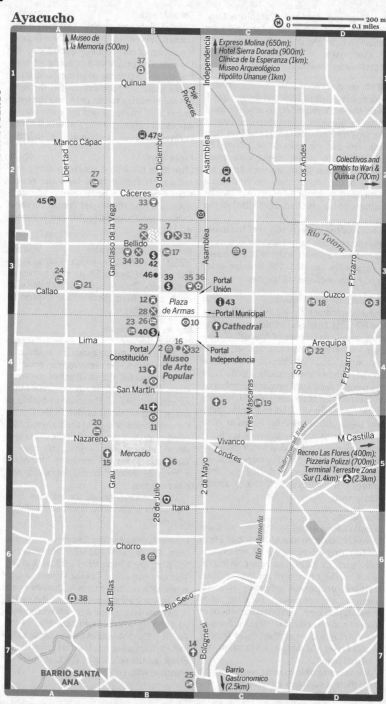

Ayacucho

◎ **Churches**

Ayacucho, the 'Ciudad de las Iglesias' (City of Churches), boasts more than 30 churches and temples.

When it comes to opening hours, churches are a law unto themselves. Some list their visiting times on the doors; with others you will have to take your chances. During Semana Santa (p309) churches are open for most of the day; at other times ask at the tourist office (p312), which publishes the guide *Circuito religioso* with information on opening hours.

Joining the congregation for mass (usually between 6am to 8am Monday to Saturday depending on the church) is an interesting way of seeing inside these buildings. Entrance to the churches is free but donations are appreciated.

★ **Cathedral**   CHURCH
(Portal Municipal; ☉10am-noon & 4-6pm) FREE
This spectacular 17th-century cathedral on the Plaza de Armas has a religious-art museum inside. The moody facade doesn't quite prepare you for the intricacy of the interior, with its elaborate gold-leaf altar being one of the best examples of the baroque-*churrigueresque* style (in which cornices and other intricate, Spanish-influenced workmanship mingled with Andean influences, often evinced by the wildlife depicted).

These altars also demonstrate how the concept of the *retablo*, the ornamental religious dioramas that are Ayacucho's most famous export, came about. The word originally meant 'behind the altar' in reference to the statues placed within cases and set behind early altars. Ten such altars are contained here. Ask at the shop at the entrance about visiting the cathedral's catacombs.

Iglesia de San Francisco de Asis   CHURCH

(Jirón 28 de Julio cuadra 3) **FREE** Visually striking stone church containing *retablos* and an attractive adjoining convent dating to the 17th century. Located opposite the market, it boasts the city's largest bell, and several *escuela cuzqueña* and *escuela ayacuchana* works of art.

Templo Compañía de Jesús   CHURCH

(Jirón 28 de Julio s/n) **FREE** This church has two fine bell towers and, in the body of the structure supporting them, striking embossings and motifs. It sits on the site of its 1605 predecessor, and took more than a century and a half to complete fully (from the 1640s to the early 1800s).

Iglesia de Santo Domingo   CHURCH

(Jirón 9 de Diciembre at Bellido) **FREE** One of Ayacucho's most photogenic churches, dating from 1548. Purportedly built with the stone of a former Inca fortress, it contains some superb examples of *churrigueresque*-style painting.

Iglesia de La Merced   CHURCH

(Jirón 2 de Mayo at San Martín) **FREE** This church, built in the mid-16th century, is full of colonial art and has one of Peru's oldest convents attached, dating from the same period.

Templo y Monasterio de Santa Clara   CHURCH

(Grau at Nazareno) **FREE** Attracts thousands of pilgrims annually for a glimpse of the image of Jesus of Nazareth supposedly inside on one of the altars.

Templo de San Cristóbal   CHURCH

(Jirón 28 de Julio, cuadra 6) **FREE** This is the oldest city church, dating from shortly after Ayacucho's founding in 1540.

Courses

Via Via   COOKING

(066-31-2834; http://viavia.world/en/south-america/ayacucho; Portal Constitución 4) Runs a cooking course where you can make a *lomo saltado* (strips of beef stir-fried with onions, tomatoes, potatoes and chili) and a pisco sour – and then consume them. The cost is S60 per person for 1½ hours.

Tours

Urpillay Tours   OUTDOORS

(066-31-5074; www.ayacuchoviajes.com; Portal Independencia 67; S120) This professional outfit is a good choice for the standard selection of tours around Ayacucho, including to the Wari ruins (p313) and Quinua or Vilcashuamán (p313). A full-day tour is S120 per person for these trips.

Mama Alice   CULTURAL

(Mama Alice 066-31-7963, Via Via 066-31-2834; www.mamaaliceperu.com; Via Via Hotel & Restaurant) The wonderful nonprofit organization Mama Alice, which works with local street children, has its shop window at leading Ayacucho hotel and restaurant Via Via Plaza. New tours, conducted by disadvantaged locals, take you beyond the pretty center into the real city; check with Via Via Plaza for more information.

Sleeping

Ayacucho isn't short on accommodations. In addition to the myriad small hotels and *hospedajes* (small, family-owned inns) with generally limited facilities, there is an ever-growing number of plusher (yet still reasonably priced) options with creature comforts such as round-the-clock hot water. During Semana Santa prices rise markedly – by 25% to even 75%.

Hostal Tres Máscaras   GUESTHOUSE $

(066-31-2921; hoteltresmascaras@yahoo.com; Tres Máscaras 194; s/d S60/80, without bathroom S30/50) The pleasing walled garden and friendly owner render this an enjoyable place to stay, and garden-facing rooms are generously sized. Hot water is on in the morning and later on request. A room with TV is S5 extra. Continental and American breakfasts are available for S8 and S10, respectively. All these things have made it a longtime backpacker favorite.

Hostal Florida   GUESTHOUSE $

(066-31-2565; Cuzco 310; s/d S40/70) This traveler-friendly *hostal* (guesthouse) has a relaxing courtyard garden and clean rooms (those on the upper level are better) with bathrooms and TV, hot water in the morning and later on request. There is a basic cafeteria too, and a laundry service.

★ Via Via Plaza   HOTEL $$

(066-31-2834; http://viavia.world/en/south-america/ayacucho; Portal Constitución 4; s/d S130/190;) One of the more imaginative sleeping options in central Ayacucho is Via Via, with an enviable plaza location and cool, vibrantly decorated rooms themed around different countries and continents.

DON'T MISS

PERU'S FINEST RELIGIOUS FESTIVAL

Held the week before Easter, Semana Santa (⊘ Mar or Apr) is Peru's finest religious festival and attracts visitors from all over the country. Each succeeding day sees solemn yet colorful processions and Catholic religious rites. Ayacucho's Semana Santa celebrations also include art shows, folk-dancing competitions, local music concerts, street events, sporting events (especially equestrian ones), agricultural fairs and the loving preparation of traditional meals.

Each year, iPerú (p312) prints a free brochure describing the Semana Santa events with street maps showing the main processions. Celebrations begin on the Friday before Palm Sunday and continue for 10 days until Easter Sunday. The first day is marked by a procession in honor of La Virgen de los Dolores (Our Lady of Sorrows), during which it is customary to inflict 'sorrows' on bystanders by firing pebbles out of slingshots. Gringos have been targets, so be warned.

The celebrations culminate on the Saturday before Easter Sunday with a huge all-night party including dawn fireworks to celebrate the resurrection of Christ. If you want to party too, stay on your guard, as proceedings are notoriously wild. Crime in the city escalates dramatically during festivities: robbery and rape are not unheard of.

Rooms in most hotels fill far in advance so book well ahead. The tourist office has lists of local families who provide accommodations for the overflow.

Travelers will feel like they've landed in a veritable oasis, all centered on a plant-filled courtyard. English and Dutch are spoken, and there's a popular 2nd-floor restaurant hangout alongside.

The owners have now opened a second hotel, Via Via Alameda, in the colonial property formerly known as Hotel El Marqués de Valdelirios.

Via Via Alameda
HOTEL $$

(☑ 066-31-7040; http://viavia.world/en/south-america/ayacucho; Bolognesi 720, Parque Alameda; s/d incl breakfast S100/130; P) This colonial building in a quiet, lovely location has rooms with beautiful furniture, and there is a grassy garden-courtyard where you can sit outside and enjoy the on-site restaurant's wonderful cooking. Now under ownership of the city center's famous Via Via company, the hotel is about 700m from the center; the walk back at night involves passing some dark neighborhoods.

Hotel Sierra Dorada
BUSINESS HOTEL $$

(☑ 066-31-9639; Parque del Colegio de Ingenieros; incl breakfast s S120-160, d S170-215; 🕏) It's more ochre than *dorada* (golden) but if your number-one priority in Ayacucho is a quiet night's sleep, this is the hotel for you. The rooms are nice if not particularly big, but the location, sequestered away in a park a short distance from the center, is tranquil indeed.

The park is also known as Parque Mariscal Cáceres. It's easiest to take a *mototaxi* here (S2).

Yañez Inn
HOTEL $$

(☑ 066-31-3431; Av Cáceres 1214; s/d incl breakfast S60/90; 🕏) Rivals any of the other midrange options in town, with rooms the size of two or three rooms at many other hotels. There are also appealing public areas including a courtyard and small cafeteria, where a complimentary American breakfast is served. The staff here are friendlier than at most Ayacucho hotels, too.

Hotel Sevilla
HOTEL $$

(☑ 066-31-4388; www.hotelsevillaperu.com/english; Libertad 635; incl breakfast s S100, d S130-150; 🕏) A long entranceway hung with hanging baskets leads back to this four-story establishment, one of the nicest, brightest, best-value hotels in Ayacucho. When it first opened, it was the deal of the Central Andes but has since realized what prices it can charge – though these are still a bargain. Ample, cozy, quiet rooms have desks, mini-bars and microwaves.

Breakfast is served in a top-floor cafe commanding great city views; there is a restaurant, too.

Hotel Santa Rosa
HOTEL $$

(☑ 066-31-4614; Lima 166; r incl breakfast from S120; 🕏) This capacious hotel with twin courtyards has spacious, airy rooms in need of a decor update. Some come with a fridge (a luxury in the Central Andes) and all have TV, DVD player and phone. The bathrooms are large and the showers have oodles of hot water. It's less than a block from the Plaza de Armas.

There's also a decent and well-priced on-site restaurant. The Santa Rosa ia a looker, even by Ayacucho's exemplary standards.

Hotel San Francisco de Paula
HOTEL $$

(☑066-31-2353; www.hotelsanfranciscodepaula.com; Callao 270; incl breakfast s S80, d S110-130; 🛜) This rather rambling, oldish hotel isn't flashy, but it is presentable, with public areas decorated with indigenous art. It has a restaurant and bar and the decent-sized, tiled rooms get the usual midrange facilities. Outside doubles are better as the inside singles can be very poky. Ask about the Jacuzzi suite, for which you will part with more cash.

Hotel Santa María
HOTEL $$

(☑tel/fax 066-31-4988; Arequipa 320; incl breakfast s S120, d S140-180, t S210; 🛜) The large, three-floor yellow edifice looks impressive from the outside and the rooms are very comfortable, quite spacious and tastefully decorated in bright Andean hues (proof that purples and oranges *can* work in harmony). Of the places opened during the hotel rush of the late '90s, this one seems to have got it right.

Hotel La Crillonesa
HOTEL $$

(☑066-31-2350; www.hotelcrillonesa.com; Nazareno 165; s/d from S60/85; 🛜) A popular hotel with helpful staff, La Crillonesa offers a rooftop terrace with photogenic views, a TV room, tour information and 24-hour hot water. Its rather small, clean rooms have comfy beds and generally functioning cable TV. The best rooms are right at the top.

DM Hoteles Ayacucho
HOTEL $$$

(☑066-31-2202; fax 066-31-2314; 9 de Diciembre 184; d/ste incl breakfast S345/511; P🛜) The interior of this impressive-looking colonial building exudes a certain kind of charm, but for what you pay, the rooms are oh-so-plain and merely adequate. Better rooms have balconies (request one); some have plaza views. It was once considered the best in town, and few centrally located top-end hotels have yet given it a run for its money in scale or in facilities.

There is a restaurant, very big and usually empty.

Eating

Standards are high, with many regional specialties on offer. There are some quality restaurants on the Plaza de Armas and at-

mospheric, if slightly touristy, dining within the Centro Turístico Cultural San Cristóbal (Jirón 28 de Julio 178). Meanwhile, Plaza Moré (p305) offers eateries that are positively gourmet: signs of the changing Ayacucho, perhaps. After all, how many Andean towns can boast their own 'Barrio Gastronómico' (Gastronomic Neighborhood)?

Frutelli
ICE CREAM $

(Bellido 356; ice creams from S3; ⊙9am-10pm) The closest central outlet stocking the delicious CREAM'Z ice creams and really unusual hard candies. Doesn't look much from outside, but let your taste buds have their say.

Café La Miel
CAFE $

(Portal Constitución 11; snacks from S3; ⊙10am-10pm) Café La Miel spent years trying to make the Plaza de Armas a convivial place to eat. Now, it has competition, but with its chirpy atmosphere strangely reminiscent of an English tearoom, it should still be on your radar. Breakfast is the time to visit – we're talking great fruit salads and some of Ayacucho's best (fresh-brewed) coffee.

It serves hearty lunches and phenomenal chocolate cake, too.

La Casona
PERUVIAN $$

(Bellido 463; menús S14, mains S18-30; ⊙7am-10:30pm) This popular, ambience-filled courtyard restaurant has been recommended by several travelers for its big portions. It focuses on Peruvian food, such as the excellent *trucha* (river trout) and *lomo saltado*, and often has regional specialties.

★ Via Via
INTERNATIONAL $$

(Portal Constitución 4; mains S19-34; ⊙7:30am-10pm Mon-Thu, to midnight Fri & Sat; 🛜☑) 🖉 The upstairs plaza-facing balcony has the best views in Ayacucho to accompany your meal of Peruvian-European fusion cuisine, made from ethically sourced, organic ingredients. You're sure to find something to sate you – perhaps *quinnoto* (risotto with quinoa) or *salteado de alpaca* (strips of alpaca meat stir-fried with onions, tomatoes, potatoes and chili) – alongside a crisp South American wine.

This is a traveler-friendly hangout, the likes of which the city had never seen before, and still does everything right a decade on from its founding, from the feistiness of its morning coffee to the originality of its dinners. Downstairs in the courtyard, and bought separately from a booth at the entrance, amazing cakes, ice creams and coffees are sold from 9am to 10:30pm.

Sukre Cocina Peruana · PERUVIAN $$
(Portal Constitución 9; mains S20-35; ⊙ 7am-11pm) This bustling and stylish hangout advertises Peruvian food but what it serves is almost fusion cuisine. Get ready for the likes of the house *lomo saltado* (with broccoli) and *pollo albardado* (chicken rolled around ham and vegetables in a creamy Mediterranean mushroom sauce). There's balcony seating on the Portal Constitución side of the Plaza de Armas.

Pizzeria Polizzi · PIZZA $$
(⌨ 066-31-7255; Tarapaca 210, cnr Av del Ejercito; pizzas S20-30; ⊙ 6-11pm) Not all of the culinary stars that shine in Ayacucho shine in the center. This pizzeria twinkles in a galaxy all of its own out on Av del Ejercito (although it's planning a second central branch). The food is superb but even that pales into insignificance besides the gushing Italian-style service at this Italian-Peruvian enterprise. Takeout is available.

Get a taxi here, and tell the driver to head to the gas station Grifo Santa Rosa.

Las Tinajas · STEAK $$
(https://lastinajas.pe; Portal Independencia 65; mains S18-46; ⊙ noon-midnight) An elegant choice with plaza- or courtyard-facing dining, ultra-professional service and, well, damned good steak. Part of the mini-chain found in other Peruvian cities. Takeout is available.

Recreo Las Flores · PERUVIAN $$
(José Olaya 106; meals S15-35; ⊙ 8am-5pm Mon-Thu, to 6:30pm Fri-Sun) *Cuy, cuy* and more *cuy*: let's hope you like it if you're eating here. It mostly comes fried with various accompaniments. Fried *trucha* (river trout) and *puca picante* (a spicy potato and beef stew served over rice) are also on offer. The inside resembles a vast Communist-style cafeteria but over by the windows that feeling is less apparent.

This and several other places nearby form a 'Barrio Gastronómico' in Conchapata district, south of the center.

Mamma Mia · ITALIAN $$
(Jirón 28 de Julio 262; medium pizzas S25; ⊙ 6pm-midnight) An exceptional pizza shop, run by a Ukrainian, no less. He has taken his extensive catering experience and come

REGIONAL SPECIALTIES

Local dishes to try include *puca picante* (potato and beef stew in a spicy red peanut-and-pepper sauce, served over rice), *patachi* (wheat soup with various beans, dried potatoes and lamb or beef) and *sopa de mondongo* (corn soup cooked with pork or beef, red chili peppers and fresh mint; the dish is found elsewhere in varying forms but is most typical of Ayacucho). *Chicharrón* (deep-fried pork) and *cuy* (guinea pig) are also popular. Vegetarians may accordingly be challenged to find meatless fare: *chifas* (Chinese restaurants) are a good bet.

up with an atmospheric place for delicious pizza and pasta. Round off your meal with a 'Mamma Mia' cocktail: vodka, coconut rum, peach schnapps and melon. The restaurant is in Plaza Moré (p305).

El Niño · PARRILLA $$
(9 de Diciembre 205; mains S17-45; ⊙ 11am-2pm & 5-11pm) The specialty at this large restaurant is grilled meat – often cooked over a wood fire on the sheltered patio in the evenings – but a variety of Peruvian dishes, as well as pasta and pizza, are dished up, too. Inside seating is also available. After years in the game, this remains one of the city's better restaurants.

The individual *parrillada* (grilled-meat platter) for S55 is good, and in practice sufficient for two modest eaters.

Drinking & Nightlife

This is an important university city, so you'll find a few bar-clubs to dance or hang out in, mostly favored by students.

Yaku · BAR
(Portal Unión 30; ⊙ 11am-11:30pm) First things first: enthusiastically run Yaku is not just a bar with a lovely balcony overlooking the Plaza de Armas: it's a live-music venue, it's a restaurant, it brews its own beer, it has table football – and its owners are ever-developing more plans. There are some of Ayacucho's best burgers (S15 to S20) here, too: wolf down a 'Cancún' (with guacamole).

Fridays and Saturdays are rock-music nights. If you want to go on to someplace wilder afterwards, staff here will tell you where.

Museo
COCKTAIL BAR

(cnr 9 de Diciembre & Av Cáceres; ☺6pm-3am) An intriguing mix of cocktails are served, DJs provide the music (*reggaetón*, salsa) most nights and the atmosphere is buzzing.

Taberna Magía Negra
BAR

(www.facebook.com/TabernaMagiaNegra; Bellido 349; ☺4pm-midnight Mon-Sat) It's been around longer than most and the youth of today prefer the newer venues but this bar-gallery still has local art, beer, pizza and great music.

☆ Entertainment

Centro Cultural
LIVE PERFORMANCE

(Portal Unión) Students and hipsters flock here for regular open-air performances (music, comedy, the works) in the courtyard.

Shopping

Ayacucho is a renowned handicraft center: a visit to the Museo de Arte Popular (p305) will give you an idea of local products. The tourist office can recommend local artisans who will welcome you to their workshops. The Santa Ana *barrio* (neighborhood) is particularly well known for its crafts.

There is a rather tamer **craft market** (Quinua s/n) close to the city center.

Edwin Pizarro
ARTS & CRAFTS

(☎966-180-666; Barrio Belén) The *retablos* from Edwin Pizarro's workshop in Barrio Belén are highly recommended. He's renowned locally as one of the best artisans in the business and will personalize his lovingly made creations by adding figures appropriate to the customer.

The workshop is a tough 15-minute walk above central Ayacucho (opposite Templo de Belén) and can be hard to find: a taxi's not a bad idea.

❶ Information

EMERGENCY

Police (Jirón 28 de Julio 325; ☺24hr)

MEDICAL SERVICES

Clínica de la Esperanza (Hospital Regional de Ayacucho; ☎066-31-7436; www.hospital-regionalayacucho.gob.pe; Independencia 355; ☺8am-8pm) English is spoken.

Inka Farma (Jirón 28 de Julio 250; ☺7am-10:30pm) Pharmacy.

MONEY

BBVA Banco Continental (Portal Unión 28) Has a Visa ATM.

Casa de Cambio (Portal Constitución) On the southwest corner of the Plaza de Armas.

Interbank (Jirón 9 de Diciembre 183)

POST

Serpost (Asamblea 293) Near the Plaza de Armas.

TOURIST INFORMATION

iPerú (☎066-31-8305; cnr Cusco & Asamblea; ☺9am-6pm Mon-Sat, to 1pm Sun) Helpful advice; English spoken.

❶ Getting There & Away

Air travel is certainly the easiest means of approach to Ayacucho, although arrival by bus is most popular.

AIR

The **airport** is 3.5km from the town center. Taxis charge about S10. Flight times and airlines can change without warning, so check airline websites for the latest schedules. Daily flights to Lima are with **LC Peru** (☎066-31-2151; Jirón 9 de Diciembre 139; ☺9am-7pm Mon-Fri, to 1pm Sat), with departures alternating between early morning and mid-afternoon depending on the day. There are morning and afternoon departures on Sundays.

BUS

Most buses (to long-distance north- and southbound destinations, including Lima) arrive and depart from the grandiosely named **Terrapuerto Libertadores de America** (Terminal Terrestre; end of Perez de Cuellar) bus terminal to the north of the city center, although you can still buy tickets at the downtown offices (it's best to ask when buying your ticket where your bus departs from). A taxi to the terminal costs S8.

Transport connections with Lima are via the relatively fast and spectacular Hwy 24 that traverses the Andes via Rumichaca to Pisco. Night departures outnumber day departures, but day trips are naturally more interesting for the wild scenery en route. Choose your bus and company carefully. Ticket prices to/from Lima are wide-ranging – from S40 for a regular seat to S90 for a reclining armchair that you can sleep in. The trip takes around nine hours. Take warm clothing if traveling by night.

Heading north to Huancayo (S30 to S40, seven hours), the road is poor, featuring vertiginous drops with precious little protection: a heart-in-mouth, spectacular old-school Andean bus ride. The main service is with **Expreso Molina** (☎066-31-9989; Universitaria 160). Change in Huancayo for onward services to Huánuco, Tingo María, Pucallpa and Satipo.

Heading southeast, the road to Andahuaylas (S30, five to six hours) and on to Cuzco (S50 to S60, 14 to 15 hours) is fully paved, but few

---

AROUND AYACUCHO

Ayacucho has several interesting excursions in its vicinity, running the gamut of regional history from the pre-Inca to Peruvian independence. You can reach them via day tours with agencies in Ayacucho for about S60 per person.

The extensive **Wari ruins** (S3; ☺8am-5:30pm), 20km above Ayacucho on the road to Quinua, are among the most significant surviving remains of the Wari culture, scattered among fields of bizarre opuntia cacti: a moody spot to contemplate this once-powerful civilization. Information is in Spanish only.

A further 17km beyond the Wari ruins is the pretty village of **Quinua**, with a museum, **Casa de la Capitulación** (Bolivar s/n, Quinua; admission S5), with erratic hours. Next to that is the room where Spanish royalist troops signed their surrender after the War of Peruvian Independence, leading to the end of colonialism in Peru. A 40m-high white **obelisk** (Quinua; admission S1; ☺dawn-dusk), intermittently visible for several kilometers as you approach Quinua, commemorates the Battle of Ayacucho, the decisive conflict in the war. It lies 15 minutes' walk above town via Jirón Sucre The whole area is protected as the 300-hectare **Santuario Histórico Pampas de Ayacucho**.

The ruins of **Vilcashuamán** (Vilcashuamán; admission S2), a former Inca stronghold (considered the geographical center of the Inca empire) lie some 110km south of Ayacucho, near **Vischongo**. Little remains of the city's early magnificence but an intact, five-tier pyramid called an *usnu* survives, topped by a huge stone-carved double throne.

---

companies thus far have the licenses to run the route, meaning there are limited choices. For Cuzco, buses run from Terrapuerto Libertadores de America, but for Andahuaylas the best option is to take a **combi** (S30) from Pasaje Cáceres in central Ayacucho. These trips boast fantastic scenery, and are worth doing in daylight.

From **Terminal Terrestre Zona Sur** (Av Cuzco), which handles southbound regional departures, the main destinations of note to travelers are Vischongo and the ruins of Vilcashuamán. All manner of vehicles here will offer the route, with Vilcashuamán rates ranging from S20 in a *combi* to S30 in a *coletivo* (shared transportation). Departures are early in the morning: get here around 5am to stake your claim to a spot. A taxi to the terminal is S4.

Combis and colectivo taxis (Pasaje Flores, btwn Melgar & Chocano) go to many local villages, including Quinua (S5, one hour), and to the Wari ruins (S5, 40 minutes), departing from northeast of the center on a yard on Pasaje Flores.

Northwest-bound *colectivos* to Julcamarca (2½ hours) from where you can also travel via Lircay (a further two hours) to Huancavelica (another three to four hours) leave from **Terminal Terrestre Totora** (Carr Huanta–Ayacucho), 4km northeast of the center. With changeovers in Julcamarca and Lircay, likely travel time to Huancavelica is eight to nine hours and costs about S120 in total.

Cruz del Sur (☎ information only 066-31-2813, reservations 01-311-5050; www.cruzdelsur. com.pe; Cáceres s/n, btwn Libertad & Sucre) Top-notch, executive-style service to Lima, with comfortable seats and meals thrown in.

Departs from its own terminal, with a bakery across the way to stock up on snacks. Prices vary depending on when and how you purchase the ticket, but start around the S70 mark.

Expreso Molina (☎ 066-31-9989; Universitaria 160) A good company to know about, with departures from its own terminal not too far from the center. Not tops for comfort, but serves Lima (two daily departures and no less than seven night departures), Huancayo (one daily, five night departures) and Huancavelica (nightly departures).

Expreso Turismo Los Chankas (☎ 066-31-2391; Terrapuerto Libertadores de America) Currently one of the only through services to Cuzco (otherwise, you need to change in Andahuaylas) – departures are at 7:30am (Monday to Saturday) and 8:30pm (daily). Even though the road is now paved, breaking this long journey in Andahuaylas is a good idea.

Turismo Libertadores (☎ 962-889-142; Manco Cápac, btwn Calle de la Vega & 9 de Diciembre) One of the best of the cheap options to Lima: the one daytime and four nightly departures cost S40 to S60.

Andahuaylas

☎ 083 / POP 6800 / ELEV 2980M

Andahuaylas is normally used as a brief stopover between Ayacucho and Cuzco. But it's a good base for exploring the dramatic nearby Chanka ruins of Sondor, plus a host of natural attractions, from lakes to rock formations.

THE SHINING PATH: A DEADLY CONFLICT

The Sendero Luminoso's (Shining Path's) activities in the 1980s focused on deadly political, economic and social upheaval. They caused violent disruption, particularly across the Central Highlands and Amazon jungle, which were almost completely off-limits to travelers at the time. Things finally changed when the group's founder, Abimael Guzmán, a former Ayacucho university professor, was captured and imprisoned for life in 1992 – followed quickly by his top lieutenants. This led to a lull in activities, as Guzmán had not had time to prepare a direct successor.

But fragmented groups of Sendero Luminoso revolutionaries carried on in far remoter areas of Peru, albeit sporadically and with vastly reduced numbers. These groups split from the original Maoist philosophy of Guzmán, and in recent years their most notable activity has been drug trafficking (the US State Department confirms the group's links with the drug trade).

The last major clash in the Ayacucho region was in April 2009, when Shining Path rebels killed 13 army officers. A high-profile incident in August 2011 saw tourists on a high-end tour to Choquequirao, a major Inca site in the Cuzco region, politely asked to hand over valuables to help the cause of the revolution.

This sparked media reports of a Sendero Luminoso reemergence, which proved to be an exaggeration, particularly when its last remaining high-profile leaders were captured during 2012 and 2013. Since then, no major incidents involving the group have been reported.

Today the number of remaining Sendero Luminoso members is, according to the *Wall Street Journal*, only around 500. Activity is mostly in remote Amazon valleys such as the Upper Huallaga Valley north of Tingo María which, not by coincidence, contain significant cocaine production areas and are not safe for tourists to visit.

Outside the areas referred to above, the threat to tourists remains minor, and most places can be visited as safely as anywhere else in Peru. The overwhelming majority of Peruvians, it should be emphasized, have no allegiance to any faction of the Sendero Luminoso or to the military searching for the remainder of their followers.

The city was the capital of the Chanka people, who put up the fiercest resistance to the Incas before eventually falling in battle in around 1430. And the Chanka spirit of independence still burns in the second-most important city of Apurímac department.

It takes a while to make sense of the place, especially if you are here on a Sunday when one of the biggest and most bizarre markets in the Andes sprawls through the city center.

◉ Sights

Sondor RUIN

(admission S2; ⊙8am-5pm) The imposing hilltop site of Sondor, constructed by the Chanka people, stands a couple of kilometers past the end of Laguna de Pacucha. The Chanka were traditional enemies of the Incas, but evidently shared their appreciation of a good view. Evidence suggests the top of the impressive central pyramid in this extensive complex of ruins was an important sacrifice spot. Bring a picnic and spend an afternoon up here.

Buses to Laguna de Pacucha from Puente Nuevo on Av Ejercito in Andahuaylas run up as far as the beginning of the track to Sondor, from where it is a 20-minute uphill walk to the site entrance.

Bosque de Piedras de Pampachiri ROCK FORMATION

(Pabellones) **FREE** A stunning *bosque de piedras* (rock forest) standing out of a plain in surreal, conical shapes. The village of Pampachiri, about 2½ hours' drive south of Andahuaylas, is the jump-off point for visits; you can ask at the municipal offices about getting a guide for the *bosque de piedras*, or you can go solo (bring your own gear and seek advice in the municipal offices prior to embarking).

A *colectivo* (shared transportation) taxi to Pampachiri costs about S20 per passenger. From there, you will need further transport (S5 per person) to Pabellones, right by the *bosque de piedras*.

Laguna de Pacucha LAKE

FREE Backed by sweeping pine forests, this lake is a wonderful watery weekend escape for locals; the rest of the time, it's a very quiet place. In the lakeside village of Pacucha, and then heading counterclockwise around the lake, there are a few fun restaurants, boat-hire places and even foosball tables to entertain you.

Public transport runs up here from Puente Nuevo by the river on Av Ejercito in the center of Andahuaylas.

Sleeping

El Encanto de Oro Hotel HOTEL $
(☑083-42-3066; Av Casafranca 424; s/d incl breakfast from S40/60; ☏) Features spotlessly clean rooms of varying shapes and sizes, all with frilly curtains and phones. Friendly and welcoming, with the best tourist information around, and located near the indoor market.

Imperio Chanka HOTEL $$
(☑083-42-3065; Vallejo 384; s/d incl breakfast S60/90; ☏) With a modern, vaguely appealing look, this multistory cement building features good, clean rooms that are well looked after. There's also an on-site restaurant.

Eating

★ Pizzeria il Gato ITALIAN $$
(Cáceres Tresierra 342; S10-36; ⊙6pm-midnight) The coziest, friendliest pizzeria you ever did see. Chunky wood tables, heavenly pizza served on boards, and pictures of the department (province) of Apurímac on the walls, interspersed with local children's drawings of *gatos* (cats). Often a complimentary nightcap is served before your departure.

Puma de Piedra PERUVIAN $$
(www.facebook.com/pumadpiedra; Los Sauces s/n; mains S15-34; ⊙9am-11pm) Simply the best for local grub, whether that is *trucha* (trout) from a local lake or *pachamanca*. This is where you want to be when it gets hot in Andahuaylas – a lovely landscaped garden where sensational Andean cuisine is served.

ⓘ Information

BCP (Av Peru 318; ⊙9am-6pm Mon-Fri) has an ATM and changes US dollars. There's a Western Union office and several *casas de cambio* on Ramón Castilla.

ⓘ Getting There & Away

AIR
LC Peru (☑in Lima 083-20-1259; www.lcperu.pe; Plaza de Armas) flies daily to Lima. A taxi to the airport, lying south of town on Hwy 308, costs about S30.

BUS
The **Terminal Terrestre** (Malecón Mil Amores s/n) is Andahuaylas' ramshackle main bus station, though some companies depart from their own stations (all conveniently located nearby).

Heading east, **Expreso los Chankas** (Malecón Mil Amores 135, Terminal los Chankas), among a host of other companies with minivans, runs daily services to Cuzco (S35, 10 hours) via Abancay (S15, five hours).

Several companies with offices in Terminal Terrestre run faster, more comfortable and expensive minibuses throughout the day to Abancay (S15 to S20, four hours) where many more Cuzco-bound services await.

Heading west, Expreso los Chankas has daily services to Ayacucho at around 7am and 8pm (S25, five to six hours), although Sunday services are unreliable. **Transportes Sarmiento Silvera** (Terminal Terrestre) does the same route in similar time for S30 and runs more regularly, but its minivans are more cramped.

For Lima (S60 to S130, 20 hours), the best direct services are run by **Expreso Internacional Palomino** (☑083-42-1850; cnr Av del Ejercito, Av Ayacucho & Jirón Palma).

For Laguna de Pacucha and Sondor, you can catch a **minibus** to the approach track to Sondor, which passes counterclockwise around the lake first (S4, one hour). Go in the morning – transport peters out by 4pm. You can also take a taxi.

TAXI
If you're in a hurry, *colectivos* (shared transportation) leave throughout the day to Abancay (S30, three hours) and, should there be demand, Cuzco. They depart from the Expreso los Chankas bus terminal.

AT A GLANCE

★

POPULATION
Piura: 755,500

OLDEST PRE-COLUMBIAN RUINS
Caral: c 2600BC

BEST BEACH HOSTEL
Loki del Mar (p360)

BEST BREAKFAST
Bottega Capuccino
(p354)

BEST SEAFOOD
La Sirena d'Juan
(p362)

📅

WHEN TO GO
Mar
Summer's sizzling
sun remains, but
prices smolder back
down to earth.

Apr–Nov
The further north
you go, the shinier
the sun and the fewer
the people.

Nov–Feb
Surf's up (and so are
summer prices) in
Máncora, Huanchaco
and Puerto Chicama.

Caballitos de tortora boats (p339), Huanchaco
CHRISTIAN VINCES/SHUTTERSTOCK ©

North Coast

This staggering shore has some of the world's best surfing, a jaw-dropping array of archaeological sites and evocative desertscapes straight out of *Mad Max*. In this land of rock and desert sand, you'll also find a few verdant valleys, while Peru's only mangrove forests cling for their lives up north. There's a lot of hyperbole to be had – one of the world's longest left breaks challenges surfers in Puerto Chicama, South America's oldest civilization vexes archaeological explorers at Caral, and the massive pre-Columbian adobe complex at Chan Chan was once the largest city in the Americas. The backpacker hubs of Máncora and Huanchaco kick into full party mode from November to March.

North Coast Highlights

1 **Chan Chan**
(p331) Wandering the high-walled adobe ruins and marveling at 700-year-old friezes.

2 **Máncora** (p359) Indulging in sun, surf and sand in Peru's premier beachside hot spot.

3 **Huaca de la Luna** (p334) Discovering hidden messages in the colorful walls of one of the north's most fascinating archaeological complexes.

4 **Museo Tumbas Reales de Sipán** (p348) Marveling at the vast wealth of once-buried booty at the North Coast's best museum.

5 **Playa Lobitos** (p357) Dragging your board up the coast in search of that elusive perfect swell.

6 **Trujillo** (p322) Getting to know the friendly locals and showing off your dance moves at some of the north's best bars.

7 **Restaurante Big Ben** (p339) Finding ceviche salvation in the coastal desert.

8 **Reserva Ecológica Chaparrí Wildlife** (p350) Settling in on a search for the elusive South American spectacled bear at this rustic nature reserve.

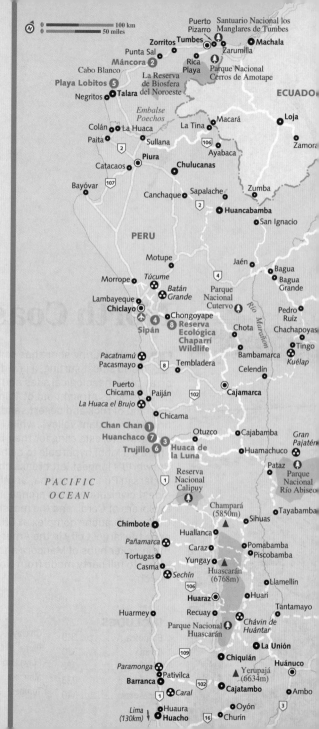

Barranca

♪ 01 / POP 146,200

Loud and unruly Barranca is used primarily as a transit hub to Huaraz, or as a stopover for visits to the nearby Caral archaeological site. The town's action centers on the plaza, where you'll find groups of rollerskating kids, couples taking romantic *paseos* (strolls), a yellow church and a spouting fountain.

Neighboring Pativilca, 10km further north, is where the road branches off to Huaraz and the Cordillera Blanca. This spectacular route climbs inland past cactus-laden cliffs and cathedrals of sheer rock, with desert brown slowly turning into a carpet of greenery as you climb to Huaraz.

◎ Sights

★ **Caral** ARCHAEOLOGICAL SITE
(www.zonacaral.gob.pe; admission S11, guide S20; ⊘ 9am-6pm) Caral culture arose in the Supe Valley some 4500 to 5000 years ago, making it one of the world's earliest large cities, alongside those in Mesopotamia, Egypt, India and China. This ancient culture was a conglomeration of 18 city-states and controlled the three valleys of Supe, Pativilca and Fortaleza, with the main seat of government at Caral. At the site, six stone pyramids have been found alongside amphitheaters, ceremonial rooms, altars, adobe complexes and several sunken circular plazas.

The monumental ruins are located about 25km inland from Barranca. Considering how few people visit Caral, the site is well set out for visitors. There are plaques in Spanish and English illustrating points of interest. Weekends are a great time to visit because handicrafts and local food are for sale at the site.

These ruins confounded Peruvian archaeologists when they proved to be part of the oldest civilization in South America. Before Caral's discovery the city of Chavín de Huántar near Huaraz, built around 900 BC, held that particular title.

The pyramids at Caral, most of which have been at least partially excavated, all have stairways leading to their peaks, where offerings were once made; there are also two separate lookouts offering great views of the lush Supe Valley. Looking down on the farmland surrounded by dramatic barren mountains, it becomes immediately obvious why this location was chosen for the city.

The people of Caral-Supe were experts in agriculture, construction, public administration and making calendars and musical instruments. Evidence of elaborate religious ceremonies among elites suggests a highly stratified culture in which classes were organized according to their labor in society. Archaeologists at Caral believe that men and women may have enjoyed considerable equality. A large geoglyph – a design carved into earth – called Chupacigaro attests to the Caral people's sophisticated measurements of the movements of the stars. Unesco declared the Sacred City of Caral a World Heritage site in 2009.

Unfortunately there is no site museum here and many of the most interesting items found at the site, including millennia-old bone flutes and Peru's oldest quipus (a system among Andean cultures of tying cords in knots to convey information), have been whisked off to Lima. However, there is a small interpretation center with some interesting artifacts.

Lima Tours (p540) arranges expensive private tours to Caral and Paramonga from Lima on request.

The 'paved' road to Caral is in very poor condition and is full of craters. Road access to the archaeological site is 3.5km down a dirt spur road that veers off the main road a few kilometers before town. The road crosses a river and is often impassable during the December to March wet season. If it's raining don't cross, even if the river is low – water levels can rise rapidly, trapping vehicles on the far side.

An alternative all-weather access is a footbridge on the outskirts of Caral town, from where it's a 30-minute walk to the site.

Irregular *colectivos* (shared transportation) depart from Calle Berenice Davila in Barranca to Caral town fairly regularly (S6, two hours), from where it's about a 45-minute walk to the site. For a few soles extra they will drop visitors at the footbridge. More frequent *colectivos* leave from the port of Supe (10 minutes' drive from Barranca), which can be reached in a shared taxi from the market area. If there are enough visitors, *colectivos* from Supe will run all the way to the Caral site for S10 a head.

Alternatively, elusive private taxis cost around S100 for the return journey (including waiting time). If you can't find a taxi in town, the *colectivo* drivers are usually willing to offer express services.

Paramonga RUINS
(♪ 012-36-0894; www.muniparamonga.gob.pe; admission S10, guide S10; ⊘ Tue-Sun 9am-5pm) The

adobe temple of Paramonga, known locally as La Fortaleza, is situated beside the Panamericana Norte, 4km beyond the turnoff for the Huaraz road, and was built by the Chimú culture, which was the ruling power on the north coast before it was conquered by the Incas. The fine details of the massive temple have long been eroded, but the multitiered construction is nonetheless impressive and affords fantastic panoramas of the lush valley.

Colectivos from Barranca (S2.50, 25 minutes) leave from the corner of Ugarte and Lima and will drop you off in the town of Paramonga, 3km from the entrance. Alternatively take a nonexpress Huarmey-bound bus and ask to be let off at the access way. A private return taxi from Barranca, including wait time, will cost about S80, but they're hard to come by.

🛏️ Sleeping & Eating

Hostal Continental　　　　HOTEL $
(☑ 012-35-2458; Ugarte 190; s/d from S40/55; 🌐)
Recently renovated, but still fairly basic, this is the best budget choice in town, offering clean rooms in a solid location a block from Plaza de Armas. Weak water pressure means some yoga skills are required to get a proper shower. Ask for a room in the back to save on street noise. Don't count on internet access.

Hotel Chavín　　　　HOTEL $$
(☑ 012-35-5025; www.hotelchavin.com.pe; Gálvez 222; s/d from S85/165; 🌐🅿) Barranca's bigshot hotel has comfortable rooms that are perfectly preserved in a resplendent 1970s style, contrasting with striking new hardwood floors and flat-screen TVs. There's a karaoke bar and pool area out back, plus a decent attached restaurant, making this a one-stop shop for Barranca stopovers.

Gran Chifa Central　　　　PERUVIAN $
(☑ 015-89-1461; Reyes Barboza 137; meals S10-17.50)
While ostensibly a *chifa* (Chinese) restaurant this busy place, a couple of blocks from the plaza, also serves up some topnotch traditional Peruvian plates. Take your pick from more than 40 different top-value menus.

ℹ️ Getting There & Away

Turismo Barranca (☑ 996-136-847; Belissario Suarez 102) buses leave every 10 minutes for Lima (S15, six hours) from 2:30am to 1am. Less frequent, but a far better option, is **Movil Bus** (☑ 012-35-9230; www.moviltours.com. pe; Lima 122), which has comfortable express buses (S20 to S30, four hours).

Alternatively flag down one of the many buses heading in the direction of Lima. Most buses from Lima going up the coast can also drop you in Barranca.

For Huaraz catch a *colectivo* (S2) to the Pecsa gas station in Pativilca, 3km from the Huaraz turnoff. From there *colectivos* leave when full (S30, three hours); infrequent buses from Lima also stop to pick up passengers.

Casma

☑ 043 / POP 32,800

Casma's big draw is the archaeological site of Sechín, about 5km away. Its once-important colonial port (11km from town) was sacked by various pirates during the 17th century, and the town today is merely a friendly blip on the historical radar.

From Casma the Pan-American Hwy branches off for Huaraz via the Callán Pass (4225m). This route is tough on your backside but offers excellent panoramic views of the Cordillera Blanca. Most points of interest in town lie along the Pan-American Hwy, between the Plaza de Armas in the west and the petrol station in the east.

👁️ Sights

Sechín　　　　ARCHAEOLOGICAL SITE
(admission S6; ⊙ 9am-5pm) One of Peru's granddaddy archaeological sites, Sechín is located 5km southeast of Casma and dates from about 1600 BC. It is among the more important and well-preserved ruins along this coast, though it has suffered some damage from grave robbers and natural disasters.

The warlike people who built this temple remain shrouded in mystery. The site consists of three exterior walls of the main temple, which are completely covered in gruesome, 4m-high bas-relief carvings of warriors and captives being vividly eviscerated. Ouch! Inside the main temple are earlier mud structures that are still being excavated: you can't go in, but there is a model in the small on-site **museum**. Stop by the museum first if you're in need of a guide, as you may be able to hire a Spanish-speaking caretaker for S30.

To get here, a *mototaxi* (three-wheeled motorcycle rickshaw taxi) from Casma costs around S2 each way, or S6 round trip if you want your driver to hang around.

Other early sites in the Sechín area have not been excavated due to a lack of funds. From the museum you can see the large, flat-topped hill of **Sechín Alto** in the distance.

The nearby fortress of **Chanquillo** consists of several towers surrounded by concentric walls, but it is best appreciated from the air. Aerial photographs are on display at the museum.

🍴 Sleeping & Eating

Hostal Gregori HOTEL $
(☎ 043-58-0573; Ormeño 579; s/d/tr from S25/60/70; ☐) Your best bet in town has a pretty interior courtyard punctuated by a handful of statues. The rooms have firmish beds and refurbished bathrooms with cement and glass sink vanities. Pop on the flat-screen for a late-night escape to TV land.

El Tío Sam PERUVIAN $$
(☎ 043-71-1447; Huarmey 138; mains S20-38) Offering big plates of delicious regional cuisine, this is your best bet in Casma. The menu is diverse, but go for one of the seafood options, which are outrageously good – its ceviche, which outclasses the town, was voted Ancash's best at one point (Ancash is a region of northern Peru). There are also some good-looking steak dishes.

ℹ️ Information

MONEY

There's a branch of **BCP** (Bolívar 111) with ATMs.

ℹ️ Getting There & Away

Colectivo taxis to Chimbote leave frequently from a spot a half-block east of Plaza de Armas.

Most bus companies are on Ormeño in front of the petrol station at the eastern end of town. Many buses stop here to pick up extra passengers.

Cruz del Norte (☎ 043-41-1633; www.transportescruzdelnorte.com; Panamericana Norte) offers frequent services to Lima. **Tepsa** (☎ 043-41-2275; www.tepsa.com.pe; Auxiliar Panamericana; ◷ 8am-11pm) has a comfortable bus to Lima departing at 11:15pm daily. **Erick El Rojo** (☎ 044-47-4957; www.turismoerickelrojo.pe; Ormeño 145) has various daily departures to Trujillo and one 7:30pm departure to Tumbes.

Yungay Express (Panamericana Norte) has three daily buses that take the scenic route to Huaraz via the Callán Pass. Faster minivans to Huaraz leave from near the traffic circle on the Panamericana when full.

Mototaxis (S2) make the run to Sechín. They are all around town, but there's an honest cluster operating as Motocars Virgen de Fatima on Plaza San Martín.

Ticket prices fluctuate with the quality of the bus/classes.

CASMA BUSES

DESTINATION	COST (S)	DURATION (HR)
Chimbote	6	1
Huaraz	20-30	2½-3
Lima	20-65	5½-7
Máncora	50-60	11
Trujillo	15	3
Tumbes	50-60	12-13

Chimbote

☎ 043 / POP 214,800

Chimbote is Peru's largest fishing port. With fish-processing factories lining the roads in and out of town, you'll probably smell it before you see it. The odor of fermenting fish may take a while to get used to, but the vibrant open plaza in the town's heart is less overwhelming. The fishing industry has declined from its 1960s glory days due to overfishing, but you'll still see flotillas moored offshore every evening as you take a sunset walk along the *malecón* (boardwalk).

This roughish port town is a transit hub, not a tourist destination, but you may have to stay overnight if you're catching an early morning bus to Huaraz along the hair-raising Cañón del Pato route.

🛏️ Sleeping

Hospedaje Chimbote HOTEL $
(☎ 043-35-6588; Pardo 205; s/d S30/40, without bathroom S20/30; ☐) A team of siblings owns this lovely budget option, which has been in the family since opening in 1959. Cell-like rooms have windows onto the corridor, which is a bright, freshly painted joy for these prices. And despite his name, manager Willie Malo (Bad Willie) is a wonderfully friendly English-speaking chef who just loves to receive international visitors.

Some shared bathrooms have only cold water, but you can use the hot-water shower upstairs if you desire.

Hotel San Felipe HOTEL $$
(☎ 043-32-3401; www.hotelcasinosanfelipe.com; Pardo 514; s/d/ste incl breakfast S80/115/160; ☐@☐) Across from the Plaza de Armas, the town's most comfortable option is run with a helpful smile. Equipped with elevators, this hotel, with its gaudy facade, offers clean, business-style rooms with strong hot showers and cable TV. Be sure to take your

continental breakfast on the 5th-floor terrace with plaza views.

A glitzy downstairs casino will help you live out your Las Vegas card-shark fantasies.

Real Hotel Gran Chimú HOTEL **$$**
(☑ 043-32-8104, 043-32-3721; www.realhotelgran chimu.com; Gálvez 109; s/d S100/120, r with view S150) This charming and dignified old building is roomy and aloof, lazing by the sea and espousing a laissez-faire life philosophy that's a welcome reprieve from Chimbote's buzzing streets. Upstairs, 76 spacious rooms and three suites are decked out with the essential mod cons and bathtubs; some come with a view over the trawler-filled bay.

It has a decent restaurant and bar.

Eating

The *chifa* at **Hostal Chifa Canton** (Bolognesi 498; mains $8.50-35.50) is top quality. There are plenty of good spots along Bolognesi and Pardo in the vicinity of Plaza de Armas as well.

Mar & Luna SEAFOOD **$$**
(cnr Villavicencio & Malecón; mains S20-25; ☺ 9am-11pm) This retro-pop pub cranks out the hits from the '70s, '80s and '90s, and serves up plentiful seafood favorites such as ceviche and *chupe de cangrejo* (crab chowder). There's a giant guitar on the ceiling that pays tribute to *Sgt Pepper's Lonely Hearts Club Band* and rock posters throughout. It's probably the liveliest spot in town and has good ocean views.

Restaurant Paola PERUVIAN **$$**
(☑ 043-34-5428; Bolognesi 401; mains S16-34; ☺ 8am-midnight) This popular corner bistro is decked out in smart red and black motifs and serves sandwiches and light meals, in addition to more filling traditional plates. High quality and very reasonable prices.

❶ Getting There & Away

Colectivos for Casma (S6, 45 minutes) depart from the corner of Pardo and Balta.

All long-distance buses leave from the Terminal Terrestre 'El Chimbador,' about 5km east of town, across from the municipal stadium (a S6 taxi ride, or catch *colectivo* 25 on Pardo for S2.50). There's an internet cafe in the terminal.

Many companies run buses to Lima. There are hourly services on ordinary buses during the day, but these make many stops and are generally not very comfortable. Most luxury express buses depart between 10pm and midnight, though a few leave in daylight. Reputable companies, several of which also have offices lined up with the banks along Bolognesi, include **Oltursa** (☑ 017-08-5000; www.oltursa.pe), **Línea** (☑ 043-35-4000; www.linea.pe), **Civa** (☑ 014-18-1111; www.excluciva.pe) and **Cruz Del Sur** (☑ 080-11-1111; www.cruzdelsur.com.pe), the last of which has the most comfortable Lima buses, with departures at 11:15am, 3pm, 11pm, 11:15pm, 11:20pm and 11:45pm.

America Express (☑ 014-24-1352; www.amer icaexpress.com.pe) has buses leaving for Trujillo every 15 minutes from 5:25am to 9:30pm.

Buses to Huaraz and the Cordillera Blanca run along one of three routes: the dazzling yet rough road through the Cañón del Pato; an equally rough road that climbs through the mountains from Casma; or the longer, comfortably paved route through Pativilca. Travel times on these routes range from seven to nine hours.

Yungay Express (☑ 043-35-0855) has buses to Caraz and Huaraz through the Cañón del Pato at 8:30am, 12:30pm and 3pm and via Casma at 7am, 8am, 1pm and 2:45pm. It pays to book Huaraz buses a day in advance.

More comfortable are the **Movil Tours** (☑ 017-16-8000; www.moviltours.com.pe) buses, which run via Pativilca at 11:30pm and midnight, with the former continuing on to Caraz.

For the northern mountains, **Caxamarca Express** (☑ 969-070-999; Terminal Terrestre El Chimbador) has one direct 10pm bus to Cajamarca.

CHIMBOTE BUSES

DESTINATION	COST (S)	DURATION (HR)
Cajamarca	60	8
Caraz	20-30	6-7
Chiclayo	23-40	6
Huaraz	20-65	5-8
Lima	35-85	6-7
Máncora	90-120	11
Piura	35-80	8
Trujillo	12-15	2
Tumbes	40-120	12

Trujillo

☑ 044 / POP 709,500

Stand in the right spot and the glamorous streets of old Trujillo look like they've barely changed in hundreds of years. Well, there are more honking taxis now, but the city still manages to put on a dashing show with its polychrome buildings and profusion of colonial-era churches. Most people come here to visit the remarkable pre-Incan archaeological sites nearby, spending just a short time wandering the compact city center.

The behemoth Chimú capital of Chan Chan (p331) is nearby. It was the largest pre-Columbian city in the Americas, making it the top attraction in the region. Other Chimú sites bake in the surrounding desert, among them the immense and suitably impressive Huacas del Sol y de la Luna (p334) (Temples of the Sun and Moon), which date back 1500 years.

Beach bums may consider staying in the laid-back surfer village of Huanchaco (p335), just 20 minutes up the road.

History

The area has been inhabited for millennia, with several prominent pre-Incan civilizations popping up in the fertile oasis.

Francisco Pizarro founded Trujillo in 1534, and he thought so highly of this patch of desert he named it after his birthplace in Spain's Estremadura. Spoiled by the fruits of the fertile Moche valley, Trujillo never had to worry about money – wealth came easily. With life's essentials taken care of, thoughts turned to politics and life's grander schemes, and so the city's reputation for being a hotbed of revolt began. The town was besieged during the Inca rebellion of 1536 and in 1820 was the first Peruvian city to declare independence from Spain.

The tradition continued into the 20th century, as bohemians flocked, poets put pen to paper (including Peru's best poet, César Vallejo) and rebels raised their fists defiantly in the air. It was here that the Alianza Popular Revolution Americana (APRA) workers' party was formed – and where many of its members were later massacred.

◉ Sights

Trujillo's colonial mansions and churches, most of which are near the Plaza de Armas, are worth seeing, though they don't keep very regular opening hours.

Hiring a good local guide is recommended if you are seriously interested in history. Many churches are often only open for early morning mass, usually from 6am to 8am, but visitors at those times should respect worshippers and not wander around. Those with an interest in colonial churches should swing by iPerú (p330) to pick up a *Recorridos Religiosos* walking guide.

The creamy pastel shades and beautiful wrought-iron grillwork fronting almost every colonial building are unique Trujillo touches.

◉ Plaza de Armas

Trujillo's spacious and spit-shined main square, surely the cleanest in the Americas and definitely one of the prettiest, hosts a colorful assembly of preserved colonial buildings and an impressive statue dedicated to work, the arts and liberty. Elegant mansions abound, including Hotel Libertador (p328).

On Friday mornings from 10:30am to 11:30am there are *'marinera para todos'* events where participants can take *marinera* classes (a typical coastal Peruvian dance involving much romantic waving of handkerchiefs), while on Saturday evenings performances of traditional dances from Trujillo and other departments are held.

Casa de Urquiaga   HISTORIC BUILDING
(Pizarro 446; ⊙9:15am-3:15pm Mon-Fri, 10am-1pm Sat) **FREE** Owned and maintained by Banco Central de la Reserva del Perú since 1972, this beautiful colonial mansion's history dates to 1604, though the original house was completely destroyed in the earthquake of 1619. Rebuilt and preserved since, it now houses exquisite period furniture, including a striking writer's desk once used by Simón Bolívar, who organized much of his final campaign to liberate Peru from the Spanish empire from Trujillo in 1824.

There is also a small collection of Moche, Nazca, Chimú and Vicús pottery. It's a working bank, so security is high for a free attraction.

Basilica Menor Catedral   CHURCH
(Plaza de Armas s/n; admission to museum S4; ⊙church 7am-1pm & 4-8pm daily, museum 9am-1pm & 4-7pm Mon-Fri, 9am-1pm Sat) Known simply as 'La Catedral,' this bright, canary-yellow church fronting the plaza was begun in 1647, destroyed in 1759, and rebuilt soon afterward. The cathedral has a famous basilica, which is generally open to visitors, and a museum of religious and colonial art, though there are intriguing frescoes in the basement (along with a few bats).

◉ East of the Plaza de Armas

Museo de Arqueología   MUSEUM
(Junín 682; S5; ⊙9am-2:30pm Mon, to 4:30pm Tue-Sat) This well-curated museum features a rundown of Peruvian history from 12,000 BC to the present day, with an emphasis on Moche, Chimú and Inca civilizations as well as the lesser-known Cupisnique and Salinar

Trujillo

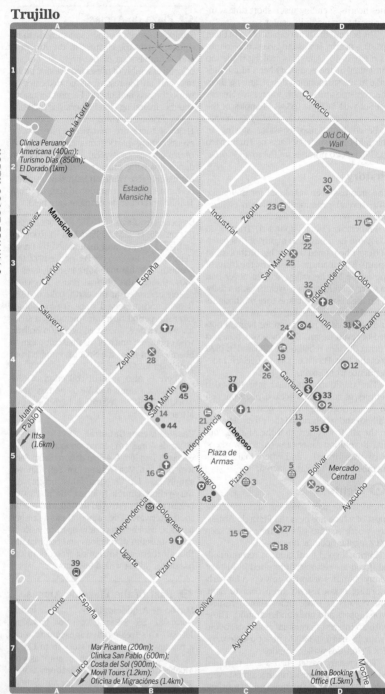

Clínica Peruano
Americana (400m);
Turismo Días (850m);
El Dorado (1km)

Old City
Wall

Estadio
Mansiche

Ittsa
(1.6km)

Plaza de
Armas

Mercado
Central

Mar Picante (200m);
Clínica San Pablo (600m);
Costa del Sol (900m);
Movil Tours (1.2km);
Oficina de Migraciónes (1.4km)

Línea Booking
Office (1.5km)

cultures. It's also worth popping in for the house itself: a restored 17th-century mansion known as La Casa Risco, which features striking cedar pillars and gorgeous painted courtyard walls.

There are sometimes traditional dance performances in the courtyard, which are well worth checking out; ask staff for details.

Palacio Iturregui
NOTABLE BUILDING

(Pizarro 688; admission S5; ⊙8-10am daily) This imposing gray early 19th-century mansion is impossible to ignore. Built in neoclassical style, it has beautiful window gratings, 36 slender interior columns and gold moldings on the ceilings. General Juan Manuel Iturregui lived here after he famously proclaimed independence.

Today it's a private social club, so visits are restricted to between 8am and 10am; ring the bell to get access. There are also often temporary exhibits here that extend the opening hours for visits.

Casa de la Emancipación
NOTABLE BUILDING

(Pizarro 610; ⊙9am-1pm & 4-8pm) Now the Banco BBVA Continental, this building features a mishmash of colonial and Republican styles and is best known as the site where Trujillo's independence from colonial rule was formally declared on December 29, 1820. Check out the unique cubic Cajabamba marble stone flooring; there are also galleries dedicated to revolving art exhibitions, Peruvian poet César Vallejo and period furniture. It hosts live-music events as well – look for posters around town.

Iglesia del Carmen
CHURCH

(☑044-24-1823; cnr Colón & Bolívar; ⊙4-5:15pm Mon-Fri) The Iglesia del Carmen and its charming monastery is home to an impressive Carmelite museum – the **Pinacoteca El Carmen** – but visiting is a real mission. You'll need to make an advance reservation and have a minimum of three visitors and even then must come in the specified hours of visitation.

Casona Orbegoso
HISTORIC BUILDING

(Orbegoso 553) Named after a former president of Peru, this beautiful 18th-century corner manor is home to a collection of well-worn and period furnishings, but its stuck-in-time feel is being increasingly insured by its ongoing closure for renovations. There was still no estimated reopening date when we came through.

Trujillo

⊙ North & West of the Plaza de Armas

There are several interesting churches near the Plaza de Armas that are well worth viewing from the outside on a walking tour of the city even when they are not open for visitors: **Iglesia de la Compañía** (Independencia), now part of the Universidad Nacional de Trujillo; **Iglesia de Santa Ana** (cnr Orbegoso & Zepita); **Iglesia de Santo Domingo** (cnr Pizarro & Bolognesi) and **Iglesia de Santa Clara** (cnr Junín & Independencia).

Casa Ganoza Chopitea   NOTABLE BUILDING
(Independencia 630; ⊙ 5:30-11:30pm Mon-Sat) Northeast of the cathedral, this c 1735 mansion, also known as Casa de los Léones, is considered to be the best-preserved mansion of the colonial period in Trujillo. The details are stunning, from the elaborate gateway at the entrance to 300-year-old frescoes and Oregon-pine pillars.

Take note of the 'JHS' insignia above the entrance, between the male and female lions (from which the Casa de los Léones

name derives). It stands for 'Jesus,' 'Hombre' (Man), 'Salvador' (Savior) and stems from the building's time as a convent. Best of all, perhaps, is that it now houses the wonderful Casona Deza cafe (p329).

⊙ Tours

There are dozens of tour agencies in Trujillo. Some supply guides who speak English but don't know much about the area; some supply guides who are well informed but don't speak English. Entrance fees are *not* included in the listed tour prices. Most full-day tours cost around S35 to S60, including transport and guide. If you prefer your own guide, it's best to go with a certified official guide who knows the area well. Ask at iPerú (p330) for a list of certified guides and contact details.

Trujillo Tours   CULTURAL
(☎ 044-23-3091; www.trujillotours.com; Almagro 301; ⊙ 7:30am-1pm & 4-8pm) This friendly operation has three- to four-hour tours to Chan Chan, Huanchaco and Huacas del Sol y de la Luna, as well as city tours. Tours are available in English, French, Portuguese and German.

Colonial Tours TOUR
(📞044-29-1034; www.colonialtoursnorteperu.com; Independencia 616) Full-day guided tours to all the major archaeological sites. Tends to offer big discounts when things are slow.

Peru Together Travel TOURS
(📞044-22-1421; www.perutogethertravel.com; Plzarro 562; ⊘8am-8pm) A popular tour operator with regular departures to the main sights in the region.

🎉 Festivals & Events

El Festival Internacional de la Primavera FESTIVAL
(International Spring Festival) Trujillo's major festival is celebrated with parades, national dancing competitions (including, of course, the *marinera*), *caballos de paso* (Peruvian parade horses) displays, sports, international beauty contests and other cultural activities. It all happens in the last week in September and better hotels are booked out well in advance.

🛏 Sleeping

Some travelers prefer to stay in the nearby beach town of Huanchaco. Many budget and midrange hotels can be noisy if you get streetside rooms. For a city of its size and history, Trujillo lags way behind when it comes to design and boutique hotels.

Hospedaje El Mochilero HOSTEL $
(📞044-29-7842; elmochileroperu@gmail.com; Independencia 887; dm/s/d from S25/35/50; 🛜) It feels more like a youth hostel than anything else in Trujillo. It has hammocks out back, three big dorm rooms that sleep 10 to 12 (bring your earplugs), a guest kitchen and cool common areas for chillaxing megathons. There are basic cane cabins out back if you want to sleep in the open air. All in all, good vibes.

Enkanta Hostal HOSTEL $
(📞044-34-6553; Independencia 341; dm/r S32/74; 🛜) This old-school arty backpackers has a choice location just a block off the plaza and basic but clean facilities centered on courtyard common areas. It's a bit improvised and some dorms don't have windows, which can be a plus depending on how hard you party.

There's no sign, but look for the little backpack logo hanging off the door.

Hotel Chimor HOTEL $$
(📞044-20-2252; www.hotelchimor.com; Almagro 631; s/d/tr S110/160/220; 🛜) This is a very solid midrange choice for comfort and modernity. The contempo rooms can get a little hot, but they are quite sharp, with built-in desks, flat-screen TVs and leather headboards. It's friendly and central, and borders on boutique cool.

Hotel El Brujo HOTEL $$
(📞044-20-8120; www.elbrujohotel.com; Independencia 978; s/d/tr incl breakfast S151/201/251; ❄@🛜) This is a solid (though slightly boring) midrange option. It is clean and quiet, and its location close to several northern bus stations adds to the convenience factor. Despite the rad Brujo wall sculpture in the lobby, it's very businesslike, with spacious modern rooms and all the requisite amenities (minibar, cable TV and writing desk).

There's another branch outside the city center in Urbanización La Merced, so make sure to specify the address to taxi drivers.

Hotel Colonial HISTORIC HOTEL $$
(📞044-25-8261; www.hotelcolonial.com.pe; Independencia 618; s/d/tr S100/120/150; 🛜) This tastefully renovated, rose-colored colonial mansion has a great location just a block from the Plaza de Armas. It's a top contender in both the midrange and budget categories. It no longer offers dorms, but has plenty of good-value private rooms with solar hot water spread out over three levels.

Chatty and helpful staff, a tour desk, popular cafe, gorgeous courtyards, open spaces and a garden come together to keep attracting travelers. Some of the cozy rooms have balconies and great views of Iglesia de San Francisco opposite.

La Hacienda HISTORIC HOTEL $$
(📞044-23-2234; www.lahaciendatrujillo.pe; San Martín 780; s/d/tr S85/115/185; 🛜🏊) This Republican-era historic hotel has a gorgeous al fresco interior patio with its own singing lion-head fountain. The rooms could be nicer, but you get plenty of space and flat-screen TVs, plus a hodgepodge of furniture that could have been picked up at any number of estate sales throughout the ages.

There's a dip pool, Jacuzzi and sauna in the slightly ghetto grotto spa area.

Munay Wasi Hostel GUESTHOUSE $$
(📞992-249-074, 044-23-1462; munaywasi@hotmail.com; Colón 250; dm S30, d/tr S90/110, s/d/tr without bathroom S50/70/90; @🛜) A pleasant, family-run budget option with just nine rooms that woos travelers with a nice courtyard, a small communal lounge, a guest kitchen, included breakfast and a wholly different

atmosphere than most spots in Trujillo. Most rooms share decent hot-water bathrooms, but there is one with private facilities.

The owners are attentive and security is a priority.

★ **Hotel Libertador** HISTORIC HOTEL $$$
(📞 044-23-2741; www.hotellibertador.com.pe; Independencia 485; r incl breakfast from S442; 🅿 ❄ @ 🤶 ☎) The classy dame of the city's hotels, the 79-room Libertador is in a beautiful building that's the Audrey Hepburn of Trujillo – it wears its age with refined grace. It earns its four stars with a beautiful and lush courtyard pool, archways aplenty and modern rooms with all expected amenities.

Rooms are centered on a bright atrium that encompasses the three floors, but try to avoid the streetside rooms unless you want to watch the goings-on, as they tend to be noisy.

Costa del Sol RESORT $$$
(📞 044-48-4150; www.costadelsolperu.com; Los Cocoteros 505; s/d incl breakfast S670/730; 🅿 ❄ @ 🤶 ☎) This chain hotel has a large resort compound about a 10-minute taxi ride from the city center. The resort has a grand circular pool, spa with Jacuzzi, treatment rooms and steam baths, and expansive grounds patrolled by a troupe of alpacas (that must hate the heat). Rooms are classy and elegant. The downside? It's in the middle of freaking nowhere.

You won't feel like you are in Trujillo at all, but it offers facilities unmatched elsewhere in town. It's usually possible to get rooms for less than half the published rates.

Casa Andino Standard Plaza HOTEL $$$
(📞 044-48-1650; www.losconquistadoreshotel.com; Almagro 586; r incl breakfast S295; 🅿 ❄ @ 🤶) A few steps from the Plaza de Armas, this art-deco-inspired hotel has some of the best contemporary rooms in the city center. The newly remodeled baths have concrete and ceramic touches, though the air fresheners can be a little overpowering. All in all, it's a strong top-end contender, but if you want a pool, you should look elsewhere.

✖ Eating

The 700 *cuadra* (block) of Pizarro is where Trujillo's power brokers hang out and families converge, and they're kept well fed by a row of trendy yet reasonably priced cafes and restaurants. Some of the best eateries in Trujillo are a short taxi ride outside the town center.

If you're here on Monday look out for *shambar,* a traditional soup made with wheat, legumes, onions, pork and herbs and served all over town.

Jugería San Agustín SANDWICHES $
(Bolívar 526; sandwiches S3.50-7.50; ⏰ 8:30am-1pm & 4-8pm Mon-Sat, 9am-1pm Sun) You can spot this place by the near-constant lines snaking around the corner in summer as locals queue for the drool-inducing juices. But don't leave it at that. The chicken and *lechón* (suckling pig) sandwiches, slathered with all the fixings, are what you'll be telling friends back home about.

The house juice, consisting of pineapple, apple, peach and papaya, is a real winner.

Dulcería San Martín DESSERTS $
(📞 982-086-729; San Martín 714; items S5-6; ⏰ 9am-8pm) This simple family-run affair pulls a crowd for its traditional local desserts, including *mazamorra* (made from boiled purple corn with dried fruits), *crema volteada, tres leches, arroz zambito* (a mix of cooked rice and spices) and *arroz con leche* (made from rice, vanilla and milk). For the most part they're not overly sweet, which makes it easy to try more than one.

★ **El Celler de Cler** PERUVIAN $$
(📞 044-31-7191; cnr Gamarra & Independencia; mains S38-58; ⏰ 6pm-1am) This atmospheric spot is the only place in Trujillo to enjoy dinner (coupled with an amazing cocktail) on a 2nd-floor balcony – the wraparound number dates to the early 19th century. The food is upscale, featuring pasta and grills, and delicious. Antiques fuel the decor, from a 1950s-era American cash register to an extraordinary industrial-revolution pulley lamp from the UK.

While the food and ambience are great, it's the creative cocktails that really shine. Don't miss the classic *chilcano* (pisco, ginger ale and lime juice), souped up here with any number of twists (*rocoto, ají limo, maracuya* etc). Try to go after rush hour or on a weekend as, ambience notwithstanding, the streets below are noisy.

★ **Mar Picante** PERUVIAN $$
(www.marpicante.com; Húsares de Junín 412; mains S20-40; ⏰ 10am-5pm) This hugely popular place has recently undergone an overhaul and is now all polished concrete and industrial metal beams, but the food remains outrageously good. If you come to Trujillo without sampling its *ceviche mixto* (mixed

ceviche) ordered with a side of something spicy, you haven't lived life on the edge.

You'll get raw fish, crab, scallops and onions, marinated as usual in lime juice, piled on top of yucca and sweet potato, with a side of *canchas* (toasted corn) and corn on the cob.

This is the North Coast's best ceviche! Service is swift and friendly as well, no small feat considering it's always packed. Take a taxi (S4) or leg it southwest on Larco from the center. Húsares de Junín splits off to the southeast 200m south of España.

Patio Rojo   HEALTH FOOD **$$**
(☑044-24-2339; San Martín 873; mains S15-28; ☺8am-11pm Mon-Thu, to 1pm Fri & Sat, 10am-4pm Sun; 🖊) You wouldn't expect to find it in this part of town, but this hip, healthy cafe serves great snacks, sandwiches, main meals and desserts with plenty of vegan options. If the sun is out, pull up a chair in the pleasant patio; if not, there is an art-covered dining room with great tunes.

Casona Deza   PERUVIAN **$$**
(Independencia 630; mains S23-46; ☺5:30-11:30pm Mon-Sat; 🖊) 🖊 Expect excellent espresso, house-made desserts and tasty pizzas and pasta, often sourced organically, at this spacious cafe that occupies one of the city's most fiercely preserved colonial homes.

The Casa Ganoza Chopitea (p326) mansion (c 1735) was resurrected via auction by a local team of brothers passionate about Trujillo. Whether you're here for coffee, wine, sustenance or architectural oohing and aahing, it's an addictive spot.

El Mochica   PERUVIAN **$$**
(☑044-29-3441; Bolívar 462; mains S25-90; ☺noon-10pm) With bow-tied waiters and art scattered throughout, this place is aiming for high end, but the fancy seat covers and tablecloths thrown over plastic tables with cardboard taped to the bottom make it feel like a cut-priced wedding reception. But locals love it for the big plates of steaks, seafood and traditional dishes, which are indeed fairly tasty.

The *causas* (layers of mashed yellow potato with savory fillings) here are particularly good and are big enough to be a meal on their own. It also has a branch on the main strip in Huanchaco.

Restaurant Demarco   PERUVIAN **$$**
(☑044-23-4251; Pizarro 725; mains S15-47; ☺7:30am-11pm; 🖊) An elegant choice, with veteran cummerbund-bound waiters who fawn over you like in the 1940s, this tableclothed

classic offers a long list of sophisticated meat and seafood dishes, along with good-value lunch specials (S13.50 to S18.50) and pizzas.

It has mouthwatering *chupe de camarones,* a seafood stew of jumbo shrimp simmering in a buttery broth with hints of garlic, cumin and oregano, and the desserts are excellent, from classic tiramisu to mile-high *tres leches* (a spongy cake made with evaporated milk).

El Valentino   ITALIAN **$$**
(☑044-22-1328; Orbegoso 224; mains S34-49; ☺5pm-1am) This popular, long-running place is the best of the offerings on a block crowded with pizzerias, though the prices are at the high end of the spectrum for Trujillo. Pasta and meat dishes are on the menu, too, and there's an elegant formal dining area upstairs.

🍷 Drinking & Entertainment

⭐**El Tragsu**   BAR
(Las Hortencias 588; ☺9pm-4am Mon-Sat) This popular place south of the center is one of the best pubs in Peru, with a classic themed front room complete with elf decorations and an elegant wooden bar for those who want to converse. There's also a steamy split-level band room where the dial is stuck on 'full party' mode.

Café Bar Museo   BAR
(cnr Junín & Independencia; ☺5pm-late Mon-Sat) This locals' favorite shouldn't be a secret. The tall, wood-paneled walls covered in artsy posters and the classic marble-top bar feel like a cross between an English pub and a Left Bank cafe. Hands down the most interesting place to drink in Trujillo. There's a limited menu of bar snacks if you want to make a night of it.

Wachaque   LIVE MUSIC
(☑943-779-327; Los Algarrobos 574; ☺7pm-3am Thu-Sat) Overlooking pleasant Parque California, this welcoming modern place is billed as a gastrobar, but while the food is pretty good, it's more of an upmarket bar/disco hybrid. Get there early to grab one of the tables on the mezzanine, overlooking the stage where live bands belt out varied Latin music.

It's a good one-stop destination: you can eat, drink and dance here with a fun-loving, mostly local crowd.

ℹ Information

EMERGENCY
Policía de Turismo (☑044-29-1705; Almagro 442; ☺8am-11pm) Shockingly helpful. Tourist

police wear white shirts around town and some deputies speak English, Italian and/or French.

IMMIGRATION

Oficina de Migraciónes (☑ 044-28-2217; www.migraciones.com.pe; Larco, cuadra 12; ☺ 8am-4:15pm Mon-Fri, 9am-1pm Sat) Handles visas for foreign residents and tourist visa extensions.

MEDICAL SERVICES

Clínica Peruano Americana (☑ 044-24-2400; Mansiche 802) An established clinic offering general medical care with English-speaking doctors.

Clinica San Pablo (☑ 044-48-5244; www.sanpablotrujillo.com.pe; Húsares de Junin 690; ☺ 24hr) This modern clinic is considered one of the best in town and offers outpatient and emergency services.

MONEY

Changing money in Trujillo is a distinct pleasure – some of the banks are housed in well-preserved colonial buildings and all have ATMs that accept Visa and MasterCard. If lines are long, visit the *casas de cambio* (foreign-exchange bureaus) near Gamarra and Bolívar, which give good rates for cash.

Banco BBVA Continental (Pizarro 620) Bank housed in the handsome Casa de la Emancipación.

Banco de La Nacion (cnr San Martin & Almagro) Bank with fee-free ATM.

BCP (Gamarra 562) Bank with ATM.

Interbank (cnr Gamarra & Pizarro) Bank with ATMs.

POST

Serpost (Independencia 286) Postal services.

SAFE TRAVEL

Single women tend to receive a lot of attention from males in Trujillo – to exasperating, even harassing, levels. If untoward advances are made, firmly state that you aren't interested. Inventing a boyfriend or husband sometimes helps get the message across.

At night it's advisable to take cabs. Ask your hotel or restaurant to find you a *taxi de confianza* (trustworthy cab – generally with a bubble on top). A good rule: if no women or kids are around, it's probably not safe to be walking about.

Like many other cities, the noise-pollution levels in Trujillo are high. Civic groups have attempted to protest the constant bleating of taxi horns.

TOURIST INFORMATION

iPerú (☑ 044-29-4561; www.peru.travel; Independencia 467, oficina 106; ☺ 9am-6pm Mon-Sat, to 1pm Sun) Provides tourist information, maps, bus schedules and a list of certified guides and travel agencies.

Local tour companies can also provide you with some basic information on the area.

❶ Getting There & Away

AIR

The **airport** (TRU) is 10km northwest of town. **LATAM** (☑ 044-22-1469; www.latam.com; Almagro 480) has three daily flights between Lima and Trujillo. **Avianca** (☑ 080-01-8222; www.avianca.com; Real Plaza, César Vallejo Oeste 1345; ☺ 10am-9pm) flies the same route twice a day, while **LC Perú** (☑ 044-29-0299; www.lcperu.com; Almagro 305; ☺ 9am-8pm) has one evening flight.

BUS

Buses often leave Trujillo full, so booking a little earlier is advised. Several companies that go to southern destinations have terminals on the Panamericana Sur, the southern extension of Moche, and Ejército; check where your bus actually leaves from when buying a ticket.

Línea has services to most destinations of interest to travelers and is one of the more comfortable bus lines.

There's an enclave of bus companies around España and Amazonas offering Lima-bound night buses (eight hours).

If you want to travel to Huaraz by day, you'll need to go to Chimbote and catch a bus from there. For more frequent buses to Cajamarca and the Northern Highlands, head to Chiclayo.

For Otuzco *combis* (minibuses) depart between the 17th and 18th *cuadras* of Prolongacíon Unión, northeast of town. **Tours Pacifico** (☑ 044-42-7137; Prolongacíon Unión, cuadra 22) buses head up the mountain six times a day.

America Express (☑ 044-26-1906; www.americaexpress.com.pe; La Marina 315) A S5 taxi ride south of town, with buses to Chimbote every 20 minutes between 4am and 10:30pm.

Civa (☑ 044-25-1402; www.civa.com.pe; Ejército 285) Offers 8:30pm and 9:30pm buses to Lima.

Cruz del Sur (☑ 080-11-1111; www.cruzdelsur.com.pe; Amazonas 437) One of the biggest and priciest bus companies in Peru. It goes to Lima six times a day and has evening buses to Guayaquil from Monday to Saturday.

El Dorado (☑ 044-29-1778; Nicolás de Piérola 1070) Has rudimentary buses to Piura five times daily (12:30pm, 8pm, 8:30pm, 10:20pm and 11pm) and three to Máncora and Tumbes (7:30pm, 8:30pm and 9pm).

Emtrafesa (☑ 044-48-4120; www.emtrafesa.com; Tupac Amaru 185) Regular departures to Chiclayo and points further north.

Ittsa (☑ 044-28-4644; www.ittsabus.com; Juan Pablo II 1110) Buses for Piura (9am, 1:30pm, 11:15pm, 11:30pm and 11:45pm), as well as a Tumbes bus at 7pm and regular Lima-bound departures from 9am to 11:15pm.

Línea (☎ 044-29-7000; www.linea.pe) The company's **booking office** (☎ 044-24-5181; www.linea.pe; cnr San Martín & Obregoso; ☺ 8am-9pm Mon-Sat) is conveniently located in the historic center, although all buses leave from its **terminal** (☎ 044-29-9666; Panamerica Sur 2857) on Panamericana Sur, a S6 taxi ride away. Línea goes to Lima nine times daily between 9am and 10:45pm; to Piura at 1:30pm and 11pm; to Cajamarca at 10:30am, 1pm, 10pm, 10:30pm and 10:40pm; and to Huaraz at 9:30am and 9:30pm.

Móvil Tours (☎ 017-16-8000; www.moviltours. com.pe; Panamerica Sur 3955) Specializes in very comfortable long-haul tourist services. It has a 10pm service to Lima, and 9:40pm and 10:10pm departures to Huaraz, the first of which continues on to Caraz. There's a bus at 4pm to Chachapoyas and a 3pm bus to Tarapoto. A taxi to the station is S6, or catch a *combi* (California/Esperanza) on Av España and hop off at Ovalo Larco.

Oltursa (☎ 044-26-3055; www.oltursa.pe; Ejército 342) Offers five daily departures to Lima on comfortable buses at 11:30am, 8:45pm, 9pm, 9:30pm and 10:30pm.

Turismo Días (☎ 044-20-1237; www.turdias. com; Nicolás de Piérola 1079) Has four departures to Cajamarca (10am, 1:15pm, 10pm and 11pm) and two to Cajabamba (8pm and 9pm).

Around Trujillo

Microbuses marked 'H' and *combis* 'A' and 'B' for Huaca Esmeralda (S1.50), Chan Chan (S1.50) and Huanchaco (S2) pass the corners of **España and Ejército**, and **España and Independencia**, every few minutes. Buses for La Huaca Arco Iris, marked 'Parque Arco Iris,' run from the same corners.

For Huacas del Sol y de la Luna, head to the corner of Orbegoso and Avenida Los Incas southeast of the centre, where 'Campiña de Moche' *combis* (S1.50) pass every 15 minutes or so. Note that these buses are worked by professional thieves; keep valuables hidden and watch your bags carefully. A taxi to most of these sites will cost S15 to S20.

El Complejo Arqueológico la Huaca el Brujo, about 60km northwest of Trujillo, is harder to reach. The safest route is to catch a bus to Chocope (S4.50, 1½ hours) from Ovalo del Papa, southwest of Trujillo's center. Switch to a *colectivo* to Magdalena de Cao (S2.50, 20 minutes), where you'll need to negotiate with a *mototaxi* to take you to and from the site with waiting time (S15 for the round trip is about the going rate, depending on how long you want at the site). There are also Chocope-bound buses from the Provincial Bus Terminal Interurbano, southeast of central Trujillo, but this neighborhood is best avoided by tourists.

Trujillo Buses

DESTINATION	COST (S)	DURATION (HR)
Cajabamba	25-35	12
Cajamarca	25-80	6-7
Caraz	50-65	8
Chachapoyas	70-90	15
Chiclayo	20-45	3-4
Chimbote	12-60	2
Guayaquil (Ecuador)	130-200	18
Huaraz	45-65	5-9
Lima	30-120	8-9
Máncora	40-90	8-9
Otuzco	8	2
Piura	35-80	6
Tarapoto	90-120	18
Tumbes	40-95	9-12

❶ Getting Around

The airport is 10km northwest of Trujillo and reached cheaply on the Huanchaco *combi*, though you'll have to walk the last 1km. It takes around 30 minutes. A taxi from the city center costs S20.

A short taxi ride around town costs about S4. For sightseeing, taxis charge about S30 (in town) to S40 (out of town) per hour.

Around Trujillo

Five major archaeological sites can be easily reached from Trujillo by local bus or taxi. Two of these are principally Moche, dating from about 200 BC to AD 850. The other three, from the Chimú culture, date from about AD 850 to 1500. The relatively recently excavated Moche ruin of La Huaca el Brujo (p334) can also be visited, but it's not as convenient.

The Moche and Chimú cultures left the greatest marks on the Trujillo area, but they were by no means the only cultures in the region. In a March 1973 *National Geographic* article, Drs ME Moseley and CJ Mackey claimed knowledge of more than 2000 sites in the Río Moche valley and many more have been discovered since.

◉ Sights

Chan Chan ARCHAEOLOGICAL SITE
(www.chanchan.gob.pe; admission S10, guide for groups of 1-5 S40; ☺ 9am-4pm, museum closed Mon) Built around AD 1300 and covering

Around Trujillo

20 sq km, Chan Chan is the largest pre-Columbian city in the Americas and the largest adobe city in the world. Although it must have been a dazzling sight at one time, devastating El Niño floods and heavy rainfall have severely eroded much of the city's outer portions. You can still visit the impressive restored Palacio Nik An complex and revel in the broad plazas, royal burial chamber and intricate designs that remain.

At the height of the Chimú empire, Chan Chan was home to an estimated 60,000 people and contained a vast wealth of gold, silver and ceramics. The wealth remained more or less undisturbed after the Incas conquered the city, but once the Spaniards hit the stage, the looting began. Within a few decades little but gold dust remained. Remnants of what was found can be seen in museums nearby.

The Chimú capital consisted of 10 walled citadels, also called royal compounds. Each contained a royal burial mound filled with vast quantities of funerary offerings, including dozens of sacrificed young women and chambers full of ceramics, weavings and jewelry.

The Palacio Nik An (also called the Tschudi Complex, after a Swiss naturalist) is the only section of Chan Chan that's partially restored. Parts of the site are covered with tent-like structures to protect from erosion. It is possible that other areas will open in the future, but until they are properly policed and signed, you run the risk of being mugged if you visit them.

At the Palacio Nik An you'll find an entrance area with tickets, souvenirs, guides, bathrooms and drinks, but there's no longer a cafe so bring snacks. Guides hang around next to the ticket office.

The best option for a visit is with an organized guided tour from Trujillo or with a local site tour guide, as signage is extremely limited. There are usually English-, French-, German- and Italian-speaking guides available here. If you want to go it alone, the path is marked out with fish-shaped pointers and you can purchase a small booklet for S2 at the ticket checkpoint with descriptions of the different areas of the complex and a map.

The complex's centerpiece is a massive, restored **ceremonial courtyard**, where the 4m-thick interior walls are mostly decorated with re-created geometric designs. The ground-level designs closest to the door, representing three or four sea otters, are the only originals left and remarkably better preserved than many of the re-creations. A ramp at the far side of the high-walled plaza rises to the 2nd level (early wheelchair access?). Though all the Chan Chan walls have crumbled with time, parts of Nik-An's walls once stood more than 10m high.

Head out of the ceremonial courtyard and walk along the outside wall, which is one of the most highly decorated and best restored of Palacio Nik-An's walls. The adobe friezes show waves of fish rippling along the entire length of the wall above a line of seabirds. Despite their time-worn appearance, the few rougher-looking originals retain a fluidity and character somehow lacking in the contemporary version.

At the end of this wall, the marked path goes through the labyrinthine **audience rooms**. Their function is unclear, but their importance is evident in both the quantity and quality of the decorations – the rooms have the most interesting friezes in Palacio Nik An. Living so close to the ocean, the Chimú based much of their diet on seafood, and the importance of the sea reached venerable proportions. Fish, waves, seabirds and sea mammals are represented throughout the city, and in the audience rooms you'll find all of them in the one place. For the Chimú, both the moon and the sea were of religious importance (unlike the Incas, who worshipped the sun and venerated the earth).

Further on, the **second ceremonial courtyard** also has a ramp to the second level. West of this plaza you visit the **Gran Hachaque Ceremonial**, a freshwater pool surrounded by a verdant border of reeds and grasses. This was no doubt an important space for ceremonial life.

To the left is an area of several dozen small, crumbling cells that has been called the **Almacenes** (warehouses). Perhaps soldiers lived here, or the cells may have been used for storage. Next is the **mausoleum**, where a king was buried along with human sacrifices and ceremonial objects. To the left of the main tomb, a pyramid containing the bodies of dozens of young women was found.

The final area is the **assembly room**. This large rectangular room has 24 seats set into niches in the walls, and its amazing acoustic properties are such that speakers sitting in any one of the niches can be clearly heard all over the room.

The **site museum** (www.chanchan.gob.pe; admission free with Chan Chan ticket; ☺9am-4pm Tue-Sun) is out on the main road, about 500m before the main Chan Chan turnoff, and contains exhibits explaining Chan Chan and the Chimú culture. It has a few signs in Spanish and English, but a guide is still useful. The aerial photos and maps showing the huge extension of Chan Chan are fascinating, as tourists can only visit a tiny portion of the site.

Combis and buses to Chan Chan (S1.50) leave Trujillo every few minutes, passing the corners of España and Ejército, and España and Industrial. They'll drop you off at the turnoff, from where it's a 10-minute walk down to the ticket office. From Huanchaco take any Trujillo-bound transport.

A taxi from Trujillo or Huanchaco runs around S12.

Huaca Esmeralda   ARCHAEOLOGICAL SITE
(☑044-20-6304; www.chanchan.gob.pe; admission free with Chan Chan ticket; ☺9am-4pm) Halfway between Trujillo and Chan Chan, this Chimú temple is south of the main road, four blocks behind the Mansiche Church. Huaca Esmeralda was buried by sand and discovered by a local landowner in 1923. He attempted to uncover the ruins, but the 1925 El Niño began the process of erosion, which was exacerbated by floods. Although little restoration work has been done, it's still possible to make out characteristic Chimú designs of fish, seabirds, waves and fishing nets.

Green-signed B *combis* to Huaca Esmeralda leave Trujillo every few minutes; they pass the corners of España and Ejército. España and Independencia. The area is not always the safest, so consider going in a group or taking a taxi to the door. Esmeralda is the only temple in the combined ticket where you cannot pay admission, so don't visit it first.

Huaca Arco Iris   ARCHAEOLOGICAL SITE
(Rainbow Temple; ☑044-27-3281; www.chanchan.gob.pe; admission free with Chan Chan ticket, guides for groups of 1-5 S25) Also known locally as Huaca del Dragón, Huaca Arco Iris is in the suburb of La Esperanza, about 4km northwest of Trujillo. Dating from the 12th century, it is one of the better preserved of the Chimú temples – simply because it was buried under sand until the 1960s. Its location was known to a handful of archaeologists and *huaqueros* (grave robbers), but excavation did not begin until 1963. Unfortunately the 1983 El Niño caused damage to the friezes.

The *huaca* used to be painted, but these days only faint traces of yellow hues remain. It consists of a defensive wall more than 2m thick enclosing an area of about 3000 sq meters, which houses the temple itself. The building covers about 800 sq meters on two levels, with a combined height of about 7.5m. The walls are slightly pyramidal and covered with repeated rainbow designs, some of which have been restored. Ramps lead visitors to the very top of the temple, from where a series of large bins, found to contain the bones of infants – possibly human sacrifices – can be seen. This may have been a fertility temple since in many ancient cultures the rainbow represents rain, considered to be the bringer of life.

Local guides are sometimes available to show you around but don't count on it. If you want any sort of explanation it's best to come with a prearranged guide.

Buses from Trujillo to La Esperanza go northwest along the Panamericana and can drop you off at Huaca Arco Iris, or look for a *combi* marked 'Parque Industrial Arco Iris' on Av España.

★ Huacas del Sol y de la Luna
ARCHAEOLOGICAL SITE

(www.huacasdemoche.pe; site admission S10, museum S5; ☺ 9am-4pm) If there's one must-see archaeological site in the region, this is it. The Temples of the Sun and the Moon, attributed to the Moche period, are more than 700 years older than Chan Chan, yet parts of the complex are remarkably well preserved. Located on the south bank of the Río Moche, the main attraction here is the **Huaca de la Luna** with its phenomenal multicolored friezes. The entrance price includes an English-speaking guide; individual travelers need to wait for a group to fill. The larger **Huaca del Sol** is closed to visitors.

Archaeologists believe the Huaca de La Luna was the religious and ceremonial center of the Moche capital, while the Huaca del Sol was the administrative center. The two edifices are separated by 500m of open desert that once contained the dwellings and other buildings of the common residents.

While Huaca de la Luna is smaller than its neighbor, it proves that, in Moche pyramids at least, size isn't everything. The structure is riddled with rooms that contained ceramics and precious metals and are adorned with some of the beautiful polychrome friezes for which the Moche were famous. The *huaca* was built over six centuries to AD 600, with six succeeding generations expanding on it and completely covering the previous structure.

Archaeologists onion-skinning selected parts of the *huaca* have discovered that there are friezes of stylized figures on every level, some of which have been perfectly preserved by the later levels built around them.

Enthusiastic local guides will walk you through different parts of the complex and explain the richly colored motifs depicting Moche gods and zoomorphic figures, before leading you to the spectacular finale: the magnificent, richly decorated external wall. Don't even think of dropping out early. Many of the guides are volunteers, so tips are appreciated.

From the Huaca de la Luna site there are good views of the Huaca del Sol, which is the largest single pre-Columbian structure in Peru, though about a third of it has been washed away. The structure was built with an estimated 140 million adobe bricks, many of them marked with symbols representing the workers who made them. At one time

the pyramid consisted of several different levels connected by steep flights of stairs, huge ramps and walls sloping at 77 degrees. The last 1500 years have wrought their inevitable damage, and today the pyramid looks like a giant pile of crude bricks partially covered with sand. Despite this, its size alone makes the pyramid an awesome sight. The Huaca del Sol is not currently open to visitors as only minimal research has been conducted on the site.

Around 600m from the Huaca de la Luna car park, the excellent **Museo Huacas de Moche** (☎ 044-60-0457; admission S5; ☺ 9am-4pm) is a fascinating and well-planned museum with three rooms of objects excavated from the site and explanations in Spanish and English. Visitors need to check in here to buy a ticket and schedule a tour before heading over to the Huaca de la Luna. Entry to the museum costs an additional S5, and it's well worth popping in while you wait for your tour departure.

As you leave look around for *biringos,* the native Peruvian hairless dogs that hang out here. Their body temperature is higher than that of normal dogs and they have traditionally been used as body warmers for people with arthritis.

Combis (S1.50) for the Huacas del Sol y de la Luna leave from Av Los Incas in Trujillo every 15 minutes or so. It's also possible to take a taxi (S15).

Complejo Arqueológico la Huaca el Brujo
ARCHAEOLOGICAL SITE

(www.elbrujo.pe; admission to site & museum S10; ☺ 9am-5pm) This archaeological complex right on the coast, about 60km from Trujillo, consists of the Huaca Prieta site, the Huaca El Brujo, which has only been minimally studied, and the magnificent excavated Moche site of Huaca Cao. At the last, with its brilliant mural reliefs, investigators made one of the most important discoveries in Peruvian archaeology in 2005, uncovering the elaborate tomb of a female governor, shaking up theories about gender roles in pre-Columbian cultures. The site has an excellent modern museum.

The complex is named El Brujo because local shamans used to meet at the site to practice ceremonies and rituals. The people who live near this *huaca* (mystical site) insist that it has positive energy and ceremonies are still occasionally performed here when someone needs to soak up good vibes.

Huaca Cao is the largest of the site's ruins. It was constructed in various phases between AD 100 and 700 and its main section houses a 27m-high truncated pyramid with some of the best friezes in the area. They show magnificently multicolored reliefs with stylized life-sized warriors, prisoners, priests and human sacrifices. There are also many burial sites from the Lambayeque culture, which followed the Moche.

It was here that the tomb of the Señora de Cao was discovered. The governor was buried with more than 100 metal objects, including crowns, necklaces and earrings, which can be observed along with the mummified remains of the leader in the well-designed **Museo de Cao** next to the site. A new exhibit includes a computer-generated, life-like bust of the Señora de Cao created by international forensic experts.

The **Huaca El Brujo**, or Huaca Cortada (the Cut Ruin), is the second most important structure in the complex and is so called for the large deep cut in its facade made by *huaqueros* looking for treasure. Like Huaca Cao it was occupied by the Moche from around AD 100 to 700. It's believed that it could have been an administrative center.

Also in the complex is the **Huaca Prieta**, which is said to date back to 12,000 BC and marks the first settlement in the area. It has been one of the most intensively studied early Peruvian sites. For non-archaeologists, however, it's generally more interesting to read about than to tour. Although it's simply a prehistoric pile of refuse, it does afford extensive views over the coastal area and can be visited along with the other *huacas* in the archaeological complex.

Local residents are available to guide visitors around the site for a voluntary contribution.

Reaching the complex on your own is complicated. The safest route is to catch a bus in Trujillo bound for Chocope (S3.50, 1½ hours) from Ovalo del Papa southwest of town. Switch to a *colectivo* to Magdalena de Cao (S2.50, 20 minutes), where you'll need to negotiate with a *mototaxi* to take you to and from the site with waiting time. There is very little public transportation out this way.

Museo Arqueológico
Municipal de Moche MUSEUM
(☑044-46-5471; Bolognesi 359, Moche; admission S5; ⊙8am-1pm & 2-4:45pm Mon-Fri, 2-5pm Sun) Not to be confused with the Museo Huacas de Moche at the Huaca de la Luna site, this

museum on the main square in the town of Moche houses around 500 ceramic pieces from the Chavin, Chimú, Lambayeque and Moche cultures curated from a private collection owned by Italian immigrants. The pieces were formerly on display at the Museo Cassinelli under a gritty gas station in Trujillo, but their new home is far more conducive to contemplation.

Have a look at the bird-shaped whistling pots, which produce clear notes when air is blown into them. Superficially the pots are very similar, but when they are blown each one produces a completely different note that corresponds to the calls of the male and female birds.

🛏 Sleeping

All of the main attractions in the region can be visited on a day trip from either Trujillo or Huanchaco. Staying in Trujillo affords greater choice of tour operators and transportation, while Huanchaco is a more relaxed base.

ⓘ Getting There & Away

Most of the major archaeological sites can easily be reached by local bus or taxi with the exception of Complejo Arqueológico la Huaca el Brujo, which requires several changes of transport. For Chan Chan, Huaca Esmeralda and Huaca Arco Iris, it's possible to call or flag down another taxi after your visit, while for Huacas del Sol y de La Luna it's best to ask your driver to wait or arrange a pick-up time in advance.

Huanchaco

☑044 / POP 68,100

This once-tranquil fishing hamlet, 12km outside Trujillo, woke up one morning to find itself a brightly highlighted paragraph on Peru's Gringo Trail. Its fame came in large part from the long, narrow reed boats you'll see lining the *malecón*. A small number of local fishers still use these age-old crafts, and you may even sight some surfing in with the day's catch. Though you can almost picture Huanchaco on postcards of days gone by, the beach is distinctly average. Nevertheless, the slow pace of life attracts a certain type of beach bum and the town has managed to retain much of its villagey appeal.

Today Huanchaco dishes up a long menu of accommodations and dining options, and great waves for budding surfers. Come summertime, legions of local and foreign tourists descend on its lapping shores, and this

PRE-COLUMBIAN PEOPLES OF THE NORTH COAST

Moche

Evolving from around AD 100 to AD 800, the Moche created ceramics, textiles and metal-work, developed the architectural skills to construct massive pyramids while still having enough time for art and a highly organized religion.

Among all their expert productions, it's the ceramics that earn the Moche a ranking in Peru's pre-Inca-civilization hall of fame. Considered the most artistically sensitive and technically developed of any ceramics found in Peru, Moche pots are realistically decorated with figures and scenes that leave us with a very descriptive look at everyday life. Pots were modeled into lifelike representations of people, crops, domestic and wild animals, marine life and monumental architecture. Other pots were painted with scenes of ceremonial activities and everyday objects.

Some facets of Moche life illustrated on pots include punishments, surgical procedures (such as amputations and the setting of broken limbs) and copulation. One room in Lima's Museo Larco (p73) is devoted to pots depicting a cornucopia of sexual practices, some the products of very fertile imaginations. The Museo Arqueológico Municipal de Moche (p335), just outside Trujillo, also has a fine collection.

A few kilometers south of Trujillo, there are two main Moche sites: Huaca del Sol y Huaca de la Luna (p334), though only Huaca de la Luna is open to visitors.

The Moche period declined around AD 700, and the next few centuries are somewhat confusing. The Wari culture, based in the Ayacucho area of the central Peruvian Andes, began to expand after this time, and its influence was reflected in both the Sicán and Chimú cultures.

Sicán

The Sicán were probably descendants of the Moche and flourished in the same region from about AD 750 to 1375. Avid agriculturalists, the Sicán were also infatuated with metallurgy and all that glitters. The Sicán are known to many archaeologists for their lost-wax (mold-cast) gold ornaments and the manufacture of arsenical copper, which is the closest material to bronze found in pre-Columbian New World archaeology. These great smiths produced alloys of gold, silver and arsenic copper in vast quantities, using little more than hearths fired by *algarrobo* (carob tree) wood and pipe-blown air to achieve the incredible 1000°C temperatures needed for such work.

---

fast-growing resort town makes a great base for exploring the ruins surrounding Trujillo.

⊙ Sights

There is a S1 charge between 10:30am and 6:30pm to enter the town pier, which is a picturesque sight with a gazebo at its terminus.

You don't need to go to Trujillo to visit the archaeological sites of the region – tour operators on the main road here organize direct trips from Huanchaco.

Santuario de la Virgen del Socorro CHURCH (⊙9am-12:30pm & 4-7pm) This church above town is worth a visit. Built between 1535 and 1540, it is said to be the second-oldest church in Peru. There are sweeping views from the restored belfry.

🏃 Activities & Tours

The curving, gray-sand beach here is fine for swimming during the December to April summer, but expect serious teeth chatter during the rest of the year. The good surf, perfect for beginners, draws its fair share of followers and you'll see armies of bleached-blond surfer types ambling the streets with boards under their arms. Expect decent waves year-round. The beach break starts about 800m south of the pier – with a rock and sand bottom. It rarely connects for longer rides, but you can get plenty of fun lefts and shortish rights anywhere on the beach.

You can rent surfing gear (S35 per day for a wetsuit and surfboard) from several places along the main drag. Lessons cost about S70 for a 1½-hour to two-hour session. Check at **Otra Cosa** (☑044-46-1302; www.otracosa. org; Las Camelias 431) for local volunteering opportunities.

Muchik Surf School SURFING (☑044-63-3487; www.escueladetablamuchik.com; Independencia 100) Huanchaco's longest-

Artifacts found at Sicán archaeological sites suggest that this culture loved to shop, or at least trade. They were actively engaged in long-distance trade with peoples along the length and breadth of the continent, acquiring shells and snails from Ecuador, emeralds and diamonds from Colombia, bluestone from Chile and gold from the Peruvian highlands.

With a structured and religiously controlled social organization, the Sicán engaged in bizarre and elaborate funerary practices, examples of which can be seen at the Museo Nacional Sicán (p350) in Ferreñafe.

Unfortunately, as was the case with many pre-Inca societies, the weather was the ultimate undoing of the Sicán. Originally building their main city at Batán Grande, northeast of Trujillo, they were forced to move to Túcume (p350) when El Niño rains devastated the area in the 13th century.

Chimú

The Chimú were contemporaries of the Sicán and were active from about AD 850 to 1470. They were responsible for the huge capital at Chan Chan (p331), just north of Trujillo. The artwork of the Chimú was less exciting than that of the Moche, tending more to functional mass production than artistic achievement. Gone for the most part was the technique of painting pots. Instead they were fired by a simpler method than that used by the Moche, producing the typical blackware seen in many Chimú pottery collections. While the quality of the ceramics declined, skills in metallurgy developed, with gold and various alloys being worked.

The Chimú are best remembered as an urban society. Their huge capital contained about 10,000 dwellings of varying quality and importance. Buildings were decorated with friezes, the designs molded into mud walls, and important areas were layered with precious metals. There were storage bins for food and other products from across the kingdom, which stretched along the coast from Chancay to the Gulf of Guayaquil (southern Ecuador). There were huge walk-in wells, canals, workshops and temples. The royal dead were buried in mounds with a wealth of offerings.

The Chimú were conquered by the Incas in 1471 and heavy rainfall has severely damaged the adobe moldings of their once-vast metropolis.

running surf school is said to be the most reliable and offers an 'if you don't stand, you don't pay' guarantee.

Un Lugar SURFING
(☑ 997-099-001; www.unlugarsurfschoolperu.com; Atahualpa 225) Two blocks back from the main beach road, this rustic surf school/guesthouse is run by highly skilled Juan Carlos and provides private two-hour lessons. It also rents boards and suits, and organizes surfing safaris to Puerto Chicama and other iconic Peruvian surf spots. Bare-bones bamboo treehouse-style rooms are also available for S15 per person.

Huanchaco Tours TOURS
(☑ 998-975-639; www.huanchacotours.com; La Ribera 726) Offers daily departures from Huanchaco to the main archaeological sites of the region, including Chan Chan (p331) and Huaca de la Luna (p334).

🛏 Sleeping

Most guesthouses are located at the southern end of town in the small streets running perpendicular to the beach. You can get discounts of up to 50% outside festival and holiday times, so be sure to ask.

★ **Naylamp** GUESTHOUSE $
(☑ 044-46-1022; www.hostalnaylamp.com; Larco 1420; camping with/without tent rental S18/15, dm/s/d from S20/40/60; @ 🛜) At the northern end of Huanchaco, and top of the pops in the budget stakes, Naylamp has one building on the waterfront and a second, larger building behind the hotel. Great budget rooms share a spacious sea-view patio, and the lush camping area has perfect sunset views. Kitchen, laundry service, hammocking zone and a cafe are all thrown in.

The beds have mosquito nets, so you can leave your windows open at night. Ask for a room up top to catch cooling ocean breezes.

Moksha
HOSTEL $

(☑ 973-713-628; La Ribera 224; dm/s/d from S15/45/50; 📶) Right across the road from the water, this spacious hostel run by a hip young couple is a great place to hang out. Rooms are basic but homey and there are plenty of public places to chill, including a sea-view terrace and rear courtyard with open kitchen for guests. Offers surf and yoga classes and there's a vegetarian cafe.

The two private rooms with private bathrooms in a quiet corner out the back are the pick of the accommodations. Free salsa classes are run on Thursdays on the large porch upstairs.

Hospedaje Oceano
GUESTHOUSE $

(☑ 044-46-1653; www.hospedaje-oceano.com; Los Cerezos 105; r S40; @ 📶) Ideally located between one of the town's most lush and pleasant *plazoletas* (small squares) and the ocean, this superbly welcoming, family-run spot will have you feeling like kin within minutes of arrival. From the outside it's indistinguishable from any number of dismissible Peruvian guesthouses, but the great Mediterranean-inspired rooms offer a pleasant surprise.

There a guest kitchen and proper hot water. Best of all? The family makes addictive homemade *cremoladas* (artisanal ice creams, S4). Take your pick from 25 different flavors and ask don Carlos to explain their health benefits (cappuccino and coconut are extraordinary).

Hospedaje My Friend
HOSTEL $

(☑ 044-46-1080; www.myfriendsurfhostal.com; Los Pinos 158; dm/r S15/30; 📶) This hole-in-the-wall attracts droves of backpackers and surfers with only a few *nuevo soles* left in their pockets. The little cafe downstairs serves breakfast, there's a peaced-out upstairs terrace and you can arrange surf lessons here, too. The dorms have five beds, and you get electric showers, lockers and plenty of travelers to hang out with.

La Casa Suiza
HOSTEL $

(☑ 044-63-9713; www.lacasasuiza.com; Los Pinos 308; dm/s/d S25/35/85; @ 📶) The Swiss House's spacious and sparkling rooms have Peru-themed, airbrushed murals. The little cafe downstairs prepares crunchy-crust pizzas, and the patio upstairs hosts a nice view and the occasional barbecue. It's less of a surfer hangout than the other budget spots in town, but retains a cool vibe nevertheless.

Hotel Bracamonte
HOTEL $$

(☑ 044-46-1162; www.hotelbracamonte.com.pe; Los Olivos 160; s/d incl breakfast from S120/165; @ 📶 ☒) Popular, friendly, welcoming and secure behind high walls and a locked gate, the Bracamonte is one of the oldest of Huanchaco's nicer hotels and it remains one of the top choices. Nice gardens, a games room, barbecue, restaurant, bar and toddlers' playground make it great for families, and the executive rooms are probably the best maintained in Huanchaco.

Ask for a higher room to catch ocean breezes. It's located at the entrance to town, by the riverbed. Overall it's the most equipped and near-resort-like choice.

Hotel Caballito de Totora
BOUTIQUE HOTEL $$

(☑ 044-46-2636; www.hotelcaballitodetotora. com.pe; La Ribera 348; s/d/tr incl breakfast S145/205/290; ✳ @ 📶 ☒) Bright modern rooms surrounding an inviting pool area make this professionally run place a top choice. The suites are the best single rooms in Huanchaco, decked in modern motifs that wouldn't be out of place in Miami. They offer perfect sea views, Jacuzzis, 100cm TVs and private patios to boot.

A cozy bar adds to the ambience. It's the one hotel in Huanchaco that feels truly boutique.

Huanchaco Hostal
HOTEL $$

(☑ 044-46-1272; www.huanchacohostal.com; Victor Larco 184; s/d S73/120; 🅿 📶 ☒) On the town's small Plaza de Armas, this cozy little place has spartan rooms and a handsome backyard concealing a secluded pool and garden. There are plenty of arty touches to make it feel homey, and it has a decidedly family-friendly air.

🍴 Eating

Not surprisingly, Huanchaco has oodles of seafood restaurants, especially near the *caballitos de tortora* (traditional indigenous reed boats) stacked at the north end of the beach.

Umi Sushi
SUSHI $

(☑ 976-361-624; Las Orquideas 317; sushi S10.50-23; ⏲ 7-11pm Tue-Sun) Many of Huanchaco's better restaurants close early, but fortunately this great little sushi place, tucked away on a quiet road at the southern end of town, is here to cater to visitors looking for something different. It serves gourmet *makis* with a Peruvian twist – try the Spicy Kani made with avocado and shrimp covered in crab sauce.

CABALLITOS DE TOTORA

Huanchaco's defining characteristic is that a small number of local fishers are still using the very same narrow reed boats depicted on 2000-year-old Moche pottery. The fishers paddle and surf these neatly crafted boats like seafaring gauchos, with their legs dangling on either side – which explains the nickname given to these elegantly curving steeds: *caballitos de tortora* (little horses). The inhabitants of Huanchaco are among the few remaining people on the coast who remember how to construct and use the boats, each one only lasting a few months before becoming waterlogged. The fishers paddle out as far as a mile, but can only bring in limited catches because of the size of their vessels (which now also integrate styrofoam for buoyancy).

The days of Huanchaco's reed-boat fishers are likely numbered. Recent reports say that erosion and other environmental factors are affecting the beds where the fishers plant and harvest the reeds, and many youngsters are opting to become surf instructors, professionals or commercial fishers rather than following in their parents' hard-paddled wakes.

Service is attentive and there's good house music pumped out at non-annoying volume. It generally looks closed, but just knock on the wooden door with the Japanese characters and you'll be let into a delicious hidden world of flavors.

Otra Cosa VEGETARIAN $
(Larco 921; dishes S6-22; ⊙8am-10pm; 🛜🖉) 🌿 This Dutch-Peruvian beachside pad is Huanchaco's requisite travelers' hub, serving up yummy vegetarian victuals such as falafel, crepes, Spanish tortillas, Dutch apple pie and tasty curry-laced burritos (one of which is *almost* a breakfast burrito). Coffee is sourced from a rural women's cooperative and the restaurant has a great record for giving back to the community.

It also offers a good-value plate of the day for S13.50 and set menu for S16.50.

★Restaurante Mococho PERUVIAN, SEAFOOD $$
(www.facebook.com/restaurantemococho; Bolognesi 535; mains S36, whole fish per 1kg S110; ⊙1-3pm, closed Mon) This tiny place sits secluded in a walled garden where the legend of chef don Victor is carried on by his widow and son, Wen. It's not cheap, but it's fresh and excellent. The specialty is steamed whole fish in sauce, which is big enough to serve three. Come early – it closes once the fresh fish runs out.

The menu is decided each morning when local fishers knock on the door shouting, 'Hey Chinese! The catch of the day is...'. Wen, the only Chinese-Peruvian restaurateur in town, makes just two dishes with whatever's fresh that day: ceviche and steamed fish (with fillets available for solo diners). He offers six sauces, but go for the traditional,

sharply colored, wildly flavorful criollo sauce or the delicate pecan option.

La Esquina PERUVIAN $$
(📞044-46-1081; Union 120; mains S25-50; ⊙6-11pm) This split-level modern corner restaurant a block back from the *malecón* specializes in whole barbecued fish, which is cooked just right on the grill out the front. Take your pick from the fresh options in the display, which are priced by the kilogram. There are also more economicalk fish fillets, veggie and meat mains on the menu.

El Caribe PERUVIAN $$
(Atahualpa 150; mains S35-37; ⊙10am-5pm) This local favorite, tucked away off the main strip, is a fair bit cheaper than the other quality seafood places, but is no also-ran in quality. It serves big portions of excellent seafood and *comida criolla* (local cuisine). Its grouper (*mero*) ceviche was featured in *Saveur* magazine.

★Restaurante Big Ben PERUVIAN $$$
(📞044-46-1378; www.bigbenhuanchaco.com; Larco 1184; mains S49-70; ⊙11:30am-5:30pm; 🛜) This sophisticated seafooder at the far north end of town specializes in lunchtime ceviches and is the best place in town for top-notch seafood. Though ceviche is the main draw, the menu is also heavy on fresh fish, *sudados* (seafood stews) and prawn dishes, all of which go down best on the 3rd-floor patio with ocean views.

🍸 Drinking & Nightlife

Jungle Bar Bily BAR
(📞044-22-8949; Larco 420; ⊙10am-late; 🛜) Travelers gravitate to this quasi-Polynesian-themed bar due to location (across from the pier), good music and a popular cheap ceviche

(S20), among other good-value seafood. Happy hour (6pm to 10pm) nets a 50% discount on selected cocktails.

There's live music on Friday evenings, with genres ranging from rock to traditional Andean.

ⓘ Information

Internet Huanchaco (Atahualpa 233; per hour $1; ☺8am-10pm) A one-stop shop where you can do your laundry and get online, or even get a haircut while you wait. Cheapest laundry in town – if you are prepared to wait for natural drying, it's just S10 per load, or S16 with machine drying.

ⓘ Getting There & Away

Some bus companies have ticket agents in Huanchaco, but buses depart from Trujillo. Combis and yellow and red micro buses to Huanchaco frequently leave from Trujillo (S2). To return, just wait on the beachfront road for the bus as it comes back from the north end.

A taxi from Trujillo to Huanchaco should cost S18 to S20, but returning you should be able to get a cheaper ride as drivers are keen to get back to where the action is.

Puerto Chicama (Puerto Malabrigo)

📞 044 / POP 90100

The small fishing outpost of Puerto Chicama might not look like all that much, but it's the offshore action that draws a dedicated following. Puerto Chicama, also known as Puerto Malabrigo, lays claim to one of the longest left-hand point breaks in the world. Originally a busy port for the sugar and cotton grown on nearby haciendas, Puerto Chicama now draws adrenaline-seeking surfers who try their luck catching that rare, long ride.

While the town itself is a fairly standard Peruvian town, the bluff above the settlement has a lovely new malecón with wooden benches, sculptures, lookout points and an as-yet-empty surf museum.

The beach here is wide and cleaner than some others in the region, while the desolate, otherworldly hilly landscapes behind, where not even a weed grows, have a certain rugged beauty of their own and are an interesting place for a stroll.

🛌 Sleeping & Eating

All the hotels are located south of the muelle (pier) on the outcrop overlooking the beach.

Los Delfines de Chicama HOTEL $$
(📞044-34-3044; delfinesdechicama@gmail.com; d/tr/ste S200/295/470; 🅿🛜🏊) This large surfer hotel has simple painted brick rooms, all with private balconies, that somehow feel more formal than their counterparts in the village. There's a pool, plenty of parking out back and a 2nd-story restaurant (mains S20 to S35) with views out to sea.

It organizes three-hour boat trips to surfing spots around the region.

El Hombre HOSTEL $$
(📞044-57-6077; www.facebook.com/hotelelhombre; s/d S70/140, without bathroom S30/60) El Hombre is the original surfers' hostel and is run by the daughter of local legend 'El Hombre,' a surfer guru who's now into his 90s but still resides here. Facing the ocean, the hostel has dead-simple rooms with communal bathrooms and more spacious options with private bathrooms in an annex with a great lounge overlooking the town's famous wave.

There's a shared kitchen and communal TVs often seen flickering with surf videos.

Picanteria Palma SEAFOOD $$
(Tacna; mains S20-22; ☺8am-8pm) This great little family-run restaurant in town looks unremarkable, but serves a couple of dozen different seafood plates, all of which are delicious. It only uses fresh produce from the Chicama dock – there's no frozen fish here – so if the fisherfolk aren't working, sometimes it closes up shop.

ⓘ Getting There & Away

Some surf shops in Huanchaco, including Un Lugar (p337) and **Wave** (📞044-58-7005; Larco 850; ☺8am-6pm), arrange surfing safaris to Puerto Chicama. The easiest independent route is catching an El Dorado bus from Trujillo direct to Puerto Chicama (S6, 2¼ hours). A faster route is taking a more comfortable Emtrafesa express bus to the town of Paiján, 40km further north on the Panamericana (S6, 1¼ hours). From here you can catch colectivos for the 16km ride to Puerto Chicama (S2.50, 20 minutes).

Pacasmayo

📞 044 / POP 27,400

This lively, mostly forgotten beach town is crammed with colonial buildings in various states of disrepair and is blessed with a pretty stretch of beach and a throwback malecón. Dedicated surfers often drop in, particularly from May to August, when there is a decent offshore break. It's also a great place to spend some time away from the more popular resort towns and get swept up in the aging nostalgia of the whole place.

Sights

Puemape
BEACH

This clean beach, accessed by a spur road south of the town of San Pedro de Lloc, has a fine long left break and has become a popular spot for those in the know. While the small village here is a bit of a ghost town, the arrival of electricity, set to happen by the time this edition is printed, is likely to lead to new construction. But for now it's blissfully quiet, with a couple of accommodations options and basic eateries.

The access road branches off the Panamericana at Km 656. You can hire a taxi from Pacasmayo or Puerto Chicama to get here.

Pacatnamú
ARCHAEOLOGICAL SITE

(⊙24hr) FREE A few kilometers north of Pacasmayo, just before the village of Guadalupe, a track leads toward the ocean and the little-visited ruins of Pacatnamú, a large site that was inhabited by the Gallinazo, Moche and Chimú cultures and is regarded by archaeologists as one of the coast's most important ruins.

The best way to visit the ruins is to take a bus to Guadalupe and hire a taxi for the final stretch to the site; it should cost around S30 round trip with waiting time. In Guadalupe there is a small museum dedicated to the ruins where you can obtain additional information.

Muelle Pacasmayo
PIER

What was once the longest pier in Peru has a storied history. Constructed between 1870 and 1874, it initially clocked in at a whopping 743.4m in length. Today it stands at around 500m after a chunk was swept out to sea in 1924 and another piece was lost in 2015. In the 1940s two overloaded train cars fell into the sea from the pier as well. It's now very rickety looking and access is prohibited.

Activities

There are decent waves close to town and even better breaks a short drive away, though the water can be cold. Several places around town rent surfboards for S20 to S30.

There are often decent winds for kitesurfing here, with the best spot being below the lighthouse on the point.

El Faro Adventure Resort
KITESURFING

(☎976-638-956; www.elfaropacasmayo.com; Playa El Faro; ⊙8am-6pm) This resort, a 15-minute walk south of town, is a one-stop adventure shop with kite rentals for S250 and stand-up paddleboards (SUP) for S100 per day. Adventure buffs might consider staying here in one of the comfortable ocean-view rooms (US$120). There is a decent restaurant on site.

Sleeping & Eating

Hotel El Mirador
HOSTAL $

(☎044-52-1883; www.pacasmayoperu.com; Aurelio Herrera 10; s/d/tr/q from S40/60/80/100; P🛜) All tiles and bricks, this surfers' hangpad has good rooms varying from *económico* (basic) to *de lujo* (luxury). All have hot water, communal balconies and wall-mounted flatscreen TVs with international channels; the nicest rooms have kitchens and DVD players. It's located just one block inland, below the Christ statue.

Downstairs there's a good common area with a pool table and foosball, which is just as well as there's nothing much going on in town after dark.

La Estación Gran Hotel
HOTEL $$

(☎044-52-1515; www.hotellaestacion.com.pe; Malecón Grau 69; s/d/ste incl breakfast S110/160/200; @🛜🏊) The majestic, restored, Republican-era facade doesn't carry over to the interiors, but there is a great rooftop terrace, small pool and ground-floor bar-restaurant (mains S25 to S45). The rooms are smallish but have fresh paint jobs and good bedding.

The restaurant is one of the best in town – try the fabulous *pescado a lo macho* (catch of the day topped with a creamy shellfish sauce with chili and garlic).

Restaurante Pastimar
INTERNATIONAL $$

(Aurelio Herrera 10; mains S16-40; ⊙noon-10pm) Serving a wide menu of Peruvian and international dishes, including risottos, pizzas and burgers, this popular place beneath a hostel is a good bet for a meal when many of the other places around town are closed. The fried-fish sandwiches are extra tasty.

Getting There & Away

All buses and many shared vans leave from the new Terrapuerto bus station near the entrance to town.

Emtrafesa (www.emtrafesa.com.pe; Terrapuerto) has frequent buses to Trujillo (S9, 1¾ hours) and Chiclayo (S10, two hours). It also has direct services to Lima (S50, nine hours,

6:30pm) and Cajamarca (S25 to S35, 4½ hours, 2pm and 11:40pm) as well as points further north.

Civa (☑ 014-18-1111; www.civa.com.pe; Terrapuerto) offers comfortable direct buses to Lima, with one departure at 9:30am and several in the evening. Prices range from S40 to S130, depending on bus class.

To get to Puerto Chicama take any Trujillo bound bus to Paiján and pick up a *colectivo*.

Chiclayo

☑ 074 / POP 553,200

Spanish missionaries founded a small rural community on this site in the 16th century. Either by chance or through help from above, Chiclayo has prospered ever since. In one of the first sharp moves in Peruvian real estate, the missionaries chose a spot that sits at the hub of vital trade routes connecting the coast, the highlands and the deep jungle. Chiclayo's role as the commercial heart of the district has allowed it to overtake other once-vital organs of the region.

La Ciudad de la Amistad (The City of Friendship) holds a friendly, outstretched hand to the wayward venturer. While it's shaking hands in greeting, it will probably slip in a bold mix of unique regional dishes to tickle your taste buds. The town itself is pretty light on tourist attractions, but the dozens of tombs with Moche and Chimú archaeological booty surrounding the area should not be missed.

⊙ Sights

Mercado Modelo   MARKET

(Arica btwn Balta & Cugilevan; ⊙ 7am-8pm Mon-Sat, to 2pm Sun) This is one of Peru's most interesting markets, sprawling over several blocks. Most notable for tourists is the *mercado de brujos* (witch doctors' market) in the southwest corner. This area is a one-stop shop for *brujos* (witch doctors) and has everything you might need for a potent brew: whale bones, amulets, snake skins, vials of indeterminate tonics, hallucinogenic cacti and piles of aromatic herbs.

If you'd like to make contact with a *brujo* for a healing session, this is a good place to start, but be wary of sham shamans. It's best to go with a reliable recommendation.

Cathedral   CHURCH

(Plaza de Armas) This cathedral was built in the late 19th century. In contrast the Plaza de Armas (Parque Principal) wasn't inaugurated

until 1916, which gives an idea of how new the city is by Peruvian standards. It's usually open for morning mass, but its rather plain interior doesn't really match the fine facade.

Tours

Agencies offer frequent inexpensive tours of Sipán, Túcume, Ferreñafe, Batán Grande, Pimental/Santa Rosa, Reserva Ecológica Chaparrí and the museums in Lambayeque. Full-day tours to the archaeological sites cost between S50 and S60 and usually call at three or four different locations. Reserva Ecológica Chaparrí tours cost around S140. Prices do not include admission fees.

Sipán Tours   CULTURAL

(☑ 074-22-9053; www.sipantours.com; Calle 7 de Enero 772; ⊙ 8:30am-1:30pm & 4:30-8:30pm) This well-established agency offers guided tours to all the major archaeological sites and nearby beach towns. Ask about a new rural tourism project that takes you on a culinary tour through the countryside with homestays en route.

Moche Tours   TOURS

(☑ 074-23-2184; www.mochetourschiclayo.com.pe; Calle 7 de Enero 638; ⊙ 8am-8pm Mon-Sat, to noon Sun) Highly recommended for cheap tours with Spanish- or English-speaking guides.

🛏 Sleeping

Hostal Colibrí   HOTEL $

(☑ 074-22-1918; www.hotelcolibriperu.com; Balta 010-A; s/d incl breakfast S60/80; ☞) Overlooking the leafy Paseo de las Musas, the neat Colibrí is a longish walk from the center but is top value. Brightly lit and brightly painted, it's a modern choice, with a burger joint in the bottom and a 2nd floor coffee/cocktail bar with patio views of the park. Funky bathrooms, too.

Hostal Sicán   HOTEL $

(☑ 074-20-8741; hsican@hotmail.com; Izaga 356; s/d/tr incl breakfast S45/70/100; ☞) This appealing pick has lots of polished wood and wrought iron, creating an illusion of grandeur. The rooms are small, comfortable and cool. All feature wood paneling as well as tasteful bits of art and a TV. A great choice, sitting on one of Chiclayo's most charming brick-lined streets.

Hostal Victoria   HOTEL $

(☑ 074-22-5642; victoriastar2008@hotmail.com; Izaga 933; s/d/tr S35/50/80; ☞) A great find just east of the main plaza. It's quiet, sanitary and has colorful rooms spruced up by tiny ceramics and textiles here and there. There's a friendly family vibe to the whole place.

Pirámide Real HOTEL **$**

(☎ 074-22-4036; piramidereal@hotmail.com; Izaga 726; s/d/tw S40/50/70; ☎) Blink and you'll miss the entrance to this place. Things don't get any bigger inside, but if you're willing to forgo space, there are clean and tidy rooms with writing desks, hot water and cable TV – a reasonably good deal at this price point.

Hotel Mochiks BOUTIQUE HOTEL **$$**

(☎ 074-20-6620; www.hotelmochiks.com; Tacna 615; s/d incl breakfast S165/210; ✿@☎) This polished upstart made an immediate impression on the city's hotel scene, owing much of its success to a sense of style that was previously MIA. Tall and narrow, the lobby, cafe and 2nd-floor bar are decked out in chromes and moody reds, which contrast perfectly with the smallish but soothing beige-toned rooms.

Everything is shiny and well maintained, and the trendiness is held in check with small indigenous Moche touches here and there. At 25 rooms, it's the perfect size.

Hotel Embajador HOTEL **$$**

(☎ 074-20-4729; www.hotelembajadorchiclayo.com; Calle 7 de Enero 1368; s/d incl breakfast S120/140; @☎) This fab 23-room choice makes no bones about it: lime and tangerine are its favorite colors and you will be pummeled with them at every turn – like being churned in an art-deco frosty-freeze machine.

It makes for a fun and festive choice that's top-loaded with value and personality: a minimalist cafe, trapezoidal bathroom mirrors, Jacuzzi tubs in suites, and efficient and friendly staff.

Latinos Hostal HOTEL **$$**

(☎ 074-23-5437; latinohotelsac@hotmail.com; Izaga 600; s/d S90/120; ✿@☎) An excellent choice, with a top location close to the plaza, this hotel is thoroughly maintained with perfect little rooms. Some of the corner rooms have giant curving floor-to-ceiling windows for great street views and plenty of light. The staff are very helpful.

Hotel Paraíso HOTEL **$$**

(☎ 074-22-8161; www.hotelesparaiso.com.pe; Ruiz 1064; s/d incl breakfast from S100/120; ✿@☎) Brighter and cheerier than its immediate neighbors, the value equation falls in Hotel Paraíso's favor. It boasts all the mod cons of far fancier hotels for a fraction of the price. Spotless, cell-like rooms have decent furniture, hot showers and cable TV.

Casa Andina Select Chiclayo HOTEL **$$$**

(☎ 074-23-4911; www.casa-andina.com; Villarreal 115; r/ste incl breakfast S803/1071; P✿@☎❄) The Peruvian boutique chain Casa Andina swooped in and gobbled up this aging relic, formerly the Gran Hotel Chiclayo. It's like a business hotel with an Andean pulse. There's a pleasant terrace and pool area, spa, fitness center and restaurant, plus modern, clean rooms that are sparkly new.

Costa Del Sol BUSINESS HOTEL **$$$**

(☎ 074-22-7272; www.costadelsolperu.com; Balta 399; s/d incl breakfast S454/492; P✿@☎❄) This fully loaded business hotel, run by the Wyndham group, is one of Chiclayo's best. All the creature comforts are here, including pool, gym, sauna and massage rooms. We aren't chain-hotel fans, mind you, but this is Chiclayo and there are few places in town offering this level of comfort.

✗ Eating

El Pescador SEAFOOD, PERUVIAN **$**

(San José 1236; mains S15-20; ◷ 11:30am-5:30pm) This little locals' secret packs in the droves for outstanding seafood and regional dishes at fantastic prices. The ceviches are every bit as good as places charging double or even triple the price, and weekend specials such as *cabrito con frijoles* (goat with beans; Saturday) and *arroz con pato* (duck with rice; Sunday) are steals.

Owner Oscar and his brother (the chef) work hard to make sure you're happy. There's no sign outside and if you blink you'll miss it.

Cevicheria Pez Chevere PERUVIAN **$**

(☎ 963-754-146; Torres Paz 600; mains S10-16; ◷ 11am-4pm) This busy corner ceviche bar serves cheap, fresh and fast ceviche and seafood rice dishes to hordes of local office workers. Seating is limited to bar stools at shared benches, so you'll get to ogle the diners in front but it's hard to find better value anywhere downtown.

Mi Tia BURGERS **$**

(Aguirre 662; burgers S2-5, mains S13-44; ◷ 8am-10pm) Lines run deep at this no-frills Peruvian haunt, where the burger stand draws legions of céntimo pinchers for burgers and sandwiches that are practically free if

Chiclayo

Terrapuerto Plaza Norte (2km)

Fiesta Chiclayo Gourmet (2km)

Children's Playground

Lora y Lora

Ruíz

San Martín

Bolívar

L Gonzales

Arica

Ruíz

Ferre

Prado

Lora y Cordero

Vicente de la Vega

San José Plaza Aguirre

Aguirre

Ortiz

Ugarte

Carrion

Mercado Central

Plaza de Armas

Izaga

Torres Paz

Cabrera

Tacna

Dall'Orso

Bolognesi

Las Americas

Las Americas

Grau

Sesquicentenario

Villarreal

Saco

Ortiz

Grau

Gonzales

Cuglievan

La Point

Colón

Balta

Balta

G de la Vega

Paseo de las Musas

you take them away. Inside, sandwiches are pricier (S5 to S12), but you get them on a plate with salad and chips. Smiling staff also serve a long list of country staples.

It does a *suspiro de limeña* (milk caramel and meringue) that's just big enough to ease the craving.

Copo Artisan   ICE CREAM **$**
(San José; ice cream S6-9.50; ⊙1-9:30pm) If you don't fancy the nasty industrial 'ice cream' sold from kiosks and on street corners all over the city, head to this friendly parlor a couple of blocks from the Plaza de Armas. It has a wide selection of flavors, including

exposed wood and adobe that connects you with the elements are the hallmarks of the best bar-cafe-restaurant in Chiclayo. It's certainly tops on ambience, and the food is simple, direct, unpretentious and affordable.

Restaurant Romana
PERUVIAN $$

(512 Romana; Balta 512; mains S20-37, menú S16; ⊙7am-1am; 🐾) This popular place serves a bunch of different dishes, all of them local favorites. If you're feeling brave, try the *chirimpico* for breakfast – it's stewed goat tripe and organs and is guaranteed to either cure a hangover or give you one.

The *humitas* (steamed dough with corn and cheese wrapped in corn husks) are also a cheap and tasty treat. For other meals there's pasta, steaks, seafood, chicken or pork *chicharróns* (breaded and fried) with yucca – you name it.

Hebron
PERUVIAN $$

(📋074-22-2709; www.hebron.com.pe; Balta 605; mains S17-40; ⊙7am-midnight; 🐾) This flashy, contemporary and bright two-story restaurant is a luxury *pollería* (restaurant specializing in roast chicken), but it also serves a variety of other mains, including plenty of fish and many options from the grill.

Fiesta Chiclayo Gourmet
PERUVIAN $$$

(📋074-20-1970; www.restaurantfiestagourmet.com; Salaverry 1820; mains S40-90) Few things are as satisfying as scraping those last bits of slightly charred rice off the bottom of an iron-clad pan and savoring all that's great about a rice dish such as *arroz con pato a la chiclayana,* made here with farm-raised duck that must be a black-feathered quacker not a day over three months of age.

Blindsiding your palette with a wholly unexpected delight is *ceviche a la brasa* (traditional raw fish served warm in corn husks after an 11th-hour searing). The pisco sours are constructed tableside, service is exquisite and the best of this region's world-famous cuisine is outrageously great. Call for a reservation, or visit the sister restaurant in Lima. A S6 taxi ride covers the 2km from the centre.

🍷 Drinking & Nightlife

Magno
CLUB

(Ortiz 490; ⊙10pm-6am) Look no further than this happening entertainment complex for a one-stop night out where locals stagger between three bars and two clubs without

local hits Pisco Sours and Aguaymanto. It's not gourmet, but it's the best there is.

★ Cafe 900
PERUVIAN $$

(www.cafe900.com; Izaga 900; mains S25-32; ⊙8am-11pm Mon-Thu, 1pm-1am Fri & Sat; 🐾) Live music, slowly spinning ceiling fans,

Chiclayo

having to leave the premises. Begin the night in the open-air Zamba bar upstairs, which has live bands playing *cumbia* (Colombian salsa-style music) and salsa and an ample terrace from which to watch the action below.

Javier Velasco Cafe   CAFE
(www.javiervelascocafe.com; Balta 400; ☺8:30am-11pm Mon-Sat) Finding a decent mug of java in Chiclayo can be a mission, so this little corner cafe is a real treat. It serves all kinds of hot and cold beverages made with gourmet Peruvian beans. It even sells bags of beans to take on your travels.

ⓘ Information

EMERGENCIES
Policía de Turismo (☏074-23-8658; Saenz Peña 830; ☺24hr) Useful for reporting problems.

IMMIGRATION
Oficina de Migraciónes (☏074-20-6838; www.migraciones.gob.pe; La Plata 30; ☺8:30am-12:30pm & 2-4pm) Near Paseo de Las Museos; handles visa issues.

MEDICAL SERVICES
Clínica del Pacífico (☏074-22-8585; www.clinicadelpacifico.com.pe; Ortiz 420) The best medical assistance in town.

MONEY
There are several banks on cuadra 6 of Balta as well as a bevy of ATMs convenient to the bus stations inside Supermarcado Metro, across from the Emtrafesa station. Money changers outside the banks change cash quickly at good rates.
Banco Continental (Balta 643) Bank with ATMs.
BCP (Balta 630) Has a 24-hour Visa and MasterCard ATM.
Interbank (cnr Colón & Aguirre)

POST
Serpost (Aguirre 140; ☺9am-7pm Mon-Fri, to 1pm Sat) West of Plaza Aguirre.

TOURIST INFORMATION
iPerú (Edificio Municipal, cnr San José & Balta; ☺9am-6pm Mon-Sat, to 1pm Sun) The best spot for tourist info in town. There's an additional office at the airport and one at the Museo de Tumbas Reales in Lambayeque. If it's closed, hit up the tour agencies.
Dircetur (☏074-23-8112; Sáenz Peña 838; ☺7:30am-1pm & 2-4:30pm Mon-Fri) Regional tourism information.

ℹ Getting There & Away

AIR

The airport (CIX) is 1.5km east of town; a taxi ride there is S6. **LATAM** (☑ 074-27-4875; www. latam.com; Izaga 770) has five daily flights in each direction between Lima and Chiclayo, while **LC Peru** (☑ 074-27-1478; www.lcperu.pe; Tacna 578; ⊙ 9am-7pm Mon-Fri, to 1pm Sat) has fewer flights but can often be cheaper.

BUS

Cruz del Sur, Móvil Tours, Línea, Ittsa and Oltursa usually have the most comfortable buses and have their own terminals.

There are a couple of large collective bus terminals that serve as bases for numerous companies. The **Terrapuerto Plaza Norte** (Av Leguia) terminal on the northern outskirts of town hosts a couple of major companies, and a load of smaller ones, with services to Cajamarca, Tumbes, Chachapoyas, Tarapoto, Yurimaguas and Jaén. Closer to the center, the **Terminal Terrestre Chiclayo Ormeño** (☑ 074-23-4206; Haya de la Torre 242) has numerous small companies serving Lima for the most part.

Civa (☑ 01-418-1111; www.civa.com.pe; Bolognesi 714) Has the cheapest comfortable Lima bus at 7pm, with more expensive options at 7:20pm and 7:40pm; Jaén buses at 9am, 9pm and 11pm; Tarapoto buses at 5pm and 5:45pm; and Chachapoyas buses at 6pm and 8:30pm. It also serves Guayaquil at 4:30pm, which is a convenient and comfortable option. Buses leave from the Terrapuerto Plaza Norte.

Cruz del Sur (☑ 080-11-1111; www.cruzdelsur.com.pe; Bolognesi 888) Has four departures to Lima between 8am and 8pm.

Emtrafesa (☑ 074-22-5538; www.emtrafesa.com; Balta 110) Has nightly buses to Tumbes and Jaén (both at 11pm) and many departures for Trujillo and Pacasmayo.

Ittsa (☑ 074-23-3612; www.ittsabus.com; Grau 497) *Bus-cama* (bed bus) departures to Lima at 7pm, 7:30pm and 8pm.

Línea (☑ 074-23-2951; Bolognesi 638) Has a comfortable Lima service at 7:30pm and regular services every couple of hours to Piura, in addition to buses to Cajamarca and Jaén.

Móvil Tours (☑ 01-716-8000; www.moviltours.com.pe; Bolognesi 199) Has three good Lima buses at 6:20pm, 6:30pm and 7pm; Tarapoto buses at 5pm and 6:30pm; a Cajamarca bus at 10:30pm; a Jaen bus at 11pm; and a Chachapoyas bus at 9pm.

Oltursa (☑ 01-716-5000; www.oltursa.pe; Vicente de la Vega 101) Five *bus-cama* services to Lima between 6:30pm and 9pm and to Máncora and Tumbes at 11:45pm; you can purchase tickets at the terminal or at its downtown **sales office** (cnr Balta & Izaga).

Tepsa (☑ 074-23-6981; www.tepsa.com.pe; Bolognesi 504) Downtown sales office for *bus-cama* services to Lima at 6:30pm, 7:30pm and 8:30pm, with the last two being the most comfortable. Buses leave from the Terrapuerto Plaza Norte terminal on the outskirts of town.

Transportes Chiclayo (☑ 074-22-3632; www.transporteschiclayo.com; Ortiz 10) Buses to Piura every half hour from 4:30am to 8:30pm, and to Máncora and Tumbes at 9:30am and 10am. There is also a Cajamarca departure at 11pm and a bus to Tarapoto at 5:30pm.

Turismo Dias (☑ 074-23-3538; www.turdias.com; Cuglievan 190) This affordable carrier heads to Lima at 6pm, also offering trips to Cajamarca at 6:45am, 5pm and 10:45pm, with the last departure being the most comfortable.

Chiclayo Long-Distance Buses

DESTINATION	COST (S)	DURATION (HR)
Cajamarca	25-50	6
Chachapoyas	30-75	10
Chimbote	20-25	6
Guayaquil (Ecuador)	90-110	15
Jaén	20-40	6
Lima	50-130	12-14
Máncora	30-90	7
Pacasmayo	11	2
Piura	16-67	3
Tarapoto	50-110	14
Trujillo	20-45	3-4
Tumbes	30-90	9
Yurimaguas	70	20

Chiclayo Regional Buses

DESTINATION	COST (S)	DURATION
Batán Grande	5	45min
Chongoyape	5	1½hr
Ferreñafe	2.50	30min
Lambayeque	2.50	15min
Monsefú	2	15min
Pimentel	2	30min
Sipán	3.50	15min
Túcume	2.50	1hr

Around Chiclayo

The countryside around Chiclayo is home to an immense wealth of archaeological sites, many of which have yet to be fully excavated. While many of the ruins are not as impressive as some other sites elsewhere in the north, the riches recovered from the tombs are absolutely magnificent and are now housed in several fantastic museums.

While busy Chiclayo is the most convenient base from which to explore the region, there are several more tranquil options, including a string of three peaceful beach towns – Puerto Etén, Santa Rosa and Pimentel – just a short drive away.

Sipán

The story of Sipán (Huaca Rajada; ☑ 978-977-622; museohrsipan@gmail.com; S8; ☺9am-5pm) reads like an Indiana Jones movie script: buried treasure, *huaqueros,* police, archaeologists and at least one killing. The archaeological site was discovered by *huaqueros* from the nearby hamlet of Sipán. The Moche site is located about 30km southwest of Chiclayo. The story of Sipán's discovery is almost as interesting as the remarkable collection of artifacts that were found in its tombs.

When local archaeologist Dr Walter Alva saw a huge influx of intricate objects on the black market in early 1987, he realized that an incredible burial site was being ransacked in the Chiclayo area. Careful questioning led Dr Alva to the Sipán mounds. To the untrained eye the mounds look like earthen hills, but in AD 300 these were huge truncated pyramids constructed from millions of adobe bricks.

At least one tomb had already been pillaged, but fast protective action by local archaeologists and police stopped further plundering. Luckily several other tombs that the grave robbers had missed were unearthed, including an exceptional royal Moche burial that became known as the Lord of Sipán. One *huaquero* was shot and killed by police in the early, tense days of the struggle over the graves. The Sipán locals were not happy at losing what they considered their treasure trove. To solve this problem, the locals were invited to train to become excavators, researchers and guards at the site, which now provides steady employment for many. The full story was detailed by Dr Alva in the October 1988 and June 1990 issues of *National Geographic,* and the May 1994 issue of *Natural History.*

The Lord of Sipán turned out to be a major leader of the Moche people, indicated by his elaborate burial in a wooden coffin surrounded by hundreds of gold, ceramic and semiprecious mineral objects, as well as an entourage consisting of his wife, two girls, a boy, a military chief, a flag bearer, two guards, two dogs

and a llama. Another important tomb held the *sacerdote* (priest), who was accompanied into the afterlife with an equally impressive quantity of treasures, as well as a few children, a guardian whose feet were cut off and a headless llama. Archaeologists don't understand why the body parts were removed, but they believe that important members of the Moche upper class took with them in death those who composed their retinues in life.

Some of the tombs have been restored with replicas to show what they looked like just before being closed up more than 1500 years ago. Opposite the entrance is the Museo de Sitio Sipán, opened in January 2009, which is worth a visit – but note that the most impressive artifacts, such as the Lord of Sipán and the Sacerdote, were placed in the Museo Tumbas Reales de Sipán in Lambayeque after going on world tour. Spanish- and English-speaking guides can be hired at the gate for S40 and parts of the sight are accessible to wheelchairs.

Daily guided tours are available from tour agencies in Chiclayo for around S40, including transportation and a guide; they usually also stop at Tucumé (p350). If you want to go independently, buses for Sipán (S3, 45 minutes) leave frequently from Chiclayo's **Terminal de Microbuses Epsel** (Nicolás de Píerola, at Oriente).

Lambayeque
☑ 074 / POP 47,900

About 11km north of Chiclayo, Lambayeque was once the main town in the area, but now plays second fiddle to Chiclayo. It's a pleasant town with narrow streets and some crumbling colonial buildings, but the main reason to stop is for a visit to the town's world-class museums, which are among the best in Peru.

◉ Sights

★Museo Tumbas Reales de Sipán   MUSEUM
(Museum of the Royal Tombs of Sipán; ☑ 074-28-3978, 074-28-3977; www.museotumbasreales.com; Vizcardo y Guzman 895; S10; ☺9am-5pm Tue-Sun) Opened in November 2002, the Museum of the Royal Tombs of Sipán is the pride of northern Peru – as well it should be. With its burgundy pyramid construction rising gently out of the earth, it's a world-class facility specifically designed to showcase the marvelous finds from Sipán. Photography is not permitted and all bags must be checked.

Visitors are guided through the museum from the top down and are shown some of

PUERTO ETÉN, SANTA ROSA & PIMENTEL

Just 20 minutes from Chiclayo there's a string of three lovely beach towns – Puerto Etén, Santa Rosa and Pimentel. Puerto Etén and Pimentel make noteworthy alternatives to staying in busy Chiclayo. The towns are listed here from south to north.

Puerto Etén. Sporting a brand-new *malecón* (boardwalk), a long honey-brown beach and slightly muddied waters, this little village has a handful of beach-view seafood joints, pretty Republican-era architecture and a few downbeat hotels.

Santa Rosa. A more modern set of ruins than the nearby pre-Hispanic sites, this rough, dilapidated fishing village is organic, pungent, powerful and quite entrancing. The dry-docked ships make for interesting Instagram opps, and there are still some *caballitos de tortora* (traditional indigenous reed boats) used here. Miracles have been reported at the cozy church.

Pimentel. The poshest of the beach towns, Pimentel has a long pier, a broad *malecón* fronted by high-end, glassed-in houses, and the nicest beach for miles. Unfortunately the waves here are rarely surfable – conversely they are highly swimmable – but an afternoon stroll along the boardwalk and through some of the stick-frame, centuries-old houses is a fun retreat. One block inland from the pier is the **Hostal Garuda** (☑ 074-61-9850; Quiñones 109, Pimentel; r incl breakfast S70-100; ☎), a yellow-fronted, 100-year-old house with a clutch of guest rooms; the rooms out back are more modern and sit around a playful garden.

Combis to the towns from Chiclayo cost S1.50 to S3, departing from several small terminals around town.

the numerous discoveries from the tomb in the same order that the archaeologists found them – this small detail alone, rare in the museum world, adds a fascinating context to visits. The first hall contains detailed ceramics representing gods, people, plants, llamas and other animals.

On the 2nd floor there are delicate objects such as impossibly fine turquoise-and-gold ear ornaments showing ducks, deer and the Lord of Sipán himself. The painstaking and advanced techniques necessary to create this jewelry place them among the most beautiful and important objects of pre-Columbian America.

Finally the ground floor features exact reproductions of the tombs as they were found. Numerous dazzling objects are displayed, the most remarkable of which are the gold pectoral plates representing sea creatures such as octopus and crabs. Even the sandals of the Lord of Sipán were made of precious metals, as he was carried everywhere and never had to walk. Interestingly, since nobility were seen as part-animal gods, they used the *nariguera* (a distinctive nose shield) to conceal their very human teeth – and the fact that they were no different from everyone else.

As interesting as the artifacts on display are the exhibits on this remarkable archaeological find was excavated.

The lighting and layout is exceptional (though it takes a minute to get used to the dark interior lighting). The signage is all in Spanish, but English-speaking guides are available for S45 to S60 per group.

Brüning Museum MUSEUM
(☑ 074-28-2110; www.museobruning.com; Huamachuco Cuadra 7; S8; ☺9am-5pm Tue-Sun) This museum, once the regional archaeological showcase, is now overshadowed by the Museo Tumbas Reales de Sipán, but it still houses an excellent collection of artifacts from the Inca, Chimú, Moche, Lambayeque, Vicus and Chavín cultures, amassed by Hans Heinrich Brüning, after whom the museum is named. It is a good place to get an overview of the different groups that have inhabited the region.

There are some excellent gold pieces and budding archaeologists will enjoy the displays showing the development of ceramics from different cultures and the exhibits explaining how ceramics and metalwork were made. Architecture and sculpture lovers may find some interest in the Corbusier-inspired building. Models of several important sites are genuinely valuable as a way to put the archaeology of the region into perspective.

The museum also houses a fascinating new exhibit dedicated to the tomb of the Sacredotisa de Chornancap, a Sicán noblewoman and governor whose burial spot loaded with intricate gold and silver artifacts was discovered in 2011 at the Chotuna-Chornancap site near the town of San José. The richly decorated tomb has given researchers new insights into gender equality in Lambeyeque society.

English-speaking guides charge S30.

ⓘ Getting There & Away

The terminals on Calle San José, near the Plazuela Elias Aguirre, in Chiclayo have regular *colectivos* and *combis* to Lambayeque (S2 to S2.50, 20 minutes), which will drop you off a block from the Brüning Museum.

Ferreñafe

Located in Ferreñafe, the splendid Museo Nacional Sicán (☑ 074-28-6469; Av Batangrande Cuadra 9, Ferreñafe; S8; ☺ 9am-5pm Tue-Sun) displays replicas of the 12m-deep tombs found at the Sicán site at Batán Grande, among the largest tombs found in South America. Enigmatic burials were discovered within – the Lord of Sicán was buried upside down, in a fetal position, with his head separated from his body. Beside him were the bodies of two women and two adolescents, as well a sophisticated security system – the red *sinabrio* dust, toxic if inhaled – to ward off grave robbers.

Another important tomb contained a nobleman sitting in a cross-legged position and wearing a mask and headdress of gold and feathers, surrounded by smaller tombs and niches containing the bodies of one man and 22 young women. The museum is worth the journey, and it's never crowded. Guided tours from Chiclayo to Ferreñafe and on to the Santuario Histórico Bosque de Pomac cost around S40 per person. Alternatively buses for Ferreñafe (S1.50) leave frequently from Chiclayo's Terminal de Microbuses Epsel (p348).

Túcume

The site of Túcume (www.tucume.com; single/combined circuit S8/12; ☺ 8am-4:30pm), around 30km north of Lambayeque on the Panamericana, is not particularly well known, but it's the most impressive collection of ruins in the region. A vast area, with more than 200 hectares of crumbling walls, plazas and 26 pyramids, it was the final capital of the Sicán culture, who moved their city from nearby Batán Grande around AD 1050 after that area was devastated by the effects of El Niño.

The pyramids you see today are a composite of structures made by several civilizations. The lower levels belonged to the Sicán, while the next two levels, along with the distinctive surrounding walls, were added by the Chimú. While little excavation has been done and no spectacular tombs have been found, it's the sheer size of the site that makes it a memorable visit.

There is a small but attractive on-site museum with some interesting tidbits, including some fine carved rocks. Guides are available for S30.

There are a couple of circuits available to visitors. The first loop includes a visit to the museum and the Huaca Las Balsas ruins, while on the second the site can be surveyed from a stunning *mirador* (lookout) atop Cerro Purgatorio (Purgatory Hill). The hill was originally called Cerro la Raya (Stingray Hill), but the name was changed after the Spaniards tried to convert local people to Christianity by dressing as demons atop the hill and throwing nonbelievers to their deaths.

From Chiclayo *combis* (S2.50) depart from the corner of Leguia and Belaúnde, north of the center, every 10 minutes from 5am to 9pm. You can also catch one from Lambayeque (ask at the Brüning Museum). Guided tours from Chiclayo cost around S40 per person, excluding admission fees.

Reserva Ecológica Chaparrí

This 34,000-hectare private reserve (☑ 978-836-377; www.chaparri.org; admission S10, reservations required, guides S50 per group; ☺ 7am-5pm), located 75km east of Chiclayo, was established in 2000 by the community of Santa Catalina and the famous Peruvian wildlife photographer Heinz Plenge. It offers a unique atmosphere for this coast – it's one of the few places in the world where you can spot the rare spectacled bear in its natural habitat; 25 or so have been accounted for (there are also two in rehabilitation captivity).

This area is an ornithologist's dream, with more than 237 species of bird, including rare white-winged guans, Andean condors, king vultures and several species of eagle. A large number of threatened animal species is also found here, including pumas, collared anteaters and Andean weasels. Nearly a third of these vertebrates are not found anywhere else in the world. There's also a friendly fox or two.

The reserve is under threat from illegal invasions by land speculators and in late 2017 one of the community leaders was killed in his home as a result of his conservation efforts. Tourism is vitally important to ensure the local community has the resources to protect the reserve.

Access to the reserve is via a rough 4WD-only track from the town of Chongoyape. Guides are obligatory and advance reservations are required. Get in touch with guide association ACOTURCH through the reserve's phone number to organize a trip. if you can't get through, call local guide Juan Carrasco (☑ 978-519-857, 074-43-3194; Chongoyape).

If you don't have your own vehicle, you can access the reserve on your own as a day trip by catching a bus from Chiclayo's Terminal de Microbuses Epsel (p348) to Chongoyape (S5, one hour), from where Juan can arrange transport for S120 round trip.

Far easier, but less adventurous, is to take a guided tour from Chiclayo. Moche Tours (p342) and Sipán Tours (p342) arrange day trips, including transportation and guide, for S130 to S140 per person (minimum four people). They include plenty of time exploring the park.

If you want to stay longer, good rustic accommodations can be found at Chaparrí EcoLodge (☑ 074-45-2299; www.chaparrilodge. com; r per person incl three meals & one-day guide S392-483). Alternatively Juan Carrasco can set campers up in a very rustic campground in a beautiful setting above Chongoyape.

Santuario Histórico Bosque de Pomac

About 22km north of Ferreñafe, a minor road leads to the Sicán ruins of Batán Grande, a major archaeological site where about 50 pyramids have been identified and several burials have been excavated. The site lies within the Santuario Histórico Bosque de Pomac (Ruinas de Batán Grande; ☑ 074-20-6466; admission Peruvian/foreign visitors S11/30; ⊙ 8:30am-5:30pm), which is both an archaeological and a nature destination. The area is huge, with an average walking tour taking around five hours, but it's also possible to complete the loop with bicycles or in a *mototaxi*.

The protected reserve incorporates one of the largest dry tropical forests on the continent and hosts more than 50 species of birds; healthy stands of *algarrobo* (carob tree) offer beautiful shade along the way. Pick up a map in iPerú (p346) in Chiclayo before setting out. Guides are available for S30 per group. Bicycles can be rented at the visitor center for S20.

Combis to Batán Grande leave from Chiclayo's Terminal de Microbuses Epsel (p348) (S5, 45 minutes). Ask the driver to let you off at the 'Entrada de Bosque de Pomac,' which is on a curve in the highway before Batán Grande town. It's also possible to access the area from the western side of the reserve on horseback rides organized through Rancho Santana (☑ 979-712-145; www.cabalga tasperu.com; Pacora; horseback tours from S75) in Pacora, about 45km northeast of Chiclayo.

Organized tours from Chiclayo combine a visit to the Santuario with the Museo Nacional Sicán for S40, including guide and transport.

Piura

☑ 073 / POP 755,500

After several hours of crossing the vast emptiness of the Sechura Desert, Piura materializes like a mirage on the horizon, enveloped in quivering waves of heat. It's hard to ignore the sense of physical isolation forced on you by this unforgiving environment – the self-sufficiency imposed upon early settlers may explain why they identify as Piuran rather than Peruvian.

Being so far inland, the scorching summer months will have you honing your radar for air-conditioning, as you seek out chilled venues in which to soothe sweltering skin. It's not a hugely attractive city, a fact not helped by severe flooding in 2017 that damaged some urban areas, but remnants of narrow cobbled streets and some colonial houses make up for the fact that there's little else for visitors to do here.

Its role as a hub for the northern towns means you'll probably end up spending some time here.

◉ Sights

Jirón Lima, a block east of the Plaza de Armas, has preserved its colonial character more than most areas in Piura.

◉ In Town

Cathedral   CHURCH
(Plaza de Armas) The cathedral was originally constructed in 1588, when Piura was finally built in its current location. The impressive early 17th-century, gold-covered side altar of the Virgin of Fatima was once the main altar in the church. Famed local artist Ignacio

Piura

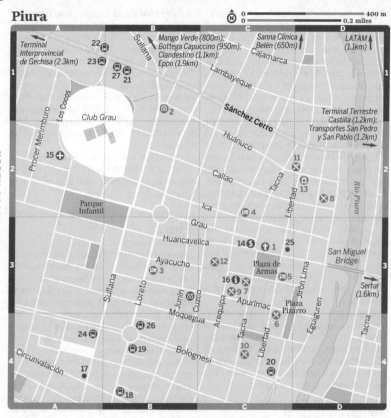

Piura

◎ Sights

🛏 Sleeping

🍴 Eating

🛍 Shopping

ℹ Information

ℹ Transport

Merino painted the canvas of San Martín de Porres in the mid-19th century.

Museo Municipal Vicus

MUSEUM

(http://mvicus.blogspot.com; Huánuco 893; ⊙9am-5pm Tue-Sat, to 1pm Sun) FREE This four-story monolith offers a sparse but decent look into Vicus culture, highlighted by the underground Sala de Oro (admission S4, 9am to 4pm Tuesday to Saturday), where some excellent pieces are displayed, including a gold belt decorated with a life-sized gold cat head that puts today's belt buckles to shame.

⊙ Outside Town

Narihualá

ARCHAEOLOGICAL SITE

(☑073-32-2307; Calle Olmos s/n; admission S2; ⊙8:30am-4:30pm Tue-Sun) Narihualá was the capital of the pre-Inca Tallán culture and is one of the premier archaeological sites around Piura. Covering 6 hectares just south of Catacaos, it's centered on a fairly well preserved adobe fortress. An attached museum features artifacts discovered in the excavation of the site.

A *mototaxi* from Catacaos costs around S15 round trip, including wait time.

Chulucanas

VILLAGE

Located about 55km east of Piura, just before the Sechura Desert starts rising into the Andean slopes, Chulucanas is known Peru-wide for its distinctive ceramics – rounded, glazed, earth-colored pots that depict humans. Chulucanas' ceramics have officially been declared a part of Peru's cultural heritage and are becoming famous outside the country.

The best place to buy ceramics around here is in La Encantada, a quiet rural outpost just outside of Chulucanas, whose inhabitants work almost exclusively in *artesanía* (handicrafts). La Encantada was home to the late Max Inga, a local legend who studied ceramic artifacts from the ancient Tallan and Vicus cultures and sparked a resurgence in the art form. The friendly artisans are often happy to demonstrate the production process, from the 'harvesting' of the clay to the application of mango-leaf smoke to get that distinctive black-and-white design. The village is reached from Chulucanas by a 30-minute *mototaxi* ride (S10) down a 7km dirt road.

While it's an interesting place, shopping in Chulucanas is probably for diehards only, as lugging this excellent but fragile pottery with you around Peru would be less than ideal.

Civa has buses to Chulucanas (S6, one hour) from Piura's Terminal Terrestre Castilla.

Catacaos

VILLAGE

A bustling small town 12km southwest of Piura, Catacaos is the self-proclaimed capital of *artesanía* in the region. And justifiably so: its arts market is the best in northern Peru. Sprawling for several blocks near the Plaza de Armas, the market has traditional sombreros, excellent weavings, gold and silver filigree jewelry, wood carvings, ceramics (including lots of pieces from Chulucanas), leather goods and more. Weekends are the best and busiest time to visit.

🛏 Sleeping

Mango Verde

B&B $$

(☑073-32-1768; www.mangoverde.com.pe; Country 248; s/d/tw/tr incl breakfast S140/160/180/230; ❄🐱) About 2km north of Plaza de Armas, on a lively street surrounded by bars and restaurants, this smart B&B has far more charm than most offerings in this price bracket. It manages to be industrial and cozy at the same time, with wonderfully inviting common terraces with plush patio furniture next to steel staircases and exposed concrete.

Pottery from local artisans and well-curated art add a bit of color to things and rooms are simple-ish with all the mod cons.

Hotel Las Arenas

HOTEL $$

(☑073-30-7583; hotellasarenaspiura@hotmail.com; Loreto 945; s/d incl breakfast S90/110, with air-con S110/130; ❄@🐱🏊) It was a low bar, but this remodeled *casona* (mansion) now offers a smidgeon more character than other spots in town. It earns its top Piura honors for the small but enchanting pool with inviting wicker love seats and copious potted plants, mismatched (depending on the era) but endearing flooring and well-maintained-if-ever-so-dated rooms.

Los Portales

HISTORIC HOTEL $$$

(☑073-32-8887; www.losportaleshoteles.com.pe/hotel-piura; Libertad 875; r incl breakfast S440-660; ❄@🐱🏊) This beautiful and fully refurbished colonial building on the Plaza de Armas delivers with its exquisite details. Handsome public areas with iron grillwork and black-and-white checkered floors lead to a poolside restaurant and rooms with large cable TV, minibar and great beds.

The new rooms out back are quieter, but lack the artisanship of the historic chambers. Discounts are available online.

Intiotel

BUSINESS HOTEL $$$

(☎073-28-7600; www.intiotel.com; Arequipa 691; s/d/ste incl breakfast S210/275/400; ❄@🛜) This modern hotel is the trendy choice, with industrially sterile hallways that lead to spotless-but-dark rooms with tasteful art and retro silver minibars, flat-screen TVs and nice bathrooms. There's a business center and round-the-clock room service.

Eating

To tuck into some regional delicacies, a lunchtime trip to the nearby town of Catacaos is a must. Vegetarians will be pleased by Piura's wealth of meatless options.

Snack Bar Romano

PERUVIAN $

(Ayacucho 580; mains S7.50-29.50, menú S14; ⊙7am-11pm Mon-Sat) With an excellent list of several daily *menús* (set meals), this local favorite has been around as long as its middle-aged waiters. It gets the double thumbs-up for ceviches, *sudados* (traditional slow-cooked meats in sauce) and other local specialties. Great ambience, great value.

Ganimedes

VEGETARIAN $

(☎912-555-757; Apurimac 486; menús S9, mains S15-35; ⊙7am-10pm Mon-Sat, 11am-9pm Sun; 🍴) No goat-head soups here, but plenty of refreshing fruit juices, yummy yogurts, wholegrain biscuits and lots and lots of salads in addition to hearty meat-free mains. Ganimedes doubles as a whole-grain bakery, making it a great place to stock your picnic basket.

D'Pauli

DESSERTS $

(Jirón Lima 541; cakes & pastries from S3; ⊙9am-9pm Mon-Sat, to 4pm Sun) Easily the best place in the center for coffee and dessert, this fantastic cafe prepares top-quality cakes and pies, real espresso and good juices. It also offers light meals, including hot and cold sandwiches and crepes.

Matheo's

VEGETARIAN $

(☎948-659-518; Libertad 487; meals S14-18; ⊙7am-11pm; 🍴) With two central locations and another in the north of town, Matheo's serves as an antidote to the hills of *parrillada* (grilled meats) found all over Peru. The all-veggie menu has lots of I-can't-believe-it's-not-meat versions of local dishes and it opens early for filling breakfast offerings. The second center branch is at Tacna 532.

★ Bottega Capuccino

CAFE $$

(Santa Maria 287, Santa Isabel; breakfast S11-21, mains S18-40; ⊙9am-11pm Mon-Sat, 5-10pm Sun; 🛜) The real deal. This bright, modern cafe in bustling Santa Isabel, a 10-minute taxi from the center, offers wholesome breakfasts and gourmet sandwiches and salads that are great for lunch. It also serves more sophisticated fare for a fine night out with a bottle of wine at dinner and, for caffeine freaks, one of the best espressos (S6.50) in Piura.

Another compelling reason to come here is for the desserts that you might be missing from home (Toblerone cheesecake, pecan pie), which are worth a taxi ride on their own.

La Tomasita

PERUVIAN $$

(☎073-32-1957; Tacna 853; mains S19-58; ⊙11am-11pm) This excellent restaurant looks unremarkable from the outside, but the interior is set up like a traditional country house, complete with adobe walls, palm ceilings and knickknacks on the walls that, along with the music, help create a wonderful atmosphere. The traditional dishes from throughout the region are no letdown, either. A fine place to try Piurana cuisine.

Carburmer

ITALIAN $$

(Los Santitos; ☎073-30-9475; Libertad 1001; mains S15-35; ⊙11am-11pm Mon-Sat, to 5pm Sun) This cozy and romantic place serves up quality traditional dishes for lunch, and in the evening morphs into the best Italian restaurant in town (though you can still go Peruvian if you fancy). Dripping with moodily lit ambience (check out the wacky pulley

COLÁN

If you want to lose a few days in an authentic Peruvian beach town that foreigners haven't yet embraced, look no further than Colán, 15km north of Paita, Piura's main port.

Paita itself is a dusty and unattractive port town that looks like it sprouted organically from the desert and has a roguish, Wild West feel to it, but as soon as Colán comes into view after you've turned off the main highway, you'll feel that often-lost sense of discovery.

Colán is home to the oldest colonial church in Peru (it looks like something out of a Cormac McCarthy novel), and the long beach is a trendy summer destination for the Peruvian jet set – and is practically deserted the rest of the year. The curving bay has a shallow beach that's excellent for swimming.

Playa Colán Lodge (☑073-32-6778; www.playacolanlodge.com.pe; 2-/4-/5-person bungalows S280/346/445; P 🛜 ⛲) The best place to stay in Colán. Built from a combination of natural materials, it has an upmarket, Robinson Crusoe feel and hosts cute, pastel-colored bungalows along the beach. There are lots of hammocks, shady palm trees, a volleyball court and a curvy and delicious pool, plus an excellent on-site restaurant. It's 1.5km south of town, on the beach.

system that opens the door), this is a fine choice for that special night out.

Don Parce PERUVIAN **$$**
(☑969-092-812; Tacna 642; mains S18-40; ◷7am-midnight; 🛜) Immensely pleasant spot serving a long list of Peruvian standards and typical northern dishes, as well as good light meals in a colonial atmosphere off the Plaza de Armas. Its selection of frozen fruit juices is an ideal way to beat the Piura heat. Daily set lunch menus are excellent value.

 Drinking & Nightlife

Clandestino BAR
(Caceres 230; ◷11am-5pm & 7pm-2am) A chilled, unpretentious bar near the university that's popular with students, Clandestino is a good place to mix with interesting young locals and practice a bit of Spanish in the process.

 Shopping

Centro Artesanal Norte ARTS & CRAFTS
(cnr Huánuco & Libertad; ◷9am-7pm Mon-Sat) This artisan center is actually a tiny mall with a collection of different craft shops featuring regional specialties from baskets to weavings to Chulucanas pottery. While it feels a bit abandoned – you'll have to get the manager to unlock each of the stalls – it's a decent option if you don't have time to go to the outlying craft towns.

 Information

IMMIGRATION

Oficina de Migraciónes (☑073-33-5536; www.migraciones.gob.pe; cnr Sullana & Circunvalación) Handles visa issues.

MEDICAL SERVICES

Clínica San Miguel (www.clinicasanmiguel piura.com; Los Cocos 111-153; ◷24hr) A long-established private clinic with 24-hour emergency ward.

Sanna Clínica Belén (☑073-62-6100; www.sanna.pe; San Cristobal 267) A recommended private clinic for outpatient needs.

MONEY

Casas de cambio (foreign exchange bureaus) are at the Ica and Arequipa intersection.
BCP (Grau 133) Bank with ATM.

POST

Serpost (Apurimac 657; ◷9am-7pm Mon-Fri, to 1pm Sat) Main post office.

TOURIST INFORMATION

iPerú (☑073-32-0249; Ayacucho 459, oficina 102; ◷9am-6pm Mon-Sat, to 1pm Sun) Has tourist information; the airport also has an iPerú counter.

🛈 Getting There & Away

AIR

The airport (PIU) is on the southeastern bank of the Río Piura, 2km from the city center. Schedules change often. An official taxi into town costs S15. Those hanging around outside charge about S10, although we don't recommend taking an unofficial taxi.

LATAM (☑073-39-4379; www.latam.com; Centro Commercial Open Plaza, Tienda 51, 1era Nivel; ◷10am-10pm Mon-Fri, to 2pm Sat) flies from Lima to Piura six times daily from 5am to 7:40pm, with return flights from 7am to 10pm. Often cheaper is **Peruvian Airlines** (☑073-32-4206; www.peruvian.pe; Libertad 777; ◷9am-7pm Mon-Fri, to 2pm Sat), which has a

WORTH A TRIP

HUANCABAMBA

For the daring adventurer Huancabamba, deep in the eastern mountains, is well worth the rough seven-hour journey from Piura. This region is famed in Peru for the powerful *brujos* (witch doctors) and *curanderos* (healers) who live and work at the nearby lakes of Huaringas. Peruvians from all over the country flock to partake in their ancient healing techniques.

When people from the West think of witchcraft, visions of pointed hats, broomsticks and bubbling brews are rarely far away, but in Peru consulting *brujos* and *curanderos* is widely accepted.

Peruvians from all walks of life visit *brujos* and *curanderos* and often pay sizable amounts of money for their services. These shamans are employed to cure an endless list of ailments, from headaches to cancer to chronic bad luck, and are particularly popular in matters of love – whether it's love lost, love found, love desired or love scorned.

The **Huaringas** lake area near Huancabamba, almost 4000m above sea level, is said to have potent curative powers and attracts a steady stream of visitors from around the continent. The most famous lake is **Laguna El Shimbe**, though nearby **Laguna Negra** is also frequently used by *curanderos*.

Ceremonies can last all night and entail hallucinogenic plants (such as the San Pedro cactus), singing, chanting, dancing and a dip in the lakes' painfully freezing waters. The *curanderos* will also use *ícaros*, which are mystical songs and chants. Serious *curanderos* will spend many years studying the art, striving for the hard-earned title of *maestro curandero*. Some ceremonies involve more powerful substances such as *ayahuasca* (Quechua for 'vine of the soul'), a potent and vile mix of jungle vines used to induce strong hallucinations. Vomiting is a common side effect. Many reports of dangerous *ayahuasca* practices (especially around Iquitos in the Amazon) are surfacing, and it pays to think once, twice and three times before ingesting the substance. Bringing a friend is also recommended, especially for single female travelers. Lonely Planet does not recommend taking *ayahuasca* and those who do so do it at their own risk.

If you're interested in visiting a *curandero* while in Huancabamba, be warned that this tradition is taken very seriously and gawkers or skeptics will get a hostile reception. The small **tourist information office** (Prolongación Calle Centenario 300, Huancabamba; ⊙8am-5pm) at the bus station has an elementary map of the area and a list of accredited *brujos* and *curanderos*. In Salala, closer to the lakes, you will be approached by *curanderos* or their 'agents,' but be wary of scam artists – try to get a reference before you arrive. Know also that there are some *brujos* who are said to work *en el lado oscuro* (on the dark side). Expect to pay around S300 for a basic visit and up to S1500 for a master *curandero*.

Note that hotels in Huancabamba are rudimentary and many share cold-water bathrooms.

From Piura, Transportes San Pedro y San Pablo and Civa have a morning and evening service to Huancabamba (S20 to S25, seven hours). Note that the road is mountainous and in poor condition and during heavy rains it's often closed by landslides.

To visit the lakes catch an early *colectivo* from the Huancabamba terminal to Salala (S10, 1½ hours), from where you can arrange treks to Laguna El Shimbe on foot or horseback (S30, 2½ hours). For Laguna Negra take a *colectivo* to El Porvenir (S15, three hours), from where it's a one-hour hike or horseback ride.

These days busy Peruvian professionals can get online and consult savvy, business-minded shamans via WhatsApp – not quite the same thing as midnight chants and icy dunks in remote Andean lakes.

morning and afternoon flight between the two cities.

BUS

International

The standard route to Ecuador goes along the Panamericana via Tumbes to Machala. **Civa** (☎073-33-1944; www.civa.com.pe; Loreto 1400) is the most comfortable option, departing at 7:45pm daily. Alternatively **Cooperativa de Transporte Loja** (☎073-33-3260; Loreto 1241, Adentro Terminal Ronco) goes via La Tina to Macará (S24, four hours) and Loja (S48, eight hours) at 1pm and 9pm. These buses stop for border formalities, then continue.

Domestic

Several companies have offices on cuadra 1100 of Sánchez Cerro, though for Cajamarca and across the northern Andes, it's best to go to Chiclayo and get a connection there.

Buses and *combis* leave for Catacaos (S1.50 to S2, 15 minutes) from east of the San Miguel pedestrian bridge. Buses to Sullana, Paita and Tarapoto leave from **Terminal Interprovincial de Gechisa** (Prolongación Sánchez Cerro), a S5 taxi ride west of town. Chulucanas and Huancabamba buses leave from **Terminal Terrestre Castilla** (Terminal El Bosque; Av Guardia Civil), aka 'El Bosque,' a S3.50 *mototaxi* ride east of town.

Civa Has 4:15pm, 5pm and 5:30pm buses to Lima, frequent buses to Chulucanas and buses to Huancabamba at 10am and 6pm, the last two leaving from Terminal Terrestre Castilla.

Cruz del Sur (☑ 073-33-7094; www.cruzdelsur. com.pe; cnr Bolognesi & Lima) Comfortable Lima buses at 3pm, 5:30pm, 6:30pm and 7:30pm, as well as a lone shot to Trujillo at 3pm.

El Dorado (☑ 073-32-5875; www.transporte-seldorado.com.pe; Cerro 1119) Comfortable buses to Tumbes every hour between 6:30am and 12:30am; all stop in Máncora. Also runs buses to Chiclayo at 1pm and 10:30pm, while there are 1pm, 11:30pm and midnight departures to Trujillo.

Eppo (☑ 073-30-4543; www.eppo.com.pe; Panamericana Manzana 243) Services to Máncora every half hour from 5:30am to 7:15pm from its huge private station behind Real Plaza on the Panamericana.

Ittsa (☑ 073-30-8645; www.ittsabus.com; Cerro 1142) Buses to Trujillo (9:30am, 1:30pm, 10:45pm, 11pm, 11:15pm and 11:30pm), Chiclayo (9:30am) and Chimbote (10pm), and comfortable buses to Lima at 5pm and 5:30pm, with an additional service at 7:30pm on demand. Buses leave from its new terminal in the industrial zone on the outskirts of town, but for the time being you can purchase tickets at this older location in the center.

Linea (☑ 073-30-3894; www.linea.pe; Cerro 1215) Hourly buses to Chiclayo between 5am and 8pm, and a 1:30pm and 11pm bus to Trujillo.

Oltursa (☑ 073-32-6666; www.oltursa.pe; Bolognesi 801) Runs some of the most comfortable buses to Lima, with regular departures between 4pm and 9:15pm from its centrally located terminal.

Tepsa (☑ 073-30-6345; www.tepsa.com.pe; Loreto 1198) Lima buses at 5pm and 6pm.

Transportes Chiclayo (☑ 074-30-8455; www. transporteschiclayo.com; Cerro 1121) Buses to Chiclayo leave roughly every half hour from 4am to 9pm from its terminal on Sanchez Cerro, near the market.

Transportes San Pedro y San Pablo (☑ 073-34-9271; Terminal Terrestre Castilla) Has a *semi-cama* for Huancabamba at 8am and 6pm.

Piura Buses

DESTINATION	COST (S)	DURATION (HR)
Chiclayo	20-26	3
Chimbote	45-55	8
Guayaquil (Ecuador)	90-110	10-12
Huancabamba	25	7
Lima	90-150	12-16
Loja (Ecuador)	46-48	8
Mancará (Ecuador)	24	4
Máncora	16-25	3
Trujillo	35-55	6
Tumbes	25-40	5

TAXI

If you are heading to Máncora, Punta Sal or Tumbes, you can catch express vans and taxis with **Sertur** (☑ 016-58-0071; www.serturperu. com; Aeropuerto), which offers both collective and private transfers departing from the airport in Piura. It's faster but significantly more expensive than local buses.

Playa Lobitos

 073 / POP 8600

Set around a desolate bay, Lobitos at first glance looks like the site of some post-industrial apocalypse, with the shells of abandoned houses sharing space with rusted pumpjacks that hammer away like a horde of lost *maneki-neko* cats, and with abandoned offshore platforms in the distance.

A virgin paradise it most definitely is not, so why visit? Waves, of course. This relative newcomer on Peru's surf scene has a ton of great breaks and has developed a parallel infrastructure of hotels and hostels to cater to those who arrive with board in tow.

If you're not going to take to the waves with a board, you probably wont dig it much and are better off looking for your slice of tranquility elsewhere.

🏃 Activities

The surf is best here in October, and April through June, but expect some waves year-round. When it's cooking, you can get 2m waves that peel for several hundred meters. Expect mostly big barreling point breaks.

ⓘ BORDER CROSSING: ECUADOR VIA LA TINA

The border post of La Tina lacks accommodations, but the Ecuadorean town of Macará (3km from the border) has adequate facilities. La Tina is reached by *colectivos* (S12, 2½ hours) leaving from Sullana, 40km north of Piura, throughout the day. A better option is Transporte Loja (p356), which has two daily buses from Piura (1pm and 9pm) that conveniently go straight through the border and on to Loja (S48, eight hours).

The border is the international bridge over the Río Calvas and is open 24 hours. Formalities are relaxed as long as your documents are all in order. There are no banks, though you'll find money changers at the border or in Macará. The Peruvian and Ecuadorean immigration offices share the same building on the bridge, which makes the crossing easy peasy.

Travelers entering Ecuador will find taxis (US$1) and *colectivos* (US$0.50) to take them to Macará. There is a Peruvian consulate in Macará. See Lonely Planet's *Ecuador & the Galápagos Islands* for further information on Ecuador.

Beginners should check out the shore breaks near the pier.

🛏 Sleeping & Eating

Los Muelles Surf Camp   HOSTEL $
(📞 978-693-003; www.facebook.com/losmuelles surfcamp; Frente los Muelles; camping S15 per person, r S20 per person) While there's a slight Jonestown vibe, this place is pretty damn cool. Housed in the skeleton of a run-down 1920s-era bodega, the open-air surfer hangout has a 2nd-floor tent area with tents pre-installed, simple rooms with mattresses and little else, and a surfer-roots feel that harks back to the sport's anti-establishment heyday.

From the 2nd-floor platform you can see a handful of breaks, sip a *mate* and share tales with surfers and hangers-on from across the globe. There is a kitchen for guest use and a couple of cheap local places to eat nearby.

Lobitos Lodge   LODGE $$
(📞 073-67-8723; www.lobitoslodge.com.pe; r S100-148; P ⓢ) Hands-down the town's nicest hotel, Lobitos Lodge has just eight rooms on a swath of beachfront property. The rooms have flat-screen TVs, balconies with hammocks and a few photographs of the surfer-owner-business-magnate and his kin ripping it up. If you ask in advance they can prepare a homemade meal. It's 300m south of the pier.

It's worth springing for the oceanfront rooms as the back rooms get hot.

El Ancla   PERUVIAN $$
(Av Nueva Lobitos; mains from S15; ⊙ 9am-10pm) This popular local hangout on a corner in town is the one place that's always guaranteed to be open for a good, filling meal. The menu is extensive and everything is prepared with gusto, which makes up for the somewhat limited ambience.

ⓘ Getting There & Away

To get here from Piura, take an Eppo (p357) bus to Talara (S10, two hours), then grab a *combi* (S4, 30 minutes) north to Playa Lobitos from the stop two blocks in front of the Eppo terminal.

During peak periods a S3 fee for cleaning and maintenance is sometimes charged to visitors entering the village.

Cabo Blanco
📞 073 / POP 7000

The Panamericana runs parallel to the ocean north of Talara, with frequent glimpses of the coast. This area is one of Peru's main oil fields, and pumps are often seen scarring both the land and the sea with offshore oil rigs.

About 40km north of Talara is the sleepy town of Cabo Blanco, one of the world's most famous fishing spots. Set on a gently curving bay strewn with rocks, the town has a flotilla of fishing vessels floating offshore, where the confluence of warm Humboldt currents and El Niño waters creates a unique microcosm filled with marine life.

Ernest Hemingway was supposedly inspired to write his famous tale *The Old Man and the Sea* after fishing here in the early 1950s.

🏃 Activities

From November to January, magnificent 3m-high, fast-charging left tubes attract hard-core surfers.

The largest fish ever landed on a rod here was a 710kg black marlin, caught in 1953 by Alfred Glassell Jr. The angling is still good, though 20kg tuna are a more likely catch than black marlin, which have declined and are now rarely over 100kg. Fishing competitions are held here and 300kg specimens are still occasionally caught.

Deep-sea fishing boats with high-quality tackle can be rented through Hotel El Merlin and other hotels in the area for S800 to S1350 per six-hour day, including drinks and lunch. January, February and September are considered the best fishing months.

Sleeping & Eating

Hotel El Merlin HOTEL **$$**
(☑ 073-25-6188; www.elmerlin.webs.com; Malecón s/n; s/d incl breakfast from S70/120; P ✿ ✿) The rooms here could do with some upkeep, but retain an elegant feel and catch fresh breezes. They have handsome flagstone floors, electric showers and balconies with ocean views. With Cabo Blanco's limited visitor numbers, this cavernous hotel can seem quite empty.

Restaurante El Mero SEAFOOD **$**
(Malecón s/n; mains S15, menú S8; ☉ 8am-5pm) For great seafood prepared in classic Peruvian ways, go no further than this humble little family-run diner on the main strip. It's right across from the fishers' cooperative, so you know its pretty darn fresh. Fantastic value.

Getting There & Away

Cabo Blanco is several kilometers down a winding road from the Pan-American Hwy town of El Alto. From Máncora you can take a bus or *combi* to El Alto (S3.50, 30 minutes), then grab a truck or *combi* down to Cabo Blanco (S2, 15 minutes).

Máncora

☑ 073 / POP 12,600

Máncora is *the* place to see and be seen along the Peruvian coast – in summer foreigners flock here to rub sunburned shoulders with the Peruvian jet set. It's not hard to see why – Peru's best sandy beach stretches for several kilometers in the sunniest region of the country, while dozens of plush resorts and their budget-conscious brethren offer up rooms just steps from the rolling waves. On shore most of the action is focused on the noisy main street, with plenty of good seafood restaurants and international flavors from which to choose.

The consistently good surf and bathtub-warm waters draw a sun-bleached, board-toting bunch, and raucous nightlife keeps visitors busy after the sun dips into the sea in a ball of fiery flames.

Year-round sun means this is one of the few resort towns on the coast that doesn't turn into a ghost town at less popular times.

Activities

There are remote, deserted beaches around Máncora that are superior to the town beach; ask your hotel to arrange a taxi or give you directions by bus and foot, but be prepared to walk several kilometers.

Diving & Snorkeling

The snorkeling and diving aren't great here, but an afternoon excursion can be fun. Snorkeling tours (S80) take you out to swim with sea turtles along the pier of a small fishing village called El Ñuro (Caleta El Ñuro, Talara; admission with/without water access S10/5; ☉ 7am-6pm), 23km south of Máncora at the end of Los Organos beach. Most of the diving is done from nearby petroleum platforms, with dives to depths of around 70m. Expect limited visibility and schools of fish and octopus.

Spondylus Dive Center DIVING
(☑ 999-891-268; www.spondylusdc.com; Piura 216; ☉ 10am-1pm & 3-7pm) Máncora's only dive shop was the first PADI-certified operation in Peru and is a professionally run operation. It offers three-day open-water courses for US$425, half-day try dives for S365 (no diving credentials required) and two fun dives for S330 for certified divers.

Mud Baths

About 11km east of town, up the wooded Fernández valley, a natural **hot spring** (admission S5; ☉ dawn-dusk) has bubbling water and powder-fine mud – perfect for a face pack. The slightly sulfurous water and mud is said to have curative properties. The hot spring can be reached by *mototaxi* (S60, including waiting time).

Surfing & Kitesurfing

Surf here is best from November to February, although good waves are found year-round and always draw dedicated surfers. The best expert break in town is Punta Ballenas, a steep point break with a rocky bottom that's located about five minutes' walk south of the main beach. Máncora beach itself has great beach breaks that are suitable for all abilities (but can get pretty crowded). Definitely consider taking long day or overnight trips to nearby breaks such as Los Organos, Lobitos, Talara and Cabo Blanco.

You can rent surfboards (per hour/day S10/20) from several places at the southern end of the beach in Máncora – in front of Del Wawa is the most convenient. Classes are offered around town for S50 to S60 per hour, including equipment.

May through September offers the best kitesurfing in Máncora and there are several schools at the southern end of town.

Geko Kite
KITESURFING

(☑ 983-438-696; www.gekokiteandsurf.com; 3-day course S990) Experienced instructor Paulo knows these shores extremely well and offers intensive three-day, nine-hour courses for beginners in addition to kite trips all over the region. Also organizes surfing classes.

Máncora Surf Shop
SURFING

(☑ 073-41-1450; www.mancorasurfshop.com; Piura 352; ⊙ 8am-8pm) Máncora Surf Shop sells boards, surf clothing and organizes lessons.

🢂 Tours

Several operators in town offer a mix of tours, including snorkeling (S70 to S80) and a nine-hour trip north to the Manglares (p368; S70 to S100) near Tumbes.

★ Pacifico Adventures
WHALE WATCHING

(☑ 998-391-428; www.pacificoadventures.com; Rivera del Mar, 150m Sur del Muelle, Los Organos) A professionally run outfit that operates whale-watching tours leaving from Los Organos, a short drive south of Máncora. It uses good boats and carries submarine audio equipment to listen to the cetacean calls. Also offers bird-watching tours.

Discovery Mancora
ADVENTURE

(☑ 073-62-8807; www.discoverymancora.com; Grau 217) Mainstream operator offering all the major tours.

🛏 Sleeping

Rates for accommodations in Máncora are seasonal, with the January to mid-March high season commanding prices up to 50% higher than the rest of the year, especially at weekends. During the three major holiday periods (Christmas to New Year, Semana Santa and Fiestas Patrias), accommodations can cost triple the low-season rate, require multinight stays and be very crowded – this time is generally best avoided. We list high-season rates.

South of town, along the Antigua Panamericana, you'll find fewer crowds, prettier landscapes and great midrange and high-end accommodation. A *mototaxi* between here and town costs between S5 and S10.

★ Loki del Mar
HOSTEL $$

(☑ 073-25-8484; www.lokihostel.com; Piura 262; dm S28-39, r S96, all incl breakfast; ❄@🗟🗷) Social butterflies flock to this mother of all beach hostels, which is really a self-contained resort masquerading as a backpackers' hangout. Tucked away in the whitewashed building are spacious dorm rooms with extrawide beds and minimalist private rooms for those seeking a hostel vibe without the communal snoring.

The party revolves around the massive pool, bar and lounge area, where beer pong rules are clearly laid out and a running board of (mostly) free activities keeps everyone entertained. As far as hostels go, it's punching above its weight class.

Aloha Lina
GUESTHOUSE $$

(☑ 982-732-284; linamollehuanca@gmail.com; 8 de Noviembre s/n; r S50-100; 🗟) Offering excellent value down a quiet alley just steps from the main beach, this small guesthouse has 11 spotless, fan-cooled rooms with fresh paint jobs set over two floors around a central courtyard. Rooms 6 to 8 on the top floor are the best, with windows on both sides that let in a breeze and glimpses of the sea.

Marcilia Beach Bungalows
BUNGALOW $$

(☑ 991-212-831; Antigua Panamericana Km 1212; r incl breakfast with/without sea view S180/100; @🗟) A friendly trilingual Peruvian couple started these rustic bungalows on Vichay-ito Beach after years working the cruise-ship circuit. Each bungalow has electric hot water and very nice bathrooms, but the real coups here are the bungalows that sit seaside: book one and you'll feel like the entire stretch of beach is your own private paradise.

Hotel Laguna Máncora
BUNGALOW $$

(☑ 994-015-628; lagunamancora@gmail.com; Veraniego s/n; dm/r incl breakfast from S48/140; 🗟🗷) This laid-back pad is a great find, one block back from the beach in its own little rustic oasis. Older Indonesian-style bamboo bungalows sit around a pleasant sandy garden right near the water and lots of swinging, shady hammocks will provide days of entertainment.

The cheery owner, Pilar, who is also a **surf instructor** (☑ 994-015-628; Veraniego s/n), is a joy and nailed the essence of Máncora years ago.

THE NORTH COAST'S TOP FIVE SURF BREAKS

Dedicated surfers will find plenty of action on Peru's North Coast, from the longest break in the world at Puerto Chicama to consistently good surf at Máncora. Most spots have reliable swell year-round, and there are plenty of spots for beginners in between.

Los Organos Located about 14km south of Máncora. Has a rocky break with well-formed tubular waves reaching up to 2m; it's for experienced surfers only.

Cabo Blanco (p358) A perfect pipeline ranging between 1m and 3m in height and breaking on rocks; experienced surfers only.

Puerto Chicama (p340) On a good day this is the longest break in the world (up to 3.2km!); it has good year-round surfing for all skill levels.

Máncora (p359) Popular and easily accessible, with consistently decent surf up to 2m high; it's appropriate for all skill levels.

Huanchaco (p335) Long and well-formed waves with a pipeline; it's suitable for all levels.

Playa Lobitos (p357) More than eight named breaks in a back-to-basics surf setting.

Hostal Las Olas
HOTEL **$$**

(☎073-25-8099; www.lasolasmancora.com; 8 de Octubre s/n; s/d incl breakfast from S160/190; ☎) This great couples spot sports a Mediterranean-esque olive-skin tone on the outside and minimalist white rooms with wood accents on the inside. The small, cozy restaurant looks onto the beach's best breaks and is a surf-spotter's dream.

Newer 2nd- and 3rd-floor rooms are larger, with expansive terraces and ocean views, but the cheapest rooms sit under a staircase that sounds like an earthquake when people who've sprung for the best rooms bound up to revel in their better abodes.

★ Sunset Hotel
BOUTIQUE HOTEL **$$$**

(☎073-25-8111; www.sunsetmancora.com; Antigua Panamericana 196; r/tr incl breakfast S320/480; ❀☎☎) The intimate, boutique-styled Sunset wouldn't be out of place on the cover of a glossy travel mag. It has beautifully furnished interiors and great aqua-themed rock sculptures, while the good-sized rooms supply solid mattresses, hot showers, balconies and views of the seascape.

The pool is diminutive and ocean access is rocky, though a short walk brings you to a sandy beach...if you can tear yourself away from the hotel's Italian restaurant (p362), one of the area's best.

Casa de Playa
RESORT **$$$**

(☎073-25-8005; www.casadeplayamancora.net; Antigua Panamericana Km 1217, Playa Los Pocitas; r incl breakfast S495-560; P☎☎) This elegant and friendly place is popular with well-to-do Peruvians and offers up modern, slick dwellings with bamboo ceilings and warm tones opening onto private balconies. Half the room interiors are dressed in smoothed exposed concrete, which contrasts well with the plethora of colorful common areas – all are reached along lush corridors strewn with all manner of vibrant plants.

All the large rooms have hot water, arty bits and a balcony with a hammock and fine sea views. An inviting two-story lounge hangs out over the sea. It's about a five-minute drive south of town.

DCO Suites
BOUTIQUE HOTEL **$$$**

(☎073-25-8171; www.hoteldco.com; Playa Los Pocitas; ste incl breakfast from S777; ❀@☎☎) This relative newcomer upped the ante into the stratosphere for trendsetters and remains the discerning choice of honeymooners and other deep-pocketed nomads. Though the color scheme – a jarring turquoise and white – is seriously polarizing, the spacious rooms come with kimono-style robes, rain-style showers and lovely curved sandstone walls that fit together like an architectural jigsaw puzzle.

Service, privacy and luxury are the trump cards here, whether in the curtained beach *cabañas,* at the remarkable outdoor spa or in the small infinity pool.

Hotelier
HOTEL **$$$**

(☎073-25-8702; www.hotelier.pe; Antigua Panamericana Km 1217; s/d incl breakfast from S220/315; ❀☎☎) If you travel for food, this artsy choice is your resting spot. The owner, Javier Ruzo, is the son of one of Peru's most famous chefs and he carries on the family tradition at the fabulous restaurant here, but beyond that, he's also an artist and photographer whose work (poems, paintings, photos) gives unique personality to the bright modern rooms.

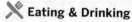 Eating & Drinking

Seafood rules the culinary roost in Máncora. Other ingredients tend to be pricier due to transportation costs. There are several mini-markets for self-caterers along the strip.

Most restaurants offer two-for-one happy-hour specials, with the party starting along Piura, then moving to the dance-hall bars along the beach. Loki (p360) has parties most nights open to nonguests (you'll need to present ID and get a wristband to get in).

Green Eggs & Ham   BREAKFAST $

(The Bird House Centro Comercial, Pasaje 8 de Noviembre; meals S12-18; ⊙7:30am-4:30pm) There's nothing silly about this Dr Seuss–inspired breakfast spot, which counts a battalion of fans for its homesick-remedy breakfasts (pancakes, French toast, hash browns). Yes, you'll like them Sam I Am, but the real coup is the 2nd-floor patio – with a view through a thatch of tall palms to the crashing waves.

Angela's Place   BREAKFAST $

(Piura 396; breakfast S13-18, mains S14-30; ⊙8am-10pm; ☌) Angela the Austrian bread wizard started selling her delicious sweet potato, yucca and wheat breads from her bicycle years ago. Now you can get them at this cheery cafe on the main drag, along with creative and substantial vegetarian (and vegan) dishes, energizing breakfast combos and sweet pastries.

La Bajadita   DESSERTS $

(☑073-25-8385; Piura 424; dishes S3-8; ⊙10am-10pm Tue-Sun) This is the place to sink your sweet tooth into some great cakes, including tiramisu, pecan pie, and the ever-popular apple pie. It also does small meals and all-day breakfasts and serves artisanal beers.

★ Donde Teresa   PERUVIAN $$

(☑073-25-8702; Antigua Panamericana Km 1217, Hotelier; mains S28-38; ⊙noon-9pm; ☎) Before Gastón Acurio there was Teresa Ocampo, Peru's most recognizable celebrity chef (famous before Peruvian food was even famous). She lives in Texas now, but her son, Javier, keeps the dream alive with gourmet takes on Peruvian classics served overlooking Los Pocitas Beach.

Recommended dishes include the smoked *ají de gallina* (chicken in spicy cream sauce) and *arroz chaufa con mariscos* (Chinese rice with seafood), but it's all fantastic.

Javier has lived in France, China and God knows where else, so his skills are honed and he even spears his own catches of the day on occasion! There's a children's menu and homemade ice creams.

★ La Sirena d'Juan   PERUVIAN $$

(☑073-25-8173; Piura 316; mains S40-45; ⊙noon-3pm & 6-11pm Wed-Mon; ☎) Local boy done good Juan has turned his intimate little main-drag seafooder into northern Peru's best restaurant. Yellowfin tuna fresh from Máncora's waters is the showstopper, whether it's prepared as a *tiradito* (a sort of Peruvian sashimi) in yellow curry or grilled with a mango-*rocoto*-red pepper chutney.

Also on the menu are creative raviolis and Peruvian classics given a foodie upgrade (baby goat in black beer, for example). Service in the small, French-farmhouse-style space is personalized and on point. It's expensive for Máncora, but you'd probably pay triple this at home. Reservations are not a bad idea in high season.

Restaurante Jasuzi   PERUVIAN $$

(☑982-541-333; Frente Colegio Pallete; mains S15-40; ⊙10am-7pm) It's a bit of a mission to reach this bright little family-run restaurant in front of a busy school on the northern edge of town, but it's well worth it for fabulous fresh ceviche that local foodies rate as the best in town. Make sure to order the *especial* with octopus, which takes the dish to a whole new level.

Ají   MEXICAN $$

(Piura Interna s/n; mains S20-38; ⊙noon-11pm; ☎) Away from the honks and exaust of the main drag, this friendly retreat serves up ample Mexican dishes and a smattering of standard pub fare such as hot wings and BBQ chicken. The open-air restaurant has a small bar, and the owner, Eric, is a cool surfer dude with plenty of tips.

Sunset   ITALIAN $$

(☑073-25-8111; Antigua Panamericana 196, Sunset Hotel; mains S40-45; ⊙8am-11pm) With a short menu of excellent Italian food, this is the most gourmet restaurant in town when the Italian chef is on, but disappointing when he isn't. It's in the hotel of the same name.

❶ Information

SAFE TRAVEL

All in all, it's fairly safe here, but there have been multiple reports of late-night robberies. Be wary of your bags in *mototaxis*, as there are some reports of taxi drivers running off with people's bags. Don't walk the beach late at night, even in groups.

Many travelers extend their stay by volunteering in hostels or finding employment in a restaurant or bar – fun for the traveler, but not great for locals who also compete for these jobs.

MEDICAL SERVICES

Medical Center (☑ 073-25-8601; www.medicalcentermancora.com; Panamericana s/n; ☺ 24hr) If you get stung by a ray or break a bone, head to this full-service clinic at the far northern entrance to town.

MONEY

Banco de la Nación (Piura 625) Change US dollars here. Has an ATM.

BCP (Piura 520) Has ATMs.

TOURIST INFORMATION

There is a fairly basic **information office** (Piura s/n, Edificio Municipal; ☺ 8am-3:45pm) in the local government building. The website www.vivamancora.com has tons of useful information.

ⓘ Getting There & Away

AIR

The best way to Máncora by plane is to fly to Piura with LATAM (p355) or Peruvian Airlines (p355), or to Tumbes with LATAM (p367), catching ground transportation from there.

BUS

Many bus offices are in the center, though most southbound trips originate in Tumbes. *Combis* leave for Tumbes (S12, two hours) regularly; they drive along the main drag until full. *Bus-camas* from Máncora go direct to Lima (14 hours); other services can drop you in intermediate cities on the way to Lima (18 hours). Regular minibuses run between Máncora and Punta Sal (S5 to S7, 30 minutes).

Cifa (☑ 941-816-863; www.cifainternacional.com; Grau 313) Cheap daily buses to Guayaquil (S65) and Cuenca (S65) in Ecuador.

Civa (☑ 014-18-1111; www.excluciva.pe; Piura 472) Has an economical 3:30pm service to Lima, as well as nicer buses at 5:30pm and 6:30pm. Also has a midnight bus to Guayaquil.

Cruz del Sur (☑ 0-801-11111; www.cruzdelsur.com.pe; Grau 208) Has *bus-cama* services to Lima at 5pm and 5:30pm; buses to Trujillo and Chimbote on Tuesday, Wednesday, Friday and Saturday at 10:30pm; and you can catch its Guayaquil-bound bus from Lima at 9am on Monday, Tuesday, Thursday and Saturday.

El Dorado (www.transporteseldorado.com.pe; Grau 198) Six buses a day to Piura between 9:30am and 9:30pm, as well as buses for Chiclayo (9:30am, 9:30pm, 11:30pm and midnight) and Trujillo (9:30am, 9:30pm and 11pm).

A Tumbes-bound bus also grabs passengers seven times a day.

Emtrafesa (☑ 072-52-5850; www.emtrafesa.com; Grau 193) Heads to Chiclayo at 9:30pm and 10pm, and Trujillo at 8:30pm, 9:30pm and 10pm.

Eppo (☑ 073-25-6262; Piura 679) Fast and regular hourly buses to Sullana and Piura between 4am and 8pm. They will also drop you at Los Organos for S2.

Ittsa (☑ 073-29-0651; Grau 624) Direct buses to Lima at 4:15pm and 9:15pm. Other services include Trujillo at 9:15pm, Chimbote at 4:15pm and Chiclayo at 9:15pm.

Oltursa (☑ 017-08-5000; www.oltursa.pe; Grau 505; ☎) Lima *bus-cama* (with wi-fi) at 5pm and 5:30pm. Has a direct bus to Trujillo at 10pm.

Sertur (☑ 073-25-8582; www.serturperu.com; Grau 111) Fast *colectivo* vans to Piura (departing hourly from 8am to 8pm) and Tumbes (departing hourly from 8am to 6pm).

Tepsa (☑ 016-17-9000; www.tepsa.com.pe; Grau 113) Lima bus at 6pm.

Transportes Chiclayo (☑ 073-25-8050; www.transporteschiclayo.pe; Grau 213) Direct services to Chiclayo at noon, 4:30pm, 10pm and 11pm in comfortable buses.

Transportes Flores (☑ 972-719-631; Grau 565) One of the more economical buses running to Lima, with departures at 10am, 1pm, 5pm and 7pm.

Máncora Buses

DESTINATION	COST (S)	DURATION (HR)
Chiclayo	40-45	7
Chimbote	90-140	14
Guayaquil (Ecuador)	60-65	8
Lima	80-180	14-18
Piura	21-95	3½
Sullana	17	2½
Trujillo	40-90	9-10
Tumbes	12-60	2

Punta Sal

☑ 072 / POP 3300

The long, curvy bay at Punta Sal, 25km north of Máncora, is prettier and far more chilled than its noisy neighbor. It's a quiet little town with sandy streets leading to a wide beach with fine sand that is home to great eateries, and there are no trucks powering through to shatter the peace.

The sea here is calm, and while there are some rocky bits it's still great for a dip in the ocean. The lack of surfer types means that this tranquil oasis of resorts is particularly popular with families.

Note that there are two towns here: Punta Sal is located down a spur road off the Panamericana, while busier and less attractive Canoas de Punta Sal straddles the highway.

Sleeping & Eating

Las Terrazas de Punta Sal HOTEL $
(☑ 910-295-022, 072-50-7701; s/d from S35/70, without bathroom S20/40; @ 🛜) One of the few budget options on this beach, friendly Las Terrazas has solid rooms inside the main house, as well as some poky small bamboo rooms at the front that are pretty much just good for crashing out in – choose wisely! The terrace restaurant here has awesome sunset views.

**★ Punta Sal
Suites & Bungalows** RESORT $$$
(☑ 072-59-6700; www.puntasal.com.pe; s/d from S380/477; P ❄ @ 🛜 ⊠) Off the Panamericana at Km 1192 – about 10 minutes' drive north of Punta Sal proper – this seaside oasis has all the good stuff you'd expect from a resort retreat. The way to go are the bungalows that can sleep up to five and are fully decked out with tropical furnishings and have excellent beach vibes.

The individual rooms lack beach views. Overall it's perfect for families, with minigolf, laundry facilities, banana-boat rides, water skiing, tennis, volleyball, table tennis, billiards and a wooden-decked pool – and what resort would be complete without a near-life-size replica of a galleon?

La Piramide PERUVIAN $$
(☑ 072-54-0006; mains S15-60; ⊙ 9am-10pm) This funky bar-restaurant right on the sand serves up some of Punta Sal's best seafood in uber-relaxed surroundings. It also has vegetarian options and is a good place for cocktails, too. Organizes movie nights.

❶ Getting There & Away

Regular minibuses run between Máncora and Punta Sal (S5 to S7, 30 minutes). A private taxi costs around S60 to S80.

Zorritos

☑ 072 / POP 9400
About 35km south of Tumbes, Zorritos is the biggest fishing village along this section of coast. While the coarse beach here isn't as nice

as beaches further south – it's unfortunately often covered with a fair amount of litter – the area is home to interesting coastal birdlife. Look for frigate birds, pelicans, egrets and other migratory birds.

Zorritos isn't so much a town as a collection of buildings spread out along a long stretch of highway, which means there is not much of a village atmosphere and the lack of footpaths make it a tough place to get around.

Sleeping

Zorritos has no center and accommodations are spread over several kilometers, so make sure to specify to your bus or *combi* driver where you need to be dropped.

Noelani HOTEL $$
(☑ 072-28-3815; reservasnuevacostazulnoelani@gmail.com; Piaggio 115; r S165-198; ❄ 🛜 ⊠) Offering two floors of modern air-con rooms surrounding an infinity pool overlooking the sand, this tidy place offers plenty of comfort for the price.

Grillo Tres Puntas Ecohostel LODGE $$
(☑ 072-79-4830; www.casagrillo.net; Panamericana Km 1235; campsites S15, r with/without bathroom per person incl breakfast from S65/35; @ 🛜 ⊠) 🌿 Grillo Tres Puntas Ecohostel was constructed (mainly by volunteers) from natural materials such as bamboo and cane. Everything here, including water, is recycled. Breezy, rustic cabins with balconies and hammocks sit on the beach and campsites have a shade roof. It's supremely rustic and not for every type of traveler, but if you value location over luxury it's pretty idyllic.

There is an artistic elevated patio fashioned from driftwood – great for sunset beers. Cheaper rooms share interesting outdoor communal bathrooms covered in mosaic tiles and seashells. Hikes to nearby mud baths can be arranged and it also runs popular tours that take in mangroves and nature reserves.

Eating

Sazon y Sabor PERUVIAN $$
(Panamericana Norte 1229; mains S28-50; ⊙ 9am-midnight) On an open deck across the road from the beach, this popular place serves up quality Peruvian classics in addition to some international plates.

ℹ️ Getting There & Away

Combis and *colectivos* to Zorritos leave regularly from Tumbes (S4, about one hour). Coming from the south, catch any bus heading toward Tumbes.

Tumbes

🎵 072 / POP 111,700

Only 30km from the Ecuadorean border, Tumbes sits in a uniquely green part of coastal Peru, where dry deserts magically turn into mangroves and an expanse of ecological reserves stretches in all directions. You'll need to pass through if you are headed to Ecuador, and the nearby eco-reserves are worth a visit (though many people are choosing to visit them on a day tour from Máncora).

There are some very interesting, kitsch mosaic structures, a river walk and a sweet Jesus statue that may just spark your imagination with their garishness.

A flashpoint for conflict during the 1940–41 border war between Ecuador and Peru, Tumbes remains a garrison town with a strong military presence.

◉ Sights

Museo de Cabeza de Vaca MUSEUM
(Caserio Cabeza de Vaca, Corrales; admission S4; ⊙8:30am-4pm Mon-Sat) About 6km south of Tumbes, off the Pan-American Hwy, is an archaeological site that was the home of the Tumpis people and, later, the site of the Inca fort visited by Pizarro. Excavations have unearthed the adobe and stone walls of the Huaca del Sol and the story of the site is told in this tiny site museum, which also displays some 1500-year-old ceramic vessels, including Chimú and Inca ones.

To get here take a *colectivo* from Parque Indecopi in Tumbes to Corrales, from where you can pick up a *mototaxi* to the museum just south of town.

☞ Tours

Preference Tours TOURS
(📞072-52-5518; turismomundial@hotmail.com; Grau 427; ⊙9am-7pm Mon-Fri, to 3pm Sat) This friendly shop runs some of the most economical tours in town. Puerto Pizarro tours cost S60 per person, Santuario Nacional Los Manglares de Tumbes tours are S90 per person and Cerros de Amotape costs S95 a head. All rates are for two visitors and fall with larger groups.

Mayte Tours HIKING
(📞072-52-3219; www.maytetours.com; Bolognesi 196, Plaza de Armas; ⊙8am-8pm) An enthusiastic local operator that offers a full range of tours with a nature and adventure focus, including a tour to the Santuario Los Manglares de Tumbes that includes the chance to harvest fresh shellfish and make ceviche right on the spot, and a multiday trip to Parque Nacional Cerros de Amotape (p367), spending the night in tents.

🛏️ Sleeping

Be sure your room has a working fan if you're here in the sweltering summer (December to March). During the wet season and the twice-yearly rice harvests, mosquitoes can be a big problem, and there are frequent water and electricity outages. At the lower end of the budget range, watch your valuables carefully.

Hotel Roma HOTEL $
(📞072-52-4137; hotelromatumbes@hotmail.com; Bolognesi 425, Plaza de Armas; s/d/t S45/70/95; 🛜) In a great location, the Roma is an upper-level budget option and provides guests with clean, comfortable rooms with hot shower, high-octane fans, phone and cable TV. Accustomed to dealing with foreigners, it extends a warm welcome, but can be noisy.

Hospedaje Lourdes GUESTHOUSE $
(📞072-52-2966; Mayor Bodero 118; s/d S40/60, with air-con S70/90; ❄️🛜) Clean, safe and friendly, the Lourdes offers austere (for Tumbes) rooms with fans, phones, TV and hot showers.

★Casa César BOUTIQUE HOTEL $$
(📞072-52-2883; www.casacesartumbes.com; Huáscar 311; s/d incl breakfast from S130/170; ❄️🛜) These former budget digs got the kind of makeover normally reserved for *Queer Eye for the Straight Guy*. It's now a full-on midrange boutique hotel that is professional, friendly and easy on the eyes. Sleek, high-design furniture colors up the minimalist white aesthetic at play here.

The 20 rooms are named after local fauna and are split between less sleek standards and colorful and bright executives. For Tumbes it's a step up and the price is right.

Hotel Rizzo Plaza HOTEL $$
(📞072-52-3991; www.rizzoplazahotel.com; Bolognesi 216; s/d incl breakfast S126/148; ❄️@🛜)

Just steps from the Plaza de Armas, the ritzy Rizzo gets solid reviews from travelers. With a business center, it leans vaguely suit-and-tie-like, with professional staff, neat, freshly painted rooms with smallish bathrooms and way too many faux plants.

Hotel Costa del Sol BUSINESS HOTEL **$$**
(☑ 072-52-3991; www.costadelsolperu.com; San Martín 275; r incl breakfast from S210; ✱ @ 🛜 🛋) The most upscale hotel in town, providing a decent restaurant, a pleasant bar and garden, and a Jacuzzi, swimming pool with a children's section, small casino and gym. The comfortable rooms could be way better – and don't compare to the other offerings by the chain – but it's about as good as you get.

It offers free airport transfers.

 ## Eating

There are several bars and restaurants on Plaza de Armas, many with shaded tables and chairs outside – a real boon in hot weather. It's a pleasant place to sit and watch the world go by as you drink a cold beer and wait for your bus.

Many restaurants in the center close early.

Moka CAFE **$**
(Bolognesi 252; snacks S6-12; ⊙ 8am-1pm & 4:30-11pm) This modern cafe is so wildly out of place in Tumbes that it turns heads. You'll find loads of scrumptious cakes, flavored frappuccinos, juices, milkshakes and not-quite-right espresso (but from a proper machine, nonetheless). The good menu of *croissantwiches* makes for a lovely quick bite or breakfast (try chicken salad with avocado).

Cappucino Panes & Mas PERUVIAN **$$**
(☑ 072-63-3214; www.capuccinotumbes.com; Feijoo 111; mains S18-30, menú S25; ⊙ 8am-9pm) At first glance this flash corner place near the Plaza Bolognesi looks like just a posh bakery, but up on the mezzanine it serves some of the best gourmet meals in town. Go for the outrageously filling set meal served with a great fresh-squeezed juice. It's paradise for weary border-crossing foodies accustomed to bus-station offerings.

Also prepares pizzas and great breakfasts.

Las Terrazas PERUVIAN **$$**
(☑ 072-52-1575; Araujo 549; mains S30-40) A little bit out of the town center, this popular place is well worth the S2 *mototaxi* ride. Packed with hungry diners daily, it serves up heaping plates of seafood, and will ceviche

or cook anything from fish to lobster and octopus. It's all prepared in the northern-coastal style and it has music upstairs Friday through Monday from 3pm.

Sí Señor PERUVIAN **$$**
(Bolívar 115; mains S18-41; ⊙ 8am-7pm; ✱) On a quiet corner of the plaza, with pleasant streetside tables outside and quixotic, slow-turning fans inside, Sí Señor is the long-standing staple doing all manner of everything, with a heavy emphasis on fish and seafood. The dizzying menu of Peruvian faves and seafood dishes will leave you giddy.

There's a good *menú* for S9 that offers great flavors at a discount.

❶ Information

IMMIGRATION

Ecuadorian Consulate (☑ 072-52-5949; Bolívar 129, 3rd fl, Plaza de Armas)

Oficina de Migraciónes (☑ 072-52-3422; www.migraciones.gob.pe; Panamericana Km 1275.5; ⊙ 8am-4:30pm Mon-Fri, to noon Sat) Along the Pan-American Hwy, 2km north of town. Handles visa issues.

MEDICAL SERVICES

Clinica Feijoo (☑ 072-52-5341; Castilla 305) One of the better medical clinics in Tumbes.

MONEY

Banco BBVA (Bolívar 129) Bank and ATM.
BCP (Bolívar 261) Changes traveler's checks and has an ATM.

POST

Serpost (San Martín 208; ⊙ 9am-7pm Mon-Fri, to 1pm Sat) Postal service on the block south of Plaza Bolognesi.

SAFE TRAVEL

The border crossing has a bad reputation, but relatively new infrastructure and immigration offices have improved the situation somewhat.

Tumbes is not the safest city – don't walk around with your phone in your hand, and ask hotels and restaurants to organize a taxi rather than hailing one on the road.

TOURIST INFORMATION

iPerú (☑ 016-16-7300 ext 3049; www.peru.travel; Bolognesi 194, Centro Civico; ⊙ 9am-6pm Mon-Sat, to 1pm Sun) Provides useful tourist information. It's on the main plaza.

Sernanp (☑ 072-52-6489; www.sernanp.gob.pe; Panamericana Norte 1739; ⊙ 8:30am-12:30pm & 3:30-5:30pm Mon-Fri) Arranges permits and provides information on visits to regional nature reserves.

PARQUE NACIONAL CERROS DE AMOTAPE

The tropical dry forest ecosystem of **Parque Nacional Cerros de Amotape** is protected by this 1515-sq-km national park, which makes up the lion's share of the Reserva de Biosfera de Noroeste. It's home to flora and fauna that includes jaguars, condors and anteaters, though parrots, deer and peccaries are more commonly sighted. Large-scale logging, illegal hunting and overgrazing are some of the threats facing this rare habitat. Independent visitors must get advance permission from the Sernanp office in Tumbes and contract a guide.

The best place to spot a wide range of wild animals is the Zona Reservada de Tumbes, now encompassed within Amotape itself. The forest is similar to the tropical dry forest of other parts of Amotape, but because it lies more on the easterly side of the hills, it is wetter and has slightly different flora and fauna, including crocodiles, howler monkeys and nutria. You can also see various orchids and a wide variety of birds.

Local guides skilled in spotting wildlife can be arranged in the town of Rica Playa, a small, friendly village located just within the park. You can camp here and local families will sell you meals.

Agencies in Tumbes also organize tours from S95 per person (minimum two), including transportation, permits and a guide.

❶ Getting There & Away

AIR

The airport (TBP) is 8km north of town. **LATAM** (☑ 072-52-4481; www.latam.com; Centro Commercial Costa Mar; ◷ 10am-10pm Mon-Fri, 11am-8pm Sat & Sun) has up to two daily flights from Lima to Tumbes.

BUS

You can usually find a bus to Lima within 24 hours of your arrival in Tumbes, but they're sometimes (especially major holidays) sold out a few days in advance. You can take a bus south to another major city and try again from there. Most bus companies have offices along Av Tumbes in the center of town.

Some companies offer a limited-stop service, with air-con, bathrooms and very loud video; and some have deluxe, nonstop *bus-cama* services.

Slower services stop at Piura, Chiclayo and Trujillo. If you are heading to Máncora or Piura, much faster *colectivo* minivans are the best way to go.

If you're going to Ecuador, it's easiest to go with Cifa, an Ecuadorean company, or Ormeño. The high-end Peruvian companies have more comfortable buses, but inconvenient schedules. Furthermore their buses come from Lima and sometimes pass in the middle of the night and if there is traffic along the way, travelers often sit around in Tumbes waiting for the bus. All stop at the border for you to complete passport formalities.

From around the market area, *colectivos* for Puerto Pizarro leave from Huascar, half a block south of Feijoo; for Zorritos *combis* depart from Castilla, near Ugarte; for Rica Playa *combis* depart from Ugarte, near Castilla; for Corrales

colectivos leave from the Parque Indecopi. Ask locals as most of the stops aren't marked.

For Máncora air-conditioned minivan services congregate around the corner of Tumbes and Piura. On the southwest corner of the same intersection, slower, cheaper *combis* also depart regularly.

Cifa (☑ 972-894-619; www.cifainternacional. com; Tumbes 572) Heads to Machala and Guayaquil in Ecuador seven times daily, about every two hours from 8am to 2:30am.

Civa (☑ 072-52-5120; www.civa.com.pe; Tumbes 518) Cheaper Lima services at 1:30pm and 3pm, midlevel service at 3:30pm and a *bus-cama* at 4pm. A comfortable Guayaquil bus departs at 12:30am.

Cruz del Sur (☑ 072-52-6200; www.cruzdel sur.com.pe; Tumbes 319) *Bus-cama* to Lima at 3pm and 4pm and Guayaquil on Monday, Tuesday, Thursday and Saturday at 1pm.

El Sol (☑ 072-50-8619; Tacna 343) Economy buses to Chiclayo at 7:30pm and 8pm and to Trujillo at 7:30pm, 8pm and 8:30pm.

Oltursa (☑ 017-08-5000; www.oltursa.pe; Tumbes 948) *Bus-cama* service to Lima at 2:30pm, 3pm and 3:30pm. Also heads to Trujillo and Chiclayo daily at 7:30pm.

Sertur (☑ 016-58-0071; www.serturperu.com; Tumbes 502) Fast minivans to Máncora and Piura every hour or so between 5:30am and 8:30pm.

Tepsa (☑ 072-52-2428; www.tepsa.com.pe; Tumbes 781) To Lima at 4pm.

Transportes Chiclayo (☑ 074-50-3548; www. transporteschiclayo.com; Tumbes 570) Daily buses to Chiclayo via Máncora at 10am, 2:30pm and 9pm.

Transportes El Dorado (☎ 072-63-5701; www.transporteseldorado.com.pe; Tacna 351) Eleven daily buses to Piura and departures to Chiclayo at 7:30pm and 9:30pm and Trujillo at 7:30pm, 8pm, 8:30pm and 9pm with economical buses.

Tumbe Buses

DESTINATION	COST (S)	DURATION
Chiclayo	30-90	9hr
Guayaquil (Ecuador)	33-131	6hr
Lima	100-200	16-18hr
Machala (Ecuador)	15-20	3hr
Máncora	12-60	1½-2hr
Piura	35-95	4-5hr
Puerto Pizarro	2.50	15min
Rica Playa	5	1½hr
Trujillo	40-95	11hr
Zorritos	2.50-5	45min

ⓘ Getting Around

Take precautions when hailing *mototaxis* on the street in Tumbes – always look for a driver wearing a vest identifying one of the different stands around the city. If in doubt ask a local business to call one. Taxis with painted logos and lights on top are generally safer.

There is no public transport to the airport; a taxi to the terminal is about S25.

Puerto Pizarro

☎ 072

North of Tumbes the character of the ocean-front changes from the coastal desert, which stretches more than 3000km north from central Chile to northern Peru, to the mangrove swamps that dominate much of the Ecuadorean and Colombian coastlines. There's an explosion of birdlife here, with up to 200 different migrating species visiting these areas.

The most convenient place from which to explore the mangroves is the tranquil little town of Puerto Pizarro, which has a pleasant waterfront area with a plaza and a dock lined with tour boats, and is a welcome change from nearby, bustling Tumbes.

◉ Sights

Santuario Nacional los Manglares de Tumbes WILDLIFE RESERVE
(Puerto 25, Zarumilla; Peruvian/foreign visitors S11/30) This national sanctuary was established in 1988 and lies on the coast, separate from the other three dry-forest areas. Only

about 30 sq km in size, it plays an essential role in conserving Peru's only region of mangroves. The sanctuary and the surrounding area is one of the few *zona-rojas* (red zones) left in Peru and it's imperative to check the security situation before heading out. It's best to visit at low tide, when the animals come out to feed.

Agencies in Tumbes also arrange tours for S90 per person (minimum two), including transport. If you want to go it alone, the best way to arrange a visit is through the iPeru office in nearby Aguas Verdes, which can arrange *mototaxis* and a local guide to meet you at the gate.

Guided mangrove tours are available from Puerto Pizarro as well, though the mangroves here are not technically within the protection of the sanctuary and are not as dense.

🏃 Activities

Boats can be hired to tour the mangroves – one tour goes to a crocodile sanctuary where you can see Peru's only crocodiles being nursed back from near extinction. The nearby Isla de Aves can be visited (but not landed on) to see the many nesting seabirds, especially between 5pm and 6pm, when huge flocks of birds return to roost for the night. Boats for rent line the waterfront of Puerto Pizarro; you can do a tour of the mangroves and the other sites for S70 to S80 per boat for up to six people. You pay a boarding fee of S1 to access the Puerto Pizarro dock.

Two good options are Turmi (Grau s/n), the boat operators' association, which is your best bet for small groups and independent travelers; and Manglaris Tours (☎ 972-634-241; Grau s/n), which has bigger boats and prices as cheap as S10 per person for the standard tour. Both hang out along the walkway to the pier. Tour companies in Tumbes also provide guided tours to the area.

If you don't want to go on a tour, a quick and easy independent trip is a visit to Isla Hueso de Ballena just offshore, which has a few lunch restaurants and inflatables in the water to keep younger travelers amused.

🍴 Eating

Restaurante Hueso de Ballena PERUVIAN **$$**
(mains S25-28; ⊙9am-6pm) On Isla Hueso de Ballena, Restaurante Hueso de Ballena is pretty ideal, right on the sand with a few hammocks and aquatic inflatables to keep young travelers amused. It promises an 'orgy

ℹ BORDER CROSSING: ECUADOR VIA TUMBES

Shady practices at the original Aguas Verdes border crossing between Ecuador and Peru earned it the dubious title of 'the worst border crossing in South America.' However, a revamped border with integrated one-stop offices and increased police presence a few kilometers away in Pocitos has made the crossing safer and easier, but keep on your toes.

Border Crossing

There are two integrated border facilities 3km apart on either side of the border at Pocitos/Huaquillas called Centro Binacional de Atención de Frontera, or CEBAF. When leaving Peru you do not need to stop at the Peruvian facility, but rather go direct to the **CEBAF Ecuador office** (Centro Binacional de Atención de Frontera; ⊙24hr) across the river, where guest Peruvian officials will give an exit stamp, then step a few meters over to have your passport stamped for Ecuador.

In theory coming into Peru the process should work in reverse, with immigration formalities taking place at the **CEBAF Peru office** (☎ 072-63-2537; Panamerica Norte Km 1293, Eje Vial No 1, Pocitos; ⊙24hr) on the Peruvian side of the border and no need to stop at the Ecuadorean office. At the time of research, however, a spat over the quality of internet in the Peruvian facility has seen the Ecuadorean officials pack up and head back to their own building so it's necessary to stamp out there before heading to the Peruvian side for entry procedures.

There are no fees to enter or exit Peru, but if you bring your own vehicle you will be required to purchase obligatory insurance.

Very few nationalities need a visa, but exit tickets out of Ecuador and sufficient funds (US$20 per day) are legally required, although rarely asked for. Tourists are allowed only 90 days per year in Ecuador without officially extending their stay at a consulate – if you have stayed longer, you may be fined quite heavily when you leave.

You are strongly advised to take a direct bus across the border with a long-distance bus company such as Cruz del Sur (p367), Civa (p367) or Cifa (p367). The slightly cheaper option is to take a *colectivo* or local bus to the border and switch busses after passing immigration; it'll save you a few bucks, but can cost you dearly (see Scams, below) and is a real hassle.

Aguas Verdes is basically a long, dusty street full of vendors that continues into the similar, but sightly more developed, Ecuadorean border town of Huaquillas via the international bridge across the Río Zarumilla. If you are forced to stay the night at the border, there are a few basic hotels in Aguas Verdes, but they're all noisy and pretty sketchy. There are some nicer options in Huaquillas, which is also better security wise, but really you're better off hanging back in Tumbes for the night or making the two-hour bus trip to the city of Machala, where there are much better facilities, or better still continuing on to Guayaquil.

Scams

By taking a direct bus, and simply getting off and on the bus at just one stop, you can avoid many scams. One common scam run in the past happens if you take local transit to the border, where you may be hoodwinked into switching buses, where you'll be eventually convinced that you need to contribute to bribe the border police.

You're also likely to encounter plenty of touts and money changers passing false bills. Don't change your money here.

See Lonely Planet's *Ecuador & the Galápagos Islands* for more information about the other side of the border.

of shellfish' and is a good place to try the local specialty, *conchas negras* (black shells) as well as ceviche, seafood rices, *chicharrónes* and soups, with ingredients plucked fresh from the water.

Boats will take you out from Puerto Pizarro and back for S25.

ℹ Getting There & Away

If you just want to eat, boats will take you out to the restaurants for S25 to S30 each way. There are regular *colectivos* between Puerto Pizarro and Tumbes (S2.50, 15 minutes).

AT A GLANCE

POPULATION
Huaraz: 127,000

TALLEST MOUNTAIN
Huascarán: 6766m

BEST MOUNTAIN TOWN
Chacas (p408)

BEST PIZZA
Mi Comedia (p381)

BEST CRAFT BEER
Los 13 Buhos (p382)

WHEN TO GO

May–Sep
Cordillera's dry season offers the best trekking conditions.

Oct–Dec
A relaxed post-season atmosphere in Huaraz; more quality guides available.

Dec–Apr
Wet and rainy, but appropriately geared trekkers enjoy the silence.

Cordillera Huayhuash (p393)
GALYNA ANDRUSHKO/SHUTTERSTOCK ©

Huaraz & the Cordilleras

G round zero for outdoor-adventure worship in Peru, the Cordilleras are one of the preeminent hiking, trekking and backpacking spots in South America. Wherever you throw your gaze, perennially frozen white peaks razor their way through expansive mantles of lime-green valleys. In the recesses of these prodigious giants huddle scores of pristine jade lakes, ice caves and torrid springs. Huaraz is the urban decompression chamber through which practically all hikers, trekkers and mountaineers pass and swap stories. Plans of daring ice climbs, mountain-biking exploits and rock-climbing expeditions are hatched over ice-cold beers in fireplace-warmed hostels and bars. Lurking quietly on the sidelines, and worth a day of quiet contemplation, are the enigmatic 3000-year-old ruins of Chavín de Huántar.

HUARAZ

☎ 043 / POP 127,000 / ELEV 3091M

Huaraz is the restless capital of this Andean adventure kingdom and its rooftops command exhaustive panoramas of the city's dominion: one of the most impressive mountain ranges in the world. Nearly wiped out by the earthquake of 1970, Huaraz isn't going to win any Andean-village beauty contests anytime soon, but it does have personality – and personality goes a long way.

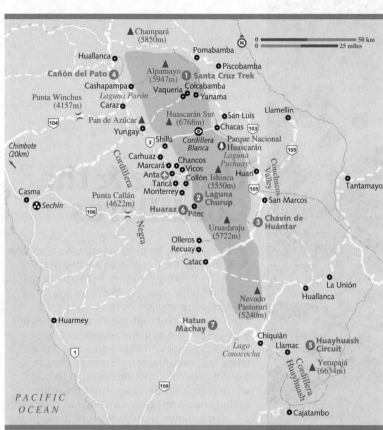

Huaraz & the Cordilleras Highlights

1 Santa Cruz Trek (p387) Getting high with a little help from your friends at 4760m on one of the Andes' classic treks, up Punta Union.

2 Laguna Churup (p384) Climbing out of Huaraz on this gritty acclimatization hike to an icy cirque adorned with an azure mountain lake.

3 Chavín de Huántar (p405) Going way way back in time in the subterranean galleries of one of Peru's oldest ruins.

4 Cañón del Pato (p400) Hiring a bike and shooting downhill through 35 tunnels in a steep-sided canyon.

5 Huayhuash Circuit (p393) Disappearing for two weeks with only mules and mountains for company in this densely packed Andean wilderness.

6 Huaraz' bars (p381) Bragging about your trekking prowess over a well-earned craft beer in the Cordillera's nightlife nexus.

7 Hatun Machay (p397) Scrambling up boulders or climbing sheer rock faces in this veritable rock forest.

This is first and foremost a trekking metropolis. During high season the streets buzz with hundreds of backpackers and adventurers freshly returned from arduous hikes or planning their next expedition as they huddle in one of the town's many fine watering holes. Dozens of outfits help plan trips, rent equipment and organize a list of adventure sports as long as your arm. An endless lineup of quality restaurants and hopping bars keep the belly full and the place lively till long after the tents have been put away. Mountain adventures in the off-season can be equally rewarding, but the vibe is more subdued and some places go into hibernation once the rains set in.

○ Sights

⊙ In Town

Museo Regional de Ancash   MUSEUM
(Plaza de Armas; adult/child S5/1; ⊘8:30am-5:15pm Tue-Sat, 9am-2pm Sun) The Museo Regional de Ancash houses one of the most significant collections of ancient stone sculptures in South America lined up in a garden out back. Most of them are from the Recuay culture (400 BC–AD 600) and the Wari culture (AD 600–1100). Otherwise the collection is limited to a few mummies and some trepanned skulls.

Jirón José Olaya   ARCHITECTURE
On the east side of town, Jirón José Olaya is the only street that remained intact through the earthquakes and provides a glimpse of what old Huaraz looked like; go on Sunday when a street market sells regional foods.

⊙ Outside Town

Monumento Nacional Wilkahuaín   RUINS
(adult/student S5/2; ⊘9am-5pm Tue-Sun) This small Wari ruin about 8km north of Huaraz is remarkably well preserved, dating from about AD 600 to 900. It's an imitation of the temple at Chavín done in the Tiwanaku style (square temples on raised platforms). Wilkahuaín means 'grandson's house' in Quechua. The three-story temple has seven rooms on each floor, each originally filled with bundles of mummies. The bodies were kept dry using a sophisticated system of ventilation ducts. A one-room museum gives some basic background information in English and Spanish.

To get here by foot take a taxi to 'El Pinar' (S7) from where there are two paths leading to the ruins – a direct route via the main road (6km) or a longer but more scenic route via Marian. Alternatively, a taxi direct to the ruins will set you back around S25.

There are actually two sets of ruins. Buy your ticket at the lower complex. It's a 10-minute walk along a dirt road to the smaller second complex (Wilkahuaín Pequeno).

Avoid taking the path from the ruins down to the baths at Monterrey as robberies have been reported on this stretch.

Mirador de Retaqeñua   VIEWPOINT
Mirador de Retaqeñua is about a 45-minute walk southeast of the center and has great views of the city and its mountainous backdrop. Unfortunately, robberies in the area in recent years have made walking here less enticing. Check information on the ground before setting out. If in doubt, take a taxi (S15).

Activities

Mountain Biking

Mountain Bike Adventures (✆972-616-008; www.chakinaniperu.com; Lúcar y Torre 530, 2nd fl; 2-day tours from US$380; ⊘9am-1pm & 3-8pm) has been in business for well over a decade and receives repeat visits from mountain bikers for its decent selection of bikes, knowledgeable and friendly service, and good safety record. It offers guided tours, ranging from an easy five-hour cruise to 12-day circuits around the Cordillera Blanca.

Involved owner, Julio, is a lifelong resident of Huaraz who speaks English and will tailor-make a trip for your specific requirements. No one knows the region's single-track possibilities better than he does.

Trekking & Mountaineering

All activity within Parque Nacional Huascarán – whether mountaineering or hiking – technically requires that you are accompanied by a certified guide, although in practice this is not enforced at most park entrances. Even so, it is well worth taking a guide even for nontechnical activities as conditions change rapidly in the mountains and altitude sickness can seriously debilitate even experienced hikers. Furthermore, a good guide will ensure you see things you otherwise may have missed.

All guides must be licensed by the Peruvian authorities and registered with the national-parks office. Mountaineers and

Huaraz

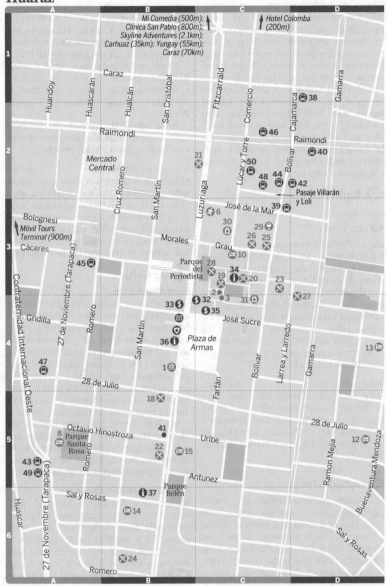

trekkers should check out **Casa de Guías** (☎043-42-1811; www.agmp.pe; Parque Ginebra 28G; ⊙9am-1pm & 4-8pm Mon-Fri, 8am-noon Sat), the headquarters of the Mountain Guide Association of Peru. It maintains a list of its internationally certified guides, all of whom are graduates of a rigorous training program. Bear in mind that international certification is not necessary to work in the park and there are also some excellent independent guides from other associations certified to work in the region.

Many agencies arrange full trekking and climbing expeditions that include guides,

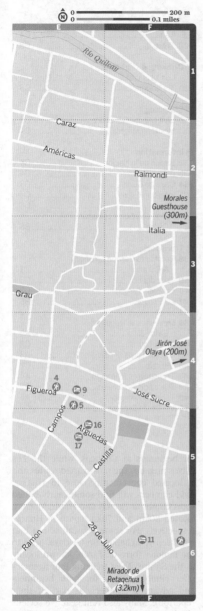

often get what you pay for. Do your research; things change, good places go bad and bad places get good.

One of the best resources for guides in Huaraz is other travelers who have just come back from a trek and can recommend (or not recommend) their guides based on recent experience. The South American Explorers Club in Lima is also an excellent source of information and maps.

★ Quechuandes
TREKKING

(☏ 943-386-147; www.quechuandes.com; Santa Gadea 995; ☺ 9am-8pm Mon-Sat, from 11am Sun) A very well organized agency that gets rave reviews for its quality guides and ethical approach to treks. Management will assess your level before sending you out into the mountains or renting gear, to ensure you are up to the task. In addition to offering treks, summit expeditions and mountaineering courses, its staff are experts in rock climbing and bouldering.

Owners Marie and David researched and wrote the Cordillera's definitive climbing guidebook. Prices vary depending on activity, number of people and type of trip. Contact them via their website for a quote.

★ Eco Ice Peru
TREKKING

(www.ecoice-peru.com; Figueroa 1185; 3- to 4-day treks from US$240; ☺ 8am-6pm) Run by a gregarious and passionate young guide, this agency gets top reviews from travelers for its customer service, guides, *arrieros* (mule drives) and food. Treks often end with a dinner at the owner's pad in Huaraz.

Climber Land
TREKKING

(☏ 943-976-886; Parque Ginebra; treks from US$60; ☺ 8am-9pm Mon-Sat, 8am-1pm & 5-9pm Sun) Attentive trekking and tour outfit based in the thick of the action in Parque Ginebra offering climbing backup or full multiday trekking trips, including the Santa Cruz trail, Los Cedro-Alpamayo and the Huayhuash Circuit.

Andean Kingdom
ADVENTURE

(☏ 944-913-011; www.andeankingdomhuaraz. com; Parque Ginebra; climbing trips from S120; ☺ 9am-9pm Mon-Sat) A laid-back but enthusiastic agency offering day courses for aspiring climbers, logistical support for experts and the usual day excursions, with an obvious bias toward climbing trips (Los Olivos and Hatun Machay feature highly).

equipment, food, cooks, porters and transportion. Depending on the number of people, the length of your trip and what's included, expect to pay from under S100 for an easy day out to up to S750 for more technical mountains per person per day. Try not to base your selection solely on price, as you

Huaraz

Skyline Adventures   MOUNTAINEERING
(☏ 043-42-7097; www.skyline-adventures.com;
Pasaje Industrial 137) Based just outside
Huaraz, this high-end operator comes
highly recommended and provides guides
for treks and mountain climbs. Leads six-
and 12-day mountaineering courses (from
US$1000).

Huascarán   TREKKING
(☏ 043-42-2523; www.huascaran-peru.com; Cam-
pos 711; treks from US$40; ◷ 7:30am-8pm) A
well-established operator offering the full
gamut of excursions.

Rock Climbing

Rock climbing is one of the Cordillera
Blanca's biggest pastimes and its popularity is growing. Huaraz is an ideal place
to plan excursions, rent gear and set off
from on day trips. There are good climbs
for beginners at Chancos, while the Los
Olivos area has the most varied routes and
is located conveniently close to Huaraz.
Avid climbers will find some gnarly bolted
sport climbs at Recuay and Hatun Machay,
located 30km and 70km south of Huaraz
respectively. For some big-wall action that
will keep you chalked up for days, head to
the famous Torre de Parón, known locally
as the Sphinx. Most trekking tour agencies
offer climbing trips, for both beginners
and advanced climbers, as part of their
repertoire. Many also rent gear. No serious
climber should leave base camp without
a copy of *Huaraz: The Climbing Guide*
(2014) by David Lazo and Marie Timmermans, with detailed descriptions of over
1000 climbing routes backed up with photos and color-coded maps.

Tours

Dozens of agencies along Luzuriaga can organize outings to local sites, including several day excursions. Most of the trips are run by the transportation companies so regardless of who you book through, you'll probably end up on the same bus.

One popular tour visits the ruins at Chavín de Huántar; another passes through Yungay to the beautiful Lagunas Llanganuco, where there are superb vistas of Huascarán and other mountains; a third takes you through Caraz to Laguna Parón, which is surrounded by ravishing glaciated peaks; and a fourth travels to the glacier at Nevado Pastoruri, the most accessible in the Cordillera.

All of these trips cost between S50 and S60 each; prices may vary depending on the number of people going, but typically include transporta (usually in minibuses) and a guide (who often doesn't speak English). Admission fees and lunch are extra. Trips take a full day; bring a packed lunch, warm clothes, drinking water and sunblock. Tours depart daily during the high season, but at other times departures depend on demand. Do not take a day trip to Chavín de Huántar on a Monday – the ruins and museum are closed.

Pablo Tours   SIGHTSEEING TOURS
(043-42-1145; www.pablotours.com; Luzuriaga 501; 9am-8pm) An agency selling the standard Huaraz day tours to places like Chavín de Huántar (S40), Lagunas Llanganuco (S40) and Laguna 69 (S45).

Festivals & Events

Carnaval   RELIGIOUS
(Feb) Carnaval in Huaraz is very busy, with Peruvian tourists flooding to town, many of whom will get soaked on the city's take on Mardi Gras (Fat Tuesday). On Ash Wednesday colorful funeral processions for ño carnavalón (king of carnival) converge on the Plaza de Armas.

Sleeping

Hotel prices can double during holiday periods and rooms become very scarce. Perhaps because Huaraz is seen as a trekking, climbing and backpacking center, budget hotels predominate.

Hostels employ individuals to meet buses, but beware of overpricing – don't pay anybody until you've seen the room.

In Town

El Jacal Backpacker   HOSTAL $
(043-23-2924; www.eljacalhostel.com; 28 de Julio 1066; dm S40, dS130, s/d without bathroom S65/100; P) A kind of cross between a *hostal* (guesthouse) and hostel, the 'Backpacker' is run by the same family as the wonderful El Jacal Classic (p379), meaning you get warm welcomes, ultraclean rooms and simple but very comfortable decor. There are dorm rooms available here, but also some doubles with private bathroom, plus a lovely lounge, modern kitchen and free parking.

As the name suggests, this is a great place to plan trips and meet other backpackers.

Albergue Benkawasi   GUESTHOUSE $
(043-43-3150; www.huarazbenkawasi.com; Parque Santa Rosa 928; dm/s/d S25/50/80;) With Coke-bottle glass windows, plaid bedspreads and cherry-red brick walls, the Benkawasi has a kind of '70s mountain chalet feel to it. It's not the most deluxe abode, but even if the furnishings are old and unfashionable, they're clean. The owner and his English-speaking Peruvian-Lebanese wife are young and fun, and there's a distracting ping-pong table in the lobby.

Dorm rooms are a good deal.

Familia Meza Lodging   GUESTHOUSE $
(943-695-908; Lúcar y Torre 538; r per person S30;) In the same building as Café Andino (p381), this charming family guesthouse has cheery rooms and is decorated throughout with homey touches. What's more, the owners are friendly and helpful enough to cure the worst bout of homesickness. Bathrooms and hot showers are shared and there's a top-floor communal area with a small kitchen.

Aldo's Guest House   GUESTHOUSE $
(043-42-5355; Morales 650; dm/s/d/tr S15/40/50/75;) Aldo's is a friendly if rudimentary hostel, decorated with cheery colors and located right in the (noisy) center of town. Dorms are a good deal and there are private rooms too, although the communal facilities (kitchen, bathrooms) can get a little overwhelmed at times. Notwithstanding, this is a good place to meet other travelers and exchange trekking tales.

Albergue Churup   HOSTEL $$
(043-42-4200; www.churup.com; Figueroa 1257; dm S45, s/d incl breakfast S120/185;) This

CHOOSING A TREK OPERATOR

Before you lay out your cold, hard cash for a guided trek make sure you know what you're getting. Ask the company or guide to list the services, products and price they're offering on your contract. In the event that they don't live up to their promises you may or may not be able to do anything about it, but a list ensures that the company understands exactly what you expect.

On your end, it is critical that you are crystal clear with your guides about your experience and fitness level. Also important is that you are properly acclimatized before setting out on a trek. All too often, parties set out for big treks and climbs just after arriving in Huaraz, with the predictable result of altitude sickness and having to turn back. Take the time to adjust in Huaraz, do a couple of acclimatization hikes, and *then* enjoy a trouble-free, multiday trek.

It is standard to provide food and shelter for the guides, cooks and *arrieros* (mule drivers), which should be discussed beforehand. Remember that prepackaged dehydrated meals are not staples in the Cordillera Blanca. You will almost certainly be eating non-shrink-wrapped local foods that weigh more and require more effort to carry.

Below are some suggested questions to ask before choosing your guide; keep in mind that the answers will make a difference in the price.

➡ Can I meet our guide ahead of time? This is an opportunity to meet the person you'll spend multiple days and nights with, and if necessary, to confirm ahead of time that he/she speaks English.

➡ Will we use public or private transportation?

➡ Will there be a cook and an *arriero*?

➡ Will there be a separate cooking tent and a separate bathroom tent?

➡ How many meals and snacks will we get every day? Many trekkers complain about inadequate breakfasts and too few energizing repasts.

➡ How many people will be on our trek? Larger numbers mean lower prices, but make sure you're comfortable trekking with a dozen strangers.

➡ Can I check the equipment before we set off? If you don't have your own sleeping bag, make sure that the one provided is long enough and warm enough (good to -15°C), and inspect the tents for holes and rain resistance.

immensely popular family-run hostel has spick-and-span rooms with sharp color accents and plenty of bright space, plus invitingly comfortable lounging areas on *every* floor. The building is topped by a massive, fireplace-warmed lounge space with magnificent 180-degree views of the Cordillera.

If that isn't enough, the affable Quirós family are consummate hosts and offer a communal kitchen and a travel office that rents out trekking gear. If you're coming back down to earth after a high-altitude trekking trip, this is where you'll want to land.

Morales Guesthouse   HOTEL **$$**
(☏ 043-42-5105; www.moralesguesthouse.com; Pasaje Ucanan 232; s/d incl breakfast S115/150; ☎) Accessed via a green gate at the end of Jirón José Olaya, the Morales has been so successful that it recently commissioned a large but architecturally thoughtful extension. Its large rooms jump out at you with pinewood furnishings and an orange-yellow color scheme and there's a terrace where you can contemplate your cooked-to-order breakfast eggs over a dozen Andean peaks.

The Morales' trump card is its amiable and knowledgeable staff who are happy to provide little extras like free bus station pick-up, same-day laundry service and help with tours and flights.

La Aurora   HOTEL **$$**
(☏ 043-42-6824; www.hotelaurorahuaraz.com; Luzuriaga 915; s/d/tr incl breakfast from S120/220/310; ☎) A midrange traveler's favorite, the Aurora makes a pleasant bookend to a trekking trip where you can wash the dust from your hair (with hot water) and sink deservedly into a soft, comfortable bed. Bright upgraded rooms feature wooden floors, luxurious bathrooms with marble

sinks, and flourishes of local flavor such as straw lampshades and woven bedspreads.

Breakfast is served on the fantastic terrace with views of Huascarán and Churup. Outstanding value.

El Jacal Classic
HOTEL $$

(☑ 043-42-4612; www.eljacalhostel.com; José Sucre 1044; s/d incl breakfast S80/105; 🛜) Family-run, friendly and a favorite with travelers on a budget who consider themselves too old (or uncool) for hosteling, El Jacal is a great decompression chamber if you've just arrived from Lima and need a few days to get acclimatized both physically and mentally to Huaraz' rhythms. Rooms are simple but comfortable and made up meticulously every day.

Generous breakfasts on the covered roof terrace with the tallest mountain in Peru for company are an additional tonic.

Olaza's Bed & Breakfast
GUESTHOUSE $$

(☑ 043-42-2529; www.olazas.com; Arguedas 1242; s/d/tr incl breakfast S90/120/160; 🅿) This smart little hotel with a distinctly orange decor has spacious bathrooms and comfortable beds, but the best part is the big lounge area and massive panoramic terrace where you get a ginormous breakfast. Owner Julio is Huaraz' most experienced cycling guide and can provide advice no matter where you want to go (if he's around). Bus-station pickup is included.

La Casa de Zarela
GUESTHOUSE $$

(☑ 043-42-1694; www.lacasadezarelahuaraz.com; Arguedas 1263; dm/s/d/tr S40/80/120/150; 🛜) The helpfulness of Zarela, the owner, is legendary and the 18 rooms here are neat and comfortable, but the best thing about this quality guesthouse is the abundance of patios, terraces and common areas that mean even when full it never feels crowded. There is a bright kitchen on the top floor for guests. No TVs.

Hotel El Tumi
HOTEL $$

(☑ 043-42-1784; www.hoteleseltumi.com.pe; San Martín 1121; s/d incl breakfast S130/230; 🛜) Tumi is one of those mid-range big city hotels that lures you in with a plush lobby and then plants you in slightly darker, less inspiring rooms. The overall picture, however, isn't bad, with a fancy spa, a bright lounge space on the 4th floor and a modern restaurant that sometimes offers sushi. Aimed more at business travelers than backpackers.

Hotel Colomba
HOTEL $$$

(☑ 043-42-1501; www.huarazhotel.com; Francisco de Zela 210; s/d/tr/q incl breakfast S225/312/475/560; 🅿🅰🛜) Hidden behind a high wall in a scruffy part of town, the Colomba is Huaraz' surprise package, a green oasis replete with compulsively trimmed hedges, neatly mowed lawns and a long colonnaded veranda. Rooms are comfy, if a little old-fashioned, secure parking is included and the sprawling gardens conceal a kids' playground with a climbing wall.

Andino Club Hotel
HOTEL $$$

(☑ 043-42-1662; www.hotelandino.com; Pedro Cochachín 357; s/d from S430/550; 🅰🛜) The structure itself feels a little bit too much like a chain hotel, so you sacrifice on cozy charm at this 54-room, Swiss-run hotel, but the immaculate rooms all have great views and are packed with the requisite mod cons. Balcony rooms are worth the investment for the wood-burning fireplaces, plant-lined terraces and in-your-face views to Huascarán peak.

The excellent on-site restaurant, Chalet Suisse, serves international and Peruvian food in addition to Swiss specialties.

🛏 Outside Town

★ Cuesta Serena
BOUTIQUE HOTEL $$$

(☑ 981-400-038; www.cuestaserena.pe; via Carhuaz, Anta; r incl 2 meals from S870) Out near the airport, this high-end hotel is a great place to stay to avoid the noise of Huaraz while remaining accessible to transportation and local attractions. The elegant rooms with subtle Peruvian touches are set in lovely manicured gardens, which offer fantastic views of Huascarán and its Cordillera siblings. The balance between luxury and homeliness is perfectly maintained.

Here you get welcome drinks, a glass-surrounded indoor pool, yoga classes, exquisite food and the refined air of a country retreat. Reservations, unsurprisingly, are essential.

The lodge is in Anta near the airport, 21km north of Huaraz.

★ Lazy Dog Inn
LODGE $$$

(☑ 943-789-330; www.thelazydoginn.com; Km 3, Cachipampa Alto; s US$79-139, d US$99-159, all incl breakfast & dinner; 🅰🛜) 🗲 Run by rugged and proud Canadians Diana and Wayne, this deluxe ecolodge steeped in sustainable and community tourism is at the mouth of the Quebrada Llaca, 8km east of Huaraz. It's made entirely of adobe and built by hand. You can either stay in comfortable double rooms in the main lodge or in fancier private cabins, with fireplaces and bathtubs.

Lots of trekking opportunities are available, including numerous day hikes right from the lodge, as well as day trips on horseback. For a post-hiking bonus, there's a sauna and communal lounge with a real fire. Dinners made from ingredients plucked from their own greenhouse are included in the price.

The inn can arrange taxi pick-ups from central Huaraz and/or the airport.

✕ Eating

Restaurant hours are flexible in Huaraz, with shorter opening times during low-season slow spells and longer hours at busy times.

Dining is casual – think hiking boots and fleeces. There is a plethora of international places offering filling pizzas and burgers for exhausted hikers.

 Manka PERUVIAN, ITALIAN $

(☑043-23-4306; Bautista 840; menú S10; ⊙8:30am-11pm) If you were curious about what happens when Peruvian *cocina* (cuisine) collides with Italian *cucina* then, let us tell you, it's a taste worth savoring. For proof, head straight to this simply decorated restaurant whose mix-and-match menu can deliver bruschetta for starters, *lomo saltado* (strips of beef stir-fried with onions, tomatoes, potatoes and chili) for a main and a delectable chocolate mousse for desert.

The food, which includes pasta, pizzas and desserts, is all made from scratch – and there's an excellent-value S10 lunch *menú* as well (also fastidiously homemade).

Mi Comedia Gelatería GELATO $

(☑043-22-1542; San Martín 1213; ice cream S4-8; ⊙noon-9pm) Not satisfied with producing Huaraz' (and maybe Peru's) best pizzas, the guys at Mi Comedia have recently opened what some are already hailing as the city's best spot for ice cream – or, to be more accurate, gelato. Choose from a small but select lineup of interesting flavors that is big on pure fruits.

If you're feeling greedy, you can combine the ice cream with an excellent cake. They also serve the fantastic Mi Comedia pizzas here as well.

Campo Base BREAKFAST $

(☑043-23-3654; Parque Ginebra 120; breakfast S11-16; ⊙7am-10pm; 🛜🍴) Make a temporary camp for breakfast at this diminutive cafe affiliated to the Andean Kingdom climbing shop that does wonderful fruit salads, egg concoctions and coffee. Lunch ain't bad either, with burritos and several vegan options.

Taita PERUVIAN $

(Larrea y Laredo 633, 2nd fl; mains S6-20; ⊙11am-3pm; 🍴) This intimate red-bricked local's haunt is like a museum to the Huaraz that once was. The walls are covered floor-to-ceiling in historical photos of a pre-earthquake, pre-trekking-era city living out its daily life. The food is an equally photo-worthy pastiche of unusual *cordillera* cuisine, including *chocho*, the alpine answer to *ceviche*, with the fish replaced with *lupine* (an Andean legume).

It also does traditional Peruvian ceviche (with fish), *leche de tigre* (ceviche juice) and *chicharrónes* (deep-fried pork rinds) – perfect fodder if you need an away day from the ubiquitous pizzas and burgers of the standard post-trekking restaurants.

California Café BREAKFAST $

(www.huaylas.com; Jiron 28 de Julio 562; breakfast S15-25; ⊙7:30am-6:30pm, to 2pm Sun; 🛜🍴) Managed by a Californian, this hip traveler magnet does breakfasts at any time, plus light lunches and salads. It's a funky, chilled space to while away many hours with a library of ancient guidebooks, well-used sofas, a sublime world-music collection and usually plenty of backpacks spread across the floor.

Check the noticeboard for hiking partner searches and upcoming Ultimate Frisbee games (every Friday).

La Brasa Roja CHICKEN $

(Luzuriaga 915; mains S12-30; ⊙noon-11pm) This upscale *pollería* (restaurant specializing in roast chicken) is the ultimate budget refueling stop. Not only is the chicken perfect, but you get five sauces – count 'em, five! – instead of the usual three (black olive and mustard make a surprise appearance). The other mains are hit and miss but if you're lucky you'll get a live violinist.

It's underneath the wonderful Aurora hotel.

Novaplaza SUPERMARKET $

(cnr Bolivar & Morales; ⊙7am-11:30pm) A good supermarket to pick up supplies for trekking or self-catering.

Mi Comedia   ITALIAN $$

(☎043-58-7954; Centenario 351; mains S22-38; ⏰5-11pm Mon-Sat) Many restaurants claim great pizzas with some even uttering the word 'Naples' blasphemously in the description. But at Mi Comedia the Italian boasts are no exaggeration. This is about as Neapolitan as a pizza can get in Peru without the DOC Campania ingredients.

Situated a 500m walk from the center in a romantically lit upstairs space complete with that all-important pizza oven (where they also cook great lasagna), the restaurant offers friendly service and fine wines to back up its chewy pies. In contrast to Italy, margherita pizzas are more expensive here due to the cost of procuring specialist ingredients.

Trivio   INTERNATIONAL $$

(☎043-22-0416; Parque del Periodista; mains S21-37; ⏰8am-midnight) ◢ Cementing a three-way marriage of craft beer, micro-roasted coffee and food made with local ingredients, Trivio joins a few Huaraz restaurants that wouldn't be alien in Lima. The decor is North America hip, the clientele predominantly gringo, and the food clever enough to excite the taste buds but filling enough to cover the hole left by your recent four-day trek.

Treat it as a bar, coffee shop or casual restaurant. Hiking boots, fleeces and backpacks are de rigueuer.

Chili Heaven   INDIAN, THAI $$

(Parque Ginebra; mains S17-35; ⏰noon-11pm) Whether you send your appetite to India or Thailand, the fiery curries at this hot spot will seize your taste buds upon arrival, mercilessly shake them up and then spit them back out the other side as if you've died and gone to chili heaven (hence the name).

Curries are graded Anglo-style from Madras (mildish) to Phal (which is like culinary fire eating). They also do a good chicken tikka masala.

Musicians often drop by for spontaneous pan-flute performances.

Café Andino   CAFE $$

(www.cafeandino.com; Lúcar y Torre 530, 3rd fl; breakfast S8-24, mains S18-35; ⏰9am-10pm; ☎◢) This modern top-floor cafe has space and light in spades, comfy lounges, art, photos, crackling fireplace, books and groovy tunes – it's the ultimate South American traveler hangout and meeting spot. You can get breakfast anytime (Belgian waffles, huevos rancheros), and snacks you miss (nachos). It's also the best place in town for information about trekking in the area.

American owner Chris is the go-to java junkie in the Cordilleras and roasts his own organic beans here. He was responsible for first bringing excellent brew to town in 1997 – he showed up a year earlier and had to resort to using a rock to smash organic beans he'd brought from Alaska, straining it through a bandanna for his morning jolt. Seriously.

Rinconcito Mineiro   PERUVIAN $$

(Morales 757; menú S8-16, mains S12-35; ⏰7am-11pm; ☎) This popular place is *the* spot to tuck into homey and cheap Peruvian daily *menús* (set meals). The daily blackboard of 10 or so options includes an excellent *lomo saltado*, plus grilled trout, *tacu-tacu* (a Peruvian fusion dish of rice, beans and a protein) and the like.

It's all served in a welcoming and clean space, tastefully decorated with regional crafts.

El Fogón   STEAK $$

(www.elfogon.com.pe; Luzuriaga 928, 2nd fl; mains S11-39; ⏰noon-3pm & 6-11pm) A bright, modern and slightly upscale twist on the traditional Peruvian grill house, this place will grill anything that moves – including the usual chicken, trout and rabbit, plus great *anticuchos* (shish kebabs). It also does a fine lunch *menú* for S10. Vegetarians will go hungry though.

Crêperie Patrick   FRENCH $$

(☎043-42-6037; www.creperiepatrick.com; Luzuriaga 422; mains S24-30; ⏰4-11pm) This French-run place is far more than just a crêperie (although both sweet and savory crepes are good). Decked out like an old-fashioned French bistro, it flaunts an extensive menu including *cuy* (guinea pig), trout, fondue, pasta, burgers, and the ultimate in Franco-Peruvian fusion: alpaca bourguignon.

🍷 Drinking & Nightlife

Huaraz is the best place in this part of the Andes to take a load off and get pleasantly inebriated. Craft beer has made a recent appearance and there are a couple of local microbreweries.

The best area for nightlife is Parque del Periodista and the adjacent Parque Ginebra.

★ **Los 13 Buhos** BAR

(Parque Ginebra; ⊙11am-2am) Halfway up some monstrous Andean pass with a 15kg pack on your back, it's not uncommon to start dreaming of 13 Buhos with its Luchos craft beer, pool table and delectable afternoon 'snacks' (waffles anyone?).

If you needed an incentive to finish your trek, this could be it – the chance to flop down at an alfresco table outside Huaraz' finest craft beer bar with a plate of Thai curry and a *blondie ale* exaggerating (but only slightly) about your rugged adventures in the Cordillera Blanca.

Tio Enrique BAR

(Bolivar 572; ⊙4-11pm) In an energy-sapping mountain town like Huaraz, this cozy Swiss-themed drinking hole with a long bar and communal pine tables is just what the doctor ordered. Popular with hardcore climbers, it serves around three dozen varieties of imported beers from the UK, Belgium and Germany as well as sausages grilled at the door by the charismatic apron-toting owner.

 Shopping

Montaña Magica SPORTS & OUTDOORS

(⊡949-680-107; Parque Ginebra 25; ⊙10am-2pm & 4-8pm Mon-Sat) Forget your kit? Head to Mountain Magic where you can stock up on a full gamut of decent trekking and mountaineering gear from rain jackets to camping stoves.

Last Minute Gift Store GIFTS & SOUVENIRS

(Lucar y Torre 530; ⊙10am-1pm & 4-8pm Mon-Sat) High-quality, attractive T-shirts with appropriately mountainous designs are made by Andean Expressions and sold at the Last Minute Gift Store, which shares digs with Mountain Bike Adventures (p373). It sells good maps too

ⓘ Information

EMERGENCIES

Casa de Guías (p374) runs mountain safety and rescue courses and maintains a list of internationally certified guides. Also mounts rescue operations to assist climbers in emergencies. If you are heading out on a risky ascent, it's worth consulting with these folks first.

Policía de Turismo (⊡043-42-1341; Luzuriaga 724; ⊙24hr) On the west side of the Plaza de Armas. Moderately helpful.

MEDICAL SERVICES

Clínica San Pablo (⊡043-42-8811; Huaylas 172; ⊙24hr) North of town, this is the best medical care in Huaraz. Some doctors speak English.

MONEY

These banks have ATMs and will exchange US dollars and euros.

Banco de la Nación (Luzuriaga 653; ⊙8am-5:30pm Mon-Fri, 9am-1pm Sat)

BCP (Luzuriaga 691; ⊙9am-6pm Mon-Fri, to 1pm Sat)

Interbank (José Sucre 320; ⊙9am-6pm Mon-Fri, to 1pm Sat)

POST

Serpost (Plaza de Armas 702; ⊙8:30am-8pm Mon-Fri, to 5:30pm Sat)

TOURIST INFORMATION

English newspaperthe *Huaraz Telegraph* (www. huaraztelegraph.com) is a good source of information about the region.

iPerú (⊡043-42-8812; iperuhuaraz@ promperu.gob.pe; Pasaje Atusparia, Oficina 1, Plaza de Armas; ⊙9am-6pm Mon-Sat, to 1pm Sun) Has general tourist information but little in the way of trekking info.

Parque Nacional Huascarán Office (⊡043-42-2086; www.sernanp.gob.pe; Sal y Rosas 555; ⊙8:30am-1pm & 2:30-6pm Mon-Fri) Staff have some limited information about visiting the park. You can also pay your park fees here.

ⓘ Getting There & Away

AIR

The Huaraz **airport** (ATA) is actually at Anta, 23km north of town. A taxi will cost about S40.

LC Perú (⊡043-42-4734; www.lcperu.pe; Luzuriaga 904; ⊙9am-7pm Mon-Fri, to 6pm Sat) is currently the only company offering service, with flights to/from Lima (US$120, one hour) on Tuesdays, Thursdays and Saturdays. Flights leave in the morning, but they are often cancelled at short notice.

BUS

Huaraz has no central bus station. Rather buses leave from different company offices, most of which are located in and around Raimondi and Bolívar streets a couple of blocks north of the Plaza de Armas.

Combis (minibuses) for **Carhuaz, Yungay and Caraz** (cnr Cajamarca and Caraz) leave every few minutes during the day from a lot on Cajamarca near Raimondi. These will drop you in any of the towns along the way. **Minibuses** (cnr Calle 27 de Noviembre & Confraternidad Internacional Oeste) head south along the Callejón de Huaylas to Recuay, Catac and other villages.

A plethora of companies have departures for Lima. The top four for comfort and reliability are Cruz del Sur, Oltursa, Linea and Movil Tours. Most depart midmorning or late evening. Some buses begin in Caraz and stop in Huaraz to pick up passengers. During high season it is recommended that you book your seats at least a day in advance.

Buses to Chimbote cross the 4225m-high Punta Callán, which provides spectacular views of the Cordillera Blanca before plummeting down to Casma and pushing north.

Many small companies with well-used, beat-up buses cross the Cordillera Blanca to the towns east of Huaraz.

Cruz del Sur (☑ 043-42-8726; Bolívar 491) Has 11am and 10pm luxury nonstop services to Lima (S35 to S75, eight hours). Arguably, the most comfortable and reliable buses.

Expreso Yungay (☑ 043-42-4377; Raimondi 930) Has departures to Chimbote (S20, five hours, five daily) via Casma.

Línea (☑ 043-42-6666; Bolívar 450) Has excellent buses to Lima (S35 to S80, eight hours, twice daily) and Trujillo (S30 to S55, seven hours, once daily).

Movil Tours (www.moviltours.com.pe; Bolívar 452) Buses to Lima (S35 to S135, eight hours, 10 daily), Chimbote (S40 to S60, five hours, one daily) and Trujillo (S45 to S75, seven hours, two daily). They leave from a **terminal** (☑ 043-42-2555; www.moviltours.com.pe; Confraternidad Internacional Oeste 451) 1.5km northwest of the Plaza de Armas.

Olguita Tours (☑ 043-39-6309, 943-644-051; Mariscal Caceres 338) Runs half-a-dozen daily buses to Chavín de Huántar (S12, 2½ hours) and Huari (S15, 4½ hours).

Oltursa (☑ 043-42-3717; www.oltursa.pe; Raimondi 825) One daily ultra-comfortable Lima-bound bus at5 12:15pm (S60 to S90, eight hours).

Transportes El Rápido (☑ 043-42-2887; Calle 28 de Julio, cuadra 1) Buses leave at 5am and 2pm to Chiquián (S25, three hours) where you can find connections onto Llamac. Also services to Huallanca and La Unión.

Transportes El Veloz (☑ 043-22-1225; Pasaja Villarán y Loli 143) Bus to Pomabamba (S20, seven hours) at 7am and Chacas (S15, three hours) at 10am, 2:30pm and 5pm

Turismo Nazario (☑ 043-77-0311; Tarapaca 1436) Has a 5am bus to Chiquián (S25, three hours) which continues on to Llamac (S30, five hours).

Via Costa Express (☑ 920-659-988; Lucar y Torre 444) Buses to Chimbote (S20, 4½ hours, 11 daily) via Casma. Convenient for onward connections to Trujillo.

ⓘ Getting Around

A taxi ride around central Huaraz costs from S3 to S4, rising a couple of soles to reach the outer neighborhoods.

Walking in the main parts of town is generally safe in the daytime. Use common sense in the evening and think about taking taxis after 10pm. If you've just arrived from sea level, some of the steeper streets will be hard work for a day or two due to the altitude.

THE CORDILLERAS

Peru's Cordillera region consists of three main mountain ranges – the Cordillera Blanca, the Cordillera Negra and the Cordillera Huayhuash – bisected by populated valleys and best accessed through the medium-sized city of Huaraz.

The Cordillera Negra, though an attractive range in its own right, is snowless and often eclipsed by the stunning, snow-covered crown of the Cordillera Blanca.

The Cordillera Blanca, about 20km wide and 180km long, is an elaborate collection of toothed summits, razor-sharp ridges, turquoise-colored lakes and green valleys draped with crawling glaciers. More than 50 peaks of 5700m or higher grace this fairly small area. Huascarán, at 6768m, is Peru's highest mountain and the highest pinnacle in the tropics anywhere in the world.

South of the Cordillera Blanca is the smaller, more remote, but no less spectacular Cordillera Huayhuash. It contains Peru's second-highest mountain, the 6634m Yerupajá, and is a more rugged and less frequently visited range.

Trekking & Mountaineering

When to Go

People hike year-round, but the dry season of mid-May to mid-September is the most popular time to visit, with good weather and the clearest views. It's still advisable to check the latest weather forecasts, however, as random heavy snowfalls, winds and electrical storms are not uncommon during this period. December to April is the wettest time, when it is often overcast and wet in the afternoons and trails become boggy. With the appropriate gear and some preparation, hiking is still possible and some trekkers find this season more rewarding, as many of the most popular trails are empty. For serious

ACCLIMATIZATION HIKES

It is important that trekkers freshly arrived in the Cordilleras spend several days in Huaraz acclimatizing before sallying forth into the mountains. Huaraz is located at an altitude of 3091m – a sharp jump in elevation if you're arriving from sea level – but most Cordillera hikes go much higher, climbing to altitudes between 3500m and 5000m.

Rush into the high country and it's possible you'll end up suffering from dizziness, nausea or worse, putting a premature end to your trekking trip or, at best, turning the whole thing into one long miserable pain-fest. It's a scenario that plays out all too often in these parts, yet it's easily avoided if you follow a few simple steps.

On your first day, take it easy by pursuing some gentle, flat walks around town. On day two, depending on how you feel (everyone is different), you might want to try the **Laguna Wilkacocha** hike, one of the few trails around Huaraz that doesn't climb above 4000m.

On day three, well-trained hikers may feel strong enough to break the 4000m barrier by shinning it up to **Laguna Churup**. A popular secondary acclimatization hike for many aspiring trekkers, Churup takes you pretty high (4450m) pretty quickly and has a tricky scrambling section toward the end. As a compromise, some people do the hike in stages, going halfway up on their first attempt and then coming back the next day to complete the final section. In terms of scenery, it's well worth two visits.

All being well, after four or five days of careful acclimatization, you should be ready to tackle the Santa Cruz, the Huayhuash Circuit or an even loftier Andean summit. The sky's the limit

mountaineering, climbers pretty much stick to the dry season.

The management body for Parque Nacional Huascarán, Sernamp (Servicio Nacional de Áreas Naturales Protegidas por el Estado; the government agency administering national parks, reserves, historical sanctuaries and other protected areas under the Ministry of Environment), technically requires the use of local licensed guides for all activity in Parque Nacional Huascarán, including day hikes, trekking and climbing.

Trail Guidebooks & Maps

The most comprehensive guide to trekking in the region is *Peru's Cordilleras Blancas & Huayhuash* (2015) by Neil and Harriet Pike. It contains detailed route maps and altitude charts, and ranks treks by difficulty. Another great resource for the Huayhuash region is the detailed *Climbs and Treks in the Cordillera Huayhuash of Peru* (2005) by Jeremy Frimer, though it's sold out and only available for consultation in Huaraz (good hostels should have a copy).

The best overview of climbing glaciers in the Cordillera Blanca is Brad Johnson's *Classic Climbs of the Cordillera Blanca Peru* (2003), which was reprinted in 2009. For rock climbing and bouldering, check out *Huaraz: The Climbing Guide* (2014) by David Lazo and Marie Timmermans.

Felipe Díaz' 1:300,000 *Cordilleras Blanca & Huayhuash* is a popular map for an overview of the land, with towns, major trails and town plans, though it's not detailed enough for remote treks.

The Alpenvereinskarte (Austrian Alpine Club) produces the most detailed and accurate maps of the region; look for the regularly updated 1:100,000 *Cordillera Blanca Nord, Cordillera Blanca Sur* and *Cordillera Huayhuash*. These maps are available in Caraz, Huaraz and at South American Explorers' clubhouses for around S80 each. Cheaper, but with a similar scale, are the Cordillera Blanca and Cordillera Huayhuash topo maps distributed by Skyline Adventures, available at Café Andino and agencies around Huaraz.

Tours & Guides

Even experienced mountaineers would do well to add a local guide, who knows exactly what has been happening in the mountains, to their group. The Casa de Guías and trekking agencies in Huaraz and Caraz are good places to start your search for qualified mountain guides, *arrieros* and cooks. Qualified guides and *arrieros* are issued with photo identification by the tourism authority – ask for credentials. Not all registered guides are of the same level, but for a small commission, many agencies will put you in touch with one of their recommended guides, although in high season they will usually be tied up with organized trips.

If your Spanish is up to it and you're not in a great hurry, you can hire *arrieros* and mules in trailhead villages, particularly Cashapampa, Colcabamba and Vaqueria, among others. Horses, donkeys and mules are used as pack animals, and while llamas are occasionally provided, they are expensive and cannot carry as much weight. Try to get a reference for a good *arriero* and establish your trekking goals (ie pace, routes) before you depart. Check the state of the pack animals before you hire them – some *arrieros* overwork their beasts of burden or use sick or injured animals.

The Dirección de Turismo and the guides' union generally set prices, but not all guides respect them. Mountain guides can charge anything from US$120 to US$250 per day – the more technical the peak the higher the price. Trekking guides charge between US$40 and US$60 per day. Agencies offering the Santa Cruz trek usually charge S20 for a donkey, S40 for a horse and S40 for an *arriero*. Expect more variable prices if you book independently. All of these prices are guidelines only.

Prices do not include food and it is customary that you provide meals and shelter for any hired staff – confirm what's included before you set off. In the case of *arrieros* you may have to pay for their return journey if your trek does not begin and end at the same point.

Equipment & Rentals

If you lack the experience or equipment required to mountain it, fear not, as dozens of 'savoir faire' businesses offer guides and gear rental, and organize entire adventures for you, right down to the *burros* (donkeys). If you go on a tour, trekking agencies will supply everything from tents to ice axes. Most of them also rent out gear independently.

Reliable rental agencies for decent climbing gear are Quechuandes (p375), Andean Kingdom (p375) and Huascarán (p376).

It often freezes at night, so make sure you have an adequately warm sleeping bag, wet-weather gear (needed year-round), and a brimmed hat and sunglasses. Strong sunblock and good insect repellent are also a must and can be found easily in Huaraz if you've left them at home.

Cordillera Blanca

One of the most breathtaking parts of the continent (both figuratively and literally), the Cordillera Blanca is the world's highest tropical mountain range and encompasses some of South America's highest mountains. Andean leviathans include the majestic Nevado Alpamayo (5947m), once termed 'the most beautiful mountain in the world' by the Austrian Alpine Club. Others include Nevado Huascarán (at 6768m, Peru's highest), Pucajirca (6046m), Nevado Quitaraju (6036m) and Nevado Santa Cruz (Nevado Pucaraju; 6259m).

Situated in the tropical zone, the Cordillera Blanca stands to be affected greatly as global warming increases; there exists significant evidence that the glaciers of the Cordillera Blanca show a measurable decrease in their volume and that the snow line has receded in recent decades. Other threats to the park include litter and high-altitude livestock grazing on endangered *qeñua* (Polylepis) trees.

Parque Nacional Huascarán

Peruvian mountaineer César Morales Arnao first suggested protecting the flora, fauna and archaeological sites of the Cordillera Blanca in the early 1960s, but it didn't become a reality until 1975, when the national park was established. This 3400-sq-km park encompasses practically the entire area of the Cordillera Blanca above 4000m, including more than 600 glaciers and nearly 300 lakes, and protects such extraordinary and endangered species as the giant *Puya raimondii* plant, the spectacled bear and the Andean condor.

Visitors to the park can register (bring your passport) and pay the park fee at the park office (p382) in Huaraz, although most of the main entrances to the park also sell tickets. Fees are S30 per person for a day visit, S60 for a three-day visit and S150 for a month.

Note, the park doesn't include the Cordillera Huayhuash, which are protected in a separate reserve.

◉ Sights

★ **Laguna Parón**   LAKE

(S5) Silent awe enters people's expressions when they talk of Laguna Parón. Nestled at 4185m above sea level, along a bumpy road

25km east of Caraz, and surrounded by spectacular snow-covered peaks, this lake is heralded by many as the most beautiful in the Cordillera Blanca. It is certainly the largest, despite its water levels being lowered from 75m to 15m in the mid-1980s to prevent a collapse of Huandoy's moraine.

Ringed by formidable peaks, Parón offers close-up views of Pirámide de Garcilaso (5885m), Huandoy (6395m), Chacraraju (6112m) and several 1000m granite rock walls. The challenging rock-climbing wall of Torre de Parón, known as the Sphinx, is also found here.

A trail rambles along the lake's north shore on flat terrain for about two hours and then up the valley to another smaller lake and the foot of Artesonraju. There is also a steep climb to a mirador that could prove difficult if you haven't acclimatized to the thin air. If you go on your own, note that it's not possible to circumnavigate the lake – the northern side is fine, but on the southern side there is a very dangerous section where the path disappears and slippery vegetation grows flush against the mountain surface. The potential for falls is huge and foreigners have died attempting to cross here.

Most people see the lake as part of an organized tour out of Huaraz or Caraz (from S50). Going solo, you can organize a taxi in Caraz for around S150 round-trip with wait. The journey from Caraz takes 1½ hours on an unpaved road.

BEWARE OF THE DOGS

Dogs are the bane of hikers in the Cordilleras. Walk into any rural village and you'll likely be 'greeted' by an unwelcome consortium of feral canines. Unfortunately, none of these dogs have leashes, kennels or regular appointments with the vet. Hikers in rural areas should thus be prepared for lots of barking and occasional confrontations with one or more untethered dogs. In most events, it's a case of all bark and no bite. Ignore a dog completely and it'll usually back off. If the barking persists, stop walking, talk in a soft tone and move slowly away. As a last resort, bend down as if to pick up a stone. If a dog bites you, seek immediate medical attention. Rabies is rare in Peru, but fatal if left untreated.

Despite being inside the national park, Parón falls under a separate justification and is run by a local community group who charge S5 admission.

Pastoruri Glacier GLACIER

Still hanging on by the skin of its teeth high up in the Cordillera Blanca, the rapidly retreating Pastoruri glacier is one of the few remaining glaciers in tropical South America. Despite its lofty vantage (5050m), it is the only icy monolith in the Peruvian Cordillera accessible by road. Due to its remoteness and the lack of public transportation serving it, the glacier is usually tackled as part of an organized day trip from Huaraz.

The tour involves a 40-minute hike from the car park to the shores of the small lake into which the ice disgorges – a challenging walk considering the altitude (horses can be hired).

The Pastoruri, like many Andean glaciers, has lost nearly a third of its size in the last 30 years. Within the next decade, it's likely it will disappear altogether. Not surprisingly, the visitor numbers have receded with the ice. Back in the 1990s, it was one of Huaraz' main tourist attractions. People came to walk, climb and ski on the immense ice field. These days, walking on the glacier is prohibited and the ice flow is promoted more as a poster-child for climate change than for its grand physical presence. Day tours have padded out their Pastoruri itinerary to include other sights on the way out and back.

The glacier is located 70km southeast of Huaraz and reached by turning east off PE-3N several kilometers south of Catac.

Lagunas Llanganuco LAKE

A dirt road ascends 1350m from Yungay, winding over 28km to the Llanganuco Valley and its two robin-egg blue lakes, which are also known as Laguna Chinancocha and Laguna Orconcocha. Nestled in a glacial valley just 1000m below the snow line, these pristine lagoons practically glow under the sun in their bright turquoise and emerald hues. There's a half-hour trail hugging Chinancocha past a jetty and picnic area to where sheer cliffs plunge into the lake.

You can take a boat out on the lake for S5. Continuing on the road past the lake you'll see a *mirador* with killer views of the mountain giants of Huascarán (6768m), Chopicalqui (6345m), Chacraraju (6108m), Huandoy (6395m) and others. The road continues over the pass of Portachuelo (4760m) to Yanama on the other side of the Cordillera Blanca.

The Lagunas Llanganuco is a popular day trip from Huaraz (from around S60) and can get relatively crowded. Bear in mind that this tour is primarily tailored around sightseeing *not* hiking, with a fair degree of shopping stops included along the way. You'll be able to stop briefly by the lakes on the more hiking-orientated Laguna 69 trip.

The lakes can also be reached by *colectivo* (shared transportation) or taxi from Yungay. Round-trip *colectivos* leave from Yungay's small terminal on the main highway (S30), allowing about two hours in the lake area. A national-park admission fee of S30 is charged. Alternatively you can take a *combi* heading to Yanama, but it costs the same and you may have difficulty getting back to town. A private round-trip taxi from Yungay will cost around S100 to S120. Go in the early morning for the clearest views, especially in the low season.

Santa Cruz Trek

Start Vaqueria

End Cashapampa

Duration Three to four days

Distance 45km

Difficulty Moderate–Demanding

The Santa Cruz is one of South America's classic multiday treks: lightly trodden, spectacular from start to finish, and achievable by anyone of decent fitness who's had adequate time to acclimatize. Running for 45km through the Cordillera Blanca between the villages of Vaqueria and Cashapampa, the trek takes hikers along the verdant Quebrada Huarípampa, over the (literally) dizzying Punta Union Pass (4760m/15617ft) and down through the deeply gouged Quebrada Santa Cruz Valley.

Unlike the Inca trail, no permit system exists for the Santa Cruz, and you can undertake it solo without a guide (although many Huaraz agencies offer the trip). The trail can be hiked in either direction but the easiest and recommended route is to head east–west from Vaqueria to Cashapampa. By starting in Vaqueria, you avoid a grueling, hot and dusty ascent at the very beginning of the hike. Finishing in Cashapampa leaves you with more transportation options at the end.

Head-turning sights along the way include emerald lakes, sensational views of many of the Cordillera's peaks, beds of brightly colored alpine wildflowers and stands of red qeñua trees.

The Santa Cruz is one of the most popular routes in Peru for international trekkers. Most days of the year there are enough other people around to keep you on track. Signposting is sporadic, but sufficient. Take care on your approach to Punta Union if it's misty (small piles of stones act as markers) and stay alert around the dried-up lakes in the Santa Cruz Valley where the path has been redirected.

It's not difficult to complete the trail in three days. However, four days offer more opportunities for side trips, the most popular being the short punt up to Alpamayo Base Camp. Water is available from rivers en route, though you'll need to treat it as grazing livestock is everywhere. There are no dangerous animals or tricky climbing sections to worry about. Instead, the main challenge is altitude, particularly as you approach Punta Union.

Heading out from Vaqueria, the first day involves a short and relatively easy ascent through the hamlet of Huarípampa and its traditional thatched-roof Quechua houses. Guinea pigs (destined for the dinner table) can often be seen running around in shallow wooden platforms underneath the roofs. After passing the village, the trail follows the Quebrada Huarípampa past the park checkpoint (where you must pay your fee and show your passport) to a campsite at Paria (3850m/12631ft) where most hikers spend the first night.

The second day is the toughest as the path starts to gain height, pushing up past Laguna Morococha and through a spiralling rocky buttress over the Punta Union Pass, which appears from below as an angular notch in a seemingly unbroken rocky wall. The panoramas from both sides of the pass are captivating should the weather cooperate, but beware: it can be cold on top year-round with occasional snow. After crossing the pass it's usual, after a steep descent, to pitch tents at Taullipampa (4250m/13944ft), which sits in a gorgeous meadow at the foot of the majestic Nevado Taulliraju (5830m/19127ft) where large chunks of ice regularly break off, especially in the afternoon sun. To the south, Nevado Paria

Santa Cruz Trek

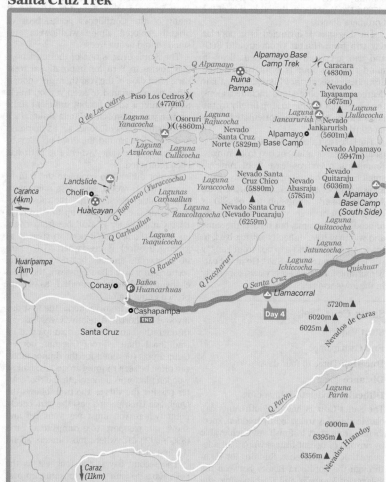

(5600m/18373ft) and Nevado Artesonraju (6025m/19767ft) dominate the skyline.

The reward on day three for the hard legwork so far is a long but easy hike through some spectacular mountain scenery, past small waterfalls, lakes and interconnected marshy areas. From Taullipampa, the trail heads across a dried-up lake bed that was drained after a 2012 avalanche blew out an ice-and-mud dam. The rebuilt path runs along the former lake's southern shore, or you can cut directly across the sandy valley.

Before you reach Laguna Jatuncocha, it is possible to take a side trip to Alpamayo Base Camp (South Side) underneath the magnificent Nevado Alpamayo (5947m/19511ft). Although from here you are not able to appreciate the perfect pyramid form of the north side of Alpamayo, there is an enchanting laguna and the vantage point offers phenomenal views of other peaks across the valley.

Beyond Laguna Jatuncocha lies the once extensive Laguna Icchicocha, now little more than a marshy area. The trail's last official campsite, Llamacorral is perched on its west 'shore.'

The final day involves more dramatic scenery and a steep 9.3km descent down Santa Cruz canyon to Cashapampa.

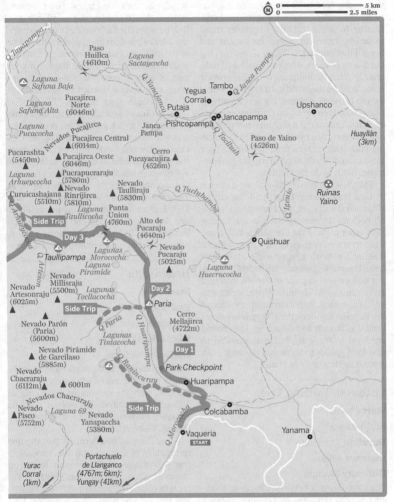

Combis leave from Yungay for Yanama at 7am and 1pm and can drop you at Vaqueria (S15, three hours). *Colectivo* (shared transportation) taxis run frequently between Caraz and the trailhead at Cashapampa (S10, 1½ hours).

Other Cordillera Blanca Treks & Hikes

While the Santa Cruz Trek attracts the lion's share of visitors, dozens of other trekking possibilities in the Cordillera Blanca supply scenery and vistas just as jaw-dropping (minus the crowds). A series of *quebradas* (valleys) – Ishinca, Cojup, Quilcayhuanca, Shallap and Rajucolta (listed north to south) – run parallel to each other from the area around Huaraz up into the heart of the Cordillera Blanca, and most of them have a high-altitude lake (or two) somewhere along the way. Each offers trekking opportunities ranging from one day to several – there are many possibilities. Interested trekkers can inquire with local agencies about connecting these valley treks with high-altitude traverses, but they are generally explored individually.

Some – but not all – trails on most of the multiday treks aren't clearly marked yet, so it's best to either go with a guide or have excellent reference maps on hand. Getting to some trailheads requires travel to nearby towns or along the rugged and beautiful Conchucos Valley (east of the Cordillera Blanca), where a handful of ludicrously friendly indigenous towns provide basic facilities and vivid cultural experiences for the intrepid explorer. For less ambitious hikers who aren't keen on camping or refuges, consider making a day hike out of some of the longer trips by starting early and turning back with enough time to transfer back to your hotel. You'll need to pay the park entrance (S30) to do these hikes.

The three- to six-day hike along a stretch of Inca trail linking Huari and the city of Huánuco doesn't get much attention, possibly because the scenery is not as spectacular as in other parts of the Cordillera. But, if you want to get away from other hikers without busting a gut, it's a worthwhile alternative trek. The walk proceeds fairly gently crossing well-preserved parts of the old Inca trail and ending up in Huánuco Viejo, which was one of the most important military sites of the Incas in northern Peru. Very few visitors walk this stretch and details on the ground are hard to come by, but it is possible to find local guides to show you the way – ask around in Huaraz or in Huari.

Chacas to Yanama Trek

Start Chacas

End Yanama

Duration Three days

Distance 49km

Difficulty Medium

The three-day trek between Chacas and Yanama is relatively easy by Cordillera Blanca

---

RUNNING IN THE ANDES

First run in 2016, the 45km-long **Sierra Andina Mountain Trail** (www.sierraandinamarathon.com; ⊘ mid-August) high-altitude 'marathon' (3km longer and a lot harder than a traditional 42km marathon) follows the standard Santa Cruz trail route between Vaqueria (where it starts) and Cashapampa. There are six aid stations en route – and, by jove, you'll need them. The course record is an astounding 4¼ hours.

---

standards, with the highest point a 'mere' 4050m (13287ft). This route provides a good link between the Callejón de Conchucos and the Santa Cruz trail and provides fine views of the glaciated valleys that radiate from Nevado Contrahierbas. These mountains are part of a big cheese-producing region and you'll spot several *queserías* (cheese factories) in villages along the way.

From Chacas, you hike through the municipalities of Sapcha and Potaca crisscrossing a paved mountain road up to Pupash Pass. Once on the other side, you can either finish the trek at Yanama or continue to the Keshu Valley, which has several good places to camp. Colcabamba, a few hours further on from Yanama, is near one end of the Santa Cruz Trek. Endurance hikers can tag the well-trodden Santa Cruz onto the end of the Chacas–Yanama hike to create a Herculean eight- to nine-day circuit before returning to Huaraz.

Honda-Ulta

Start Vicos

End Shilla

Duration Seven days

Distance 84km

Difficulty Medium

This loop starting at Vicos and ending at the village of Shilla, near Carhuaz, is a moderate trek, with the exception of a couple of difficult high-altitude passes at Laguna Yanayacu (4850m/15912ft) and Portachuelo Honda (4750m/15584ft).

Along the way, hikers can stop at the tiny community of Juitush and the impossibly precious village of Chacas and linger on views of Yanaragra (5987m/19642ft), Pucaranra (6156m), Palcaraju (6274m/20197ft) and two remote lakes. This is a great hike if you want to experience an off-the-beaten-track route and enjoy a few charismatic indigenous villages along the way. It's usually spread over seven days.

Huari to Chacas Trek

Start Laguna Purhuay

End Chacas

Duration Two to three days

Distance 30km

Difficulty Medium

This relatively easy trek makes its way along the eastern flanks of the Cordillera Blanca, roughly paralleling the Callejón de Conchucos south to north. The path starts at Laguna Purhuay (p407), 8km above Huari (S25 in a taxi), a lovely spot little visited by international hikers, with a rustic restaurant and kayaks for rent.

The route passes several other lakes, reaches its zenith at 4550m San Bartolomé Pass and finishes in the misty high-altitude tropical forests of the Parhua Valley (3500m).

Laguna 69

Start Yurac Corral

End Yurac Coral

Duration Five to six hours

Distance 14km

Difficulty Medium

This vivid blue lake surrounded by snow-covered peaks is the jewel of the Cordilleras. Set at 4600m, it's a challenging second acclimatization hike. 'Sixty-nine' is most commonly visited as a day trip from Huaraz and has become increasingly popular in recent years. Don't expect to have the place to yourself. Swimming in the lake is prohibited.

It's a fairly long and tough three-hour ascent from the trailhead to the lake, which sits right at the base of Chacraraju (6112m). However, you will be rewarded with great views of Chopicalqui (6345m), Huascarán Sur (6768m) and Norte (6655m) along the way. Allow around two hours for the descent.

The trail to Laguna 69 starts near the Yurac Corral (3800m), on the northern tip of a big bend in the Llanganuco road.

Some agencies in Huaraz offer a guided hike to the lake including transportation, breakfast and a guide for as little as S35, making it cheaper than public transportation, although you'll likely be joining a group of up to 30 people.

If you want to hike on your own, you can hunt around the agencies for a transportation-only option that will drop you at the trailhead and wait for you to return. Alternatively, a taxi from Huaraz will charge from S180 round-trip. All of these will stop on request at the Lagunas Llanganuco, which are right next to the road on the way up.

Going with public transportation, you'll need to catch a *combi* or *colectivo* to Yungay and then another one heading toward Yanama. The main issue is getting back to the trailhead by around 3pm to catch the last *combi* to Yungay – you'll need to start the trek early.

Laguna Churup

Start Pitec

End Pitec

Duration Six hours

Distance 7km

Difficulty Medium–Demanding

The hamlet of Pitec (3850m), just above Huaraz, is the official start of this hike to drop-dead gorgeous Laguna Churup (4450m) at the base of Nevado Churup. The tranquil cobalt blue lake nestles high in a natural amphitheater, surrounded by snow-frosted peaks.

The path is steep, but sweet. You can choose to approach along either the left- or right-hand side of the valley; most hikers opt for the left approach where a series of cables have been installed to assist your progress up a steep rock wall (the climb may test those who have issues with heights).

This day hike is often chosen as an acclimatization hike, but note the altitudes and the 600m ascent – make sure you're ready before charging into this one.

A taxi from Huaraz to Pitec (which is just a couple of houses with no facilities) will cost about S60 one-way. Alternatively, you can start and/or finish lower down in the village of Llupa (which has a couple of shops). *Combis* for Llupa (S3, 30 minutes) leave Huaraz from the corner of Gamarra and Las Americas about every 30 minutes (ask to be dropped off at the path to Pitec); from there it's a one-hour 3km walk to Pitec. You'll need to be back at Llupa by 5pm to catch the last *combi* to Huaraz.

Los Cedros-Alpamayo

Start Huancarhuaz

End Cashapampa

Duration 10 days

Distance 120km

Difficulty Demanding

This is one of the more dazzling and demanding treks of the Cordillera Blanca and an alternative to the epic Huayhuash circuit further south. There are numerous variations, from seven- to 14-day itineraries, measuring 90km to 120km in length, so study the alternatives carefully before you set out.

Whichever route you take, prepare for very long ascents to high passes (up to 4850m), incredible alpine scenery (including the regal north side of Nevado Alpamayo), and traditional Quechua communities with no road access.

Popular starting and/or finishing points are Cashapampa or nearby Huancarhuaz. The shorter seven-day itinerary ends in Pomabamba; other itineraries incorporate parts of the iconic Santa Cruz Trek.

The trek is only recommended for experienced and acclimatized hikers who are familiar with navigation. The route is relatively straightforward, but not signposted. If in doubt, go with a reputable agency. Quechuandes (p375) offers a good 10-day version of this trek and its website has a useful map.

Olleros to Chavín de Huántar Trek

Start Olleros

End Chavín de Huántar

Duration Two to three days

Distance 37km

Difficulty Medium

If you're short on time but still want to cross the Cordillera, the relatively easy Olleros to Chavín de Huántar trek (sometimes known as the 'Llama Trek') is a good choice, although you'll be further from the big peaks here and the mountain views aren't as impressive as in other parts of the park.

You can start thetrek in either town, though most people start at the trailhead in Canray Chico, just outside Olleros in the Callejón de Huáylas, on the western side of the Cordillera Blanca. You can arrange llamas here as pack animals. Pretty villages and pre-Inca roads with great views of the Uruashraju (5722m), Rurec (5700m) and Cashan (5716m) mountains dot the landscape as you follow the Ríío Negro up the Uquian Valley to the 4700m Punta Yanashallash Pass. The finishing point on the Callejón de Conchucos side is absolutely gorgeous. Best of all, in Chavín you can soak your weary bones in hot springs and get up early the next day to visit the ruins, without the usual throng of tourists. The ascents on this route aren't too arduous and dedicated mountain bikers have been known to tackle it successfully. Taxis from Huaraz to Canray (40 minutes) cost around S50.

Quebrada Akillipo

Start Joncopampa

End Cochan Pampa

Duration Three days

Distance 34km

Difficulty Demanding

Despite its proximity to Huaraz, the beautiful Quebrada Akillpo is somewhat off the tour radar, making this tough circuit a great choice for experienced trekkers who want to get away from the high-season crowds.

The trail begins at Joncopampa and ascends through a forest of *qeñua* trees before emerging near Laguna Akillpo at the base of the Akillpo glacier. From here there is a tricky 4900m pass beneath Nevado Tocllaraju with difficult descents bordered by precipices. Following this, the trail continues down past the Refugio Ishinca (4390m) into the Ishinca valley finishing in the hamlet of Cochan Pampa, very close to where you started . Donkeys are not able to cross the pass. The path is not well marked and the difficult terrain means a knowledgeable guide is essential.

If you don't have the experience to complete the full circuit, a one- or two-day trek up into the Quebrada Akillpo and back allows you to see the remarkable forest, and also serves as a good acclimatization hike. The former will take you to the end of the forest before turning back, while the latter reaches the laguna but not the pass.

For even easier access to the valley you can rent horses in Joncopampa to explore part of the trail. Taxis from Huaraz to Joncopampa (1¼ hours) cost around S180 round-trip.

Quebrada Quilcayhuanca

Start Pitec

End Pitec

Duration Three to four days

Distance 29km

Difficulty Demanding

This hiking circuit leaving from Pitec (a short taxi ride from Huaraz) is one of the most beautiful in the Cordillera, but it's a difficult trek. You'll need to be well acclimatized to tackle it, as pack animals don't make it up over the 5000m Paso Choco. It's one thing to hike at altitude, and another altogether with a 15kg pack on your back.

The path winds up the Quebrada Quilcayhuanca through *qeñua* trees and grassy meadows until reaching the Laguna Cuchillacocha and Tullpacocha. Along the way, you pass unforgettable views: Nevado Cayesh (5721m), Maparaju (5326m), Tumarinaraju (5668m) and a half-dozen other peaks over 5700m. It then climbs to the soaring Paso Choco and descends through the Quebrada Cojup, past another pair of lagunas. Because this trek is not well marked, it's best to go with a guide (or have advanced navigation skills and a good topo map).

An easier version is a hike up the Quilcayhuanca valley to the first two lagunas before returning to Pitec on a two-day trek with a night in tents at 4000m. You'll still need to carry your gear but your backpack will be much lighter. This good alternative is less strenuous than the Santa Cruz Trek, but also takes in spectacular mountain vistas.

Cordillera Huayhuash

Often playing second fiddle to Cordillera Blanca, its limelight-stealing cousin, the Huayhuash hosts an equally impressive medley of glaciers, summits and lakes – all packed tightly into a hardy area only 30km across. Increasing numbers of travelers are discovering this rugged and remote territory, where trails skirt around the outer edges of stirring sharp-sided peaks. Strenuous high-altitude passes reaching up to 5000m throw down a gauntlet to the hardiest of trekkers, but the gut busting is worth it. The sight of majestic Andean condors coupled with the feeling of utter solitude once you're five days into your journey make the region's two-week Huayhuash Circuit one of the world's finest high-altitude treks.

The Huayhuash gained international attention in 1985 when Joe Simpson and Simon Yates became the first climbers to scale the west face of Siula Grande (6344m) and nearly perished on the descent. The experience inspired the book and film *Touching the Void* (p396).

Huayhuash Circuit

Start Pocpa/Matacancha

End Llamac

Duration Nine days

Distance 115km

Difficulty Demanding

The finest trek in the Andes? South America? The World? The rugged, remote, unnervingly mysterious Huayhuash would make many people's top tens.

Circling a tight cluster of high peaks, including Yerupajá (6634m), the world's second-highest tropical mountain, this lengthy trek crosses multiple high-altitude passes with spine-tingling views. The dramatic lakes along the eastern flanks provide great campsites (and are good for trout fishing) and give hikers a wide choice of routes to make this trek as difficult as they want.

Daily ascents range from 500m to 1200m, but a couple of days in the middle and at the end of the trek involve major descents, which can be just as tough as going uphill. The average day involves about 12km on the trail, or anywhere from four to eight hours of hiking, although you may experience at least one 10- to 12-hour day.

Most trekkers take extra rest days along the way, partly because the length and altitude make the entire circuit very demanding, and partly to allow for the sensational sights to sink in. Others prefer a shorter version: it's possible to hike for as few as five days along the remote eastern side of the Huayhuash.

Described here is the classic Huayhuash Circuit trek, but many side trips and alternate routes along the way can add a day or two to your trekking time.

If you are trekking with an agency you may begin your trek at Matacancha, but if you don't have private transportation you will need to begin from Pocpa near **Llamac**, the last town for several days as the trail leaves 'civilization.' In Pocpa it's possible to arrange *arrieros* and pack animals, and there are several local families offering accommodations and basic meals.

On the first stretch of the trek, you'll follow the Río Llamac through the village of Palca to Matacancha, where you'll spend the night. The second day takes you over a 4700m pass and down to Laguna Mitacocha (4230m). On day three, you'll see more excellent mountain panoramas and eventually reach a cliff that overlooks Laguna Carhuacocha (4138m) and the glaciated mountains behind Siula Grande (6344m) and Yerupajá looming in the distance.

Continuing on the main trail, you hit a short section of paved Inca trail, about 1.5m wide and 50m long, the remnants of an Inca road heading south from the archaeological

Cordillera Huayhuash Circuit

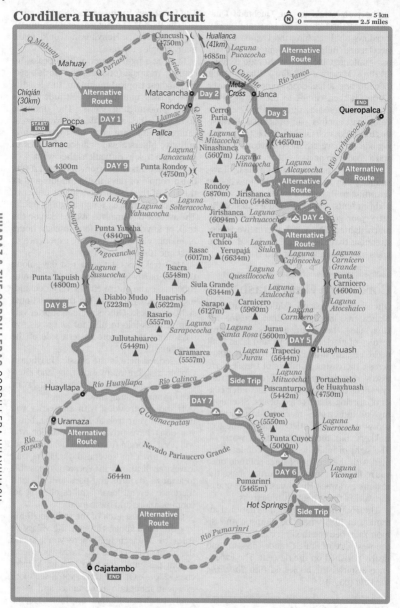

site of Huánuco Viejo near La Unión. Over the next couple of days, work your way toward Laguna Carnicero (4430m), Laguna Mitucocha, the top of Portachuelo de Huayhuash (4750m), and Laguna Viconga (4407m). After several glaciated mountain crowns come into view, including the double-peaked Cuyoc (5550m), you can either camp and continue the main circuit, or you can head southwest along the Río Pumarinri Valley toward Cajatambo, leaving the circuit early.

If you keep going, get ready for the challenging 5000m-plus Punta Cuyoc Pass. On day six, the trail crests a small ridge on Pumarinri (5465m), giving trekkers face-on views of Cuyoc. Look out for the hardy *Stangea henricii*, a grayish-green, flat, rosette-shaped plant of overlapping tongue-like leaves that only grows above 4700m.

On the seventh day you can continue the direct circuit by hiking past the village of Huayllapa; exit the circuit through Huayllapa and the town of Uramaza to Cajatambo; or make a side trip up the Río Calinca Valley to Lagunas Jurau, Santa Rosa and Sarapococha, where there are some of the best mountain panoramas of the entire trek. The traditional circuit will take you past the glacier-clad pyramid of Jullutahuarco (5449m) and a stupendous 100m-high waterfall. Push on to a small lake near Punta Tapuish (4800m) for good high-altitude camping.

The following day the trail drops gently to Laguna Susucocha (4750m) shortly before a junction (4400m) with Quebrada Angocancha. The trail skirts boggy meadows and climbs into rock and scree before reaching Punta Yaucha (4840m), offering wonderful views of the range's major peaks, including Yerupajá to the east and many of the minor glaciated high points to the southeast. Go fossil-hunting in this area for imprints of ammonites and other creatures that once dwelled under the sea – and imagine the Andes relegated to the ocean's bottom. Finally, the path descends to the wonderfully scenic Laguna Yahuacocha.

The last day is short, with an early arrival in Llamac, from where public transportation to Chiquián and on to Huaraz leaves at 11:15am. Trekkers should be prepared for aggressively territorial dogs (p386) along the way.

ℹ Information

CAMPING FEES

In the waning moments of 2001, Peru's Ministry of Agriculture declared the Cordillera Huayhuash a 'reserved zone,' giving a transitory measure of protection to nearly 700 sq km of almost-pristine land. Since then, the ministry has backed away from official support as a unique, private- and community-managed conservation effort has taken root. Several communities whose traditional territory lies at the heart of the Huayhuash range are formally recognized as 'Private Conservation Areas.' Nine settlements along the circuit – **Llamac**, **Pocpa**, **Jirishanca**, **Quishuarcancha**, **Tupac Amaru**, **Guñog**, **Uramasa**, **Huayllapa** and **Pacllón**, now charge user fees of S20 to S40, plus an extra S1.50 per pack animal per night for grazing. Costs for the

basic circuit were around S200 to S230 at the time of writing and continuing to rise on a yearly basis. Part of the fees goes toward improved security for hikers and part goes to continued conservation work and improved facilities, although the standard of toilets in some parts of the circuit remain far from acceptable. Support this grassroots preservation attempt by paying your fees, carrying enough small change and by always asking for an official receipt (to ensure you are dealing with the right people).

Note that open fires are prohibited throughout the Huayhuash region as wood is scarce. If you're hiking independently, make sure you bring a gas cooker.

ℹ Getting There & Away

The vast majority of travelers planning hiking expeditions in the Cordillera Huayhuash proceed first of all to Huaraz to acclimatize, meet with guides and/or set up their own solo trip. However, it is possible to travel direct from Lima to the village of Chiquián and then onto the village of Llamac where many of the Huayhuash treks begin.

Turismo Cavassa (📞 043-44-7036; www.turismocavassa.com.pe; Bolognesi 421) has several daily buses from Lima to Chiquián (S35, eight hours).

Turismo Nazario (p383) has a daily bus leaving Huaraz at 5am for Chiquián, Llamac and Pocpa (S30, 5½ hours), the starting point for most treks. The bus turns around and heads back to Huaraz at around 10:30am.

Cordillera Negra

The poor little Cordillera Negra lives literally in the shadows of its big-brother range, the Cordillera Blanca, whose towering glaciated peaks to the east block the morning sun and loom dramatically over everything around them. The 'Black Range,' which gets its name from its obvious contrast to the more beautiful 'White Range,' will probably always look a bit dressed down – with its arid, mud-brown, merely hilly silhouette – against the Cordillera Blanca's stunning icy and craggy profile. Still, the Negra has an important role to play in the area's ecology as it blocks warm Pacific winds from hitting the Blanca's glaciers and contributing to their thaw. It's also an important agricultural and mining area for the local population.

◎ Sights

Punta Winchus   NATURE RESERVE
A remote 4157m pass in the Cordillera Negra is the center of a huge stand of 5000 rare

SIULA GRANDE & 'TOUCHING THE VOID'

The story of British climbers Joe Simpson and Simon Yates and their heroic but nearly fatal ascent of Siula Grande in the Cordillera Huayhuash has entered mountaineering folklore, not purely for the drama of the climb, but for the eloquence with which it was later recounted by Simpson in his hugely popular book, *Touching the Void* (1988).

At 6344m, Siula Grande is the eighth-highest mountain in Peru and the second-highest in the Cordillera Huayhuash. Rather like its near neighbor, Yerupajá (6617m) it is considered a difficult mountain to climb due to the sheerness of its rock walls and the fickle weather that enshrouds its upper slopes. Siula was first climbed in 1936 via its north ridge by two Austrian alpinists. Simpson and Yates' audacious expedition in 1985 tackled the then unclimbed west face. Although they were successful in reaching the summit, they got into trouble while descending the north ridge when Simpson slipped on an ice cliff and broke his leg. With the weather closing in, Yates bravely tried to belay Simpson down the mountain, but, as darkness fell, he only succeeded in inadvertently lowering his colleague over a cliff. Open to the elements and with an agonizing broken leg, Simpson was left dangling in mid-air unable to move up or down. Yates, who was only 21 at the time and completely exhausted, found himself facing a horrible dilemma. He was being gradually pulled off the mountain by Simpson's weight. Unable to communicate with his climbing partner or pull him back up, he was left with only two options: cut the rope and live, or get pulled off the mountain and die along with Simpson. Yates cut the rope, sending Simpson falling 100m into a deep crevasse. Despite being initially given up for dead by Yates, Simpson miraculously survived, but his desperate plight in the icy crevasse and his subsequent 5-mile crawl back to base camp in a state of almost total delirium remains one of mountaineering's greatest survival stories.

Siula Grande has continued to prove difficult in the years since. By the late 1980s, a new danger had emerged. The Maoist guerilla group, the Sendero Luminoso (Shining Path) was active in the area and the Cordillera Huayhuash was considered unsafe – even for intrepid climbers. With the decline of the Shining Path in the late 1990s the area reopened and, by the early 2000s, the Huayhuash Circuit had established itself as a quieter trekking alternative to the Cordillera Blanca. Meanwhile, thanks to the success of *Touching the Void* and a subsequent 2003 film adaptation of the book, Siula Grande has become Peru's most famous mountain. It still attracts ambitious alpinists to its precipitous slopes, most of them seemingly impervious to its hidden menace, and in 2016 two Frenchmen became the first climbers to successfully scale its east face.

Puya raimondii plants; the biggest known for these 10m-tall members of the pineapple family, which take 100 years to mature and in full bloom flaunt up to 20,000 flowers each. On a clear day you have an astounding 145km panorama from the Cordillera Blanca all the way to the Pacific Ocean. It's 45km west of Caraz and reached by tour vehicles.

The Punta makes for a fabulous 45km bike ride – most of it downhill (catch a *colectivo* from Caraz to the top).

 Activities

Laguna Wilkacocha

Start Puente Santa Cruz
End Laguna Wilkacocha
Duration Three hours

Distance 6.5km round-trip
Difficulty Medium

In the Cordillera Negra, just 10km from Huaraz, the tranquil Laguna Wilkacocha (3700m) is a popular first acclimitization hike. It's well worth a visit in its own right, but is often frequented by visitors who plan bigger outings in the Cordillera Blanca.

The views from here across to the Cordillera Blanca are absolutely spectacular and take in many snow-covered peaks including Huantsan, Shaqsha, Vallunaraju and Ranrapalca.

The trail begins at the Puente Santa Cruz on the highway south of Huaraz and is easy to follow, winding up along a dirt road through a small village. At a junction just past the village, fork right and then turn left onto a stony path (with some steps) opposite a small sports pitch. It takes around two hours going up and an hour on the return.

Colectivos heading from Huaraz to Recuay will drop you at Puente Santa Cruz (S2, 20 minutes). Alternatively, a taxi from Huaraz can take you all the way to the lake for S40 – you can then wander down at your own pace to take one of the frequently passing *colectivos* back to town from the Puente Santa Cruz.

Rock Climbing

Los Olivos
CLIMBING

The Cordillera's most accessible sport-climbing zone is conveniently located 10 minutes from Huaraz by *colectivo* (S1) and has up to 60 routes ranging from intermediate to super-elite. Set at 3120m, Los Olivos is an ideal place for warming up and/or acclimatizing for the tougher walls of Hatun Machuay and the Sphinx.

You can go it alone if you have the expertise or sign up with a guide. Andean Kingdom (p375) and Quechuandes (p375) run guided trips from S120 per day.

Hatun Machay
CLIMBING

(admission S10) Hatun is a veritable rock forest located 70km south of Huaraz, on the road to Lima and in the vicinity of the village of Pampas Chico. Well hidden from the main road, it was fairly obscure spot until the early 2000s, when foreign sport-climbers discovered it. Today, there are about 300 marked routes, plus a rudimentary **campground** (campsites S10).

A basic refuge on the site was awaiting renovation at last visit.

Two treks around the area take you past archaeological remains of rock carvings and a view of the Pacific Ocean (on a clear day), and make for great half-day acclimatization hikes.

Hatun is located 6km west of the PE-3N highway up a dirt road. You can get a *combi* from Catac (S10) to drop you at the junction and walk up. A taxi from Catac will cost S50; from Huaraz nearer S150.

NORTH OF HUARAZ

Monterrey

☎ 043 / POP 1100 / ELEV 2800M

Huddled around a scattered spine of tourist facilities, this tiny *pueblo* (village), 7km north of Huaraz, earns a spot on the map for its natural hot springs, small cluster of restaurants and lovely hacienda-style hotel, all pleasantly detached from the bustle of the big city.

 ## Activities

Hot Springs
HOT SPRINGS

(Av Monterrey; admission S4; ⏱7am-4:30pm) These hot springs are divided into two public pools, which are sometimes far from warm, and private rooms that offer the sort of scalding action you're looking for. Amenities are very basic and the private facilities have a distinct public hospital feel – don't expect a romantic soak. It's best to visit early in the morning, before the crowds.

There is no need to wrinkle your nose at the brown color of the water, it's due to high iron content rather than questionable hygiene practices.

Sleeping

★ El Patio de Monterrey
HOTEL $$$

(☎043-42-4965; www.elpatio.com.pe; Av Cordillera Blanca; s/d incl breakfast S270/335; @☎) A relic in an area rather short on them (due to devastating earthquakes), El Patio is a handsome hacienda that's been carefully modernized without abandoning its colonial style. Ship-shape rooms have a pleasant 'olde' vibe with beamed ceilings and bathtubs, but the real deal-swinger is the communal areas.

Enjoy the country-style lounge with its charred fireplace, the well-tended mature gardens, and the cobbled patio sprinkled with fountains, wagon wheels and the odd rocking chair creaking in the breeze.

Eating

On Sundays, many restaurants serve a traditional Peruvian feast called *pachamanca* (*pacha* means 'earth' and *manca* means 'oven' in Quechua), a magnificent bounty of chicken, pork, lamb, guinea pig, corn, potatoes and other vegetables cooked for several hours over hot stones.

El Cortijo
PERUVIAN $$

(☎043-42-3813; Av Cordillera Blanca; mains S25-60; ⏱8am-7pm; 🖼) This excellent restaurant grills Angus beef on its outdoor *parrilla* (grill) alongside *cuy* and other meats. Outdoor tables are arranged around a fountain (complete with a little boy peeing) in a grassy flower-filled garden, with swings for children. There are good pasta dishes – including one in a Peruvian *huancaína* (spicy cheese) sauce – and a kids' menu.

Getting There & Away

Local *combis* from Huaraz go north along Luzuriaga, west on Calle 28 de Julio, north on Calle 27 de Noviembre, east on Raymondi and north on Fitzcarrald. Try to catch a bus early in the route, as they fill up quickly. The fare for the 25-minute ride is S1. A taxi ride between Huaraz and Monterrey costs about S8.

Carhuaz

043 / POP 15,400 / ELEV 2638M

Carhuaz, 35km north of Huaraz, lays claim to one of the prettiest plazas in the valley, with a combination of rose gardens and towering palms that make lingering here a pleasure. The Sunday **market** is a kaleidoscopic treat as *campesinos* (farmers) descend from surrounding villages to sell a medley of fresh fruits, herbs and handicrafts. A paved road passes over the Cordillera Blanca from Carhuaz, via the beautiful Quebrada Ulta and the more recently constructed Punta Olímpica tunnel, to Chacas and San Luis.

Sleeping

Hotel La Merced HOTEL $

(043-39-4280; Ucayali 724; s/d S40/50) One of the town's longest-running ventures is starting to show the wrinkles of age, though it's safe and friendly enough with plenty of religious pamplets and the odd ABBA poster thrown in. Some rooms have shared bathrooms and there's no internet.

★**Hotel El Abuelo** INN $$$

(043-39-4456; www.elabuelohotel.com; Calle 9 de Diciembre 257; s/d incl breakfast S230/288; P@) El Abuelo is the Huascarán of Cordillera accommodations, towering over all opposition. The design features are impeccable, melding Inca-style trapezoidal windows with minimalist rooms to provide an open and comfortable accommodation space, replete with lemon trees, a produce garden, a fine restaurant and – pride of place – a 3D model of the Cordillera.

Owner Felipe Díaz is a talented cartographer who produces his own maps and guides of the Cordillera and other parts of Peru. Check them out, along with other local crafts, at the hotel's small, tasteful shop.

Hearty buffet breakfasts are laid on in the restaurant.

Montaña Jazz HOTEL $$$

(043-63-0023; www.montanajazzperu.com; Via Chucchun s/n; bungalows S360-500;) Within walking distance from Carhuaz but with a distinctly rural vibe, these comfortable and well-equipped bungalows make a great base for exploring the Callejon de Huaylas. Set in an ample garden with mountain vistas flooded with birdsong, rooms are elegant and spacious and most feature fireplaces, modern bathrooms and functional private kitchens.

If you don't feel like cooking, the friendly owners serve Italian-style meals on the porch. They can also arrange activities throughout the region.

It must be reserved in advance.

Eating

Don't miss the town's ubiquitous treat, *raspadilla,* a slurpee of ice slathered in fruity syrup.

Carhuaz has a surfeit of ice-cream sellers, most of them lining the Plaza de Armas.

Heladería Porvenir ICE CREAM $

(943-106-740; Progreso 729; ice cream S2.50-8; 8am-8pm) Carhuaz is an ice-cream town and its Plaza de Armas is ringed with about half a dozen *helado*-serving establishments. You can save time testing them all by heading straight to Porvenir which seems to draw the biggest crowd and stock the widest range of flavors.

Pakta Restaurante FUSION $$

(043-26-1672; Comercio 449; mains S12-28; 7:30am-11pm) Easy to miss in Carhuaz is this uncharacteristically modern restaurant that opened in 2016, serving Peruvian food with a few Asian and European twists. A colorful ever-changing blackboard menu greets you at the door. Inside, the well-priced, well-presented food mixes fried rice dishes with most people's favorite – giant homemade hamburgers served with chunky fries.

Getting There & Away

Passing minibuses to Yungay (S3, 30 minutes) and Caraz (S3.50, 45 minutes) pick up on the highway near the corner of La Merced. *Combis* to Huaraz (S3, 50 minutes) leave from a **small terminal** on the first block of La Merced. Buses and *colectivos* from Huaraz to Chacas and San Luis stop on the corner of La Merced and Amazonas, one block from the plaza.

Movil Tours (043-39-4141; www.moviltours.com.pe; Progreso 757) runs buses to Lima (S40 to S80, nine hours, six daily).

YANAMA

Yanama is a tiny, mountain-enveloped *pueblo*, where the most exciting thing to happen in the past decade is a connection to the electricity grid in 2005. The town is about a 1½-hour walk (or a 20-minute drive) from the start of the popular Santa Cruz trek and makes a good stopover point for trekkers and mountain-bikers to refuel and recharge. The town **Festival of Santa Rosa** is held here in August.

Facilities are rudimentary in Yanama and showers can be as frosty as the mountain air. It might be in back-of-beyond Yanama, hemmed in by massive mountains, but the **Andes Lodge Peru** (☑043-76-5579; www.andeslodgeperu.com; Jirón Gran Chavín s/n; s with/without bathroom S65/75, d S120-150, all incl breakfast; @🛜) feels like home sweet home thanks to the generosity of its amiable owner, Zacharias. Small but handsome country rooms come with traditional blankets (you'll need them here) and snowcapped views. Some have shared bathrooms. All are spotless.

The highlight are the hearty dinners, cooked by Zacharias' lovely wife, Esperanza, who'll chat to you like you're one of the family.

Combis link Yanama with Yungay (S15, three hours), passing the famed Lagunas Llanganuco and the village of Vaqueria, the starting point for the Santa Cruz trekking circuit. *Colectivos* from Yungay to Yanama leave from one block east of the police station at 7am and 1pm, although the latter service is less punctual. Return services leave Yanama from the plaza around 3am and between noon and 1pm (S15, three hours). The ride – obviously – is stunning.

Yungay

☑ 043 / POP 21,900 / ELEV 2458M

Light on overnight visitors, serene little Yungay has relatively few tourist services but is a well-organized and neat little town. It is the access point for the popular Lagunas Llanganuco and Laguna 69, via a dirt road that continues over the Cordillera to Yanama and beyond. Surrounded on all sides by lush hills wafting brisk mountain air, it's difficult to believe the heart-wrenching history of this little junction in the road.

The original village of Yungay is now a rubble-strewn zone about 2km south of the new town and marks the site of the single worst natural disaster in the Andes. The earthquake of May 31, 1970, loosened 15 million cubic meters of granite and ice from the west wall of Huascarán Norte. The resulting *aluvión* (debris avalanche) dropped over three vertical kilometers on its way to Yungay, 15km away. The town and almost all its 25,000 inhabitants were buried beneath 8m to 12m of soil.

◉ Sights

Campo Santo MEMORIAL
(PE-3N; admission S5; ⊘7am-6:30pm) A giant cemetery and memorial to the former town of Yungay (Yungay Viejo), Campo Santo is an attractive yet poignant spot that lies beneath the giant hulk of Mt Huscarán. Vast rose gardens bloom where busy thoroughfares once stood while gravestones and monuments mark the names of people and streets lost in the catastrophe.

You can follow a grassy path through the gardens to the site of the erstwhile Plaza de Armas, now overlooked by a replica of the old cathedral's facade built to honor the dead. A ruined arch from the original church stands nearby. The site is dominated by a towering white statue of Christ standing on a knoll above the path of the *aluvión*.

🛏 Sleeping

Hostal Gledel GUESTHOUSE $
(☑043-39-3048; Arias Grazziani; s/d without bathroom S25/30; 🛜) The gregarious and generous Señora Gamboa rents out 13 spartan rooms with decent mattresses brightened by colorful bedspreads, plus there's hot water. Expect at least one hug and a sample of her cooking during your stay. This is both the cheapest and best place to stay in town – it's deservedly popular.

Hotel Rima Rima HOTEL $$
(☑043-39-3257; www.hotelrimarima.com; Grau 275; s/d S85/140; 🛜) The most comfortable hotel in town, Rima Rima has spacious rooms that don't lack light or color. The rooms at the back have great views of the Cordillera Negra, but there's a rooftop

LLANGANUCO MOUNTAIN LODGE

About 45 minutes by taxi from Yungay toward the Lagunas Llanganuco, this recommended **lodge** (☏943-669-580; www.llanganucolodge.com; d incl all meals US$195-234; ☏) run by Brit Charlie Good is in a prime position for serious acclimatization, exploring the lakes area or the Santa Cruz Trek. It is perched at 3500m next to Keushu ruins on the shore of a translucent lagoon and offers guided hikes right from the door.

Lodge rooms are big on space and comfort with down-feather beds, Don Bosco wooden furniture (made in Chacas), traditional rugs and old-fashioned stoves. Balconies afford great views of the three highest peaks in the range and the food, usually taken outside on the terraced lawn, is legendary. Unusually for Peru, the super-fresh tap water is drinkable.

From Yungay, taxis departing in front of the town hospital charge S50 for the ride here. Reservations are essential.

terrace with even better vistas in case you don't snare one. Management is very involved and can help out with advice and trip planning in the area.

✖ Eating

Pilar's
PERUVIAN $

(Plaza de Armas; mains S8-30; ⊙8am-9pm Thu-Tue) Right on the plaza, friendly Pilar's knocks up good-quality typical Peruvian dishes like trout and *lomo saltado*, along with international breakfasts, burgers, sandwiches and coffee. There's another branch a block to the southeast.

Restaurant Turístico Alpamayo
PERUVIAN $$

(☏043-39-3090; Carretera Central; mains S14-26, menú S10; ⊙8am-6:30pm; ☐) Surrounded by gardens, just off the main highway at the north end of town, Alpamayo is a pleasant touristic restaurant, complete with a garden gazebo, table football, music on Sundays and Peruvian classics like trout, *cuy* or *chicharrónes* to dig into. The clincher: homemade ice cream for dessert. It's popular with hungry post-hiking tour groups.

ⓘ Getting There & Away

Minibuses run from a small **terminal** (PE-3N) along the highway to Caraz (S2, 15 minutes), Carhuaz (S3.50, 30 minutes) and Huaraz (S5, 1¼ hours). Buses from Caraz to Lima (S45 to S80, nine hours, seven daily), including **Movil Tours** (☏043-39-3512; www.moviltours.com. pe; Av Grazziani), pick up passengers one block north of the Plaza de Armas. A couple of *combis* leave from the terminal heading for Yanama (S15, 7am, three hours) via the dirt road over the Cordillera Blanca, with another service leaving from near the police station around 1pm. They

pass through Vaqueria, the launching point for the Santa Cruz Trek.

Caraz

☏043 / POP 26,200 / ELEV 2270M

With an extra helping of superb panoramas of the surrounding mountains and a perfectly adequate serving of cheap hotels, food-as-fuel restaurants and travel agencies, Caraz might be called 'little Huaraz.' If the honking taxis of the big Cordillera city were too much for you, base yourself here. Trekking and hiking trails meander in all directions – some are day trips, others are much longer sojourns.

One of the few places in the valley spared total destruction by earthquakes or *aluvión*, the town still has a gentle whiff of history. Its lazy Plaza de Armas wouldn't be out of place in a much smaller *pueblo*.

Located 70km north of Huaraz, Caraz offers a head start for rugged treks into the remote northern parts of the Cordillera Blanca, which are some of the best in the region. The north side of Alpamayo (5947m), considered by some to be the most beautiful mountain in the world, is accessible from here.

◉ Sights & Activities

Cañón del Pato
CANYON

If you continue north from Caraz along the Callejón de Huaylas, you will wind your way through the outstanding Cañón del Pato. It's here that the Cordillera Blanca and the Cordillera Negra come to within kissing distance for a battle of bedrock wills, separated by only 15m in parts and plummeting to vertigo-inducing depths of up to 1000m. The harrowing road snakes along a path hewn out of sheer rock, over a precipitous gorge and passing through 54 tunnels.

Gargantuan, crude walls tower above the road on all sides, and as the valley's hydro-electric plant comes into sight you realize that it's dramatic enough to house the secret lair of a James Bond arch-villain. The most dramatic stretch of the road is between Caraz and Huallanca, especially between tunnels 10 and 18, where the canyon is at its narrowest point.

If you're passing through on a bus, sit so that you're looking out of the right-hand side of the vehicle (as you face the driver) for the best views along the way. However, the best way to see the canyon is by bike. Report to Pony Expeditions in Caraz for bikes and maps.

Pony Expeditions OUTDOORS

(☑043-39-1642; www.ponyexpeditions.com; José Sucre 1266) English- and French-speaking regional expert Alberto Cafferata provides equipment rental (including bicycles, S10/50 per hour/day), transportation, guides and *arrieros*, and organizes various excursions including mountaineering expeditions, mountain treks, and vehicle and cycling trips through the Cañón del Pato. Books, maps, fuel and other items are for sale at the shop below the excellent Café de Rat (p402).

🛏 Sleeping

Hostal Chavín HOTEL $

(☑043-39-1171; chavinhostel@hotmail.com; San Martín 1135; s/d incl breakfast S50/100; 🛜) With its old sofas and dark lobby, the Chavín couldn't be described as a hip and happening hotel, but the central plaza location is good and the spacious, simple rooms have decent bathrooms with free-flowing hot water (although the cleanliness can be hit or miss). Breakfast is laid out in a small downstairs cafe.

Grand Hostal Caraz Dulzura HOTEL $

(☑043-39-1523; Sáenz Peña 212; s/d/tr incl breakfast S45/70/120; 🛜) About 10 blocks north of the plaza along Cordova, this quiet lodge provides a glow of relative luxury if you've just emerged from the Cordillera outback. Rooms are bright and have electric hot showers and comfortable beds. The congenial owners are on hand with hearty breakfasts and plenty of trekking information.

★ Los Pinos Lodge LODGE $$

(☑043-39-1130; www.lospinoslodge.com; Pasaje 9 No 116; s/d/ste incl breakfast S140/170/280;

P@🛜) This rustic-chic inn in a gated mansion set back from the road has been thoughtfully decorated inside and out. It offers outstanding rooms verging on boutique standard that could easily compete with anything in Huaraz. There are several great courtyards, a relaxing garden and a wonderful little cocktail bar in which to sit and chat.

The tasteful local paintings compete with the colorful Andean flowers in the grounds outside

Pony's Lodge LODGE $$

(☑043-39-1642; José Sucre 1266; s/d incl breakfast S45/90; 🛜) Upstairs at Pony Expeditions is this simple little lodge with small, cozy rooms and a equally diminutive terrace. Under the tutelage of owner Alberto you can plan practically any excursion in the Cordilleras. Also on-site is the wonderfully named Cafe de Rat (p402).

🍴 Eating

Of all the small towns north of Huaraz, Caraz offers the best places to eat – from unadorned roast chicken to the comfort food of tired hikers (pizzas, burgers and pasta).

The town is also known for its cakes and the manufacture of *manjar blanco* (homemade caramel spread).

Cafetería El Turista BREAKFAST $

(San Martín 1127; breakfast S7-18; ⊙6:30am-noon & 5-8pm) A super place to grab an early breakfast, this tiny five-table cafe is a one-woman show run by the exuberant Maria. She'll talk your ear off about your travels and hers while plonking down eggs, freshly-blended fruit juice and steaming coffee.

★ La Pizza del Abuelo PIZZA $$

(☑987-318-077; San Martín 1029; pizzas S31-40; ⊙6-11pm; 🍴) Most visitors to Caraz, descending from the clouds after trekking at high altitudes, crave carbohydrates. Enter the Abuelo (grandfather), a dark woody restaurant that plies what they call Argentinian-style pizzas with some fruity ingredients – just the ticket after a week surviving on camp food. Vegan options are available and they also serve two or three pasta dishes including lasagna.

There's another branch in Huaraz.

Entre Panes INTERNATIONAL $$

(Villar 211; mains S20-25; ⊙1-4pm & 6:30-10pm Mon-Sat) This gourmet bistro with checkered tablecloths and colorful blackboard menus is a respite from the usual suspects. It serves

Caraz

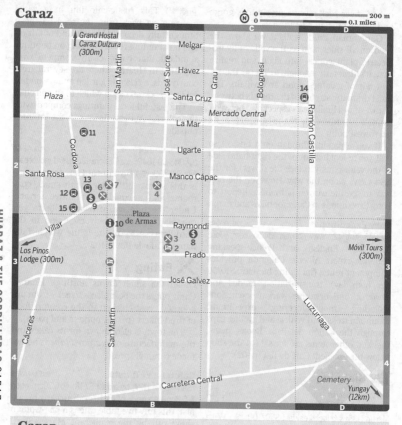

Caraz

🗘 Activities, Courses & Tours

Pony Expeditions ....(see 3)

🛏 Sleeping

1 Hostal Chavín B3
2 Pony's Lodge B3

🍽 Eating

3 Café de Rat B3
4 Café La Terraza B2
5 Cafetería El Turista................................ B3
6 Entre Panes A2
7 La Pizza del Abuelo.............................. B2

ℹ Information

8 Banco de la Nación B3
9 BCP A2
10 Oficina de Turismo................................. B3

ℹ Transport

11 Colectivos to Huallanca........................ A2
12 Cooperativa Ancash.............................. A2
13 Expreso Yungay.................................... A2
14 Terminal Santa Cruz............................. D1
15 Transportes Julio Cesar....................... A2

up interesting sandwiches (as its name implies) including sesame pork and *lomo salado*, plus more substantial fare such as beef in Roquefort sauce and quinoa curry.

Café de Rat   CAFE $$

(José Sucre 1266; pizza S17-32; ⏰ 8-11am & 6-10pm Mon-Sat) Don't mind the name, the menu

has been cleared of rodents. What remains are sandwiches, pasta and, most popular of all, pizza. The cafe is run by Alberto of the downstairs Pony Expeditions (p401) and is something of a traveler's hub with a book exchange, darts, a bar and music.

Opt for a pew by the fireplace or sit on the upstairs balcony with plaza views.

You'll need to ring the doorbell to gain entry.

Café La Terraza
CAFE $$

(☎043-30-1226; José Sucre 1107; mains S13-18; ⊙7am-10pm Tue-Sun) The ambiance might be a bit wooden, but this doesn't stop the locally loved Terraza filling up at lunchtime for three-course S8 meals, or anything else on its extensive but reasonably priced menu (pizza, pancakes, trout and desserts). Affiliated to the Grand Hostal Caraz Dulzura (p401), it also pedals the town's best coffee and has a handy side-window dispatching ice cream.

ℹ Information

MONEY

Both **BCP** (cnr Villar & Cordova; ⊙9am-6pm Mon-Fri, to 1pm Sat) and **Banco de la Nación** (Raymondi 1051; ⊙9am-5:30pm Mon-Fri, to 1pm Sat) change cash and have ATMs.

TOURIST INFORMATION

The staff at the **Oficina de Turismo** (☎043-48-3860 ext 143; Plaza de Armas; ⊙7:45am-1pm & 2:30-7pm) are very helpful and will give advice about the entire region.

ℹ Getting There & Away

BUS

Transportes Julio Cesar (☎94-492-8824; www.transportesjuliocesar.com.pe; cnr Cordova y Villar) Has bus services to Lima (S45 to S60, 10 hours, twice daily) and Trujillo (S45 to S55, 5½ hours, once daily).

Móvil Tours (☎043-39-1184; Pasaje Santa Teresita 334) Has luxury bus service to Lima (S40 to S70, 10 hours, six daily) via Huaraz. Another bus heads to Trujillo (S50 to S65, nine hours) via Chimbote at 8:20pm

Cooperativa Ancash (☎043-39-1126; www.transportesancash.pe; Cordova 915) Has three daily buses to Lima (S45, 9½ hours) via Yungay, Carhuaz and Huaraz, leaving at 11am, 7pm and 8pm.

Expreso Yungay (☎043-39-1492; Cordova 830) Has a service to Chimbote (S25, six hours, once daily) via the Cañón del Pato and other buses via Casma (S20, four hours, three daily).

TAXI

Colectivo taxis for Cashapampa (S10, 1½ hours) for the northern end of the Santa Cruz Trek leave when full from the **Terminal Santa Cruz** (Ramón Castilla), near the market. Colectivos to Pueblo Parón (S10, one hour), which is about 9km from the famous Laguna Parón, leave from the same terminal. It's best to get there early in the morning when departures are more frequent.

Colectivos to Huallanca (S10, one hour), for the Cañón del Pato, leave from the small **terminal** (Córdova 818) on Jirón Cordova when full.

Mototaxis (S1.50) trundle around town, but Caraz is easily managed on foot.

SOUTH OF HUARAZ

Covering the southern extent of the Cordillera Blanca and the majestic Cordillera Huayhuash, this part of the Andes refuses to be outdone in the 'breathtaking mountain scenery' stakes. Several peaks here pass the 6000m mark, huddling to form a near-continuous, saw-toothed ridge of precipitous summits. Yerupajá (6617m), Peru's second-highest mountain, is the icing on the Cordillera cake and is followed in height by its second lieutenant Siula Grande (6344m). The rugged and rewarding 10-day Cordillera Huayhuash Circuit (p393), accessed through the town of Llamac, is the glittering star attraction.

Recuay (population 2900), a town 25km from Huaraz, is one of the few municipalities to have survived the 1970 earthquake largely unscathed. Catac (population 2300), 10km south of Recuay, is an even smaller hamlet and the starting point for trips to see the remarkable *Puya raimondii* plant.

Chiquián

☎043 / POP 3641 / ELEV 3400M

A subdued hill town, Chiquián was traditionally the base of operations for folk trekking the Cordillera Huayhuash Circuit. Now, however, it is frequently bypassed by hikers heading directly to the trailheads at Pocpa and Llamac on a much improved road, though if you plan on spending the night in the area, you will be infinitesimally more comfortable here. Spectacular eyefuls of the Huayhuash come into view as you drive into town.

⊙ Sights

Mirador de San Juan Cruz
VIEWPOINT

Many Peruvian towns have a cross on a hill with a path leading tantalizingly to the top, but no others have a pinch-yourself view of the snowy Huayhuash range rising above a sea of lesser peaks. To get to the giant cross above Chiquián, follow Jirón Tacna from the Plaza de Armas, take the staircase uphill, veer right at the top and follow the path round.

The tallest peak, Yanupajá (the second-highest mountain in Peru), rises like an icy meat cleaver above all opposition. The peak to the right is the infamous Siula Grande.

🛏 Sleeping

★ Hotel Los Nogales
GUESTHOUSE $

(📞 043-44-7121; www.hotelnogaleschiquian.com; Comercio 1301; s/d from S50/80; 🔌) The big surprise in regularly bypassed Chiquián is not its gaping lack of restaurants, but this pretty flower-bedizened hotel that might have materialized from Cartagena or some other well-trodden colonial city. Rooms in the bright hacienda-style building are clustered warmly around a gorgeous patio stuffed with plants and statues. They marry modern fixtures (some have jacuzzi tubs) with a pleasant rural feel.

You can arrange the best dinners in town here (guests only), plus there's a cute little shop in the reception that sells local crafts. Staff are charming and a resident harpist regularly strokes the strings for tired-out trekkers enjoying their dinner.

Gran Hotel Huayhuash
HOTEL $

(📞 043-44-7049; cnr 28 de Julio & Amadeo; s/d S40/60, d without bathroom S45, all incl breakfast; @🔌) The 'Gran' (great) might be a bit of a euphemism, but what this multistory building lacks in atmosphere, it makes up for in basic comforts. Large rooms have hot water and flat-screen TVs as standard, although there is no cable. Some rooms also afford fine mountain vistas.

🍴 Eating

Panadería y Pastelería
Sierra Andina
BAKERY, CAFE $

(Comercio 780; cakes S2-3; ⊙9am-9pm) Apart from the Hotel Nogales, Chiquián lacks any restaurant that looks half inviting. At a pinch, you can decamp to this bakery where the cakes and breads look nicer than the decor. Expect local stray dogs to come wandering in as you tuck into your caramel roll.

ℹ Getting There & Away

If you're interested in heading straight to Chiquián and the Cordillera Huayhuash, you'll find direct buses from Lima. However, as you'll probably need a few days to acclimatize, note that Huaraz offers a wider selection of distractions. Turismo Cavassa (p395) has buses direct to Lima (S30, eight hours) at 8am and 8pm as well as services to La Unión, from where there are connections to Huánuco.

If you're starting the Huayhuash Circuit, catch the 8am **Turismo Nazario** (📞 043-77-0311;

Comercio 1050) bus to Pocpa via Llamac (S15, 1¼ hours). The same company runs a bus to Huaraz at 2pm (S10, 2½ hours) that connects with the bus arriving from Pocpa and Llamac. **Transportes El Rapido** (📞 043-44-7096; Comercio) goes to Huaraz at 5am and 2pm (S15).

The ride between Huaraz and Chiquián, whether the fogged-in morning run from Huaraz (sit on the left) or the afternoon ride back from Chiquián (sit on the right), affords some of the most beautiful scenery you will see in Peru.

Llamac
📍 043 / POP 200 / ELEV 3300M

The ramshackle brick-and-mud village of Llamac was once the launching point for the Huayhuash Circuit, but now that the public bus continues on to the trailhead at Pocpa, closer to the Matacancha rest site, many hikers only visit Llamac to pick up transportation back to Chiquián upon exiting the circuit.

There are few services here, though there's a small Plaza de Armas with a diminutive church draped in bougainvillea. The trail leading to Laguna Yahuacocha sits behind the municipal building on the same plaza.

There is a S20 entry fee for foreigners to enter Huayhuash, the first in the fee circuit. You will be expected to pay even if just passing through on the bus – hold on to your receipt to avoid paying again when you finish your trek.

🛏 Sleeping & Eating

Hotel Nazario
GUESTHOUSE $

(📞 990-300-731; Grau s/n; r per person with/without bathroom S20/15) In an unmissable large concrete building, Hotel Nazario has neat rooms with good natural light and mountain views. There is a communal TV room and it also serves meals (S5 to S10). The helpful owners can organize *arrieros* and pack animals for treks.

Hotel Nazario can prepare a meal with a few hours' notice. There are few other options.

ℹ Getting There & Away

A fair percentage of trekkers in these parts arrive on organized trips with transport provided.

If you're venturing out solo, **Turismo Nazario** (📞 990-300-731; Grau s/n) departs Huaraz for Chiquián daily at 5am where you can connect onto Llamac and Pocpa (S30, 5½ hours). Upon arrival in Pocpa, the bus turns right around and passes back through Llamac at 11:15am, before continuing to Chiquián and Huaraz.

CALLEJÓN DE CONCHUCOS

The Conchucos Valley (locally called the Callejón de Conchucos) runs parallel to the Callejón de Huaylas on the eastern side of the Cordillera. Sprinkled liberally with remote and rarely visited towns and archaeological sites, this captivating valley is steeped in history and blessed with postcard-perfect Andean villages so tranquil that they'd fall into comas if they were any sleepier. Interlaced with excellent yet rarely visited hiking trails, this untapped region begs for exploration. Tourist infrastructure is still in its infancy, with a handful of welcoming but modest hotels and erratic transportation along rough, unpaved roads that can be impassable in the wet season – and are plagued by breakdowns and accidents. If you do make the effort to get here, the highland hospitality of Quechua-speaking *campesinos* and awe-inspiring scenery will more than make up for the butt-smacking, time-consuming bumps in the road.

Chavín de Huántar

☑ 043 / POP 9220 / ELEV 3250M

In most people's minds, Chavín is less a town and more a set of ruins – not any old ruins, but the erstwhile ceremonial center of one of Peru's most sophisticated early civilizations, and a Unesco World Heritage Site to boot.

Most visitors zip by on a day trip, ignoring the diminutive colonial town with its whimsical plaza and somnolent streets that sits somewhere on the charm-o-meter between gorgeous Chacas and slightly less gorgeous Huari. If you decide to overnight here, you can visit the impressive archaeological site in the early morning and have it all to yourself.

⊙ Sights & Activities

From Chavín you can hike for a few hours into a lofty valley, in the direction of Olleros, to a high pass with stirring views of Huantsán (6395m) – the highest mountain in the southern Cordillera Blanca.

Longer hiking trips with mules and guides can be organized through Cafetería Renato (p406).

★ **Chavín de Huántar** ARCHAEOLOGICAL SITE (admission S15; ⊙9am-4pm Tue-Sun) The quintessential site of Peru's Mid-Late Formative Period (c 1200–500 BC), Chavín de Huántar is the most intriguing of the many relatively independent, competitive ceremonial centers constructed throughout the central Andes. It is a phenomenal achievement of ancient construction, with large temple-like structures above ground and labyrinthine (now electronically lit) underground passageways. Although not as initially impressive as sites like Machu Picchu and Kuélap, Chavín tells an engrossing story when combined with its excellent affiliated museum (p406).

Chavín is a series of older and newer temple arrangements built between 1200 BC and 500 BC, but most structures visible today came from a big building effort between 900 and 700 BC. In the middle is a massive Plaza Mayor (central square), slightly sunken below ground level, which like the overall site has an intricate, extensive and well-engineered system of channels for drainage. From the square, a broad staircase, the Escalinata Blanca y Negra, leads up to the portal in front of the largest and most important building, called Edificio A, which has withstood some mighty earthquakes over the years. Built on three different levels of stone-and-mortar masonry (sometimes incorporating cut stone blocks), the walls here were at one time embellished with tenon heads (blocks carved to resemble human heads with animal or perhaps hallucinogen-induced characteristics backed by stone spikes for insertion into a wall). Only one of these remains in its original place, although around 30 others may be seen in the local museum related to the site.

A series of tunnels underneath Edificio A are an exceptional feat of engineering, comprising a maze of complex corridors, ducts and chambers. In the heart of this complex is an exquisitely carved, 4.5m monolith of white granite known as the Lanzón de Chavín. In typical terrifying Chavín fashion, the low-relief carvings on the Lanzón represent a person with snakes radiating from his head and a ferocious set of fangs, most likely feline. The Lanzón, almost certainly an object of worship given its prominent, central placement in this ceremonial center, is sometimes referred to as the Smiling God – but its aura feels anything but friendly.

Several beguiling construction quirks, such as the strange positioning of water channels and the use of highly polished mineral mirrors to reflect light, led Stanford archaeologists to believe that the complex was used as an instrument of shock and awe. To instill fear in nonbelievers, priests manipulated sights and sounds. They blew on echoing Strombus trumpets (made from shells), amplified the sounds of water running through specially designed channels and reflected sunlight through ventilation shafts. The disoriented cult novitiates were probably given hallucinogens such as San Pedro cactus shortly before entering the darkened maze. These tactics endowed the priests with awe-inspiring power.

To get the most from your visit, it's worth hiring a local guide to show you around (S40) or go on a guided day trip (including transportation) from Huaraz; this latter option is by far the most budget-friendly way to see these ruins, although it means you'll be wandering with the crowds. For more solitude, stay in town overnight and view the ruins before midday. The Sala de Interpretación Marino González near the entrance is also a good source of background information.

Museo Nacional de Chavín
MUSEUM
(☑043-45-4011; 17 de Enero s/n; ☺9am-5pm Tue-Sun) FREE This outstanding museum, funded jointly by the Peruvian and Japanese governments, houses most of the intricate tenon heads carved with horror-stricken expressions from Chavín de Huántar (p405), as well as the magnificent Tello Obelisk, another stone object of worship with low relief carvings of a caiman and other fierce animals. The obelisk had been housed in a Lima museum since the 1945 earthquake that destroyed much of the original museum, and was only returned to Chavín in 2008.

The museum is located around 2km from the ruins on the north side of town – an easy 25-minute walk.

🛏 Sleeping

Hostal Inca
GUESTHOUSE $
(☑043-45-4021; Plaza de Armas; s/d S40/75) The street profile is alluring enough – a whitewashed colonial building in Chavín's main square with some flowery arrangements in the courtyard. However, when you get down to the nitty-gritty the Inca is overdue a refurb, with dusty rooms, slightly lumpy beds and no hot water. Breakfast is S12 extra.

Hostal Chavín Turístico
GUESTHOUSE $$
(☑043-45-4051; chavinturistico1@gmail.com; Mayta Capac 120; r S90) This go-to, family-run

option for the few travelers who stay overnight in Chavín has well-appointed rooms with cute bedspreads, large bathrooms and – perhaps most refreshingly – no chipped paint or rusty pipes. The rooms are one block away from the same-name restaurant where you check in. No wi-fi.

🍴 Eating

Cafetería Renato
BREAKFAST, PERUVIAN $
(☑943-974-062; Plaza de Armas; breakfast S9-15; ☺8am-9pm) For simple international breakfasts alongside homemade yogurt, cheese and *manjar blanco*, head to this better-than-it-looks cafe done out like a cowboy corral with saddles slung over walls and maps decorating the walls. The owners also organize horseback riding and hiking trips in the area.

★Buongiorno
PERUVIAN $$
(Calle 17 de Enero Sur s/n; mains S20-35; ☺7am-7pm Tue-Sun) Churning out sophisticated dishes that outpunch its location's weight class, Buongiorno is a pleasant surprise in a cordial garden setting. The *lomo a la pimienta*, a Peruvian fave of grilled steak in wine, cream and cracked-pepper sauce (S35), is three-star Lima quality and the menu also has some strong Italian inflections courtesy of the owner who spent several years abroad.

The cooks here often dart out to the extensive gardens and grab some fresh organic herbs – a nice touch. It's 50m across the bridge from the entrance to the ruins. The restaurant mainly focuses on the busy dinner trade (when it fills with tour groups). If you're planning on dinner, check ahead as closing times are flexible.

🛍 Shopping

Artesania Rumi Tzaka
ARTS & CRAFTS
(☑999-657-443; 17 de Enero; ☺9am-4pm) Of the several shops that cluster around the ruins site, this one could be the best, selling unique Chavín souvenirs from textile and wool items to huge replicas of the Lanzón de Chavín rendered in granite. Most of the crafts are homemade by the owners – the textile work by the señora and the carvings by the señor.

ℹ Information

MONEY

The **Banco de la Nación** (Plaza de Armas; ☺7am-5:30pm Mon-Fri, 9am-1pm Sat) ohas an ATM and will change US dollars.

In the municipal building next to the plaza, the **tourist information office** (☑ ext 106 043-45-4235; Bolivar s/n; ⊙ 8am-12:30pm & 2:30-5:30pm Mon-Fri) has details about attractions throughout the area.

❶ Getting There & Away

The paved road across the Cordillera Blanca to Chavín passes the Laguna Querococha at 3980m from where there are views of the peaks of Pucaraju (5322m) and Yanamarey (5237m). The road continues through the Kahuish Tunnel (4516m above sea level), which cuts through the Kahuish Pass. As you exit the tunnel and descend toward Chavín, look out for the massive statue of Christ blessing your journey. It was built by Italian missionaries.

In Chavín, most transportation leaves from the ugly new **bus station** (AN-110) several blocks south of the plaza. All local buses pick up and drop off where the highway bends at the plaza. **Olguita Tours** (☑ 941-870-525; Gran Terminal Terrestre, AN-110) has regular departures to Huaraz (S12, 2½ hours, six daily) as well as Huari (S5, two hours, four daily) to the north. **Transportes Sandoval** (☑ 043-42-8069; Gran Terminal Terrestre, AN-110) offers similar services. *Combis/colectivos* head to Huaraz (S20/25, 2½ hours) from the oddly named Plaza Chupa, a block north of the quaint Plaza de Armas.

Both **Movil Tours** (☑ 958-809-378; www.moviltours.com.pe; Gran Terminal Terrestre, AN-110) and **Turismo Rosario** (☑ 944-988-425; Gran Terminal Terrestre, AN-110) have 7:40pm departures to Lima (S55 to S75, nine hours). The former is far superior, with comfortable and reliable coaches equipped with reclining seats.

To continue north along the east side of the Cordillera Blanca, most of the buses originating in Huaraz continue to Huari (S5, two hours). *Colectivos* leave frequently from near the Plaza de Armas to San Marcos (S2, 20 minutes) from where you can catch *colectivos* to Huari (S5, 45 minutes). Other than these buses, there is no other public transportation beyond Huari.

Hikers can walk to Chavín from Olleros in the Callejón de Hualyas in about three days; it's an uncrowded **trek** (p392).

Huari

☑ 043 / POP 10,300 / ELEV 3150M

A small Quechua-speaking town barely clinging to the mountainside, Huari has nearly 360-degree mountain panoramas from its steep streets. Market day here is Sunday, when *campesinos* from surrounding towns descend on Huari to hawk fruits

and vegetables. The annual town fiesta, Señora del Rosario, is held in early October and has a strange tradition of cat consumption (residents from Huari are jokingly referred to in Quechua as *Mishikanka*, which literally means 'Deep-Fried Cats' but more figuratively 'Cat Eaters'). The town has a small and modern Plaza de Armas and a larger Plaza Vigil (known as El Parque) one block away, where you'll find the bus-company offices (buses leave from a terminal a few blocks away) and banks.

◉ Sights & Activities

Laguna Purhuay   LAKE

In a scoop of a valley 8km above Huari and just inside the Parque Nacional Huascarán, this idyllic lake is well set up for day excursions, but is surprisingly little visited. You can rent kayaks from the friendly park attendant (S10 per hour), follow the lakeshore to the pre-Hispanic ruins of Mama Shoco, or enjoy local trout at a lakeside restaurant. Camping (S40 per night) is also available.

It's possible to walk to the lake from Huari along an unpaved road (a path cuts off some of the corners). Alternatively, hire a taxi for around S60 round-trip. Be sure to stop in the village of Acopalca on the way up, known for its trout farms and plethora of fish restaurants specializing in cerviche.

The two- or three-day **Huari to Chacas trek** (p390) that forges across the mountains via the San Bartolomé Pass starts on the lakeshore.

🛏 Sleeping & Eating

Hospedaje Genais   HOTEL $

(cnr Condamine & Ancash; r S45; 🛜) Just getting off the ground at last visit, the Genais has filled a run-of-the-mill Huari tenement with small but wonderfully comfortable rooms, all with plush bedspreads, tiled floors and modern bathrooms. The stand-out features, however, are the wooden doors, carved and hand-painted with various intricate designs. Hands down Huari's best hotel.

Chifa Dragón Andino   CHINESE $

(☑043 45-4110; Libertad 660; mains S10-18; ⊙noon-10pm Mon-Sat) Decked out in classic *chifa* style (bland canteen-style tables and zilch decor except for a couple of Chinese lanterns), Dragón Andino is better than it looks and serves some of the tastiest Chinese food in the eastern Cordillera.

ℹ️ Information

Turismo Andino (☎ 99-342-7102; Ancash 836, Plaza Vigil; ⊙ 9am-noon & 2-5pm Mon-Sat) Has a town map and info on surrounding attractions.

ℹ️ Getting There & Away

For fast connections to Chavín and Huaraz, get a *colectivo* to San Marcos from behind the **market** (Magisterial; S6, 45 minutes). **Olguita Tours** (☎ 954-470-914; Plaza Vigil) has six daily buses from Huari to Huaraz (S15, 4½ hours) via Chavín (S5, two hours).

Movil Tours (Av Circunvalación) have recently introduced a comfortable daily bus to Lima

(S65 to S85, 11 hours) via Chavín de Huántar, leaving at 6:20pm.

If you want to forge ahead on your own timeframe to San Luis, where you can catch onward travel to Chacas and Pomabomba, a taxi will cost anywhere between S250 and S300 depending on your negotiation skills. The road is rough but beautiful.

Chacas

☎ 043 / POP 2100 / ELEV 3360M

This ornate mountain town sits atop a hillcrest at 3360m, surrounded by fertile hills and with guest appearances by the

---

THE DON BOSCO WOOD-CARVING COOPERATIVE

It's hard to separate the recent history of Chacas from the name of the late Padre Ugo De Censi, an Italian priest of the Salesian order who founded the esteemed Don Bosco wood-carving cooperative (www.artesanosdonbosco.org) in the town in the late 1970s.

De Censi first came to Peru in 1976 after several years working as a missionary in Brazil where he established Operación Mato Grosso, a non-governmental organization dedicated to tackling poverty. Entranced by the rugged mountain terrain of the Andes (which reminded him of the Italian Alps), but troubled by the high levels of poverty in the region, De Censi settled in Chacas where he became the parish priest and founded a school for young people to pursue the art of wood carving. It was an inspired decision. Calling on a network of volunteers and fund-raisers he had already built up in Brazil, the school quickly prospered, matriculating 25 new pupils a year – young boys (and later girls) aged between 12 and 18 drawn from the region's poorest families – and offering them five years of free study. The pupils were trained in everything from wood carving to furniture making by international volunteers, mostly drawn from Italy, and their new skills were quickly put to good use.

Don Bosco's first big project was the rebuilding of Chacas' **Santuario de Mama Ashu** (Ancash; ⊙ 7am-7pm), badly damaged in the 1970 earthquake. Rather than rebuild the church in a bland modern style common to so many other earthquake-wracked Cordillera towns, the santuario re-emerged, under De Censi's expert tutelage, as a handsome Renaissance-inspired structure adorned with beautiful wooden doors and embellished inside with rich choir stalls and a meticulously restored baroque altarpiece.

With the church complete, the co-op turned its attention to the town, restoring Chacas' signature white houses characterized by their intricately carved wooden balustrades and balconies. During the 1980s and '90s, the Don Bosco school mushroomed to include workshops for stonecutting, glass making, art restoration, textiles, and even mountain guiding; five tourist **refuges** (☎ 971-110-088; www.rifugi-omg.org; dm S100 per bed; ⊙ May-Sep) 🅿 were built in the Cordillera Blanca. The work continues today, not just in Chacas but all across the Ancash region, with profits from the Don Bosco schemes plowed directly back into the local community. Over the years, the funds have helped to finance power stations, medical clinics and irrigation projects.

The Don Bosco co-op continues to list over 500 active graduates on its books and makes its artisan products for churches, public buildings and private homes, many of them for export. It is supported by numerous international volunteers who come out to Peru on long- and short-term secondments to lend their help and expertise and, in 2016, an Italian Consulate opened in Chacas to cater for the need.

Padre Ugo De Censi became a Peruvian citizen in 2007 and his work has been recognized and rewarded by the government many times. In Chacas, his legacy is everywhere, from the grand Mama Ashu church where a huge painting illustrates his story, to the thriving artisan workshops and schools that give this town its special flavor.

occasional snowcapped Cordillera peak. The charismatic main plaza is dominated by a brilliant church built by a religious non-profit Italian aid organization, Don Bosco, based in Marcará and established by the pioneering Padre Ugo De Censi, a priest of the Salesian order. As a result, the town has a strong Italian influence; since 2016, it has even had its own Italian consulate.

Chacas' architecture is very distinctive, its white-walled houses adorned with intricate wooden balconies and brightly colored doors and window shutters lovingly preserved by Don Bosco. Look out for the Andean women who sit meditatively spinning wool on every second corner. This is an excellent place to while away a few days enjoying what is possibly the most alluring small town in the Cordilleras.

🛏 Sleeping

Accommodations in Chacas are on the up. The current crop of hotels, while modest, don't lack atmosphere, while the plush new Hotel Plaza in the Plaza de Armas could stand shoulder to shoulder with any midrange option in Huaraz.

Hotel Plaza   HOTEL **$**
(📞921-970-956; cnr Bolognesi & Lima; s/d incl breakfast S35/80; 🛜) Leading Chacas' recent renaissance, the Plaza is a new hotel (you can still smell the paint) set in an old, quintessential Chacas building with whitewashed adobe walls and rich wooden balconies. The rooms play for function over features, but are clean, comfortable and spacious. It also includes a restaurant and tour agency, and can help with any transportation conundrums.

Hostal Asunción   GUESTHOUSE **$**
(📞956-490-064; Bolognesi 370; s/d with bathroom S30/50, without bathroom S25/40; 🛜) This place on the Plaza de Armas, in a typical Chacas house with ornate wooden balconies, has neat and appealing rooms, especially the pair at the front whose windows open onto the plaza with church views.

Eating

Restaurante-Cevichería D'Faveg   CEVICHE **$**
(cnr Buenos Aires & Ancash; menus S6; ⏰noon-4pm) You're in small-town Peru with no fancy restaurants and no diners, drive-ins or dives – just places like D'Faveg with its half-dozen tables, friendly usher-you-in staff and ultra-cheap three-course lunches that include *seco de pollo* (spicy stewed chicken), flattened steaks and, obviously, ceviche.

Pizzeria San Francisco   PIZZA **$$**
(Ancash; pizzas S20; ⏰6-10pm Sat & Sun) Proper artisan pizzas made by a local Italian religious mission in a space next to the church. It's only open on weekend evenings (alas!), but the sizable pies are large and authentic. Worth timing your trip to Chacas around.

ℹ Information

There is a small, friendly branch of Banco de la Nación, but no ATM. The closest is in San Luis.

ℹ Getting There & Away

Transportes El Veloz (Buenos Aires s/n) goes to Huaraz (S15 to S20, 3½ hours) around three times a day, via the Tunel Punta Olímpica and Carhuaz.

Both companies also have services to Pomabamba (S20, four hours), which originate in Huaraz and pass through around 10am. There is a further Pomabamba service at around 10pm, but it's not recommended to travel on this road at night due to robberies and accidents.

Combis for San Luis (S5, one hour) depart from **Bolognesi at Buenos Aires**, one block east of the plaza. There is no transportation from this side of the valley to Yanama, although any Pomabamba-bound bus can drop you at the turnoff, from where it's a 22km trek up to the town. A taxi from San Luis will set you back at least S200.

Several agencies in town advertize Lima-bound buses passing through Chacas (S45, 14 hours), but these companies don't always have good safety records. You're better off traveling to Huaraz and transferring to a more reputable company there, such as Cruz del Sur (p383).

AT A GLANCE

POPULATION
Cajamarca: 249,000

**TALLEST
WATERFALL**
Gocta: 771m (p429)

**BEST AMAZONIAN
FOOD**
La Patarashca
(p443)

BEST COFFEE
Aromacafé (p438)

**BEST
ACCOMMODATION
WITH A VIEW**
Gocta Andes Lodge
(p429)

WHEN TO GO
Jan–Apr
Rain-soaked but
vibrantly lush and full
of life, with waterfalls
in great gushing
glory.

Feb & Mar
Let the rowdy may-
hem commence:
Carnaval is on in
Cajamarca.

Jun–Oct
The rains – and the
landslides – are a
thing of the past.
Enjoy the sunshine.

Leimebamba (p432)
MATYAS REHAK/SHUTTERSTOCK ©

Northern Highlands

V ast tracts of unexplored jungle and mist-shrouded mountain ranges guard the secrets of the Northern Highlands like a suspicious custodian. Interspersed with the relics of Inca kings and the jungle-encrusted ruins of cloud-forest-dwelling warriors, connections to these outposts are just emerging from their infancy.

Cajamarca's cobbled streets testify to the beginning of the end of the once-powerful Inca Empire, and remnants of the work of these famed Andean masons still remain. The hazy forests of Chachapoyas have only recently revealed their archaeological bounty. At the jungle gateway of Tarapoto, the Amazon waits patiently on the periphery, as it has for centuries, endowed with a cornucopia of wildlife and exquisite good looks.

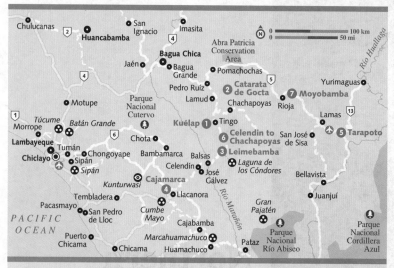

Northern Highlands Highlights

1 Kuélap (p431) Taking a spectacular cable-car ride up to this immense stone citadel founded by the pre-Inca Chachapoyas civilization.

2 Catarata de Gocta (p429) Trekking through the cloud forest to this lofty but still little-visited waterfall near Chachapoyas.

3 Leimebamba (p432) Enjoying hummingbirds,

good coffee and one of the best museums in northern Peru in this ultrafriendly small mountain town.

4 Cajamarca Exploring the story of America's great clash of civilizations in the 'capital' of the Northern Highlands.

5 Tarapoto (p439) Booking into a jungle lodge and bathing in a pristine river on the edge of the Amazon rainforest.

6 Celendín to Chachapoyas (p422) Traveling with your heart in your mouth on one of Peru's narrowest and most spine-chilling roads.

7 Moyobamba (p436) Stopping for the night to soak up orchids, Amazonian cuisine and laid-back jungle ambience.

Cajamarca

📞 076 / POP 249,000 / ELEV 2750M

A dainty but strong-willed metropolis, Cajamarca is cradled in a languid valley and stonewalled by brawny mountains in every direction. The most important town in the Northern Highlands, its mushroom field of red-tile-roofed abodes surely confesses a secret desire to cling to its village roots. Fertile farmland carpets the entire valley and Cajamarca's streets belong as much to the wide-brimmed-hat-wearing *campesinos* (peasants) bundled in brightly colored scarves as they do to the young city slickers who frequent the town's boutique restaurants and bars.

In the colonial center, majestic churches border the capacious Plaza de Armas. From

here, once-decadent baroque mansions spread out along the narrow streets, many housing elegant hotels and fine restaurants. Cajamarca is famous for its cheese, gold (one of the world's largest mines lies nearby), baroque churches – and as the place where Inca emperor Atahualpa faced off against the Spanish colonizers. It's a potent brew.

⊙ Sights

Catedral de Cajamarca CATHEDRAL
(Batán; ⊙ 8am-noon & 3-6pm) This squat but ornate building was begun in the late 17th century and only recently finished. Like most of Cajamarca's churches, the cathedral has no belfry. This is because the Spanish Crown levied a tax on finished churches and so the belfries were not built, leaving

the church unfinished and thereby avoiding the tax.

The church's interior lacks the ornamentation of its exterior – until you near the rich baroque altarpiece covered in gold leaf.

El Cuarto del Rescate
RUINS

(Ransom Chamber; Puga; S5; ⊘9am-1pm & 3-8pm Tue & Wed, 9am-8pm Thu-Sat, 9am-1pm Sun) The Ransom Chamber, the only Inca building still standing in Cajamarca, is where Inca ruler Atahualpa (p416) was imprisoned. The small room has three trapezoidal doorways and a few similarly shaped niches in the inner walls – signature Inca construction. Visitors are not permitted to enter the room, but from outside it's possible to observe the red line marking the original ceiling of the structure – the point to which it was to be filled with treasure to secure Atahualpa's release.

At the entrance to the site are a couple of modern paintings depicting Atahualpa's capture and imprisonment. The stone of the building is weathered as it has only recently been covered by a large protective dome. The ticket to El Cuarto del Rescate includes El Complejo de Belén and Museo de Arqueológico & Etnográfico if they are all visited on the same day.

El Complejo de Belén
HISTORIC BUILDING

(cnr Belén & Comercio; S5; ⊘9am-1pm & 3-8pm Tue & Wed, 9am-8pm Thu-Sat, 9am-1pm Sun) Construction of this sprawling colonial complex, comprising a church and hospital made entirely from volcanic rock, occurred between 1627 and 1774. The hospital was run by nuns and 31 tiny, cell-like bedrooms line the walls of the T-shaped building. The baroque church next door is one of Cajamarca's finest and has a prominent cupola and a well-carved pulpit. Art exhibitions usually adorn the interior.

Among several interesting wood carvings in the church is one of an extremely tired-looking Christ sitting cross-legged on a throne, propping up his chin with a double-jointed wrist and looking as though he could do with a pisco sour after a hard day's miracle-working. Look out for the oversized cherubs supporting the elaborate centerpiece, which represents the weight of heaven. The outside walls of the church are lavishly decorated.

Iglesia de San Francisco
CHURCH, MUSEUM

(Calle 2 de Mayo; S5; ⊘museum 10am-2pm & 4-6pm, church 10am-2pm & 5-8pm) Outgunning the cathedral on Plaza de Armas is this elaborate church with striking stone carvings and decadent altars. Unlike other illustrious Cajamarca churches, the San Francisco has two belfries. It houses the slightly dog-eared **Museo de Arte Religioso** full of 17th-century religious paintings by indigenous artists. The museum includes some creepy catacombs – in one room you'll see the orderly tombs of monks, and in another are skeletons recovered from indigenous graves found at the site, lying bare and without ceremony.

The intricately sculpted Capilla de la Dolorosa located to the right of the nave is considered one of the finest chapels in the city. Look out for a depiction of the Last Supper carved in stone on the left side of the altar.

Museo de Arqueológico & Etnográfico
MUSEUM

(cnr Belén y Commercio; admission S5; ⊘9am-1pm & 3-6pm Tue-Sat, 9am-1pm Sun) This small museum has exhibits of pre-Columbian pottery and stone statues, as well as displays on local costumes and clothing, domestic and agricultural implements and musical instruments. The most disturbing exhibit is the mummified remains of a baby in a ceramic vase.

The museum is housed inside the Antigua Hospital de Mujeres, just a few meters from El Complejo de Belén. Its ornate facade has a fascinating statue of a woman with four breasts – carved by local artisans, it supposedly represents an affliction (supernumerary nipples, that is) commonly found in one of the nearby towns.

Cerro Santa Apolonia
VIEWPOINT

(admission S1; ⊘7am-7pm) This garden-covered viewpoint, overlooking the city from the southwest, is a prominent Cajamarca landmark. It is easily reached by climbing the stairs at the end of Calle 2 de Mayo and following the path that spirals around the hilltop. The pre-Hispanic carved rocks at the summit are mainly from the Inca period, but some are thought to originally date back to the Chavín period.

☞ Tours

Plaza de Armas is ringed by tour agencies all offering pretty much the same full- and half-day trips. Many companies claim to have English-speaking guides, but, as most

Cajamarca

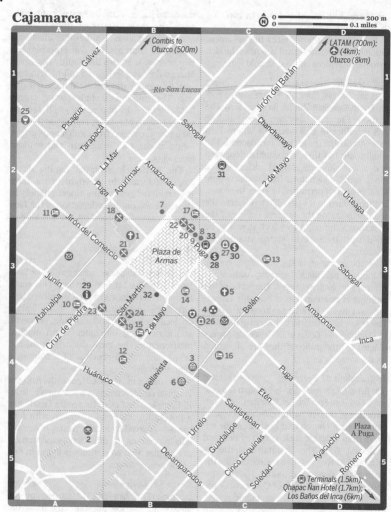

tourism in these parts is Peruvian, the reality is a little different.

Tours (S20) to Cumbemayo (p420) run from 9am to 1:30pm daily, meaning you can squeeze in a 3:30pm to 7pm tour (S17) to the Ventanillas de Otuzco (p420) in the afternoon. Tours (S70) to the ruins of Kuntur Wasi (p421) take all day, but run less frequently. Check ahead of time.

There are several other half-day tours to cheese factories, mini zoos (containing mostly domesticated animals) and local lakes, all costing in the vicinity of S20.

Sergio Tours   SIGHTSEEING TOUR
(📞 076-36-7598; www.sergiotours.com; Puga 643; ⏰ 8am-10pm) One of a dozen tour agencies on Plaza de Armas. This outfit often runs day trips to the ruins of Kuntur Wasi (p421).

Clarín Tours   SIGHTSEEING TOUR
(📞 076-36-6829; www.clarintours.com; Del Batán 161) Friendly tour company with low prices and good customer service.

Mega Tours   SIGHTSEEING TOUR
(📞 076-34-1876; www.megatours.org; Puga 691) A popular option for cheap sightseeing tours.

Cajamarca

⚞ Festivals & Events

Carnaval   FESTIVAL

The Peru-wide pageantry of Carnaval is celebrated at the beginning of Lent, usually in February. Not all Carnavals are created equal, however. Ask any Peruvian where the wildest celebrations are, and Cajamarca will invariably come up trumps. The festival here is nine days of dancing, eating, singing, partying, costumes, parades and general rowdy mayhem.

🛏 Sleeping

Hatuchay Inka-Aparthotel   APARTMENT **$$**

(☑076-35-7059; Calle 2 de Mayo 221; s/d incl breakfast S120/168, apt S220-320; ☎) These classy apartments characterized by their sloping ceilings, elegant arches and eclectic paintings combine the convenience of a hotel (there's a reception area and substantial breakfasts are provided) and the intimacy of a B&B (the owners are very involved and congenial), with the space and independence of an apartment (you get your own lounge and full-service kitchen).

It's tantalizingly located on the flight of stairs that leads up to the Cerro Santa Apolonia (p413).

Hotel Sol de Belén   HOTEL **$$**

(☑076-36-2196; www.hotelsoldebelen.com; Belén 636; s/d incl breakfast S100/135; ☐☎) The 'Sol' mixes smart rooms with an old-town Cajamarca feel – and a perfect location on a pedestrian street opposite the Complejo de Belén (p413). Quiet rooms are set back from the road and come with good lighting along with customized sheets and towels. Bonus: there's a small gym on the top floor.

Qhapac Ñan Hotel   HOTEL **$$**

(☑956-037-357; www.qhapacnanhotel.com; Nogales, Villa Universitaria; s/d S140/220; ☎) This smart hotel in a residential neighborhood offers very comfortable modern rooms with firm beds, well-equipped bathrooms and fast internet. Service is very efficient and there is an on-site restaurant (handy in these parts). It's convenient to the bus offices, too.

Hospedaje los Jazmines   HOTEL **$$**

(☑076-36-1812; Amazonas 775; s/d/tr S60/90/120, without bathroom S50/70/90; @☎) In a land of ubiquitous colonial courtyards, this friendly inn is a value standout. Compared to Cajamarca's grander mansions, the Jazmines appears a little quainter, more intimate and more lived-in. Small rooms set around a lush garden are simple but perfectly comfortable. Even better, the

WHEN PIZARRO MET ATAHUALPA

The city of Cajamarca predates both the Spanish and the Incas (it was probably founded around 1320), but it was the face off between these two cultures – the so-called clash of civilizations in 1532 – that cemented the city in popular legend and changed the course of world history forever.

After the death of Huayna Capac in 1525, the remaining Inca Empire, which then stretched from southern Colombia to central Chile, was pragmatically divided between his sons, with Atahualpa ruling the north and Huascar the south. Obviously not everyone was in concord, as civil war soon broke out and in 1532 Atahualpa and his victorious troops marched southward toward Cuzco to take complete control of the empire. Parked at Cajamarca to rest for a few days, Atahualpa, the new Inca emperor, was camped at the natural thermal springs known today as Los Baños del Inca when he heard the news that the Spanish were nearby.

Francisco Pizarro and his force of 168 Spaniards arrived in Cajamarca on November 15, 1532, to a deserted city; most of its 2000 inhabitants were with Atahualpa at his hot-springs encampment. The Spaniards spent an anxious night, fully aware that they were severely outnumbered by the nearby Inca troops, who were estimated to be between 40,000 and 80,000. The Spaniards plotted to entice Atahualpa into the plaza and, at a prearranged signal, capture the emperor should the opportunity present itself.

Upon Atahualpa's arrival, he ordered most of his troops to stay outside while he entered the plaza with a retinue of nobles and about 6000 men armed with slings and hand axes. He was met by the Spanish friar Vicente de Valverde, who attempted to explain his position as a man of God and presented the Inca emperor with a Bible. Reputedly, Atahualpa angrily threw the book to the ground and Valverde needed little more justification to sound the attack.

Cannons were fired and the Spanish cavalry attacked Atahualpa and his troops. The indigenous people were terrified and bewildered by the fearsome onslaught of never-be-fore-seen cannons and horses. Their small hand axes and slings were no match for the well-armored Spaniards, who swung razor-sharp swords from the advantageous height of horseback to slaughter 7000 indigenous people and capture Atahualpa. The small band of Spaniards was now literally conquistadors (conquerors).

Atahualpa soon became aware of the Spaniards' lust for gold and offered to fill a large room in the town once with gold and twice with silver in return for his freedom. The Spanish agreed and slowly the gold and silver began pouring into Cajamarca. Nearly a year later the ransom was complete – about 6000kg of gold and 12,000kg of silver had been melted down into gold and silver bullion. At today's prices, this ransom would be worth almost $180 million, but the artistic value of the ornaments and implements that were melted down to create the bullion is impossible to estimate.

Atahualpa, suspecting he was still not going to be released, sent desperate messages to his followers in Quito to come to Cajamarca and rescue him. The Spaniards, panic-stricken by these messages, sentenced Atahualpa to death. On July 26, 1533, Atahualpa was led out to the center of the Cajamarca plaza to be burned at the stake. At the last hour, Atahualpa 'accepted' baptism and, as a reward, his sentence was changed to a quicker death by strangulation.

Most of the great stone Inca buildings in Cajamarca were torn down and the stones used in the construction of Spanish homes and churches. The great plaza where Atahualpa was captured and later killed was in roughly the same location as today's Plaza de Armas. The Ransom Chamber, or El Cuarto del Rescate (p413), where Atahualpa was imprisoned, is the only Inca building still standing.

hotel's profits help sustain an orphanage for special-needs children in Los Baños del Inca.

In keeping with the social vibe, there's an on-site espresso bar that makes some of the best coffee in town, and has become a small traveler hangout and work space.

El Cabildo　　　　HISTORIC HOTEL $$
(☏ 076-36-7025; www.elcabildohostal.pe; Junín 1062; s/d incl breakfast S110/140; @ 🛜) Like a

favorite old sweater, El Cabildo is a pleasantly lived-in colonial abode that has retained a bit of its old mustiness but added plenty of style: there's elegantly carved wooden balustrades, charred brick fireplaces, a lounge area with dented armchairs and a courtyard splashed with natural greenery. The better rooms have mezzanine floors, decent art and deluxe bedding.

Las Americas Hotel BUSINESS HOTEL $$
(📞076-36-3951; www.lasamericashotel.com.pe; Amazonas 622; s/d incl breakfast S165/215; @ 🛜) Breaking away from the 'cozy colonial hotel' pack, this contemporary property is all business. The 38 rooms face onto a central atrium dripping with plants. All rooms have mini-fridges, cable TV and excellent mattresses; three have Jacuzzi tubs and six have balconies. A restaurant provides room service and there's an underused rooftop terrace and small on-site gym.

Hostal Casona del Inca HISTORIC HOTEL $$
(📞076-36-7524; Calle 2 de Mayo 458; s/d incl breakfast S90/130; @ 🛜) This hotel on the central plaza is located in a not-unpleasant colonial building that's nonetheless getting a bit long in the tooth. Common areas retain color and character and the affiliated restaurant can grill up some good chicken, but the rooms here, while large, can be drab with beds minus headboards and pre-internet-age TVs.

Some rooms have tiny bathrooms so ask to compare options.

★**Posada del Purhuay** HISTORIC HOTEL $$$
(📞076-36-7028; www.facebook.com/Posada Puruay; Km 4.5 Carr Porcón; s/d/t incl breakfast S210/260/315; @ 🛜) This luxuriously restored 1822 hacienda, sitting on 23 hectares off the road to Granja Porcón, is a true find. The relaxing grounds are meticulously groomed, leading to a lovely hotel offering discerning service and a step-back-in-time appeal. Spacious rooms, chock-full of antiquated charm and period furnishings, surround an impeccable courtyard and fountain.

The Posada del Purhuay somehow manages to balance the benefits of a family getaway (kids' playground, gardens and horses) with the appeal of a romantic retreat. A taxi here will cost around S15 from the city center.

El Portal del Marques HISTORIC HOTEL $$$
(📞076-36-8464; www.portaldelmarques.com; Jirón del Comercio 644; s/d incl breakfast S200/257; @ 🛜) The erstwhile marquis who once owned this handsome house must have reigned over a veritable palace. It's now a smart hotel with 41 rooms. When you've finished admiring the ornate portal, enter through the modern reception and behold the huge colonial courtyard. Rooms are a mix of modern and traditional with woven Peruvian art pieces adorning the walls.

There's a conference suite for business travelers, and a cool little restobar with shapely stools out front that keeps things from becoming too stuffy.

Hotel Cajamarca HISTORIC HOTEL $$$
(📞076-36-2532; www.hotelcajamarca.com.pe; Calle 2 de Mayo 311; s/d incl breakfast S180/250; @ 🛜) The grand covered courtyard with its soft settees makes a perfect introduction, while the sleek rooms with parquet floors, crisp duvets and shiny bathrooms give an encouraging second impression. Obviously designed by someone with an eye for function *and* history, the Cajamarca strikes a good balance between modernity and colonial character.

There's a classy on-site restaurant that spills into the central courtyard.

🍴 Eating

★**Cascanuez Café Bar** CAFE $
(📞076-36-6089; Puga 554; cakes S7.50; ⏱7:30am-10pm; 🛜) Every city needs a Cascanuez, a place where you can go at 4pm for your tea or *merienda* (afternoon snack) and have a bow-tied waiter serve you a hot drink and a sweet treat. In Cajamarca this means *cafe pasado* (coffee made by mixing thick coffee essence with boiling water) and a choice of nine varieties of *tres leches* (a cake made with three types of milk).

Decor is British tearoom meets-French bistro, music is (yawn) Kenny G, and service is slightly over formal.

Heladería Holanda DESSERTS $
(📞076-34-0113; Puga 657; ice creams S2-4; ⏱9am-7pm) 🍦 The tiny entrance on the Plaza de Armas opens into a large, Dutch-orange cafe selling the best ice cream in Cajamarca. The staff will shower you with samples of the 20 or so changing flavors, the best of which are based on local and regional fruits. The Dutch owner buys them direct from family farms following a fair-trade philosophy.

Staff members are single mothers and the deaf, an ongoing social project started by the owner. Heladería Holanda has locations at **El Quinde Shopping Center** (Av Hoyos Rubio, cuadra 7; ⊘ 10am-10pm) and in Los Baños del Inca as well.

Sanguchon.com
FAST FOOD $

(www.facebook.com/sanguchonpuntocom; Junín 1137; burgers S9-12; ⊘ 6pm-midnight; 🛜🍴) This wildly popular hamburger-and-sandwich joint features an extensive menu of hand-held snacks. It has 16 varieties of burgers (including vegetarian) and a dozen sauces – adding up to almost 200 different menu choices. The thick-cut chips are more than just filling. Walk in through the kitchen and grab your pew in the rowdy bar hidden behind a stained-glass partition.

El Marengo
PIZZA $

(Junín 1201; pizzas S11-20; ⊘ 7-11pm) Marengo is the smallest, hottest and most fun of the melee of pizza places in the blocks west of Plaza de Armas. With six wooden tables and a brick pizza oven squeezed into a space the size of a dentist's waiting room, it feels more like a blacksmith's forge than a restaurant. Choose from 14 pizza flavors.

The white-asparagus-and-pineapple pizza is an intriguing option. Watch you don't get whacked around the head by the pizza shovel (the place is *that* small).

Vaca Loca
PIZZA $$

(San Martín 330; pizzas S14-40; ⊘ 6-11pm) Set in an inviting colonial house with a warm paint job, the 'Mad Cow' pays homage to the local dairy culture with bovine-print furniture and cow art. But the reason to come here is for the quality pies – they're dripping with local cheese and a wide selection of toppings including gourmet offerings such as artichoke and wild mushroom.

Salas
PERUVIAN $$

(Puga 637; mains S14-35; ⊘ 8am-10pm) This old-school diner is a weird juxtaposition of bland cafeteria-style tables and ostentatiously outfitted wait staff (with bow-ties, no less). It's located down a narrow entrance off the Plaza de Armas and has been in business since 1947. Most of the clientele look like they've been around just as long, enjoying typical *Cajamarquino* dishes like *lomo saltado* (a beef stir-fry), tamales and chicken soup.

Granted, it's a tad old-fashioned and probably hasn't changed its menu since it opened, but for a basic appreciation of Cajamarca's culinary bedrock (pre-pizza era), Salas is worth a brief breakfast or lightning lunch.

Paprika
PERUVIAN $$$

(☑ 076-36-2472; www.costadelsolperu.com; Cruz de Piedra 707; mains S25-50; ⊘ noon-11pm) Cajamarca's poshest restaurant is located in its fanciest hotel and – no surprise – offers the most inventive food in the city. Large windows look out onto the main plaza, starched white tablecloths lend a formal edge and food arrives artistically arranged on a variety of slates, boards, spoons and sometimes even plates.

More unconventional menu options include fish in a *lomo saltado* sauce, roast beef salad and *piqueo marino*, a taster dish consisting of various fish items presented in glasses or on bite-sized spoons.

🍷 Drinking & Nightlife

★ Usha-Usha
BAR

(Puga 142; cover S5; ⊘ 9pm-late) For an intimate local experience, head to this hole-in-the-wall dive bar run by eccentric local musician Jaime Valera, who has managed to cultivate a heap of charisma in such a small space. He sings his heart out with his musician friends and you walk out with an unforgettable travel memory.

🔒 Shopping

Quesos Chugur El Tambo
CHEESE

(☑ 076- 340-178; Calle 2 de Mayo 576; ⊘ 7:30am-9pm) Cajamarca is known nationwide for its cheese and this place sells the best mini-wheels. Ask for a taste first. The shop also serves excellent frozen yogurt.

There are numerous other cheese shops on the same block.

Artesanias El Rescate
ARTS & CRAFTS

(Jirón del Commercio 1029; ⊘ 9am-8pm) This open-air arcade has around a dozen small shops selling handicrafts from around the region, including woven bags and ponchos.

ℹ️ Information

EMERGENCIES

Policía de Turismo (Tourist Police; ☑ 076-36-4515; Jirón del Comercio 1013) Special force dealing with crimes against tourists.

MONEY

Interbank (☑ 076-36-2460; Calle 2 de Mayo 546; ⊘ 9am-6pm Mon-Fri)

Scotiabank (Amazonas 750; ⊘ 8am-6pm Mon-Fri, 9am-noon Sat)

POST

Post Office (☏ 076-36-4065; Puga 668; ◷9am-7pm Mon-Fri, to 1pm Sat) Behind the Iglesia de San Francisco.

Serpost (Apurimac 624; ◷8am-7pm Mon-Sat) Postal service.

TOURIST INFORMATION

iPerú (☏ 076-36-5166; Cruz de Piedra 601; ◷9am-6pm Mon-Sat, to 1pm Sun) Incredibly helpful tourist office that has detailed maps outlining how to visit attractions around town and beyond.

The **Dirección de Turismo** (☏ 076-36-2997; El Complejo de Belén; ◷7:30am-1pm & 2:30-5pm Mon-Fri) in the Complejo de Belén has local maps for sale (S1.50).

❶ Getting There & Away

The quickest way to get to Huaraz from Cajamarca is via Trujillo where you'll need to change buses. Cajamarca–Trujillo is six hours and Trujillo–Huaraz is eight hours. Línea has good connections.

Alternatively, you can fly between the cities in one day, though you'll have to change planes in Lima.

AIR

The **airport** is 4km outside town off the road to Otuzco. Taxis charge S10 into downtown. The combination of difficult terrain and frequent heavy rains mean cancellations and delays are fairly common here. Reconfirm your flight before heading out to the airport. It would be unwise to book tight connections when leaving from Cajamarca.

Frequent *combis* (minibuses) heading for Otuzco pass the airport (S1, 10 minutes). You can catch them from the corner of Tayabambo and Los Gladiolos, near the market district. Warning: they can be crowded.

LC Perú (☏ 076-36-3115; www.lcperu.pe; Jirón del Comercio 1024; ◷9am-7pm Mon-Fri, to 1pm Sat) Most economical but least reliable operator with two daily flights to Lima (US$100, 1¼ hours) leaving at 7:15am and 5pm.

LATAM (www.latam.com; Centro Commercial El Quinde; ◷10am-10pm) Has two to three daily flights from Cajamarca to Lima (US$135, 1¼ hours).

BUS

Cajamarca continues its ancient role as a crossroads, with buses heading to all four points of the compass. Most bus terminals are close to *cuadra* (block) 3 of Atahualpa, about 1.5km southeast of the center (not to be confused with the Atahualpa in the town center), on the road to Los Baños del Inca.

The major route is westbound to the Carretera Panamericana near Pacasmayo on the coast, then north to Chiclayo (six hours) or south to Trujillo (six hours) and Lima (15 hours).

The old southbound road is paved and travel on this route is no longer a bone-rattling nightmare. Frequent services head to Cajabamba (three hours) from where onward buses travel to Huamachuco and Trujillo.

The rough northbound road to Chota (five hours) passes through wild and attractive countryside via Bambamarca, which has a busy market on Sunday morning. Buses connect Chota to Chiclayo along a rough road.

The staggeringly scenic eastbound road winds to Celendín, then bumps its way across the Andes, past Chachapoyas and down into the Amazon lowlands.

Combis for **Ventanillas de Otuzco** (cnr Los Gladiolos & Tayabambo) (S1, 20 minutes) leave from the corner of Tayabambo and Los Gladiolos, near the market district. These pass the airport, although jamming yourself into a crowded van with your backpack will require some finesse and diplomacy. *Combis* for **Los Baños del Inca** (S1, 25 minutes) leave frequently from the corner of Del Batán and Chanchamayo. Both Otuzco (8km) and Baños del Inca (6km) are walkable if you've got the legs for it.

Civa (☏ 076-36-1460; www.civa.com.pe; Av Atahualpa 335) Daily bus to Lima (S60 to S80, 15 hours) at 6:30pm.

Cruz del Sur (☏ 076-36-2024; Atahualpa 884) Nice *bus-cama* (bed bus) with seat-back screens to Lima (S100 to S120, 16 hours) at 6:30pm.

Línea (☏ 076-34-0753; www.linea.pe; Atahualpa 316) Has a comfortable Lima-bound *bus-cama* (S120 to S140, 15 hours) with a departure at 6pm. There are departures to Chiclayo (S25 to S46, six hours) at 10:45am, 1:30pm, 10:50pm and 11pm, and Trujillo (S25 to S50, six hours) at 10:30am, 1pm, 10pm, 10:15pm, 10:30pm and 10:40pm. Línea also has a **ticket office** (Puga 691; ◷9am-7pm) on the Plaza de Armas.

Movil Tours (☏ 076-28-0093; www.moviltours.com.pe; Av Atahualpa 686) Daily bus to Lima (S90 to S110, 15 hours) at 3:50pm. Also a daily bus to Piura (S50 to S70, eight hours) via Chiclayo at 8:45pm.

Tepsa (☏ 076-36-3306; Sucre 422; 📶) Comfortable *bus-cama* to Lima (S45, 15 hours) at 6pm.

Transportes Chiclayo (☏ 076-36-4628; www.facebook.com/TransportesChiclayoSA; Atahualpa 283) Has a Chiclayo-bound bus (S30 to S40, six hours) at 11pm which is good for transferring north to Máncora or Tumbes.

Transportes Rojas (☏ 076-34-0548; Atahualpa 309) Service to Celendín (S10, 2½ hours) at 10am and 3pm. Also service to Cajabamba (S15, three hours, six daily).

Turismo Dias (☑ 076-34-4322; Atahualpa 307) Regular buses to Lima (S50 to S100, 15 hours, four daily), Trujillo (S25 to S40, six hours, four daily) and Chiclayo (S25, 5½ hours, four daily). Buses leave from the Terminal Via de Evitamiento 1370.

Virgen del Carmen (☑ 98-391-5869; www. turismovirgendelcarmen.com.pe; Atahualpa 333A) Departs at 5am and 5pm daily for Chachapoyas (S50, 11½ hours) via Celendín and Leimebamba. The 5am service carries on to Tarapoto (S80, 19 hours).

Cajamarca Buses

DESTINATION	COST (S)	TIME (HR)
Cajabamba	10-20	3
Celendín	10	2½
Chachapoyas	50	11½
Chiclayo	20-45	5½
Leimebamba	35	9
Lima	80-136	15
Piura	50-70	8
Tarapoto	80	19
Trujillo	20-40	6

Around Cajamarca

Los Baños del Inca HOT SPRINGS

(www.ctbinca.com.pe; admission S2; ⊙ 5am-8pm) History was made at these thermal baths in 1532 when Inca emperor Atahualpa camped out here as Spanish conquistador Pizarro (p416) marched boldly into Cajamarca with his army of 168 men. The pools are a little more hygienic these days, but you can still take a dip in the same waters that an Inca king used to bathe his war wounds.

Set in flower-bedizened grounds, the attractive compound channels its hot water (a practically boiling 72°C) into private cubicles (S20 per 30 minutes), some large enough for up to six people at a time. Unfortunately all the private baths are indoors, which makes it impossible to admire the mountain scenery while soaking. The steaming outdoor pools are just for show, although there's a public swimming pool (S3) designed using generic concrete and reminiscent of a dated 1930s lido. There are also steam rooms and massages available for S10 and S20 each.

The place is hugely popular with a mainly Peruvian clientele. Come in the morning to avoid the rush. A major extension to the baths was underway at last visit and should be up and running by the time you read this.

The baths are 6km from Cajamarca. *Combis* for Los Baños del Inca (S1, 25 minutes) leave from Chanchamayo and Plaza a Puga in Cajamarca; or take an organized tour from Cajamarca (S15). Alternatively, you can walk. There's a *cyclovia* (bike lane) all the way starting at the Plazuela Bolognesi in Cajamarca.

Cumbemayo ARCHAEOLOGICAL SITE

(S8) Cumbemayo (derived from the Quechua *kumpi mayo*, meaning 'well-made water channel') is an astounding feat of pre-Inca engineering. These perfectly smooth aqueducts were carved around 2000 years ago and zigzag at right angles for 9km, for a purpose that is as yet unclear, since Cajamarca has an abundant water supply. Other rock formations are carved to look like altars and thrones. Nearby caves contain petroglyphs, including some that resemble woolly mammoths. The site is located about 20km southwest of Cajamarca.

The surrounding countryside is high, windswept and slightly eerie. Superstitious stories are told about the area's eroded rock formations, which look like groups of shrouded mountain climbers.

Public transport to Cumbemayo is sporadic and getting there on your own takes some planning. *Combis* serving the village of Chetilla pass by the entrance to the site and leave Av Perú between Jirón Ica and Jirón Loreta in Cajamarca at 4:30am, 6am, noon and 1:30pm. The last *combi* back to Cajamarca passes Cumbemayo around 1:40pm.

The site can be reached on foot via a signed road from behind Cerro Santa Apolonia in Cajamarca. The hike follows sections of the *Qhapac Ñan* (Inca paths) and takes about four hours. Most people visit as part of a guided tour (S20, 4½ hours) that runs every morning out of Cajamarca.

Ventanillas de Otuzco ARCHAEOLOGICAL SITE

(S5; ⊙ 9am-6pm) This pre-Inca necropolis has scores of funerary niches built into the hillside, hence the name *ventanillas* (windows). Set in alluring countryside, 8km northeast of Cajamarca, the site is easily walkable from either Cajamarca or Los Baños del Inca (ask for directions). Alternatively, *combis* to Ventanillas de Otuzco (S1, 20 minutes) leave frequently from the corner of Jirón Los

WORTH A TRIP

HUAMACHUCO AND ITS RUINS

Despite being in the enviable position of having two first-class pre-Hispanic ruins on its doorstep, the pleasant mountain town of Huamachuco receives very few visitors.

Without doubt the major star is the massive pre-Inca mountain fort of **Marcahuamachuco** (☉dawn-dusk) **FREE**, a spectacular collection of rugged ruins dating from around 400 BC that sprawls over a windswept plateau at a dizzying 3600m.

Although dwarfed by its famous neighbor, the easily accessed ruins of **Wiracochapampa** are also well worth a visit. Despite the close proximity of the sites, the structures here are not directly connected to those at Marcahuamachuco. Research suggests the buildings here were completed around AD 700 and served as a ceremonial center of the Wari culture.

Unlike many other large pre-Hispanic settlements in the region that cling to soaring peaks, these structures were built low in a valley. The ruins are centered on a large central plaza, surrounded on three sides by a compact maze of rooms, and divided by high rock walls, which contain numerous tombs. From the center of Huamachuco it's a 45-minute hike to Wiracochapampa. Otherwise a *mototaxi* should cost around S8.

The **tourism office** (☎076-44-0048; www.munihuamachuco.gob.pe; Castilla 564, Huamachuco) can organize guides to both archaeological sites, as well as other attractions in the area. A block from the plaza in Huamachuco, the small **Museo Municipal Wamachuko** (cnr Sucre & San Martin, Huamachuco; ☉9am-noon & 2-5pm Mon-Fri) **FREE** houses ceramics from the Huamachuco period.

For accommodations, try **Hostal Plaza** (☎044-441-303; cnr José Balta & San Martín, Huamachuco; r S40-50), which offers good-value rooms right on the main square. For eats, head to **Antojitos Grill** (Ramón Castilla 534, Huamachuco; mains S15; ☉7-11am & 6-11pm), which does a tasty mixed grill, as well as filling traditional breakfasts.

Colectivos (shared transportation) leave for Cajabamba (S10, 1½ hours) when full from the small terminal on the east side of town. **Tunesa Express** (☎076-44-1157; www.turismonegreiros.com; cnr José Balta & Suarez, Huamachuco) has regular express services linking Huamachuco with Trujillo (S15 to S25, five hours, five daily).

Gladiolos and Jirón Tayabamba, north of the Plaza de Armas in Cajamarca.

Ventanillas de Combayo   ARCHAEOLOGICAL SITE

FREE Combayo is the largest and most impressive collection of funerary niches in the region, although its location 30km northeast of Cajamarca means it's less visited than more accessible Otuzco. The site is best incorporated into a tour from Cajamarca (between S20 and S25). If you want to go on your own, irregular *colectivos* (shared transportation; S5, 1½ hours) depart when full from the second block of Av Hoyos Rubio 2 from 5am to 4pm. Leave early to ensure return transport.

Kuntur Wasi   ARCHAEOLOGICAL SITE
(adult/child S5/1;   ☉9am-5:30pm Tue-Sun) Perched on a mountaintop overlooking the small town of San Pablo, these seldom-visited pre-Inca ruins are well worth the trip from Cajamarca. The site is considered one of the cradles of Andean culture; four distinct cultures used the area for their ceremonies, with the first constructions taking

place around 1100 BC. The main structure is a large U-shaped temple consisting of three elevated platforms around which are located numerous tombs.

While the ruins are not the most spectacular in the region – apart from the walls and central plaza, most of the excavated structures have been filled in – the views from the site are spectacular.

The real drawcard here is the **museum** (☎976-679-484;   museo.kunturwasi@gmail.com; admission adult/child S4/1; ☉9am-5pm Tue-Sun), located at the foot of the ruins in the hamlet of Kuntur Wasi. It displays many of the fascinating relics unearthed by archaeologists at the site.

Kuntur Wasi is just outside the sleepy town of San Pablo. A *mototaxi* (three-wheeled motorcycle rickshaw taxi) from San Pablo to the museum costs S3. The archaeological site is a steep 800m hike up the trail behind the museum.

Combis to San Pablo (S10, 1½ hours) depart regularly from the small terminal on Jirón Angamos, in front of Grifo Continental

THE ROAD TO CHACHAPOYAS: BETWEEN A ROCK AND A HARD PLACE

Having sufficiently soaked up both the coastal sun and highland historical atmosphere in the mountains, travelers often find themselves itching for a little cloud forest and jungle action. Off to Tarapoto and Chachapoyas you go, right? Not so fast. First, you must decide: do you have the heart, patience and nerves of steel to brave the astonishingly spectacular but hopelessly harrowing mountain route via Celendín and Leimebamba? Or would you be more comfortable taking the long way round on the highway from Chiclayo? Decisions, decisions.

Via Celendín

This rough but beautiful road climbs over a 3085m pass before plummeting steeply to the Río Marañón at the shabby and infernally hot village of **Balsas** (975m), 55km from Celendín. The road climbs again, through gorgeous cloud forests and countryside swathed in a lush quilt a million shades of green. It emerges 57km later at **Abra de Barro Negro** (Black Mud Pass; 3678m), which offers the highest viewing point of the drive, over the Río Marañón, more than three vertical kilometers below. Ghostly low-level clouds and mists hug the dispersed communities in this part of the trip and creep eerily among the hills.

The road then drops for 32km to Leimebamba at the head of the Río Utcubamba Valley and follows the river as it descends past Tingo and on to Chachapoyas. Although the road has recently been paved, it remains a narrow, high-altitude twist fest. With no guardrails in sight, your life teeters precariously on the edge around every corner. Your only hope is that the driver knows the nuances of the road intimately. Travelers should carry water and food (and maybe a valium), as the few restaurants en route are poor.

Despite the thrills, accidents involving buses on this route are very rare, with most drivers taking a very slow and steady approach. Heading north, the left side of the bus affords the most scenic viewing time, but the right side is less nauseating for those who fear heights.

Via Chiclayo

Considerably longer and immeasurably less thrilling is the usual route for travelers to Chachapoyas. From the old Pan-American Hwy 100km north of Chiclayo, a paved road heads east over the Andes via the 2145m PorcuIla Pass, the lowest Peruvian pass going over the Andean continental divide. The route then tumbles to the Río Marañón valley. About 190km from the Carretera Panamericana turnoff, you reach the turnoff to the town of Jaén, the beginning of the route to Ecuador. Continuing east, a short side road reaches the town of Bagua Chica in a low, enclosed valley (elevation about 500m), which Peruvians claim is the hottest town in the country. The bus usually goes through Bagua Grande (population 28,830) on the main road, and follows the Río Utcubamba Valley to the crossroads town of Pedro Ruíz, about 1½ hours from Bagua Grande. From here, a paved southbound road branches to Chachapoyas, 54km and about one hour away.

in Cajamarca. The last van back leaves San Pablo at 5:30pm; you may want to reserve your place in advance.

Celendín

☏ 076 / POP 28,000 / ELEV 2625M

A delightfully sleepy little town that receives few travelers except for those taking the wild and scenic route to Chachapoyas, Celendín is particularly known for high-quality straw hats, which can be bought at its interesting Sunday market. It's an ideal place to observe traditional highland life and interact with local indigenous people. Celendín is easily reached by a paved road from Cajamarca.

🛏 Sleeping & Eating

As an overnight stop between Cajamarca and Chachapoyas, Celendín can deliver the goods with at least two passable cheap hotels.

Hotel Villa Madrid   HOTEL $

(☑076-55-5123; villamadridcelendin@hotmail.com; cnr Pardo & Dos de Mayo; s/d S50/60; 🅿🛜) Hotel Villa Madrid is the best choice in town with spacious modern rooms set around an internal courtyard that serves as a large restaurant (and can get noisy). It's just off the Plaza de Armas.

Restaurant Turístico La Reserve   PERUVIAN $$

(Gálvez 420; meals S6-32; ⊘7am-10pm) A popular eating choice, with multilevel seating and a warm ambience. The menu is ample and filled with small-town Peruvian classics like *cau cau* (tripe and potato stew) and *ají de gallina* (spicy chicken and walnut stew).

🍺 Drinking & Nightlife

Tiesto Café Bar   BAR, CAFE

(☑997-478-450; Calle 2 de Mayo 410; ⊘4pm-midnight) Celendín has sprouted a bit of trendy nightlife with this slick little bar, best visited for its multicolored cocktails including the ubiquitous pisco sours. On weekend evenings DJs spin ambient sounds and the local 20-somethings crowd in to claim their 2-for-1s.

ℹ Getting There & Away

Virgen del Carmen (☑076-55-5187; www.turismovirgendelcarmen.com.pe; Cáceres 112) Goes to Chachapoyas (S35, nine hours) via Leimebamba (S25, seven hours) at 8am and 8pm. Also runs services to Cajamarca (S10, 2½ hours) at 4:30am and 5pm.

Movil Tours (www.moviltours.com.pe; Cáceres 112) Has recently installed its executive-VIP buses in Celendín with one daily departure to Lima (S100 to S120, 18 hours) via Cajamarca at 1pm.

Transportes Rojas (☑076-55-5108; Cáceres 125) Two daily buses to Cajamarca (S10, 2½ hours).

Chachapoyas

☑041 / POP 29,000 / ELEV 2335M

Isolated for centuries in the cloud forests of northern Peru, mellow Chachapoyas appears to be a town on the cusp of wider discovery. For vintage travelers, the ignition of interest will come as no surprise. Straddling the transitional zone between the high Andes and the Amazon Basin, 'Chacha' and its surroundings have long felt like a box of hidden treasure waiting to be dug up.

Founded early in the Spanish conquest as the base from which the exploitation of the Amazon region was launched, contemporary Chacha is a relatively unremarkable town, a tight grid of whitewashed houses with red-tiled roofs whose individualistic history means that few of the populace speak Quechua. Instead, Chacha's jewels lie scattered across the surrounding countryside: a crinkled web of cloud-enveloped mountains and valleys, inhabited by colossal waterfalls, remarkable birdlife and a mysterious raft of pre-Columbian, pre-Inca ruins, half of them still covered by tangled undergrowth.

◉ Sights

Church   CHURCH

(Plaza de Armas) This whitewashed church, officially known as the Catedral San Juan Bautista, sits on the Plaza de Armas. Its heavy black wooden doors rarely seem to open outside mass.

Instituto Nacional de Cultura Museo   MUSEUM

(INC; Ayacucho 904; ⊘9am-1pm & 3-5:45pm Mon-Fri) FREE This small museum on the Plaza de Armas houses mummies found throughout the region, plus ceramics from several pre-Columbian periods and one of the original sarcophagi from Karajía (p430).

Huancas   VILLAGE

The tiny and agreeably unkempt village of Huancas (pronounced like the English 'wankers'!) has a small artisan community making clay pots the old-fashioned way. You can watch the local potters at work in a couple of houses on the diminutive Plaza de Armas. Huancas is also famed for its two magnificent *miradores* (lookouts), both a short walk from its main square.

Mirador Huancas has soaring views of the Utcubamba Valley. Mirador Cañón del Sonche has equally impressive vistas over a deeply gouged river canyon.

A S30 round-trip taxi ride will take you the 8km north to Huancas from Chachapoyas. It's also possible to take a *colectivo* (shared transportation; S3, 25 minutes) from the bus terminal. To get there on foot, walk up to the **Mirador Luya Urco** (Carr Aeropuerto) and keep heading north, turning left at a fork in the road after 1km.

Mirador Cañón del Sonche   VIEWPOINT

(Huancas; admission S3; ⊘8am-5pm) The joy of this steep-sided canyon that cuts like a deep gash through the Northern Highlands

Chachapoyas

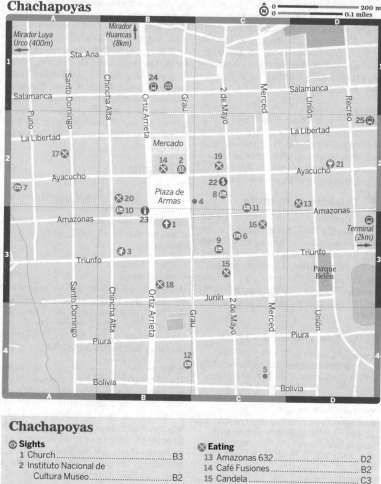

Chachapoyas

is that you're barely aware it's there until you are practically standing on its lip. Pay the entry fee at a small cabin a short 500m walk east of the tiny village of Huancas (p423) and proceed up a short path to a wooden tower for spectacular views of the hidden 962m-deep valley.

Courses

International Language Center LANGUAGE
(☑ 041-47-8807; www.ilc-peru.com.pe; Triunfo 1098; ☺ 8am-10pm) Well-established school offering Spanish lessons from S20 per hour. There are also daily group lessons between 2:30pm and 3:30pm (S20).The friendly owner freely doles out tourist information and sometimes has paid positions for English teachers.

Tours

All the budget tour agencies are found near or on the Plaza de Armas. Ask around for other travelers' experiences before you choose an agency. Expect to pay S100 to S150 per person for multiday treks (a little more for groups of less than four) and between S50 and S80 for day tours.

Standard day tours include Kuélap (p431) for S100, Karajía (p430) to Caverna de Quiocta (p430) for S100, Gocta (p429) for S60 and Revash (p431) to Leimebamba for S120. Prices might vary.

Turismo Explorer TOURS
(☑ 041-47-8162; www.turismoexplorerperu.com; Grau 549) This company has a great reputation among travelers and offers short trips and multiday treks. It has professional guides who speak excellent English.

Vilaya Tours TOURS
(☑ 941-70-8798; www.vilayatours.com; Merced 1096) A recommended high-end operator run by experienced British guide Rob Dover. It offers tailor-made multiday tours and treks focusing on archaeological sites and nature destinations.

Sleeping

Most places in Chachapoyas fall squarely in the budget category. A couple of more upperscale hotels inhabit traditional Chacha houses adorned with courtyards and wooden balconies.

★ Chachapoyas Backpackers HOSTEL **$**
(☑ 041-47-8879; www.chachapoyasbackpackers.com; Calle 2 de Mayo 639; d S70, dm/s/d without bathroom S20/35/45; @ ⍤) A godsend in a region not overflowing with hosteling options, this travelers' nexus doesn't just go through the motions, it excels. Offering clean, uncluttered rooms and dorms ignited by splashes of color plus a well-stocked communal kitchen and hot showers, it doubles up as a local information portal masterfully overseen by keen multilingual staff.

If you're still vacillating, say hello to owner and former guide José, an expert on the burgeoning Chacha scene who can organize tours through his agency or provide detailed explanations if you want to go it alone.

Hotel Karajía HOTEL **$**
(☑ 041-31-2606; Calle 2 de Mayo 546; s/d S50/80, without bathroom S35/60; ⍤) A simple cheapie with a bright paint job and the occasional frilly touch such as toilet-seat covers and kaleidoscopic bedspreads. Rooms are basic and some are a little dark but they are adequate to crash for the night after a hard trek.

La Casona Monsante HOTEL **$$**
(☑ 041-47-7702; www.casonamonsante.com; Amazonas 746; s/d/tr S200/250/350; ⍤) One of Chacha's more deluxe offerings, the Monsante takes advantage of a large colonial mansion centered on an atmospheric plant-filled courtyard. Rooms are mansion-house-large with wood beams, modern bathrooms and above-average soaps and scents. Some have mezzanines. There's also a restaurant and plenty of nooks and crannies where you can hide and relax.

La Casona de Chachapoyas HISTORIC HOTEL **$$**
(☑ 041-47-7353; www.lacasonadechachapoyas peru.com; Chincha Alta 569; s/d/tr incl breakfast S140/190/240; @ ⍤) One of Chachapoyas' newest hotels continues the city's charm offensive to lure more tourists to understated northern Peru. It piles on plenty of colonial style in a sympathetically renovated old *casona* (large house) with a verdant central patio that attracts hummingbirds. Rooms are tasteful with interesting design motifs and the common areas encourage communal lingering. Breakfasts are substantial.

Miraculously, the whole place manages to be agreeably somnolent despite being only one block from the main square.

La Casa de los Balcones B&B **$$**
(☑ 982-180-794; Jirón Triunfo 828; s/d S95/115; ⍤) It doesn't look much from the outside, but open that innocuous wooden door on Jirón Triunfo and enter one of Chacha's best

family-run hotels. Rooms are simple but meticulously maintained (a different chocolate adorns your pillow every morning), breakfast is served around a communal family table, and every request is greeted by a smile.

Hostal La Villa de Paris HOTEL $$

(☑ 041-63-1310; www.hotelvilladeparis.com; Prolongación 2 de Mayo, cuadra 5; s/d/tr incl breakfast S130/170/240; P@🐕❄) This lovely colonial-style hotel, furnished with lots of wood and antiques, has the feel of a much more expensive place. Large windows and balconies bring in the light and there's a tiny pool and restaurant. It's 1.5km south from the main square.

The only letdown is the location, on a rather scruffy road, meaning it's not a particularly pleasant walk into town.

Hostal Las Orquídeas GUESTHOUSE $$

(☑ 041-47-8271; www.hostallasorquideas.com; Ayacucho 1231; s/d incl breakfast S90/140; @🐕) Midrange guesthouse with tile-floor rooms decorated in safe whites and creams. The public area offers a bit more color with wood features and artsy accents. Some rooms are more appealing than others; the renovated rooms at the front of the building have carpeted walls and more-modern granite-slab bathrooms.

★ La Xalca HOTEL $$$

(☑ 041-47-9106; www.laxalcahotel.com; Grau 940; s/d/tr incl breakfast S290/360/530; P🐕) It's hard to believe that this drop-dead-handsome colonial edifice was built from scratch only a few years ago – the elegant wood and adobe walls and balconies are gloriously authentic. Melding modern minimalism with sturdy tradition, the hotel abounds with inviting communal spaces decked out with comfy sofas, hand-carved furniture and curious art. Best hotel in town, hands down.

Rooms are huge with terra-cotta-tiled floors, glass bricks to allow natural light, and dark-wood furniture. Breakfast is buffet style and there's gratis tea and coffee available all day.

Eating

Moving east across the Andes, Chachapoyas is the first place where you begin finding Amazonian-style dishes, though with local

---

THE PEOPLE OF THE CLOUDS

The Chachapoyas, or 'People of the Clouds,' controlled the vast swath of land around present-day Chachapoyas from AD 500 to around 1493, when the Incas conquered the area and ended the Chacha isolation. Very little is known about this civilization, whose inhabitants were thought to be great warriors, powerful shamans and prolific builders who were responsible for one of the most advanced civilizations of Peru's tropical jungles. Today, among the many dozens of cliff tombs and hamlets of circular structures left behind, archaeologists match wits with grave robbers in a race to uncover the heritage of the Chachapoyas.

The Chachapoyas were heavily engaged in trade with other parts of Peru. However, isolated in their cloud-forest realm, they developed independently of these surrounding civilizations. The Chachapoyas speculatively cultivated a fierce warrior cult; depicted trophy heads as well as uncovered human skulls show evidence of trepanation and intentional scalping. The eventual expansion of the Inca Empire in the 15th century was met with fierce resistance, and sporadic fighting continued well after the initial conquest.

Environmentalists long before Greenpeace, the Chachapoyas built structures that were in perfect harmony with their surroundings and that took advantage of nature's aesthetic and practical contributions. The Chachapoyas religion is believed to have venerated some of the salient natural features of these territories; the serpent, the condor and the puma were worshipped as powerful representatives of the natural world, as were caves, lakes and mountains.

The unique use of circular construction was complemented by intricate masonry friezes, which used zigzags and rhomboids. The buildings were covered by thatch roofs, which were tall and steep to facilitate the runoff of the area's frequent rains. Hundreds of ruins illustrate Chachapoyas architecture, but none stands out as much as the impressive fortified citadel of Kuélap (p431), surrounded by a colossal 20m-high wall and encompassing hundreds of dwellings and temples.

variations. *Juanes* (banana leaves stuffed with chicken or pork) are made with yucca instead of rice. *Cecina,* a dish made from dehydrated pork in the lowlands, is often made with beef here. There's a good and growing selection of casual cafes.

Café Fusiones   CAFE $
(www.cafefusiones.com; Ayacucho, Plaza de Armas; breakfasts S8-11, light meals S6-17; ⊗ 7am-10pm; 🛜🅿) 🍽 One of those comfortable 'Gringo Trail' cafes that offer everything necessary to keep a peanut-butter-deprived backpacker happy – vegetarian omelets, multilingual book exchange, Pearl Jam on repeat, organic coffee and leaflets advertising the nearest yoga studio. If you're dying to meet a gringo, this is where they'll be. It's also one of the few Chacha cafes that stays open all day.

Terra Mia Café   BREAKFAST, PERUVIAN $
(Chincha Alta 557; breakfasts S11-14; ⊗ 7:30am-12:30pm & 3-10pm; 🛜) A chic spot with the fanciest espresso machine in town, Terra Mia's wonderful menu has regional and international breakfasts (ahem...waffles!), plus sandwiches and salads all served up in a cozy and clean atmosphere with colonial archways and indigenous-motif seat cushions. Service is as sweet as the cakes.

There's a recently opened new **branch** (snacks S7-10; ⊗ 8am-5pm) at the top cable-car station in Kuélap.

Panificadora San José   BAKERY, INTERNATIONAL $
(Ayacucho 816; breakfasts S2-5; ⊗ 7am-10pm) The town's biggest bakery is a two-story affair featuring a downstairs takeout counter filled with savory *humitas* (mashed corn dumplings filled with spiced beef, vegetables and potatoes) and sweet chocolate cups infused with cream. Upstairs, a large featureless restaurant offers a full menu of international meat-and-chips dishes.

⭐ **Amazonas 632**   CAFE, INTERNATIONAL $$
(🖉 979-877-031; Amazonas 632; mains S10-22; ⊗ 7:30am-2:30pm & 5-11pm; 🛜) This smart new coffee shop and casual dining spot attracts a mix of laptop campers (free wi-fi and power outlets) and locals tucking into the thick, juicy burgers – the best in town. Strong coffee, gigantic fruit salads, and small but unusually flavored artisanal pizzas, too. The underlying owl motif lends the place a warm quirkiness despite the otherwise Starbucks-y decor.

CANYONING

The intrepid sport of rappelling down rivers and waterfalls has found a natural home in northern Peru, which has an impressive collection of spectacular water flumes, including some of the highest in South America. Canyoning (or *barranquismo* as it's known in Spanish) is still in its infancy in these parts but has recently sprouted a professional operator, **Canyoning Explorer** (🖉 997-583-804; www.canyoningexplorer. com; Bongará 220, Cuispes; from S160 per person). Under the enthusiastic tutelage of Andalucian Juan Pérez you can arrange trips to up to five local waterfalls in the vicinity of Cuispes, 60km north of Chachapoyas, including 896m-tall **Catarata Yumbilla**, considered the fifth-tallest waterfall in the world.

Candela   PIZZA $$
(🖉 961-867-428; Calle 2 de Mayo 728; pizzas S14-28; ⊗ 6-11pm) Candela marries colorful Chachapoyas culture (indigenous-style murals adorn the walls) with decent Italian-influenced food. The focus is the giant pizza oven stoked industriously by a hard-working chef who turns out crunchy thin-crust pies with generous toppings. A theatrical sideshow is provided by the wait staff, some of whom appear to have a talent for dancing.

A selection of homemade pastas (rolled in full view through the pasta-maker) is also available.

El Tejado   PERUVIAN $$
(Santo Domingo 426; mains S15-25; ⊗ noon-4pm) This charming little lunch spot doesn't look much from the outside, but a lovely interior courtyard and dining room await. Set menus rarely go north of S10 from Monday to Friday for three courses and a drink. The specialty is *tacu-tacu* (a Peruvian fusion dish of rice, beans and a protein), seen here in nine varieties.

Its version of *lomo saltado* is conversation-stopping good.

La Tushpa   STEAKHOUSE, PERUVIAN $$
(🖉 041-77-71-98; Ortiz Arrieta 753; mains S18-35; ⊗ 6:30-11pm Mon-Sat) Classic local steakhouse serving large portions supplemented by some chunky side dishes (excellent plantains). The meat-heavy menu is highlighted by the *cuadril* (tri-tip), a succulent beef cut,

and interesting creations such as *lomo fino* (sirloin) with a spicy pisco sauce. There's a good deal of pork and chicken to choose from as well, all with homemade house sauces.

★ **El Batan de Tayta**   AMAZONIAN $$
(☑959-865-539; La Merced 604; mains S20-46; ☺11am-11pm Sun-Thu, to midnight Fri & Sat) Exotic is the word here, from the decor (Amazonian creepers, bamboo table umbrellas and furry seat covers), to the food ('drunk' guinea pig, duck and edible ants in a vanilla and cognac cocktail!) and the implements it's served on (model boats, mini-drums, or if you're lucky, a terra-cotta roof tile). Despite the theatrics, the food is plentiful and well executed.

Try the *arroz shutito con bife y chica de jora* (creamy rice with tenderloin and a touch of maize liquor) or house specialty *cuy borracho* (literally 'drunk guinea pig' with Andean potatoes and herb sauce).

There's even a few boring dishes (eg pasta) on the menu if you don't happen to like insects or inebriated rodents.

🍷 Drinking & Nightlife

★ **La Reina**   BAR
(Ayacucho 520; ☺9am-1pm & 3pm-1am Mon-Sat, 7pm-midnight Sun) An artsy spot to lubricate your mind very cheaply on exotic fruit drinks and Amazonian liqueurs by the shot (S1.50) or the jar (from S18). The 11 options include *mora* (blackberry), the most popular; *maracuyá* (passion fruit), the best; and seven *raíces* and *chuchuhuasi*, two notorious Amazonian aphrodisiacs. The bar inhabits an elegantly aging courtyard in a traditional Chacha mansion.

The same owners run the best **disco** in town, a few blocks down at Ayacucho 345.

ℹ️ Information

MONEY

Banco de la Nación (cnr Ayacucho & Calle 2 de Mayo; ☺8am-5:30pm Mon-Fri, 9am-1pm Sat) Has a Visa/MasterCard ATM.

BCP (Plaza Burgos; ☺9am-6pm Mon-Fri, to 1pm Sat) Changes US dollars and has an ATM.

POST

Serpost (Salamanca 940; ☺8am-1pm & 2-7pm Mon-Fri, 8am-1pm Sat) Postal services; in the market district.

TOURIST INFORMATION

iPerú (☑041-47-7292; Ortiz Arrieta 582; ☺9am-6pm Mon-Sat, to 1pm Sun) Extremely helpful like most iPerú offices, this place on Plaza de Armas hands out excellent maps, transportation information and brochures.

ℹ️ Getting There & Away

AIR

Chachapoyas Airport is located 4km northeast of the city center. **ATSA Airlines** (☑717-3268; www.atsaairlines.com) has five flights a week to and from Lima (US$140, 1¾ hours) leaving Chachapoyas at 11:30am. Book tickets online or at the Turismo Explorer (p425) office in Plaza de Armas.

BUS

All local and regional transport leaves from Chachapoyas' scruffy beehive of a **bus terminal** (Triunfo cuadra 2), 1km east of Plaza de Armas. Note that long-distance express buses leave from private terminals around the city.

The frequently traveled route to Chiclayo and on to Lima starts on the vista-lined route to Pedro Ruíz along the Río Utcubamba. The very comfortable **Movil Tours** (☑041-47-8545; www.moviltours.com.pe; La Libertad 464) has buses to Lima (S130 to S165, 22 hours) at 4pm, Chiclayo (S55 to S75, nine hours) at 8pm, Trujillo (S65 to S85, 14 hours) at 7:30pm, and Jaén (S50, four hours) at 4:30am. **Civa** (☑041-47-8048; cnr Ortiz Arrieta y Salamanca) has slightly cheaper buses to Chiclayo (S30 to S70, 10 hours, twice daily) and Lima (S100 to S120, 24 hours, once daily).

Virgen del Carmen (☑041-79-7707; www.turismovirgendelcarmen.com.pe; Terminal Terrestre) is the safest operator for the thrilling scenic route between Chachapoyas and Cajamarca (S50, 11 hours) via Leimebamba (S10, 2½ hours) and Celendín (S40, nine hours). There's one bus daily usually leaving in the evening. Another bus heads east to Tarapoto (S35, eight hours).

Also continuing into the Amazon Basin is **Turismo Selva** (☑961-659-443; Terminal de Transporte) running less comfortable minivans to Tarapoto (S35, eight hours) via Moyobamba (S24, six hours) at 6:30am, 8:30am, 10:30am and 12:30pm. There is also a 2:30pm service just to Moyobamba.

For Jaén and its airport, Turismo Explorer (p425) runs daily transfer buses (S50, four hours) leaving Chachapoyas at 7am. Buses pick up passengers from the 12:30pm flight and return to Chachapoyas.

Turismo Kuélap (Terminal Terrestre) runs frequent minibuses from Chachapoyas' main bus terminal to the base of the cable-car station in

Nuevo Tingo (S7, one hour). Buses leave when full approximately every half hour.

Transportes Trotamundo (☑947-507-787; Terminal Terrestre) goes several times a day to Leimebamba (S10, two hours) stopping off at Yerbabuena (S8, 1½ hours) and Tingo Viejo (S7, one hour) en route. **Mi Cautivo** (☑951-076-019; Terminal Terrestre) runs a similar service.

ETSA (☑950-046-809; Terminal Terrestre) Runs *combis* (minibuses) between Chachapoyas and Pedro Ruíz (S5, one hour) with a stop at Cocahuayco (S3, 45 minutes) for the Gocta waterfalls. Buses leave when full.

Yalape

The largely unexcavated archaeological site of Yalape dates from around AD 1100 and is located 17km south of Chachapoyas near the village of Levanto. Yalape was once the Chachapoyas' second-largest settlement after Kuélap (p431). A visit here won't appeal to everyone – there are no panels, guides or well-defined paths to aid you on your misty mountain hop – but for those who like their ruins well and truly ruined, Yalape will leave you imagining how explorer Hiram Bingham must have felt when he rediscovered Machu Picchu in 1911.

To get to Yalape you need to take a *combi* (S5, one hour, twice daily) or taxi (S50) from Chachapoyas to Levanto and get off at the Km 17 post. An orange sign beside the road marks the site's entry. It's a 200m climb to the ruins through a cow field to a cluster of stone structures, some of which still sport visible trapezoid friezes.

A visit to the ruins can be combined with a hike along part of an old Inca trail back down to Chachapoyas afterwards. The trail starts 2km further up the Levanto road next to an orange sign saying '*camino prehispanico*' (beware, this is the first and last sign you'll see). The ancient path intersperses irregular paving with muddy sections and can be slippery when wet. Navigation is a little tricky, but stay on the main trail and, after about 3km, you'll see Chachapoyas laid out below you. It's a total of 13km of mainly downhill walking to the city center.

Gocta

★ **Catarata de Gocta** WATERFALL

(1/both falls S10/20; ⏰8am-5pm) This 771m waterfall somehow escaped the notice of the Peruvian government, international

LUXURY IN THE HIGHLANDS

The classy **Gocta Andes Lodge** (☑041-63-0552; www.goctalodge.com; Cocachimba; d/tr/ste S325/395/460; ☎☒) in Cocachimba is one of the special spots in the Northern Highlands, sitting in a supremely idyllic setting with unimpeded views to the falls, both from the rooms and the small infinity pool. Said rooms feature lovely kaleidoscopic textiles, cozy down comforters, vaulted ceilings and balconies that frame the falls like a painting.

There's a sophisticated restaurant on-site, as well as a tour agency. Grounds and gardens are meticulously manicured to enhance the natural setting.

explorers and prying satellite images until 2005, when German Stefan Ziemendorff and a group of locals put together an expedition to map the falls. Various claims ranging from the third-loftiest waterfall on earth to the 15th highest resulted in an international firestorm. Whatever its rank, Gocta is mighty impressive and, thanks to a web of well-signposted, forested trails, it's now pretty accessible, too.

To get to the falls from Chachapoyas, catch an ETSA *combi* heading toward Pedro Ruíz (S3, 45 minutes) and get off at Cocahuayaco (a bridge on the main road). *Mototaxis* (three-wheeled motorcycle rickshaw taxis) usually wait here offering to take hikers up to the villages of Cocachimba (5.3km) or San Pablo (6km) for S10. Alternatively, you can hike up to either village. San Pablo provides best access to the upper falls. Cocachimba is the start of the trail to the lower falls. Both villages have community tourist offices where you must pay your entrance fee. Cocachimba has more in the way of places to stay and eat.

For a full day out, it's possible to visit both the upper and lower falls on one 15km circuit. Start in San Pablo village, from where a 6km trail leads to the base of the 231m-high upper cascade. Double back on the same path for 1.8km and then turn left heading down the mountain to a fantastic lookout with a clear view of both cascades, and then across a suspension bridge to the base of the taller 540m-high lower falls. From here you exit along the main trail to Cocachimba

(6.2km), where you can catch a *mototaxi* back to Cocahuayco. From the road bridge, *combis* for Chachapoyas pass every 30 minutes.

For die-hard athletes wanting to do the full circuit, starting and finishing in Cocahuaycos, you're looking at a 26km hike over hilly, sometimes-muddy terrain. Start early.

Gran Vilaya

The name Gran Vilaya refers to the bountiful valleys that spread out west of Chachapoyas, reaching toward the rushing Río Marañón. Abutting the humid Amazon, this region sits in a unique microcosm of perennially moist high-altitude tropics and cloud forests – an ecological anomaly that gave rise to the moniker of the Chachapoyas culture, 'People of the Clouds.'

The fertility of this lush area was never a big secret – the valleys successfully supported the huge populations of the Chachapoyas and Inca cultures, and to date more than 30 archaeological sites have been found dotting the mountains. Important sites such as Paxamarca, Pueblo Alto, Pueblo Nuevo and Pirquilla lie connected by winding goat-tracks as they did hundreds of years ago, completely unexcavated, and can be visited on multiday hikes. Immaculately constructed Inca roads weave up and around the hills, past many ruined cities camouflaged by centuries of jungle.

The impossibly green and silt-filled Valle de Belén lies at the entrance of Gran Vilaya. The flat valley floor here is dissected by the mouth of the widely meandering Río Huaylla, coiled like a languid serpent. Filled with grazing cattle and horses, and surrounded on all sides by mist-covered hills, the vistas here are mesmerizing.

Most travel agencies in Chachapoyas offer multiday trekking tours of this region with the classic four-day circuit (S720 per person) beginning at Cohechán and ending at Kuélap via Choctámal. Hikers should be in good physical condition as the trek requires some serious ascents at altitude.

Karajía

This extraordinary funerary site (admission S10) hosts six sarcophagi perched high up a sheer cliff face. Each long-faced tomb is constructed from wood, clay and straw and uniquely shaped like a stylized forlorn individual. The characters stare intently over the valley below, where a Chachapoyas village once stood; you can see stone ruins scattered among the fields today.

Originally there were eight coupled sarcophagi, but two have collapsed, opening up the adjoining coffins – which were found to contain mummies, plus various crafts and artifacts relating to the deceased. Look out for scattered bones below the coffins. Only important individuals were buried with such reverence: shamans, warriors and chieftains. The skulls above the tombs are thought to have been trophies of enemies or possibly human sacrifices.

Karajía is a 25-minute downhill walk from the tiny outpost of Cruz Pata, or you can hire a horse for S15 roun -trip. Minibuses from Chachapoyas travel to Luya (S8, 50 minutes), and then to Cruz Pata (S8, 50 minutes) on a bumpy road.

All said and done, a day tour from Chachapoyas (S80) is the way to go. The trip usually incorporates a visit to the Caverna de Quiocta on the way. Take binoculars and a camera with a good zoom.

Caverna de Quiocta   CAVE
(admission S5; ⊘8am-5pm) This large cave is 545m long and guards a spooky selection of stalagmites, stalactites and other trippy rock formations. Also visible around the entrance are some pre-Inca cave paintings along with scattered human remains. Quiocta is located around 40km northwest of Chachapoyas on the way to Karajía, and a visit here is usually included in the trip to Karajía sold by most agencies in Chachapoyas. You'll be given boots and a flashlight before going in. Guides are mandatory.

La Jalca (Jalca Grande)

Lovely little mountain town La Jalca, also known as Jalca Grande, is a small, cobble-stoned municipality that has managed to retain much of its historical roots, though modernization is slowly creeping its way in. Quechua is still spoken by older residents here and Chachapoyas-influenced architecture can be seen around the town. Look for Choza Redonda, a traditional Chachapoyas house that was supposedly continually inhabited until 1964. It was used as a model for the re-creation of Chachapoyas houses in Kuélap and Levanto. The roof has collapsed but remains one of the best preserved indigenous houses in the region.

At the ruins of **Ollape**, a 30-minute walk west of La Jalca, you can see several house platforms and circular balconies decorated with complex designs.

There is one direct *combi* from Chachapoyas to La Jalca (S10, two hours) leaving at 3pm from the bus terminal and returning to Chachapoyas at 5am. Otherwise take a Chachapoyas–Leimebamba bus and ask to be let off at the La Jalca turnoff, from where it's a three-hour hike up the hill.

Revash

The historic site of **Revash** (admission S10; ⊘ ticket office 8am-1pm & 2-5pm) protects several brightly colored funerary buildings tucked into limestone cliff ledges high above a valley near the town of Santo Tomás. Looking a bit like attractive, yet inaccessible, cottages, these *chullpas* (ancient Andean funerary towers) are made of small, mud-set stones that were plastered over and embellished with red and cream paints. They are thought to date from the 14th century, but their bright taste in decor is still clearly visible today.

While much of the site was looted long ago, the skeletons of 11 adults and one child, along with a wealth of artifacts such as musical instruments and tools made from bones, were found inside by archaeologists. A number of pictographs decorate the walls of the cliff behind the tombs, and a now empty **funerary cave**, originally containing more than 200 funerary bundles, lies 1km from the main set of tombs. You can't enter the *chullpas* anymore, but a wooden *mirador* about 30m below offers excellent views.

The shortest route to the site is to take a Leimebamba-bound *combi* from Chachapoyas and get off in Yerbabuena (S8, 1½ hours, five daily). From here, you can try to find a *mototaxi* to take you a further 16km along a solid but unpaved road to the hamlet of Cruz de San Bartolo (S20, 30 minutes). Pay your entrance fee at the office in San Bartolo from where it's a 2km hike to the archaeological site along a partly paved and well-marked path. Spanish-speaking guides can be hired for S25.

Alternatively, you can hike up from Yerbabuena. Follow the San Bartolo road to just past the 5km marker where a signposted trail heads into the hills. From here it's a rough two-hour climb to the *chullpas* (total elevation gain 1000m).

A day tour from Chachapoyas is about S80 and also visits the museum (p433) in Leimebamba.

Kuélap

ELEV 3100M

The so-called 'Machu Picchu of the north,' once home to the mysterious 'warriors of the cloud forest,' sits like a giant medieval castle on a craggy mountain ridge 60km southwest of Chachapoyas, close to the village of Tingo. It is the best preserved and most dramatic of the district's many archaeological sites and – with the recent construction of a cable car – is fast becoming northern Peru's biggest attraction (annual tourist numbers doubled to 120,000 within a year of the cable-car opening). Situated at a higher altitude to Machu Picchu and built a good 500 years earlier, Kuélap predates the Inca Empire and was probably never conquered by Peru's most famous pre-Columbian culture. Sometimes described as a fortress, it was more likely a walled city (but what walls!) which at its peak might have been home to up to 300,000 people.

Kuélap (adult/child S20/10; ⊘ 8am-5pm) is made up of millions of cubic feet of remarkably preserved stone. The 700m-long oval fortress was constructed between AD 900 and 1100, and rediscovered in 1843. Shaped like an ocean liner atop a 3000m-high limestone ridge, it is surrounded by an imposing, near-impenetrable wall that towers up to 20m high in places. Entrance into this stronghold is via three deep, narrow gates designed like funnels – an ingenious security system that forced attacking parties into easily defeated single files.

The main entrance, **Acceso 3**, is reached by walking along the east side of the fortress. A wooden boardwalk takes visitors on a winding route inside with newly installed panels giving basic explanations in Spanish and English. You'll be directed first to the raised **Pueblo Alto**, site of a 7m-high **Torreón** (tower) that sits like a sentry guarding Kuélap's northern bows. Despite its name, the tower's role was probably ritualistic rather than military – burials have been unearthed in its entrails. Nearby is the **Callanca**, one of the complex's few rectangular buildings, thought to have been a hostel and ritualistic center where pieces of Inca-influenced ceramics have been found.

The center of the fort is scattered with the remnants of more than 400 circular dwellings. Some are decorated with zigzag and rhomboid friezes, and all were once topped by soaring thatched roofs. A variety of trees grow in and around the ruins, many heavy with epiphytes that attract hundreds of hungry hummingbirds.

The most impressive and enigmatic structure, named the **Templo Mayor** or El Tintero (Inkpot), sits near the south end of Kuélap and has been fashioned in the shape of a large inverted cone. Inside, an underground chamber houses the remains of animal sacrifices, leading archaeologists to believe that it was a religious building of some kind. Kuélap resident archaeologist Alfredo Narvez has now excavated graves and llama skeletons around El Tintero to further support this theory. A 1996 hypothesis by a team from the University of San Diego suggests it may have also been a solar calendar.

Since 2017, access to the ruins has been made infinitely easier by the building of a cable car, or **Telecabinas** (www.telecabinaskuelap.com; S20 round-trip; ⏰8am-3:30pm). Eight-berth cabins take visitors on a 20-minute journey across a V-shaped river valley and up a steep treeless hillside to within a 20-minute walk of the ruins. The bottom station is located just above the village of Nuevo Tingo. From here minibuses shuttle visitors up a 3km road to where the cable-car ride starts. At the top station there is a cafeteria (p427), interpretation center and a ticket office for the site itself. A stone path leads 1.5 km directly to the ruins from the top station. Community guides can be hired for S50 from the top station. Bank on two hours to view the ruins properly.

Tour groups usually arrive at the ruins around 11:30am and leave by 3pm, so consider setting off from Chachapoyas at around 8am to avoid the rush.

It is still possible to hike down (or up) the 9km-long **Camino Herradura** between the ruins and Tingo Viejo. Pick up the path by the old ticket office outside Acceso 1 (if going down), or by the river bridge in Tingo Viejo (if going up).

🛏 Sleeping

Hospedaje Imperio Kuelapino HOTEL $
(☑941-735-833; d S85, dm/d without bathroom S25/65) The closest you can get to the Kuélap

ruins without staying in them (they're about 250m away) is this fetching lodge on the opposite side of the hill to the cable car in the pinprick community of Longuita. It's a basic hike-in affair with good bedding and meals available. The mountain views are *Lord of the Rings*–worthy.

Breakfast is S5 extra.

Hospedaje León GUESTHOUSE $
(☑941-715-685; Tingo Viejo; d S30, without bathroom S25) This basic place with tiny, very simple rooms and electric hot water (if you pay S5 a night extra) is run by a friendly older couple who capitalized on a tourism vision years ago. About as good as it gets in this neck of the woods. It's 3km below Tingo Nuevo at the start point for the Camino Herradura.

Combis from Chachapoyas stop right outside.

Marvelous Spatuletail Lodge LODGE $$
(☑995-237-268; www.marvelousspatuletail.com; Choctanal; s/d/tr S150/180/230) 🍃 The name isn't a boast about the lodge's quality (although it *is* pretty marvelous) but rather a reference to the Marvelous Spatuletail Hummingbirds that frequent its flowery grounds. The birds aren't the only allure at this isolated retreat built in the style of an old country hacienda and located within shouting distance of the Kuélap (p431) ruins.

The location means you can pop over to the ruins early before the crowds. Additional appeal comes with the meals (by prior arrangement) and views of mystical mountains topped by clouds and ruins. The lodge is run as a co-op in association with the local village of Choctanal. A taxi pickup from Pedro Ruíz costs S160; arrange in advance through the lodge.

ℹ Getting There & Away

Getting to Kuélap is now easy in a day trip from Chachapoyas arriving either independently or as part of an organized group.

Several bus companies, including Turismo Kuélap (p428), run frequent minibuses from Chachapoyas' main bus terminal to the base of the cable-car station in Nuevo Tingo (S7, one hour). Buses leave when full approximately every half hour.

Leimebamba

📞041 / POP 4200 / ELEV 2050M

This convivial cobblestoned town – often spelled 'Leymebamba' – lies at the head of the Río Utcubamba, with a mellow town square and ample local attractions. It has an endearingly laid-back allure that is maintained by its relative isolation: it is flanked by towering mountains and the nearest big city is a couple of hours away via a narrow road. Horses are still a popular form of transport around town and the friendliness of the locals is legendary in the region. Surrounded by a multitude of archaeological sites from the Chachapoyas era, peaceful, community-focused Leimebamba is a great place to base yourself for a few days while exploring the province.

Sights

★ Museo Leimebamba   MUSEUM
(www.museoleymebamba.org; admission S15; ⊙10am-4:30pm) The mummies found at Laguna de los Cóndores are housed in the Museo Leimebamba, 5km south of town. The museum is owned by the local community and located in a wonderfully constructed complex with multitiered roofs that pays tribute to indigenous architecture. The mummies are stored behind glass in a climate-controlled room. Most are wrapped in bundles although some have been unwrapped for your gruesome viewing pleasure.

Other well-presented artifacts on display include ceramics, textiles, wood figures and photos of Laguna de los Cóndores. A taxi/*mototaxi* from town costs S7/5.

Laguna de los Cóndores   ARCHAEOLOGICAL SITE
This part of Peru hit the spotlight in 1996 when a group of farmers found six *chullpas* on a ledge 100m above a cloud-forest lake. The burial site was a windfall for archaeologists, and its 219 mummies and more than 2000 artifacts have given researchers a glimpse past the heavy curtain of history that conceals the details of the Chachapoyas civilization.

So spectacular was the find that a Discovery Channel film was made about it and a museum was built in Leimebamba to house the mummies and cultural treasures. Some of the tombs, plastered and painted in white or red-and-yellow ochre, are decorated with signature Chachapoyas zigzag friezes. All lie huddled against the cliff on a natural ledge overlooking the stunning Laguna de los Cóndores.

The only way to get to the lagoon is by a strenuous nine- to 10-hour journey on foot or horseback from Leimebamba. The standard tour is three days: one day to hike in, a day of sightseeing (including fishing and boating on the lake) and a day hiking out. Horses and guides can be arranged either in Leimebamba or at travel agencies in Chachapoyas. Bank on paying S850 per person.

La Congona   RUINS
The most captivating of the many ancient ruins strewn around Leimebamba, La Congona is definitely worth the three-hour hike needed to get here. The flora-covered site contains several well-preserved circular houses, one of which, oddly for Chachapoyas culture, sits on a square base. Inside, the houses are adorned with intricate niches; outside, wide circular terraces surround each residence.

This archaeological site is renowned for the symbolic decoration on its buildings and particularly for the numerous sophisticated masonry friezes. A tall **tower** can be climbed by a remarkable set of curving steps for wide-angle panoramas of the surrounding valley.

The site is reached from Leimebamba along a track beginning at the lower end of Calle 16 de Julio. The track zigzags up a hillside to a hamlet called **La Fila**, from where a narrower path continues to the ruins. There are no signposts, but you can hire a guide at the Asociación Comunal de Turismo. Expect to pay around S150 for the eight-hour circuit.

Activities

★ Asociación Comunal de Turismo   HIKING
(☑95-107-2028; jabierfarje@hotmail.com; Parque Principal; ⊙8am-noon & 2-5pm) Ultrahelpful community tourist office able to impart info on all of Leimebamba's fascinating sites. Here you can arrange guides for treks to archaeological sites such as La Congona and the Laguna de los Cóndores.

Sleeping

La Casona   GUESTHOUSE $$
(☑041-83-0106; www.casonadeleymebamba.com; Amazonas 221; s/d/tr incl breakfast S145/245/290; ⊛) This friendly, rambling guesthouse run by a brother-sister team is chock-full of antiquated character and homespun charm. Old rooms feature polished hardwood floors while all have modern bathrooms with hot water. Some also sport little balconies looking onto the quiet street below, while others

have views over the town's tiled roofs and surrounding mountains.

Nelly, the matriarch here, runs a mean kitchen for guests. Breakfast is a real treat, with an espresso machine along with homemade cheese, butter and milk from the proprietors' own cows.

★**Kentitambo** GUESTHOUSE **$$$**
(☑97-111-8273; www.kentitambo.com; s/d incl breakfast S380/550; ☎) 🖋 This wonderfully romantic guesthouse is an exclusive getaway for discerning nature lovers. King-sized beds and filtered rainwater showers are highlights of the colorful, rustic bungalows built in earthquake-proof *quincho* (mud hut) style. But the real coup is the spacious front porch with hammocks that reach into the surrounding nature – perfect for ogling the exotic birdlife congregating on the property.

Reservations are essential. It's located next to equally delectable KentiKafé, and in front of the museum (p433).

✖ Eating

KentiKafé CAFE **$**
(snacks S3.50-10; ⊙8:30am-5:30pm; ☎) Perched on a hill with views of the valley below, alfresco KentiKafé serves gourmet coffee, homemade cakes and sandwiches with avocado and local cheese. The surrounding garden is visited by 17 hummingbird species – including the Marvelous Spatuletail Hummingbird. It's just a short stroll across the street from Museo Leimebamba (p433).

The cafe maintains about a dozen feeders through which the local hummingbirds drink some 5kg of sugar per day. You can lie in wait for glimpses of the spatuletail while sipping your espresso.

**Restaurante Turísitico
Rumi Wasi** PERUVIAN **$$**
(☑966-545-695; San Agustín 465; mains S15-25; ⊙11am-9pm) It's not often that tiny Leimebamba gets a new restaurant, so all hail Rumi Wasi on the main plaza, whose congenial owner, Eliott, scrawls his daily menu on a whiteboard and invites you in. Specialties don't stray far from local favorites, including trout, *cuy* (guinea pig) and chorizo.

Despite the name it's not at all touristy, although Eliott is happy to direct you toward the area's wonderfully understated sights.

🛍 Shopping

AMAL ARTS & CRAFTS
(San Augustín 429; ⊙9am-6pm) This women's artisan cooperative located on the plaza sells top-grade handicrafts and local weavings. Better than the shop, however, is the co-op's small workshop, about a five-minute walk along the road to the museum (p433). Here, you can see the women in action and choose your own material to custom-design anything from purses to backpacks.

❶ Information

MONEY
Leimebamba doesn't have an ATM; bring cash.

❶ Getting There & Away

Various minibuses run between Chachapoyas (S10) and Leimebamba. The trip takes around two hours. The most comprehensive service is offered by **Raymi Express** (☑942-152-181; Amazonas 420) with about five minivans daily. The last bus leaves Leimebamba for Chachapoyas at around 1pm. **Mi Cautivo** (☑94-194-0571; Parque Principal) is another company operating on this route for similar prices.

Virgen del Carmen (☑96-483-3033; www.turismovirgendelcarmen.com.pe; Plaza de Armas) has two daily buses to Chachapoyas (S15, 2½ hours) from Cajamarca/Celendín that pass through at about 2pm or 2am. In the reverse direction, heading toward Celendín (S25, six hours) and Cajamarca (S35, eight hours), the buses pass at about 10pm.

Pedro Ruíz

☑041 / POP 2700 / ELEV 1313M
This transit town sits at the junction of the Chiclayo–Tarapoto road and the turnoff to Chachapoyas. When traveling from Chachapoyas, you can board east- or westbound buses here.

The journey east from Pedro Ruíz is spectacular, climbing over two high passes, traveling by a beautiful lake and dropping into fantastic high-jungle vegetation in between. Keep the binoculars handy. You're passing through northern Peru's famous 'bird corridor.'

◉ Sights

**Abra Patricia-Alto Nieva
Private Conservation Area** NATURE RESERVE
(☑041-81-6814; www.ecoanperu.org; Carr Fernando Balaunde Km 365.5; admission S75) The

2960-hectare Abra Patricia-Alto Nieva Private Conservation Area is a bird-watcher's paradise managed by the Association of Andean Ecosystems (ECOAN). More than 300 species call this area home, 23 of which are considered globally threatened. There are a half-dozen named trails in the reserve. None of them are particularly long, but all offer perfect conditions for observing the native birds.

The conservation area is located about 40 minutes east of Pedro Ruíz on the road to Moyobamba. ECOAN maintains two lodges in the area: the **Owlet Lodge** (☏984-564-884; www.ecoanperu.org; Carr Fernando Balaunde Km 365.5; s/d incl admission & all meals S485/795) on the main Anra Patricia site and the **Huembo Lodge** (☏984-564-884; www.ecoan-peru.org; Carr Fernando Balaunde Km 315; s/d incl admission & all meals S290/545), 50km west in the direction of Pedro Ruíz.

This is a fabulous spot to enjoy mountainous cloud forest that has never seen the swipe of a chainsaw. Although an obvious favorite of bird-watching tour groups – who come to see such endemic species as yellow-scarfed tanager, Lulu's tody-flycatcher and the extremely rare long-whiskered owlet – it's also the best place to see the critically endangered yellow-tailed woolly monkey.

Huembo Interpretation Center

WILDLIFE RESERVE

(www.ecoanperu.org; Carr Fernando Balaunde Km 315; ⊙7:30am-6pm) This interpretation center 15 minutes west of the village of San Lucas de Pomacochas maintains feeders on a private reserve that attracts the Marvelous Spatuletail (*Loddigesia mirabilis*) and many other hummingbirds; the views over the valley and the plunging road from here are also spectacular. The center's administrator, Santos Montenegro, may show you the spatuletail at the breeding ground on his property, on the west edge of town and 15 minutes' hike up into the scrub forest.

Santos' family does not formally charge for the spatuletail excursion, but a donation is appropriate.

The reserve also harbors accommodation courtesy of the Huembo Lodge run by Peru's ECOAN.

🍴 Sleeping & Eating

Casablanca Hotel HOTEL $

(☏941-902-878; Marginal 122; s/d/tr S30/70/90) The pick of the none-too-inspiring hotels in Pedro Ruíz is by the road junction, but try to get a room away from the noisy highway. Rooms are basic but perfectly decent with cable TV and hot water.

A HAVEN FOR HUMMINGBIRDS

You don't have to be a big-time bird-watcher to get turned on by the Marvelous Spatuletail Hummingbird, a rare and exquisitely beautiful bird that lives in limited habitats of scrubby forest between 2000m and 2900m in northern Peru's Utcubamba Valley. As with most bird species, the males get the prize in the looks category, and the Marvelous male is no exception, with his shimmering blue crown and green throat, and a sexy set of curved and freakishly long quills that splay out from his backside and end in wide, feather 'rackets' or 'spatules.' He can independently maneuver these long plumes into extravagant mating displays, crossing the two spatuletail feathers over each other or swinging them in front of his head as he hovers in front of a female.

According to some Peruvians in the Utcubamba Valley, the spatuletail's most spectacular anatomical feature is its heart, which is considered an aphrodisiac when eaten. The hunting of the birds for this purpose has probably contributed to keeping its numbers low – perhaps less than 1000 pairs remain – although conservation efforts in the region have led to increased awareness about the precarious status of the bird, whose habitat is quickly diminishing due to deforestation and agricultural development, and the need to protect it. Leading this effort are local conservation centers such as KentiKafé in Leimebamba, the Marvelous Spatuletail Lodge (p432) near Kuélap and the Huembo Interpretation Center, 15 minutes west of Pomacochas on the road to Pedro Ruíz. The views over the valley and the plunging road from the center are also spectacular – you can spend the night here as well.

Virgen de Chuquichaca PERUVIAN $

(Av Marginal; menús S6-9, mains S10-15; ⊙8am-9pm) Your best bet for a filling meal in Pedro Ruíz. Manage your expectations.

ℹ Information

Pedro Ruíz has a Visa/MasterCard ATM on Av Marginal across from the PetroPeru gas station.

SAFE TRAVEL

The highway on both sides of the town is particularly susceptible to landslides. If it's wet, check on conditions before making plans.

ℹ Getting There & Away

Buses from the coast pick up passengers heading to Rioja or Moyobamba (S30 to S35, five hours) and Tarapoto (S40 to S50, seven hours), and in the opposite direction to Chiclayo (S55, seven hours) and Lima (S90 to S170, 21 hours). The most comfortable choice is **Movil Tours** (🕿 041-83-5188; www.moviltours.com.pe; Av Cahuide 653), which departs east at noon and west for Lima at 5pm and 8pm. **Civa** (🕿 941-727-323; Av Marginal s/n) heads east at midnight and west to Chiclayo and Lima at midnight.

Turismo Selva (🕿 998-455-075; www.turismoselva.com; PE-5N) runs a half-dozen daily eastbound minivans to Moyobamba (S20, five hours), Tarapoto (S30, seven hours) and Yurimaguas (S40, eight hours).

If coming from Tarapoto, **ETSA** (🕿 950-046-809; Av Marginal s/n), next to the PetroPeru gas station, runs *combis* to Chachapoyas (S5, one hour) from 4am to 6pm every 30 minutes or so.

Jaén

🕿 076 / POP 93,600 / ELEV 729M

For visitors to the Northern Highlands the fast-growing agricultural center of Jaén is little more than a gateway town. Its airport is only a three-hour bus ride from Chachapoyas, while roads north head to the border with Ecuador. Jaén has all the services of a mid-size town...along with a reputation for street crime and, judging by the signs, a serious dengue problem (bring repellent).

🛏 Sleeping & Eating

Business Class

Prim's Hotel BUSINESS HOTEL $$

(🕿 076-43-1039; www.bcprimshotel.com; San Martín 1261; s/d incl breakfast S150/200; P ❄ 🛜 🐾) Prim's will do just nicely for an overnight stay in Jaén on the way to and from Ecuador or Chachapoyas. Claiming to be a business-boutique hotel, its large

rooms are slick and shiny in an austere business-bland way. There's an attached restaurant, a parking garage and use of a small outdoor swimming pool at a sister property a block away.

Cafetería Apu CAFE $

(www.cafeteriasapu.com; Pasaje Bracamoros; snacks S8-15; ⊙7am-11pm) Let's cut to the chase: Apu serves the best coffee in Jaén using beans plucked from the nearby hills. The cafeteria is a jolly good place to imbibe it, too, with comfortable seating, colorful modern decor and crispy sandwiches to soak it up.

ℹ Getting There & Away

AIR

Located 20km northeast of the town, Jaén's **airport** is often used by travelers heading to and from the Chachapoyas region.

LATAM (www.latam.com; Bolívar 1458; ⊙8am-8pm Mon-Sat) offers one to two daily flights to and from Lima (S60 to S80, 1½ hours).

BUS

The solidly reliable **Movil Tours** (🕿 076-43-3963; www.moviltours.com.pe; Av Mesones Muro cuadra 7) has one daily bus to Chachapoyas (S50, 3½ hours) at 1:30pm, and two daily to Chiclayo (S30 to S40, six hours) at 1:30pm and 11pm.

Turismo Explorer (p425) runs daily transfer buses (S50, four hours) between Jaén airport and Chachapoyas. Buses leave Chachapoyas at 7am, pick up passengers from the 12:30pm flight in Jaén, and then return to Chachapoyas.

Moyobamba

🕿 042 / POP 86,000 / ELEV 860M

The 'City of Orchids' welcomes you to Peru's jungle region with a florid flourish. Moyobamba, the capital of the department of San Martín, might not be Arequipa or even Cajamarca in the architectural stakes (earthquakes have contributed to the demise of most of its historic buildings), but with its intimate Plaza de Armas, easily accessible viewpoints and little hidden secrets (excellent coffee!), it's worth a stopover.

Tourist authorities, working together with local communities, have developed a number of ecological activities in the area, including hiking, riverboat trips and appreciation of the town's emblematic orchids. To many travelers, Moyobamba offers a quieter,

---

ⓘ BORDER CROSSING: ECUADOR VIA JAÉN

....

If your next port of call is Ecuador, remember that you don't have to spend days on winding roads to get back to the Peruvian coast. From Jaén, a good northbound road heads 107km to San Ignacio (population 10,720) near the Ecuadorian border, on the other side of which you'll find the town of Zumba.

From Jaén, *autos* (shared taxis; S20, 2½ hours) and *combis* (minibuses; S15, 2½ hours) leave for **San Ignacio** from **Empresa Transporte Jaén–San Ignacio** (Pakumuros 2093, Pueblo Libre; ☉4am-8pm). In San Ignacio there's a simple hotel and places to eat. Change in San Ignacio for a *colectivo* (shared transportation) on the rough road to **La Balsa** (S15, two hours) on the Río Blanco, dividing Peru from Ecuador. There used to be a *balsa* (ferry) here – hence the name – but there's now an international bridge linking the two countries.

Once in Ecuador, curious yet typical *rancheras* (trucks with rows of wooden seats) await to take you on the uncomfortable and unpredictable (because of the weather) 10km drive to **Zumba** (US$2.75, 1½ to 2½ hours). From here, buses go to **Loja** (US$7.50, six hours), where you can continue on to the famed 'valley of longevity' of **Vilcabamba**. If you leave Jaén at dawn, you should be able to make it to Vilcabamba in one day.

---

more intimate antidote to Tarapoto – the town's larger, much noisier eastern cousin.

⊙ Sights

Morro de Calzada
HILL
(admission S3; ☉dawn-dusk) Drawing your eye on your way into Moyobamba from the west is a craggy hill rising abruptly out of the flat forest. This is the Morro de Calzada (550m), a wildlife-rich natural feature encased in a protected reserve with a clear if sometimes rocky trail to the summit. On the way up, you'll pass through thick jungle-like vegetation and, with luck, see an abundance of birdlife, including owls.

To get to the trailhead, take a *combi* from Jirón Callao in Moyobamba to the village of Calzada (S2.50, 15 minutes), 12km to the west. From here you can either walk 2.5km or get a *mototaxi* (S10) to the start point. Pay your entry at the visitor center and join the trail. It takes around 90 minutes to get to the top where the views over Moyobamba and its surroundings are stupendous. On the way down, be sure to pay a visit to **Calzada village**, known for its hat-making stores and dairy products.

Reserva Tingana
NATURE RESERVE
(☏042-78-2803, 942-958-538; www.tingana.org; Calle 20 de Abril 1092; day tours from S135) This community-run nature reserve protects a swath of forest on the upper Río Mayo that is home to monkeys and a wide variety of birds, frogs and butterflies. The tourism cooperative offers day tours that include transport, guide, breakfast, lunch and a 3½ rowboat trip. Reservations are essential.

Contact the cooperative online or call into its office in Barrio Zaragoza.

Waqanki Orchid Center
GARDENS
(www.waqanki.com; Carr a Baños de San Mateo; admission S10; ☉7:30am-5pm) This showcase garden replete with some 400 species of orchid growing in a beautiful forest is located 5km south of the 'City of Orchids.' Providing a wonderful natural alliance is an adjacent hummingbird garden where around 26 species of the tiny birds can be seen. Professional guides can take you round a 40-minute walking circuit or you can stroll alone.

Mirador Tahuishco
VIEWPOINT
(Malecon San Juan) Head to this viewpoint seven blocks northeast of the plaza for supreme panoramas of the Mayo River valley below. (Stairs head down the mountainside to the river port.) It's a potentially tranquil spot, depending on how many local teenagers are playing rap on their iPhones when you arrive. Forget the evenings, as the road behind appears to be Moyobamaba's main nightclub quarter. Another, quieter lookout is located a few blocks downstream at **Mirador San Juan**.

Museo Departamental de San Martín
MUSEUM
(☏042-56-2281; Benavides 352; admission S2; ☉8am-1pm & 2:30-5pm Mon-Fri) Moyobamba's tiny museum devotes most of its space to the Chachapoyas culture and its history including some unearthed ceramics and textile work.

🏃 Activities

Baños Termales de San Mateo　HOT SPRINGS
(admission S3; ⏰5am-8pm) These well-maintained hot springs, 5km south of town, have six *pozos* (large baths) of varying temperatures in a pleasant garden setting. A *mototaxi* ride here will cost S6. On weekends the baths get crowded with locals.

👉 Tours

Upper Río Mayo　BOATING
(Puerto de Tahuishco; 30min/1hr trip S30/60) Short sightseeing trips in narrow motorboats on the Río Mayo are run out of the impressive Embarcadero Turístico 2km north of the plaza. It's best to go in the early morning or evening when you'll see more birdlife.

A *mototaxi* to the port costs around S7 or you can walk down the stairs from Mirador Tahuishco (p437).

🛏 Sleeping

⭐ El Portón　GUESTHOUSE $$
(☎042-56-2900; casahospedajeelporton@hotmail.com; San Martín 449; s/d S80/90; 📶) In the middle of downtown, seemingly oblivious to the honks of 100 *mototaxis*, El Portón hides a heavenly little garden full of exotic jungle plants behind a high wall. Surrounding the greenery are the small but charming rooms, each equipped with an alfresco hammock, comfy beds and bright Peruvian paintings on the walls.

All said, it's an unexpected and spirit-reviving little hideaway of which the friendly owner is rightly proud. Breakfast costs S10 extra.

Hospedaje Moyobamba　HOTEL $$
(☎042-56-1025; Alfonso de Alvarado 493; s/d S80/100; 📶) Friendly midranger with some notable bright spots, namely the foliage-crammed mini garden that makes a refreshing antidote to the hot, *mototaxi*-filled streets outside. Rooms, set around said garden, have fans but no air-con. Breakfast isn't included.

La Casa de Seizo　BUNGALOW $$
(☎042-78-4766; www.lacasadeseizo.com; Contiguo a Los Baños de San Mateo; s/d S80/100; 📶) In a verdant and idyllic setting outside Moyobamba overlooking a couple of Japanese-style ponds and with a soundtrack of birdsong from the feathered fauna that frequent the grounds. The well-appointed, but rustic rooms have exposed-brick walls, but

no TVs. However, the highlight here is the food. La Casa de Seizo is a short walk from the San Mateo hot springs.

The Japanese-Peruvian/Venezuelan couple running the show couldn't be sweeter or better cooks: whether Seizo plucks a tilapia from the pond and turns it into sashimi before your eyes, whips up his garlic-ginger fish or feeds you his cafe-smoked chicken, you are in for a real treat.

Plenty of *mototaxis* ferry the 5km between Moyobamaba and the hot springs (S6).

🍴 Eating

⭐ Aromacafé　COFFEE $
(☎042-56-2733; Jirón San Martín 183; snacks S2-5; ⏰8am-1pm & 4-10pm) The coffee is exquisite – made by people who know how to bring out the best flavors – at this coffee bar full of pop-culture collectibles. While you're waiting for the steam to heat up your cappuccino, examine the mini-museum's Texaco petrol pump, vintage rock posters, Wild West iconography and an assemblage of coffee pots, jars, bags and grinders.

Café Bet-El　CAFE $
(☎042-56-2796; Jirón Callao 537; breakfasts S10-12; ⏰7:30am-10:30pm Mon-Sat, from 3:30pm Sun; 📶) Serving up truly excellent coffee (including frappuccinos), Bet-el is affiliated to a small hotel. A large coffee roaster greets you at the door (always a good sign), and inside there's plenty of room to commune with the wi-fi or sit down for something to eat with a fellow traveler. Filling breakfasts, hearty sandwiches and alluring cakes are served with casual aplomb.

⭐ La Olla de Barro　AMAZONIAN $$
(☎042-56-3450; cnr Canga & Filomeno; mains S8-34; ⏰8am-midnight) Don't miss this local institution, set up tiki-lounge-style, where you can double-dare your friends to try fried ants or alligator, all while you savor the phenomenal *inchicapi* (chicken soup with peanuts, cilantro and yucca). This is the best place in town to sample local jungle dishes and river fish, plus exotic regional fruit sours such as *camu-camu* and *cocona*.

Avoid endangered wild *paiche* (local river fish) from October to February, when its commercial fishing is prohibited due to near extinction.

ℹ️ Information

MONEY

BCP (Calle de Alvarado 903; ⊙ 9am-6pm Mon-Fri, to 1pm Sat)

TOURIST INFORMATION

Oficina de Información Turística (Plaza de Armas; ⊙ 8am-1pm & 2:30-5:15pm Mon-Sat)

ℹ️ Getting There & Away

Turismo Selva (Jirón Callao 394) runs frequent minivans to Rioja (S2, 30 minutes), Chachapoyas (S24, six hours) and Tarapoto (S10, two hours). Vans leave when full.

Movil Tours (☑ 042-56-3720; www.moviltours.com.pe; Av Grau 320) has two daily departures for Lima (S130 to S170, 26 hours) at 2pm and 3pm. Also a daily bus to Tujillo (S90 to S120, 17 hours) at 5pm, and another one to Chiclayo (S80 to S105, 13 hours) at 6pm.

Tarapoto

☑ 042 / POP 144,200 / ELEV 356M

Tarapoto straddles the base of the Andean foothills, providing an unlikely entry ticket into the vast jungles of eastern Peru. A sweltering rainforest metropolis, it dips its toe into the Amazon Basin while managing to cling to the rest of Peru by the umbilical cord of a long paved road back to civilization. People come here more for the sights that surround the town than the town itself – although it's by no means an unpleasant place. From Tarapoto you can take the plunge deeper into the Amazon, or just enjoy the easily accessible jungle-lite, with plenty of places to stay and eat, and reliable connections to the coast. There's a bunch of natural sights to explore nearby, from waterfalls to lagoons, while river-running opportunities will entertain the adventure-seeking contingent.

◎ Sights

Alto Shilcayo   NATURE RESERVE
(fin Prolongación Alerta; admission S10; ⊙ 7am-6pm) 🖋 Dense jungle lies just 3km from the city limits of the crazy, cacophonous metropolis of Tarapoto. This section of the Área de Conservación Regional Cordillera Escalera protects the thick foliage around the upper Río Shilcayo. The zone is populated by monkeys and many bird species, and there are five rarely visited **waterfalls** plus a fantastic **natural lookout**. Some trails become impassable when very wet.

The local community has formed a tourism cooperative and offers guides for a number of **treks**, ranging from short trips to the waterfalls to two-night treks – utilizing a simple jungle *hostal* (guesthouse) – finishing on the other side of the reserve at the Yurimaguas highway. It's possible to venture in solo although signage is practically non-existent. One trail, the short **Circuito de Aves**, is easy enough to navigate, but the others are longer and require multiple river crossings. Bring appropriate footwear.

To get to the reserve, follow Alegría Arias de Morey northeast to a T-junction, turn left opposite **La Collpa** (☑ 042 52-2644; Circunvalación 164; mains S14-35; ⊙ 10am-11pm) and take the dirt road downhill. The entrance to the reserve is 2.5 km along the road.

Lamas   VILLAGE
This town, a short drive from Tarapoto, is remarkable in the way that it is split into two distinct halves with *mestizo* (person of mixed indigenous and Spanish descent) residents positioned on the upper plateau while the indigenous community resides on the lower. A large faux-European castle (p442) has been constructed on the edge of the upper town, a bizarre sight that serves to reinforce the weird colonial vibe.

The large indigenous population of Lamas has a strong folkloric tradition manifested in music and dance and celebrates an annual **Feast of Santa Rosa de Lima** in the last week of August. The local **Museo Chanka y de la Diversidad Lamista** (San Martín 1165; admission S6; ⊙ 8:30am-7pm) explains the origins of the festival and other distinct elements of the folkloric culture.

It's very easy to visit the town on your own; minibuses and *colectivos* (shared transportation; S5, 30 minutes) leave for Lamas regularly from the 10th *cuadra* (block) of Jirón Urgarte. Alternatively, three-hour guided tours from Tarapoto cost around S35.

Cataratas de Ahuashiyacu   WATERFALL
(Carr Yurimaguas, Km 13) This 40m waterfall has a small restaurant nearby and a locally favored swimming spot. Four-hour tours cost around S35 per person. It's possible to reach the entrance, a short walk from the falls, on public *combis* heading toward Yurimaguas. Heading back to town can be a problem, though, as most vans return full and you may have to wait for a ride. The falls are about 45 minutes from Tarapoto toward Yurimaguas.

Tarapoto

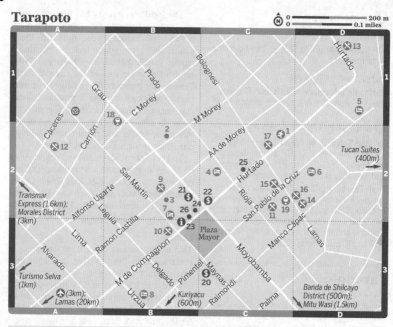

Tarapoto

Also popular are the **Cataratas de Hua-camaillo**, which involve two hours of hiking and wading across the river several times – as a result, they're far less crowded. Tours cost around S85 per person.

To reach the falls on your own, take a *colectivo* (shared transportation) from Jirón Comandante Chirinos to the Puente de San Antonio de Cumbaza, from where the trail begins. Hiring a guide is recommended.

Laguna Azul
LAKE

You'll find good swimming, boating and fishing at this popular local spot, also called Laguna de Sauce. Day tours (S85 per person, minimum two people) and overnight excursions are available, as are accommodations, from camping to upscale bungalows. There are also a couple of **waterfalls** nearby and some fairly undeveloped **thermal springs**, just after the river crossing. Reach the lake by crossing the Río Huallaga, 45km away, on a vehicle raft ferry and continuing by car or taxi for another 45 minutes.

Several *combis* (S15, two hours) go each day to nearby Sauce from a bus stop on Marginal Sur *cuadra* (block) 7 in the Banda de Shilcayo district, east of the town. Taxi drivers know it.

Chazuta
VILLAGE

This small village is famed throughout the region for its elegant pottery. It has artisan workshops, a small museum showcasing pre-Inca funerary urns, and a port on the Río Huallaga with great fishing. Nearby are the impressive 40m, three-level **Tununtunumba waterfalls** and the **Chazutayacu thermal baths**.

Combis (S10, two hours) leave from Jirón Olaya *cuadra* (block) 13. The paved road is subject to landslides so check conditions before making plans.

Activities

Rafting

The local river-running specialists run rafting trips on the **Río Mayo**, 30km from Tarapoto, and for those with experience, on the wilder **Río Huallaga**.

The Río Mayo (half-day trips, from S50 per person) is mostly class II and III, and is more of a sightseeing trip than a full-on adventure. Kayaks are available for rent with mandatory guide (half day S100).

Try safety-first **Ecorutas** (☑945-294-945; www.facebook.com/ecorutas; Hurtado 435) whose owner, Julio, speaks a bit of English; or **Kuriyacu** (☑942-793-388, 042-52-1511; Libertad 265), which can arrange guides in English and French.

☞ Tours

There are dozens of licensed agencies selling almost identical tours mostly catering for national (Peruvian) tourists. Prices are low and pretty generic, but don't expect your guide to speak anything but Spanish.

Popular half-day tours include outings to Lamas (p439) and the Cataratas de Ahuashiyacu (p439). Both cost around S35 and run most days. Full-day tours include Laguna Azul (S85) and trips on the **Alto Mayo River** (S120).

Shilcayo Travel Tours
TOURS

(☑042-78-2832; www.shilcayotraveltours.com; Morey 118) An experienced and reliable local operator offering the full set of tours in the area. The tour desk is located inside the handicrafts market on the plaza.

Martín Zamora Tours
TOURS

(☑042-52-5148; Morey 247; ⊙8am-1pm & 4-7:30pm) Tarapoto's go-to operator for day tours, cultural trips and longer excursions to local lakes and waterfalls.

🛏 Sleeping

You don't need to go far from town to find lush jungle surrounds. There are a string of nature lodges on the banks of the Río Shilcayo just north of the center.

In town, expect your digs to be a little less exotic.

🛏 In Town

El Mirador
GUESTHOUSE $

(☑042-52-2177; www.elmiradortarapoto.com; San Pablo de la Cruz 517; s/d incl breakfast S60/80, with air-con S100/150; ❊ ☞) Travelers swoon over this budget spot. Maybe it's because the family owners offer up the warmest welcome in Tarapoto; or perhaps it's about the excellent breakfast served on the terrace with hammocks and jungle views? Rooms in the main house are basic, with fans and white decor; those in the newer annex are bright, air-conditioned and sport very yellow bathrooms.

As it's a few blocks from the center, you won't suffer as much *mototaxi* noise here.

La Posada Inn
GUESTHOUSE $

(☑042-52-2234; laposada_inn@latinmail.com; San Martín 146; s/d incl breakfast S60/80, with air-con S75/95; ❊ ☞) This quaint hotel has beamed ceilings and a rickety wooden staircase. The rooms are a mixed bag: some have balconies, some have air-con. Even though it's right in the town center, La Posada manages to remain quiet. A pleasant little cafe out front lays on breakfast.

★ La Patarashca
GUESTHOUSE $$

(☑042-52-7554; www.lapatarashca.com; Calle de la Cruz 362; s/d/tr incl breakfast S120/160/190; ❊ ☞ ☁) It must be hard to recreate a tranquil jungle resort in the middle of hot, honking Tarapoto, but La Patarashca pulls it off with aplomb. The key(s): sprawling grounds with jungle-like fauna, a curvaceous turquoise swimming pool, spacious common areas replete with books and art, and comfortable rooms adorned with florescent paintings and crafty lamps that feel homey and welcoming.

DON'T MISS

CASTILLO DE LAMAS

Some deride **Castillo de Lamas** (☑955-933-531; Martin de la Riva y Herrera; admission adult/child S6/3; ⊗9am-6:30pm), a short drive from Tarapoto, as a tasteless white elephant; others laud it for its eccentricity. Whatever your position, this 'mock' Italian castle that rises out of jungle-like vegetation on the edge of the town of Lamas is certainly – ahem – different. It was built in the early 2000s by Italian industrialist Nicola Felice Aquilano, originally from Turin, who employed a local painter to decorate the walls and ceilings with frescos of Dante, Christian saints and Amazonian birds.

The renaissance-style castle has five floors, a pool, battlements, two towers and a cafe. Piped opera music fills its frescoed interior most days. You can wander around at will.

A few ornery macaws drive home a sense of place, as does the best regional restaurant in town, attached by a walkway.

Add S30 per night for rooms with air-conditioning.

Sol de Selva HOTEL **$$**
(☑042-52-4817; Pedro de Urzúa 161; s/d/tr incl breakfast S80/100/150; ❋🐾) Cross the threshold of calm, collected and clean Sol de Selva and you'll feel instantly freed from the noisy, dusty streets outside. Rooms have modern air-con units, shampoos restocked every day and furnishings colored by pale yellows and subtle oranges. The family operators extend a warm welcome and the breakfast sandwiches are substantially tastier than your average Peruvian omelets.

Mitu Wasi HOTEL **$$**
(☑042-67-0027; www.mituwasiecohospedaje.com; Jorge Chavez 1153, Barrio Huayco; s/d/t incl breakfast S90/120/140; ❋🐾) Mitu Wasi pulls off that wonderful Tarapoto trick of hiding a peaceful jungle-like retreat inside the city limits. Traditional thatched bungalows with simple but color-splashed rooms inhabit a seemingly endless garden packed with flowers and foliage. Taking breakfast alfresco while chatting to the friendly hosts, Roberto and Anna, is what makes this place special.

Mitu Wasi is 2km from the city center, not far from the airport (p444).

Casa de Palos GUESTHOUSE **$$**
(☑940-317-681; www.casadepalos.pe; Prado 155; s/d/tr incl breakfast S120/185/220; ❋🐾) The small, nine-room 'house of sticks' harbors simple, modern rooms with unfinished concrete flooring and rustic woven headboards, giving it a smidgen more character for this price range. Rooms surround a jungle-like makeshift courtyard full of chirping canaries and tiny gawking monkeys. The attached cafe on the expansive open-air terrace roasts its own coffee and offers free tastings to guests.

Tucan Suites HOTEL **$$$**
(☑042-52-8383; www.tucansuites.com; Calle 1 de Abril 315; apt from S439; ❋@🐾❋) This chic apartment-hotel in the *barrio* (neighborhood) of Banda de Shilcayo is Tarapoto's only four-star accommodations. Spacious one- and two-bedroom suites feature chrome-tiled kitchenettes and soundproof glass, another city first (and wholly welcomed). Eight of the duplex rooms have open-air kitchenettes and the restaurant drops out onto a tri-level pool terrace. You'll sleep no sounder in town than here.

The attached restaurant is run by a skilled *Nikkei* (Peruvian of Japanese descent) chef who serves up wonderfully executed creative cuisine. Worth a visit even if you're not staying here.

🛏 Outside Town

Chirapa Manta LODGE **$$**
(☑997-435-611; www.chirapamanta.com; San Roque de Cumbaza; dm/d/tr S60/140/215) 🍃 Staying at this tranquil ecological retreat, surrounded by birdlife and butterflies, is like taking a chill pill and waking up in a new, less frenetic dimension. Set among lush vegetation on the banks of the upper Río Cumbaza, a 40-minute drive northwest of Tarapoto, this is where people come for 'wellness,' yoga, detoxification and 'spiritual reconnection.'

The lodge feels totally isolated yet is just a short walk to the charming village of San Roque. The comfortable rooms have electric hot water and well-functioning dry toilets, plus they feature clay walls embedded with colored glass. Guests have access to the kitchen and vegetarian meals are also available. The friendly management also organizes hikes and ecological excursions in the area.

Shimiyacu Lodge   LODGE **$$**

(☑966-609-151;   www.shimiyaculodgetarapoto.
com; s/d incl breakfast S150/180) This small
lodge offers an authentic Amazon experi-
ence just 3km from town, next to the Alto
Shilcayo (p439) nature reserve and accessed
by a narrow suspension bridge. Perched on
a hillside are a handful of well-designed,
thatched A-frame bungalows that look out
over the lush jungle canopy. Each has a
screened dining area and an enclosed main
bedroom with polished wooden floors.

Bungalows also have hot-water bath-
rooms and a small room upstairs. Apart
from breakfast – which features home-baked
wholewheat bread – no meals are offered,
but there is a small kitchen hut for guests
and delivery from town can be arranged.
Airport pickup is included in the room price.

⭐**Pumarinri Amazon Lodge**   LODGE **$$$**

(☑042-52-6694; www.pumarinri.com; Carr Chazu-
ta Km 16; d/ste incl breakfast S280/390; ❇🌐≋)
This thatched-roof retreat on the banks of
the Río Huallaga and surrounded by transitional mountain rainforest is a perfect escape from the *mototaxi* blues. Most rooms
are upscale-basic but very comfortable with
expansive river-view terraces. It's located
30km east of Tarapoto.

Excursions from the tranquil setting include nearby waterfalls, treks to spot the
poison dart frog, boat tours, and bird-spot-
ting some 260 recorded species within a
16km radius. Upon return, the kitchen staff
fish your *gamitana* straight from their own
breeding pond.

Cordillera Escalera Lodge   LODGE **$$$**

(☑042-78-1672; www.cordilleraescalera.com; Pro-
log Alerta 1521; s/d S195/260) Set in a beauti-
ful garden surrounded by jungle around
1.5km out of town, this well-run lodge has
cute little bungalows with sweeping views of
forested mountains. The rooms are simple
yet functional with good mattresses, fans
and hot water, and they reverberate with the
sounds of the jungle.

It's a bit of a hike up the hill to the bunga-
lows, but worth it for the panoramic views
from the hammock on your balcony. Apart
from breakfast there are no meals served,
but guests are free to use the well-equipped
kitchen. A *mototaxi* from town costs S8.

✖ **Eating**

Don't leave Tarapoto without trying *inchi-
capi* or *juanes*.

There's a growing band of experimental
restaurants in town including new gourmet
offering Natural (p444) – Tarapoto's first.

Zygo Café   CAFE **$**

(☑042-58-6382; Hurtado 417; small plates S8-20;
⊙8am-8pm Mon-Fri, 9am-2pm Sat; 🌐🖊) 🖊
New coffee bar with a strong emphasis on
vegetarian and vegan food where you can
enjoy fresh porridge (not common in Peru)
and vegan muffins alongside gap-year travel-
lers in tie-dye t-shirts. The coffee is the best
in town and the French-Peruvian owners
are friendly and knowledgeable about their
brews.

Café Plaza   CAFE **$**

(San Martín 109; small plates S6-12; ⊙7:30am-
11pm; 🌐) Classic central-plaza corner cafe
stocked full of people sipping espressos,
breaking the no-smoking policy, and dis-
cussing 'deals' hunched over wooden tables.
Open to the street, it offers a front-row seat
into the film that is Tarapoto. Good for cof-
fee, cakes, snacks and milkshakes.

Suchiche   AMAZONIAN **$$**

(☑042-52-7554; www.lapatarashca.com; Lamas
245, La Patarashca Hotel; mains S11-20; ⊙7am-
11pm) A relatively new addition to Tarapoto's colony of bars and clubs on and around
Jirón Lamas, Suchiche positions itself as a
restobar, with good food, from Peruvian-Japanese (Amazonian sushi, aka *maki*) to Peru-
vian-Italian (pasta with *lomo saltado*). The
long, handsome bar dispatches coffee, craft
beer, pisco sours or freshly blended juice.

The interior paints a pretty picture with
flashing neon, symbolic paintings of Che
Guevara and Charlie Chaplin, and some
woody Amazonian flourishes.

⭐**Doña Zully**   AMAZONIAN **$$**

(☑042-53-0670; San Pablo de la Cruz 244; mains
S20-42; ⊙11am-midnight) The *parrilla* (char-
coal grill) masters here rustle up some of
the best barbecues in the Peruvian Amazon
using the staple ingredients of *cecina* and
doncella, among others. The tilapia, steam-
cooked in a banana leaf with sides of fried
plantain and avocado salad, is sensational.
Service is attentive and the atmosphere qui-
etly refined.

⭐**La Patarashca**   AMAZONIAN **$$**

(www.lapatarashca.com; Lamas 261, La Patarashca Hotel; mains S26-44; ⊙noon-11pm; 🌐) Come
to Patarashca for an Amazonian culinary
awakening. Outstanding regional cuisine is

on tap at this woody open-sided restaurant replete with pre-Columbian iconography. Don't miss the salad of *chonta,* thin strips of local hearts of palm, with avocados; or the namesake *patarashcas,* fish served in a warm bath of tomatoes, peppers, onions, garlic and cilantro wrapped in a *bijao* leaf.

Then there's the *juanes* (here, balls of rice, meat, egg and olives boiled in a *bijao* leaf), the *tacu tacu* (fried rice and beans topped with plantain and an egg or meat), and the succulent river fish such as *doncella*. Bring a big appetite and dig into the exotic tastes.

Natural AMAZONIAN $$

(☑ 042-60-1741; Lamas 142; meals S35-56; ☺ 6-11pm Mon-Sat) Brand new and boldly experimental, Natural is the first attempt at a true gourmet restaurant in Tarapoto and possibly one of the first to focus wholly on Amazonian food. Six-course tasting menus examine the delights of fried *doncella* (a type of freshwater fish) with *queso de cuñumbuque* (local cheese) and *chicharrón de pescado* (crisp fish skins).

The interior is modern and deftly designed and the staff are keen to share their love of their (as yet) little-traveled local flavors.

Café d' Mundo ITALIAN $$

(☑ 042-52-4918; Calle de Morey 157; mains S28-49; ☺ 6:30pm-midnight) This dark and sexy restaurant-bar is illuminated nightly by moody candlelight. It has outdoor seating and snug indoor lounges – and sophisticated live piano on Friday and Saturday evenings. Italian-style pizzas are the mainstay (try the caprese with avocado), but interesting regional lasagnas (with *cecina*) and pastas adorn the small menu.

The owner is also the proprietor of the Castillo de Lamas (p442), where there is another cafe-style branch of the restaurant.

El Rincón Sureño STEAK $$$

(☑ 042-52-2785; Leguia 458; steaks S20-85; ☺ noon-midnight) Tarapoto loves a steak and this is where most of the town comes to get it along with all number of other meats fresh off the grill (vegetarians stay away!). For a northern Peru flavor you might want to go for *cecina* (smoked pork), chorizo, *chicharrón* (deep-fried pork) or that old Peruvian stand-by, chicken. The wine list is impressive, too.

🍷 Drinking & Nightlife

★ La Alternativa BAR

(Grau 401; ☺ 4pm-1am) Like drinking in a medieval pharmacy or maybe a Tarantino film, a night out here hearkens back to a time when alcohol was literally medicine (like, for ailments, not for your emotional problems) and your local apothecary was the place to get sauced on God-knows-what elixir that happened to be inside the bottle.

Shelves here are stacked pharmaceutical-style with dusty bottles of natural concoctions combining roots and vines, and cane liquor including 15 different aphrodisiac varieties. It's a recipe for total mayhem.

Stonewasi Taberna BAR

(Lamas 218; ☺ noon-3am) Pretenders come and go, but this local institution is still the place to see and be seen in Tarapoto. Recycled sewing tables street-side are chock-full of punters, *mototaxi* drivers and the town's à la mode crowd thronging to a theme of international rock and house music.

ℹ Information

MONEY

BCP (Maynas 130; ☺ 9am-6pm Mon-Fri, to 1pm Sat) Has several ATMs.

Interbank (Grau 119; ☺ 9am-6pm Mon-Fri, to 1pm Sat) Has an ATM.

Scotiabank (Hurtado 215; ☺ 9:15am-6pm Mon-Fri) Cashes traveler's checks and has an ATM.

POST

Serpost (San Martín 482; ☺ 8am-6pm Mon-Sat) Postal services.

SAFE TRAVEL

Tarapoto is a wasp's hive of honking, speeding *mototaxis* and, as a pedestrian, you'll find yourself at the bottom of the food chain. Take care when crossing roads – no one yields (ever) – and consider wearing earplugs.

TOURIST INFORMATION

Tourist Information Office (☑ 042-52-6188; Hurtado s/n; ☺ 7:30am-11pm) The municipal tourist office on Plaza Mayor. Local police keep it open when tourism officials go home.

ℹ Getting There & Away

AIR

The **airport** (TPP; ☑ 042-53-1165) is 3km southwest of the center, a S5 *mototaxi* ride or a 30-minute walk.

LATAM (☑ 042-52-9318; www.latam.com; Hurtado 183) has four to five daily flights to Lima (US$60, 1¼ hours).

Star Perú (☑ 042-52-1056; www.starperu.com; Plaza Mayor 325; ☻9am-7pm Mon-Fri, to 5pm Sat) has one daily flight to Lima (US$60, 1¼ hours) and another to Iquitos (US$80, one hour).

Peruvian (www.peruvian.pe; Hurtado 277; ☻9am-7pm) has three daily flights to Lima (US$50, 1¼ hours).

BUS

Several companies head west on the paved road to Lima via Moyobamba, Chiclayo and Trujillo, generally leaving between 8am and 4pm. All these companies can be found along the same *cuadra* (block) of Salaverry and its cross streets in the Morales district, an S3 *mototaxi* ride from the town center.

Civa (☑ 042-52-2269; www.civa.com.pe; Salaverry 840) Has a comfortable 12:45pm bus to Lima (S100 to S120, 30 hours), stopping at Chiclayo and Trujillo.

Movil Tours (☑ 042-52-9193; www.moviltours.com.pe; Salaverry 880) Top-end express buses to Lima (S120 to S170, 29 hours) leave at 8am and 1pm, with a 3pm departure to Trujillo (S90 to S120, 17 hours), a 4pm bus to Chiclayo (S80 to S105, 13 hours), a 5pm bus to Piura (S80 to S105, 14 hours) and a 3:45pm bus to Pucallpa (S75 to S95, 11 hours).

Transmar Express (☑ 042-53-2392; Amoraca 117) Departs at 9:30am on Monday, Wednesday and Friday for the ride to Pucallpa (S70, 15 hours) via Juanjuí, Tocache Nuevo and Tingo María.

Turismo Selva (☑ 042-52-5682; Alfonso Ugarte 1130) Runs frequent minivans to Yurimaguas (S15, 2¾ hours), Moyobamba (S10, two hours) and Chachapoyas (S35, eight hours).

Virgen del Carmen (☑ 976-015-514; www.turismovirgendelcarmen.com.pe; cnr Calles 1 de Mayo & Callao) Daily buses to Cajamarca (S80, 20 hours) at 8:30am via Chachapoyas (S35, nine hours) and Celendín (S60, 18 hours).

Tarapoto Buses

DESTINATION	COST (S)	TIME
Cajamarca	80	20hr
Celendín	60	18hr
Chachapoyas	35	9hr
Chazuta	10	2hr
Chiclayo	80-105	13hr
Jaén	40	9-12hr
Lamas	5	30min
Lima	100-170	26-30hr
Moyobamba	10	2hr
Pedro Ruíz	40-45	7hr
Piura	80-105	14hr
Pucallpa	80-95	11-15hr
Trujillo	90-120	17hr
Yurimaguas	15	2¾hr

ⓘ Getting Around

Mototaxis cruise the streets like circling sharks. A short ride in town is around S2, to the bus stations S3 to S4.

AT A GLANCE

POPULATION
Iquitos: 472,000

LARGEST PROTECTED AREA
Reserva Nacional Pacaya-Samiria: 20,800 sq km (p481)

BEST JUNGLE LODGE
Inkaterra Reserva Amazonica (p461)

BEST VEGETARIAN FOOD
Cafe Elixir (p479)

BEST VIEWPOINT
Tres Cruces (p465)

WHEN TO GO

Jan
Rising temperatures and water levels; perfect for chilling in waterfalls near La Merced.

Apr & May
Rains subside, heralding courtship season for many birds in Parque Nacional Manu.

Jun
The rainy season ends: cue the jungle's best parties, like debauched San Juan in Iquitos.

Trekking in Parque Nacional Manu (p468)
RPBAIAO/SHUTTERSTOCK ©

Amazon Basin

The best-protected tract of the world's most biodiverse forest, the strange, sweltering, seductive country-within-a-country that is Peru's Amazon Basin, is changing. Its vastness and impenetrability have long protected its indigenous communities and diverse wildlife from external eyes. But as the 21st century encroaches on this expanse of arboreal wilderness, exploitation of the rainforest's abundant resources threatens to irreversibly damage it. Sure: the Peruvian Amazon offers phenomenal wildlife-spotting, dalliances into untamed forest from the jungle's best selection of lodges and raucous city life, but it also begs for ongoing protection. Remember that as, forging through it by rough road and raging river, you emulate the explorers who first brought international attention to this region.

Amazon Basin Highlights

1 **Río Tambopata** (p455)
Spotting birds and animals on
a river trip.

2 **Parque Nacional Manu**
(p468) Traveling overland
through a smorgasbord
of Peruvian scenery via
mountains, cloud forest and
jungle.

3 **Oxapampa** (p473)
Discovering the Central
Amazon's German heritage
from the sweet treats to the
Tyrolean architecture.

4 **Iquitos** (p482) Swinging
in a hammock on a multiday
riverboat trip.

5 **Belén Mercado** (p483)
Haggling in Peru's premier

jungle market within the
floating district of Belén in
Iquitos.

6 **Iquitos** (p488) Tucking
into the diverse, wondrous
eating scene.

7 **Pevas** (p497) Admiring
world-class art at the remote
rainforest gallery of Francisco
Grippa.

SOUTHERN AMAZON

Abutting the neighboring nations of Bolivia and Brazil, the vast tract of the southern Amazon Basin is among Peru's remotest territories: comparatively little is either inhabited or explored. That said, this is changing almost as fast as a Peruvian bus timetable, thanks to the Carr Interocéanica (Transoceanic Hwy) transecting much of the region. Yet with well-developed facilities for ecotravelers, the benefits of travel here are clear: visitors will, with relatively little effort, be rewarded with a treasure trove of unforgettable close encounters of the wild kind.

Puerto Maldonado

📞 082 / POP 56,000 / ELEV 250M

Visibly blossoming from its road connection to the outside world, Puerto Maldonado, capital of the southern jungle, has an increasingly smart sheen to the bedlam of its central streets, abuzz with tooting *mototaxis* (three-wheeled motorcycle rickshaw taxis).

The city's money-spinning proximity to the most easily visited animal-rich jungle in the entire Amazon Basin is its blessing but also its curse: travelers arrive, yet quickly leave again to the lodges and wildlife on the nearby rivers.

Yet Puerto Maldonado's languid laid-back ambience invites you to linger. Although a shock to the system, with its sweltering climate and mosquitoes aplenty, its beautiful plaza, burgeoning accommodation options and lively nightlife provide reason enough to hang around.

It remains of foremost importance to travelers, however, as a jumping-off point for voyaging on Ríos Tambopata and Madre de Dios, converging here: watery wonderlands that offer the most accessible primary jungle-locales in the country.

🔴 Sights

Mariposario Tambopata Butterfly Farm FARM

(http://perubutterfly.com; Av Elmer Faucett Km 7; admission S18; ☺ 8am-5pm) Peru has the greatest number of butterfly species in the world (some 3700) and you can see many of them here at this well-run butterfly conservation project, one of Peru's best, initiated in 1996. There are also displays on rainforest conservation. Butterflies are nice, but at this price remember you'll see lots of species for free in the jungle proper.

Río Madre de Dios Ferry Dock PORT

(Puerto Capitanía) This dock close to the Plaza de Armas is a cheap way of seeing a little of the action on a major Peruvian jungle river (the Río Madre de Dios), which is about 500m wide at this point. River traffic is colorful – multiple *peki-pekis* (canoes powered by two-stroke motorcycle engines with outlandishly long propeller shafts) set off from here.

However, the number of boats is vastly reduced since the opening of **Puente Guillermo Billinghurst (Puente Intercontinental)** (Puente Intercontinental), the bridge now carrying the Carr Interocéanica across the river a few hundred meters to the northwest. Gone are the days when a fleet of decrepit catamarans ferried Brazil-bound drivers and their vehicles across the river alongside a flotilla of smaller craft coming and going to this-or-that port amid a splutter of wheezing engines. *Bienvenido* to the 21st century.

Mirador de la Biodiversidad TOWER

(cnr Fitzcarrald & Madre de Dios; admission S3; ☺ 8am-noon & 1-9pm Mon-Sat, 8am-noon Sun) Although this strangely cosmic blue building, surrounded by statues of locals in various poses of labor outside, was designed as a modern *mirador* (lookout tower), its 30m height unfortunately does not rise high enough above the city for viewers to glimpse the rivers. The view is still fantastic: a distant glimmer of jungle and many corrugated-metal roofs can be admired!

Photos displayed on the way up document the region's history and culture, proudly concluded by a mention of the Carr Interocéanica. Formerly known just as the *obelisco* (obelisk) it has now been grandiosely rebranded thus.

🏃 Activities

Corredor Turístico Bajo Tambopata DRIVING TOUR

This largely river-hugging minor road winds for some 15km out toward Sotupa Eco House (p457), the first lodge on the Río Tambopata. En route are several homestays; some locals along this stretch open up their houses to travelers for lunch. One for the independent adventurers.

Puerto Maldonado

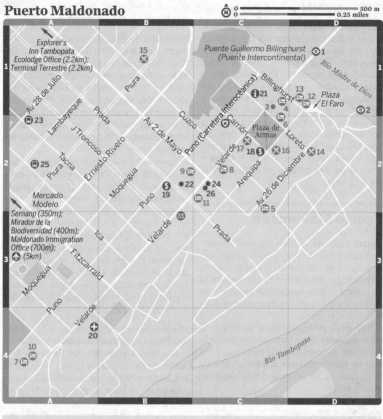

Puerto Maldonado

◎ Sights
1 Puente Guillermo Billinghurst................D1
2 Río Madre de Dios Ferry Dock D1

✪ Activities, Courses & Tours
3 Carlos Expeditions...................................C1

🛏 Sleeping
4 Corto Maltes Lodge Office.......................C1
5 Eco Amazonia Lodge Office C2
6 Estancia Bello Horizonte Lodge
    Office C2
7 Hospedaje El Gato Lodge Office...........A4
8 Hospedaje Rey Port..................................C2
9 Hospedaje Royal Inn.................................B2
10 Huarayo Lodge Office A4
    Monte Amazonico Lodge
    Office ....(see 3)
11 Paititi Hostal...C2
12 Wasai Hostel...D1
13 Wasai Lodge..D1

✗ Eating
14 Burgos's Restaurante............................D2
15 El Califa.. B1
    El Faro at Wasai Lodge ....(see 12)
16 La Semilla..C2
17 Pizzería El Hornito/Chez Maggy..........C2

🍷 Drinking & Nightlife
    Discoteca Witite ....(see 4)

ℹ Information
18 BCP..C2
19 Casa de Cambio......................................B2
20 Hospital Santa Rosa..............................A4
21 iPeru..C1

ℹ Transport
22 Anclas...B2
23 Buses to Laberinto................................A2
24 LAN...C2
25 Minivans to Iñapari...............................A2
26 Star Perú...C2

☞ Tours

Most visitors arrive with prearranged tours and stay at a jungle lodge – convenient, but by no means the only possibility. You can also arrange a tour upon arrival by going to the lodge offices in town, where you'll likely get a significant discount on a tour that would cost more in Lima or Cuzco.

You can, too, look for an independent guide. However, to enter the Reserva Nacional Tambopata (including Lago Sandoval, and anywhere upriver of Puesto Control El Torre on the Río Tambopata) all guides need licenses which are only issued if they are affiliated with a lodge or registered tour operator (this is an important thing to check). Choosing an independent guide not working for a lodge/tour operator also gives you way less recourse in the event of a disastrous trip.

With independent guides, choosing one can be a lottery. They'll offer you tours for less, yet stories of bad independent guided trips are common. Beware of guides at the airport, who often take you to a 'recommended' hotel (and collect a commission), then hound you throughout your stay. Shop around, don't prepay for any tour and, if paying an advance deposit, insist on a signed receipt. If you agree to a boat driver's price, make sure it includes the return trip, and if quoted prices are all-inclusive or exclusive of national park entrance fees.

Almost all of the best guides with official licenses granted by the Ministerio de Industria y Turismo work full time for one of the area's jungle lodges. Guides charge from S120 to S200 per person per day, depending on the destination and number of people. Going with more people reduces the cost; in fact, some guides will only take tours with a three-person minimum.

Most tours, either with a lodge or with an independent guide, leave from the Río Madre de Dios ferry dock (p449), heading downriver on the Río Madre de Dios or upriver on the Río Tambopata (meaning a large component of the expense of a jungle trip is the fuel the boat will expend).

Some lodges/independent guides now cut hours off a Río Tambopata river trip by heading to the community of Alto Tambopata Filadelfia (45 minutes on the Carr Interocéanica toward Cuzco, then an hour down a rough track).

Carlos Expeditions   ADVENTURE SPORTS
(☎082-57-1320; http://carlosexpeditions.com; Velarde 139-141; ⊗8am-6pm) Tour operator arranging the likes of zip-lining and clambering in canopy walkways, mostly at their jungle-based Monte Amazonico Lodge (p461).

Rainforest Expeditions   TOURS
(☎in Puerto Maldonado 082-57-2575, in US & Canada 1-877-231-9251; www.perunature.com; Prolongación La Joya (Av Aeropuerto) Km 6) 🚲 Coordinates various area lodges, including Refugio Amazonas (p460), Posada Amazonas (p460) and Tambopata Research Center (p457), and has reputable rainforest tours as well as budget-oriented Tambopata homestays.

Infierno   CULTURAL TOUR
About an hour southeast of Puerto Maldonado is Infierno (Hell!), home and hub of activity for the Ese'eja tribespeople. It's a lively, spread-out settlement, which has a reputation for its *ayahuasca* (derivative of a hallucinogenic jungle vine) rituals, conducted by local shamans. Lonely Planet does not recommend taking *ayahuasca* and those who do so do it at their own risk.

Arrange your own transport here via car or motorbike: *mototaxis* won't make the rough journey.

Jony Valles Rengifo   WILDLIFE
(☎982-704-736; jhony.com@hotmail.es) Speaks English and French.

Nilthon Tapia Miyashiro   WILDLIFE
(☎982-788-174; nisa_30@hotmail.com) A well-known, experienced guide.

🛌 Sleeping

Besides the plethora of basic budget places, you can also choose from pleasant backpacker accommodations or comfortable hotels/lodges in the city itself. Note that not all lodges have reservations offices in Puerto Maldonado; some only have offices in Cuzco, Lima or the USA.

Outside Puerto Maldonado there are around 30 jungle lodges.

Wasai Hostel   HOSTEL **$**
(☎082-57-2290; www.wasai.com; cnr Billinghurst & Arequipa; dm S39-52, r incl breakfast S98-117; ❄) It's quite expensive as hostels go, but it's quite nice, too, with a prime central location with the benefit of the on-site pool and tour agency offering jungle tours, as well as

TRANSOCEANIC HIGHWAY: ROAD TO RICHES & RUIN

Few events in history have had such an immediate effect on the Amazon rainforest as the construction of the Carr Interocéanica (Transoceanic Hwy) has: following its completion in July 2011, it now links the Pacific coast of Peru with the Atlantic coast of Brazil via paved road. At a cost of billions of dollars, the road is now a massive export opportunity for both countries (former Peruvian president Alejandro Toledo estimated the road would signify a 1.5% annual increase in Peru's GDP). The more than 2500km of newly constructed road breaches the dual hazards of the Andes and the rainforest to link the Peruvian coast at San Juan de Marcona near Nazca via Cuzco to the southern Amazon, through Puerto Maldonado, to the Brazilian border at Iñapari. From there the road runs to Rio Branco in Brazil and feeds into the Brazilian road system.

The effects of the road, good and bad, are being felt. Thousands of new jobs have been created and Puerto Maldonado, the main city on the route not previously connected by asphalted highway, is thriving from increased tourism (Cuzco is now only 10 hours away by road) and commerce.

But for the estimated 15 uncontacted tribes that inhabit the once-isolated southeastern corner of Peru, the road now slicing through their territory heralds the risk of disease and the loss of hunting grounds. According to one NGO, Survival International, the possibility of migration a road creates without the facilities to back it up would, along with the destruction of natural habitat, have a disastrous effect on such peoples. And if there are 15 human groups at risk, there are infinitely more species of plants and animals. The total area of destroyed rainforest as a result of the Transoceanic's construction equates to a third of the size of the UK and, according to various studies on roads in the Brazilian Amazon, is likely to have a significant effect on rainforest deforestation for 40km to 60km on either side.

Yet the devastation the building of the road has caused is less significant than the devastation that people who now have improved access to the remote rainforest could bring. Newspapers from the *Peruvian Times* to the *Guardian* have reported on the *prosibars* (bars with often underage prostitutes) springing up along routes that can now be traversed with greater ease by the loggers and miners that already posed an ecological threat to this part of the Amazon. Illegal mining has since become a serious enough issue to call in the army to quell it. Ecosystems here are renowned for being among the world's most diverse and undisturbed. They still are. But, one wonders, for how much longer.

---

the lovely El Faro restaurant. Breakfast is included with the rooms but not with the dorms.

Hospedaje Rey Port   GUESTHOUSE **$**
(☑ 082-57-3464; Velarde 457; s S15-30, d S30; 🛜) This one's for bargain hunters, generations of which have been sniffing out the Rey Port's 'charms.' Rooms are a tad grubby, with fans/cable TV. Ground-floor courtyard rooms with shared bathrooms may be cheapest and dingiest, but the top floor has large rooms with private bathrooms starting at S20: lots of light, which shows up the views... and the dirt.

Hospedaje Royal Inn   GUESTHOUSE **$**
(☑ 082-57-3464; 2 Av de Mayo 333; s with/without air-con S70/50, d with/without air-con S100/70; ❄🛜) A good choice for travelers, sporting lots of large, clean rooms with fans or air-con. The courtyard has seen better days, but still, get a room here as street-facing digs are noisy. Cable TV comes with each room.

⭐ **Anaconda Lodge**   LODGE **$$**
(☑ 982-611-039, 082-79-2726; http://anaconda-junglelodge.com; cnr Prolongación La Joya/ Av Aeropuerto & Elmer Faucett; s/d/tr 100/160/80/220, s/d without bathroom S50/80; ℗🛜🏊) The most original airport hotel in South America? Cocooned in its own tropical garden on the edge of town, and with its own Thai restaurant, too, this lodge has a more remote feel than its location would suggest. There are eight double-room bungalows with shared bathroom and four luxury bungalows with private facilities; all are mosquito netted.

There's also camping space (per person S20), a small pool and a spacious two-floor restaurant-bar serving sensational Thai food and pancake breakfasts (it is one of only three Thai restaurants in all Peru!). And we *luuurve* the honeymoon suite – erotic furniture with an oriental theme! These guys also organize kayak trips.

Wasai Lodge　　　　　　　　LODGE **$$**
(☑082-57-2290; www.wasai.com; cnr Billinghurst & Arequipa; s incl breakfast S183-215, d incl breakfast S245-278; ✳🔊🖥) This lodge is a striking complex of comfortable wooden bungalows overlooking the Río Madre de Dios (and its flash bridge!). Higher tariffs are for air-con. Minibars, hot showers, cable TV and river views, however, are standard. Room lighting is pretty abysmal: consider bringing a flashlight! There is a good ground floor restaurant, room service, a bar and a pool.

The lodge arranges various trips on the region's rivers – usually involving a stay at its well-regarded Wasai Alto Tambopata Lodge (p459).

Paititi Hostal　　　　　　　　HOTEL **$$**
(☑082-57-4667; Prada 290; s S90-120, d S120-140, all incl breakfast; ✳🔊) A relatively flash, central place, the Paititi has a series of spacious, airy rooms, many full of attractive old wooden furniture, along with telephones and cable TV. A continental breakfast is included, and there's even hot water at night – very un-Amazon. Higher tariffs are for air-con.

🍴 Eating

Regional specialties include *juanes* (banana leaves stuffed with chicken or pork and rice), *chilcano* (a broth of fish chunks flavored with cilantro) and *parrillada de la selva* (barbecued marinated meat, often game, in a Brazil-nut sauce). *Plátano* (plantain) is served as an accompaniment to many meals.

Other culinary options are Wasai Lodge's restaurant, El Faro, or delicious Thai food at Anaconda Lodge.

★La Semilla　　　　　　　VEGETARIAN **$**
(Arequipa, btwn Carrión & Loreto; light meals S10-20; ⊙10am-1pm & 4-9pm Mon-Sat, 10am-1pm Sun; 🍴) Clamber up three flights of stairs to this welcoming open-sided vegetarian restaurant with views over the Plaza de Armas. Here you can get about the best coffee in town, *pie de maracuya* (like lemon meringue pie with a fruit change) and lovingly prepared salads.

El Califa　　　　　　　　PERUVIAN **$**
(Piura 266; mains S10-25; ⊙9am-5pm Mon-Fri) *The* local restaurant in town: in the game for decades. An ocean of tables are attended with no-nonsense service. Portions are large, cheap and tasty, and you can try a variety of jungle classics, from *chancho* (rainforest pig) to *parrillada de la selva*.

El Faro at Wasai Lodge　　　　PERUVIAN **$$**
(cnr Billinghurst & Arequipa; mains S25; ⊙7am-9:30pm) A pleasing and popular little spot that charges above-average prices for way-above-average Amazonian food, with a few surprises such as the divine ceviche with camu camu fruit. It overlooks the little plaza with the statue of the *faro* (lighthouse), hence the name.

★Burgos's Restaurante　　　PERUVIAN **$$**
(cnr 26 de Diciembre & Loreto; mains S19-38; ⊙11am-11pm; 🍴) This has quickly developed into Puerto Maldonado's standout restaurant. It calls itself an exponent of Novo Amazonica cuisine – that's like Novo Andino, only making those bold culinary adaptations to jungle dishes – but this is still more about dependable Peruvian Amazon staples, cooked to perfection rather than with particular innovation.

It's a huge, airy, courteously staffed restaurant, with a couple of terraces sporting lush river views, and serves plenty of vegetarian options alongside its fish-focused specialties.

Pizzería El Hornito/Chez Maggy　PIZZA **$$**
(Carrión 271; large pizzas S30; ⊙6pm-late) 'I get knocked down, but I get up again...' this could well be the anthem to this popular upstairs hangout on the Plaza de Armas, which burned to the ground but has gamely risen from the ashes, built with rather less wood this time too. It serves pasta and amply sized, wood-fired pizzas – the best in town.

It puts on the loud *telenovelas* (Peruvian soap operas) on large, obtrusive TVs for free. Yeah, it does takeaway.

🍷 Drinking & Nightlife

The city's nightlife, while nothing beside that of Lima or Cuzco, is some of the Amazon's liveliest. Discos mostly just have recorded music, but bars and clubs pound away until the early hours of a weekend.

Discoteca Witite CLUB

(Velarde 151; ☺9pm-late Fri & Sat) Well, we preferred Witite with the gaudy clapboard but the smartened-up version is still the classic place to party, jungle-style – a party that goes on all night. It's on the pedestrianized street near the plaza.

☆ Entertainment

El Huayruro LIVE MUSIC

(Prolongación La Joya s/n; ☺6pm-late Fri & Sat) The best place for live music and dancing, away out of the city. Brazilian music is favored.

🛍 Shopping

Proximity to local tribes means many lodges around town, such as Posadas Amazonas on the Río Tambopata, are better for purchasing local handicrafts than the town itself.

ℹ Information

EMERGENCY

Police Station (Police Station; ☑082-80-3504; cnr Carrión & Puno)

IMMIGRATION

The border town of Iñapari, 233km north of Puerto Maldonado, has regular border-crossing facilities to enter Brazil.

Maldonado Immigration Office (☑082-57-1069; Av 15 de Agosto 658; ☺8am-1pm & 2:30-4pm Mon-Fri, 8am-noon Sat) To leave Peru via Puerto Heath (river) or Iberia (road) for Bolivia, get your passport stamped here (morning's best). Travelers can also extend their visas or tourist cards here.

INTERNET ACCESS

Internet is slower here than in other Peruvian cities and costs about S2 per hour. There are multiple cybercafe choices along Velarde, heading southwest from the plaza. About half of the accommodations in town have decent wi-fi.

MEDICAL SERVICES

Hospital Santa Rosa (☑082-57-1019, 082-57-1046; www.hospitalsantarosa.gob.pe; cnr Cajamarca & Velarde) Provides basic services.

MONEY

Perhaps unsurprisingly, Brazilian reais and Bolivian bolivianos have become much easier to exchange here since the opening of the Carr Interoceánica: ask where is currently giving the best exchange rate.

BCP (Plaza de Armas) Changes US cash or traveler's checks and has a Visa ATM.

Casa de Cambio (Puno, at Prada) Standard rates for US dollars.

POST

Post Office (Velarde 675; ☺8am-noon & 2-7pm Mon-Fri) Southwest of the Plaza de Armas.

TOURIST INFORMATION

iPerú (☑082-57-1830; Loreto 390; ☺9am-6pm Mon-Sat, to 1pm Sun) Good office in the center of town.

Tourist Booth (Airport)

Ayaadvisors Advice on places that hold *ayahuasca* ceremonies, plus general info about *ayahuasca*.

ℹ Getting There & Away

AIR

The **airport** (PEM) is 7km outside town. Scheduled flights leave every day to/from Lima via Cuzco with **LAN** (LATAM; ☑082-57-3677; Velarde 503; ☺9am-7pm Mon-Fri, to 1pm Sat) and **Star Perú** (☑082-57-3564; Velarde 505; ☺8:30am-7pm Mon-Sat). Schedules and airlines change from one year to the next, but the airline offices, as well as numerous travel agents in the town center, have the latest details.

BOAT

Hire boats at the Río Madre de Dios ferry dock (p449) for local excursions or to take you downriver to destinations like Lago Sandoval, Río Heath and the Bolivian border – see the advice under Tours (p451). It's difficult to find boats going up the Madre de Dios (against the current) to Manu; Cuzco is currently a better departure point for Manu. Occasionally, people reach Puerto Maldonado by boat from Manu (with the current) or from the Bolivian border (against the current). However, transportation is infrequent unless you are on an arranged Manu excursion that includes this option in its itinerary.

The **Tambopata ferry dock** is 2km south of the center and reachable by *mototaxi*. Here, a public boat leaves on Mondays at 8am, chugging upriver to Baltimore. It returns from Baltimore on Friday morning. Passage costs S20 or thereabouts depending on how far you go.

Heading upriver on Río Tambopata, all passengers must stop at **Puesto Control El Torre** (checkpoint), where passports and Sernanp (p457) permits (S30 or S65 depending on the duration of your stay) are needed.

Boats to jungle lodges leave from both docks, depending on the lodge location. When transporting visitors upriver, some Río Tambopata lodges avoid several hours of river travel by taking a road and then a rough track to Alto Tambopata Filadelfia (about 1¾ hours), and

WARNING: AYAHUASCA

Throughout your travel in the Peruvian Amazon, you will come across numerous places offering the chance to partake of *ayahuasca*. This is the derivative of a hallucinogenic jungle vine, used to attain a purgative trancelike state by shamans for centuries and now very popular with Westerners. *Ayahuasca* is invariably taken as part of a ceremony that can last anything from hours to days, depending upon who is conducting the rituals.

Be wary of taking *ayahuasca*: it can have serious side effects, including severe dehydration, convulsions, dramatic rises in blood pressure and – if taken regularly – blindness. If mixed with the wrong substances, it has even been known to be fatal. Also, for the purists, know that some places mix LSD in with the *ayahuasca* to intensify the 'trip.'

Be sure, too, to do research into the type of ceremony you're signing up for. Among some shamans offering a genuine ritualistic experience (although even so the aforementioned health risks still apply), there are charlatans out there who have also been known to rob and on occasion rape unsuspecting gringos under the influence. And such cases are reported on a yearly basis.

Lonely Planet does not recommend taking *ayahuasca* and those who wish to do so, do so at their own risk.

If you are convinced an *ayahuasca* ceremony is nevertheless for you, remember that doing so properly involves a necessary dietary adjustment beforehand. Read up about it, too: resources such as **Ayaadvisors** (https://ayaadvisors.org) can provide helpful feedback on the places that offer *ayahuasca* to tourists. Regarding where to do it, as well as a number of independently operating shamans, the majority of jungle lodges offer *ayahuasca* ceremonies – and in the last few years many dedicated *ayahuasca* retreats have sprung up.

---

continuing by boat from there. This needs to be arranged in advance, however.

BUS

Terminal Terrestre (Av Circunvalación Nte s/n) is 6km northwest of the center; from there, buses ply the Carr Interoceánica (Transoceanic Hwy) southwest to Cuzco and northeast to Rio Branco, Brazil. Numerous companies leave either during the morning or at night (around 8pm) to Cuzco (S35 to S70, 10 hours). Top tariffs are for fully reclining seats. Other options heading southwest include Juliaca (S35, 12 hours) and Arequipa (S50, 17 hours), both destinations being served by **Transportes Julsa** (☑951-751-246; Terminal Terrestre). Options from Terminal Terrestre to Río Branco (S100, nine to 10 hours) are more scant and do not depart every day. It's advisable to buy your ticket as far in advance of travel as possible.

MINIBUS & TAXI

Trucks, minibuses and *colectivos* (shared taxis) leave Puerto Maldonado for Laberinto (1½ hours), passing the turnoff to Baltimore at Km 37 on the Cuzco road (from here you can walk three hours to the Río Tambopata where, if you're staying at a Baltimore homestay, boats will pick you up if it's been arranged in advance). **Laberinto-bound transport** (cnr Tacna & 28 de Julio) leaves frequently from the corner of Av 28 de Julio and Tacna.

For Iñapari (S25, three hours), near the borders with Brazil and Bolivia, take a **minivan** (cnr Ica & Lambayeque; S25) departing from the corner of Ica and Lambayeque. Other companies on the same block also advertise this trip.

❶ Getting Around

Mototaxis take two or three passengers (and light luggage) to the airport for S7. Short rides around town cost S2 or less.

Motorcycle-rental places, mainly on Prada between Velarde and Puno, charge S5-S10 per hour and have mainly small, 100cc bikes: go in pairs in case of breakdowns or accident. Driving one is fun, but crazed local drivers and awful road conditions can make this option intimidating.

Anclas (cnr Prada & Puno; per hour/day S6/45)

AROUND PUERTO MALDONADO

Río Tambopata

With its headwaters actually in Bolivia, the Río Tambopata churns through a large portion of southern Peru. Upriver (southwest) of Puerto Maldonado, it winds through

ℹ️ BORDER CROSSINGS

Brazil via Puerto Maldonado

A good paved road, part of the Carr Interocéanica, goes from Puerto Maldonado to Iberia and on to Iñapari, 233km from Puerto Maldonado, on the Brazilian border. Along the road are small settlements of people involved in the Brazil nut farming, cattle ranching and logging industries. After about 170km you reach **Iberia**, which has very basic hotels. The village of **Iñapari** is another 70km beyond Iberia.

Peruvian border formalities can be carried out in Iñapari. Stores around the main plaza accept and change both Peruvian and Brazilian currency; if leaving Peru, it's best to get rid of any nuevos soles here. Small denominations of US cash are negotiable, and hotels and buses often quote rates in US dollars. From Iñapari, you can cross over the bridge to **Assis Brasil**, which has better hotels (starting from around US$15 per room).

US citizens need to get a Brazilian visa beforehand, either in the USA or Lima. It's 325km (six to seven hours) by paved road from here to the important Brazilian city of Rio Branco, via Brasiléia (100km, two hours).

For more detailed coverage of Brazil, pick up Lonely Planet's *Brazil*, from the Lonely Planet online shop (http://shop.lonelyplanet.com).

Bolivia via Puerto Maldonado

There are three ways of reaching Bolivia from the Puerto Maldonado area.

First and easiest is to go to Brasiléia in Brazil and cross the Río Acre by ferry or bridge to **Cobija** in Bolivia, where there are hotels, banks, an airstrip with erratically scheduled flights further into Bolivia, and a rough gravel road with several river crossings to the city of **Riberalta** (seven to 12 hours depending on season).

From **Iberia** in Peru on the Carr Interocéanica to Iñapari, a road also runs to Cobija, but public transportation mostly uses the Iñapari/Assis Brasil route.

Alternatively, hire a boat at Puerto Maldonado's Madre de Dios dock to take you to the Peru–Bolivia border at **Puerto Pardo**. A few minutes from Puerto Pardo by boat is **Puerto Heath**, a military camp on the Bolivian side. The trip takes half a day and can cost up to US$100 (but is negotiable) – the boat will carry several people. With time and luck, you may also be able to find a cargo boat that's going there anyway and will take passengers much more cheaply.

It's possible to continue down the river on the Bolivian side, but this can take days (even weeks) to arrange and isn't cheap. Travel in a group to share costs, and avoid the dry months of July to September, when the river is too low. From Puerto Heath, continue down the Río Madre de Dios as far as Riberalta (at the confluence of the Madre de Dios and Beni, far into northern Bolivia), where road and air connections can be made: a classic (if tough) Amazon adventure the like of which no road trip can compete with. Basic food and shelter (bring a hammock) can be found en route. When river levels allow, a cargo and passenger boat runs from Puerto Maldonado to Riberalta and back about twice a month, but this trip is rarely done by foreigners.

If you've had your fill of river transport by Puerto Heath, you can switch to a dirt road which runs to **Chivé** (1½ hours by bus), where there are very basic accommodations and from where minivans depart each morning around 8am to Cobija (six hours).

Always get your Peruvian exit stamp in Puerto Maldonado. Bolivian entry stamps can be obtained in Puerto Heath or Cobija. Visas are not available, however, so get one ahead of time in Lima or your home country if you need it. US citizens need to pay US$135 in cash for a visa to enter Bolivia (US$160 if purchased in the US).

Formalities are generally slow and relaxed.

For more detailed coverage of Bolivia, pick up Lonely Planet's *Bolivia* from the Lonely Planet online shop (http://shop.lonelyplanet.com).

much of Reserva Nacional Tambopata, and on balance contains the region's best selection of jungle lodges.

The river has been well protected, and wildlife sightings are correspondingly high. Enticingly, sightings of the bigger rainforest animals, such as the tapir and the jaguar, have been increasing along this stretch of river.

One of the reserve's highlights is Collpa Chuncho, one of the country's largest natural macaw clay licks. It attracts hundreds of birds and is a spectacular sight.

◉ Sights

Collpa Chuncho   WILDLIFE RESERVE
(admission S60) One of the best clay licks in the Reserva Nacional Tambopata, where you can see the colorful cacophony of feeding macaws for which the Tambopata region is renowned. The admission charge is what you need to pay to get into the reserved zone for two to three days, but covers you for Collpa Chuncho however long you want to stay.

**Reserva Nacional
Tambopata**   WILDLIFE RESERVE
(admission per day S30, 2-3 days S65) The wildlife-rich Río Tambopata is a major tributary of the Río Madre de Dios, joining it at Puerto Maldonado. Boats go up the river, past several good lodges, and into Reserva Nacional Tambopata, an important protected area divided into the reserve itself and the *zona de amortiguamiento* (buffer zone). The big draw is the birdlife: chattering groups of macaws and parrots gather to feed at clay licks here. Sightings of jaguars on the riverbanks are not unusual, either.

Park entrance fees must be paid at Puerto Maldonado's **Sernanp** (☏082-57-1247; www.sernanp.gob.pe; Cajamarca, btwn Ancash & Madre de Dios) office if you are not on a guided tour, in which case you'll pay at the relevant lodge office. An additional fee is required if you are heading into the reserve proper (such as to the Tambopata Research Center) rather than just the buffer zone.

Baltimore   VILLAGE
The community of Baltimore, just after Refugio Amazonas lodge, is the only real settlement on the river, and has a few simple *hospedajes* (homestays). Baltimore is accessible by taking a Laberinto-bound bus from Puerto Maldonado and getting off at Km 37. From there, a footpath goes to Baltimore (about three hours). No public transport exists to points further upriver.

You can also reach Baltimore by the snail-paced weekly public boat.

🛏 Sleeping

The best selection of lodges in the Peruvian Amazon can be found on this stretch of the Río Tambopata. You can also stay in a homestay in or around the community of Baltimore. Either way, you will need to arrange your stay in advance.

Sotupa Eco House   LODGE $$
(☏950-416-257; www.sotupa.pe; dm/r per person per night US$54/120) The first lodge on the Río Tambopata, accessible by road, is close enough to Puerto Maldonado for a one-night break. Perched on a pea-green grassy expanse atop a cliff, it feels isolated. The cabins are idyllic, 9.5km of trails beckon, and as you swing from your garden hammock, know no other lodges boast a chill-out area with these river views.

A bungalow on stilts, separate from the rest of the complex, is great for families. Sotupo Eco House sits at the end of the Corredor Turístico Bajo Tambopata (p449). As it is before the first of the reserve checkpoints, no Reserva Nacional Tambopata entrance fees are necessary.

Reserve online or by phone.

Tambopata Research Center   LODGE $$$
(www.perunature.com; s/d 5 days & 4 nights per person US$1592/2412) About seven hours' river travel from Puerto Maldonado, this important research facility and lodge is known for a famous salt lick nearby that attracts four to 10 species of parrots and macaws on most mornings. The lodge itself is fairly simple, with 18 double rooms sharing four showers and four toilets.

As for the research, this focuses on why macaws eat clay, their migration patterns, their diet, nesting macaws and techniques for building artificial nests. If you're interested in seeing more macaws than you ever thought possible, this lodge is worth the expense, although the owners point out that occasionally, due to poor weather or other factors, macaws aren't found at the lick. Nevertheless, wildlife sightings are high here.

A stopover is usually made at Refugio Amazonas (p460) on the first and last nights of a trip here, for which you really do need five days and four nights' total stay. The last section of the ride is through remote country, with excellent chances of seeing capybaras and maybe more-unusual animals.

AMAZON BASIN RÍO TAMBOPATA

Around Puerto Maldonado

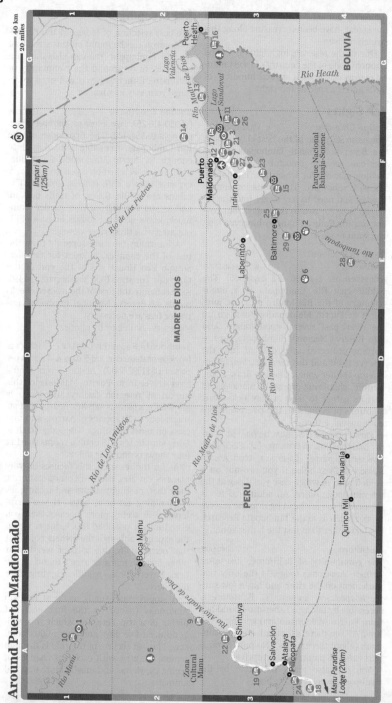

0 40 km
0 20 miles

BOLIVIA

Río Heath

Puerto Heath

Lago Valencia

Lago Sandoval

Río Madre de Dios

Puerto Maldonado

Ihapari (125km)

Infierno

Parque Nacional Bahuaja-Sonene

Río de Los Piedras

MADRE DE DIOS

Laberinto

Baltimore

Río Tambopata

Río Inambari

PERU

Río de Los Amigos

Río Madre de Dios

Río Alto Madre de Dios

Boca Manu

Zona Cultural Manu

Río Manu

Shintuya

Salvación

Atalaya

Pillcopata

Manu Paradise Lodge (20km)

Itahuania

Quince Mil

Around Puerto Maldonado

Have your passport ready at the **Puesto Control Malinowski**, entrance point to the reserve proper.

Book online or at the Rainforest Expeditions (p451) in Puerto Maldonado, and remember that the Reserva Nacional Tambopata reserve entrance fee is payable.

Explorer's Inn
Tambopata Ecolodge   LODGE $$$

(www.explorersinn.com; s/d 4 days & 3 nights per person US$731/1462) About 58km from Puerto Maldonado (three to four hours by river) and featuring 15 rustic double and 15 triple rooms, sleeping 70 people, all with bathrooms and screened windows. Around since the 1970s, this is a more open lodge than most, in a pleasant grassy clearing dotted by fruit trees near the confluence of Ríos Tambopata and La Torre.

The central lodge room sports a restaurant, a bar and a small museum; outside is a soccer pitch and a medicinal garden.

The place is located in the former 55-sq-km Zona Preservada Tambopata (itself now surrounded by the much larger Reserva Nacional Tambopata, and just inside the reserve buffer zone). More than 600 species of bird have been recorded in this preserved zone, which is a world record for bird species sighted in one area. Despite such (scientifically documented) records, the average tourist won't see much more here than at any of the other Río Tambopata lodges during the standard two-night visit, which misses out on the macaw clay

lick at Collpa Chuncho. The 38km of trails around the lodge can be explored independently or with naturalist guides. German, English and French are spoken.

Book online or at the **Puerto Maldonado office** (☎082-57-3029, 950-186-820; Terminal Terreste piso 2, Av Circunvalación s/n).

Wasai Alto Tambopata Ecolodge LODGE $$$

(www.wasai.com; d 4 days & 3 nights per person from US$410) Just after Baltimore, this reasonably priced lodge is one of the furthest from Puerto Maldonado along the Río Tambopata. Unlike most others hereabouts, it doesn't feature programmed eco-activities. Just relax, read a book, enjoy a beer or amble around 20km of well-signed trails. The lodge itself consists of 21 lovely rustic wooden cabins, and can accommodate up to 50 guests.

Fishing and canoe paddling are other optional pursuits. There is a tall observation tower, too, from where you get good views of the surrounding jungle, and a chill-out room that boasts a library and wi-fi!

Guests can now arrive by road/rough track to Filadelfia and continue by boat from there to cut down transportation time and costs (meaning one-night stays are possible). Four-day, three-night tours take in Tambopata and Lago Sandoval, but not the Tambopata reserved zone.

Book online or at Wasai Lodge (p453) in Puerto Maldonado. The cheapest prices are often only available online.

AMAZON BASIN RÍO TAMBOPATA

Refugio Amazonas
LODGE $$$

(www.perunature.com; s/d 4 days & 3 nights per person US$960/1416) This lodge is a fairly lengthy (80km) boat ride upriver, meaning a three-night tour is recommended. It's on a 20-sq-km private reserve in the buffer zone of Reserva Nacional Tambopata. While it feels isolated, this is one of the sleekest lodges in the southern jungle. Rooms are very comfortable, complemented by a large, impressive reception, dining and drinking area.

Neatly varnished walkways lead off to the rooms. There is even an art gallery and massage available.

Activities include a Brazil-nut trail and camp and, for children, a dedicated rainforest trail. The increased remoteness usually means better opportunities for spotting wildlife. Book online or with Rainforest Expeditions (p451) in Puerto Maldonado.

Posada Amazonas
LODGE $$$

(www.perunature.com; s/d 3 days & 2 nights per person from US$640/944) About two hours from Puerto Maldonado along Río Tambopata, followed by a 10-minute uphill walk, this *posada* (hostel) is on the land of the Ese'eja tribespeople, and tribal members are among the guides. At or near the lodge, which has 30 rooms including two suites, macaws, parrots and giant river otters can be spotted.

There are excellent chances of seeing macaws and parrots on a small salt lick nearby, and giant river otters are often found swimming in lakes close to the lodge. Guides at the lodge are mainly English-speaking Peruvian naturalists with varying interests. Your assigned guide stays with you throughout the duration of your stay.

Visits are also made to the Centro Ñape ethnobotanical center, where medicine is produced for the Ese'eja community. There is a medicinal-plant trail and a 30m-high observation platform giving superb views of the rainforest canopy. Lodge rooms have private showers and open (unglazed) windows overlooking the rainforest. Mosquito nets are provided. Electricity is available in the evenings; otherwise everything is candle- or lamp-lit.

Book online or at Rainforest Expeditions (p451) in Puerto Maldonado. Not even the Reserva Nacional Tambopata buffer zone entrance fee is payable, as the reserve is before the first checkpoint, Puesto Control La Torre.

The same outfit has two other lodges on the Tambopata: Refugio Amazonas and the Tambopata Research Center (p457).

ⓘ Getting There & Away

Transport to almost all lodges, as well as all sights, will be taken care of by the lodge you are staying at.

The only exception is with the community of Baltimore, which you can arrive at independently. Take a Laberinto-bound bus from Puerto Maldonado and get off at Km 37. From there, a footpath goes to Baltimore (about three hours). You can also reach Baltimore by snail-paced weekly public boat.

Río Madre de Dios

In Puerto Maldonado the Río Madre de Dios meets the Río Tambopata and, having widened considerably since having come from Parque Nacional Manu, the vast torrent of water now zigzags east, skirting the fringes of Reserva Nacional Tambopata, toward the Peru–Bolivia border at Puerto Heath. The parts of interest to Puerto Maldonado travelers are all downriver of the city: its mix of fun and fancy lodges, and the lovely lakes of Lago Sandoval and Lago Valencia awaiting close to its banks. Accordingly, reaching the several lodges on this river, including the southern jungle's best, is much easier than getting to Río Tambopata's lodges.

◉ Sights

Lago Sandoval is easily accessible from many lodges here. A couple of canopy walkways – Inkaterra Reserva Amazonica and Monte Amazonico Lodge – provide a distraction from normal jungle activities. Monte Amazónico Lodge even has a zipline!

Hacienda Concepción Research Center
VISITOR CENTER

(www.wcupa.edu/aceer) **FREE** Formerly the ITA Aceer Tambopata Research Center, Inkaterra's reconstructed lodge, 8km downriver from Puerto Maldonado, is an important research center of interest to ecotourists, with an exhibition on conservation, occasional lectures and a laboratory for scientists. It's built on the site of the house of one of the first doctors to practice in the Amazon.

Next door, the Hacienda Concepción lodge has a good restaurant and accommodations. Inkaterra's Reserva Amazonica lodge is only 7km away.

🛏 Sleeping

There is a healthy choice of lodges on this river. These range from the budget to the elite to those that focus more on adventure sports and activities.

Hacienda Concepción LODGE $$$
(☑ in UK 0044-800-458-7506, in US 1-800-442-5042; www.inkaterra.com; s/d 3 days & 2 nights per person US$521/844) 🌿 This bright, enticing lodge is one of the southern Amazon's best. Facilities might be classic top-end Inkaterra but the big draw is that its prices are not. Its spacious rooms, fashioned out of reclaimed timber, exude an early 20th-century glamor, and there's a securely mosquito-netted bar, chill-out area and restaurant (serving incredible food).

The serene location could hardly be better, with an on-site rainforest learning center and laboratory, its own private *cocha* (an indigenous word for lagoon) nearby and Lago Sandoval a stone's throw away. Electricity is from 5:30am to 9:30am and 6pm to 11pm: it's one of the few jungle lodges with cell-phone reception and wifi. Rooms are spread around the 2nd floor surveying the forest clearing with a broad wraparound terrace, while cabins have secluded *cocha* views – good enough, according to staff, for celebrities such as Mick Jagger to favor.

Book online or at Inkaterra in **Lima** (Map p70; ☑ in Lima 01-610-0400, in UK 0-800-458-7506, in US & Canada 1-800-442-5042; www.inkaterra.com; Andalucía 174, Miraflores) or Cuzco (p224).

⭐ **Inkaterra**
Reserva Amazonica LODGE $$$
(www.inkaterra.com; s 3 days & 2 nights per person US$818-950, d US$1290-1478) 🌿 Down the Madre de Dios, almost 16km from Puerto Maldonado, this top-end lodge offers a luxurious look at the jungle. About 40 rustic individual cabins have bathrooms and porches with two hammocks. Tours here include 10km of private hiking trails, and a series of swaying, narrow, jungle canopy walkways up to 35m above the jungle floor for flora and fauna observation.

A huge, traditionally thatched, cone-shaped, two-story reception, restaurant, bar (built spectacularly around a fig tree), library and relaxation area greet the traveler. Some of the southern Amazon's best meals are served here; travelers with special dietary needs can be accommodated. There are occasional alfresco barbecues, sitting areas upstairs for imbibing views or spotting birdlife, and a separate building housing a good interpretation center. Guides speak English, French or Italian. Higher tariffs listed are for the six suites, with huge bathrooms, writing desks and two queen-size beds each.

Book online or at Inkaterra in Lima or Cuzco (p224).

Estancia Bello Horizonte LODGE $$$
(www.estanciabellohorizonte.com; d or tr bungalow 3 days & 2 nights per person US$285-320; ❄) 🌿 A superb getaway 20km from Puerto Maldonado on the east side of the Río Madre de Dios. Accommodations, which comprise of bungalows with smallish, comfortable rooms with bathrooms, are built in local wood and poised on a ridge overlooking the rainforest; each has a hammock for lounging in.

The main building contains a relaxing dining, reading, drinking and chill-out space, and child-friendly grounds include a soccer pitch, a volleyball court, a swimming pool and signposted jungle walks.

The final approach to the lodge is along a 6km private road through dense jungle.

Book online or at the **Puerto Maldonado office** (☑ 082-57-2748; www.estanciabello horizonte.com; Loreto 252; d or tr bungalow 3 days & 2 nights per person US$285-320).

Monte Amazonico Lodge LODGE $$$
(http://monteamazonico.com; r 3 days & 2 nights per person US$408; ❄) Adrenalin-pumping adventures take priority over wildlife watching here. This popular lodge near Lago Sandoval, with its two spick-and-span blocks of wooden, tin-roofed rooms, has canopy walkways and a zipline. A decent pool, a resident tapir and a nicely done common area with table football completes the agreeable overall effect.

Kayaking and fishing are also possibilities, alongside other more conventional jungle activities. You can head here just for the day for US$80 per person. Book through their **Puerto Maldonado office** (☑ 082-57-1320; http://monteamazonico.com; Velarde 141; r 3 days & 2 nights per person US$408), part of Carlos Expeditions.

AMAZON BASIN RÍO MADRE DE DIOS

Eco Amazonia Lodge
LODGE $$$

(www.ecoamazonia.com; bungalow 3 days & 2 nights per person US$325; ☒) Roughly 30km from Puerto Maldonado this lodge sports a huge, thatch-roofed restaurant and bar, with fine river views from the 2nd floor. Guides speak English, French and Italian; the knowledgeable manager also speaks Japanese. Fifty rustic, tin-roofed completely screened bungalows each have a bathroom and a small sitting room.

There is also a games room and a pool here. Several trails lead from this lodge, including a tough 14km hike to a lake, and several shorter walks. Boat tours to local lakes and along the rivers are also offered, and *ayahuasca* ceremonies can be arranged by advance request. Lonely Planet does not recommend taking *ayahuasca* and those who do so do it at their own risk.

Book online or at Eco Amazonia in **Puerto Maldonado** (☏ 082-57-3491; www.ecoamazonia.com; 26 de Diciembre 435; bungalow 3 days & 2 nights per person US$325) or **Lima** (Map p74; ☏ 01-242-2708; www.ecoamazonia.com; Palacios 292, Miraflores; bungalow 3 days & 2 nights per person US$325).

Corto Maltes
LODGE $$$

(www.cortomaltes-amazonia.com; d 3 days & 2 nights per person US$290; ☒) The closest lodge to Puerto Maldonado on the Río Madre de Dios is traveler friendly and upbeat. Only 5km from town, this lodge offers 27 comfortable, fully screened, high-ceilinged bungalows with solid mattresses: some bungalows even have king-size beds!

Eye-catching Shipibo indigenous wall art and hammock-laced patios light up all the bungalows, as do cheerful decorative touches in the public areas. Electricity is available from dusk until 10:30pm, and showers have hot water. The French owners pride themselves on the excellent European–Peruvian fusion cuisine. *Ayahuasca* ceremonies can be arranged, too, though Lonely Planet does not recommend taking *ayahuasca*. Prices are based on a two-person minimum group size.

Book online or at the **Puerto Maldonado office** (☏ 082-57-3831; http://cortomaltes-amazonia.com; Billinghurst 229; d 3 days & 2 nights per person from US$290).

ⓘ Getting There & Away

Many visitors come for the day, as boats can go with the current and distances to many locales from Puerto Maldonado are not huge. Lodges will take care of transport in and out, returning you to Puerto Maldonado.

Lago Sandoval

Lago Sandoval is an idyllic lake east of Puerto Maldonado, accessed from the Río Madre de Dios. It's a wildlife-watching haven, particularly known for its giant river otters, and has a couple of good lodges.

Surrounded by different types of rainforest, Lago Sandoval is about two hours from Puerto Maldonado by boat down the Madre de Dios, followed by a 3km hike, which has its own appeal for the wildlife-watching opportunities it yields. With luck, either on the trail or at the lake, you might see caiman, turtles, brightly colored birds, monkeys and, more thrillingly yet, maybe the endangered giant river otters.

◉ Sights

As with other jungle regions, you really need a guide to glimpse the best flora and fauna.

Those resolved to see Lago Sandoval independently can, for about S100 (bargain; several people can travel for this price), hire a boat from Puerto Maldonado that drops you at the beginning of the hiking trail to the lake and picks you up later. From the dock, the trail is marked, although poorly maintained.

⌂ Sleeping

The choice, for an isolated jungle lake, is really not bad: there is a plush lodge and appealing homestays around the shores.

Casa Sandoval
LODGE $$$

(☏ 982-613-293; www.casasandovallodge.com; s/d 3 days & 2 nights US$300/460) The friendly owners are proud that it took two years to construct this lodge, Lago Sandoval's newest, because the materials were brought in along a 3km trail then ferried across the lake. The result is pleasing: a convivial five-room lodge with a lovely dining and hammock area, run by a family who have known the lake their whole lives.

This lodge irons out a lot of the things that can rankle on jungle trips: it has single-language tours, very good quality boats and a mine of local knowledge. How about the unforgettable sight of giant otters cavorting in the water for a pre-breakfast treat?!

Sandoval Lake Lodge LODGE $$$
(www.inkanatura.com; s/d 3 days & 2 nights per person US$660/874) These spacious premises crest a hilltop about 30m above Lago Sandoval and are surrounded by primary forest. The big draw is the lake itself, which provides excellent wildlife-watching opportunities. Rooms, with heated showers and ceiling fans, are of high standards. The restaurant-bar area is huge, airy and conducive to relaxing and chatting.

Another big attraction is getting there. After hiking the 3km to the lake, you board canoes to negotiate narrow canals through a flooded palm-tree forest inhabited by red-bellied macaws, then silently paddle across the beautiful lake to the lodge.

With luck, you may spot the endangered giant river otter, several pairs of which live in the lake (early morning is best). Various monkey species and a host of birds and reptiles can also be seen. Hikes into the forest are offered, and the knowledgeable guides are multilingual.

The lodge was built from salvaged driftwood; the owners pride themselves on the fact that no primary forest was cut during construction (this is also true of some other lodges, though not always mentioned). Sadly, travelers have reported a drop in the quality of service.

Book online or with InkaNatura (p80) in Lima.

ⓘ Information
To see Lago Sandoval, you'll need to pay the Reserva Nacional Tambopata entrance fee. Permits to visit the lake (included in licensed guide tours and lodge stays) are S30 for the day, or S60 for two to three day visits.

ⓘ Getting There & Away
Lodges take care of transport in and out. Show your permits for entering Lago Sandoval at **Puesto de Control Lago Sandoval**.

Lago Valencia
Just off the Río Madre de Dios and near the Bolivian border, Lago Valencia is about 60km from Puerto Maldonado. At least two days are needed for a visit here (staying at Lago Sandoval, which is quite close, is best for this, as is basing yourself at nearer Huarayo Lodge), though three or four days are recommended. This lake offers the region's best fishing, as well as good bird-watching and wildlife-watching (bring your binoculars). There are trails into the jungle around the lake.

Lodges around Puerto Maldonado can arrange tours, as can independent guides.

🛏 Sleeping
Huarayo Lodge LODGE $$$
(http://perunaturepro.com; r 3 days & 2 nights per person US$160) Handsome Huarayo Lodge enjoys the closest position to Lago Valencia, about halfway between this lake and Lago Sandoval. It has use of its own private creek, the Briolo, where it carries out activities like fishing and kayaking. The lodge has six rooms, a large dining room/common area and a hammock area.

Programs include a mix of Lago Sandoval and Lago Valencia activities (the former good for spying animals like the giant otter, the latter more conducive to fishing or merely paddling across). The price, at such a distance from Puerto Maldonado, should be a deal-clincher.

Reserve online or through its **Puerto Maldonado office** (Huarayo Expeditions; ☑ 980-973-736; www.perunaturepro.com; Junin cuadra 1 s/n, behind IPD Stadium; r 3 days & 2 nights per person US$160).

ⓘ Getting There & Away
Your elected lodge, especially if you are staying at Huarayo Lodge or one of the Lago Sandoval lodges, will ferry you in and out.

Río Heath
Forging on down the Río Madre de Dios from Puerto Maldonado, you hit Puerto Heath, the Peru–Bolivia border, and with it the Río Heath. Running approximately north–south, this river forms the border for much of its length and offers access to one of Peru's largest, remotest wilderness reserves and just one basic lodge.

This, of course, far from being a disadvantage, is the region's allure. Here, unlike other jungle locales open to tourism, development has been minimal indeed. This means acre for acre wildlife sightings are not only greater, but the species spotted, including the maned wolf and spider monkey, are much rarer than elsewhere.

The reserve in question, **Parque Nacional Bahuaja-Sonene** (admission per day S30, 2-3 days S60), comprises only a part of the still-vaster Tambopata-Madidi wilderness reserve that spans a nigh-on 14,000 sq km tract across Peru and Bolivia.

About two hours south of the Río Madre de Dios and along the Río Heath (the latter forming the Peru–Bolivia border), the national park has some of the best wildlife in Peru's Amazon region, including such rarities as the maned wolf and the spider monkey, although these are hard to see. Infrastructure in the park, one of the nation's largest, is limited, and wildlife-watching trips are in their infancy here, rendering the experience all the more genuine.

The park entrance fee should be paid at Sernanp (p457) in Puerto Maldonado, because checkpoints along the way don't sell tickets.

🛏 Sleeping

Heath River Wildlife Center　　　LODGE $$$
(www.inkanatura.com; s/d 5 days & 4 nights per person US$1478/2438) This simple, 10-room lodge is owned by the Ese'eja indigenous people of Sonene, who provide guiding and cultural services. Trails into the isolated Parque Nacional Bahuaja-Sonene are available, and field biologists have assessed this area as one of the most biodiverse in southeastern Peru. Capybaras are frequently seen, and guided tours to a nearby macaw clay lick are arranged.

Hot water is provided and park entrance fees are included. The first and/or last nights of tours are sometimes spent at Sandoval Lake Lodge (p463). Tour prices are notoriously hard to understand because tours involve staying at more than one lodge, so do check at the time of reserving.

Reserve online or through InkaNatura (p80) in Lima.

ⓘ Information

If by any chance you are continuing into Bolivia by boat from here rather than returning to Puerto Maldonado, ensure you have the necessary exit and entry formalities resolved in Puerto Maldonado or, for US citizens entering Bolivia, Lima.

ⓘ Getting There & Away

Getting in and out will almost certainly be organized courtesy of your likely accommodation possibility and the region's lone lodge, Heath River Wildlife Center.

MANU AREA

The Manu area encompasses Parque Nacional Manu and much of the surrounding jungle and cloud forest. Covering almost 20,000 sq km (about the size of Wales), the park is one of the best places in South America to scout out a whole shebang of tropical wildlife.

The official **Parque Nacional Manu website** (www.visitmanu.com) has more information.

☞ Tours

It's important to check exactly where the tours are going: Manu is a catchall word that includes the national park and much of the surrounding area. Some tours, such as to the Manu Wildlife Center (p469), don't actually enter Parque Nacional Manu at all (although the wildlife center is recommended for wildlife-watching, nonetheless). Some companies aren't allowed to enter the park, but offer what they call 'Manu tours' outside the park or act as agents for other operators. Other companies work together and share resources such as lodges, guides and transportation services. This can mean the agency in whose office you sign up for the tour isn't the agency you end up going with. Most will combine a Manu experience with a full Peru tour on request. Confusing? You bet!

The companies we recommend are all authorized to operate within Manu by the national park service and maintain some level of conservation and low-impact practices. The number of permits to operate tours into Parque Nacional Manu is limited; only a few thousand visitors are allowed in annually. Intending visitors must book well in advance. Be flexible with onward travel plans as delays are common. Entering by bus and boat (on the Río Alto Madre de Dios) and returning by boat (the Río Madre de Dios) and flight from Puerto Maldonado is the best means of seeing Manu. Some agencies now return by continuing down the Río Madre de Dios by boat to Puerto Maldonado and flying back from there.

Tour costs depend on whether you camp or stay in a lodge, whether you arrive and depart overland or by air and whether you

TRES CRUCES

About two hours beyond Paucartambo is the extraordinary jungle view at **Tres Cruces**, a lookout off the Paucartambo–Shintuya road. The sight of the mountains dropping away into the Amazon Basin is gorgeous in itself, but is made more magical by the sunrise phenomenon that occurs from May to July (other months are cloudy), especially around the winter solstice on June 21. The sunrise here gets optically distorted, causing double images, halos and an incredible multicolored light show.

At this time of year, many travel agencies and outdoor adventure outfitters run sunrise-watching trips from Cuzco. During Paucartambo's Fiesta de la Virgen del Carmen, minibuses run back and forth between Paucartambo and Tres Cruces all night long. You can also take a truck en route to Pillcopata and ask to be let off at the turnoff to Tres Cruces (a further 13km walk). Alternatively, ask around in Paucartambo to hire a truck. Make sure you leave in the middle of the night to catch the dawn, and take plenty of warm clothing. Camping is possible but take all your own supplies.

Tres Cruces lies (just) within the Parque Nacional Manu *zona cultural* but is always visited from Paucartambo.

enter the *zona reservada*. A tour inside the zone won't necessarily get you better wildlife viewing – although, since it's virgin jungle here, the chances of seeing larger animals are greater. If your budget allows, the more expensive companies really are worth considering. They offer more reliable and trained multilingual guides, better equipment, a wider variety of food, suitable insurance and emergency procedures. Perhaps most importantly, there are more guarantees that your money is going partly toward preserving Manu, as many of these companies fund conservation costs.

All companies provide transportation, food, purified drinking water, guides, permits and camping equipment or screens in lodge rooms. Personal items such as a sleeping bag (unless staying in a lodge), insect repellent, sunblock, flashlight with spare batteries, suitable clothing and bottled drinks are the traveler's responsibility. Binoculars and a camera with a zoom lens are highly recommended.

All lodges and tour operators in the big-money business of Manu excursions quote prices in US dollars.

Cuzco to Manu

⊙ Sights

This spectacular journey provides opportunities for some excellent bird-watching at the lodges en route, as well as some of Peru's most dramatic scenery changes. The route runs from bare Andean mountains into cloud forest before dropping into a steamy tangle of lowland jungle. Whilst undertaken usually as a necessary part of the long trip through to Parque Nacional Manu, this leg is a memorable adventure in itself.

You can get from Cuzco as far as Boca Manu, an hour before the entrance point for the *zona reservada,* independently. This is challenging but possible: most lodges en route will let you stay, but giving them advance notice is advised. However, to either enter the *zona reservada* or maximize your chances of seeing wildlife, you will still need a guide and therefore a tour.

Traveling overland, the first stage of the journey involves taking a bus or truck (or minivan if you are on a tour) from Cuzco via Paucartambo (S12, three hours) to Pilcopata, then Atalaya and Shintuya. Buses run by Transportes Corazon Serraño (p468) leave at 5am on Monday, Wednesday and Friday for Pilcopata (S26, 10 to 12 hours in good weather), returning from Pilcopata on the same days at 6pm.

Be aware that breakdowns, extreme overcrowding and delays are common on this route, and during the rainy season (even during the dry) vehicles slide off the road. It's safer, more comfortable and more reliable to take the costlier tourist buses offered by Cuzco tour operators. Many tour companies in Cuzco offer trips to Manu.

After the pretty town of **Paucartambo**, the road continues for 1½ hours to the entrance to Parque Nacional Manu (p468) (*zona cultural*; admission S10 for independent travelers, at the turnoff to the mesmeric jungle viewpoint of Tres Cruces (p465), a further 13km).

The next six hours to Pilcopata are through spectacular cloud forest, occupying a humid elevation of some 1600m and home to thousands of bird species, many of which are yet to be officially identified. There are several lodges at which you can enjoy phenomenal bird-watching (including, if you are lucky, the rarely glimpsed cock-of-the-rock, with striking scarlet plumage and elaborate mating dances).

The next village, Pilcopata, is the end of the public bus route and indeed contact with the outside world of all kinds: the last public phone (and cell-phone reception) before Manu is here, along with Manu's main police station. There are basic hotels (beds around S20) and stores, too. Pickup trucks leave early every morning for Atalaya (45 minutes) and Shintuya (three hours).

The road beyond Pilcopata can be nigh-on impassable in wet season, which is why most vehicles give up the ghost at Atalaya, and switch to boat (all Manu tour agencies continue by boat from here).

To continue by rough road beyond here to Salvación (where there is a national park office) and Shintuya (with limited basic accommodations) is possible, but slightly pointless, as there are more boats available for continuing downriver in Atalaya. Just past Shintuya, Itahuanía has Manu's emergency hospital. Then the road really does peter out, although there is talk of extending it as far as Boca Manu.

The long boat journey down the Río Alto Madre de Dios from Atalaya to Boca Manu, known for building the region's best riverboats, and at the junction with the Río Manu, can take almost a day. Independent travelers: again, bear in mind that if you are not on a tour with a licensed Manu tour agency you will not be permitted entry into the *zona reservada*, although continuing on down the Río Manu to the Manu Wildlife Center (p469) and Puerto Maldonado may be possible.

Because of this long process of reaching Boca Manu from Cuzco, some companies prefer using the other route to Manu (a flight into Puerto Maldonado followed by a road trip on the Carr Interoceánica and a trip up the Madre de Dios): quicker maybe, but not nearly as spectacular.

🛏 Sleeping

There are several good lodges on this route. While none are in the *zona reservada* or the *zona natural* of Parque Nacional Manu, they nevertheless can provide great wildlife-watching opportunities. Lodges are congregated either in the cloud forest or on the Río Alto Madre de Dios after Atalaya: most let independent tourists stay, but tour groups on lodge-affiliated tours get priority.

🛏 Cloud Forest

Several spectacular lodges for bird-watching are tucked away in the cloud forest here.

Rainforest Lodge — LODGE $$
(www.bonanzatoursperu.com; d per person incl meals US$40) 🍃 A cheap option, and a good journey-breaker, is this rustic lodge around 10 hours from Cuzco near Pilcopata (you could almost hit the village nightlife from here). The 12 cabins here sleep up to 40 people; of these eight have private bathrooms. It's at the base of the cloud forest (one hour's drive from the best cloud forest bird-watching).

Owned by a local family, the lodge supports many admirable practices, such as getting guests out volunteering clearing the road to Manu of rubbish. It's an opportunity to give something back to the jungle, as well as participating in the usual jungle activities.

Book through Bonanza Tours (p468).

Manu Paradise Lodge — LODGE $$$
(✆984-765-659; www.manuparadiselodge. com; s/d per person per night room only from US$70/110, s/d 4 days & 3 nights specialized nature-watching tours from US$1921/2228) 🍃 Around six hours from Cuzco and overlooking the scenic Río Kosñipata valley, this lodge sleeps 16 people in spacious rooms with private hot-water bathrooms. It looks quite modern, unlike the more rustic lodges further into the park. Among its assets are an attractive dining room–bar with a fireplace and telescopes for wildlife viewing.

It advertises its wide variety of tours (three to six nights) on its website. Rafting and mountain-biking tours can be arranged, but the primary attraction is bird-watching (its classic bird-watching tour is what is priced).

Book online.

Manu Cloud Forest Lodge   LODGE $$$

(☎084-63-2081; www.manuperu.com; d 3 days & 2 nights per person US$550) Six to seven hours' drive from Cuzco, Manu Cloud Forest Lodge is a basic 16- to 20-bed lodge providing six rooms with hot showers, a sauna (!), a restaurant and bird-watching opportunities in the high cloud forest. Rates can decrease if you arrive independently: ask. Book online or by phone.

Río Alto Madre de Dios

This is the upper echelons of the Río Madre de Dios; upriver of Boca Manu. It is harder to stay at some of these lodges independently, as you need a boat to reach them, and there are few available boats not affiliated with a particular tour agency. Guests at the lodges themselves, however, report wildlife sightings nigh on as good as those within Parque Nacional Manu.

Pantiacolla Lodge   LODGE $$$

(www.pantiacolla.com; s/d per day per person incl meals US$150/200, r 5 days & 4 nights per person incl meals & activities US$815) ✐ There are 11 double rooms here, eight with shared bathrooms and three with private. Both rates include meals; only the five-day option is a tour with all activities included. However, for DIY adventurers, there are forest trails (some re-ascending into cloud forest at 900m) near the lodge, a parrot lick and hot springs. Various transportation and guided-tour options are available.

Independent travelers: it is necessary to give advance notice if you need the boat to the lodge (about 1½ hours from Atalaya by boat, or 12½ hours' journey from Cuzco), which is on the fringe of the national park, just before Itahuanía village. You could hope to find a boat in Atalaya by just turning up and asking, but it is not guaranteed.

Book with Pantiacolla Tours (p468) in Cuzco.

Manu Learning Center   LODGE $$$

(www.crees-manu.org; s/d 4 days & 3 nights US$1045/1630) This smart new lodge on the Río Alto Madre de Dios is owned by Crees, and where its week-long volunteer programs are based. Shorter trips, without the volunteering, are also run. Either way it is a great place for learning more about the jungle and its associated issues in the 21st century.

Reserve online or with Crees' Cusco office (p224).

Bonanza Ecological Reserve   LODGE $$$

(www.bonanzatoursperu.com; d per person incl meals US$85) Past Itahuanía toward the community of Bonanza, this family-run 40-person capacity lodge has cabins abutting a large clearing that also has a large restaurant area with sofas and a two-floor hammock-strung chill-out zone; bathrooms are shared and there's solar-paneled electricity throughout. From here trails lead off into dense jungle that backs onto Manu's zona natural.

The highlight here is the tree house peeping out on a clay lick that tapirs visit, and two 15m observation towers for improved animal viewing. There are also canoes available for nearby river trips. The lodge is around three hours from Atalaya by boat, or 14 hours' journey from Cuzco.

Book through Bonanza Tours (p468).

Amazonia Lodge   LODGE $$$

(www.amazonialodge.com; s/d with private bathroom incl meals US$140/210) In an old colonial hacienda in the Andean foothills, Amazonia provides travelers with slightly different environs to bed down: and agreeable ones, too, following a refurbishment. Expect clean, comfortable beds and hot showers. The lodge has forest trails, including one to an observation tower, excellent bird-watching (guided tours are offered), and limited electricity.

There are slightly cheaper rates for rooms with shared bathrooms.

As it's just across the river from Atalaya (itself about 11 hours from Cuzco), you can usually charter a local boat to ferry you across, making this one of the very few jungle lodges it is possible to visit independently (if you do so, arrange a discounted price, but be aware you still have to reserve in advance).

Reserve online or with Amazon Trails Peru in Cuzco.

❶ Getting There & Away

Buses run by **Transportes Corazon Serraño** (☑984-608-469; Via Expresa s/n, behind Sanidad de la Policía Nacional, Urbanizacion Enaco) go from Cuzco via Paucartambo (S12, three hours) to Pilcopata (S26, 10 to 12 hours in good weather), then Atalaya, Shintuya and Salvación. They leave at 11am daily. For points anywhere beyond Atalaya you really need to be part of a tour and traveling on a tour boat.

Parque Nacional Manu

This vast **national park** (entry per 1/2-3/4+ days S30/60/150) 🏊 in the Amazon Basin covers almost 20,000 sq km and is one of the best places in South America to see a stunning variety of tropical wildlife. Progressive in its emphasis on preservation, Unesco declared Manu a Biosphere Reserve in 1977 and a World Natural Heritage Site in 1987. Entry is only with guide and permit.

One reason the park is so successful in preserving such a large tract of virgin jungle and its wildlife is that it's remote and relatively inaccessible to people, and therefore has not been exploited by rubber tappers, loggers, oil companies or hunters.

At **Cocha Salvador**, one of the park's largest and most beautiful lakes, you'll find camping and guided hiking possibilities, as well as wonderful wildlife viewing.

With patience, wildlife is seen in most areas. During a one-week trip, you can reasonably expect to see scores of different bird species, several kinds of monkey and a few other mammals.

The best time to go is during the dry season (June to November); much of Manu may be inaccessible or closed during the rainiest months (January to April). Going with an organized group is best arranged in Cuzco, from where trips depart almost daily, or with international tour operators.

☞ Tours

It is illegal to enter the park's *zona reservada* without a guide, and difficult to arrange a tour independently that will get you good wildlife sightings even in the *zona cultural*. Going with an organized group can be arranged in Cuzco or with international tour operators.

It's an expensive trip; budget travelers should arrange their trip in Cuzco and be flexible with travel plans. Travelers often report returning from Manu several days late. Don't plan an international airline connection the day after a Manu trip!

Permits, which are necessary to enter the park, are arranged by tour agencies. Transportation, accommodations, food and guides are also part of tour packages. Most visits are for a week, although three-night stays at a lodge can be arranged.

Bonanza Tours   ADVENTURE
(Map p206; ☑084-50-7871, 985-371-500; www.bonanzatoursperu.com; Suecia 343; 3 nights & 4 days per person from US$510; ⊙8am-5pm) 🏊 Run by Ryse Choquepuma and his brothers, who grew up in Manu and know it better than most. Tours are to the family home, which has been converted into the well-appointed Bonanza Ecological Reserve (p467). The land here virtually backs onto the park proper and there are trails as well as a clay lick that attracts plenty of wildlife.

Pantiacolla Tours   ADVENTURE
(Map p206; ☑084-23-8323; www.pantiacolla.com; Garcilaso 265 interior, 2nd fl, Cuzco; ⊙8am-6pm Mon-Sat) 🏊 Pantiacolla is frequently recommended by a variety of travelers for its knowledgeable and responsibly executed tours, helped by the fact that its staff members were raised in the area. It also helps fund conservation of Manu, so ecologically, there's no better bet. Runs shorter trips, but it's the seven-day tours to Manu that are the real crowd-puller (per person US$1550).

★**InkaNatura**   ADVENTURE
(☑084-25-5255,   084-23-1138,   984-691-838; www.inkanatura.com; Ricardo Palma J1 Urb Santa Mónica & Plateros 361) InkaNatura is a highly

PARQUE NACIONAL MANU'S DIFFERENT ZONES

The park is divided into three zones:

The largest sector is the *zona natural*, comprising 80% of the total park area and closed to unauthorized visitors. Entry to this sector is restricted to a few indigenous groups, mainly the Matsiguenka (also spelled Machiguenga), some of whom continue to live here as they have for generations; some groups have had almost no contact with outsiders and do not seem to want any. Fortunately, this wish is largely respected – although tensions and clashes between tribes and settled villages have been reported more of late. A handful of researchers with permits are also allowed in to study the wildlife.

The second sector, still within the park proper, is the *zona reservada* (reserved zone, recently rebranded as the Manu river sector), where controlled research and tourism are permitted. There are a couple of official accommodation options here. This is the northeastern sector, comprising about 10% of the park area.

The third sector, covering the southeastern area, is the *zona cultural* (cultural zone, rebranded as the cultural history zone), where most other visitor activity is concentrated.

To travel between the *zona cultural* and the *zona reservada*, you'll need to take the Río Alto Madre de Dios to the park's main transit village, Boca Manu. Finally, outside the national park boundaries southeast of Boca Manu are, ironically, some of the very best wildlife-watching opportunities, especially at the macaw and tapir salt licks around the Manu Wildlife Center.

respected international agency and co-owner of the Manu Wildlife Center. The operators can combine a visit here with trips to other parts of the southern Peruvian rainforest, including Lago Sandoval, where it has its Sandoval Lake Lodge (p463), and Pampas del Heath near Puerto Maldonado, where it also has a lodge (the Heath River Wildlife Center (p464)).

But its main office is in Lima (p80) and it is better to book there, or online.

Amazon Trails Peru ADVENTURE (Map p206; ☎ 084-43-7374; www.amazontrailsperu.com; Tandapata 660; 2 nights & 3 days from US$540) ∥ This outfit has a growing reputation for providing the best service among the cheaper tour operators. Tours provide a deal of quirky insider information en route. High-power binoculars are also provided, increasing chances of wildlife sightings. Four-night, five-day tours to the *zona reservada* start from US$1350 per person. Any shorter trips concentrate on either cloud forest or Manu's *zona cultural*.

🛏 Sleeping

There are a couple of lodges within the park, plus a tented camp: you can't stay at any of these independently, but all are included on tours – with the owners or with other agencies. There is also more basic camping on and around the riverbanks,

offered as an option with many Manu operators: ask about.

Many other lodges are located within a few hours by boat of the park entrance.

Built in traditional style by the Matsiguenka tribespeople, the rustic, 19-room rustic **Casa Matsiguenka** ∥ lodge is the deepest into the reserved zone of any, on the other side of serene Cocha Salvador. Money spent here goes in part to the Matsiguenka. Several tour operators factor in stays here on their range of tours, almost always in combination with another lodge closer to Cuzco.

Operators staying here include Bonanza Tours.

❶ Getting There & Away

You can only enter Parque Nacional Manu on a guided tour, which means the lodge or tour company with which you are coming here will take care of all transport, and deposit you safely back in Cuzco at the end of it all.

Getting a portion of the way here independently is possible, however, although rarely done: see Cuzco to Manu (p465) for more on this.

Manu Wildlife Center & Around

A two-hour boat ride southeast of Boca Manu on Río Madre de Dios takes you to **Manu Wildlife Center** (www.manuexpeditions.com;

ℹ️ JUNGLE CHECKLIST

First jungle voyage? You'll find things far more relaxing than the movies make out. The jungle, you'll see, has largely been packaged to protect delicate tourists. With lodge facilities and the below kit list, you should be ready for most eventualities.

➡ Two pairs of shoes, one for jungle traipsing, one for camp.

➡ Spare clothes – in this humidity clothes get wet quickly; take a spare towel, too.

➡ Binoculars and a zoom lens camera, for wildlife in close-up.

➡ Flashlight for night walks.

➡ Mosquito repellent with DEET – bugs are everywhere.

➡ Sunblock and sunglasses – despite that foliage, you'll often be in direct sun.

➡ First-aid kit for basics such as bites, stings or diarrhea.

➡ Plastic bags to waterproof gear and pack nonbiodegradable litter to take back with you.

➡ Lightweight rainproof jacket.

➡ Sleeping bag, mat or hammock if sleeping outside.

➡ Books – cell phones rarely work and neither do TVs; electricity is often limited to several hours daily.

s/d 4 days & 3 nights from US$1430/2136) 🖋. This is a lodge owned by Manu Expeditions and co-run by InkaNatura Travel (www.inka-natura.com; Ricardo Palma J-1 Urbanización Santa Monica, Cuzco), among others, either of which take reservations. There are 22 screened double cabins with hot showers, a dining room and a bar-hammock room, and the lodge is set in tropical gardens.

The lodge is not in the Parque Nacional Manu *zona reservada*, but is recommended for its exceptional wildlife-watching opportunities.

There are 48km of trails around the wildlife center, where 12 species of monkey, as well as other wildlife, can be seen. Two canopy platforms are a short walk away, and one is always available for guests wishing to view the top of the rainforest and look for birds that frequent the canopy.

A 3km walk through the forest brings you to a natural salt lick, where there is a raised platform with mosquito nets for viewing the nightly activities of the tapirs. This hike is for visitors who can negotiate forest trails by flashlight. Chances to see animals are excellent if you have the patience, although visitors may wait for hours. Note that there isn't much happening at the lick during the day.

A short boat ride along the Madre de Dios brings visitors to another well-known salt lick that attracts various species of parrot and macaw. Most mornings you can see flocks in the hundreds. The largest flocks are seen from late July to September. As the rainy season kicks in, the numbers diminish and in June birds don't visit the salt lick at all. May and early July aren't reliable either, though ornithologists report the presence of the birds in other nearby areas during these months, which birders can usually spot.

The macaw lick is visited on a floating catamaran blind, with the blind providing a concealed enclosure from which 20 people can view the wildlife. The catamaran is stable enough to allow the use of a tripod and scope or a telephoto lens, and gets about halfway across the river. Boat drivers won't bring the blind too close to avoid disturbing the birds. In addition to the trails and salt licks, there are a couple of nearby lakes accessible by catamaran where giant otters may be seen (as well as other wildlife). If you wish to see the macaw and tapir lick, the lakes and the canopy, and hike the trails in search of wildlife, you should plan on a three-night stay at the Manu Wildlife Center. Shorter and longer stays are workable.

Note that some tours start with a flight into Puerto Maldonado and travel up the Río Madre de Dios to reach Manu Wildlife Center from there. This is a great opportunity to explore a little-plied section of this majestic river. Other options can also include one to two nights camping within the park itself in addition to a stay at the Manu Wildlife Center, and in any case at least one night of any tour will be spent at another lodge en route because of the distances involved.

CENTRAL AMAZON

For a quick Amazon fix on long weekends and holidays, *limeños* (inhabitants of Lima) usually head for this relatively accessible area of the Amazon, reachable in eight hours by bus. The tropical Chanchamayo Province, which accounts for most of this region, is as different to the coastal desert or the Andean mountains as can be. The last hour of the journey here is particularly remarkable for the change in vegetation and climate as you slip down the Andes into the vibrant green of La Selva Central, as it is known in Spanish. Comprising the two towns of La Merced and San Ramón, plus a scattering of remoter communities, the area is noted for coffee and fruit production. The region offers the traveler a good insight into Amazon life in all its sweaty clamor. An adventurous back route also awaits the intrepid: forging ahead via Satipo to the port of Pucallpa, a jumping-off point for river trips deeper into the jungle.

San Ramón & La Merced

064 / POP 52,000 / ELEV 800M

San Ramón is 295km east of Lima, and La Merced is 11km further along. Chanchamayo's two key settlements are quite likable in a languid sort of way. Resistance to colonists by the local Asháninka people meant that these towns were not founded until the 19th century. Today they are popular Peruvian holiday destinations, good for cooling off with many swimming pools and natural swimming holes in the vicinity, and great bases for exploring the luxuriant countryside nearby. The lush surrounds are characterized by photogenic forested hills and waterfalls that tumble into the Río Chanchamayo valley.

Sights

Puente Kimiri   BRIDGE
Three kilometers north of La Merced on the Satipo road is this attractive bridge over the Río Chanchamayo, where indigenous rebel leader Juan Santos Atahualpa had a stand-off with authorities about the encroaching missions in Peru. It is a pleasant spot for a bite of lunch.

Viewpoints   VIEWPOINT
(Av 2 de Mayo, La Merced) The stairs at the northwest end of Av 2 de Mayo afford a good view of the town, and from the balcony at the southeast end there's a photogenic river viewpoint.

Catarata El Tirol   WATERFALL
There are many impressive waterfalls around San Ramón, but this 35m cascade is the most visited. El Tirol crashes down 5km east of San Ramón off the La Merced road. You can take a taxi the first 2km; the last 3km is along shady forest paths and streams.

Off the Pichanaqui road, beyond La Merced at Puente Yurinaki, are the higher waterfalls of **Catarata Velo de la Novia** and **Catarata Bayoz**. Agencies in La Merced or Tarma arrange tours to all three falls.

Activities

Isla Las Turunas   ADVENTURE SPORTS
(942-600-089; Las Guanábanas, La Merced; S35 per day; 8am-6pm Tue-Fri) At the southern end of Calle las Guanábanas, south of the San Ramón–La Merced road, this leafy, lagoon-dotted enclave has been made into a fun, well-run adventure park, with kayaking and a zipline, plus an inviting pool. The restaurant rustles up mean *tacacho con cecina* (roasted banana and meat balls with smoked pork).

Entry gets you access to the activities; food is extra.

Sleeping

La Merced harbors most decent digs; some luxury lodges beckon just outside San Ramón. Accommodations bookings are recommended at busy periods, when room rates almost double.

La Merced

You don't have to look far in the central blocks to find a cheap *hospedaje* for S30 per person or less; plenty of newer, fancier options have now joined the fray.

Hotel Rey
HOTEL $

(☑064-53-1185; www.hotelrey.net; Junín 103, La Merced; s/d S60/80) A popular place, this old stalwart has been in the midrange accommodations game for awhile. Bright, inviting hallways (public phones on each) lead to rooms with fans, cable TV and hot showers. Ask to see a couple of rooms: some are quite dark.

Hotel Elio's
HOTEL $

(☑064-53-1229; Palca 281, La Merced; s/d S50/70) Just off the plaza with spacious rooms that make the beds look almost lost; there are writing desks, fans, cable TV and spotless bathrooms at this friendly old hotel. Street-facing rooms can be noisy.

Tropical Hotel Suite
HOTEL $$

(☑064-53-2069; www.tropicalhotelsuite.com; Arica 282, La Merced; s/d incl breakfast S80/120; ❄️🅿️📶) Bandying about a lime-green colour scheme to support the 'tropical' part of its title, this is the only hotel in town with sufficient height to write its name lengthways down the building (seven floors, lofty by La Merced standards). Rooms are sizable and very clean – and green, of course.

A sparkling midrange choice: and now with a top-floor restaurant with great views over town.

Aviró Hotel
HOTEL $$

(☑064-53-1394; www.avirohotel.com; Junín 992, La Merced; s/d/tr incl breakfast S100/150/200; ❄️🅿️📶) Just about the best of La Merced's hotels and formerly known as Hotel Heliconia, the air-conditioned rooms here are ginormous and all come with fridges and sparkling bathrooms. Breakfast is enjoyed in a cheerful setting and views are mostly onto Parque Integración.

🛏 San Ramón

The town itself is unexceptional. However, the best places to stay in this region lie outside, on the La Merced road.

★ Gad Gha Kum Lodge
LODGE $$

(☑064-33-1935; www.facebook.com/elmensajero lodge; Carr Central Km 98; s/d cabins S180/250; 🅿️❄️) This is the nicest of several good lodges on the La Merced–San Ramón road: vast peaceful grounds, its own private waterfall trail, large well-appointed cabins with terraces, a pretty pool and a central thatched restaurant. There is also camping space, and the lodge is well known for its massage treatments. Another world altogether from the frenetic La Selva Central towns nearby.

La Merced–San Ramón minibuses run past the entrance.

🍴 Eating

Restaurant Shambari Campa
PERUVIAN $$

(Tarma 389, La Merced; mains S27-34; ⊘7am-12:30am) On the plaza, this famous hole-in-the-wall restaurant provides an Amazon-centric menu so extensive you can be lost for choice, but includes sensational *chancho*. It has been the best restaurant in town for donkey's years.

Chifa Felipe Siu
CHINESE $$

(Junín 121, La Merced; meals S20-40; ⊘noon-11pm) The best place to eat Chinese food in the Amazon has a branch in La Merced and in San Ramón, but this clean, smart address is the most convenient.

🍷 Drinking & Nightlife

Chanchamayo Highland Coffee Café Misha
CAFE

(cnr Ancash & Palca; coffees S2-7; ⊘8am-10pm) The region's waterfalls are splashed across the walls and the coffee served is first-rate – Chanchamayo coffee is now well known and well regarded – but the service is lackadaisical.

🛍 Shopping

Chanchamayo Highland Coffee
COFFEE

(☑064-53-1198; http://highlandproducts.com. pe; 7 de Junio s/n, La Merced; ⊘9am-7:30pm Mon-Fri) Here you can sample and buy the coffee for which Chanchamayo is famous. (Peru is one of the world's largest coffee producers but nearly all gets exported.) It's a tad gimmicky but enjoyable, and besides the shop, you can browse displays on coffee production and check out old coffee-producing machinery. There is a tour (free) if you prefer.

Most singular of the caffeinated products is the Café Misha, billed as the world's most expensive coffee. The price tag is due to the coffee cherries being processed in the digestive system of the coati, a raccoon-like animal (the coati only chooses the best cherries, and the coffee bean is released in the animal's stool). It's 1km northeast of the main bus terminal on the Satipo road. These days the shop does a tempting range of local jams and ice creams, too.

ⓘ Information

MEDICAL SERVICES

Hospital Selva Central (☑ 064-53-1408; cnr Los Robles & Calle Los Cauchos, La Merced)

MONEY

Both towns have a BCP with an ATM.

ⓘ Getting There & Away

AIR

The Chanchamayo airstrip is on the east side of the river in San Ramón. Small planes can theoretically be chartered to almost anywhere in the region but the strip is deserted most days. This makes Jauja in the Central Highlands the closest practical airport (p299).

BUS

The **main bus terminal** (Terminal Terrestre; cnr Prolongación Tarma & Av Fray Jeronimo Jiménez) is a 1km downhill walk east of the center of La Merced. Bus companies have offices here for booking tickets but the big buses leave from their own yards outside the center. The transport that actually leaves from here is minibuses and *colectivos*.

Direct buses go from Lima to Chanchamayo, though many travelers break the journey at Tarma. Try to travel the 70km stretch from Tarma to San Ramón in daylight for the views during the spectacular 2200m descent.

Many companies run to Lima (S35 to S75, eight hours) from La Merced, including **Expreso Molina Unión** (☑ 988-893-599; Av José De Aguirrezabal s/n), with its own separate terminal 1km from the main bus terminal along the San Ramón road. Other outfits like **Cruz del Sur** (☑ 993-555-399) also go to Lima, with nightly and/or daily departures. Their offices are all located at the main bus terminal.

Frequent buses from various companies go to Tarma (around S10, 2½ hours) and on to Huancayo (S20 to S25, 4½ hours) via Jauja.

Transportation into the jungle is by large minibus or pickup truck. *Colectivo* taxis ply some routes for a slightly higher price. Minibuses leave for Satipo (S15, 2½ hours) about every half hour; minibuses also depart frequently to Oxapampa (S15, 2½ hours), where you can change for services to Pozuzo (two to three hours further on).

TAXI

Colectivos seating four passengers go to Tarma (S18, about two hours), Oxapampa (S18, two hours) and Satipo (S20, two hours) from marked stands within the bus terminal complex.

ⓘ Getting Around

Minibuses linking La Merced with San Ramón and the hotels in between leave frequently (S1.50, 15 minutes) from outside the bus terminal. Drivers try charging more if they think you're staying at one of the flash hotels outside San Ramón. *Mototaxis* charge S2 to drive you from the terminal up into La Merced center.

Oxapampa

☑ 063 / POP 14,000 / ELEV 1800M

Oxapampa, a pretty ranching and coffee center 75km north of La Merced, sports some superb wilderness lodges and luxury accommodations. When you add a cracking nearby national park and Peru's best music fest you are left with one of the most intriguing locales in the Amazon. Buildings have a Tyrolean look, Austrian-German food is prepared, an old-fashioned form of German is still spoken, and numerous Germanic customs are preserved. Two key periods in history have shaped this region. The first was during the mid-19th century when it attracted some 200 settlers from Germany, the descendants of which (many still blonde-haired and blue-eyed) inhabit Oxapampa and its surrounds. The second? The last decade! Local land has been sold off at basement prices, enticing a new wave of settlers: this time largely from Lima. New businesses have opened, many of which are attractive guesthouses and restaurants, keeping the town's tourist appeal buoyant.

⊙ Sights

Museo Schafferer MUSEUM
(Av Los Colonos 220, Pozuzo; S3; ⊙9am-1pm & 2:30-4pm Mon-Sat, 9am-noon Sun) One of the most typically Tyrolean buildings in Pozuzo, wood-panelled and with a steeply pitched roof, this museum contains the intriguing history of the Germanic adventurers (OK, there were a few Belgians, too) who voyaged all the way out to this part of the Amazon to settle it in the mid-19th century.

Parque Nacional Yanachaga-Chemillén NATIONAL PARK
(admission S5) North of Oxapampa rear the cloud-capped hills of this little-visited park, preserving spectacular cloud forest and diverse flora and fauna, including the rare spectacled bear. The most accessible entrance is from a turning near Carolina Egg

Guesthaus on the eastern edge of town. A 7km track, of which 5km is doable by car, corkscrews up to the reserve entrance. A glorious two-hour hike then leads to the top of the forest at Abra Esperanza (2420m and chilly).

A second park entrance lies at Yurritunqui (take a Pozuzo-bound minibus for 60km and ask the driver where to get off). Basic *refugios* (refuges) can be found at each entrance, and just below Abra Esperanza. Further information can be obtained at Oxapampa's **INRENA office** (☎063-46-2544; Jr Pozuzo cuadra 3 s/n).

Pozuzo VILLAGE
The inexorably Germanic Pozuzo, three hours north of Oxapampa by daily minibus, is picturebook Tyrolean, from the architecture to the residents, straight out of a Grimms fairy tale (well almost). Its pretty plaza remembers Josef Egg and the 300 Tyrolean and Prussian adventurers who settled here in the 1850s, with an impressive model of the boat they traveled on to South America. Check out the history of the settlers at Museo Schafferer (p473).

🎆 Festivals & Events

Selvámonos MUSIC
(http://selvamonos.org; full ticket S110) Held against the backdrop of Parque Nacional Yanachaga-Chemillén (p473) every June since 2010, this is one of Peru's most talked-about festivals. A great showcase of Peruvian contemporary music: new rock, electronica, reggae and wacky takes on *cumbia* (a Colombian salsa-like dance and musical style), it's also a force behind simultaneously run Semana Kultura, where musical and cultural events occur in towns around here.

🛏 Sleeping

⭐**Carolina Egg Gasthaus** GUESTHOUSE $$
(☎063-46-2331; http://carolinaegg.com; Av San Martin 1085; s/d incl breakfast S100/160; P✱🛜🛏) Across from Oxapampa's bus station, this is an oasis of pretty wooden cabins and rooms run by descendants of one of the town's original German settlers. It's set way back from the road in a gorgeous garden, with a couple of shady terraces, a pool and a restaurant. Perhaps the only breakfast in Peru where you're served strudel!

TaKuRaNiCha LODGE $$
(☎064-39-3298; luchoh1959@gmail.com; near Mesapata; S145 incl meals; 🦟) ✏ This beautifully located rustic lodge, accessible via a fun jeep ride along a rough track coiling up from the La Merced–Oxapampa road, nestles around 1200m up in waterfall-laced cloud forest. It's a place for true adventurers: here you will trek on precipitous high jungle paths, observe cocks-of-the- rock and other birdlife and help gather firewood or plants for dinner.

Mountain-biking and waterfall-climbing are available for S80 per person extra. The journey back to civilization is particularly unique, on a mini cable car that whizzes across the river far below the property. The unusual name derives from the beginnings of the names of all the owner's children.

Cabañas El Trapiche CABINS $$
(☎063-46-2049; http://trapichelodge.com; Av San Martín cuadra 1 s/n; cabins from S100 inc breakfast; P) On the western entrance of town is this smart and spacious complex of 20 wooden cabins, dotted across a swath of lush, spacious parkland. Cabins have fridges, microwaves, porches and private bathrooms. An on-site restaurant specializes in *parrillas* (grilled meats).

⭐**Ulcumano Ecolodge** LODGE $$$
(☎972-679-060; http://ulcumanoecolodge.com; near Chonabamba; s/d incl breakfast, lunch & dinner S410/558; P) ✏ A birders' paradise in Chontabamba district, 10km outside Oxapampa, this lodge is perched in the forest and is named for the endangered Ulcumano tree. The species was sought after to build many houses hereabouts, but survives in the grounds here. Beautiful, light, wooden cabins sleep 18 people, the property's bird list surpasses 150 and there's a restaurant strung with hammocks.

Tailored hiking tours are offered into Parque Nacional Yanachaga-Chemillén (p473), and there are mountain-biking excursions, too.

🍴 Eating

Biergarten GRILL $
(Mullembruck 548; grills S20; ⏱noon-4pm Thu-Sat) Formerly dealing in just teas, coffees and light snacks, this enterprising German-Peruvian-owned establishment now combines a first-class butchers with, sensibly, a garden restaurant serving grilled meat. This place brews good beers: a pale

ale, a weiss bier and a red ale. Plans are afoot to open Saturday evenings, too.

Mamá Frida CAFE $
(Bolivar 274; light meals S6-15; ⊙5-9pm Tue-Sun) Keeping the flame burning for good machine coffee and tantalizing cakes in Oxapampa is this 2nd-floor plaza-fronting gem. It serves simple, tasty lunches like yucca with scrambled eggs and homemade chorizo, and whilst you wait for the grub you can people-watch from the balcony or survey the many photographs interestingly and sometimes hilariously charting the town's recent past.

Drinking & Nightlife

Vatter Otto BAR
(cnr Grau & Mariscal Castilla; ⊙6pm-late) Stays open, reputedly, until the last punter fancies leaving. A classic.

Shopping

Floralp FOOD
(www.floralp-sa.com; Carr á Chontabamba Km 2; ⊙9am-9pm) Peru won't wow you with its cheese – unless you find your whey to Oxapampa. Come to the factory shop here and, besides purchasing a few flavorsome cheeses, you might get lucky with a factory tour.

❶ Getting There & Away

Pozuzo minibuses (S25) run the three-hour route from Oxapampa's Plaza de Armas at 6am, 10am and 2pm along a part-paved road. *Colectivos* leave for the same journey, charging similar prices, from the **Parada de Colectivos a Pozuzo** (cnr Ruffner & Malecón Yanachaga). Oxapampa's **bus station** is eight blocks from the center on the paved La Merced road. La Merced transportation (buses S15, *colectivos* S18) leaves from here. Direct Lima buses run in the evenings.

Pucallpa

☑ 061 / POP 205,000 / ELEV 154M

The busy port of Pucallpa is enjoying something of a renaissance. It has an attractive pedestrianized boulevard, and is a starting point for a spectacular river adventure north to Iquitos – and, if time and inclination allow, on to Brazil and the Atlantic.

However, the city has a distinctly less junglelike appearance than other Amazonian towns. Although this is an important distribution center for goods along the broad, brown Río Ucayali, which sweeps past the city en route to join the Río Amazonas, the rainforest feels far away.

There is reason for the traveler to linger: the lovely, more traveler-friendly oxbow lake of Yarinacocha, with river lodges to relax at and interesting indigenous communities to visit.

Pucallpa's only cultural attraction as such is the free **Museo Agustín Rivas** (Tarapaca 861; ⊙8am-4pm Mon-Fri, to noon Sat). Its namesake specializes in wooden sculptures of mythical Amazonian creatures and beings. Rivas does not live in Pucallpa but his work is internationally regarded. The place is on the 2nd floor: a woman on the 1st floor will open up for you.

Sleeping

Most places here have rooms with bathrooms, fans and cable TV. Only midrange and top-end places offer air-con. Accommodations overall have improved noticeably, and there are several top-end options these days.

★ Manish Hotel Ecológico CABINS $$
(☑061-57-7167; www.manishhotel.com.pe; Jirón Vargas Guerra s/n; s/d/ste incl breakfast S180/230/270, 4-person bungalows incl breakfast S420; ⑨❄☎☒) Escape Pucallpa's dusty thoroughfares in this serene expanse of leafy grounds, dotted with terra-cotta-roofed cabins. For families, taking one of the bungalows can mean downtime on the terrace for the grown-ups while the kids can safely run wild betwixt the palms and the pool.

Airport pickup is included in the price.

Hostal Arequipa GUESTHOUSE $$
(☑061-57-1348; Progreso 573; s S60-100, d S70-120; ❄☎) This is a popular, professional and often full midrange choice, and has hot water, minibars, a restaurant, and aesthetic public areas decorated with Shipibo art. The pricier rooms with air-con also include a continental breakfast.

Hospedaje Komby GUESTHOUSE $$
(☑061-59-2074, 061-57-1562; www.elkomby pucallpa.com; Ucayali 360; s S65-75, d S80-100; ❄☎☒) In a quandary about whether to aim for budget or luxury? Komby has rooms that veer between the two brackets. Accommodations overall are clean but basic, brightened by the small pool. Higher tariffs are for rooms with air-con.

Pucallpa

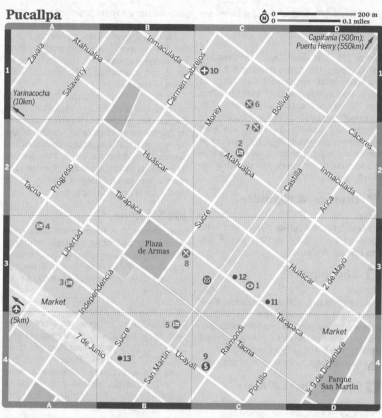

Capitanía (500m);
Puerto Henry (550km)

Pucallpa

Casa Andina Select HOTEL $$$
(☏ 061-58-6600; Sucre 198, cnr Atahualpa; s/d
incl breakfast from S236/259; 🅿❄🛜🏊) Spick
and span, spacious and quiet as a tomb,
Casa Andina Select is a bit of a novelty for
Pucallpa, but has raised the game as far as
accommodations go. Never before was there
such a decent, modern hotel hereabouts. It
opens up into a leafy pool area at the rear.

The hotel restaurant, **La Plaza Bar &
Grill** (mains S20-30; ⏱ 6am-11pm), adjoining,
would not look out of place in New York.

Hotel Sol del Oriente HOTEL $$$
(☏ 061-57-5510; www.hotelessoldeloriente.
com; San Martín 552; s/d/ste S230/285/460;
🅿❄@🛜🏊) This sizeable central hotel is
not nearly as flash as it fancies itself, but

it's comfortable. Set around a swimming pool, the somewhat old-fashioned rooms are of a decent size and have cable TV, minibars and good, always-hot showers. You get a welcome cocktail on arrival. A gym is on-site.

✖ Eating

Pucallpa does cafes and ice-cream parlors well, but noteworthy restaurants less so. Yarinacocha is better for food, as it can be enjoyed there in a lakeside setting. The heat in the middle of the day means restaurants tend to open by 7am for breakfast. Delicious cakes and ice cream can be found at cafes, plus there's a supermarket for groceries.

Fuente Soda Tropitop   CAFE $
(Sucre 401; snacks from S3-15; ⊘ 7am-midnight) Mean cakes, ice cream and tried and test ed breakfasts and mains can be found at Fuente Soda Tropitop, along with a lineup of rainforest juices.

Chez Maggy   PIZZA $$
(www.chezmaggylosmaderos.com.pe; Inmaculada 643; medium pizzas S24-27; ⊘ 5pm-midnight) Maggy whips up pizzas nothing short of superb, and from a wood-burning oven. The flavors play up to their names: an 'Amazónico' for example comes with smoked *cecina* (pork) and pineapple. The interior is cozy, modern and not plasticized like some neighboring restaurants. The unusual, tropical-tasting sangria goes down well with all dishes.

Chifa Mey Lin   CHINESE $$
(Inmaculada 698; mains S19-29; ⊘ 6-11pm) This place gets the gong for being the best of Pucallpa's *chifas* (Chinese restaurants). Choosing where to sit in the roomy interior can be a challenge. Plates are BIG: to top it off there is also karaoke next door. It could improve the service, though: there are other *chifas* snapping at its ankles to get to the number one spot.

Drinking & Nightlife

Gold Bar   BAR
(www.facebook.com/pg/goldbarkaraoke; cnr Av Miraflores & Arborizacón; ⊘ 7pm-6am) A great, lively bar playing pop and rock from the last 30-odd years. It does karaoke and has a dance floor.

❶ Information

MEDICAL SERVICES
Clínica Monte Horeb (☑ 061-57-1689; www.clinicamontehoreb.com.pe; Inmaculada 529; ⊘ 24hr) Good medical services.

MONEY
Several banks have ATMs and change money and traveler's checks. Foreign-exchange bureaus are found along the fourth, fifth and sixth *cuadras* (blocks) of Raimondi.
Banco Continental (cnr Raimondi & Ucayali)
Western Union (Raimondi 399, In Viajes Laser)

POST
Post Office (Castilla, btwn Tacna & Tarapaca)

TRAVEL AGENCIES
For jungle guides, go to Yarinacocha (p479).
Viajes Laser (☑ 061-57-1120, 961-900-512; www.laserviajes.pe; Raimondi 399) Western Union is here, at one of Pucallpa's better travel agencies.

❶ Getting There & Away

AIR
Pucallpa's decent-sized **airport** is 5km west of town. The best connection is with **Star Perú** (☑ 061-59-0585; 7 de Junio 865; ⊘ 8:30am-6:30pm Mon-Fri, to 5pm Sat) with a direct flight leaving from Lima at 7:15am – the flight continues to Iquitos. For Pucallpa–Lima, the time is 12:15pm. Another option is **LAN** (LATAM; Tarapacá 805) with three daily (but pricier) flights to Lima.

Other towns and settlements – including Atalaya (on the Río Ucayali), Contamaná, Tarapoto and Yurimaguas – are served by small local airlines using light aircraft; ask at the airport.

BOAT
Pucallpa's port moves depending on water levels. During high water (January to April) boats moor at the dock abutting Parque San Martín in central Pucallpa itself.

As water levels drop, the port falls back to several spots along the banks, including **Puerto Henry** (Manco Capác s/n) and eventually to about 3km northeast of the town center, reached by *mototaxi* (S3). The town port stretches some way: different boats for different destinations depart from different areas, usually referred to by the name of the nearest intersecting road.

Wherever the port is, riverboats sail the Río Ucayali from Pucallpa to Iquitos (S80 to S100, slinging your own hammock and with basic meals, three to five days). Cabins with two or

AMAZON BASIN PUCALLPA

> **① WARNING: PUERTO BERMÚDEZ**
>
> Although it is possible to travel via Puerto Bermúdez to Pucallpa from La Merced, we do not currently recommend it.

four bunks and private bathrooms come with better food service and cost anything from about S150 to S400, depending on the quality and indeed your powers of negotiation.

Boats announce their departure dates and destinations on chalkboards on the boats themselves, but these can be unreliable. Talk to the captain or the cargo loadmaster for greater dependability. They must present boat documents on the morning of their departure day at the **Capitanía** (☎ 061-59-0193; M Castilla 754) – come here to check for the latest reliable sailing information. Many people work here, but only the official in charge of documents knows the real scoop and can give you accurate sailing information. Passages are daily when the river is high, but in the dry season low water levels result in slower, less frequent passages.

The quality of the boats varies greatly both in size and comfort. Choose a boat that looks good. The *Henry V* is one of the better-equipped outfits, with a 250-passenger capacity.

This is not a trip for everyone. Come prepared – the market in Pucallpa sells hammocks, but mosquito repellent may be of poor quality. Bottled drinks are sold on board, but it's worth bringing some large bottles of water or juice.

When negotiating prices for a riverboat passage, ask at any likely boat, but don't pay until you and your luggage are aboard your boat of choice, then pay the captain and no one else. Always get to the port well in advance of when you want to leave: it can take hours hunting for a suitable vessel. Most boats leave either at first light, or in the late afternoon or evening.

The river journey to Iquitos can be broken at various communities, including Contamaná (about S30, 15 to 20 hours) and Requena, and continued on the next vessel coming through (although there's precious little to do in these villages). Alternatively, ask around for speedboats to Contamaná (about S100, five hours), which depart at 6am most days. The return trip (six to seven hours) goes against the current.

Smaller boats occasionally head upriver toward Atalaya; ask at the Capitanía or the town port.

Jungle 'guides' approaching you on the Pucallpa waterfront are not recommended. For jungle excursions, look for a reliable service in Yarinacocha.

BUS

The sprucing up of Pucallpa's center hasn't been quite so sexy for bus companies – all of which now depart from disparate terminals straggled along the airport road around 4km from the center, after Parque Natural. One or two companies still have central booking offices. For departures, get a taxi (about S5) out to the relevant bus terminal.

A direct bus to Lima (S65 to S90) takes 18 to 20 hours in the dry season; the journey can be broken in Tingo María (S20, six hours) or Huánuco (S25, eight hours). The road is paved but vulnerable to flooding and erosion. This journey has become safer since the posting of armed police units along parts of the route: still, it's better to do the Pucallpa–Tingo María section in daylight.

León de Huánuco (☎ 061-44-0815; Centenario s/n), with a central booking office, serves Lima at 7:30pm, stopping at Tingo María and Huánuco. It's often best to get a taxi out to Km 4 of the airport road and do the rounds of the offices for the service best suiting your schedule.

MINIBUS & TAXI

The reorganization of Pucallpa's transportation has seen all the *colectivo* taxis and minivans to all destinations from Pucallpa bundled together so that they arrive and depart from the same terminal, 8km outside the center: **Terminal Terrestre Pucallpa** (cnr Habilitacion Urbana Municipal & Túpac Amaru).

① Getting Around

Mototaxis to Yarinacocha are S6, the airport about S8 and the Terminal Terrestre S9. Taxis to the airport are S15.

Yarinacocha

About 10km northwest of central Pucallpa, Yarinacocha is an enticing oxbow lake where you can go boating, observe wildlife and visit indigenous communities and purchase their handicrafts. The lake, once part of the Río Ucayali, is now landlocked, though a small canal links the two bodies of water during rainy season.

The lakeside village, **Puerto Callao**, is a welcome relief from the chaos of downtown Pucallpa. Buzzards amble among pedestrians, and *peki-pekis* (canoes powered by a two-stroke motorcycle engine with a long propeller shaft) come and go to their various destinations all day. Travelers stop by, too, to check out either the wildlife or the *ayahuasca* ceremonies for which Yarinacocha area is known.

In Puerto Callao you'll find limited accommodations, as well as the Central Amazon's best food. Hire boats here to further explore the lake, too. Overall, it is worth spending a couple of days hereabouts.

Tours

You'll be nabbed as soon as you turn up by boat touts and *peki-peki* boat owners seeking to lure you to their vessel. Choose your boat carefully: make sure it has new-looking life jackets and enough petrol for the voyage, and pay at the end of the tour. Wildlife to watch out for includes freshwater pink dolphins, sloths and meter-long green iguanas, as well as birds such as the curiously long-toed wattled jacana (which walks on lily pads) and the metallic-green Amazon kingfisher. If you like fishing, the dry season is apparently the best time. Guides are also available for walking trips into the surrounding forest.

A highly recommended guide is **Gilber Reategui Sangama** (☑ messages 936-508-090; http://ayakruna.com; Puerto Callao; per hour S40), who owns the boat *La Normita* in Yarinacocha. Contact him in advance to arrange a tour. Some other guides will claim Gilber is unavailable or no longer works. Don't believe all you hear.

A good boat driver will float slowly along, so that you can look for birdlife at the water's edge, or *perezosos* (sloths) in the trees. Sunset is a good time to be on the lake.

Boat trips to the Shipibo villages of either **San Francisco** (also reached by road) or, better, **Santa Clara** (reached only by boat), are also popular. For short trips, boat drivers charge around S30 an hour for the boat; these can carry several people. Bargaining over the price is acceptable.

San Francisco is also known these days for its *ayahuasca* ceremonies. Lonely Planet does not recommend taking ayahuasca (p455) and those who do so do it at their own risk.

Eating

Several inexpensive restaurants and lively bars line the Puerto Callao waterfront.

Overall, Yarinacocha's eateries are not only Pucallpa's, but the entire Central Amazon's best.

★ Cafe Elixir   CAFE $
(Aguaytia cuadra 3 s/n, Yarinacocha; breakfast & lunch S10-18; ☺10am-6pm Tue-Sun; 🛜🍴) 🍴
You don't find this sort of cafe very often in Peru, let alone in Yarinacocha. Lovely coffee (the city's best), freshly squeezed juices and 100% homemade food are all served at reasonable prices. Some of the creative, veggie and vegan-friendly concoctions include Peruvian or Jamaican curry (go and find out) as well as the house take on pad thai.

In colorful, cozy, traveler-friendly environs, local products from artworks to herbal remedies to *ayahuasca* soap are also sold.

Parrilladas Orlando's   PARRILLA $$
(cnr Aguaytia & 28 de Julio; mains S20-35; ☺11:30am-3:30pm & 6-10:30pm Tue-Fri, 11:30am-10:30pm Sat, to 8pm Sun; 🌐) This *parrilla* place does grilled meat every bit as wonderfully as it claims to: its smoked chicken and pork are particularly divine. That's what 45 years of experience can give you: the edge over the competition!

❶ Getting There & Away

Offer any passing *mototaxi* driver in central Pucallpa S6 and they will bring you to Puerto Callao.

NORTHERN AMAZON

Raw, vast and encapsulating the real spirit of the Amazon, the northern Amazon Basin is home to the eponymous river that wells up from the depths of the Peruvian jungle before making its long, languorous passage through Brazil to the distant Atlantic Ocean. Settlements are scarce in this remote region: Yurimaguas in the west and Iquitos in the northeast are the only two of any size.

Yurimaguas

☑ 065 / POP 72,000 / ELEV 181M
This sleepy port is one of the Peruvian Amazon's best-connected towns and the gateway to the northern tract of the Amazonas. It's visited by travelers looking for boats down the Río Huallaga to Iquitos and the Amazon proper or by those wanting to

experience one of Peru's most animal-rich paradises, the Reserva Nacional Pacaya-Samiria, accessible from here. Go to Lagunas for a jungle guide, although touts will approach you in Yurimaguas. A paved road connects Yurimaguas with Tarapoto to the south.

🛏 Sleeping & Eating

You might have better luck encountering El Dorado than a hotel with hot water. Budget hotels flank the *cuadras* of Jauregui west of the plaza. On the plus side, several accommodations have swimming pools.

Río Huallaga Hotel & Business Center   BUSINESS HOTEL $$$
(☑ 065-35-3951; www.facebook.com/riohuallaga hotel; Arica 111; s/d S195/295; ☀ 🛜 🏊) Courteous service; spacious, clean, well-designed rooms; a swimming pool and bar; a three-floor restaurant (perhaps the best in town) with cracking Río Huallaga views from the top deck, and even its own tour agency. For all this, the town's best hotel has a high asking price.

The whole place is built on multiple levels, and tucked away at the bottom are cheapie rooms (still not bad) for a mere S50 per person.

Cebicheria El Dorado   PERUVIAN $$
(Aguirre 113; mains S20-35; ⊘9am-6pm) Getting a taxi to this spot, slightly out of the center, is the best idea for breakfast or lunch. Nothing fancy, mind, but agreeable enough – and the portions are exceedingly generous.

ℹ Information

It is better to arrange Pacaya-Samiria tours in nearby Lagunas. Otherwise, try **Huayruro Tours** (☑ 965-662-555; www.peruselva.com; Río Huallaga Hotel, Arica 111).

ℹ Getting There & Away

AIR
No airline company currently serves Yurimaguas. The nearest mainline airport is at Tarapoto (p444), with connections to Lima and Iquitos.

BOAT
The main port 'La Boca (Mariscal Castilla s/n)' is 13 blocks north of the center. Cargo boats from Yurimaguas follow the Río Huallaga onto the Río Marañón and Iquitos, taking between two and four days with numerous stops for loading and unloading cargo. There are usually departures daily, except Sunday. Passages cost about S100 on deck to Nauta for Iquitos (sling your own hammock and receive basic food) or around S130 for a bunk in double or quadruple cabins on the top deck, where the food is better and your gear safer; at Nauta, switch to road for the remainder of the journey to Iquitos (one hour). Bottled water, soft drinks and snacks are sold on board; bring insect repellent and a hat. Taking your own food and water supplies is also advisable. The **Eduardo** (☑ 965-635-351, 065-35-1270; Elena Pardo 104) boats (the company has five cargo boats) are considered the best (although readers have reported graphic animal cruelty on these). The journey can be broken at Lagunas (S30, 10 to 12 hours), just before the Río Huallaga meets the Marañón.

Fast boats to Lagunas, which continue on to Iquitos, also leave from the La Boca port. Usually leaving Yurimaguas at the ungodly hour of 2:30am to 3am daily, they hit Lagunas around 7:30am or 8am, getting to Iquitos if all goes to plan about 6pm.

BUS
The paved road to Tarapoto makes Yurimaguas easily accessible by Amazon standards.

Buses and taxis arrive and depart from offices 2km southwest of the center. For Tarapoto (S15, three hours), several companies leave from numberless offices on the Tarapoto road, or nearby on Calle Pastaza. Take a taxi to do the rounds for the company best suiting your schedule.

Likewise, there are multiple companies with *colectivos* to Tarapoto (S20, two hours) from *cuadra* 5 and *cuadra* 6 of Sifuentes. These include **Autos San Martin** (☑ 065-35-1438; Victor Siffuentes, Carr á Yurimaguas s/n) but there is nothing really to choose between them: it's a matter of which one leaves first, which will happen only when they've touted four passengers.

ℹ Getting Around
Mototaxis charge around S2 to take you anywhere around town.

Lagunas
☑ 065 / POP 14,300 / ELEV 148M

Travelers come to Lagunas because it is the best embarkation point for a trip to the western portion of the Reserva Nacional Pacaya-Samiria. The town is a spread-out, remote place; there are stores, but stock (slightly pricier than elsewhere in Peru) is limited, so it's wise to bring your own supplies as backup. There are no mon-

RESERVA NACIONAL PACAYA-SAMIRIA

At 20,800 sq km, this is the most immense of Peru's parks and reserves. **Reserva Nacional Pacaya-Samiria** (per person per day S30, incl entrance fee, guide, food & accommodations S150) provides local people with food and a home, and protects ecologically important habitats. An estimated 42,000 people live on and around the reserve; juggling the needs of human inhabitants while protecting wildlife is the responsibility of some 30 rangers. Staff also teach inhabitants how to best harvest the natural renewable resources to benefit the local people and to maintain thriving populations of plants and animals.

The reserve is the home of aquatic animals such as Amazon manatees, pink and grey river dolphins, two species of caiman, giant South American river turtles and many other bird and animal species.

Lagunas is the reserve's western entry point; it is also possible to access the eastern side of the reserve from Iquitos/Nauta. The area close to Lagunas has suffered from depletion: allow several days to get deep into the least-disturbed areas. With 15 days, you can reach Lago Cocha Pasto, where there are reasonable chances of seeing jaguars and larger mammals. Other noteworthy points in the reserve include Quebrada Yanayacu, where the river water is black from dissolved plants; Lago Pantean, where you can check out caimans and go medicinal-plant collecting; and Tipischa de Huana, where you can see the giant *Victoria amazonica* waterlilies, big enough for a small child to sleep upon without sinking.

Official information is available at the agencies offering Pacaya-Samiria tours in Iquitos and Lagunas.

The best way to visit the reserve is to go by dugout canoe with a guide from Lagunas and spend several days camping and exploring. Alternatively, comfortable ships visit from Iquitos.

If coming from Lagunas, Santa Rosa is the main entry point, where you pay the park entrance fee (often included in tour prices).

The best time to go is during the dry season, when you are more likely to see animals along the riverbanks. Rains ease off in late May; it then takes a month for water levels to drop, making July and August the best months to visit (with excellent fishing). September to November isn't too bad, and the heaviest rains begin in January. The months of February to May are the worst times to go. February to June tend to be the hottest months, with animal viewing best in the early morning and late afternoon.

Travelers should bring plenty of insect repellent and plastic bags (to cover luggage), and be prepared to camp out.

ey-changing facilities and hardly any public phones or restaurants.

Tours

Reserva Nacional Pacaya-Samiria is also visitable from Iquitos, but Lagunas is closer to the reserve. A trip here comes with no frills, unlike the trips from Iquitos: it is a back-to-basics adventure, but with high chances of spying a range of wildlife.

Spanish-speaking guides are locally available to visit Pacaya-Samiria. It is illegal to hunt within the reserve (though fishing for the pot is OK). The going rate is S150 per person per day for a guide, a boat and accommodations in huts, tents and ranger stations (for short trips prices could be slightly higher). Food and park fees are extra, although the guides can cook for you.

In the past, there was such a plethora of guides in Lagunas that to avoid harassment and price cutting, an official guides association was formed. This then split into separate organizations. Good options include **Acatupel** (☑948-976-610; www.acatupel.com; Padre Lucero 1324) and **Huayruro Tours** (☑965-662-555, 065-40-1186; www.peruselva.com; Alfonso Aiscorbe 424), an increasingly prominent association that is great for helping plan tours (agency staff speak English; its guides are Spanish-speaking but know the reserve extremely well). It offers tours of up to 22 days and is involved in programs like turtle reintroduction within the reserve.

🛏 Sleeping

Hostal Paraíso Verde   GUESTHOUSE **$**
(📞959-941-566; contacto@hostalaparaisoverde.
com; Daniel A Carrión 320; r per person from S25)
Clean tiled rooms typify the upper end of
the upward curve in Lagunas accommodations standards. There are fans and TVs –
but of course both stop with the almost
nightly electricity cut-offs, like elsewhere
in town.

Hotel Samiria   GUESTHOUSE **$**
(📞947-903-519, 065-40-1061; Fitzcarrald s/n;
s/tr S25/50) This is probably Lagunas'
best option. Rooms are smallish but clean
enough, with Spanish-language TV and OK
bathrooms. The best feature is the secluded
central courtyard that the rooms face onto,
which includes a hammock area. Situated
near the market.

❶ Getting There & Away

Regular boats downriver from Yurimaguas to
Lagunas take about 10 to 12 hours and leave
Yurimaguas' La Boca (p480) port between
7am and 8am most days. Times are posted
on boards at the port in both Yurimaguas and
Lagunas for a day in advance. Fast boats from
Yurimaguas usually head off around 2:30am
(from La Boca): they take 4½ to 5½ hours to
arrive in Lagunas.

Action time is, indeed, between 7am and
8am in Lagunas' ramshackle **port**. This is when
many fast boats rock up for the journey upriver
to Yurimaguas (S40, 5½ to 6½ hours) and
downriver to Iquitos (S100, 10 hours).

Iquitos

📞 065 / POP 472,000 / ELEV 130M

Linked to the outside world by air and
by river, Iquitos is the world's largest city
that cannot be reached by road. It's a prosperous, vibrant jungle metropolis and the
northern Amazon Basin's chief city, teeming with the usual, inexplicably addictive
Amazonian anomalies. Unadulterated jungle encroaches beyond town in view of the
air-conditioned, elegant restaurants that
flank the riverside; motorized tricycles
whiz manically through the streets yet locals mill around the central plazas eating
ice cream like there is all the time in the
world. Mud huts mingle with magnificent
tiled mansions; tiny dugout canoes ply the
water alongside colossal cruise ships. You
may well arrive in Iquitos for the greater
adventure of a boat trip down the Amazon,
but whether it's sampling rainforest cuisine, the buzzing nightlife or one of Peru's
most fascinating markets in the floating
shantytown of Belén, this thriving city will
entice you to stay awhile.

History

Iquitos was founded in 1757 as a Jesuit
mission, though indigenous tribes actively resisted conversion. In the 1870s the
great rubber boom boosted the population
16-fold and for the next 30 years, Iquitos was at once the scene of ostentatious
wealth and abject poverty. Rubber barons
became fabulously rich, while rubber tap-
pers (mainly local tribespeople and poor
mestizos – people of mixed indigenous and
Spanish descent) suffered virtual enslave-
ment and sometimes death from disease or
harsh treatment.

By WWI, the bottom fell out of the rubber boom as suddenly as it had begun. A
British entrepreneur smuggled some rub-
ber-tree seeds out of Brazil, and plantations
were seeded in the Malay Peninsula. It was
much cheaper and easier to collect the rubber from orderly rubber tree plantations
than from wild trees scattered in the Amazon Basin.

Iquitos suffered subsequent economic
decline, supporting itself with a combination of logging, agriculture (Brazil nuts,
tobacco, bananas and *barbasco* – a poi-
sonous vine used by indigenous peoples
to hunt fish and now exported for use in
insecticides) and the export of wild animals
to zoos. Then, in the 1960s, a second boom
revitalized the area. This time the resource
was oil, and its discovery made Iquitos a
prosperous modern town. In recent years
tourism has also played an important part
in the area's economy.

◉ Sights

Iquitos' cultural attractions, while limited,
dwarf those of other Amazon cities: especially boosted by the arrival of two new
museums in the period between 2013 and
2014. The cheery Malecón (riverside walk)
runs between Nauta and Ricardo Palma:
perhaps the most diverting sight of all!

Remnants of the rubber-boom days
include *azulejos*, tiles imported from
Portugal to decorate the rubber barons'
mansions. Many buildings along Raimondi

and Malecón Tarapaca are decorated with these tiles.

★ **Belén Mercado** MARKET

FREE At the southeast end of town is the floating shantytown of Belén, consisting of scores of huts, built on rafts, which rise and fall with the river. During the low-water months, these rafts sit on the river mud, but for most of the year they float on the river – a colorful and chaotic sight. Seven thousand people live here, and canoes float from hut to hut selling and trading jungle produce.

The best time to visit the area is at 7am, when people from the jungle villages arrive to sell their produce. To get here, take a cab to 'Los Chinos,' walk to the port and rent a canoe to take you around.

The market here, located within the city blocks in front of Belén, is the raucous, crowded affair common to most Peruvian towns. In fact, because of the fluctuating water levels that make this market so muddy and mosquito-plagued, Belén is a level more squalid again. All kinds of strange and exotic products, from bottled *ayahuasca* to insect grubs are sold among the more mundane bags of rice, sugar, flour and cheap household goods. Look for the bark of the *chuchuhuasi* tree, which is soaked in rum for weeks and used as a tonic (it's served in many of the local bars). *Chuchuhuasi* and other Amazon plants are common ingredients in herbal pain-reducing and arthritis formulas manufactured in Europe and the USA.

The market makes for exciting shopping and sightseeing, but do remember to watch your wallet.

★ **Historical Ships Museum** MUSEUM
(Plaza Castilla; S10; ⊗8am-8pm) Moored below Plaza Castilla is the diverting Historical Ships Museum, on a 1906 Amazon riverboat, the gorgeously restored three-deck *Ayapua*. The exhibitions reflect the Amazon River's hodgepodge past: explorers, tribes, rubber barons and the filming of the 1982 Werner Herzog movie *Fitzcarraldo*. Included in the entrance price is a half-hour historic-boat ride on the river (Río Itaya out to the Río Amazonas proper).

Malecón VIEWPOINT
(Malecóns Maldonado & Tarapaca) The sight of Iquitos' sophisticated riverside walkway,

edged by swanky bars and restaurants and yet cut off from the rest of the world by hundreds of kilometers of jungle river, is as spectacular as it is surreal. Tours are touted and jungle food is served from stalls, while below are decaying old riverboats, and the lower town's huts on stilts are at the mercy of rapidly changing river levels.

Museum of Indigenous Amazon Cultures MUSEUM
(Malecón Tarapaca 332; S15; ⊗8am-7:30pm) This intuitively presented museum takes you through the traits, traditions and beliefs of the tribes of the Amazon Basin, with a focus on the Peruvian Amazon. Some 40 Amazonian cultures are represented.

Casa de Fierro HISTORIC BUILDING
(Iron House; cnr Putumayo & Raymondi) FREE
Every guidebook mentions the 'majestic' Casa de Fierro (Iron House), designed by Gustave Eiffel (of Eiffel Tower fame). It was made in Paris in 1860 and imported piece by piece into Iquitos around 1890, during the rubber-boom days, to beautify the city. It's the only survivor of three different iron houses originally imported here. It resembles a bunch of scrap-metal sheets bolted together, was once the location of the Iquitos Club and is now, in humbler times, a general store.

It is a building to appreciate from the outside only.

UPROOTING BELÉN

The order has come from on high: Belén – perhaps the character-defining district of Iquitos – needs to be moved. The main reason cited is sanitation. When water levels are high, this shantytown-cum-market on the river floats, but it sits on the stinking mud when the water drops. But how do you relocate an entire district, and to where? It's proving a headache. At the time of writing, a few families of the hundreds living here have signed up for the scheme. The rest have strongly opposed it and, as you will see if you visit the market here, staying put. Without residents' consent, and with a relocation threatening the only livelihood most of them know (fishing and river trade), any uprooting of Belén will be a struggle taking many years.

Iquitos

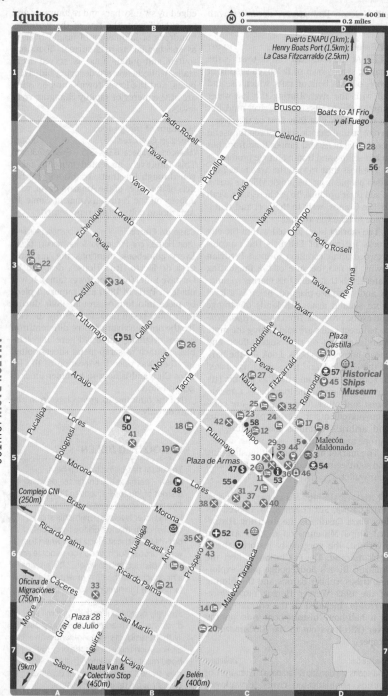

N
0 ———————— 400 m
0 ———————— 0.2 miles

Puerto ENAPU (1km);
Henry Boats Port (1.5km);
La Casa Fitzcarraldo (2.5km)

Brusco

Boats to Al Frio
y al Fuego

Celendin

Pedro Rosell

Tavara

Pucallpa

Yavari

Callao

Nanay

Ocampo

Pedro Rosell

Loreto

Echenique

Pevas

Tavara

Requena

Yavari

Castilla

Putumayo

Callao

Moore

Condamine

Loreto

Plaza
Castilla

Araujo

Tacna

Pevas

Fitzcarrald

Nauta

Raimondi

Historical
Ships
Museum

Pucallpa

Lores

Bolognesi

Morona

Condamine

Napo

Putumayo

Malecón
Maldonado

Complejo CNI
(250m)

Brasil

Plaza de Armas

Lores

Ricardo Palma

Morona

Huallaga

Brasil

Arica

Próspero

Oficina de
Migraciónes
(750m)

Cáceres

Ricardo Palma

Plaza 28
de Julio

San Martín

Malecón Tarapaca

Grau

Aguirre

Ucayali

Belén
(400m)

Nauta Van &
Colectivo Stop
(450m)

(9km)

Moore

Sáenz

Iquitos

AMAZON BASIN IQUITOS

☞ Tours

River Cruises

Cruising the Amazon is an expensive business: the shortest trips can cost over US$1000. It's a popular pastime, too, and advance reservations are often necessary (and often mean discounts). Cruises naturally focus on the Río Amazonas, both downriver (northeast) toward the Brazil–Colombia border and upriver to Nauta, where the Ríos Marañón and Ucayali converge. Beyond Nauta, trips continue up these two rivers to the Reserva Nacional Pacaya-Samiria. Trips can also be arranged on the three rivers surrounding Iquitos: the Itaya, the Amazonas and the Nanay. Operators quote prices in US dollars. A useful booking website is www.amazoncruise.net.

★ Dawn on the Amazon
Tours & Cruises   CRUISE
(☏ 065-22-3730; www.dawnontheamazon.com; Malecón Maldonado 185; day trips incl lunch per person from US$85, multiday cruises per day from US$225) This small outfit offers a great deal for independent travelers. The *Amazon I* is a beautiful 11m wooden craft with modern furnishings, available for either day trips or river cruises up to two weeks. Included are a bilingual guide, all meals and transfers.

You can travel along the Amazon, or along its quieter tributaries (larger cruise ships will stick to the main waterways). While many cruise operators have fixed departures and itineraries, Dawn on the Amazon's can be adapted to accommodate individual needs. The tri-river cruise is a favorite local trip: while on board, fishing and bird-watching are the most popular activities.

Aqua Expeditions

CRUISE

(☎965-832-517, 065-60-1053, in US 1-866-603-3687; www.aquaexpeditions.com; 3-night Marañón & Ucayali cruise per person in ste from US$3825) Aqua operates luxury riverboat cruises, departing weekly for Reserva Nacional Pacaya-Samiria. The vessel, MV *Aria Amazon,* has splendid accommodations, in 16 similarly sized suites and with an on-board spa and beautiful observation lounge. Cruises last three, five or seven days, departing from Nauta.

Its Peru office (p80) is headquartered in Lima, not Iquitos, and you will need to reserve in advance.

Cruise boats come with a full crew and bilingual guides. Meals are included and small launches are carried for side trips. Activities can involve visiting indigenous communities (for dancing and craft sales), hikes, and bird- and pink dolphin-watching (on big ships, don't expect to see too much rare wildlife).

R & F Expeditions

CRUISE

(☎999-954-004; www.rfexpeditions.com; 4 days & 3 nights per person from US$3150) The RF *Amazonas* (brand new in 2016) is a wood-built four-deck vessel offering cruises along the Río Amazonas from Iquitos, sporting an observation deck, spa, lovely bar-restaurant and 13 stunning cedar-paneled suites varying between 33 and 48 sq meters. This, then, is your ticket to enjoy cruise activities like community visits, wildlife-watching forays and even a visit to a rum distillery.

Cruises depart from Puerto Bellavista-Nanay.

🎇 Festivals & Events

San Juan

TRADITIONAL MUSIC

(⊙Jun 22-27) This is the big annual debauch, a festival that has grown around the saint's day of San Juan Bautista (St John the Baptist) on June 24 (the main party day). It's celebrated in most Amazon towns but Iquitos honors the saint most fervently with dancing, and above all feasting and frivolity.

Juanes are the typical food consumed. On the night of June 23 locals partake in the river dunk, as this is the day of the year when the waters of the Itaya are said to have healing properties.

Great Amazon River Raft Race

SPECTATOR SPORT

(www.facebook.com/carreradebalsas2017) Held in September or October, this is an annual race down the river between Nauta and Iquitos in hand-built craft.

🛏 Sleeping

The range of accommodations here is broad. Basic budget to five-star luxury are catered for, with a plethora of enterprises attempting top-end and failing. The best hotels fill fast at weekends and on major festivals. The busiest season is May to September, when prices may rise marginally. Due to the competition, even budget hotels have quite decent standards. Mosquitoes are rarely problematic in town, but be aware that mosquito netting is not always provided.

Casa Celestial

HOSTEL $

(☎978-801-728; www.hablayoga.com/casacelestial; Brasil 277; dm/d incl breakfast S30/80-100) This bright new hostel-cum-guesthouse has a dorm room and three comfortable private rooms (two of which have private bathrooms). The guys in charge have cut their teeth working in various Latin American hostels and it shows: traveler-friendly service, wickedly strong coffee at the complimentary breakfast and (if you're lucky) even stronger pisco sours are the hallmarks of this three-floor place.

There is a yoga studio up top, and plans are afoot for a cafe, too.

La Casa Chacruna

GUESTHOUSE $

(☎065-24-2920; www.facebook.com/lacasachacruna; Napo 312; dm S30, d S70-100) Hard to believe, but across the way from Iquitos' most expensive hotel, you could save a sweet 400 nuevos soles and stay in a place with the same plaza views. A constant supply of good coffee is available in the common room. Clean and friendly, but a tad cramped and prone to suffer from plaza noise.

This place fills a niche between the hostels and the hotels, and fills it attractively.

Hospedaje Golondrinas

GUESTHOUSE $

(☎065-23-6428; www.hospedajegolondrinas.com; Putumayo 1024; dm/s/d S23/40/50; 🖥) Quickly growing in clout as a backpacker hangout because of a combination of reasonable prices and well-maintained rooms, Hospedaje Golondrinas manages to throw in a pool and offer great budget jungle tours out to its lodge, Jungle Wolf (p497).

Flying Dog Hostel
HOSTEL **$**

(☑ 065-22-3755; www.flyingdogperu.com; Malecón Tarapaca, btwn Brasil & Ricardo Palma; dm/s/d incl breakfast S28/85/99; @ ❂) The Flying Dog, part of the same hostel chain you'll find in Lima and Cuzco, is leader of the pack for traditional backpacker digs: clean, bright rooms, hot water and kitchen facilities. The singles and doubles are a tad pricey for what you get but have private bathrooms.

La Maison
GUESTHOUSE **$**

(☑ 065-23-4146; www.lamaison-iquitos.com; Raimondi 183; dm S18-25, r S50-60) A secure, hammock-strung courtyard leads back to this decent budget choice, a halfway house between a hostel and a guesthouse. The colonial rooms show the wear and tear of generations of budget-minded backpackers, but they're alright.

Hostal Florentina
GUESTHOUSE **$**

(☑ 065-23-3591; Huallaga 212; r S60-90; ❄) Rooms in this old colonial house are smallish but very quiet. They come with cable TV, mosquito nets and sparkling bathrooms, and are tucked well back from the road with a hammock-hung courtyard at the rear. Lower rates are for rooms with fans, higher for rooms with air-con. A bit stuffy overall but there is far worse around.

Hostal El Colibrí
GUESTHOUSE **$**

(☑ 065-24-1737; Nauta 172; s S60, d S70-90; ❄) A so-so budget choice close to the river and the main square, with pleasant, airy singles and doubles sporting fans and TVs. It has three floors of rooms, and with its small cafeteria has the air of a hotel. Higher tariffs are for air-con; otherwise you just have a fan. Breakfast is available for an extra S8.

★ Boulevard 251 Riverside Apartments
APARTMENT **$$**

(☑ 965-730-491; www.iquitosapartments.com; Malecón Maldonado 251; apt S157-230; ❄ ❂) We'll tell it to you straight: there is no better place to stay in Iquitos, either for the exceptional location, high above the banks of the river, or for the chic environs that those who check in enjoy here. There are three categories of accommodations, but

we recommend the riverside apartments, on the upper floors gazing out at the river.

The spaces are light and sleek (some apartments have floor-to-ceiling windows) and there is an outside upper terrace with a barbecue. Apartments come with very well-equipped kitchenettes, which make completely shutting yourself off from the city's hectic goings-on a tempting possibility.

Hotel La Época
BOUTIQUE HOTEL **$$**

(☑ 065-22-4172; www.epoca.com.pe; cnr Ramirez Hurtado & Ricardo Palma; s/d/tr incl breakfast S198/231/330; ❄) At the apex of the colonial boutique sector of Iquitos' many luxury sleeps, Hotel La Época is great value for all that guests get. There are the high ceilings, lofty rooms, beautiful tile work and art nouveau flourishes that are the rubber boom era's raison d'être, plus minibars and cable TV in the bedrooms, and a lovely 2nd-floor restaurant.

In places, with its photographs depicting turn-of-the-century Iquitos, La Época resembles as much a museum as a hotel. Find it on Ramirez Hurtado, which at this point is still known as the Malecón Tarapaca.

La Casa Fitzcarraldo
GUESTHOUSE **$$**

(☑ 065-60-1139, 065-60-1138; www.casafitzcarraldo.com; Av La Marina 2153; r incl breakfast S170-315; P ❄ ❂ ❄) Sequestered within a serene walled garden 3km north of the city, this is most interesting accommodation. The house takes its title from Werner Herzog's film (p490) – Herzog and co stayed here during the filming of *Fitzcarraldo*. Stay in the mahogany-floored blue room, the luxuriantly green Klaus Kinski suite (with its beautiful butterfly picture) or five other individually designed rooms.

There is a tree house (with wi-fi!), a lovely swimming pool (nonresidents S10) and a huge breakfast included in the price, as well as a bar-restaurant, mini-cinema and several four-legged residents to check out. Unique stills from the filming of *Fitzcarraldo* line the walls of the public areas. The place is a S3 *mototaxi* ride from the center; airport pickup is included in room prices, however.

Nativa Apartments
APARTMENT **$$**

(☑ 065-60-0270; https://nativaapartments.com; Nanay 144; apt S150-390; ❄ ❂) If what you want in Iquitos is a clean, safe, quiet, friendly home-from-home where you can do your own cooking in a generously sized apartment, there is no need to keep searching.

Hotel Acosta
HOTEL $$

(☎065-23-1761; www.terraverde.pe/acosta-hotel; cnr Araujo & Huallaga; s/d S120/145; ❋ 🛜) The Acosta has dropped its prices because, frankly, its standards have dropped, too, from upper-end business hotel to lower midrange. Still, decent-sized rooms are finished in delicate earthy tones; they all come with minibars, air-con, safes and writing desks; the best have balconies. There is a ground-floor restaurant, too. But a somewhat dead atmosphere wafts through this place.

Marañón Hotel
HOTEL $$

(☎065-24-2673; www.hotelmaranon.com; Nauta 289; s/d incl continental breakfast S99/150; ❋ 🛜 🏊) Inhale. Through the strong odor of cleaning products, there it is, unmistakably: tumbleweed. This place, looking a little like a stranded ferry but feeling more like the *Mary Celeste*, has light tiles everywhere and rooms with good-sized bathrooms, minibars and indeed all the usual amenities. Good value if you don't mind abandoning all hope of atmosphere.

Casa Morey
BOUTIQUE HOTEL $$$

(☎065-23-1913; www.casamorey.com; Loreto 200; s/d incl breakfast S230/310; ❋ 🛜 🏊) This former mansion of the rubber baron Luis F Morey dates from 1910 and has been renovated to its former elegance, with 14 extravagantly large suites, plenty of original *azulejos*, voluminous bathrooms with baths, river views, a courtyard with a small pool and a library with a stupendous collection of Amazon-related literature.

The grandiose dining area makes for charming breakfast environs (though the tiling here isn't original).

Hotel Victoria Regia
HOTEL $$$

(☎065-23-1983; www.terraverde.pe/victoria -regia-hotel-suites; Ricardo Palma 252; s/d incl breakfast S373/420; ❋ @ 🏊) A blast of icy, air-conditioned air welcomes guests to this comfortable hostelry. It has excellent beds and sizable rooms that include fancy reading lights and minibars, plus hair dryers and baths in the bathrooms. One of the suites has a spa. The indoor pool and fine restaurant-bar attract upscale guests and business people.

The reality, though, is that this is not significantly better than several city hotels that charge S100 or more less. Various promotions can reduce the quoted rates by almost half, however: check the website for offers.

DoubleTree by Hilton Hotel Iquitos
BUSINESS HOTEL $$$

(☎065-22-2555; http://doubletree3.hilton.com; Napo 258; s/d incl breakfast from S423/455; ❋ 🛜 🏊) With a prime plaza location, this modern hotel is the town's priciest (undoubtedly) and best (hmm... possibly), now switched to become part of the Hilton group. Over 60 well-equipped rooms (some with plaza views, others overlooking the pool), a spa, sauna, gym, nice lower-ground floor restaurant, several suites, 24-hour room service, two bars and attentive staff make this hotel top-notch.

Rates for rooms are often discounted when the hotel is not busy: check the website for offers.

🍴 Eating

The city has excellent restaurants. However, many regional specialties feature endangered animals, such as *chicharrón de lagarto* (fried alligator) and *sopa de tortuga* (turtle soup). More environmentally friendly dishes include ceviche made with river fish, *chupín de pollo* (a tasty soup of chicken, egg and rice) and *juanes*.

★ Belén Mercado
MARKET $

(cnr Próspero & Jirón 9 de Diciembre; menús from S5) There are great eats at Iquitos' markets, particularly the Belén mercado where a *menú*, including jugo especial (jungle juice) costs S5. Look out for specialties including meaty Amazon worms, ishpa (simmered sabalo fish intestines and fat) and sikisapa (fried leafcutter ants; abdomens are supposedly tastiest), and watch your valuables. Another good market for cheap eats is Mercado Central (Lores cuadra 5; snacks from S1).

Cafezinho
CAFE $

(Nauta 250; coffees S2.50-10; ⊙7am-1pm & 4-11pm Mon-Sat, 5-9pm Sun) Taking on the big boys in town and beating them hands down as far as caffeine fixes go, this agreeable little air-conditioned place will do anything from ristretto to Oreo frappes, and do them supremely well.

Cafe Express
CAFE $

(Próspero 285; snacks/breakfasts S3-10; ⊙7am-4pm Mon-Sat) Wondering what to do for breakfast? Don't wonder. This is the spot; has been for decades. Grab a newspaper from the old dude outside and pull up a pew with the locals for a dose of the infamously curt service (part of the fun) and then the tasty grub. If it ain't broke, don't fix it.

Ari's Burger   AMERICAN $

(☑065-23-1470; Próspero 127; meals $10-25; ⊘7am-3am) On the corner of the Plaza de Armas, this clean, chirpy and brightly lit joint is known locally as *gringolandia* (gringo land).Two walls are open to the street, allowing great plaza- and people-watching. It's almost always open and serves American-style fast-food (with cute Amazonian caveats like the burger with *paiche,* a local fish). Popular with tourists and locals alike.

Ivalú   PERUVIAN $

(Lores 215; snacks from $3; ⊘8am-early afternoon) One of the most popular local spots for juice, and cake and tamales (corn cakes filled with chicken or fish and wrapped in jungle leaves). The juices are sensational, many going by names of jungle fruits you have never heard of. Go early, before they sell out!

Chifa Long Fung   CHINESE $

(San Martín 454; mains $15-30; ⊘noon-2:30pm & 7pm-midnight) Once you have gotten over the miserable service, the mountains of tasty Chinese food at this most legendary of the *chifas* near the Plaza 28 de Julio might make you grin again.

Supermercado Los Portales SUPERMARKET $

(Próspero at Morona; ⊘7:30am-11:30pm) For self-catering supplies, visit this supermarket, which has a surprisingly diverse wine section and a clean, dirt-cheap cafe (from 7:30am to 10pm; you sit next to the pet food aisle).

★Dawn on the Amazon Cafe   INTERNATIONAL $$

(http://dawnontheamazoncafe.com; Malecón Maldonado 185; mains $10-30; ⊘7:30am-10pm Mon-Sat; 🕾) This traveler magnet on the Malecón, with its tempting row of street-front tables, sports a menu divided up into North American, Peruvian, Spanish and Chinese. Travel wherever your taste buds desire but bear in mind that the steamed fresh fish is very good. Ingredients are all non-MSG and those on gluten-free diets are catered for.

They do acai bowls: a sumptuous and refreshing start to the sticky day.

ChillOut Carnes y Pescados   CEVICHE $$

(Napo 834; mains $20-32; ⊘10am-5pm Sun-Tue, 7-10pm Thu-Sat; ❄) This gets our nod for first prize in the keenly contested battle for number one in the city's *cevichería* (ceviche restaurant) contest. An air-conditioned interior, a little street-front courtyard and, most crucially of all, delicious, huge platters of ceviche.

Espresso Cafe-Bar   CAFE $$

(www.facebook.com/espressocafeiquitos; cnr Próspero & Morona; mains $21-32; ⊘noon-midnight) Elegant rubber boom-style refurbishments are all the rage in Iquitos and this 2nd-floor people-watching spot has nailed the vibe. Airy, high-ceilinged and stylishly furnished, the service here is also gracious. Cue, then, the partaking of a delightful range of coffees, infusions, cocktails and cakes as well as sandwiches, well-presented grazing plates of barbecue wings, bruschetta and the like.

There is live music at weekends and a gallery (where you can also sit) next door.

Karma Cafe   CAFE $$

(www.facebook.com/karmacafeiquitos; Napo 138; mains $19-34; ⊘9am-12:30am; 🕾✏) This chilled atmospheric place does a little bit of everything and does it well: Thai, Greek, Indian, vegetarian, Peruvian, cocktails. It offers a 'make your own' breakfast, a popular happy hour, displays local art and has great live music several nights per week. Travelers seem to adore it: it's always packed.

★Le Bateau Ivre   INTERNATIONAL $$

(Malecón Tarapaca 268; mains $20-40; ⊘6am-midnight; 🕾) This is laid out with TLC by the Belgian owner with a New York–style breakfast bar (OK, Amazon version thereof) and upper-level mezzanine seating looking down on the main eating area. The cuisine refuses to be pigeon-holed: there's Argentine steaks, not to mention the Belgian influence, creeping across in the crepes, the escargot and the range of Belgian beers.

Then there is some of the city's best coffee, which goes down rather nicely in conjunction with a fresh croissant. The bistro is best for breakfast but not bad for an evening drink, either. A separate garden courtyard is toward the rear of the main restaurant.

HERGOG'S AMAZON

Eccentric German director Werner Herzog, often seen as obsessive and bent on filming 'reality itself,' shot two movies in Peru's jungle: *Aguirre, the Wrath of God* (1972) and *Fitzcarraldo* (1982). Herzog's accomplishments in getting these movies made at all – during havoc-fraught filming conditions – are in some ways more remarkable than the finished products.

Klaus Kinski, the lead actor in *Aguirre,* was a volatile man prone to extreme fits of rage. Herzog's documentary *My Best Fiend* details such incidents as Kinski beating a conquistador extra so severely that his helmet, donned for the part, was all that saved him from being killed. Then there was the time near the end of shooting when, after altercations with a cameraman on the Río Nanay, Kinski prepared to desert the film crew on a speedboat. Herzog had to threaten to shoot him with a rifle to make him stay. (To tell both sides of the story, however, *My Best Fiend* also reveals that Herzog admitted to once trying to firebomb Kinski in his house and according to other members of the film crew Herzog often over exaggerated.) Kinski's biography, *Kinski Uncut* (albeit partly ghostwritten by Herzog) paints a picture of the director as a buffoon who had no idea how to make movies.

Filming *Fitzcarraldo,* the first choice for the lead fell ill and the second, Mick Jagger, abandoned the set to do a Rolling Stones tour. With a year's filming already wasted, Herzog called upon Kinski once more. Kinski soon antagonized the Matsiguenka tribespeople being used as extras: one even offered to murder him for Herzog. While filming near the Peru–Ecuador frontier, a war between the two nations erupted and soldiers destroyed the film set. Then there was the weather: droughts so dire that the rivers dried and stranded the film's steamship for weeks, followed by flash floods that wrecked the boat entirely. (Some of these are chronicled in *Conquest of the Useless: Reflections from the Making of Fitzcarraldo,* Herzog's film diaries, translated into English in 2009.) To hear another side to events during filming, chat to the folks at La Casa Fitzcarraldo (p487), owned by the daughter of the executive producer of *Fitzcarraldo.*

Herzog could certainly be a hard man to work with, filming many on-set catastrophes and using them as footage in the final cut. The director once said he saw filming in the Amazon as 'challenging nature itself.' The fact that he completed two films in the Peruvian jungle against such odds is evidence that in some ways, Herzog did challenge nature – and triumphed.

Al Frio y al Fuego
FUSION $$

(☑ 965-607-474; www.facebook.com/alfrioyalfuegorestaurante; Embarcadero Av La Marina 138; mains S40-50; ⊙noon-11pm Mon-Sat, to 6pm Sun; ⧈) Take a boat out to this floating foodie paradise in the middle of the mouth of the Río Itaya to sample some of the city's best food. The emphasis is on river fish (such as the delectable *doncella*), but the *parrillas* are inviting, too. The address given is the boat embarkation point.

Come here at night for the best overall view of Iquitos, beautifully lit up beyond the restaurant's swimming pool.

Mitos y Cubiertos
PERUVIAN $$

(Napo 337; mains S20-35; ⊙11am-11:30pm; ⧈) Resembling the inside of an *ayahuasca* vision, Mitos y Cubiertos is one of *the* places to be cool in an understated way in Iquitos. The menu loosely hinges on the national classics, but there are veggie options, bruschetta and imaginative pasta to add a tad of pizzazz.

Gran Maloca
PERUVIAN $$

(Lores 170; mains S25-45; ⊙noon-4pm & 7-11pm; ⧈) Enter the bygone world of the rubber-boom days at this atmospheric Amazonian restaurant. Expect silk tablecloths, wall-length mirrors and imaginative regional delicacies such as *chupín de pollo,* Amazon venison with toasted coconut and the scrumptious Loretan omelet (omelet from the Loreto region) with jungle leaves.

The air-con will leave you wondering why you didn't just plan a vacation to Antarctica.

Antica
ITALIAN $$

(☑ 065-24-1988; www.facebook.com/antica pizzeriaiquitos; Napo 159; mains S25-49; ⊙8am-11:45pm) The Antica is the best Italian restaurant in town. Primarily a pizza place – there's an impressive wood-fired pizza oven – pasta also takes a predominant spot on the menu with the lasagna being another excellent choice. Chow down at solid wooden tables and choose from the range of fine imported Italian wines.

Fitzcarraldo

Restaurant-Bar   INTERNATIONAL **$$**
(☎ 065-50-7545; www.restaurantefitzcarraldo. com; Napo 100; mains S20-35; ⊗7am-midnight; ❋) The Fitzcarraldo is an upscale option on the riverside strip, with very good food, but occasionally dopey service. It does various local and international dishes, like alpaca steak or ceviche made with Amazon river fish. Beware the icy air-con.

Drinking & Nightlife

Iquitos is a party city. The Malecón is the cornerstone of the lively nightlife scene and you can dance until dawn and beyond at the discos just outside the center.

Arandú Bar   BAR

(Malecón Maldonado 113; ⊗till late) The liveliest of several thumping Malecón bars, full of funky art, great for people-watching and always churning out loud rock-and-roll classics.

Musmuqui   BAR

(Raimondi 382; ⊗5pm-midnight Sun-Thu, to 3am Fri & Sat) Locally popular lively bar with two floors and an extensive range of aphrodisiac cocktails concocted from wondrous Amazon plants.

Entertainment

Complejo CNI   LIVE MUSIC
(cnr Ricardo Palma & Echenique; admission S5; ⊗till late Thu-Sat) Well-known local group Illusion play here at Iquitos' best disco, where hundreds and hundreds of *iquiteños* end up dancing on a weekend evening.

Shopping

There are a few **craft stands** (cnr Malecón Maldonado & Napo; ⊗7am-9pm) along the Malecón selling jungle crafts. Another good place for crafts is **Mercado de Artesanía San Juan** (Av José Abelardo Quiñones), on the airport road. Don't buy items made from animal bones and skins, as they are made from jungle wildlife. It's illegal to import many such items into the US and Europe.

ⓘ Information

EMERGENCY

National police (☎ 065-23-1131; Morona 126) Most central police station.

Policía de Turismo (Main Hall, Francisco Secada Vignetta Airport)

IMMIGRATION

If arriving from or departing for Brazil or Colombia, get your entry/exit stamp at the border.

Brazilian Consulate (☎ 065-23-5151; Lores 363; ⊗9am-1pm Mon-Fri)

Colombian Consulate (☎ 065-23-1461; Moore 249, cnr Calvo de Aurajo)

Oficina de Migraciónes (☎ 065-23-5173; Mariscal Cáceres cuadra 18; ⊗8am-4pm Mon-Fri, to noon Sat)

MEDICAL SERVICES

Clínica Ana Stahl (☎ 065-25-2535; www. facebook.com/caas.iquitos; La Marina 285; ⊗24hr) Private clinic 2km north of the center.

Happydent (Putumayo 786) Dentist.

InkaFarma (Próspero 397, cnr Morona; ⊗7am-midnight) Reliable.

MONEY

Several banks provide an ATM, including BCP, which has secure ATMs.

BCP (Próspero & Putamayo)

POST

Serpost (Arica 402; ⊗8am-6pm Mon-Fri, to 5pm Sat)

SAFE TRAVEL

Street touts and self-styled jungle guides tend to be aggressive, and many are both irritatingly insistent and dishonest. They are working for commissions, and usually for bog-standard establishments. It is best to make your own decisions by contacting hotels, lodges and tour companies directly. Exercise particular caution around Belén, which is very poor and where petty thieving is quite common. That said, violent crime is almost unknown in Iquitos.

TOURIST INFORMATION

Various jungle guides and jungle lodges also give tourist information, obviously promoting their services, which is fine if you are looking for them but otherwise rarely helpful.

iPerú (☎ 065-26-0251; Main Hall, Francisco Secada Vignetta Airport; ⊗when flights are arriving/departing) Airport branch.

iPerú (☎ 065-23-6144; Napo 161; ⊗9am-6pm Mon-Sat, to 1pm Sun) On Napo.

❶ Getting There & Away

Approaching the largest city not to be connected by road to the rest of the world is, of course, done by either air or, for the plucky, by river.

AIR

Iquitos' small but busy **airport**, 7km from the center, receives flights from Lima, Pucallpa and Tarapoto.

Charter companies at the airport have five-seat passenger planes to almost anywhere in the Amazon, if you have a few hundred US bucks going spare.

LATAM (LAN; ☎ 065-23-2421; Próspero 232; ☻9am-6:30pm Mon-Fri, to 1pm Sat) Direct daily runs to Lima, plus flights to Cuzco on Mondays, Wednesdays and Saturdays.

Star Perú (☎065-23-6208; Napo 260; ☻8:30am-6:30pm Mon-Fri, to 5:30pm Sat) Star Perú operates two daily flights to and from Lima: the morning flight stops at Pucallpa and the afternoon flight at Tarapoto. Fares are about US$70 to Lima and US$60 to Pucallpa or Tarapoto.

BOAT

Iquitos is Peru's largest, best-organized river port. You can theoretically travel all the way from Iquitos to the Atlantic Ocean, but most boats out of Iquitos ply only Peruvian waters, and voyagers necessarily change boats at the tri-border with Colombia and Brazil. If you choose to arrive or depart by river, you'll end up at one of six ports, which are between 2km and 3km north of the city center.

---

❶ BORDER CROSSING: THE PERU–COLOMBIA–BRAZIL BORDER ZONE

Even in the middle of the Amazon, border officials adhere to formalities and will refuse passage if documents are not in order. With a valid passport and visa or tourist card, border crossing is not a problem. It is highly advisable to check what immigration policies are for your country prior to showing up at the border.

When leaving Peru for Brazil or Colombia, you'll get an exit stamp at a Peruvian guard post just before the border (boats stop there long enough for this; ask the captain).

The ports at the three-way border are several kilometers apart, connected by public ferries. They are reached by air or boat, but not by road.

At this point, Peru occupies the south side of the river, where currents create a constantly shifting bank. Peru's border town (OK, tiny village) is **Santa Rosa**, which has Peruvian immigration facilities.

From here, motor canoes reach **Leticia**, in Colombia, in about 15 minutes. The biggest, nicest border town, Leticia has by far the best hotels and restaurants, and a hospital. You can fly from Leticia to Bogotá on almost-daily commercial flights. Otherwise, infrequent boats go to **Puerto Asis** on the Río Putumayo; the trip takes up to 12 days. From Puerto Asis, buses go further into Colombia.

The two small ports in Brazil are **Tabatinga** and **Benjamin Constant**; both have basic hotels. Tabatinga has an airport with flights to Manaus. Get your official Brazilian entry stamp from the Tabatinga police station if flying on to Manaus. Tabatinga is a continuation of Leticia, and you can walk or take a taxi between the two with no immigration hassles, unless you are planning on traveling further into Brazil or Colombia. Cargo boats leave from Tabatinga downriver, usually stopping in Benjamin Constant for a night, then continuing on to Manaus, a week away. It takes about an hour to reach Benjamin Constant by public ferry. US citizens need a visa to enter Brazil. Make sure you apply in good time – either in the USA or in Lima.

For travelers to Colombia or Brazil, Lonely Planet has guidebooks for both countries.

If you are arriving from Colombia or Brazil, you'll find boats in Leticia and Tabatinga for Iquitos. You will have to first voyage to Santa Rosa. From here, you should pay US$10 to US$15 for the nigh-on two-day trip on a cargo riverboat. Happily, since the arrival of the Consorcio Fluvial del Amazonas ferry, fast boats upriver have become much more dependable. For a *mas rápido* (fast boat), prices begin at US$25 and run all the way up to about US$50. Prices are the same for the opposite journey (downriver), too, although downriver from Iquitos to the tri-border is quicker. Upriver or downriver, you *may* be able to get passage on a cruise ship, but note that this will make stops en route.

Remember that however disorganized things may appear, you can always get meals, money changed, beds and boats simply by asking around.

Six main ports are of interest to travelers:

Puerto Bellavista-Nanay (Av La Marina s/n), furthest from the center at the end of Av La Marina, is mainly used by smaller craft to destinations local to Iquitos, such as to Pilpintuwasi Butterfly Farm (p494). However, cruise ships as well as some jungle expedition boats use this as a departure port. A *mototaxi* ride here is S4.

Puerto Masusa (Los Rosales), about 3km north of the town center, is where cargo boats depart for Yurimaguas (upriver; three to six days) and Pucallpa (upriver; four to seven days); but these trips are better undertaken in the other direction, with the current. Fares cost S80 to S100 for hammock space and S130 to S180 for a tiny (often cell-like) cabin. Boats leave most days for both places: there are more frequent departures for the closer intermediate ports en route. For Yurimaguas, the Eduardo boats have the best reputation.

Downriver boats to the Peruvian border with Brazil and Colombia leave from Puerto Masusa, too. There are about two or three departures weekly for the two-day journey (per person S80). Boats will stop at Pevas (hammock space S40, about 15 hours) and other ports en route. Boats may dock closer to the center if the water is very high (from May to July).

Closer to the center, the more organized **Henry Boats Port** (Av La Marina 1640; ⊙7am-7pm) runs services along the Iquitos–Pucallpa route.

At both ports chalkboards tell you which boats are leaving when, for where, and whether they accept passengers. Although there are agencies in town, it's usually best to go to the dock and look around; don't trust anyone except the captain for an estimate of departure time. Be wary: the chalkboards have a habit of changing dates overnight! Boats often leave hours or even days late.

You can often sleep aboard the boat while waiting for departure, and this enables you to get the best hammock space. Never leave gear unattended – ask to have your bags locked up when you sleep.

Puerto ENAPU (Av La Marina s/n), on Av La Marina near the crossroads with 28 de Julio, is mainly of interest as it's where the Consorcio Fluvial del Amazonas ferry leaves from heading downriver to Pevas and Santa Rosa, on the Colombia–Brazil border.

Tiny **Puerto Embarcadero** (Puerto LAO; off Requena near Ocampo), closest to the center, near the join of Av La Marina/Calle Ocampo, is for speedboats to the tri-border (with Colombia and Brazil). These depart between 5am and 6am daily. You'll need to purchase your ticket in advance. **Speedboat offices** (Raimondi at Plaza Castilla; ⊙6am-8pm) are bunched together on Raimondi near the Plaza Castilla. Standard fares are S150 to Pevas or Santa Rosa, on the Peruvian side of the border, including meals.

Finally, some tours still depart from the **dock** (Malecón Maldonado s/n) right on Malecón Maldonado.

You *may* be able to book a berth on a Leticia-bound cruise ship if space is available, although this is more likely coming from Leticia to Iquitos (the captain is more likely to take pity on you if you're stranded in Leticia).

ⓘ Getting Around

BOAT

There is an overwhelming number of ports around town; for local trips, those worth knowing about include Puerto Bellavista-Nanay and Puerto Embarcadero.

BUS

Colectivos and minivans to Nauta take 1½ hours and depart from the **Nauta Van & Colectivo Stop** (Aguirre 1550). There are swimming opportunities at the creeks and beaches en route.

Buses and trucks for several nearby destinations, including the airport, leave from near Plaza 28 de Julio. Airport buses are marked Nanay–Belén–Aeropuerto: they head south down Arica to the airport.

LOCAL TRANSPORT

Squadrons of *mototaxis* are the bona fide transport round town. They are fun to ride, though they don't provide much protection in an accident. Always enter *mototaxis* from the sidewalk side – passing traffic pays scant heed to embarking passengers – and keep your limbs inside at all times. Scrapes and fender benders are common. Most rides around Iquitos cost a standard S1.50 to S3; to the airport it's about S8 for a *mototaxi* and S15 for the harder-to-spot cabs. Your accommodation will always order you a taxi on request.

Around Iquitos

The northern Amazon Basin fanning out from Iquitos is home to the Amazon River (Río Amazonas) itself. Should you so choose, you can follow this waterway all the way through to Brazil and on again to the Atlantic.

The way to experience the jungle here is to take a tour from Iquitos for a minimum of three days, staying out in one of the many wilderness lodges.

Heading upriver (southwest from Iquitos) you encounter the wilderness reserve of Reserva Nacional Pacaya-Samiria. Heading downriver (east from Iquitos) on the

ROAD TO NOWHERE?

Talk of a road connecting Iquitos to the rest of Peru, through the jungle to the current terminus of the Peruvian road network at Saramiriza, has long been the goal of developers. Those in favor were particularly buoyed by the construction of the Carr Interocéanica, which now connects Puerto Maldonado with Cuzco in Peru and with Brazil, and has been cited as a major contributor to that city's recent prosperity. Backers of the Iquitos–Saramiriza road included Pedro Pablo Kuczynski, 66th President of Peru. He vowed to complete the road link by the end of his term in 2021; but Kuczynski resigned from office in March 2018. For now at least, Iquitos will continue to rely on air and river for its links to the outside world.

Río Amazonas takes you toward the border with Colombia and Brazil, and possible continuation on a river voyage all the way down to the Atlantic.

⊙ Sights

Yanamono Rum Distillery DISTILLERY
(⊙dawn-dusk) **FREE** For three generations the Guerra family has been operating this traditional rum distillery in Yanamono, in the middle of nowhere in the northern Peruvian Amazon. There is nothing different about the rum-making process here to how it would have been in the conquistador era. Sugarcane is crushed in a huge hand-turned press (there is a donkey to assist). Battered wooden vats then finish the fermentation.

The owner, don Guerra, will explain the process (in Spanish) and after such a wonderful insight into traditional Amazonian distilling it would be churlish not to purchase a bottle of the finished product. Several jungle tours, including those run by Otorongo Expeditions, stop off here.

Laguna Quistacocha LAKE
(Carr Iquitos–Nauta Km 6; admission S6) This lake, 15km south of Iquitos, is served by minibus (S2) several times an hour from near Plaza 28 de Julio (corner of Bermúdez and Moore), as well as *mototaxis* (S15). There's a small **zoo** of local fauna (much improved of recent years) and an adjoining **fish hatchery**, which has 2m-long *paiche*,

endangered until recently, due to habitat loss and its popularity as food; attempts to rectify the situation are being made with the breeding program here.

A pedestrian walk circles the lake, swimming is possible and paddle boats are available for hire (S5 to S10). There are several restaurants and a hiking trail to the Río Itaya. It's fairly crowded with locals on the weekend but not midweek.

Pilpintuwasi Butterfly Farm WILDLIFE RESERVE
(☎065-23-2665; www.amazonanimalorphanage.org; Padre Cocha; adult/student S20/10; ⊙9:30am-2:45pm Tue-Sun) Ostensibly, the Pilpintuwasi Butterfly Farm is a conservation and breeding center for Amazonian butterflies. Butterflies aplenty there certainly are, including the striking blue morpho *(Morpho menelaus)* and the fearsome-looking owl butterfly *(Caligo eurilochus)*. But it's the farm's exotic animals that steal the show. Raised as orphans and protected within the property are several mischievous monkeys, a tapir, an anteater and Pedro Bello, a majestic jaguar. Some animals have to be kept caged as Peruvian law states they cannot be released into the wild without precise ideas of their origin.

To get to Pilpintuwasi , take a boat from Puerto Bellavista-Nanay (p493), 4km north of Iquitos, to the village of Padre Cocha. Boats run all day. The farm is signposted: it's a 15-minute walk through the village from the Padre Cocha boat dock (keep to the paths that stick close to the river, bearing left at all opportunities).

Activities

RAREC WILDLIFE
(Rainforest Awareness Rescue Education Center; ☎925-165-682; www.facebook.com/pg/rescueparks; Carr Iquitos Km 47; day visit incl pickup from Iquitos & lunch S100; ⊙8:30am-4pm) This is the most highly regarded of several animal rescue centers dotted around Iquitos. Ill, mistreated animals are nursed back to health and cared for and visitors can either observe (day visit) or stay over and volunteer (US$50 per day) depending on their time and inclination. A moving but uplifting experience; reserve in advance to guarantee the best possible visit.

An education center for locals and a study center for scientists are in the pipeline at this ever-expanding and ever-evolving site, set in pretty environs between Iquitos and Nauta.

Tours

Jungle 'guides' will approach you everywhere in Iquitos. Some will be independent operators, and many will be working on behalf of a lodge. Travelers have mixed experiences with private guides. All guides should have a permit or license – if they don't, check with the tourist office. Get references for any guide, and proceed with caution. The better lodges often snap up the best guides quickly.

Oswaldo Icahuate ADVENTURE
(965-660-389; reizeu51@hotmail.com; per day US$20) Oswaldo Icahuate is fluent in English and extremely knowledgable about the Reserva Nacional Pacaya-Samiria. He also brings the experience of many years' work on the region's leading luxury river cruises to the trips he offers here, but perhaps the key advantage with Oswaldo is his flexibility: tell him your requirements and an itinerary can be individually tailored.

Amazon King ADVENTURE
(www.amazonkinglodge.com; per person per day from US$150;) Amazon King calls its tours adventures, and with just one night in its comfortable lodge and two nights camping 60km downriver on the banks of the Amazon on its most budget-friendly trip, the phraseology is appropriate. Activities include visiting a Yagua indigenous community – the experience is enhanced because the owners themselves grew up on the remote riverbanks here.

Its office (065-22-1581; www.amazonkinglodge.com; Nauta 298; per person per day from US$150) is in Iquitos.

Walter Soplin ADVENTURE
(965-303-113; per person per night from US$50) Walter's hardcore adventure trips go deep into the incredibly flora-and-fauna-rich Tamshiyacu-Tahuayo Reserve, around seven to eight hours' boat ride from Iquitos. This is back-to-basics stuff – sleeping is in small-scale cabins scattered around a blackwater lake, near one of the Amazon's remotest communities, Nuevo Jerusalén.

Because of the distances involved, you really need to sign up for the seven-day and six-night tour. Trips under four days cost slightly more.

Sleeping

Sleeping will be exclusively at the lodge you choose to stay at, or, in certain cases, at a camp out in the jungle affiliated with your chosen lodge and included in the tour price.

★**Samiria Ecolodge** LODGE $$$
(www.samiriaecolodge.com; cabin 3 days & 2 nights per person US$400;) It's not significantly more 'eco' than other lodges, but this beauty on the Río Marañón is significantly flashier. Shiny, dark-wood 56 sq meter cabins, with cotton-sheeted king beds, futons, huge windows and balconies, form part of an exquisite thatched complex – which also has a restaurant, bar and inviting swimming pool. Activities, including crash courses in local botany, get good reports.

★**Otorongo Lodge** LODGE $$$
(950-542-907; www.otorongoexpeditions.com; s/d 4 days & 3 nights per person US$700/1080) Travelers give great feedback about this rustic-style lodge, 100km from Iquitos, and no wonder. It's set down a peaceful tributary off the Amazon and surrounded by walkways to maximize appreciation of the surrounding wildlife, and has 12 rooms with private bathrooms and a relaxing common area. It's run by a falconer who imitates an incredible number of bird sounds.

This gets you up close and personal to a huge variety of wildlife, and so this lodge comes recommended for a magical, personal experience of the Amazonian wilderness. What is more, the lodge land encompasses what is known as a Pleistocene refuge (an area of the jungle that has historically remained unchanged for millennia despite surrounding ecosystems oscillating between dry savannah and wetland, and thus contains tremendous biodiversity).

There are also two stand-alone houses (a family house and a honeymoon suite!) tucked away in the trees with exemplary bathrooms by the Amazon's standards. The five-day, four-night tour can include lots of off-the-beaten-path visits to nearby communities, and camping trips deeper in the jungle. Also ask about Otorongo's 'extreme fishing' and jungle survival programs: the owner is an expert on these.

The lodge office (950-542-907, 971-019-170; https://otorongoexpeditions.com; Nauta 350) is in Iquitos.

AMAZON BASIN AROUND IQUITOS

ExplorNapo Lodge
LODGE $$$

(http://explorama.com; s/d 5 days & 4 nights per person US$1235/2430) 🏊 On the Río Napo, 157km from Iquitos, this simple lodge has 30 rooms with shared cold-shower facilities. The highlights are guided trail hikes in remote primary forest, bird-watching, an ethno-botanical garden of useful plants (curated by a local shaman) and a visit to the nearby canopy walkway (a half-hour walk away). Run by **Explorama** (☑065-25-2530; www.explorama.com; Av La Marina 340; d 3 days & 2 nights per person from US$544).

A major highlight of any trip to the Peruvian Amazon, the canopy walkway is suspended 35m above the forest floor to give visitors a bird's-eye view of the rainforest canopy and its wildlife. Bear in mind that because of the distance involved, you spend the first and last night of a five-day/four-night package at the Explorama Lodge.

The other cool thing about ExplorNapo is the chance to combine a stay here with a visit to the **ACTS Field Station** (srmadigosky@widener.edu) 🏊 where wildlife sightings are that much better; this costs an extra US$130 per person per night spent at ACTS.

Sample rates are given; contact Explorama for other options and combinations – and discounts.

Tahuayo Lodge
LODGE $$$

(☑US 1-813-907-8475, US or Canada toll-free 1-800-262-9669; www.perujungle.com; cabin 6 days & 5 nights per person US$1295) 🏊 This lodge, 140km from Iquitos, is the only one with immediate access to the 2500-sq-km Tamshiyacu-Tahuayo Reserve, an area of pristine jungle where a record 93 species of mammal have been recorded. The 17 lodge cabins are located 65km up an Amazon tributary, built on high stilts and connected by walkways; half have private bathrooms.

There is a laboratory with a library here, too. Wildlife-viewing opportunities are among the best of any lodge: they usually include a peek at the pygmy marmosets that nest near the lodge. On the recommended six-day/five-night tour from Iquitos, visitors also get a chance to stay at the nearby Amazon Research Center Lodge, which is remoter and has an extensive trail network.

Travel is by speedboat from Iquitos. Reserve online or through its Iquitos **office** (Av La Marina 100).

Friends of the Amazon Jungle Lodge
LODGE $$$

(www.friendsoftheamazonjungle.com; bungalows per night US$185) Friends of the Amazon Jungle has cornered the budget jungle tour market. As well as offering dirt-cheap digs at its Iquitos **office** (☑065-22-1998; www.friendsoftheamazonjungle.com; Pevas 186; jungle trips per night US$185), it has neat bungalows a 45-minute boat ride from Iquitos – the price is for the whole bungalow, which sleeps two, so per person it's cheap. Enjoy hiking to waterfalls, kayaking and visiting jungle communities around its 1.6-hectare grounds.

Ayahuasca and *kambo* (Amazon tree frog poison, used to cleanse and treat pain) ceremonies are conducted; both should be undertaken with extreme caution. If backpackers choose to make their own way there (ask about directions first!) and self-cater, the prices come tumbling down to under S100 per person.

Cumaceba Botanical Garden
LODGE $$$

(www.cumaceba.com; s/d 3 days & 2 nights per person US$431/690) This lodge, run by Cumaceba, has an extensive botanical garden showcasing rainforest plants and herbs. It has a lodge office in Iquitos. There are 18 rooms, all with private bathrooms, raised about a metre above the ground and connected by walkways, as well as a hammock house, dining room and a large *maloca,* or place for undertaking *ayahuasca* ceremonies.

The lodge is 80km downriver from Iquitos.

Avatar Amazon Lodge
LODGE $$$

(www.avataramazonlodge.com; 2 days & 1 night for 1/2-4 people per person US$200/190; 🐾) Avatar makes no claims to guarantee you the best wildlife sightings: instead, in pleasant secondary jungle you can stay in comfort in well-appointed bungalows, monkey around on the superb canopy tower, whoosh through the trees on ziplines or splash about in a lovely pool. The lodge is under an hour's boat journey downriver from Iquitos; the **office** (☑065-50-0055; https://avataramazonlodge.com; Putumayo 133; 2 days & 1 night 1/2-4 people per person US$200/190) is in Iquitos.

Llaquipallay
LODGE $$$

(☑959-338-607; https://llaquipallay.com; 3 days & 2 nights per person US$270) Just before the mouth of the Río Yarapa, a tributary of

PEVAS

Pevas, about 180km downriver from Iquitos, is Peru's oldest European settlement on the Amazon and most interesting stop between Iquitos and the border. Founded by Jesuit missionaries in 1735, Pevas has about 5000 inhabitants but no cars, post office or banks (or attorneys!); the first telephone was installed in 1998. Most residents are *mestizos* (persons of mixed indigenous and Spanish descent) or indigenous people from one of four tribes.

The main attraction in Pevas is the studio-gallery of one of Peru's best-known living artists, **Francisco Grippa** (Pevas) `FREE`. Grippa specialises in portraying the Amazonian people, places and customs in his work – he has been living out in the Peruvian Amazon observing its ways of life for over two decades.

the Ucayali on the edge of Reserva Nacional Pacaya-Samiria, this lodge remains surrounded by water for most of the year, meaning a more intimate, isolated experience than many other lodges. Rooms are simple but securely netted against mosquitoes, and the bathrooms probably have the best views in the jungle!

Jungle Wolf Lodge   LODGE **$$$**
(☑ 065-23-6428; http://junglewolfexpedition. com; Putumayo 1024; r per person 2 days & 1 night US$180) One for the budget hunters! This lodge is very nice for the price, offering basic but clean rustic wood-built rooms in blocks raised on stilts above the forest floor. It's right up the Río Cumaceba, a tributary of the Yarapa, and gets no passing river traffic, which can mean more serenity and wildlife sightings.

Travel is by bus to Nauta, then boat. Its **office** (☑ 065-23-6428; http://junglewolfexpedition.com; Putumayo 1024) is in Iquitos.

Cumaceba Amazon Lodge   LODGE **$$$**
(☑ 065-23-2229; www.cumaceba.com; s 3 days & 2 nights per person US$358-431, d US$572-690) Rustic Cumaceba Lodge, in operation since 1995, is about 35km downriver from Iquitos. It has 15 screened rooms with private showers, and focuses on local adventure trips – although not in primary jungle. Guides speak English, French and even Japanese.

The same company also runs Cumaceba Botanical Garden, which places an emphasis on studying rainforest plants in addition to wildlife watching.

It has an **office** (☑ 065-23-2229, 984-915-155; www.cumaceba.com; Putumayo 188; s 3 days & 2 nights US$358-431, d US$572-690) in Iquitos.

Ceiba Tops   LODGE **$$$**
(☑ 065-25-2530; http://explorama.com; s/d 3 days & 2 nights per person US$596/1072; ✸ @ ☒) About 40km northeast of Iquitos downriver on the Amazon, this is still probably the area's most well-appointed lodge and resort. There are 75 luxurious rooms and suites, all featuring comfortable beds and furniture, fans, screened windows, porches and spacious bathrooms with hot showers. Landscaped grounds surround a pool complex, complete with hydromassage, waterslide and hammock house.

The restaurant adjoins a bar with live Amazon music daily. Short guided walks and boat rides are available for a taste of the jungle; there is primary forest nearby containing *Victoria amazonica* (giant Amazon waterlilies). This lodge is a recommended option for people who really don't want to rough it. It even hosts business incentive meetings.

One of a number of Explorama lodges, it has an office in Iquitos.

Explorama   LODGE **$$$**
(☑ 065-25-2530; http://explorama.com; s/d 3 days & 2 nights per person US$544/1028) About 80km from Iquitos on the Amazon, near its junction with the Río Napo, this was among the first lodges constructed in the Iquitos area (1964) and remains attractively rustic. The lodge has several large, palm-thatched buildings; the 55 rooms have private cold-water bathrooms. Covered walkways join the buildings and lighting is by kerosene lantern. Lodge offices are in Iquitos.

Guides accompany visitors on several trails that go deeper into the forest. You could arrange a trip to visit this along with one or more of Explorama's other lodges (each of which is very different) combined with a visit to the canopy walkway located near the company's ExplorNapo Lodge (p496). Sample rates are given; contact Explorama for other options and combinations – and discounts.

Muyuna Amazon Lodge   LODGE $$$

(☎ 065-24-2858; www.muyuna.com; s/d in bungalow 4 days & 3 nights per person US$1920/3200) 🍃 About 140km upriver from Iquitos on the Río Yanayacu, this intimate lodge is surrounded by 10 well-conserved lakes in a remote area less colonized than jungle downriver. It makes for a great rainforest experience – and a luxurious one. Fifteen trim, stilted, thatched bungalows each sleep between two and six people and have lovely bathrooms and a balcony with a hammock.

The helpful Peruvian owners have a very hands-on approach to maintaining their lodge, ensuring that recycling occurs and staff set an ecofriendly example to visitors. During high water, the river rises up to the bungalows, which are connected to the lodge's dining building with sweeping covered, raised walkways. Lighting is by kerosene lanterns.

The bilingual guides are excellent and they guarantee observation of monkeys, sloths and dolphins, as well as rich avian fauna typical of the nearby Amazonian *varzea* (flooded forest), including the *piuri* (wattled curassow, *crax globulosa*), a critically endangered bird restricted to western Amazonia, which can only be seen in Peru at Muyuna. One of the most unforgettable activities, however, is setting out from here by canoe at night and paddling through the maze of blackwater tributaries, where the foliage – and often the wildlife – gets within touching distance.

ℹ Getting There & Away

This is an isolated region, mostly accessible only by boat (except Laguna Quistacocha, on the Iquitos–Nauta road). Because of the remote location of the lodges, transportation in and out is generally by the particular lodge's own boat (included in the tour price). Regular public transport does run downriver from Iquitos towards the tri-border with Colombia and Brazil, but this is not practical for visiting lodges or seeing the surrounding scenery.

Understand
Peru

History

In 1532, when Francisco Pizarro landed to conquer Peru in the name of God and the Spanish Crown, the region had already seen the epic rise and fall of civilizations. Yet the conquest changed everything: the economy, political systems, religion and language. Modern history experienced a series of aftershocks from that seismic clash between Inca and Spaniard. It's a conflict embedded in the Peruvian psyche. With it came new cultures, new races, new voices, new cuisines – ultimately, a new civilization.

Earliest Settlers

There is some debate about how long, exactly, there has been a human presence in Peru. Some scholars have suggested that humans occupied the Andes as far back as 14,000 BC (with at least one academic reporting that it could precede even that early date). The most definitive archaeological evidence, however, puts humans in the region at around 8000 BC. Caves in Lauricocha (near Huánuco) and Toquepala (outside Tacna) bear paintings that record hunting scenes from that era. The latter shows a group of hunters cornering and killing what appears to be a group of camelid animals.

In 4000 BC, domestication of llamas and guinea pigs began in the highlands – followed by the farming of potatoes, gourds, cotton, *lúcuma* (an earthy Andean fruit), quinoa, corn and beans. By 2500 BC, once-nomadic hunters and gatherers clustered into settlements along the Pacific, surviving on fishing and agriculture. These early Peruvians lived in simple one-room dwellings, but also built many structures for ceremonial or ritual purposes. Some of the oldest – raised temple platforms facing the ocean and containing human burials – date from the third millennium BC.

In recent years, studies at some of these archaeological sites have revealed that these early societies were far more developed than previously imagined. Along with Egypt, India and China, Peru is considered one of the six cradles of civilization (a site where urbanization accompanied agricultural innovation) – the only one located in the southern hemisphere. Ongoing excavations at Caral, on the coast about 200km north

TIMELINE	8000 BC	c 3000 BC	3000 BC
	Hunting scenes are painted in caves by hunter-gatherers near Huánuco in the central highlands and in Toquepala in the south – early evidence of humans in Peru.	Settlement of Peru's coastal oases begins; some of the first structures are built at the ceremonial center of Caral, north of present-day Lima.	Potatoes, squash, cotton, corn, *lúcuma* fruit and quinoa begin to be farmed; at this point, llamas, alpacas and guinea pigs had likely been domesticated for 1000 years.

of Lima, continue to uncover evidence of what is the oldest civilization in the Americas.

Roughly contemporary to these developments on the coast, a group in the highlands built the enigmatic Temple of Kotosh near Huánuco, whose structures are an estimated 4000 years old. The site features two temple mounds with wall niches and decorative friezes. It represents some of the most sophisticated architecture produced in the highlands during the period.

Clay & Cloth

In the centuries from 1800 BC to about 900 BC, a more sophisticated ceramics and textile production came into being. Some of the earliest pottery from this time comes from coastal archaeological sites at Las Haldas in the Casma Valley, south of Chimbote, and the Huaca La Florida, an unmapped temple structure in the heart of Lima. During this time, ceramics developed from basic undecorated bowls to sculpted, incised vessels of high quality. In the highlands, the people of Kotosh produced skilled pieces fashioned from black, red or brown clay.

The epoch also saw the introduction of looms, which were used to produce plain cotton cloths, as well as improvements in agriculture, including early experimentation with the terrace system.

Chavín Horizon

Lasting roughly from 1000 BC to 300 BC, and named after the site of Chavín de Huántar, this was a rich period of development for Andean culture – when artistic and religious cultures appeared, perhaps independently, over a broad swath of the central and northern highlands, as well as the coast. The salient feature of this era is the repeated representation of a stylized feline deity, perhaps symbolizing spiritual transformations experienced under the influence of hallucinogenic plants. One of the most famous depictions of this many-headed figure can be found on the Raimondi Stela, a bas relief carving that is kept at the Museo Nacional de Antropología, Arqueología e Historia del Perú in Lima.

Chavín's feline also figures prominently in ceramics of the era, particularly the stark, black-clay specimens referred to as Cupisnique, a style that flourished on the northern coast.

Methods of working with gold, silver and copper were also developed during this time, and there were important advances in weaving and architecture. In short, this was a period when culture truly began to blossom in the Andes.

The Tiwanaku were a pre-Inca cultural group that settled the area around Lake Titicaca and are, in many ways, closely linked with the Wari. Margaret Young-Sanchez's *Tiwanaku: Ancestors of the Inca*, provides a lushly illustrated compendium of their art and history.

1000 BC	200 BC	AD 1	200
The Chavín Horizon begins, a period in which various highland and coastal communities share uniform religious deities.	The coastal Nazca culture starts construction of a series of giant glyphs that adorn the desert to this day.	The southern coast sees the rise of the Paracas Necropolis culture, known for its intricate textiles that depict stylized images of warriors, animals and gods.	The Tiwanaku begin their 400-year domination of the area around Lake Titicaca, into what is today Bolivia and northern Chile.

Birth of Local Cultures

After 300 BC, numerous local settlements achieved importance at a regional level. South of Lima, in the area surrounding the Península de Paracas, lived a coastal community whose most significant phase is referred to as Paracas Necropolis (AD 1–400), after a large burial site. It is here that some of the finest pre-Columbian textiles in the Americas have been unearthed: colorful, intricate fabrics that depict oceanic creatures, feline warriors and stylized anthropomorphic figures.

To the south, the people of the Nazca culture (200 BC–AD 600) carved giant, enigmatic designs into the desert landscape that can only be seen from the air. Known as the Nazca Lines, these were mapped early in the 20th century – though their exact purpose remains up for debate. The culture is also known for its fine textile and pottery works, the latter of which used – for the first time in Peruvian history – a polychrome (multicolored) paint technique.

During this time, the Moche culture settled the area around Trujillo between AD 100 and 800. This was an especially artistic group (they produced some of the most remarkable portrait art in history), leaving behind important temple mounds, such as the Huacas del Sol y de la Luna (Temples of the Sun and Moon), near Trujillo, and the burial site of Sipán, outside Chiclayo. The latter contains a series of tombs that have been under excavation since 1987 – one of the most important archaeological discoveries in South America since Machu Picchu.

A catastrophic drought in the latter half of the 6th century may have contributed to the demise of the Moche as a culture.

The portrayal of indigenous people in pop culture tends to be that of benign stewards of a vast wilderness. But Charles C Mann's *1491: New Revelations of the Americas Before Columbus* reveals that the continent was a place of great urbanization and high technological skill. The Incas are prominently featured.

Wari Expansion

As the influence of regional states waned, the Wari, an ethnic group from the Ayacucho Basin, emerged as a force to be reckoned with for 500 years beginning in AD 600. They were vigorous military conquerors who built and maintained important outposts throughout a vast territory that covered an area from Chiclayo to Cuzco. Though their ancient capital lay outside present-day Ayacucho – the ruins of which can still be visited – they also operated the major lowland ceremonial center of Pachacamac, just outside Lima, where people from all over the region came to pay tribute.

As with many conquering cultures, the Wari attempted to suppress other groups by emphasizing their own traditions over local belief. Thus from about AD 700 to 1100, Wari influence is noted in the art, technology and architecture of most areas in Peru. These include elaborate, tie-dyed tunics, and finely woven textiles featuring stylized human figures and geometric patterns, some of which contained a record-breaking 398

500	600	c 800	c 850
In the north, the Moche culture begins construction of the Huacas del Sol y de la Luna, adobe temples situated outside present-day Trujillo.	The Wari emerge from the Ayacucho area and consolidate an empire that covers a territory from Cuzco to Chiclayo; they are closely linked, stylistically, to the Tiwanaku culture of Bolivia.	The fiercely independent Chachapoyas build Kuélap, a citadel in the northern highlands comprising upwards of 400 constructions – including their trademark circular dwellings.	The Chimú begin development of Chan Chan, outside present-day Trujillo, a sprawling adobe urban center.

threads per linear inch. The Wari are most significant, however, for developing an extensive network of roadways and for greatly expanding the terrace agriculture system – an infrastructure that would serve the Inca well when they came into power just a few centuries later.

Regional Kingdoms

The Wari were eventually replaced by a gaggle of small nation-states that thrived from about 1000 until the Inca conquest of the early 15th century. One of the biggest and best studied of these are the Chimú of the Trujillo area, whose capital was the famed Chan Chan, the largest adobe city in the world. Their economy was based on agriculture and they had a heavily stratified society with a healthy craftsman class, which produced painted textiles and beautifully fashioned pottery that is distinctive for its black stain.

Closely connected to the Chimú are the Sicán from the Lambayeque area, renowned metallurgists who produced the *tumi* – a ceremonial knife with a rounded blade used in sacrifices. (The knife has since become a national symbol in Peru and replicas can be found in crafts markets everywhere.)

To the south, in the environs of Lima, the Chancay people (1000–1500) produced fine, geometrically patterned lace and crudely humorous pottery, in which just about every figure seems to be drinking.

In the highlands, several other cultures were significant during this time. In a relatively isolated and inaccessible patch of the Utcubamba Valley in the northern Andes, the cloud-forest-dwelling Chachapoyas people built the expansive mountain settlement of Kuélap, one of the most intriguing and significant highland ruins in the country. To the south, several small altiplano (Andean plateau) kingdoms near Lake Titicaca left impressive *chullpas* (funerary towers). The best remaining examples are at Sillustani and Cutimbo.

The formation of chiefdoms in the Amazon also began during this period.

Enter the Incas

According to Inca lore, their civilization was born when Manco Cápac and his sister Mama Ocllo, children of the sun, emerged from Lake Titicaca to establish a civilization in the Cuzco Valley. Whether Manco Cápac was a historical figure is up for debate, but what is certain is that the Inca civilization was established in the area of Cuzco at some point in the 12th century. The reign of the first several *incas* (kings) is largely unremarkable – and for a couple of centuries it remained a small, regional state.

Guns, Germs & Steel, the Pulitzer Prize–winning book by Jared Diamond, is a thoughtful, biological examination of why some European societies triumphed over so many others. The battle for Cajamarca and Atahualpa's capture by the Spanish is discussed at length.

A classic of the genre, John Hemming's *The Conquest of the Incas,* first published in 1970, is a must-read for anyone wanting to understand the rise and fall of the short-lived Inca empire.

1100–1200	1438–71	1492	1493
The Incas emerge as a presence in Cuzco; according to legend, they were led to the area by a divine figure known as Manco Cápac and his sister Mama Ocllo.	The reign of Inca Yupanqui – also known as Pachacutec – represents a period of aggressive empire-building for the Incas; during this time, Machu Picchu and Saqsaywamán are built.	Funded by the Spanish Crown, Genoa-born Christopher Columbus arrives in the Americas.	Inca Huayna Cápac begins his reign, pushing the empire north to Colombia; his untimely death in 1525 – probably from smallpox – leaves the kingdom fatally divided.

Expansion took off in the early 15th century, when the ninth king, Inca Yupanqui, defended Cuzco – against incredible odds – from the invading Chanka people to the north. After the victory, he took on the boastful new name of 'Pachacutec' ('Transformer of the Earth') and spent the next 25 years bringing much of the Andes under his control. Under his reign, the Inca grew from a regional fiefdom in the Cuzco Valley into a broad empire of about 10 million people known as Tawantinsuyo (Land of Four Quarters). The kingdom covered most of modern Peru, in addition to pieces of Ecuador, Bolivia and Chile. This was made more remarkable by the fact that the Inca, as an ethnicity, never numbered more than about 100,000.

Pachacutec allegedly gave Cuzco its layout in the form of a puma and built fabulous stone monuments in honor of Inca victories, including Sacsaywamán, the temple-fortress at Ollantaytambo and possibly Machu Picchu. He also improved the network of roads that connected the empire, further developed terrace agricultural systems and made Quechua the lingua franca.

Atahualpa's Brief Reign

Inca kings continued the expansions of the empire, first started by Pachacutec. Pachacutec's grandson, Huayna Cápac, who began his rule in 1493, took over much of modern-day Ecuador all the way into Colombia. Consequently, he spent much of his life living, governing and commanding his armies from the north, rather than Cuzco.

By this time, the Spanish presence was already being felt in the Andes. Smallpox and other epidemics transmitted by European soldiers were sweeping through the entire American continent. These were so swift, in fact, that they arrived in Peru before the Spanish themselves, claiming thousands of indigenous lives – including, in all likelihood, that of Huayna Cápac, who succumbed to some sort of plague in 1525.

Without a clear plan of succession, the emperor's untimely death left a power vacuum. The contest turned into a face-off between two of his many children: the Quito-born Atahualpa, who commanded his father's army in the north, and Huáscar, who was based in Cuzco. The ensuing struggle plunged the empire into a bloody civil war, reducing entire cities to rubble. Atahualpa emerged as the victor in April 1532. But the vicious nature of the conflict left the Inca with a lot of enemies throughout the Andes – which is why some tribes were so willing to cooperate with the Spanish when they arrived just five months later.

The Spanish Invade

In 1528 Spaniard Francisco Pizarro and his right-hand-man Diego de Almagro landed in Tumbes, a far-flung outpost on the north coast of Peru.

1532	1572	1609	1611
Atahualpa wins a protracted struggle for control over Inca territories; at virtually the same time, the Spanish land in Peru – in less than a year, Atahualpa is dead, executed by Francisco Pizarro.	Túpac Amaru, the monarch who had established an Inca state independent of the Spanish at Vilcabamba, is captured and beheaded by colonial authorities.	*Mestizo* writer and thinker El Inca Garcilaso de la Vega publishes *Los comentarios reales* (The Royal Commentaries), a celebrated narrative of Inca life before and after the conquest.	Diego Quispe Tito, one of the most renowned painters of the so-called 'Cuzco School' movement of religious painting, is born in the southern highlands.

There, a group of locals offered them meat, fruit, fish and corn beer. A cursory examination of the city revealed an abundance of silver and gold, and Pizarro and De Almagro quickly returned to Spain to court royal support for a bigger expedition.

They returned to Tumbes in September 1532, with a shipload of arms, horses and slaves, as well as a battalion of 168 men. Tumbes, the rich town Pizarro had visited just four years earlier, had been devastated by epidemics, as well as the recent Inca civil war. Atahualpa, in the meantime, was in the process of making his way down from Quito to Cuzco to claim his hard-won throne. When the Spanish arrived, he was in the highland settlement of Cajamarca, enjoying the area's mineral baths.

Pizarro quickly deduced that the empire was in a fractious state. He and his men charted a course to Cajamarca and approached Atahualpa with royal greetings and promises of brotherhood. But the well-mannered overtures quickly devolved into a surprise attack that left thousands of Incas dead and Atahualpa a prisoner of war. (Between their horses, their armor and the steel of their blades, the Spanish were practically invincible against fighters armed only with clubs, slings and wicker helmets.)

In an attempt to regain his freedom, Atahualpa offered the Spanish a bounty of gold and silver. Thus began one of the most infamous ransoms in history – with the Incas attempting to fill an entire room with the precious metals in order to placate the unrelenting appetites of the Spanish. But it was not enough. The Spanish held Atahualpa for eight months before executing him with a garrote at the age of 31.

The Inca empire never recovered from this fateful encounter. The arrival of the Spanish brought on a cataclysmic collapse of indigenous society. One scholar estimates that the native population – around 10 million when Pizarro arrived – was reduced to 600,000 within a century.

Tumultuous Colony

Following Atahualpa's death, the Spanish got to work consolidating their power. On January 6, 1535, Pizarro sketched out his new administrative center in the sands that bordered the Río Rímac on the central coast. This would be Lima, the so-called 'City of Kings' (named in honor of Three Kings' Day), the new capital of the viceroyalty of Peru, an empire that for more than 200 years would cover much of South America.

It was a period of great turmoil. As elsewhere in the Americas, the Spanish ruled by terror. Rebellions erupted regularly. Atahualpa's half-brother Manco Inca (who had originally sided with the Spanish and served as a puppet emperor under Pizarro) tried to regain control of the highlands in 1536 – laying siege to the city of Cuzco for almost a

A full scan of Guamán Poma de Ayala's 17th-century manuscript (complete with illustrations), in which he documents colonial atrocities against indigenous people, can be found on the Danish National Library's website at www.kb.dk/permalink/2006/poma/info/en/frontpage.htm.

1613	1671	1717	1781
Guamán Poma de Ayala pens a 1200-page missive to the Spanish king detailing poor treatment of indigenous people; it lies forgotten until 1908, when it's discovered in a Danish archive.	Santa Rosa de Lima, the patron saint of Peru and the Americas, is canonized by Pope Clement X.	The Spanish Crown establishes the Viceroyalty of New Granada, covering modern-day Ecuador, Colombia and Panama – reducing the Peruvian viceroyalty's power and reach.	Inca noble Túpac Amaru II (born José Gabriel Condorcanqui) is executed by the Spanish in Cuzco after leading an unsuccessful indigenous rebellion.

THE MAKING OF PERU'S SAINTS

The first century of the Peruvian colony produced an unusual number of Catholic saints – five in all. There was the highly venerated Santa Rosa of Lima (1556–1617), a devout *criolla* (Spaniard born in Peru) who took a vow of chastity and practiced physical mortification. (She wore a cilice and slept on a bed of broken glass and pottery.) In addition, there was San Juan Macías (1585–1645), who counseled the needy; and San Martín de Porres (1579–1639), the New World's first black saint.

Why so many? A lot of it had to do with the Spanish program to systematically replace the old indigenous order with its own traditions. Catholic authorities, through a process known as the Extirpation, aimed to eradicate indigenous religious belief by prohibiting ancestor worship and holding ceremonies in which pre-Columbian religious idols were burned. The whole process gave rise to a crop of holy figures that Catholic officials could hold up as examples of piousness. Priests preached the wonders of everyday people who rejected worldly possessions and displayed extreme humility – qualities that the Church was eager to cultivate in its newfound flock. Countless figures were canonized during this time, and those who attained sainthood remain an integral part of Peruvian spiritual culture to this day.

You can see relics from these saints at the Iglesia de Santo Domingo in Lima.

year – but was ultimately forced to retreat. He was stabbed to death by a contingent of Spanish soldiers in 1544.

Throughout this, the Spanish were doing plenty of fighting among themselves, splitting into a complicated series of rival factions, each wanting control of the new empire. In 1538 De Almagro was sentenced to death by strangulation for attempting to take over Cuzco. Three years later, Pizarro was assassinated in Lima by a band of disgruntled De Almagro supporters. Other conquistadors met equally violent fates. Things grew relatively more stable after the arrival of Francisco de Toledo as viceroy, an efficient administrator who brought some order to the emergent colony.

Until independence, Peru was ruled by a series of Spanish-born viceroys, all of whom were appointed by the Crown. Immigrants from Spain held the most prestigious positions, while *criollos* (Spaniards born in Peru) were confined to middle management. *Mestizos* – people of mixed descent – were placed even further down the social scale. Full-blooded *indígenas* resided at the bottom, exploited as *peones* (expendable laborers) in *encomiendas,* a feudal system that granted Spanish colonists land titles that included the property of all the indigenous people living in that area.

Tensions between *indígenas* and Spaniards reached boiling point in the late 18th century, when the Spanish Crown levied a series of new

1810	1821	1826	1845
Painter Pancho Fierro, a watercolorist known for recording daily life, is born in Lima; his paintings helped define a uniquely Peruvian identity.	José de San Martín declares Peru independent, but true sovereignty doesn't come until Simón Bolívar's forces vanquish the Spanish in battles at Junín and Ayacucho three years later.	The last of the Spanish military forces depart from Callao, after which the country descends into a period of anarchy.	Ramón Castilla begins the first of four nonconsecutive presidential terms, bringing some degree of stability to Peru.

taxes that hit indigenous people the hardest. In 1780 José Gabriel Condorcanqui – a descendant of the Inca monarch Túpac Amaru – arrested and executed a Spanish administrator on charges of cruelty. His act unleashed an indigenous rebellion that spread into Bolivia and Argentina. Condorcanqui adopted the name Túpac Amaru II and traveled the region fomenting revolution.

The Spanish reprisal was swift – and brutal. In 1781 the captured indigenous leader was dragged to the main plaza in Cuzco, where he would watch his followers, his wife and his sons killed in a day-long bout of violence, before being drawn and quartered himself. Pieces of his remains were displayed in towns around the Andes as a way of discouraging further insurrection.

Independence

By the early 19th century, *criollos* in many Spanish colonies had grown increasingly dissatisfied with their lack of administrative power and the Crown's heavy taxes, leading to revolutions all over the continent. In Peru, the winds of change arrived from two directions. Argentine revolutionary José de San Martín led independence campaigns in Argentina and Chile, before entering Peru by sea at the port of Pisco in 1820. With San Martín's arrival, royalist forces retreated into the highlands, allowing him to ride into Lima unobstructed. On July 28, 1821, independence was declared. But real independence wouldn't materialize for another three years. With Spanish forces still at large in the interior, San Martín would need more troops to fully defeat the Spanish.

Then came Simón Bolívar, the Venezuelan revolutionary who had been leading independence fights in Venezuela, Colombia and Ecuador. In 1823 the Peruvians gave Bolívar dictatorial powers (an honor that had been bestowed on him in other countries). By the latter half of 1824, he and his lieutenant, Antonio José de Sucre, had routed the Spanish in decisive battles at Junín and Ayacucho. The revolutionaries had faced staggering odds, but nonetheless managed to capture the viceroy and negotiate a surrender. As part of the deal, the Spanish would withdraw all of their forces from Peru and Bolivia.

New Republic

The lofty idealism of the revolution was soon followed by the harsh reality of having to govern. Peru, the young nation, proved to be just as anarchic as Peru, the viceroyalty. Between 1825 and 1841, there was a revolving door of regime changes (two dozen) as regional *caudillos* (chieftains) scrambled for power. The situation improved in the 1840s with the mining of vast deposits of guano off the Peruvian coast; the

Historic Churches

Iglesia de Santo Domingo (Lima)

Catedral de Ayacucho (Ayacucho)

Iglesia de La Compañía de Jesús (Cuzco)

Iglesia de San Pedro (Andahuaylillas)

Monasterio de Santa Catalina (Arequipa)

Basilica Menor Catedral (Trujillo)

1872	1879–83	1892	1895
Scholar Ricardo Palma publishes the first of a series of books – known as the *Tradiciones peruanas* – that chronicle a distinctly *criollo* (Creole) folklore.	Chile wages war against Peru and Bolivia over nitrate-rich lands in the Atacama Desert; Peru loses the conflict – in addition to its southernmost region of Tarapacá.	Poet César Vallejo is born in the highlands; he lives for only 46 years, but his spare phrasing and socially conscious themes make him one of the continent's transformative literary figures.	Nicolás de Piérola is elected president, beginning a period of relative stability buoyed by a booming world economy.

nitrate-rich bird droppings reaped unheard-of profits as fertilizer on the international market.

The country would find some measure of stability under the governance of Ramón Castilla (a *mestizo*), who would be elected to his first term in 1845. The income from the guano boom – which he had been key in exploiting – helped Castilla make needed economic improvements. He abolished slavery, paid off some of Peru's debt and established a public school system. Castilla served as president three more times over the course of two decades – at times, by force; at others, in an interim capacity; at one point, for less than a week. Following his final term, he was exiled by competitors who wanted to neutralize him politically.

He died in 1867, in northern Chile, attempting to make his way back to Peru. (Visitors can see his impressive crypt at the Panteón de los Proceres in Central Lima.)

In Lima from the 16th to 19th centuries many women donned head scarves that obscured everything but one eye, leading locals to dub them *las tapadas* (the covered ones). The origins of the tradition are unclear (some say it is Moorish), but the practice allowed women to venture out alone in public.

War of the Pacific

With Castilla's passing, the country once again descended into chaos. A succession of *caudillos* squandered the enormous profits of the guano boom and, in general, managed the economy in a deplorable fashion. Moreover, military skirmishes would ensue with Ecuador (over border issues) and Spain (which was trying to dominate its former South American colonies). The conflicts left the nation's coffers empty. By 1874 Peru was bankrupt.

This left the country in a weak position to deal with the expanding clash between Chile and Bolivia over nitrate-rich lands in the Atacama Desert. Borders in this area had never been clearly defined and escalating tensions eventually led to military engagement. To make matters worse for the Peruvians, President Mariano Prado abandoned the country for Europe on the eve of the conflict. The war was a disaster for Peru at every level (not to mention Bolivia, which lost its entire coastline).

Despite the brave actions of military figures such as Admiral Miguel Grau, the Chileans were simply better organized and had more resources, including the support of the British. In 1881 they led a land campaign deep into Peru, occupying the capital of Lima, during which time they ransacked the city, making off with the priceless contents of the National Library. By the time the conflict came to a close in 1883, Peru had permanently lost its southernmost region of Tarapacá – and it wouldn't regain the area around Tacna until 1929.

A New Intellectual Era

As the 20th century loomed, things were looking up for Peru. A buoyant world economy helped fuel an economic recovery through the export of sugar, cotton, rubber, wool and silver. And, in 1895, Nicolás de Piérola

1911	1924	1928	1932
US historian Hiram Bingham arrives at the ruins of Machu Picchu; his 'discovery' of the ancient city is chronicled in *National Geographic*.	Northern political leader Víctor Raúl Haya de la Torre founds APRA, a populist, anti-imperialist political party that is immediately declared illegal.	Journalist and thinker José Carlos Mariátegui publishes the *Seven Interpretive Essays on Peruvian Reality*, which heavily critiques the feudal nature of his country's society.	More than 1000 APRA party followers are executed by the military at the ancient ruins of Chan Chan, following an uprising in Trujillo.

was elected president – beginning an era known as the 'Aristocratic Republic.' Hospitals and schools were constructed and de Piérola undertook a campaign to build highways and railroads.

This period would witness a sea change in Peruvian intellectual thought. The late 19th century had been an era in which many thinkers (primarily in Lima) had tried to carve out the notion of an inherently Peruvian identity – one largely based on *criollo* experience. Key among them was Ricardo Palma, a scholar and writer renowned for rebuilding Lima's ransacked National Library. Beginning in 1872, he published a series of books on *criollo* folklore known as the *Tradiciones peruanas* (Peruvian Traditions) – now required reading for every Peruvian schoolchild.

But as one century gave way to the next, intellectual circles saw the rise of *indigenismo,* a continent-wide movement that advocated for a dominant social and political role for indigenous people. In Peru this translated into a wide-ranging (if fragmented) cultural movement. Historian Luis Valcárcel attacked his society's degradation of the indigenous class. Poet César Vallejo wrote critically acclaimed works that took on indigenous oppression as themes. And José Sabogal led a generation of visual artists who explored indigenous themes in their paintings. In 1928 journalist and thinker José Carlos Mariátegui penned a seminal Marxist work – *Seven Interpretive Essays on Peruvian Reality* – in which he criticized the feudal nature of Peruvian society and celebrated the communal aspects of the Inca social order. (It remains vital reading for the Latin American Left to this day.)

In this climate, in 1924, Trujillo-born political leader Victor Raúl Haya de la Torre founded the Alianza Popular Revolucionaria Americana (American Popular Revolutionary Alliance) – otherwise known as APRA. The party espoused populist values, celebrated 'Indo-America' and rallied against US imperialism. It was quickly declared illegal by the autocratic regime of Augusto Leguía – and remained illegal for long stretches of the 20th century. Haya de la Torre, at various points in his life, lived in hiding and in exile and, during one period, endured a 15-month stint as a political prisoner.

Dictatorships & Revolutionaries

After the start of the Great Depression in 1929, the country's history becomes a blur of dictatorships punctuated by periods of democracy. Leguía, a sugar baron from the north coast, ruled on a couple of occasions: for his first period in office (1908–12) he was elected; for the second (1919–30), he made it in via a coup d'état. He spent his first term dealing with a morass of border conflicts and the second, stifling press freedom and political dissidents.

It is possible to browse original research materials dating back to the colony (from simple text to scanned communiqués) on the website of the Biblioteca Nacional (National Library). Go to www.bnp.gob.pe and click on 'Biblioteca Digital.'

Peru's exports of guano in the mid-19th century totaled more than US$20 million a year – more than US$517 million a year by today's standards. In 1869 the country was exporting more than half a million tons of the nitrate-rich fertilizer per year.

1948	1962	1968	1970
General Manuel Odría assumes power for eight years, encouraging foreign investment and cracking down on the APRA movement.	Mario Vargas Llosa publishes *La ciudad y los perros* (*The Time of the Hero*), an experimental novel set at a military academy in Lima.	General Juan Velasco Alvarado takes power in a coup d'état; in his seven years in office, he promulgates a populist agenda that involves 'Peruvianization' of all industry.	A 7.7-magnitude earthquake in northern Peru kills almost 80,000 people, and leaves 140,000 injured and another 500,000 homeless.

Legúia was followed by Colonel Luis Sánchez Cerro, who served a couple of short terms in the 1930s. (Though his time in office was turbulent, Sánchez would be celebrated in some sectors for abolishing a conscription law that required able-bodied men to labor on road-building projects. The law affected poor indigenous men disproportionately, as they couldn't afford to pay the exemption fee.) By 1948 another dictator had taken power: former army colonel Manuel Odría, who spent his time in office cracking down on the APRA and encouraging US foreign investment.

The most fascinating of Peru's 20th-century dictators, however, is Juan Velasco Alvarado, the former commander-in-chief of the army who took control in 1968. Though he was expected to lead a conservative regime, Velasco turned out to be an inveterate populist – so much so that some APRA members complained that he had stolen their party platform away from them. He established a nationalist agenda that included 'Peruvianizing' (securing Peruvian majority ownership) various industries. In his rhetoric he celebrated the indigenous peasantry, championed a radical program of agrarian reform and made Quechua an official language. He also severely restricted press freedom, which drew the wrath of the power structure in Lima. Ultimately, his economic policies were failures – and in 1975, in declining health, he was replaced by another, more conservative military regime.

Internal Conflict

Peru returned to civilian rule in 1980, when President Fernando Belaúnde Terry was elected to office – the first election in which leftist parties were allowed to participate – including APRA, which was now legal. Belaúnde's term was anything but smooth. Agrarian and other social reforms took a back seat as the president tried desperately to jump-start the moribund economy.

It was at this time that a radical Maoist group from the poor region of Ayacucho began its unprecedented rise. Founded by philosophy professor Abimael Guzmán, Sendero Luminoso (Shining Path) wanted nothing less than an overthrow of the social order via violent armed struggle. Over the next two decades, the situation escalated into a phantasmagoria of violence, with the group assassinating political leaders and community activists, carrying out attacks on police stations and universities and, at one point, stringing up dead dogs all over downtown Lima. (Its actions earned the group a place on the US State Department's list of foreign terrorist organizations.) At the same time, another leftist guerrilla group sprang into action – the Movimiento Revolucionario Túpac Amaru (MRTA), which focused its attacks on the police and the armed forces.

Most Influential Writers

El Inca Garcilaso de la Vega, chronicler

Ricardo Palma, folklorist

Abraham Valdelomar, essayist

César Vallejo, poet

José Carlos Mariátegui, political theorist

Mario Vargas Llosa, novelist

1980	1980	1983	1985
Guerrilla group Sendero Luminoso (Shining Path) takes its first violent action – burning ballot boxes – in the Ayacucho region; the incident draws little notice from the press.	Fernando Belaúnde Terry becomes the first democratically elected president after a 12-year military dictatorship, but his term is plagued by economic instability and violence in the Andes.	In one of the more high-profile massacres of the internal conflict, eight journalists are murdered in the Andean town of Uchuraccay.	Alan García becomes president, but his term is marked by hyperinflation and increased attacks by terrorist groups; he flees the country in 1992, plagued by allegations of embezzlement.

To quell the violence, the government sent in the military, a heavy-handed outfit that knew little about handling a guerrilla insurgency. There was torture and rape, plus disappearances and massacres, none of which did anything to put a stop to Sendero Luminoso. Caught in the middle were tens of thousands of poor *campesinos* (peasants), who bore the brunt of the violence.

In the midst of this, Alan García was elected to the presidency in 1985. Initially, his ascent generated a great deal of hope. Young, a gifted public speaker and popular, he was the first member of the storied APRA party to win a presidential election. But his economic program was catastrophic (his decision to nationalize the banks and suspend foreign-debt payments led to economic ruin), and, by the late 1980s, Peru faced a staggering hyperinflation rate of 7500%. Thousands of people were plunged into poverty. There were food shortages and riots. Throughout this, Sendero Luminoso and MRTA stepped up attacks. The government was forced to declare a state of emergency.

Two years after completing his term, García fled the country after being accused of embezzling millions of dollars. He would return to Peru in 2001, when the statute of limitations on his case finally ran out.

Fujishock

With the country in a state of chaos, the 1990 presidential elections took on more importance than ever. The contest was between famed novelist Mario Vargas Llosa and Alberto Fujimori, a little-known agronomist of Japanese descent. During the campaign, Vargas Llosa promoted an economic 'shock treatment' program that many feared would send more Peruvians into poverty, while Fujimori positioned himself as an alternative to the status quo. Fujimori won handily. But as soon as he got into office, he implemented an even more austere economic plan that, among other things, drove up the price of gasoline by 3000%. The measures, known as 'Fujishock,' ultimately succeeded in reducing inflation and stabilizing the economy – but not without costing the average Peruvian dearly.

Fujimori followed this, in April 1992, with an *autogolpe* (coup from within). He dissolved the legislature and generated an entirely new congress, one stocked with his allies. Peruvians, not unused to *caudillos*, tolerated the power grab, hoping that Fujimori might help stabilize the economic and political situation – which he did. The economy grew. And by the end of the year, leaders of both Sendero Luminoso and MRTA had been apprehended (though, not before Sendero Luminoso had assassinated community activist María Elena Moyano and detonated lethal truck bombs in Lima's tony Miraflores district).

The Internal Conflict, however, wasn't over. In December 1996, 14 members of MRTA stormed the Japanese ambassador's residence,

Shining Path founder Abimael Guzmán took the name 'Sendero Luminoso' from a maxim by writer and Communist Party founder José Carlos Mariátegui: 'Marxism-Leninism will open the shining path to revolution.'

1987	1990	1992	1992
Archaeologists working near Lambayeque uncover a rare, undisturbed tomb of a Moche warrior-priest known as El Señor de Sipán.	Alberto Fujimori is elected president; his authoritarian rule leads to improvements in the economy, but charges of corruption plague his administration.	Sendero Luminoso detonates truck bombs in Miraflores, Lima, killing 25 and wounding scores more; following this act, public opinion turns decisively against the guerrillas.	Abimael Guzmán, the founder of Sendero Luminoso, is captured in Lima after he is found hiding out above a dance studio in the well-to-do neighborhood of Surco.

A NOBEL FOR PERU

In 2010 Mario Vargas Llosa (b 1936), Peru's most famous living writer, was awarded the Nobel Prize for Literature for work that explored the vagaries of love, power and corruption. The honorific caps an extraordinary life: as a young man, Vargas Llosa had an affair with an uncle's sister-in-law, whom he later married (an incident he fictionalized in *Aunt Julia and the Scriptwriter*). In the 1970s, he came to blows with Colombian Nobel Laureate Gabriel García Márquez for reasons that have never been revealed. The following decade he ran for the presidency – and lost. Over his life he has produced novels, short stories, plays and political essays. Upon winning the Nobel Prize, he told a reporter: 'Death will find me with my pen in hand.'

taking hundreds of prominent people hostage, and demanding that the government release imprisoned MRTA members, among other things. Most of the hostages were released early on, though 72 men were held until the following April – at which point, Peruvian commandos stormed the embassy, killing all the captors and releasing the surviving hostages.

By the end of his second term, Fujimori's administration was plagued by allegations of corruption. He ran for a third term in 2000 (which was technically unconstitutional) and remained in power despite the fact that he didn't have the simple majority necessary to claim the election. Within the year, however, he was forced to flee the country after it was revealed that his security chief Vladimiro Montesinos had been embezzling government funds and bribing elected officials and the media. (Many of these acts were caught on film: the 'Vladivideos' – all 2700 of them – riveted the nation when they first aired in 2001.) Fujimori formally resigned the presidency from abroad, but the legislature rejected the gesture, voting him out of office and declaring him 'morally unfit' to govern.

Peru, however, hadn't heard the last of Fujimori. In 2005 he returned to South America, only to be arrested in Chile on long-standing charges of corruption, kidnapping and human-rights violations. He was extradited to Peru in 2007 and, that same year, was convicted of ordering an illegal search. Two years later, he was convicted of ordering extrajudicial killings, and three months after that, he was convicted of channeling millions of dollars in state funds to Montesinos. Montesinos was sentenced to 20 years for bribery and selling arms to Colombian rebels. In 2009 Fujimori also pleaded guilty to wiretapping and bribery. He was serving 25 years in prison when he was pardoned in 2017 by President Pedro Pablo Kuczynski.

For students of Peruvian history, *The Peru Reader* by Orin Starn, Carlos Iván Degregori and Robin Kirk (Duke University Press, 2005) provides an indispensable collection of articles covering every historical era – from excerpts of Spanish chronicles to essays on the cocaine economy.

1994	1996	2000	2001
Chef Gastón Acurio opens Astrid y Gastón in the Lima neighborhood of Miraflores; the restaurant helps catapult Peruvian cuisine to international levels.	Guerrillas from the Movimiento Revolucionario Túpac Amaru (MRTA) storm the Japanese ambassador's residence in Lima and hold 72 hostages for four months.	Fujimori flees to Japan after videos surface showing his intelligence chief bribing officials and the media; the Peruvian legislature votes him out of office.	Alejandro Toledo becomes the first indigenous person to govern an Andean country.

The 21st Century

The new millennium has, thus far, been pretty good to Peru. In 2001, shoeshine-boy-turned-Stanford-economist Alejandro Toledo became the first person of Quechua ethnicity to be elected to the presidency. (Until then, Peru had had *mestizo* presidents, but never an *indígena*.) Unfortunately, Toledo inherited a political and economic mess. This was amplified by the fact that he lacked a majority in congress, hampering his effectiveness in the midst of an economic recession.

Toledo was followed in office by – of all people – the APRA's Alan García, who was re-elected in 2006. His second term was infinitely more stable than the first. The economy performed well and the government invested money in upgrading infrastructure such as ports, highways and the electricity grid. But it wasn't without problems. For one, there was the issue of corruption (García's entire cabinet was forced to resign in 2008 after widespread allegations of bribery) and the touchy issue of how to manage the country's mineral wealth was an ongoing problem. In 2008 García signed a law that allowed foreign companies to exploit natural resources in the Amazon. The legislation generated a backlash among various Amazon tribes and led to a fatal standoff in the northern city of Bagua in 2009.

The Peruvian congress quickly revoked the law, but this issue remained a challenge for President Ollanta Humala, elected in 2011. Having campaigned on a broader inclusion of all social classes, he passed the Prior Consultation Law, historic new legislation to guarantee indigenous

Forgotten Continent: The Battle for Latin America's Soul is an acclaimed (if dense) political tome by *Economist* contributor Michael Reid. Published in 2009, it examines the continent's strained relations with the US and Europe, as well as its economic and political development in the last three decades.

IN THE WAKE OF THE INTERNAL CONFLICT

One of the most remarkable things to come out of Alejandro Toledo's presidency (2001–06) was the establishment of the country's Comisión de la Verdad y Reconciliación (Truth and Reconciliation Commission), which examined the innumerable acts of mass violence from the Internal Conflict (1980–2000). Though the panel wasn't endowed with prosecutorial powers, its public hearings nonetheless proved to be an emotional and cathartic act. Men and women of all ages and races came forward to testify to the massacres, rapes and disappearances that had occurred at the hands of the military and various guerrilla groups during this period.

In August 2003, the commission issued its final report, revealing that the death toll from that era was more than twice the original estimate: almost 70,000 people had been killed or disappeared. Along with the final report, the commission also staged an exhibit of photography called *Yuyanapaq* ('to remember' in Quechua) that is now housed at Lima's Museo de la Nación. Even as the years pass, this poignant installation remains a profoundly moving experience.

2003	2005	2009	2011
The country's Truth and Reconciliation Commission releases its final report on Peru's internal conflict; estimates of the dead reach 70,000.	Construction of the Interoceánica (Trans-oceanic Hwy), which opens an overland trade route between Peru and Brazil, begins in the southern Amazon Basin.	Fujimori is convicted of embezzlement; this is in addition to prior convictions for authorizing an illegal search and ordering military death squads to carry out extrajudicial killings.	Populist former army officer Ollanta Humala assumes the presidency after winning a tight run-off election against Fujimori's daughter Keiko.

people rights to consent to projects affecting them and their lands. The former army officer was initially thought to be a populist in the vein of former Venzuelan president Hugo Chávez (the Lima stock exchange dropped precipitously when he was first elected). But his administration was quite friendly to business. Though the economy functioned well under his governance, civil unrest over a proposed gold mine in the north, as well as a botched raid on a Sendero Luminoso encampment in the highlands, sent his approval rating into a tailspin by the middle of 2012.

While the explosive growth spurt of the early part of the millennium has slowed down, the country has become far more stable than in previous decades. The 2016 elections saw Pedro Pablo Kuczynski beat Keiko Fujimori, daughter of the former president.

In 2017, Kuczynski was involved in a corruption scandal in which he was found to have taken payoffs from a construction company. He avoided impeachment due to a lack of votes – despite later evidence which showed his supporters were buying votes to save his presidency. He resigned prior to a second scheduled impeachment vote and was replaced by Vice President Martin Vizcarra in 2018.

Scandals continued into 2020 compounded by the emergence of the coronavirus pandemic that hit Peru early and hard. With GDP falling 30% and the country logging a higher death rate per million than any other South American nation except Brazil, problems quickly mounted.

President Vizcarra was impeached twice in 2020 on charges of 'influence peddling' and 'moral incapacity'. He was ultimately removed from office on the second charge in November 2020 and replaced by far-right leader, Manuel Merino.

Accused of staging a 'coup', Merino lasted a mere five days in office after a violent crackdown marred massive protests in several Peruvian cities. It was left to centrist leader Francisco Sagasti to pick up the pieces and try to restore some calm.

At the time of writing, Peru's long-term future was to be decided in the 2021 presidential elections, a close run-off between left-leaning Pedro Castillo and right-wing populist Keiko Fujimori (daughter of former president, Alberto Fujimori). A winner had not been formally announced by electoral authorities in the weeks after the ballet of 6 June.

2011	2016	2018	2020
A state of emergency is declared in four provinces following massive protests against mining projects, due to environmental concerns.	Economist Pedro Pablo Kuczynski wins the presidential race against Keiko Fujimori.	Facing scandals and impeachment, President Kuczynski resigns from office and is succeeded by Vice President Martín Vizcarra.	Political crises, violent protests and the coronavirus pandemic see Peru getting through three presidents in less than two weeks.

Peru's Cuisine

In Peru, fusion is a natural part of everyday cooking. Over the past 400 years, Andean stews have mingled with Asian stir-fries, and Spanish rice dishes have absorbed Amazonian flavors, to produce the country's famed *criollo* cooking. More recently, a generation of experimental young innovators has pushed local fare to gastronomic heights. You'll never go hungry in Peru: from humble spots in Moyobamba to trendy boîtes in Miraflores, this is a country devoted to creatively keeping the human palate entertained.

Embracing Local Cuisine

Peru, once a country where important guests were treated to French meals and Scotch whiskey, is now a place where high-end restaurants spotlight deft interpretations of Andean favorites, including quinoa and *cuy* (guinea pig). The dining scene has blossomed. And tourism outfits have swept in to incorporate a culinary something as part of every tour. In 2000 the country became the site of the first Cordon Bleu academy in Latin America, and in 2009 *Bon Appétit* magazine named Lima the 'next great food city.' In 2017 three Lima restaurants made the list of the World's Best Restaurants, with Virgilio Martínez earning the Chefs Choice Award. And the honors roll on. Of Peru's 3.1 million annual visitors, 40% do gastronomic tourism. And maybe you should too.

Foodie fever has infected Peruvians at every level, with even the most humble *chicharrón* (fried pork) vendor hyperattentive to the vagaries of preparation and presentation. No small part of this is due to mediagenic celebrity chef Gastón Acurio, whose culinary skill and business acumen (he owns dozens of restaurants around the globe) have given him rock-star status.

First published in 2001, *The Exotic Kitchens of Peru* by Copeland Marks is not only a comprehensive guide to traditional cooking, but a good source of insight into the history of many dishes.

Staples & Specialties

Given the country's craggy topography, there's an infinite variety in regional cuisines. But at a national level much of the country's cooking begins and ends with the humble potato – which originally hails from the Andes. (All potatoes can be traced back to a single progenitor from Peru.)

Standout dishes include *ocopa* (potatoes with a spicy peanut sauce), *papa a la huancaína* (potato topped with a creamy cheese sauce) and *causa* (mashed potato terrines stuffed with seafood, vegetables or chicken). Also popular is *papa rellena*, a mashed potato filled with ground beef and then deep-fried. Potatoes are also found in the chowder-like soups known as *chupe* and in *lomo saltado,* the simple beef stir-fries that headline every Peruvian menu.

Other popular items include tamales (corn cakes), which are made in various regional variations – such as *humitas* (created with fresh corn) and *juanes* (made with rice or cassava).

Coast

The coast is all about seafood – and ceviche, naturally, plays a starring role. A chilled concoction of fish, shrimp or other seafood marinated in lime juice, onions, cilantro and chili peppers, it is typically served with a wedge of boiled corn and sweet potato. The fish is cooked in the citrus juices through a process of oxidation. (Some chefs, however, have begun to cut back on their marinating time, which means that some ceviches are served at a sushi-like consistency.) Another popular seafood cocktail is *tiradito,* a Japanese-inflected ceviche consisting of thin slices of fish served without onions, sometimes bathed in a creamy hot-pepper sauce.

Cooked fish can be prepared dozens of ways: *al ajo* (in garlic), *frito* (fried) or *a la chorrillana* (cooked in white wine, tomatoes and onions), the latter of which hails from the city of Chorrillos, south of Lima. Soups and stews are also a popular staple, including *aguadito* (a soupy risotto), *picante* (a spicy stew) and *chupe* (bisque) – all of which can feature fish, seafood and other ingredients.

Other items that make a regular appearance on seafood menus are *conchitas a la parmesana* (scallops baked with cheese), *pulpo al olivo* (octopus in a smashed olive sauce) and *choros a la chalaca* (chilled mussels with fresh corn salsa). On the north coast, around Chiclayo, omelets made with manta ray *(tortilla de manta raya)* are a typical dish.

None of this means that pork, chicken or beef aren't popular. *Aji de gallina* (shredded chicken-walnut stew) is a Peruvian classic. In the north, a couple of local dishes bear repeat sampling: *arroz con pato a la chiclayana* (duck and rice simmered in cilantro), typical of Chiclayo) and *seco de cabrito* (goat stewed in cilantro, chilis and beer).

Along the coast, where the Asian presence is most significant, you will also find the Peruvian-Chinese restaurants known as *chifas*. The cuisine is largely Cantonese-influenced: simple dishes low on heavy sauces.

Highlands

In the chilly highlands, it's all about soups – which tend to be a generous, gut-warming experience, filled with vegetables, squash, potatoes, locally grown herbs and a variety of meats. *Sopa a la criolla* (a mild, creamy noodle soup with beef and peppers) is a regular item on menus, as is *caldo de gallina* (a nourishing chicken soup with potatoes and herbs). In the area around Arequipa, *chupe de camarones* (chowder made from river shrimp) is also a mainstay.

The highlands are also known as the source of all things *cuy*. It is often served roasted or *chactado* (pressed under hot rocks). It tastes very similar to rabbit and is often served whole. River trout – prepared myriad ways – is also popular.

Arequipa has a particularly dynamic regional cuisine. The area is renowned for its *picantes* (spicy stews served with chunks of white cheese), *rocoto relleno* (red chilis stuffed with meat) and *solterito* (bean salad).

For special occasions and weddings, families will gather to make *pachamanca:* a mix of marinated meats, vegetables, cheese, chilis and fragrant herbs baked on hot rocks in the ground.

Amazon

Though not as popular throughout the entire country, Amazon ingredients have begun to make headway in recent years. Several high-end restaurants in Lima have started giving gourmet treatment to jungle mainstays, to wide acclaim. This includes the increased use of river snails and fish (including *paiche* and *doncella*), as well as produce such as *aguaje* (the fruit of the moriche palm), yucca (cassava) and *chonta* (hearts of palm). *Juanes* (a bijao leaf stuffed with rice, yucca, chicken and/or pork) is a savory area staple.

Sumptuous photographs and recipes are available in Tony Custer and Miguel Etchepare's hardback two-volume tome *The Art of Peruvian Cuisine.* Visit www.art perucuisine.com for mouthwatering previews.

Cuy – otherwise known as guinea pig – was an important source of protein for pre-Columbian people all over the Andes. In recent years Peru has begun testing the export market: the guinea pig is high in protein, but low in fat and cholesterol.

Desserts

Desserts tend to be hypersweet concoctions. *Suspiro limeño* is the most famous, consisting of *manjar blanco* (caramel) topped with sweet meringue. Also popular are *alfajores* (cookie sandwiches with caramel) and *crema volteada* (flan). Lighter and fruitier is *mazamorra morada,* a purple-corn pudding of Afro-Peruvian origin that comes with chunks of fruit.

During October, bakeries sell *turrón de Doña Pepa,* a sticky, molasses-drenched cake eaten in honor of the Lord of Miracles.

Drinks

Beer & Wine

The craft-beer trend has come to Peru, with interesting innovations such as quinoa beer. Small-batch brewers have popped up in Huaraz, Cuzco and Lima. The best-known mainstream brands of beer are Pilsen Callao, Brahma, Cristal and Cusqueña, all of which are light lagers. Arequipeña and Trujillana are regional brews served in and around those cities. In the Andes, homemade *chicha* (fermented corn beer) is very popular. It tastes lightly sweet and is low in alcoholic content. In rural Andes villages, a red flag posted near a door indicates that *chicha* is available.

Local wines have improved greatly over the years. The best local labels are Tabernero, Tacama, Ocucaje and Vista Alegre.

Pisco

It is the national beverage – the omnipresent grape brandy served at events from the insignificant to the momentous.

Production dates back to the early days of the Spanish colony in Ica, where it was distilled on private haciendas and then sold to sailors making their way through the port of Pisco. In its early years, pisco

The dessert turrón de Doña Pepa was first made by a slave woman, in 1800, to honor the Christ of Miracles after she regained the use of her paralyzed arms.

PERU'S CUISINE DESSERTS

TOP EATS

Collectively, Lonely Planet's writers spent months on the road and ate hundreds of meals. Herewith, a list of the places so good they brought tears to our eyes and unbridled joy to our palates:

Arequipa At Zig Zag (p159), the succulent combination meat plate of alpaca, beef and lamb, cooked over hot volcanic rocks, is a carnivore's delight.

Cajamarca Antifusion restaurant Salas (p418) meticulously prepares the full gamut of typical *Cajamarquiño* dishes according to classic recipes.

Cuzco Elegant Uchu (p233) serves stone-grilled alpaca with piquant sauces. You can also order off the menu of Marcelo Batata – twice-baked Andean potatoes are a must!

Huancayo Dip into the creamiest *papas a la huancaína* (steamed potatoes served with a cheese sauce) in a flower-filled courtyard at Huancahuasi (p297).

Iquitos Set at the mouth of the Río Itaya, Al Frío y al Fuego (p490) has excellent night-time views of Iquitos and scrumptious dishes crafted from Amazon river fish.

Lima The aphrodisiacal ceviche found in Barra Chalaca (p88), El Punto Azul (p92) and La Mar (p93).

Máncora Hyperfresh yellowfin tuna drawn straight from the Pacific is worth the price at La Sirena d'Juan (p362).

Tarapoto At La Patarashca (p443) don't miss the namesake dish – traditional platters of fresh-grilled Amazon fish or shrimp doused in tomatoes, garlic and cilantro.

Trujillo The bamboo-lined Mar Picante (p328) is known for serving behemoth orders of divine *ceviche mixto,* piled high with shrimp, fish, crab and scallops.

NOVOANDINA & THE PERUVIAN NEW WAVE

Today's Peruvian gastronomic renaissance has its roots in the 1980s. The country was in turmoil. The economy was in a free-fall. And newspaper publisher Bernardo Roca Rey was experimenting with Andean ingredients in his kitchen – roasting *cuy*, using rare strains of potatoes and producing risottos made with quinoa (a dish now known as *quinotto*). At the same time, Cucho La Rosa, the chef at El Comensal (since closed), was upgrading Peruvian recipes by improving cooking techniques: gentle steaming instead of boiling; searing instead of frying. These early figures detailed their discoveries in newspaper articles and recipe booklets. The cuisine was dubbed *novoandina* (Peruvian nouvelle cuisine) – but given the challenges of that period, it never quite ignited as a full-blown movement.

By 1994, however, circumstances had changed. The economy was in recovery and the political situation was beginning to improve. When Gastón Acurio (who studied cooking at Le Cordon Bleu in Paris) opened Astrid y Gastón in Lima, he applied many of the same principles as the *novoandina* pioneers before him: interpreting Peruvian cooking through the lens of haute cuisine. The restaurant quickly became a place of pilgrimage. Other innovative new-wave chefs have since followed, including Rafael Piqueras and Pedro Miguel Schiaffino. Collectively, they have expanded the definition of *novoandina*, adding European, Chinese and Japanese ingredients and influences – in the process, transforming Peruvian food into a global cultural phenomenon.

Novoandina is now pushing even further, experimenting with molecular gastronomy, and ancient foods and growing techniques. Chef Virgilio Martínez of Central is developing terraced crops to experiment with growing practices similar to those used by the Incas. Meanwhile, even among everyday diners, the local palette is becoming ever bolder.

Most Influential Chefs

Gastón Acurio at Astrid y Gastón and others

Virgilio Martínez at Central and MIL

Mitsuharu Tsumura at Maido

Francesca Ferreyros at IK

Pedro Miguel Schiaffino at Malabar and ámaZ

Rafael Osterling at Rafael and El Mercado

Marilú Madueño at Huaca Pucllana

was the local firewater: a great way to get ripped – and wake up the following morning feeling as if you had been hammered over the head. By the early 20th century, the pisco sour (pisco with lime juice and sugar) arrived on the scene, and quickly became the national drink. In recent decades, as production has become more sophisticated, piscos have become more nuanced and flavorful (without the morning-after effects).

The three principal types of Peruvian pisco are Quebranta, Italia and Acholado. Quebranta (a pure-smelling pisco) and Italia (slightly aromatic) are each named for the varieties of grape from which they are crafted, while Acholado is a blend of varietals that has more of an alcohol top note (best for mixed drinks). There are many small-batch specialty piscos made from grape must (pressed juice with skins), known as *mosto verde*. These have a fragrant smell and are best sipped straight.

The most common brands include Tres Generaciones, Ocucaje, Ferreyros and La Botija, while Viñas de Oro, Viejo Tonel, Estirpe Peruano, LaBlanco and Gran Cruz are among the finest. Any pisco purchased in a bottle that resembles the head of an Inca will make for an unusual piece of home decor – and not much else.

Where to Eat & Drink

For the most part, restaurants in Peru are a community affair, and local places will cater to a combination of families, tourists, teenagers and packs of chatty businesspeople. At lunchtime, many eateries offer a *menú* – a set meal consisting of two or three courses. This is generally good value. (Note: if you request the *menú*, you'll get the special. If you want the menu, ask for *la carta*.)

Cevicherías – places where ceviche is sold – are popular along the coast, and most commonly open for lunchtime service, as most places proudly serve fish that is at its freshest. In the countryside, informal local restaurants known as *picanterías* are a staple. In some cases these operate right out of someone's home.

Quick Eats

Peru has a vibrant street-food culture. The most popular items are *anticuchos* (beef-heart skewers), ceviche, tamales, boiled quail eggs and *choclo con queso* (corn with cheese). Also popular, and quite delicious, are *picarones* (sweet doughnut fritters) usually served with sweet syrup.

For a cheap and tasty meal, check out the many *pollerías* (spit-roasted chicken joints) found just about everywhere.

Vegetarians & Vegans

In a country where many folks survive on nothing but potatoes, there can be a general befuddlement over why anyone would choose to be vegetarian. This attitude has started to change, however, and some of the bigger cities have restaurants catering exclusively to vegetarians. In recent years, Lima and Cuzco have become progressive centers for vegetarian and sustainable dining, with raw food, organic and vegan options that finally befit their ambitious fine-dining scenes.

In addition, you can always find vegetarian dishes at a regular Peruvian restaurant. Many of the potato salads, such as *papas a la huancaína, ocopa* and *causa* are made without meat, as is *palta a la jardinera,* an avocado stuffed with vegetables. *Sopa de verduras* (vegetable soup), *tortilla* (Spanish omelet) and *tacu-tacu* (beans and rice pan-fried together) are other options. *Chifas* can also be a good source of vegetarian meals. Before ordering, however, ask if these are *platos vegetarianos* (vegetarian dishes). The term *sin carne* (without meat) refers only to red meat or pork, so you could end up with chicken or seafood instead.

Vegans will have a harder time in conventional restaurants. Peruvian cuisine is based on eggs and dairy and infinite combinations thereof. There are grocery stores and a handful of eateries with gluten-free options, mostly in tourist centers.

If you want an encyclopedic primer on Peruvian cooking, look no further than Gaston Acurio's *Peru: The Cookbook,* published in 2015.

Ancient Peru

A *pachacuti,* **according to the Incas, was a cataclysmic event dividing the different ages of history. For the indigenous cultures of 16th-century Peru, the arrival of the Spanish was the most earth-shattering** *pachacuti* **imaginable. The conquerors obliterated native history: melting gold objects, immolating religious icons and banning long-held traditions. Not a single Andean culture left behind a written language. Historians are still piecing together Peru's pre-Columbian history. Thankfully, the physical legacy – from sumptuous textiles and striking ceramics to monumental structures – is bountiful.**

Caral

Just a couple of hundred kilometers north of Lima is one of the most exciting archaeological sites in Peru. It may not look like much – half a dozen dusty temple mounds, a few sunken amphitheaters and remnants of structures crafted from adobe and stone – but it is. This is the oldest known city in the Americas: Caral.

Situated in the Supe Valley, this early society developed almost simultaneously with the cultures of Mesopotamia and Egypt about 5000 years ago, and it predates the earliest civilizations in Mexico by about 1500 years. Little is known about the people who built this impressive 626-hectare urban center. However, archaeologists, led by Ruth Shady Solís (the former director of Lima's Museo Nacional de Antropología, Arqueología e Historia del Perú) have managed to unearth a few precious details.

For an excellent primer to Peru's pre-Hispanic art, pick up Ferdinand Anton's *The Art of Ancient Peru.* The descriptions are concise and accessible and the book is laden with almost 300 large-scale photographs.

Caral was a religious center that venerated its holy men and paid tribute to unknown agricultural deities. They cultivated crops, such as cotton, squash, beans and chilies, collected fruits and were knowledgeable fishers. Archaeological finds include pieces of textile, necklaces, ceremonial burials and crude, unbaked clay figurines depicting female forms. The first serious digs began in the area in 1996 and much of the complex has yet to be excavated – expect further discoveries.

Chavín

If Caral is evidence of early urbanization, then Chavín de Huántar, near Huaraz, represents the spread of a unified religious and artistic iconography. In a broad swath of the northern Andes, from roughly 1000 BC to 300 BC, a stylized feline deity began to appear on carvings, friezes, pottery and textiles. As with Caral, there is only patchy information available about the era's societies, but its importance is without question: in Peru, this moment heralds the true birth of art.

It is still debated whether the temple at Chavín de Huántar represented a capital or merely an important ceremonial site, but what is without doubt is that the setting is extraordinary. With the stunning Cordillera Blanca as a backdrop, the remnants of this elaborate ceremonial complex – built over hundreds of years – include a number of temple structures, as well as a sunken court with stone friezes of jaguars. Here, archaeologists have found pottery from all over the region filled with *ofrendas* (offerings), including shells from as far away as the Ecuadorean coast, and carved bones (some human) featuring supernatural motifs. The site's most remarkable feature is a maze of disorienting galleries beneath the temple complex, one of which boasts a nearly 5m-tall rock carving of a fanged anthropomorphic deity known as the Lanzón – just the sort of fierce-looking creature that is bound to turn anyone into a believer.

Paracas & Nazca

The Chavín Horizon, when Chavín civilization emerged, was followed by the development of a number of smaller, regional ethnicities. Along the country's south coast, from about 700 BC to AD 400, the Paracas culture – situated around modern-day Ica – produced some of the most renowned textiles ever created. The most impressive of these were woven during the period known as the Paracas Necropolis (AD 1 to 400), so named for a massive grave site on the Península de Paracas uncovered by famed Peruvian archaeologist Julio Tello in the 1920s.

The historical data on the culture is thin, but the magnificent textiles recovered from the graves – layers of finely woven fabrics wrapped around mummy bundles – provide important clues about day-to-day life and beliefs. Cloths feature flowers, fish, birds, knives and cats, with some animals represented as two-headed creatures. Also significant are the human figures: warriors carry shrunken trophy heads and supernatural anthropomorphic creatures are equipped with wings, snake tongues and lots of claws. (There are some fantastic examples at the Museo Larco in Lima.) Many of the mummies found at this site had cranial deformations, most of which showed that the head had been intentionally flattened using two boards.

During roughly the same period, the Nazca culture (200 BC to AD 600), to the south, was producing an array of painted pottery, as well as incredible weavings that showcased everyday objects (beans, birds and fish), in addition to supernatural cat- and falcon-men in an array of explosive colors. The Nazca were skilled embroiderers: some weavings feature tiny dangling figurines that must have induced blindness in their creators. (Well-preserved examples can be seen at the Museo Andrés del Castillo in Lima.)

The culture is best known, however, for the Nazca Lines, a series of mysterious geoglyphs carved into a 500-sq-km area in the southern Peruvian desert. Recently, new Japanese research suggests that two different groups made the glyphs. The lines became the center of a worldwide scandal in 2014. When Greenpeace activists entered the site on foot without authorization to leave an environmental message (saying 'Time for change, the future is renewable'), which inadvertently damaged the site.

Moche

When it comes to ceramics, there is no Andean civilization that compares to the Moche, a culture that inhabited the Peruvian north coast from about AD 100 to AD 800. Though not inherently urban, they built sophisticated

The website www.arqueologia.com.ar gathers useful links (in Spanish) related to archaeology news in Peru. The site contains timelines and some basic photo galleries devoted to different cultural groups.

Top Ruins Sites

Machu Picchu (p257)

Chan Chan (Trujillo; p333)

Sillustani (Puno; p187)

Chavín de Huántar (p408)

Huacas del Sol y de la Luna (Trujillo; p335)

Kuélap (p434)

DRONES & RUINS

When the Nazca Lines were damaged in a Greenpeace climate-change protest, the Peruvian government dispatched drones to survey the damage. They're also being used to protect ancient sites in other ways, such as to document the encroachment of developers and squatters into protected areas. Drones have proved handy in conservation, tracing the effects of El Niño storms on Chan Chan. State-of-the-art technology called octocopters are outfitted with a high-definition swivel camera for precision monitoring – that's a lot of high tech in service to the ancients.

ceremonial centers, such as the frieze-laden Huacas del Sol y de la Luna, outside modern-day Trujillo, and the elaborate burial site of Sipán, near Chiclayo. They had a well-maintained network of roads and a system of relay runners who carried messages, probably in the form of symbols carved onto beans.

But it's their portrait pottery that makes the Moche stand out: lifelike depictions of individuals (scars and all) are so skillfully rendered they seem as if they are about to speak. Artisans often created multiple portraits of a single person over the course of a lifetime. One scholar, in fact, recorded 45 different pieces depicting the same model. Other ceramics showcase macho activities such as hunting, combat and ritual sacrifice. This doesn't mean, however, that the Moche didn't know a thing or two about love – they are famous for their downright acrobatic depictions of human sex (on view at Lima's Museo Larco).

Published by Harvard University's Peabody Museum, *The Moche of Ancient Peru: Media and Messages,* by Jeffrey Quilter, is an outstanding introduction to the history, art and architecture of the Moche culture of the north coast.

Wari

From about AD 600 to 1100, the Andes saw the rise of the first truly expansive kingdom. The Wari were avid empire builders, expanding from their base around Ayacucho to a territory that occupied most of the highlands, in addition to a piece of the northern coast. Expert agriculturalists, they improved production by developing the terrace system and creating complex networks of canals for irrigation.

Like many conquering cultures in the region, the Wari built on what was already there, usurping and adding to extant infrastructure created by smaller regional states. The coastal ceremonial center of Pachacamac, for instance, was originated by the Lima culture but expanded by the Wari.

This doesn't mean that there aren't definitive Wari sites to be seen. The remains of what was once a 15-sq-km city is located outside Ayacucho, and there is a Wari ceremonial center in Piquillacta, near Cuzco. Unfortunately, the Wari's architecture was cruder than that of the Incas and so the buildings have not aged gracefully.

The Wari culture was highly skilled in weaving, producing elegant fabrics with elaborate, stylized designs. The Wari were masters of color, using as many as 150 distinct shades which they incorporated into woven

FATHER OF PERUVIAN ARCHAEOLOGY

Much of what we know about some of Peru's most important pre-Columbian cultures we owe to a single man: Julio C Tello (1880–1947), the acclaimed 'Father of Peruvian Archaeology.' A self-described 'mountain Indian,' Tello was born in the highland village of Huarochirí, in the mountains east of Lima. He earned a medical degree at the Universidad Nacional Mayor de San Marcos in Lima and later studied archaeology at Harvard University – no small achievement for a poor, indigenous man in turn-of-the-20th-century Peru.

In the 1920s he undertook a series of groundbreaking archaeological studies of the Wari centers around Ayacucho and the temple complex at Chavín de Huántar, where an ornate stela – the Tello Obelisk – is named in his honor (it's on view at the Museo Nacional de Chavín). He also discovered hundreds of mummy bundles on the Península de Paracas in 1927 – one of the most important sources of information about this pre-Inca culture. Most significantly, Tello brought scientific rigor to Peru's burgeoning archaeological efforts. In the 19th century, digs often resulted in more destruction than conservation, and looting was widely accepted. Tello helped get laws passed that offered legal protection to important archaeological sites.

For more on this charismatic figure, pick up a copy of *The Life and Writings of Julio C Tello: America's First Indigenous Archaeologist,* published by University of Iowa Press. The publication is the first to gather his key writings.

and tie-dyed patterns. Many textiles feature abstract, geometric designs, as well as supernatural figures – most common is a winged deity holding a staff.

In 2013 the first unlooted Wari imperial tomb to be discovered intact was a 1200-year-old royal tomb, north of Lima at El Castillo de Huarmey. In what has been described as the 'Temple of the Dead,' three Wari queens were accompanied by numbers of seated mummies, alabaster drinking cups, decorated ceramic vessels and gold weaving tools. Thirty tons of loose stone fill had been protecting the site from grave robbers. In 2015 another ceremonial site known as Tenahaha in the Cotahuasi Valley was unearthed, revealing hundreds of mummies and artifacts which will eventually illuminate more of the Wari culture.

Chimú & Chachapoyas

Following the demise of the Wari, a number of small nation-states emerged in different corners of the country. They are too numerous to detail here, but there are two that merit discussion because of the art and architecture they left behind.

The first of these is the Chimú culture, once based around present-day Trujillo. Between about AD 1000 and AD 1400, this sophisticated society built the largest known pre-Columbian city in the Americas. Chan Chan is a sprawling, 36-sq-km complex which once housed an estimated 60,000 people. Though over the centuries this adobe city has been worn down by the elements, parts of the complex's geometric friezes have been restored, giving a small inkling of what this metropolis must have been like in its heyday. The Chimú were accomplished artisans and metallurgists – producing, among other things, some absolutely outrageous-looking textiles covered top-to-bottom in tassels.

In the interior of the northern highlands is the cloud-forest citadel of Kuélap, built by the Chachapoyas culture in the remote Utcubamba Valley, beginning around AD 800. It is an incredible structure – or, more accurately, series of structures. The site is composed of more than 400 circular dwellings in addition to unusual, gravity-defying pieces of architecture, such as an inverted cone known as El Tintero (The Inkpot). The compound caps a narrow ridge and is surrounded, on all sides, by a 6m- to 12m-high wall, making the city practically impenetrable. This has led at least one historian to theorize that if the Incas had made their last stand against the Spanish here, rather than outside Cuzco, history might have been quite different.

Tejidos Milenarios del Perú: Ancient Peruvian Textiles is a sumptuously illustrated encyclopedia of Peruvian textiles, from Chavín and the Incas. It's a legacy so rich that the tome spans more than 800 pages and weighs more than 10kg.

Incas

Peru's greatest engineers were also its greatest empire builders. Because the Incas made direct contact with the Spanish, they also happen to be the pre-Columbian Andean culture that is best documented – not only through Spanish chronicles, but also through narratives produced by descendants of the Incas themselves. (The most famous of these scribes is El Inca Garcilaso de la Vega, who lived in the 16th century.)

The Incas were a Quechua civilization descended from alpaca farmers in the southern Andes. Over several generations, from AD 1100 until the arrival of the Spanish in 1532, they steadfastly grew into a highly organized empire that extended over more than 37° latitude from present-day Colombia to Chile. This was an absolutist state with a strong army, where ultimate power resided with the *inca* (emperor). The political history is fascinating.

The society was bound by a rigid caste system: there were nobles, an artisan and merchant class, and peasants. The latter supplied the workers for the Incas' many public-works projects. Citizens were expected to pay tribute to the crown in the form of labor (typically three months of the year), enabling the development and maintenance of monuments, canals and roadways. The Incas also kept a highly efficient communications system consisting of a body of *chasquis* (relay runners), who could make the 1600km trip between Quito and Cuzco in just seven days. (By comparison, it takes the average traveler three to four days to hike the Inca Trail from Ollantaytambo to Machu Picchu – a mere 43km!) As brutal as the regime was (with bloody wars and human sacrifice), the Incas also had a notable social-welfare system, warehousing surplus food for distribution to areas and people in need.

On the cultural front, the Incas had a strong tradition of music, oral literature and textiles. Their fabrics were generally composed of bold, solid colors in an array of abstract, geometric prints. But they are best known for their monumental architecture. The capital of Cuzco, along with a series of constructions at Sacsaywamán, Pisac, Ollantaytambo and the fabled Machu Picchu, are all incredible examples of the imperial style of building. Carved pieces of rock, without mortar, are fitted together so tightly that it is impossible to fit a knife between the stones. Most interestingly, walls are built at an angle and windows in a trapezoidal form, to resist seismic activity. The Incas kept the exteriors of their buildings austere, opting to put the decoration on the inside, in the form of rich wall hangings made of precious metals.

Nestled into spectacular natural locales, these structures, even in their ruined state, are an unforgettable sight. Their great majesty was something the Spanish acknowledged, even as they pried them apart to build their own monuments. 'Now that the Inca rulers have lost their power,' wrote Spanish chronicler Pedro Cieza de León in the 16th century, 'all these palaces and gardens, together with their other great works, have fallen, so that only the remains survive. Since they were built of good stone and the masonry is excellent, they will stand as memorials for centuries to come.' León was right. The Inca civilization did not survive the Spanish *pachacuti,* but its architecture did – a reminder of the many grand societies we are just beginning to understand.

At its acme, the Inca empire was larger than imperial Rome and boasted 40,000km of roadways. A network of *chasquis* (relay runners) kept the kingdom connected, relaying fresh-caught fish from the coast to Cuzco in 24 hours.

Indigenous Peru

While Peru's social order has been molded by Spanish custom, its soul remains indigenous. According to the country's census bureau, this crinkled piece of the South American Andes harbors 52 different ethnicities, 13 distinct linguistic families and 1786 indigenous communities. In fact, almost half of Peru's population of more than 30 million identifies as indigenous. Together, these groups account for a plethora of rituals, artistic traditions and ways of life – a cultural legacy that's as rich as it is long running.

Post-Conquest Life

In the wake of the Spanish conquest, colonial authorities transformed the ways in which people lived in the Andes. Indigenous people who had only ever known an agricultural life were forced to live on *reducciones* (mission towns) by colonial authorities. These urbanized 'reductions' provided the Church with a centralized place for evangelism and allowed the Spanish to control the natives politically and culturally. In these *reducciones*, indigenous people were often prohibited from speaking their native language or wearing traditional dress.

By the 17th century, after the Spanish had consolidated their power, many indigenous people were dispersed back to the countryside. But rather than work in the self-sustaining collectives (*ayllus*) that had existed in pre-Columbian times, they were forced into a system of debt peonage. For example: a native family was granted a subsistence plot on a Spanish landowner's holdings. In exchange, the family provided labor for the *patrón* (boss). In many cases, these *campesinos* (farmers) were not allowed to leave the land on which they lived.

This system remained firmly in place into the 20th century.

A 20th-Century Shift

The last 100 years have marked a number of significant steps forward. Since the indigenist social movements of the 1920s, various constitutions and laws have granted legal protection to communal lands (at least on paper, if not always in practice). In 1979, the Peruvian constitution officially recognized the right of people to adhere to their own 'cultural identities,' and the right to bilingual education was officially established. (Until then, the public school system had made a systematic effort to eliminate the use of native languages and pressured indigenous people to acculturate to Spanish *criollo* society.) And, the following year, literacy voting restrictions were finally lifted – allowing indigenous people to fully participate in the political process.

In 2011, President Humala passed a law that required native peoples be consulted on all mining and extraction activities on their territories. Yet, conflict still runs deep. In September, 2014, four indigenous activists were murdered en route to a meeting to discuss illegal logging.

Pressures of Poverty & Environment

Even as *indígenas* continue to make strides, there are obstacles. Indigenous people make up almost twice as many of the country's extreme poverty

English Words Derived from Quechua
Coca
Condor
Guano
Llama
Pampa
Puma
Quinoa

cases as Peruvians of European descent. In addition, access to basic services is problematic. Nearly 60% of indigenous communities do not have access to a health facility, and the country has a high maternal mortality ratio (higher than Iraq or the Gaza Strip). This affects indigenous women disproportionately.

Perhaps the biggest issue facing some ethnicities is the loss of land. Drug trafficking and the exploitation of natural resources in ever more remote areas are putting increased pressure on indigenous communities whose territories are often ill-defined and whose needs are poorly represented by the federal government in Lima. According to Aidesep, a Peruvian indigenous organization representing various rainforest ethnic groups, oil prospecting and extraction is occurring in more than 80% of indigenous territories in the Amazon. In late 2014, the remote Mashco-Piro, a tribe that had never been contacted until recently, raided a *mestizo* (mixed descent) village for supplies after being displaced from their own lands by logging and drug trafficking. In 2017, Achuar people seized 50 oil wells in their territory to protest the renewal of a Canadian company's contract despite a history of pollution.

In Spanish, *indígena* (indigenous) is the appropriate term. The word *indio* – 'Indian' in English – can be insulting, especially when used by outsiders. The slang *cholo* (translating roughly to 'Indian peasant') has long been considered derogatory, though some Peruvians use it as a term of empowerment.

Multitude of Cultures

Indigenous cultures are identified by their region or name, such as the Arequipa or Chachapoyas. But with more than 1000 highly localized regional cultures in the Peruvian Andes alone, it is easiest to identify groups by the language they speak. Quechua – the lingua franca of the Incas – is predominant. It is the most commonly spoken native language in the Americas and is heard all over the Andes. In Peru, more than 13% of the national population claims it as a birth language.

Aymara is the second-most spoken indigenous language – with nearly 2% of Peruvians speaking it from birth, primarily in the area around Lake Titicaca. Nearly 1% of Peruvians speak one of another 50 or so smaller, regional dialects. These include the numerous Amazon cultures that inhabit the rainforest.

Quechua

The descendants of the Incas (along with the myriad peoples the Incas conquered) inhabit much of Peru's Andean spine, representing the biggest indigenous cohort in the country. The department of Cuzco, however, remains the symbolic center of Quechua life. Traditional

OLLANTAY: QUECHUA'S GREAT LITERARY EPIC

Ollantay tells the story of a pair of star-crossed lovers: Ollanta, a celebrated warrior of humble birth, and Cusi Cuyllur, a captivating Inca princess. Because Ollanta is not a noble, societal mores dictate that he cannot marry his beloved. But he nonetheless draws up the courage to ask Emperor Pachacutec for his daughter's hand in marriage. The emperor becomes enraged at the audacity of the young lovers, and expels Ollanta from Cuzco and throws his daughter in jail. Battles ensue, a child is born and after much palace intrigue, the lovers are reunited.

Ollantay is a work of classic Quechua – the version of Quechua spoken at the time of the conquest. But because the Incas didn't leave behind a written language, its origins are quite murky: no one knows who composed it, or when. Its first recorded appearance is in the manuscripts of an 18th-century priest named Antonio Valdés, who worked in the department of Cuzco. Some scholars have surmised that Valdés may have written *Ollantay*. Others say that it was one of the many epic poems transmitted orally among the Incas, and that Valdés simply recorded it. Others figure Valdés may have tailored an indigenous work to suit Spanish tastes. Regardless, it is a popular theater drama in Peru – and remains one of the great works of art in Quechua.

Quechua refer to themselves as *runakuna* and refer to mixed-raced *mestizos* or indigenous people who adopt Spanish-Peruvian culture as *mistikuna*. The ritual chewing of coca is regarded as a major point of self-identification among *runakuna*. However, such distinguishing characteristics are becoming increasingly blurred as more indigenous people adopt at least some *criollo* customs in order to participate in the greater economy.

Regardless, many people continue to speak the language, chew coca and wear traditional dress. For men, this generally consists of brightly woven ponchos and the ear-flap hats known as *chullos*. Women's outfits are more elaborate and flamboyant: a bowler or flat-topped hat accompanies some sort of woven wrap or sweater, and multiple layers of handwoven or shiny skirts. (The layered skirt look is considered very feminine.) Elements of traditional and Western dress are often combined.

Aymara

Though subjugated by the Quechua-speaking Incas in the 15th century, the Aymara have maintained a distinct language group and identity. Traditionally an agricultural society, they were reduced to near-slave status through debt peonage and, later, in the silver mines of Bolivia. Within Peru, they are clustered in the area around Puno and Lake Titicaca.

While identification with indigenous custom is strong, Spanish elements are present in spiritual life. *Indígenas* have largely adapted Catholic deities to their own beliefs. Like the Quechua, many Aymara practice syncretic religious beliefs that closely link indigenous custom to Catholic thought. In Puno, there is a large festival in honor of La Virgen de la Candelaria every February 2 (Candlemas). The Virgin, however, is closely identified with Pachamama, as well as natural elements such as lightning and fertility.

Cultures of the Amazon

The vast Peruvian Amazon is home to more than 330,000 indigenous people, representing more than five dozen different ethnicities – some are closely related while others couldn't be more different in terms of tradition and language.

Within this group, the biggest demographic is comprised of the Asháninka people (also known as Campa). Comprising roughly a quarter of the indigenous population in the Peruvian Amazon, they inhabit numerous river valleys east of the central highlands. (Because of this location, the Asháninka suffered mightily during the Internal Conflict, when the Sendero Luminoso – Shining Path – made incursions to the east.)

The second-largest Amazon group is the Aguaruna, who occupy the Marañón, Nieva and Santiago River valleys to the north. The group not only resisted Inca attempts at conquest, they also fended off the Spanish. In fact, they still occupy their preconquest lands, and survive by practicing horticulture, hunting and fishing.

There are countless other smaller ethnic groups, including the Shipibo, Matsiguenka and the small, so-called 'uncontacted tribes' that have made headlines in recent years. These groups are extremely vulnerable to land loss and pollution caused by oil and mineral extraction. For the most remote groups, the biggest problem can boil down to simple immunity: in the 1980s, more than half of the Nahua people in the southern Amazon died after contracting diseases from loggers and oil-company agents.

INDIGENOUS PERU MULTITUDE OF CULTURES

Racism remains a potent societal force in Peru. Yet a DNA study recently published by *National Geographic* shows that the inhabitants of Lima have 68% indigenous blood.

For a well-written examination of Quechua life in Peru, read Catherine Allen's *The Hold Life Has: Coca and Cultural Identity in an Andean Community*. This intriguing ethnography, last updated in 2002, covers everything from belief systems to the rituals of daily life in the southern highlands.

The Natural World

Few countries have topographies as rugged, forbidding and wildly diverse as Peru. It lies in the tropics, south of the equator, straddling three strikingly different geographic zones: the arid Pacific coast, the craggy Andes and a good portion of the Amazon Basin. Regardless of which part you visit, you'll never travel a straight line. Between snaking rivers, plunging canyons and zigzagging mountain roads, navigating Peru's landscape is about circumventing natural obstacles along a path of excitement and jaw-dropping beauty.

The Land

The third-largest country in South America – at 1,285,220 sq km – Peru is five times larger than the UK, almost twice the size of Texas and one-sixth the size of Australia. On the coast, a narrow strip of land, which lies below 1000m in elevation, hugs the country's 3000km-long shoreline. Consisting primarily of scrubland and desert, it eventually merges, in the south, with Chile's Atacama Desert, one of the driest places on earth. The coast includes Lima, the capital, and several major agricultural centers – oases watered by dozens of rivers that cascade down from the Andes. These settlements make for a strange sight: barren desert can give way to bursts of green fields within the course of a few meters. The coast contains some of Peru's flattest terrain, so it's no surprise that the country's best road, the Carretera Panamericana (Pan-American Hwy), borders much of the Pacific from Ecuador to Chile.

The origin of the word 'Andes' is uncertain. Some historians believe it comes from the Quechua *anti*, meaning 'east,' or *anta*, an Aymara-derived term that signifies 'copper-colored.' Interestingly, the mountains don't stop at the Pacific coast; 100km offshore is a trench that is as deep as the Andes are high.

The Andes form the spine of the country. Rising steeply from the coast, and growing sharply in height and gradient from north to south, they reach spectacular heights of more than 6000m just 100km inland. Peru's highest peak, Huascarán (6768m), located northeast of Huaraz, is the world's highest tropical summit and the sixth-tallest mountain in the Americas. Though the Peruvian Andes resides in the tropics, the mountains are laced with a web of glaciers above elevations of 5000m. Between 3000m and 4000m lie the agricultural highlands, which support more than a third of Peru's population.

The eastern Andean slopes receive much more rainfall than the dry western slopes and are draped in lush cloud forests as they descend into the lowland rainforest of the Amazon. Here, the undulating landscape rarely rises more than 500m above sea level as various tributary systems feed into the mighty Río Amazonas (Amazon River), the largest river in the world. Weather conditions are hot and humid year-round, with most precipitation falling between December and May.

Wildlife

With its folds, bends and plunging river valleys, Peru is home to countless ecosystems, each with its own unique climate, elevation, vegetation and soil type. As a result, it has a spectacular variety of plant and animal life. Colonies of sea lions occupy rocky outcroppings on the coast, while raucous flocks of brightly colored macaws descend on clay licks in the

Amazon. In the Andes, rare vicuñas (endangered relatives of the alpaca) trot about in packs as condors take to the wind currents. Peru is one of only a dozen or so countries in the world considered to be 'megadiverse.'

Birds

Peru has more than 1800 bird species – that's more than the number of species found in North America and Europe together. From the tiniest hummingbirds to the majestic Andean condor, the variety is colorful and seemingly endless; new species are discovered regularly.

Along the Pacific, marine birds of all kinds are most visible, especially in the south, where they can be found clustered along the shore. Here you'll see exuberant Chilean flamingos, oversized Peruvian pelicans, plump Inca terns sporting white-feather moustaches and bright orange beaks, colonies of brown boobies engaged in elaborate mating dances, cormorants, and endangered Humboldt penguins, which can be spotted waddling around the Islas Ballestas.

In the highlands, the most famous bird of all is the Andean condor. Weighing up to 10kg, with a 3m-plus wingspan, this monarch of the air (a member of the vulture family) once ranged over the entire Andean mountain chain from Venezuela to Tierra del Fuego. Considered the largest flying bird in the world, the condor was put on the endangered species list in the 1970s, due mostly to loss of habitat and pollution. But it was also hunted to the brink of extinction because its body parts were believed to increase male virility and ward off nightmares. Condors usually nest in impossibly high mountain cliffs that prevent predators from snatching their young. Their main food source is carrion and they're most easily spotted riding thermal air currents in the canyons around Arequipa.

Other prominent high-altitude birds include the Andean gull (don't call it a seagull!), which is commonly sighted along lakes and rivers as high as 4500m. The mountains are also home to several species of ibis, such as the puna ibis, which inhabits lakeside marshes, as well as roughly a dozen types of cinclodes, a type of ovenbird (their clay nests resemble ovens) endemic to the Andes. Other species include torrent ducks, which nest in small waterside caves, Andean geese, spotted Andean flickers, black-and-yellow Andean siskins and, of course, a panoply of hummingbirds.

Swoop down toward the Amazon and you'll catch sight of the world's most iconic tropical birds, including boisterous flocks of parrots and macaws festooned in brightly plumed regalia. You'll also see clusters of aracaris, toucans, parakeets, toucanets, ibises, regal gray-winged trumpeters, umbrella birds donning gravity-defying feathered hairdos,

A Neotropical Companion (1989), by John Kricher, provides an introduction to the wildlife and ecosystems of the New World tropics, including coastal and highland regions.

A comprehensive overview of Peru's avian life is contained in the 656-page Princeton Field Guide *Birds of Peru* (2010) by Thomas Schulenberg.

THE NATURAL WORLD WILDLIFE

WATCHING WILDLIFE IN PERU

➜ Be willing to travel – the coast has limited fauna and some highland areas have been hunted out; remote is the way to go

➜ Hire a knowledgeable local guide – they know what to look for, when to look and where to go

➜ Get up *really* early – animals tend to be most active at dawn and dusk

➜ Bring a pair of lightweight binoculars – they improve wildlife observation tremendously

➜ Be quiet: animals tend to avoid loud packs of chatty humans, so keep chitchat to a whisper; in the Amazon, opt for canoes instead of motorboats – you'll see much more

➜ Have realistic expectations: vegetation can be thick and animals shy – you're not going to see everything in a single hike

crimson colored cocks-of-the-rock, soaring hawks and harpy eagles. The list goes on.

Mammals

The Amazon is home to a bounty of mammals. More than two dozen species of monkeys are found here, including howlers, acrobatic spider monkeys and wide-eyed marmosets. With the help of a guide, you may also see sloths, bats, piglike peccaries, anteaters, armadillos and coatis (ring-tailed members of the raccoon family). And if you're really lucky, you'll find giant river otters, capybaras (a rodent of unusual size), river dolphins, tapirs and maybe one of half a dozen elusive felines, including the fabled jaguar.

Toward the west, the cloud forests straddling the Amazon and the eastern slopes of the Andean highlands are home to the endangered spectacled bear. South America's only bear is a black, shaggy mammal that grows up to 1.8m in length, and is known for its white, masklike face markings.

The highlands are home to roving packs of camelids: llamas and alpacas are the most easily spotted since they are domesticated, and used as pack animals or for their wool; vicuñas and guanacos live exclusively in the wild. On highland talus slopes, watch out for the viscacha, which looks like the world's most cuddly rabbit. Foxes, deer and domesticated *cuy* (guinea pigs) are also highland dwellers, as is the puma (cougar or mountain lion).

On the coast, huge numbers of sea lions and seals are easily seen on the Islas Ballestas. While whales are very rarely seen offshore, dolphins are commonly seen. In the coastal desert strip, there are few unique species of land animals. One is the near-threatened Sechuran fox, the smallest of the South American foxes (found in northern Peru), which has a black-tipped tail, pale, sand-colored fur, and an omnivorous appetite for small rodents and seed pods.

Travellers' Wildlife Guides: Peru (2014), by David Pearson and Les Beletsky, helpfully lists the country's most important and frequently seen birds, mammals, amphibians, reptiles and ecosystem habitats.

Reptiles, Amphibians, Insects & Marine Life

The greatest variety of reptiles, amphibians, insects and marine life can be found in the Amazon Basin. Here, you'll find hundreds of species, including toads, tree frogs and thumbnail-sized poison dart frogs (indigenous peoples once used the frogs' deadly poison on the points of their blow-pipe darts). Rivers teem with schools of piranhas, *paiche* and *doncella* (both are types of freshwater fish), while the air buzzes with the activity of thousands of insects: armies of ants, squadrons of beetles, as well as katydids, stick insects, caterpillars, spiders, praying mantises, transparent moths, and butterflies of all shapes and sizes. A blue morpho butterfly in flight is a remarkable sight: with wingspans of up to 10cm, their iridescent-blue coloring can seem downright hallucinogenic.

Naturally, there are all kinds of reptiles, too, including tortoises, river turtles, lizards, caimans and, of course, that jungle-movie favorite: the anaconda. An aquatic boa snake that can measure more than 10m in length, it will often ambush its prey by the water's edge, constrict its body around it and then drown it in the river. Caimans, tapirs, deer, turtles and peccaries are all tasty meals for this killer snake; human victims are almost unheard of (unless you're Jennifer Lopez and Ice Cube in a low-rent Hollywood production). Far more worrisome to the average human is the bushmaster, a deadly, reddish-brown viper that likes to hang out inside rotting logs and among the buttress roots of trees. Thankfully, it's a retiring creature, and is rarely found on popular trails.

One of the most engaging books on rainforest life is Adrian Forsyth and Ken Miyata's *Tropical Nature: Life and Death in the Rain Forests of Central and South America* (1984). Partially researched in the Amazon Basin, it is an essential, highly enjoyable primer on life in the lowland tropics.

THE NATURAL WORLD PLANTS

Plants

At high elevations in the Andes, especially in the Cordilleras Blanca and Huayhuash, outside Huaraz, there is a cornucopia of distinctive alpine flora and fauna. Plants encountered in this region include native lupins, spiky tussocks of ichu grass, striking queñua (Polylepis) trees with their distinctive curly, red paper-like bark, in addition to unusual bromeliads. Many alpine wildflowers bloom during the trekking season, between May and September.

In the south, you'll find the distinctive *puna* ecosystem. These areas have a fairly limited flora of hard grasses, cushion plants, small herbaceous plants, shrubs and dwarf trees. Many plants in this environment have developed small, thick leaves that are less susceptible to frost and radiation. In the north, you can find some *páramo* (high-altitude Andean grasslands), which have a harsher climate, are less grassy and have an odd mixture of landscapes, including peat bogs, glacier-formed valleys, alpine lakes, wet grasslands, and patches of scrubland and forest.

Vegetation of the Cloud & Rainforest

As the eastern Andean slopes descend into the western Amazon uplands, the scenery once again changes. Here, tropical cloud forests – so named because they trap (and help create) clouds that drench the forest in a fine mist – allow delicate forms of plant life to survive. Cloud-forest trees are adapted to steep slopes, rocky soils and a rugged climate. They are characterized by low, gnarled growth, dense small-leafed canopies and moss-covered branches supporting a host of plants such as orchids, ferns and bromeliads. The mist and the dense vegetation give the cloud forest a mysterious, fairy-tale appearance.

In the Amazon rainforest, the density is astonishing: tens of thousands of species of plant can be found living on top of and around each other. There are strangler figs (known as *matapalos*), palms, ferns, epiphytes, bromeliads, flowering orchids, fungi, mosses and lianas, to name a few.

GIANT FLOWERS OF THE MOUNTAINS

Reaching the staggering height of more than 10m, with an explosive, flower-encrusted cigar shape that looks to be straight out of a Dr Seuss book, the *Puya raimondii* certainly takes the award for most unusual flora. The world's tallest flowering plant is a member of the pineapple family and can take up to a century or more to mature. In full bloom, each plant flaunts up to 8000 white flowers, each resembling a lily. It blooms only once in its lifetime, after which the plant dies. Some of the most famous stands of *Puya raimondii* can be found in the Peruvian Andes, in the rocky mountains outside Huaraz, near Catac and Punta Winchus.

Some rainforest trees – such as the 'walking palm' – are supported by strange roots that look like stilts. These are most frequently found where periodic floods occur; the stilt roots are thought to play a role in keeping the tree upright during the inundation.

One thing that often astounds visitors is the sheer immensity of many trees. A good example is the *ceiba* (also called the 'kapok' or cotton silk tree), which has huge flattened trunk supports, known as buttresses, around its base. The trunk of a ceiba can easily measure 3m across and will grow straight up for 50m before the first branches are reached. These spread out into a huge crown with a slightly flattened appearance. The staggering height of many Amazon trees, some reaching a height of 80m-plus, creates a whole ecosystem of life at the canopy level, inhabited by creatures that never descend to the forest floor.

Andean Botanical Information System (www.sacha.org) is a veritable online encyclopedia of flowering plants in Peru's coastal areas and the Andes.

Desert Coast

In stark contrast to the Amazon, the coastal desert is generally barren of vegetation, apart from around water sources, which may spring into palm-fringed lagoons. Otherwise, the limited plant life you'll glimpse will consist of cacti and other succulents, as well as *lomas* (a blend of grasses and herbaceous species in mist-prone areas). On the far north coast, in the ecological reserves around Tumbes, is a small cluster of mangrove forests, as well as a tropical dry-forest ecosystem, of which there is little in Peru.

National Parks

Peru's vast wealth of wildlife is protected by a system of national parks and reserves with 60 areas covering almost 15% of the country. The newest is the Sierra del Divisor Reserve Zone, created in 2006 to protect 1.5 million hectares of rainforest on the Brazilian border. All of these protected areas are administered by the Instituto Nacional de Recursos Nacionales (Inrena; www.inrena.gob.pe), a division of the Ministry of Agriculture.

Unfortunately, resources are lacking to conserve protected areas, which are subject to illegal hunting, fishing, logging and mining. The government simply doesn't have the funds to hire enough rangers and provide them with the equipment necessary to patrol the parks. That said, a number of international agencies and not-for-profit organizations contribute money, staff and resources to help with conservation and education projects.

Environmental Issues

Peru faces major challenges in the stewardship of its natural resources, with problems compounded by a lack of law enforcement and its

FREQUENT FLYERS

For many bird enthusiasts in Peru, the diminutive hummingbirds are among the most delightful to observe. More than 100 species have been recorded in the country, and their exquisite beauty is matched by their extravagant names. There's the 'green-tailed gold-enthroat,' the 'spangled coquette,' the 'fawn-breasted brilliant' and 'amethyst-throated sunangel.' Species such as the redheaded Andean hillstar, living in the *puna* (high Andean grasslands), have evolved an amazing strategy to survive a cold night. They go into a state of torpor, which is like a nightly hibernation, by lowering their body temperature by up to 30°C, thus drastically slowing their metabolism.

One of the most unusual species of hummingbird is the marvelous spatuletail, found in the Utcubamba Valley in northern Peru. Full-grown adult males are adorned with two extravagant feathery spatules on the tail, which are used during mating displays to attract females.

COCA CULTIVATION PAST & PRESENT

Cultivation of the coca plant dates back at least 5000 years and its traditional uses have always included the practical and the divine. In pre-Hispanic times, chewing coca was a traditional treatment for everything from a simple toothache to exhaustion. It has also long been used in religious rituals as a sacred offering. When the Spaniards arrived in the 15th century, they attempted to outlaw the 'heathen' practice of cultivating this 'diabolical' plant. However, with coca-chewing an essential part of life for the colony's indigenous labor pool (it is a mild appetite suppressant and stimulant – on par with coffee), the Spanish ultimately reversed their policies.

Today, there continues to be a struggle surrounding coca, but it has to do with its derivative product, cocaine (in which a paste derived from coca leaves is treated with kerosene and refined into a powder). In an attempt to stem the flow of this narcotic, the US led eradication programs of coca plants in Peru in the early 2000s. These programs have done little to curb coca's cultivation (or the cocaine trade), but the herbicides employed have damaged some agricultural lands in indigenous communities. Critics of the US-sponsored programs – including Peruvian *cocaleros* (coca-growers' associations) and President Evo Morales of Bolivia – have called for regulation of eradication.

In 2014, President Ollanta Humala announced that Peru would stop its coca-eradication campaign, while stepping up promoting other crops in coca-heavy regions, such as coffee and cocoa. The Peru Coca Survey reported that the surface area of coca crops increased by 9% in 2016 – an alarming number, but it's actually the lowest increase in the region.

impenetrable geography. Deforestation and erosion are major issues, as is industrial pollution, urban sprawl and the continuing attempted eradication of coca plantations on some Andean slopes. In addition, the Carr Interoceánica through the heart of the Amazon may imperil thousands of square kilometers of rainforest.

Reduced growth in mining earnings in the 21st century has led the government to install protectionist measures, much to the detriment of the environment. A law enacted in July 2014 weakened environmental protections by removing Peru's environmental ministry's jurisdiction over air, soil, and water quality standards.

Deforestation & Water Problems

At the ground level, clear-cutting of the highlands for firewood, of the rainforests for valuable hardwoods, and of both to clear land for agriculture, oil drilling and mining, has led to severe erosion. In the highlands, where deforestation and overgrazing of Andean woodlands and *puna* grass is severe, soil quality is rapidly deteriorating. In the Amazon rainforest, deforestation has led to erosion and a decline in bellwether species such as frogs. Erosion has also led to decreased water quality in this area, where silt-laden water is unable to support microorganisms at the base of the food chain.

Potable water is an issue for a large number of Peruvians: in urban areas 87% of the population has access to clean water; in rural areas, the percentage drops to 62% of residents. There is also the problem of water pollution caused by mining in the highlands. Sewage contamination along the coast has led to many beaches around some coastal cities being declared unfit for swimming. In the south, pollution and overfishing have led to the continued decline of the Humboldt penguin (its numbers have declined by more than a third since the 1980s).

Air pollution is another grave issue in Peru, especially in Lima, the continent's worst offender. In 2018, Google's pollution tracker tool found pollutants from industry and vehicle emissions at almost double the healthy limit set by the World Health Organization.

Top Protected Areas

Cañón del Colca
(Arequipa; p166)

Cordillera Blanca
(Ancash; p385)

Lake Titicaca
(Puno; p177)

Parque Nacional
Manu (Amazon
Basin; p468)

Islas Ballestas
(Pisco; p117)

Protective Steps

In the early 1990s, Peru took steps to formulate a national environmental and natural resource code, but the government (occupied with a bloody guerrilla war in the highlands) lacked the funding and political will to enforce it. In 1995 Peru's congress created a National Environmental Council (Conam) to manage the country's national environmental policy. Though there have been some success stories (eg flagrant polluters being fined for poor practices), enforcement remains weak.

Some positive measures are being taken to help protect the country's environment. Peruvian government and private interests within the tourism industry have come together to develop sustainable travel projects in the Amazon. In 2012, the Peruvian government created three new protected areas in the northern Amazon territory of Loreto, spanning nearly 600,000 hectares. The areas represent a world hot spot of biological and cultural diversity known as the Putumayo Trinational Conservation Corridor, a joint effort at regional-style management by the governments of Peru, Ecuador and Colombia.

Monga Bay (www.mongabay.com) is an online resource for news and information related to the Amazon and rainforests around the world.

Peru's first Environment Minister Antonio Brack, who died in 2014, took an aggressive stance on deforestation, copying other Amazonian nations in a plea for Western help in conservation, and pledging to curb forest fires and reduce logging rates. Unfortunately, official policy tends to have little relevancy in remote, unmonitored areas.

Illegal mining is a major environmental hazard. In 2014, an economic emergency was declared by the government in 17 indigenous communities along the Río Marañón in the Amazon Basin because oil contamination posed a significant threat to the population. Liquid mercury, used to extract gold, contaminates water sources and kills fish.

Lima has started using a local technology known as Super Tree to combat air pollution. The device (not an actual tree) uses thermodynamic pressure to purify the air; it's the equivalent of having 1200 trees, not a small number in this deforested country. By-products are mud and nonpotable water.

Survival Guide

Directory A–Z

Accessible Travel

Peru offers few conveniences for travelers with disabilities. Features such as signs in Braille or phones for the hearing-impaired are virtually nonexistent, while wheelchair ramps and lifts are few and far between, and the pavement is often badly potholed and cracked. Most hotels do not have wheelchair accessible rooms, at least not rooms specially designated as such. Bathrooms are often barely large enough for an able-bodied person to walk into, so few are accessible to wheelchairs.

Nevertheless there are Peruvians with disabilities who get around, mainly through the help of others.

Apumayo Expediciones (☑914-169-665; www.apumayo. com; Jr Ricardo Palma Ñ-11, Urb Santa Monica Wanchaq, Cuzco; ⊙9am-6pm Mon-Fri) An adventure-tour company that takes disabled travelers to Machu Picchu and other historic sites in the Sacred Valley.

Conadis (Map p66; ☑01-332-0808; www.conadisperu.gob. pe; Av Arequipa 375, Santa Beatriz, Lima; ⊙8am-5pm Mon-Fri) Governmental agency for Spanish-language information and advocacy for people with disabilities.

Emerging Horizons (www. emerginghorizons.com) Travel magazine for the mobility impaired, with handy advice columns and news articles.

Mobility International (☑USA 541-343-1284; www.miusa. org; 132 E Broadway, Suite 343, USA; ⊙9am-4pm Mon-Fri) Advises disabled travelers on mobility issues and runs an educational exchange program.

Online Resources

Download Lonely Planet's free Accessible Travel guides from http://lptravel.to/Accessible Travel.

Accommodations

➡ Many lodgings offer laundry service and free short-term luggage storage (ask for a receipt).

➡ *Habitación simple* refers to a single room. A *habitación doble* features twin beds while a *habitación matrimonial* has a double or a queen-sized bed.

➡ Street noise can be an issue in any lodging, so select your room accordingly.

➡ It's always OK to ask to see a room before committing.

➡ Homestays are sometimes offered by Spanish-language schools.

➡ Campgrounds are rare.

Rates

Note that prices may fluctuate with exchange rates.

Extra charges Foreigners do not have to pay the 18% hotel tax (sometimes included in rates quoted in soles), but may have to present their passport and tourist card to photocopy. A credit card transaction surcharge of 7% or more does not include the home bank's foreign-currency exchange fee. US dollars may be accepted, but the exchange rate may be poor.

Packages In the remote jungle lodges of the Amazon and in popular beach destinations such as Máncora, all-inclusive resort-style pricing is more the norm.

High season In Cuzco, demand is very high during the high season (June to August). Other busy times include Inti Raymi, Semana Santa and Fiestas

Patrias, when advance reservations are a must. In Lima, prices remain steady throughout the year; look for last-minute specials online. Paying cash always helps; ask for discounts for long-term stays.

Apartments

Short-term rentals, primarily in Lima, increasingly attend mid- to high-end needs.

Hostels

Hostels are diverse and plentiful in Peru, from rundown to boutique, from party hostel to mellow haven with the gamut of amenities. There are also Hostelling International (www.hihostels.com) affiliates.

Hotels
BUDGET

Hostales, *hospedajes* and *albergues* are Peru's cheapest accommodations. In this price range, expect to find small rooms, with a shared or private bathroom. In the major cities, these options will generally include hot showers; in more rural and remote areas, they likely will not. Some budget inns will include a very simple breakfast in the rate, such as instant coffee with toast.

Avoid rooms that appear insecure; test the locks on doors and windows. Shopping around makes a difference.

MIDRANGE

Rooms generally have private bathrooms with hot-water showers and small portable heaters or fans. Some are also equipped with air-conditioning. Amenities may include cable TV, in-room telephones and safes. Continental or American-style breakfasts are usually included.

TOP END

Peru's top hotels are generally equipped with en suite

bathrooms with bathtubs, international direct-dial phones, handy dual-voltage outlets, central heating or air-conditioning, hairdryers, in-room safes, cable TV and internet access (either through high-speed cable or wi-fi); some may come with minifridges, microwaves or coffee makers.

A large high-end spot may also feature a bar, cafe or restaurant (or several), as well as room service, concierge services and an obliging, multilingual staff.

Expect the biggest places (particularly in Lima) to come with business centers, spas and beauty salons. In the Amazon, where conditions tend to be isolated, high-end lodgings have fewer amenities and are more rustic.

Customs Regulations

➡ Peru allows duty-free importation of 3L of alcohol and 20 packs of cigarettes, 50 cigars or 250g of tobacco. You can import US$300 of gifts. Legally, you are allowed to bring in such items as a laptop,

camera, portable music player, kayak, climbing gear, mountain bike or similar items for personal use.

➡ It is illegal to take pre-Columbian or colonial artifacts out of Peru, and it is illegal to bring them into most countries. If purchasing reproductions, buy only from a reputable dealer and ask for a detailed receipt. Purchasing animal products made from endangered species or even just transporting them around Peru is also illegal.

➡ Coca leaves are legal in Peru, but not in most other countries, even in the form of tea bags. People subject to random drug testing should be aware that coca, even in the form of tea, may leave trace amounts in urine.

➡ Check with your own home government about customs restrictions and duties on any expensive or rare items you intend to bring back. Most countries allow their citizens to import a limited number of items duty-free, though these regulations are subject to change.

Electricity

Type A
220V/60Hz

Type C
220V/60Hz

Embassies & Consulates

Most foreign embassies are in Lima, with some consular services in major tourist centers such as Cuzco.

It is important to realize what your embassy can and can't do if you get into trouble. Your embassy will not be sympathetic if you end up in jail after committing a crime, even if such actions are legal in your own country. If all your money and documents are stolen, the embassy can help you get a new passport.

Call in advance to double-check operating hours or schedule an appointment. While many consulates and embassies are staffed during regular business hours, attention to the public is often more limited. For after-hours and emergency contact numbers, check individual websites.

Oficinas de migraciónes (immigration offices) are where you'll need to go to receive an exit stamp or secure a new entry card, which can also be done online through the website.

Australian Embassy (Map p74; ☑01-630-0500; www.peru. embassy.gov.au; Av La Paz 1049, piso 10, Miraflores)

Belgian Embassy (Map p74; ☑01-241-7566; www.peru. diplomatie.belgium.be; Av Angamos Oeste 380, Miraflores; ⊙8:30am-4pm Mon-Fri)

Bolivian Embassy (Map p70; ☑01-440-2095; www.bolivia enperu.com; Los Castaños 235, San Isidro; ⊙8:30am-12:30pm Mon-Fri) There's a consulate in **Puno** (Map p180;☑051-20-5400; www.consuladopuno. simplesite.com; Cajamarca 664; ⊙8am-4pm Mon-Fri).

Brazilian Embassy (Map p74; ☑01-512-0830; www.embajada brasil.org.pe; Av José Pardo 850, Miraflores; ⊙8:15am-4pm Mon-Fri)

Canadian Embassy (Map p74;☑01-319-3200; www. canadainternational.gc.ca/ peru-perou; Bolognesi 228, Miraflores; ⊙8am-12:30pm & 1:15-5pm Mon-Thu, 8am-12:30pm Fri) With a helpful website.

Chilean Embassy (Map p70; ☑01-710-2211; www.chile.gob. cl/peru; Javier Prado Oeste 790, San Isidro)

Colombian Embassy (Map p70; ☑01-201-9830; http://peru. embajada.gov.co/embajada; Av Víctor Andrés Belaúnde 340, San Isidro; ⊙8am-1pm & 2-5pm Mon-Fri) There's a consulate in **Iquitos** (Map p484; ☑065-23-1461; Moore 249, cnr Calvo de Aurajo).

Ecuadorian Embassy (Map p70;☑01-212-4027; www.peru. embajada.gob.ec; Las Palmeras 356, San Isidro; ⊙8:30am-4pm Mon-Fri) There's a consulate in **Tumbes** (☑072-52-5949; Bolívar 129, 3rd fl, Plaza de Armas).

French Embassy (Map p70; ☑01-215-8400; www.amba france-pe.org; Av Arequipa 3415, San Isidro; ⊙8:30am-12:15pm Mon-Thu, to noon Fri)

German Embassy (☑01-203-5940; www.lima.diplo.de; Av Dionisio Derteano 144, 7th & 8th fl, San Isidro; ⊙8am-4:30pm Mon-Thu, to 1:30pm Fri)

Israeli Embassy (Map p70; ☑01-418-0500; www.em-bassies.gov.il/lima; Centro Empresarial Platinum Plaza II, Av Andres Reyes 437, piso 13, San Isidro; ⊙9am-12:30pm Mon-Fri)

Italian Embassy (☑01-463-2727; www.amblima.esteri. it; Av Guiseppe Garibaldi 298, Jesús María; ⊙8:30am-5:30pm Mon & Thu, 8am-2pm Tue, Wed & Fri)

Netherlands Embassy (Map p74;☑01-213-9800; www. dutch-embassy.com/contact-details/netherlands-in-lima; Av José Larco 1301, Torre Parque Mar, 13th fl, Miraflores; ⊙8:30am-12:45pm & 1:30-5pm Mon-Thu, 8:30am-1pm Fri)

Spanish Consulate (Map p70; ☑01-513-7930; www.consulado lima.com.pe; Calle Los Pinos, San Isidro; ⊙8:30am-1pm Mon-Fri)

Swiss Embassy (☑01-264-0305; www.eda.admin.ch/lima; Av Salaverry 3240, San Isidro; ⊙8am-1pm & 2-4:30pm Mon-Thu, 8am-2pm Fri)

UK Embassy (Map p74;☑01-617-3000; www.gov.uk/world/ organisations/british-embassy-peru; Av José Larco 1301, Edificio Parquemar, 22nd fl, Miraflores; ◷8am-1pm & 2-4:30pm Mon-Thu, 8am-1pm Fri)

US Embassy (☏01-618-2000; https://pe.usembassy.gov/ embassy/lima; Av Encalada, cuadra 17, Surco; ◷8am-5pm) Call before showing up in person.

Insurance

Having a travel-insurance policy to cover theft, loss, accidents and illness is highly recommended. Always carry your insurance card with you. Not all policies compensate travelers for misrouted or lost luggage. Check the fine print to see if it excludes 'dangerous activities,' which can include scuba diving, motorcycling and even trekking. Also check if the policy coverage includes worst-case scenarios, such as evacuations and flights home.

You must usually report any loss or theft to local police (or airport authorities) within 24 hours. Make sure you keep all documentation to make any claim.

Internet Access

➡ Most regions have excellent internet connections and reasonable prices; it is typical for hotels and hostels to have wi-fi or computer terminals.

➡ Family guesthouses, particularly outside urban areas, lag behind in this area.

➡ Internet cafes are widespread.

Language Courses

Peru has schools in Lima, Cuzco, Arequipa, Huaraz, Puerto Maldonado and Huancayo. You can also study Quechua with private teachers or at one of the various language institutes in Lima, Cuzco and Huancayo.

Legal Matters

Legal assistance Your own embassy is of limited help if you get into trouble with the law in Peru, where you are presumed guilty until proven innocent. If you are the victim, the *policía de turismo* (tourist police; Poltur) can help, with limited English. Poltur stations are found in major cities.

Bribery Though some police officers (even tourist police) have a reputation for corruption, bribery is illegal. Beyond traffic police, the most likely place officials might request a little extra is at land borders. Since this too is illegal, those with time and fortitude can and should stick to their guns.

Drugs Avoid having any conversation with someone who offers you drugs. Peru has draconian penalties for possessing even a small amount of drugs; minimum sentences are several years in jail.

Police Should you be stopped by a plainclothes officer, don't hand over any documents or money. Never get into a vehicle with someone claiming to be a police officer, but insist on going to a real police station on foot.

Protests It's not recommended to attend political protests or to get too close to blockades – these are places to avoid.

Detention If you are imprisoned for any reason, make sure that someone else knows about it as soon as possible. Extended pretrial detentions are not uncommon. Peruvians bring food and clothing to family members who are in prison, where conditions are extremely harsh.

Complaints For issues with a hotel or a tour operator, register your complaint with the **National Institute for the Defense of Competition and the Protection of Intellectual Property** (Indecopi; ☏01-224-7800; www. indecopi.gob.pe) in Lima.

LGBTIQ+ Travelers

Peru is a strongly conservative, Catholic country. While most believe that legalizing same-sex civil unions will happen soon, the initiative has met resistance from the Peruvian Congress in the past, despite the adoption of similar measures in neighboring countries in the Southern Cone. While many Peruvians will tolerate homosexuality on a 'don't ask; don't tell' level when dealing with foreign travelers, LGBTIQ+ rights remain a struggle. As a result, many Peruvians don't publicly identify.

Public displays of affection among homosexual couples is rarely seen. Outside gay clubs, it is advisable to keep a low profile. Lima is the most accepting of gay people, but this is on a relative scale. Beyond that, the tourist towns of Cuzco, Arequipa and Trujillo tend to be more tolerant than the norm. Social media platforms Tinder and Grindr can connect travelers to the gay scene.

FYI: the rainbow flag seen around Cuzco and in the Andes is *not* a gay pride flag – it's the flag of the Inca empire.

FOOD PRICE RANGES

Mid- to high-end restaurants charge a 10% service fee and 19% tax. The following price ranges refer to a main dish.

$ less than S20

$$ S20–S60

$$$ more than S60

Information

Gay Lima (http://lima.gaycities.com) A handy guide to the latest gay and gay-friendly spots in the capital, along with plenty of links.

Gay Peru (www.gayperu.pe) A magazine-style website covering news, fashion and events.

Global Gayz (www.globalgayz.com) Excellent, country-specific information about Peru's gay scene and politics, with links to international resources.

Purpleroofs.com (www.purpleroofs.com) Massive LGBT portal with links to a few tour operators and gay-friendly accommodations in Peru.

Tours

Lima Tours (Map p60; ☎01-619-6900; www.limatours.com.pe; Nicolás de Piérola 589, 18th fl, Lima Centro; ⏲9:30am-6pm Mon-Fri, to 1pm Sat) A travel agency that is not exclusively gay, but organizes gay-friendly group trips around the country.

Maps

The best road map of Peru is the 1:2,000,000 *Mapa Vial* published by Lima 2000 and available in better bookstores. The 1:1,500,000 *Peru South and Lima* country map, published by International Travel Maps, covers the country in good detail south of a line drawn east to west through Tingo María, and has a good street map of Lima, San Isidro, Miraflores and Barranco on the reverse side.

For topographical maps, go to the **Instituto Geográfico Nacional** (IGN; ☎ext 119 01-475-3030; www.ign.gob.pe; Aramburu 1190-98, Surquillo; ⏲8:30am-5pm Mon-Fri), with reference maps and others for sale. In January the IGN closes early, so call ahead. High-scale topographic maps for trekking are available, though sheets of border areas might be hard to get. Geological and demographic maps and CD-ROMs are also sold.

Up-to-date topo maps are often available from outdoor outfitters in major trekking centers such as Cuzco, Huaraz and Arequipa. If you are bringing along a GPS unit, ensure that your power source adheres to Peru's 220V, 60Hz AC standard and always carry a compass.

Money

Prices are generally listed in Peruvian nuevos soles. However, many package lodgings and higher-end hotels will only quote prices in US dollars, as will many travel agencies and tour operators. In these cases, we list prices in US dollars.

Both currencies have experienced fluctuations in recent years, so expect many figures to be different from what you have read.

ATMs

- *Cajeros automáticos* (ATMs) proliferate in nearly every city and town in Peru, as well as at major airports, bus terminals and shopping areas.
- ATMs are linked to the international Plus (Visa) and Cirrus (Maestro/MasterCard) systems, as well as American Express and other networks.
- Users should have a four-digit PIN. To avoid problems, notify your bank that you'll be using your ATM card abroad.
- If your card works with Banco de la Nación, it may be the best option as it doesn't charge fees (at least at the time of writing).
- Both US dollars and nuevos soles are readily available from Peruvian ATMs.
- Your home bank may charge an additional fee for each foreign ATM transaction.
- ATMs are normally open 24 hours.
- For safety reasons use ATMs inside banks with security guards, preferably during daylight hours. Cover the keyboard for PIN entry.

Cash

The nuevo sol ('new sun') comes in bills of S10, S20, S50, S100 and (rarely) S200. It is divided into 100 céntimos, with copper-colored coins of S0.05, S0.10 and S0.20, and silver-colored S0.50 and S1 coins. In addition, there are bimetallic S2 and S5 coins with a copper-colored center inside a silver-colored ring.

US dollars are accepted by many tourist-oriented businesses, though you'll need nuevos soles to pay for local transportation, meals and other incidentals.

Counterfeit bills (in both US dollars and nuevo soles) often circulate in Peru. Merchants question both beat-up and large-denomination bills. Consumers should refuse them too.

To detect fakes check for a sheer watermark and examine a metal strip crossing the note that repeats Peru in neat, not misshapen, letters. Colored thread, holographs and writing along the top of the bill should be embossed, not glued on.

Changing Money

The best currency for exchange is the US dollar, although the euro is accepted in major tourist centers. Other hard currencies can be exchanged, but usually with difficulty and only in major cities. All foreign currencies must be in flawless condition.

Cambistas (money changers) hang out on street corners near banks and *casas de cambio* (foreign exchange bureaus) nand give competitive rates (there's only a little flexibility for bargaining), but are not always honest. Officially, they should wear a vest and badge identifying themselves as legal. They're useful after regular business hours or at borders where there aren't any other options.

PRACTICALITIES

Media

➡ Peru's government-leaning *El Comercio* (www.elcomercioperu.com.pe) is the leading daily newspaper. There's also the slightly left-of-center *La República* (www.elcomercioperu.com.pe) and the *Peruvian Times* (www.peruviantimes.com) and *Peru this Week* (www.peruthisweek.com) in English.

➡ A helpful online resource for expats in English is www.expatperu.com.

➡ *Etiqueta Negra* (www.etiquetanegra.com.pe) magazine focuses on culture. A good bilingual travel publication is the monthly *Rumbos* (www.rumbosdelperu.com).

➡ Cable and satellite TV are widely available for a fix of CNN or even Japanese news.

Smoking

➡ It's illegal to smoke in any establishment dedicated to health or education (schools, hospitals etc).

➡ Smoking is prohibited in all forms of public transport.

➡ Workplaces, hotels, restaurants and bars allow smoking only in designated smoking areas with a physically separate location.

Weights & Measures

➡ Peru uses the metric system but gas (petrol) is measured in US gallons.

Credit Cards

Midrange and top-end hotels and shops accept *tarjetas de crédito* (credit cards) with a 7% (or greater) fee. Your bank may also tack on a surcharge and additional fees for each foreign-currency transaction. The most widely accepted cards in Peru are Visa and MasterCard.

Post

The privatized postal system is run by Serpost (www.serpost.com.pe). Its service is fairly efficient and reliable, but surprisingly expensive. Most international mail will take about two weeks to arrive from Lima; longer from the provinces.

Public Holidays

Major holidays may be celebrated for days around the official date.

Fiestas Patrias (National Independence Days) is the biggest national holiday, when the entire nation seems to be on the move.

New Year's Day January 1

Good Friday March/April

Labor Day May 1

Inti Raymi June 24

Feast of Sts Peter & Paul June 29

National Independence Days July 28–29

Feast of Santa Rosa de Lima August 30

Battle of Angamos Day October 8

All Saints Day November 1

Feast of the Immaculate Conception December 8

Christmas December 25

Safe Travel

For newcomers, Peru can be busy and disorienting at first, making it easy to be caught off guard. Some things to be aware of:

➡ Travelers may experience periodic protests and strikes that can cut off transportation.

➡ While safety has improved, especially in Lima, street crimes such as pickpocketing, bag snatching and muggings are still common.

➡ Sneak theft is by far the most widespread type of crime.

➡ Bus drivers often act as if every bend in the road should be assaulted at Autobahn speeds.

Important Documents

All important documents (passport, credit cards, travel insurance policy, driver's license etc) should be photocopied or photographed before you leave home. Leave one copy at home or on a cloud drive and keep another with you, separate from the originals.

Thefts, Muggings & Other Crimes

Use basic precautions and a reasonable amount of awareness to avoid a robbery. Some tips:

➡ Crowded places such as bus terminals, train stations, markets and fiestas are the haunts of pickpockets; wear your day pack in front of you or carry a bag that fits snugly under your arm.

➡ Thieves look for easy targets, such as a bulging wallet in a back pocket or a camera held out in the open; keep spending money in your front pocket and your camera stowed when it's not in use.

➡ Passports and larger sums of cash are best carried in a money belt or an inside pocket that can be zipped or closed – or better yet, stowed in a safe at your hotel.

➡ Snatch theft can occur if you place a bag on the ground (even for a few seconds), or while you're asleep on an overnight bus; never leave a bag with your wallet and passport in the overhead rack of a bus.

➡ Don't keep valuables in bags that will be unattended.

➡ Blending in helps: walking around town in brand-new hiking gear or a shiny leather jacket will draw attention; stick to simple clothing.

➡ Leave jewelry and fancy watches at home.

➡ Hotels – especially cheap ones – aren't always trustworthy; lock valuables inside your luggage or use safety deposit services.

➡ Walk purposefully wherever you are going, even if you are lost; if you need to examine your map, duck into a shop or restaurant.

➡ Always take an official taxi at night and from the airport or bus terminals. If threatened, it's better just to give up your goods than face harm.

CRIMINAL TACTICS

Distraction Some thieves work in pairs or groups. One person creates a distraction as another robs. This can take the form of a bunch of kids fighting in front of you, an elderly person 'accidentally' bumping into you or perhaps someone spilling something on your clothes. Some may slit open your bag,

whether it's on your back or on the luggage rack of a bus.

Armed muggings In some cases, there have been robberies and armed muggings of trekkers on popular hiking trails around Huaraz, and jungle treks in the south. Going as part of a group with a local guide may help prevent this. In addition, the area around Tingo María, on the eastern edge of the central highlands, is a renowned bandit area, with armed robberies and other crimes regular occurrences. Keep any activities in the area, including bus rides, to daylight hours.

Express kidnapping 'Express' kidnappings have been recorded, particularly in some of the unsavory neighborhoods that surround the airport in Lima, and even just outside the airport. An armed attacker (or attackers) grabs someone out of a taxi or abducts them off the street, then forces them to go to the nearest bank to withdraw cash using their ATM cards. Victims who do not resist their attackers generally don't suffer serious physical harm.

REPORTING CRIME

The *policía de turismo* (tourist police, aka Poltur) can be found in major cities and tourist areas and can be helpful with criminal matters. If you are unsure how to locate them, contact the main office in Lima. If you are the victim of a crime, file a report with the tourist police immediately. At some point, inform your country's embassy about what has

happened. They won't be able to do much, but embassies do keep track of crime geared at foreigners as a way of alerting other travelers to potential dangers.

If you have taken out travel insurance and need to make a claim, Poltur will provide you with a police report. Stolen passports can be reissued at your embassy, though you may be asked for an alternative form of identification first. After receiving your new passport, go to the nearest Peruvian immigration office to get a new tourist card.

Corruption & Scams

Police The military and police (even sometimes the tourist police) have a reputation for corruption. While a foreigner may experience petty harassment (usually to procure payment of a bribe), most police officers are courteous to tourists or just leave them alone.

Touts Perhaps the most pernicious things travelers face are the persistent touts that gather at bus terminals, train stations, airports and other tourist spots to offer everything from discounted hotel rooms to local tours. Many touts – among them, many taxi drivers – will say just about anything to steer you to places they represent. They will tell you the establishment you've chosen is a notorious drug den, it's closed down or is overbooked. Do not believe everything you hear. If you have doubts about a place you've decided to stay at, ask to see a room before paying up.

GOVERNMENT TRAVEL ADVICE

The following government websites offer travel advisories and information on current hotspots.

Australian Department of Foreign Affairs (www.smartraveller.gov.au)

British Foreign Office (www.gov.uk/foreign-travel-advice/peru)

Canadian Department of Foreign Affairs (www.dfait-maeci.gc.ca)

US State Department (www.travel.state.gov)

Travel agents It's not advisable to book hotels, travel arrangements or transportation through independent agents. Often, they will demand cash upfront for services that never materialize. Stick to reputable, well-recommended agencies and you'll be assured a good time.

Transportation Issues

When taking buses, choose operators carefully. The cheapest companies will be the most likely to employ reckless drivers and have roadside breakdowns. Overnight travel by bus can get brutally cold in the highlands (take a blanket or a sleeping bag). In some parts, nighttime trips are also subject to the vagaries of roadside bandits, who create impromptu road blocks, then relieve passengers of their valuables. Armed robberies have been reported on the night buses between Trujillo and Cajabamba and Lima and Cuzco.

Environmental Hazards

Some of Peru's natural hazards include earthquakes and avalanches. Rescues in remote regions are often done on foot because of the inability of helicopters to reach some of the country's more challenging topography. Perhaps the most common hazard is travelers' diarrhea, which comes from consuming contaminated food or water. Other problems include altitude sickness, animal and insect bites, sunburn, heat exhaustion and even hypothermia. You can take precautions for most of these.

Protests & Other Conflict

Protests During the Internal Conflict, through the 1980s and into the 1990s, terrorism, civil strife and kidnappings meant that entire regions were off-limits to both foreign and domestic travelers. Now travelers visit much

of the country without problems. Even so, public protests remain a familiar sight. Generally speaking, these have little effect on tourists. It is worth staying aware of current events while in the country; and if a road is blocked or an area cut off, respect the situation. Being a foreigner will not grant you immunity from violence.

Shining Path In the news, a Sendero Luminoso (Shining Path) resurgence has brought isolated incidents of violence in the main coca growing areas in the provinces of Ayacucho, Cuzco (the trekking route to Espíritu Pampa), Huancavelica, Huánuco, Junín and San Martín. These are generally directed at the Peruvian military or the police. Even so, it is worth exercising caution: avoid transit through isolated areas in these regions at night and always check with reputable tour operators before heading out on a remote trekking route.

Drug trafficking Likewise, drug trafficking areas can be dangerous, especially at night. Travelers should avoid the upper Río Huallaga valley between Tingo María and Juanjuí, Puerto Bermúdez, and near Ayacucho, where the majority of Peru's illegal drug-growing takes place. Exercise similar caution near the Colombian border, where trafficking also goes on.

Landmines

A half century of armed conflict over the Cordillera del Condor region on Peru's northeastern border with Ecuador was finally resolved in 1998. However, unexploded ordnance (UXO) in the area has not been completely cleaned up. Only use official border crossings and don't stray from the beaten path when traveling in this region.

Telephone

A few public pay phones operated by Movistar and Claro are still around, especially in small towns. They work with coins or phone cards, which can be purchased at

supermarkets and groceries. Often internet cafes have 'net-to-net' capabilities (such as Skype), to talk for free.

Cell Phones

In Lima and other larger cities you can buy SIM cards for unlocked phones for about S15. Credit can be purchased in pharmacies and supermarkets. Cell-phone reception may be poor in the mountains or jungle.

Phone Codes

When calling Peru from abroad, dial the international access code for the country you're in, then Peru's country code (51), then the area code without the 0 and finally, the local number. When making international calls from Peru, dial the international access code (00), then the country code of where you're calling to, then the area code and finally, the local phone number.

In Peru, any telephone number beginning with a 9 is a cell-phone number. Numbers beginning with 0800 are often toll-free only when dialed from private phones. To make a credit-card or collect call using AT&T, dial 0800-50288. For an online telephone directory, see www.paginasamarillas.com.pe.

Time

➡ Peru is five hours behind Greenwich Mean Time (GMT). It's the same as Eastern Standard Time (EST) in North America. At noon in Lima, it's 9am in Los Angeles, 11am in Mexico City, noon in New York, 5pm in London and 4am (following day) in Sydney.

➡ Daylight Saving Time (DST) isn't used in Peru.

➡ Punctuality is not one of the things that Latin America is famous for, so be prepared to wait around. Buses rarely depart or arrive on time. Savvy travelers should allow some flexibility in their itineraries.

Toilets

Peruvian plumbing leaves something to be desired. There's always a chance that flushing a toilet will cause it to overflow, so you should avoid putting anything other than human waste into the toilet. Even a small amount of toilet paper can muck up the entire system – that's why a small, plastic bin is routinely provided for disposing of the paper. This may not seem sanitary, but it is definitely better than the alternative of clogged toilets and flooded floors. A well-run hotel or restaurant, even a cheap one, will empty the bin and clean the toilet daily. In rural areas, there may be just a rickety wooden outhouse built around a hole in the ground.

Public toilets are rare outside of transportation terminals, restaurants and museums, but restaurants will generally let travelers use a restroom (sometimes for a charge). Those in terminals usually have an attendant who will charge you about S0.75 to enter and then give you a few sheets of toilet paper. Public restrooms frequently run out of toilet paper, so always carry extra.

Tourist Information

➡ The Ministry of Culture and Tourism has a network of tourist information offices throughout the country.

➡ iPeru (www.peru.travel) A great resource for travelers. It can supply schedules for public transportation and information on lodgings and attractions.

Visas

Tourists are permitted a 183-day, non-extendable stay, stamped into passports and onto a tourist card called a Tarjeta Andina de Migración (Andean Immigration Card).

Keep it – it must be returned upon exiting the country. If you will need it, request the full amount of time to the immigration officer at the point of entry, since they have a tendency to issue 30- or 90-day stays.

Those who enter Peru via the Lima airport or cruise ship do not receive a tourist card; their visits are processed online.

If you lose your tourist card, visit the **Oficina de Migraciónes** (Immigration Office; Map p64; ☑01-200-1000; www.migraciones.gob.pe; Prolongación España 734, Breña; ◷8am-1pm Mon-Fri) or obtain a replacement copy via the website. Information in English can be found online. Extensions are no longer officially available.

Anyone who plans to work, attend school or reside in Peru for any length of time must obtain a visa in advance. Do this through the Peruvian embassy or consulate in your home country.

Carry your passport and tourist card on your person at all times, especially in remote areas (it's required by law on the Inca Trail). For security, make a photocopy of both documents and keep them in a separate place from the originals.

Volunteering

General advice for finding volunteer work is to ask at language schools; they usually know of several programs suitable for their students. Both nonprofit and for-profit organizations can arrange volunteer opportunities, if you contact them in advance.

Action Without Borders (www.idealist.org) Online database of social-work-oriented jobs, internships and volunteer opportunities.

Cross-Cultural Solutions (www.crossculturalsolutions.org) Educational and social-service projects in Lima and Ayacucho; program fees include professional in-country support.

Earthwatch Institute (www.earthwatch.org) Pay to help scientists on archaeological, ecological and other real-life expeditions in the Amazon Basin and the Andes.

Global Crossroad (☑in UK 0800-310-1821, in USA 866-387-7816; www.globalcrossroad.com) Volunteer, internship and job programs in the Andes. Summer cultural immersion programs for 18- to 29-year-olds include language instruction, homestays, volunteer work and sightseeing.

Global Volunteers (www.globalvolunteers.org) Offers short-term volunteer opportunities helping orphans in Lima.

Kiya Survivors/Peru Positive Action (☑in UK 1273-721902; www.kiyasurvivors.org; 1 Sussex Rd, Hove, UK) Organizes two- to six-month volunteer placements for assistant teachers and therapists to work with special-needs children in Cuzco, Urubamba in the Sacred Valley and Máncora on the north coast.

Women Travelers

Machismo is alive and well in Latin America. Most female travelers to Peru will experience little more than shouts of *mi amor* (my love) or an appreciative hiss. If you are fair-skinned with blond hair, however, be prepared to be the center of attention. Peruvian men consider foreign women to have looser morals and be easier sexual conquests than Peruvian women and will often make flirtatious comments to single women.

Unwanted attention Staring, whistling, hissing and catcalls in the streets is common and best ignored. Most men rarely, if ever, follow up on the idle chatter (unless they feel you've insulted their manhood). Ignoring all provocation and staring ahead is generally the best response. If someone is particularly persistent, try a potentially ardor-smothering phrase such as *soy casada* (I'm married). If you appeal directly to locals, you'll find most Peruvians to be protective of lone women, expressing surprise and concern if you tell them you're traveling without your family or husband.

Bricheros It's not uncommon for fast-talking charmers, especially in tourist towns such as Cuzco, to attach themselves to gringas. Known in Peru as bricheros, many of these young Casanovas are looking for a meal ticket, so approach any professions of undying love with extreme skepticism. This happens to men too.

First impressions Use common sense when meeting men in public places. In Peru, outside of a few big cities, it is rare for a woman to belly up to a bar for a beer, and the ones that do tend to be prostitutes. If you feel the need for an evening cocktail, opt for a restaurant. Likewise, heavy drinking by women might be misinterpreted by some men as a sign of promiscuity. When meeting someone, make it very clear if only friendship is intended. This goes double for tour and activity guides. When meeting someone for the first time, it is also wise not to divulge where you are staying until you feel sure that you are with someone you can trust.

Practicalities

➡ In highland towns, dress is generally fairly conservative and women rarely wear shorts, opting instead for long skirts. Shorts, miniskirts and revealing blouses may draw unwanted attention.

➡ Tampons are difficult to find in smaller towns, so stock up in major cities.

➡ Birth-control pills and other contraceptives (even condoms) are scarce outside metropolitan areas and not always reliable, so bring your own supply from home. Rates of HIV infection are on the rise, especially among young women.

➡ Abortions are illegal, except to save the life of the mother.

Sexual Assault

Travelers who are sexually assaulted can report it to the nearest police station or to the tourist police. However, Peruvian attitudes toward sexual assaults favor the attackers, not the survivors. Rape is often seen as a disgrace, and it is difficult to prosecute. Because the police tend to be unhelpful, we recommend calling your own embassy or consulate to ask for advice, including on where to seek medical treatment, which should be an immediate priority.

A few tips:

➡ Skip the hitchhiking.

➡ Do not take unlicensed taxis, especially at night (licensed taxis have a number on the door and an authorization sticker on the windshield).

➡ Avoid walking alone in unfamiliar places at night.

➡ If a stranger approaches you on the street and asks a question, answer it if you feel comfortable – but don't stop walking as it could allow potential attackers to surround you.

➡ Avoid overnight buses through bandit-ridden areas.

➡ Be aware of your surroundings; attacks have occurred in broad daylight around well-touristed sites and popular trekking trails.

➡ When hiring a private tour or activity guide, seek someone who comes from a recommended or reliable agency.

Useful Organizations

Centro de La Mujer Peruana Flora Tristán (Map p64; ☏01-433-1457; www.flora.org.pe; Parque Hernán Velarde 14,

Lima; ⊙9am-6pm Mon-Fri) Feminist social and political advocacy group for women's and human rights in Peru, with a Spanish-language website and a library in Lima.

Instituto Peruano de Paternidad Responsable (Inppares; ☏01-480-1626; www.inppares.org) Planned Parenthood–affiliated organization that runs a dozen sexual and reproductive health clinics for both women and men around the country, including in Lima.

Work

It's increasingly difficult to obtain residence and work permits for Peru, and likewise to get jobs without a proper work visa. Some jobs teaching English in language schools may not require one, but this is illegal. Occasionally, schools advertise for teachers, but more often, jobs are found by word of mouth. Schools expect you to be a native English speaker, and the pay is low. If you have teaching credentials, so much the better.

American and British schools in Lima sometimes hire teachers of math, biology and other subjects, but usually only if you apply in advance. They pay much better than the language schools, and might possibly be able to help you get a work visa if you want to stay. In Lima, the South American Explorers clubhouse and international cultural centers may have contacts with schools that are looking for teachers.

Most other jobs are obtained by word of mouth (eg bartenders, hostel staff, jungle guides), but the possibilities are limited. Volunteer organizations offer internships and short-term job opportunities.

Transportation

GETTING THERE & AWAY

Flights, cars and tours can be booked online at lonelyplanet.com/bookings.

Entering the Country

Travelers' passports should be valid for at least six months beyond their departure date. When arriving by air, US citizens must show a return ticket or an open-jaw onward ticket.

Upon arrival, immigration officials may only stamp 30 days into a passport though the limit is 180 days. If this happens, explain how many more days you need, supported by an exit ticket for onward or return travel.

Bribery (known colloquially as *coima*) is illegal, but some officials may try to procure extra 'fees' at land borders.

Air

Peru (mainly Lima) has direct flights to and from cities all over the Americas, as well as continental Europe. Other locations require a connection.

Airports & Airlines

Located in the port city of Callao, Lima's **Aeropuerto Internacional Jorge Chávez** (☑01-517-3500, schedules 01-511-6055; www.lima-airport.com) has terminals sparkling with shopping and services. A major hub, it's serviced by flights from North, Central and South America, and two regular direct flights from Europe (Madrid and Amsterdam). Check the airport website or call for updated departure and arrival schedules for domestic and international flights. Cuzco has the only other airport with international services (within South America).

Tickets

Peak season From most places in the world, South America can be a relatively costly destination. The high season for air travel to and within Peru is late May to early September, as well as around major holidays. Look for lower fares outside peak periods.

Discounts Shopping around online can turn up cheaper tickets. Students with international student ID cards – the International Student Identity Card (ISIC) is one widely recognized card – and anyone under 26 years can often get discounts with budget or specialty travel agencies. A good option to check out is STA Travel (www.statravel.com), with offices around the globe.

Tax Tickets bought in Peru are subject to a 19% tax (included in the ticket price).

Reconfirming flights It is essential to reconfirm all flights 72 hours in advance, either by phone or online, or you may get bumped off the flight. If you are traveling in remote areas, have a reputable travel agent do this for you.

Australia & New Zealand

Santiago (Chile) tends to be the most common gateway city from Australia and New Zealand, though some carriers connect through the US as well.

South American Travel Centre (☑03-9642-5353; www.satc.com.au) In Melbourne, this agency specializes in travel to Latin America.

Canada

There are direct flights to Lima from Toronto, but most trips require a connection in the US or Mexico City.

Continental Europe

There are direct flights from Amsterdam and Madrid, but connections through the USA, Central America or Colombia are often cheaper.

Latin America

There are direct flights to Peru from a large number of Latin American cities, including Bogotá, Leticia, Buenos Aires, Caracas, Guayaquil, La Paz, Mexico City, Panama City, Quito, Rio de Janeiro, San José (Costa Rica), Santiago (Chile) and São Paulo.

LATAM, Copa and TACA are the principal Latin American airlines that fly to Lima.

UK & Ireland

Flights from the UK or Ireland connect through gateway cities in continental Europe, North America and Brazil.

USA

There are direct (nonstop) flights to Lima from Atlanta, Dallas-Fort Worth, Houston, Los Angeles, Miami and New York. In other cases, flights will connect either in the US or in Latin American gateway cities such as Mexico City and Bogotá.

Land & River

Because no roads bridge the Darien Gap, it is not possible to travel to South America by land from the north. Driving overland from neighboring Bolivia, Brazil, Chile, Colombia and Ecuador requires careful logistical planning.

Bus and train International bus companies go to Chile, Ecuador, Colombia, Bolivia, Brazil and Argentina. Smaller regional companies do cross-border travel, but on a more-limited basis. The only rail service that crosses the Peru border is the train between Arica (Chile) and Tacna on Peru's south coast.

Boat Getting to Peru by boat is possible from points on the Amazon River in Brazil and from Leticia (Colombia). There are also port cities on Peru's Pacific coast.

Tickets With any form of transport, it may be a bit cheaper to buy tickets to the border, cross over and then buy onward tickets on the other side, but it's usually much easier, faster and safer to buy a cross-border through ticket. When traveling by bus, check carefully with the company about what is included in the price of the ticket, and whether the service is direct or involves a transfer, and possibly a long wait, at the border.

Bolivia

Peru is normally reached overland from Bolivia via Lake Titicaca; the border crossing at Yunguyo is much safer and a lot less chaotic than its counterpart at Desaguadero. There are many transportation options for both of these routes, most of which involve changing buses at the Peru–Bolivia border before reaching Puno. It's possible, but a logistical feat, to cross into Bolivia from Puerto Maldonado.

Brazil

You can travel overland between Peru and Brazil via Iñapari. Traveling from Iquitos, it's more straightforward to go along the Amazon to Tabatinga in Brazil via Leticia (Colombia).

Chile

Traveling on the Pan-American Hwy, the major crossing point is between Arica (Chile) and Tacna on Peru's south coast.

Long-distance buses to Tacna depart from Lima, Arequipa and Puno. Colectivo (shared) taxis are the fastest and most reliable way to travel between Tacna and Arica. It's also possible to make the crossing, albeit much more slowly, by train; border formalities are done at the respective stations. Flights to Tacna from Arequipa are cheap but book up quickly. Alternatively, buses go from Lima all the way to Santiago, Chile. From Arequipa, buses go to Santiago (Chile) and Buenos Aires (Argentina).

Colombia

It is easiest to travel between Peru and Colombia via Ecuador. Ormeño has through buses between Lima and Bogotá via Ecuador. This long-haul trip is better done in stages, though.

If you are in the rainforest, it is more straightforward to voyage along the Amazon by boat between Iquitos and Leticia (Colombia) from where there are flights to Bogotá.

Ecuador

The most common way to get to or from Ecuador is along the Pan-American Hwy via Tumbes (Peru), where there is a border-crossing station. Another route is via La Tina to Loja in Ecuador. A third way is via Jaén. **Cifa** (☎972-894-619; www.cifainternacional.com; Tumbes 572) runs buses between Tumbes and Machala or Guayaquil in Ecuador. From Piura, **Transportes Loja** (Map p354; ☎073-33-3260; Loreto 1241, Adentro Terminal Ronco) goes via La Tina to Macará and Loja. **Ormeño** (☎01-472-1710; www.grupo-ormeno.com.pe; Av Javier Prado Este 1057) has weekly through buses between Lima and Quito.

Tours

Travelers who prefer not to travel on their own, or have a limited amount of time, have ample tours to choose from. Travel with knowledgeable guides comes at a premium. It's worth it for highly specialized outdoor activities like rafting, mountaineering, bird-watching or mountain biking.

If you want to book a tour locally, Lima, Cuzco, Arequipa, Puno, Trujillo, Huaraz, Puerto Maldonado and Iquitos have the most travel agencies offering organized tours. For more specialized, individual or small-group tours, you can generally hire a bilingual guide starting at US$20/80 per hour/day plus expenses (keep in mind exchange rates may affect this); tours in other languages may be more expensive. Some students or unregistered guides are cheaper, but the usual caveat applies – some are good, others aren't.

For more guide listings, check out www.leaplocal.org, a resource promoting socially responsible tourism.

From Australia & New Zealand

Aspiring Adventures (☑in US & Canada 1-877-438-1354, in New Zealand 03-489-7474; www.aspiringadventures.com) A small, enthusiastic outfit that's Kiwi-Australian run with extensive experience in Cuzco and the Sacred Valley. Offers biking, classic trips and food-focused tours.

From Canada & the USA

With easy flight connections, the USA has more companies offering tours of Peru than the rest of the world.

Adventure Life (☑406-541-2677, in USA 800-344-6118; www.adventure-life.com; 712 W Spruce St, Ste 1, Missoula, MT 5980) Andean trekking, Amazon exploring and multisport itineraries; a reputable agency that uses bilingual guides, family-run hotels and local transportation.

Explorations (www.explorations inc.com) Amazon trips include biologist-escorted cruises, lodge-based expeditions and fishing trips in the Reserva Nacional Pacaya-Samiria.

G Adventures (☑1-416-260-0999; www.gadventures.com; 19 Charlotte St, Toronto, ON, M5V 2H5; ⑤St Andrew) The premier Canadian agency with offices in Vancouver, Boston and London, UK. Budget-priced tours include hotel-based, trekking, Amazon and cultural trips.

International Expeditions (☑800-230-7665, 205-428-

1700; www.ietravel.com; One Environs Park, Helena, AL 35080) Offers Amazon tours, staying in jungle lodges or on river boats, with an emphasis on natural history and bird-watching.

Mountain Travel Sobek (☑510-594-6000, in USA 888-831-7526; www.mtsobek.com; 1266 66th St, Emeryville, CA 94608) Luxury trekking tours along the Inca Trail or in the Cordillera Blanca, and occasional rafting trips on the Río Tambopata.

Sacred Rides (☑647-999-7955; http://sacredrides.com; 261 Markham St, Toronto, ON M6J 2G7; ⑤Bathurst) A mountain-biking specialist that organizes various multiday bike tours throughout the Peruvian Andes.

SA Expeditions (☑in USA 1-415-549-8049; www.sa expeditions.com) High-end tour operator offering standard tours and is the flagship operator developing treks for the Qhapaq Ñan, the Inca road system which became a World Heritage Site in 2014. It has a five-day route from Castillo to Guanaco Pampa and plans to add more.

Wilderness Travel (☑510-558-2488, 800-368-2794; www.wildernesstravel.com; 1102 Ninth St, Berkeley, CA 94710) Offers luxury treks, from four nights to two weeks, throughout the highlands and the Amazon.

From the UK & Continental Europe

Andean Trails (☑in Scotland 0131-467 7086; www.andean trails.co.uk; 33 Sandport St, Leith, Edinburgh, EH6 5QG) Mountain-biking, climbing,

trekking and rafting tours in some unusual spots.

Exodus (www.exodus.co.uk) Award-winning, responsible-travel operator offering long-distance overland trips and shorter cultural and trekking adventures.

Hauser Exkursionen (www.hauser-exkursionen.de) A German sustainable tour operator.

Huwans Clubaventure (☑in France 01 44 32 09 30; www.clubaventure.fr; 18 rue Séguier, 75006 Paris) A reputable French company organizing treks and tours.

Journey Latin America (☑in UK 020-3131-5349; www.journeylatinamerica.co.uk; 401 King St, London, W6 9NJ) ☀ Cultural trips and treks in the Cordilleras Blanca and Huayhuash and to Machu Picchu.

GETTING AROUND

Air

Domestic-flight schedules and prices change frequently. New airlines open every year, as those with poor safety records close. Most big cities are served by modern jets, while smaller towns are served by propeller aircraft.

Airlines in Peru

Most domestic airlines have offices in Lima. Smaller carriers and charters are also an option. The most remote towns may require connecting flights, and smaller towns are not served every day. Many

---

CLIMATE CHANGE & TRAVEL

Every form of transport that relies on carbon-based fuel generates CO_2, the main cause of human-induced climate change. Modern travel is dependent on airplanes, which might use less fuel per kilometer per person than most cars but travel much greater distances. The altitude at which aircraft emit gases (including CO_2) and particles also contributes to their climate change impact. Many websites offer 'carbon calculators' that allow people to estimate the carbon emissions generated by their journey and, for those who wish to do so, to offset the impact of the greenhouse gases emitted with contributions to portfolios of climate-friendly initiatives throughout the world. Lonely Planet offsets the carbon footprint of all staff and author travel.

airports for these places are no more than a dirt strip.

Be at the airport two hours before your flight departs. Flights may be overbooked, baggage handling and check-in procedures tend to be chaotic, and flights may even leave *before* their official departure time because bad weather is predicted.

Most airlines fly from Lima to regional capitals, but service between provincial cities is limited.

LATAM (Map p72; ☑01-213-8200; www.latam.com; Av José Pardo 513, Miraflores) Reliable service to Arequipa, Chiclayo, Cuzco, Iquitos, Juliaca, Piura, Puerto Maldonado, Tacna, Tarapoto and Trujillo. Additionally it offers link services between Arequipa and Cuzco, Arequipa and Juliaca, Arequipa and Tacna, Cuzco and Juliaca, and Cuzco and Puerto Maldonado. With international services as well.

LC Perú (☑01-204-1300; www.lcperu.pe; Av Pablo Carriquirry 857, San Isidro; ⊙9am-7pm Mon-Fri, to 5pm Sat) Flies from Lima to Andahuaylas, Arequipa, Ayacucho, Chachapoyas, Chiclayo, Cajamarca, Huánuco, Huaraz, Iquitos, Trujillo and Huancayo (Jauja) on smaller turbo-prop aircraft. Gets low marks for frequent cancellations and the difficulty in obtaining a refund.

Peruvian Airlines (Map p72; ☑01-715-6122; www.peruvianairlines.pe; Av José Pardo 495, Miraflores; ⊙9am-7pm Mon-Fri, to 5pm Sat) Flies to Arequipa, Cuzco, Piura, Iquitos, Jauja, Pucallpa, Tarapoto, Tacna and internationally to La Paz, Bolivia.

Star Perú (Map p72; ☑01-213-8813; www.starperu.com; Av Espinar 331, Miraflores; ⊙9am-6:45pm Mon-Fri, to 1pm Sat) Domestic carrier, flying to Ayacucho, Cuzco, Huanuco, Iquitos, Pucallpa, Puerto Maldonado and Tarapoto.

Viva Air (☑01-705-0107; www.vivaair.com; Aeropuerto Internacional Jorge Chávez; ⊙hours vary) Budget flights to Arequipa, Piura, Cuzco, Iquitos and Tarapato.

Tickets

Most travelers travel in one direction overland and save time returning by air. You can sometimes buy tickets at the airport on a space-available basis, but don't count on it.

Peak season The peak season for air travel within Peru is late May to early September, as well as around major holidays. Buy tickets for less popular destinations as far in advance as possible, as these infrequent flights book up quickly. It's almost impossible to buy tickets just before major holidays, notably Semana Santa (the week leading up to Easter) and Fiestas Patrias (the last week in July). Overbooking is the norm.

Discounts Domestic flights are usually cheaper when advertised on the Peruvian website (versus its international version), so if you can wait until you arrive to Peru to buy regional tickets, you may save money.

Reconfirming flights In remote areas, buying tickets and reconfirming flights is best done at airline offices; otherwise, you can do so online or via a recommended travel agent. Ensure all flight reservations are *confirmed and reconfirmed* 72 and 24 hours in advance; airlines are notorious for overbooking and flights are changed or canceled with surprising frequency, so it's even worth calling the airport or the airline just before leaving for the airport. Confirmation is especially essential during the peak travel season.

Bicycle

Safety The major drawback to cycling in Peru is the country's bounty of kamikaze motorists. On narrow, two-lane highways, drivers can be a serious hazard to cyclists. Cycling is more enjoyable and safer, though very challenging, off paved roads. Mountain bikes are recommended, as road bikes won't stand up to the rough conditions.

Rentals Reasonably priced rentals (mostly mountain bikes) are available in popular tourist destinations, including Cuzco, Arequipa, Huaraz and Huancayo. These bikes are rented to travelers for local excursions, not to make trips all over the country. For long-distance touring, bring your own bike from home.

Transporting bicycles Airline policies on carrying bicycles vary, so shop around.

Boat

There are no passenger services along the Peruvian coast. In the Andean highlands, there are boat services on Lake Titicaca. Small motorized vessels take passengers from the port in Puno to visit various islands on the lake, while catamarans zip over to Bolivia.

In Peru's Amazon Basin, boat travel is of major importance. Larger vessels ply the wider rivers. Dugout canoes powered by outboard engines act as water taxis on smaller rivers. Those called *peki-pekis* are slow and rather noisy. In some places, modern aluminum launches are used.

Cargo Boat

Some travelers dream of plying the Amazon while swinging in a hammock aboard a banana boat with cargo on the lower deck. It's possible to travel from Pucallpa or Yurimaguas to Iquitos and on into Brazil this way.

Departures At ports, chalkboards with ships' names, destinations and departure times are displayed; these are usually optimistic. The captain has to clear documents with the *capitanía* (harbor master's office) on the day of departure, so ask the captain directly for updates. Nobody else really knows. Departure time often depends on a full cargo. Usually, you can sleep on the boat while waiting if you want to save on hotel bills. Never leave your luggage unattended.

Sleeping Bring your own hammock, or rent a cabin for the journey. If using a hammock hang it away from the noisy engine room and not directly under a light, as these are often lit late at night, precluding sleep and attracting insects. Cabins are often hot, airless boxes, but are lockable. Sanitary facilities are basic and there's usually a pump shower on board.

Eating Basic food is usually included in the price of the passage, and may be marginally better on the bigger ships or if you are in cabin class. Finicky eaters or people with dietary restrictions should bring their own food. Bottled soft drinks are usually available.

Bus

Buses are the usual form of transportation for most Peruvians and many travelers. Fares are cheap and services are frequent on the major long-distance routes, but buses are of varying quality. Don't always go with the cheapest option – check their safety records first. Remote rural routes are often served by older, worn-out vehicles. Seats at the back of the bus yield a bumpier ride.

Many cities do not have a main bus terminal. Buses rarely arrive or depart on time, so consider most average trip times as best-case scenarios. Buses can be significantly delayed during the rainy season, particularly in the highlands and the jungle. From January to April, journey times may double or face indefinite delays because of landslides and bad road conditions.

Fatal accidents are not unusual in Peru.

Avoid overnight buses, on which muggings and assaults are more likely to occur.

Classes

Luxury buses Invariably called Imperial, Royal, Business or Executive, these higher-priced express services feature toilets, videos and air-conditioning. Luxury buses serve paltry snacks and don't stop.

Bus-camas Feature seats which recline halfway or almost fully. Better long-distance buses stop for bathroom breaks and meals in special rest areas with inexpensive but sometimes unappetizing fare. Almost every bus terminal has a few kiosks with basic provisions.

Económico For trips under six hours, you may have no choice but to take an *económico* bus, and these are usually pretty beaten up. While *económico* services don't stop for meals, vendors will board and sell snacks.

Costs & Reservations

Schedules and fares change frequently and vary from company to company; therefore, quoted prices are only approximations.

Fares fluctuate during peak and off-peak travel times. For long-distance or overnight journeys, or travel to remote areas with only limited services, buy your ticket at least the day before. Most travel agencies offer reservations but overcharge shockingly for the ticket. Except in Lima, it's cheaper to take a taxi to the bus terminal and buy the tickets yourself.

You can check schedules online (but not make reservations, at least not yet) for the major players, including the following:

Cruz del Sur (www.cruzdelsur. com.pe)

Oltursa (www.oltursa.com.pe)

Ormeño (☎01-472-1710; www. grupo-ormeno.com.pe; Av Javier Prado Este 1057)

Transportes Línea (www.linea.pe)

Luggage

➡ Watch your luggage in bus terminals very carefully. Some terminals have left-luggage facilities.

➡ Bags put into the luggage compartment are generally safe. Hand luggage is a different matter. Items may be taken while you sleep. For this reason, never use the overhead compartments and bring only items that can fit at your feet or on your lap.

Car & Motorcycle

➡ Distances in Peru are long so it's best to bus or fly to a region and rent a car from there. Hiring a taxi is often cheaper and easier.

➡ At roadside checkpoints, police or military conduct meticulous document checks. Drivers who offer an officer some money to smooth things along consider it a 'gift' or 'on-the-spot fine' to get on their way. Readers should know that these transactions are an unsavory reality in Peru and Lonely Planet does not condone them.

➡ When filling up, make sure the meter starts at zero.

Driver's License

A driver's license from your own home country is sufficient for renting a car. An International Driving Permit (IDP) is only required if you'll be driving in Peru for more than 30 days.

Car Rental

Major rental companies have offices in Lima and a few other large cities. Renting a motorcycle is an option mainly in jungle towns, where you can go for short runs around town on dirt bikes, but not much further.

Economy car rental starts at US$25 a day without the 19% sales tax, 'super' collision-damage waiver, personal accident insurance and so on, which together can climb to more than US$100 per day, not including excess mileage. Vehicles with 4WD are more expensive.

Make sure you completely understand the rental agreement before you sign. A credit card is required, and renters normally need to be over 25 years of age.

Road Rules & Hazards

Bear in mind that the condition of rental cars is often poor, roads are potholed (even the paved Pan-American Hwy), gas is expensive, and drivers are aggressive, regarding speed limits, road signs and traffic signals as mere guides, not the law. Moreover, road signs are often small and unclear.

➡ Driving is on the right-hand side of the road.

➡ Driving at night is not recommended because of poor conditions, speeding buses and slow-moving, poorly lit trucks.

➡ Theft is all too common, so you should not leave your vehicle parked on the street. When stopping overnight, park the car in a guarded lot (common in better hotels).

➡ Gas or petrol stations (called *grifos*) are few and far between.

Hitchhiking

Hitching is never entirely safe, and we don't recommend it. Travelers who hitch should understand that they are taking a small but potentially serious risk. Hitchhikers will be safer if they travel in pairs and let someone know where they are planning to go. In Peru hitching is not very practical, as there are few private cars, buses are so cheap and trucks are often used as paid public transportation in remote areas.

Local Transportation

In most towns and cities, it's easy to walk everywhere or take a taxi. Using local buses, *micros* and *combis* can be tricky, but is very inexpensive.

Bus

Local buses are slow and crowded but cheap. Ask locals for help, as there aren't any obvious bus lines in most towns.

A faster, more hair-raising alternative is to take *micros* or *combis*, sometimes called *colectivos* (though the term usually refers to taxis). Typically, *micros* and *combis* are minibuses or minivans stuffed full of passengers. They can be identified by stickers along the outside panels and destination placards in the front windows. You can flag one down or get off anywhere on the route. A conductor usually leans out of the vehicle, shouting out destinations. Once inside, you must quickly squeeze into any available seat, or be prepared to stand. The conductor comes around to collect the fare, or you can pay when getting off.

Safety is not a high priority for *combi* drivers. The only place for a passenger to safely buckle up is the front seat, but in the event of a head-on collision (not an unusual occurrence), that's the last place you'd want to be.

Taxi

Taxis seem to be everywhere. Private cars that have a small taxi sticker in the windshield aren't necessarily regulated. Safer, regulated taxis usually have a lit company number on the roof and are contacted by phone. These are more expensive than taxis flagged down on the street, but are more reliable.

Fares Always ask the fare in advance, as there are no meters. It's acceptable to haggle; try to find out what the going rate is before taking a cab, especially for long trips. The standard fare for short runs in most cities is around S5.

Tipping Tipping is not the norm, unless you have hired a driver for a long period or he has helped you with luggage or other lifting.

Long-distance trips Hiring a private taxi for long-distance trips costs less than renting a car and takes care of many of the problems with car rental. Not all taxi drivers will agree to drive long distances, but if one does, you should carefully check their credentials and vehicle before hiring.

Train

The privatized rail system, PeruRail (www.perurail.com), has daily services between Cuzco and Aguas Calientes, aka Machu Picchu Pueblo, and thrice-weekly services between Cuzco and Puno on the shores of Lake Titicaca. There are also luxury passenger services between Cuzco, Puno and Arequipa twice weekly. **Inca Rail** (Map p204; ☎084-25-2974; www. incarail.com; Portal de Panes 105, Plaza de Armas; 1 way S231-330; ⏰8am-9pm Mon-Fri, 9am-7pm Sat, to 2pm Sun) 🚆 also offers a service between Ollantaytambo and Aguas Calientes.

Train buffs won't want to miss the lovely **Ferrocarril Central Andino** (Map p60; ☎01-226-6363; www.ferrocarrilcentral.com. pe; Estación Desamparados; round-trip adult/child 12 & under tourist class S600/300, standard class S450/225), which reaches an altitude of 4829m. It usually runs between Lima and Huancayo from mid-April to mid-November. In Huancayo, cheaper trains to Huancavelica leave daily from a different station. Another charmingly historic railway makes inexpensive daily runs between Tacna on Peru's south coast and Arica, Chile.

Health

It's not unusual to suffer from altitude sickness in the Andes or have tummy problems, despite Peru's wonderful culinary reputation. Peru's many climates mean that travelers will face different risks in different areas. While food-borne as well as mosquito-borne infections happen, many of these illnesses are not life-threatening – but they can certainly ruin your trip. Besides getting the proper vaccinations, it's important that you take insect repellent and exercise care in what you eat and drink.

BEFORE YOU GO

Since most vaccines don't produce immunity until at least two weeks after they're given, visit a physician four to eight weeks before departure. Ask your doctor for an International Certificate of Vaccination (otherwise known as the 'yellow booklet'), which will list all the vaccinations you've received. This is mandatory for countries that require proof of yellow-fever vaccination upon entry, but it's a good idea to carry it wherever you travel.

Bring medications in their original containers, clearly labeled. A signed, dated letter from your physician describing all medical conditions and medications, including generic names, is also a good idea. If carrying syringes or needles, be sure to have a physician's letter documenting their medical necessity.

Most doctors and hospitals expect payment in cash, regardless of whether you have travel health insurance.

The World Health Organization (www.who.int/ith) offers a free download of its International Travel and Health booklet.

Health Insurance

All travelers should have health insurance. If yours does not cover medical expenses abroad, consider supplemental insurance. Find out in advance if your insurance plan will make payments directly to providers or reimburse you later for overseas health expenditures.

Recommended Vaccinations

The only required vaccine for Peru is yellow fever, and that's only if you're arriving from a yellow-fever-infected country in Africa or the Americas. It is strongly advised, though, for those visiting the jungle, as are malaria pills.

Diseases found in Peru include mosquito-borne infections, such as malaria, Zika virus, yellow fever and dengue fever, although these are rare in temperate regions.

Medical Checklist

- ➡ antibiotics
- ➡ antidiarrheal drugs (eg loperamide)
- ➡ acetaminophen (Tylenol) or aspirin
- ➡ anti-inflammatory drugs (eg ibuprofen)
- ➡ antihistamines (for hay fever and allergic reactions)
- ➡ antibacterial ointment (eg Bactroban; for cuts and abrasions)
- ➡ steroid cream or cortisone (for poison ivy and other allergic rashes)
- ➡ bandages, gauze, gauze rolls, adhesive or paper tape
- ➡ scissors, safety pins, tweezers, thermometer, pocketknife
- ➡ insect repellent containing DEET (for the skin); insect spray containing permethrin (for clothing, tents and bed nets)
- ➡ sunblock, oral rehydration salts
- ➡ iodine tablets (for water purification)
- ➡ acetazolamide (Diamox; for altitude sickness)

IN PERU

Availability & Cost of Health Care

Lima has high-quality 24-hour medical clinics, and

English-speaking doctors and dentists. Often embassies have a list of providers. Rural areas may have the most basic medical services. You may have to pay in cash, regardless of whether or not you have travel insurance.

Life-threatening medical problems may require evacuation if you are in a remote area.

Pharmacies are known as *farmacias* or *boticas* and are identified by a green or red cross. They offer most of the medications available in other countries. Usually each city has one pharmacy open all night.

Diseases

Many of the following diseases are spread by mosquitoes. Take precautions to minimize your chances of being bitten. These precautions also protect against other insect-borne diseases like Baronellois (Oroya fever), Leishmaniasis and Chagas' disease.

Cholera

An intestinal infection, cholera is acquired through contaminated food or water, resulting in profuse diarrhea, which may cause life-threatening dehydration. Treatment includes oral rehydration and possibly antibiotics.

Dengue Fever

A viral infection, dengue is transmitted by mosquitoes which breed primarily in puddles and artificial water containers. It is especially common in densely populated, urban environments, including Lima and Cuzco.

Flu-like symptoms include fever, muscle aches, joint pains, headaches, nausea and vomiting, often followed by a rash. The body aches may be quite uncomfortable, but most cases resolve in a few days.

Take analgesics, such as acetaminophen/paracetamol (Tylenol), and drink plenty of fluids. Severe cases may require hospitalization.

Malaria

Malaria is transmitted by mosquito bites, usually between dusk and dawn. High spiking fevers may be accompanied by chills, sweats, headache, body aches, weakness, vomiting or diarrhea. Severe cases may lead to seizures, confusion, coma and death.

Taking malaria pills is strongly recommended for all areas in Peru except Lima and its vicinity, the coastal areas south of Lima, and the highland areas (including around Cuzco, Machu Picchu, Lake Titicaca and Arequipa). Most cases in Peru occur in Loreto, in the country's northeast, where transmission has reached epidemic levels.

Typhoid Fever

Caused by ingestion of food or water contaminated by *Salmonella typhi*, fever occurs in virtually all cases. Other symptoms may include headache, malaise, muscle aches, dizziness, loss of appetite, nausea and abdominal pain. Either diarrhea or constipation may occur. Possible complications include intestinal perforation or bleeding, confusion, delirium or, rarely, coma.

The vaccine is usually given orally, but is also available as an injection. The treatment drug is usually a quinolone antibiotic, such as ciprofloxacin (Cipro) or levofloxacin (Levaquin).

REQUIRED & RECOMMENDED VACCINATIONS

VACCINE	RECOMMENDED FOR	DOSAGE	SIDE EFFECTS
chickenpox	travelers who've never had chickenpox	2 doses one month apart	fever; mild case of chicken-pox
hepatitis A	all travelers	1 dose before trip; booster 6–12 months later	soreness at injection site; headaches; body aches
hepatitis B	long-term travelers in close contact with the local population	3 doses over 6-month period	soreness at injection site; low-grade fever
measles	travelers born after 1956 who have had only one measles vaccination	1 dose	fever; rash; joint pains; allergic reactions
rabies	travelers who may have contact with animals and may not have access to medical care	3 doses over 3–4 week period	soreness at injection site; headaches; body aches
tetanus-diphtheria	all travelers who haven't had a booster within 10 years	1 dose lasts 10 years	soreness at injection site
typhoid	all travelers	4 capsules by mouth, 1 taken every other day	abdominal pain; nausea; rash
yellow fever	all travelers	1 dose lasts 10 years	headaches; body aches; severe reactions are rare

Yellow Fever

A life-threatening viral infection, yellow fever is transmitted by mosquitoes in forested areas. Flu-like symptoms may include fever, chills, headache, muscle aches, backache, loss of appetite, nausea and vomiting. They usually subside in a few days, but one person in six enters a second, toxic phase characterized by recurrent fever, vomiting, listlessness, jaundice, kidney failure and hemorrhage which can lead to death. There is no treatment except for supportive care.

Yellow-fever vaccination is strongly recommended for all those who visit any jungle area of Peru at altitudes less than 2300m (7546ft). Most cases occur in the departments in the central jungle. Get vaccinated at least 10 days before any potential exposure; it remains effective for about 10 years. The vaccine should not be given during pregnancy.

Zika Virus

Zika virus is primarily transmitted by infected mosquitoes, typically active from dawn to dusk. It can be transmitted from a pregnant woman to her fetus. Human transmission can also occur through unprotected sex, and on occasion through saliva and urine. Symptoms include mild fever, headache, muscle and joint pain, nausea, vomiting and general malaise. Symptoms may present three to 12 days after being bitten.

The best prevention is to use long sleeves, repellent with 20% to 30% DEET and avoid being outdoors at dawn and dusk when mosquitos are most common. High-altitude destinations like Cuzco, Lake Titicaca and Machu Picchu are not considered a risk.

Environmental Hazards

Altitude Sickness

Altitude sickness may result from rapid ascents to altitudes greater than 2500m (8100ft). In Peru, this includes Cuzco, Machu Picchu and Lake Titicaca. Being physically fit offers no protection. Symptoms may include headaches, nausea, vomiting, dizziness, malaise, insomnia and loss of appetite. Severe cases may be complicated by fluid in the lungs (high-altitude pulmonary edema) or swelling of the brain (high-altitude cerebral edema). If symptoms persist for more than 24 hours, descend immediately by at least 500m and see a doctor.

The best prevention is to spend two nights or more at each rise of 1000m. Diamox may be taken starting 24 hours before ascent. A natural alternative is ginkgo.

It's also important to avoid overexertion, eat light meals and abstain from alcohol. Altitude sickness should be taken seriously; it can be life threatening when severe.

Hypothermia

To prevent hypothermia, dress in layers: silk, wool and synthetic thermals are all good insulators. Essentials include a hat and a waterproof outer layer. Carry food and lots of fluid. An emergency space blanket can be highly useful.

Symptoms are exhaustion, numbness (particularly toes and fingers), shivering, slurred speech, irrational or violent behavior, lethargy, stumbling, dizzy spells, muscle cramps and violent bursts of energy.

To treat, go indoors and replace wet clothing with dry. Take hot liquids – no alcohol – and some high-calorie, easily digestible food. Do not rub victims, as rough handling may cause cardiac arrest.

Mosquito Bites

The best prevention is wearing long sleeves, long pants, hats and shoes (rather than sandals). Use insect repellent with DEET. Protection usually lasts about six hours. Children aged two to 12 should use formulas with no more than 10% to 30% DEET, which lasts about three hours.

Insect repellents containing certain botanical products, including eucalyptus oil and soybean oil, are effective but last only 1½ to two hours.

If sleeping outdoors or in accommodations where mosquitoes can enter, use a mosquito net with 1.5mm mesh, preferably treated with permethrin, tucking edges under the mattress.

Sunburn & Heat Exhaustion

Stay out of the midday sun, wear sunglasses and a wide-brimmed sun hat, and use sunblock with high SPF, UVA and UVB protection. Be aware that the sun is more intense at higher altitudes.

Dehydration or salt deficiency can cause heat exhaustion. Drink plenty of fluids and avoid excessive alcohol or strenuous activity when you first arrive in a hot climate. Long, continuous periods of exposure can leave you vulnerable to heatstroke.

Tap Water

Tap water in Peru is not safe to drink. Boiling water vigorously for one minute is the most effective means of water purification. At altitudes over 2000m (6500ft), boil for three minutes.

You can also disinfect water with iodine or water-purification pills or use a water filter or Steripen. Consult with outdoor retailers on the best option for your travel situation.

Women's Health

Travel to Lima is reasonably safe if you're pregnant, but finding quality obstetric care outside the capital may be difficult. Tampons are not available in rural areas. It isn't advisable for pregnant women to spend time at high altitudes. The yellow-fever vaccine should not be given during pregnancy.

Language

Latin American Spanish pronunciation is easy, as most sounds have equivalents in English. Read our colored pronunciation guides as if they were English, and you'll be understood. Note that kh is a throaty sound (like the 'ch' in the Scottish loch), v and b are like a soft English 'v' (between a 'v' and a 'b'), and r is strongly rolled. There are also some variations in spoken Spanish across Latin America, the most notable being the pronunciation of the letters ll and y. In our pronunciation guides these are represented with y because they are pronounced like the 'y' in 'yes' in much of Latin America. Note, however, that in some parts of Peru (and the rest of the continent) they sound like the 'lli' in 'million'. The stressed syllables are indicated with italics in our pronunciation guides.

The polite form is used in this chapter; where both polite and informal options are given, they are indicated by the abbreviations 'pol' and 'inf'. Where necessary, both masculine and feminine forms of words are included, separated by a slash and with the masculine form first, eg perdido/a (m/f).

BASICS

Hello.	Hola.	o·la
Goodbye.	Adiós.	a·dyos
How are you?	¿Qué tal?	ke tal
Fine, thanks.	Bien, gracias.	byen gra·syas
Excuse me.	Perdón.	per·don
Sorry.	Lo siento.	lo syen·to
Please.	Por favor.	por fa·vor
Thank you.	Gracias.	gra·syas
You're welcome.	De nada.	de na·da
Yes./No.	Sí./No.	see/no

My name is ...
Me llamo ...   me ya·mo ...

What's your name?
¿Cómo se llama Usted? ko·mo se ya·ma oo·ste (pol)
¿Cómo te llamas?   ko·mo te ya·mas (inf)

Do you speak English?
¿Habla inglés?   a·bla een·gles (pol)
¿Hablas inglés?   a·blas een·gles (inf)

I don't understand.
Yo no entiendo.   yo no en·tyen·do

ACCOMMODATIONS

I'd like a single/double room.
Quisiera una   kee·sye·ra oo·na
habitación   a·bee·ta·syon
individual/doble.   een·dee·vee·dwal/do·ble

How much is it per night/person?
¿Cuánto cuesta por   kwan·to kwes·ta por
noche/persona?   no·che/per·so·na

Does it include breakfast?
¿Incluye el desayuno?   een·kloo·ye el de·sa·yoo·no

campsite	terreno de cámping	te·re·no de kam·peeng
guesthouse	pensión	pen·syon
hotel	hotel	o·tel
youth hostel	albergue juvenil	al·ber·ge khoo·ve·neel
air-con	aire acondicionado	ai·re a·kon·dee·syo·na·do
bathroom	baño	ba·nyo
bed	cama	ka·ma
window	ventana	ven·ta·na

WANT MORE?

For in-depth language information and handy phrases, check out Lonely Planet's *Latin American Spanish Phrasebook*. You'll find it at **shop.lonelyplanet.com**, or you can buy Lonely Planet's iPhone phrasebooks at the Apple App Store.

KEY PATTERNS

To get by in Spanish, mix and match these simple patterns with words of your choice:

When's (the next flight)?
¿Cuándo sale   kwan·do sa·le
(el próximo vuelo)?   (el prok·see·mo vwe·lo)

Where's (the station)?
¿Dónde está   don·de es·ta
(la estación)?   (la es·ta·syon)

Where can I (buy a ticket)?
¿Dónde puedo   don·de pwe·do
(comprar un billete)?   (kom·prar oon bee·ye·te)

Do you have (a map)?
¿Tiene (un mapa)?   tye·ne (oon ma·pa)

Is there (a toilet)?
¿Hay (servicios)?   ai (ser·vee·syos)

I'd like (a coffee).
Quisiera (un café).   kee·sye·ra (oon ka·fe)

I'd like (to hire a car).
Quisiera (alquilar   kee·sye·ra (al·kee·lar
un coche).   oon ko·che)

Can I (enter)?
¿Se puede (entrar)?   se pwe·de (en·trar)

Could you please (help me)?
¿Puede (ayudarme),   pwe·de (a·yoo·dar·me)
por favor?   por fa·vor

Do I have to (get a visa)?
¿Necesito   ne·se·see·to
(obtener   (ob·te·ner
un visado)?   oon vee·sa·do)

DIRECTIONS

Where's ...?
¿Dónde está ...?   don·de es·ta ...

What's the address?
¿Cuál es la dirección?   kwal es la dee·rek·syon

Could you please write it down?
¿Puede escribirlo,   pwe·de es·kree·beer·lo
por favor?   por fa·vor

Can you show me (on the map)?
¿Me lo puede indicar   me lo pwe·de een·dee·kar
(en el mapa)?   (en el ma·pa)

at the corner	en la esquina	en la es·kee·na
at the traffic lights	en el semáforo	en el se·ma·fo·ro
behind ...	detrás de ...	de·tras de ...
in front of ...	enfrente de ...	en·fren·te de ...
left	izquierda	ees·kyer·da
next to ...	al lado de ...	al la·do de ...
opposite ...	frente a ...	fren·te a ...
right	derecha	de·re·cha
straight ahead	todo recto	to·do rek·to

EATING & DRINKING

Can I see the menu, please?
¿Puedo ver el menú,   pwe·do ver el me·noo
por favor?   por fa·vor

What would you recommend?
¿Qué recomienda?   ke re·ko·myen·da

Do you have vegetarian food?
¿Tienen comida   tye·nen ko·mee·da
vegetariana?   ve·khe·ta·rya·na

I don't eat (red meat).
No como (carne roja).   no ko·mo (kar·ne ro·kha)

That was delicious!
¡Estaba buenísimo!   es·ta·ba bwe·nee·see·mo

Cheers!
¡Salud!   sa·loo

The bill, please.
La cuenta, por favor.   la kwen·ta por fa·vor

I'd like a	Quisiera una	kee·sye·ra oo·na
table for ...	mesa para ...	me·sa pa·ra ...
(eight) o'clock	las (ocho)	las (o·cho)
(two) people	(dos) personas	(dos) per·so·nas

Key Words

appetisers	aperitivos	a·pe·ree·tee·vos
bottle	botella	bo·te·ya
bowl	bol	bol
breakfast	desayuno	de·sa·yoo·no
children's menu	menú infantil	me·noo een·fan·teel
(too) cold	(muy) frío	(mooy) free·o
dinner	cena	se·na
food	comida	ko·mee·da
fork	tenedor	te·ne·dor
glass	vaso	va·so
hot (warm)	caliente	kal·yen·te
knife	cuchillo	koo·chee·yo
lunch	comida	ko·mee·da
main course	segundo plato	se·goon·do pla·to
plate	plato	pla·to
restaurant	restaurante	res·tow·ran·te
spoon	cuchara	koo·cha·ra
with	con	kon
without	sin	seen

Meat & Fish

beef	carne de vaca	kar·ne de va·ka
chicken	pollo	po·yo
duck	pato	pa·to
fish	pescado	pes·ka·do
lamb	cordero	kor·de·ro
pork	cerdo	ser·do
turkey	pavo	pa·vo
veal	ternera	ter·ne·ra

Fruit & Vegetables

apple	manzana	man·sa·na
apricot	albaricoque	al·ba·ree·ko·ke
artichoke	alcachofa	al·ka·cho·fa
asparagus	espárragos	es·pa·ra·gos
banana	plátano	pla·ta·no
beans	judías	khoo·dee·as
beetroot	remolacha	re·mo·la·cha
cabbage	col	kol
carrot	zanahoria	sa·na·o·rya
celery	apio	a·pyo
cherry	cereza	se·re·sa
corn	maíz	ma·ees
cucumber	pepino	pe·pee·no
fruit	fruta	froo·ta
grape	uvas	oo·vas
lemon	limón	lee·mon
lentils	lentejas	len·te·khas
lettuce	lechuga	le·choo·ga
mushroom	champiñón	cham·pee·nyon
nuts	nueces	nwe·ses
onion	cebolla	se·bo·ya
orange	naranja	na·ran·kha
peach	melocotón	me·lo·ko·ton
peas	guisantes	gee·san·tes
(red/green) pepper	pimiento (rojo/verde)	pee·myen·to (ro·kho/ver·de)
pineapple	piña	pee·nya
plum	ciruela	seer·we·la
potato	patata	pa·ta·ta
pumpkin	calabaza	ka·la·ba·sa
spinach	espinacas	es·pee·na·kas
strawberry	fresa	fre·sa
tomato	tomate	to·ma·te
vegetable	verdura	ver·doo·ra
watermelon	sandía	san·dee·a

QUESTION WORDS

What?	¿Qué?	ke
When?	¿Cuándo?	kwan·do
Where?	¿Dónde?	don·de
Who?	¿Quién?	kyen
Why?	¿Por qué?	por ke

Other

bread	pan	pan
butter	mantequilla	man·te·kee·ya
cheese	queso	ke·so
egg	huevo	we·vo
honey	miel	myel
jam	mermelada	mer·me·la·da
oil	aceite	a·sey·te
pasta	pasta	pas·ta
pepper	pimienta	pee·myen·ta
rice	arroz	a·ros
salt	sal	sal
sugar	azúcar	a·soo·kar
vinegar	vinagre	vee·na·gre

Drinks

beer	cerveza	ser·ve·sa
coffee	café	ka·fe
(orange) juice	zumo (de naranja)	soo·mo (de na·ran·kha)
milk	leche	le·che
red wine	vino tinto	vee·no teen·to
tea	té	te
(mineral) water	agua (mineral)	a·gwa (mee·ne·ral)
white wine	vino blanco	vee·no blan·ko

SIGNS

Abierto	Open
Cerrado	Closed
Entrada	Entrance
Hombres/Varones	Men
Mujeres/Damas	Women
Prohibido	Prohibited
Salida	Exit
Servicios/Baños	Toilets

NUMBERS

1	uno	oo·no
2	dos	dos
3	tres	tres
4	cuatro	kwa·tro
5	cinco	seen·ko
6	seis	seys
7	siete	sye·te
8	ocho	o·cho
9	nueve	nwe·ve
10	diez	dyes
20	veinte	veyn·te
30	treinta	treyn·ta
40	cuarenta	kwa·ren·ta
50	cincuenta	seen·kwen·ta
60	sesenta	se·sen·ta
70	setenta	se·ten·ta
80	ochenta	o·chen·ta
90	noventa	no·ven·ta
100	cien	syen
1000	mil	meel

EMERGENCIES

Help!
¡Socorro! so·ko·ro

Go away!
¡Vete! ve·te

Call ...!
¡Llame a ...! ya·me a ...
  a doctor
  un médico oon me·dee·ko
  the police
  la policía la po·lee·see·a

I'm lost.
Estoy perdido/a. es·toy per·dee·do/a (m/f)

I'm ill.
Estoy enfermo/a. es·toy en·fer·mo/a (m/f)

I'm allergic to (antibiotics).
Soy alérgico/a a soy a·ler·khee·ko/a a
(los antibióticos). (los an·tee·byo·tee·kos) (m/f)

Where are the toilets?
¿Dónde están los don·de es·tan los
baños? ba·nyos

SHOPPING & SERVICES

I'd like to buy ...
Quisiera comprar ... kee·sye·ra kom·prar ...

I'm just looking.
Sólo estoy mirando. so·lo es·toy mee·ran·do

Can I look at it?
¿Puedo verlo? pwe·do ver·lo

I don't like it.
No me gusta. no me goos·ta

How much is it?
¿Cuánto cuesta? kwan·to kwes·ta

That's too expensive.
Es muy caro. es mooy ka·ro

Can you lower the price?
¿Podría bajar un po·dree·a ba·khar oon
poco el precio? po·ko el pre·syo

There's a mistake in the bill.
Hay un error ai oon e·ror
en la cuenta. en la kwen·ta

ATM	cajero	ka·khe·ro
	automático	ow·to·ma·tee·ko
internet cafe	cibercafé	see·ber·ka·fe
market	mercado	mer·ka·do
post office	correos	ko·re·os
tourist office	oficina	o·fee·see·na
	de turismo	de too·rees·mo

TIME & DATES

What time is it? *¿Qué hora es?* ke o·ra es

It's (10) o'clock. *Son (las diez).* son (las dyes)

It's half past *Es (la una)* es (la oo·na)
(one). *y media.* ee me·dya

morning	mañana	ma·nya·na
afternoon	tarde	tar·de
evening	noche	no·che
yesterday	ayer	a·yer
today	hoy	oy
tomorrow	mañana	ma·nya·na
Monday	lunes	loo·nes
Tuesday	martes	mar·tes
Wednesday	miércoles	myer·ko·les
Thursday	jueves	khwe·ves
Friday	viernes	vyer·nes
Saturday	sábado	sa·ba·do
Sunday	domingo	do·meen·go

TRANSPORTATION

boat	barco	bar·ko
bus		autobús
ow·to·boos		
plane	avión	a·vyon
train	tren	tren
first	primero	pree·me·ro

AYMARA & QUECHUA

The few Aymara and Quechua words and phrases included here will be useful for those traveling in the Andes. Aymara is spoken by the Aymara people, who inhabit the area around Lake Titicaca. While the Quechua included here is from the Cuzco dialect, it should prove helpful wherever you travel in the highlands too.

In the following lists, Aymara is the second column, Quechua the third. The principles of pronunciation for both languages are similar to those found in Spanish. An apostrophe (') represents a glottal stop, which is the 'nonsound' that occurs in the middle of 'uh-oh.'

Hello.	Kamisaraki.	Napaykullayki.	father	auqui	tayta
Please.	Mirá.	Allichu.	mother	taica	mama
Thank you.	Yuspagara.	Yusulipayki.	food	manka	mikíuy
Yes.	Jisa.	Ari.	river	jawira	mayu
No.	Janiwa.	Mana.	snowy peak	kollu	riti-orko
			water	uma	yacu

How do you say ...?	Cun saña-sauca'ha ...?	Imainata nincha chaita ...?	1	maya	u'
It's called ...	Ucan sutipa'h ...	Chaipa'g sutin'ha ...	2	paya	iskai
			3	quimsa	quinsa
			4	pusi	tahua
Please repeat.	Uastata sita.	Ua'manta niway.	5	pesca	phiska
How much?	K'gauka?	Maik'ata'g?	6	zo'hta	so'gta
			7	pakalko	khanchis
			8	quimsakalko	pusa'g
			9	yatunca	iskon
			10	tunca	chunca

last	último	ool·tee·mo
ticket office	taquilla	ta·kee·ya
timetable	horario	o·ra·ryo
bus stop	parada de autobuses	pa·ra·da de ow·to·boo·ses
train station	estación de trenes	es·ta·syon de tre·nes

A ... ticket, please.	Un billete de ..., por favor.	oon bee·ye·te de ... por fa·vor
1st-class	primera clase	pree·me·ra kla·se
2nd-class	segunda clase	se·goon·da kla·se
one-way	ida	ee·da
return	ida y vuelta	ee·da ee vwel·ta

Does it stop at ...?
¿Para en ...?   pa·ra en ...

What stop is this?
¿Cuál es esta parada?   kwal es es·ta pa·ra·da

What time does it arrive/leave?
¿A qué hora llega/sale?   a ke o·ra ye·ga/sa·le

Please tell me when we get to ...
¿Puede avisarme   pwe·de a·vee·sar·me
cuando lleguemos a ...?   kwan·do ye·ge·mos a ...

I want to get off here.
Quiero bajarme aquí.   kye·ro ba·khar·me a·kee

I'd like to hire a ...	Quisiera alquilar ...	kee·sye·ra al·kee·lar ...
4WD	un todo-terreno	oon to·do·te·re·no
bicycle	una bicicleta	oo·na bee·see·kle·ta
car	un coche	oon ko·che
motorcycle	una moto	oo·na mo·to

helmet	casco	kas·ko
hitchhike	hacer botella	a·ser bo·te·ya
mechanic	mecánico	me·ka·nee·ko
petrol/gas	gasolina	ga·so·lee·na
service station	gasolinera	ga·so·lee·ne·ra
truck	camion	ka·myon

Is this the road to ...?
¿Se va a ... por | se va a ... por
esta carretera? | es·ta ka·re·te·ra

Can I park here?
¿Puedo aparcar aquí? | pwe·do a·par·kar a·kee

The car has broken down.
El coche se
ha averiado. | el ko·che se a a·ve·rya·do

I have a flat tyre.
Tengo un
pinchazo. | ten·go oon peen·cha·sot

GLOSSARY

albergue – family-owned inn

altiplano – literally, a high plateau or plain; specifically, it refers to the vast, desolate Andean flatlands of southern Peru, Bolivia, northern Chile and northern Argentina

aluvión – fast-moving flood of ice, water, rocks, mud and debris caused by an earthquake or a bursting dam in the mountains

arequipeño – inhabitant of Arequipa

arriero – animal driver, usually of burros or mulas (mules)

avenida – avenue (Av)

ayahuasca – potent hallucinogenic brew made from jungle vines and used by shamans and traditional healers

barrio – neighborhood

bodega – winery, wine shop, wine cellar or tasting bar

boleto turístico – tourism ticket

bruja/brujo – shaman, witch doctor, or medicine person

burro – donkey

bus-cama – long-distance, double-decker buses with seats reclining almost into beds; toilets, videos and snacks are provided on board

caballito – high-ended, cigar-shaped boat; found near Huanchaco

calle – street

campesino – peasant, farmer or rural inhabitant

cañón – canyon

carretera – highway

casa – home, house

casa de cambio – foreign-exchange bureau

cerro – hill, mountain

chullpa – ancient Andean burial tower, found around Lake Titicaca

cocha – lake, from the indigenous Quechua language; often appended to many lake names

colectivo – shared transportation; usually taxis, but also minibuses, minivans or boats

combi – minivan or minibus (usually with tiny seats, and as many passengers as possible)

cordillera – mountain chain

criolla/criollo – Creole or native of Peru; also applies to coastal Peruvians, music and dance; criollo food refers to spicy Peruvian fare with Spanish, Asian and African influences

cuadra – city block

curandera/curandero – traditional healer

cuzqueño – inhabitant of Cuzco (also Cusco or Qosq'o)

escuela cuzqueña – Cuzco school; colonial art movement that combined Spanish and Andean artistic styles

feria – street market with vendor booths

garúa – coastal fog or mist

grifo – gas (petrol) station

gringa/gringo – all foreigners who are not from South or Central America and Mexico

guanaco – large, wild camelid that ranges throughout South America, now an endangered species in Peru

hospedaje – small, family-owned inn

hostal – guesthouse, smaller than a hotel and with fewer amenities

huaca – sacred pyramid, temple or burial site

huaquero – grave robber

huayno – traditional Andean music using instrumentation with roots in pre-Columbian times

iglesia – church

inca – king

indígena – indigenous person (male or female)

Inrena – Insituto Nacional de Recursos Naturales (National Institute for Natural Resources); government agency that administers national parks, reserves, historical sanctuaries and other protected areas

Inti – ancient Peruvian sun god; husband of the earth goddess Pachamama

isla – island, isle

jirón – road (abbreviated Jr)

lavandería – laundry

limeño – inhabitant of Lima

lomo saltado – stir-fried beef with onions, tomatoes, potatoes and chili

marinera – a typical coastal Peruvian dance involving the flirtatious waving of handkerchiefs

mestizo – person of mixed indigenous and Spanish descent

micro – a small bus used as public transport

mirador – watchtower, observatory, viewpoint

mototaxi – three-wheeled motorcycle rickshaw taxi; also called motocarro or taximoto

museo – museum

nevado – glaciated or snow-covered mountain peak

nuevo sol – the national currency of Peru

oficina de migraciónes – immigration office

Pachamama – ancient Peruvian earth goddess; wife of the sun god Inti

pampa – large, flat area, usually of grasslands

Panamericana – Pan-American Highway (aka Interamericana); main route joining Latin American countries

parque – park

peña – bar or club featuring live folkloric music

playa – beach

pongo – narrow, steep-walled, rocky, jungle river canyon that can be a dangerous maelstrom during high water

pueblo – town, village

puna – high Andean grasslands of the *altiplano*

puya – spiky-leafed plant of the bromeliad family

quebrada – literally, a break; often refers to a steep ravine or gulch

quero – ceremonial Inca wooden drinking vessel

río – river

selva – jungle, tropical rainforest

sillar – off-white volcanic rock, often used for buildings around Arequipa

soroche – altitude sickness

taximoto – see *mototaxi*

terminal terrestre – bus station

totora – reed of the papyrus family; used to build the 'floating islands' and traditional boats of Lake Titicaca

turismo vivencial – homestay tourism

vals peruano – Peruvian waltz, an upbeat, guitar-driven waltz played and danced to in coastal areas

vicuña – threatened wild relative of the alpaca; smallest living member of the camelid family

LANGUAGE GLOSSARY

Behind the Scenes

SEND US YOUR FEEDBACK

We love to hear from travelers – your comments keep us on our toes and help make our books better. Our well-traveled team reads every word on what you loved or loathed about this book. Although we cannot reply individually to your submissions, we always guarantee that your feedback goes straight to the appropriate authors, in time for the next edition. Each person who sends us information is thanked in the next edition – the most useful submissions are rewarded with a selection of digital PDF chapters.

Visit **lonelyplanet.com/contact** to submit your updates and suggestions or to ask for help. Our award-winning website also features inspirational travel stories, news and discussions.

Note: We may edit, reproduce and incorporate your comments in Lonely Planet products such as guidebooks, websites and digital products, so let us know if you don't want your comments reproduced or your name acknowledged. For a copy of our privacy policy visit lonelyplanet.com/privacy.

OUR READERS

Many thanks to the travelers who used the last edition and wrote to us with helpful hints, useful advice and interesting anecdotes: Amanda Hill, Danielle Wolbers, David Brown, Jeff White, Johannes Hirvonen, Sarah Brooks, Seda

WRITER THANKS

Brendan Sainsbury

Muchas gracias to all the skilled bus drivers, helpful tourist information staff, generous hotel owners, expert lomo saltado makers, and innocent passers-by who helped me, unwittingly or otherwise, during my research trip. Special thanks to Marie Timmermans at Quechuandes, Fredy, my superb driver in the Cordilleras, José at Chachapoyas Backpackers, and fellow LP scribe, Luke Waterson for his company hiking around Huaraz.

Alex Egerton

Major gratitude to all the wonderful staff from Promperu who went above and beyond in every way imaginable and all the ordinary Peruvians whose pride for their country is infectious and makes working on the ground such a pleasure. And big props for Olga Mosquera for keeping things running at home and Nicholas Kazu for the patience.

Mark Johanson

Muchas gracias to all the Bolivian people who warmed my heart and filled my belly. Thanks to Felipe Bascuñán for allowing me to be gone from home for so many weeks and to Tomas Sivila, María Fernanda Alandia, Alex Villca Limaco, Raul Mendoza, Augusto Aruquipa Coromi, Rosa Maria Ruiz and Jose Antonio Diaz for being fountains of knowledge along the way.

Carolyn McCarthy

Many thanks go out to the Peruvian chefs and street vendors who played a key role in my contentment. I am also grateful for the friendship, advice and assistance of Jorge Riveros Cayo, Arturo Rojas, Mandy Kalitsis, Louise Norton, Elizabeth Shumaker, John Leivers and Illa Liendo. To my hardworking co-authors, a chilled pisco sour and cheers.

Phillip Tang

Muchísimas gracias a Bernardo Ocsa y Raúl por Sibayo y cañones. In Arequipa, thanks to Kevin for the uber great night, Manuel Anthony Carpio Ortiz for Callejón del Solar, Felipe for music, Matt for a bridge with a view, and Moral for hospitality. In Lima, gracias Giancarlo Ramírez Mazza for stylish moves and Chin for welcoming me. En Puno, gracias Joaquín Eduardo por el frappe y 15 minutos de fama, desde chini; gracias Omar y Verónica en iPerú.

Luke Waterson

The honors list of those who gave a helping hand this edition is as great as the Amazon is vast. Special mentions are as follows. In Iquitos: Marmelita and the guys at Casa Celestial; in Pucallpa: Kyle; in Oxapampa: Bertl; in Manu: Ryse; in Puerto Maldonado: Gerson; in Tingo Maria: Graciela; in Tarma: Pepe and Inge; in Huancayo: Lucho; in Ayacucho: Pauline and Emilie. *Gracias* too to all the bus, minivan, colectivo and boat drivers for not crashing.

ACKNOWLEDGEMENTS

Cover photograph: Rainbow Mountain (Vinicunca), Daniel Prudek/Shutterstock ©

Illustration p260-1 by Michael Weldon

THIS BOOK

This 11th edition of Lonely Planet's *Peru* guidebook was researched and written by Brendan Sainsbury, Alex Egerton, Mark Johanson, Carolyn McCarthy, Phillip Tang and Luke Waterson. This guidebook was produced by the following:

Senior Product Editor Sandie Kestell

Product Editors Joel Cotterell, Saralinda Turner

Cartographer Corey Hutchison

Book Designers Hannah Blackie, Gwen Cotter

Assisting Editors Andrew Bain, Michelle Coxall, Andrea Dobbin, Emma Gibbs, Jennifer Hattam, Amy Lynch, Louise McGregor, Alison Morris, Kristin Odijk, Monique Perrin, Claire Rourke, Fionnuala Twomey

Cover Researcher Gwen Cotter

Thanks to Ronan Abayawickrema, Imogen Bannister, Daniel Bolger, Heather Champion, Karen Henderson, Sandie Kestell, Lauren O'Connell, Genna Patterson, Gabrielle Stefanos, Angela Tinson

Index

Map Legend

Sights
- Beach
- Bird Sanctuary
- Buddhist
- Castle/Palace
- Christian
- Confucian
- Hindu
- Islamic
- Jain
- Jewish
- Monument
- Museum/Gallery/Historic Building
- Ruin
- Shinto
- Sikh
- Taoist
- Winery/Vineyard
- Zoo/Wildlife Sanctuary
- Other Sight

Activities, Courses & Tours
- Bodysurfing
- Diving
- Canoeing/Kayaking
- Course/Tour
- Sento Hot Baths/Onsen
- Skiing
- Snorkeling
- Surfing
- Swimming/Pool
- Walking
- Windsurfing
- Other Activity

Sleeping
- Sleeping
- Camping
- Hut/Shelter

Eating
- Eating

Drinking & Nightlife
- Drinking & Nightlife
- Cafe

Entertainment
- Entertainment

Shopping
- Shopping

Information
- Bank
- Embassy/Consulate
- Hospital/Medical
- Internet
- Police
- Post Office
- Telephone
- Toilet
- Tourist Information
- Other Information

Geographic
- Beach
- Gate
- Hut/Shelter
- Lighthouse
- Lookout
- Mountain/Volcano
- Oasis
- Park
- Pass
- Picnic Area
- Waterfall

Population
- Capital (National)
- Capital (State/Province)
- City/Large Town
- Town/Village

Transport
- Airport
- Border crossing
- Bus
- Cable car/Funicular
- Cycling
- Ferry
- Metro station
- Monorail
- Parking
- Petrol station
- Subway/Subte station
- Taxi
- Train station/Railway
- Tram
- Underground station
- Other Transport

Routes
- Tollway
- Freeway
- Primary
- Secondary
- Tertiary
- Lane
- Unsealed road
- Road under construction
- Plaza/Mall
- Steps
- Tunnel
- Pedestrian overpass
- Walking Tour
- Walking Tour detour
- Path/Walking Trail

Boundaries
- International
- State/Province
- Disputed
- Regional/Suburb
- Marine Park
- Cliff
- Wall

Hydrography
- River, Creek
- Intermittent River
- Canal
- Water
- Dry/Salt/Intermittent Lake
- Reef

Areas
- Airport/Runway
- Beach/Desert
- Cemetery (Christian)
- Cemetery (Other)
- Glacier
- Mudflat
- Park/Forest
- Sight (Building)
- Sportsground
- Swamp/Mangrove

Note: Not all symbols displayed above appear on the maps in this book

Phillip Tang

Arequipa & Canyon Country, Lake Titicaca Phillip grew up on a typically Australian diet of *pho* and fish'n'chips before moving to Mexico City. A degree in Chinese and Latin-American cultures launched him into travel and then writing about it for Lonely Planet's *Canada*, *China*, *Japan*, *Korea*, *Mexico* and *Vietnam* guides. See his writing at vihellophillip.com; photos @mrtangtangtang; and tweets @ philliptang.

Luke Waterson

Amazon Basin, Central Highlands Raised in southwest England, Luke quickly became addicted to exploring out-of-the-way places. Completing a Creative Writing degree at the University of East Anglia, he shouldered his backpack and vowed to see as much of the world as possible. Luke specialises in writing on South America – he contributes to the LP *Ecuador* guide, and his debut novel *Roebuck*, set in the 16th-century Amazon jungle, was published in December 2015. For updates about his writing, fact and fiction, visit lukeandhiswords.com.

OUR STORY

A beat-up old car, a few dollars in the pocket and a sense of adventure. In 1972 that's all Tony and Maureen Wheeler needed for the trip of a lifetime – across Europe and Asia overland to Australia. It took several months, and at the end – broke but inspired – they sat at their kitchen table writing and stapling together their first travel guide, *Across Asia on the Cheap*. Within a week they'd sold 1500 copies. Lonely Planet was born.

Today, Lonely Planet has offices in Franklin, Dublin and Beijing, with a network of over 2000 contributors in every corner of the globe. We share Tony's belief that 'a great guidebook should do three things: inform, educate and amuse'.

OUR WRITERS

Brendan Sainsbury

Northern Highlands, Huaraz & the Cordilleras Born and raised in the UK in a town that never merits a mention in any guidebook (Andover, Hampshire), Brendan didn't leave Blighty until he was 19. Making up for lost time, he's since squeezed 70 countries into a sometimes precarious existence as a writer and professional vagabond. His rocking-chair memories will probably include staging a performance of *A Comedy of Errors* at a school in war-torn Angola and running 150 miles across the Sahara Desert in the Marathon des Sable. In the last 11 years, he has written over 40 books for Lonely Planet, covering everything from Castro's Cuba to the canyons of Peru.

Alex Egerton

North Coast, South Coast A news journalist by trade, Alex has worked for magazines, newspapers and media outlets on five continents. He spends most of his time on the road checking under mattresses, sampling suspicious street food and chatting with locals as part of the research process for travel articles and guidebooks. When he is not traveling, you'll find him at home in Popayán, southern Colombia.

Mark Johanson

Lake Titicaca Mark grew up in Virginia and has called five different countries home over the last decade while circling the globe reporting for British newspapers (*The Guardian*), American magazines (*Men's Journal*) and global media outlets (CNN, BBC). When he is not on the road, you'll find him gazing at the Andes from his current home in Santiago, Chile. Follow the adventures at www.markjohanson.com

Carolyn McCarthy

Lima & Around, Cuzco & the Sacred Valley Carolyn specializes in travel, culture and adventure in the Americas. She has written for *National Geographic*, *Outside*, *BBC Magazine*, *Sierra Magazine*, *Boston Globe* and other publications. Carolyn has contributed to 40 guidebooks and anthologies for Lonely Planet. For more information, visit www.carolynmccarthy.org or follow her Instagram travels @mccarthyoffmap. Carolyn also wrote the Plan and Understand sections.

OVER PAGE MORE WRITERS

1/2022

DISCARD